THE
PHYSICAL CHEMISTRY
OF
ELECTROLYTIC
SOLUTIONS

BY

HERBERT S. HARNED

Professor of Chemistry, Yale University   Emeritus,

and

BENTON B. OWEN

Professor of Chemistry, Yale University

American Chemical Society
Monograph Series

THIRD EDITION

REINHOLD PUBLISHING CORPORATION
A SUBSIDIARY OF CHAPMAN-REINHOLD, INC.
NEW YORK

Library of Congress Catalog Card No. *58-6863*

REINHOLD PUBLISHING CORPORATION

Publishers of Chemical Engineering Catalog, Chemical Materials Catalog, Materials in Design Engineering, Progressive Architecture, Automatic Control; Advertising Management of American Chemical Society

Printed in the U.S.A. by The Guinn Co., Inc., New York

To those institutions which have fostered free inquiry through these troubled times, this book is gratefully dedicated.

GENERAL INTRODUCTION

American Chemical Society's Series of Chemical Monographs

By arrangement with the Interallied Conference of Pure and Applied Chemistry, which met in London and Brussels in July, 1919, the American Chemical Society was to undertake the production and publication of Scientific and Technologic Monographs on chemical subjects. At the same time it was agreed that the National Research Council, in cooperation with the American Chemical Society and the American Physical Society, should undertake the production and publication of Critical Tables of Chemical and Physical Constants. The American Chemical Society and the National Research Council mutually agreed to care for these two fields of chemical progress. The American Chemical Society named as Trustees, to make the necessary arrangements of the publication of the Monographs, Charles L. Parsons, secretary of the Society, Washington, D. C.; the late John E. Teeple, then treasurer of the Society, New York; and the late Professor Gellert Alleman of Swarthmore College. The Trustees arranged for the publication of the ACS Series of (a) Scientific and (b) Technological Monographs by the Chemical Catalog Company, Inc. (Reinhold Publishing Corporation, successor) of New York.

The Council of the American Chemical Society, acting through its Committee on National Policy, appointed editors (the present list of whom appears at the close of this sketch) to select authors of competent authority in their respective fields and to consider critically the manuscripts submitted.

The first Monograph of the Series appeared in 1921. After twenty-three years of experience certain modifications of general policy were indicated. In the beginning there still remained from the preceding five decades a distinct though arbitrary differentiation between so-called "pure science" publications and technologic or applied science literature. By 1944 this differentiation was fast becoming nebulous. Research in private enterprise had grown apace and not a little of it was pursued on the frontiers of knowledge. Furthermore, most workers in the sciences were coming to see the artificiality of the separation. The methods of both groups of workers are the same. They employ the same instrumentalities, and frankly recognize that their objectives are common, namely, the search for new knowledge for the service of man. The officers of the Society therefore combined the two editorial Boards in a single Board of twelve representative members.

Also in the beginning of the Series, it seemed expedient to construe rather broadly the definition of a Monograph. Needs of workers had to be recognized. Consequently among the first hundred Monographs appeared works in the form of treatises covering in some instances rather broad areas. Because such necessary works do not now want for publishers, it is considered advisable to hew more strictly to the line of the Monograph character, which means more complete and critical treatment of relatively restricted areas, and, where a broader field needs coverage, to subdivide it into logical subareas. The prodigious expansion of new knowledge makes such a change desirable.

These Monographs are intended to serve two principal purposes: first, to make available to chemists a thorough treatment of a selected area in form usable by persons working in more or less unrelated fields to the end that they may correlate their own work with a larger area of physical science discipline; second, to stimulate further research in the specific field treated. To implement this purpose the authors of Monographs are expected to give extended references to the literature. Where the literature is of such volume that a complete bibliography is impracticable, the authors are expected to append a list of references critically selected on the basis of their relative importance and significance.

Preface to Third Edition

The present edition is a drastic revision of the second edition. Chapter (1) now includes a section on Irreversible Thermodynamics to supplement the treatment on Reversible Thermodynamics. The theoretical portion in Chapters (2) to (5) has been expanded. Mayer's cluster-sum theory of thermodynamic properties is outlined in Chapter (3), and tables for numerical computation by this theory are included in Chapter (5). In Chapter (4), the theory of Onsager and Kim for the conductivity of solutions containing s-ions and their general theory of the Wien effect for strong electrolytes are outlined. Their table for computing the Wien effect is incorporated in Chapter (5). The conductance theory of Fuoss and Onsager which includes inhomogeneous terms and the a-parameter, and suitable tables for applying this theory are presented in Chapters (4) and (5). Detailed applications of this theory are illustrated in Chapter (6).

The tables in Chapter (5) and the numerical coefficients in all *numbered* equations throughout the book have been recalculated to conform with the values recommended by the Subcommittee on Fundamental Constants, National Research Council, 1952.

In the experimental chapters (6) through (15), the sections on diffusion, mixtures of electrolytes, mixed solvents and apparent molal quantities have been extended considerably. Applications of the new theoretical advances in conductivity and thermodynamic properties have been discussed. New experimental results on the Wien effect of both strong and weak electrolytes have been considered, and the equilibrium and electromotive force centrifuges have received attention.

Appendices A and B of the second edition have been consolidated, and much new material added. Some tables in the appendix were revised or completely recalculated as improvements in standards or methods of extrapolation seemed to warrant. For convenience of reference, three indices, author, subject and chemical are included.

In preparing this edition, we are grateful for the help of Professor John G. Kirkwood on irreversible thermodynamics, for the use of notes and manuscripts by Professor Raymond M. Fuoss on the theory of conductance, and for the aid of Doctor S. K. Kim in outlining the theory of the Wien effect.

HERBERT S. HARNED
BENTON B. OWEN

December, 1957

Preface to Second Edition

During the years of the war, the tremendous emphasis upon technology caused a diminution in the volume of fundamental scientific research. The science of electrolytic solutions has not escaped this influence, but since 1945 the pre-war momentum of the laboratories is beginning to be restored. In view of this retardation and of the expense entailed in a thoroughgoing revision of the original text, a compromise has been adopted in preparing a second edition of this work. An appendix has been added which contains revisions of the tables of the theoretical functions, extensions of some of the tables of data, and discussions of some recent experimental and theoretical contributions.

While part of our original text was in press in 1941, revised tables of fundamental constants were published by Birge. At that time, it was decided to make no change in the numerical tables of physical constants, characteristic slopes and mathematical functions in Chapter (5). Had we decided to make this change, all of the numerical tables would have been inconsistent with the actual calculations in the book. In this edition we have not altered the tables in Chapter (5) for the same reason, but have incorporated in Appendix B revised values of those quantities affected by changes in the fundamental constants. This procedure leaves the original text representative of the calculations during the three decades preceding 1940, and we believe that this is the most unequivocal way of meeting this unfortunate complication.

Appendix B is comparatively short, so no subject index for it has been included. Instead, a detailed Table of Contents and a separate Author Index are supplied. The sections in Appendix B are designated consecutively, (B-1), (B-2), etc., and the equations are numbered, (B-1-1), (B-10-4), etc., where (B-1-1) is the first equation in Section (1), (B-10-4) is the fourth equation in Section (10), etc. The Figures and Tables are similarly designated. Cross references between tables in the main body of the book and Appendix B have been introduced.

Every effort has been made to eliminate the errors of typography, of sign, of factor omission, and of misstatements in the text. We are grateful to those of our colleagues who have called our attention to these mistakes. In particular we extent our thanks to Dr. Albert Sprague Coolidge of Harvard University, and to Dr. Roger G. Bates of the Bureau of Standards for lists of corrections which were the result of meticulous examination of many chapters of our work.

HERBERT S. HARNED
BENTON B. OWEN

New Haven, Conn.
June, 1949

Preface to First Edition

The science of solutions is very complex. It has evolved its own numerous experimental methods, and has required for its clarification many branches of mathematical physics, such as thermodynamics, statistical mechanics, electrostatics, and hydrodynamics. A great deal has been achieved by theory, but this achievement has been by no means enough to warrant the neglect of further experimental investigation. In writing this treatise on electrolytic solutions, we have tried to stress the importance of theory without neglecting that part of the subject which is empirical. At the same time, we have not hesitated to state the limitations of theory, or to criticize the accuracy of experimental data. We trust that the result approaches a well-balanced treatment, and hope that many of our readers will become aware of the many parts of the subject which are obscure, and which require further constructive effort. If we succeed in suggesting new and profitable fields of study to them, we shall be greatly repaid for our labor.

Although many of the important fundamental principles of electrochemistry had been discovered in the last decades of the eighteenth century and the first eighty years of the nineteenth century, it was not until 1887 that an organized theoretical and experimental investigation of conducting solutions was begun. This was brought about by the monumental discovery of van't Hoff[1] that solutions which readily conduct electric current possess freezing points, boiling points, osmotic pressures, and vapor pressures characteristic of a special class of systems, and the simultaneous and even more important discovery of Arrhenius[2] that such systems contain electrically charged particles, or ions.

It was van't Hoff who first applied the powerful methods of thermodynamics to solutions in a systematic manner. His treatment, however, lacked the generality which might have been achieved at that time if the system of thermodynamics developed by Gibbs[3] ten years earlier had been employed. Gibbs' great treatise provides all the essential basic principles required for the thermodynamics of solutions. The most important contribution of thermodynamics has been to reduce all measurements of systems in equilibrium to the determination of a single thermodynamic function. Measurements of the elevation of the boiling point and the lowering

---

[1] J. H. van't Hoff, *Z. physik, Chem.*, **1**, 481 (1887).

[2] S. Arrhenius, *Z. physik. Chem.*, **1**, 631 (1887).

[3] J. W. Gibbs, *Transactions of Connecticut Academy of Sciences*, **2**, 309, 382 (1873); **3**, 108, 343 (1875–1878). "Scientific Papers of J. Willard Gibbs," Vol. I, New York, Longmans, Green and Co., 1906. "The Collected Work of J. Willard Gibbs," Vol. I, New York, Longmans, Green and Co., 1928.

of the freezing point and vapor pressure of a solvent, caused by the addition of solute, and measurements of solubility, osmotic pressure, and the electromotive forces of suitable cells may all be used to determine the Gibbs chemical potentials of electrolytes.

From 1887 to the present, the knowledge of ionic solutions has increased immensely. Steady improvement has been made in the experimental methods of measuring the properties associated with thermodynamic equilibrium, and those such as conductivity, viscosity, and diffusion, which involve ions under the influence of externally imposed fields. This development has led to an immense volume of information (some of very high accuracy) concerning a large number of ionic systems. Simultaneously with this more and more detailed study, an electrostatic and hydrodynamic theory, depending upon the methods of statistics, has been evolved.

Soon after the discovery that ions exist in solutions, it was realized that the electrostatic forces between the ions must play an important role in determining their properties. Although attempts were made to deduce a theory of interionic attraction in the first two decades of this century, it was not until 1923 that an exact thorey of dilute solutions of electrolytes was evolved. After Debye's[4] formulation of the interionic attraction theory, a large literature developed, which includes theories of all the properties of electrolytic solutions.

The structure of this treatise is different from that of any other general treatment of the properties of ionic solutions. We are convinced that the interionic attraction theory is sufficiently well established to permit the development of the purely theoretical aspects of the subject before the discussion of the experimental methods and properties. This order of presentation has the advantage of allowing a logical development of the theory without the interpolation of extraneous material. Further, by presenting the basic theory first, the fundamental equations of theory become available both for the numerical treatment of the data and for subsequent discussions of the various properties of electrolytes.

The work is divided into three general parts of five chapters each. Chapters (1) to (5) are theoretical. The first chapter contains a thermodynamic introduction. Chapter (2) introduces the concept of the ionic atmosphere, and the foundations of the interionic attraction theory. Chapters (3) and (4) contain the theory of ionic solutions in equilibrium, and in perturbed states, respectively. A numerical summary of the theoretical results, in which the theoretical equations are reduced to their simplest form, is given in Chapter (5). For facilitating practical calculations, numerous tables of constants and theoretical functions are given. We believe that a thorough understanding of this chapter will be of con-

P. Debye and E. Hückel, *Physik. Z.*, **24**, 185, 305 (1923).

siderable practical value to those interested in numerical calculations which involve ionic solutions.

The second general division of the work [Chapters (6) to (10)] contains a discussion of experimental methods. No apparatus or experimental technique is described in detail. Chapters (6) and (7) contain a description of the use of the conductance method in the study of strong and weak electrolytes in aqueous and non-aqueous solutions, respectively. The effects of high frequencies and high fields upon conductances are also considered. Viscosity and diffusion of electrolytic solutions are included in this part. Chapter (8) contains a treatment of partial molal quantities with the exception of the partial molal free energy, work content, and entropy. In Chapter (9) freezing point, boiling point, and vapor pressure measurements are developed, and in Chapter (10) a general discussion of the electromotive force method is presented.

In the last third of the book, the emphasis is upon the properties of electrolytes rather than upon the methods by which they were obtained. Chapters (11), (12), and (13) deal with solutions of hydrochloric acid, 1-1 electrolytes, and polyvalent electrolytes, respectively. Thermodynamic properties, their interpretation, and special theories of these solutions are discussed. Mixtures of strong electrolytes in water form the subject of Chapter (14). Ionization constants of weak electrolytes, their temperature coefficients, and the ionization of weak electrolytes in salt solutions are considered in Chapter (15).

In all these discussions, we have tried to incorporate the most accurate results. Rather extensive tables of quantities derived from the best available data are given in an Appendix. These will prove useful for both theorists and experimental investigators. The former will find much to explain, and the latter will have at hand material which can be employed in practical calculations, and in comparisons with future data.

Each of the last ten chapters is of the nature of a short monograph. This has involved a certain amount of repetition which we felt was necessary to increase the value of the work as a reference book. Theoretical equations, deduced in the first part, have frequently been restated in subsequent sections. This procedure has been followed in order that the immediate subject under consideration may be more clearly discussed. The most pronounced example of such repetition occurs in Chapter (8) in which the properties of partial molal quantities are considered. Here, each section, devoted to the discussion of one of these quantities, is treated as a separate subject. This has the advantage of keeping the attention of the reader focussed on the immediate subject matter, although it may have the effect of rendering continuous reading of the chapter somewhat tiresome.

In the theoretical treatment of irreversible processes, we have had to remain content with the statement of fundamental principles and boundary conditions, and with the deduction of the differential equations. Detailed descriptions of the methods of integration would have led to a mathematical treatise. Our principal object has been the discussion and treatment of data, and both theoretical and empirical methods for computing them. Detailed descriptions of methods of extrapolation have been made with the risk that continued reading of these parts will be tedious. However, we trust that this procedure will be of help to experimenters in the calculation of their material.

Our original intention was to include a comprehensive discussion of ionic reaction velocities and homogeneous catalysis in liquid systems containing ions. This project was abandoned after careful consideration of the scope of the subject. It seemed that an adequate treatment could not be effected without increasing the volume of the book beyond convenient limits.

Some further restrictions have been imposed. Since we have devoted ourselves principally to the electrostatic theory and properties of ions in solutions, little attention has been paid to electrode processes, standard free energies and entropies of ions, or quantum theories of electrode processes. Nor have the Raman spectra and refractive indices of ionic solutions been considered. Further, we have omitted detailed discussion of solutions containing electrolytes of complicated structure, such as higher-order cobalt compounds, complex organic acids, bases, ampholytes, etc. The theory of the properties of dipolar ions is omitted because it has been thoroughly treated by Kirkwood in this series of monographs.[5] Even with these restrictions, an adequate treatment of all the excellent experimental material was found to be difficult to keep within the limits of a single volume

The choice of symbols and conventions in a complicated field is always a source of considerable trouble. For the thermodynamic parts, we have used to a large extent the nomenclature of Lewis and Randall,[6] because it is commonly employed in this country. We have adopted, with modification, the symbols of Onsager and Fuoss[7] in developing the interionic attraction theory. These conform fairly well to those in general use. In a number of special deductions we have used symbols which conform closely to the original articles in the literature. In such cases, confusion has been avoided by careful explanatory notes. A complete glossary of symbols is given immediately before Chapter (1).

A large number of equations, figures and tables occur. All these are characterized by three numbers. The first number indicates the chapter,

[5] Chapter 12 of E. J. Cohn and J. T. Edsall, "Proteins, Amino Acids and Peptides," A. C. Monograph, No. 90, Reinhold Publishing Corporation, New York (1943).

[6] G. N. Lewis and M. Randall, "Thermodynamics," New York, McGraw-Hill Book Co., 1923.

[7] L. Onsager and R. M. Fuoss, *J. Phys. Chem.*, **36**, 2689 (1932).

the second, the section of the chapter, and the third, the number of the equation, etc., in this section [Equation (4-4-22), Fig. (13-9-1), Table (12-2-3), etc.]. Tables which occur in the appendix are indicated by an A following the last number, and refer to the chapter and section of the text in a similar manner [Table (12-6-1A)].

It is impossible to acknowledge all the help we have received from the publications, the private correspondence, and conversations with our colleagues in this and other countries. The influences from all these pleasant associations will appear in innumerable ways throughout the work. We are grateful for a number of suggestions and corrections made by members of the committee of the American Chemical Society Monograph Series and to Professor T. F. Young of the University of Chicago.

Among our immediate associates at Yale University, we are particularly aware of our indebtedness to Dr. Gösta Åkerlöf for his generous coöperation over many years in matters pertaining to the experimental side of the subject. We have been greatly influenced by our association with Dr. Lars Onsager, whose masterly treatment of the theory of irreversible processes has been closely followed. We are also greatly indebted to Dr. Robert A. Robinson of the University of New Zealand, who has allowed us access to experimental material on polyvalent electrolytes prior to publication, and who has generously helped with the calculation of the properties of weak electrolytes.

Above all, we thank our colleagues, the fellows and students, whose hard work and spirit of coöperation have made the last five chapters of this treatise possible.

HERBERT S. HARNED
BENTON B. OWEN

New Haven, Conn.
October, 1943.

Glossary of Symbols

The complexity of the subject has made it necessary frequently to use the same symbol for different quantities. For example, the principal use of A is to represent the work content, but in some instances, it is used to represent an area, special functions, or an empirical parameter. No confusion should arise from this source because all special uses are described carefully in the text.

In accordance with the procedure of Lewis and Randall, a bar over a thermodynamic quantity has been used to represent its partial derivative with respect to the number of mols at constant pressure and temperature. Thus $\bar{F}$ is the partial molal free energy, $\bar{V}$ the partial molal volume.

A circle directly over a symbol representing distance indicates that it is expressed in Ångström units. Thus, if "a" is used for distance in centimeters, $\overset{\circ}{a}$ will represent this distance in Ångströms.

All vectors are in bold face type with the exception of the operator ∇. The dot and cross representations of products of vectors are used. Only four scalar quantities, **E**, **F**, **N** and **c**, representing electromotive force, Faraday charge, number of equivalents and the velocity of light are printed in bold face type.

Subscripts represent (a) ionic or molecular constituents. For example, $+$, $-$, i, j represent ionic constituents, 1, 2, $\cdots$ c, molecular components, w denotes water, v, vapor, etc. (b) The subscript $\pm$ is used to indicate a mean ionic quantity of an electrolyte. Thus, $\gamma_{\pm}$ is the mean molal activity coefficient, $m_{\pm}$ the mean molality. (c) The subscript zero is used to designate a property of the pure solvent. For example, d_0 and η_0 are the density and viscosity of a solvent.

The superscript zero has been used to indicate the value of a function in the standard state. The standard state is understood to be unit activity in aqueous solutions unless otherwise indicated (*e.g.*, by an asterisk).

There is, however, one use of the superscript zero which is not consistent with the above rules. We have represented the equivalent conductance of an electrolyte, and the equivalent conductance and transference number of an ion at infinite dilution by Λ^0, λ_i^0 and T_i^0, respectively. This choice of superscript rather than subscript was governed by the difficulty of describing all the conductance phenomena without multiple subscripts.

There is one innovation in symbols which is of considerable importance. A large number of the limiting theoretical equations reduce to a simple form. For example,

$$\log f_{\pm} = -\mathcal{S}_{(f)}\sqrt{\Gamma} = -\mathfrak{S}_{(f)}\sqrt{c}$$
$$L_2 = \mathcal{S}_{(L)}\sqrt{\Gamma} = \mathfrak{S}_{(L)}\sqrt{c}$$

and so forth for many properties. In these equations $\mathfrak{F}_{(f)}$, $\mathfrak{F}_{(L)}$, $\mathfrak{S}_{(f)}$, etc., are theoretical constants at constant pressure and temperature in a given medium. The subscript denotes the property under consideration. Since numerous graphs occur in which the left sides of these equations are plotted against the square root of concentration variables, these constants are limiting slopes and are referred to as such. We believe that the consistent use of this method of expression will avoid unnecessary confusion if generally adopted.

Not all of the symbols introduced into the text since the first edition will be found in the revised glossary. Many symbols representing special functions and complicated integrals, which appear only briefly in the course of mathematical deductions, have been excluded in order to keep the glossary from becoming unduly extended.

A, work content per mol.

$\bar{A}$, partial molal work content.

$\bar{A}_1$, $\bar{A}_2$, etc., $\bar{A}_i$, $\bar{A}_j$, etc., partial molal work content of components, etc., and ion constituents, etc., indicated by subscripts.

A, contribution to, (1) ΔA (el), electrical contribution to the work content [Equation (3–2–1)]; (2) $\Delta A_{(s)}$, contribution to the work content caused by addition of electrolyte [Equation (3–10–7)].

A^*_w, van der Waals co-volume contribution to the work content [Chapter (12), Section (8)].

A, A', characteristic parameters of equations (5–2–7) and (5–2–9). Important functions. Note that $A'_m = A' \sqrt{d_0}$.

A, area

A, special function given by equation (4–7–19).

A, special function [Chapter (12), Section (7)].

$A\Delta\alpha$, special function in Table (5–2–6), defined by equation (5–2–17).

A, A_n, A_{n-1}, A^*_{n-1}, A', A^*, etc., empirical coefficients.

A, characteristic parameter defined by equation (3-6-9).

$A(a)$, $A(k, m, a)$, functions in the theory of the Wien effect, Chapter (4), Section (8).

A_{ji}, A_{ij}, $A_{ji}(0)$, $A_{ij}(0)$, functions employed in Chapter (1), Section (14).

$\mathfrak{a}$, theoretical conductance parameter, equation (6-11-34).

a, field parameter in the theory of the Wien effect, equation (4-8-13).

a, activity.

a_1, a_2, $\cdots$, activities of components indicated.

a_+, a_-, a_i, a_j, conventional activities of ionic constituents indicated.

$a_\pm$, mean ionic activity of an electrolyte [Equation (1–6–3)].

a_R, activity of a component in a reference solution.

a_w, activity of water.

a_H, a_{OH}, etc., activities of ionic constituents indicated.

a_N, a_m, a_c, activity on N-, m-, and c-, concentration scales.

a'_s, activity of solid solvent at T'.

$a_1^{0'}$, activity of pure liquid solvent at T'.

a'_1, activity of solvent in solution at T'.

a'_2, activity of solute in solution at T'.

a'_v, activity of solvent vapor at T'.

a, mean distance of approach of ions defined by equation (14–1–5).

$\overset{\circ}{a}$, same in Ångström units.

a_i, a_j, mean ionic distances of approach of ions indicated.

$\overset{\circ}{a}_i$, $\overset{\circ}{a}_j$, same in Ångström units.

a, distance of approach of ions in theory of ionic pair formation [Chapter (3), Section (7)].

a_3, distance in triple ion formation equation (3–7–21).

a_4, distance in quadrupole formation equation (3–7–28).

a_{12}, a_{10}, a_{20}, mutual cohesive energy densities [Chapter (12), Section (7)].

a_μ^λ, element of rate of strain dyadic [Chapter (4), Section (2)].

a, a_0, a_1, a', a'', etc., coefficients of empirical equations.

$B_2(\kappa a)$, $B_3^*(\kappa a)$, $B_3(\kappa a)$, functions of extended theory [Equation (3–6–6)].

B, B', B'', B_{RI}, etc., coefficients of empirical equations.

$B_j(a)$, $B_j(k, m, a)$, functions in the theory of the Wien effect, Chapter (4), Section (8).

$B(\kappa a)$, conductance function defined by equation (4-9-16).

$b_\mu(\kappa a)$, function defined by equation (3-6-10).

b, characteristic parameter, Bjerrum's theory of ionic pair formation [Equation (3–7–7)].

b_3, characteristic parameter in theory of triple ion formation [Equation (3–7–21a)].

$\bar{b}$, function used in theory of effect of field on the dissociation of weak electrolytes, and given by equation (4–7–27).

b_j, ionic radius in salting theory [Chapter (3), Section (10)].

b, b_0, b_1, b', b'', b_c, b_m, etc., coefficients of empirical equations.

C_p, molal heat capacity at constant pressure.

C_{p_s}, molal heat capacity of solid.

C_{p_v}, molal heat capacity of vapor.

C_{p_1}, molal heat capacity of solvent.

$\bar{C}_p$, partial molal heat capacity.

$\bar{C}_{p_1}$, $\bar{C}_{p_2}$, partial molal heat capacities of components indicated.

$\bar{C}_p^0$, $\bar{C}_{p_1}^0$, $\bar{C}_{p_2}^0$, standard partial molal heat capacities.

C_n, function defined by equation (9–2–9).

C_n^*, function defined by equation (9–3–6).

C_{-2}, C_{-1}, C_0, C_1, C_2, coefficients in equation (11–9–3).

C', C^*, etc., coefficients of empirical equations.

c, velocity of light.

c_p, c_p^0, c_v, etc., specific heat capacities at constant pressure, or volume.

c, molar concentration in mols per 1000 cc. solution.

c_+, c_-, c_i, c_j, molar concentrations of constituents indicated.

$c_{\pm}$, mean molar concentration [Equation (1–8–8)].

c^*, concentration in equivalents per 1000 cc. solution.

c_u, molar concentration of undissociated electrolyte.

c_A^*, normality of ion constituent, A.

c_I^*, normality of indicator solution.

$c_I^{*\prime}$, initial normality of indicator solution.

$c(x)$, concentration of solute at a distance, x, from boundary of solution [Chapter (3), Section (11)].

c, number of components (Gibbs) in a system.

c_0, c_1, c_2, c_n, etc., coefficients defined by equations (4–3–52) and (4–3–53).

c, c_0, c', c'', c''', c_1, etc., coefficients of empirical equations.

D, dielectric constant of solution.

D_1, D_2, etc., dielectric constants of components indicated.

D_0, dielectric constant of solvent.

$\mathfrak{D}$, coefficient of diffusion [Equation (6–10–1)].

$\mathfrak{D}^v$, $\mathfrak{D}_A$, $\mathfrak{D}_{0,A}$, etc., special diffusion coefficients, Chapter (6), Section (10).

$\mathfrak{D}'$, diffusion function defined by equation (6-10-21).

$\mathfrak{D}^0$, coefficient of diffusion at infinite dilution.

$D_{\lambda\mu}^2$, second differential coefficients.

D', D^*, coefficients of empirical equations.

d, density of solution.

d_0, density of solvent.

$d(\ )$, complete differential.

d_1, d_2, d_{12}, d_+, d_-, $d_{\pm}$, diameters of constituents indicated [Chapter (12), Section (8)].

$d(\omega_j)$, function defined by equation (6-10-9).

$\mathbf{E}$, electromotive force of cell.

$\mathbf{E}^0$, standard electromotive force of cell.

$\mathbf{E}_N^0$, $\mathbf{E}_m^0$, $\mathbf{E}_c^0$, standard electromotive force of cell on the N-, m-, and c-scales.

$\mathbf{E}^{0*}$, standard electromotive force of cell in a mixed, or non-aqueous solvent.

$\mathbf{E}_{1(T)}$, $\mathbf{E}_{2(T)}$, electromotive forces of cells with transference.

$\mathbf{E}_{12}$, $\mathbf{E}_{21}$, etc., electromotive forces of certain cells without transference.

$\mathbf{E}_J$, liquid junction electromotive force.

$\mathbf{E}_{Ext.}$, contribution of extended terms of electromotive force.

$\mathbf{E}_{pH}^0$, constant in equation (10–7–2).

$\bar{E}_1$, $\bar{E}_2$, partial molal expansibilities of components indicated.

$\bar{E}_1^0$, $\bar{E}_2^0$, standard partial molal expansibilities.

$\bar{E}_2 - \bar{E}_2^0$, relative partial molal expansibility of component (2).

ξ, light absorption coefficient [Equation (15–4–11a)].

$Ei(\ )$, exponential integral function.

e, base of natural logarithm.

e, electrical charge.

$e_1, e_2, \cdots . e_s, e_i, e_j$, total electrical charge of ions indicated (carry sign).

$|e_1|, |e_2|, \cdots |e_s|, |e_i|, |e_j|$, magnitudes of charges on ions.

$\mathbf{F}$, Faraday charge.

$\mathbf{F}$, force per unit volume in equations (4-2-9) to (4-2-13).

$F(\kappa a)$, function defined by equation (6-11-14).

F, molal free energy.

F^0, standard molal free energy.

$F_1, F_2, \cdots F_c$, molal free energies of components indicated.

$F_1^0, F_2^0, \cdots F_c^0$, standard molal free energies of components indicated.

$\bar{F}_1, \bar{F}_2, \cdots \bar{F}_c$, partial molal free energies of components indicated.

$\bar{F}_1^0, \bar{F}_2^0, \cdots \bar{F}_c^0$, standard partial molal free energies of components indicated.

$\bar{F}_i, \bar{F}_j$, conventional partial molal free energies of ions indicated.

$\bar{F}_i^0, \bar{F}_j^0$, same in standard states.

$\bar{F}_N^0, \bar{F}_m^0, \bar{F}_c^0$, standard partial molal free energies on the N-, m-, and c-scales.

F_w^*, van der Waals' co-volume contribution to free energy [Chapter (12), Section (8)].

$\mathcal{F}$, force.

$F(\bar{b})$, special function given by equation (4–7–30).

$F(Z)$, special function given by equation (7–2–5).

$F_{ji}(\Omega)$, number of ions leaving interior, Ω, of region, S [Equation (4–6–7)].

f, rational activity coefficient.

$f_{(s)}$, rational activity coefficient of non-electrolyte.

f_+, f_-, f_i, f_j, conventional rational activity coefficients of ions indicated.

$f_\pm$, mean rational activity coefficient [Equation (1–8–4)].

$f_{\pm(s)}$, rational activity coefficient of electrolyte in salting equation (3–10–10).

$f_{\pm(t)}$, rational activity coefficient of electrolyte in equation (3–10–13) for transfer of electrolyte.

$f_{ij}(\mathbf{r}_2, \mathbf{r}_{12}), f_{ji}(\mathbf{r}_1, \mathbf{r}_{21}), f_{ji}, f_{ij}$, distribution functions according to equation (2–1–4).

f_{ji}^0, f_{ij}^0, distribution functions for solution in unperturbed state.

f_{ji}', f_{ij}', distribution functions for perturbed solutions.

f_c, f_m, special functions given by equation (12–10–7).

$f(x)$, function in theory of Wien effect [Equation (4–6–45), Table (5–3–6)]

f, f_p, functions of displacements, Chapter (1), Section (14).

G_{ji}, G_{ij}, G_{12}, G_{21}, G_{11}, G_{22}, $G(\mathbf{r})$, functions used in theory of frequency and field effects (Wien effect) upon conductance [Chapter (4), Sections (5) and (6)].

G_{r1}, G_{rn}, etc., coefficients of forces in the theory of irreversible processes, equation (1-14-10).

g, acceleration of gravity.

g, rational osmotic coefficient [Equation (1–9–5)].

$g(x)$, function in theory of Wien effect [Equation (4–6–48), Table (5–3–5)].

$g(c)$, special function in equation (7–4–10).

g, special function [Chapter (4), Section (7)].

H, molal heat content.

H_1, H_2, $\cdots H_c$, molal heat contents of components indicated.

$\bar{H}_1$, $\bar{H}_2$, $\cdots \bar{H}_c$, partial molal heat contents of components indicated.

$\bar{H}_i$, $\bar{H}_j$, conventional partial molal heat contents of ions indicated.

H^0, standard molal heat content.

H_1^0, H_2^0, $\cdots H_c^0$, standard molal heat contents of components indicated.

$\bar{H}_1^0$, $\bar{H}_2^0$, $\cdots \bar{H}_c^0$, standard partial molal heat contents of components indicated.

$\bar{H}_i^0$, $\bar{H}_j^0$, conventional standard partial molal heat contents of ions indicated.

h, height.

h, function of κa defined by equation (5-2-24).

h_{ji}, h'_{ji}, elements of matrix [Chapter (4), Section (3)].

H, changes in, ΔH_D, heat of dilution; $\Delta H_{D(s)}$, $\Delta H_{D(a)}$, $\Delta H_{D(b)}$, heats of dilution of salt, acid and base; ΔH_n, heat of neutralization; $\Delta H_n^* = \Delta H_n - \Delta H_{D(s)}(m \rightarrow m')$; ΔH_i^0, heat of ionization.

I_0, intensity of light before traversing solution.

I, intensity of light after traversing solution.

$I(b_3)$, special function in theory of triple ion formation [Equation (3–7–25), Table (5–2–4)].

$\imath$, electric current.

$\mathbf{i}$, vector electric current.

i, characteristic constant in equation (8–7–28b)

$J (\equiv \bar{C}_p - \bar{C}_p^0)$, relative partial molal heat capacity.

J_1, J_2, $\cdots J_c$, relative partial molal heat capacities of components indicated.

$J_{2(T_R)} = J_2$, at a reference temperature, T_R.

$\mathbf{J}$, flow of ions [Equation (4–4–1)].

$\mathbf{J}_i$, $\mathbf{J}_j$, flow of i ion, j ion.

$(J_i)_I$, $(J_i)_{II}$, $(J_i)_I(\kappa)$, special functions in Debye's theory of salting effect [Equations (3–10–44) to (3–10–49)].

$J(b_3, x)$, special function in theory of triple ion formation [Equation (3–7–26)].

J, function defined by equation (6-11-35).

J_1, J_2, functions defined by equations (6-11-21) and (6-11-22).

J, mole number, equation (6-12-7).

j, valence factor, equation (14-10-5); hydration number, equation (12-9-1).

j, function in freezing point theory [Equation (9–5–21)].

$\bar{K}_1$, $\bar{K}_2$, $\cdots \bar{K}_c$, partial molal compressibilities of components indicated.

$\mathbf{K}_i$, $\mathbf{K}_j$, total forces on ions.

K, equilibrium constant.

K_A, acid ionization constant.

K_B, base ionization constant.

K_w, ionization constant of water.

K_{2A}, second ionization constant of dibasic acid.

K_h, equilibrium constant of hydrolytic reaction.

K_θ, maximum value of ionization constant at temperature, θ.

K_A^*, specially defined ionization constants used in treatment of medium effects [Chapter (15), Section (7)].

K^*, K_A^*, $\bar{K}_2^{0*}$, etc., indicated quantities defined in terms of unusual reference state.

K_3, dissociation constants for triple ions.

K_4, dissociation constants for quadruple ion aggregates.

$K(X)$, $K(0)$, ionization constants with, and without external field.

K^2, special function given by equation (4–5–9).

$\mathcal{K}_{(H)}$, special function given by equation (3–8–8).

$\mathcal{K}_{(V)}$, special function given by equation (3–9–5).

k, Boltzmann constant.

k, valence factor, equation (14-10-5).

k, valence factor in the theory of the Wien effect, equation (4-8-19).

k, function of κa defined by equation (5-2-26).

k_{AB}, k_{BA}, k_{BC}, etc., kinetic constants, equation (1-13-26).

$\mathbf{k}_i$, $\mathbf{k}_j$, external forces on ions.

$\mathbf{k}_0$, force acting in molecules of solvent.

k, k_0, bulk compression of solution and solvent [Equation (8-7–16)].

$k(\equiv 2.3026\ RT/\mathbf{NF})$ [Equation (11–2–3), etc.].

k_1, constant in equation (4–1–18).

k_1, k_2, kinetic constants in equation (14–1–3).

k_s, k_m, k_N, salting coefficients on c-, m-, and N-scales.

$k_w(\equiv m_H m_{OH})$.

$k_A(\equiv m_H m_R/m_{HR})$.

$k_h\ (\equiv m_{HR} m_{OH}/m_R)$.

k_A', k_{0A}', special functions [Chapter (15), Section (7)].

$\bar{L}_1$, $\bar{L}_2$, relative partial molal heat contents of components indicated.

$\bar{L}_{2(T_R)}$, $\bar{L}_2$ at reference temperature, T_R.

L_s', relative molal heat content of solid at T'.

$L_{s(0)}$, relative molal heat content of solid at T_0.
L'_v, heat of vaporization at T'.
$L_{v(0)}$, heat of vaporization at T_0.
L, specific conductivity of solution.
L_0, specific conductivity of solvent.
$L^*(\equiv L - L_0)$.
L, constant in equation (8–7–28b).
l, length.
l, wave length [Equation (5–3–13)].

M, molecular weight.
M_1, M_2, molecular weight of components indicated.
M_X, M_Y, molecular weights of components of a binary mixture of solvents.
M_{XY}, mean molecular weight [Equation (1–8–16)].
M'_j, effective molecular weight defined by equation (1-15-47).
$\mathfrak{M}_{ij}$, $\mathfrak{M}_{12}$, etc., admittance matrix notation used in Chapter (1), Section (13).
$\mathfrak{M}$, $\Delta\mathfrak{M}$, $\mathfrak{M}_{ik}$, $\mathfrak{M}_{ki}$, $\Delta\overline{\mathfrak{M}}'$, $\Delta\overline{\mathfrak{M}}''$, functions in diffusion theory [Chapter (4), Section (4)].
m, molality (concentration in mols per 1000 g. of solvent).
m, mobility function defined by equation (4-8-19).
m_R, reference molality.
m_1, $m_2, \cdots m_c$, molalities of components indicated.
m_i, m_j, m_+, m_-, molalities of ions indicated.
$m_\pm$, mean molality of ions of an electrolyte [Equation (1–8–7)].
m_H, m_{Cl}, m_{HSO_4}, etc., molalities of ions indicated.
m'_H, etc., apparent hydrogen ion. etc.. concentration.
$\mathbf{N}$, number of Faraday equivalents.
N, Avogadro's number.
N_1, $N_2 \cdots N_c$, mol fractions of components indicated.
N_w, mol fraction of water.
$N_\pm$, mean mol fraction of electrolytic component [Equation (1–8–3)].
N_1^0, N_2^0, mol fractions at great distance from ion [Chapter (3), Section (10)].
n, revolutions per second in centrifuge equations.
$\bar{n}_A$, $\bar{n}_B$, $\bar{n}_C$, equilibrium concentrations, equation (1-13-27).
n, valence function defined by equation (3-6-8).
n_1, $n_2, \cdots n_c$, number of mols of components indicated.
$\mathfrak{n}_1$, $\mathfrak{n}_2, \cdots \mathfrak{n}_s$, number of ions of kind indicated per cc.
n, n', number of mols of non-electrolyte, and electrolyte [Chapter (3), Section (10)].
n_{ji}, number of i ions in the presence of j ion.
n_{ij}, number of j ions in the presence of i ion.
n_{ji}^0, n_{ij}^0, same (solution unperturbed)
n'_{ji}, n'_{ij}, same (solution perturbed).

P, total external pressure.

P_0, initial total external pressure [Chapter (8), Section (7)].

P_e, effective pressure [Chapter (8), Section (7)].

P_2, molecular polarization [Equation (7-4-22)].

P_i, experimental slope at x_i [Equation (8-2-17)].

$\bar{P}_i$, defined by equation (8-2-15).

$\mathscr{P}(\equiv m_+'^{+}m_-'^{-})$ where m_+, m_- are molalities of ions of saturating salt.

$\mathscr{P}_{(0)}(\equiv\mathscr{P})$ in pure solvent.

$\mathscr{P}_1(\equiv\mathscr{P})$ of component 1 in salt solution.

$\mathscr{P}_{1(0)}(\equiv\mathscr{P})$ of component 1 in pure solvent.

p_1, p_2, $\cdots p_c$, partial pressures of components indicated.

p_1, p_2, p_3, parameters defined by equations (6·11-11) to (6-11-13).

p_{jn}, p_{j1}, p_{j3}^{*}, coefficients in the series equation (4-8-38). Table (5-3-7).

p_0, vapor pressure of solvent.

p, vapor pressure of solution.

pH($\equiv \log 1/a_{H^+}$).

p, constant of equation (15-6-6).

Q, current density of heat, equation (1-15-4).

$\tilde{Q}_i$, heat of transport of an ion, equation (1-15-7).

Q_i^{*}, total heat of transport of an ion including partial ionic heat content, equation (1-15-14).

Q, quantity of heat.

Q, special function given by equation (5-3-6).

$\bar{Q}$, special function given by equation (4-5-24).

$Q(b)$, function in theory of ion pair formation [Equation (3-7-10), Table (5-2-3)].

q, function in theory of ionic association [Equation (3-7-4)].

q^{*}, function in theory of irreversible processes [Equation (4-3-34)].

R, gas constant per mol.

$R_{\tilde{\omega}}$, electrical resistance at frequency, $\tilde{\omega}$.

R_∞, electrical resistance at infinite frequency.

$\bar{R}$, characteristic distance given by equation (3-10-27)

$\bar{R}_j$, special function given by (3-10-38).

$\bar{R}$, special function in theory of frequency effects given by equation (4-5-24).

R, distance in equation (3-7-21).

$\mathfrak{R}$, concentration ratio, equation (6-12-12).

R_{11}, R_{12}, R_{ij}, etc., resistance matrix notation used in Chapter (1), Section (15).

R_n, R_3^{*}, coefficients in the series equation (4-8-37). Table (5-3-7).

r, distance.

$\mathbf{r}$, vector distance.

$\mathbf{r}_1, \mathbf{r}_2, \mathbf{r}_3, \cdots \mathbf{r}_{12}, \mathbf{r}_{21}$, variable vector distances.

r_+, r_-, ionic radii.

$r_j, r_j^0, r_j^{(n)}$, functions defined by equations (4–3–54) and (4–3–55).

S, entropy.

S, solubility of neutral molecule in salt solution.

S^0, solubility of neutral molecule in pure solvent.

S, experimental slope of plot.

S^0, experimental slope when $x_i = 0$ [Equation (8–2–17)].

S_{C_p}, S_V, S_E, S_K, experimental slopes for partial molal heat capacity, apparent molal volume, apparent molal expansibility and apparent molal compressibility.

$\mathcal{S}_{(f)}, \mathcal{S}_{(L)}, \mathcal{S}_{(J)}, \mathcal{S}_{(\lambda)}, \mathcal{S}_{(T+)}$, etc., limiting theoretical slopes of quantities indicated. Variable is $\sqrt{c}$.

$\pmb{\mathcal{S}}_{(f)}, \pmb{\mathcal{S}}_{(L)}, \pmb{\mathcal{S}}_{(J)}, \pmb{\mathcal{S}}_{(\lambda)}, \pmb{\mathcal{S}}_{(T+)}$, etc., limiting theoretical slopes of quantities indicated. Variable is $\sqrt{\Gamma}$.

$S_{xy}, S_{yx}, S_{mn}, S_{nm}$, etc., elements of stress dyadic.

$S_{xy}^*, S_{yx}^*, S_{mn}^*, S_{nm}^*$, etc., electrostatic contribution to stresses.

$\check{S}(\mathbf{J}_n)$, entropy change defined by equation (1-13-20).

$\check{S}^*(\mathbf{J}_n)$, entropy change defined by equation (1-13-19).

S_{xy}^0, S_{mn}^0, etc., stress elements between neutral solvent molecules.

$S(Z)$, special conductance function given by equation (7–2–13).

T, absolute temperature.

T', freezing point, or boiling point of solution.

T_0, freezing point, or boiling point of solvent.

T_R, reference temperature.

$T_1, T_2, \cdots T_+, T_-, T_i, T_j$, transference numbers of constituents indicated.

$T_+^0, T_-^0, T_i^0, T_j^0$, limiting transference numbers of ions indicated.

T_A, transference number [Equation (6–5–2)].

T_A', apparent transference number [Equation (6–5–1)].

T_R, transference number at reference concentration.

$T_+^{0'}$, transference number function given by equation (6–7–1).

t, degrees centigrade.

t, time in seconds.

t_i, t_j, time in which i ion, or j ion is in element of volume [Chapter (2), Section (1)].

t_{ij}, t_{ji}, time in which j ions or i ions are in given elements of volume, respectively [Chapter (2), Section (1)].

t_{ji}, matrix element defined by equation (4–3–56).

U, energy.

U^0, standard energy.

U_{ij}, U_{ji}, potential energy of j ion in presence of i ion, and vice versa.

U_0, energy of triple ion when $\theta = 0$ [Equation (3–7–17)].

$U(\mathfrak{r})$, function in theory of Wien effect [Equation (4–6–27)].

u, velocity of sound [Equation (8–7–29)].

u_i, u_j, mobilities of ions ($\equiv v_i/X$), for unit potential gradient (c.g.s. units).

$\bar{u}_i$, $\bar{u}_j$, mobilities of ions (practical units).

$\bar{u}_i^0$, $\bar{u}_j^0$, limiting mobilities of ions (practical units).

$\mathbf{V}(\mathfrak{r}_1)$, $\mathbf{V}(\mathfrak{r}_2)$, velocity of solution as a whole.

V, total volume.

V, molal volume.

V, potential in volts/cm.

V_1, V_2, $\cdots$, molal volumes of components indicated.

$\bar{V}_1$, $\bar{V}_2$, $\cdots$, partial molal volumes of components indicated.

$\bar{V}_i$, $\bar{V}_j$, conventional partial molal volumes of ions indicated.

$\bar{V}_1^0$, $\bar{V}_2^0$, $\cdots$, $\bar{V}_i^0$, $\bar{V}_j^0$, $\cdots$, partial molal volumes in standard states.

V^*, critical disruptive volume [(Chapter (8), Section (5)].

$V_s (\equiv \nu_1 V_1 + \nu_2 V_2)$ [Chapter (12), Section (7)].

$\bar{V}_2^{0*}$, ΔV^*, etc., indicated quantities defined in terms of an unusual reference state.

v, velocity.

$\mathbf{v}$, vector velocity.

$\mathbf{v}_i$, $\mathbf{v}_j$, velocities of ions indicated.

$\mathbf{v}_{ji}$, velocity of i ion in the presence of the j ion.

$\mathbf{v}_{ij}$, velocity of j ion in the presence of the i ion.

v_x, v_y, v_z, components of velocity.

v_1, v_2, volume constants in theory of salting effects [Chapter (3), Section (10)].

v, v_0, specific volume of solution, of pure solvent.

W, work.

W(el), electrical work.

$W_{ji}(r)$, mutual potential of the average forces between ions, i and j [Equation (4–7–3)].

$W(x)$, work required to bring a molecule, or ion, from interior of solution (depth $= x$) to surface [Equation (3–11–1)].

$W(n_j)$, $W'(n)$, $W(\kappa)$, electrical work expressions [Equations (3–10–1), (3–10–2), and (3–10–3)].

W_t, electrical work of transfer [Equation (3–10–12)].

$\mathfrak{W}_{(H)}$, special function defined by equation (3–8–7).

$\mathfrak{W}_{(r)}$, special function defined by equation (3–9–4).

w, function given by equation (5-2-1).

w', function given by equation (5-2-4).

w'', function given by equation (5-2-10).

w^*, function given by equation (5-3-7).

X, electrical field.

$\mathbf{X}$, vector electric field.

$\mathbf{X}_1$, $\mathbf{X}_2$, etc., vector forces, Chapter (1), Section (13).

X_1, X_A, etc., components of forces, Chapter (1), Section (13).

$X_{\bar{\omega}}$, electrical field strength at frequency, $\bar{\omega}$.

ΔX_j, field acting upon j ion due to both ionic atmosphere and electrophoresis effects.

$X_{2m+1}(\kappa a)$, $X_3(\kappa a)$, $X_5(\kappa a)$, $X_2(\kappa a)$, $X_3^*(\kappa a)$, functions in extended theory [Equations (3-6-4), (3-6-6), Table (5-2-2)].

X, represents various special functions given by equations (3-7-21), (3-8-12), (9-5-17), and (11-9-2).

X_T, special function given by equation (11-9-2).

X, Y, weight percentages of components of a mixture of two miscible solvents.

$x_1, y_1, \cdots X_1, Y_1, \cdots x_1', y_1', \cdots X_1', Y_1' \cdots$, numbers of mols. Special use [Chapter (1), Section (10)].

x, various functions used as variables.

x, special function given by equation (4-6-43).

x_A, x_B, x_C, concentration displacements, Chapter (1), Section (13).

$Y_{2m+1}(\kappa a)$, $Y_3(\kappa a)$, $Y_5(\kappa a)$, functions in extended term theory [Equations (3-6-4), (3-6-6), Table (5-2-2)].

Y, Y_c, Y_f, Y', Y_c', Y_f', y^2, function in surface tension theory [Equations (3-11-14), (3-11-15), Table (5-2-6)].

Y, variable defined by equation (3-7-6).

$Y(r)$, function given by equation (4-6-18).

y, molar activity coefficient.

$y_\pm'$, special molar activity coefficient defined by equation (3-6-7).

y_+, y_-, y_1, y_2, y_H, etc., molar activity coefficients of constituents indicated.

$y_\pm$, mean molar activity coefficient of an electrolyte [Equation (1-8-6)].

y_u, molar activity coefficient of an undissociated molecule.

y, various functions used as variables.

Z, special function given by equation (7-2-6).

Z_2', average number of molecules surrounding an ion. [Chapter (3), Section (10)].

Z_2^0, number of molecules of component (2) at disposal of ion [Chapter (3), Section (10)].

Z_2, number of molecules in solution after addition of electrolyte [Chapter (3), Section (10)].

z, valence.

z_i, z_j, valences of ions indicated (carry sign of charge).

$|z_i|$, $|z_j|$, $|z_+|$, $|z_-|$, magnitudes of valences of ions indicated.

z, function given by equation (12-4-5).

z, various functions used as variables. See equations (6-11-47) and (12-4-5).

α, degree of dissociation in general.

α_0, degree of dissociation in absence of external field [Chapter (4), Section (7)].

α, coefficient of expansion of solution [Chapter (8)].

α_0, coefficient of expansion of solvent [Chapter (8)].

α^*, coefficient of conductance equation (5-3-4).

α, empirical coefficient in equations for heat data.

$\bar{\alpha}$, special function defined by equation (3-10-37).

α_{12}, α_{21}, empirical coefficients in equations for mixed electrolytes [Chapter (14)].

α', function defined by equation (6-11-5).

α_j, α_p, α_1^r, α_2^r, $\cdots$, α_1', α_2', etc., displacements in the theory of irreversible processes, Chapter (1), Section (14).

α_1, α_2, $\cdots$, α_s, α_p, special quantities used in Chapter (4), Section (3A).

β, coefficient of compression of solution [Chapter (8)].

β_s, adiabatic coefficient of compression [Equation (8-7-29)].

β_0, coefficient of compression of solvent [Chapter (8)].

β^*, coefficient of conductance equation (5-3-5).

β, empirical coefficient in equations for heat data.

$\bar{\beta}$, $\bar{\beta}'$, empirical constants, salting theory [Chapter (3), Section (10)].

β_{12}, β_{21}, empirical coefficients in equations for mixed electrolytes [Chapter (14)].

β, special function defined by equation (4-7-14).

β', function defined by equation (6-11-6).

$\Gamma(\equiv \Sigma c_i z_i^2)$, ional concentration.

Γ_2, mols of solute negatively absorbed per unit increase in surface tension [Equation (1-11-1)].

$\Gamma(r)$, special function in theory of Wien effect [Equations (4-6-24)].

Γ_1, Γ_2, etc., $\Gamma'_{1\ldots n}$, special representation of states in Chapter (1), Section (14).

γ, molal activity coefficient.

γ_+, γ_-, γ_i, γ_j, conventional activity coefficients of ions indicated.

$\gamma_\pm$, mean molal activity coefficient of an electrolyte [Equation (1-8-5)].

γ_R, reference activity coefficient at a concentration, m_R.

γ_u, activity coefficient of an undissociated molecule.

$\gamma_{(s)}$, activity coefficient of a non-electrolyte.

$\gamma'_{\pm}$, $\gamma''_{\pm}$, activity coefficients at temperatures T' and T''.

$\gamma_{H(H)}$, $\gamma_{Cl(H)}$, $\gamma_{H(K)}$, etc., interaction coefficients [Chapter (14), Section (5)].

$\gamma_{(H+K)}$, $\gamma_{(Cl)}$, etc., salting out coefficient [Chapter (14), Section (5)].

$\gamma_{HCl(MCl)}$, etc., activity coefficient of HCl in a solution of MCl, etc., for other mixtures.

γ_0, γ^0, γ_0^0, γ^*, γ_A, γ_{0A}, γ_A^*, γ'_A, γ'_{0A}, specially defined activity coefficients used in theory of medium effects [Chapter (15), Section (7)].

$\gamma_{(0)1}$, $\gamma_{0(2)}$, $\gamma_{1(0)}$, $\gamma_{2(0)}$, special activity coefficients used in theory of mixed electrolytes [Equations (14–5–1) and (14–5–2)].

γ_a, special activity coefficient used in Chapters (11) and (13).

$\Delta(\ )$, finite increase in quantity, ( ).

∇, ∇_1, ∇_2, vector operator, nabla or del.

$\nabla\cdot\nabla$, Laplacian operator.

Δ, conductance deficiency [Chapter (6), Section (3)].

Δ, deviation.

$\Delta_{\text{ave.}}$, average deviation.

$\partial(\ )$, partial differential

$\delta(\ )$, variation.

$\delta_{ji} = \begin{Bmatrix} 1; j=i \\ 0; j\neq i \end{Bmatrix}$, Kronecker symbol.

δ, special function given by equation (5–2–13).

δ_i, special function given by equation (8–2–18).

δ, special functions. See equations (5-2-13) and (6-11-32).

δ, δ_0, functions given by equation (8-7-30).

δ_+, δ_-, functions given by equation (12-13-1).

ϵ, electronic charge.

ζ, special activity coefficient, a/n [Chapter (4), Section (4)].

η, viscosity of solution.

η_0, viscosity of solvent.

η^*, contribution to viscosity of solution caused by ionic interaction.

η', special function defined by equation (4–6–35).

$\cdot\vartheta$, freezing point depression.

ϑ, empirical constant [Equation (15–8–2)], temperature at which ionization constant is a maximum in salt solution.

θ, boiling point elevation.

θ, empirical constant [Equation (15–6–6)], temperature at which ionization constant is a maximum.

θ, angle variable.

θ, function defined by equation (8-8-16).

$\theta_1(a)$, $\theta_2(a)$, $\theta_3(a)$, functions defined by equations (6-11-23) to (6-11-25).

$\theta(k, m, a)$, function defined by equation (5-3-21).

κ, reciprocal of average radius of ionic atmosphere. Defined by equation (2-4-11).

$\kappa_1^2 (\equiv q^* \kappa^2)$ by equation (4-3-33).

κ_I, κ_{II}, functions in equation (4-5-14).

Λ, equivalent conductance of electrolyte.

Λ^0, limiting equivalent conductance of electrolyte at infinite dilution.

Λ_m, molar conductance.

Λ_m^0, limiting molar conductance.

$\Lambda_{\tilde{\omega}}$, molar conductance at frequency, $\tilde{\omega}$.

$\Lambda_{I\tilde{\omega}}$, contribution to molar conductance due to frequency, $\tilde{\omega}$.

Λ_{II}, contribution to molar conductance caused by electrophoresis.

$\Lambda_{I(0)}$ is $\Lambda_{I\tilde{\omega}}$ when $\tilde{\omega}=0$.

$\Lambda^{0\prime}$, special conductance function given by equation (6-3-7).

Λ', special conductance function given by equation (6-6-3).

Λ'', conductance function given by equation (6-11-20).

Λ''', conductance function given by equation (6-11-19).

Λ_X, conductance in field of strength, X.

λ, λ_1, λ_2, $\cdots \lambda_i$, functions used in Chapter (1), Section (15).

λ_+, λ_-, λ_i, λ_j, λ_1, λ_2, equivalent conductance of ions indicated.

λ_+^0, λ_-^0, λ_i^0, λ_j^0, λ_1^0, λ_2^0, limiting equivalent conductances of ions indicated at infinite dilution.

λ, molal freezing point lowering.

λ^*, molal boiling point elevation.

λ, wave length of light.

λ_1, λ_2, λ_3, λ_4, special variables defined by equation (4-6-39) and (4-6-40).

λ, λ_1, λ_2, empirical constants in equations (12-6-3) and (12-6-4).

μ, chemical potential.

μ^0, chemical potential of standard state.

μ_1, μ_2, $\cdots \mu_c$, chemical potentials of components indicated.

μ_i, μ_j, conventional chemical potentials of ions indicated.

μ_1^0, μ_2^0, $\cdots \mu_c^0$, μ_i^0, μ_j^0, chemical potentials in standard states.

μ_1', μ_1'', $\cdots \mu_1^p$, chemical potentials of component (1) in each of p phases.

μ_2', μ_2'', $\cdots \mu_2^p$, same for component (2).

$\bar{\mu}_i$, $\bar{\mu}_j$, electrochemical potentials [Equation (10-6-19)].

$\bar{\mu}$, chemical potential in ergs per mol [Chapter (4), Section (4)].

$\bar{\mu}_j$, special chemical potential, equation (1-15-2).

μ, running index used in Chapter (3), Section (6).

μ, μ_s, dipole strength, equations (6-11-49), (7-3-9) and (7-4-22).

μ, dipole strength [Chapter (7), Section (4)].

μ, contributions to, (1) $\Delta\mu_j(\text{el})$, electrical contribution to chemical potential, (2) $\Delta\mu_{(s)}$, contribution to chemical potential of nonelectrolyte caused by addition of electrolyte [Equation (3-10-8)].

$\mu(\equiv\frac{1}{2}\Sigma m_i z_i^2)$, ionic strength.

μ', approximated "real" ionic strength [Equation (13–3–6) *et seq.*

$\mu'(\equiv eX/kT)$, special use in theory of Wien effect [Equation (4–6–36)].

$\mu_i(\equiv\Gamma_i/\Gamma)$ [Equation (4–3–57)].

ν_+, ν_-, numbers of cations, anions produced by dissociation of one molecule of electrolyte.

$\nu(\equiv\nu_++\nu_-)$.

ν_R, ν of a reference solute.

ν_{ji}, number of molecules which dissociate [Chapter (4), Sections (1) and (7)].

ξ_1, ξ_2, $\cdots$ ξ_6, space coordinates.

$\dot{\xi}_1$, $\dot{\xi}_2$, $\cdots$ $\dot{\xi}_6$, corresponding velocities.

$\xi(r)$, special function given by equation (4–2–20).

Π, product

$\pi(=3.1416)$.

π^0, standard electrode potential.

ρ, density in general.

ρ_i, ρ_j, coefficients of friction of ions indicated.

$\bar{\rho}$, $\bar{\rho}^2$, functions defined by equations (4–2–25) and (4–2–26).

$\overline{1/\rho}$, function defined by equation (4–1–9).

Σ, summation.

σ, as a subscript, represents summation.

σ, surface tension of solution.

σ_0, surface tension of solvent.

σ, electrical conductance, special use [Chapter (4), Sections (1) and (7)].

σ, special function given by equation (3–10–34).

σ, special function defined by equation (9–5–7).

σ_m, special function defined by equation (9–5–11).

σ, $\sigma(\alpha_1, \alpha_2, \cdots)$, entropy in Chapter (1), Section (14).

σ_A, σ_B, characteristic parameters used in Chapter (6), Section (10).

$\sigma_{1...n}$, function used in the theory of irreversible processes, equation (1-14-14).

τ, τ_0, τ_f, time intervals, Chapter (1), Section (14).

τ, function of κa defined by equation (8-8-2).

τ, time of relaxation.

τ', Langevin time lags [Chapter (4), Sections (1) and (7)].

$\bar{\tau}(\equiv\tau q^*)$, equation (4–5–8).

Φ, total free energy in salting theory [Equation (3–10–17)].

Φ_V, mean apparent molal volume, equation (8-9-5).

$\Phi(\mathbf{J}, \mathbf{J})$, $\phi(\mathbf{J}, \mathbf{J})$, dissipation functions, equations (1-13-21) and (1-13-13).

ϕ, gravitational potential, equations (1-15-2) and (1-15-45).

ϕ_1, ϕ_2, ϕ_3, ϕ_4, functions used in Chapter (4), Section (9). See Table (5-3-1a).

ϕ, practical osmotic coefficient, defined by equation (1-9-6).

ϕ', osmotic coefficient at freezing, or boiling point.

ϕ_R, osmotic coefficient of reference solution.

ϕ_x, $\phi_{2(0)}$, $\phi_{1(0)}$, osmotic coefficients used in describing mixtures [Chapter (14), Section (5)].

ϕ_H, ϕ_L, ϕ_{Cp}, ϕ_V, ϕ_K, etc., apparent molal quantities as indicated.

ϕ_H^0, ϕ^0, etc., standard apparent molal quantities at infinite dilution.

$\phi'_{H(s)}$, $\phi_{H(a)}$, $\phi_{H(b)}$, apparent molal heat contents of salt, acid, and base [Equation (8-3-2)].

ϕ'_H, ϕ''_H, apparent molal heats of dilution at concentrations, m' and m''.

ϕ_1, ϕ_2, free energies per molecule in salting effect theory [Chapter (3), Section (10)].

$\phi(\kappa a)$, special function given by equation (4-3-23a).

ϕ, special variable in equation (4-6-51).

ϕ_V^*, function in equation (8-5-14).

ϕ, angle variable.

$\psi^*(\equiv \phi_V^*/V^*)$, function used in Chapter (8), Section (5).

ψ, electrical potential.

$\psi'-\psi''$, difference in electrical potential.

ψ_i, ψ_j, electrical potentials of ions and their atmospheres.

ψ_i^0, ψ_j^0, electrical potentials of ions and their atmospheres for unperturbed solution.

ψ'_i, ψ'_j, electrical potentials of ions and their atmospheres for perturbed solution.

$\psi_{i(0)} = \psi_{i(r=0)}$.

ψ_{ij}, potential of i ion in the presence of j ions.

ψ_{ji}, potential of j ion in the presence of i ions.

ψ_{ij}^0, ψ_{ji}^0, same for unperturbed solutions.

ψ'_{ij}, ψ'_{ji}, same for perturbed solution.

ψ_j^{0*}, potential due to ionic atmosphere.

ψ_1, ψ_2, apparent specific volumes of solvent and solute in solution

ψ, volume change on mixing, equation (8-9-8).

$\psi(d)$, function defined by equation (6-10-4).

$\chi(q_i^*, \tilde{\omega}\tau)$, function given by equation (4-5-19).

χ_R, function given by equation (4-5-23).

Ω, $\Omega_{\tilde{\omega}}$, functions used in conductance equations [Chapter (4), Section (5)].

$\Omega_{(H)}$, $\Omega_{(V)}$, functions of κa defined by equations (5-2-23) and (5-2-25).

ω, angular velocity.

ω_2, ω_3, valence factors, equation (8-9-7).

ω, mobility in general.

ω_i, ω_j, mobilities of ions in general ($\omega_i = 1/\rho_i$; $\omega_j = 1/\rho_j$).

$\tilde{\omega}$, frequency of alternating electrical field.

Contents

Chapter (1)

General Thermodynamic Introduction

The properties of electrolytic solutions fall naturally into two groups: (1) those determined by measurements of systems in equilibrium, and (2) those determined by measurements of systems in disturbed states. To the first group belong such properties as those derived from measurements of vapor pressure lowering, boiling point rise, freezing point lowering, solubility, specific heat, heat content, the potentials of galvanic cells, and surface tension. Properties derived from measurements of diffusion, electrical conductance, and viscosity comprise the second group, consideration of which will be reserved for later chapters. Reversible thermodynamics provides the formal method for treating systems in equilibrium and irreversible thermodynamics provides the basis for the treatment of steady state processes of which transport phenomena in electrolytic solutions are special cases. In this chapter, fundamental relations of both reversible and irreversible thermodynamics essential for subsequent developments are presented.

Reversible Thermodynamics

(1) Energy, Entropy, and the Chemical Potentials of Gibbs

The first law of thermodynamics will be expressed in a sufficiently general way if we regard the energy, U, of a phase as a function of the pressure, P, the volume, V, the temperature, T, the electrical charge, e, and the numbers of mols of each of the c components, n_1, n_2, $\cdots n_c$, in the phase. All other variables, such as surface, the force of gravity, external fields, etc., will be kept constant throughout the immediate discussions to follow. Later, the thermodynamic equation which involves surfaces of discontinuity will receive special attention. The energy of a phase in terms of these variables is

$$U = f(P, V, T, n_1, n_2, \cdots n_c, e) + U^0 \qquad (1\text{-}1\text{-}1)$$

in which U^0 is the energy in some arbitrary standard state. Since any one of the variables may be eliminated by the equation of state of the phase, the number of independent variables in the above expression is $c + 3$. The first law of thermodynamics requires that the increase in energy of a system, of constant composition and mass, is equal to the heat absorbed by the system plus the mechanical and electrical work done on the system by the surroundings. In the thermodynamic developments to

1

follow, the mechanical work will be confined to the effect of changes in the volume of the system; therefore

$$dU = dQ - PdV + dW(el) \qquad (1\text{-}1\text{-}2)$$

By further limiting this treatment to reversible processes only, P represents the equilibrium pressure of the system, and $dW(el)$ is the reversible electrical work. The second law of thermodynamics requires that the reversible heat absorbed by the system is

$$dQ = TdS \qquad (1\text{-}1\text{-}3)$$

whereby the entropy, S, is introduced. The combination of equations (1-1-2) and (1-1-3) can be extended[1] to include variations in composition by introducing the chemical potentials, $\mu_1 = \dfrac{\partial U}{\partial n_1}$, $\mu_2 = \dfrac{\partial U}{\partial n_2}$, etc., representing rates of change in energy per mol. Accordingly, our generalized representation of the first and second laws becomes

$$dU = TdS - PdV + \mu_1 \, dn_1 + \cdots \mu_c \, dn_c + \frac{\partial U}{\partial e} \, de \qquad (1\text{-}1\text{-}4)$$

for reversible processes. The term $\dfrac{\partial U}{\partial e} \, de$ is the reversible electrical work expressed in terms of the charge as independent variable.

(2) Heat Content, Work Content, and Free Energy

The heat content, H, work content, A, and free energy, F,[2] are defined by the equations

$$H = U + PV \qquad (1\text{-}2\text{-}1)$$

$$A = U - TS \qquad (1\text{-}2\text{-}2)$$

$$F = U - TS + PV = H - TS \qquad (1\text{-}2\text{-}3)$$

The differentials of these quantities can be written in the forms

$$dH = +TdS + VdP + \mu_1 \, dn_1 + \cdots \mu_c \, dn_c + \frac{\partial H}{\partial e} \, de \qquad (1\text{-}2\text{-}4)$$

$$dA = -SdT - PdV + \mu_1 \, dn_1 + \cdots \mu_c \, dn_c + \frac{\partial A}{\partial e} \, de \qquad (1\text{-}2\text{-}5)$$

$$dF = -SdT + VdP + \mu_1 \, dn_1 + \cdots \mu_c \, dn_c + \frac{\partial F}{\partial e} \, de \qquad (1\text{-}2\text{-}6)$$

---

[1] "The Scientific Papers of J. Willard Gibbs," Vol. I, p. 63, equation (12), and p. 338, equation (691). New York, Longmans, Green and Co. 1906.

[2] H, A, and F are the χ, ψ, and ζ functions of Gibbs, *loc. cit.*

consistent with the relations

$$\mu_1 = \left(\frac{\partial U}{\partial n_1}\right)_{S,V,n_2\cdots n_{c,e}} = \left(\frac{\partial H}{\partial n_1}\right)_{S,P,n_2\cdots n_{c,e}}$$
$$= \left(\frac{\partial A}{\partial n_1}\right)_{V,T,n_2\cdots n_{c,e}} = \left(\frac{\partial F}{\partial n_1}\right)_{P,T,n_2\cdots n_{c,e}} \cdots \tag{1-2-7}$$

Analogous definitional equations may be written for μ_2, $\cdots$ μ_c. Since μ_1 is less specific than any of the above differential coefficients, it is preferred as a basis for certain theoretical deductions.

By considering a system composed of p phases at constant temperature, pressure and charge, Gibbs was able to prove by equation (1-1-4), valid for each phase, that at equilibrium

$$\mu_1' = \mu_1'' = \cdots \mu_1^p$$
$$\mu_2' = \mu_2'' = \cdots \mu_2^p \tag{1-2-8}$$
$$\cdots\cdots\cdots\cdots\cdots$$
$$\mu_c' = \mu_c'' = \cdots \mu_c^p$$

if μ_1', μ_1'', $\cdots$ μ_1^p represents the chemical potentials of the first component, μ_2', μ_2'', $\cdots$ μ_2^p those of the second component, etc., throughout the p phases.

(3) Systems at Constant Composition and Charge

Since U, H, A, F, and S are always referred to some standard state, which in almost all applications is arbitrarily selected, we are especially interested in changes in these quantities, and introduce the operator symbol Δ to indicate such changes. Thus, $\Delta F \equiv \int_1^2 dF$, where the integration is from state 1 to state 2, and ΔF, ΔH, etc., may replace, F, H, etc., in the fundamental equations.

At constant composition and charge, equation (1-1-4) reduces to

$$dS = \frac{dU + PdV}{T} \tag{1-3-1}$$

By completely differentiating equation (1-2-3) and combining it with the above, we obtain

$$\left(\frac{\partial F}{\partial T}\right)_P = -S, \quad \text{or} \quad \left(\frac{\partial \Delta F}{\partial T}\right)_P = -\Delta S \tag{1-3-2}$$

and

$$\left(\frac{\partial F}{\partial P}\right)_T = V, \quad \text{or} \quad \left(\frac{\partial \Delta F}{\partial P}\right)_T = \Delta V \tag{1-3-3}$$

As a consequence of (1-3-2), equation (1-2-3) may be written as

$$\Delta F = \Delta H + T \left(\frac{\partial \Delta F}{\partial T} \right)_P$$

or

$$\left(\frac{\partial (\Delta F / T)}{\partial T} \right)_P = -\frac{\Delta H}{T^2} \tag{1-3-4}$$

(4) Systems at Constant Pressure, Temperature, and Charge. Partial Molal Quantities

Under these conditions, equation (1-2-6) reduces to

$$dF = \mu_1 \, dn_1 + \mu_2 \, dn_2 + \cdots \mu_c \, dn_c = \sum_1^c \mu_i \, dn_i \tag{1-4-1}$$

Since this equation is homogeneous and of the first degree in the extensive variables, n_1, n_2, $\cdots n_c$, it may be integrated at constant μ_1, μ_2, $\cdots \mu_c$ to yield[3]

$$F = \mu_1 n_1 + \mu_2 n_2 + \cdots \mu_c n_c = \sum_1^c \mu_i n_i \tag{1-4-2}$$

If this be divided by $(n_1 + n_2 + \cdots n_c) = \sum_1^c n_i$, we obtain

$$\frac{F}{\Sigma n_i} = \mu_1 N_1 + \mu_2 N_2 + \cdots \mu_c N_c = \sum_1^c \mu_i N_i \tag{1-4-3}$$

where

$$N_i = \frac{n_i}{\Sigma n_i} \tag{1-4-3a}$$

N_1, N_2, $\cdots N_c$ are the mol fractions of the c components, and $(F/\Sigma n_i)$ is the free energy per mol of phase. Because the terms μ_1, μ_2, $\cdots \mu_c$, at constant temperature and pressure, are the partial derivatives of the free energy with respect to the number of mols, they are designated as the partial molal free energies, and written $\bar{F}_1$, $\bar{F}_2$, $\cdots \bar{F}_c$. For typographical reasons, $F/\Sigma n_i$ will be written F, since we are usually concerned with molal quantities. When this is not the case, it will be made clear by the context.[4]

Complete differentiation of equation (1-4-2) gives

$$dF = \sum_1^c \mu_i \, dn_i + \sum_1^c n_i \, d\mu_i \tag{1-4-4}$$

[3] P. S. Epstein, "Textbook of Thermodynamics," p. 103, John Wiley and Sons, New York, 1937.

[4] This symbolism has been adopted to conform to the system of chemical thermodynamics most prevalent in the United States.

which, by combination with (1-4-1), yields the important equation

$$\sum_1^c n_i \, d\mu_i = 0, \quad \text{or} \quad \sum_1^c N_i \, d\mu_i = 0 \qquad (1\text{-}4\text{-}5)$$

interrelating the chemical potentials of the components of a phase, at constant temperature and pressure.

(5) SYSTEMS AT CONSTANT TEMPERATURE AND PRESSURE

THE REVERSIBLE GALVANIC CELL[5]

Consider a cell consisting of two electrodes connected by a solution of an electrolyte. Let $(\psi' - \psi'')$ be the difference in electrical potential between two pieces of the same metal attached to the two electrodes. Thus, if the cell is charged reversibly at constant temperature and pressure, the electrical work done upon the system will be $(\psi' - \psi'') \, de$, and this will equal the total increase in free energy. At constant temperature, pressure, and potential within each phase

$$dF_e = \sum_1^p \left(\frac{\partial F}{\partial e} \right)_{P,T,n_1 \cdots n_c} de = (\psi' - \psi'') \, de \qquad (1\text{-}5\text{-}1)$$

for the total electrical contribution to dF. It is important to note that the difference in potential, as defined above, is the quantity which is measured, and that the individual differences in potential between each of the two electrodes and the solution are not subject to separate measurement.[6]

At constant temperature and pressure, equation (1-2-6) yields for the total change in free energy of p phases the expression

$$dF = \sum_1^p \sum_1^c \mu_i \, dn_i + (\psi' - \psi'') \, de \qquad (1\text{-}5\text{-}2)$$

If all the changes in composition occur in one phase,

$$dF = \sum_1^c \mu_i \, dn_i + (\psi' - \psi'') \, de \qquad (1\text{-}5\text{-}2a)$$

As in the derivation of (1-4-2), this equation may be integrated to give

$$F = \sum_1^c \mu_i n_i + (\psi' - \psi'')e \qquad (1\text{-}5\text{-}3)$$

Complete differentiation of this expression yields

$$dF = \sum_1^c \mu_i \, dn_i + \sum_1^c n_i \, d\mu_i + (\psi' - \psi'') \, de + e \, d(\psi' - \psi'') \qquad (1\text{-}5\text{-}4)$$

---

[5] Such a cell, operating reversibly, has been termed "the perfect electrochemical apparatus" by Gibbs, *loc. cit.*, p. 338.

[6] "The Scientific Papers of J. Willard Gibbs," Vol. I, pp. 338–349, New York, Longmans, Green and Co., 1906.

which, by combination with (1-5-2a), becomes

$$\sum_1^c n_i \, d\mu_i + e \, d(\psi' - \psi'') = 0 \qquad (1\text{-}5\text{-}5)$$

This equation may be applied, under suitable conditions, to electrochemical cells containing liquid junctions.

An important feature of this equation is that only the whole of the electrical term is measurable. Consequently, the measurement of the electromotive force of a concentration cell permits the evaluation of the chemical potentials of the components as defined by Gibbs. It does not allow a similar evaluation of the potentials of each of the constituents of the components, or to be more specific, the potentials of the ions.

(6) THE ACTIVITY FUNCTION. THE ACTIVITY OF AN ELECTROLYTE

The equations appearing in the preceding sections contain all the variables, and are sufficiently general to provide thermodynamic background for all the systems which we shall discuss, except those which involve surface tension. By the use of the chemical potentials, it is possible to develop an adequate thermodynamics of solutions if suitable restrictions are imposed. In order to conform to the system most generally adopted in recent years, it is desirable to introduce additional, more restricted functions. In the application of thermodynamics to this subject, G. N. Lewis[7] introduced two new functions, *i.e.*, fugacity and activity. The latter has been employed extensively in solution thermodynamics, and its definition and general characteristics will be presented. For the sake of simplicity, we shall omit any considerations of the fugacity.[8] The activity, a_i, of a pure chemical species or constituent of a solution may be given general definition by the equation

$$\mu_i = RT \ln a_i + \mu_i^0 \qquad (1\text{-}6\text{-}1)$$

in which μ_i^0 is its chemical potential in some arbitrary standard state. We shall find that the value of μ_i^0 will depend on the concentration scales (molalities, mol fractions, etc.) in which a_i is expressed [Section (8)].

Expressing equation (1-6-1) by its equivalent in the notation of Section (4), the activity of a constituent of a solution may be defined by

$$\bar{F}_i = RT \ln a_i + \bar{F}_i^0 \qquad (1\text{-}6\text{-}2)$$

[7] G. N. Lewis, *Proc. Am. Acad. Sci.*, **37**, 45 (1901); **43**, 259 (1907).

[8] Detailed discussions of the general thermodynamics of these functions may be found in the following works: G. N. Lewis and M. Randall, "Thermodynamics," McGraw-Hill Book Co., New York, 1923; J. N. Brönsted, *J. Am. Chem. Soc.*, **42**, 761 (1920); N. Bjerrum, *Z. physik. Chem.*, **104**, 406 (1923); H. S. Harned, Chap. XII in H. S. Taylor, "Treatise on Physical Chemistry," First Edition, 1924, Second Edition, 1930, New York, D. Van Nostrand Co.

where $\bar{F}_i$ is the partial molal free energy of the constituent, and $\bar{F}_i^0$ is its value in some arbitrary standard state.

In solutions of an electrolyte, electro-neutrality imposes the condition that the number of mols of the individual ionic species cannot be varied independently. We must be careful, therefore, to refer to ionic species as constituents of the solution rather than as components, so that the latter term may retain the precise meaning assigned to it by Gibbs. A component is an independently variable constituent of a solution. Thus, in the system NaCl and H_2O there are two components whose chemical potentials can be measured by the application of thermodynamics alone. They are, of course, NaCl and H_2O. Although the ionic constituents Na^+ and Cl^- are of fundamental importance in determining the behavior and properties of the system, their concentrations are not independent variables. Thermodynamics does not permit the evaluation of the chemical potentials, free energies, activities, etc., of the individual ionic species. In spite of this limitation it is advantageous to express a number of thermodynamic developments in terms of "hypothetical" ionic activities, with the strict understanding that only certain ionic activity products, or ratios, have any real physical significance.

Convenient alternative expressions for the activity of an electrolyte are obtained upon consideration of the formal representation of its dissociation in solution.[9] This device has rendered important service in correlating the properties of electrolytes of different valence types. Thus, if an electrolyte, $C_{\nu_+}A_{\nu_-}$, dissociates into ν_+ cations and ν_- anions according to $C_{\nu_+}A_{\nu_-} \rightarrow \nu_+ C + \nu_- A$, then its activity may be written

$$a = a_+^{\nu_+} a_-^{\nu_-} = a_\pm^\nu \qquad (1\text{-}6\text{-}3)$$

where $\nu = \nu_+ + \nu_-$, a_+ and a_- are the conventional individual activities of the ionic constituents, and $a_\pm$ is termed the mean activity of the ions. Accordingly, the chemical potential and partial molal free energy of an electrolytic component of a solution may both be written

$$\mu - \mu^0 = RT \ln (a_+^{\nu_+} a_-^{\nu_-}) = \nu RT \ln a_\pm \qquad (1\text{-}6\text{-}4)$$

and

$$\bar{F} - \bar{F}^0 = RT \ln (a_+^{\nu_+} a_-^{\nu_-}) = \nu RT \ln a_\pm \qquad (1\text{-}6\text{-}5)$$

It is important to note that the activity function is more restricted than the chemical potential or partial molal free energy, because its definition usually involves the introduction of a separate standard state for each phase. Obviously the standard state must be clearly and unambiguously defined before the activity can be given a definite numerical value. To illustrate this matter, let us consider equation (1-2-8), which states that at

[9] G. N. Lewis and M. Randall, "Thermodynamics," New York, McGraw-Hill Book Co., 1923.

constant temperature, pressure, and charge the chemical potential of a component is the same in every phase. The definition of activity, however, requires that the statement of a similar proposition regarding the activity of a component be accompanied by the proper proviso. Thus, the activity of a component of a system at constant temperature, pressure, and charge is the same in every phase, *provided that it is defined in each phase in reference to the same standard state.* If this proviso is borne in mind, no real difficulty will be experienced in the investigation of polyphase systems by solubility, distribution, freezing point lowering, and similar means.

(7) VARIATION OF THE ACTIVITY WITH TEMPERATURE AND PRESSURE

According to equation (1-4-3), the relative free energy of one mol of solution will be given by

$$F - F^0 = N_1(\bar{F}_1 - \bar{F}_1^0) + N_2(\bar{F}_2 - \bar{F}_2^0) + \cdots \qquad (1\text{-}7\text{-}1)$$

and likewise, the relative heat content per mol of solution, by

$$H - H^0 = N_1(\bar{H}_1 - \bar{H}_1^0) + N_2(\bar{H}_2 - \bar{H}_2^0) + \cdots \qquad (1\text{-}7\text{-}2)$$

respectively. The first of these equations may be combined with the definition of activity in the preceding section to give

$$F - \bar{F}^0 = N_1 RT \ln a_1 + N_2 RT \ln a_2 + \cdots \qquad (1\text{-}7\text{-}3)$$

By substitution of these values for ΔF and ΔH in equation (1-3-4) and by performing the indicated partial differentiation with respect to temperature at constant composition and charge, we obtain

$$\left[\frac{N_1 \partial \ln a_1 + N_2 \partial \ln a_2 + \cdots}{\partial T} \right]_P$$
$$= -\frac{N_1(\bar{H}_1 - \bar{H}_1^0) + N_2(\bar{H}_2 - \bar{H}_2^0) + \cdots}{RT^2} \qquad (1\text{-}7\text{-}4)$$

This general equation is rarely used. It is more usual to limit the investigation to each component separately. Thus,

$$\left(\frac{\partial \ln a_i}{\partial T} \right)_P = \frac{-(\bar{H}_i - \bar{H}_i^0)}{RT^2} \qquad (1\text{-}7\text{-}5)$$

The relative partial molal heat content of the component, i, $(\bar{H}_i - \bar{H}_i^0)$ will be represented by $\bar{L}_i$ according to

$$\bar{L}_i \equiv \bar{H}_i - \bar{H}_i^0 \qquad (1\text{-}7\text{-}6)$$

Differentiation of this equation with respect to temperature at constant pressure serves to define the important quantities, the partial molal heat capacity, $\bar{C}_{p_i}$, and relative partial molal heat capacity, $\bar{C}_{p_i} - \bar{C}_{p_i}^0$, at constant pressure. Thus,

$$\left(\frac{\partial \bar{H}_i}{\partial T}\right)_P - \left(\frac{\partial \bar{H}_i^0}{\partial T}\right)_P = \bar{C}_{p_i} - \bar{C}_{p_i}^0 = \left(\frac{\partial \bar{L}_i}{\partial T}\right)_P \equiv \bar{J}_i \qquad (1\text{-}7\text{-}7)$$

At constant composition, temperature, and charge,

$$\left(\frac{\partial (F - F^0)}{\partial P}\right)_T = V - V^0 \qquad (1\text{-}7\text{-}8)$$

according to equation (1-3-3), where V, the total volume of the phase, is given by

$$V = \sum_1^c N_i \bar{V}_i \qquad (1\text{-}7\text{-}9)$$

in which $\bar{V}_1$, etc., are the partial molal volumes of the components. Combining these equations with equation (1-6-2), which defines the activity, we obtain

$$\left[\frac{N_1 \partial \ln a_1 + N_2 \partial \ln a_2 + \cdots}{\partial P}\right]_T$$
$$= \frac{N_1(\bar{V}_1 - \bar{V}_1^0) + N_2(\bar{V}_2 - \bar{V}_2^0) + \cdots}{RT} \qquad (1\text{-}7\text{-}10)$$

and for each individual component,

$$\left(\frac{\partial \ln a_i}{\partial P}\right)_T = \frac{\bar{V}_i - \bar{V}_i^0}{RT} \qquad (1\text{-}7\text{-}11)$$

(8) Variation of Activity with Composition at Constant
Temperature and Pressure. Definitions of Activity
Coefficients

By combining equation (1-4-5) with (1-6-1) or 1-6-4) we obtain the equation

$$\sum_1^c N_i d \ln a_i = 0 \qquad (1\text{-}8\text{-}1)$$

at constant temperature, pressure and charge. This important relation permits the calculation of the activity of one component of a solution from the known activities of the remaining components. In binary solutions it is most frequently used to estimate the activity of the solute from measurements of the so-called colligative properties of the solvent.

In solutions of such high dilution that the mutual interaction between solute particles can be ignored, it has been shown experimentally[10] and by

[10] Cf., for example, H. S. Harned, Chapter XII, in H. S. Taylor, "Treatise on Physical Chemistry," New York, D. Van Nostrand and Co., 1930.

theoretical considerations[11] that the activities of solutes approach proportionality to their concentrations as the latter approach zero. Thus, as a limiting law for any electrolyte in infinitely dilute solution,

$$\bar{F} - \bar{F}_N^0 = \nu RT \ln N_\pm \tag{1-8-2}$$

This equation has the same form as (1-6-5), and introduces the mean ionic mol fraction defined by the equation

$$N_\pm \equiv (N_+^{\nu+} N_-^{\nu-})^{1/\nu} \tag{1-8-3}$$

analogous to (1-6-3). The partial molal free energy in the standard state has been written $\bar{F}_N^0$ to indicate that activities have been expressed on the mol fraction scale. Mol fractional activities are of particular theoretical importance because equation (1-8-2) is used to define the behavior of the hypothetical "ideal" or "perfect" ionized solute at all concentrations. It is convenient to describe the departures of real solutes from ideality in terms of the factor

$$f_\pm \equiv \frac{a_{N\pm}}{N_\pm} = (f_+^{\nu+} f_-^{\nu-})^{1/\nu} \tag{1-8-4}$$

called the rational activity coefficient. This name will be retained for the sake of brevity, but a more adequate designation would be the stoichiometric mean ionic mol fractional activity coefficient.

For many purposes it will prove more convenient to employ activities expressed in terms of molalities (mols per 1000 g. solvent) or molarities (mols per 1000 cc. solution), and define the corresponding activity coefficients,

$$\gamma_\pm \equiv \frac{a_{m\pm}}{m_\pm} = (\gamma_+^{\nu+} \gamma_-^{\nu-})^{1/\nu} \tag{1-8-5}$$

and

$$y_\pm \equiv \frac{a_{c\pm}}{c_\pm} = (y_+^{\nu+} y_-^{\nu-})^{1/\nu} \tag{1-8-6}$$

The mean ionic molality and mean ionic molarity are defined by

$$m_\pm \equiv [m_+^{\nu+} m_-^{\nu-}]^{1/\nu} = [(\nu_+ m)^{\nu+} (\nu_- m)^{\nu-}]^{1/\nu} = m[\nu_+^{\nu+} \nu_-^{\nu-}]^{1/\nu} \tag{1-8-7}$$

and

$$c_\pm \equiv [c_+^{\nu+} c_-^{\nu-}]^{1/\nu} = [(\nu_+ c)^{\nu+} (\nu_- c)^{\nu-}]^{1/\nu} = c[\nu_+^{\nu+} \nu_-^{\nu-}]^{1/\nu} \tag{1-8-8}$$

respectively. The stoichiometric mean ionic molal activity coefficient, $\gamma_\pm$, is most often encountered in experimental work and is usually called the practical activity coefficient. The stoichiometric mean ionic molar activity coefficient, $y_\pm$, has not come into sufficiently general use to

[11] E. A. Guggenheim, *Proc. Roy. Soc. London*, **A 135**, 181 (1932).

acquire a scientific sobriquet. In later chapters, it will be possible without ambiguity to refer to any one of the three as "the" activity coefficient.

Following the discussion in Section (6), it is essential that the values of μ_i^0 or $\bar{F}_i^0$ in the reference state should be assigned so that the value of μ_i or $\bar{F}_i$ of a component is independent of the concentration scale in which a_i is expressed. Bearing this in mind, we may combine equation (1-6-2), (1-8-4), (1-8-5) and (1-8-6) and express the partial molal free energy of an electrolyte as follows:

$$\bar{F} = \bar{F}_N^0 + \nu RT \ln f_\pm N_\pm = \bar{F}_m^0 + \nu RT \ln \gamma_\pm m_\pm$$
$$ \cdot = \bar{F}_c^0 + \nu RT \ln y_\pm c_\pm \tag{1-8-9}$$

In practically all thermodynamic studies of electrolytic solutions except some of those in which mixed solvents are involved, it is customary to select the reference states so that $f_\pm = \gamma_\pm = y_\pm = 1$ at infinite dilution of solute at all temperatures and all pressures. As long as this convention is adhered to, we may introduce the limiting values of $N_\pm/m_\pm$ and $c_\pm/m_\pm$ at infinite dilution, and obtain the relation

$$\bar{F}_N^0 = \bar{F}_m^0 + \nu RT \ln \frac{1000}{M_1} = \bar{F}_c^0 + \nu RT \ln \frac{1000 \, d_0}{M_1} \tag{1-8-10}$$

from (1-8-9). Here M_1 is the molecular weight of the solvent, and d_0 is its density. The appearance of d_0 in the last member of this equation brings out an important distinction between the weight and volume concentration units. The concentration (composition) of a phase, in the sense in which the term is used in the development of fundamental thermodynamic relations, is an *independent* variable. When a process, or partial differentiation, takes place at constant composition, the weight concentration units, m, N, etc., remain constant, but the volume concentration unit c can, and usually does, vary. The constancy of c ordinarily imposes two conditions: constant composition and constant volume. Accordingly, when $\bar{F}_c^0$ (and other thermodynamic functions on the c-scale) are differentiated with respect to T or P at constant composition, it should not be forgottem that c is variable. The confusion which can be produced by overlooking this point makes it undesirable to use the c-scale except at constant temperature and pressure.

Combination of equations (1-8-9) and (1-8-10) leads to

$$\ln f_\pm = \ln \gamma_\pm + \ln \frac{m_\pm}{N_\pm}\left(\frac{M_1}{1000}\right) = \ln y_\pm + \ln \frac{c_\pm}{N_\pm}\left(\frac{M_1}{1000 \, d_0}\right) \tag{1-8-11}$$

The concentration ratios are given at all dilutions by the general expressions

$$N_\pm = \frac{m_\pm}{\nu m + 1000/M_1} = \frac{c_\pm}{\nu c + (1000 \, d - cM_2)/M_1} \tag{1-8-12}$$

in which m and c are the stoichiometric molality and molarity of the electrolyte, M_2 its molecular weight, and d is the density of the solution. Substitution of (1-8-12) in (1-8-11) leads to the important relationships

$$\ln f_{\pm} = \ln \gamma_{\pm} + \ln (1 + m\nu M_1/1000) \tag{1-8-13}$$

$$\ln f_{\pm} = \ln y_{\pm} + \ln (d/d_0 + c(\nu M_1 - M_2)/1000 \, d_0) \tag{1-8-14}$$

$$\ln \gamma_{\pm} = \ln y_{\pm} + \ln (d/d_0 - cM_2/1000 \, d_0) \tag{1-8-15}$$

Although the dependence of equations (1-8-13) to (1-8-15) upon (1-8-10) is of negligible interest in studies concerned only with the variation of the various activity coefficients with concentration, it will prove to be of fundamental importance in investigating the effects of changes in the solvent medium upon the thermodynamic behavior of the solute. Mixed solvents have come into general use in such investigations because their properties can be varied in a regular and continuous manner. If M_X and M_Y are the molecular weights of the components of a binary solvent mixture, and X and Y represent the composition in weight per cent, then the average molecular weight of the mixed solvent,

$$M_{XY} = \frac{100}{(X/M_X + Y/M_Y)} \tag{1-8-16}$$

must be substituted in the preceding equations for M_1.

(9) Activity Coefficient and Osmotic Coefficient of the Solvent

The rational activity coefficient of the solvent is defined by the equation

$$\bar{F}_1 - \bar{F}_1^0 = RT \ln f_1 N_1 \tag{1-9-1}$$

which is formally the same for any component of a solution, but the subscript 1 will always be used to designate the solvent. In dilute solutions, where the preponderance of the solvent is very pronounced, the activity coefficient of the solvent is subject to practical disadvantages for numerical computations. For the solute, represented by the subscript 2, we have according to (1-6-2) and the definition of rational activity coefficient, the equation

$$\bar{F}_2 - \bar{F}_2^0 = RT \ln f_2 N_2 \tag{1-9-2}$$

Differentiating these two equations, at constant temperature and pressure and combining with equation (1-8-1), we obtain

$$N_1 \, d \ln f_1 N_1 + N_2 \, d \ln f_2 N_2 = 0 \tag{1-9-3}$$

Since $(N_1 + N_2 = 1)$, this readily reduces to

$$d \ln f_1 = -\frac{N_2}{N_1} \, d \ln f_2 \tag{1-9-4}$$

from which it follows that in dilute solutions the departure of f_1 from unity is much less than that of f_2. To obtain a more sensitive measure of the non-ideality of solutions in terms of the solvent, Bjerrum[12] introduced the concept of osmotic coefficient. The rational osmotic coefficient, g, is defined by

$$\bar{F}_1 - \bar{F}_1^0 = gRT \ln N_1 \qquad (1\text{-}9\text{-}5)$$

and the practical osmotic coefficient, ϕ, by

$$\bar{F}_1 - \bar{F}_1^0 = -\phi RT \sum^s m_i M_1/1000 \qquad (1\text{-}9\text{-}6)$$

where M_1 is molecular weight of solvent. The relation between the two coefficients is clearly

$$\phi = \frac{-g \ln N_1}{\sum^s m_i M_1/1000} \qquad (1\text{-}9\text{-}7)$$

which becomes

$$\phi = g[1 - \tfrac{1}{2} \sum^s m_i M_1/1000 + \tfrac{1}{3}(\sum^s m_i M_1/1000)^2 - \cdots] \qquad (1\text{-}9\text{-}8)$$

in dilute solutions by introducing the relation $-\ln N_1 = \ln (1 + \sum^s m_i M_1/1000)$ and expanding the logarithm. The factor $\sum^s m_i$ represents the summation over all the solute species present. For a single electrolyte dissociating into ν ions, $\sum^s m_i$ equals νm. In this case, equation (1-9-6) reduces to

$$\ln a_1 = -\phi \nu m \frac{M_1}{1000} \qquad (1\text{-}9\text{-}9)$$

Differentiating to obtain $d \ln a_1$ and substituting in equation (1-8-1) in the form

$$N_1 d \ln a_1 + N_2 d \ln a_2 = 0; \quad \text{or} \quad \frac{1000}{M_1} d \ln a_1 + \nu m \, d \ln \gamma_{\pm} m = 0 \qquad (1\text{-}9\text{-}10)$$

leads to the important relation first derived by Bjerrum for the relation between the practical osmotic coefficient and the activity coefficient, namely

$$d[m(1 - \phi)] + m \, d \ln \gamma_{\pm} = 0 \qquad (1\text{-}9\text{-}11)$$

For the more general case, we obtain

$$d\{\sum^s m_i(1 - \phi)\} + \sum^s m_i \, d \ln \gamma_i = 0 \qquad (1\text{-}9\text{-}11a)$$

In integrated form, these equations become

[12] N. Bjerrum, *Z. Elektrochem.*, **24**, 259 (1907); *Proc. Internat. Congr. Appl. Chem.*, *Sect. X*, London, 1909.

$$\phi = 1 + 1/m \int m \, d \ln \gamma_{\pm} \qquad (1\text{-}9\text{-}12)$$

and

$$\phi = 1 + 1/\sum m_i \int \sum m_i \, d \ln \gamma_i \qquad (1\text{-}9\text{-}12a)$$

(10) The Equilibrium Constant of a Chemical Reaction

Consider any chemical reaction at constant temperature, pressure and charge in which x_1, x_2, $\cdots$ mols of X_1, X_2, $\cdots$ and y_1, y_2, $\cdots$ mols of Y_1, Y_2, $\cdots$ react to form x_1', x_2', $\cdots$ mols of X_1', X_2', $\cdots$ and y_1', y_2', $\cdots$ mols of Y_1', Y_2', $\cdots$ where the X's indicate pure substances and the Y's indicate the components of any polycomponent phase present. Then

$$x_1 X_1 + x_2 X_2 + \cdots + y_1 Y_1 + y_2 Y_2 + \cdots$$
$$\rightleftarrows x_1' X_1' + x_2' X_2' + \cdots + y_1' Y_1' + y_2' Y_2' + \cdots \qquad (1\text{-}10\text{-}1)$$

and from the definition of activity we may write

$$x_1 F_{X_1} - x_1 F^0_{X_1} = x_1 RT \ln a_{X_1} \text{, etc.,}$$

$$y_1 \bar{F}_{Y_1} - y_1 \bar{F}^0_{Y_1} = y_1 RT \ln a_{Y_1} \text{, etc.,}$$

and
$$x_1' F_{X_1'} - x_1' F^0_{X_1'} = x_1' RT \ln a_{X_1'} \text{, etc.,} \qquad (1\text{-}10\text{-}2)$$

$$y_1' \bar{F}_{Y_1'} - y_1' \bar{F}^0_{Y_1'} = y_1' RT \ln a_{Y_1'} \text{, etc.}$$

The total change in free energy for the reaction will be

$$\Delta F - \Delta F^0 = RT \ln \frac{(a_{X_1'})^{x_1'}(a_{X_2'})^{x_2'} \cdots (a_{Y_1'})^{y_i'} \cdots}{(a_{X_1})^{x_1}(a_{X_2})^{x_2} \cdots (a_{Y_1})^{y_1} \cdots} \qquad (1\text{-}10\text{-}3)$$

where

$$\Delta F = (x_1' F_{X_1'} + x_2' F_{X_2'} \cdots + y_1' \bar{F}_{Y_1'} + y_2' \bar{F}_{Y_2'} \cdots)$$
$$- (x_1 F_{X_1} + x_2 F_{X_2} \cdots + y_1 \bar{F}_{Y_1} + y_2 \bar{F}_{Y_2} \cdots) \qquad (1\text{-}10\text{-}4)$$

and

$$\Delta F^0 = (x_1' F^0_{X_1'} + x_2' F^0_{X_2'} \cdots + y_1' \bar{F}^0_{Y_1'} + y_2' \bar{F}^0_{Y_2'} \cdots)$$
$$- (x_1 F^0_{X_1} + x_2 F^0_{X_2} \cdots + y_1 \bar{F}^0_{Y_1} + y_2 \bar{F}^0_{Y_2} \cdots) \qquad (1\text{-}10\text{-}5)$$

ΔF is obviously the free energy change of the reaction in general, and ΔF^0 the free energy change when all the products and reactants are in their standard states.

When the reaction is in equilibrium at constant temperature, pressure, and charge, the composition of each phase is fixed. Then, from equation (1-2-6), it follows that the condition

$$\Delta F = 0$$

must prevail. As a consequence,

$$\Delta F^0 = -RT \ln \frac{(a_{x_1'})^{x_1'}(a_{x_2'})^{x_2'} \cdots (a_{Y_1'})^{y_1'} \cdots}{(a_{x_1})^{x_1}(a_{x_2})^{x_2} \cdots (a_{Y_1})^{y_1} \cdots} \qquad (1\text{-}10\text{-}6)$$

Since ΔF^0 is a constant[13] at constant temperature and pressure, we may write

$$K = \frac{(a_{x_1'})^{x_1'}(a_{x_2'})^{x_2'} \cdots (a_{Y_1'})^{y_1'} \cdots}{(a_{x_1})^{x_1}(a_{x_2})^{x_2} \cdots (a_{Y_1})^{y_1} \cdots} \qquad (1\text{-}10\text{-}7)$$

where K is the equilibrium constant of the reaction. The relation stated in equation (1-10-7) forms the basis of the study of ionic equilibria. In another form it may be written

$$K = \frac{(a_{x_1'})^{x_1'}(a_{x_2'})^{x_2'} \cdots (m_{Y_1'})^{y_1'} \cdots \Pi\gamma'}{(a_{x_1})^{x_1}(a_{x_2})^{x_2} \cdots (m_{Y_1})^{y_1} \cdots \Pi\gamma} \qquad (1\text{-}10\text{-}8)$$

where $\Pi\gamma'$ and $\Pi\gamma$ are the appropriate activity coefficient products. If we adopt the convention that all activity coefficients of pure phases (the species X_1, X_2, $\cdots$) are chosen so that their activities are unity, and the activity coefficients of all components of polycomponent phases (the species Y_1, Y_2, $\cdots$) are unity at infinite dilution of the corresponding components, then the classical mass action law,

$$K_m = \frac{(m_{Y_1'})^{y_1'} \cdots}{(m_{Y_1})^{y_1} \cdots} \qquad (1\text{-}9\text{-}10)$$

results at infinite dilution.

Since the important relation

$$\Delta F^0 = -RT \ln K \qquad (1\text{-}10\text{-}10)$$

follows from (1-10-6) and (1-10-7), the variations of the equilibrium constant with pressure and temperature are given by equations (1-3-3) and (1-3-4). Thus,

$$\left(\frac{\partial \ln K}{\partial P}\right)_T = -\frac{\Delta V^0}{RT} \qquad (1\text{-}10\text{-}11)$$

and

$$\left(\frac{\partial \ln K}{\partial T}\right)_P = \frac{\Delta H^0}{RT^2}. \qquad (1\text{-}10\text{-}12)$$

The latter expression is sometimes referred to as the van't Hoff equation.

---

[13] ΔF^0 is arbitrary to the extent that its value depends upon the selection of standard states for the components, and upon the units in which the activities are expressed. In the special case where the reaction is symmetrical, and confined to a single phase, ΔF^0 is independent of these arbitrary considerations.

(11) SURFACE TENSION. THE ADSORPTION EQUATION OF GIBBS

In the subsequent treatment of the variation of surface tension with electrolyte concentration, we shall have occasion to use the adsorption equation of Gibbs in the form

$$- \Gamma_2 = \left(\frac{\partial \sigma}{\partial \mu_2}\right)_{T,P} = \frac{a_2}{RT}\left(\frac{\partial \sigma}{\partial a_2}\right)_{T,P} \qquad (1\text{-}11\text{-}1)$$

Here, Γ_2 is the number of mols of solute "negatively" adsorbed per unit increase in surface energy, and σ is the surface tension. The derivation and discussion of this relation would cause too great a digression from our principal objectives and will not be attempted.[14]

(12) CROSS-DIFFERENTIATION EQUATIONS

The condition of integrability of equation (1-2-6) and the definitions (1-2-7) require that at constant temperature and pressure the chemical potentials are related by equations of the type

$$\left(\frac{\partial \mu_1}{\partial n_2}\right)_{n_1, n_3 \cdots n_c} = \left(\frac{\partial \mu_2}{\partial n_1}\right)_{n_2, \cdots n_c}, \qquad \text{etc.} \qquad (1\text{-}12\text{-}1)$$

In the important special case of mixtures composed of solvent (component 0) and two or more electrolytes (components 1, 2, $\cdots$ c) it is convenient to express concentrations on the m-scale, for by this means the number of moles of solvent, n_0, remains constant, and n_1, n_2, $\cdots$ n_c become the independent variables, m_1, m_2, $\cdots$ m_c, and equations (1-12-1) may be rewritten in the form

$$\nu_1 \left(\frac{\partial \log \gamma_1}{\partial m_2}\right)_{m_1, m_3 \cdots m_c} = \nu_2 \left(\frac{\partial \log \gamma_2}{\partial m_1}\right)_{m_2, \cdots m_c}, \qquad \text{etc.} \qquad (1\text{-}12\text{-}2)$$

Irreversible Thermodynamics

The laws of Fourier, Ohm, and Fick describe the flows of heat, electricity and matter in terms of the gradients of temperature, electromotive force and concentration, respectively. There are many phenomena in which two or more flow processes proceed simultaneously such as the Peltier effect, heat conduction in anisotropic media and transport processes in electrolytic solutions. In the Peltier effect the flow of electric current in a system of conductors of different metals will produce heat, and conversely, if such metallic junctions are maintained at different temperatures, electricity will flow. In anisotropic solids, the temperature gradients and corresponding flows of heat will be different along the three space co-ordinates required to express the phenomenon. In gases or solutions where two or

---

[14] J. W. Gibbs, "Collected Works," Vol. I, pp. 219–233, Longmans, Green and Co., New York, 1928; "Commentary on the Scientific Writings of J. Willard Gibbs," Section by James Rice, Vol. I, pp. 504 ff., Yale University Press, New Haven, 1936; E. A. Guggenheim, *J. Chem. Phys.*, **4**, 689 (1936).

more species are present, simultaneous transport of the components will take place. Consideration of these combined steady state processes lead to a whole group of phenomenological relations which form the fundamental basis for irreversible thermodynamics.

(13) RECIPROCAL RELATIONS IN SIMULTANEOUS IRREVERSIBLE PROCESSES. THEORY OF ONSAGER[15]

Interacting Steady State Processes

As early as 1854, William Thomson (Lord Kelvin)[16] recognized the reciprocal relation of the coupled processes involved in the Peltier effect. In this thermoelectric circuit, let J_1 represent the flow of electricity and J_2 the flow of heat. Let X_1, and X_2 represent the "forces" which drive the electric current and cause the flow of heat, respectively. If X_1 is the electrical force, then X_2 in corresponding units will be

$$\mathbf{X_2} = -\frac{1}{T} \nabla T \qquad (1\text{-}13\text{-}1)$$

where T is the absolute temperature and ∇T its gradient. If the flow of current is independent of the flow of heat

$$\mathbf{X_1} = R_1 J_1$$
$$\mathbf{X_2} = R_2 J_2 \qquad (1\text{-}13\text{-}2)$$

where R_1 and R_2 are the electrical and thermal resistances. However since the thermal and electrical processes may interact, Thomson concluded that the more complicated phenomenological equations

$$\mathbf{X_1} = R_{11} J_1 + R_{12} J_2$$
$$\mathbf{X_2} = R_{21} J_1 + R_{22} J_2 \qquad (1\text{-}13\text{-}3)$$

are required to describe the situation. He also thought it plausible that the assumption of the reciprocal relation

$$R_{12} = R_{21} \qquad (1\text{-}13\text{-}4)$$

is correct. This assumption proved to be in accord with the best available measurements.

The extension of the conception involved in the simple coupled processes of the Peltier effect to systems involving steady state processes in general is due to Onsager.

A function which expresses the time rate of production of the entropy

---

[15] L. Onsager, *Phys. Rev.*, 37, 405, 2265 (1931). The following presentation of the theory follows very closely the original presentation by Onsager as recorded in these references.

[16] W. Thomson, *Proc. Roy. Soc. Edinburgh*, p. 123 (1854); "Collected Papers," 237–241.

of a system in which simultaneous irreversible processes occur is defined. Multiplied by T, this function yields the rate of dissipation of the free energy. The employment of this dissipation function $\Phi(\mathbf{J}, \mathbf{J})$ and the reciprocal relations lead to a variation principal of the form

$$\delta\{\dot{S} - \Phi(\mathbf{J}, \mathbf{J})\} \geqq 0 \qquad (1\text{-}13\text{-}4a)$$

similar to that of the entropy in reversible thermodynamics. The application of these fundamental relations leads to a group of phenomenological equations which form the basis of the subject of irreversible thermodynamics which has had a marked development in recent years as witnessed by the monographs of Prigogine,[17] de Groot[18] and Denbigh.[19]

Thermoelectrical phenomena in electrolytes are examples which illustrate the interaction of three simultaneous processes superimposed upon thermodynamic equilibrium. As an illustration, imagine a vertical glass tube filled with a sodium chloride solution and containing two identical silver-silver chloride electrodes reversible to the chloride ion placed at the top and bottom of the tube. Let a temperature gradient be established through this solution and connect the electrodes through a suitable resistance. There will result a simultaneous flow of electricity, matter and heat. If the temperature gradient be removed, the whole system will approach a state of equilibrium in which no bulk motion will occur. Let $\mathbf{J}_1$, $\mathbf{J}_2$ and $\mathbf{J}_3$ represent the flows of the two ions and energy (heat) and $\mathbf{X}_1$, $\mathbf{X}_2$ and $\mathbf{X}_3$ the "forces" that produce these flows. By analogy with Thomson's equations for the Peltier effect, we expect that the phenomenological equations

$$\mathbf{J}_1 = \mathfrak{M}_{11}\mathbf{X}_1 + \mathfrak{M}_{12}\mathbf{X}_2 + \mathfrak{M}_{13}\mathbf{X}_3$$

$$\mathbf{J}_2 = \mathfrak{M}_{21}\mathbf{X}_1 + \mathfrak{M}_{22}\mathbf{X}_2 + \mathfrak{M}_{23}\mathbf{X}_3 \qquad (1\text{-}13\text{-}5)$$

$$\mathbf{J}_3 = \mathfrak{M}_{31}\mathbf{X}_1 + \mathfrak{M}_{32}\mathbf{X}_2 + \mathfrak{M}_{33}\mathbf{X}_3$$

and the reciprocal relations

$$\mathfrak{M}_{12} = \mathfrak{M}_{21}; \qquad \mathfrak{M}_{13} = \mathfrak{M}_{31}; \qquad \mathfrak{M}_{23} = \mathfrak{M}_{32} \qquad (1\text{-}13\text{-}6)$$

will represent the behavior of these simultaneous transport processes. Indeed, as early as 1926, Eastman[20] had derived a reciprocal theorem for the interaction between heat conduction and diffusion. Diffusion brought about by temperature gradients is denoted as the Soret effect while the

[17] I. Prigogine, "Etude Thermodynamique des Processes Irréversibles," Desoer, Liege (1947).

[18] S. R. de Groot, "Thermodynamics of Irreversible Processes," Interscience Publishers, Inc., New York (1951).

[19] K. G. Denbigh, "Thermodynamics of the Steady State," John Wiley and Sons, Inc., New York (1951).

[20] E. D. Eastman, *J. Am. Chem. Soc.*, **44**, 1482 (1926); *Ibid.*, **50**, 283, 292 (1928).

production of a temperature gradient as a result of diffusion is known as the Dufour effect.

Diffusion of s kinds of ions in a liquid medium is another phenomenon which may be expected to follow a similar pattern. For this type of system, equations (1-13-5) may be written in the condensed form

$$\mathbf{J}_i = -\sum_{k=1}^{s} \mathfrak{M}_{ik} \nabla \mu_k \;; \qquad i = 1, \cdots s \qquad (1\text{-}13\text{-}7)$$

where $\nabla \mu_k$, the gradient of the chemical potential of each ion, represents the "force" which causes mass flow and $\mathfrak{M}_{ik}$ is an element of the "admittance" matrix. Here again we expect that

$$\mathfrak{M}_{ik} = \mathfrak{M}_{ki} \qquad (1\text{-}13\text{-}8)$$

The Dissipation Function and the Formulation of a Variation Principle

For the present, we shall adopt the intuitional concept that the formulation of the behavior of simultaneous irreversible processes is correctly represented by equations of the types (1-13-5) and (1-13-6) and investigate the consequences of this concept as applied to the flow of heat in anisotropic crystals of arbitrary symmetry. This specialized procedure will reveal the nature of the functions involved and their relation to the thermodynamic functions.

For heat conduction in the x_1, x_2 and x_3 directions in the crystal, the forces are

$$\mathbf{X}_1 = -\frac{1}{T}\frac{\partial T}{\partial x_1}\;; \qquad \mathbf{X}_2 = -\frac{1}{T}\frac{\partial T}{\partial x_2}\;; \qquad \mathbf{X}_3 = -\frac{1}{T}\frac{\partial T}{\partial x_3} \qquad (1\text{-}13\text{-}9)$$

These forces can be expressed in terms of the flows, $\mathbf{J}_1$, $\mathbf{J}_2$ and $\mathbf{J}_3$ by transformation of equation (1-13-5). Thus

$$-\frac{1}{T}\frac{\partial T}{\partial x_1} = \mathbf{X}_1 = R_{11}\mathbf{J}_1 + R_{12}\mathbf{J}_2 + R_{13}\mathbf{J}_3$$

$$-\frac{1}{T}\frac{\partial T}{\partial x_2} = \mathbf{X}_2 = R_{21}\mathbf{J}_{11} + R_{22}\mathbf{J}_2 + R_{23}\mathbf{J}_3 \qquad (1\text{-}13\text{-}10)$$

$$-\frac{1}{T}\frac{\partial T}{\partial x_3} = \mathbf{X}_3 = R_{31}\mathbf{J}_1 + R_{32}\mathbf{J}_2 + R_{33}\mathbf{J}_3$$

In general forms equations (1-13-5) and (1-13-10) may be expressed

$$\mathbf{J}_i = \sum_{j=1}^{\nu} \mathfrak{M}_{ij}\mathbf{X}_j\;; \qquad i = 1, \cdots \nu$$

$$\mathbf{X}_j = \sum_{i=1}^{\nu} R_{ji}\mathbf{J}_i\;; \qquad j = 1, \cdots \nu \qquad (1\text{-}13\text{-}11)$$

where $\mathfrak{M}_{ij}$ and R_{ji} are elements of the corresponding admittance and resistance matrices.   For heat flow in anisotropic crystals, ν equals 3 and

$$R_{12} = R_{21} \; ; \qquad R_{13} = R_{31} \; ; \qquad R_{23} = R_{32} \qquad (1\text{-}13\text{-}12)$$

At this point, Onsager introduces a *dissipation function*, $\phi(\mathbf{J}, \mathbf{J})$, defined by

$$2T\phi(\mathbf{J}, \mathbf{J}) \equiv \sum_{i,k} R_{ik}\mathbf{J}_i\mathbf{J}_k \qquad (1\text{-}13\text{-}13)$$

With the help of the reciprocal relations it can be shown that

$$T^{-1}X_k = \frac{\partial T^{-1}}{\partial x_k} = \frac{\partial \phi\,(\mathbf{J}, \mathbf{J})}{\partial J_k} \qquad (1\text{-}13\text{-}14)$$

with the result that $\phi(\mathbf{J}, \mathbf{J})$ can be expressed by products of the flows and forces.   Thus,

$$2\,T\phi\,(\mathbf{J}, \mathbf{J}) = \sum_{k=1}^{3} J_k T \frac{\partial \phi\,(\mathbf{J}, \mathbf{J})}{\partial J_k} = \sum_{k=1}^{s} J_k X_k \qquad (1\text{-}13\text{-}15)$$

Onsager shows by the following elegant method that $2\phi(\mathbf{J}, \mathbf{J})$ equals the rate of production of entropy caused by heat flow through a volume element of unit size.   Since the heat content of the element is constant under the conditions of a steady state very close to thermodynamic equilibrium, the product of the temperature and the increase in entropy determines the rate of decrease in free energy, or

$$2T\phi(\mathbf{J}, \mathbf{J}) = -dF/dt = 2F(\mathbf{J}, \mathbf{J}) \qquad (1\text{-}13\text{-}16)$$

The quantity $2F(\mathbf{J}, \mathbf{J})$ is the *rate of dissipation of free energy.**

If s is the local entropy density, then the local accumulation of heat is $T\,ds/dt = -\nabla.\mathbf{J}$ and the total rate of increase in entropy of the system of volume V is given by

$$dS/dt = \iiint (-\nabla.\mathbf{J})\,T^{-1}\,dV \qquad (1\text{-}13\text{-}17)$$

According to Green's theorem

$$\iiint (\nabla.\mathbf{J})\,T^{-1}\,dV + \iint J_n\,T^{-1}\,d\Omega = \iiint (\mathbf{J}.\nabla\,T^{-1})\,dV$$

$$= \iiint \sum_{k=1} J_k \frac{\partial T^{-1}}{\partial x_k} \qquad (1\text{-}13\text{-}18)$$

where the double integral extends over the boundary of the system, and

---

* Lord Raleigh used the function $F(J, J) = T\phi(J, J)$, and called $F(J, J)$ the dissipation function. Since Onsager applies this name to $\phi(J, J)$ alone, we prefer to make use of the less ambiguous expression "dissipation of free energy" applied to the function $2T\phi(J, J)$ and to represent it by either of the ordinary symbols, $-dF/dt$ or $\dot{F}$, for time rate of change for the free energy.

J_n is the normal component of flow at its surface. Let

$$\dot{S}^* \, (\mathbf{J}_n) \equiv \iint J_n \, T^{-1} d\Omega \qquad (1\text{-}13\text{-}19)$$

for the entropy given off to the surroundings and

$$\dot{S} \, (\mathbf{J}) \equiv \iiint \left(-\frac{1}{T} \nabla . \mathbf{J} \right) dV \qquad (1\text{-}13\text{-}20)$$

for the entropy change of the system, then

$$\dot{S} \, (\mathbf{J}) + \dot{S} \, (\mathbf{J}_n) = \iiint \sum_k J_k \frac{\partial}{\partial x_k} \left(\frac{1}{T} \right) dV$$

$$= \iiint \frac{1}{T} \sum_k J_k \, X_k \, dV = \iiint \sum_k J_k \frac{\partial \phi \, (\mathbf{J}, \mathbf{J})}{\partial J_k} dV \qquad (1\text{-}13\text{-}21)$$

$$= \iiint 2\phi \, (\mathbf{J}, \mathbf{J}) \, dV \equiv 2 \, \Phi \, (\mathbf{J}, \mathbf{J})$$

Thus, $2\phi(\mathbf{J}, \mathbf{J})$ and $2\Phi(\mathbf{J}, \mathbf{J})$ equal the rates of production of entropy caused by heat flow through unit volume and a volume V, respectively. It immediately follows that $2\dot{F} = 2\Phi T$ equals the rate of dissipation of free energy.

A variation principal may now be derived from the preceding relations. From equation (1-13-21), it follows that

$$\delta \, [\dot{S} \, (\mathbf{J}) + \dot{S}^* \, (\mathbf{J}_n) - \Phi \, (\mathbf{J}, \mathbf{J})]$$

$$= \delta \int \left[\sum_k J_k \frac{\partial}{\partial x_k} \left(\frac{1}{T} \right) - \phi \, (\mathbf{J}, \mathbf{J}) \right] dV \qquad (1\text{-}13\text{-}22)$$

$$= \int \sum_k \left[\frac{\partial}{\partial x_k} \left(\frac{1}{T} \right) - \frac{\partial}{\partial J_k} \phi \, (\mathbf{J}, \mathbf{J}) \right] \delta J_k dV$$

By equation (1-13-14), the bracketed term in this last expression equals zero, and therefore

$$\delta[\dot{S}(\mathbf{J}) + \dot{S}^*(\mathbf{J}) - \Phi(\mathbf{J}, \mathbf{J})] = 0 \qquad (1\text{-}13\text{-}23)$$

Since $\dot{S}(\mathbf{J})$ and $\dot{S}(\mathbf{J}_n^*)$ are linear functions of J, and $\Phi(\mathbf{J}, \mathbf{J})$ is a positive definite homogeneous quadratic form, the bracketed expression can have only one maximum or minimum. Also, since $2\Phi(\mathbf{J}, \mathbf{J})$ is a positive definite homogeneous quadratic form, the bracketed expression can have only one maximum or minimum. Also, since $2\Phi(\mathbf{J}, \mathbf{J}) = \dot{S}(\mathbf{J}_n)$, the second law of thermodynamics requires that it be positive, and consequently

$$\dot{S}(\mathbf{J}) + \dot{S}^*(\mathbf{J}_n) - \Phi(\mathbf{J}, \mathbf{J}) = \text{maximum} \qquad (1\text{-}13\text{-}24)$$

and when $J_n = 0$, or the body under consideration is isolated

$$\dot{S}(\mathbf{J}) - \Phi(\mathbf{J}, \mathbf{J}) = \text{maximum} \qquad (1\text{-}13\text{-}25)$$

The relations between the flows and "forces" expressed by equations (1-13-5) and (1-13-10) and the accompanying reciprocal relations, the identification of a "dissipation function" with the time rate of change of entropy and the statement of a variation principle represent the operational basis of the theory of irreversible thermodynamics. The statement regarding the simultaneous flows of heat, matter and electricity given by equations (1-13-5) and (1-13-6) is intuitional following as it does upon the extension of Thomson's theory of the Peltier effect. The result expressed by equations (1-13-10) and (1-13-12) for the "forces" and flows of heat in a crystal is the simplest case of simultaneous flows in three directions. The problem now arises both as to the validity of these relations and upon what hypothesis they can be derived from a microscopic point of view. A clue to a possible procedure may be obtained from the consideration of an appropriate system of chemical reactions.

Reciprocal Relations in Chemical Reactions

Imagine a triangular monomolecular chemical reaction represented by

$$\begin{array}{c} A \\ \diagup \quad \diagdown \\ C \;\rightleftharpoons\; B \end{array}$$

in which three forms of the same substance exist simultaneously in the same phase. According to the mass action law, the fraction of A molecules which changes into B in a short time Δt will be $k_{BA}\Delta t$ where k_{BA} is the proportionality constant. The time rates of change of the concentrations, n_A, n_B, n_C in terms of the other velocity constants, will be

$$dn_A = -(k_{BA} + k_{CA})n_A + k_{AB}n_B + k_{AC}n_C$$

$$dn_B = k_{BA}n_A - (k_{AB} + k_{CB})n_B + k_{BC}n_C \qquad (1\text{-}13\text{-}26)$$

$$dn_C = k_{CA}n_A + k_{CB}n_B - (k_{AC} + k_{BC})n_C$$

If all the coefficients are $\geqq 0$, then at equilibrium finite concentrations, $\bar{n}_A$, $\bar{n}_B$, $\bar{n}_C$, are assured and interrelated by equations of the types

$$\frac{d\bar{n}_A}{dt} = -(k_{BA} + k_{CA})\bar{n}_A + k_{AB}\bar{n}_B + k_{AC}\bar{n}_C = 0 \qquad (1\text{-}13\text{-}27)$$

and

$$\bar{n}_A + \bar{n}_B + \bar{n}_C = n_A + n_B + n_C = n \qquad (1\text{-}13\text{-}28)$$

In addition to these restrictions, it is important to note that physical chemists have assumed that when equilibrium is reached each individual reaction must be balanced microscopically. Thus, every transition from A to B will occur as frequently as the reverse transition from B to A. As a result of this microscopic reversibility, three additional relations

$$k_{BA}\bar{n}_A = k_{AB}\bar{n}_B$$

$$k_{CB}\bar{n}_B = k_{BC}\bar{n}_C \tag{1-13-29}$$

$$k_{AC}\bar{n}_C = k_{CA}\bar{n}_A$$

are imposed. These correspond to the reciprocal relations in equations (1-13-6) and (1-13-12) and lead to one relation between the velocity constants,

$$k_{AC}k_{CB}k_{BA} = k_{AB}k_{BC}k_{CA} \tag{1-13-30}$$

Now this relation is not necessary to meet the thermodynamic requirement which will be satisfied when equilibrium is established by a set of positive values of the velocity constants. Indeed, other mechanisms may be postulated in which a detailed balancing of all the reactions does not occur as, for example, the scheme

But this type of mechanism is not in accord with the idea that molecular mechanics and the ordinary mechanics of conservative systems are fundamentally similar. With the exception of cases which involve Coriolis forces and external magnetic fields, the law of dynamic reversibility requires that if all the velocities of all the particles of a conservative dynamical system be reversed, the particles will retrace their former paths, thus reversing the previous succession of configurations. Applied to molecular mechanics, the assumption of dynamic reversibility implies that every type of motion has a probability equal to that of its reverse. This implies the assumption made above that when the molecule A changes a given number of times to molecule B, the reverse transition of B to A takes place just as often.

In order to complete the comparison between this chemical system and the phenomenological equations relating the flows to the forces, we must construct expressions for J_1, J_2, J_3 and X_1, X_2, X_3 which are the analogues of equations (1-13-5) or (1-13-10). To this end we employ the thermodynamic equation for the free energy at constant temperature and pressure of a single reaction in a perfect gas system. (Section (10) of this chapter).

$$\Delta F_{P,T} = RT\left[n_A \ln \frac{n_A}{\bar{n}_A} + n_B \ln \frac{n_B}{\bar{n}_B} + n_C \ln \frac{n_C}{\bar{n}_C} \right] \tag{1-13-31}$$

Using the condition specified by equation (1-13-28), it follows that

$$dF_{P,T,n} = RT\left[\ln \frac{n_A}{\bar{n}_A} dn_A + \ln \frac{n_B}{\bar{n}_B} dn_B + \ln \frac{n_C}{\bar{n}_C} dn_C \right] \tag{1-13-32}$$

Let the displacements of the concentration, X_A etc., be

$$X_A = n_A - \bar{n}_A \text{, etc.} \tag{1-13-33}$$

and write dF in the form

$$dF = -X_A \, dx_A - X_B \, dx_B - X_C \, dx_C \tag{1-13-34}$$

In order to obtain proportionality between the "forces", X_A, X_B, X_C, and the displacements x_A, x_B, x_C, it is necessary to impose the restriction that the system is not far from equilibrium. Thus

$$x_A \ll \bar{n}_A \text{, etc.} \tag{1-13-35}$$

and

$$X_A = - RT \ln \frac{n_A}{\bar{n}_A} \cong - \frac{RT}{\bar{n}_A} x_A$$

$$X_B \cong - \frac{RT}{\bar{n}_B} x_B \tag{1-13-36}$$

$$X_C \cong - \frac{RT}{\bar{n}_C} x_C$$

From equations (1-13-27) and (1-13-33), it follows that

$$\dot{x}_A = \frac{dx_A}{dt} = - (k_{BA} + k_{CA})x_A + k_{AB} x_B + k_{AC} x_C \tag{1-13-37}$$

and, finally by the use of (1-13-36)

$$\dot{x}_A = (k_{BA} + k_{CA}) \frac{\bar{n}_A}{RT} X_A - \frac{k_{AB} \bar{n}_B}{RT} X_B - \frac{k_{AC} \bar{n}_C}{RT} X_C$$

$$\dot{x}_B = - \frac{k_{BA} \bar{n}_A}{RT} X_A + (k_{AB} + k_{CB}) \frac{\bar{n}_B}{RT} X_B - \frac{k_{BC} \bar{n}_C}{RT} X_C \tag{1-13-38}$$

$$\dot{x}_C = - \frac{k_{CA} \bar{n}_A}{RT} X_A - \frac{k_{CB} \bar{n}_B}{RT} X_B + (k_{AC} + k_{BC}) \frac{\bar{n}_C}{RT} X_C$$

If this set of equations be compared with (1-13-5) it is immediately apparent that the analogy is complete, including all the reciprocal relations given by equations (1-13-6) and (1-13-29). In equations (1-13-38) $\dot{x}_A$, $\dot{x}_B$, $\dot{x}_C$ and the coefficients of X_A, X_B, X_C correspond to J_1, J_2, J_3 and $\mathfrak{M}_{11}$, $\cdots$ $\mathfrak{M}_{ik}$ $\cdots$ $\mathfrak{M}_{33}$ in equation (1-13-5).

That a deduction based upon linear laws for velocities and the principle of microscopic reversibility yields reciprocal relations between the coefficients of the "forces" in a closed system of chemical reactions suggests that a general theory of irreversible processes may be developed by the use of the same principle. Since x_A, x_B, x_C represent small displacements from equilibrium, it is to be expected that the problem should serve to reveal the more profound assumptions upon which the phenomenological equations rest.

(14) Derivation of Reciprocal Relations in Irreversible Processes from a Theory of Fluctuations, the Principle of Microscopic Reversibility and the Hypothesis of the Regression of Fluctuations.

Theory of Onsager

Forces, Displacements and Flows

We shall first define the quantities which correspond to the flows, **J**, and the forces, **X**, in the preceding phenomenological equations, (1-13-5) and (1-13-10). To express the entropy we choose a set of variables, α_1, α_2, $\cdots$ α_n which measure the displacements of heat, matter and electricity so that

$$S = \sigma(\alpha_1, \alpha_2, \cdots \alpha_n) \tag{1-14-1}$$

The nature of the displacements and the "forces" can be readily understood from consideration of the thermodynamic functions in equations (1-1-2) and (1-2-4)

$$dS = \frac{1}{T}(dE - P\,dV) + \frac{\mu}{T}\,dm + dW_{\mathrm{E}} \tag{1-1-4}$$

where

$$dW_{\mathrm{E}} = (\psi' - \psi'')\,de \quad \text{and} \quad \nabla\psi = \mathbf{X}$$

For example, if there exists a uniform gradient of T^{-1} in the x-direction, a quantity of heat dQ will be transferred a distance Δx_r and

$$dS = dQ\,\Delta x_r\,\frac{\partial T^{-1}}{\partial x_r} = d\alpha_r\,\frac{\partial T^{-1}}{\partial x_r} \tag{1-14-2}$$

and as a result

$$\frac{\partial S}{\partial \alpha_r} = \frac{\partial T^{-1}}{\partial x_r} \tag{1-14-3}$$

Similarly, if α_r represents a displacement of matter

$$\frac{\partial S}{\partial \alpha_r} = -\frac{\partial(\mu/T)}{\partial x_r} \tag{1-14-4}$$

and if α_r is a displacement of electric charge and X the field intensity

$$\partial S/\partial \alpha_r = X \tag{1-14-5}$$

The right members of these equations correspond to the forces in the phenomenological equations (1-13-5) and (1-13-10).

The flows of heat, matter and charge are proportional to these forces. Thus

$$\mathbf{J} \sim -\nabla T^{-1} \tag{1-14-6}$$

$$\mathbf{J} \sim T^{-1}\nabla\mu \tag{1-14-7}$$

$$\mathbf{J} \sim \nabla\psi \tag{1-14-8}$$

for the transport of heat, matter and electricity, respectively. In general, these relations may be expressed by

$$d\alpha_r/dt = \dot{\alpha}_r \sim \partial S/\partial\alpha_r \tag{1-14-9}$$

where $\dot{\alpha}_r$ is the flow $\mathbf{J}$ except for a volume factor. When a number, n, of transport processes take place simultaneously and interfere with one another, the flow is a function of the different displacements (α_1, α_2, $\cdots$ α_n) and

$$\dot{\alpha}_r = G_{r1}\frac{\partial\sigma}{\partial\alpha_r} + \cdots G_{rn}\frac{\partial\sigma}{\partial\alpha_n} \qquad (r = 1, 2, \cdots n) \tag{1-14-10}$$

where we follow the symbolism of Onsager in representing the entropy by σ [See equation (1-14-1)]. We shall proceed to show upon what assumptions general reciprocal relations of the type

$$G_{rs} = G_{sr} \tag{1-14-11}$$

may be derived from the principle of the microscopic reversibility and the general statistical theory of the fluctuations.

The General Theory of Fluctuations

The central idea of Onsager's theory of irreversible processes is to explore the conditions under which an initial thermodynamic state can be employed to predetermine the course of an irreversible process which proceeds according to definite empirical laws such as those for the flows of heat, electricity and matter. Towards this end, we choose the measurable extensive quantities, α_1, α_2, $\cdots$ α_n, which represent displacements of heat, matter, etc. as state variables. As indicated by equations (1-14-2) to (1-14-5), these variables are suitable for expressing the changes in entropy.

Statistical mechanics provides an explanation of thermodynamic equilibrium as a statistical equilibrium of elementary processes among a large number of molecules. Since the present theory involves the changes in entropy, the fundamental equation of Boltzmann

$$S = k \log W + \text{constant} \tag{1-14-12}$$

relating the entropy with the probability W is the most suitable as a basis for a theory of fluctuations from a state of equilibrium. It is to be observed that the probability involving a deviation in entropy, ΔS, is exp

($\Delta S/k$) where ΔS is necessarily negative. A fluctuation from an equilibrium state is appreciable when ΔS and k are of the same order of magnitude. Fluctuations of this order have been observed in some cases, for example, with liquids near the critical point.

The probability in terms of the measurable variables, α_1, α_2, $\cdots$ α_n will be expressed by a distribution function, $f(\alpha_1^r, \alpha_2^r, \cdots \alpha_n^r)$, so that in general the entropy of a given state will be

$$S^r = k \log f(\alpha_1^r, \alpha_2^r, \cdots \alpha_n^r) \qquad (1\text{-}14\text{-}13)$$

Now consider a system at constant energy in which the volume, pressure and the number of molecules are fixed. If this system is isolated for a sufficient length of time to reach equilibruim, then we may expect it will have passed through all the states, Γ_1, Γ_2, $\cdots$ Γ_l consistent with the conditions of isolation. Over a long time, t, the system will have spent a time t_r in the state Γ_r and t_1, t_2, $\cdots$ t_l will be proportional to the phase regions W_1, W_2, $\cdots$ W_l. It is to be noted that the ratios W_r/W_s are important and not W_r itself.

Of all these thermodynamic states given by a set of variables α_1, α_2, $\cdots$ α_n there will be one which will occur more frequently than all the others. We shall adopt the convention that this state of greatest entropy occurs when the variables have the values α_1', α_2', $\cdots$ α_n' and denote this entropy by

$$\sigma_{1 \ldots n}(\alpha_1', \alpha_2', \cdots \alpha_n') \qquad (1\text{-}14\text{-}14)$$

and the corresponding thermodynamic state

$$\Gamma_{1 \ldots n}'(\alpha_1', \alpha_2', \cdots \alpha_n') \qquad (1\text{-}14\text{-}15)$$

Then

$$\sigma_{1 \ldots n}(\alpha_1', \alpha_2', \cdots \alpha_n') = k \log f(\alpha_1', \alpha_2', \cdots \alpha_n') \qquad (1\text{-}14\text{-}16)$$

measures the probability of finding the variables, α_1, $\cdots$ α_n with the values α_1', $\cdots$ α_n'.

We shall now derive a valuable relation for the average values of the products of fluctuations and forces, $d\sigma/d\alpha_r$. For a single variable equation (1-14-16) becomes

$$\sigma_p(\alpha_p) = k \log f_p(\alpha_p) + \text{constant} \qquad (1\text{-}14\text{-}17)$$

Upon differentiation, we obtain

$$k \frac{df(\alpha_p)}{d\alpha_p} = f_p(\alpha_p) \frac{d\sigma_p}{d\alpha_p} \qquad (1\text{-}14\text{-}18)$$

Further

$$\int_{-\infty}^{\infty} f_p(\alpha_p) \, d\alpha_p = 1 \qquad (1\text{-}14\text{-}19)$$

since the sum of all the probabilities is unity. Now, let the entropy be a maximum when α_p equals α_p^0 and assume that $(\alpha_p - \alpha_p^0)f(\alpha_p)$ approaches zero for large positive or negative values of the fluctuation $(\alpha_p - \alpha_p^0)$. If this latter assumption is not true, the function must have an infinite number of maxima. With these premises, a simple result may be obtained by evaluating the average product of the fluctuation and the force. Thus

$$\overline{(\alpha_p - \alpha_p^0)\, d\sigma/d\alpha_p} = \int_{-\infty}^{\infty} (\alpha_p - \alpha_p^0)(d\sigma_p/d\alpha_p)f(\alpha_p)d\alpha_p \qquad (1\text{-}14\text{-}20)$$

$$= k \int_{-\infty}^{\infty} (\alpha_p - \alpha_p^0)(df(\alpha_p)/d\alpha_p)d\alpha_p \qquad (1\text{-}14\text{-}21)$$

which upon integration by parts becomes

$$\overline{(\alpha_p - \alpha_p^0)d\sigma/d\alpha_p} = k(\alpha_p - \alpha_p^0)f(\alpha_p)\Big]_{-\infty}^{\infty} - k \int_{-\infty}^{\infty} f_p(\alpha_p)d\alpha_p \qquad (1\text{-}14\text{-}22)$$

The first term on the right vanishes, and since the integral which remains equals unity

$$\overline{(\alpha_p - \alpha_p^0)\, d\sigma/d\alpha_p} = -k \qquad (1\text{-}14\text{-}23)$$

In a similar manner, it can be shown that

$$\overline{(\alpha_p - \alpha_p^0)\, d\sigma/d\alpha_p} = \begin{cases} -k; & p = q \\ 0; & p \neq q \end{cases} \qquad (1\text{-}14\text{-}24)$$

The Hypothesis of the Regression of Fluctuations and the Principle of Microscopic Reversibility

An understanding of the nature of the concepts and the assumptions involved in the theory may perhaps best be obtained by considering a process of flow in one direction. Over a long period of time, we observe the displacements, and whenever $\alpha = \alpha'$ we record its value t seconds later. The average of a large number of such observations shall be designated $\bar{\alpha}(t, \alpha')$. We recall that α' corresponds to an equilibrium state of maximum entropy. The flow

$$\frac{\bar{\alpha}(t + \tau, \alpha') - \bar{\alpha}(t, \alpha')}{\tau} \sim \frac{d\bar{\alpha}}{dt} = \dot{\alpha} \qquad (1\text{-}14\text{-}25)$$

is to be regarded as a quotient of differences.

The assumption is now made that *the average decay of fluctuations will obey the ordinary macroscopic phenomenological laws of transport.* Thus, for a displacement $\bar{\alpha}$ the flow $\dot{\alpha}$ is given by the linear equation

$$\dot{\alpha} = d\bar{\alpha}/dt = -K\bar{\alpha} = \frac{\bar{\alpha}(t + \tau) - \bar{\alpha}(t)}{\tau} \qquad (1\text{-}14\text{-}26)$$

which upon the integration yields

$$\bar{\alpha} = \bar{\alpha}_0 e^{-Kt} \tag{1-14-27}$$

For *positive t*, this equation is assumed to express the rate at which an average fluctuation caused by a force X diminishes. In Fig. (1-14-1), the upper portion of a graph of equation (1-14-26) for positive values of t is represented by the solid line. For convenience we let $\bar{\alpha} = \bar{\alpha}_0$ when $t = 0$. The magnitudes of the times involved are indicated in seconds on the ab-

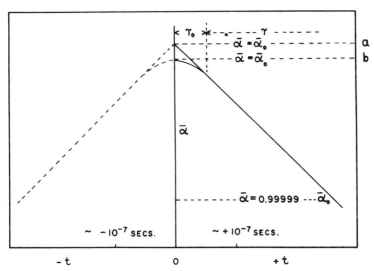

Fig. (1-14-1)
The hypothesis of the regression of fluctuations and microscopic reversibility.
(a) Equation (1-14-25)
(b) Adjusted for time of acceleration

scissa and the minuteness of the change in $\bar{\alpha}$ is indicated roughly on the ordinate.

Now, microscopic reversibility requires that

$$\bar{\alpha}(\tau, \alpha') = \bar{\alpha}(-\tau, \alpha')$$

$$\dot{\alpha}(\tau, \alpha') = -\dot{\alpha}(-\tau, \alpha') \tag{1-14-28}$$

$$\dot{\alpha}(0, \alpha') = -\dot{\alpha}(0, \alpha')$$

According to the macroscopic law of conduction, $\bar{\alpha}$ decreases for positive τ. According to microscopic reversibility $\dot{\alpha}$ decreases for positive τ and increases for negative τ, a condition illustrated by the dashed line in Fig. (1-14-1). If then the phenomenological law is to be substituted for the average values which occur in the equations for microscopic reversibility, it will be necessary to always express this latter principle in a form involving positive τ. This object is readily achieved when two suitable variables

α_i and α_j are considered simultaneously. Then, at equilibrium according to equation (1-14-28)

$$\overline{\alpha_j(t)\alpha_i(t + \tau)} = \overline{\alpha_j(t)\alpha_i(t - \tau)} \tag{1-14-29}$$

Now, this equation can be written in the alternative form

$$A_{ji} = \overline{\alpha_j(t)\alpha_i(t + \tau)} = \overline{\alpha_i(t)\alpha_j(t + \tau)} = A_{ij} \tag{1-14-30}$$

which means that the event $\alpha_j = \alpha_j'$, followed τ seconds later by $\alpha_i(t + \tau)$ takes place just as frequently as $\alpha_i = \alpha_i'$ followed τ seconds later by $\alpha_j'(t + \tau)$.

The straight solid and dashed lines in Fig. (1-14-1) according to equation (1-14-27) and its reverse (1-14-28) are discontinuous at τ equals 0. This is due to the neglect of the acceleration of the flow during a very short time interval τ_0. This effect is taken into account by the curve at the top of the figure. After the time, τ_0, there exists a time τ during which $\bar{\alpha}$ is proportional to τ within the narrowest of limits. During this latter time interval the flow is certainly given $\bar{\alpha}(t + \tau, \alpha') - \bar{\alpha}(t, \alpha')$ divided by τ. The time of acceleration, τ_0, is very much less than τ. It is of the order of magnitude of the time spent by a molecule between two collisions of molecules, or the time required to establish a steady state. Therefore, for most anticipated cases of conduction, τ_0 may be neglected and the law of conduction represented by the straight line.

In addition to the condition that $\tau \gg \tau_0$, we note the extremely small change in $\bar{\alpha}$ with the increase of t. In other words, the system is always near a condition of equilibrium so that $\bar{\alpha}(\tau, \alpha')$ may be inserted in the equations which express microscopic reversibility. As expressed by DeGroot,[21] τ_f the time during which a decay of a fluctuation is appreciable, or a deviation from equilibrium is sensibly reduced, is very much greater than τ. Thus,

$$\tau_0 \ll \tau \ll \tau_f \tag{1-14-31}$$

These considerations may easily be generalized. Consider the fluctuations of the variables of an isolated system over a long period of time. Whenever $\alpha_1, \alpha_2, \cdots \alpha_n$ have the values $\alpha_1', \alpha_2', \cdots \alpha_n'$ we record their values τ seconds later. The average of these recordings will be denoted

$$\bar{\alpha}_1(\tau, \alpha_1', \alpha_2', \cdots \alpha_n'), \cdots \bar{\alpha}_n(\tau, \alpha_1', \alpha_2', \cdots \alpha_n') \tag{1-14-32}$$

Almost every time $\alpha_1 = \alpha_1', \cdots \alpha_n = \alpha_n'$, the system will be in a phenomenological state

$$\Gamma_{1,\cdots n}' = \Gamma(\alpha_1', \cdots \alpha_n') \tag{1-14-33}$$

[21] S. R. DeGroot, "Thermodynamics of Irreversible Processes," p. 17, Interscience, Publishers, Inc., New York (1951); see also H. B. G. Casimir, *Rev. Modern Phys.*, **17**, 343 (1945).

and the average course of an irreversible process following this state and described by the averages

$$\bar{\alpha}_1(\tau, \Gamma'_{1\cdots n}), \quad \cdots \quad \bar{\alpha}_n(\tau, \Gamma'_{1\cdots n}) \tag{1-14-34}$$

will be known from macroscopic measurements and may be regarded as properties of the state $\Gamma'_{1\cdots n}$. The "normal" properties corresponding to $\alpha'_1, \cdots \alpha'_n$ are certainly those of the state $\Gamma'_{1,\cdots n}$. *Whether these normal and average values are interchangeable must be determined by consideration of each case.* If this interchange is valid, then the relation

$$\bar{\alpha}_i(\tau, \alpha'_1, \cdots \alpha'_n) = \bar{\alpha}_i(\tau, \Gamma'_{1\cdots n}) \tag{1-14-35}$$

may be adopted as a rule for predicting the average decay of fluctuations from the phenomenological laws of irreversible processes.

The Derivation of Reciprocal Relations in Simultaneous Irreversible Processes from Microscopic Reversibility and the Hypothesis for the Average Decay of Fluctuations

For mathematical convenience, we shall let the variables $\alpha_1, \cdots \alpha_n$ represent deviations from the state of equilibrium. We shall consider that the course of an irreversible process starting from an equilibrium state can be represented by the linear differential equation (1-14-10)

$$\frac{d\bar{\alpha}_i}{dt} = \dot{\alpha}_i = G_{ir} \frac{\partial \sigma_{1,\cdots n}(\alpha_1, \cdots \alpha_n)}{\partial \alpha_r}; \qquad i = 1, \cdots n \tag{1-14-36}$$

Microscopic reversibility will be expressed in the form

$$A_{ji} = \alpha_j(t)\alpha_i(t + \tau) = \alpha_i(t)a_j(t + \tau) = A_{ij} \tag{1-14-37}$$

Now consider a state of maximum entropy in which only a fluctuation in α_j occurs and which is specified by the conditions

$$\alpha_j = \alpha'_j \tag{1-14-38}$$

$$\frac{\partial \sigma_{1,\cdots n}}{\partial \alpha_r} = \begin{cases} 0; & r \neq j \\ d\sigma_j/d\alpha_r; & r = j \end{cases} \tag{1-14-39}$$

For a time interval τ following the equilibrium value of $\alpha_j = \alpha'_j$

$$\bar{\alpha}_i(\tau, \alpha'_j) = \bar{\alpha}_i(0, \alpha'_j) + \dot{\alpha}_i \tau \tag{1-14-40}$$

$$= \bar{\alpha}_i(0, \alpha'_j) + \sum_{r=1}^{n} G_{ir} \frac{\partial \sigma_{1,\cdots n}}{\partial \alpha_r} \tau \tag{1-14-41}$$

$$= \bar{\alpha}_i(0, \alpha'_j) + G_{ij} \frac{d\sigma_j}{d\alpha_r} \tau \tag{1-14-42}$$

The hypothesis of the regression of fluctuations permits the substitution of α'_i and α'_j for $\bar{\alpha}_i$ and $\bar{\alpha}_j$ in the expressions for microscopic reversibility.

Thus

$$A_{ji} = \overline{\alpha_j(t)\alpha_i(t + \tau)} = \overline{\alpha_j'(t)\alpha_i(0, \alpha_j')} + \overline{G_{ij}\alpha_j'\frac{d\sigma_j}{\partial\alpha_j}}\tau \quad (1\text{-}14\text{-}43)$$

Similarly

$$A_{ij} = \overline{\alpha_i(t)\alpha_j(t + \tau)} = \overline{\alpha_i'(t)\alpha_j(0, \alpha_j')} + \overline{G_{ji}\alpha_j'\frac{d\sigma_i}{d\alpha_i}}\tau \quad (1\text{-}14\text{-}44)$$

Since α_j and α_i are small fluctuations corresponding to $(\alpha_p - \alpha_p^0)$ in equation (1-14-23)

$$\overline{\alpha_j'\frac{d\sigma_j}{d\alpha_j}} = \overline{\alpha_i'\frac{d\sigma_i}{d\alpha_i}} = -k \quad (1\text{-}14\text{-}45)$$

Microscopic reversibility requires the equality of A_{ji} and A_{ij} and therefore

$$A_{ji} = A_{ji}(0) - kTG_{ij} = A_{ij}(0) - k\tau G_{ji} = A_{ij} \quad (1\text{-}14\text{-}46)$$

whence

$$G_{ij} = G_{ji} \quad (1\text{-}14\text{-}47)$$

the reciprocal relations for the coefficients of the flows.

If we now substitute $\dot{\alpha}_i$, G_{ir} and $\dfrac{\partial\sigma}{\partial\alpha_r}$ by their corresponding quantities J_i, $\mathfrak{M}_{ir}$ and X_r, equation (1-14-36) reduces to equation (1-13-5) and equation (1-14-47) yields the reciprocal relations, $\mathfrak{M}_{ij} = \mathfrak{M}_{ji}$, of equation (1-13-6).

The preceding statements and deductions include the principal results of Onsager's theory as presented in his original contributions. More recently, the statistical theory of irreversible processes has been extended.[22, 23] Upon the additional assumption that the fluctuating thermodynamic variables are Gaussian random variables, the probability of a given succession of non-equilibrium states in a fluctuating thermodynamic system is calculated. This probability can be expressed in terms of the dissipation function and as a result the statistical significance of the dissipation function is revealed. For systems in which the kinetic energies of the various flows contributes to the entropy (e.g., magnetic energy in electric circuits), it is necessary to add velocity variables to the displacements used in the previous development of the theory. This matter is treated in the contribution by Machlup and Onsager.*

For the thorough application of this theory to numerous steady state

[22] L. Onsager and S. Machlup, *Phys. Rev.*, 91, 1505 (1953).
[23] S. Maclup and L. Onsager, *Ibid*, **91**, 1512 (1953).
* In a recent contribution [*J. Phys. Chem.* **61**, 622 (1957)] O. K. Rice has presented a general kinetic treatment directed to the elucidation of the thermodynamics of irreversible processes.

processes we recommend the treatise of DeGroot.[24]   We shall restrict our discussion to processes which involve ions in solution.

(15) Applications to Processes Involving the Simultaneous Flows of Ions and Heat*

We shall consider a system in which the current densities of matter, J_i, are initiated by the presence of gradients of the chemical potentials of the ions, μ_i, the temperature, T, the electrical potential, ψ, and the gravitational potential, ϕ.   In order to avoid the difficulty of defining separately the electrostatic and the chemical potentials of the ions, the electrochemical potential

$$\bar{\mu}_j \equiv \mu_j + z_j F\psi \qquad (1\text{-}15\text{-}1)$$

as defined by Brönsted[25] and Guggenheim[26] will be employed for cases where the gravitational potential may be neglected.   To include the gravitational field, we shall introduce the quantity defined by

$$\tilde{\mu}_j = \mu_j + z_j F\psi + M_j\phi \qquad (1\text{-}15\text{-}2)$$

where ϕ is the gravitational potential and M_j the molecular weight of the ion.   The potential $\phi = gx$ where g is the acceleration of gravitation and $\phi = -\frac{1}{2}\omega^2 x$ in the centrifugal field.

After a sufficient length of time, a closed system will reach a stationary state in which heat transport will be present but in which the currents of matter will vanish.   The derivation of the equations which describe the staionary state of a solution in which gradients of concentrations, temperature, electrical and gravitational potentials exist will serve to illustrate the importance of the reciprocal relations in obtaining unambiguous solutions of problems of this nature.

The current density of the ith species, J_i, and the current density of heat, Q, are given by

$$J_i = -\mathfrak{M}_{i0}\nabla \ln T - \sum_{j=1}^{s} \mathfrak{M}_{ij}\nabla_T \tilde{\mu}_j \qquad (1\text{-}15\text{-}3)$$

and

$$Q = -\mathfrak{M}_{00}\nabla \ln T - \sum_{j=1}^{s} \mathfrak{M}_{0j}\nabla_T \tilde{\mu}_j \qquad (1\text{-}15\text{-}4)$$

* A thorough formulation of the macroscopic equations of transport based upon a postulate of local thermodynamic equilibrium has been presented by J. G. Kirkwood and B. Crawford, Jr., *J. Phys. Chem.*, **56**, 1048 (1952).   For the treatment of the subject in this section, we are greatly indebted to Professor John G. Kirkwood.

[24] S. R. DeGroot, "Thermodynamics of Irreversible Processes," Interscience Publishers, Inc., New York (1951).

[25] J. N. Brönsted, *Z. physik. Chem.*, **143**, 301 (1929).

[26] E. A. Guggenheim, *J. Phys. Chem.*, **33**, 842 (1929); **34**, 1540 (1930).

$\mathfrak{M}_{ij}$ is the admittance matrix for mass flow. By inversion, equation (1-15-3) yields

$$\nabla_T \tilde{\mu}_j = -\sum_{i=1}^{s} R_{ji}[\mathbf{J}_i + \mathfrak{M}_{i0}\nabla \ln T] \qquad (1\text{-}15\text{-}5)$$

$R_{ij}|\mathfrak{M}| = |\mathfrak{M}|_{ij}$, where $|\mathfrak{M}|$ is the determinant of the coefficients $\mathfrak{M}_{ij}$, and $|\mathfrak{M}|_{ij}$ is the appropriate cofactor. Combination with (1-15-4) yields

$$\mathbf{Q} = -\left[\mathfrak{M}_{00} - \sum_{i=1}^{s} \mathfrak{M}_{i0}\tilde{Q}_i\right]\nabla \ln T + \sum_{i=1}^{s} \tilde{Q}_i \mathbf{J}_i \qquad (1\text{-}15\text{-}6)$$

where

$$\tilde{Q}_i \equiv \sum_{j=1}^{s} R_{ij}\mathfrak{M}_{0j} \qquad (1\text{-}15\text{-}7)$$

This equation defines the heats of transport.[27]

At this stage, the value of the reciprocal relations, $R_{ij} = R_{ji}$ is revealed, for by their use equation (1-15-5) may be written

$$\nabla_{P,T}\tilde{\mu}_j = -\sum_{i=1}^{s} R_{ij}\mathfrak{M}_{0i}\nabla \ln T - \sum_{i=1}^{s} R_{ij}\mathbf{J}_i \qquad (1\text{-}15\text{-}8)$$

or

$$\nabla_{P,T}\tilde{\mu}_j = -\tilde{Q}_j\nabla \ln T - \sum_{i=1}^{s} R_{ij}\mathbf{J}_i \qquad (1\text{-}15\text{-}9)$$

The chemical potential is a function of the pressure and temperature so that

$$d\mu_j = d\mu_j]_{P,T} + \frac{\partial\mu_j}{\partial T}dT + \frac{\partial\mu_j}{\partial P}dP$$

or

$$d\mu_j = d\mu_j]_{P,T} - \bar{S}_j dT + \bar{V}_j dP \qquad (1\text{-}15\text{-}10)$$

where $\bar{S}_j$ and $\bar{V}_j$ are the partial entropy and volume, respectively. Therefore, differentiation of equation (1-15-2) and substitution yields

$$\nabla\tilde{\mu}_j = \nabla_T\mu_j - \bar{S}_j\nabla T + z_j\mathbf{F}\nabla\psi + M_j\nabla\phi \qquad (1\text{-}15\text{-}11)$$

or in the absence of a pressure gradient

$$\nabla_P\tilde{\mu}_j = \nabla_{P,T}\mu_j - \bar{S}_j\nabla T + z_j\mathbf{F}\nabla\psi \qquad (1\text{-}15\text{-}12)$$

Since the partial heat content, $\bar{H}_j$, equals $\mu_j + T\bar{S}_j$, equation (1-15-8)

---

[27] Thermal quantities of this kind were introduced by Eastman in his pioneer investigations of the Soret effect [*J. Am. Chem. Soc.*, **50**, 283, 290 (1932)]. DeGroot employs the symbol Q_i^{**} for the quantity $\tilde{Q}_i$ [*Thermodynamics of Irreversible Processes*, Interscience Publishers, Inc., New York (1951)].

may be written in the alternative forms

$$T\nabla\left(\frac{\mu_j}{T}\right) = -z_j \mathbf{F}\nabla\psi - Q_j^* \nabla \ln T - M_j\nabla\phi - \sum_{i=1}^{s} R_{ij} \mathbf{J}_i \quad (1\text{-}15\text{-}13)$$

or, at constant pressure

$$T\nabla_P\left(\frac{\mu_j}{T}\right) = -z_j \mathbf{F}\nabla\psi - Q_j^* \nabla \ln T - \sum_{i=1}^{s} R_{ij} \mathbf{J}_i \quad (1\text{-}15\text{-}14)$$

where $Q_j^* = \tilde{Q}_j + \bar{H}_j$. Recalling the definitional equation (1-6-2), we may change this latter equation to

$$\nabla_P \ln a_j = -\frac{z_j \mathbf{F}\nabla\psi}{RT} - \frac{(\tilde{Q}_j - \bar{L}_j)}{RT} \nabla \ln T - \sum_{i=1}^{s} R_{ij} \mathbf{J}_i \quad (1\text{-}15\text{-}15)$$

where $\bar{L}_j$ is the relative partial heat content.

The Soret Effect

Consider a vertical tube containing a solution of s ions evenly distributed. Let this system be subjected to a temperature gradient positive downwards which will cause a flow of heat. This temperature gradient will produce ionic currents until a stationary state of the mass currents occurs, or when the J_i are zero. Under this stationary condition heat will continue to enter and leave the system. Since the pressure may be regarded as constant, the electrical potential gradient may be obtained by multiplying both sides of equation (1-15-14) by T_j/z_j, where T_j is the transference number, and z_j the valence of the ion. Upon summing over j, we obtain

$$-\mathbf{F}\nabla\psi = \sum_{j=1}^{s} \frac{T_j}{z_j} T\nabla_P\left(\frac{\mu_j}{T}\right) + \sum_{j=1}^{s} \frac{T_j}{z_j} Q_j^* \nabla \ln T \quad (1\text{-}15\text{-}16)$$

It is important to note that this result does not require the vanishing of the individual mass currents, $\mathbf{J}_j$, but is valid when

$$\sum_{i=1}^{s} \sum_{j=1}^{s} \frac{T_j}{z_j} R_{ij} \mathbf{J}_j = 0 \quad (1\text{-}15\text{-}17)$$

The transference numbers are defined in terms of admittance matrix by

$$T_j \equiv \frac{\displaystyle\sum_{i=1}^{s} z_i z_j \mathfrak{M}_{ij}}{\displaystyle\sum_{i,j=1}^{s} z_i z_j \mathfrak{M}_{ij}} \quad (1\text{-}15\text{-}18)$$

Then, it follows that

$$\sum_{j=1}^{s} \frac{T_j}{z_j} R_{ij} = \frac{z_i}{\displaystyle\sum_{r,p=1}^{s} z_r z_p \mathfrak{M}_{rp}} \quad (1\text{-}15\text{-}19)$$

and equation (1-15-17) is consistent with the condition

$$\sum_{i=1}^{s} z_i J_i = 0 \qquad (1\text{-}15\text{-}20)$$

which implies that the electric current, i, vanishes, or that

$$i = \sum_{i=1}^{s} z_i F J_i = 0 \qquad (1\text{-}15\text{-}21)$$

In the stationary state, $J_i = 0$, equation (1-15-14) becomes

$$-z_j F \nabla \psi = T \nabla \left(\frac{\mu_j}{T}\right) + Q_j^* \nabla \ln T \qquad (1\text{-}15\text{-}22)$$

By substitution of the value of $\nabla \psi$ in equation (1-15-16), we obtain

$$\sum_{i=1}^{s} \left(\delta_{ij} - z_j \frac{T_i}{z_i}\right)\left(T \nabla \left(\frac{\mu_i}{T}\right) + Q_i^* \nabla \ln T\right) = 0; \qquad j = 1, 2, \cdots s \quad (1\text{-}15\text{-}23)$$

where δ_{ij} is the Kroenecker symbol. Let $\lambda_i z_i$ replace the second parenthesis in this equation with the result

$$\sum_{i=1}^{s} \left(\delta_{ij} - z_j \frac{T_i}{z_i}\right)\lambda_i z_i ; \qquad j = 1, 2, \cdots s \qquad (1\text{-}15\text{-}24)$$

We note that $\sum_{i=1}^{s} \delta_{ij}(\lambda_j z_j) = \lambda_i z_i$. Solution of the system of equations (1-15-24) shows that

$$\lambda_1 = \lambda_2 = \cdots = \lambda_s = \lambda = -F \nabla \psi \qquad (1\text{-}15\text{-}25)$$

Further, the determinant of equation (1-15-24) vanishes and consequently $(s - 1)$ of the desired quantities, λ_i, are independent and only the ratios of their values are determined. Therefore in order to evaluate the quantities, λ_i, themselves, an additional condition such as electrical neutrality

$$\sum_{i=1}^{s} c_i z_i = 0 \qquad (1\text{-}15\text{-}26)$$

is required.

The Soret Coefficient

It is now possible to compute the distribution of the ionic chemical potentials and show the restricted conditions under which the Soret coefficient, $d\ln c_i/dT$, is related to the heats of transport. From equation (1-15-23) and (1-15-25), we have

$$T \nabla_P \left(\frac{\mu_i}{T}\right) + Q_i^* \nabla \ln T = \nabla_{P,T} \mu_i + \tilde{Q}_i \nabla \ln T = \lambda_i z_i; \qquad \lambda_i = \lambda \quad (1\text{-}15\text{-}27)$$

Multiplying by $c_i z_i$ and summing yields

$$\sum_{i=1}^{s} c_i z_i \nabla_{P,T} \mu_i + \sum_{i=1}^{s} c_i z_i \tilde{Q}_i \nabla \ln T = \lambda \sum_{i=1}^{s} c_i z_i^2 \qquad (1\text{-}15\text{-}28)$$

so that

$$-\mathbf{F} \nabla \psi = \lambda = \frac{\displaystyle\sum_{j=1}^{s} c_j z_j \nabla_{P;T} \mu_j + \sum_{j=1}^{s} c_j z_j \tilde{Q}_j \nabla \ln T}{\displaystyle\sum_{j=1}^{s} c_j z_j^2} \qquad (1\text{-}15\text{-}29)$$

Substituting for λ in equation (1-15-27) and rearranging gives

$$\nabla_{P,T} \mu_i = -\left[\tilde{Q}_i - \frac{z_i \displaystyle\sum_{j=1}^{s} c_j z_j \tilde{Q}_j}{\displaystyle\sum_{j=1}^{s} c_j z_j^2} \right] \nabla \ln T + z_i \frac{\displaystyle\sum_{j=1}^{s} c_j z_j}{\displaystyle\sum_{j=1}^{s} c_j z_j^2} \nabla_{P,T} \mu_j \qquad (1\text{-}15\text{-}30)$$

To introduce the ionic concentrations, we employ the relation (1-6-1)

$$\mu_j - \mu_j^0 = RT \ln a_j = RT \ln c_j y_j \qquad (1\text{-}6\text{-}1)$$

where a_j, c_j and y_j represent the activity, concentration and activity coefficient of the ion. Upon differentiation, multiplication by $c_j z_j$ and summation we obtain

$$\sum_{j=1}^{s} c_j z_j \nabla_{P,T} \mu_j = RT \sum_{j=1}^{s} c_j z_j \nabla_{P,T} \ln y_j \qquad (1\text{-}15\text{-}31)$$

since electrical neutrality requires that

$$\sum_{j=1}^{s} c_j z_j \nabla_{P,T} \ln c_j = 0 \qquad (1\text{-}15\text{-}32)$$

Equation (1-15-30) now becomes

$$\nabla_{P,T} \ln c_i = -\frac{1}{RT} \left[\tilde{Q}_i - z_i \frac{\displaystyle\sum_{j=1}^{s} c_j z_j \tilde{Q}_j}{\displaystyle\sum_{j=1}^{s} c_j z_j^2} \right] \nabla \ln T$$

$$\qquad (1\text{-}15\text{-}33)$$

$$- z_i \frac{\displaystyle\sum_{j=1}^{s} c_j z_j}{\displaystyle\sum_{j=1}^{s} c_j z_j^2} \nabla_{P,T} \ln y_j - \nabla_{P,T} \ln y_i$$

The terms containing the individual ionic activity coefficients are not capable of evaluation until the difficulty of the source of the electrical potential at single boundaries is solved (See Chapter (10), Sections (6) and

(7)). Since, however, the standard potentials μ_i^0 are so chosen as to cause all activity coefficients to approach unity as the concentrations approach zero, these terms vanish at the limit of zero concentration and equation (1-15-33) may be reduced to[28]

$$\frac{1}{c_i}\frac{dc_i}{dT} = -\frac{1}{RT^2}\left[\tilde{Q}_i - \frac{z_i \sum_{j=1}^{s} c_j z_j \tilde{Q}_j}{\sum_{j=1}^{s} c_j z_j^2}\right] \tag{1-15-34}$$

The Liquid Junction Potential

Equation (1-15-16) is an expression for the gradient of the electrical potential, $\nabla\psi$, produced within the solution by ordinary and thermal diffusion. At constant pressure and temperature, this equation reduces to

$$\mathbf{F}\nabla\psi = -\left(\sum_{j=1}^{s} \frac{T_j}{z_j}\frac{d\mu_j}{dx}\right)dx \tag{1-15-35}$$

In the above form or in the form

$$\psi = -\frac{RT}{F}\int_{\mathrm{I}}^{\mathrm{II}}\sum_{j=1}^{s}\frac{T_j}{z_j}d\ln a_j \tag{1-15-36}$$

we have obtained the well-known expressions for the liquid junction of diffusion potential.[29] The integration is extended over the entire range or concentration.

We have noted that equation (1-15-16) and consequently equation (1-15-36) do not depend on the vanishing of the individual mass currents, but do depend on the vanishing of the electric current. Therefore, a potentiometric measurement in which ψ is exactly balanced by an external potential yields an exact value of ψ even though a diffusion process is proceeding.

An alternative method[30] of deducing equation (1-15-16) based upon the condition of the vanishing of the electric current density is revealing.

From equation (1-15-8), upon neglecting the gravitational field, we obtain

$$\mathbf{J}_i = -\sum_{j=1}^{s}\mathfrak{M}_{ij}[\nabla_{P,T}\bar{\mu}_j + \tilde{Q}_j\nabla\ln T] \tag{1-15-37}$$

or upon rearrangement

$$\sum_{j=1}^{s} z_j\mathfrak{M}_{ij}\mathbf{F}\nabla\psi + \mathbf{J}_i = -\sum_{j=1}^{s}\mathfrak{M}_{ij}\left[T\nabla_P\left(\frac{\mu_j}{T}\right) + Q_j^*\nabla\ln T\right] \tag{1-15-38}$$

---

[28] This equation is given by H. J. V. Tyrrell, Chap. 13, p. 119, "Electrochemical Constants," National Bureau of Standards Circular, 524 (1953). This contribution contains a comprehensive bibliography relating to the Soret effect.

[29] For further discussion of equation (1-15-36), see Chapter (10), Section (6).

[30] This treatment was pointed out to us by Prof. John G. Kirkwood.

Multiplying by z_i, summing over i, and recalling that the electric current density, $\mathbf{i} = \sum_{i=1}^{s} z_i \mathbf{F} \mathbf{J}_i$, we obtain

$$\sum_{i,j=1}^{s} z_i z_j \mathfrak{M}_{ij} \mathbf{F} \nabla \psi + \mathbf{i}/\mathbf{F}$$

$$= - \sum_{i,j=1}^{s} z_i \mathfrak{M}_{ij} \left[T \nabla_P \left(\frac{\mu_j}{T} \right) + Q_j^* \nabla \ln T \right] \qquad (1\text{-}15\text{-}39)$$

Introducing the definitions of the transference numbers (Equation 1-15-18) and the specific resistance, L,

$$L \equiv \frac{1}{\mathbf{F}^2 \sum\limits_{i,j=1}^{s} z_i z_j \mathfrak{M}_{ij}} \qquad (1\text{-}15\text{-}40)$$

we find that

$$\mathbf{F} \left[\nabla \psi + L \mathbf{i} \right] = - \sum_{i,j=1}^{s} \frac{T_j}{z_j} \left[T \nabla_P \left(\frac{\mu_j}{T} \right) + Q_j^* \nabla \ln T \right] \qquad (1\text{-}15\text{-}41)$$

which becomes equation (1-15-16) subject only to the vanishing of the electric current density.

Defining the vector electromotive force by

$$\mathbf{E} = \nabla \psi + L \mathbf{i} \qquad (1\text{-}15\text{-}42)$$

and replacing $\nabla \psi$ by the electrical field, $\mathbf{X}$, we have

$$L \mathbf{i} = (\mathbf{E} - \mathbf{X}), \qquad \text{or } \mathbf{E} = \mathbf{X} \text{ when } L \mathbf{i} = 0 \qquad (1\text{-}15\text{-}43)$$

The Equilibrium Centrifuge

The high velocity centrifuge as developed by Svedberg[31, 32] has been employed for the determination of the molecular weights and the thermodynamic properties of solutions by Peterson,[33] Drucker,[34] Tiselius[35] and by Johnson, Kraus and Young.[36] A lower velocity centrifuge by which accurate measurements of the electromotive forces of cells in a centrifugal field has been perfected by MacInnes[37], and described by MacInnes and Ray.[38]

[31] Th. Svedberg, *Kolloid Z.*, **36**, 53 (1925); *Z. physik Chem.*, **121**, 65 (1926).

[32] Th. Svedberg and K. O. Peterson, *The Ultracentrifuge*, The Clarendon Press, Oxford (1940).

[33] K. O. Peterson, *Z. physik. Chem.*, **A170**, 41 (1934).

[34] C. Drucker, *Ibid.*, **A180**, 359, 378 (1937).

[35] A. Tiselius, *Ibid.*, **124**, 449 (1926).

[36] J. S. Johnson, K. A. Kraus and T. F. Young, *J. Am. Chem. Soc.* **76**, 1436 (1954); *J. Chem. Phys.*, **22**, 878 (1954).

[37] D. A. MacInnes, *Ann. N. Y. Acad. Sci.*, **43**, 243 (1942); *Electrochemical Constants*, p. 41, Nat. Bur. Standards Circular 524 (1953).

[38] D. A. MacInnes and B. R. Ray, *J. Am. Chem. Soc.*, **71**, 2987 (1949).

We may develop the theory of the equilibrium centrifuge from equation (1-15-11) by introducing condition that at equilibrium,

$$\nabla_T \bar{\mu}_j = 0; \qquad j = 1, \cdots s \qquad (1\text{-}15\text{-}44)$$

At constant temperature

$$\nabla_T \bar{\mu}_j = \bar{V}_j \nabla P + z_j \mathbf{F} \nabla \psi + M_j \nabla \phi + \nabla_{P,T} \mu_j \qquad (1\text{-}15\text{-}45)$$

If ρ is the density of the solution then

$$\nabla P = -\rho \nabla \phi \qquad (1\text{-}15\text{-}46)$$

so that if

$$M'_j \equiv M_j - \rho \bar{V}_j \qquad (1\text{-}15\text{-}47)$$

we obtain at equilibrium

$$\nabla_T \bar{\mu}_j = 0 = \nabla_{P,T} \mu_j + M'_j \nabla \phi + z_j \mathbf{F} \nabla \psi \qquad (1\text{-}15\text{-}48)$$

For any neutral combination of ions, $\sum_{j=1}^{s} \nu_j z_j = 0$, and

$$\sum_{j=1}^{s} \nabla_{P,T}(\nu_j \mu_j) = -\sum_{j=1}^{s} \nu_j M'_j \nabla \phi \qquad (1\text{-}15\text{-}49)$$

or since at constant pressure and temperature

$$d\mu_j = \sum_{j=1}^{s} \left(\frac{\partial \mu_j}{\partial c_j} \right)_{P,T,c_r} dc_j = RT d \ln a_j \qquad (1\text{-}15\text{-}50)$$

we obtain

$$RT \sum_{j=1}^{s} \nu_j d \ln a_j \bigg]_{P,T,c_r} = -\sum_{j=1}^{s} \nu_j (M_j - \rho \bar{V}_j) d\phi \qquad (1\text{-}15\text{-}51)$$

The sedimentation potential, ψ, may be obtained by multiplying equation (1-15-48) by T_j/z_j and summing over j with the result

$$-\mathbf{F} \nabla \psi = \sum_{j=1}^{s} \frac{T_j}{z_j} [\nabla_{P,T} \mu_j + M'_j \nabla \phi] \qquad (1\text{-}15\text{-}52)$$

Adopting the procedure used in deriving equation (1-15-23), we substitute this latter value of $\mathbf{F} \nabla \psi$ in equation (1-15-48) and obtain the set of linear equations

$$\sum_{i=1}^{s} \left(\delta_{ij} - z_j \frac{T_i}{z_i} \right) (\nabla_{P,T} \mu_i + M'_i \nabla \phi) = 0 \qquad (1\text{-}15\text{-}53)$$

Since the determinant of this system of equations is zero, $(s - 1)$ relations of the kind

$$\frac{\nabla_{P,T} \mu_i + M'_i \nabla \phi}{z_i} = \lambda'_i \ (i = 1, \cdots s) = -\mathbf{F} \nabla \psi \qquad (1\text{-}15\text{-}54)$$

are obtained which fix the ratios of the required quantities but which do not permit the evaluation of the quantities themselves. To effect this determination the supplementary condition of electrical neutrality

$$\sum_{j=1}^{s} c_j z_j = 0 \qquad (\text{I-15-55})$$

must be employed to evaluate a given λ_i'.

Chapter (2)

General Statement of the Interionic Attraction Theory and Properties of Ionic Atmospheres

Progress in developing the modern theory of ionic solutions has depended on one factor, namely, that the law of the force of attraction between ions is known. Upon the basis of this law, and by the specialized application of the fundamental concepts of electrostatics, hydrodynamics and statistical mechanics, an exact theory has been developed which will describe the properties of electrolytes under circumstances where these forces are the predominating factor and where other influences, such as intermolecular forces and short-range repulsive forces between ions, may be considered negligible. Consequently, the first step in constructing a theory requires a quantitative investigation of the effects of the forces between the ions on all the known properties of ionic solutions. If this is done correctly, and if under suitable conditions the results are verified experimentally, the next step in elucidating the electrolytic state of matter from the observed deviations from these laws may be undertaken with some hope of success.

Fortunately, it is possible to test the conclusions of the interionic attraction theory directly, since there exists a class of strong electrolytes which at moderate concentrations in water seem to be completely dissociated, and which conform to the simple electrostatic picture of charged ions in a medium of a given dielectric constant. It has been suspected for a long time that the behavior of strong electrolytes in dilute solution could be accounted for by the hypothesis of complete dissociation and an adequate consideration of the effects of interionic attraction. Sutherland,[1] Noyes,[2] and particularly Bjerrum[3] were among the first to adopt this point of view. Before this van Laar[4] had emphasized the importance of electrostatic forces in explaining the characteristics of ionic solutions. Hertz[5] and

[1] W. Sutherland, *Phil. Mag.* (6), **3**, 167 (1902); **7**, 1 (1906).

[2] A. A. Noyes, *Congress Arts Sci., St. Louis Exposition*, **4**, 317 (1904).

[3] N. Bjerrum, *D. Kgl. Danske Vidensk. Selsk. Skrifter* (7), **4**, 1 (1906); Proc. 7th Intern. Congr. Applied Chemistry, Sect. X, London (1909); 16 *Skand. Naturforsk. Forhandl.*, 226, 1916; *Z. Electrochem.*, **24**, 321 (1918); *Meddel. Kgl. Vet. Akad. Nobel-inst.*, **5**, No. 16 (1919); *Z. anorg. Chem.*, **109**, 275 (1920).

[4] J. J. van Laar, *Z. physik. Chem.*, **15**, 457 (1894); **17**, 245 (1895); **19**, 318 (1896); *Z. anorg. Chem.*, **139**, 108 (1924).

[5] P. Hertz, *Ann. Physik.* (4), **37**, 1 (1912).

Ghosh[6] attempted to give the effects of interionic attraction mathematical expression, but the basis of their treatments proved to be inadequate. Milner[7] successfully analyzed the problem, but his mathematical treatment was exceedingly involved and did not yield an entirely satisfactory result.

The conception of the ionic "atmosphere" introduced by Debye, and his use of Poisson's equation, effected an ingenious mathematical short cut which leads to exact relations from which the behaviors of dilute solutions of electrolytes may be quantitatively predicted. In their first contribution to this theory, Debye and Hückel[8] computed successfully the limiting law for the activity coefficient, that is to say, an exact theoretical expression for the behavior of this property in extremely dilute solutions.

Upon the basis of their theory, they[9] were able also to make an important contribution to the theory of electrolytic conductance. Somewhat later, by developing a general treatment of the motion of ions, Onsager[10] derived the limiting law for electrolytic conductance. Later, Onsager's theory of conductance was extended by Debye and Falkenhagen[11] so that the effects of high frequency upon the conductance and dielectric constant were taken into account. The limiting law for the viscosity of an electrolytic solution has been deduced by Falkenhagen,[12] and the general laws of the diffusion of electrolytes have been investigated by Onsager and Fuoss.[13] Further, the Wien effect, or the influence of fields of high intensity upon the properties of these solutions, has been investigated from the theoretical point of view by Joos and Blumentritt.[14] More recently, Wilson[15a] has obtained a complete solution of this problem for the case of electrolytes which dissociate into two ions, and Kim[15b] has extended the treatment to electrolytes of all valence types. The theoretical treatment of the effects of high fields upon the ionization of weak electrolytes has been developed in a very interesting manner by Onsager.[16]

[6] I. C. Ghosh, *J. Chem. Soc.*, **113**, 449, 627, 707, 790 (1918); *Trans. Faraday Soc.*, **15**, 154 (1919); *J. Chem. Soc.*, **117**, 823, 1390 (1920); *Z. physik. Chem.*, **98**, 211 (1921).

[7] R. Milner, *Phil. Mag.*, **23**, 551 (1912); **25**, 742 (1913).

[8] P. Debye and E. Hückel, *Physik. Z.*, **24**, 185 (1923). The statistical basis of this theory has been examined by R. H. Fowler, *Trans. Faraday Soc.*, **23**, 434 (1927); L. Onsager, *Chem. Rev.*, **13**, 73 (1933); H. A. Kramers, *Proc. Royal Acad. Sci. Amsterdam*, **30**, 145 (1927); J. G. Kirkwood, *J. Chem. Phys.*, **2**, 767 (1934).

[9] P. Debye and E. Hückel, *Physik. Z.*, **24**, 305 (1923).

[10] L. Onsager, *Physik. Z.*, **28**, 277 (1927).

[11] P. Debye and H. Falkenhagen, *Physik. Z.*, **29**, 121, 401 (1928).

[12] H. Falkenhagen and M. Dole, *Z. physik. Chem.*, **6**, 159 (1929); *Physik. Z.*, **30**, 611 (1929); H. Falkenhagen, *Physik. Z.*, **32**, 365, 745 (1931).

[13] L. Onsager and R. M. Fuoss, *J. Physical Chem.*, **34**, 2689 (1932).

[14] G. Joos and M. Blumentritt, *Physik. Z.*, **28**, 836 (1927).

[15a] W. S. Wilson, *Dissertation*, Yale University, June, 1936.

[15b] Shoon K. Kim, *Dissertation*, Yale University, June, 1956; L. Onsager and Shoon K. Kim, *J. Phys. Chem.*, **61**, 198, (1957).

[16] L. Onsager, *J. Chem. Phys.*, **2**, 599 (1934).

This brief survey of the history of the theory shows that it has now reached an advanced stage of development and has been applied successfully to most of the thermodynamic properties and irreversible processes in solutions. In this chapter, we shall examine the fundamental basis of the theory and derive the general equations for its application to various phenomena. In Chapters (3) and (4), we shall consider the reversible and irreversible properties, respectively.

The Ionic Atmosphere

In considering an ionic solution, two factors are of fundamental and equal importance. The first of these is the distribution of the ions with respect to one another, and the second the forces acting on the ions due to the presence of the ions themselves and external forces. These factors are not mutually exclusive, since the forces affect the distribution of the ions and the distribution of the ions determines the forces. The first step in developing the theory will be the formulation of distribution functions which are sufficiently general for the treatment of an ionic solution in equilibrium or in a perturbed state, the latter being caused by external disturbances such as imposed electrical fields or the flow of the solution as a whole.

Since the original contribution of Debye and Hückel, the theory for the solution in the absence of external fields has been frequently presented in a simple manner.[17] Although this simplified treatment is satisfactory for the equilibrium case, it is not general enough for the theory of solutions under the influence of external forces, e.g., for the calculation of the conductance. Further, unless the symbolism is made more specific, a number of important fundamental theoretical assumptions are not brought to light. This situation may be remedied by employing the more elaborate symbolism of Onsager and Fuoss. Although the adoption of this symbolism increases the difficulty at the start, it ultimately leads to a more rigorous and a clearer understanding of the theory.

(1) The Distribution Functions

Consider an electrolytic solution containing n_1, n_2, $\cdots$ n_s ions per cc. of the ion species denoted by subscripts, and with charges, e_1, e_2, $\cdots$ e_s,

---

[17] A. A. Noyes, *J. Am. Chem. Soc.*, **46**, 1080 (1924).

H. S. Harned in Taylor, "Treatise on Physical Chemistry," p. 784, D. Van Nostrand and Company, New York, 1930.

A. Eucken, "Fundamentals of Physical Chemistry," Translated by E. R. Jette and V. K. LaMer, McGraw-Hill Book Co., New York, 1925.

M. Dole, "Principles of Experimental and Theoretical Electrochemistry," McGraw-Hill Book Co., New York, 1935.

D. A. MacInnes, "The Principles of Electrochemistry," Reinhold Publishing Corporation, New York, 1939.

W. M. Clark, "The Determination of Hydrogen Ions," 3rd Edition, Williams and Wilkins Co., Baltimore, 1928.

respectively. Since Coulomb forces, $e_j e_i / D r^2$, act between all pairs of ions of charges e_j and e_i, the motion of the ions is not entirely a random one. As a result, the presence of an ion at a given point in the solution will affect the space distribution of the other ions in its immediate vicinity. For example, each positive ion, by inducing a negative charge density in its vicinity, will be surrounded by an "atmosphere" which contains on the average more negative ions and less positive ions than the bulk of the solution. In a similar manner a negative ion will be surrounded with a positively charged "atmosphere." In order to treat the problem of ionic distribution in a manner sufficiently general for a theory of both the equilibrium conditions and of irreversible processes such as electrolytic conductance, diffusion, and visocsty, a function is required which will

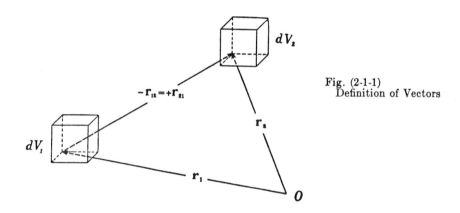

Fig. (2-1-1)
Definition of Vectors

describe the chance of finding two ions in two given volume elements in the solution simultaneously.

This chance can readily be found if we specify two volume elements [Fig. (2-1-1)], located by the termini of the vectors, r_1 and r_2, drawn from some arbitrary origin. The distance between the two volume elements is given by

$$\mathbf{r}_{21} = \mathbf{r}_2 - \mathbf{r}_1 = -\mathbf{r}_{12} \qquad (2\text{-}1\text{-}1)$$

We shall denote the concentrations (ions per cc.) of ions of kinds j and i by n_j and n_i, respectively. Further, we let n_{ji} be the time average concentration of i ions in dV_2 in the vicinity of a single j ion in dV_1; *vice versa* we let n_{ij} equal the time average concentration of j ions in dV_1 in the neighborhood of an ion of kind i in dV_2.

In general, these concentrations will depend on several variables.

(1) They will be a function of the distance r between the j ion and the point where the concentration of the i ion is required, and *vice versa*.

(2) When external forces act on the ions, a particular direction in space

is specified, and n_{ji} and n_{ij} will depend on the direction of $\mathbf{r}$ as well as on its magnitude. For example, when an electrical field is applied, the ions may be considered to move in a specified direction, *i.e.*, the x direction. Thus, the conductance will involve the direction x, as well as the distance between the ions, r.

(3) If a variable velocity gradient is applied to the solution as a whole, n_{ji} will depend on the location of the j ion and n_{ij} on that of the i ion. These conditions may be expressed adequately by the functional expressions

$$n_{ji} = n_{ji}(\mathbf{r}_1, \mathbf{r}_{21})$$
$$n_{ij} = n_{ij}(\mathbf{r}_2, \mathbf{r}_{12})$$

(2-1-2)

These general relations are required in the theory of viscosity.

It is now necessary to obtain the distribution functions. We consider the two volume elements, dV_1 and dV_2, temporarily fixed in space during a time t, and the two species of ions j and i. Out of the total time, t, we record a time, t_j, during which the j ion is in dV_1, and also the time, t_i, in which the i ion is in dV_2. The chance, t_j/t, of finding a j ion in dV_1 and the chance, t_i/t, of finding an i ion in dV_2 are related to the concentrations n_j and n_i by the expressions

$$\frac{t_j}{t} = n_j dV_1; \qquad \frac{t_i}{t} = n_i dV_2$$

Further, we note the time, t_{ji}, during which a j ion and an i ion are in dV_1 and dV_2 simultaneously. Then,

$$\frac{t_{ji}}{t_j} = n_{ji} dV_2; \qquad \frac{t_{ij}}{t_i} = n_{ij} dV_1$$

By eliminating t_j and t_i from the preceding two sets of equations, we find that

$$\frac{t_{ji}}{t} = n_j n_{ji} dV_1 dV_2 = \frac{t_{ij}}{t} = n_i n_{ij} dV_1 dV_2$$

(2-1-3)

Since t_{ji}/t is the chance of finding a j ion in dV_1 and an i ion in dV_2 simultaneously, the foregoing relation can be employed to define the required distribution functions, namely

$$f_{ji}(\mathbf{r}_1, \mathbf{r}_{21}) \equiv n_j n_{ji}(\mathbf{r}_1, \mathbf{r}_{21}) = n_i n_{ij}(\mathbf{r}_2, \mathbf{r}_{12}) \equiv f_{ij}(\mathbf{r}_2, \mathbf{r}_{12}) \quad (2\text{-}1\text{-}4)$$

Note that f_{ji} is the concentration (number of ions per cc.) of the i ions at a distance $\mathbf{r}_{21}$ from the j ion multiplied by n_j, the number of ions per cc. of the kind j, located in space by $\mathbf{r}_1$. In others words, f_{ji} is the concentration of the i ions in the atmospheres of n_j ions of the kind j. Also note the important symmetry condition represented by the equality in this equation which causes f_{ji} to equal the reciprocal quantity f_{ij}. It is a quantity which must be known if the problem of the distribution of ions is to be solved. Now, n_j and n_i are known, but $n_{ji}(\mathbf{r}_1, \mathbf{r}_{21})$ and $n_{ij}(\mathbf{r}_2, \mathbf{r}_{12})$ must be found from further statistical considerations. In the equilibrium case, when the only forces considered are the Coulombic forces between the ions, the Maxwell-Boltzmann distribution law will be sufficient to determine these quantities.

A satisfactory conception of the "ionic atmosphere" may be obtained by considering a positive ion as fixed in dV_1. Due to the force of attraction between positive and negative ions, the latter (on the average) will be in dV_2 more frequently than the former. This excess of negative ions around a positive ion, or *vice versa*, constitutes an ionic atmosphere. In an electrolytic solution undisturbed by external forces, the field around an ion is the same in all directions and is therefore a function of the distance, r, and not the direction. In this case, the ionic atmosphere possesses spherical symmetry. When external forces act on the ions, as in the case of an applied electrical field, the ionic atmosphere is asymmetrical.

(2) The Time Rate of Change of the Distribution Function

We let $\mathbf{v}_{ji}$ equal the velocity of an i ion in the neighborhood of a j ion and write

$$\mathbf{v}_{ji} = \mathbf{v}_{ji}(\mathbf{r}_1, \mathbf{r}_{21})$$

Similarly

$$\mathbf{v}_{ij} = \mathbf{v}_{ij}(\mathbf{r}_2, \mathbf{r}_{12}) \tag{2-2-1}$$

Further, if we let $\xi_1, \cdots \xi_6$ represent six space coördinates which locate two points in the solution, we can follow dV_1 and dV_2 simultaneously. Thus, the components of the velocity of the j ion in dV_1 are $\dot{\xi}_1, \dot{\xi}_2$, and $\dot{\xi}_3$, and of the i ion in dV_2 they are $\dot{\xi}_4, \dot{\xi}_5$, and $\dot{\xi}_6$, where the dots have the usual connotation of differentiation with respect to time. In this six-dimensional space, consider a six-dimensional element of volume whose center is located at $\xi_1, \cdots \xi_6$. Since f_{ji} is the concentration (in six-dimensional space) at this point, the flow of i ions, $f_{ji}\mathbf{v}_{ji}$, at ξ_1 through the five-dimensional area $d\xi_2 \cdots d\xi_6$ perpendicular to ξ_1 into the volume element is

$$\dot{\xi}_1 f_{ji} d\xi_2 \cdots d\xi_6$$

and at $\xi_1 + d\xi_1$ the flow out is

$$\left[\dot{\xi}_1 f_{ji} + \frac{\partial(\dot{\xi}_1 f_{ji})}{\partial \xi_1} d\xi_1 \right] d\xi_2 \cdots d\xi_6$$

and hence the net increase in the number of ions in the volume element due to flow in the direction of the coördinate ξ_1 is

$$- \frac{\partial(\dot{\xi}_1 f_{ji})}{\partial \xi_1} d\xi_1 \cdots d\xi_6$$

per unit time. Division of the sum of the corresponding differences along the six coördinates by the volume of the element, $d\xi_1 \cdots d\xi_6$ gives the time rate of change of concentration in the volume element,

$$\frac{\partial f_{ji}}{\partial t} = -\sum_{r=1}^{6} \frac{\partial(\dot{\xi}_r f_{ji})}{\partial \xi_r} \qquad (2\text{-}2\text{-}2)$$

Now, the differential operator on the right represents a six-dimensional divergence which may be written

$$\sum_{r=1}^{6} \frac{\partial}{\partial \xi_r} \equiv \nabla_1 \cdot + \nabla_2 \cdot$$

where the subscripts 1 and 2 represent differentiation with respect to the components of r_1 and r_2 respectively. Since $f_{ji}(r_1, r_{21}) = f_{ij}(r_2, r_{12})$, equation (2-2-2) may be written

$$-\frac{\partial f_{ji}(r_1, r_{21})}{\partial t} = \nabla_1 \cdot (f_{ij} \mathbf{v}_{ij}) + \nabla_2 \cdot (f_{ji} \mathbf{v}_{ji}) = -\frac{\partial f_{ij}(r_2, r_{12})}{\partial t} \qquad (2\text{-}2\text{-}3)$$

which is the equation of continuity in an adequate form for the theory of ionic motion. In a steady state, $\dfrac{\partial f_{ij}}{\partial t} = 0$, and consequently

$$\nabla_1 \cdot (f_{ij}\mathbf{v}_{ij}) + \nabla_2 \cdot (f_{ji}\mathbf{v}_{ji}) = 0 \qquad (2\text{-}2\text{-}4)$$

These fundamental hydrodynamic equations form the basis for the theory of irreversible processes. Before they can be used, however, it will be necessary to evaluate both the distribution functions and the velocities

(3) The Equations of Motion

The factors which cause the ions to move can be reduced to three: (1) forces on the ions, (2) thermal (random) motion, and (3) flow of solution as a whole. The forces which influence the ions may be external (outside electrical field), and internal (concentration gradients and electrostatic forces due to the presence of the ions themselves). If the mobility of an i ion be ω_i, then a force, $\mathbf{K}_i$, acting upon it will produce a velocity equal to $\mathbf{K}_i \omega_i$. The coefficient of friction of this ion is given by $\rho_i = 1/\omega_i$. If the diffusion constant for an ion is taken to be $kT\omega$,[18] then a concentration gradient of ∇f will produce a current of strength $-kT\omega\nabla f$. Since this current is equal to $\mathbf{v}f$, the diffusion velocity is $-kT\omega\nabla \ln f$. Therefore, if the velocity of the solution as a whole at a point located by r_2 is $\mathbf{V}(r_2)$, then the total velocity, $\mathbf{v}_{ji}$, at this point is

$$\mathbf{v}_{ji} = \mathbf{V}(r_2) + \omega_i(\mathbf{K}_{ji} - kT\nabla_2 \ln f_{ji}) \qquad (2\text{-}3\text{-}1)$$

[18] W. Nernst, *Z. physik. Chem.*, **2**, 613 (1888); "Theoretical Chemistry," p. 368–374, Translation by H. T. Tizard, Macmillan Co., London, 1911; R. C. Tolman, "Statistical Mechanics," p. 231, Equation (535), Chemical Catalog Co. (Reinhold Publishing Corp.), New York, 1927.

Similarly

$$\mathbf{v}_{ij} = \mathbf{V}(\mathbf{r}_1) + \omega_j(\mathbf{K}_{ij} - kT\nabla_1 \ln f_{ij})$$

Substituting these values of the velocities, equation (2-2-4) for the steady state becomes

$$\nabla_1 \cdot [f_{ij}\mathbf{V}(\mathbf{r}_1) + \omega_j(f_{ij}\mathbf{K}_{ij} - kT\nabla_1 f_{ij})]$$
$$+ \nabla_2 \cdot [f_{ji}\mathbf{V}(\mathbf{r}_2) + \omega_i(f_{ji}\mathbf{K}_{ji} - kT\nabla_2 f_{ji})] = 0 \qquad (2\text{-}3\text{-}2)$$

In order to apply this equation to the theory of the irreversible processes, it will now be necessary to introduce considerations of the interionic forces. This will first require a careful examination of the electrolytic solution in the absence of external fields. We have delayed the discussion of this comparatively simple case because the expressions for the ionic velocities given by equation (2-3-1) are required to explain certain basic assumptions underlying the entire theory.

(4) The Fundamental Equations for the Potentials of an Ion and Its Atmosphere in the Absence of External Fields. Theory of Debye

If the electrolyte is stationary and not acted upon by external forces, the ionic atmospheres possess spherical symmetry and the distribution functions become functions of the distance $r = |\mathbf{r}_{12}| = |\mathbf{r}_{21}|$ only. The vertical bars indicate magnitude. The distribution functions for this case will be specified by the superscript zero, and therefore

$$f^0_{ji}(r) = n_j n^0_{ji}(r) = n_i n^0_{ij}(r) = f^0_{ij}(r) \qquad (2\text{-}4\text{-}1)$$

We shall now examine carefully the effects of Coulombic forces and thermal motion of the ions upon the distribution functions and the potentials. We shall assume that the ions are point charges, and reserve until later the computation of the effects due to the finite sizes of the ions. An ion of charge e_j in a liquid of dielectric constant D possesses an electrical potential e_j/Dr at a distance r from the ion. In a solution containing an electrolyte, ionic atmospheres are formed and the fields of the ions derivable from the potential superpose. The potential due to an ion and its atmosphere will be represented by $\psi_j(\mathbf{r}_1, \mathbf{r}_{21})$ in general, and by $\psi^0_j(r)$ in the static (unperturbed) case.

In a medium containing electrical charges (or other sources of fields) subject to forces which vary inversely as the square of the distance, the relation between the charge density, ρ, and the potential is given in general by Poisson's equation

$$\nabla \cdot \nabla \psi = -\frac{4\pi\rho}{D}$$

This equation states that at any point in a medium located by three space coördinates $(x, y, z; r, \theta, \phi)$ the divergence of the gradient of the potential, or the total outward flux of the force at this point, is proportional to the charge density at this point. In an electrolytic solution, the charge density (concentration or charge per cc.) at a distance r from the j ion is $\sum\limits_{i=1}^{s} n_{ji}e_i$, where the summation is over all the kinds of ions in the solution. The potential at this point is that due to the j ion and its atmosphere. Thus, in general

$$\nabla\cdot\nabla\psi_j(\mathbf{r}_1, \mathbf{r}_{21}) = -\frac{4\pi}{D}\sum_{i=1}^{s} n_{ji}\, e_i \tag{2-4-2}$$

For the unperturbed electrolyte

$$\nabla\cdot\nabla\psi_j^0(r) = -\frac{4\pi}{D}\sum_{i=1}^{s} n_{ji}^0\, e_i \tag{2-4-3}$$

ψ_j^0 is a function of r only.

From consideration of the thermal motion of the ions, we assume that the concentration of an ion in the neighborhood of another ion is determined by the Maxwell-Boltzmann distribution law in the forms

$$n_{ji}^0 = n_i e^{-U_{ji}/kT}$$
$$n_{ij}^0 = n_j e^{-U_{ij}/kT} \tag{2-4-4}$$

U_{ji} is the potential energy of the i ion in the vicinity of the j ion and kT its kinetic energy.

An important insight into the fundamental assumption underlying the theory will appear upon examining these relations and the equations of motion. It is characteristic of the equilibrium case that the average values of the velocities $\mathbf{v}_{ji}$ and $\mathbf{v}_{ij}$ vanish. Hence, from equations (2-3-1), it follows that

$$\mathbf{K}_{ji} = kT\nabla \ln f_{ji}^0 = kT\nabla \ln f_{ij}^0 = \mathbf{K}_{ij} \tag{2-4-5}$$

According to equation (2-1-4), $f_{ji}^0 = n_j n_{ji}^0 = n_i n_{ij}^0 = f_{ij}^0$, and hence equations (2-4-4) yield

$$f_{ji}^0 = n_j n_i e^{-U_{ji}/kT} = n_i n_j e^{-U_{ij}/kT} = f_{ij}^0$$

Since n_j and n_i are constant concentrations, it follows by introducing this relation in equation (2-4-5) that

$$kT\nabla \ln f_{ji}^0 = -\nabla U_{ji} = -\nabla U_{ij} = kT\nabla \ln f_{ij}^0 \tag{2-4-6}$$

at constant temperature.

If it is assumed that the average force acting upon one ion is given by the potential of the other ion, which is equivalent to the assumption of the linear superposition of the fields, then the potential energies, U_{ji} , and U_{ij}

will equal $\psi_j^0(r)e_i$ and $\psi_i^0(r)e_j$, respectively, and according to equation (2-4-6)

$$U_{ji} = \psi_j^0(r)e_i = \psi_i^0(r)e_j = U_{ij} \tag{2-4-7}$$

Thus, the potential energy of the i ion at a distance r from the j ion is assumed to be equal to the potential due to the j ion and its atmosphere at this point, multiplied by the charge on the i ion, and is equal to the work done in charging the i ion in a field of potential $\psi_j^0(r)$. The reciprocal relations given by equation (2-4-7) require that the potential of the ion and its atmosphere be proportional to its charge.

It is important to realize that the assumption of the linear superposition of the fields has always been employed in the development of the theory. For example, the theoretical calculation of the thermodynamic properties (chemical potentials, activity coefficients etc.) has been derived upon the assumption that $\psi_j^0(r) \propto e_j$. In the discussion which follows, we shall examine the conditions under which the relation of proportionality of potential to charge is compatible with the Maxwell-Boltzmann distribution.[19]

By the combination of equations (2-4-3) and (2-4-4) and by substitution of $\psi_j^0(r)e_i$ for U_{ji}, we obtain

$$\nabla \cdot \nabla \psi_j^0(r) = -\frac{4\pi}{D} \sum_{i=1}^{s} n_i e_i \exp\left(-\psi_j^0(r)e_i/kT\right) \tag{2-4-8}$$

Now this equation does not fulfill the requirement that $\psi_j^0(r)$ is proportional to e_j, since the term on the left is linear in e_j by hypothesis, while that on the right is not. This contradiction is remedied by making the approximation

$$\exp\left(-\psi_j^0(r)e_i/kT\right) \simeq 1 - \psi_j^0(r)e_i/kT \tag{2-4-9}$$

which neglects the terms in the expansion of higher order than the first. This approximation is justifiable only when $\psi_j^0(r)e_i$ is small, or when $\psi_j^0(r)$ is small, a condition approached at very low concentrations. For electrolytes of high-valence type and for electrolytes in media of low dielectric constant, $\psi_j^0(r)e_i$ becomes larger and the approximation is not good.

If we now substitute the approximation given by equation (2-4-9) in (2-4-8), we obtain

$$\nabla \cdot \nabla \psi_j^0(r) = \frac{4\pi}{DkT} \sum_{i=1}^{s} n_i e_i^2 \psi_j^0(r) \tag{2-4-10}$$

since electroneutrality of the solution as a whole requires that

$$\frac{4\pi}{D} \sum_{i=1}^{s} e_i n_i = 0 \tag{2-4-10a}$$

[19] L. Onsager, *Chem. Rev.*, **13**, 73 (1933).

We now let $e_i^2 = z_i^2 \epsilon^2$, where z_i is the valence of the ion and ϵ the electronic charge, and define the quantity κ by

$$\kappa^2 \equiv \frac{4\pi\epsilon^2}{DkT} \sum_{i=1}^{s} n_i z_i^2 \qquad (2\text{-}4\text{-}11)$$

whence equation (2-4-10) reduces to

$$\nabla \cdot \nabla \psi_j^0(r) = \kappa^2 \psi_j^0(r) \qquad (2\text{-}4\text{-}12)$$

In the unperturbed electrolyte, the ionic atmospheres are spherical and it is most convenient to express $\nabla \cdot \nabla \psi_j^0(r)$ in spherical coördinates. Hence

$$\frac{1}{r^2} \frac{\partial}{\partial r}\left(r^2 \frac{\partial \psi_j^0(r)}{\partial r}\right) = \kappa^2 \psi_j^0(r) \qquad (2\text{-}4\text{-}13)$$

since $\psi_j^0(r)$ is a function of r only. The integration of this equation will give $\psi_j^0(r)$ as a function of r and κ, where κ is seen to be a function of the dielectric constant of the medium, the temperature and the concentration of electrolyte.

A general solution of equation (2-4-13) is

$$\psi_j^0(r) = \frac{A e^{-\kappa r}}{r} + \frac{A' e^{\kappa r}}{r} \qquad (2\text{-}4\text{-}14)$$

where A and A' are integration constants. The constant A' must be zero since $\psi_j^0(r)$ equals zero when r is infinite, i.e., $\psi_j^0(\infty) = 0$. For small values of κr, the equation remaining may be expanded to yield

$$\psi_j^0(r) = \frac{A}{r} - A\kappa \qquad (2\text{-}4\text{-}14a)$$

if the higher terms be neglected. It will be shown in Chapter (3), Section (5), that A is independent of both r and κ. Hence A/r is a function of r only, and $A\kappa$ is a function of κ only, and vanishes at infinite dilution. Thus, A/r is the potential at a distance r from a point charge, e_j, of magnitude AD at the origin, and $\psi_j^0(r)$ is the potential corresponding to a point charge (ion) of magnitude AD at the origin, plus the potential due to the space charge of the atmosphere. Thus, A, may be replaced by e_j/D. From equations (2-4-3), (2-4-12), and (2-4-14), it follows that

$$\nabla \cdot \nabla \psi_j^0(r) = -\frac{4\pi}{D} \sum_{i=1}^{s} n_{ji}^0 e_i = \kappa^2 \psi_j^0(r) = \kappa^2 \frac{e_j e^{-\kappa r}}{Dr} \qquad (2\text{-}4\text{-}15)$$

and hence the space charge of the i ion in the atmosphere of the j ion and at a distance r is given by

$$\sum_{i=1}^{s} n_{ji}^0 e_i = -\frac{D}{4\pi} \kappa^2 \frac{e_j e^{-\kappa r}}{Dr} \qquad (2\text{-}4\text{-}16)$$

The very important equations for the potentials follow from (2-4-14) upon substitution of e_j/D or $z_j\epsilon/D$ for A. Thus

$$\psi_i^0(r) = \frac{z_j \epsilon e^{-\kappa r}}{Dr} \tag{2-4-17}$$

or in another form

$$\psi_i^0(r) = \frac{z_j \epsilon}{Dr} - \frac{z_j \epsilon (1 - e^{-\kappa r})}{Dr} \tag{2-4-18}$$

The first term on the right of this equation is simply the potential at a distance r from an isolated ion in a medium of dielectric constant D. The second term is the potential of the ionic atmosphere. The first term will not be required in the expression for the variation of the thermodynamic properties of electroytes with concentration of ions. However, in certain cases when the influence of change of media is required, the first term is retained. Since $(1 - e^{-\kappa r})$ approaches the value κr for small values of κr, the potential of the ion and its atmosphere becomes

$$\psi_i^0(r) = \frac{z_j \epsilon}{Dr} - \frac{z_j \epsilon \kappa}{D} \tag{2-4-18a}$$

an equation which also follows directly from (2-4-14a). The second term on the right is simply the potential of the ionic atmosphere, ψ_j^{0*}, for small values of κr, a condition fulfilled when, at a finite value of r, κ approaches 0, *i.e.*, the concentration approaches zero. It is apparent that $1/\kappa$ in the last term of equation (2-4-18a)

$$\psi_j^{0*} = - \frac{z_j \epsilon \kappa}{D} \tag{2-4-19}$$

is analogous to the distance r in the first term on the right of this equation and possesses the dimension of length. Thus, $1/\kappa$ is the mean radius of the ionic atmosphere, a property which makes κ an extremely important quantity in the theory.

In order to render the equation of continuity (2-3-2) suitable for the specialized theories of irreversible processes in electrolytes, the distribution functions f_{ji}^0 and f_{ij}^0 must be expressed as a function of r. The desired expressions may be obtained from equations (2-4-1), (2-4-4), (2-4-7), (2-4-9) and (2-4-17) and are

$$f_{ji}^0 = n_j n_{ji}^0 = n_j n_i \exp\left(- \psi_i^0(r) e_i/kT\right) \simeq n_j n_i \left(1 - \frac{\psi_i^0(r) e_i}{kT}\right) \tag{2-4-20}$$

$$= n_j n_i \left(1 - \frac{e_j e_i}{DkTr} e^{-\kappa r}\right)$$

Three of these equations are fundamental for various subsequent developments. Equation (2-4-19) is the basic equation of the theory for computing the limiting laws for activity and osmotic coefficients and, subsequently, partial molal heats of dilution and heat capacities [Chapter (3), Sections (1–4)]. Equation (2-4-17) is fundamental for the derivation of the Debye and Hückel equation for the activity coefficient which involves the mean distance of approach of the ions [Chapter (3), Section (5)]. The last of these equations (2-4-20) will be employed in the next section in adapting equation (2-3-2) to meet the requirements of the theory of irreversible processes in electrolytic solutions.

(5) General Equations for the Perturbations of ionic Atmospheres

If the electrolyte is disturbed by external forces both the potentials and distribution functions become asymmetric. Thus

$$\psi_j(\mathbf{r}_1, \mathbf{r}_{21}) = \psi_j'(\mathbf{r}_1, \mathbf{r}_{21}) + \psi_j^0(r)$$
$$f_{ji}(\mathbf{r}_1, \mathbf{r}_{21}) = f_{ji}'(\mathbf{r}_1, \mathbf{r}_{21}) + f_{ji}^0(r)$$

(2-5-1)

where the primed terms represent the effects of the perturbations. The potentials and distributions are related according to Poisson's equation in the following manner

$$\nabla \cdot \nabla \psi_j' = -\frac{4\pi}{D} \sum_{i=1}^{s} \frac{f_{ji}' e_i}{n_j}$$

(2-5-2)

For simplicity, we frequently write ψ_j' and f_{ji}' in place of $\psi_j'(\mathbf{r}_1, \mathbf{r}_{21})$ and $f_{ji}'(\mathbf{r}_1, \mathbf{r}_{21})$, respectively.

The perturbing factors bring about irreversible processes in the solution and the distribution is not given by the Maxwell-Boltzmann equation. We must therefore resort to the equation of continuity (2-3-2), since the average values of the velocities $\mathbf{v}_{ji}$ and $\mathbf{v}_{ij}$ do not equal zero.

The total force, $\mathbf{K}_{ji}$, acting on the i ion will be given by

$$\mathbf{K}_{ji} = \mathbf{k}_i - e_i \nabla_2 \psi_i'(0) - e_i \nabla_2 \psi_j(\mathbf{r}_1, \mathbf{r}_{21})$$

(2-5-3)

In this equation, $\mathbf{k}_i$ is the applied external force. The second term on the right is the force (gradient of potential) on the i ion due to the atmosphere of this ion. Note that it is the potential at the origin ($r = 0$) or at the point occupied by the i ion. The third term is the force acting on the i ion due to the potential of the j ion (as origin) and its atmosphere. It is important to note that this estimate of the total force involves the assumption that the total field due to the ions and their atmospheres may be obtained by linear superposition of the separate fields.

Upon substituting equation (2-5-3) in (2-3-1), multiplying by f_{ji} and taking the divergence, we obtain

$$\nabla_2 \cdot (f_{ji} \mathbf{v}_{ji}) = \nabla_2 \cdot [(f_{ji} \mathbf{V}(\mathbf{r}_2)) + \omega_i(f_{ji} \mathbf{k}_i - e_i f_{ji} \nabla_2 \psi_i'(0) - e_i f_{ji} \nabla_2 \psi_j - kT \nabla_2 f_{ji})]$$

(2-5-4)

Upon expansion, a few terms may be eliminated. For all cases to be considered, both the velocity of the solution as a whole and the external electrical field are maintained constant, and therefore, since $\nabla_2 \cdot \mathbf{V}(\mathbf{r}_2) = 0$, and $\nabla_2 \cdot \mathbf{k}_i = 0$, two terms vanish. The term containing $\nabla_2 \psi_i'(0)$ may be neglected since it is of the order of e_i^2, and the terms retained are of the order e_i [See Equation (2-4-17)]. Further, according to equation (2-4-20), $f_{ji} - n_j n_i$ is of the order of e_i. Hence, in the expression $e_i f_{ji} \nabla_2 \psi_j$, f_{ji} may be replaced by $n_j n_i$, and since $\nabla_2 n_j n_i$ is zero, the term $\nabla_2 \cdot [e_i \omega_i n_j n_i \nabla_2 \psi_j]$ reduces to $e_i \omega_i n_j n_i \nabla_2 \cdot \nabla_2 \psi_j$. Upon making these reductions, equation (2-5-4) becomes

$$\nabla_2 \cdot (f_{ji}\mathbf{v}_{ji}) = \mathbf{V}(\mathbf{r}_2) \cdot \nabla_2 f_{ji} + \omega_i(\mathbf{k}_i \cdot \nabla_2 f_{ji})$$
$$- e_i \omega_i n_j n_i \nabla_2 \cdot \nabla_2 \psi_j - \omega_i k T \nabla_2 \cdot \nabla_2 f_{ji} \tag{2-5-5}$$

A similar equation for $\nabla_1 \cdot (f_{ij}\mathbf{v}_{ij})$ may be obtained. In order to obtain the desired form of the equation of continuity, these values are substituted in equation (2-2-3), and some further reductions made. Both f_{ji}, f_{ij}, and ψ_j, ψ_i are replaced by use of equations (2-5-1). Since for the equilibrium state $\mathbf{k}_i = 0$, $\mathbf{k}_j = 0$, when $\mathbf{v}_{ji} = 0$ and $\mathbf{v}_{ij} = 0$, we find by use of equations (2-3-1) and (2-5-3) that $\omega_i k T \nabla_2 \cdot \nabla_2 f_{ji}^0 = -\omega_i n_j n_i e_i \nabla_2 \cdot \nabla_2 \psi_i^0$ and $\omega_j k T \nabla_1 \cdot \nabla_1 f_{ij}^0 = -\omega_j n_i n_j e_j \nabla_1 \cdot \nabla_1 \psi_j^0$, whence four terms disappear by cancellation. The final equation of continuity, which is sufficiently general for all further discussion of irreversible processes in electrolytic solutions, is

$$\mathbf{V}(\mathbf{r}_2) \cdot \nabla_2 f_{ji} + \mathbf{V}(\mathbf{r}_1) \cdot \nabla_1 f_{ij}$$
$$+ \omega_i(\mathbf{k}_i \cdot \nabla_2 f_{ji}) + \omega_j(\mathbf{k}_j \cdot \nabla_1 f_{ij})$$
$$- e_i \omega_i n_j n_i \nabla_2 \cdot \nabla_2 \psi_j' - e_j \omega_j n_i n_j \nabla_1 \cdot \nabla_1 \psi_i' \tag{2-5-6}$$
$$- \omega_i k T \nabla_2 \cdot \nabla_2 f_{ji}' - \omega_j k T \nabla_1 \cdot \nabla_1 f_{ij}'$$
$$= -\frac{\partial f_{ji}(\mathbf{r}_1, \mathbf{r}_{21})}{\partial t} = -\frac{\partial f_{ij}(\mathbf{r}_2, \mathbf{r}_{12})}{\partial t} \quad \text{(For non-stationary fields)}$$

$$= 0 \quad \text{(For stationary fields)}$$

With the exception of the theory of the Wien effect [Chapter (4), Section (5)], $\mathbf{V}(\mathbf{r}_1)$, $\mathbf{V}(\mathbf{r}_2)$, $\mathbf{k}_i$ and $\mathbf{k}_j$ are sufficiently small to permit the replacement of f by f^0 in the first four terms.

(6) GENERAL CONSIDERATION OF THE BEHAVIOR OF IONIC ATMOSPHERES IN PERTUBED STATES

Equation (2-5-6) is of sufficient generality for treating the theory of viscosity, conductance and diffusion of electroytes. The first four terms contain the perturbing factors and the last four the asymmetric contributions to the potentials. The differential equations for the potentials, from which the forces causing the motion of the ions may be computed, can be obtained by elimination of the distribution functions f'_{ji} and f'_{ij} by means of the Poisson equation (2-5-2).

Equation (2-5-6) may be specialized for a particular problem. Thus, in the case of viscosity, the terms containing the bulk velocities $V(r_2)$ and $V(r_1)$ are retained, while those containing the external perturbing forces, k_i and k_j, are omitted. The contribution to the viscosity due to the ions can be shown to be related to the potentials derivable from equation (2-5-6), and can be computed by suitable mathematical procedures.

In dealing with conductance and diffusion, the first two terms of equation (2-5-6), which contain the bulk velocities, may be omitted. The perturbing forces, k_i and k_j, are the applied external fields in the case of conductance, and the gradients of the thermodynamic potentials in the case of diffusion. As the ion moves in the field, it drags its atmosphere with it and the resulting effect is a lowering of its mobility. The extent of this effect may be computed by evaluating the potentials by equation (2-5-6), and subsequently the forces upon the ions. However, there is another effect due to the motion of solvent with respect to the ion, called "electrophoresis," which must be computed independently and added to the influence of the asymmetric ionic atmospheres.

All these considerations apply to the stationary cases of constant external fields, where f_{ij} and f_{ji} do not vary with time. However, there are some phenomena which necessitate an investigation of the non-stationary case, and which require that the left side of equation (2-5-6) equal $\dfrac{-\partial f_{ji}(r_1, r_{21})}{\partial t}$ instead of zero.

If the ionic atmosphere becomes asymmetric because of a perturbing field and if this field is removed, the atmosphere will revert to its original spherical form. This reverse change will require a finite time which is denoted "the time of relaxation" of the atmosphere.

If the electrolytic solution is exposed to an alternating field of a frequency of the order of magnitude of this time of relaxation, the atmosphere will not have a chance to assume an asymmetric distribution, and the change in mobility of the ions, due to asymmetry of the atmospheres, will be less than in the stationary case. This idea is fundamental in the theory of Debye and Falkenhagen of the effect of high frequencies upon the conductances of the ions. Equation (2-5-6), modified for the non-stationary case, is the starting point for this theory.

There is still another important phenomenon which will require our attention. If a solution of an electrolyte is subjected to a high field, the central ions will be drawn out of their atmospheres. This will increase the conductances of the ions, since they no longer drag their atmospheres with them. This phenomenon, known as the Wien effect, may be treated theoretically by means of equation (2-5-5).

The application of equation (2-5-6) to the viscosity, conductance and diffusion will be undertaken in Chapter (4). The simpler theories of the thermodynamic properties will be presented in detail in the next chapter.

(7) STATISTICAL MECHANICS AND THE INTERIONIC ATTRACTION THEORY

In the preceding account of the theory which records the unique characteristics of solutions of ions, we have stated the fundamental relations necessary for the derivation of the limiting laws for both the thermodynamic properties and the irreversible phenomena. These limiting laws have been verified by all the experimental data and there seems to be no doubt that as the concentration of the ions approaches zero the theory becomes increasingly exact. Nevertheless, it is desirable to subject the theory to the criticism which the exact science of statistical mechanics provides.

Fowler[20] in a critical examination of the theory showed that the Poisson-Boltzmann equation (2-4-8) was not in accord with the criteria of statistical mechanics. It was recognized that the equality represented by equation (2-4-7) is an approximation and that the Poisson-Boltzmann equation is only valid when certain "fluctuation terms" can be ignored as small. In Section (4) of this chapter we have shown that the validity of equation (2-4-7) rests upon the assumption of the linear superposition of the fields of the separate ions and if the Poisson-Boltzmann equation is linearized to yield equation (2-4-9) the conditions of integrability of this latter equation are satisfied. We also mentioned that the condition that the potential, $\psi_j^0(r)$, is proportional to the charge e_j is consistent with the usual calculation of the chemical potential by means of the charging process equation (3-2-3).

Onsager[21] and Kirkwood[22] showed that statistical mechanical methods lead to a provisional conclusion that the errors caused by derivations from the principle of superposition are of the same order in the ionic charges as the non-linear terms of the Poisson-Boltzman equation.

Recently, Kirkwood and Poirier[23] have stressed a weakness in the preceding theory on the grounds that it only demonstrates "that the use of the approximate principle of superposition was consistent with the rigorous validity of the linearized Poisson-Boltzmann equation, not that this equation was in fact valid." For the purpose of remedying this weakness, Kirkwood and Poirier have subjected the theory to a thorough and systematic examination by the methods of statistical mechanics. They were able to express the potentials of mean force of sets of n ions as a power series of a charging parameter. The linearized Poisson-Boltzmann equation is proved to be valid for the coefficient of the first power of the charging

[20] R. H. Fowler, *Proc. Camb. Phil. Soc.*, **22**, 861 (1925); *Trans. Far. Soc.*, **23**, 434 (1927); "Statistical Mechanics," Chap. XIII, Cambridge University Press (1929).

[21] L. Onsager, *Chem. Rev.*, **13**, 73 (1933).

[22] J. G. Kirkwood, *J. Phys. Chem.*, **3**, 767 (1934).

[23] J. G. Kirkwood and J. C. Poirier, *J. Phys. Chem.*, **58**, 591 (1954).

parameter in the expansion of the potential of the mean force of an ion-pair, when ion size is neglected. This procedure demonstrates the validity of the limiting law of the theory.

The preceding discussion has shown that the application of statistical mechanics to the theory of electrolytes has clarified the profound basis of the theory and has served to prove the exact validity of the limiting law. The contribution of Kirkwood and Poirier contains a new and additional element that is well calculated to be of considerable value in revealing the structure of concentrated solutions of electrolytes and of fused salts. Upon introducing the ion size parameter in their statistical mechanical development, "the linearized integral equation for the potential of average force of a pair of ions possesses oscillating solutions at high ionic strength, corresponding to stratifications of average space-charge of alternating sign in the neighborhood of each ion."

Mayer[24] by adapting his cluster theory of imperfect gases[25] to solutions of electrolytes has derived equations for the computation of the osmotic pressure and the activity coefficient. By restricting the clusters to ring types and by multiplying the Coulomb potential by the factor $e^{-\alpha r}$, where α is finite and positive, Mayer succeeded in obtaining a slow convergence for the cluster sums. He was also able to show that these conditions are consistent with the limiting equations of the Debye and Hückel theory. At higher concentrations, the differences in energy of two oppositely charged ions, at an infinite distance and at closest approach, is sufficient to cause considerable ion-pair formation in water at concentrations of the order of 0.01 or 0.1 molar. Interaction of a third ion with an ion-pair will not be an important factor at concentrations below one molar. In Chap. 3, Section (6), we shall state the equations which result from this theory in a form suitable for the calculation of the activity coefficient as a function of concentration.[26] In chapter (12) the predictions of this theory will be compared with experimental results for some electrolytes of different valence types.

[24] J. E. Mayer, *J. Chem. Phys.*, **18,** 1426 (1950).

[25] J. E. Mayer and M. G. Mayer, "Statistical Mechanics," Chap. 13, Wiley and Sons, New York (1940).

[26] J. C. Poirier, *J. Chem. Phys.*, **21,** 965 (1953); **21,** 972 (1953).

Chapter 3

Theory of Thermodynamic Properties of Electrolytic Solutions

A comprehensive theory of the thermodynamic properties of dilute ionic solutions will now be developed by combination and extension of the theoretical equations for the equilibrium case [Chapter (2), Section (4)] with the thermodynamic relations given in Chapter (1). The limiting laws for the variation with concentration of the activity and osmotic coefficients, relative partial molal heat content, heat capacity, expansibility and compressibility will be derived. Extension of the theory to include the effect of the finite sizes of the ions will be made. Further extension of the theory which avoids the approximation made in neglecting the higher terms in the expansion of the exponential function in equation (2-4-8) will be stated, and the theory which attempts to estimate the effect of ionic association will be discussed. The theory of the electrostatic contribution to the surface tension of the solution will be given in a condensed form. Finally, the theories of the salting effect of ions upon neutral molecules will be discussed.

(1) PROPERTIES OF $1/\kappa$

Considerations of the distribution of ions regarded as point charges have led to the conception that on the average each ion has in its neighborhood an excess of ions of opposite sign, and that this condition produces an electrical potential which, in the electrolyte solution undisturbed by external forces, we have designated ψ_j^{0*}. Upon the assumption that the Maxwell-Boltzmann distribution is maintained, and by employing the approximation represented by equation (2-4-9), we arrived at the very important first approximation of the Debye and Hückel theory represented by equation (2-4-19),

$$\psi_j^{0*} = \frac{-z_j \epsilon \kappa}{D} \tag{2-4-19}$$

where κ was defined by

$$\kappa^2 \equiv \frac{4\pi\epsilon^2}{DkT} \sum_{i=1}^{s} n_i z_i^2 \tag{2-4-11}$$

The quantity, κ, possesses the dimensions of a reciprocal distance, and $1/\kappa$ is related to the potential of the ionic atmosphere, ψ_j^{0*}, as r is related to the

59

potential ψ of a lone particle of charge e_j in a medium of dielectric constant D.

The concentration, c_i, of an ion in mols per liter of solution is related to n_i (ions per cc.) by

$$c_i = \frac{1000 \, n_i}{N} \tag{3-1-1}$$

where N is Avogadro's number. Consequently, by (2-4-11),

$$\kappa = \left(\frac{4\pi\epsilon^2 N}{1000 \, DkT} \, \Gamma \right)^{1/2} \tag{3-1-2}$$

if we represent the so-called "ional" concentration by

$$\Gamma \equiv \sum_1^s c_i z_i^2 \tag{3-1-3}$$

Upon substitution of the numerical values of the constants, we fine that

$$\frac{1}{\kappa} = 2.812 \times 10^{-10} \sqrt{\frac{DT}{\Gamma}} \text{ cm} \tag{3-1-4}$$

in general, and for the particular case of a 1-1 electrolyte in water at 25°

$$\frac{1}{\kappa} = \frac{3.043 \times 10^{-8}}{\sqrt{c}} \tag{3-1-5}$$

Thus in a normal solution $1/\kappa$ is of the order of a molecular diameter. Owing to the relation involving the square root of c, we note that $1/\kappa$ increases ten times for a hundredfold decrease in concentration.

(2) Methods of Computing the Work Content and Chemical Potential

The electrical contribution to the work content, ΔA, [Equation (1-2-2)] of n_j ions and their atmospheres is given by

$$W(\text{el}) = \Delta A(\text{el}) = \sum_{j=1}^{nj} \int_0^{ej} \psi(e_j) \, de. \tag{3-2-1}$$

Thus, if an uncharged ion at constant composition is charged reversibly in a field of a potential, $\psi(e_j)$ depends on the instantaneous charge e. The charging process of Debye, which is represented by

$$W(\text{el}) = \Delta A(\text{el}) = \sum_{j=1}^{nj} \int_{\lambda=0}^{\lambda=1} e_j \psi(\lambda e_j) \, d\lambda \tag{3-2-2}$$

follows directly from this equation if we represent the instantaneous charge by λe_j.

From the definition of the chemical potential, μ_j, given by equation (1-2-7), another "charging process" follows immediately from (3-2-1) such that the electrical contribution to this quantity for an ion is

$$\Delta\mu_j(\text{el}) = \left(\frac{\partial \Delta A(\text{el})}{\partial n_j}\right)_{v,T} = \int_0^{z_j\epsilon} \psi(e_j)\, de \qquad (3\text{-}2\text{-}3)$$

which was pointed out by Güntelberg.[1] Provided the approximation represented by equation (2-4-9) and the first approximation for ψ_j^{0*} given by equation (2-4-19) are employed, these two charging processes lead to the same result. On the other hand, if the integration of the Poisson-Boltzmann equation (2-4-8) is made without using this approximation, the Debye and Güntelberg charging processes lead to somewhat different results. This fact was mentioned by Gronwall, LaMer and Sandved[2], who developed the complete integration and employed the Debye charging process. They obtained a somewhat different result than Müller[3], who used the simpler Güntelberg method. In a theoretical analysis of this difficulty, Onsager[4] arrived at the conclusion that the discrepancy is due to the limitation of the Poisson-Boltzmann equation at higher concentrations where the potentials of the ionic atmospheres can no longer be expected to be additive.

(3) The Charging Process and the Calculation of the Electrostatic Contribution to the Chemical Potential

From the fundamental assumption of the linear superposition of ionic atmospheres, it followed that the potential of the ionic atmosphere is proportional to the charge, or

$$a\psi_j^{0*} = e_j \qquad (3\text{-}3\text{-}1)$$

where a is a proportionality factor. If the charging process given by equation (3-2-3) is employed, the electrostatic contribution to the chemical potential of a j ion is given by

$$\Delta\mu_j(\text{el}) = \int_0^{z_j\epsilon} \psi_j^{0*}(e_j)\, de_j = \int_0^{\psi_j^{0*}} a\psi_j^{0*}\, d\psi_j^{0*} = \frac{a\psi_j^{0*}\psi_j^{0*}}{2} = \frac{z_j\epsilon\psi_j^{0*}}{2} \qquad (3\text{-}3\text{-}2)$$

Upon substitution of the value of ψ_j^{0*} obtained from (2–4–19),

$$\Delta\mu_j(\text{el}) = -\frac{(z_j\epsilon)^2\kappa}{2D} \qquad (3\text{-}3\text{-}3)$$

(4) The Limiting Law for the Variation of the Activity Coefficient

According to equation (1-8-9), we have

$$\bar{F} = \nu RT \ln f_\pm + \nu RT \ln N_\pm + \bar{F}_N^0 \qquad (1\text{-}8\text{-}5)$$

[1] E. Güntelberg, *Z. physik. Chem.*, **123**, 199 (1926).
[2] T. H. Gronwall, V. K. LaMer and K. Sandved, *Physik. Z.*, **29**, 358 (1928).
[3] H. Müller, *Ibid.*, **28**, 324 (1927); **29**, 78 (1928).
[4] L. Onsager, *Chem. Rev.*, **13**, 73 (1933).

$\bar{F}$ can be divided into two parts, as follows:

$$\bar{F}_N = \nu RT \ln N_{\pm} + \bar{F}_N^0 \qquad (3\text{-}4\text{-}1)$$

$$\bar{F}_f = \nu RT \ln f_{\pm} \qquad (3\text{-}4\text{-}2)$$

The first of these relations is of the form of the limiting law for dilute solutions of un-ionized solutes, and would presumably apply to solutions of electrolytes as well, were it not for the charges on the ions.

It is therefore assumed that, for completely ionized electrolytes in dilute solution, the deviation of electrolytic solutions from ideality can be attributed entirely to electrostatic forces between the ions. This is equivalent to identifying $\bar{F}_f$ with $N\Delta\mu(\text{el})$ for any ion. Hence

$$\Delta\mu_j(\text{el}) = kT \ln f_j = -\frac{(z_j\epsilon)^2\kappa}{2D} \qquad (3\text{-}4\text{-}3)$$

By substituting the value of κ from (3-1-2) and rearranging terms, we obtain

$$\ln f_j = -z_j^2 \left(\frac{\pi N\epsilon^6}{1000 \ (DkT)^3}\right)^{1/2} \sqrt{\Gamma} \qquad (3\text{-}4\text{-}4)$$

as the limiting expression for the activity coefficient of an ion (of an arbitrary kind j) in a solution containing s kinds of ions at concentrations $n_1, n_2, \cdots n_s$ per cc.

The mean activity coefficient of an electrolyte dissociating into p kinds of ions is

$$\ln f_{\pm} = \frac{1}{\nu} \sum_1^p \nu_j \ln f_j \qquad (3\text{-}4\text{-}5)$$

by (1-8-4), where the dissociation of one molecule of electrolyte produces a total number of ions, ν, of which ν_j are of the j kind. Combining this equation with (3-4-4), we obtain

$$\ln f_{\pm} = -\frac{1}{\nu} \sum_1^p \nu_j z_j^2 \left(\frac{\pi N\epsilon^6}{1000 \ (kDT)^3}\right)^{1/2} \sqrt{\Gamma} \qquad (3\text{-}4\text{-}6)$$

For convenience we convert this equation to decadic logarithms, and introduce the numerical values of the constants, writing

$$\log f_{\pm} = -\mathfrak{S}_{(f)} \sqrt{\Gamma} \qquad (3\text{-}4\text{-}7)$$

where

$$\mathfrak{S}_{(f)} = \frac{1}{\nu} \sum_1^p \nu_j z_j^2 (DT)^{-3/2} 1.290 \times 10^6 \qquad (3\text{-}4\text{-}8)$$

The symbol $\mathfrak{S}$, with appropriate subscripts, will be used exclusively to represent the limiting slopes of the theoretical equations, in their most general form, which are derived from considerations of interionic attraction. $\maltese$ is always associated with $\sqrt{\Gamma}$, and is usually applicable to solutions of mixed electrolytes. In solutions containing a single electrolyte, Γ is proportional to c, and it is convenient to rewrite the theoretical equations in terms of $\sqrt{c}$. This requires a redefinition of the limiting slopes, and we employ the symbol $\mathfrak{S}$ for this purpose in Chapter (5).

In the very important, though special, case for which $p = 2$, the valence factor in $\maltese_{(f)}$ reduces to $|z_1z_2|$†, and we write

$$\maltese_{(f)} = |z_1z_2| (DT)^{-3/2} 1.290 \times 10^6; \quad p = 2 \qquad (3\text{-}4\text{-}8a)$$

Equations (3-4-6) to (3-4-8) represent the Debye-Hückel "limiting law" for activity coefficients in its most general form. It requires that the logarithm of the activity coefficient of an electrolyte, at extreme dilution, decreases linearly with the square root of Γ. It is important to remember that Γ is a function of *all* the ions $1, \cdots i, \cdots s$ in the solution, regardless of source, while the summation involved in $\maltese$ is confined to the ions $1, \cdots j, \cdots p$ resulting from the dissociation of the electrolyte to which $f_{\pm}$ refers. Since we have retained only two terms in the expansion used to evaluate ψ_j^0, and assumed that the deviation in the behavior of electrolytic solutions from ideality may be attributed entirely to Coulomb forces between the ions, we cannot expect these equations to be *strictly* valid at measurable concentrations. We have, however, good reason to expect them to represent accurately the limiting behavior of electrolytes as the ional concentration is made to approach zero.

An important feature of "the limiting slope," $\maltese_{(f)}$, is its unambiguous definition in terms of fundamental physical constants: the absolute temperature, the dielectric constant of the solvent, and the valence type of the electrolyte under consideration.

Before leaving this section it will be necessary to rewrite the limiting law in several very useful forms for future reference. For many purposes it is convenient to employ γ, the activity coefficient corresponding to molal concentrations (mols per kilo of solvent), rather than the rational activity coefficient f. By equations (1-8-13) and (3-4-7),

$$\log \gamma_{\pm} = - \maltese_{(f)} \sqrt{\Gamma} - \log\left(1 + \frac{vmM_1}{1000}\right) \qquad (3\text{-}4\text{-}9)$$

but for dilutions at which this equation approaches validity, the last term on the right‡ may be dropped. Since $c_i = m_i\left(d - \frac{c_iM_1}{1000}\right)$, $c_i = m_id_0$,

---

† The presence of bars in the expression $|z_1z_2|$ indicates the magnitude of the valence product irrespective of the signs of the valencies.

‡ This term is written for the single electrolyte in solution. · If the solution contains several electrolytes of concentrations, $m_1, m_2, \cdots$, it may be generalized to read:

$$-\log\left(1 + \frac{\Sigma vmM_1}{1000}\right)$$

at extreme dilution. Γ, the ional concentration, is therefore related to the "ionic strength,"

$$\mu \equiv \frac{1}{2} \sum_{1}^{s} m_i z_i^2 , \qquad (3\text{-}4\text{-}10)$$

by

$$\Gamma = \sum_{1}^{s} c_i z_i^2 = d_0 \sum_{1}^{s} m_i z_i^2 = 2d_0\mu; \qquad c \ll 1 \qquad (3\text{-}4\text{-}10a)$$

Consequently,

$$\log \gamma_\pm = - \; \text{\spadesuit}_{(f)} \sqrt{2d_0\mu} \qquad (3\text{-}4\text{-}11)$$

Finally, by rearranging equation (3-4-6), or by combining (3-4-3) directly with (3-4-5), we may write

$$\ln f_\pm = -\left(\frac{1}{\nu} \sum_{1}^{p} \nu_j z_j^2\right) \frac{\epsilon^2 \kappa}{2kDT} \qquad (3\text{-}4\text{-}12)$$

in general, and

$$\ln f_\pm = - \frac{|z_1 z_2| \, \epsilon^2 \kappa}{2kDT} \qquad (3\text{-}4\text{-}13)$$

for an electrolyte dissociating into two kinds of ions only. In applying the limiting equations for calculating partial molal quantities, we shall require equation (3-4-6) in the form

$$\ln f_\pm = - \frac{1}{\nu} \sum_{1}^{p} \nu_j z_j^2 \frac{2.470 \times 10^{14}}{R(DT)^{3/2}} \sqrt{\Gamma} \qquad (3\text{-}4\text{-}14)$$

containing R in erg deg^{-1}, mole^{-1}, and, by combination with (3-4-8), obtain the useful relation

$$2.303\nu R \; \text{\spadesuit}_{(f)} = \sum_{1}^{p} \nu_j z_j^2 \frac{2.470 \times 10^{14}}{(DT)^{3/2}} \qquad (3\text{-}4\text{-}15)$$

(5) The Effect of the Apparent Diameters of the Ions. Equations for the Activity and Osmotic Coefficients

In the previous discussion of the Debye and Hückel development of the Poisson-Boltzmann equation, we regarded the ions as point charges. We shall now consider a modification of the theory, which does not disregard the finite size of the ions, and introduce an ionic parameter "a." This parameter is the minimum average distance to which ions, both positive and negative, can approach one another. It has been pointed out that the primitive of the Poisson-Boltzmann equation is

$$\psi_j^0(r) = \frac{Ae^{-\kappa r}}{r} \qquad (2\text{-}4\text{-}14)$$

$\psi_j^0(r)$ is the potential of the ion and its atmosphere, and may also be written

$$\psi_j^0(r) = \frac{z_j\epsilon}{Dr} + \psi^*(r) \tag{3-5-1}$$

where the first term on the right is the potential at r due to point charge $z_j\epsilon$ and $\psi^*(r)$ represents the potential of the ionic atmosphere at this distance.

Consequently,

$$\psi^*(r) = \frac{Ae^{-\kappa r}}{r} - \frac{z_j\epsilon}{Dr} \tag{3-5-2}$$

In order that the field be continuous when r equals the average minimum distance of approach a_j, it is necessary for the field of the ion and its atmosphere, $\partial\psi_j^0(r)/\partial r$, to equal the field of the ion alone, $-z_j\epsilon/Dr^2$, when $r = a_j$. This condition is satisfied if

$$\left(\frac{\partial\psi^*(r)}{\partial r}\right)_{r=a_j} = -\frac{Ae^{-\kappa a_j}}{a_j^2}(1 + \kappa a_j) + \frac{z_j\epsilon}{Da_j^2} = 0$$

whence

$$A = \frac{z_j\epsilon}{D}\frac{e^{\kappa a_j}}{1 + \kappa a_j} \tag{3-5-3}$$

Consequently,

$$\psi^*(r) = \frac{z_j\epsilon}{Dr}\left(\frac{e^{\kappa a_j}}{1 + \kappa a_j}e^{-\kappa r} - 1\right) \tag{3-5-4}$$

and

$$\psi^*(a_j) = -\frac{z_j\epsilon}{D}\frac{\kappa}{1 + \kappa a_j} \tag{3-5-5}$$

It is to be noted that this differs from the value of ψ_j^* given by (2-4-19) by a factor $\dfrac{1}{1 + \kappa a_j}$. If we now assume that the potential is proportional to the charge, and employ the Güntelberg charging process [Equation (3-2-3)], we obtain

$$\Delta\mu_j(\mathrm{el}) = -\frac{(z_j\epsilon)^2}{2D}\frac{\kappa}{1 + \kappa a_j} \tag{3-5-6}$$

for the chemical potential and

$$\ln f_j = -\frac{(z_j\epsilon)^2}{2DkT}\frac{\kappa}{1 + \kappa a_j} \tag{3-5-7}$$

for the activity coefficient of an ion. By the same procedure by which equation (3-4-7) was obtained, log $f_\pm$ of an electrolyte (dissociating into two kinds of ions) is given by

$$\log f_\pm = - \frac{\mathcal{S}_{(f)} \sqrt{\Gamma}}{1 + A\sqrt{\Gamma}} \tag{3-5-8}$$

where $\mathcal{S}_{(f)}$ is given by equations (3-4-8) and (3-4-8a) and

$$A \equiv \frac{a\kappa}{\sqrt{\Gamma}} = \frac{35.56 \times 10^8 a}{(DT)^{1/2}}; \qquad a \text{ in cm.}$$
$$= \frac{35.56 \times \mathring{a}}{(DT)^{1/2}}; \qquad \mathring{a} \text{ in Ångstrom units} \tag{3-5-9}$$

It is important to note that as Γ approaches zero, equation (3-5-8) approaches the limiting law derived for point charges.

The theoretical equations for the osmotic coefficient may be derived by combining any of the above expressions for $\ln f_j$ with equation (1-9-12), or (1-9-12a). Thus, equation (1-9-12a) can be written

$$\phi = 1 + \frac{1}{\sum c_j} \int \sum c_j \, d \ln f_i \tag{3-5-10}$$

because $c_j = m_j d_0$, and $\gamma_j = f_j$ at high dilution. Introducing the value of $d \ln f_j$ obtainable from (3-4-4), integration leads to the general limiting equation

$$\phi = 1 - \left(\frac{\pi N \epsilon^6}{1000 \ (DkT)^3}\right)^{1/2} \frac{(\sum c_j z_j^2)^{3/2}}{3 \sum c_j} \tag{3-5-11}$$

for ϕ (or g) which is applicable to solutions containing any number of ionized solutes. This equation is rarely used. If we consider the important special case of solutions of a single electrolyte, where $\sum c_j = \nu c$, and $\sum c_j z_j^2 = c \sum \nu_j z_j^2 = \Gamma$, equations (3-4-6) and (3-4-8) may be introduced to simplify the result. In this case, equation (3-5-11) reduces to

$$\phi = 1 + (\tfrac{1}{3}) \ln f_\pm = 1 - (\tfrac{1}{3}) 2.303 \mathcal{S}_{(f)} \sqrt{\Gamma} \tag{3-5-12}$$

This result is also obtained by combining equations (3-4-6) and (3-4-8) directly with (1-9-12), and performing the integration.

A more detailed derivation and discussion of the theoretical equations for ϕ will be given in Chapter (9), Section (5), where the dependence of ϕ upon the parameter A of equation (3-5-8) is considered.

(6) The Development of the Extended Terms of the Debye and Hückel Theory According to Gronwall, LaMer and Sandved

The fundamental equation of the Debye and Hückel theory has been shown to be

$$\nabla \cdot \nabla \psi_j^0 = - \frac{4\pi}{D} \sum_{i=1}^{s} n_i e_i \exp\left(- \psi_j^0 e_i / kT\right) \tag{2-4-8}$$

Up to the present, we have employed the approximation

$$\exp(-e_i\psi_j^0/kT) \simeq 1 - e_i\psi_j^0/kT \qquad (2\text{-}4\text{-}9)$$

obtained from the first two terms of the expansion of the exponential function. Let us consider an electrolyte at a concentration of n molecules per cc. which dissociates into two kinds of ions. Then

$$\sum_1^2 n\nu_i e_i \exp(-e_i\psi_j^0/kT)$$

$$= n\nu_1|e_1|\,[\exp(-|e_1|\psi_j^0/kT) - \nu_2|e_2|\exp(|e_2|\psi_j^0/kT)] \quad (3\text{-}6\text{-}1)$$

$$= n\nu_1|e_1|\,[\exp(-|e_1|\psi_j^0/kT) - \exp(|e_2|\psi_j^0/kT)]$$

since $\nu_1|e_1| = \nu_2|e_2|$.

Now if $|e_1|$ equals $|e_2|$, the expression in brackets is the negative of twice the hyperbolic sine of $|e_1|\psi_j^0/kT$ and consequently, the summation is given by

$$-2n\nu|e_1|\left[\frac{|e_1|\psi_j^0}{kT} + \frac{1}{\underline{3}}\left(\frac{|e_1|\psi_j^0}{kT}\right)^3 + \frac{1}{\underline{5}}\left(\frac{|e_1|\psi_j^0}{kT}\right)^5 + \cdots\right] \quad (3\text{-}6\text{-}2)$$

It becomes apparent that for symmetrical types of electrolytes we have previously neglected the effects of terms of the 3rd, 5th and higher odd-numbered orders. Further, it is likewise apparent that for cases of unsymmetrical valence type electrolytes terms of even as well as odd-numbered orders must be considered. The complete treatment of this problem is to be found in the contributions of Gronwall, LaMer, and Sandved,[5] who developed the equation for the symmetrical type of electrolyte, and of LaMer, Gronwall, and Greiff,[6] who considered the unsymmetrical type. Because of the mathematical complexity, we shall not consider this development in detail, but shall write their final equations and discuss the character of the effects which can be attributed to the inclusion of the higher terms.

For electrolytes of symmetrical valence types, $(|z_1| = |z_2|)$, the extended equation for $\ln f_\pm$ is found to be

$$\ln f_\pm = -\frac{(\epsilon z)^2}{2DkT}\frac{\kappa}{1 + \kappa a}$$

$$+ \sum_{m=1}^\infty \left(\frac{\epsilon^2 z^2}{DkTa}\right)^{2m+1}\left[\frac{1}{2}X_{2m+1}(\kappa a) - 2mY_{2m+1}(\kappa a)\right] \quad (3\text{-}6\text{-}3)$$

[5] T. H. Gronwall, V. K. LaMer, and K. Sandved, *Physik. Z.*, **29**, 358 (1928).

[6] V. K. LaMer, T. H. Gronwall and L. J. Greiff, *J. Physical Chemistry*, **35**, 2245 (1931).

which when expanded to include all terms up to the fifth order becomes

$$\ln f_\pm = -\frac{(\epsilon z)^2}{2DkT}\frac{\kappa}{1+\kappa a} + \left(\frac{\epsilon^2 z^2}{DkTa}\right)^3\left[\frac{1}{2}X_3(\kappa a) - 2Y_3(\kappa a)\right]$$
$$+ \left(\frac{\epsilon^2 z^2}{DkTa}\right)^5\left[\frac{1}{2}X_5(\kappa a) - 4\,Y_5(\kappa a)\right] \tag{3-6-4}$$

The first term on the right is identical with (3-5-7) and (3-5-8), and represents the first approximation obtained by Debye and Hückel. The next two terms represent the contribution of the third and fifth order terms. $X_3(\kappa a)$, $Y_3(\kappa a)$, $X_5(\kappa a)$, and $Y_5(\kappa a)$ are complicated series functions of κa, the values of which have been obtained and tabulated by Gronwall, La-Mer, and Sandved. The terms of the seventh order and higher were omitted by them.

From the character of the coefficients of the terms in brackets, the conditions for departure from the original Debye and Hückel theory become apparent. For electrolytes of high valence types (e.g., 2-2, 3-3), and for electrolytes whose a values are small, deviations are to be expected. Further, in solvents of low dielectric constant, wide departure from the first approximation should be found.

For cases of unsymmetrical valence type electrolytes the situation, as found by LaMer, Gronwall and Grieff, is even more complicated. Thus,

$$\ln f_\pm = -\frac{|z_1 z_2|\,\epsilon^2}{2DkT}\frac{\kappa}{1+\kappa a} - |z_1 z_2|\left\{\frac{1}{(10^8 a)^2}(z_1 + z_2)^2 B_2(\kappa a)\right.$$
$$-\frac{1}{(10^8 a)^3}(z_1^2 - |z_1 z_2| + z_2^2)(z_1 + z_2)^2 B_3^*(\kappa a) \tag{3-6-5}$$
$$\left.-\frac{1}{(10^8 a)^3}(z_1^2 - |z_1 z_2| + z_2^2)^2 B_3(\kappa a) - \cdots\right\}$$

where

$$B_2(\kappa a) = \left(\frac{10^8\epsilon^2}{DkT}\right)^2\left[\frac{1}{2}X_2(\kappa a) - Y_2(\kappa a)\right]$$
$$B_3^*(\kappa a) = \left(\frac{10^8\epsilon^2}{DkT}\right)^3\left[\frac{1}{2}X_3^*(\kappa a) - 2Y_3^*(\kappa a)\right] \tag{3-6-6}$$
$$B_3(\kappa a) = \left(\frac{10^8\epsilon^2}{DkT}\right)^3\left[\frac{1}{2}X_3(\kappa a) - 2Y_3(\kappa a)\right]$$

Numerical values of the bracketed terms have been tabulated by LaMer, Gronwall and Greiff. As a result of this equation, large departures from the Debye and Hückel first approximation are to be expected for cases of electrolytes of unsymmetrical types of higher valences, even in a medium of high dielectric constant such as water. Tables of all these special functions will be given in Chapter (5), Section (2).

(6A) The Development of the Cluster Sum Theory of Mayer for the Computation of Activity Coefficients

The equations resulting from the theory of Mayer [Chap. 2, Section (7)] have been reduced to forms suitable for practical calculations of the thermodynamic functions of electrolytes by Poirier.[7] The explicit formula for a specially defined molar activity coefficient, $y'_\pm$, is

$$\ln y'_\pm = - \frac{n_2 \epsilon^2 \kappa}{2\,DkT} - \frac{A}{n_2} \sum_{\mu \geq 0} \frac{(-1)^\mu n_\mu^2}{A^\mu} b_\mu(\kappa a) \tag{3-6-7}$$

in which μ is a running index. The first term on the right of this equation represents the Debye and Hückel limiting law. The valence factors n_μ are defined by

$$n_\mu \equiv \frac{1}{\nu} \sum_s z_i^\mu \nu_i \tag{3-6-8}$$

so that when μ equals two, n_2 is the factor which when multiplied by c gives the ional concentration, or when multiplied by m yields twice the ionic strength. The quantity, A, is defined by the equation

$$A \equiv aDkT/\epsilon^2 \tag{3-6-9}$$

where a is the distance of closest approach of oppositely charged ions. The theory in general form assumes a distance a_{rs} which is different for each "ion-pair" type, and consequently $a_{rs} = a_r + a_s$. Since repulsive forces make the close approach of ions of like sign a rare event, the assumption is made that $a_{rs} = a$ for solutions containing one species of cation and one species of anion.

The function $b_\mu(\kappa a)$ is expressed by the integral

$$b_\mu(\kappa a) = \frac{(\kappa a)^2}{\lfloor \mu} \int_1^{l\mu} e^{-\mu\kappa a y} y^{2-\mu} (1 - \mu\kappa a y)\, dy \tag{3-6-10}$$

with limits $l\mu = 0$, when $\mu \leq 2$ and $l\mu = \infty$ for $\mu \geq 3$. Poirier has recorded values of $b_\mu(\kappa a)$ for $\mu = 0$ to $\mu = 16$ in a table, part of which is reproduced in Chap. 5, Table (5-2-2a).

The activity coefficient, $y'_\pm$, differs from the usual molar activity coefficient $y_\pm$ since it is referred to a standard state at a pressure equal to the external pressure, P_0 , plus the osmotic pressure of the solution, P. The coefficient, $y_\pm$, may be obtained from $y'_\pm$, by the equation

$$\ln y_\pm = \ln y'_\pm - \frac{1}{RT} \int_{P_0}^{P_0+P} \bar{V}_2 \, dP \tag{3-6-11}$$

where $\bar{V}_2$ is the partial molal volume of the solute. The equations and tables required for this complicated calculation are given by Poirier and

[7] J. C. Poirier, *J. Chem. Phys.*, **21**, 965, 972 (1953).

will not be reproduced here. However, the magnitudes of the correction for a few electrolytes as estimated by Poirier are assembled in Table (3-6-1).

Although the summation represented by the second term on the right side of equation (3-6-7) converges, this convergence is very slow. As evidenced by Table (5-2-2a), Poirier found it necessary to carry the computation to sixteen terms of this power series. Scatchard[8a] has made a very detailed critical survey of the methods of computing the extended terms of the Debye and Hückel Theory. He suggests that the tedious calculation due to the slow convergence of the summation in Mayer's theory can be expedited by employing the closed series approximation of Kirkwood.[8b]

Scatchard applied the theory to influences of concentrations upon reaction velocities and equilibrium constants. For reactions between ions all of the same sign, he was able to explain that the concentration of ions of opposite sign is more important than the ionic strength. This deduction resolves the problem raised by the experiments of Olson and Simonson.[8c]

TABLE (3-6-1). THE OSMOTIC PRESSURE CORRECTION, $\ln y_{\pm} - \ln y'_{\pm}$

c	NaCl	CaCl$_2$	ZnSO$_4$	LaCl$_3$
0.01	-0.00014	-0.00015	0.00005	-0.000015
.3	-0.0044	-0.0054	—	-0.0047
1.0	-0.017	-0.027	—	-0.031

Further, in agreement with the results of LaMer and Fessenden,[8d] the valence of ions of opposite sign is very important.

(7) BJERRUM'S THEORY OF IONIC ASSOCIATION[9]

Soon after Debye and Hückel proposed their theory, Bjerrum, who realized the mathematical difficulties which would accompany the complete solution of the Poisson-Boltzmann equation as developed by Gronwall, LaMer and Sandved, suggested a much simpler improvement. The theory of Bjerrum develops from the consideration of the factors which determine the extent of ionic association or, more particularly, the formation of ion pairs under the influence of Coulombic forces. The simplest model is assumed. The ions are taken to be rigid unpolarizable spheres contained in a medium of a fixed macroscopic dielectric constant. Non-

[8a] G. Scatchard, "Electrochemical Constants," p. 185 National Bureau of Standards Circular 524 (1953).

[8b] J. G. Kirkwood, *Chem. Rev.*, **19**, 275 (1936).

[8c] A. R. Olson and T. R. Simonson, *J. Chem. Phys.*, **17**, 1167 (1949).

[8d] V. K. LaMer and R. W. Fessenden, *J. Am. Chem. Soc.*, **54**, 2351 (1932).

[9] N. Bjerrum, *Kgl. Danske Vidensk. Selskab.*, **7**, No. 9 (1926).

polar quantum bonds between ions as well as ion-solvent interactions are excluded.

The probability that an i ion is at a distance r from a j ion is given according to the Maxwell-Boltzmann distribution law by

$$\text{Probability} \;=\; \frac{Nc_i}{1000}\, e^{U/kT} 4\pi r^2\, dr \qquad (3\text{-}7\text{-}1)$$

$Nc_i/1000$ is the number of i ions per cc. of solution, and $4\pi r^2\, dr$ is the volume of a spherical shell of thickness dr and radius r, circumscribing the j ion. U is the potential energy, or work of separating an i and j ion from r to infinity. At certain distances, U may be replaced by the simple Coulomb law,

$$U \;=\; -\,\frac{z_1 z_2 \epsilon^2}{Dr} \qquad (3\text{-}7\text{-}2)$$

with the result that the probability is given by

$$\text{Probability} \;=\; \frac{Nc_i}{1000}\left[\exp\left(\frac{-z_1 z_2 \epsilon^2}{DrkT} \right) \right] 4\pi r^2\, dr \qquad (3\text{-}7\text{-}3)$$

This function possesses some interesting properties. If the ions are of like sign, the probability of ionic association is very low. If the ions are of opposite sign, the probability can be shown to possess a minimum at a distance q, such that,

$$r(\text{min}) \;=\; q \;=\; \frac{\epsilon^2\, |\, z_1 z_2\, |}{2DkT} \qquad (3\text{-}7\text{-}4)$$

from which it follows that q is the distance at which the energy of separation of the ions is $2kT$. For values of r less than q, the probability increases rapidly as r decreases. At values of r greater than q, the probability increases slowly. Bjerrum assumes that two ions at a distance of $r < q$ are associated.* For 1-1 electrolytes in water at 18°, q equals 3.52 Å, and consequently electrolytes of this type, possessing values of the mean distance of approach of the ions, $å$, less than 3.5, will form short-range ion pairs. For 1-1 electrolytes, possessing values of $å$ greater than 3.5 Å, the theory of Debye and Hückel is valid.

Upon the basis of these considerations, two ions at a distance, r, less than q, will be associating, and the extent of ion pair formation will in-

---

* This definition of association is limited to high dilutions. Fuoss [*Chem. Rev.*, **17**, 27 (1935); *J. Am. Chem. Soc.*, **57**, 2604 (1935)] has made a more detailed analysis of the formation of ion pairs, and derived a convergent distribution function, $G(r)$, for them. From this he has shown that above a critical concentration, $c_0 = 1.2 \times 10^{-14}\, (DT)^3$ for 1-1 electrolytes, interactions of higher order become significant, and pairwise coulomb attraction no longer serves as a basis for distinguishing between free and associated ions because of space crowding.

crease very rapidly with decreasing r. The degree of association, or $(1 - \alpha)$, will be given by the definite integral

$$(1 - \alpha) = \frac{4\pi Nc}{1000} \int_a^q e^{\frac{|z_1 z_2| \epsilon^2}{DrkT}} r^2 \, dr \tag{3-7-5}$$

The distance between the centers of the two ions forming the ion pair at their closest distance of approach is a. If we let

$$Y \equiv \frac{|z_1 z_2| \epsilon^2}{rDkT} \tag{3-7-6}$$

$$b \equiv \frac{|z_1 z_2| \epsilon^2}{aDkT} \tag{3-7-7}$$

and substitute in equation (3-7-5), we obtain

$$(1 - \alpha) = \frac{4\pi Nc}{1000} \left(\frac{|z_1 z_2| \epsilon^2}{DkT} \right)^3 \int_2^b e^Y Y^{-4} \, dY \tag{3-7-8}$$

$$= \frac{4\pi Nc}{1000} \left(\frac{|z_1 z_2| \epsilon^2}{DkT} \right)^3 Q(b) \tag{3-7-9}$$

where $Q(b)$ is defined by the integral

$$Q(b) \equiv \int_2^b e^Y Y^{-4} \, dY \tag{3-7-10}$$

From equations (1-10-7) and (1-10-8), the equilibrium constant, K^{-1}, for the formation of an ion pair is given by

$$K^{-1} = \frac{y_{12}(1 - \alpha)}{y_1 y_2 \alpha^2 c} \tag{3-7-11}$$

As the concentration decreases, the activity coefficient ratio approaches unity, α^2 approaches unity, and therefore

$$(1 - \alpha) = K^{-1} c \tag{3-7-12}$$

Thus, the reciprocal of the ionization constant of the associated ion pair is given by

$$K^{-1} = \frac{4\pi N}{1000} \left(\frac{|z_1 z_2| \epsilon^2}{DkT} \right)^3 Q(b) \tag{3-7-13}$$

Another deduction of this equation has been made by Fuoss and Kraus[10] by employing the somewhat less familiar, but more general, phase integral. The integral $Q(b)$ reduces to

$$Q(b) = \int_2^b e^Y Y^{-4} \, dY = \frac{1}{6} \left\{ e^2 - Ei(2) + Ei(b) - \frac{e^b}{b} \left(1 + \frac{1}{b} + \frac{2}{b^2} \right) \right\} \tag{3-7-14}$$

[10] R. M. Fuoss and C. A. Kraus, *J. Am. Chem. Soc.*, **55**, 1019 (1933).

where $Ei(x)$ is the integral exponential function,

$$Ei(x) = \int_{\infty}^{-x} e^{-t}t^{-1}\,dt \qquad (3\text{-}7\text{-}15)$$

Values of $Q(b)$ for the range, $1 \leq b \leq 15$, have been tabulated by Bjerrum from tables.[11] Values of $Q(b)$ in the range $15 \leq b \leq 80$ were obtained by Fuoss and Kraus by employing an asymptotic expansion of $Ei(x)$. The latter are not correct when b equals 15, but the error decreases rapidly with increasing b. Values of $Q(b)$ are given in Table (5-2-3).

In order to keep clearly in mind the various aspects of the phenomena of ionic association, or electrolyte dissociation, and to state the conditions under which Bjerrum's theory may be expected to be valid, a few general considerations will be of interest. We shall distinguish between two kinds of binding which will remove ions from the solution with the formation of neutral particles. For singly charged ions we may represent an association by

$$C^+ + A^- \rightleftharpoons [C^+A^-]^0 \rightleftharpoons CA$$

Here $[C^+A^-]^0$ denotes an ion pair and CA an undissociated molecule with a non-polar bond, the former being produced by the action of Coulombic forces only, and the latter by electronic linkage. Further reactions are possible such as the formation of a triple ion,

$$[C^+A^-]^0 + A^- \rightleftharpoons [A^-C^+A^-]^-$$
$$[C^+A^-]^0 + C^+ \rightleftharpoons [C^+A^-C^+]^+$$

and more complex ion aggregates.

Bjerrum's theory is based entirely upon the range of validity of Coulombic forces, where the potential is given by $\psi(r) = \dfrac{e_1e_2}{Dr}$, and upon the assumption that the ions act as rigid bodies. The variation of the potential as a function of r for this case is shown by Fig. (3-7-1) (a). Since e_1e_2 is negative and constant, $\psi(r)$ is negative and the plot is a hyperbola. At the minimum distance of approach of the positive and negative ions, $\psi(r)$ rises perpendicularly, indicating an infinite potential barrier. The distance for ion pair formation is that represented by $(q - a)$.

Bjerrum's theory cannot be expected to be valid if undissociated molecules with non-polar linkages are found. For, consider a dissociation such as

$$HAc + H_2O \rightleftharpoons H_3O^+ + Ac^-$$

In this case, the variation of $\psi(r)$ with r, when $r < f$, is determined by

[11] E. Jahnke and F. Emde, "Tables of Functions," Teubner, Berlin and Leipzig, 1938.

quantum conditions, and is of the nature of the curve in Fig. (3-7-1) (b). Here, the molecular system on the left of the above reaction must possess sufficient energy to escape as ionic species, H_3O^+ and Ac^-, over the potential maximum at d.

These considerations lead to the conclusion that for weak electrolytes $\psi(r)$ is a much more complicated function of r than that postulated by Bjerrum's theory. On the other hand, we may expect this theory to hold in media of low dielectric constant for electrolytes which have sufficiently large a values. Indeed, we shall find numerous examples of its essential validity in subsequent discussions.

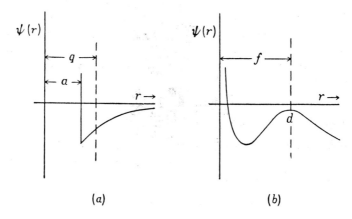

(a)   (b)

Fig. (3-7-1).   Illustrating (a) Ionic association, and (b), Non-polar bond formation

(7A) The Theory of the Formation of Triple Ions and Quadrupoles According to Fuoss and Kraus[12]

By following the method of Bjerrum for the computation of ionic association, it is possible to obtain an expression for the dissociation constant, K_3, of the reactions

$$[A^-C^+A^-]^- \rightleftharpoons A^- + [A^-C^+]^0$$

$$[C^+A^-C^+]^+ \rightleftharpoons C^+ + [C^+A^-]^0$$

Consider a triple ion consisting of two negative and one positive ion, and assume the ions to be charged spheres. Of the various ways by which a triple ion can form, consider the approach of a negative ion to an ion pair. Let the distance between the ions of a pair be a; let θ be the angle between the extended axis of the pair and the line drawn to the center of the nearest negative ion from the center of the positive ion of the pair; and let r be the distance of the approaching negative ion from the positive ion. Then,

[12] R. M. Fuoss and C. A. Kraus, *J. Am. Chem. Soc.*, **55**, 2387 (1933); **57**, 1 (1935).

the distance between the approaching negative ion and the negative ion of the pair will be $(r^2 + a^2 + 2ar \cos \theta)^{1/2}$, and the potential energy, U, of the negative ion will be

$$U = -\frac{e^2}{D}\left[\frac{1}{r} - \frac{1}{\sqrt{r^2 + a^2 + 2ar \cos \theta}}\right] \tag{3-7-16}$$

Considered as a function of θ, the minimum of potential energy, U_0, will occur when θ equals zero, so that

$$U_0 = -\frac{e^2}{D}\left[\frac{1}{r} - \frac{1}{a + r}\right] \tag{3-7-17}$$

Since the minimum in potential energy determines the maximum stability, the most favorable condition for triple ion formation occurs when all three ions lie in the same line.

The probability of finding a negative ion in dV_2 at a distance from the positive ion of an ion pair in dV_1 is given by

$$\text{Probability} = ne^{-U/kT} \, dV_1 \, dV_2$$
$$= ne^{-U_0/kT} e^{(U_0-U)/kT} \, dV_1 \, dV_2 \tag{3-7-18}$$

where n is the number of free ions per unit volume. In polar coördinates, with the origin at the center of the positive ion, this expression may be changed to

$$\text{Probability} = ne^{-U_0/kT} e^{(U_0-U)/kT} 2\pi r^2 \sin \theta \, d\theta \, dr \, dV_1 \tag{3-7-19}$$

The function $r^2 e^{-U_0/kT}$ is a minimum at $r = R$, which is a root of the equation

$$\frac{1}{r} = \frac{2DkT}{e^2} + \frac{r}{(r + a)^2} \tag{3-7-20}$$

If

$$x \equiv r/a_3 ; \qquad X \equiv R/a_3 \tag{3-7-21}$$

$$q = \frac{e^2}{2DkT} ; \qquad b_3 \equiv \frac{e^2}{a_3 DkT} \tag{3-7-21a}$$

be substituted in equation (3-7-20), we obtain

$$\frac{1 + 2x}{x(x + 1)^2} = \frac{a_3}{q} = \frac{2}{b_3} \tag{3-7-22}$$

The minimum corresponds to the root, X, of this equation. The parameters, a_3 and b_3, play the same part in triple ion formation as a and b in the theory of ion pairs.

In a manner analogous to that employed by Bjerrum for ion pair formation, we assume that triple ions are formed when $r \leq R$ and $\theta = 0$. When

$r > R$, the triple ion is dissociated into an ion pair and an ion. The dissociation constant, K_3, of the triple ions is obtained from these considerations and equation (3-7-19) by the following integral:

$$K_3^{-1} = \frac{2\pi N}{1000} \int_{a_3}^{R} e^{-U_0/kT} r^2 dr \int_0^{\pi} e^{(U_0-U/kT)} \sin \theta \, d\theta \qquad (3\text{-}7\text{-}23)$$

Upon introducing the variable, x, defined by equation (3-7-21), this equation may be reduced to a form more suitable for numerical computation. Thus,

$$K_3^{-1} = \frac{2\pi N a_3^3}{1000} \int_1^{x} x^2 \exp\left(\frac{b_3}{x(x+1)}\right) J(b_3, x) \, dx \qquad (3\text{-}7\text{-}24)$$

$$= \frac{2\pi D a_3^3}{1000} I(b_3) \qquad (3\text{-}7\text{-}25)$$

$J(b_3, x)$ includes the integration over θ, and is given by

$$J(b_3, x) = \int_{-1}^{+1} \exp\left[\frac{b_3}{x+1}\left(1 - \frac{x+1}{\sqrt{x^2+1+2xz}}\right)\right] dz \qquad (3\text{-}7\text{-}26)$$

where $z = \cos \theta$. Fuoss and Kraus evaluated $J(b_3, x)$ as a function of x graphically, and then computed $I(b_3)$. In Table (5-2-4), their values of $I(b_3)$ are reproduced.

Fuoss and Kraus[13] have also developed a theory of ionic cluster dissociation represented by the scheme

$$\begin{bmatrix} C^+A^- \\ A^-C^+ \end{bmatrix}^0 \rightleftharpoons 2[C^+A^-]^0$$

Introducing the assumption that the quadrupole is an ellipsoid with axes a_4 and λa_4, with $\lambda < \sqrt{2}$, containing a dipole of strength μ at the center and parallel to the major axis, they derived the expression

$$K_4^{-1} = \frac{N}{2000} \left(\frac{\pi}{3}\right)^{3/2} \frac{\mu^2}{DkT} \frac{e^y}{y^{7/2}} \left(\frac{1}{2\lambda^2} - 1\right)^{-1/2} \qquad (3\text{-}7\text{-}27)$$

y is defined by the equation,

$$y \equiv \frac{\mu^2}{(\lambda a_4)^3 DkT} \qquad (3\text{-}7\text{-}28)$$

(8) The Limiting Equations for the Relative Partial Molal Heat Content and Relative Partial Molal Heat Capacity

From equation (1-7-5), and the definition of the activity coefficient, f, it follows that the relative partial molal heat content of one mol of electro-

[13] R. M. Fuoss, J. Am. Chem. Soc., **56**, 2017 (1934); R. M. Fuoss and C. A. Kraus, Ibid., **57**, 1 (1935).

lyte at a given temperature is given by

$$\bar{L}_2 \equiv \bar{H}_2 - \bar{H}_2^0 = -\nu RT^2 \left(\frac{\partial \ln f_\pm}{\partial T}\right)_{P,N} \tag{3-8-1}$$

If we extend the concentration range of equation (3-5-8) by the addition of an empirical linear term, $B\Gamma$, the expression for $\ln f_\pm$ becomes

$$\ln f_\pm = -\frac{2.303\mathfrak{S}_{(f)}\sqrt{\Gamma}}{1 + A\sqrt{\Gamma}} + 2.303 B\Gamma \tag{3-8-2}$$

where

$$\mathfrak{S}_{(f)} = \frac{1}{\nu}\sum_1^p \nu_j z_j^2 (DT)^{-3/2} 1.290 \times 10^6 \tag{3-8-3}$$

and

$$A = \mathring{a}(DT)^{-1/2} 35.56 \tag{3-8-4}$$

by equations (3-4-8) and (3-5-9). In performing the differentiation of equation (3-8-2) with respect to T and substitution into (3-8-1), the temperature variations of D, Γ, $\mathring{a}$ and B must all be considered, but it is convenient to have the familiar quantities $\mathfrak{S}_{(f)}$ and A appear in the final result. Accordingly,

$$\bar{L}_2 = \frac{\mathfrak{S}_{(H)}\sqrt{\Gamma}}{1 + A\sqrt{\Gamma}} + \frac{\mathfrak{W}_{(H)}\Gamma}{(1 + A\sqrt{\Gamma})^2} + \mathfrak{K}_{(H)}\Gamma \tag{3-8-5}$$

where

$$\mathfrak{S}_{(H)} = -2.303\nu RT^2 \mathfrak{S}_{(f)} \frac{3}{2}\left\{\frac{1}{T} + \frac{\partial \ln D}{\partial T} + \frac{\alpha}{3}\right\} \tag{3-8-6}$$

$$\mathfrak{W}_{(H)} = 2.303\nu RT^2 \mathfrak{S}_{(f)} A \frac{1}{2}\left\{\frac{1}{T} + \frac{\partial \ln D}{\partial T} + \alpha - \frac{2\partial \ln \mathring{a}}{\partial T}\right\} \tag{3-8-7}$$

and

$$\mathfrak{K}_{(H)} = -2.303\nu RT^2 B \left\{\frac{\partial \ln B}{\partial T} - \alpha\right\} \tag{3-8-8}$$

Numerical values of the above parameters in aqueous solutions are given in Table (5-2-5). The term α is the coefficient of thermal expansion of the solution, which by equation (8-6-5) has been written for $-\partial\ln\Gamma/\partial T$. Complete expressions analogous to equation (3-8-5) were derived by Harned and Ehlers[14] and Harned and Hecker[15] who demonstrated the importance of the contribution of the term containing B in moderately dilute solutions.

[14] H. S. Harned and R. W. Ehlers, *J. Am. Chem. Soc.*, **55**, 2179 (1933).
[15] H. S. Harned and J. C. Hecker, *Ibid.*, **55**, 4838 (1933). The variable y which the authors define in their equation (11) should have an a written in the numerator.

At extreme dilutions the equation reduces to the limiting law

$$\bar{L}_2 = \mathcal{S}_{(H)} \sqrt{\Gamma} \qquad (3\text{-}8\text{-}9)$$

which was originally derived by Bjerrum[16] without consideration for the variation of Γ with temperature, but later corrected for this effect.[17,18] The sign of $\mathcal{S}_{(H)}$ is governed by ther term $\partial \ln D/\partial T$, which is negative, and usually greater than $1/T$ by an amount exceeding $\alpha/3$. Therefore, for water and most (if not all) other solvents, the Debye-Hückel theory requires that $\bar{L}_2$ increases with the square root of the ional concentration at extreme dilution.

The relative partial molal heat capacity, $\bar{C}_{p_2} - \bar{C}_{p_2}^0 \equiv \bar{J}_2$, is determined by differentiation of equations (3-8-1) or (3-8-5) with respect to temperature at constant pressure and composition. Thus, in general

$$\bar{J}_2 = \left(\frac{\partial \bar{L}_2}{\partial T}\right)_{P,N} = -\nu R \frac{\partial}{\partial T} \left\{ T^2 \frac{\partial \ln f_\pm}{\partial T} \right\} \qquad (3\text{-}8\text{-}9a)$$

To avoid obtaining a too unwieldy expression for practical purposes, we shall consider only the limiting law

$$\bar{J}_2 = \mathcal{S}_{(Cp)} \sqrt{\Gamma} \qquad (3\text{-}8\text{-}10)$$

derived by differentiation of (3-4-7) or (3-8-9). The limiting slope is given by

$$\mathcal{S}_{(Cp)} = 2.303 \nu R \, \mathcal{S}_{(f)} \left\{ X^2 - T \frac{\partial X}{\partial T} - \frac{1}{4} \right\} \qquad (3\text{-}8\text{-}11)$$

where

$$X \equiv 1 + \frac{3}{2} T \frac{\partial \ln D}{\partial T} + \frac{1}{2} T\alpha \qquad (3\text{-}8\text{-}12)$$

This expression is in suitable form for the evaluation of $\mathcal{S}_{(cp)}$ in most solvents because it has been shown[19] that $\ln D$ is linear in T over a wide temperature range. The bracketed term of (3-8-11) may be written,

$$\frac{3}{4} \left\{ 1 + 2 \frac{T}{D} \frac{\partial D}{\partial T} + 5 \left(\frac{T}{D} \frac{\partial D}{\partial T} \right)^2 + \frac{2T^2}{DV} \frac{\partial D}{\partial T} \frac{\partial V}{\partial T} + \frac{2}{3} \frac{T}{V} \frac{\partial V}{\partial T} \right.$$
$$\left. + \left(\frac{T}{V} \frac{\partial V}{\partial T} \right)^2 - \frac{2T^2}{D} \frac{\partial^2 D}{\partial T^2} - \frac{2}{3} \frac{T^2}{V} \frac{\partial^2 V}{\partial T^2} \right\} \qquad (3\text{-}8\text{-}13)$$

which is the form usually appearing in the literature.[20, 21] In this ex-

[16] N. Bjerrum, *Z. physik. Chem.*, **119**, 145 (1926).
[17] G. Scatchard, *J. Am. Chem. Soc.*, **53**, 2037 (1931).
[18] O. Gatty, *Phil. Mag.* [7], **11**, 1082 (1931).
[19] G. Åkerlöf, *J. Am. Chem. Soc.*, **54**, 4125 (1932).
[20] V. K. LaMer and I. A. Cowperthwaite, *J. Am. Chem. Soc.*, **55**, 1004 (1933).
[21] F. T. Gucker, Jr., *Chem. Rev.*, **13**, 111 (1933).

pression α has been replaced by equivalent functions of V, which may be either the specific volume or the total volume of the solution.

(9) The Limiting Equations for the Relative Partial Molal Volume, Expansibility and Compressibility of an Electrolyte

According to equation (1-7-8), differentiated with respect to n_2, the partial molal volume of an electrolyte in solution is

$$\bar{V}_2 - \bar{V}_2^0 = \left(\frac{\partial(\bar{F}_2 - \bar{F}_2^0)}{\partial P}\right)_{T,N} = \nu RT \frac{\partial \ln f_\pm}{\partial P} \qquad (3\text{-}9\text{-}1)$$

which by combination with (3-8-2) yields the general expression

$$\bar{V}_2 - \bar{V}_2^0 = \frac{\mathcal{S}_{(v)}\sqrt{\Gamma}}{1 + A\sqrt{\Gamma}} + \frac{\mathcal{W}_{(v)}\Gamma}{(1 + A\sqrt{\Gamma})^2} + \mathcal{K}_{(v)}\Gamma \qquad (3\text{-}9\text{-}2)$$

Equations (3-8-3) and (3-8-4) are used in evaluating the parameters

$$\mathcal{S}_{(v)} = 2.303\nu RT \, \mathcal{S}_{(f)} \cdot \frac{1}{2}\left\{\frac{3\partial \ln D}{\partial P} - \beta\right\} \qquad (3\text{-}9\text{-}3)$$

$$\mathcal{W}_{(v)} = -2.303\nu RT \, \mathcal{S}_{(f)}A \, \frac{1}{2}\left\{\frac{\partial \ln D}{\partial P} - \frac{2\partial \ln \mathring{a}}{\partial P} - \beta\right\} \qquad (3\text{-}9\text{-}4)$$

and

$$\mathcal{K}_{(v)} = 2.303\nu RTB\left\{\frac{\partial \ln B}{\partial P} + \beta\right\} \qquad (3\text{-}9\text{-}5)$$

The coefficient of compressibility, $\beta = \partial \ln \Gamma/\partial P$, is known for a number of solvents, but numerical values of $\partial \ln D/\partial P$ are generally not available. Fortunately, $\partial \ln D/\partial P$ is known for water at room temperatures. At present, we have no information whatever regarding the coefficients, $\partial \ln \mathring{a}/\partial P$ and $\partial \ln B/\partial P$, so that the last two terms of equation (3-9-2) cannot be evaluated. Accordingly, our use of this equation will often be confined to extreme dilutions where the limiting law

$$\bar{V}_2 - \bar{V}_2^0 = \mathcal{S}_{(v)}\sqrt{\bar{\Gamma}} \qquad (3\text{-}9\text{-}6)$$

is applicable.

The relative partial molal expansibility of an electrolyte in solution is defined by

$$\bar{E}_2 - \bar{E}_2^0 = \left(\frac{\partial(\bar{V}_2 - \bar{V}_2^0)}{\partial T}\right)_{P,N} \qquad (3\text{-}9\text{-}7)$$

Differentiation of equation (3-9-6) with respect to temperature gives the corresponding limiting equation

$$\bar{E}_2 - \bar{E}_2^0 = \mathcal{S}_{(E)} \sqrt{\Gamma} \tag{3-9-8}$$

in which[22]

$$\mathcal{S}_{(E)} = -2.303\nu RT \; \mathcal{S}_{(f)} \frac{1}{2} \left\{ \frac{1}{2} \left(\frac{3\partial \ln D}{\partial P} - \beta \right) \left(\frac{3\partial \ln D}{\partial T} + \frac{1}{T} + \alpha \right) \right.$$
$$\left. - \frac{\partial}{\partial T} \left(\frac{3\partial \ln D}{\partial P} - \beta \right) \right\} \tag{3-9-9}$$

At this point, it would be quite useless to derive a more general expression, similar to equation (3-9-2), because even the limiting slope, $\mathcal{S}_{(E)}$, already contains the unknown temperature derivative of $\partial \ln D/\partial P$.   Estimates[23,24] of this term lead to values of $10^3 \mathcal{S}_{(E)} (\sum \nu_j z_j^2)^{-1}$ between 2.5 and 4.3 at 20°.

Similar considerations lead to a limiting expression for the relative partial molal compressibility, defined by

$$\bar{K}_2 - \bar{K}_2^0 = -\frac{\partial(\bar{V}_2 - \bar{V}_2^0)}{\partial P} = \mathcal{S}_{(K)} \sqrt{\Gamma} \tag{3-9-10}$$

The limiting slope[25] is given by

$$\mathcal{S}_{(K)} = 2.303\nu RT \; \mathcal{S}_{(f)} \frac{1}{4} \left\{ \beta^2 + 2 \frac{\partial \beta}{\partial P} - \frac{6\beta \partial \ln D}{\partial P} \right.$$
$$\left. + 15 \left(\frac{\partial \ln D}{\partial P} \right)^2 - \frac{6}{D} \frac{\partial^2 D}{\partial P^2} \right\} \tag{3-9-11}$$

Estimates[21,24,25] of the terms in this equation lead to values of $10^4 \mathcal{S}_{(K)} (\sum \nu_j z_j^2)^{-1}$ between 3.2 and 5.3 at 25° when pressures are expressed in bars.

(10) Salting Out and Salting In of Molecules or Electrolytes

It is well known that the addition of a salt to an aqueous solution containing a neutral molecule frequently tends to decrease its solubility. This corresponds to an increase in activity coefficient of the molecule. "Salting out" of this kind is not general, and examples of the reverse behavior, "salting in", may be found.   A complete and reliable theory of these effects has not been developed, but it can be shown that the order of magnitude of the experimental results can be computed theoretically from the action of Coulombic forces without the inclusion of other factors.

Debye and McAulay[26] computed the partial free energy of a molecule

[22] F. T. Gucker, Jr., J. Am. Chem. Soc., 56, 1017 (1934).
[23] The lower figure corresponds to $\mathcal{S}_{(E)}$ from Table (5-2-5).
[24] The higher figure corresponds to $\mathcal{S}_{(K)}$ from Table (5-2-5).
[25] F. T. Gucker, Jr., Chem. Rev., 13, 111 (1933).
[26] P. Debye and J. McAulay, Physik. Z., 26, 22 (1925).

relative to the pure solvent from the reversible electrical work. The ions are assumed to be rigid spheres. Later, Debye[27] developed a theory which is based upon the influence of ions on the distribution of the non-electrolyte molecules, and derived an expression for the concentration of these molecules as a function of the distance from an ion. This theory has been extended by Gross,[28] who incorporates the effect of the ionic atmosphere.

(a) Theory of Debye and McAulay

Consider an ion as a perfect sphere of radius b_j. Then, the potential at its surface will be given by e_j/Db_j. The work of charging n_j ions of this kind may be obtained from equation (3-2-2).

$$W(n_j) = \sum_1^{n_j} \int_{\lambda=0}^{\lambda=1} \frac{e_j^2 \lambda \, d\lambda}{Db_j} = \frac{n_j e_j^2}{2Db_j} \qquad (3\text{-}10\text{-}1)$$

Let us consider a solution containing $n_1, \cdots n_j, \cdots n_s$ ions per cc., resulting from the dissociation of n' molecules of electrolyte, and compute the electrical work of discharging the ions at high dilution in a solvent (water) of dielectric constant D_0, and recharging them in a medium of dielectric constant D. The change in dielectric constant from D_0 to D may be produced by addition of either an electrolyte or a non-electrolyte to the solution. The net electrical work done on the system is

$$W'(n) = \sum_1^s \frac{n_j e_j^2}{2Db_j} - \sum_1^s \frac{n_j e_j^2}{2D_0 b_j} \qquad (3\text{-}10\text{-}2)$$

Equation (2-4-19) permits a calculation of the additional electrical work done against the potential due to ionic atmospheres. Thus

$$W(\kappa) = \sum_1^s \sum_1^{n_j} \int_{\lambda=0}^{\lambda=1} \psi_j^{0*}(e_j\lambda)e_j \, d\lambda$$

$$= -\sum_1^s \sum_1^{n_j} \int_{\lambda=0}^{\lambda=1} (\kappa\lambda) \frac{\lambda e_j}{D_0} e_j \, d\lambda = -\frac{\kappa}{3D} \sum_1^s n_j e_j^2 \qquad (3\text{-}10\text{-}3)$$

The appearance of $\kappa\lambda$ in the next to last member of this expression results from the fact that κ is proportional to e. To a first approximation, the total electrical work of the charging process, obtained by adding the above equations, may be set equal to the increase in work content of the system. Thus

$$\Delta A = \frac{1}{2D} \sum_1^s \frac{n_j e_j^2}{b_j} - \frac{1}{2D_0} \sum_1^s \frac{n_j e_j^2}{b_j} - \frac{\kappa}{3D} \sum_1^s n_j e_j^2 \qquad (3\text{-}10\text{-}4)$$

Again, as a first approximation, we may represent the dielectric constant of the mixture by the equation

$$D = D_0(1 - \bar{\beta}n - \bar{\beta}'n') \qquad (3\text{-}10\text{-}5)$$

[27] P. Debye, *Z. physik. Chem.*, **130**, 55 (1927).
[28] P. Gross, *Monatsh. d. Chem.*, **53**, 54 (1929).

where n and n' are the number of molecules of non-electrolyte and electro-lyte respectively, and $\bar{\beta}$ and $\bar{\beta}'$ are empirical constants. From these last two equations, we obtain

$$\Delta A = \frac{\bar{\beta}n}{2D_0} \sum_1^s \frac{n_j e_j^2}{b_j} + \frac{\bar{\beta}'n'}{2D_0} \sum_1^s \frac{n_j e_j^2}{b_j} - \frac{\kappa}{3D_0} \sum_1^s n_j e_j^2 \qquad (3\text{-}10\text{-}6)$$

if terms containing higher powers of n and n' are neglected. The last term leads to the limiting law of Debye and Hückel under the conditions, $n' = 0$ and $\bar{\beta} = 0$. In the discussion to follow we are concerned only with the "salting out" or "salting in" of electrolytes or non-electrolytes at ex-treme dilutions caused by alterations in dielectric constant according to equation (3-10-5). Under these conditions,

$$\Delta A_{(s)} = \frac{\bar{\beta}n}{2D_0} \sum_1^s \frac{n_j e_j^2}{b_j} + \frac{\bar{\beta}'n'}{2D_0} \sum_1^s \frac{n_j e_j^2}{b_j} \qquad (3\text{-}10\text{-}7)$$

which represents a pure salting-out (-in) term independent of terms in-volving κ.

From this equation we may determine the contribution to the chemical potential of the non-electrolyte ($\Delta\mu_{(s)}$ per molecule) caused by the addition of electrolyte, or *vice versa*. Thus for a neutral molecule

$$\Delta\mu_{(s)} = \frac{\partial \Delta A_{(s)}}{\partial n} = \frac{\bar{\beta}}{2D_0} \sum_1^s \frac{n_j e_j^2}{b_j} = kT \ln f_{(s)} \qquad (3\text{-}10\text{-}8)$$

or

$$\ln f_{(s)} = \frac{\bar{\beta}}{2kTD_0} \sum_1^s \frac{n_j e_j^2}{b_j} \qquad (3\text{-}10\text{-}9)$$

which is the equation of Debye and McAulay. It is apparent that when $\bar{\beta}$ is positive the macroscopic dielectric constant of the medium is decreased. Accordingly, f is increased, and "salting out" occurs. When $\bar{\beta}$ is negative, "salting in" takes place. Considering the simplified picture, and the approximations made during the deduction, it is clear that (3-10-9) is a limiting equation, and can be regarded as only a first approximation.

An expression for the "salt effect" of an electrolyte upon itself may be readily obtained from equation (3-10-7) by differentiation with respect to n'. In performing this differentiation, it should be observed that $n_j = \nu_j n'$. Accordingly,

$$\ln f_{\pm(s)} = \frac{\bar{\beta}'n'\epsilon^2}{\nu kTD_0} \sum_1^s \frac{\nu_j z_j^2}{b_j} \qquad (3\text{-}10\text{-}10)$$

Eliminating $\bar{\beta}'n'$ by (3-10-5), we obtain

$$\ln f_{\pm(s)} = \frac{(D_0 - D)\epsilon^2}{\nu kTD_0^2} \sum_1^s \frac{\nu_j z_j^2}{b_j} \qquad (3\text{-}10\text{-}11)$$

if no non-electrolyte is present except the solvent (water). This equation also gives the salt effect of one electrolyte upon another at high dilution. In this case the summation is taken over all the ions of both electrolytes.

Other equations for the salt effects of ions have been derived by means of a similarly simplified picture. Butler[29] obtained an equation identical with (3-10-9) except that D and not D_0 appears in the denominator. His equation for the mutual salting out of ions differs from (3-10-11) by replacement of D_0^2 and D^2 in the denominator.

An expression for the effect of a non-electrolyte upon the activity coefficient of an electrolyte at extreme dilution is readily obtained from equation (3-10-2). Thus the electrical work, W_t, of transferring the charges from n' molecules of electrolyte from pure water, of dielectric constant D_0, to a water-non-electrolyte mixture of dielectric constant D, is

$$W_t = \frac{n'\epsilon^2}{2D} \sum_1^s \frac{\nu_j z_j^2}{b_j} - \frac{n'\epsilon^2}{2D_0} \sum_1^s \frac{\nu_j z_j^2}{b_j} \qquad (3\text{-}10\text{-}12)$$

Setting this work equal to the increase in work content, and differentiating with respect to n', we obtain

$$\nu k T \ln f_{\pm(t)} = \frac{\epsilon^2}{2D} \sum_1^s \frac{\nu_j z_j^2}{b_j} - \frac{\epsilon^2}{2D_0} \sum_1^s \frac{\nu_j z_j^2}{b_j}$$

or

$$\ln f_{\pm(t)} = \frac{(D_0 - D)\epsilon^2}{2\nu k T D D_0} \sum_1^s \frac{\nu_j z_j^2}{b_j} \qquad (3\text{-}10\text{-}13)$$

which is the equation derived by Born.[30] The quantity $\log f_{\pm(t)}$ is the primary medium effect, $\log f_0$, discussed in Chapter (15), Section (7).

(b) Theory of Debye

We shall now obtain an expression for the concentration of a neutral molecule in presence of an ion as a function of its distance from the ion by a method developed by Debye.[31] Consider a spherical ion of radius, b, in a medium composed of two miscible non-electrolytes. For an ideal mixture of these substances,

$$n_1 v_1 + n_2 v_2 = 1 \qquad (3\text{-}10\text{-}14)$$

where v_1 and v_2 are the molal volumes of the pure components divided by Avogadro's number, and n_1 and n_2 the number of molecules of each species

[29] J. A. V. Butler, *J. Phys. Chem.*, **33**, 1015 (1929).

[30] M. Born, *Z. Physik.*, **1**, 45 (1920). See also H. S. Harned and N. N. T. Samaras, *J. Am. Chem. Soc.*, **54**, 1 (1932).

[31] P. Debye, *Z. physik. Chem.*, **130**, 56 (1927).

per cc. The free energy of an element of volume, according to equation (1-9-1), is given by

$$[n_1(\phi_1 + kT \ln N_1) + n_2(\phi_2 + kT \ln N_2)]dV \qquad (3\text{-}10\text{-}15)$$

where N_1 and N_2 are the mol fractions, and ϕ_1 and ϕ_2 are the standard free energies per molecule on the mol fraction scale. We are adhering to Debye's symbols to allow F_1, $\bar{F}_1^0$, etc. to be free energies or partial free energies per mol. Since the ideal solution is assumed, the activity coefficients are unity. In order to obtain the total free energy of the solution, it is necessary to add to this the contribution due to the field of the ion. From electrostatics, this quantity is found to be the energy of the volume element at a distance r from the ion, and is given by the expression

$$\frac{(DX)^2}{8\pi D}dV = \frac{\left[\dfrac{d}{dr}\left(\dfrac{e}{r}\right)\right]^2}{8\pi D}dV = \frac{e^2}{8\pi r^4 D}dV \qquad (3\text{-}10\text{-}16)$$

where X is electric field strength, $\dfrac{e}{Dr^2}$. The total free energy of the system is, therefore,

$$\Phi = \int\left[n_1(\phi_1 + kT \ln N_1) + n_2(\phi_2 + kT \ln N_2) + \frac{e^2}{8\pi r^4 D}\right]dV \qquad (3\text{-}10\text{-}17)$$

if the integration is extended over the entire volume of the solution. Let n_1 and n_2 be varied by δn_1 and δn_2. Then

$$\delta\Phi = \int\left[\delta n_1\left(\phi_1 + kT \ln N_1 - \frac{e^2}{8\pi r^4}\frac{1}{D^2}\frac{\partial D}{\partial n_1}\right)\right.$$
$$\left. + \delta n_2\left(\phi_2 + kT \ln N_2 - \frac{e^2}{8\pi r^4}\frac{1}{D^2}\frac{\partial D}{\partial n_2}\right)\right]dV \qquad (3\text{-}10\text{-}18)$$

The condition of equilibrium requires that $\delta\Phi = 0$, or Φ is a minimum subject to the condition that the total number of molecules does not change, or that $\int n_1 dV$ and $\int n_2 dV$ are constant. From equation (3-10-14)

$$v_1\delta n_1 + v_2\delta n_2 = 0$$

Now let

$$\delta n_1 = v_2\delta x; \qquad \delta n_2 = -v_1\delta x$$

where δx is an arbitrary variation. As a result, equation (3-10-18) becomes

$$\delta\Phi = \int \delta x\left[v_2\left(\phi_1 + kT \ln N_1 - \frac{e^2}{8\pi r^4}\frac{1}{D^2}\frac{\partial D}{\partial n_1}\right)\right.$$
$$\left. - v_1\left(\phi_2 + kT \ln N_2 - \frac{e^2}{8\pi r^4}\frac{1}{D^2}\frac{\partial D}{\partial n_2}\right)\right]dV \qquad (3\text{-}10\text{-}19)$$

Since

$$\int \delta n_1 \, dV + \int \delta n_2 \, dV = (v_2 - v_1) \int \delta x \, dV = 0,$$

we find that

$$\int \delta x \, dV = 0 \qquad (3\text{-}10\text{-}20)$$

This requires that for zero variation, $(\delta x = 0)$ and $(\delta \Phi = 0)$, the bracketed term under the integral in equation (3-10-19) equals a constant, or

$$v_2 \left(\phi_1 + kT \ln N_1 - \frac{e^2}{8\pi r^4} \frac{1}{D^2} \frac{\partial D}{\partial n_1} \right)$$

$$- v_1 \left(\phi_2 + kT \ln N_2 - \frac{e^2}{8\pi r^4} \frac{1}{D^2} \frac{\partial D}{\partial n_2} \right) = \text{constant} \qquad (3\text{-}10\text{-}21)$$

Let N_1^0 and N_2^0 represent the mol fractions at great distances from the ion $(r = \infty)$. Then,

$$\text{constant} = v_2(\phi_1 + kT \ln N_1^0) - v_1(\phi_2 + kT \ln N_2^0)$$

and

$$v_2 \ln \frac{N_1}{N_1^0} - v_1 \ln \frac{N_2}{N_2^0} = \frac{e^2}{8\pi kT D^2} \left(v_2 \frac{\partial D}{\partial n_1} - v_1 \frac{\partial D}{\partial n_2} \right) \frac{1}{r^4} \qquad (3\text{-}10\text{-}22)$$

From this result, it is clear that if D is known as a function of the composition, the concentrations of both components at a distance, r, from the ion may be computed. It is important to note that this theory excludes a variation of D as a function of r.

A simple and useful result may be obtained by considering a mixture which contains a small quantity of component (2). Since $N_1 = 1 - N_2$, and $N_1^0 = 1 - N_2^0$, the left of equation (3-10-22) becomes

$$v_2 \ln \frac{1 - N_2}{1 - N_2^0} - v_1 \ln \frac{N_2}{N_2^0}$$

We now assume that component (2) is salted out, and therefore $N_2/N_2^0 < 1$, and assume further that N_2^0 itself is small. Under these conditions, we retain only the term $-v_1 \ln N_2/N_2^0$, and equation (3-10-22) becomes

$$\ln \frac{N_2}{N_2^0} = - \frac{e^2}{8\pi kT} \frac{1}{v_1 D^2} \left(v_2 \frac{\partial D}{\partial n_1} - v_1 \frac{\partial D}{\partial n_2} \right) \frac{1}{r^4} \qquad (3\text{-}10\text{-}23)$$

Let

$$\bar{R}^4 = \frac{e^2}{8\pi kT v_1} \frac{1}{D^2} \left(v_2 \frac{\partial D}{\partial n_1} - v_1 \frac{\partial D}{\partial n_2} \right) \qquad (3\text{-}10\text{-}24)$$

then

$$N_2 = N_2^0 e^{-(\bar{R}/r)^4} \qquad (3\text{-}10\text{-}25)$$

and $\bar{R}$ is seen to be a characteristic length. The last two equations represent the basic result of Debye's theory. If D is a linear function of N_1 and N_2, or

$$D = N_1 D_1 + N_2 D_2 \tag{3-10-26}$$

$$\bar{R}^4 = \frac{e^2 V_1}{8\pi RT} \frac{(D_1 - D_2)}{D_1^2} \tag{3-10-27}$$

where V_1 is the volume of one mol of component (1).

From this result, it is clear that the salting out effect increases very rapidly with decreasing r. Salting out, or salting in, will depend upon whether $D_1 - D_2 < 0$, or $D_1 - D_2 > 0$.

Numerically useful equations for salting effects may be obtained from the preceding equations. From equation (3-10-14), we obtain in general,

$$n_1 = \frac{N_1}{v_1 N_1 + v_2 N_2} \; ; \quad n_2 = \frac{N_2}{v_1 N_1 + v_2 N_2} \tag{3-10-28}$$

which for small amounts of component (2) reduces to

$$n_2 = \frac{N_2}{v_1 N_1} \backsimeq \frac{N_2}{v_1} \tag{3-10-29}$$

Consider a solution saturated with component (2) in component (1), in the presence of $\sum n_i$ ions per unit volume. Then, according to equation (3-10-25), the average number of molecules surrounding an ion is given by

$$Z_2^1 = \int n_2 \, dV = \frac{N_2^0}{v_1} \int e^{-(\bar{R}/r)^4} \, dV$$

$$= \frac{N_2^0}{v_1} \left[\int dV - \int (1 - e^{-(\bar{R}/r)^4}) \, dV \right] \tag{3-10-30}$$

The integration is over the volume at the disposal of the ion. When r is ∞, N_2 equals N_2^0, and represents the concentration at any point containing no ions. The number of molecules of component (2), Z_2^0, at the disposal of one ion and before the addition of electrolyte will, consequently, be given by

$$Z_2^0 = \frac{N_2^0}{v_1} \int dV \tag{3-10-31}$$

The ratio of Z_2, the number of molecules present in the solution after the addition of electrolyte, to Z_2^0 is therefore

$$\frac{Z_2}{Z_2^0} = 1 - \frac{\int (1 - e^{-(\bar{R}/r)^4}) \, dV}{\int dV} \tag{3-10-32}$$

The integration of the term in the numerator is over the volume at the disposal of one ion. Therefore

$$\sum n_j \int dV = 1 \tag{3-10-33}$$

where $\sum n_j$ is the total number of ions per cubic centimeter.
Let

$$\sigma = 4\pi \int_b^\infty (1 - e^{-(\bar{R}/r)^4}) r^2 \, dr \tag{3-10-34}$$

then

$$\frac{Z_2}{Z_2^0} = \frac{f_2^0}{f_2} = 1 - \sum \sigma n_j \tag{3-10-35}$$

where f_2 and f_2^0 are, respectively, the rational activity coefficients of component (2) in the presence and absence of ions. Since non-ionic solutions are assumed ideal in the study of salt effects, f_2^0 is usually set equal to unity.

In the statement and derivation of equation (3-10-35), we have closely followed Debye,[32] but in the numerical evaluation of the term $\sum \sigma n_j$ it seems preferable to modify it slightly so as to distinguish between the various physical conditions under which it will be used. According to equation (3-10-26)

$$D = D_1 \left[1 - \left(\frac{D_1 - D_2}{D_1} \right) N_2 \right] = D_1 \left[1 - \left(\frac{D_1 - D_2}{D_1} \right) V_1 c \right] \tag{3-10-36}$$

since the concentration of component (2) in dilute solution is N_2/V_1. It is convenient to define the numerical magnitude

$$|\bar{\alpha}| = \left(\frac{D_1 - D_2}{D_1} \right) V_1 \tag{3-10-37}$$

so that

$$\bar{R}_j^4 = \frac{z_j^2 \epsilon^2 1000}{8\pi RTD_1} |\bar{\alpha}| \tag{3-10-38}$$

and the sign of the term $\sum \sigma n_j$ depends upon whether D_1 is greater or less than D_2. In the first case (I), $D_1 > D_2$

$$D = D_1(1 - |\bar{\alpha}| c) \tag{3-10-39}$$

and we define

$$(J_j)_\text{I} = \int_{b_j}^\infty (1 - e^{-(\bar{R}_j/r)^4}) r^2 \, dr \tag{3-10-40}$$

---

[32] P. Debye, *Z. physik. Chem.*, **130**, 56 (1927).

In the second case (II), $D_1 < D_2$

$$D = D_1(1 + |\bar{\alpha}| c) \tag{3-10-41}$$

and we define

$$(J_j)_{II} = \int_{b_j}^{\infty} (1 - e^{+(\bar{R}_j/r)^4}) r^2 \, dr \tag{3-10-42}$$

The equation for the salt effect (3-10-35) and therefore takes the form

$$\frac{f_2^0}{f_2} = 1 - \frac{4\pi N}{1000} \sum J_j c_j \tag{3-10-43}$$

The integrals involved in the evaluation of J_j are given by the series[33, 34]

$$(J_j)_I = \bar{R}_j^3 \left[1.21 - \frac{1}{3} \left(\frac{b_j}{\bar{R}_j} \right)^3 \cdots \right]; \qquad \bar{R}_j > b_j \tag{3-10-44}$$

$$(J_j)_I = \frac{\bar{R}_j^4}{b_j} \left[1 - \frac{1}{|25} \left(\frac{\bar{R}_j}{b_j} \right)^4 \cdots \right]; \qquad \bar{R}_j < b_j \tag{3-10-45}$$

and

$$(J_j)_{II} = - \frac{\bar{R}_j^4}{b_j} \left[1 + \frac{1}{|25} \left(\frac{\bar{R}_j}{b_j} \right)^4 \cdots \right]; \qquad \bar{R}_j < b_j \tag{3-10-46}$$

Gross[35] has extended this theory to include the effect of the ionic atmosphere. This effect requires that the energy of the volume element at a distance r from the ion [see equations (2-4-17) and (3-10-16)] increases by the amount

$$\frac{e^2}{8\pi D} \left[\frac{\partial}{\partial r} \left(\frac{e^{-\kappa r}}{r} \right) \right]^2 dV = \frac{e^2(1 + \kappa a)e^{-2\kappa r}}{8\pi r^4 D} dV \tag{3-10-47}$$

The result of this inclusion is to change equations (3-10-44) and (3-10-45) to

$$(J_j)_I(\kappa) = \bar{R}_j^3 \left[1.21 - \frac{1}{3} \left(\frac{a_j}{\bar{R}_j} \right)^3 - \frac{3}{2} \kappa \bar{R}_j + \cdots \right]; \qquad \bar{R}_j > a_j \tag{3-10-48}$$

and

$$(J_j)_I(\kappa) = \frac{\bar{R}_j^4}{a_j} \left[1 - \frac{3}{2} \kappa a_j \right]; \qquad \bar{R}_j < a_j \tag{3-10-49}$$

[33] P. Gross and and K. Schwarz, *Monats. Chem.*, **55**, 287 (1930); *Sitz. Akad. Wiss. Wien.*, **139**, 179 (1930).

[34] P. Gross, *Ibid.*, **138**, 449 (1929).

[35] P. Gross, *Monatsh. Chem.*, **53**, 445 (1929); **55**, 287 (1930).

(11) The Theoretical Limiting Law for Surface Tension of Electrolytic Solutions

Wagner,[36] and Onsager and Samaras[37] have developed the theory of the effect of interionic attraction on the surface tension of electrolytic solutions. The solution of this problem requires the computation of the deficiency of solute in the interfacial region

$$-\Gamma_2 = \left(\frac{d\sigma}{d\mu_2}\right)_{P,T} = \frac{a_2}{RT}\left(\frac{\partial\sigma}{\partial a_2}\right)_{P,T} \tag{1-11-1}$$

and subsequently, the surface tension increase, $\sigma - \sigma_0$, by integration of this equation.

Owing to the forces of attraction of the ions in the interior of the solution, or, more specifically, the repulsion of the ions from the surface by the electrostatic image force, there will be a deficiency of the solute near the surface. The screening effect of the ionic atmospheres of radii, $1/\kappa$, limits the depth at which these forces are operative. Wagner's formulation led to equations which were very difficult to solve. Onsager and Samaras, by adding one further simplifying assumption to Wagner's treatment, were able to obtain an explicit solution which, upon analysis, appears to be a good first approximation.

The Interfacial Layer and the Adsorption Potential

The concentration of solute, $c(x)$, at a distance, x, from a boundary is given by the Maxwell-Boltzmann equation,

$$c(x) = ce^{-W(x)/kT} \tag{3-11-1}$$

Here, c is the concentration of solute in the interior of solution $[c = c(\infty)]$ and $W(x)$ is the work required to bring a molecule of solute, or ion, from the interior of the solution to a point at a depth, x, from the boundary. The quantity $W(x)$ is the "adsorption potential." Each ionic species will be considered to possess an adsorption potential to be designated $W_i(x)$.

To compute $W(x)$, Wagner employed the method of electrical images. Consider an ion of charge e at a distance, x, from a fixed boundary. The ion is in a medium of dielectric constant, D, in contact with air of dielectric constant, D', equal to unity. Construct its electrical image as in Fig. (3-11-1). The electrostatic potential, ψ, at any point in the medium will be given by

$$\psi = \frac{e_j}{Dr_1} + \frac{(D-D')}{(D+D')}\frac{e_j}{Dr_2} = \frac{e_j}{Dr_1} + \frac{(D-1)}{(D+1)}\frac{e_j}{Dr_2} \tag{3-11-2}$$

[36] C. Wagner, *Physik. Z.*, **25**, 474 (1924).

[37] L. Onsager and N. N. T. Samaras, *J. Chem. Phys.*, **2**, 528 (1934).

where r_1 is the distance from the ion and r_2 the distance from the electrical image.[38]　The second term on the right of this equation is the potential caused by the presence of the boundary, and is expressed in terms of charge $[(D - 1)/(D + 1)]e_j$ of the image.　This exerts a force

$$-\frac{\partial W(x)}{\partial x} = \left[\frac{(D - 1)e_j^2}{(D + 1)Dr_2^2}\right]_{r_2 = 2x} = \frac{(D - 1)}{(D + 1)}\frac{e_j^2}{4Dx^2}$$

on the ion, and the potential of this force is

$$W(x) = \frac{(D - 1)}{(D + 1)}\frac{e_j^2}{4Dx} \tag{3-11-3}$$

Wagner showed that such an adsorption potential would cause an in-

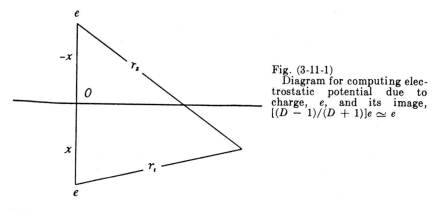

Fig. (3-11-1)
Diagram for computing electrostatic potential due to charge, e, and its image, $[(D - 1)/(D + 1)]e \simeq e$

finite increase in surface tension because the adsorbed amount of solute would be infinite

$$-\Gamma_2 = c\int_0^\infty (1 - e^{-W(x)/kT})\, dx = \infty \tag{3-11-4}$$

which is indeed a paradoxical situation.　For ionic solutions, the screening effect of the ionic atmosphere limits the effective range of the electrostatic forces to a distance, $1/\kappa$, and, consequently, the above difficulty disappears.　For electrolytic solutions, the potential has been found to obey equation (2-4-12)

$$\nabla \cdot \nabla \psi = \kappa^2 \psi \tag{3-11-5}$$

Further, since the concentration at the surface is different from that in the interior, κ^2 is a function of z if this equation is expressed in cylindrical

[38] A simple deduction of equation (3-11-2) is to be found in J. J. Thomson, "Elements of Electricity and Magnetism," Fourth Edition, p. 169–171, Cambridge University Press, 1909.

coördinates, as follows

$$\nabla \cdot \nabla \psi \; = \; \frac{\partial^2 \psi}{\partial z^2} + \frac{1}{r} \frac{\partial}{\partial r} \left(r \frac{\partial \psi}{\partial r} \right) = \kappa^2(z) \psi \qquad (3\text{-}11\text{-}6)$$

The solution is restricted by the conditions that when $z = x$, $r = 0$; when $z = -x$, $r = 0$; when $z > 0$, $\kappa^2(z)$ is given by equation (3-11-1), and the equation for the definition of κ^2 [Equation (2-4-11)]; and when $z < 0$, $\kappa^2(z) = 0$. At the boundary, $z = 0$, ψ is continuous, and $\partial\psi/\partial z$ changes by a factor D.

To obtain an approximate solution of this equation, Wagner let $D' = 0$ instead of unity. Furthermore, he replaced $\kappa^2(z)$ by $\kappa^2(x)$. Onsager and Samaras simplified the problem by the additional approximation that

$$\kappa^2(z) \sim \kappa^2(\infty) = \kappa^2 \qquad (3\text{-}11\text{-}7)$$

Under these conditions, $W(x)$ is given by

$$W(x) \; = \; \frac{e_j^2 e^{-2\kappa x}}{4Dx} \qquad (3\text{-}11\text{-}8)$$

which is seen to differ from equation (3-11-3) by the factor $e^{-2\kappa x}$, provided that $D'(= 1)$ is neglected. By combining equation (3-11-8) with equation (3-11-1), we obtain for the concentration, at a depth x from the boundary, the expression,

$$c(x) \; = \; c \exp \left(\frac{-e_j^2}{4DkTx} e^{-2\kappa x} \right) = c \exp \left(\frac{-q}{2x} e^{-2\kappa x} \right) \qquad (3\text{-}11\text{-}9)$$

where

$$q \; = \; e_j^2 / 2DkT \qquad (3\text{-}11\text{-}10)$$

is the characteristic distance employed in Bjerrum's theory of ionic association [Equation (3-7-6)]. This is the simplest limiting equation. If the mean ionic distance of approach of the ions is introduced, then

$$W(x) \; = \; \frac{e^{\kappa a}}{1 + \kappa a} \frac{e_j^2}{4Dx} e^{-2\kappa x} \qquad (3\text{-}11\text{-}11)$$

$$c(x) \; = \; c \exp \left(\frac{-q e^{\kappa a}}{1 + \kappa a} \frac{e^{-2\kappa x}}{2x} \right) \qquad (3\text{-}11\text{-}12)$$

and

$$-\Gamma_2 \; = \; c \int_0^\infty \left[1 - \exp \left(\frac{-q e^{\kappa a}}{1 + \kappa a} \frac{e^{-2\kappa x}}{2x} \right) \right] dx \qquad (3\text{-}11\text{-}13)$$

Onsager and Samaras succeeded in solving equation (3-11-13). Γ_2, obtained in this manner, was then substituted in equation (1-11-1). Upon integration, the increase in surface tension, $\Delta\sigma$, or $\sigma - \sigma_0$, where σ_0 is the surface tension of the solvent, was obtained.

In the limiting case (mean distance of approach of ions omitted), they expressed their result in the form

$$\sigma - \sigma_0 = \frac{kT}{16\pi q^2} (Y_c + Y_j) = \frac{kT}{16\pi q^2} Y \qquad (3\text{-}11\text{-}14)$$

Similarly, the equation which includes the sizes of the ions is

$$\sigma - \sigma_0 = \frac{kT}{16\pi q^2} (Y'_c + Y'_j) = \frac{kT}{16\pi q^2} Y' \qquad (3\text{-}11\text{-}15)$$

Y and Y' are complicated functions [Chapter 5, Table (5-2-6)].

For 1-1 electrolytes, the limiting law becomes

$$\sigma - \sigma_0 = \frac{79.517}{D} c \log \frac{1.143 \times 10^{-13}(DT)^3}{c} \qquad (3\text{-}11\text{-}16)$$

With water as solvent at 25°

$$\sigma - \sigma_0 = 1.0124 \, c \log \frac{1.467}{c} \qquad (3\text{-}11\text{-}17)$$

Chapter (4)

The Theory of Irreversible Processes in Electrolytic Solutions

In Chapter (2), we discussed the fundamental theory necessary for the treatment of the dynamics of ionic atmospheres. By adaptation of the general equation of continuity (2-5-6) to the special problem under consideration, and by the addition of further important concepts, it is possible to deduce exact equations by means of which the electrostatic contribution of Coulomb forces to viscosity, conductance and diffusion of dilute electrolytic solutions may be computed. The development of this difficult theory is due to Debye and Hückel, Falkenhagen, and Onsager. Since the solution of any of these problems requires considerable highly specialized mathematics, a complete treatment will not be given. However, a discussion of the fundamental physical foundations of the theory and an outline of the important steps of the deductions will be presented. This will introduce the reader to the literature which must be consulted if a thorough knowledge of the field is to be acquired. Following the theory of viscosity, conductance and diffusion, the theory of the effects of frequency and of high electrical fields upon the conductance will receive consideration. The final laws in forms adaptable for actual calculation will be stated. The more practical numerical aspects of the subject will receive detailed consideration in Chapter (5), where simplified equations and their numerical constants will be tabulated.

(1) Time Lags

(a) The Time of Relaxation of the Ionic Atmosphere (Debye and Hückel)

Whenever the ions of an electrolyte are subjected to a disturbance, such as an electrical field or a concentration gradient, the central ion moves relative to its atmosphere and the latter no longer will possess a symmetrical (spherical) structure. If the disturbing force is suddenly removed, the ionic atmosphere will tend to revert to its normal equilibrium condition. This change from the perturbed to the normal condition will require a finite time.

Let us suppose that a disturbance has taken place which causes a change in the density of charge, ρ. If the source of disturbance is suddenly removed, the system will revert to its original condition with a velocity, $\frac{d\rho}{dt}$, proportional to ρ

$$-\frac{d\rho}{dt} = k\rho = \frac{1}{\tau}\rho$$

The time, τ, which will be denoted the "time of relaxation," is the reciprocal of a velocity constant.

For consider a disturbance of electrical charges and the corresponding changes in density. If ψ is the disturbing potential and σ the conductance, then the current, according to Ohm's law, is

$$\mathbf{i} = -\sigma\nabla\psi \tag{4-1-1}$$

The time rate of density changes is given by the equation of continuity or

$$\frac{d\rho}{dt} = -\nabla\cdot\mathbf{i} = \sigma\nabla\cdot\nabla\psi \tag{4-1-2}$$

Further, according to Poisson's equation

$$\nabla\cdot\nabla\psi = -\frac{4\pi}{D}\rho \tag{4-1-3}$$

which relation, when combined with equation (4-1-2), yields

$$-\frac{d\rho}{dt} = +\frac{4\pi\sigma\rho}{D} = \frac{1}{\tau}\rho \tag{4-1-4}$$

Upon integration

$$\rho(t) = \rho(0)e^{-4\pi\sigma t/D} = \rho(0)e^{-t/\tau} \tag{4-1-5}$$

We note that

$$\tau = \frac{D}{4\pi\sigma} \tag{4-1-6}$$

a result first obtained by Maxwell.

From these considerations, we can readily obtain an expression for the time of relaxation of the ionic atmosphere. Since a force, $-\nabla\psi_j$, will cause an i ion to move with a velocity $-\omega_i e_i \nabla\psi_j$, or $\frac{-e_i\nabla\psi_j}{\rho_i}$, and since the current is equal to the velocity times the total charge,

$$\mathbf{i} = -\sum_{i=1}^{s}\frac{n_i e_i^2}{\rho_i}\nabla\psi_j \tag{4-1-7}$$

and consequently

$$\sigma = \sum_{i=1}^{s}\frac{n_i e_i^2}{\rho_i} \tag{4-1-8}$$

where ω_i and ρ_i represent the mobilities and frictional coefficients of the ion defined in Chapter (2), Section (3). Let

$$\overline{1/\rho} = \frac{\sum\limits_{i=1}^{s} \dfrac{n_i e_i^2}{\rho_i}}{\sum\limits_{i=1}^{s} n_i e_i^2} \tag{4-1-9}$$

then

$$\sigma = \overline{1/\rho} \sum_{i=1}^{s} n_i e_i^2 = \frac{\kappa^2 D k T}{4\pi} \overline{1/\rho} \tag{4-1-10}$$

upon introducing the value of κ^2 given by equation (2-4-11). Consequently, the time of relaxation, according to equation (4-1-6), will be given by

$$\tau = \frac{1}{\kappa^2 k T \overline{1/\rho}} \tag{4-1-11}$$

If $\rho_1 = \rho_2 = \rho_3 = \rho_i$, then $\overline{1/\rho} = 1/\rho_i$, and

$$\tau = \frac{\rho_i}{\kappa^2 k T} \tag{4-1-12}$$

This simplified equation will prove useful in the preliminary discussion of viscosity. $\dfrac{kT}{\rho_i}$ is the coefficient of diffusion.

In order to estimate the magnitude of the time of relaxation, we shall write equation (4-1-11) in terms of known quantities for an electrolyte which dissociates into two kinds of ions. The equivalent conductance of an ion, λ_i, is equal to the current at a potential gradient of one volt per cm. produced by one gram equivalent of the ion. Hence,

$$\lambda_i = F\bar{u}_i = F\,|\,e_i\,|/\rho_i = F\,|\,e_i\,|\,\omega_i \tag{4-1-13}$$

and consequently

$$1/\rho_i = \omega_i = u_i/|\,z_i\,|\,\epsilon = c \times 10^{-8} \bar{u}_j/|\,z_j\,|\epsilon \tag{4-1-14}$$

where the mobility, u_i, is in electrostatic units, and $\bar{u}_i$ refers to a potential gradient of one volt per cm., and c is the velocity of light. Therefore,

$$\omega_i = \frac{1}{\rho_i} = \frac{c \times 10^{-8} \lambda_i}{F\,|\,z_i\,|\,\epsilon} \tag{4-1-15}$$

Upon introducing this value of ρ_i in equation (4-1-9), we find that for a symmetrical electrolyte which dissociates into two ions,

$$\overline{1/\rho} = \frac{c \times 10^{-8}}{\epsilon F} \left(\frac{\lambda_1 + \lambda_2}{|\,z_1\,| + |\,z_2\,|} \right) \tag{4-1-16}$$

whence by equation (4-1-11)

$$\tau = \left(\frac{|z_1| + |z_2|}{\lambda_1 + \lambda_2}\right) 15.46 \times 10^{-8}/kT\kappa^2 \qquad (4\text{-}1\text{-}17)$$

$z_1 = |z_1|$ times the sign of z_1 ; $z_2 = |z_2|$ times the sign of z_2 .

It is apparent that, at a given temperature, this equation reduces to the simple form

$$\tau \simeq \frac{k_1}{c} 10^{-10} \text{ sec.} \qquad (4\text{-}1\text{-}18)$$

upon introducing the value of κ^2. The normal concentration is c, and k_1 is a constant characteristic of each electrolyte in a given solvent. Thus, for potassium chloride and hydrochloric acid at 18°, k_1 equals 0.55 and 0.19, respectively. In a $0.001N$ solution of electrolytes in water, τ is of the order of 10^{-7} to 10^{-8} sec.

(b) Time Lags of Processes of Ionic Combination

In some of our subsequent discussions of rates of dissociation and recombination of ions to form neutral molecules, we shall require a knowledge of the rate constant and time lags of such reactions. If n_i and n_j represent the number of the two species of ions which combine, and ν_{ji} the number of molecules which dissociate, then the chemical rate equations become

$$\frac{d\nu_{ji}}{dt} = -\frac{dn_j}{dt} = -\frac{dn_i}{dt} = An_jn_i - KA\nu_{ji} \qquad (4\text{-}1\text{-}19)$$

where A and KA are the rate constants for combination and dissociation, respectively, K is the ionization constant, $\dfrac{\alpha_0^2 n}{1 - \alpha_0}$, and, consequently α_0 is the degree of dissociation in the unperturbed state. If n is the number of molecules of electrolyte and α the degree of dissociation in general, then

$$\nu_{ji} = (1 - \alpha)n; \quad \text{and} \quad n_j = \alpha n = n_i$$

From equation (4-1-19) and these relations, it follows that

$$\frac{d\nu_{ji}}{An_jn_i - KA\nu_{ji}} = -\frac{d\alpha}{AK\left(\dfrac{n}{K}\alpha^2 + \alpha - 1\right)} = dt \qquad (4\text{-}1\text{-}20)$$

Upon integration, it is found that

$$\frac{(1 - \alpha_0)}{An(2 - \alpha_0)\alpha_0} \log \frac{\alpha - \alpha_0}{\alpha + \alpha_0/(1 - \alpha_0)} = -t + c', \quad \text{or} \quad (4\text{-}1\text{-}21)$$

$$\frac{\alpha - \alpha_0}{\alpha + \alpha_0/(1 - \alpha_0)} = ce^{-t/\tau'} \qquad (4\text{-}1\text{-}22)$$

where

$$\tau' = \frac{1 - \alpha_0}{An(2 - \alpha_0)\alpha_0} \qquad (4\text{-}1\text{-}23)$$

Thus, if an ionization equilibrium is disturbed by an external force, and if this disturbing influence is suddenly released, the system will proceed to a steady unperturbed state. The quantity, τ', is a measure of the time required for this process to take place and is analogous to the time of relaxation of the ionic atmosphere. Since the theory of such processes was originally studied by Langevin,[1] we shall refer to τ' as "the Langevin time lag." We shall find these fundamental considerations of value in discussions of the effect of high fields on the ionization of weak electrolytes. [This Chapter, Section (7)]

(2) Viscosity. Theory of Falkenhagen*

(a) A Preliminary Discussion of Velocity

The theory of the change in viscosity of a medium brought about by the presence of Coulomb forces between the ions was first successfully developed by Falkenhagen[2] for the case of binary electrolytes. In the following outline of the theory, the method of treatment of Onsager and Fuoss[3] will be followed. They succeeded in obtaining a general solution applicable to mixtures as well as individual electrolytes. Since the equation for the potentials is of the same general form and somewhat simpler than the one involved in the computation of the conductance, the theory of viscosity will be treated first.

In the first place, a simplified treatment will be considered which will serve to show how the electrostatic forces between the ions influence the viscosity, and roughly estimate the order of magnitude of the effect. This procedure will serve to introduce the fundamentals of the theory of the dynamics of viscous fluids necessary for the development of the general theory.[4]

As illustrated by Fig. (4-2-1), we consider a solution between two parallel plates, A and B, which are h cms. apart. A is fixed and B moves with a

---

* The theory of conductance in Section (3) is easier to comprehend than this difficult theory of viscosity and can be studied without reference to the latter. The present order is that adopted for logical reasons by Onsager and Fuoss.

[1] P. Langevin, *Ann. Chim. Phys.*, **28**, 433 (1903); L. Onsager, *J. Chem. Phys.*, **2**, 599 (1934).

[2] H. Falkenhagen and M. Dole, *Z. physik. Chem.* [B], **6**, 159 (1929); *Physik. Z.*, **30**, 611 (1929); H. Falkenhagen, *Ibid.*, **30**, 611 (1929); H. Falkenhagen and E. L. Vernon, *Ibid.*, **33**, 140 (1932).

[3] L. Onsager and R. M. Fuoss, *J. Phys. Chem.*, **36**, 2689 (1932).

[4] An excellent and comprehensive presentation of this subject is to be found in L. Page, "Introduction to Theoretical Physics," pp. 225–229, Van Nostrand Co., New York, 1928.

constant velocity v' in the x direction.   A constant velocity gradient in the y direction described by

$$\frac{v'}{h} = \frac{\partial v_x}{\partial y}; \qquad v_y = 0; \qquad v_z = 0, \qquad (4\text{-}2\text{-}1)$$

will be assumed.   The coefficient of the ij element of the stress dyadic[5], S_{xy}, is related to the corresponding element of the rate of strain dyadic[6] by the equation which defines the viscosity, η, namely,

$$S_{xy} = \eta \left(\frac{\partial v_y}{\partial x} + \frac{\partial v_x}{\partial y} \right) = S_{yz} \qquad (4\text{-}2\text{-}2)$$

In the case of a simple laminar flow

$$S_{xy} = \eta \frac{\partial v_x}{\partial y} \qquad (4\text{-}2\text{-}3)$$

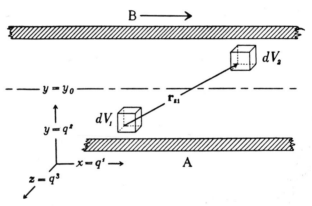

Fig. (4-2-1). Diagram for viscosity computation

The coefficient of viscosity, η, is the stress transferred per unit velocity gradient per unit area from each layer of liquid to the layer beneath it, or the force exerted by the portion of the medium above the plane on the portion of the medium below the plane per unit area of surface of separation.

In an electrolytic solution, part of the stress is caused by the deformation of the ionic atmosphere.   In the unperturbed solution, each ion will be surrounded by an atmosphere of ions of opposite sign at an average distance of $1/\kappa$, and as previously shown [Chapter (2)], this distribution will possess a spherical symmetry.   A velocity gradient in the solution will deform these atmospheres from a spherical to an ellipsoidal form.   The electrostatic forces and thermal motion will tend to restore the atmos-

---

[5] L. Page, *loc. cit.*, Equation (43–13).
[6] L. Page, *loc. cit.*, Equation (71-3).

pheres to their original form. As a result of these two opposite tendencies, and because the time relaxation, τ, is finite, a stationary deformation will persist. If the relative rate of deformation is taken to be $\partial v_x/\partial y$, then a stationary deformation, $\tau \partial v_x/\partial y$ will prevail. Since by equation (4-1-12), $\tau = \rho_i/\kappa^2 kT$, the deformation of the ionic atmospheres will be of the order of magnitude

$$\frac{\rho_i}{\kappa^2 kT} \frac{\partial v_x}{\partial y} \tag{4-2-4}$$

The forces between two ions of charge e at a distance $1/\kappa$ is $e^2\kappa^2/D$, and the total transfer of force between the ion and its atmosphere is $1/\kappa$ times this quantity, or $e^2\kappa/D$. This quantity, multiplied by the displacement of the ionic atmosphere, represented by equation (4-2-4), or,

$$\frac{e^2 \rho_i}{\kappa D kT} \frac{\partial v_x}{\partial y}$$

should be of the order of magnitude of the stress transferred between the ion and its atmosphere. Upon substitution of the value of κ^2 given by equation (2-4-11), we obtain for the electrostatic contribution to the stress, S_{yx}^*,

$$S_{yx}^* \sim \kappa \rho_i \frac{\partial v_x}{\partial y} \tag{4-2-5}$$

This equation is correct except for a proportionality factor, $1/480\pi$ which can only be obtained by the more general consideration of the exact deformation of the ionic atmosphere. Thus for the case where $\frac{1}{\rho_i} = \omega_i = \omega_2 = \cdots \omega_s$,

$$S_{yx}^* = \frac{1}{480\pi} \rho_i \kappa \frac{\partial v_x}{\partial y} \tag{4-2-6}$$

The stress between the solvent molecules is given by the equation

$$S_{yx}^0 = \eta_0 \frac{\partial v_x}{\partial y} \tag{4-2-7}$$

where η_0 is the viscosity of the solvent. Hence, the ionic atmosphere contributes,

$$\eta^* = \frac{\rho_i \kappa}{480\pi} \tag{4-2-8}$$

to the viscosity. This is Falkenhagen's result, which verifies the conclusion reached experimentally by Jones and Dole[7] that in dilute solution η^* is proportional to the square root of the concentration.

[7] G. Jones and M. Dole, *J. Am. Chem. Soc.*, **51**, 2950 (1929).

(b) Outline of the General Solution of the Viscosity Problem

The general equation of motion of a viscous fluid[8] is

$$\frac{\partial \mathbf{v}}{\partial t} d + \mathbf{v} \cdot \nabla \mathbf{v} d = \mathbf{F} d - \nabla P + \frac{1}{3} \eta \nabla \nabla \cdot \mathbf{v} + \eta \nabla \cdot \nabla \mathbf{v} \qquad (4\text{-}2\text{-}9)$$

where $\mathbf{F}$ is the force per unit volume and P is the pressure. According to the equation of continuity, if the fluid is incompressible, $\nabla \cdot \mathbf{v} = \operatorname{div} \mathbf{v} = 0$. If the density "$d$" is taken to be unity, and the second term on the left is neglected for slow rates of flow since it involves the square of the velocity, $\mathbf{v}$, we obtain for constant rates of flow

$$\eta \nabla \cdot \nabla \mathbf{v} = \nabla P - \mathbf{F} \qquad (4\text{-}2\text{-}10)$$

For the case of the general motion at a point in a liquid located by $\mathbf{r}$, where the velocity $\mathbf{v}$ has the components v_x, v_y, v_z, the y component of the stress, S_{xy}, per unit area across a plane perpendicular to x, is given by equation (4-2-2). There are two factors which contribute to the stress. One is the friction of molecules of solvent on solvent molecules, and the second is the interaction of the electrostatic forces between the ions. As a result, if S_{mn}^0 is the general coefficient of the stress matrix for force transfer in the pure solvent, and S_{mn} the same for motion in the solution, then

$$S_{mn} - S_{mn}^0 = S_{mn}^* \qquad (4\text{-}2\text{-}11)$$

is the contribution by the ions to the stress. Further

$$\eta - \eta_0 = \eta^* \qquad (4\text{-}2\text{-}12)$$

is the increase in viscosity caused by the addition of solute. Upon substitution of this last relation in equation (4-2-10)

$$\eta_0 \nabla \cdot \nabla \mathbf{v} = \nabla P - (\mathbf{F} + \eta^* \nabla \cdot \nabla \mathbf{v}) \qquad (4\text{-}2\text{-}13)$$

is obtained. *This important result shows that the electrostatic forces between the ions may be interpreted as an addition to the volume force.*

Stresses are transferred from the ions to the solvent by friction, and there will be a relative motion between the ions and the solvent. Now, if in the interior of the solution $\nabla \cdot \nabla \mathbf{v}$ is 0, no stress is transferred between the solvent and the ions. In this case, the forces acting at the boundaries [A and B, Fig. (4-2-1)] equal $\pm \eta \, \partial v_x / \partial y$, and not $\pm \eta_0 \, \partial v_x / \partial y$. The difference, $\eta^* \, \partial v_x / \partial y$ can be explained if the ions move relative to the solvent along the boundaries up to distances, $1/\kappa$, and nowhere else.

These special considerations and the general equation of continuity (2-5-6) contain all the fundamental physical concepts for the solution of the viscosity problem. The mathematical treatment is quite complicated, and if the method of Onsager and Fuoss is to be followed a knowledge of

---

[8] L. Page, *loc. cit.*, p. 229, Equation (71-18); note special use of $\mathbf{F}$ for total force.

the linear transformation of quadratic forms is essential. In this discussion, a few steps of the deduction will be given, which will show how the computation of the stress, S_{yx}^*, as a volume force requires a knowledge of the potentials of the ionic atmospheres, which for the irreversible process in question can be evaluated only from the general equation of continuity.

We shall now calculate the stress by computing the total volume force. To accomplish this, we return to consideration of Fig. (4-2-1), and compute the total transfer of electrostatic force in the x direction, AS_{yx}^*, across an area, A, of a plane at $y = y_0$, and assume a constant velocity gradient of one component,

$$\frac{\partial v_x}{\partial y} = a_2^1$$

where the notations 1 and 2 characterize the variables x and y. The electrostatic force between any two ions is

$$\frac{e_j e_i}{D} \frac{\mathbf{r}_{21}}{r^3}$$

where $\mathbf{r}_{21}$ or r, is the distance separating them. Only those which are on opposite sides of the plane, $y = y_0$, contribute to the stress, so our considerations are limited to pairs of ions which satisfy the condition,

$$y_1 < y_0 < y_2 \qquad (4\text{-}2\text{-}14)$$

where $\mathbf{r}_1$ and $\mathbf{r}_2$ locate the ions, respectively. The force transferred from a j ion in dV_1 to the ions in dV_2 is

$$\frac{e_j}{D} \sum_i e_i n_{ji}(\mathbf{r}_{21}) \, dV_2 \frac{\mathbf{r}_{21}}{r^3}$$

and the total force of all pairs of ions in dV_1 and dV_2 will be

$$\sum_j \frac{n_j e_j}{D} \, dV_1 \sum_i e_i n_{ji}(\mathbf{r}_{21}) \, dV_2 \frac{\mathbf{r}_{21}}{r^3} = \sum_{ji} \frac{e_j e_i}{D} f_{ji}(\mathbf{r}_{21}) \, dV_1 \, dV_2 \frac{\mathbf{r}_{21}}{r^3}$$

$$\qquad (4\text{-}2\text{-}15)$$

$$= -\sum_{ij} \frac{e_i e_j}{D} f_{ij}(\mathbf{r}_{12}) \, dV_1 \, dV_2 \frac{\mathbf{r}_{12}}{r^3}$$

Thus, according to equation (2-1-4), the distribution function $f_{ji}(\mathbf{r}_{21})$ now appears in the equation. By integrating over all the volume elements which satisfy the restriction (4-2-14), the total stress may be computed. Thus, if $A = \int dx \, dz$, the x component of the force transferred is:

$$-AS_{yx}^* = \underset{y_1 < y_0 < y_2}{\int\!\!\int\!\!\int\!\!\int\!\!\int} \sum_{ji} \frac{e_i e_j}{D} f_{ji}(\mathbf{r}_{21}) \frac{x_{21}}{r^3} \, dV_1 \, dV_2 \qquad (4\text{-}2\text{-}16)$$

Integration over x_1 and z_1 gives a factor A, and integration over y_1, keeping

y_{21} constant, gives a factor y_{21}. By suitable manipulation of the limits of integration, and upon dropping the subscripts of x_{21}, y_{21}, dV_1, and dV_2, the integral becomes

$$S_{yz}^* = -\frac{1}{2} \iiint\limits_{-\infty}^{+\infty} \frac{xy}{r^3} \sum_{ji} \frac{e_j e_i}{D} f_{ji}(\mathbf{r}) \, dV \tag{4-2-17}$$

Upon elimination of $f_{ji}(\mathbf{r})$ by Poisson's equation, the potential in the environment of the j ions may be introduced, and the integral

$$S_{yz}^* = \frac{1}{8\pi} \iiint\limits_{-\infty}^{+\infty} \sum_j n_j e_j \nabla \cdot \nabla \psi_j'(\mathbf{r}) \frac{xy}{r^3} \, dV \tag{4-2-18}$$

is obtained. For purposes of mathematical convenience, another function, $\xi_j(r)$ which is related to the potential is introduced. The integral then becomes

$$S_{yz}^* = \frac{1}{8\pi} \iiint\limits_{-\infty}^{+\infty} \sum_j n_j e_j (a_\mu^\lambda D_{\lambda\mu}^2 \nabla \cdot \nabla \xi_j(r)) \frac{xy}{r^3} \, dV \tag{4-2-19}$$

in which a_μ^λ is the designated element of the rate of strain dyadic, and $D_{\lambda\mu}^2$ a second differential. For the case now under consideration a_2^1 is the only element of the strain dyadic, a_μ^λ, which does not vanish. Consequently,

$$\psi_j'(\mathbf{r}) = a_2^1 \frac{\partial^2}{\partial x \partial y} (\xi_j(r)) \tag{4-2-20}$$

Therefore

$$S_{yz}^* = \frac{1}{8\pi} \iiint\limits_{-\infty}^{+\infty} \sum_j n_j e_j \frac{xy}{r^3} a_2^1 \frac{\partial^2}{\partial x \partial y} \nabla \cdot \nabla \xi_j(r) \, dV$$

Upon changing to polar coördinates, and integrating the angles, we obtain

$$S_{yz}^* = \frac{a_2^1}{30} \sum_j n_j e_j \int_0^\infty \frac{d^2 \nabla \cdot \nabla \xi_j(r)}{(r \, dr)^2} r^3 \, dr$$

which, upon integration by parts becomes

$$S_{yz}^* = \frac{a_2^1}{15} \sum_j n_j e_j \nabla \cdot \nabla \xi_j(0)$$

Consequently, the electrostatic contribution of the viscosity, η^*, is given by

$$\eta^* = \frac{1}{15} \sum_j n_j e_j \nabla \cdot \nabla \xi_j(0) \tag{4-2-21}$$

It is apparent from these considerations that the solution of the viscosity problem requires the evaluation of $\nabla \cdot \nabla \xi_j(0)$. This can be obtained only by means of the general equation of continuity (2-5-6). In order to obtain the differential equation for the potentials in a suitable form from equation (2-5-6), it is necessary to employ a few rather complicated transformations of variables.

Since this part of the deduction is concerned largely with matters of mathematical convenience, only a very brief outline is necessary for our purpose.

In the viscosity problem, the third and fourth terms of the general equation of continuity (2-5-6) are eliminated, since no external forces of the character of $\mathbf{k}_i$ and $\mathbf{k}_j$ are present. In order to convert equation (2-5-6) to a workable form, it is necessary to express the velocities in an appropriate manner. In the present case of the flow of the solution, both the distance between the ions, $\mathbf{r}_{21} = -\mathbf{r}_{12}$, and the distances $\mathbf{r}_1$ and $\mathbf{r}_2$ are independent variables. Since

$$\mathbf{r}_2 - \mathbf{r}_1 = \mathbf{r}_{21} = -\mathbf{r}_{12}$$

all the terms may be transformed to functions of two of these $(\mathbf{r}_1, \mathbf{r}_{21})$, or $(\mathbf{r}_2, \mathbf{r}_{12})$. Such transformation functions are devised. In all these problems, it turns out that it is more advantageous to employ the potentials, ψ_j', instead of the distribution functions, f_{ji}', since this substitution gives s functions, rather than $\dfrac{s(s+1)}{2}$. By means of Poisson's equation f_{ji}' and f_{ij}' are replaced by the potentials ψ_j' and ψ_i', and these in turn are replaced by ξ_j' and ξ_i' by means of the relation

$$\nabla \cdot \nabla \psi_j'(\mathbf{r}) = a_\mu^\lambda D_{\lambda\mu}^2 \nabla \cdot \nabla \xi_j(r) \qquad (4\text{-}2\text{-}22)$$

With these transformations, the equation of continuity (2-5-6) reduces to the specialized form

$$(\nabla \cdot \nabla)^2 \xi_j(r) - \frac{4\pi}{DkT} \sum_{i=1}^{s} \frac{n_i e_i^2 \omega_i}{\omega_i + \omega_j} \nabla \cdot \nabla \xi_j(r)$$

$$- \frac{4\pi}{DkT} \sum_{i=1}^{s} \frac{e_i e_j \omega_j n_i}{\omega_i + \omega_j} \nabla \cdot \nabla \xi_i(r) = - \frac{4\pi}{(DkT)^2} \frac{e^{-\kappa r}}{\kappa} \sum_{i=1}^{s} \frac{n_i e_i^2 e_j}{\omega_i + \omega_j} \qquad (4\text{-}2\text{-}23)$$

As we shall learn, the left side of this equation is identical with the left side of equation (4-3-27) for ψ_j' which appears in the conductance problem. This consideration shows the reason for the complicated transformations and the introduction of ξ_j.

The general solutions of some complicated differential equations involving summations can best be obtained by the use of matrix algebra.[9] By matrix methods, Onsager and Fuoss obtained a general solution of

[9] Chapter I in R. Courant and D. Hilbert, "Methoden der Mathematischen Physik," Vol. I, Springer, Berlin, 1924, contains the necessary standard methods for the treatment of the present problem.

equation (4-2-23) subject to the natural boundary conditions of the problem. An adequate treatment of the complicated algebra involved in the solution of this, and other differential equations resulting from the theory of irreversible processes in electrolytic solutions, would require much space and would divert attention from the physical aspects of the subject. Details are to be found in the contribution of Onsager and Fuoss, and in other papers to which we shall refer as occasion arises.

For the case of an electrolyte which dissociates into two kinds of ions ($s = 2$), the solution of equation (4-2-23) may be expressed in the form

$$\nabla \cdot \nabla \xi_j(0) = \frac{\kappa e_j}{2DkT} \left\{ \frac{\bar{\rho}}{4\kappa^2} - \left(\rho_j - \frac{\overline{\rho^2}}{\bar{\rho}} \right) \frac{(1 - \sqrt{q^*})}{(1 - \sqrt{q^*})} \frac{1}{\kappa^2} \right\} \quad (4\text{-}2\text{-}24)$$

where $\bar{\rho}$, $\overline{\rho^2}$ and q^* are defined by the relations

$$\bar{\rho} = \frac{n_1 e_1^2/\omega_1 + n_2 e_2^2/\omega_2}{n_1 e_1^2 + n_2 e_2^2} \quad (4\text{-}2\text{-}25)$$

$$\overline{\rho^2} = \frac{n_1 e_1^2/\omega_1^2 + n_2 e_2^2/\omega_2^2}{n_1 e_1^2 + n_2 e_2^2} \quad (4\text{-}2\text{-}26)$$

$$q^* = \frac{n_1 e_1^2 \omega_1 + n_2 e_2^2 \omega_2}{(n_1 e_1^2 + n_2 e_2^2)(\omega_1 + \omega_2)} \quad (4\text{-}2\text{-}27)$$

From equation (4-2-24), the electrostatic contribution to the viscosity, η^*, given by equation (4-2-21) may readily be obtained. Thus,

$$\eta^* = \frac{1}{15} \sum_j n_j e_j \nabla \cdot \nabla \xi_j(0) = \frac{\kappa}{480\pi} \left\{ \bar{\rho} + 4 \left(\frac{\overline{\rho^2}}{\bar{\rho}} - \bar{\rho} \right) \frac{1 - \sqrt{q^*}}{1 + \sqrt{q^*}} \right\} \quad (4\text{-}2\text{-}28)$$

if equation (2-4-11) used to define κ, is employed to eliminate $\sum n_j e_j^2$.[10] We note that, if the second term on the right of equation (4-2-28) is omitted, the result is identical with equation (4-2-8), which we derived by approximate methods. The second term in the brackets involves $\overline{\rho^2}$, or the second power of the mobilities, or equivalent conductances. As stated, equation (4-2-28) is in a form convenient for conversion to practical units, and is the same as Falkenhagen's equation.[11] If $\omega_1 = \omega_2 = \cdots \omega_s = \omega$, the second term on the right vanishes, and Onsager and Fuoss convert this equation

$$\eta^* = \frac{\kappa}{480\pi\omega} \quad (4\text{-}2\text{-}29)$$

to an interesting form by substituting the value of the coefficient of fric-

---

[10] Equation (4-2-28) is not given in the article of Onsager and Fuoss. We are indebted to Professor Onsager for this symmetrical and convenient result which was obtained through consultation with him.

[11] H. Falkenhagen, "Electrolyte," Equations (580) and (581), S. Hirzel, Leipzig, 1932.

tion ρ, given by Stokes formula [Equation (4-3-9)]. Thus

$$\frac{1}{\omega} = \rho = 6\pi\eta r$$

where r is the radius of the ion. Combining this relation with equation (4-2-29), we obtain

$$\frac{\eta^*}{\eta} = \frac{\kappa r}{80} = \frac{\eta - \eta_0}{\eta} \tag{4-2-30}$$

This shows that, in the first approximation, the relative increase in the viscosity is proportional to the ratio of the radius of the ion to that of its atmosphere.

(3) CONDUCTANCE. THEORY OF ONSAGER[12]

A. General Considerations and Preliminary Theory

In order to develop both the problems of conductance and diffusion from a common point of view, Onsager and Fuoss begin with a general treatment of the migration of ions in a homogeneous field of forces represented by $\mathbf{k}_1$, $\mathbf{k}_2$, $\cdots$ $\mathbf{k}_s$ (per ion) acting upon the ionic species 1, $\cdots$ s and a force, $\mathbf{k}_0$, acting upon molecules of the solvent, which balances the former according to

$$n_0\mathbf{k}_0 = -\sum_{i=1}^{s} n_i\mathbf{k}_i \tag{4-3-1}$$

Such a system of forces is equivalent to a combination of an electric field, $E = -\nabla\psi$, where ψ is the electrical potential, and the concentration gradients, ∇n_1, ∇n_2, $\cdots$ ∇n_s, provided that electrical neutrality is maintained according to

$$\sum_{i=1}^{s} e_i\nabla n_i \equiv \nabla \sum_{i=1}^{s} n_i e_i = \nabla(0) = 0 \tag{4-3-2}$$

This can be shown by the following thermodynamic reasoning.

Equilibrium can be maintained with this system of electrical forces and gradients by superimposing forces of another nature, and of opposite sign, $-\mathbf{k}_0$, $-\mathbf{k}_1$, $\cdots$ $-\mathbf{k}_s$, such that

$$\mathbf{k}_i = -\nabla\mu_i = -\nabla(\mu_i' + e_i\psi) \tag{4-3-3}$$

where μ_i' is the ordinary chemical potential, and μ_i the total chemical potential or the "electrochemical potential" [Chap. (10), Section (7)]. The velocities due to the various causes of migration may be assumed to be superimposable. Consequently, the velocities caused by the gradients, $-\nabla\mu_i$, must be the same as those caused by the forces, $\mathbf{k}_0$, $\mathbf{k}_1$, $\cdots$ $\mathbf{k}_s$,

---

[12] L. Onsager and R. M. Fuoss, *J. Phys. Chem.*, **36**, 2689 (1932).

because they balance the superimposed forces, $-\mathbf{k}_0$, $-\mathbf{k}_1$, $\cdots -\mathbf{k}_s$. Since at constant pressure and temperature, the Gibbs-Duhem equation requires that $\sum_i n_i d\mu_i' = 0$, the equilibrium condition given by equation (4-3-1) can be shown to be consistent with the nature of the forces given by (4-3-3).

The very important part of the theory which is concerned with migration velocities of the ions will now be considered. If there were no Coulomb forces between the ions, or if the ion was isolated, the velocity relative to the medium in which the ion moves would be given by

$$\mathbf{v}_i = \frac{\mathbf{k}_i}{\rho_i} = \mathbf{k}_i \omega_i \qquad (4\text{-}3\text{-}4)$$

This law would be valid for the ideal solution in which the forces between the ions are not sufficient to interfere. For actual electrolytic solutions, it is necessary to consider two effects:

(1) The direct transfer of forces between the ions. The complete treatment of this effect which includes allowance for the Brownian movement of the ions is due to Onsager.

(2) Electrophoresis, whereby an ion does not move in a medium at rest. Since it is surrounded by an ionic atmosphere which moves in the opposite direction, it migrates in respect to a moving medium. The effect of electrophoresis was first recognized by Debye and Hückel.

(a) **Preliminary Estimate of Force Transfer.** An ion under the influence of a force, $\mathbf{k}_j$, will move with a velocity equal approximately to

$$\mathbf{v}_j = \frac{\mathbf{k}_j}{\rho_j} \qquad (4\text{-}3\text{-}5)$$

When the force is applied, the ion tends to move away from its atmosphere, but the displaced ion will still attract the lagging atmosphere which will continue to form around the ion as it moves. If τ is the time of relaxation, the ion will be ahead of its atmosphere by a distance of the order

$$\mathbf{v}_j \tau = \frac{\mathbf{k}_j \tau}{\rho_j} \qquad (4\text{-}3\text{-}6)$$

The ratio of this distance to the thickness of the ionic atmosphere, $\mathbf{k}_j \tau \kappa / \rho_j$, will measure the relative dissymmetry of the atmosphere. The directed force, $\Delta \mathbf{k}_j$, due to this dissymmetry, is obtained approximately by multiplying this quantity by the total force between the ion and its atmosphere. Thus,

$$\Delta \mathbf{k}_j \approx -\frac{e_j^2 \kappa^2}{D} \frac{\kappa \mathbf{k}_j \tau}{\rho_j} = -\frac{e_j^2 \kappa \mathbf{k}_j}{DkT} \qquad (4\text{-}3\text{-}7)$$

upon substituting the value of τ given by equation (4-1-12). This value of $\Delta \mathbf{k}_j$, except for a numerical factor, will prove to be in agreement with the result obtained by the general method of procedure.

This force is caused by the dissymmetry of the atmosphere relative to the central ion. If some of the ions of the atmosphere migrate under the influence of external forces, the central ion becomes a part of the atmospheres of these. The relationship of these forces is reciprocal, and in order to take this reciprocity completely into account, the Brownian movement of the central ion must be considered, since it contributes to the relaxation of its own atmosphere. The fundamental equation (2-5-6) of Onsager takes care of this important effect.

(b) **Preliminary Treatment of Electrophoresis.** The calculation of electrophoresis is most easily made for electrical conductance, where the electrical field is $\mathbf{X}$, and where

$$\mathbf{k}_0 = 0; \qquad \mathbf{k}_j = e_j\mathbf{X}(j = 1, \cdots s) \qquad (4\text{-}3\text{-}8)$$

The ion of charge e_j will possess an ionic atmosphere of charge $-e_j$, and this atmosphere will be subjected to a force, $-\mathbf{X}e_j$. This force will tend to move the atmosphere, and along with it liquid containing the atmosphere, in the direction of the force, $-\mathbf{X}e_j$. The central ion will also be carried by the medium in a direction opposite to its motion under the force, $-\mathbf{X}e_j$. The velocity of this counter-current may be calculated if it be assumed that the entire charge, $-e_j$, of the atmosphere is situated at a distance, $1/\kappa$, from the central ion, is distributed on a spherical shell of radius $1/\kappa$, and that the motion of this sphere is governed by Stokes law for the motion of a sphere in a viscous fluid. Thus,

$$\Delta\mathbf{v}_j = -\frac{\mathbf{k}_j\kappa}{6\pi\eta} = -\frac{\mathbf{X}e_j\kappa}{6\pi\eta} \qquad (4\text{-}3\text{-}9)$$

where $\Delta\mathbf{v}_j$ is the velocity of the interior of the shell, and η is the viscosity of the medium. We are led to the result that the medium in the interior of the shell will be travelling with this velocity, and that the central ion will migrate against a current of this magnitude. This expression is the correct equation for the most important part of the effect of electrophoresis although certain refinements are not present.

If the central ion possessed no atmosphere it would migrate with a velocity $\mathbf{k}_j/\rho_j$, but due to its atmosphere, the ion is subjected to a force, $\mathbf{k}_j - \Delta\mathbf{k}_j$, and will move with a velocity, relative to its environment, of a magnitude, $(\mathbf{k}_j - \Delta\mathbf{k}_j)/\rho_j$. Consequently, the net velocity, $\mathbf{v}_j$, is given by

$$\mathbf{v}_j = \Delta\mathbf{v}_j + \frac{(\mathbf{k}_j - \Delta\mathbf{k}_j)}{\rho_j} \qquad (4\text{-}3\text{-}10)$$

For the case of electrical conduction, we obtain

$$\mathbf{v}_j = \frac{(\mathbf{X}e_j - \Delta\mathbf{k}_j)}{\rho_j} - \frac{\mathbf{X}e_j\kappa}{6\pi\eta} \qquad (4\text{-}3\text{-}11)$$

Since both the equations of force transfer (4-3-7), and electrophoresis (4-3-9) involve the first power of κ, these effects are both proportional to the square root of the concentration. The above considerations serve as an introduction to the fundamental physical conceptions underlying the general theory.

B. Outline of the General Theory of Conductance According to Onsager

(a) **Electrophoresis.** The subsequent treatment of the general theory of conductance and diffusion will require a more general development of the theory of the electrophoretic effect than the one just reviewed. The volume force acting on the medium surrounding the ion is the cause of electrophoresis. If n_j is the average concentration of j ions, the average external force per unit volume will be

$$\sum_{j=1}^{s} n_j \mathbf{k}_j \equiv n_\sigma \mathbf{k}_\sigma$$

where the Greek index, σ, represents summation. These forces are transferred to the solvent molecules of concentration n_0 per unit volume. All the forces balance, according to equation (4-3-1), with the result that

$$n_\sigma \mathbf{k}_\sigma + n_0 \mathbf{k}_0 = 0 \tag{4-3-12}$$

In an element of volume dV near the j ion, the volume force is $n_{j\sigma}\mathbf{k}_\sigma \, dV$, since the presence of the j ion influences the average concentration of the ions in dV. The net force on dV will be given by

$$(n_{j\sigma}\mathbf{k}_\sigma + n_0 \mathbf{k}_0) \, dV = (n_{j\sigma} - n_\sigma)\mathbf{k}_\sigma \, dV \tag{4-3-13}$$

In spherical coördinates the force acting on a spherical shell at a distance, r, from the central ion will be

$$4\pi r^2 (n_{j\sigma} - n_\sigma)\mathbf{k}_\sigma \, dr \tag{4-3-14}$$

This force is in the direction of the applied force, and is distributed uniformly over the surface. These conditions are comparable to those under which Stokes Law,

$$\mathbf{v} = \frac{\mathfrak{F}}{6\pi\eta r} \tag{4-3-15}$$

is applicable,[13] and consequently, the latter may be employed. The force, $\mathfrak{F}$, will cause the points within the sphere to move with the velocity, $\mathbf{v}$.

The next step is to express $(n_{ji} - n_i)$ as a function of r by means of the Maxwell-Boltzmann distribution, or

$$n_{ji} = n_i e^{-\frac{e_i \psi_j^0}{kT}} \simeq n_i \left[1 - \frac{e_i \psi_j^0}{kT} + \frac{1}{2}\left(\frac{e_i \psi_j^0}{kT}\right)^2 \right] \tag{4-3-16}$$

[13] Compare M. J. Polissar, *J. Chem. Phys.*, **6**, 833 (1938).

The second term of the expansion of the exponential function is retained by Onsager and Fuoss as it is of interest to the theory of diffusion. For the potential, the second approximation of Debye and Hückel,

$$\psi_i^0 = \frac{e_j}{D}\left[\frac{e^{\kappa a}}{(1 + \kappa a)}\frac{e^{-\kappa r}}{r}\right] \tag{4-3-17}$$

is employed. This equation is easily derived from equations (2-4-14) and (3-5-3). Combining equations (4-3-14), (4-3-16) and (4-3-17), the desired force acting on the spherical shell is found by

$$d\mathfrak{F}(r) = 4\pi r^2\left\{-\frac{e_j e_\sigma}{DkT}\frac{e^{\kappa a}}{(1 + \kappa a)}\frac{e^{-\kappa r}}{r}\right.$$
$$\left. + \frac{1}{2}\left(\frac{e_j e_\sigma}{DkT}\frac{e^{\kappa a}}{(1 + \kappa a)}\right)^2\frac{e^{-2\kappa r}}{r^2}\right\}n_\sigma \mathbf{k}_\sigma\, dr \tag{4-3-18}$$

which may be written in the simpler form

$$d\mathfrak{F}(r) = 4\pi(-A_1 r e^{-\kappa r} + A_2 e^{-2\kappa r})\, dr \tag{3-4-19}$$

By introducing Stokes equation, we obtain for the velocity

$$d\mathbf{v}_j = \frac{d\mathfrak{F}(r)}{6\pi\eta r} = \frac{2}{3\eta}\left(-A_1 e^{-\kappa a} + \frac{A_2 e^{-2\kappa r}}{r}\right) dr \tag{4-3-20}$$

The total velocity is obtained by integrating over all values of r from a to ∞, whence

$$\Delta\mathbf{v}_j = \frac{2}{3\eta}\left\{-\frac{A_1 e^{-\kappa a}}{\kappa} + A_2 \mathrm{Ei}\,(2\kappa a)\right\} \tag{4-3-21}$$

where Ei $(2\kappa a)$ is the exponential integral function

$$\mathrm{Ei}\,(x) = \int_x^\infty e^{-t}\frac{dt}{t} = -0.5772 - \ln x + x - \frac{x^2}{2\lfloor 2} + \cdots \tag{4-3-21a}$$

By resubstituting the values of A_1 and A_2, the final estimate of the effect of electrophoresis becomes

$$\Delta\mathbf{v}_j = -\frac{2}{3\eta}\frac{e_j e_\sigma n_\sigma \mathbf{k}_\sigma}{DkT\,\kappa(1 + \kappa a)} + \frac{1}{3\eta}\left(\frac{e_j}{DkT}\frac{e_\sigma e^{\kappa a}}{(1 + \kappa a)}\right)^2 n_\sigma \mathbf{k}_\sigma \mathrm{Ei}\,(2\kappa a) \tag{4-3-22}$$

For electrical forces, where $\mathbf{k}_i = X e_i$, and at low concentrations, when κa is negligible, the first term on the right of this equation equals the term derived by the preliminary considerations and given by equation (4-3-9). This becomes apparent upon combining with equation (2-4-11) which defines κ.

For the case of diffusion of an electrolyte which dissociates into two kinds of ions, $s = 2$, and $\mathbf{k}_j = \mathbf{v}_j/\omega_j$. If $\mathbf{v}$ is the net velocity of diffusion, equation (4-3-22) reduces to

$$\Delta\mathbf{v}_j = -\frac{2}{3\eta}\left(\frac{n_1 e_1}{\omega_1} + \frac{n_2 e_2}{\omega_2}\right)\frac{e_j\mathbf{v}}{DkT}\frac{1}{\kappa(1+\kappa a)}$$
$$+\frac{1}{3\eta}\left(\frac{n_1 e_1^2}{\omega_1} + \frac{n_2 e_2^2}{\omega_2}\right)\frac{\mathbf{v}e_j^2}{(DkT)^2}\phi(\kappa a) \tag{4-3-23}$$

where

$$\phi(\kappa a) = e^{2\kappa a}\,\text{Ei}\,(2\kappa a)/(1+\kappa a)^2 \tag{4-3-23a}$$

In a subsequent discussion of diffusion, the contribution due to electrophoresis will be required. The product of the number of ions, n_j, into the electrophoretic velocity will give the flow, $\Delta\mathbf{J}_j$, or the number of ions passing unit area per second perpendicular to the direction of diffusion. Thus

$$\Delta\mathbf{J}_j = n_j\Delta\mathbf{v}_j = \left[-\frac{2}{3\eta}\frac{n_j e_j n_\sigma e_\sigma}{DkT\kappa(1+\kappa a)} + \frac{n_\sigma e_\sigma^2 n_j e_j^2\phi(\kappa a)}{3\eta(DkT)^2}\right]\mathbf{k}_\sigma \tag{4-3-24}$$

If $\Delta\mathbf{J}_j = \Delta\mathfrak{M}_{j\sigma}\mathbf{k}_\sigma$, then $\Delta\mathfrak{M}_{ji} = \partial\Delta\mathbf{J}_j/\partial\mathbf{k}_i$, or the term in the brackets in the above equation. This completes the general treatment of electrophoresis.

(b) **The General Theory of Ionic Forces Specialized for Conductance and Diffusion.** For the treatment of conductance and diffusion, the first two terms of the general equation of continuity (2-5-6) involving the velocities, $V(\mathbf{r}_2)$ and $V(\mathbf{r}_1)$, which refer to flow of the solution as a whole, vanish. This equation for the stationary fields under consideration becomes

$$\omega_i[\mathbf{k}_i\cdot\nabla_2 f_{ji}^0(r)] + \omega_j[\mathbf{k}_j\cdot\nabla_1 f_{ij}^0(r)]$$
$$- e_i\omega_i n_i n_j\nabla_2\cdot\nabla_2\psi_j'(\mathbf{r}_{21}) - e_j\omega_j n_i n_j\nabla_1\cdot\nabla_1\psi_i'(-\mathbf{r}_{21}) \tag{4-3-25}$$
$$- \omega_i kT\nabla_2\cdot\nabla_2 f_{ji}'(\mathbf{r}_{21}) - \omega_j kT\nabla_1\cdot\nabla_1 f_{ij}'(-\mathbf{r}_{21}) = 0$$

By consideration of certain symmetry relations among the variables, and because of the fact that $\mathbf{k}\cdot\nabla f_{ji}^0$ can be replaced by $k(\partial f_{ji}^0/\partial x)$, without loss of generality, this equation can be simplified to

$$(\omega_i k_i - \omega_j k_j)\frac{\partial f_{ji}^0}{\partial x} - e_i\,\omega_i\,n_i\,n_j\,\nabla\cdot\nabla\psi_j'$$
$$+ e_j\omega_j n_i n_j\nabla\cdot\nabla\psi_i' - (\omega_i + \omega_j)kT\nabla\cdot\nabla f_{ji}' = 0 \tag{4-3-26}$$

By means of the s Poisson equations

$$\nabla\cdot\nabla\psi_j' = -\frac{4\pi}{D}\sum_{i=1}^{s}\frac{e_i}{n_j}f_{ji}'$$

the distribution functions f_{ji}', may be eliminated from this equation.

Further, since by equation (2-4-20),

$$f_{ji}^0 = n_j n_i \left(1 - \frac{e_j e_i}{DkT} \frac{e^{-\kappa r}}{r}\right)$$

we can also eliminate f_{ji}^0. By performing this operation, and by employing some other simple relations involving ψ_j' and ψ_i', the final differential equation for the potentials can be expressed in the form,

$$(\nabla \cdot \nabla)^2 \psi_j' - \frac{4\pi}{DkT} \sum_{i=1}^{s} \frac{n_i e_i^2 \omega_i}{\omega_i + \omega_j} \nabla \cdot \nabla \psi_j' - \frac{4\pi}{DkT} \sum_{i=1}^{s} \frac{n_i e_i e_j \omega_i}{\omega_i + \omega_j} \nabla \cdot \nabla \psi_i'$$

$$= \frac{4\pi}{(DkT)^2} \sum_{i=1}^{s} \frac{\omega_i \mathbf{k}_i - \omega_j \mathbf{k}_j}{\omega_i + \omega_j} n_i e_i^2 e_j \frac{\partial}{\partial x}\left(\frac{e^{-\kappa r}}{r}\right)$$

(4-3-27)

We note that the left side of this equation is identical in form with that of equation (4-2-23) for the potentials encountered in the general treatment of viscosity.

(c) The Limiting Law of the Conductance of Electrolytes in Low Fields and at Low Frequency.[14] **Electrolytes Which Dissociate into Two Kinds of Ions.** Before proceeding to an outline of the general solution of the conductance problem, valid for any number of ions, s, it will clarify matters somewhat to consider the case of an electrolyte which dissociates into two ions, or for $s = 2$. To this end, we shall expand equation (4-3-27), which for the case in question is

$$(\nabla \cdot \nabla)^2 \psi_1' - \frac{4\pi}{DkT} \frac{n_2 e_2^2 \omega_2}{\omega_1 + \omega_2} \nabla \cdot \nabla \psi_1' + \frac{4\pi}{DkT} \frac{n_2 e_1 e_2 \omega_1}{\omega_i + \omega_j} \nabla \cdot \nabla \psi_2'$$

$$= \frac{4\pi X}{DkT} \frac{e_2 \omega_2 - e_1 \omega_1}{\omega_1 + \omega_2} \frac{n_2 e_2^2 e_1}{DkT} \frac{\partial}{\partial x}\left(\frac{e^{-\kappa r}}{r}\right)$$

(4-3-28)

We note that for the conductance, $\mathbf{k}_i$ and $\mathbf{k}_j$ are replaced by Xe_2 and Xe_1, where X is the x-component of the external electrical field. Further, the condition

$$n_1 e_1 \psi_1' + n_2 e_2 \psi_2' = 0$$

(4-3-29)

prevails, and also

$$\psi_1' = \psi_2'$$

(4-3-30)

must be true since electrical neutrality requires that

$$n_1 e_1 + n_2 e_2 = 0$$

(4-3-31)

Upon introducing these conditions, equation (4-3-28) becomes

$$(\nabla \cdot \nabla)^2 \psi_1' - \frac{4\pi}{DkT} \left(\frac{n_1 e_1^2 \omega_1 + n_2 e_2^2 \omega_2}{\omega_1 + \omega_2}\right) \nabla \cdot \nabla \psi_1'$$

$$= \frac{4\pi X}{DkT} \left(\frac{e_2 \omega_2 - e_1 \omega_1}{\omega_1 + \omega_2}\right) \frac{n_2 e_2^2 e_1}{DkT} \frac{\partial}{\partial x}\left(\frac{e^{-\kappa r}}{r}\right)$$

(4-3-32)

[14] L. Onsager, *Physik. Z.*, **28**, 277 (1927).

If we let

$$\kappa_1^2 = q^* \kappa^2 \tag{4-3-33}$$

$$q^* = \frac{e_1\omega_1 - e_2\omega_2}{(e_1 - e_2)(\omega_1 + \omega_2)} \tag{4-3-34}$$

and

$$\Omega = \frac{X e_1 e_2}{D k T} \tag{4-3-35}$$

then equation (4-3-32) becomes

$$(\nabla \cdot \nabla)^2 \psi_1' - \kappa_1^2 \nabla \cdot \nabla \psi_1' = \Omega \kappa_1^2 \frac{\partial}{\partial x}\left(\frac{e^{-\kappa r}}{r}\right) \tag{4-3-36}$$

Upon integration, ψ_1' may be expressed in a series of powers of r, as follows:

$$\psi_1' = \frac{\Omega \kappa_1^2 x}{\kappa^2 - \kappa_1^2}\left\{-\left(\frac{\kappa - \kappa_1}{3}\right) + \left(\frac{\kappa^2 - \kappa_1^2}{8}\right) r - \cdots\right\} \tag{4-3-37}$$

From this the field due to the perturbation of the atmosphere, ΔX_1, is given by

$$\Delta X_1 = -\nabla \psi'_{1(r=0)} = \frac{e_1 e_2}{3 D k T}\left(\frac{q^*}{1 + \sqrt{q^*}}\right) \kappa X \tag{4-3-38}$$

which is the original expression of Onsager.[15]

This result, and the result obtained for the effect of electrophoresis, are all that we shall require for the computation of the mobility, ionic conductance, and equivalent conductance of an electrolyte. The total field acting on our ion is $X + \Delta X_j$. Because of electrophoresis, the velocity of the ion will be less than $e_j \omega_j (X + \Delta X_j)$. Introducing all the effects, we find that the net velocity in the x-direction is given by

$$v_j = X\left(e_j \omega_j + \frac{\Delta X_j}{X} e_j \omega_j - \frac{e_j \kappa}{6 \pi \eta}\right) \tag{4-3-39}$$

where the last term is the correction for electrophoresis according to equation (4-3-11), or (4-3-22), upon neglecting the terms involving the squares. The mobility is the velocity for unit potential gradient, or $u_j = |v_j|/X$. Hence, in practical units,

$$\bar{u}_j = \frac{1}{c \times 10^{-8}}\left(|e_j|\,\omega_j + \frac{\Delta X_j}{X}|e_j|\,\omega_j - \frac{|e_j|\,\kappa}{6 \pi \eta}\right) \tag{4-3-40}$$

Now, $|e_j|\,\omega_j/c \times 10^{-8}$ is the limiting mobility $\bar{u}_j^0$ at infinite dilution, and

[15] L. Onsager, *Physik. Z.*, **28**, 277 (1927).

further, $\lambda_j = \mathbf{F}\bar{u}_j$. Upon substituting these relations, and the value of κ given by equation (3-1-4), we obtain

$$\lambda_j = \lambda_j^0 + \frac{\Delta X_j}{X}\lambda_j^0 - \frac{\mathbf{F}\,|\,e_j\,|\,\kappa}{6c\times 10^{-8}\pi\eta}$$

or

$$\lambda_j = \lambda_j^0 + \frac{\Delta X_j}{X}\lambda_j^0 - \frac{29.16\,|\,z_j\,|}{\eta(DT)^{1/2}}\Gamma^{1/2} \tag{4-3-41}$$

For this special case, where $s = 2$, we may substitute the value of $\Delta X_j/X$, given by equation (4-3-38), and introduce equation (3-1-4) for κ. We obtain,

$$\lambda_j = \lambda_j^0 - \mathcal{S}_{(\lambda)}\Gamma^{1/2} \tag{4-3-42}$$

where

$$\mathcal{S}_{(\lambda)} = \frac{1.981\times 10^6}{(DT)^{3/2}}\left(\frac{q^*}{1+\sqrt{q^*}}\right)|\,z_1 z_2\,|\,\lambda_j^0 + \frac{29.16\,|\,z_j\,|}{\eta(DT)^{1/2}} \tag{4-3-42a}$$

Expressing the ionic mobilities in equation (4-3-34) by the corresponding conductances, we may write,

$$q^* = \frac{|\,z_1 z_2\,|}{(|\,z_1\,| + |\,z_2\,|)}\frac{(\lambda_1^0 + \lambda_2^0)}{(|\,z_2\,|\lambda_1^0 + |\,z_1\,|\lambda_2^0)} \tag{4-3-43}$$

Rewriting equation (4-3-42) for both kinds of ions of the electrolyte, and adding, we obtain,

$$\Lambda = \Lambda^0 - \mathcal{S}_{(\Lambda)}\Gamma^{1/2} \tag{4-3-44}$$

and

$$\mathcal{S}_{(\Lambda)} = \frac{1.981\times 10^6}{(DT)^{3/2}}\left(\frac{q^*}{1+\sqrt{q^*}}\right)|\,z_1 z_2\,|\,\Lambda^0 + \frac{29.16(|\,z_1\,| + |\,z_2\,|)}{\eta(DT)^{1/2}} \tag{4-3-45}$$

by virtue of the Kohlrausch relation,

$$\Lambda^0 = \lambda_+^0 + \lambda_-^0 \tag{4-3-46}$$

This situation is further simplified if the electrolyte is a symmetrical valence type, for when $|\,z_1\,| = |\,z_2\,| = z$, $q^* = \frac{1}{2}$, $q^*/(1 + \sqrt{q^*}) = 0.2929$. and

$$\mathcal{S}_{(\Lambda)} = \frac{5.802\times 10^5}{(DT)^{3/2}}z^2\Lambda^0 + \frac{58.32z}{\eta(DT)^{1/2}} \tag{4-3-47}$$

This result has proved to be of great importance, since it renders possible the interpretation of years of accurate experimental work upon the conductance of strong electrolytes, and with its help the determination of ionization constants of weak electrolytes may be performed with far greater certainty than was possible before the interionic attraction theory was developed.

Before turning to the general application of equation (4-3-41) in the next section, we shall consider the important special case where $s = 2$, and $|z_2| = 2|z_1|$. In this case

$$\frac{q^*}{1 + \sqrt{q^*}} = \frac{0.2929 \times 2.2761}{1 + T_1^0 + 0.8165\sqrt{1 + T_1^0}} \quad (4\text{-}3\text{-}48)$$

if we introduce the transference number, $T_1^0 = \lambda_1^0/(\lambda_1^0 + \lambda_2^0)$, of the ion constituent having the smaller valence z_1. The numerator, which is exactly 2/3, has been factored into 0.2929×2.2761 to simplify the use of Table (5-3-1). Accordingly, substitution in equation (4-3-45) gives

$$\mathfrak{S}_{(\Lambda)} = \frac{5.802 \times 10^5 \times 2.276 \, |z_1 z_2| \, \Lambda^0}{(DT)^{3/2}(1 + T_1^0 + 0.8165\sqrt{1 + T_1^0})}$$
$$+ \frac{29.16(|z_1| + |z_2|)}{\eta(DT)^{1/2}} \quad (4\text{-}3\text{-}49)$$

Electrolytes Which Dissociate into any Number of Ions.[16] In order to obtain $\Delta X_j/X$, equation (4-3-41) for the general case of $s > 2$ ions, it is necessary to obtain a general solution of equation (4-3-27). This has been accomplished successfully by Onsager and Fuoss by the use of the matrix algebra in a manner similar to that employed in the case of viscosity. The final complete solution, which may be expanded into forms suitable for numerical computation, is given by

$$\frac{\Delta X_j}{X} = -\frac{1.981 \times 10^6 \Gamma^{1/2}}{(DT)^{3/2}} z_j \sum_{n=0}^{\infty} c_n r_j^{(n)} \quad (4\text{-}3\text{-}50)$$

If this is substituted in the equation for the ionic conductance (4-3-41), we obtain

$$\lambda_j = \lambda_j^0 - \left(\frac{1.981 \times 10^6}{(DT)^{3/2}} \lambda_j^0 z_j \sum_{n=0}^{\infty} c_n r_j^{(n)} + \frac{29.16\,|z_j|}{\eta(DT)^{1/2}}\right) \Gamma^{1/2} \quad (4\text{-}3\text{-}51)$$

The series function, $\sum_{n=0}^{\infty} c_n r_j^{(n)}$, may be computed from the following relations. The coefficients c_n are given by

$$c_0 = \tfrac{1}{2}(2 - \sqrt{2})$$
$$c_n = -\tfrac{1}{2}\sqrt{2}\binom{1/2}{n}; \quad n \geq 1 \quad (4\text{-}3\text{-}52)$$

where $\binom{1/2}{n}$ represents the coefficient of the terms of the expansion

[16] L. Onsager and R. M. Fuoss, *J. Phys. Chem.*, **36**, 2689 (1932).

$(1 + x)^{1/2}$, or $-1/2$, $1/8$, $-1/16$, $+5/128$, $-7/256$ for n equal to 1, 2, 3, 4, 5. Therefore, the first six coefficients are

$$c_0 = 0.2929 \qquad c_3 = -0.0442$$

$$c_1 = -0.3536 \qquad c_4 = 0.0276 \tag{4-3-53}$$

$$c_2 = 0.0884 \qquad c_5 = -0.0193$$

Further,

$$r_j = r_j^{(0)} = z_j\left(1 - \frac{\sum \mu_i z_i}{z_j \omega_j \sum \mu_i/\omega_i}\right) \tag{4-3-54}$$

$$r_j^{(n)} = \sum t_{ji} r_i^{(n-1)} \tag{4-3-55}$$

and t_{ji} is an element of a matrix and is given by

$$t_{ji} = \delta_{ji} \sum_k \mu_k \frac{\omega_k - \omega_j}{\omega_k + \omega_i} + \frac{2\mu_i \omega_i}{\omega_j + \omega_i} \tag{4-3-56}$$

In these equations, u_i is defined by

$$\mu_i = \frac{\Gamma_i}{\Gamma} = \frac{n_i e_i^2}{\sum n_j e_j^2} \tag{4-3-57}$$

and the Kronecker symbol, δ_{ji}, is given

$$\delta_{ji} = \begin{cases} 1, & \text{if } j = i \\ 0, & \text{if } j \neq i \end{cases} \tag{4-3-58}$$

t_{ji} is related to an element, h_{ji}, of a matrix H [Onsager and Fuoss, Equations (4-7-6) and (4-7-7)] according to

$$t_{ji} = 2h_{ji} - \delta_{ji} = 2h'_{ij} - \delta_{ji} \tag{4-3-59}$$

In employing these equations, it is important to observe that z_j carries the sign of the corresponding ionic charge. For the simplest case when $s = 2$ and $z_1 = -z_2$, it is clear that $r_j^0 = z_j$. It can also readily be shown that $r_j^{(n)} = 0$, and as a result $\sum c_n r_j^{(n)}$ reduces to $c_0 z_j$, or $0.2929 z_j$, and equation (4-3-51) reduces to equation (4-3-41). For the case when $s = 2$, $|z_1| = |z_2|$ and $q^* = \frac{1}{2}$, the equivalent of equation (4-3-42) can be obtained from equations (4-3-51) to (4-3-56). In cases of mixtures when $s = 3$, or higher, the algebra involved becomes quite complicated. We shall have occasion to employ these expressions when some features of electrolytic conduction in mixtures of electrolytes come under consideration.

(3a) Another Solution for a System Containing s Ions. Theory of Onsager and Kim[*],[16a]

In order to obtain a convenient and more easily workable general solution of equation (4-3-27), Onsager[16b] introduced the quantities

$$0 = \alpha_1 < \alpha_2 < \cdots < \alpha_s \tag{4-3-60}$$

which are the roots of the equation

$$\alpha_p \sum_{i=1}^{s} \frac{T_i^0}{\omega_i^2 - \alpha_p^2} = 0 \tag{4-3-61}$$

where T_i^0 is the limiting transference number of the ith ion. The solution of equation (4-3-27) is

$$\psi_j'(r) = \frac{e_j}{DkT} \sum_{p=2}^{s} \frac{\partial}{\partial x} \left(\frac{1 - e^{-\kappa r}}{\kappa^2 r} - \frac{1 - e^{-\sqrt{q_p}\kappa r}}{q_p \kappa^2 r} \right) \chi_j^p \sum_{i=1}^{s} T_i^0 \chi_i^p k_i \tag{4-3-62}$$

where

$$\chi_i^p \equiv N_p \frac{\omega_i}{\omega_i^2 - \alpha_p^2}; \qquad N_p^{-2} \equiv \sum_{i=1}^{s} \frac{T_i^0 \omega_i^2}{(\omega_i^2 - \alpha_p^2)^2} \tag{4-3-63}$$

$$q_p \equiv \bar\omega \sum_{i=1}^{s} \frac{T_i^0 \omega_i}{\omega_i^2 - \alpha_p^2}; \qquad \bar\omega \equiv \frac{\sum_{i=1}^{s} n_i e_i^2 \omega_i}{\sum_{i=1}^{s} n_i e_i^2} \tag{4-3-64}$$

The quantities α_p and q_p satisfy the inequalities

$$0 = \alpha_1 < \omega_1 < \alpha_2 < \omega_2 \cdots < \alpha_s < \omega_s \tag{4-3-65}$$

$$1 > q_1 > d(\omega_1) > q_2 > \cdots > q_s > d(\omega_s) > 0 \tag{4-3-66}$$

where

$$d(\alpha_p) \equiv \bar\omega \sum_{i=1}^{s} \frac{T_i^0}{\omega_i + \alpha_p} \tag{4-3-67}$$

For conductance, k_i in equation (4-3-62) is replaced by Xe_j, and the field

---

[*] The full details of this theory are contained in a dissertation by Dr. Shoon Kyung Kim, Yale University, June, 1956. We are grateful to Dr. Kim for the following summary of the theory.

[16a] L. Onsager and S. K. Kim, *J. Phys. Chem.*, **61**, 215 (1957).

[16b] L. Onsager, *Ann. N. Y. Acad. Sci.*, **46**, 263 (1945).

ΔX_j due to the ionic atmosphere is given by

$$\frac{\Delta X_j}{X} = - \frac{\kappa e_j}{3DkT} \sum_{p=2}^{s} (1 - \sqrt{q_p})\chi_j^p(T_\sigma^0\chi_\sigma^p z_\sigma) \qquad (4\text{-}3\text{-}68)$$

where σ implies summation over all ions present. Upon substitution of this expression in equation (4-3-40) the equivalent conductance λ_j takes the form

$$\lambda_j = \lambda_j^0 - \left\{ \frac{F N \epsilon^2 \, |z_j|}{6c \times 10^{-8} \sqrt{250\pi R} \, \eta(DT)^{1/2}} \right.$$
$$\left. + \lambda_j^0 \sqrt{\frac{\pi}{250R}} \frac{N^2\epsilon^3}{3R} \frac{z_j}{(DT)^{3/2}} \sum_{p=2}^{s} (1 - \sqrt{q_p})\chi_j^p(T_\sigma^0\chi_\sigma^p z_\sigma) \right\} \Gamma^{1/2} \qquad (4\text{-}3\text{-}69)$$

In applying this equation, computational difficulties arise only in the evaluation of the roots of equation (4-3-61). One of these roots is always zero, while the others (α_1^2, α_2^2, $\cdots \alpha_s^2$) designated by θ are obtained by

$$\sum_{i=1}^{s} \frac{T_i^0}{\omega_i^2 - \theta} = 0 \qquad (4\text{-}3\text{-}70)$$

For $s = 2$,

$$\alpha_2^2 = T_2^0\omega_1^2 + T_1^0\omega_2^2 \qquad (4\text{-}3\text{-}71)$$

For $s = 3$,

$$\alpha_2^2 = B - \sqrt{B^2 - C} \qquad (4\text{-}3\text{-}72)$$

$$\alpha_3^2 = B + \sqrt{B^2 - C} \qquad (4\text{-}3\text{-}73)$$

where

$$2B = (1 - T_1^0)\omega_1^2 + (1 - T_2^0)\omega_2^2 + (1 - T_3^0)\omega_3^2 \qquad (4\text{-}3\text{-}74)$$

$$C = \omega_1^2\omega_2^2\omega_3^2 \left(\frac{T_1^0}{\omega_1^2} + \frac{T_2^0}{\omega_2^2} + \frac{T_3^0}{\omega_3^2} \right) \qquad (4\text{-}3\text{-}75)$$

For s equals 4 or 5, explicit formulas for α_p^2 can be obtained by equation (4-3-70) by well known algebraic methods. Frequently, questions pertaining to mixtures need to be answered for a series of compositions by linear interpolation between two given extreme compositions. In such cases, it is convenient to invert the problem since equation (4-3-70) determines the mixing ratios as a simple explicit function of θ. Reasonably accurate values, α_2^2, α_3^2, $\cdots \alpha_s^2$, which belong to any specified ratio can be obtained by graphical interpolations, and these are easily improved to any required degree of accuracy by Newton's method.

(4) Diffusion of Electrolytes. Theory of Onsager[17, 18]

(a) Some General Considerations

The coefficient of diffusion, $\mathfrak{D}$, is ordinarily defined by Fick's first law, or by the relation

$$\mathbf{J} = n\mathbf{v} = -\mathfrak{D}\nabla n \qquad (4\text{-}4\text{-}1)$$

where $\mathbf{J}$ is the flow, $\mathbf{v}$ the velocity, and n is the number of molecules of solute per cc. The flow is usually defined relative to a fixed plane, assumed to be at rest. This definition is adequate for some purposes, but is not altogether convenient for the treatment of diffusion of electrolytes, since an appreciable volume change takes place upon mixing the solutions. In the present treatment, the flow of any solute species will be defined relative to a local frame of reference moving with the solvent. A bulk velocity may be defined by

$$\mathbf{v} = \sum \mathbf{J}_i \bar{V}_i = \sum n_i \mathbf{v}_i \bar{V}_i \qquad (4\text{-}4\text{-}2)$$

where $\bar{V}_0$, $\bar{V}_1$, $\cdots$ $\bar{V}_s$ are the partial volumes of the solvent molecule and the solute ions, 1, $\cdots$ s.

The law expressed by equation (4-4-1) may be written in the form

$$\mathbf{J} = -\mathfrak{D}\nabla n = -\mathfrak{M}\nabla\mu \qquad (4\text{-}4\text{-}3)^{[18a]}$$

where μ is the chemical potential, whence

$$\mathfrak{D} = \left(\frac{\partial\mu}{\partial n}\right)_{P,T} \mathfrak{M} \qquad (4\text{-}4\text{-}4)$$

For the ideal solution,

$$\frac{\partial\mu}{\partial n} = \frac{RT}{n}$$

and, consequently,

$$RT\mathfrak{M} = n\mathfrak{D}$$

[17] L. Onsager and R. M. Fuoss, *J. Phys. Chem.*, **36**, 2689 (1932). See pp. 2759–2770.

[18] J. J. Hermans [*Rec. trav. chim.*, **56**, 635 (1937)] has developed a more general theory of diffusion which is not restricted to spherical symmetry of ionic atmospheres. We have not attempted to review his generalized equations because they reduce to those of Onsager under similar conditions. Although Hermans' equations may be valid at somewhat higher concentrations than Onsager's, they could hardly be expected to apply at the concentrations for which direct diffusion data are available. Hermans bases the experimental proof of his theory upon measurements of liquid junction potentials. See J. J. Hermans, *Rec. trav. chim.*, **56**, 658 (1937); **58**, 199, 259 (1939).

[18a] "The Scientific Papers of J. Willard Gibbs," Letter to W. D. Barcroft, Vol. I, p. 430, Longmans, Green and Co., New York, 1906; E. Schreiner, *Tids. Chem. Bergvesen*, **2**, 151 (1922); G. S. Hartley, *Phil. Mag.*, 12, 473 (1931).

In concentrated solutions, the effect due to deviations from the ideal solution occurs, and the activity coefficient must be introduced, in which case

$$n\mathfrak{D} = RT\mathfrak{M}\left(1 + n\frac{\partial \ln \zeta}{\partial n}\right) \qquad (4\text{-}4\text{-}5)$$

where ζ ($\equiv a/n$) is the activity coefficient of solute when n is in molecules per cc. If the variation of $\mathfrak{D}$ with the concentration could be entirely accounted for by the deviation from the ideal solution, $\mathfrak{M}/n$ would be a constant. The theory to be developed shows that this is not the case, nor do the facts bear out such a contention. $\mathfrak{M}/n$ is the mobility, or the velocity at unit potential gradient, produced by the force $\mathbf{k} = -\nabla\mu$.

Equation (4-4-3) may be converted to the general form

$$\mathbf{J}_i = -\sum_{k=1}^{s} \mathfrak{M}_{ik}\nabla\mu_k \qquad (4\text{-}4\text{-}6)$$

upon the assumption of a linear relationship between the velocity and potential gradients of solute species. By a study of reciprocal relations in irreversible processes, Onsager,[19] on the basis of very general considerations involving the principle of microscopic reversibility, has shown that the matrix coefficients are symmetrical, or

$$\mathfrak{M}_{ik} = \mathfrak{M}_{ki} \qquad (4\text{-}4\text{-}7)$$

This important result means that *the flow of the ith species of ion under unit force per unit amount of kth species equals the flow of the kth species under unit force per unit quantity of the ith species.*

(b) The Theory of Diffusion of a Simple Electrolyte

In the case of a solution of an electrolyte containing two kinds of ions, the condition for the absence of electric current is that both cations and anions possess the same velocity, or

$$\mathbf{v}_1 = \mathbf{v}_2 = \mathbf{v}; \qquad \mathbf{J}_1 = n_1\mathbf{v}; \qquad \mathbf{J}_2 = n_2\mathbf{v} \qquad (4\text{-}4\text{-}8)$$

At low concentrations, we may neglect the interaction between the ions, and write

$$\mathbf{v} = \mathbf{k}_1\omega_1 = \mathbf{k}_2\omega_2 = -\omega_1\nabla\mu_1 = -\omega_2\nabla\mu_2 \qquad (4\text{-}4\text{-}9)$$

If μ is the chemical potential of a molecule which dissociates into ν_1 anions and ν_2 cations, we obtain

$$\mathbf{k} = \nu_1\mathbf{k}_1 + \nu_2\mathbf{k}_2 = -\nabla\mu \qquad (4\text{-}4\text{-}10)$$

[19] L. Onsager, *Physical Review*, **37**, 405 (1931); L. Onsager and R. M. Fuoss, *J. Phys. Chem.*, **36**, 2689 (1932), pp. 2760–2762.

From the last two equations, it follows that

$$\mathbf{k}_2 = \left(\frac{\rho_2}{\rho_1}\right) \mathbf{k}_1 = \left(\frac{\omega_1}{\omega_2}\right) \mathbf{k}_1$$

$$\mathbf{k}_1 = \frac{-\rho_1}{\nu_1\rho_1 + \nu_2\rho_2} \nabla\mu = -\frac{\omega_2}{\nu_1\omega_2 + \nu_2\omega_1} \nabla\mu$$

and that

$$\mathbf{v} = -\frac{\omega_1\omega_2}{\nu_1\omega_2 + \nu_2\omega_1} \nabla\mu$$

If the solution is ideal,

$$\nabla\mu = (\nu_1 + \nu_2)kT\nabla n/n$$

and consequently

$$\mathbf{J} = n\mathbf{v} = -\frac{(\nu_1 + \nu_2)\omega_1\omega_2}{\nu_1\omega_2 + \nu_2\omega_1} kT\nabla n \qquad (4\text{-}4\text{-}11)$$

which is the simple law of diffusion of electrolytes first derived by Nernst.[20] When interionic forces are considered

$$\nabla\mu = (\nu_1 + \nu_2)kT\nabla \ln (\zeta_{\pm}n)$$

where $\zeta_{\pm}$ is the activity coefficient of electrolyte.

The observation that in the case of diffusion both positive and negative ions migrate with the same velocity is important. Since

$$\mathbf{k}_1\omega_1 = \mathbf{k}_2\omega_2$$

the perturbation terms in the equation of continuity (2-5-6) can readily be shown to cancel. A consequence of this simplification is that the ionic atmospheres remain symmetrical, a fact which considerably reduces the complexity of the problem.

On the other hand electrophoresis produces an effect, since it is the result of a volume force acting in the ionic atmosphere. Equation (4-3-23), upon substitution of $1/\rho_i$ for ω_i, gives the electrophoretic correction for the velocity, and may be written

$$\Delta\mathbf{v}_j = \mathbf{v}\left[-\frac{2}{3\eta}(n_1e_1\rho_1 + n_2e_2\rho_2)\frac{e_j}{DkT\kappa(1 + \kappa a)}\right.$$
$$\left.+ \frac{1}{3\eta}(n_1e_1^2\rho_1 + n_2e_2^2\rho_2)\left(\frac{e_j}{DkT}\right)^2 \phi(\kappa a)\right] \qquad (4\text{-}4\text{-}12)$$

This influence upon the velocity alters the forces $\mathbf{k}_1$ and $\mathbf{k}_2$ in such a way that

$$\mathbf{k}_j = \rho_j(\mathbf{v} - \Delta\mathbf{v}_j); \qquad (j = 1, 2) \qquad (4\text{-}4\text{-}13)$$

[20] W. Nernst, *Z. physik. Chem.*, **2**, 613 (1888).

Upon introduction of this consideration in equation (4-4-10), we find that

$$-\nabla\mu = \mathbf{k} = \nu_1\rho_1(\mathbf{v} - \Delta\mathbf{v}_1) + \nu_2\rho_2(\mathbf{v} - \Delta\mathbf{v}_2) \qquad (4\text{-}4\text{-}14)$$

and if equation (4-4-12) is employed for the elimination of $\Delta\mathbf{v}_1$ and $\Delta\mathbf{v}_2$,

$$-\nabla\mu = \mathbf{v}\left[\nu_1\rho_1 + \nu_2\rho_2 + (\rho_1 - \rho_2)^2 \frac{\nu_1\nu_2}{(\nu_1 + \nu_2)} \frac{\kappa}{6\pi\eta(1 + \kappa a)} \right.$$
$$\left. - \left(\frac{\nu_2\rho_1 + \nu_1\rho_2}{\nu_1 + \nu_2}\right)^2 \frac{\kappa^4\phi(\kappa a)}{48\pi^2\eta n}\right] \qquad (4\text{-}4\text{-}15)$$

This is the force per molecule of solute at a concentration, $n = n_1/\nu_1 = n_2/\nu_2$ molecules per cc. The third term in the brackets on the right is the "first order" (electrophoretic) effect, and is proportional to the square root of the concentration. The last term is of the order of $c \log c$, and is negative.

By solving equation (4-4-15) for $\mathbf{v}$, and multiplying by n, we obtain **J**. If the second and higher powers of $\Delta\mathbf{v}_1$ and $\Delta\mathbf{v}_2$ are neglected, we obtain

$$\mathbf{J} = n\mathbf{v} = -\mathfrak{M}\nabla\mu = -\left(\frac{n\omega_1\omega_2}{\nu_1\omega_2 + \nu_2\omega_1} + \Delta\mathfrak{M}\right)\nabla\mu \qquad (4\text{-}4\text{-}16)$$

$\Delta\mathfrak{M}$ is given by

$$\Delta\mathfrak{M} = -\left(\frac{\omega_1 - \omega_2}{\nu_1\omega_2 + \nu_2\omega_1}\right)^2 \left(\frac{\nu_1\nu_2}{\nu_1 + \nu_2}\right) \frac{\kappa n}{6\pi\eta(1 + \kappa a)}$$
$$+ \frac{(\nu_1\omega_1 + \nu_2\omega_2)^2}{(\nu_1 + \nu_2)^2(\nu_1\omega_2 + \nu_2\omega_1)^2} \frac{\kappa^4\phi(\kappa a)}{48\pi^2\eta} \qquad (4\text{-}4\text{-}17)$$

In order to convert to more familiar units, we employ the relations

$$n = N\bar{n}; \qquad \mu N = \bar{\mu}$$

where N is Avogadro's number, $\bar{n}$ the concentration in mols per cc., and $\bar{\mu}$ the chemical potential in ergs per mol. Consequently, the flow per mol per cc. is given by

$$\mathbf{J} = \bar{n}\mathbf{v} = -\overline{\mathfrak{M}}\nabla\bar{\mu} = -\left(\frac{\mathfrak{M}}{N^2}\right)\nabla\bar{\mu} \qquad (4\text{-}4\text{-}18)$$

If we eliminate ω_1 and ω_2 from equation (4-4-17) by means of

$$\omega_j = \frac{c \times 10^{-8}\lambda_j^0}{F|z_j|\epsilon} \qquad (4\text{-}4\text{-}18a)$$

let $\Lambda^0 = \lambda_1^0 + \lambda_2^0$, and $c = 1000\bar{n}$, and introduce the numerical values of the universal constants given by Birge,[21] we obtain

$$\overline{\mathfrak{M}} = 1.0741 \times 10^{-20} \frac{\lambda_1^0\lambda_2^0 c}{\nu_1|z_1|\Lambda^0} + \Delta\overline{\mathfrak{M}}' + \Delta\overline{\mathfrak{M}}'' \qquad (4\text{-}4\text{-}19)$$

[21] R. T. Birge, *Phys. Rev. Suppl.*, **1**, 1 (1929).

where

$$-\Delta\overline{\mathfrak{M}}' \equiv \frac{(|z_2|\lambda_1^0 - |z_1|\lambda_2^0)^2}{\Lambda^{02}|z_1z_2|(\nu_1 + \nu_2)} \frac{3.132 \times 10^{-19}}{\eta_0(DT)^{1/2}} \frac{c\sqrt{\Gamma}}{(1 + \kappa a)} \qquad (4\text{-}4\text{-}20)$$

and

$$\Delta\overline{\mathfrak{M}}'' \equiv \frac{(z_2^2\lambda_1^0 + z_1^2\lambda_2^0)^2}{\Lambda^{02}} \frac{9.304 \times 10^{-13}}{\eta_0(DT)^2} c^2\phi(\kappa a) \qquad (4\text{-}4\text{-}21)$$

The function $\phi(\kappa a)$ is given by equation (4-3-23a).

According to equation (4-4-4), the coefficient of diffusion is given by

$$\mathfrak{D} = \overline{\mathfrak{M}}\frac{\partial\bar{\mu}}{\partial\bar{n}} = 1000\overline{\mathfrak{M}}\frac{\partial\bar{\mu}}{\partial c} \qquad (4\text{-}4\text{-}22)$$

For a binary electrolyte,

$$c\frac{\partial\bar{\mu}}{\partial c} = 2RT\left(1 + c\frac{\partial\ln y_\pm}{\partial c}\right) \qquad (4\text{-}4\text{-}23)$$

and therefore $\mathfrak{D}$ is given by

$$\mathfrak{D} = 2000RT\frac{\overline{\mathfrak{M}}}{c}\left(1 + c\frac{\partial\ln y_\pm}{\partial c}\right) \qquad (4\text{-}4\text{-}24)$$

which is the equation[22] for the diffusion coefficient of an electrolyte which dissociates into only two ions. The value of R in this equation must be given in ergs per degree per mol.

(5) The Dependence of Conductance and Dielectric Constants of Strong Electrolytes Upon the Frequency. Theory of Debye and Falkenhagen

(a) Equations for Potentials and Forces in an Alternating Field

We have developed the theory of the conductance of electrolytes, and computed the effect on the mobility of the ions caused by the asymmetry of their ionic atmospheres. So far no consideration has been given to the influence of the frequency of the alternating current upon the conductance, and the result obtained is valid at low frequencies and low electrical fields. The effect of high frequencies upon the conductance and dielectric constant has been successfully investigated from a theoretical point of view by Debye and Falkenhagen.[23]

In an alternating field the ions possess an oscillatory motion. At low

---

[22] In comparing this equation with the final result given by Onsager and Fuoss (*loc. cit.* p. 2767), it should be noted that their equation (4-13-19) contains a typographical error, the numerical coefficient being 1000 times too small.

[23] P. Debye and H. Falkenhagen, *Physik. z.*, **29**, 121, 401 (1928); *Z. Elektrochem.*, **34**, 562 (1928). H. Falkenhagen, "Electrolytes," p. 181–192, Clarendon Press, Oxford, 1934.

frequencies, the ionic atmospheres have an asymmetry caused by the external field. But if the frequency is so great that the period of oscillation is of the order of the time of relaxation of the atmosphere, then the asymmetric ionic atmospheres have less chance to form. As a result, the ionic atmospheres depart less and less from the spherical symmetry of the unperturbed state as the frequency is increased, and the conductance of the solution will increase accordingly.

Since the presence of an alternating external field produces a condition which is not stationary, we require the non-stationary form of the equation of continuity (2-5-6) in order to derive the equations for the potentials. Thus,

$$- \frac{\partial f_{ji}(\mathbf{r}_1, \mathbf{r}_{21})}{\partial t} = \omega_i(\mathbf{k}_i \cdot \nabla_2 f^0_{ji}(\mathbf{r})) + \omega_j(\mathbf{k}_j \cdot \nabla_1 f^0_{ij}(\mathbf{r}))$$

$$- e_i\omega_i n_i n_j \nabla_2 \cdot \nabla_2 \psi'_j(\mathbf{r}) - e_j\omega_j n_i n_j \nabla_1 \cdot \nabla_1 \psi'_i(-\mathbf{r}) \qquad (4\text{-}5\text{-}1)$$

$$- \omega_i kT \nabla_2 \cdot \nabla_2 f'_{ji}(\mathbf{r}) - \omega_j kT \nabla_1 \cdot \nabla_1 f'_{ij}(-\mathbf{r})$$

By the introduction of the relative co{rdinates, $q_{21} = q_2 - q_1$, etc., or, $x = x_2 - x_1$, $y = y_2 - y_1$, etc., it can be shown that

$$f^0_{ji}(\mathbf{r}) = f^0_{ij}(\mathbf{r}),$$

$$\nabla_1 f^0_{ij}(\mathbf{r}) = -\Delta_2 f^0_{ij}(\mathbf{r}) = -\nabla f^0_{ji}(\mathbf{r})$$

$$\nabla_2 \cdot \nabla_2 = \nabla_1 \cdot \nabla_1 = \nabla \cdot \nabla$$

$$f'_{ji}(\mathbf{r}) = -f'_{ij}(\mathbf{r}) = f'_{ij}(-\mathbf{r})$$

Also since $\mathbf{k}_i$ and $\mathbf{k}_j$ have components in the x direction only, we have

$$\mathbf{k} \cdot \nabla f^0_{ji} = k \frac{\partial f^0_{ji}}{\partial x} = Xe_j \frac{\partial f^0_{ji}}{\partial x}$$

Upon employing these relations, and also by eliminating $\nabla_2 \cdot \nabla_2 \psi'_j$, and $\nabla_1 \cdot \nabla_1 \psi'_i$ by the corresponding Poisson equations, we may transpose equation (4-5-1), and obtain[24]

$$\frac{\partial f_{ji}}{\partial t} = kT(\omega_i + \omega_j)\nabla \cdot \nabla f'_{ij} + (e_j\omega_j - e_i\omega_i)X \frac{\partial f^0_{ji}}{\partial x}$$

$$- \frac{4\pi}{D}[e_i\omega_i n_i \sum_i f'_{ji}e_i + e_j\omega_j n_j \sum_j f'_{ij}e_j] \qquad (4\text{-}5\text{-}2)$$

Now, we assume that the field strength, X, is small, and possesses a frequency $\bar{\omega}$, and let

$$X_{\bar{\omega}} = X_{(\omega=0)}e^{i\bar{\omega}t} = Xe^{i\omega t} \qquad (4\text{-}5\text{-}3)$$

[24] (4-5-2) is equation (4-3-26) of Onsager and Fuoss, after introduction of the Poisson equation, with the difference that the nonstationary form is used. It is identical with equation (411) of H. Falkenhagen, "Electrolytes," p. 172, *loc. cit.*

Further, let

$$f_{ji} = f^0_{ji} + g_{ji} = f^0_{ji} + G_{ji}e^{i\omega t} \tag{4-5-4}$$

where

$$f^0_{ji} = n_i n_j \left(1 - \frac{e_i e_j}{D_0 kT} \frac{e^{-\kappa r}}{r}\right) \tag{2-4-20}$$

Upon substitution of these relations in equation (4-5-2), we obtain[25]

$$(\omega_i + \omega_j)kT\nabla\cdot\nabla G_{ji} - i\bar{\omega}G_{ji} - \frac{4\pi n_i e_i \omega_i}{D_0} \sum_i G_{ji} e_i$$
$$\tag{4-5-5}$$
$$- \frac{4\pi n_j e_j \omega_j}{D_0} \sum_j G_{ij} e_j = (e_j \omega_j - e_i \omega_i)X \frac{\partial f^0_{ji}}{\partial x}$$

For the case of an electrolyte which dissociates into two kinds of ions, the conditions which are of interest in the present problem are:

$$G_{12} = -G_{21} ; \quad \text{and} \quad G_{11} = G_{22} = 0,$$

and, as a result, equation (4-5-5) reduces to

$$(\omega_1 + \omega_2)kT\nabla\cdot\nabla G_{12} - i\bar{\omega}G_{12} - \frac{4\pi}{D_0}(n_1 e_1^2 \omega_1 + n_2 e_2^2 \omega_2)G_{12}$$
$$\tag{4-5-6}$$
$$= -(e_1 \omega_1 - e_2 \omega_2)X \frac{\partial f^0_{12}}{\partial x}$$

We now use the relations given by equations (4-3-33) and (4-3-34), namely,

$$\kappa_1^2 = q^* \kappa^2 \tag{4-3-33}$$

$$q^* = \frac{e_1 \omega_1 - e_2 \omega_2}{(e_1 - e_2)(\omega_1 + \omega_2)} \tag{4-3-34}$$

From these relations, and equation (4-1-11), we obtain for the time of relaxation,

$$\tau = \left(\frac{\rho_1 \rho_2}{\rho_1 + \rho_2}\right) \frac{1}{kT\kappa_1^2} \tag{4-5-7}$$

Further, we let

$$q^*\tau = \bar{\tau} \tag{4-5-8}$$

and define the complex quantity K^2 by

$$K^2 = \kappa_1^2(1 + i\bar{\omega}\tau) \tag{4-5-9}$$

By substitution of all these relations in equation (4-5-6), we obtain

$$\nabla\cdot\nabla G_{12} - K^2 G_{12} = -\frac{(e_1 \rho_2 - e_2 \rho_1)X}{(\rho_1 + \rho_2)kT}\left(\frac{\partial f^0_{12}}{\partial x}\right) \tag{4-5-10}$$

[25] This corresponds to equation (462), p. 184—H. Falkenhagen, "Electrolytes." *loc. cit.* Equation (4-5-6) is equation (465), p. 185 in this text.

Further, according to equation (2-4-20), the distribution function, f_{12}^0 is given by

$$f_{12}^0 = n_1 n_2 - \frac{n_1 n_2 e_1 e_2 e^{-\kappa r}}{D_0 k T r}$$ (2-4-20)

and the asymmetric potentials, ψ_1', may be found from previous relations to be given by

$$-\frac{D_0 n_1}{4\pi e_2} \nabla \cdot \nabla \psi_1' = G_{12} e^{i\tilde{\omega} t}$$ (4-5-11)

Combining these last two relations with equation (4-5-10), we obtain the differential equation for the potential of the atmosphere around ion (1). Thus,

$$(\nabla \cdot \nabla)^2 \psi_1' - K^2 \nabla \cdot \nabla \psi_1' = \Omega \kappa_1^2 \frac{\partial}{\partial x} \left(\frac{e^{-\kappa r}}{r} \right) e^{i\omega t}$$ (4-5-12)

where Ω is defined by equation (4-3-35) when $\tilde{\omega}$ equals zero. We note that equation (4-5-12) has the same form as equation (4-3-36) derived by Onsager. K^2 is given by equation (4-5-9), or by

$$K^2 = \frac{\rho_1 \kappa_{II}^2 + \rho_2 \kappa_I^2}{\rho_1 + \rho_2} + \frac{2\rho_1 \rho_2}{(\rho_1 + \rho_2)} \frac{i\tilde{\omega}}{2kT}$$ (4-5-13)

and κ_I^2 and κ_{II}^2 are defined by

$$\kappa^2 = \kappa_I^2 + \kappa_{II}^2 = \frac{4\pi}{D_0 kT} n_1 e_1^2 + \frac{4\pi}{D_0 kT} n_2 e_2^2$$ (4-5-14)

When $\tilde{\omega}$ equals zero, equation (4-5-12) reduces to equation (4-3-36) and is sufficiently general for the computation of the frequency effect upon the conductance and dielectric constant. ψ_1' is the asymmetric potential of the oscillating ion.

ψ_1' and the corresponding value of ψ_2' may be obtained by integration of equation (4-5-12), and the fundamental relations

$$n_1 e_1 \psi_1' + n_2 e_2 \psi_2' = 0,$$

$$n_1 e_1 = -n_2 e_2 ,$$

$$\psi_1' = \psi_2'$$

The asymmetric part of the potential in the immediate neighborhood of the ions turns out to be

$$\psi_1' = -\frac{\Omega_{\tilde{\omega}} q^* \kappa^2}{3(\kappa + K)} e^{i\omega t} [r \cos \theta + o(r^2)]$$ (4-5-15)

where θ is the angle between the radius vector, r, and the direction of the field.

From this equation, the field, at the position of ion 1 for $\theta = 0$, may be obtained according to the method indicated by equation (4-3-38). Thus,

$$\Delta X_\omega = -\nabla\psi_1'(r = 0) = \frac{e_2}{3D_0kT}\left(\frac{q^*\kappa\rho_1v_1e^{i\tilde{\omega}t}}{1 + \sqrt{q^*}\sqrt{1 + i\tilde{\omega}t}}\right) \quad (4\text{-}5\text{-}16)$$

where $v_1e^{i\tilde{\omega}t}$ is the absolute velocity of ion 1.

(b) Equations for Conductance and Dielectric Constant Lowering in an Alternating Field

We now adopt a procedure similar to that which was employed in computing the conductance for the non-oscillating case. We are interested in the velocity $v_je^{i\tilde{\omega}t}$. If we modify equation (4-3-39) to meet the conditions now under consideration, we obtain

$$v_je^{i\tilde{\omega}t} = \left(Xe_j\omega_j + \Delta Xe_j\omega_j - \frac{Xe_j\kappa}{6\pi\eta}\right)e^{i\tilde{\omega}t} \quad (4\text{-}5\text{-}17)$$

By employing equation (4-5-16), replacing ρ_1v_1 by Xe_j,

$$v_je^{i\tilde{\omega}t} = X\left(e_j\omega_j + \frac{e_1e_2}{3D_0kT}\kappa e_j\omega_j\chi(q^*, \tilde{\omega}\tau) - \frac{e_j\kappa}{6\pi\eta}\right)e^{i\tilde{\omega}t} \quad (4\text{-}5\text{-}18)$$

is obtained, where

$$\chi(q^*, \tilde{\omega}\tau) = \frac{q^*}{\sqrt{q^*}\sqrt{1 + i\tilde{\omega}\tau} + 1} \quad (4\text{-}5\text{-}19)$$

From the above equation for the velocity, it is possible by suitable procedures to obtain final equations for the molar conductance, Λ_m, and the increase in the dielectric constant, $D_{\tilde{\omega}} - D_0$. In practical units, the results may be expressed as follows:

$$\Lambda_\omega = \Lambda_m^0 - \Lambda_{I\omega} - \Lambda_{II} \quad (4\text{-}5\text{-}20)$$

Λ_ω is the total molar conductance at a frequency $\tilde{\omega}$, Λ_m^0 the molar conductance at infinite dilution, $\Lambda_{I\tilde{\omega}}$ the contribution to Λ_ω due to asymmetric ionic atmosphere, and Λ_{II} the contribution due to electrophoresis. Λ_I and Λ_{II} are given by the equations,

$$\Lambda_{I\omega} = \frac{|e_1e_2|\kappa}{3D_0kT}\Lambda_m^0\chi_R \quad (4\text{-}5\text{-}21)$$

and

$$\Lambda_{II} = \sum_j \frac{n_je_j^2\kappa}{6\pi\eta_0}\left(\frac{1000}{c}\right)\frac{1}{9 \times 10^{11}} \quad (4\text{-}5\text{-}22)$$

where χ_R, or the real part of χ, may be computed from

$$\psi_R = \frac{\sqrt{q^*}}{(1 - 1/q^*)^2 + \tilde{\omega}^2\tau^2}[(1 - 1/q^*)(\bar{R} - 1/\sqrt{q^*}) + \tilde{\omega}\tau\bar{Q}] \quad (4\text{-}5\text{-}23)$$

and where

$$\bar{R} = 2^{-1/2}[(1 + \tilde{\omega}^2\tau^2)^{1/2} + 1]^{1/2}; \quad \bar{Q} = 2^{-1/2}[(1 + \tilde{\omega}^2\tau^2)^{1/2} - 1]^{1/2} \quad (4\text{-}5\text{-}24)$$

The increase in the dielectric constant caused by the alternating field turns out to be

$$D_{\tilde{\omega}} - D_0 = \frac{4\pi \mid e_1 e_2 \mid}{3D_0 kT} \kappa \sum n_j e_j^2 \omega_j \frac{\tau\sqrt{q^*}}{\bar{\omega}\tau[(1 - 1/q^*)^2 + \bar{\omega}^2\tau^2]}$$
$$\cdot[\bar{Q}(1-1/q^*) - \bar{\omega}\tau(\bar{R}-1/\sqrt{q^*})] \qquad (4\text{-}5\text{-}25)$$

Equations (4-5-20) to (4-5-24), and (4-5-25) represent the final formulation of the Debye-Falkenhagen theory of the dependence of conductance and dielectric constant upon high frequencies. For stationary fields ($\bar{\omega} = 0$), χ_R becomes $\dfrac{q^*}{1 + \sqrt{q^*}}$ in agreement with the result of Onsager's theory of conductance. Simplified equations, and tables for practical computations will be found in Chapter (5), Section (3).[26]

(6) Theory of the Effects of High Fields on the Properties of Strong Electrolytes. Wien Effect

In the previous discussion of the behaviors of ionic atmospheres [Chapter (2)], we have pointed out that, in high fields, the ions are drawn out of their atmospheres, and as a result, when they are caused to migrate, they are not retarded by having to drag their atmospheres with them. A simple calculation by Falkenhagen[27] will serve to illustrate how this condition arises. According to equation (4-1-15), we find that

$$\rho_i = \frac{1.54 \times 10^{-7} \mid z_i \mid}{\lambda_i^0} \qquad (4\text{-}6\text{-}1)$$

Let us take the case of a solution of potassium chloride in water at 18°, and consider the potassium ion. Its mobility is 0.000675 cm/sec, and therefore its absolute velocity in a field of 100,000 volts/cm is 67.5 cm/sec. Since λ_1^0 equals 65, ρ_i equals 0.236×10^{-8}. If the concentration, c, is taken to be 0.0001, then according to equation (4-1-12), the time of relaxation is 0.276×10^{-6} sec. Now, at this concentration the mean thickness of the ionic atmosphere, $1/\kappa$, is 3.06×10^{-6} cm. During the time of relaxation, the ion will have migrated 18.6×10^{-6} cm, or six times the thickness of the atmosphere. Under such conditions, it is impossible for the atmosphere to form.

From these considerations, it is apparent that in the field the ions possess greater mobilities than in the absence of the field. Consequently, the conductance of the solution is increased, and Ohm's law can be expected to have only a limited range of validity.

[26] The extension of the theory of the influence of frequency upon conductance and dielectric constant to mixtures of strong electrolytes has been made by Falkenhagen and Fischer [H. Falkenhagen and W. Fischer, *Physik. Z.*, **33**, 941 (1932); **34**, 593 (1933); *Nature* **130**, 928 (1932)].

[27] H. Falkenhagen, "Electrolytes," p. 237, Clarendon Press, Oxford, 1934.

Since the Debye-Hückel-Onsager theory of conductance was limited to low potentials, it must be modified to take into account the effects of high fields. The first attempt to extend the theory was made by Joos and Blumentritt.[28] They obtained an equation of the form

$$\frac{\Delta\Lambda}{\Lambda_{X=0}} \equiv \frac{\Lambda_X - \Lambda_{X=0}}{\Lambda_{X=0}} = AX^2(1 - BX^2) \qquad (4\text{-}6\text{-}2)$$

where Λ_X and $\Lambda_{X=0}$ represent the molar conductances in fields of potential, X, and $X = 0$, respectively. The parameters A and B are functions of T, D, c, and the ionic conductances and valences. This result was applicable for the lower values of the applied potential. On account of the assumptions premised by Joos and Blumentritt, their theory possesses qualitative value only.

Proceeding in a different manner, Falkenhagen[29] developed a qualitative theory for fields varying in potential from 0 to ∞. Later, Falkenhagen and Fleischer,[30] on the basis of this theory, introduced the non-stationary field and computed the effect of frequency upon the Wien effect.

A more exact theory of the Wien effect for strong electrolytes which takes into account both the hydrodynamic effect and electrophoresis has been developed by Onsager and Wilson[31]. The general outline and final results of this theory will now be presented.

In terms of the variable $\mathbf{r}$, it follows from equation (2-5-5) that†

$$\nabla \cdot f_{ji}(\mathbf{r})[\mathbf{v}_{ji}(\mathbf{r}) - \mathbf{v}_{ij}(-\mathbf{r})] = \omega_i[\mathbf{k}_i \cdot \nabla f_{ji}(\mathbf{r})]$$

$$- \omega_j[\mathbf{k}_j \cdot \nabla f_{ij}(\mathbf{r})] - n_j n_i[e_i \omega_i \nabla \cdot \nabla \psi_j(\mathbf{r}) + e_j \omega_j \nabla \cdot \nabla \psi_i(-\mathbf{r})] \qquad (4\text{-}6\text{-}2a)$$

$$- kT(\omega_i + \omega_j)\nabla \cdot \nabla f_{ji}(\mathbf{r}) = 0; \qquad (i, j = 1, 2, \cdots s)$$

Only the case of the binary electrolyte will be considered. The forces, $\mathbf{k}_1$ and $\mathbf{k}_2$, will be expressed by

$$\mathbf{k}_1 = \mathbf{X}e_1 ; \qquad \mathbf{k}_2 = \mathbf{X}e_2$$

where X is the component of the electric field acting in the direction of the positive x-axis. Further, for the restricted case of the binary electrolyte,

$$|e_1| = |e_2| = e$$

$$n_1 = n_2 = n$$

---

[28] G. Joos and M. Blumentritt, *Physik. Z.*, **28**, 836 (1927); M. Blumentritt, *Ann. Physik.*, **85**, 812 (1928).

[29] H. Falkenhagen, *Physik. Z.*, **30**, 163 (1929); **32**, 353 (1931).

[30] H. Falkenhagen and H. Fleischer, *Ibid.*, **39**, 305 (1938); H. Falkenhagen, F. Fröhlich, and H. Fleischer, *Naturwiss.*, **25**, 446 (1937); H. Fleischer, "Dissertation," Dresden 1938; F. Fröhlich, *Physik. Z.*, **40**, 139 (1939).

[31] W. S. Wilson, "Dissertation," Yale University, 1936; also H. C. Eckstrom and C. Schmelzer, *Chem. Rev.*, **24**, 367 (1939).

† Note that the perturbation effects are large and that f, not f^0, appears in these equations.

With these relations, the equations of motion become

$$n^2 e\{\nabla \cdot \nabla(\psi_1(\mathbf{r}) + \psi_1(-\mathbf{r}))\} + 2kT\nabla \cdot \nabla f_{11}(\mathbf{r}) = 0 \qquad (4\text{-}6\text{-}3)$$

$$-n^2 e\{\nabla \cdot \nabla(\psi_2(\mathbf{r}) + \psi_2(-\mathbf{r}))\} + 2kT\nabla \cdot \nabla f_{22}(\mathbf{r}) = 0 \qquad (4\text{-}6\text{-}4)$$

$$Xe(\omega_1 + \omega_2)\frac{\partial f_{12}(\mathbf{r})}{\partial x} - n^2 e\{\omega_1 \nabla \cdot \nabla \psi_2(\mathbf{r}) - \omega_2 \nabla \cdot \nabla \psi_1(-\mathbf{r})\}$$
$$+ kT(\omega_1 + \omega_2)\nabla \cdot \nabla f_{12}(\mathbf{r}) = 0 \qquad (4\text{-}6\text{-}5)$$

$$- Xe(\omega_1 + \omega_2)\frac{\partial f_{21}(\mathbf{r})}{\partial x} - n^2 e\{\omega_1 \nabla \cdot \nabla \psi_2(-\mathbf{r}) - \omega_2 \nabla \cdot \nabla \psi_1(\mathbf{r})\}$$
$$+ kT(\omega_2 + \omega_1)\nabla \cdot \nabla f_{21}(\mathbf{r}) = 0 \qquad (4\text{-}6\text{-}6)$$

(a) The Boundary Conditions

(i) *Flow.* The number of ions, $F_{ji}(\Omega)$, leaving the interior, Ω, of a region S is

$$-\frac{\partial F_{ji}(\Omega)}{\partial t} = \int_S f_{ji}(\mathbf{r})\{\mathbf{e}_n \cdot [\mathbf{v}_{ji}(\mathbf{r}) - \mathbf{v}_{ij}(-\mathbf{r})]\}\, dS$$
$$= \int_\Omega \nabla \cdot (f_{ji}(\mathbf{r})[\mathbf{v}_{ji}(\mathbf{r}) - \mathbf{v}_{ij}(-\mathbf{r})])\, d\Omega = 0 \qquad (4\text{-}6\text{-}7)$$

where $\mathbf{e}_n$ is the unit vector normal to the surface, S. The laws of chemical conservation require that this integral vanish for any region, Ω. This fundamental condition is usually applied in the form

$$\lim_{\Omega(s)=0} \int f_{ji}(\mathbf{r})\{\mathbf{e}_n \cdot [\mathbf{v}_{ji}(\mathbf{r}) - \mathbf{v}_{ij}(-\mathbf{r})]\}\, dS = 0 \qquad (4\text{-}6\text{-}8)$$

and states that the vector field of the flow, $f_{ji}(\mathbf{r})[\mathbf{v}_{ji}(\mathbf{r}) - \mathbf{v}_{ij}(-\mathbf{r})]$, must be without sources.

(ii) *Poisson Equations.* According to (2-4-1) and (2-4-2),

$$\nabla \cdot \nabla \psi_j(\mathbf{r}) = -\frac{4\pi}{D}\rho_j(\mathbf{r}) = -\frac{4\pi}{D}\sum_{i=1}^{s} n_{ji}(\mathbf{r})e_i$$
$$= -\frac{4\pi}{D}\frac{1}{n_j}\sum_{i=1}^{s} f_{ji}(\mathbf{r})e_i \qquad (4\text{-}6\text{-}9)$$

The expanded forms of these equations for a binary electrolyte are

$$\nabla \cdot \nabla \psi_1(\mathbf{r}) = \frac{4\pi e}{nD}[-f_{11}(\mathbf{r}) + f_{12}(\mathbf{r})] \qquad (4\text{-}6\text{-}10)$$

$$\nabla \cdot \nabla \psi_2(\mathbf{r}) = \frac{4\pi e}{nD}[-f_{21}(\mathbf{r}) + f_{22}(\mathbf{r})] \qquad (4\text{-}6\text{-}11)$$

(iii) *Ionic Fields.* The space charge within the region Ω is

$$-\frac{D}{4\pi}\int_\Omega \nabla \cdot \nabla \psi_j(\mathbf{r})\, d\Omega = \int_\Omega \rho_j(\mathbf{r})\, d\Omega$$

$\rho_j(\mathbf{r})$ is integrable except for the condition of point charge at the origin. The right side of this equation approaches zero as Ω approaches zero, unless Ω contains the origin, in which case

$$\lim_{\Omega=0} \int_\Omega \rho_j(\mathbf{r}) \, d\Omega = e_j$$

Combining these equations and applying Gauss's theorem, we obtain

$$\lim_{\Omega=0} \int_{S(\Omega)} \nabla \psi_j(\mathbf{r}) \cdot d\mathbf{S} = -\frac{4\pi e_j}{D}\delta \qquad (4\text{-}6\text{-}12)$$

where δ is unity if the origin is at central ion, and zero if origin is elsewhere·

Very near a given ion, the screening effect of the ionic atmosphere becomes negligible, and the potential of the ion is given by e_j/Dr. The potential of the ion and its atmosphere, $\psi(\mathbf{r})$, will differ from the above potential by a finite amount, whence

$$\psi_j(\mathbf{r}) - e_j/Dr < \infty \qquad (4\text{-}6\text{-}13)$$

At infinity

$$\psi_j(\mathbf{r}) = \psi_i(\mathbf{r}) = 0$$

whence for a binary electrolyte,

$$\psi_1(\mathbf{r}) - e_1/Dr \quad < \infty$$

$$\psi_2(\mathbf{r}) - e_2/Dr \quad < \infty \qquad (4\text{-}6\text{-}14)$$

$$\psi_1(\infty) = \psi_2(\infty) = 0 \qquad (4\text{-}6\text{-}15)$$

(iv) *Symmetry Conditions for the Potentials.* Two symmetry conditions may be derived for the potentials, one of which depends on the fact that $f_{11}(\mathbf{r})$ and $f_{22}(\mathbf{r})$ are even, and the other depends on the odd part of the distribution functions given by $f_{12}(\mathbf{r}) = f_{21}(-\mathbf{r})$. From this equality and the Poisson equations, (4-6-10) and (4-6-11), it follows that

$$\nabla \cdot \nabla[\psi_2(\mathbf{r}) - \psi_2(-\mathbf{r}) - \psi_1(\mathbf{r}) + \psi_1(-\mathbf{r})] = 0 \qquad (4\text{-}6\text{-}16)$$

Since the differences, $\psi_i(\mathbf{r}) - \psi_i(-)\mathbf{r}$, are finite, the quantity within the brackets is always finite. Further, this quantity is a constant, since from the theory of harmonic functions, any finite function which satisfies Laplace's equation is a constant. In addition, since $\psi_j(\infty) = \psi_i(\infty) = 0$,

$$\psi_2(\mathbf{r}) - \psi_2(-\mathbf{r}) - \psi_1(\mathbf{r}) + \psi_1(-\mathbf{r}) = 0 \qquad (4\text{-}6\text{-}17)$$

or

$$\psi_2(\mathbf{r}) - \psi_2(-\mathbf{r}) = \psi_1(\mathbf{r}) - \psi_1(-\mathbf{r}) = 2Y(\mathbf{r}) \qquad (4\text{-}6\text{-}18)$$

where $Y(\mathbf{r})$ is the odd part of the potential.

The symmetry conditions for the even part of the potential may be obtained in the following manner. From equation (4-5-1) the flow for $i = j = 1$ becomes

$$f_{11}(\mathbf{r})[\mathbf{v}_{11}(\mathbf{r}) - \mathbf{v}_{11}(-\mathbf{r})]$$
$$= \omega_1 \nabla[-n^2 e(\psi_1(\mathbf{r}) + \psi_1(-\mathbf{r})) - 2kTf_{11}(\mathbf{r})] \tag{4-6-19}$$

The boundary condition for the flow states that its vector field is source-less. The gradient in the right-hand member is zero, and the bracketed term is constant. Since $f_{ji}(\infty) = n^2$, and $\psi_i(\infty) = \psi_j(\infty) = 0$, it follows that

$$f_{11}(\mathbf{r}) = f_{11}(-\mathbf{r}) = n^2 - \frac{n^2 e}{2kT}[\psi_1(\mathbf{r}) + \psi_1(-\mathbf{r})] \tag{4-6-20}$$

and, similarly,

$$f_{22}(\mathbf{r}) = f_{22}(-\mathbf{r}) = n^2 + \frac{n^2 e}{2kT}[\psi_2(\mathbf{r}) + \psi_2(-\mathbf{r})] \tag{4-6-21}$$

By addition of the Poisson equations, (4-6-10) and (4-6-11), substitution of $f_{11}(\mathbf{r})$ and $f_{22}(\mathbf{r})$, further addition, and the use of the fundamental relation, equation (2-1-4), we obtain

$$\left(\nabla \cdot \nabla - \frac{\kappa^2}{2}\right)[\psi_1(\mathbf{r}) + \psi_1(-\mathbf{r}) + \psi_2(\mathbf{r}) + \psi_2(-\mathbf{r})] = 0 \tag{4-6-22}$$

where, for the binary electrolyte,

$$\kappa^2 = \frac{8\pi n e^2}{DkT}$$

The boundary conditions require that the bracketed term containing the sum of the potentials be finite. Since equation (4-6-22) has no solution (other than 0) that is finite everywhere and possesses no singularities, it follows that

$$\psi_1(\mathbf{r}) + \psi_1(-\mathbf{r}) + \psi_2(\mathbf{r}) + \psi_2(-\mathbf{r}) = 0$$

or

$$\psi_1(\mathbf{r}) + \psi_1(-\mathbf{r}) = -[\psi_2(\mathbf{r}) + \psi_2(-\mathbf{r})] = 2\Gamma(\mathbf{r}) \tag{4-6-23}$$

where $\Gamma(\mathbf{r})$ is the even part of the potential.

Solving (4-6-18) and (4-6-23) leads to

$$\psi_1(\mathbf{r}) = -\psi_2(-\mathbf{r}) = \Gamma(\mathbf{r}) + Y(\mathbf{r}) \tag{4-6-24}$$

$$\psi_1(-\mathbf{r}) = -\psi_2(\mathbf{r}) = \Gamma(\mathbf{r}) - Y(\mathbf{r}) \tag{4-6-25}$$

which represent the fundamental symmetry conditions of the ionic fields for the binary electrolyte. Combining with (4-6-20) and (4-6-21), we obtain

$$f_{11}(\mathbf{r}) = f_{22}(\mathbf{r}) = n^2 - \frac{n^2 e}{kT} \Gamma(\mathbf{r}) \tag{4-6-26}$$

(b) Simplification of the Fundamental Differential Equations for the Distribution Functions and Potentials

The differential equations (4-6-5) and (4-6-6), can be reduced to a convenient form by the symmetry relations, (4-6-24) and (4-6-25). Equations (4-6-3) and (4-6-4) are contained in (4-6-26), and this will serve for the elimination of $f_{11}(\mathbf{r})$ and $f_{22}(\mathbf{r})$. If we represent the even and odd parts of the distribution functions, $f_{12}(\mathbf{r})$, by $G(\mathbf{r})$ and $U(\mathbf{r})$, so that

$$f_{12}(\pm\mathbf{r}) = f_{21}(\mp\mathbf{r}) = G(\mathbf{r}) - n^2 \pm U(\mathbf{r}) \tag{4-6-27}$$

where $G(\mathbf{r}) - G(-\mathbf{r}) = U(\mathbf{r}) + U(-\mathbf{r}) = 0$, equations (4-6-5) and (4-6-6) reduce to

$$\frac{n^2 e}{kT} \nabla \cdot \nabla \Gamma(\mathbf{r}) - \nabla \cdot \nabla G(r) = \frac{eX}{kT} \frac{\partial U(\mathbf{r})}{\partial x} \tag{4-6-28}$$

$$\frac{n^2 e}{kT} \nabla \cdot \nabla Y(\mathbf{r}) - \nabla \cdot \nabla U(\mathbf{r}) = \frac{eX}{kT} \frac{\partial G(\mathbf{r})}{\partial x} \tag{4-6-29}$$

In this formula of the stationary condition, the mobilities ω_1 and ω_2 do not appear.

Upon introducing the boundary conditions for the flow and utilizing the Poisson equations, the differential equations for the distribution functions and the potentials may be expressed in the following manner:

$$\left(\nabla \cdot \nabla - \frac{\kappa^2}{2}\right) U(\mathbf{r}) = -\mu' \frac{\partial G(\mathbf{r})}{\partial x} \tag{4-6-30}$$

$$\left(\nabla \cdot \nabla - \frac{\kappa^2}{2}\right) G(\mathbf{r}) - n^2 \eta' \frac{\kappa^2}{2} \Gamma(\mathbf{r}) = -\mu' \frac{\partial U(\mathbf{r})}{\partial x} \tag{4-6-31}$$

$$\left(\nabla \cdot \nabla - \frac{\kappa^2}{2}\right) \Gamma(\mathbf{r}) = \frac{\kappa^2}{2n^2\eta'} G(\mathbf{r}) \tag{4-6-32}$$

$$\nabla \cdot \nabla Y(\mathbf{r}) = \frac{\kappa^2}{2n^2\eta'} U(\mathbf{r}) \tag{4-6-33}$$

By combining (4-6-30), (4-6-31) and (4-6-32), we obtain

$$\nabla \cdot \nabla (\nabla \cdot \nabla - \kappa^2) G(r) = \mu'^2 \frac{\partial^2 G(\mathbf{r})}{\partial x^2} \tag{4-6-34}$$

from which $G(\mathbf{r})$ may be calculated. Once $G(\mathbf{r})$ is known, $\Gamma(\mathbf{r})$, $Y(\mathbf{r})$ and

$U(\mathbf{r})$ may be evaluated by equations (4-6-27) to (4-6-29). In the above expressions,

$$\eta' = e/kT \tag{4-6-35}$$

$$\mu' = eX/kT \tag{4-6-36}$$

(c) Solution of the Differential System

The differential system may be treated conveniently in cylindrical coördinates (x, ρ, θ), and is invariant to rotation around x, so that the angle variable, θ, may be dropped. Onsager and Wilson base their solution of these equations by expressing $G(\mathbf{r})$, $U(\mathbf{r})$, $\Gamma(\mathbf{r})$ and $Y(\mathbf{r})$ in terms of their Fourier transforms.[32] The final integrals for $f_{12}(\pm\mathbf{r})$ and $\psi_{12}(\pm\mathbf{r})$ are found to be,

$$f_{12}(\pm\mathbf{r}) = f_{21}(\mp\mathbf{r}) = \frac{2}{\pi}\frac{n^2\eta'e}{D}\left[\int_0^\infty \frac{1}{\sqrt{\kappa^4 - 4\mu'^2\alpha^2}}\right.$$

$$\{(\lambda_1^2 - \alpha^2)K_0(\lambda_1\rho) - (\lambda_2^2 - \alpha^2)K_0(\lambda_2\rho)\} \cos(\alpha x)\, d\alpha$$

$$\pm \int_0^\infty \frac{\mu'\alpha}{\kappa^4 - 4\mu'^2\alpha^2}\left\{(\lambda_1^2 - \alpha^2)K_0(\lambda_1\rho) + (\lambda_2^2 - \alpha^2)K_0(\lambda_2\rho)\right. \tag{4-6-37}$$

$$\left.\left. - \frac{\kappa^2}{2}K_0(\lambda_3\rho)\right\}\sin(\alpha x)\, d\alpha\right]$$

$$\psi_{12}(\pm\mathbf{r}) = \frac{2}{\pi}\frac{e}{D}\left[\int_0^\infty \frac{\kappa^2}{\kappa^4 - 4\mu'^2\alpha^2}\left\{(\lambda_1^2 - \alpha^2)K_0(\lambda_1\rho)\right.\right.$$

$$\left. +(\lambda_2^2 - \alpha^2)K_0(\lambda_2\rho) - \frac{4\mu'^2\alpha^2}{\kappa^2}K_0(\lambda_3\rho)\right\}\cos(\alpha x)\, d\alpha \tag{4-6-38}$$

$$\pm \int_0^\infty \frac{\kappa^2\mu'\alpha}{\kappa^4 - 4\mu'^2\alpha^2}\{K_0(\lambda_1\rho) + K_0(\lambda_2\rho) - 2K_0(\lambda_3\rho)\}\sin(\alpha x)\, d\alpha\right]$$

where $K_0(\lambda\rho)$ is a modified Bessel's function of the second kind and zero order, and λ_1, λ_2 and λ_3 are given by

$$\lambda_1^2 = \lambda_2^2 = \alpha^2 + \kappa^2/2 \pm \sqrt{\kappa^4/4 - \mu'^2\alpha^2} \tag{4-6-39}$$

$$\lambda_3^2 = \alpha^2 + \kappa^2/2 \quad \text{and} \quad \lambda_4 = \alpha \tag{4-6-40}$$

The above integral forms can be used conveniently for both the solution of the ionic force effect and the effect of electrophoresis.

[32] E. T. Whitaker and G. N. Watson, "Modern Analysis," Fourth Edition, Chapter IX, p. 160ff, Cambridge University Press, 1927. R. Courant and D. Hilbert, "Methoden der Mathematischen Physik," I, Chapter II, p. 65ff, Springer, Berlin 1931.

(d) Electrophoresis

The effect of electrophoresis on the velocity of the ion in an external electric field of strength, $\mathbf{X}$, is obtained by the solution of the hydrodynamic equations

$$\eta_0 \nabla \times (\nabla \times \mathbf{v}) = -\nabla P + \mathbf{F}$$
$$\nabla \cdot \mathbf{v} = 0 \tag{4-6-41}$$

where $\mathbf{v}$ is the velocity, P the pressure, η_0 the viscosity, and $\mathbf{F}$ the force density which arises from the action of the external field upon the ionic atmosphere.

By utilizing the results of the preceding section, the velocity in the direction of the axis of the field is

$$v_x(0, 0, \theta) = -\frac{Xe}{2\pi^2\eta_0} \int_0^\infty \frac{1}{\kappa^4 - 4\mu'^2\alpha^2} \left\{ -\kappa^2\lambda_1^2 \ln\left(\frac{\lambda_1}{\alpha}\right) \right.$$

$$- \kappa^2\lambda_2^2 \ln\left(\frac{\lambda_2}{\alpha}\right) + \frac{\kappa^4 - 4\alpha^2\mu'^2}{2} \tag{4-6-42}$$

$$\left. + \frac{4\alpha^2\mu'^2(2\alpha^2 + \kappa^2)}{\kappa^2} \ln\left(\frac{\lambda_3}{\alpha}\right) \right\} d\alpha$$

By employing the variable

$$x \equiv \mu'/\kappa \tag{4-6-43}$$

where $\mu' = Xe/kT$, and integrating, (4-6-42) may be expressed in the form

$$v_x(0, 0, \theta) = -\frac{Xe\kappa}{6\sqrt{2}\,\pi\eta_0} f(x) \tag{4-6-44}$$

where $f(x)$ is given by the equation

$$f(x) = 1 + \frac{3}{4\sqrt{2}\,x^3} \left\{ 2x^2 \sinh^{-1} x + \sqrt{2}\,x - x\sqrt{1 + x^2} \right.$$

$$\left. - (1 + 2x^2) \tan^{-1} (\sqrt{2}\,x) + (1 + 2x^2) \tan^{-1} \frac{x}{\sqrt{1 + x^2}} \right\} \tag{4-6-45}$$

We note that when $x = 0$, $f(x) = \sqrt{2}$ and (4-6-44) reduces to

$$v_0(0, 0, \theta) = -\frac{Xe\kappa}{6\pi\eta_0} \tag{4-3-9}$$

which is the result previously obtained [Equation (4-3-39)]. Further, for infinite field strengths, $x = \infty$, $f(x) = 1$, and

$$v_\infty(0, 0, \theta) = -\frac{Xe\kappa}{6\sqrt{2}\,\pi\eta_0} \tag{4-6-46}$$

and the electrophoretic effect does not disappear at infinite field.

(e) The Ionic Field

As in case of conductance in low fields [Section (3)], it is necessary to obtain the ionic field due to the perturbation of the atmosphere. This requires the evaluation of $-\nabla\psi(r)$ for $r = 0$. Thus, the total force

$$ie\Delta X(0) = ie\Delta X(0, 0, \theta) = \lim_{x=\rho=0} (\nabla\psi_j(0))$$

where **i** is unit vector in the x-direction. In terms of the variable $x = \mu'/\kappa$, and by utilizing the result given by equation (4-6-38),

$$\Delta X(0, 0, \theta) = \mp\frac{e\mu'\kappa}{2D} g(x) \qquad (4\text{-}6\text{-}47)$$

where

$$g(x) = -\frac{1}{2x^3}\left\{-x\sqrt{1 + x^2} + \tan^{-1}\frac{x}{\sqrt{1 + x^2}}\right.$$
$$\left. + \sqrt{2}\,x - \tan^{-1}\sqrt{2}\,x\right\} \qquad (4\text{-}6\text{-}48)$$

and therefore

$$g(0) = \frac{2 - \sqrt{2}}{3}; \quad \text{and} \quad g(\infty) = 0 \qquad (4\text{-}6\text{-}48a)$$

(f) The functions, $f(x)$ and $g(x)$, in Convenient forms for Numerical Computation

Equations (4-6-45) and (4-6-48) may be transformed into convenient numerical forms by the following substitutions:

$$\tan\frac{\pi}{8} = \sqrt{2} - 1 = \frac{1}{\sqrt{2} + 1};$$

$$\left(\tan^{-1}s\right)\left(\cot\frac{\pi}{8}\right) + \left(\tan^{-1}s\right)\left(\tan\frac{\pi}{8}\right) = \tan^{-1}\left(\frac{2s\sqrt{2}}{1 - s^2}\right);$$

$$\left(\tan^{-1}s\right)\left(\cot\frac{\pi}{8}\right) - \left(\tan^{-1}s\right)\left(\tan\frac{\pi}{8}\right) = \tan^{-1}\left(\frac{2s}{1 + s^2}\right);$$

where,

$$s = \frac{x}{1 + \sqrt{1 + x^2}}; \qquad (4\text{-}6\text{-}49)$$

Then,

$$x = \frac{2s}{1 - s^2}; \qquad \sqrt{1 + x^2} = \frac{1 + s^2}{1 - s^2};$$

and

$$\tan^{-1}\left(\sqrt{2}\,x\right) - \tan^{-1}\frac{x}{\sqrt{1 + x^2}}$$

$$= \tan^{-1}\left(\frac{2\sqrt{2}\,s}{1 - s^2}\right) - \tan^{-1}\left(\frac{2s}{1 + s^2}\right) = 2\tan^{-1}\left(s\tan\frac{\pi}{8}\right)$$

By utilizing these expressions, equation (4-6-48) may be written in the form

$$g(x) = \left(\frac{1 - s^2}{2}\right)\left\{\frac{1}{2} - \frac{1}{2}\tan\frac{\pi}{8}\left(\frac{1 - s^2}{2}\right)\right.$$

$$\left. - 4\tan^3\frac{\pi}{8}\left(\frac{1 - s^2}{2}\right)^2\left\{\frac{1}{3} - \frac{\left(s\tan\frac{\pi}{8}\right)^2}{5} + \frac{\left(s\tan\frac{\pi}{8}\right)^4}{7} \cdots\right\}\right\}$$

(4-6-50)

which reduces to the simple numerical equation

$$g(x) = \frac{1}{\phi}\left\{\frac{1}{2} - \frac{0.20710688}{\phi} - \left(\frac{0.20710688}{\phi}\right)^2\left\{0.55228\right.\right.$$

$$\left.\left. - 0.0569\left(\frac{x}{\phi}\right)^2 + 0.00695\left(\frac{x}{\phi}\right)^4 \cdots\right\}\right\}$$

(4-6-51)

if we replace $(1 - s^2)/2$ by $1/\phi$. In a like manner, equation (4-6-45) becomes

$$f(x) = 1 + \frac{3}{4\sqrt{2}}\left(\frac{1 - s^2}{2}\right)\left\{\frac{2}{s}\ln\left(\frac{1 + s}{1 - s}\right) - \cot\left(\frac{\pi}{8}\right)\right.$$

$$\left. - \left(1 + s^2\cot^2\frac{\pi}{8}\right)\tan^3\frac{\pi}{8}\left(\frac{1}{1 \times 3} - \frac{\left(s\tan\frac{\pi}{8}\right)^2}{3 \times 5} + \frac{\left(s\tan\frac{\pi}{8}\right)^4}{5 \times 7} \cdots\right)\right\}$$

(4-6-52)

whence

$$f(0) = \sqrt{2}; \quad \text{and} \quad f(\infty) = 1 \qquad \text{(4-6-52a)}$$

Plots of $f(x)$ and $g(x)$ are shown in Fig. (4-6-1). The limits approached by these functions at high and low fields are indicated in the diagram. Tables of these functions are given in Chapter (5), Section (3).

(g) The Conductance Equation Modified for the Wien Effect

The conductance equation for strong electrolytes in presence of the field can be derived readily from the preceding expressions. Introducing equations (4-6-44) and (4-6-47) for the effects of electrophoresis and the ionic fields, as in the derivation of equation (4-3-39), the ionic velocity becomes

$$v_j = X \left[e_j \omega_j - \frac{e_j^2 \omega_j \mu' \kappa}{2DX} g(x) - \frac{e_j \kappa}{6\sqrt{2}\, \pi \eta_0} f(x) \right] \qquad (4\text{-}6\text{-}53)$$

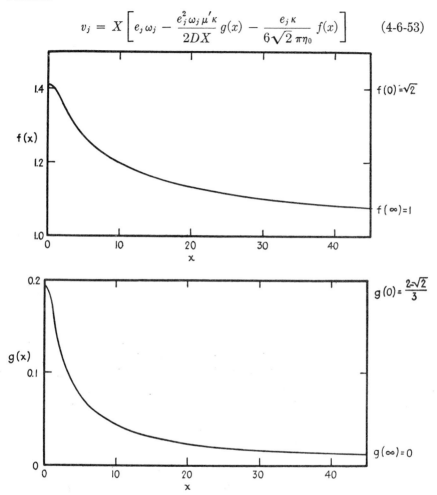

Fig. (4-6-1) (a and b). The functions, $f(x)$ and $g(x)$, for calculation of Wien effect for strong electrolytes.

and (4-3-40) may be expressed in the form

$$\bar{u}_j = \frac{10^8}{c} \left[|e_j| \omega_j - \frac{e_j^2 \omega_j \mu' \kappa}{2DX} g(x) - \frac{|e_j| \kappa}{6\sqrt{2}\, \pi \eta_0} f(x) \right] \qquad (4\text{-}6\text{-}54)$$

Consequently, the equation for λ_j takes the form

$$\lambda_j = \lambda_j^0 - \frac{e_j^2 \kappa}{2DkT} \lambda_j^0 g(x) - \frac{F |e_j| \kappa f(x)}{6\sqrt{2}\, \pi \eta_0 c \times 10^{-8}} \qquad (4\text{-}6\text{-}55)$$

upon substitution of $e_j X/kT$ for μ'. This equation reduces to (4-3-42) when x equals 0, since $f(x) = \sqrt{2}$ and $g(x) = \dfrac{2 - \sqrt{2}}{3}$.

It is now possible from inspection of Fig. (4-6-1) to understand what happens to the conductance with increase in field. Since the magnitudes of both $g(x)$ and $f(x)$ decrease with increasing field strength, and since both effects [Equation (4-6-55)] of the ionic fields and electrophoresis are subtracted from the limiting conductance, λ_j will increase with increasing field strength. However, in very high fields λ_j will not approach λ_j^0 since $f(x)$ equals unity when $(x = \infty)$. The forms of the conductance curves as functions of the field and the quantitative proof of this theory will be discussed in Chapter (7), Section (8).

Falkenhagen, Frölich and Fleischer[33] have extended the Debye and Falkenhagen theory of frequency effects [This chapter, Section (5)] upon conductance and dielectric constant in the presence of high fields. It is not as complete as the preceding theory of Onsager and Wilson for zero frequency, since the effect of electrophoresis is omitted. The equations for the frequency effects are given in the forms

$$\frac{\Lambda_{X=\infty} - \Lambda_X}{\Lambda_{X=\infty}} = \frac{e^2 \kappa^2}{2DkT} \frac{y'}{\mu'} = \frac{e\kappa^2}{X} y' \qquad (4\text{-}6\text{-}56)$$

$$D_{\tilde{\omega}} - D_{\tilde{\omega}=\infty} = - \frac{\kappa^2 e y''}{X \tilde{\omega} \tau} \qquad (4\text{-}6\text{-}57)$$

where μ' equals $2DkT/Xe$. The functions y' and y'', the real and imaginary parts of a complicated function y^*, are not given explicitly but are tabulated. Their tables contain values of y' and y'' as functions of $\mu'/\sqrt{DT/c}$ and $\tilde{\omega}\tau$.

(7) INFLUENCE OF HIGH FIELDS ON THE IONIZATION OF WEAK ELECTROLYTES. THEORY OF ONSAGER

Weak electrolytes in the presence of high fields exhibit deviations from Ohm's law which are many times greater than those of strong electrolytes.[34] The conductance is proportional to the absolute value of the field over a considerable range, and its limit corresponds to the complete dissociation of the weak electrolyte. Recently, upon the basis of the interionic attraction theory, Onsager[35] has developed a theory of this effect which promises to be a very close approach to the solution of the problem, and which has far-reaching implications.

The theory results from a detailed study of the rates of dissociation of

---

[33] H. Falkenhagen, F. Frölich, and H. Fleischer, *Naturwiss.*, **25**, 446 (1937); H. Fleischer, "Dissertation," Dresden, 1938, Effect upon conductance; F. Fröhlich, *Physik. Z.*, **40**, 139 (1939), Effect upon dielectric constant.

[34] M. Wien and J. Schiele, *Physik. Z.*, **32**, 545 (1931).

[35] L. Onsager, *J. Chem. Phys.*, **2**, 599 (1934).

electrolytes, and recombination of ions. The conventions regarding association of ions are obtained from an extension of Bjerrum's theory [Chapter (3), Section (7)]. Further, since in the presence of the field, **X**, the Boltzmann distribution law is no longer valid, the general laws of the Brownian movement of the ions as given by equation (2-5-6) for the non-stationary case are required. The complete development of this complicated problem of ionic motion requires considerable judgment regarding necessary simplifications, and involves an integral which had not previously been solved.

In the first place, Bjerrum's convention that a pair of ions of opposite sign at a distance $r < q$ is associated is assumed. Since our considerations will involve weak electrolytes, the concentration of free ions is small, and as a result, $1/\kappa$ is much greater than the "effective range" of the ions, q. Thus,

$$\kappa q = -\kappa e_1 e_2 / 2DkT \ll 1 \qquad (4\text{-}7\text{-}1)$$

and

$$\kappa^2 = \frac{4\pi(n_1 e_1^2 + n_2 e_2^2)}{DkT} \qquad (4\text{-}7\text{-}2)$$

where n_1 and n_2 are the concentrations of the free ions. In solutions of strong electrolytes, if κq is small as implied by equation (4-7-1), the effects of interionic forces are small. On the other hand, in the case of weak electrolytes, combination of ions may occur even though κq is small. Bjerrum showed that this effect is governed by the law of mass action no matter what forces are responsible for binding the ions. The variation of the mass action constant with the field becomes our primary concern.

Certain peculiarities of the ionic atmosphere, under the condition that $\kappa q \ll 1$, require examination. In the absence of an external field, the density of i ions in the presence of j ions, n_{ji}, is given by

$$n_{ji}(r) = n_i \exp\left(-W_{ji}(r)/kT\right) \qquad (4\text{-}7\text{-}3)$$

where $W_{ji}(r)$ is the mutual potential of the average force between i and j. When $r > q$, the ions are free, and when $r < q$ the ions are bound. In the case $r > q$, $W_{ji}(r)$ may be derived from the Debye and Hückel theory, and by adapting equation (3-5-4) for the mutual potential between the ions, we obtain

$$W_{ji}(r) = \frac{e_j e_i}{D} \frac{e^{\kappa q - \kappa r}}{(1 + \kappa q)r} ; \qquad r > q \qquad (4\text{-}7\text{-}4)$$

Further, according to Bjerrum, the work of separation of the ions is[*]

$$W_{ji}(r) = \frac{e_j e_i}{Dr} ; \qquad r < q \qquad (4\text{-}7\text{-}5)$$

[*] A correction term of the magnitude $\kappa q kT$ has been neglected, since we have adopted the assumption represented by equation (4-7-1).

The concentration of associated ion pairs is given by

$$\nu_{ji} = \nu_{ij} = n_j \int_a^q n_{ji}(r) 4\pi r^2 \, dr \qquad (4\text{-}7\text{-}6)$$

where a is the closest distance of approach of the positive to a negative ion. For weak electrolytes, and for all electrolytes in media of low dielectric constant, the principal effect takes place at distances, r, just greater than a. While the upper limit of q is arbitrarily fixed, it can be shown that it may be replaced by $q/2$ or $2q$ without materially affecting the results.

Some important considerations regarding limits may be derived from equations (4-7-4) and (4-7-5). $e^{-\kappa r}$ in equation (4-7-4) represents the "screening off" of the field of an ion by its atmosphere, or by the space charge which surrounds it. If this factor is omitted from equation (4-7-4), and the resulting value for $W_{ji}(r)$ is employed in equation (4-7-3), this space charge can be shown to be infinite, since the integral of equation (4-7-3) with the upper limit of ∞ does not converge. Onsager points out, however, that $e^{-\kappa r}$ may be neglected if equation (4-7-1) is assumed up to a certain distance, $r' > q$, or to be specific

$$q \ll r' \ll 1/\kappa \qquad (4\text{-}7\text{-}7)$$

These considerations make possible the extension of equation (4-7-5) to distances $r' > r$, so that

$$W_{ji}(r) = e_j e_i / Dr; \qquad r < r' \qquad (4\text{-}7\text{-}8)$$

This approximation is particularly good for weak electrolytes, since incomplete dissociation depends principally on the innermost region of the field of the ions, while the region beyond r' is of no importance.

For strong electrolytes, equation (4-7-3) may be replaced [Equation (2-4-9)] by the approximation,

$$n_{ji}(r) \sim n_i(1 - W_{ji}(r)/kT) \qquad (4\text{-}7\text{-}9)$$

which is good for large values of r, or when $W_{ji}(r)/kT \ll 1$. It is poor for small values of r. On the other hand, the approximation given by equations (4-7-8) and (4-7-6) is good at small distances, but leads to absurd consequences at $r = \infty$. Onsager finds, however, that, if r' is extended to infinity, and if the effects due to infinite total space charge at large distances are neglected, a convenient and significant solution may be obtained.

In order to compute the effects of an external field, $\mathbf{X}$, it is necessary to employ the general equations for the motion of the ions. Since the total force, $\mathbf{K}$, is the sum of the external force, $e\mathbf{X}$ acting on the ions, and $\mathbf{k}$, the average of the forces due to the ion atmosphere acting on the ions, we obtain from equation (2-3-1)

$$\mathbf{v}_{ji}(\mathbf{r}) - \mathbf{v}_{ij}(-\mathbf{r}) = -\omega_i[e_i\mathbf{X} + \mathbf{k}_{ji}(\mathbf{r}) - kT\nabla_2 \ln f_{ji}(\mathbf{r})]$$
$$- \omega_j[e_j\mathbf{X} + \mathbf{k}_{ij}(-\mathbf{r}) - kT\nabla_1 \ln f_{ij}(-\mathbf{r})] \qquad (4\text{-}7\text{-}10)$$

Further, from equation (2-2-3),

$$\frac{\partial f}{\partial t} = - \nabla_2 \cdot [f_{ji}(\mathbf{r}_2 - \mathbf{r}_1)\mathbf{v}_{ji}(\mathbf{r}_2 - \mathbf{r}_1)] - \nabla_1 \cdot [f_{ij}(\mathbf{r}_1 - \mathbf{r}_2)\mathbf{v}_{ij}(\mathbf{r}_1 - \mathbf{r}_2)]$$

$$= \nabla_2 \cdot [f_{ji}(\mathbf{r}) \{\mathbf{v}_{ij}(- \mathbf{r}) - \mathbf{v}_{ji}(\mathbf{r}) \}] = 0 \tag{4-7-11}$$

This equation can be reduced to a suitable form upon the basis of the assumptions so far premised. (1) By the assumption $\kappa q \ll 1$, the effects of the ionic atmosphere are negligible. This is particularly applicable when a strong field is present, since the atmosphere around the ion is destroyed. (2) By letting $r' = \infty$ in equation (4-7-8), it becomes possible to replace W by the Coulomb potential, $e_j e_i/Dr$. (3) By choosing an external field, $\mathbf{X}$, parallel to the x axis with a potential $-\mathbf{X}x$, and assuming $\mathbf{X}e_j > 0$, $\mathbf{X}e_i < 0$, and dropping the indices of f, the flow is given by

$$f(\mathbf{r})\mathbf{v}(\mathbf{r}) = f(\mathbf{r})[\mathbf{v}_{ji}(\mathbf{r}) - \mathbf{v}_{ij}(-\mathbf{r})]$$

$$= kT(\omega_j + \omega_i) \left(-\nabla f + f\nabla \left[\frac{2q}{r} + 2\beta x \right] \right) \tag{4-7-12}$$

where

$$q = - \frac{e_j e_i}{2DkT} \tag{4-7-13}$$

$$2\beta = \frac{X(e_j\omega_j - e_i\omega_i)}{kT(\omega_i + \omega_j)} \tag{4-7-14}$$

The stationary condition required by equation (4-7-11) is given by

$$\nabla \cdot \left[f\nabla \left(2\beta x + \frac{2q}{r} \right) \right] - \nabla \cdot \nabla f = 0$$

and since the field of the potential $\left(\frac{2q}{r} + 2\beta x \right)$ has no divergence,

$$\nabla \cdot \nabla \left(\frac{2r}{r} + 2\beta x \right) = 0,$$

and

$$\nabla \cdot \nabla f = \nabla f \cdot \nabla \left(\frac{2q}{r} + 2\beta x \right) \tag{4-7-15}$$

The net rate at which pairs of ions enter any closed surface, S, may be obtained from equation (4-7-12). Thus,

$$\int \frac{\partial f}{\partial t} dV = kT(\omega_j + \omega_i) \int \left[\nabla_n f - f\nabla_n \left(\left(\frac{2q}{r} \right) + 2\beta x \right) \right] dS \tag{4-7-16}$$

where ∇_n is the gradient normal to S.

In order to develop the theory of incomplete dissociation from the premises so far adopted, it becomes necessary to solve equation (4-7-15) with appropriate boundary conditions. Onsager has succeeded in performing for the first time the integration of this equation, but has not stated the mathematical details in his contribution to the theory of the Wien effect.* Since all the important assumptions have been stated in the preceding discussion, we shall merely outline the method and give the final results.

Onsager found it most convenient to separate the problem by computing the density, f, for the processes of combination and dissociation. The chemical rate of combination has already been given by equation (4-1-19), or

$$\frac{d\nu_{ji}}{dt} = -\frac{dn_j}{dt} = -\frac{dn_i}{dt} = An_jn_i - KA\nu_{ji} \qquad (4\text{-}7\text{-}17)$$

where A and KA are velocity constants of combination and dissociation, respectively, and K the ionization constant. When complete dissociation exists, the distribution of the ions is given by equation (4-7-15), and $n_jn_i = f(r) = $ constant. Consequently, the rate of combination of ions may be obtained from equation (4-7-16) as follows, if spherical co-ordinates, r, θ, and ϕ, are employed.

$$An_jn_i = kT(\omega_j + \omega_i) \int n_jn_i \left(\frac{2q}{r^2} - 2\beta \sin \theta\right) r^2 \sin \theta \, d\theta \, d\phi$$
$$= 8\pi qkT(\omega_j + \omega_i)n_jn_i \qquad (4\text{-}7\text{-}18)$$

For a binary electrolyte, $e_1 = -e_2$,

$$A = \frac{4\pi(e_1^2\omega_1 + e_2^2\omega_2)}{D} \qquad (4\text{-}7\text{-}19)$$

Thus, the rate constant of the recombination of ions is unaffected by the field. When there is no field, and consequently β is zero, it follows from equations (4-7-8), (4-7-3) and the relation, $f(r) = n_jn_{ji}$, that the number of undissociated molecules, ν_{ji}, is given by

$$f(r) = \nu_{ji}K(0)(e^{2q/r} - 1) = n_jn_i(e^{2q/r} - 1) \qquad (4\text{-}7\text{-}20)$$

where $K(0)$ denotes the dissociation constant in the absence of the field. This is the only solution of (4-7-15) which is satisfied by the boundary conditions, that $f = 0$ when $r = \infty$, and the flow from the origin through any space angle is finite.

When $X \neq 0$, the solution of equation (4-7-15) with these boundary

* Solutions are given elsewhere by L. Onsager, Dissertation, Mathieu Functions of Period 4π, Yale University, June 1935.

conditions is complicated. Onsager has succeeded in obtaining a unique result in the form of a definite integral, namely

$$f(r, \theta) = g e^{-\beta r + \beta r \cos \theta} \int_{s=0}^{s=2q} J_0[\sqrt{-4\beta s(1 + \cos \theta)}] \exp\left(\frac{2q - s}{r}\right) \frac{ds}{r} \quad (4\text{-}7\text{-}21)$$

where J_0 is a Bessel function of order zero. For small values of r, q may be replaced by ∞, and a good approximation

$$f(r, \theta) \simeq g e^{2q/r} e^{2\beta r \cos \theta} \quad (4\text{-}7\text{-}22)$$

is obtained. If, as mentioned in the preliminary discussion, we disregard the region $r > q$, and go a step further by replacing the second exponential term by unity, then

$$f(r) \sim g e^{2q/r} \quad (4\text{-}7\text{-}23)$$

which is the same distribution as that of the equilibrium case where $1 \ll \exp(2q/r)$. By comparison with equation (4-7-20), we find that

$$\nu_{ji} = g/K(0) \quad (4\text{-}7\text{-}24)$$

which gives the desired relation between g and $K(0)$.

In order to evaluate the rate of dissociation according to equation (4-7-21), it is necessary to substitute $f(r, \theta)$ in equation (4-7-16). If the integral is separated according to

$$\int_0^{2q} = \int_0^\infty - \int_{2q}^\infty$$

it happens that only the second integral on the right contributes anything. One obtains (most easily by specialization to small r),

$$-K(X)A\nu_{ji} = -8\pi qkT(\omega_j + \omega_i)g \frac{J_1(4\sqrt{-\beta q})}{2\sqrt{-\beta q}} \quad (4\text{-}7\text{-}25)$$

From equations (4-7-18) and (4-7-25), it is clear that the relative increase of the dissociation constant in the field is

$$\frac{AK(X)}{AK(0)} = \frac{K(X)}{K(0)} = \frac{J_1(4\sqrt{-\beta q})}{2\sqrt{-\beta q}}$$

$$= 1 + 2\beta q + \frac{(4\beta q)^2}{|2\,|3} + \frac{(4\beta q)^3}{|3\,|4} + \cdots \quad (4\text{-}7\text{-}26)$$

where J_1 is a Bessel function of the order one. Referring to equation (4-7-19), we recall that the rate constant, A, of combination of ions turned out to be independent of the field.

Equation (4-7-26) represents the principal result of Onsager's theory. The present outline of the theory suffices merely to state the grounds upon which it has been developed, and to indicate the great difficulties.

Onsager follows his outline of the derivation with a detailed critique of the approximations employed, and estimates the order of magnitude of the errors involved in these approximations. He notes that, for purposes of simplicity, the hydrodynamic interaction has been omitted, and he attempts to make an estimate of the order of magnitude of the hydrodynamic correction. His conclusion is that, in high fields, this effect may become important, but not sufficiently so to change the order of magnitude of the principal result.

According to equation (4-7-26), it appears that the relative increase of the dissociation constant is measured by the parameter $2\beta q$. From equation (4-7-14), this parameter $\bar{b}$ is given by

$$\bar{b} = 2\beta q = \frac{|z_1|\omega_1 + |z_2|\omega_2}{\omega_1 + \omega_2} |z_1 z_2| \frac{X\epsilon^3}{2Dk^2T^2}$$

$$= \frac{z_1^2 z_2^2 (\lambda_1 + \lambda_2)}{|z_2|\lambda_1 + |z_1|\lambda_2} 9.695 \frac{V}{DT^2} \tag{4-7-27}$$

where z_1, z_2 are the valences of the ions, λ_1 and λ_2 the equivalent conductances, ϵ the electronic charge, and V the field intensity in volts/cm. For 1–1 electrolytes, this reduces to the simple relation

$$\bar{b} = 9.695 \frac{V}{DT^2} \tag{4-7-28}$$

The function on the right of equation (4-7-26) is given by a power series,

$$\frac{K(X)}{K(0)} = F(\bar{b}) = 1 + \bar{b} + \frac{\bar{b}^2}{3} + \frac{\bar{b}^3}{18}$$

$$+ \frac{\bar{b}^4}{180} + \frac{\bar{b}^5}{2700} + \frac{\bar{b}^6}{56700} + \cdots \tag{4-7-29}$$

or, for large values of $\bar{b}$, by asymptotic expansion

$$F(\bar{b}) \cong \sqrt{2/\pi}\,(8\bar{b})^{-3/4} e^{\sqrt{8\bar{b}}}$$

$$\left\{1 - \frac{3}{8(8\bar{b})^{1/2}} - \frac{15}{128(8\bar{b})} - \frac{105}{1024(8\bar{b})^{3/2}} \cdots \right\} \tag{4-7-30}$$

where, for $\bar{b} \geq 3$, the remainder of the series is less than $1/130\bar{b}^2$, which is less than 10^{-3}.

We are now in a position to point out some important and far-reaching consequences of the theory.

(1) From equation (4-7-29), it is clear that the initial effect of the field is to cause $K(X)/K(0)$ to vary linearly with $\bar{b}$, or according to equation (4-7-27), linearly with the absolute value of the field, X.

(2) From these latter two equations, it is also apparent that the change in K with the field depends on two characteristics of the electrolyte, the valencies and the mobilities of its ions.

(3) From the law of mass action, it is possible to compute the effect of the field upon the concentration of the free ions, c_i. For binary electrolytes

$$\frac{c\alpha^2}{1 - \alpha} = K(X) = K(0)F(\bar{b}) \qquad (4\text{-}7\text{-}31)$$

where c is the concentration of the electrolyte, and α the degree of dissociation, c_i/c. Further,

$$\frac{\Lambda_x}{\Lambda_{x=0}} = \frac{c_i(X)}{c_i(0)} = \frac{\alpha}{\alpha_0} \qquad (4\text{-}7\text{-}32)$$

where Λ is the conductance.

From the law expressed by equation (4-7-31), the important result is obtained that the change in equilibrium, corresponding to a given change in K, depends on the initial value of the degree of dissociation, α_0.

(4) It is important to note that α/α_0 decreases with increasing α_0. For the case of small values of $\bar{b}$, and for small changes of K,

$$\frac{\Delta\Lambda}{\Lambda_{x=0}} = \frac{\Delta\alpha}{\alpha_0} = \frac{(1 - \alpha)}{(2 - \alpha)}\frac{\Delta K}{K(0)} = \frac{(1 - \alpha)}{(2 - \alpha)}\bar{b} \qquad (4\text{-}7\text{-}33)$$

if all the terms in equation (4-7-29) of order $\bar{b}^2$, or higher, are neglected. Δ denotes an increase caused by the field. When α is nearly unity, the change due to the field is proportional to $(1 - \alpha)$. When $\alpha \ll 1$, the effect approaches a maximum which is given by

$$\frac{\Lambda_x}{\Lambda_{x=0}} = \frac{\alpha}{\alpha_0} = \sqrt{\frac{K(X)}{K(0)}} = \sqrt{F(\bar{b})} = 1 + \frac{1}{2}\bar{b} + \frac{1}{24}\bar{b}^2 + \cdots \qquad (4\text{-}7\text{-}34)$$

(5) Reference to equation (4-7-27) shows that b is proportional to the cube of the electronic charge, and inversely proportional to the dielectric constant. Equation (4-7-34), valid for binary electrolytes, is of particular importance in solutions of low dielectric constant where very small ionization is the rule. The magnitudes of the maximum effects in water ($D = 78.57$), and benzene ($D = 2.28$), in fields of the order of 5×10^5 volts/cm, is found to be $\Lambda_x/\Lambda_{x=0} = 1.37$ in water, and 121 in benzene.

(6) We have shown that the time lag of an ionization equilibrium, τ', for a binary electrolyte may be computed by means of equation (4-1-23). By substituting for A in this equation the value given by equation (4-7-19), we obtain the interesting relation,

$$\tau' = \frac{1 - \alpha_0}{An(2 - \alpha_0)\alpha_0} = \frac{(1 - \alpha_0)D}{(2 - \alpha_0)4\pi\sigma} \qquad (4\text{-}7\text{-}35)$$

where σ is $\alpha_0 n(e_1^2\omega_1 + e_2^2\omega_2)$, or the specific conductance of the solution in electrostatic units. When $\alpha_0 \ll 1$, the Langevin time lag is

$$\tau' = D/8\pi\sigma = D/8\pi(9 \times 10^{11}L) \qquad (4\text{-}7\text{-}36)$$

where L is the specific conductivity in practical units [Equation (6-1-2)]. Comparison with equation (4-1-6) indicates that τ' is just one-half the value of the Maxwell time of relaxation, or the time needed for the shielding of charges.

In equation (4-7-35), α_0 and σ refer to a steady state in a field of magnitude, X. Since our theory shows that both α_0 and σ increase with increasing field, τ' must decrease with the field.

(8) Wien Effect for Simple Strong Electrolytes of Any Valence Type*

Theory of Onsager and Kim[36]

In Section (6) of this chapter, the theory of Onsager and Wilson for the Wien effect for strong binary electrolytes was outlined. The fundamental equation was solved by employing a one-dimensional Fourier transformation. The details of their theory have not been published because a general treatment by means of a three dimensional Fourier transformation was regarded as preferable to the earlier method of procedure. Onsager and Kim have now succeeded in obtaining a solution by a three-dimensional Fourier transformation. An outline of their procedure will be the subject of the present section.

Starting with the linearized equation of continuity (4-6-2a) and Poisson's equation (2-5-2) and applying the three dimensional Fourier transformation to the differential system, the transformed potential and the transformed distribution function specialized for simple electrolytes may be obtained. From the asymmetric part of the potential the ionic field, ΔX_j, may be derived by means of the Fourier inversion formula. In like manner, the Stokes hydrodynamic equation (4-6-41) can be solved upon substituting the charge density derived from the potential. By this procedure, one obtains the following double integrals for the ionic field, ΔX_j, and the electrophoretic velocity Δv_j (Equation 4-3-10).

$$\Delta X_j = X \frac{\kappa q^* e_1 e_2}{DkT} A(a) \qquad (j = 1, 2) \quad (4\text{-}8\text{-}1)$$

$$\Delta v_j = X \frac{\kappa e_1 e_2}{4\pi \eta_0 (e_j - e_i)} B_j(a) \qquad (j \neq i) \quad (4\text{-}8\text{-}2)$$

where

$A(a)$

$$= \frac{2}{\pi} \int_{t=0}^{1} \int_{\lambda=0}^{\infty} \frac{t^2 \lambda^2 (\lambda^2 + q^*)}{(\lambda^2 + 1)(\lambda^2 + q^*)^2 + a^2 t^2 (\lambda^2 + \mu_1)(\lambda^2 + \mu_2)} \, dt \, d\lambda \qquad (4\text{-}8\text{-}3)$$

---

* We are indebted to Dr. Kim for this abbreviated statement which outlines the theory of the Wien effect presented in a dissertation, Yale University, June 1956. The symbols are those used by Kim.

[36] L. Onsager and S. K. Kim, *J. Phys. Chem.*, **61**, 198 (1957).

$$B_j(a) = \frac{2}{(1 - \mu_j)\pi} \int_{t=0}^{1} \int_{\lambda=0}^{\infty}$$

$$\cdot \frac{(1 - t^2)\{(\lambda^2 + q^*)^2 + a^2t^2(\lambda^2 + 1 - \mu_j)\mu_j\}}{(\lambda^2 + 1)(\lambda^2 + q^*)^2 + a^2t^2(\lambda^2 + \mu_1)(\lambda^2 + \mu_2)} \, dt \, d\lambda \tag{4-8-4}$$

and

$$\mu_1 \equiv \frac{n_1 e_1^2}{n_1 e_1^2 + n_2 e_2^2} \; ; \qquad \mu_2 \equiv \frac{n_2 e_2^2}{n_1 e_1^2 + n_2 e_2^2} \; ; \qquad q^* \equiv \frac{\mu_1 \omega_1 + \mu_2 \omega_2}{\omega_1 + \omega_2} \tag{4-8-5}$$

$$a = \frac{X\epsilon}{\kappa kT} q^*(|z_1| + |z_2|) \tag{4-8-6}$$

The field parameter, a, has an interesting physical significance since it approximates the ratio of the time of relaxation to the time required for an ion to move out of its atmosphere.

When $a \ll 1$, the deformation of the ionic atmosphere will be small so that the first order perturbation approximation is correct. Under this condition, the integrals become

$$A(a) = \frac{1}{3(1 + \sqrt{q^*})} + o(a^2) \tag{4-8-7}$$

$$B_j(a) = \frac{2}{3(1 - \mu_j)} + o(a^2) \tag{4-8-8}$$

which yield the results obtained in Section (3) of this chapter, expressed by equations (4-3-38) and (4-3-39).

When $a \simeq \infty$, the integrals reduce to

$$A(a) = \frac{1}{2a} + o\left(\frac{1}{a^2}\right) \tag{4-8-9}$$

$$B_j(a) = \frac{2\sqrt{\mu_j}}{3(1 - \mu_j)} + a^{-1} \ln a + o\left(\frac{1}{a}\right) \tag{4-8-10}$$

These integrals as functions of a^2 are monotonic decreasing functions which do not have inflection points since

$$\frac{\partial A}{\partial(a^2)} < 0; \qquad \frac{\partial^2 A}{\partial(a^2)^2} > 0 \tag{4-8-11}$$

$$\frac{\partial B_j}{\partial(a^2)} < 0; \qquad \frac{\partial^2 B_j}{\partial(a^2)^2} > 0 \tag{4-8-12}$$

For binary electrolytes

$$\mu_1 = \mu_2 = q^* = \frac{1}{2}; \qquad a = \left(\frac{DX^2}{8\pi\kappa kT}\right)^{1/2}. \tag{4-8-13}$$

where a is the parameter, x, used by Wilson [Equation (4-6-43)]. If this expression be substituted in equations (4-8-3) and (4-8-4), the integration of these latter equations can be readily achieved. It is convenient to first integrate over λ. The result may be expressed by the functions $f(x)$ and $g(x)$ of equations (4-6-45) and (4-6-48) where

$$A(a) = g(x) \tag{4-8-14}$$

$$B_j(a) = \frac{2\sqrt{2}}{3} f(x) \tag{4-8-15}$$

For extension to all valence types of electrolytes, the integrals may be expressed in closed forms of elliptical integrals of the first and second kinds. First, the integral $B_j(a)$ will be divided into two parts

$$B_j(a) = H_j(a) - D_j(a) \tag{4-8-16}$$

where

$$H_j(a) = \frac{2}{(1 - \mu_j)\pi} \int_{t=0}^{t=1} \int_{\lambda=0}^{\lambda=\infty} \frac{(\lambda^2 + q^*)^2 + a^2 t^2}{(\lambda^2 + 1)(\lambda^2 + q^*)^2} \cdot (\lambda^2 + 1 - \mu_j)\mu_j}{+ a^2 t^2 (\lambda^2 + \mu_1)(\lambda^2 + \mu_2)} \, dt \, d\lambda \tag{4-8-17}$$

$$D_j(a) = \frac{2}{(1 - \mu_j)\pi} \int_{t=0}^{t=1} \int_{\lambda=\lambda}^{\lambda=\infty} \frac{t^2\{(\lambda^2 + q^*)^2 + a^2 t^2 (\lambda^2 + 1 - \mu_j)\mu_j\}}{(\lambda^2 + 1)(\lambda^2 + q^*)^2 + a^2 t^2 (\lambda^2 + \mu_1)(\lambda^2 + \mu_2)} \, dt \, d\lambda \tag{4-8-18}$$

The quantities

$$k \equiv \frac{|z_2| - |z_1|}{|z_2| + |z_1|} > 0; \qquad m \equiv \frac{\omega_2 - \omega_1}{\omega_2 + \omega_1} \tag{4-8-19}$$

where the convention $|z_2| > |z_1|$ is maintained.

The quantities, s_1, s_2, s_3, are defined as the roots of the cubic equation

$$(1 - ks)(s - m)^2 - 2a^2(1 - s^2) = 0 \tag{4-8-20}$$

Then s_ν satisfies the set of inequalities

$$-1 \leqslant s_1 \leqslant m \leqslant s_2 \leqslant 1 \leqslant \frac{1}{k} \leqslant s_3 \leqslant \infty \tag{4-8-21}$$

The result of the integration can now be expressed by the set of equations

$$4a^3 A(k, m, a) = -(1 + m^2)I + (2 + m^2)J - 2mkL$$
$$+ \sum_{\nu=1}^{3} \{2m - (1 + m^2)s_\nu\}r_\nu \tag{4-8-22}$$

$$2aH_1(k, m, a) = mI - \frac{1+m}{1-k}J + L - \frac{1+m}{1+k}\sum_{\nu=1}^{3}(1 - s_\nu)r_\nu$$

$$4a^3D_1(k, m, a) = -M_3I + (1 + M_3 - M_2)J - M_2kL$$

$$+ \sum_{\nu=1}^{3}\left\{(M_2 - M_1) - (M_3 - M_2)s_\nu - M_1(k'/k)^2\frac{1}{1+s_\nu}\right\}r_\nu \qquad (4\text{-}8\text{-}23)$$

$$2aH_2(k, m, a) = -mI - \frac{(1-m)}{(1-k)}J + L$$

$$+ \frac{1-m}{1-k}\sum_{\nu=1}^{3}(1 + s_\nu)r_\nu \qquad (4\text{-}8\text{-}24)$$

$$4a^3D_2(k, m, a) = -\bar{M}_3I + (1 + \bar{M}_3 - \bar{M}_2)J + \bar{M}_2kL$$

$$- \sum_{\nu=1}^{3}\left\{(\bar{M}_2 - \bar{M}_1) + (\bar{M}_3 - \bar{M}_2)s_\nu - \bar{M}_1(k'/k)^2\frac{1}{1-s_\nu}\right\}r_\nu$$

where A, H_j and D_j are designated as functions of k, m as well as a, and $k' = (1 - k^2)^{1/2}$

$$I = \int_{s_1}^{s_2}\frac{ds}{\sqrt{(1 - s^2)(1 - k^2s^2)}} - \int_{(1/ks_3)}^{1}\frac{ds}{\sqrt{(1 - s^2)(1 - k^2s^2)}}$$

$$J = \int_{s_1}^{s_2}\sqrt{\frac{(1 - k^2s^2)}{(1 - s^2)}}\,ds - \int_{(1/ks_3)}^{1}\sqrt{\frac{(1 - k^2s^2)}{(1 - s^2)}}\,ds + (s_3 - s_3^{-1})r_3$$

$$L = \frac{1}{2}\log\prod_{\nu=1}^{3}\frac{(k + r_\nu)}{(k - r_\nu)}; \qquad r_\nu = \alpha\frac{\sqrt{2(1 + ks_\nu)}}{s_\nu - m} \qquad (4\text{-}8\text{-}25)$$

$$M_1 = \tfrac{1}{3}(1 + m^3)(k/k')^2; \qquad M_2 = (1 + 3m);$$

$$M_3 = (2 + 3m + 3m^2) - \tfrac{2}{3}(1 + m)^3$$

$$\bar{M}_1 = \tfrac{1}{3}(1 - m_1^3)(k/k')^2; \qquad \bar{M}_2 = (1 - 3m);$$

$$\bar{M}_3 = (2 - 3m + 3m^2) - \tfrac{2}{3}(1 - m)^3$$

The integrals I and J are incomplete elliptic integrals of the first and second kinds, respectively. Tables of these integrals by intervals of 5° in the modular angle, $\alpha = \sin^{-1} k$, and 1° in the amplitude, $\phi = \sin^{-1} s$, are available.†

† E. Jahnke and F. Emde, Tables of Functions, 4th Edition, p. 53–97, Dover Press (1945).

The notation

$$F(k, \phi) = \int_0^\phi \frac{d\psi}{\sqrt{1 - k^2 \sin \psi}}$$

$$E(k, \phi) = \int_0^\phi \sqrt{(1 - k^2 \sin^2 \psi}\, d\psi \qquad (4\text{-}8\text{-}26)$$

$$K(k) = F(k, \tfrac{1}{2}\pi)$$

$$E(k) = E(k, \tfrac{1}{2}\pi)$$

is standard, although $F(\sin \alpha, \phi)$ is written $F(\alpha, \phi)$ etc. To use this notation one writes

$$\sin \phi_1 = s_1; \qquad \sin \phi_2 = s_2; \qquad \sin \phi_0 = 1/ks_3 \qquad (4\text{-}8\text{-}27)$$

so that

$$I = F(k, \phi_2) - F(k, \phi_1) + F(k, \phi_0) - K(k)$$
$$J = E(k, \phi_2) - E(k, \phi_1) + E(k, \phi_0) - E(k) + (s_3 - s_3^{-1})r_3 \qquad (4\text{-}8\text{-}28)$$

The variable ϕ_1 may be negative in which case

$$F(k, -\phi) = -F(k, \phi); \qquad E(k, -\phi) = -E(k, \phi)$$

The ordinary types of simple electrolytes are NaCl-type (binary)$(k = 0)$, BaCl$_2$-type $(k = \tfrac{1}{3})$, LaCl$_3$-type $(k = \tfrac{1}{2})$; K$_4$Fe(CN)$_6$-type $(k = \tfrac{2}{3})$ and Al$_2$(SO$_4$)$_3$-type $(k = \tfrac{1}{5})$. For the case of $k = 0$, one obtains Wilson's result (See Section 6 of this chapter). When $k = \tfrac{1}{2}$, the modular angle $\alpha = \sin^{-1} \tfrac{1}{2}$ equals 30°, so that the elliptic integrals (4-8-26) can be evaluated from the table of Jahnke and Emde with interpolations for the amplitude ϕ.

When $k = \tfrac{1}{3}$, it is advantageous to use Landen's transformation which relates elliptic functions of modulus k to those of the modulus

$$k_I = \frac{2 \sqrt{k}}{1 + k} \qquad (4\text{-}8\text{-}29)$$

since $k_I = \sin 60°$. The elliptic integrals transform to

$$I = \frac{1}{1 + k} \{F(k_I, \phi_2^I) - F(k_I, \phi_1^I) + F(k_I, \phi_3^I) - K(k_I)\} \qquad (4\text{-}8\text{-}30)$$

$$J = \frac{1 + k}{2} \{E(k_I, \phi_2^I) - E(k_I, \phi_2^I) + E(k_I, \phi_3^I) - E(k_I)\}$$
$$+ \frac{k'^2}{2} I - k \sum_{\nu=1}^{3} (\sin \phi_\nu^I - s_\nu)r_\nu \qquad (4\text{-}8\text{-}31)$$

where

$$\sin \phi_\nu^I = \frac{(1 + k)s_\nu}{1 + ks_\nu^2}; \qquad -\frac{\pi}{2} \leqslant \phi_\nu^I \leqslant \frac{\pi}{2} \qquad (4\text{-}8\text{-}32)$$

The solution of the cubic equation (4-8-20) may not be difficult. Onsager and Kim, however, prefer to use one of the roots, s_3, as the independent variable rather than a^2. It follows that the roots and the coefficients of the cubic equations are given by

$$s_i = \frac{C_i}{B_i + \sqrt{B_i^2 - C_i}}; \qquad s_i = B_i + \sqrt{B_i^2 - C_i} \qquad (4\text{-}8\text{-}33)$$

$$2a^2 = m^2 - ks_iC_i \qquad (4\text{-}8\text{-}34)$$

where

$$2B_i \equiv \frac{(1+k)(1+m)^2}{2k(s_i+1)} - \frac{(1-k)(1-m^2)^2}{2k(s_i-1)} \qquad (4\text{-}8\text{-}35)$$

$$C_i = \frac{(1+k)(1+m)^2}{2k(s_i+1)} + \frac{(1-k)(1-m)^2}{2k(s_i-1)} - 1 \qquad (4\text{-}8\text{-}36)$$

In actual computation, we may choose s_i in such a way that the modular angle ϕ_0 defined by equation (4-8-27) is a round number. As a consequence, rapid use may be made of the table of elliptic integrals. Since the functions A and B_j[Equations (4-8-3) and (4-8-4)] are monotonic decreasing functions of a^2 which have no inflection points, these functions may be plotted against a^2 for the purpose of interpolation.

From the results of the preceding analysis and by means of Lagrange's theorem on the expansion of functions in a power series, Onsager and Kim succeeded in expressing the functions $A(k, m, a)$ and $B_j(k, m, a)$ in a descending series of the field parameter, a. These series converge satisfactorily when and only when $a > 2$. The series equations are

$$2A(k, m, a) = \sum_{n=1}^{\infty} R_n a^{-n} + R_3^* a^{-3} \ln a \qquad (4\text{-}8\text{-}37)$$

$$B_j(k, m, a) = \sum_{n=0}^{\infty} p_{jn} a^{-n} + p_{j1} a^{-1} \ln a + p_{j3}^* a^{-3} \ln a \qquad (4\text{-}8\text{-}38)$$

valid for high field strengths. A sufficient number of terms in these series for computation for ordinary unsymmetrical valence type electrolytes are assembled in Table (5-3-7).

For lower fields when $a < 2$, the analytical method of numerical computation is exceedingly tedious and in its stead numerical quadrature is recommended. Upon substituting

$$\sigma = at \qquad (4\text{-}8\text{-}39)$$

$$R^2 = \frac{(\lambda^2 + 1)(\lambda^2 + q^*)^2}{(\lambda^2 + \mu_1)(\lambda^2 + \mu_2)} \qquad (4\text{-}8\text{-}40)$$

in equations (4-8-3) and (4-8-4) we obtain

$$A(a) = \frac{2}{\pi a^3} \int_{\sigma=0}^{a} \sigma^2 d\sigma \int_{\lambda=0}^{\infty} \frac{\lambda^2(\lambda^2 + q^*)}{(\lambda^2 + \mu_1)(\lambda^2 + \mu_2)} \frac{1}{R^2 + \sigma^2} d\lambda \qquad (4\text{-}8\text{-}41)$$

$$B_j(a) = \frac{2\sqrt{\mu_j}}{3(1 - \mu_j)} + \frac{2}{\pi a} \int_{\sigma=0}^{a} \left(1 - \frac{\sigma^2}{a^2}\right) d\sigma$$

$$\cdot \int_{\lambda=0}^{\infty} \frac{\lambda^2(\lambda^2 + q^*)^2}{(\lambda^2 + \mu_j)(\lambda^2 + \mu_1)(\lambda^2 + \mu_2)} \frac{1}{R^2 + \sigma^2} d\lambda \qquad (4\text{-}8\text{-}42)$$

According equation (4-8-10)

$$B_j(\infty) = \frac{2\sqrt{\mu_j}}{3(1 - \mu_j)} \qquad (4\text{-}8\text{-}43)$$

so that both integrals in equations (4-8-41) and (4-8-42) tend to zero as $a \to \infty$, although at different approaching rates.

Upon utilizing the substitution, $\lambda = \sqrt{\gamma} \tan \theta$, where γ is an adjustable constant, equations (4-8-41) and (4-8-42) become

$A(a)$

$$= \frac{2\gamma^{3/2}}{\pi a^3} \int_{\sigma=0}^{a} \sigma^2 d\sigma \int_{\theta=0}^{\pi/2} \frac{\tan^2 \theta \, (\tan^2 \theta + 1)}{(\gamma \tan^2 \theta + q^*)(\gamma \tan^2 \theta + 1)} \frac{1}{1 + \sigma^2 R^{-2}} d\theta \qquad (4\text{-}8\text{-}44)$$

$$B_j(a) = \frac{2\sqrt{\mu_j}}{3(1 - \mu_j)} + \frac{2\gamma^{3/2}}{\pi a} \int_{\sigma=0}^{a} \left(1 - \frac{\sigma^2}{a^2}\right) d\sigma \int_{\theta=0}^{\pi/2}$$

$$\frac{\tan^2 \theta(\tan^2 \theta + 1)}{(\gamma \tan^2 \theta + \mu_j)(\gamma \tan^2 \theta + 1)} \frac{1}{1 + \sigma^2 R^{-2}} d\theta \qquad (4\text{-}8\text{-}45)$$

where

$$R^{-2} = \frac{(\gamma \tan^2 \theta + \mu_1)(\gamma \tan^2 \theta + \mu_2)}{(\gamma \tan^2 \theta + q^*)^2(\gamma \tan^2 \theta + 1)} \qquad (4\text{-}8\text{-}46)$$

R^{-2} tends to zero as θ approaches $\pi/2$. To compute the specific conductance, the quantity $(B_1(k, m, a) + B_2(k, m, a))$ is required and is found to be given by

$$B_1(k, m, a,) + B_2(k, m, a) = \frac{2}{3}\left(\frac{\sqrt{\mu_1}}{\mu_2} + \frac{\sqrt{\mu_2}}{\mu_1}\right)$$

$$+ \frac{2\gamma^{3/2}}{\pi a} \int_{\sigma=0}^{a} \left(1 - \frac{\sigma^2}{a^2}\right) G_B(\sigma) \, d\sigma \qquad (4\text{-}8\text{-}47)$$

and in a similar terminology, $A(a)$ is expressed by

$$A(a) = \frac{2\gamma^{3/2}}{\pi a^3} \int_{\sigma=0}^{a} \sigma^2 G_A(\sigma) \, d\sigma \qquad (4\text{-}8\text{-}48)$$

where

$G_B(\sigma)$

$$= \int_{\theta=0}^{\pi/2} \frac{\tan^2 \theta (\tan^2 \theta + 1)(2\gamma \tan^2 \theta + 1)}{(\gamma \tan^2 \theta + \mu_1)(\gamma \tan^2 \theta + \mu_2)(\gamma \tan^2 \theta + 1)} \frac{1}{1 + \sigma^2 R^{-2}} d\theta \quad (4\text{-}8\text{-}49)$$

$$G_A(\sigma) = \int_{\theta=0}^{\pi/2} \frac{\tan^2 \theta (\tan^2 \theta + 1)}{(\gamma \tan^2 \theta + q^*)(\gamma \tan^2 \theta + 1)} \frac{1}{1 + \sigma^2 R^{-2}} d\theta \quad (4\text{-}8\text{-}50)$$

For the construction of a table, numerical quadrature by the trapezoidal rule is recommended at intervals of 5° and 0.1 in the variables θ and σ. Kim has computed the values of $A(k, m, a)$ and $B_j(k, m, a)$ by both the analytic expressions and the method of numerical quadrature for calcium chloride solutions and found a complete coincidence for values of a where the results overlapped.

The Conductance Equations for the Wien Effect

The values $A(a)$ and $B_j(a)$ evaluated by this analysis may be substituted in equations (4-8-1) and (4-8-2), which procedure followed by combination with equation (4-3-10), leads to the following results for the specific conductance of the electrolyte and equivalent conductance of the j-ion, respectively ($\Gamma_0 = n_1 e_1^2 + n_2 e_2^2$).

$$L = L^0 - L^0 \frac{\kappa q^* |e_1 e_2|}{DkT} A(k, m, a)$$

$$(4\text{-}8\text{-}51)$$

$$- \Gamma_0 \frac{\kappa \mu_1 \mu_2}{4\pi\eta_0} [B_1(k, m, a) + B_2(k, m, a)]$$

and

$$\lambda_j = \lambda_j^0 - \lambda_j^0 \frac{\kappa q^* |e_1 e_2|}{DkT} A(k, m, a) - \frac{965\kappa}{12\pi\eta_0} \frac{|e_1 e_2|}{|e_1| + |e_2|} B_j(k, m, a)$$

$$= \lambda_j^0 - \lambda_j^0 \sqrt{\frac{\pi}{250R}} \frac{N^2 \epsilon^3}{R} \frac{q^* |z_1 z_2|}{(DT)^{3/2}} A(k, m, a) \Gamma^{1/2} \quad (4\text{-}8\text{-}52)$$

$$- \frac{193}{12} \frac{N\epsilon^2}{\sqrt{10\pi R}} \frac{1}{\eta_0 (DT)^{1/2}} \frac{|z_1 z_2|}{|z_1| + |z_2|} B_j(k, m, a) \Gamma^{1/2}$$

In Section (3), Chapter (5), these equations are transformed to convenient forms for computing the Wien effect of single electrolytes in aqueous solutions.

(9) The Conductance Equation with Inclusion of Higher Order Inhomogeneous Terms and the Ionic Size Parameter. Theory of Fuoss and Onsager[37]

For unassociated ions, values yielded by the Onsager conductance equation (4-3-44) for point charges are smaller than the observed ones at finite electrolyte concentrations. It was soon observed[38, 39, 40] empirically that if the term, $\mathscr{B}_{(A)}\Gamma^{1/2}$, of this equation is divided by $(1 + \kappa a)$, the resulting expression, with reasonable values of the distance parameter, a, yields results in agreement with experiment at higher concentrations. Theoretical justification that terms of the first and higher order in the concentration should be present in the limiting equation is to be found in the theories of Kaneko,[39] of Falkenhagen, Leist and Kelbg,[41] and of Pitts.[42, 43]

Fuoss and Onsager point out that the differential equation employed by Falkenhagen and Pitts is an approximation in which terms have been neglected which also would have led to terms of the order c and still more important to transcendental terms of order $c \ln c$ in the relaxation field. They then proceed to justify this criticism by undertaking the formidable task of constructing a thoroughly rigorous theory based on the interionic attraction theory of Debye. This procedure requires the integration of the equation of continuity with the retention of higher terms and subject to the boundary conditions for spherical ions.

Fuoss and Onsager start with a differential equation which is an extension of equation (4-3-26) after $\nabla \cdot \nabla \psi'_j$ has been eliminated by the use of Poisson's equation and k_i has been replaced by Xe_i. Thus, for $i = 1, j = 2$

$$kT(\omega_1 + \omega_2)(\nabla \cdot \nabla)f'_{21} - [(4\pi f^0_{21}/D)(e_1^2\omega_1/n_2 + e_2^2\omega_2/n_1)]f'_{21}$$
$$= X(e_1\omega_1 - e_2\omega_2)(\partial f^0_{21}/\partial x) + T(g_1) + T(g_2) + T(g_3) + T(a) + T(v) \tag{4-9-1}$$

where the "Ts" represent the inhomogeneous terms which are all of the form $F(r) \cos \theta$. Explicitly, these terms are expressed by

$$T(g_1) = -\left\{\left(e_1\omega_1\frac{\partial}{\partial x}\left(\frac{\psi'_2}{\cos\theta}\right) - e_2\omega_2\frac{\partial}{\partial x}\left(\frac{\psi'_1}{\cos\theta}\right)\right)\right\}\frac{df^0_{21}}{dx} \tag{4-9-2}$$

$$T(g_2) = -(e_1\omega_1\psi_2^0 + e_2\omega_2\psi_1^0)\kappa^2 f'_{21} \tag{4-9-3}$$

[37] R. M. Fuoss and L. Onsager, *Proc. Nat. Acad. Sci.*, **41,** 274 (1955); *J. Phys. Chem.*, **61,** 668 (1957).

[38] R. T. Lattey, *Phil. Mag.*, **4,** 831 (1927).

[39] S. Kaneko, *J. Chem. Soc., Japan*, **56,** 793, 1320 (1935); **58,** 985 (1937).

[40] D. M. Ritson and J. B. Hasted, *J. Chem. Phys.*, **16,** 11 (1948).

[41] H. Falkenhagen, M. Leist and G. Kelbg, *Ann. Phys., Leipzig* [6], **11,** 51 (1952).

[42] E. Pitts, *Proc. Roy. Soc.*, **217A** 43 (1953).

[43] R. A. Robinson and R. H. Stokes, "Electrolyte Solutions," Butterworths Scientific Publications, London (1955), Chapter 7, contains a discussion and numerous applications of the equations containing the distance parameter.

$$T(g_3) = -\left(e_1\omega_1\frac{d\psi_2^0}{dr} + e_2\omega_2\frac{d\psi_1^0}{dr}\right)\frac{\partial}{\partial x}\left(\frac{f_{21}'}{\cos\theta}\right) \tag{4-9-4}$$

$$T(a) = \left\{e_1\omega_1\frac{\partial}{\partial x}\left(\frac{\psi_1'}{\cos\theta}\right) - e_2\omega_2\frac{\partial}{\partial x}\left(\frac{\psi_2'}{\cos\theta}\right)\right\}_{r=a}\frac{df_{21}^0}{dr} \tag{4-9-5}$$

$$T(v) = (v_{1r} - v_{2r})(df_{21}^0/dr) \tag{4-9-6}$$

For the spherical symmetrical part of the potential of the j-ion, $\psi_j^0(r)$, the Debye and Hückel result given by equation (4-3-17) is employed.

Formal expansion of (4-9-1) leads to a long list of individual terms and it was necessary to devise a test which would segregate terms of like order. The solution of equation (4-9-1) comprises the sum of solutions of equations of the form

$$\nabla\cdot\nabla u_k(r,\theta) - q^2\kappa^2 u_k = e^{-\kappa r}\cos\theta/r^k \tag{4-9-7}$$

Division by κ^2 reduces this equation to a function of the dimensionless independent variable, $\xi = \kappa r$, so that

$$\nabla\cdot\nabla u_k - q^2 u_k = \kappa^{k-2}e^{-\xi}\cos\theta/\xi^k \tag{4-9-8}$$

Hence, if $U_k(\xi,\theta)$ is a solution of

$$\nabla\cdot\nabla U_k - q^2 U_k = e^{-\xi}\cos\theta/\xi^k \tag{4-9-9}$$

the solution of (4-9-7) is $u_k = \kappa^{k-2}U_k$, where U_k is dimensionless. Consequently, a term $e^{-\kappa r}/r^k$ on the right of equation (4-9-1) will give a term κ^{k-2} in the solution multiplied by whatever powers of κ which appear in the coefficient of that term. Application of this procedure selects for the leading terms of the "Ts" of equation (4-9-1) the explicit values given by equations (4-9-2) to (4-9-6). These all yield solutions of the order κ^5 while the first inhomogeneous term in $\partial f_{21}^0/\partial x$ gives a solution of the order of κ^4. Since the latter produces the classical $\sqrt{c}$ in the conductance equation, the leading terms of the "Ts" must yield terms of the order $\kappa\sqrt{c}$ or terms linear in the concentration. They also are shown to lead to terms of the limiting order $c\ln c$, terms which are the limiting forms of exponential integrals which appear upon integration of equation (4-9-7) when $k \geqslant 2$. It is to be noted that terms of the order $c^{3/2}$ and higher are discarded.

The differential equation for the potential is obtained as in Section 3b by eliminating the distribution functions by means of Poisson's equation with the result that fourth order differential equation of the form

$$(\nabla\cdot\nabla)^2\psi_j' - q^2\kappa^2\nabla\cdot\nabla\psi_j' = \Sigma \text{ (inhomogeneous terms)} \tag{4-9-10}$$

is obtained similar to equations (4-3-27) and (4-3-28). Four boundary conditions are required for the evaluation of the four integration constants arising from the solution of this fourth order equation. Three of these may be derived from the electrostatic requirements that the field must vanish when $r = \infty$ and the field and potential must be continuous at $r = a$ (Chapter (3), Section (5)). Thus

$$(\partial\psi'/\partial r)_{r=\infty} = 0 \qquad (4\text{-}9\text{-}11)$$

$$\psi'_{(a-0)} = \psi'_{(a+0)} ; \qquad (\partial\psi'/\partial r)_{a-0} = (\partial\psi'/\partial r)_{a+0} \qquad (4\text{-}9\text{-}12)$$

The fourth boundary condition on the other hand is a hydrodynamic one and rests on the model that the ions are rigid spheres of radius, a, which cannot interpenetrate. This condition is explicitly introduced by requiring that the radial component of the relative velocity of any two ions vanishes at contact. Thus

$$[(f_{ij}\mathbf{v}_{ij} - f_{ji}\mathbf{v}_{ji})\cdot\mathbf{r}]_{r=a} = 0 \qquad (4\text{-}9\text{-}13)$$

In order to complete the integration of equation (4-9-10) including all the inhomogeneous terms, it is necessary to obtain an explicit expression for the velocity term, $T(v)$ given by equation (4-9-6). This problem was originally solved by Debye and Hückel who stated their boundary conditions in terms of Stokes' radius. Owing to the quantitative failure of Walden's rule Fuoss and Onsager regard this choice as hazardous and state their boundary conditions in terms of the distance parameter, a. An external electrical field will exert a force per unit volume on the ions of the solution which will be transmitted to the solvent. This effect will produce a velocity field v in the solution which will depend on the local concentration around each ion, n_{ji}, rather than on the average concentration, n_i. Evaluation of this velocity field and subsequent computation of $T(v)$ makes possible a complete and rigorous solution of the differential equation for the potential including all the higher inhomogeneous terms given by equations (4-9-2) to (4-9-6).

Upon the basis of this comprehensive analysis $\Delta\mathbf{X}_1 = -\nabla\psi'_{1(r=0)}$ is computed (Section (3)) and subsequently, the equation for the conductance of a symmetrical electrolyte. The electrophoresis term, $\beta^*\sqrt{c}$, is simply replaced by $\beta^*\sqrt{c}/(1 + \kappa a) = \beta^*\sqrt{c} - \beta^*\sqrt{c}\kappa a/(1 + \kappa a)$ because the coefficient of the transcendental term (Equation (4-3-22)) $n_\sigma e_\sigma^2 k_\sigma \sim n_\sigma e_\sigma^3$ vanishes. As a result, the conductance equation becomes

$$\Lambda = [\Lambda^0 - \beta^*\sqrt{c}/(1 + \kappa a)][1 + \Delta X/X] \qquad (4\text{-}9\text{-}14)$$

which upon introduction of the force term yields the final result

$$\Lambda = \Lambda^0 - (\alpha^*\Lambda^0 + \beta^*)\sqrt{c} + cB(\kappa a) \qquad (4\text{-}9\text{-}15)$$

$$B(\kappa a) = \frac{\kappa^2 a^2 b^2}{c}\left(\frac{1 + 2b}{b^2}\phi_1 - \phi_2\right)\Lambda^0$$

$$\qquad\qquad\qquad\qquad (4\text{-}9\text{-}16)$$

$$+ \frac{\beta^*\kappa ab}{\sqrt{c}}\left(\phi_3 + \frac{\phi_4}{b}\right) + \alpha^*\beta^*$$

where b is Bjerrum's function

$$b = \frac{e_1 e_2}{aDkT} > 0 \qquad (4\text{-}9\text{-}17)$$

For purposes of numerical calculation, ϕ_1, ϕ_2, ϕ_3 and ϕ_4 are given as functions of κa in Chapter (5) Table (5-3-1a).

The final result of this derivation expressed by equations (4-9-15) and (4-9-16) is not without its limitations. The effects of changes in viscosity and dielectric constant with electrolyte concentration have been discarded as well as co-volume correction. A kinetic effect due to non-zero velocity of colliding ions was omitted. The discontinous nature of the solvent has been ignored. Linear superposition of field was assumed (Chapter (2), Section (4)). These and other effects which may introduce linear and higher terms in concentration limit the use of equation (4-9-15) to the dilute solution range.

This limitation as to electrolyte concentration deserves critical analysis. It is pointed out that purely mathematical approximations limit the validity of the equations to values of κa less than about 0.3. In addition, it is pointed by Fuoss and Onsager that the interionic attraction theory has definite physical limitations at κa equals 0.3, or even less. For aqueous solutions, κa is numerically almost equal to $c^{1/2}$ for 1-1 electrolytes. As a result $c = 0.1N$ corresponds to a value of $1/\kappa$ of approximately $3a$. Now the whole theory is based on the Poisson-Boltzmann equation which presupposes that all the ions except the reference one may be replaced by a continuous charge distribution. Now $1/\kappa$ is the distance at which the charge density of the ionic atmosphere reaches its maximum. Consequently, the approximation involved in employing a continuum when $1/\kappa$ reaches the order of a few ionic diameters is indeed hazardous. In this situation, the total charge in the whole atmosphere equals one unit charge and hence the approach of any one ion to the central ion will produce a large fluctuation in potential. Because of this fundamental limitation, the application of equation (4-9-15) is limited to concentrations less than $0.02N$ which corresponds to values of $(1/\kappa) > 7a$.

Considering the very elaborate analysis required to achieve the limiting result expressed by equation (4-9-15) to (4-9-17), one must agree with the concluding statement of Fuoss and Onsager that "the problem of concentrated solutions cannot, in our opinion, be solved by any extension of the present theory based on smoothed ionic distribution. The approach must start by an adequate theory for fused salts, which must then be followed by the theoretical treatment of the effect on the radial distribution function of adding uncharged (solvent) molecules. At high concentrations, the distribution function must be a damped periodic function of interionic distances; as the concentration decreases, this function must approach the $e^{-\kappa r}$ type of function as the asymptotic limit. Unfortunately, knowledge of this limit does not permit prediction of the function of which it is the limit."

Chapter (5)

Numerical Compilations of Physical Constants, Characteristic Slopes, and Mathematical Functions

As an unique feature of this monograph, we have collected, in this chapter, the final equations resulting from the interionic attraction theory, and reduced them to forms suitable for practical applications. Numerical values of important limiting and characteristic slopes have been tabulated under the appropriate equations, and physical constants and mathematical functions which occur frequently have also been recorded. We believe that a careful study of the contents of this chapter will be of considerable value to anyone concerned with applications of the theory, because many of the expressions are in more convenient forms than those previously given, and the tables have been assembled here for the first time.

(1) Fundamental Physical Constants

In a work of this kind which involves numerical calculations extending over a period of years, it is neither possible nor desirable to maintain all of the nearly 200 tables of data, extrapolated properties and numerical parameters in complete agreement with the latest determinations of the fundamental physical constants. In the first place almost a thousand of the original papers referred to in this monograph are experimental, and a majority of these are based upon the values of the physical constants given in The International Critical Tables.[1] The first edition conformed with these values. During the past decade an increasing number of papers have reported new measurements, or recalculations of older results in terms of the values of the physical constants recommended by Birge[2] in 1941, or more recently recommended by the Subcommittee on Fundamental Constants of the National Research Council.[3] The major changes, which occurred in the Boltzman constant, the electronic charge, Avagadro's number and the ice point, are large enough to affect our calculations, but are often less than the errors in the physico-chemical data with which they are combined. Our second edition contained tables designed to begin the transition from the older[1] to the newer[2] values. In this third edition all of the theoretical constants and numerical parameters which appear in

[1] "International Critical Tables," Vol. I, p. 17, McGraw-Hill Book Co., New York, 1930.

[2] R. T. Birge, *Rev. Mod. Phys.*, **13**, 233 (1941).

[3] F. D. Rossini, F. T. Gucker, H. L. Johnston, L. Pauling and G. W. Vinal, *J. Am. Chem. Soc.*, **74**, 2699 (1952).

numbered equations throughout the text have been recalculated to conform with the values of the constants recommended by the Subcommittee.[3] Fortunately, almost identical values are obtained if the constants of Birge[2] are used. The Subcommittee's values are given in Table (5-1-1).

TABLE (5-1-1). FUNDAMENTAL PHYSICAL CONSTANTS.*

Symbol	Constant	Value	Units
c	Velocity of light	2.997902×10^{10}	cm sec^{-1}
ϵ	Electronic charge	4.80223×10^{-10}	esu
F	Faraday constant	9.64931×10^{4}	coul gm. equiv^{-1}
	" "	2.30624×10^{4}	cal volt. equiv^{-1}
	" "	2.89277×10^{14}	esu gm. equiv^{-1}
V_0	Ideal gas volume, 0°C. 1 Atm.	2.24146×10^{4}	cm^3 mole^{-1}
T_0	Ice point, 0°C. 1 Atm.	273.16	°Kelvin
R	Gas constant	8.31439	joules deg^{-1} mole^{-1}
	" "	1.98719	cal deg^{-1} mole^{-1}
	" "	82.0567	cm^3 atm deg^{-1} mole^{-1}
N	Avagadro's number	6.02380×10^{23}	molecules mole^{-1}
k	Boltzman's constant	1.380257×10^{-16}	erg deg^{-1} molecule^{-1}
h	Planck's constant	6.62377×10^{-27}	erg sec molecule^{-1}
	Atmosphere, standard normal	1.013250×10^{6}	dynes cm^{-2}
cal	Gram calorie, defined	4.184 (exact)	joules
cal$_{15}$	" "	4.1847	joules
	Liter	1.000028×10^{3}	cm^3
	Ohm	0.999505	internat ohm
	Ampere	1.000165	internat amp
	Volt	0.999670	internat volt
	Coulomb	1.000165	internat coulomb
	Joule	0.999835	internat joule

* All electrical units are absolute unless otherwise indicated. See Ref. (3).

Dielectric Constant

From the point of view of the interionic theory, the most important physical property of a solvent is its dielectric constant. Many studies of this property of water have been made, but measurements of a high dielectric constant in a liquid possessing appreciable conductance are not easy. Bridge measurements are usually conducted at frequencies below 1 or 2 megacycles and require rather elaborate corrections for conductance. Resonance and standing wave methods minimize the effects of conductance by operating at higher frequencies, but involve assumptions regarding the resonator system. Formerly, the results usually credited with the highest precision were obtained by the standing wave[4] and resonance methods[5], and during the last twenty years the majority of American writers on electrolytic solutions have used either the original values of Wyman[5] or the corrected values given by the equation

$$D = 78.54 \,[1 - 4.579 \times 10^{-3} \,(t - 25) + 11.9 \times 10^{-6} \,(t - 25)^2 + 28 \times 10^{-9} \,(t - 25)^3] \tag{5-1-1}$$

[4] F. H. Drake, G. W. Pierce and M. T. Dow, *Phys. Rev.*, **35**, 613 (1930).
[5] J. Wyman, Jr., *Ibid.*, **35**, 623 (1930).

of Wyman and Ingalls[6]. We conformed to this somewhat arbitrary choice in earlier editions. Recently doubt as to the accuracy of these values has been raised by a series of bridge measurements by Malmberg and Maryott[7]. They expressed their results (to within 0.01 unit) by the equation

$$D = 87.740 - 0.40008t + 9.398 \times 10^{-4}t^2 - 1.410 \times 10^{-6}t^3 \quad (5\text{-}1\text{-}2)$$

Comparison with equation (5-1-1) shows a difference of 0.5 % in the absolute value of D at 0°, and about 0.3 % from 20 to 100°. The temperature derivatives, dD/dT, differ by 2 % at 0°, but by less than 1 % above 20°.

TABLE (5-1-2). SOME USEFUL FUNCTIONS OF THE ABSOLUTE TEMPERATURE.
(T = 273.16 + t)

t	$\log T$	$\dfrac{1000}{T}$	$\dfrac{RT \ln 10^{(a)}}{F}$	$\dfrac{RT^2 \ln 10^{(a)}}{10^5}$	$y \times 10^{8\,(b)}$	$z \times 10^{5\,(c)}$
0	2.43642	3.6609	0.054196	3.4142	6708	86
5	2.44430	3.5951	.055188	3.5403	5270	54
10	2.45203	3.5316	.056180	3.6688	3883	30
15	2.45963	3.4703	.057172	3.7995	2543	13
18	2.46413	3.4345	.057767	3.8790	1762	6
20	2.46711	3.4111	.058164	3.9325	1250	3
25	2.47445	3.3539	.059156	4.0678	0	0
30	2.48167	3.2986	.060148	4.2053	−1209	3
35	2.48878	3.2451	.061140	4.3452	−2379	12
40	2.49577	3.1933	.062132	4.4873	−3511	26
45	2.50265	3.1431	.063124	4.6318	−4607	45
50	2.50942	3.0944	.064116	4.7785	−5670	69
55	2.51609	3.0473	.065108	4.9275	−6700	97
60	2.52265	3.0016	.061003	5.0788	−7700	130
70	2.53550	2.9141	.068084	5.3883	−9612	206
80	2.54797	2.8316	.070068	5.7069	−11415	296
90	2.56010	2.7536	.072052	6.0346	−13119	398
100	2.57190	2.6798	.074036	6.3716	−14732	511

[a] $\ln 10 = 2.3026$, $R \ln 10 = 4.5757$

[b] $y = \dfrac{298.16 - T}{2.3026R \times 298.16\,T}$

[c] $z = 298.16y - \dfrac{1}{R} \log \dfrac{298.16}{T}$

Until there has been time for an adequate explanation for the discrepancies between the best bridge and resonance techniques, we will continue to use the Wyman and Ingalls equation (5-1-1) so as to be consistent with the bulk of our source material. The difference between this equation and (5-1-2) is not large, and might be regarded for the present as a measure of the uncertainty in the values. Table (5-1-3) contains useful functions of D calculated from equation (5-1-1).

The dielectric constants of a number of organic solvent-water mixtures[8] are given in Table (5-1-4). For the dielectric constants of pure solvents the

[6] J. Wyman, Jr., and E. N. Ingalls, *J. Am. Chem. Soc.*, **60**, 1182 (1938).

[7] C. G. Malmberg and A. A. Maryott, *J. Research Nat. Bur. Stds.*, **56**, 1 (1956). Compare G. A. Vidulich and R. L. Kay, *J. Phys. Chem.*, **66**, 383 (1962) and Reference 12.

[8] G. Akerlöf, *J. Am. Chem. Soc.*, **54**, 4125 (1932).

reader is referred to the tabulation of Maryott and Smith[9]. Because of its low dielectric constant, neutral character and complete miscibility with water, dioxane is an important solvent for studies of the effect of varying

TABLE (5-1-3). PROPERTIES OF WATER USED IN THE CALCULATION OF THEORETICAL PARAMETERS.

t	D	$\dfrac{-10^6}{D}\dfrac{\partial D}{\partial T}$	DT	$10^3\,\eta$	d	$10^6\,\alpha$	$10^6\,\beta$
0	88.15	4657	24079	17.938	0.999868	−67.9	50.9
5	86.12	4641	23956	15.188	.999992	+15.9	49.4
10	84.15	4625	23828	13.097	.999728	87.9	48.14
15	82.23	4609	23696	11.447	.999129	150.8	47.12
18	81.10	4600	23614	10.603	.998625	185.1	46.61
20	80.36	4594	23559	10.087	.998234	206.6	46.30
25	78.54	4579	23417	8.949	.997075	257.0	45.65
30	76.77	4565	23272	8.004	.995678	303.1	45.14
35	75.04	4553	23123	7.208	.994064	345.7	44.77
40	73.35	4541	22970	6.536	.992247	385.4	44.53
45	71.70	4531	22813	5.970	.990244	422.8	44.39
50	70.10	4523	22653	5.492	.988065	458.0	44.36
55	68.53	4516	22490	5.072	.985722	491.5	44.42
60	67.00	4512	22323	4.699	.983223	523.4	44.56
65	65.51	4510	22153	4.368	.980578	554.2	44.81
70	64.05	4510	21979	4.071	.977791	584	45.12
75	62.62	4514	21802	3.806	.974870	613	45.52
80	61.22	4521	21621	3.570	.971816	642	45.99
85	59.85	4532	21436	3.357	.968635	670	46.53
90	58.51	4547	21248	3.166	....	...	47.13
95	57.19	4566	21055	2.994	....	...	47.8
100	55.90	4590	20859	2.839	....	...	48.5

TABLE (5-1-4). DIELECTRIC CONSTANTS AT 25° OF MIXTURES OF WATER AND (1) METHANOL, (2) ETHANOL, (3) n-PROPANOL, (4) ISO-PROPANOL, (5) ter-BUTANOL, (6) ETHYLENE GLYCOL, (7) GLYCEROL, (8) ACETONE, (9) MANNITOL, (10) SUCROSE, AND (11) DIOXANE.

Water Wt. %	(1)*	(2)	(3)	(4)	(5)	(6)	(7)	(8)	(9)	(10)	(11)
90	74.1	72.8	71.8	71.4	70.0	75.6	75.5	73.0	77.1	76.3	69.69
80	69.2	67.0	64.9	64.1	61.3	72.8	72.9	67.0	75.5	73.6	60.79
70	64.3	61.1	57.7	56.9	52.6	69.8	70.0	61.0		70.9	51.90
60	59.6	55.0	50.3	49.7	43.9	66.6	67.1	54.6		67.9	42.98
50	54.9	49.0	43.0	42.5	35.4	63.2	64.0	48.2		64.2	34.26
40	50.1	43.4	36.4	35.3	27.9	59.4	60.0	41.8		59.9	25.85
30	45.0	38.0	30.7	28.7	21.4	54.7	55.6	35.7		54.2	17.69
20	40.1	32.8	26.1	23.7	16.5	49.3	50.6	29.6			10.71
10	35.7	28.1	22.7	20.3	12.4	43.7	45.5	24.0			5.605
0	31.5	24.3	20.1	18.0	9.9	37.7	40.1	19.1			2.101

* Compare T. T. Jones and R. M. Davies, *Phil. Mag.* [7], **28**: 289, 307 (1939).

dielectric constant upon the properties of ionic solutions. For this reason many properties of dioxane-water mixtures are recorded in Tables

[9] A. A. Maryott and E. R. Smith, "Table of Dielectric Constants of Pure Liquids," National Bureau of Standards Circular 514, Washington, D. C.

(11-1-1A), (11-3-1A), (11-3-2A) and (11-9-1A). The dielectric constant of these mixtures is represented between 0 and 80° by the equation

$$\log D = A - Bt \tag{5-1-3}$$

for which the parameters[10] are given in Table (5-1-5). An equation of this simple form will also represent the dielectric constant of water[7] between 0 and 100° within 0.02 unit.

The pressure derivatives of the dielectric constants of solvents are required for calculating the theoretical parameters of partial molal volumes, compressibilities and expansibilities. For many organic solvents the equation

$$\frac{1}{D}\frac{dD}{dP} = \frac{0.4343AD^{(1)}}{B + P} \tag{5-1-4}$$

TABLE (5-1-5). PARAMETERS FOR THE CALCULATION OF DIELECTRIC CONSTANTS OF DIOXANE-WATER MIXTURES BY EQUATION (5-1-3)

Wt. % Dioxane	A	B	Wt. % Dioxane	A	B
0*	1.9461	0.00205	60	1.4747	.00249
10	1.8969	.00215	70	1.3090	.00245
20	1.8398	.00224	80	1.0860	.00225
30	1.7734	.00233	90	0.7896	.00164
40	1.6935	.00241	95	0.5923	.00100
50	1.5965	.00247	100	0.3234	.00004

* Åkerlöf's results for pure water are included here for comparison. In subsequent calculations we shall always use those given in Table (5-1-3).

proposed by Owen and Brinkley[11] represents the pressure dependence of D up to several thousand atmospheres. To a fairly close approximation, the product of the constants A and $D^{(1)}$, the dielectric constant at $P = 1$, is independent of T, and the constant B has the numerical value given by equation (5-1-7) for the compressibility. The validity of this approximation has not been verified for water for want of sufficient data[12], but the product $0.4343AD^{(1)}$ can be shown to be about 0.1754 from the data of Kyropoulos[13] at 20°, and B, evaluated from compressibility measurements, is given by equation (5-1-7). Using these values of the constants, and assuming that water behaves like organic solvents with respect to equation (5-1-4), the tentative values of the limiting slopes recorded in Table (5-2-5) have been calculated.

[10] G. Akerlöf and O. A. Short, *J. Am. Chem. Soc.*, **58**, 1241 (1936).

[11] B. B. Owen and S. R. Brinkley, Jr., *Phys. Rev.*, **64**, 32 (1943).

[12] Since this paragraph was written, an experimental determination of $d \ln D/dP$ for water from 0 to 70° [B. B. Owen, R. C. Miller, C. E. Milner and H. L. Cogan, *J. Phys. Chem.*, **65**, 2065 (1961)] has shown that equation (5-1-4) is much less satisfactory for water than for other solvents.

Viscosity, Density and Coefficients of Expansibility and Compressibility of Water

The viscosity of the solvent is a factor which often appears in the equations dealing with irreversible processes. Table (5-1-3) contains values of the viscosity of water, and Table (11-1-1A) contains the viscosities of dioxane-water mixtures. These values will be used for consistency throughout the text, but recent measurements[14] at 20° indicate that they may be too high in absolute magnitude by as much as 0.3%.

Between 0 and 42° the density (gm/ml) and coefficient of expansion of water given in Table (5-1-3) are those of Chappuis[15] as expressed by the equation[16]

$$d = 1 - \frac{(t - 3.9863)^2(t + 288.9414)}{508929.2(t + 68.12963)} \tag{5-1-5}$$

Above this range the values are the results of new measurements[17] up to 85°. The coefficient of compressibility was calculated from the Tait[18] equation

$$\beta = \frac{0.4343Cd^{(1)}}{B + P} \tag{5-1-6}$$

for $P = 1$, $0.4343\,Cd^{(1)} = 0.1368$, and values of B (in bars) given by the equation

$$B = 2996.0 + 7.5554(t - 25) - 0.17814(t - 25)^2 + 608 \times 10^{-6}(t - 25)^3 \tag{5-1-7}$$

whose parameters were derived[19] from the compression of water throughout the range 25 to 85°. Outside this range the values of B are extrapolated by this equation, and the corresponding values of β in Table (5-1-3) are less accurate than the others.

[13] S. Kyropoulos, *Z. Physik*, **40**, 507 (1926).

[14] J. F. Swindells, J. R. Coe and T. B. Godfry, *J. Research Nat. Bur. Stds.*, **48**, 1 (1952).

[15] P. Chappuis, "Travaux et Memoires Bur. International Poids et Mesures", **13**, D40 (1907).

[16] L. W. Tilton and J. K. Taylor, *J. Research Nat. Bur. Stds.*, **18**, 205 (1937).

[17] B. B. Owen, J. R. White and J. S. Smith, *J. Am. Chem. Soc.*, **48**, 356 (1956).

[18] References and an extensive discussion of this equation will be found in Chapter (8), Section (7).

[19] The most recent values of B were kindly supplied by Dr. R. E. Gibson in a private communication (1943). The coefficients of equation (5-1-7) were evaluated by Dr. S. R. Brinkley, Jr. *Cf.* R. E. Gibson and O. H. Loeffler, *J. Am. Chem. Soc.*, **63**, 898 (1941).

Ionic Radii

Table (5-1-6) contains values of the radii of some simple ions.

(2) EQUATIONS DERIVED IN CHAPTER (3) FOR THE CALCULATION OF THERMODYNAMIC PROPERTIES FROM THE ELECTROSTATICS OF IONIC ATMOSPHERES

The limiting equation for the mean rational activity coefficient of a strong electrolyte which dissociates into p kinds of ions was shown to be

$$\log f_{\pm} = -\mathcal{S}_{(f)}\sqrt{\Gamma} \tag{3-4-7}$$

where

$$\mathcal{S}_{(f)} = \frac{1}{\nu} \sum_{1}^{p} \nu_j z_j^2 \frac{1.290 \times 10^6}{(DT)^{3/2}} \tag{3-4-8}$$

and

$$\Gamma = \sum_{1}^{s} c_i z_i^2 \tag{3-1-3}$$

TABLE (5-1-6). IONIC RADII (ANGSTROM UNITS) FROM CRYSTALLOGRAPHIC DATA.*

F^- 1.341	Li^+ 0.607	Ag^+ 1.26	Cd^{++} 0.97
Cl^- 1.806	Na^+ 0.958	Mg^{++} 0.65	Zn^{++} 0.74
Br^- 1.951	K^+ 1.331	Ca^{++} 0.99	In^{+++} 0.81
I^- 2.168	Rb^+ 1.484	Sr^{++} 1.13	La^{+++} 1.15
	Cs^+ 1.656	Ba^{++} 1.35	Tl^{+++} 0.95

* L. Pauling, "Nature of the Chemical Bond," Chapter X, Cornell University Press, Ithaca, New York (1939).

Values of the theoretical limiting slope, $\mathcal{S}_{(f)}$, for aqueous solutions at various temperatures are given in Table (5-2-1). The values of (DT) employed in the calculation of these slopes were taken from column (4) of Table (5-1-3). For simplicity in tabulation the valence factor has been written

$$w \equiv \frac{1}{\nu} \sum_{1}^{p} \nu_j z_j^2 \tag{5-2-1}$$

If the electrolyte dissociates into only two kinds of ions ($p = 2$), w reduces to $|z_1 z_2|$ in general, and becomes unity for 1-1 electrolytes.

In the important special case of solutions containing only a single electrolyte, Γ equals $c \sum_{1}^{p} \nu_j z_j^2$, and the limiting law may be written

$$\log f_{\pm} = -\mathcal{S}_{(f)}\sqrt{c} \tag{5-2-2}$$

where

$$\mathcal{S}_{(f)} = \frac{1}{\nu} \left(\sum_{1}^{p} \nu_j z_j^2 \right)^{3/2} \frac{1.290 \times 10^6}{(DT)^{3/2}} \tag{5-2-3}$$

The values of $\mathfrak{S}_{(f)}$ given in Table (5-2-1) are expressed in terms of the valence factor

$$w' \equiv \frac{1}{\nu\sqrt{2}} \left(\sum_{1}^{p} \nu_j z_j^2 \right)^{3/2} \tag{5-2-4}$$

The term $\sqrt{2}$ was introduced into this factor so that w' becomes unity for 1-1 electrolytes.

At the high dilutions postulated in the derivation of the limiting law,

TABLE (5-2-1).* DEBYE AND HÜCKEL CONSTANTS FOR AQUEOUS SOLUTIONS.#

$t°C$	$\mathfrak{S}_{(f)} = \dfrac{-\log f_\pm}{\sqrt{\Gamma}}$	$\mathfrak{S}_{(f)} = \dfrac{-\log f_\pm}{\sqrt{c}}$	$A/d = \dfrac{\kappa \, 10^{-8}}{\sqrt{\Gamma}}$	$A'/d = \dfrac{\kappa \, 10^{-8}}{\sqrt{c}}$
0	$0.3453w$	$0.4883w'$	0.2292	$0.3241w''$
5	$.3480w$	$.4821w'$	$.2297$	$.3249w''$
10	$.3507w$	$.4960w'$	$.2304$	$.3258w''$
15	$.3537w$	$.5002w'$	$.2310$	$.3267w''$
18	$.3555w$	$.5028w'$	$.2314$	$.3273w''$
20	$.3568w$	$.5046w'$	$.2316$	$.3276w''$
25	$.3600w$	$.5091w'$	$.2324$	$.3286w''$
30	$.3634w$	$.5139w'$	$.2331$	$.3297w''$
35	$.3669w$	$.5189w'$	$.2338$	$.3307w''$
40	$.3706w$	$.5241w'$	$.2346$	$.3318w''$
45	$.3744w$	$.5295w'$	$.2355$	$.3330w''$
50	$.3784w$	$.5351w'$	$.2363$	$.3342w''$
55	$.3825w$	$.5410w'$	$.2372$	$.3354w''$
60	$.3868w$	$.5470w'$	$.2380$	$.3366w''$
70	$.3959w$	$.5599w'$	$.2399$	$.3392w''$
80	$.4058w$	$.5739w'$	$.2418$	$.3420w''$
90	$.4166w$	$.5891w'$	$.2440$	$.3450w''$
100	$.4282w$	$.6056w'$	$.2462$	$.3482w''$

* For definitions of w, w' and w'', see equations (5-2-1), (5-2-4) and (5-2-10).
# Limiting slopes in important mixed solvents are given in Table (11-3-1A).

the ratio of the volume and weight concentrations becomes d_0, the density of the pure solvent. Thus, by equation (3-4-10a)

$$\log f_\pm = -\sqrt{2d_0} \, \mathfrak{S}_{(f)} \sqrt{\mu} \tag{5-2-5}$$

in general, and

$$\log f_\pm = -\sqrt{d_0} \, \mathfrak{S}_{(f)} \sqrt{m} \tag{5-2-6}$$

for solutions containing only a single electrolyte

At moderate dilutions where the ionic parameter "a" (the "mean distance of nearest approach" of the ions) can no longer be neglected, the activity coefficient is given by

$$\log f_\pm = -\frac{\mathfrak{S}_{(f)} \sqrt{\Gamma}}{1 + A\sqrt{\Gamma}} \tag{3-5-8}$$

The term $A\sqrt{\Gamma}$ is equal to κa. It is convenient to express the ionic parameter in Ångstrom units, in which case it is written $\mathring{a}$. Accordingly,

$$A = \mathring{a}\kappa \frac{10^{-8}}{\sqrt{\Gamma}} = \mathring{a}\frac{35.56}{(DT)^{1/2}} \tag{5-2-7}$$

Values of $\kappa 10^{-8}\Gamma^{-1/2}$ calculated by (3-1-2) are recorded in Table (5-2-1).

In solutions containing only a single electrolyte equation (3-5-8) may be used in the restricted form

$$\log f_{\pm} = -\frac{\mathcal{S}_{(f)}\sqrt{c}}{1 + A'\sqrt{c}} \tag{5-2-8}$$

where

$$A' = \mathring{a}\frac{\kappa 10^{-8}}{\sqrt{c}} \tag{5-2-9}$$

The values of $\kappa 10^{-8}c^{-1/2}$ given in Table (5-2-1) are expressed in terms of the valence factor

$$w'' \equiv \left(\frac{1}{2}\sum_{1}^{p} \nu_j z_j^2\right)^{1/2} = \frac{w'}{w} \tag{5-2-10}$$

It should be noted that for binary electrolytes ($|z_1| = |z_2| = z$), the valence factor w'' reduces to z.

Computations involving the so-called "extended terms" of the Debye-Hückel theory are carried out with equations (3-6-4) to (3-6-6), containing the contributions to $\log f_{\pm}$ of higher terms in the expansion of the function, $\exp(-e_i\psi_i^0/kT)$, which were neglected in the derivation of equation (3-4-7). Symmetrical valence types of electrolytes are treated by equation (3-6-4). Values of

$$10^3[\tfrac{1}{2}X_3(\kappa a) - 2Y_3(\kappa a)]$$

and

$$10^5[\tfrac{1}{2}X_5(\kappa a) - 4Y_5(\kappa a)]$$

are recorded as functions of (κa) in Table (5-2-2) for values of κa varying from 0.005 to 0.4.[20] Equations (3-6-5) and (3-6-6) are used for unsymmetrical types of electrolytes. Values of

$$10^2[\tfrac{1}{2}X_2(\kappa a) - Y_2(\kappa a)]$$

and

$$10^3[\tfrac{1}{2}X_3^*(\kappa a) - 2Y_3^*(\kappa a)]$$

[20] T. H. Gronwall, V. K. LaMer, and K. Sandved, *Physik. Z.*, **29**, 358 (1928). Note that in this paper, $x_i = \kappa a$.

are also given in Table (5-2-2) for values of κa varying from 0.005 to 0.4.[21] Calculation of the extended terms is complicated by the necessity of successive arithmetical approximations. The magnitude of "a" must be

TABLE (5-2-2). EXTENDED TERMS OF THE DEBYE-HÜCKEL THEORY.

$x = \kappa a$	$10^3[\frac{1}{4}X_3 - 2Y_3]$	$10^5[\frac{1}{4}X_5 - 4Y_5]$	$10^2[\frac{1}{4}X_2 - Y_2]$	$10^3[\frac{1}{4}X_3^* - 2Y_3^*]$
0.	0.00000	0.00000	0.000000	0.000000
.005	− .00092	− .00107	− .001482	.000009
.01	− .00351	− .00416	− .004797	.000071
.02	− .01239	− .01487	− .014784	.000423
.03	− .02497	− .02985	− .027666	.001264
.04	− .04014	− .04725	− .042363	.002693
0.05	− .05711	− .06564	− .058209	.004750
.06	− .07522	− .08394	− .074748	.007457
.07	− .09403	− .10138	− .091660	.010809
.08	− .11316	− .11737	− .108703	.014766
.09	− .13231	− .13153	− .125699	.019291
0.10	− .15130	− .14363	− .142514	.024335
.11	− .16992	− .15356	− .15905	.02986
.12	− .18802	− .16126	− .17522	.03580
.13	− .20355	− .16680	− .19097	.04211
.14	− .22240	− .17023	− .20626	.04874
0.15	− .23853	− .17166	− .22105	.05563
.16	− .25391	− .17123	− .23533	.06274
.17	− .26851	− .16910	− .24908	.07002
.18	− .28231	− .16543	− .26230	.07743
.19	− .29530	− .16037	− .27497	.08493
0.20	− .30750	− .15409	− .28710	.09248
.21	− .31892	− .14674	− .29870	.10005
.22	− .32953	− .13847	− .30977	.10761
.23	− .33943	− .12942	− .32032	.11513
.24	− .34859	− .11973	− .33036	.12258
0.25	− .35703	− .10953	− .33991	.12994
.26	− .36478	− .09895	− .34896	.13720
.27	− .37187	− .08804	− .35755	.14433
.28	− .37832	− .07696	− .36567	.15132
.29	− .38416	− .06577	− .37335	.15816
0.30	− .38942	− .05453	− .38060	.16482
.31	− .39411	− .04335	− .38743	.17132
.32	− .39827	− .03222	− .39386	.17762
.33	− .40193	− .02131	− .39990	.18374
.34	− .40510	− .01053	− .40557	.18965
0.35	− .40780	− .00001	− .41087	.19536
36	− .41007	+ .01027	− .41583	.20087
.37	− .41193	+ .02022	− .42045	.20617
.38	− .41339	+ .02986	− .42475	.21116
.39	− .41448	+ .03917	− .42875	.21613
0.40	− .41525	+ .0481	− .43244	.22080

known to evaluate the functions, and they in turn must be known to determine "a." In later discussions some applications of these terms will be considered in detail. The ratios recorded in the last two columns of Table (5-2-1) readily permit the estimation of κ from Γ or c.

The application of the cluster theory led to an alternative representation of the activity coefficient in terms of the a-parameter in dilute solutions.

[21] V. K. LaMer, T. H. Gronwall, and L. J. Greiff, *J. Phys. Chem.*, **35**, 2245 (1931).

In Chapter (3) Section (6) it was shown that a special molar activity coefficient, $y'_\pm$, was given by

$$\ln y'_\pm = -\frac{n_2 \epsilon^2 \kappa}{2kDT} - \frac{A}{n_2} \sum_{\mu \geq 0} \frac{(-1)^\mu n_\mu^2}{A^\mu} b_\mu(\kappa a) \tag{3-6-7}$$

in which μ is a running index. The valence factor

$$n_\mu = \frac{1}{\nu} \sum_1^p \nu_i z_i^\mu \tag{3-6-8}$$

becomes w defined by equation (5-2-1) for $\mu = 2$, and the first term on the right in equation (3-6-7) can be identified with the limiting term, 2.303 $\mathbf{S}_{(f)}\sqrt{\Gamma}$ of the Debye-Hückel theory. The parameter A is given by the equation

$$A = akDT/\epsilon^2 \tag{3-6-9}$$

where a is the distance of closest approach. Values of the function $b_\mu(\kappa a)$ have been calculated by Poirier[22] up to b_{16}, and these are recorded in Table (5-2-2a) for round values of κa (b_1 is zero for all values of κa). The difference between the usual activity coefficient, $y_\pm$ defined by equation (1-8-6), and the $y'_\pm$ of equation (3-6-7) is defined by

$$\ln y_\pm - \ln y'_\pm = -\frac{1}{RT} \int_{P_0}^{P_0+P} \bar{V}_2 \, dP \tag{3-6-11}$$

and is very small in dilute solutions. Values of this difference for several salts of different valence types are compared in Table (3-6-1).

As in the case of other extensions of the limiting law, the practical application of the preceding equations involves evaluation of the a-parameter from activity coefficient data. The first step is to convert the values of $\ln y_\pm$ to $\ln y'_\pm$. This can usually be done with acceptable accuracy by linear interpolation of the differences $\ln y_\pm - \ln y'_\pm$ given for the same valence type salt in Table (3-6-1), or more accurately by the use of equation (3-6-11). In order to make the next step as simple as possible, Poirier has calculated $\ln y'_\pm$ for various values of A at the particular concentrations, 0.10, 0.05, 0.01 and 0.01 which he has shown to be the maximum concentrations at which equation (3-6-7) is valid for 1-1, 2-1, 3-1 and 2-2 valence type electrolytes respectively. These values of $\ln y'_\pm$ are given in Table (5-2-2b), and if $\ln y'_\pm$ has been evaluated by direct measurement, or interpolation, at the proper maximum concentration, the table furnishes an immediate means of evaluating A, and then a by equation (3-6-9). Values of the ratio a/A in aqueous solutions will be found in the last column of Table (5-3-1). Subsequently, $\ln y'_\pm$ may be calculated from equations

[22] J. C. Poirier, *J. Chem. Phys.*, **21**, 972 (1953).

(3-6-7) to (3-6-11) at any concentrations less than the maximum value used to determine A.

If the experimental values of ln $y'_\pm$ are not known at concentrations as

TABLE (5-2-2a). THE FUNCTION $10^\mu b_\mu(\kappa a)$ OF MAYER'S THEORY

κa	$b_0(\kappa a)$	$10^2 b_2(\kappa a)$	$10^3 b_3(\kappa a)$	$10^4 b_4(\kappa a)$	$10^5 b_5(\kappa a)$	$10^6 b_6(\kappa a)$	$10^7 b_7(\kappa a)$	$10^8 b_8(\kappa a)$
0.01	−0.000033	−0.004930	0.045273	0.034447	0.037056	0.041428	0.044177	0.043781
.03	−0.000300	−0.043554	0.253519	0.239245	0.268721	0.300299	0.315751	0.307176
.05	−0.000833	−0.11748	0.52052	0.534446	0.609117	0.675111	0.697587	0.665328
.07	−0.001633	−0.22471	0.800544	0.859069	0.981491	1.074299	1.090580	1.016414
.10	−0.003333	−0.44221	1.200784	1.329711	1.50674	1.609645	1.582799	1.424580
.16	−0.008533	−1.05392	1.83504	2.04343	2.22224	2.23208	2.040950	1.696036
.20	−0.013333	−1.57145	2.11451	2.31219	2.41949	2.31352	2.000368	1.562944
.26	−0.022533	−2.47908	2.33770	2.44049	2.37965	2.08847	1.636399	1.142536
.30	−0.030000	−3.15535	2.37813	2.38430	2.19952	1.80601	1.30591	0.82667
.40	−0.053333	−5.02868	2.21626	1.95204	1.51552	0.99373	0.52285	0.189250
.50	−0.083333	−7.07573	1.84322	1.36290	0.81756	0.33581	0.015386	−0.134420
.60	−0.120000	−9.21695	1.40326	0.80959	0.28518	−0.064620	−0.217732	−0.230093
.70	−0.163333	−11.39883	0.98000	0.37083	−0.053349	−0.252340	−0.276476	−0.214408
.80	−0.213333	−13.58670	0.6146	0.061394	−0.232780	−0.304238	−0.250685	−0.162947
.90	−0.270000	−15.75921	0.3217	−0.133366	−0.302670	−0.284655	−0.196198	−0.110918
1.00	−0.333333	−17.90412	0.1011	−0.242135	−0.306387	−0.235921	−0.140916	−0.070395
1.20	−0.480000	−22.09155	−0.1610	−0.292921	−0.231341	−0.133112	−0.062188	−0.024767
1.40	−0.653333	−26.14360	−0.2549	−0.243381	−0.142868	−0.064569	−0.024138	−0.007755
1.60	−0.853333	−30.08152	−0.2577	−0.172827	−0.079124	−0.028607	−0.008630	−0.002250
1.80	−1.080000	−33.93442	−0.2215	−0.112193	−0.040839	−0.011911	−0.002915	−0.000616
2.00	−1.333333	−37.72868	−0.1725	−0.068658	−0.020085	−0.004746	−0.000946	—
2.50	−2.083333	−47.08556	−0.0753	−0.017090	−0.002227	−0.000417	—	—
3.00	−3.000000	−56.38936	−0.0276	−0.003682	−0.000382	—	—	—

κa	$10^9 b_9(\kappa a)$	$10^{10} b_{10}(\kappa a)$	$10^{11} b_{11}(\kappa a)$	$10^{12} b_{12}(\kappa a)$	$10^{13} b_{13}(\kappa a)$	$10^{14} b_{14}(\kappa a)$	$10^{15} b_{15}(\kappa g)$	$10^{16} b_{16}(\kappa a)$
.01	0.040265	0.034007	0.026805	0.019619	0.013419	0.008607	0.005196	0.002961
.03	0.275601	0.228419	0.176348	0.125938	0.084022	0.052562	0.030937	0.017186
.05	0.583625	0.472350	0.356818	0.248410	0.161504	0.098423	0.056418	0.030516
.07	0.870741	0.687478	0.507275	0.343894	0.217611	0.129015	0.071915	0.037809
.10	1.17517	0.89181	0.633269	0.411424	0.249213	0.141273	0.075204	0.037712
.16	1.28468	0.89057	0.576305	0.338393	0.184127	0.093088	0.043805	0.019212
.20	1.106758	0.71279	0.425010	0.227617	0.111311	0.049598	0.019943	0.007089
.26	0.710120	0.391221	0.175056	0.077052	0.023963	0.003238	−0.002661	−0.003067
.30	0.451820	0.206443	0.058188	0.009133	−0.010646	−0.012623	−0.009140	−0.005398
.40	0.005280	−0.065893	−0.083716	−0.058515	−0.036513	−0.020023	−0.009911	−0.004499
.50	−0.163163	−0.132753	−0.094474	−0.052364	−0.026699	−0.012391	−0.005294	−0.002100
.60	−0.176809	−0.112467	−0.065850	−0.031811	−0.014187	−0.005811	−0.002204	−0.000779
.70	−0.135972	−0.074288	−0.037792	−0.016235	−0.006444	−0.002358	−0.000801	−0.000254
.80	−0.089616	−0.043146	−0.019420	−0.007475	−0.002659	−0.000874	−0.000267	−0.000076
.90	−0.053904	−0.023116	−0.009280	−0.003212	−0.001027	−0.000304	−0.000084	−0.000022
1.00	−0.030491	−0.011709	−0.004211	−0.001313	−0.000378	−0.000101	−0.000025	—
1.20	−0.008628	−0.002671	−0.000778	−0.000198	−0.000046	−0.000010	—	—
1.40	−0.002187	−0.000553	−0.000130	−0.000027	—	—	—	—
1.60	−0.000516	—	—	—	—	—	—	—

high as the maxima upon which Table (5-2-2b) is based, the determination of A involves successive approximations which make use of Table (5-2-2b) and special approximate forms of equations (3-6-7) and (3-6-11). For the details of this more complicated procedure the reader is referred to the article (II) by Poirier.[22]

TABLE (5-2-2b). THE QUANTITY, $\ln y'_\pm$ AS A FUNCTION OF THE PARAMETER, A.

A	(1 − 1) $(c = 0.1)$ $-\ln y'_\pm$	(2 − 1) $(c = 0.05)$ $-\ln y'_\pm$	(3 − 1) $(c = 0.01)$		(2 − 2) $(c = 0.01)$	
			A	$-\ln y'_\pm$	A	$-\ln y'_\pm$
0.3	0.3125	—	0.8	0.5994	0.470	1.090
.35	0.2984	—	.82	0.5984	.48	1.058
.40	0.2855	—	.84	0.5904	.49	1.029
.45	0.2731	0.6714	.86	0.5860	.50	1.003
.5	0.2604	0.6481	.88	0.5817	.51	0.980
.56	0.2444	0.6240	.90	0.5775	.52	0.959
.6	0.2331	0.6091	.94	0.5691	.53	0.941
.66	0.2147	0.5876	.98	0.5608	.54	0.924
.7	0.2014	0.5733	1.02	0.5525	.55	0.909
.76	0.1796	0.5515	1.06	0.5442	.56	0.895
.8	0.1637	0.5365	1.10	0.5357	.57	0.882
.86	0.1376	0.5129	1.14	0.5270	.58	0.870
.9	0.1185	0.4964	1.18	0.5182	.59	0.859
.94	0.0980	0.4790	1.22	0.5091	.60	0.849
1.	0.0644	0.4512	1.26	0.4998	.63	0.822
1.2	−0.0754	0.3404	1.30	0.4902	.65	0.807

Functions of Bjerrum's Theory[23] of the Association of Ions

Equation (3-7-13) relates the ionization constant with the dielectric constant and the function $Q(b)$. Thus

$$K^{-1} = \frac{4\pi N}{1000} \left(\frac{|z_1 z_2| \epsilon^2}{kDT} \right)^3 Q(b) \tag{3-7-13}$$

where b and $Q(b)$ are given by

$$b = \frac{|z_1 z_2| \epsilon^2}{aDkT} \tag{3-7-7}$$

$$Q(b) = \int_2^b e^Y Y^{-4} \, dY \tag{3-7-14}$$

$$= \frac{1}{6} \left\{ e^2 - Ei(2) + Ei(b) - \frac{e^b}{b}\left(1 + \frac{1}{b} + \frac{2}{b^2} \right) \right\}$$

Values of $Ei(b)$ to $b = 15$ were obtained by Bjerrum from tables. Values for b from 15 to 80 were obtained by Fuoss and Kraus,[24] who used the asymptotic expansion

$$Ei(x) = \frac{e^x}{x} \left(1 + \frac{1}{x} + \frac{1 \cdot 2}{x^2} + \frac{1 \cdot 2 \cdot 3}{x^3} + \cdots \right) \tag{5-2-11}$$

Taking the logarithm and neglecting the term, $(1/6\{e^2 - Ei(2)\}) = 0.41$, the equation for $\log Q(b)$ becomes

$$\log Q(b) \simeq 0.4343b - 4 \log b + \log (1 + \delta) \tag{5-2-12}$$

[23] N. Bjerrum, *Kgl. Danske Vidensk. Selskab.*, **7**, No. 9 (1926).
[24] R. M. Fuoss and C. A. Kraus, *J. Am. Chem. Soc.*, **55**, 1019 (1933).

where

$$\delta = \frac{4}{b} + \frac{4 \cdot 5}{b^2} + \frac{4 \cdot 5 \cdot 6}{b^3} + \cdots \qquad (5\text{-}2\text{-}13)$$

This approximation causes an error in log $Q(b)$ for b equals 15, but this error decreases rapidly with increasing b. Values of log $Q(b)$ in Table (5-2-3) were obtained from these results.

TABLE (5-2-3). THE FUNCTION log $Q(b)$ OF BJERRUM'S THEORY.

b	log $Q(b)$	b	log $Q(b)$	b	log $Q(b)$
2	$-\infty$	10	0.655	40	11.01
2.5	-0.728	12	1.125	45	12.99
3	-0.489	14	1.680	50	14.96
4	-0.260	16	2.275	55	16.95
5	-0.124	18	2.92	60	18.98
6	$+0.016$	20	3.59	65	21.02
7	0.152	25	5.35	70	23.05
8	0.300	30	7.19	75	25.01
9	0.470	35	9.08	80	27.15

Functions of the Fuoss and Kraus Theory of Triple Ion Formation[25]

We have shown [Chapter (3), Section (7)] that the constant, K_3, of triple ion dissociation represented by

$$[C^+A^-C^+]^+ \rightleftharpoons [C^+A^-]^0 + C^+$$
$$[A^-C^+A^-]^- \rightleftharpoons [C^+A^-]^0 + A^-$$

may be computed by the equation

$$K_3^{-1} = \frac{2\pi N a_3^3}{1000} I(b_3) \qquad (3\text{-}7\text{-}25)$$

where

$$b_3 = \frac{\epsilon^2}{a_3 D k T} \qquad (3\text{-}7\text{-}7)$$

Table (5-2-4) contains $I(b_3)$ and log $I(b_3)$ at values of b_3 from 3.5 to 36.6. The last column contains values of $X = R/a_3$ where R is the characteristic distance which determines whether or not triple ions can form.

Limiting Slopes for the Relative Partial Molal Heat Content and Heat Capacity in Aqueous Solutions

The relative partial molal heat content and heat capacity of an electrolyte have been shown to vary with the concentration according to the equations

$$\bar{L}_2 = \bar{H}_2 - \bar{H}_2^0 = \mathcal{S}_{(H)}\sqrt{\Gamma} \qquad (3\text{-}8\text{-}9)$$

and

$$\bar{J}_2 = \bar{C}_{p_2} - \bar{C}_{p_2}^0 = \mathcal{S}_{(c_p)}\sqrt{\Gamma} \qquad (3\text{-}8\text{-}10)$$

[25] R. M. Fuoss and C. A. Kraus, *J. Am. Chem. Soc.*, **55**, 2387 (1933).

According to equation (3-8-6), $\mathfrak{S}_{(H)}$ is a function of D, T and α, the coefficient of expansion of the solution. $\mathfrak{S}_{(c_p)}$ is a more complicated function of the same variables, and is calculated by equations (3-8-11) to (3-8-13). The nature of these functions is such that the magnitudes of $\mathfrak{S}_{(H)}$ and $\mathfrak{S}_{(c_p)}$ are very sensitive to experimental uncertainties in measuring the temperature coefficient of D. Consequently the values of these slopes given in the literature show considerable discrepancy, depending upon the sources of the dielectric constant data. Throughout the decades, 1920 to 1940, which witnessed phenomenal growth in the theory and techniques of thermochemistry, the values of D used in estimating theoretical slopes were based upon measurements of Kockel[26] and of Wyman.[27] Readers studying the literature of this period are referred to earlier editions of this monograph, or to Harned and Hecker[28], for values of $\mathfrak{S}_{(H)}$ and $\mathfrak{S}_{(c_p)}$ based

TABLE (5-2-4). Log $I(b_3)$, $I(b_3)$ AND $X = R/a_3$ AS FUNCTIONS OF b_3.

b_3	$\log I(b_3)$	$\log I(b_3) - 3 \log b_3$	$I(b_3)$	X
8/3	$-\infty$	$-\infty$	0	1.0
3.5	0.096	-1.536	1.25	1.225
5	.668	-1.429	4.66	1.56
10	1.534	-1.466	34.2	2.46
15	2.183	-1.345	152.4	3.17
20	2.894	-1.009	784.	3.76
25	3.732	-0.462	5.40×10^3	4.28
30	4.634	$+0.203$	4.30×10^4	4.75
35	5.565	$+0.933$	3.67×10^5	5.19
36.6	5.878	$+1.187$	7.55×10^5	5.33

$I(b_3) = 0$, when $X = 1$, so that on a plot of $\log I(b_3)$ versus b_3, $\log I(b_3)$ is asymptotic to the vertical line at $b_3 = 8/3$. This means that triple ions form when $b_3 > 8/3$, and are unstable when $b_3 \le 8/3$.

upon the measurements of Wyman.[27] In 1938, Wyman and Ingalls[29] corrected Wyman's results for expansion of the resonator used in the measurements, and these corrected values enjoyed increasingly widespread acceptance[30] up to the present.

It is also convenient to write the limiting equations in the forms

$$\bar{L}_2 = \bar{H}_2 - \bar{H}_2^0 = \mathfrak{S}_{(H)}\sqrt{c} \tag{5-2-14}$$

and

$$\bar{J}_2 = \bar{C}_{p_2} - \bar{C}_{p_2}^0 = \mathfrak{S}_{(c_p)}\sqrt{c} \tag{5-2-15}$$

[26] L. Kockel, *Ann. Physik*, **77**, 417 (1925).

[27] J. Wyman, *Phys. Rev.*, **35**, 623 (1930).

[28] H. S. Harned and J. C. Hecker, *J. Am. Chem. Soc.*, **35**, 4838 (1933).

[29] J. Wyman and E. N. Ingalls, *Ibid.*, **60**, 1182 (1938).

[30] In their survey, "Table of Dielectric Constants of Liquids", Natl. Bureau Standards Circular 514, Washington (1951), A. A. Maryott and E. R. Smith selected equation (5-1-1) to represent the dielectric constant of water. The shift to equation (5-1-2) was proposed in 1956.

which apply to solutions containing only a single electrolyte. Values of $S_{(H)}$ and $S_{(C_p)}$ are recorded in Table (5-2-5) for 1-1 type electrolytes. For higher valence types the limiting slopes must be multiplied by the factor $\nu w'/2$. These values are based upon D represented by equation (5-1-1), α from Table (5-1-3), and the physical constants given in Table (5-1-1). They are consistent with much of the recent literature on aqueous solutions between 0 and 45°, but above this range the new values of α given in Table (5-1-3) differ significantly from the widely used values in the International Critical Tables.[31]

The new measurements of D at the National Bureau of Standards[32]

TABLE (5-2-5). THEORETICAL COEFFICIENTS FOR VARIOUS PARTIAL MOLAL PROPERTIES OF UNI-UNIVALENT* ELECTROLYTES IN AQUEOUS SOLUTIONS.

$t°$	$S_{(H)}$	$S_{(C_p)}$	$S_{(V)}$	$10^3\,S_{(K)}$	$10^3\,S_{(E)}$	h
0	509	6.5	3.7	1.7	−5.0	−0.0222
5	543	7.1	3.7	1.6	−1.5	0.0051
10	580	7.7	3.7	1.6	1.6	.0275
15	620	8.2	3.7	1.5	4.5	.0462
18	645	8.5	3.7	1.5	6.1	.0559
20	663	8.7	3.7	1.5	7.1	.0619
25	708	9.2	3.8	1.5	9.6	.0752
30	756	9.7	3.8	1.5	12	.0866
35	806	10.3	3.9	1.5	14	.0966
40	860	10.9	4.0	1.5	17	.1054
45	917	11.6	4.1	1.6	19	.1130
50	978	12.4	4.2	1.6	21	.1196
55	1043	13.2	4.3	1.7	24	.1255
60	1113	14.1	4.4	1.7	26	.1306
65	1188	15.2	4.6	1.8	29	.1350
70	1268	16.4	4.7	1.9	31	.1389
75	1355	17.7	4.9	2.0	34	.1422
80	1449	19.2	5.1	2.0	37	.1449
85	1551	20.9	5.3	2.1	40	.1472

* For electrolytes of higher valence types multiply the limiting slopes by the valence factor $\nu w'/2$. Read page 162 before using the coefficients for V, E, and K.

represented by equation (5-1-2) lead to values of $S_{(H)}$ which are less than those in Table (5-1-3) below 45°, and greater above this temperature. The discrepancy is −45 cal/mole at 0° and 22 cal/mole at 75°, and it varies almost linearly with T. The discrepancy in $S_{(C_p)}$ is about twice as great on a percentage basis, and in this case the values calculated from equation (5-1-2) are greater at all temperatures than those from equation (5-1-1).

The uncertainties in these thermochemical parameters, and in $S_{(V)}$, $S_{(K)}$ and $S_{(E)}$, which involve pressure derivatives of D, emphasize the experimental nature of these theoretical slopes. This must be borne in mind when considering either the validity or the utility of the limiting

[31] "International Critical Tables", Vol. III, p. 25, McGraw-Hill Book Co., New York, 1930.
[32] C. G. Malmberg and A. A. Maryott, *J. Research Natl. Bur. Stds.*, **56**, 1 (1956).

laws for partial molal quantities. The values of the theoretical slopes tabulated in this edition are those we believe to be most useful at present. They are reported to three or four figures as a convenience to the reader who might wish to check his calculations, interpolate, or express the variation of his results with temperature analytically. Some estimates of the uncertainties in these slopes will be found in Chapter (8).

Limiting Slopes for the Relative Partial Molal Volume, Expansibility and Compressibility of an Electrolyte in Aqueous Solutions

It is clear from the equations in Chapter (3), Section (9), that the theoretical parameters which appear in the equations

$$\bar{V}_2 - \bar{V}_2^0 = \mathbb{S}_{(V)}\sqrt{c} \tag{5-2-16}$$

$$\bar{K}_2 - \bar{K}_2^0 = \mathbb{S}_{(K)}\sqrt{c} \tag{5-2-17}$$

$$\bar{E}_2 - \bar{E}_2^0 = \mathbb{S}_{(E)}\sqrt{c} \tag{5-2-18}$$

are functions of the pressure derivatives of D. In the absence of sufficiently extensive data for water, we have estimated these derivatives from equation (5-1-4) as explained in Section (1) of this chapter. Equation (5-1-1) was used as the source of D as a function of T. The resulting values of $\mathbb{S}_{(V)}$, $\mathbb{S}_{(K)}$ and $\mathbb{S}_{(E)}$ are included in Table (5-2-5). It seems likely that the uncertainty in $\mathbb{S}_{(V)}$ is not more than 25 % between 20 and 30°. Outside this short range, the values of $\mathbb{S}_{(V)}$ are little more than crude estimates, and this description applies to $\mathbb{S}_{(K)}$ and $\mathbb{S}_{(E)}$ at all temperatures.

Limiting Slopes and Limiting Equations for Relative Apparent Molal Properties

It follows from equation (8-2-7) that the limiting slopes of the apparent molal properties are two thirds of the limiting slopes for the corresponding partial molal properties. Thus, for two examples we write

$$\phi_H - \phi_H^0 = (2/3)\mathbb{S}_{(H)}\sqrt{c} \tag{5-2-19}$$

$$\phi_V = \phi_V^0 = (2/3)\mathbb{S}_{(V)}\sqrt{c} \tag{5-2-20}$$

and similar equations can be written for $\phi_{C_p} - \phi_{C_p}^0$, $\phi_K - \phi_K^0$ and $\phi_E - \phi_E^0$. The numerical values of $\mathbb{S}_{(V)}$, $\mathbb{S}_{(H)}$, etc., are given in Table (5-2-5). In Chapter (8), Section (8), where the theoretical limiting equations for $\phi_H - \phi_H^0$ and $\phi_V - \phi_V^0$ are derived, it is shown that the a-parameter makes an important contribution to these apparent molal properties, even at the lowest experimental concentrations. Neglecting the possible variations of this parameter with T and P, the limiting equations may be written

$$\phi_H - \phi_H^0 = (2/3)\mathbb{S}_{(H)}\Omega_{(H)}\sqrt{c} \tag{5-2-21}$$

$$\phi_V - \phi_V^0 = (2/3)\mathbb{S}_{(V)}\Omega_{(V)}\sqrt{c} \tag{5-2-22}$$

where

$$\Omega_{(H)} = (1 + h)/(1 + \kappa a) - \sigma h \tag{5-2-23}$$

$$h = -(\alpha/3)[\partial \ln D/\partial T + T^{-1} + \alpha/3]^{-1} \tag{5-2-24}$$

$$\Omega_{(V)} = (1 + k)/(1 + \kappa a) - \sigma k \tag{5-2-25}$$

$$k = (\beta/3)[\partial \ln D/\partial P - \beta/3]^{-1} \tag{5-2-26}$$

and

$$\sigma = 3(\kappa a)^{-3}[1 + \kappa a - (1 + \kappa a)^{-1} - 2 \ln (1 + \kappa a)] \tag{5-2-27}$$

The function $\sigma(x) = \sigma(\kappa a)$ is given in Table (5-2-6) for various values of the argument $x = \kappa a$. The numerical values of h and k depend upon the derivatives of the dielectric constant, and are not accurately calculable at present. The values of h which appear in Table (5-2-5) are based upon $\partial \ln D/\partial T$ derived from equation (5-1-1) and α from Table (5-1-3). If equation (5-1-4) is used to represent $\partial \ln D/\partial P$ and equation (5-1-6) to represent β, the estimated value of k is 0.3513 at all temperatures.

Theoretical Laws for the Increase of Surface Tension

The limiting law for surface tension for binary electrolytes was found to be

$$\Delta\sigma = \sigma - \sigma_0 = \frac{kT}{16\pi q^2} (Y_c + Y_f) = \frac{kT}{16\pi q^2} Y \tag{3-11-14}$$

where

$$q = \frac{\epsilon^2 z^2}{2DkT} \tag{3-7-4}$$

If the mean distance of approach of the ions is included, then

$$\Delta\sigma = \sigma - \sigma_0 = \frac{kT}{16\pi q^2} (Y_c' + Y_f') = \frac{kT}{16\pi q^2} Y' \tag{3-11-15}$$

Let

$$y^2 = \kappa^2 q^2 = \frac{1.765 \times 10^{13}}{(DT)^3} z^6 c \equiv Bc \tag{5-2-28}$$

and

$$\frac{Y}{y^2} = \frac{Y_c + Y_f}{y^2} = \frac{2 \times 10^3 \sigma_0 D}{N\epsilon^2 z^2} \left(\frac{\sigma - \sigma_0}{c\sigma_0}\right) \equiv A\Delta\alpha \tag{5-2-29}$$

where $\Delta\alpha$ is defined as the relative surface tension increase per mol of solute.

Numerical values of Y_c, Y_f, Y_c', and Y_f' have been obtained by Onsager and Samaras[33] for 1-1 electrolytes. Values of these quantities divided by y^2 at given values of y^2 are given in Table (5-2-7). Values of $A\Delta\alpha$ are also

[33] L. Onsager and N. N. T. Samaras, *J. Chem Phys.*, **2**, 528 (1934).

TABLE (5-2-6)*. THE FUNCTION σ

$$\sigma \equiv \frac{3}{x^3}[1 + x - (1 + x)^{-1} - 2\ln(1 + x)]$$

x	σ	x	σ	x	σ	x	σ
0.00	1.000000	0.50	0.537675	1.00	0.341117	2.00	0.176041
.01	.958178	.51	.532127	.02	.335718	.05	.171274
.02	.970704	.52	.526668	.04	.330451	.10	.166704
.03	.956568	.53	.521298	.06	.325313	.15	.162321
.04	.942758	.54	.516014	.08	.320299	.20	.158114
0.05	0.929263	0.55	0.510813	1.10	0.315405	2.25	0.154074
.06	.916074	.56	.505695	.12	.310627	.30	.150191
.07	.903182	.57	.500657	.14	.305962	.35	.146458
.08	.890577	.58	.495699	.16	.301405	.40	.142867
.09	.872250	.59	.490817	.18	.296953	.45	.139410
0.10	0.866193	0.60	0.486010	1.20	0.292604	2.50	0.136082
.11	.854399	.61	.481278	.22	.288353	.55	.132875
.12	.842859	.62	.476617	.24	.284198	.60	.129783
.13	.831565	.63	.472028	.26	.280136	.65	.126801
.14	.820510	.64	.467507	.28	.276164	.70	.123924
0.15	0.809687	0.65	0.463055	1.30	0.272279	2.75	0.121147
.16	.799090	.66	.458669	.32	.268479	.80	.118464
.17	.788712	.67	.454348	.34	.264761	.85	.115872
.18	.778547	.68	.450091	.36	.261123	.90	.113367
.19	.768589	.69	.445896	.38	.257562	.95	.110945
0.20	0.758832	0.70	0.441763	1.40	0.254077	3.00	0.108601
.21	.749271	.71	.437689	.42	.250665	.05	.106333
.22	.739900	.72	.433675	.44	.247323	.10	.104138
.23	.730714	.73	.429718	.46	.244051	.15	.102011
.24	.721707	.74	.425817	.48	.240846	.20	.099951
0.25	0.712876	0.75	0.421972	1.50	0 237705	3.25	0.097955
.26	.704216	.76	.418182	.52	.234628	.30	.096019
.27	.695721	.77	.414444	.54	.231613	.35	.094142
.28	.687388	.78	.410759	.56	.228658	.40	.092320
.29	.679212	.79	.407125	.58	.225761	.45	.090553
0.30	0.671189	0.80	0.403542	1.60	0.222921	3.50	0.088837
.31	.663316	.81	.400008	.62	.220136	.55	.087170
.32	.655588	.82	.396522	.64	.217405	.60	.085551
.33	.648002	.83	.393083	.66	.214727	.65	.083979
.34	.640554	.84	.389692	.68	.212099	.70	.082450
0.35	0.633241	0.85	0.386346	1.70	0.209521	3.75	0.080963
.36	.626060	.86	.383045	.72	.206992	.80	.079518
.37	.619007	.87	.379788	.74	.204510	.85	.078112
.38	.612078	.88	.376574	.76	.202073	.90	.076743
.39	.605272	.89	.373403	.78	.199682	.95	.075412
0.40	0.598585	0.90	0.370273	1.80	0.197335	4.00	0.074115
.41	.592014	.91	.367185	.82	.195030	.05	.072853
.42	.585557	.92	.364137	.84	.192766	.10	.071623
.43	.579210	.93	.361128	.86	.190543	.15	.070425
.44	.572971	.94	.358158	.88	.188360	.20	.069257
0.45	0.566838	0.95	0.355226	1.90	0.186216	4.25	0.068119
.46	.560809	.96	.352332	.92	.184109	.30	.067009
.47	.554880	.97	.349475	.94	.182039	.35	.065927
.48	.549049	.98	.346654	.96	.180005	.40	.064871
.49	.543315	.99	.343868	.98	.178006	.45	.063842
0.50	0.537675	1.00	0.341117	2.00	0.176041	4.50	0.062837

* We are indebted to Dr. Stuart R. Brinkley, Jr., and Ruth F. Brinkley for permission to publish this table.

included. We note that the effect caused by introducing the mean distance of approach of the ions is not great.

TABLE (5-2-7). FUNCTIONS FOR THEORETICAL COMPUTATION OF SURFACE TENSION INCREASE FOR 1-1 ELECTROLYTES AT 25°.

	I				II		
y^2	Y_c/y^2	Y_f/y^2	$A\Delta\alpha$	y^2	Y_c'/y^2	Y_f'/y^2	$A\Delta\alpha$
0			∞	0			∞
0.0063	3.048	−0.076	2.972				
0.0126	2.747	−0.097	2.650				
0.0189	2.576	−0.111	2.465				
0.0315	2.367	−0.134	2.233				
0.0378	2.295	−0.141	2.154	0.0378	2.308	−0.107	2.201
0.0630	2.095	−0.163	1.932	0.0850	2.003	−0.125	1.878
0.0944	1.944	−0.184	1.760				
0.1259	1.840	−0.203	1.637	0.1259	1.867	−0.132	1.735
0.1574	1.760	−0.217	1.543				
0.1889	1.697	−0.228	1.469	0.1963	1.718	−0.139	1.579
0.2014	1.675	−0.232	1.443				
0.2266	1.634	−0.241	1.394				

(3) EQUATIONS DERIVED IN CHAPTER (4) INVOLVING THE DYNAMICS OF IONIC ATMOSPHERES

Limiting Law for Viscosity.—The limiting law for the increase in the viscosity of a solution with addition of electrolyte dissociating into two kinds of ions is

$$\eta^* = \eta - \eta_0 = \frac{\kappa}{480\pi}\left\{\bar{\rho} + 4\left(\frac{\overline{\rho^2}}{\bar{\rho}} - \bar{\rho}\right)\frac{1 - \sqrt{q^*}}{1 + \sqrt{q^*}}\right\} \qquad (4\text{-}2\text{-}28)$$

where

$$\bar{\rho} = \frac{n_1 e_1^2/\omega_1 + n_2 e_2^2/\omega_2}{n_1 e_1^2 + n_2 e_2^2} \qquad (4\text{-}2\text{-}25)$$

$$\overline{\rho^2} = \frac{n_1 e_1^2/\omega_1^2 + n_2 e_2^2/\omega_2^2}{n_1 e_1^2 + n_2 e_2^2} \qquad (4\text{-}2\text{-}26)$$

and

$$q^* = \frac{n_1 e_1^2 \omega_1 + n_2 e_2^2 \omega_2}{(n_1 e_1^2 + n_2 e_2^2)(\omega_1 + \omega_2)} \qquad (4\text{-}2\text{-}27)$$

In all these expressions, it is important to remember that e_1 and e_2 carry the sign of the charge. Thus, for a binary electrolyte $e_1 = -e_2$. To convert to practical units, we substitute for κ and ω_i the values

$$\kappa = \left(\frac{4\pi\epsilon^2 N}{1000 DkT}\right)^{1/2}\sqrt{\Gamma} = \frac{35.56 \times 10^8\sqrt{\Gamma}}{(DT)^{1/2}} \qquad (3\text{-}1\text{-}2)$$

and

$$\omega_i = \frac{c \times 10^{-8}\lambda_i^0}{F\,|z_i|\,\epsilon} \qquad (4\text{-}1\text{-}15)$$

where Γ equals $\sum c_i z_i^2$, λ_i^0 is the limiting ionic conductance and $|z_i|$ the magnitude of the valence. Further, for electro-neutrality,

$$n_1 e_1 = -n_2 e_2 ; \qquad n_1 |z_1| \epsilon = n_2 |z_2| \epsilon$$

where ϵ is the electronic charge, and n_i is given by

$$n_i = \frac{c_i N}{1000}$$

Here c_i is the concentration of the i ion in mols per liter of the solution. For binary electrolytes, $n_1 = n_2$, and $|z_1| = |z_2|$. Consequently, $q^* = 1/2$, $\bar{p} = 1/2(1/\omega_1 + 1/\omega_2)$, and $\overline{p^2} = 1/2(1/\omega_1^2 + 1/\omega_2^2)$, which considerably simplifies equation (4-2-28) for this special case.

Limiting Slope for the Equivalent Conductance of a Strong Electrolyte

Computation of the limiting slope for the general case of conductance in solutions of mixed electrolytes is very complicated. It may be accomplished by means of equations given in Chapter (4), Sections (3) and (3A). Particular examples are discussed in Chapters (6) and (7).

In the important special case of a single electrolyte dissociating into two kinds of ions only, equation (4-3-44) for the equivalent conductance may be written

$$\Lambda = \Lambda^0 - \mathcal{S}_{(\Lambda)} \sqrt{c} \tag{5-3-1}$$

and the limiting slope expressed in the convenient form

$$\mathcal{S}_{(\Lambda)} = \alpha^* \Lambda^0 + \beta^* \tag{5-3-2}$$

The constants

$$\alpha^* = \left(\frac{1.981 \times 10^6 \times 0.2929\sqrt{2}}{(DT)^{3/2}} \right) w'Q \tag{5-3-4}$$

and

$$\beta^* = \left(\frac{29.16 \times 2\sqrt{2}}{\eta(DT)^{1/2}} \right) w^* \tag{5-3-5}$$

are recorded in Table (5-3-1), which is based upon values of the viscosity and dielectric constant given in Table (5-1-3). The quantities $0.2929\sqrt{2}$ and $2\sqrt{2}$ are introduced within the parentheses so that the factors

$$Q = \frac{q^*}{0.2929(1 + \sqrt{q^*})} \tag{5-3-6}$$

and

$$w^* = \left(\frac{|z_1| + |z_2|}{2} \right) \left(\frac{\nu |z_1 z_2|}{2} \right)^{1/2} \tag{5-3-7}$$

become unity for 1-1 electrolytes. The valence factor w' defined by equation (5-2-4) becomes

$$w' = |z_1 z_2|(|z_1 z_2|\nu/2)^{1/2} \qquad (5\text{-}3\text{-}8)$$

for the case under consideration. The parameter q^* which appears in the definition of Q is given by equation (4-3-43), or

$$q^* = \frac{|z_1 z_2|(\lambda_1^0 + \lambda_2^0)}{(|z_1| + |z_2|)(|z_2|\lambda_1^0 + |z_1|\lambda_2^0)} \qquad (4\text{-}3\text{-}43)$$

TABLE (5-3-1)[a]. VALUES OF THE CONSTANTS APPEARING IN THE LIMITING EQUATIONS FOR CONDUCTANCE IN AQUEOUS SOLUTIONS[b].

$t°C$	α^*	β^*	α'	β'	$ab \times 10^8$
0	0.2195	29.61	0.2108	4.165	6.939
5	.2212	35.07	.2140	4.970	6.975
10	.2230	40.77	.2175	5.825	7.012
15	.2249	46.78	.2211	6.740	7.051
18	.2261	50.59	.2234	7.327	7.076
20	.2268	53.24	.2250	7.738	7.092
25	.2289	60.19	.2291	8.828	7.135
30	.2311	67.51	.2334	9.994	7.180
35	.2333	75.21	.2380	11.241	7.226
40	.2356	83.21	.2428	12.562	7.274
45	.2381	91.41	.2478	13.943	7.324
50	.2406	99.72	.2531	15.371	7.376
55	.2432	108.37	.2587	16.887	7.429
60	.2460	117.41	.2645	18.501	7.485
Factor	$w'Q$	w^*	z^6	z^5	z^2

[a] For definitions of the valence factors w', Q and w^* see equations (5-3-6) to (5-3-8). Since the conductance equations involving α', β' and b are limited to symmetrical valence types, the valence factors for these parameters contain only z.
[b] Values of α^* and β^* for mixed solvents are given in Table (11-1-1A).

Q may also be expressed in terms of the limiting transference numbers of the ion constituents. Thus

$$Q = \frac{3.4141 S^2}{(T_2^0 + \nu T_1^0) + S(T_2^0 + \nu T_1^0)^{1/2}} \qquad (5\text{-}3\text{-}9)$$

where $\nu \equiv |z_2|/|z_1|$ and $S^2 \equiv \nu/(1 + \nu)$. In this equation it is immaterial whether the anion or cation is assigned the subscript 2. Consequently Q has the same form for sodium sulfate as for barium chloride. Q is unity for all symmetrical electrolytes.

The equation (4-3-42) for the equivalent conductance of the individual ion constituents in solutions containing only two kinds of ions can be written

$$\lambda_j = \lambda_j^0 - \mathcal{S}_{(\lambda)}\sqrt{c} \qquad (5\text{-}3\text{-}10)$$

where

$$\mathcal{S}_{(\lambda)} = \alpha^*\lambda_j^0 + \frac{\beta^*|z_j|}{|z_1| + |z_2|}; \qquad j = 1, 2 \qquad (5\text{-}3\text{-}10a)$$

Limiting Equation for Equivalent Conductance of Strong Electrolytes. Inclusion of the Ionic Size Parameter.

In Section (9) of Chapter (4) it was shown that inclusion of the a-parameter and terms of order c results in the limiting equation

$$\Lambda = \Lambda^0 - (\alpha^*\Lambda^0 + \beta^*)c^{1/2} + cB(\kappa a) \qquad (4\text{-}9\text{-}15)$$

where

$$B(\kappa a) = B_1\Lambda^0 + B_2 \qquad (6\text{-}11\text{-}2)$$

$$B_1 = 24\alpha'(b^{-2}(1 + 2b)\phi_1 - \phi_2) \qquad (6\text{-}11\text{-}3)$$

$$B_2 = \alpha^*\beta^* + 16\beta'(\phi_3 - b^{-1}\phi_4) \qquad (6\text{-}11\text{-}4)$$

$$\alpha' = \kappa^2 a^2 b^2/24c \qquad (6\text{-}11\text{-}5)$$

$$\beta' = \beta^*\kappa ab/16c^{1/2} \qquad (6\text{-}11\text{-}6)$$

and

$$b = z^2\epsilon^2/akDT \qquad (3\text{-}7\text{-}7)$$

Numerical values of the quantities α^*, β^*, α', β' and ab are given in Table (5-3-1), and the four functions ϕ_1, ϕ_2, ϕ_3 and ϕ_4, calculated by Fuoss and Onsager, are given in Table (5-3-1a).

TABLE (5-3-1a)*. FUNCTIONS FOR CONDUCTANCE EQUATIONS (4-9-16) AND (6-11-2).

κa	ϕ_1	ϕ_2	ϕ_3	ϕ_4
0.01	0.08275	0.30761	0.4691	0.8801
.02	.08217	.24944	.3826	.8715
.03	.08159	.21534	.3320	.8630
.04	.08102	.19114	.2963	.8547
.05	.08045	.17238	.2686	.8466
.06	.07990	.15720	.2465	.8386
.07	.07934	.14436	.2276	.8308
.08	.07879	.13333	.2116	.8230
.09	.07825	.12370	.1976	.8155
.10	.07771	.11512	.1849	.8081
.11	.07717	.10745	.1737	.8008
.12	.07664	.10050	.1637	.7937
.13	.07612	.09425	.1545	.7867
.14	.07560	.08848	.1461	.7797
.15	.07508	.08313	.1383	.7730
.16	.07458	.07824	.1313	.7663
.17	.07407	.07375	.1246	.7597
.18	.07357	.06951	.1184	.7533
.19	.07308	.06560	.1128	.7470
.20	.07258	.06191	.1073	.7407
.20	.07209	.05850	.1023	.7346
.22	.07161	.05525	.0976	.7286
.23	.07114	.05224	.0930	.7227
.24	.07066	.04937	.0888	.7169
.25	.07019	.04668	.0849	.7111

* The authors are indebted to Dr. R. M. Fuoss for supplying this table prior to its publication.

Theory of Diffusion

In Chapter (4), Section (4), it was shown that the Onsager and Fuoss theory of diffusion led to the expression

$$\mathfrak{D} = 16.629 \times 10^{10} T \frac{\overline{\mathfrak{M}}}{c} \left(1 + c \frac{\partial \ln y_{\pm}}{\partial c} \right) \qquad (4\text{-}4\text{-}24)$$

for the coefficient of diffusion of an electrolyte which dissociates into two kinds of ions. $\overline{\mathfrak{M}}$ is a complicated function which may be evaluated by means of equations (4-4-19), (4-4-20), and (4-4-21), (4-3-21a) and (4-3-23a). For symmetrical electrolytes this function may be written

$$\left(\frac{\overline{\mathfrak{M}}}{c} \right) 10^{20} = \frac{1.074}{z} \left(\frac{\lambda_+^0 \lambda_-^0}{\Lambda^0} \right) - \frac{0.4404}{\mathring{a} \eta_0} \left(\frac{\lambda_+^0 - \lambda_-^0}{\Lambda^0} \right)^2 \frac{\kappa a}{1 + \kappa a}$$
$$+ \left(\frac{z}{\mathring{a}} \right)^2 \frac{36790}{\eta_0 DT} (\kappa a)^2 \cdot \phi(\kappa a) \qquad (5\text{-}3\text{-}11)$$

TABLE (5-3-2). VALUES OF THE FUNCTIONS $\phi(\kappa a)$ AND $(\kappa a)^2 \phi(\kappa a)$ FOR USE IN EQUATIONS (4-4-21) AND (5-3-11).

(κa)	$\phi(\kappa a)$	$(\kappa a)^2 \phi(\kappa a)$	(κa)	$\phi(\kappa a)$	$(\kappa a)^2 \phi(\kappa a)$
0	∞	0	.5	.2651	.06628
.010	3.3550	.00034	.6	.2054	.07394
.025	2.4695	.00154	.7	.16304	.07989
.05	1.8273	.00457	.8	.13194	.08444
.10	1.2342	.01234	.9	.10844	.08784
.15	.9245	.02080	1.0	.09033	.09033
.20	.7277	.02911	1.2	.06477	.09327
.25	.5907	.03692	1.4	.04813	.09433
.30	.4899	.04409	1.6	.03676	.09411
.35	.4130	.05059	1.8	.02876	.09318
.40	.3527	.05643	2.0	.02292	.09168
.45	.3044	.06164	2.5	.01391	.08694
.50	.2651	.06628	3.0	.00908	.08172

which is a convenient form for numerical calculations. Values of $(\kappa a)^2 \cdot \phi(\kappa a)$ are recorded in Table (5-3-2). An equivalent equation, written in terms of $\sqrt{c}$, will be found in Chapter (6), Section (10), where the expression for the limiting slope of $\mathfrak{D}$ against $\sqrt{c}$ is also given [See equations (6-10-6) and (6-10-7)].

Theory of Frequency Effects

The molar conductance $\Lambda_{\bar{\omega}}$ in the presence of a field of frequency, $\bar{\omega}$, has been split into three parts according to equation (4-5-20), or

$$\Lambda = \Lambda_m^0 - \Lambda_{I\bar{\omega}} - \Lambda_{II} \qquad (4\text{-}5\text{-}20)$$

Λ_m^0 is the molar conductance at infinite dilution, $\Lambda_{I\bar{\omega}}$ the contribution to $\Lambda_{\bar{\omega}}$ due to asymmetric ionic atmosphere, and Λ_{II} is the contribution due to electrophoresis. $\Lambda_{I\tilde{\omega}}$ is given by equation (4-5-21), and is a complicated function of the frequency, time of relaxation, and the quantity q^*. When $\tilde{\omega}$ is zero, $\Lambda_{I(0)}$ is the contribution to the molecular conductance due to the asymmetric ionic atmosphere computed by Onsager. The numerical values of $\Lambda_{I\tilde{\omega}}/\Lambda_{I(\tilde{\omega}=0)}$ as a function of $\tilde{\omega}\tau$ and q^*, computed by Falkenhagen, are given in Table (5-3-3).

$$\text{TABLE } (5\text{-}3\text{-}3)* \quad \frac{\Lambda_{I\tilde{\omega}}}{\Lambda_{(I\tilde{\omega}=0)}}$$

$\tilde{\omega}\tau$	$q^* = 0.5$	$q^* = 0.45$	$q^* = 0.40$	$q^* = 0.35$	$q^* = 0.30$
0.	1.	1.	1.	1.	1.
0.2	0.997	0.997	0.997	0.997	0.997
.5	.980	.981	.981	.981	.981
.75	.956	.959	.962	.965	.968
1.	.930	.934	.938	.942	.946
1.25	.904	.909	.913	.918	.922
1.5	.876	.882	.888	.894	.900
2.	.826	.833	.841	.848	.856
2.5	.783	.791	.799	.808	.817
3.	.745	.753	.763	.773	.785
4.	.682	.691	.701	.713	.727
6.	.593	.603	.614	.628	.643
8.	.531	.540	.553	.565	.582
10.	.486	.496	.507	.520	.537
15.	.409	.417	.428	.442	.458
20.	.360	.368	.378	.390	.406
25.	.326	.334	.344	.354	.369
30.	.299	.307	.317	.327	.342
35.	.279	.286	.295	.305	.318
40.	.261	.267	.272	.287	.299
45.	.247	.254	.263	.272	.288
50.	.235	.242	.250	.259	.271
75.	.193	.199	.206	.214	.223
100.	.168	.173	.179	.186	.195
150.	.138	.142	.147	.153	.160
200.	.1195	.1232	.1278	.1328	.1394
300.	.0983	.1011	.1046	.1088	.1145
500.	.0759	.0783	.0812	.0844	.0888
700.	.0643	.0663	.0688	.0716	.0751
1000.	.0538	.0555	.0576	.0599	.0629
5000.	.0241	.0249	.0258	.0269	.0282
10000.	.0171	.01755	.0182	.0190	.0199

*H. Falkenhagen, "Electrolytes," Table 31, p. 213. English Translation by R. P. Bell, Oxford Press, 1934.

The effect of frequency on the dielectric constant is given by equation (4-5-24) which measures $D_{\tilde{\omega}} - D_0$ as a function of q^*, $\tilde{\omega}\tau$, T, and c. Falkenhagen has also computed $(D_{\tilde{\omega}} - D_0)/(D_{\tilde{\omega}=0} - D_0)$ as a function of $\tilde{\omega}\tau$ and q^*, and these results are compiled in Table (5-3-4).

The time of relaxation, required for these calculations, may be computed from a simple formula readily obtained from equation (4-1-17), namely,

$$\tau = \frac{8.85 \times 10^{-11}}{\Lambda^{\circ}c^*} D_0 \tag{5-3-12}$$

Here, $\Lambda^0 = \lambda_1^0 + \lambda_2^0$, $c^* = \nu_1 \mid z_1 \mid c = \nu_2 \mid z_2 \mid c$, and D_0 is the dielectric constant of the solvent; q^* is given by equation (4-3-43),

$$q^* = \frac{\mid z_1 z_2 \mid (\lambda_1^0 + \lambda_2^0)}{(\mid z_1 \mid + \mid z_2 \mid)(\mid z_2 \mid \lambda_1^0 + \mid z_1 \mid \lambda_2^0)} \qquad (4\text{-}3\text{-}43)$$

TABLE (5-3-4).* $(D_{\tilde{\omega}} - D_0)/(D_{\tilde{\omega}=0} - D_0)$.

$\tilde{\omega}\tau$	$q^* = 0.5$	$q^* = 0.45$	$q^* = 0.4$	$q^* = 0.35$	$q^* = 0.3$
0.0	1.	1.	1.	1.	1.
.1	0.999	0.999	0.999	0.999	0.999
.2	.989	.989	.989	.9895	.990
.35	.974	.974	.974	.975	.975
.5	.940	.941	.943	.944	.946
.75	.879	.882	.885	.887	.890
1.	.813	.816	.820	.824	.830
1.25	.748	.752	.757	.763	.768
1.5	.689	.694	.700	.706	.713
2.	.585	.591	.598	.605	.615
2.5	.502	.510	.517	.525	.535
3.	.437	.444	.452	.406	.471
4.	.342	.349	.356	.365	.375
6.	.231	.237	.244	.251	.261
8.	.1703	.1753	.1811	.1877	.1957
10.	.1326	.1369	.1419	.1477	.1546
15.	.0822	.0853	.0889	.0931	.0983
20.	.0576	.0600	.0627	.0660	.0700
25.	.0434	.0453	.0475	.0501	.0533
30.	.0343	.0358	.0376	.0398	.0425
35.	.0280	.0293	.0316	.0327	.0350
40.	.0235	.0246	.0259	.0275	.0298
45.	.0201	.0210	.0222	.0236	.0253
50.	.01741	.01826	.0193	.0205	.0220
75.	.01001	.01053	.01114	.01190	.01284
100.	.00672	.00707	.00750	.00803	.00869
150.	.00380	.00401	.00426	.00457	.00497
200.	.00252	.00267	.00284	.00302	.00332
300.	.001411	.001493	.001592	.001714	.001870
500.	.000674	.000713	.000762	.000822	.000899
700.	.000413	.000437	.000467	.000505	.000553
1000.	.000245	.000259	.000268	.000300	.000329
5000.	.0000227	.0000241	.0000258	.0000280	.0000308
10000.	.00000808	.00000859	.00000922	.00000999	.0000110

* H. Falkenhagen, "Electrolytes," Table 37, p. 219. English Translation by R. P. Bell, Oxford Press, 1934.

Since the wave length, l, in meters is sometimes used in these calculations, the equation for its computation

$$l = \frac{2\pi c}{\tilde{\omega}100} = \frac{18.835 \times 10^6}{\tilde{\omega}} \qquad (5\text{-}3\text{-}13)$$

will be useful.

Effect of High Fields on Conductance of Electrolytes

Equation (4-6-55) of the Onsager-Wilson theory of the Wien effect on the conductance of strong electrolytes gives for the equivalent conductances of a binary electrolyte,

$$\Lambda = \Lambda^0 - \frac{|e_j|^2 \kappa\Lambda^0}{2DkT} g(x) - \frac{Fk |e_j| 2\kappa}{6\sqrt{2}\,\pi\eta c \times 10^{-8}} f(x) \qquad (5\text{-}3\text{-}14)$$

where

$$x = \frac{\mu'}{\kappa} = \frac{Xz\epsilon}{kT\kappa} \qquad (4\text{-}6\text{-}43)$$

TABLE (5-3-5)*. THE FUNCTION $g(x)$.

x	$g(x)$	x	$g(x)$	x	$g(x)$	x	$g(x)$
0.0	0.19526	2.5	0.11977	7.5	0.05551	23.	0.02045
.1	.19492	2.6	.11721	7.6	.05491	24.	.01965
.2	.19391	2.8	.11236	8.0	.05262	25.	.01891
.3	.19228	3.0	.10786	8.5	.05002	26.	.01822
.4	.19009	3.2	.10367	9.0	.04766	27.	.01758
.5	.18742	3.4	.09977	9.5	.04550	38.	.01698
.6	.18437	3.6	.09612	10.0	.04354	29.	.01643
.7	.18102	3.8	.09272	10.5	.04173	30.	.01590
.8	.17745	4.0	.08952	11.0	.04007	31.	.01541
.9	.17373	4.2	.08656	11.5	.03853	32.	.01495
1.0	.16992	4.4	.08376	12.0	.03711	33.	.01452
1.1	.16607	4.6	.08113	12.5	.03579	34.	.01413
1.2	.16223	4.8	.07865	13.0	.03456	35.	.01372
1.3	.15842	5.0	.07632	13.5	.03341	38.	.01269
1.4	.15466	5.2	.07411	14.0	.03233	41.	.01178
1.5	.15098	5.4	.07203	14.5	.03132	44.	.01101
1.6	.14740	5.6	.07005	15.0	.03037	47.	.01032
1.7	.14390	5.8	.06818	15.5	.02948	50.	.00972
1.8	.14051	6.0	.06640	16.0	.02864	55.	.00886
1.9	.13723	6.2	.06472	17.	.02709	60.	.00814
2.0	.13406	6.4	.06311	18.	.02570	65.	.00753
2.1	.13099	6.6	.06158	19.	.02444	70.	.00700
2.2	.12803	6.8	.06012	20.	.02331	75.	.00654
2.3	.12518	7.0	.05873	21.	.02227	80.	.00614
2.4	.12242	7.2	.05740	22.	.02133	85.	.00579
		7.4	.05613				

* The authors are indebted to Dr. William S. Wilson for these values which do not occur in his Dissertation.

For practical computations, values of $g(x)$ and $f(x)$ in Tables (5-3-5) and (5-3-6) may be used. In terms of the constants α^* and β^* given in Table (5-3-1), equation (5-3-14) becomes

$$\Lambda = \Lambda^0 - \left(\frac{\alpha^* 3g(x)}{2 - \sqrt{2}} \Lambda^0 + \frac{\beta^*}{\sqrt{2}} f(x)\right) \sqrt{c} \qquad (5\text{-}3\text{-}15)$$

The Dissociation Field Effect

According to the theory of Onsager, the effects of high fields on the ionization constants are given by equations (4-7-29) and (4-7-30). Thus,

$$\frac{K(X)}{K(0)} = F(\bar{b}) = 1 + \bar{b} + \frac{\bar{b}^2}{3} + \frac{\bar{b}^3}{18} + \frac{\bar{b}^4}{180} + \cdots \qquad (4\text{-}7\text{-}29)$$

or, for large values of $\bar{b}$, by the asymptotic expansion

$$F(\bar{b}) \cong \left(\frac{2}{\pi}\right)^{1/2} (8\bar{b})^{-3/4} e^{\sqrt{8\bar{b}}} \left\{ 1 - \frac{3}{8(8\bar{b})^{1/2}} \right.$$

$$\left. - \frac{15}{128(8\bar{b})} - \frac{105}{1024(8\bar{b})^{3/2}} \cdots \right\} \qquad (4\text{-}7\text{-}30)$$

TABLE (5-3-6).* THE FUNCTION $f(x)$.

x	$f(x)$	x	$f(x)$	x	$f(x)$
0.0	1.4142	4.2	1.2895	15.5	1.1531
.1	1.4139	4.4	1.2845	16.0	1.1502
.2	1.4133	4.6	1.2797	16.5	1.1475
.3	1.4121	4.8	1.2750	17.0	1.1449
.4	1.4104	5.0	1.2705	17.5	1.1424
.5	1.4085	5.2	1.2662	18.0	1.1399
.6	1.4061	5.4	1.2622	18.5	1.1376
.7	1.4035	5.6	1.2583	19.0	1.1354
.8	1.4006	5.8	1.2545	19.5	1.1332
.9	1.3975	6.0	1.2507	20.0	1.1312
1.0	1.3942	6.2	1.2471	20.5	1.1291
1.1	1.3907	6.4	1.2437	21.0	1.1272
1.2	1.3872	6.6	1.2403	22	1.1235
1.3	1.3836	6.8	1.2370	23	1.1201
1.4	1.3799	7.0	1.2338	24	1.1168
1.5	1.3762	7.2	1.2308	25	1.1138
1.6	1.3724	7.4	1.2278	26	1.1109
1.7	1.3687	7.5	1.2263	27	1.1082
1.8	1.3650	7.6	1.2249	28	1.1057
1.9	1.3613	8.0	1.2193	29	1.1032
2.0	1.3576	8.5	1.2129	30	1.1010
2.1	1.3539	9.0	1.2068	31	1.0988
2.2	1.3503	9.5	1.2011	32	1.0969
2.3	1.3468	10.0	1.1958	33	1.0947
2.4	1.3433	10.5	1.1908	34	1.0928
2.5	1.3398	11.0	1.1860	35	1.0910
2.6	1.3364	11.5	1.1815	38	1.0861
2.8	1.3298	12.0	1.1773	41	1.0816
3.0	1.3234	12.5	1.1733	44	1.0780
3.2	1.3172	13.0	1.1695	47	1.0742
3.4	1.3112	13.5	1.1659	50	1.0710
3.6	1.3055	14.0	1.1625	55	1.0664
3.8	1.2999	14.5	1.1592	60	1.0623
4.0	1.2946	15.0	1.1561	65	1.0588

* The authors are indebted to Dr. William S. Wilson for these values which do not occur in his Dissertation.

where $\bar{b}$ is given by the equation

$$\bar{b} = \frac{z_1^2 z_2^2 (\lambda_1 + \lambda_2)}{|z_2|\lambda_1 + |z_1|\lambda_2} \frac{9.695V}{DT^2} \qquad (4\text{-}7\text{-}27)$$

For the important case where $\alpha \ll 1$, the equivalent conductance, degree of ionization, and ionization constant in the field may be computed by

$$\frac{\Lambda_x}{\Lambda_{x=0}} = \frac{\alpha}{\alpha_0} = \sqrt{\frac{K(X)}{K(0)}} = 1 + \frac{1}{2}\bar{b} + \frac{1}{24}\bar{b}^2 \cdots \qquad (4\text{-}7\text{-}37)$$

Λ_X, α, and $K(X)$ are the conductance, the degree of dissociation, and ionization constant in the field of V (volts/cm), and $\Lambda_{x=0}$, α_0, and $K(0)$, are these quantities in the absence of the field.

Numerical Equations for the Effect of High Fields on Conductance of Electrolytes According to the General Theory given in Chapter (4), Section (8)

Equation (4-8-52) for the equivalent conductance of an ion reduces to

$$\lambda_j = \lambda_j^0 - 5.942 \times 10^6 \frac{|z_1 z_2| q^*}{(DT)^{3/2}} A(k, m, a)\lambda_j^0 \Gamma^{1/2}$$

$$- \frac{43.744 |z_1 z_2|}{(|z_1| + |z_2|)\eta_0(DT)^{1/2}} B_j(k, m, a) \Gamma^{1/2} \tag{5-3-16}$$

upon introducing the values of the universal constants.

A and B_j depend explicitly upon

$$k \equiv \mu_2 - \mu_1 = \frac{|z_2| - |z_1|}{|z_1| + |z_2|} \geq 0 \tag{5-3-17}$$

$$m \equiv \omega_{21} - \omega_{12} = \frac{\omega_2 - \omega_1}{\omega_1 + \omega_2} = \frac{|z_1| \lambda_2^0 - |z_2| \lambda_1^0}{|z_1| \lambda_2^0 + |z_2| \lambda_1^0} \tag{5-3-18}$$

so that k and m are characteristic of the particular electrolyte. The field parameter, a, is given by

$$a = 3.2633 \times 10^{-6}(|z_1| + |z_2|) q^* \sqrt{\frac{D}{T}} \frac{V}{\sqrt{\Gamma}} \tag{5-3-19}$$

when V is in volts per centimeter.

In order to compute the relative increase in conductance of an electrolyte with increasing field strength, equation (4-8-51) is required. For convenience let

$$B_{12}(k, m, a) \equiv B_1(k, m, a) + B_2(k, m, a) \tag{5-3-20}$$

and

$$\Theta(k, m, a) \equiv 5.9420 \times 10^6 \frac{q^* |z_1 z_2|}{(DT)^{3/2}} A(k, m, a)$$

$$+ \frac{43.744}{\eta_0(DT)^{1/2}} \frac{|z_1 z_2|}{|z_1| + |z_2|} \frac{B_{12}(k, m, a)}{\Lambda^0} \tag{5-3-21}$$

where $\Lambda^0 = \lambda_1^0 + \lambda_2^0$. By using these substitutions in equation (4-8-51), the equivalent conductance of the electrolyte is given by

$$\Lambda(a) = \lambda_1 + \lambda_2 = \Lambda^0(1 - \Theta(k, m, a)\Gamma^{1/2}) \tag{5-3-22}$$

and the relative increase in conductance caused by the field becomes

$$\frac{\Delta\Lambda}{\Lambda(0)} = \frac{\Lambda(a) - \Lambda(0)}{\Lambda(0)} = \frac{\Theta(0) - \Theta(a)}{\Gamma^{-1/2} - \Theta(0)} \tag{5-3-23}$$

For aqueous solutions at 25°

$$\Theta(k, m, a) = 1.6572 \, q^* \mid z_1 z_2 \mid A(k, m, a)$$

$$\tag{5-3-24}$$

$$+ \frac{31.936}{\Lambda^0} \frac{\mid z_1 z_2 \mid}{\mid z_1 \mid + \mid z_2 \mid} B_{12}(k, m, a)$$

For $a = 0$, equations (4-8-7) and (4-8-8) become

$$A(0) = \frac{1}{3(1 + \sqrt{q^*})} \tag{5-3-25}$$

$$B_{12}(0) = B_1(0) + B_2(0) = \frac{2}{3}\left[\frac{1}{1 - \mu_1} + \frac{1}{1 - \mu_2}\right]$$

$$\tag{5-3-26}$$

$$= \frac{2}{3} \frac{(\mid z_1 \mid + \mid z_2 \mid)^2}{\mid z_1 z_2 \mid}$$

and

$$\Theta(0) = 0.5524 \frac{q^* \mid z_1 z_2 \mid}{1 + \sqrt{q^*}} + \frac{21.291}{\Lambda^0} (\mid z_1 \mid + \mid z_2 \mid) \tag{5-3-27}$$

For 1:1 electrolytes ($k = 0$, $q^* = \frac{1}{2}$, $a = x$), equations (4-8-14) and (4-8-15) yield

$$\Theta(x) = 0.8286g(x) + 0.2009f(x) \tag{5-3-28}$$

$$\Theta(0) = 0.4459 \quad \text{(for } \Lambda^0 = 150\text{)} \tag{5-3-29}$$

in which x is Wilson's field parameter and $g(x)$ and $f(x)$ are recorded in Tables (5-3-5) and (5-3-6).

Table (5-3-7) lists sufficient terms of the descending power series

$$2A(k, m, a) = \sum_{n=1}^{\infty} R_n a^{-n} + R_3^* a^{-3} \ln a \tag{4-8-37}$$

$$B_j(k, m, a) = \sum_{n=0}^{\infty} p_{jn} a^{-n} + p_{j1}^* a^{-1} \ln a + p_{j3}^* a^{-3} \ln a \tag{4-8-38}$$

for the calculation of the functions, $A(k, m, a)$ and $B_j(k, m, a)$ required for evaluating the Wien effect for unsymmetrical types of electrolytes. The calculations by this table are valid for high fields. For low fields, numerical quadrature as described in Chapter (4), Section (8) is recommended.

TABLE (5-3-7).   THE DESCENDING POWER SERIES OF THE FUNCTIONS $A(a)$ AND $B_i(a)$
FOR USE IN EQUATIONS (4-8-37) AND (4-8-38).   VALID WHEN $a > 2$.

$$m = \frac{\omega_2 - \omega_1}{\omega_2 + \omega_1} \; ; \qquad \omega_{12} = \frac{\omega_1}{\omega_1 + \omega_2} \; ; \qquad \omega_{21} = \frac{\omega_2}{\omega_1 + \omega_2}$$

$$z_2^2 > z_1^2 \; ; \qquad k = \mu_2 - \mu_1 = \frac{|z_2| - |z_1|}{|z_1| + |z_2|} > 0$$

(1) $k = 0$;   Type $|z_1| = |z_2|$;   MCl, MSO$_4$, etc.,

$$R_1 = 1; \qquad R_2 = -\sqrt{2}, \qquad R_3^* = 0, \qquad R_3 = \frac{1}{2} + \frac{\pi}{4}, \qquad R_4 = -\frac{\sqrt{2}}{2},$$

$$R_5 = \frac{1}{8}, \qquad R_6 = \frac{\sqrt{2}}{12}, \qquad R_7 = -\frac{1}{16}, \text{ etc.,}$$

and

$$p_{jn} = p_n, \qquad p_{jn}^* = p_n^* \qquad \text{where} \qquad p_0 = \frac{2}{3}\sqrt{2}, \qquad p_1^* = 1,$$

$$p_1 = -\left(\frac{1}{2} + \frac{\pi}{4} - \log 2\right), \qquad p_2 = \sqrt{2}, \qquad p_3^* = 0, \qquad p_3 = -\left(\frac{1}{4} + \frac{\pi}{8}\right),$$

$$p_4 = \frac{\sqrt{2}}{6}, \qquad p_5 = -\frac{1}{32}, \qquad p_6 = -\frac{\sqrt{2}}{60}, \qquad p_7 = \frac{1}{96}, \text{ etc.,}$$

(2) $k = \frac{1}{3}$. Type MCl$_2$.

$$R_1 = 1, \qquad R_2 = -\frac{2}{\sqrt{3}}\,\omega_{21} - \frac{4}{\sqrt{6}}\,\omega_{12}, \qquad R_3^* = -\frac{2}{3}\,m,$$

$$R_3 = 1.21752 + 0.18494m - 0.04558_5 m^2$$

$$R_4 = -\frac{4}{3\sqrt{3}}\,\omega_{21}^2(3 - 2\omega_{21}) - \frac{1}{3\sqrt{6}}\,\omega_{12}^2(12 - 11\omega_{12})$$

$$R_5 = -\frac{1}{18}\,(-1 + 6m + 3m^2)$$

$$R_6 = \frac{1}{27\sqrt{3}}\,\omega_{21}^3(80 - 100\omega_{21} + 33\omega_{21}^2) + \frac{5}{216\sqrt{6}}\,\omega_{12}^3(64 - 152\omega_{12} + 75\omega_{12}^2)$$

$$R_7 = \frac{1}{216}\,(-3 + 24m + 45m^2 + 10m^3) \text{ etc.,}$$

and

$$p_{10} = \frac{1}{\sqrt{3}}, \qquad p_{11}^* = 1, \qquad p_{11} = -0.47473_5 + 0.11136m$$

$$p_{12} = \frac{1}{\sqrt{3}}\,\omega_{21}(4 - 3\omega_{21}) + \frac{4}{\sqrt{6}}\,\omega_{12}^2, \qquad p_{13}^* = \frac{1}{6}\,(1 + 3m)$$

TABLE (5-3-7).—*Continued.*

$$p_{13} = -0.46136 + 0.27553m + 0.0809m^2 + 0.00417_5m^3$$

$$p_{14} = \frac{1}{18\sqrt{3}}\, \omega_{21}^2(48 - 64\omega_{21} + 21\omega_{21}^2) + \frac{1}{9\sqrt{6}}\, \omega_{12}^3(16 - 15\omega_{12})$$

$$p_{15} = \frac{1}{72}\,(1 + 10m + 5m^2)$$

$$p_{16} = -\frac{1}{270\sqrt{3}}\, \omega_{21}^3(320 - 600\omega_{21} + 396\omega_{21}^2 - 99\omega_{21}^3)$$

$$-\frac{1}{1080\sqrt{6}}\, \omega_{12}^4(480 - 1104\omega_{12} + 559\omega_{12}^2)$$

$$p_{17} = -\frac{1}{2592}\,(9 + 105m + 147m^2 + 35m^3), \text{ etc.,}$$

$$p_{20} = \frac{2}{3}\sqrt{6}\,, \qquad p_{21}^* = 1, \qquad p_{21} = -0.67205_5 + 0.08597m$$

$$p_{22} = \frac{1}{\sqrt{6}}\, \omega_{12}(8 - 3\omega_{12}) + \frac{2}{\sqrt{3}}\, \omega_{21}^2\,, \qquad p_{23}^* = \frac{1}{6}\,(-1 + 3m)$$

$$p_{23} = -0.70917 + 0.13456m + 0.06007m^2 + 0.00277m^3$$

$$p_{24} = \frac{1}{72\sqrt{6}}\, \omega_{12}^2(192 - 352\omega_{12} + 135\omega_{12}^2) + \frac{4}{9\sqrt{3}}\, \omega_{21}^3(4 - 3\omega_{21})$$

$$p_{25} = \frac{1}{72}\,(-2 + 5m + 5m^2)$$

$$p_{26} = -\frac{1}{4360\sqrt{6}}\, \omega_{12}^3(2560 - 9120\omega_{12} + 9000\omega_{12}^2 - 2763\omega_{12}^3)$$

$$-\frac{1}{135\sqrt{3}}\, \omega_{21}^4(120 - 168\omega_{21} + 61\omega_{21}^2)$$

$$p_{27} = -\frac{1}{2592}\,(-9 + 21m + 105m^2 + 35m^3) \text{ etc.,}$$

(3) $k = \frac{1}{2}$,   Type MCl_3

$$R_1 = 1, \qquad R_2 = -\omega_{21} - \sqrt{3}\,\omega_{12}\,, \qquad R_3^* = -m$$

$$R_3 = 1.12460 + 0.23493m - 0.10915m^2$$

$$R_4 = -\frac{1}{4}\, \omega_{21}^2(9 - 7\omega_{21}) - \frac{1}{4\sqrt{3}}\, \omega_{12}^2(9 - 11\omega_{12})$$

$$R_5 = -\frac{1}{32}\,(1 + 16m + 12m^2)$$

$$R_6 = \frac{5}{96}\, \omega_{21}^3(36 - 48\omega_{21} + 13\omega_{21}^2) + \frac{1}{288\sqrt{3}}\, \omega_{12}^3(180 - 600\omega_{12} + 353\omega_{12}^2)$$

TABLE (5-3-7).—*Continued.*

$$R_7 = \frac{1}{128}(6 + 33m + 60m^2 + 20m^3) \text{ etc.,}$$

and

$$p_{10} = \frac{4}{9}, \qquad p_{11}^* = 1, \qquad p_{11} = -0.39076_5 + 0.18707m$$

$$p_{12} = 2\omega_{21}(1 - \omega_{21}) + \sqrt{3}\,\omega_{12}^2, \qquad p_{13}^* = \frac{1}{4}(1 + 3m)$$

$$p_{13} = -0.29819 + 0.54233m + 0.21853m^2 + 0.01827m^3$$

$$p_{14} = \frac{1}{24}\omega_{21}^2(36 - 56\omega_{21} + 15\omega_{21}^2) + \frac{1}{6\sqrt{3}}\omega_{12}^3(6 - 7\omega_{12})$$

$$p_{15} = \frac{1}{128}(7 + 30m + 20m^2)$$

$$p_{16} = -\frac{1}{240}\omega_{21}^3(180 - 360\omega_{21} + 195\omega_{21}^2 - 49\omega_{21}^3)$$

$$-\frac{1}{1440\sqrt{3}}\omega_{12}^4(270 - 828\omega_{12} + 491\omega_{12}^2)$$

$$p_{17} = -\frac{1}{1536}(33 + 147m + 210m^2 + 70m^3) \text{ etc.,}$$

$$p_{20} = \frac{4}{\sqrt{3}}, \qquad p_{21}^* = 1, \qquad p_{21} = -0.7024 + 0.1246m$$

$$p_{22} = \frac{2}{\sqrt{3}}\omega_{12}(3 - \omega_{12}) + \omega_{21}^2, \qquad p_{23}^* = \frac{1}{4}(-1 + 3m)$$

$$p_{23} = -0.7085 + 0.1886m + 0.1352m^2 + 0.00951m^3$$

$$p_{24} = \frac{1}{72\sqrt{3}}\omega_{12}^2(108 - 264\omega_{12} + 101\omega_{12}^2) + \frac{1}{6}\omega_{21}^3(6 - 5\omega_{21})$$

$$p_{25} = \frac{1}{128}(-1 + 10m + 20m^2)$$

$$p_{26} = -\frac{1}{2160\sqrt{3}}\omega_{12}^3(540 - 2700\omega_{12} + 3177\omega_{12}^2 - 1033\omega_{12}^3)$$

$$-\frac{1}{480}\omega_{21}^4(270 - 396\omega_{21} + 131\omega_{21}^2)$$

$$p_{27} = -\frac{7}{1536}(1 + 5m + 18m^2 + 10m^3) \text{ etc.,}$$

(4) $k = \frac{1}{5}$, $Al_2(SO_4)_3$ type

TABLE (5-3-7).—*Continued.*

$$R_1 = 1, \quad R_2 = -\frac{4}{\sqrt{10}}\,\omega_{21} - \frac{6}{\sqrt{15}}\,\omega_{12}, \quad R_3^* = -\frac{2}{5}\,m,$$

$$R_3 = 1.26153 + 0.11866m - 0.01595m^2$$

$$R_4 = -\frac{1}{5\sqrt{10}}\,\omega_{21}^2(36 - 23\omega_{21}) - \frac{4}{5\sqrt{15}}\,\omega_{12}^2(9 - 7\omega_{12})$$

$$R_5 = -\frac{1}{50}\,(-5 + 10m + 3m^2)$$

$$R_6 = \frac{1}{600\sqrt{10}}\,\omega_{21}^3(2880 - 3720\omega_{21} + 1343\omega_{21}^2)$$

$$+ \frac{1}{225\sqrt{15}}\,\omega_{12}^3(720 - 1380\omega_{12} + 617\omega_{12}^2)$$

$$R_7 = \frac{1}{1000}\,(-45 + 48m + 75m^2 + 10m^3)\ \text{etc.},$$

$$p_{10} = = \frac{2}{9}\,\sqrt{10}, \quad p_{11}^* = 1, \quad p_{11} = -0.52788_5 + 0.06220m$$

$$p_{12} = \frac{1}{\sqrt{10}}\,\omega_{21}(8 - 5\omega_{21}) + \frac{6}{\sqrt{15}}\,\omega_{12}^2$$

$$p_{13}^* = \frac{1}{10}\,(1 + 3m)$$

$$p_{13} = -0.55168 + 0.13726m + 0.02625_5m^2 + 0.00078\ m^3$$

$$p_{14} = \frac{1}{120\sqrt{10}}\,\omega_{21}^2(576 - 736\omega_{21} + 261\omega_{21}^2) + \frac{8}{15\sqrt{15}}\,\omega_{12}^3(6 - 5\omega_{12})$$

$$p_{15} = \frac{1}{200}\,(-2 + 15m + 5m^2)$$

$$p_{16} = -\frac{1}{12000\sqrt{10}}\,\omega_{21}^3(23040 - 44640\omega_{21} + 32232\omega_{21}^2 - 8405\omega_{21}^3)$$

$$- \frac{1}{1125\sqrt{15}}\,\omega_{12}^4(1080 - 2088\omega_{12} + 965\omega_{12}^2)$$

$$p_{17} = -\frac{7}{12000}\,(-9 + 27m + 33m^2 + 5m^3)\ \text{etc.},$$

$$p_{20} = \frac{\sqrt{15}}{3}, \quad p_{21}^* = 1, \quad p_{21} = -0.64350_5 + 0.05342m$$

$$p_{22} = \frac{1}{\sqrt{15}}\,\omega_{12}(12 - 5\omega_{12}) + \frac{4}{\sqrt{10}}\,\omega_{21}^2, \quad p_{23}^* = \frac{1}{10}\,(-1 + 3m),$$

$$p_{23} = -0.69374 + 0.08892m + 0.02209m^2 + 0.00061m^3$$

TABLE (5-3-7).—*Continued.*

$$p_{24} = \frac{1}{90\sqrt{15}} \omega_{12}^2(432 - 672\omega_{12} + 257\omega_{12}^2) + \frac{1}{15\sqrt{10}} \omega_{21}^3(48 - 35\omega_{21})$$

$$p_{25} = \frac{1}{200} (- 7 + 10m + 5m^2)$$

$$p_{26} = - \frac{1}{6750\sqrt{15}} \omega_{12}^3(8640 - 24840\omega_{12} + 22212\omega_{12}^2 - 6545\omega_{12}^3)$$

$$- \frac{1}{3000\sqrt{10}} \omega_{21}^4(4320 - 6192\omega_{21} + 2375\omega_{21}^2)$$

$$p_{27} = - \frac{1}{12000} (- 97 + 49m + 189m^2 + 35m^3) \text{ etc.,}$$

(5) $k = \dfrac{3}{5}$, $K_4Fe(CN)_6$ type

$$R_1 = 1, \quad R_2 = - \frac{1}{\sqrt{5}} (3 - m), \quad R_3^* = - \frac{6}{5} m$$

$$R_3 = 1.04272 + 0.23434m - 0.16633m^2$$

$$R_4 = - \frac{2}{5\sqrt{5}} \omega_{21}^2(12 - 11\omega_{21}) - \frac{1}{10\sqrt{5}} \omega_{12}^2(24 - 37\omega_{12})$$

$$R_5 = - \frac{1}{50} (5 + 30m + 27m^2)$$

$$R_6 = \frac{2}{75\sqrt{5}} \omega_{21}^3(160 - 240\omega_{21} + 51\omega_{21}^2) + \frac{1}{2400\sqrt{5}} \omega_{12}^3(1280 - 5520\omega_{12} + 3783\omega_{12}^2)$$

$$R_7 = \frac{1}{1000} (95 + 396m + 675m^2 + 270m^3) \text{ etc.,}$$

$$p_{10} = \frac{\sqrt{5}}{6}, \quad p_{11}^* = 1, \quad p_{11} = - 0.32593_5 + 0.24472m$$

$$p_{12} = \frac{1}{4\sqrt{5}} (7 - 10m - m^2), \quad p_{13}^* = \frac{3}{10} (1 + 3m)$$

$$p_{13} = -0.15762 + 0.79120m + 0.36696m^2 + 0.03915_5m^3$$

$$p_{14} = \frac{2}{15\sqrt{5}} \omega_{21}^2(24 - 44\omega_{21} + 9\omega_{21}^2) + \frac{1}{30\sqrt{5}} \omega_{12}^3(32 - 45\omega_{12})$$

$$p_{15} = \frac{1}{200} (17 + 60m + 45m^2)$$

TABLE (5-3-7).—*Concluded.*

$$p_{16} = -\frac{1}{375\sqrt{5}}\,\omega_{21}^3(640 - 1440\omega_{21} + 612\omega_{21}^2 - 185\omega_{21}^3)$$

$$-\frac{1}{12000\sqrt{5}}\,\omega_{12}^4(1920 - 7392\omega_{12} + 5015\omega_{12}^2)$$

$$p_{17} = -\frac{1}{12000}\,(439 + 1743m + 2457m^2 + 945m^3)\ \text{etc.,}$$

$$p_{20} = \frac{4}{3}\,\sqrt{5}\ ,\qquad p_{21}^* = 1,\qquad p_{21} = -0.71789_5 + 0.14724m$$

$$p_{22} = \frac{1}{8\sqrt{5}}\,(31 - 14m - m^2),\qquad p_{23}^* = \frac{3}{10}\,(-1 + 3m)$$

$$p_{23} = -0.69667 + 0.22603_5 m + 0.19821m^2 + 0.01710m^3$$

$$p_{24} = \frac{1}{480\sqrt{5}}\,\omega_{12}^2(768 - 2368\omega_{12} + 903\omega_{12}^2) + \frac{2}{15\sqrt{5}}\,\omega_{21}^3(16 - 15\omega_{21})$$

$$p_{25} = \frac{1}{200}\,(2 + 15m + 45m^2)$$

$$p_{26} = -\frac{1}{96000\sqrt{5}}\,\omega_{12}^3(20480 - 132480\omega_{12} + 181584\omega_{12}^2 - 61405\omega_{12}^3)$$

$$-\frac{2}{375\sqrt{5}}\,\omega_{21}^4(240 - 384\omega_{21} + 115\omega_{21}^2)$$

$$p_{27} = -\frac{1}{12000}\,(121 + 483m + 1323m^2 + 945m^3)\ \text{etc.,}$$

Chapter (6)

Experimental Investigation of Irreversible Processes in Solutions of Strong Electrolytes. Conductance, Transference Numbers, Viscosity and Diffusion

In the preceding chapters, the theoretical equations necessary for the interpretation of dilute ionic solutions have been developed and summarized. We shall now undertake to utilize the experimental methods which have proved most fruitful in this field, considering first the conductance measurements [Chapters (6) and (7)], and then the measurements of thermodynamic properties [Chapters (8), (9) and (10)] in suitable order. From the very beginning of the study of electrolytes, conductance measurements have proved of great value, and their importance has increased as the subject has developed. This is because of the great accuracy attainable, and of the generality of the method, which can be applied to the study of strong and weak electrolytes in any stable medium which will dissolve them. Further, the conductance of electrolytic solutions has been studied as a function of the frequency and potential gradient of external electrical fields. This extends the range of variables beyond that considered by thermodynamic methods.

(1) EQUIVALENT CONDUCTANCE, Λ. PRIMARY STANDARDS

The equivalent conductance of an electrolyte in solution is defined by the equation

$$\Lambda = \frac{1000 \, L^*}{c^*} \tag{6-1-1}$$

in which c^* is the concentration of the electrolyte in equivalents per liter, and L^* is that part of the specific conductivity of the solution which is due to the electrolyte. In the simplest case, L^* is obtained by subtracting the specific conductivity of the pure solvent, L_0, from that of the solution, L. If L_0 is not very small compared to L, it may be necessary to consider the effect of the dissolved electrolyte upon the conductivity of the solvent. For example, if much of the solvent conductivity is due to the ions formed from dissolved carbon dioxide, it is clear that this quantity would be greatly decreased in the presence of a strong acid such as hydrochloric. Thus the proper estimation of L^* from observed values of L and L_0 must take account of the nature of the electrolyte as well as the solvent. The details of such calculations are discussed elsewhere.[1]

[1] C. W. Davies, "The Conductivity of Solutions," John Wiley and Sons, New York, 1930; *Trans. Faraday Soc.*, **28**, 607 (1932). W. F. K. Wynne-Jones, *J. Phys Chem.*, **31**, 1647 (1927).

Measurement of the conductivity of solutions of electrolytes depends upon the use of some modification of the Wheatstone bridge. Except in very rare cases,[2] polarization at the electrodes in contact with the solution must be reduced by the use of alternating currents[3] and platinization of the electrodes.[4] Even at moderate frequencies, alternating currents complicate the measurement of resistance by including the effects of the capacitance of the cell, and the inductance and capacitance of various parts of the bridge network. The elimination or accurate compensation of these effects requires considerable ingenuity. Since the initial development of the alternating current conductivity bridge by Kohlrausch,[5] many technical advances have been made in bridge design, and in the source and detection of the alternating current signal.[6] A large proportion of the most precise conductivity data now available was obtained with equipment based upon the designs of Jones and Josephs,[7] and of Shedlovsky.[8] In most studies of electrolytes at high dilution, the errors due to limitations of the best modern bridges are considerably less than those due to capacitance effects in conductivity cells, and uncertainty in the estimation of the proper solvent conductivity.

The problem of cell design has been very thoroughly investigated by Jones and Bollinger[9] and by Shedlovsky.[10] The capacitance of the cell is ordinarily compensated by a variable condenser in the opposite bridge arm, but Jones and Bollinger showed that if the leads to the electrodes are not widely separated from certain parts of the cell which contain solution, there is produced a capacitance by-path of such a nature that compensation is not practicable. It was shown that this fault in cell design would

[2] J. N. Brönsted and R. F. Nielsen, *Trans. Faraday Soc.*, **31**, 1478 (1935); R. M. Fuoss and C. A. Kraus, *J. Am. Chem. Soc.*, **55**, 21, 3614 (1933); L. V. Andrews and W. E. Martin, *Ibid.*, **60**, 871 (1938); H. E. Gunning and A. R. Gordon, *J. Chem. Phys.*, **10**, 126 (1942).

[3] Polarization is not eliminated at audio frequencies, but may be corrected for by extrapolating resistance readings, $R_{\tilde{\omega}}$ (at various frequencies $\tilde{\omega}$), to give the resistance, R_{∞}, at infinite frequency. G. Jones and S. M. Christian [*J. Am. Chem. Soc.*, **57**, 272 (1935)] showed that extrapolation of $R_{\tilde{\omega}}$ against $1/\sqrt{\tilde{\omega}}$ is linear.

[4] The conditions under which polarization is reduced by platinization of the electrodes have been investigated by G. Jones and D. M. Bollinger [*J. Am. Chem. Soc.*, **57**, 280 (1935)].

[5] F. Kohlrausch, *Z. physik. Chem.*, **2**, 561 (1888).

[6] A comprehensive review of the subject is given by B. Hague, "A. C. Bridge Methods," Pitman, New York, 1938.

[7] G. Jones and R. C. Josephs, *J. Am. Chem. Soc.*, **50**, 1049 (1928); P. H. Dike, *Rev. Sci. Instruments*, **2**, 379 (1931).

[8] T. Shedlovsky, *J. Am. Chem. Soc.*, **52**, 1793 (1930). These investigators make use of a ground similar to that of K. W. Wagner [*Elektrotech. Z.*, **32**, 1001 (1911)]. A. V. Astin [*Bur. Standards J. Research*, **21**, 425 (1938)] and W. F. Luder [*J. Am. Chem. Soc.*, **62**, 89 (1940)] have recently proposed a separate detector terminal balance to ground for increasing the sensitivity in measuring high resistances.

[9] G. Jones and G. M. Bollinger, *J. Am. Chem. Soc.*, **53**, 411 (1931).

[10] T. Shedlovsky, *Ibid.*, **52**, 1806 (1930). *Cf.* J. C. Nichol and R. M. Fuoss, *J. Phys. Chem.*, **58**, 15 (1954).

produce an error which must vary with the specific resistance of the solution.[11] This offered a ready explanation for the observation that the cell constants of certain cells show a slight variation[12] with the conductivity of the solution.

The relation between the measured resistance across the terminals of a conductivity cell and the specific conductivity of the solution depends upon the geometry of the cell. In the simple case, where the electrodes form the parallel ends of a cylindrical cell, X, of length, l, and uniform cross-section, a, the specific conductivity is given by

$$L = K_x/R_x \qquad\qquad (6\text{-}1\text{-}2)$$

The term K_x equals l/a, is a property of the particular cell, and is called the cell constant.[13] To avoid the necessity of always constructing cells of uniform and accurately known dimensions, K_x is calculated by equation (6-1-2) from the measured value of R_x when the cell contains a standard solution of known specific conductivity, L. The primary standard for this purpose is pure mercury, by virtue of its use in defining the international ohm. The specific conductivity of mercury is so high that solutions of potassium chloride are used as secondary standards in determining the cell constants of cells designed for the study of electrolytes. Kohlrausch[14] was the first to determine the specific conductivity of standard potassium chloride solutions in absolute units, and his results were used for many years without being seriously questioned. There was, however, some ambiguity in the manner in which Kohlrausch described the composition of his standard solutions. Parker and Parker[15] redetermined the specific conductance of potassium chloride solutions, and eliminated an inconsistency in units by defining a *demal* (written 1D) solution as one containing one gram molecule of salt dissolved in one cubic decimeter of solution at 0°. The Parker and Parker results were chosen as standards for the tabulation of conductance values in the "International Critical Tables," but objections were soon raised regarding this choice.

Jones and Bradshaw[16] made new absolute measurements of the specific conductivity of solutions of the same composition used by Parker and Parker, and Jones and Prendergast[17] reinvestigated the solutions described

[11] Compare C. W. Davies, *J. Chem. Soc.*, **138**, 432 (1937).

[12] H. C. Parker, *J. Am. Chem. Soc.*, **45**, 1366, 2017 (1923).

[13] If the cross-section, a, is not uniform, but is known as a function of the distance from one of the electrodes, the cell constant is given by

$$K_x = \int_0^l \frac{dl}{a}$$

[14] F. Kohlrausch, L. Holborn and H. Diesselhorst, *Wien. Ann.*, **64**, 417 (1898).

[15] H. C. Parker and E. W. Parker, *J. Am. Chem. Soc.*, **46**, 312 (1924).

[16] G. Jones and B. C. Bradshaw, *J. Am. Chem. Soc.*, **55**, 1780 (1933).

[17] G. Jones and M. J. Prendergast, *J. Am. Chem. Soc.*, **59**, 731 (1937).

by Kohlrausch.   The results of these new measurements tend to confirm the values of Kohlrausch rather than those of Parker and Parker, but differ substantially from both.   The results of Jones are now generally accepted as the most reliable secondary standards available for solution conductivity, and all the conductances which we compile in the text and tables have been referred to the Jones standards.   As an aid in making the conversion from one of the common standards to another, we have recorded the Kohlrausch, Parker, and Jones values of the specific conductivity for various potassium chloride solutions in Table (6-1-1).   In the lower half of this table, the concentrations are expressed as 1 demal ($1D$), tenth demal ($0.1D$), etc.   Jones has eliminated all sources of ambiguity by expressing the composition of his solutions in terms of the actual weights of salt and solution in vacuo.

TABLE (6-1-1).† SPECIFIC CONDUCTIVITY OF STANDARD POTASSIUM CHLORIDE SOLUTIONS IN OHMS⁻¹ CM.⁻¹

	0°	18°	20°	25°
$1N$ KCl 71.3828 g KCl per kg of solution in vacuum				
Kohlrausch.........	0.06541	0.09822	0.10207	0.11180
Parker.............	$.06531_2$	$.09811_6$		$.11168_7$
Jones.............	$.06543_0$	$.09820_1$	$.10202_4$	$.11173_3$
$0.1N$ KCl 7.43344 g KCl per kg of solution in vacuum				
Kohlrausch.........	0.00715	0.01119	0.01167	0.01288
Parker.............	$.007141_6$	$.011184_6$		$.012876_5$
Jones.............	$.007154_2$	$.011191_9$	$.011667_6$	$.012886_2$
$0.01N$ KCl 0.746558 g KCl per kg of solution in vacuum				
Kohlrausch.........	0.000776	0.001225	0.001278	0.001413
Parker.............	$.0007742_2$	$.0012223_8$		$.0014103_7$
Jones.............	$.0007751_2$	$.0012226_9$	$.0012757_2$	$.0014114_5$
$1D$ KCl 71.1352 g KCl per kg of solution in vacuum				
Parker.............	0.06509_8	0.09779_0		0.11132_2
Jones.............	$.06517_6*$	$.09783_8*$		$.11134_2*$
$0.1D$ KCl 7.41913 g KCl per kg of solution in vacuum				
Parker.............	0.007129_5	0.011163_8		0.012852_4
Jones.............	$.007137_9*$	$.011166_7*$		$.012856_0*$
$0.01D$ KCl 0.745263 g KCl per kg of solution in vacuum				
Parker.............	0.00077284	0.0012202_3		0.0014078_9
Jones.............	$.0007736_4*$	$.0012205_2*$		$.0014087_7*$

† A discrepancy of several parts in 10,000 between the conductivities of the normal and demal standard solutions has been pointed out by H. E. Gunning and A. R. Gordon, *J. Chem. Phys.*, **10**, 130 (1942), footnote (14).

* These values of Jones and Bradshaw are used as standards for all conductances recorded in this book.   An equation permitting standardization at other concentrations is proposed by J. E. Lind, Jr., J. J. Zwolenik and R. M. Fuoss, *J. Am. Chem. Soc.*, **81**, 1557 (1959).

(2) The Onsager Conductance Equation.   Comparison with Experiment

In the derivation of the theoretical equation (5-3-1) for the equivalent conductance,

$$\Lambda = \Lambda^0 - \mathcal{S}_{(\Lambda)}\sqrt{c} = \Lambda^0 - (\alpha^*\Lambda^0 + \beta^*)\sqrt{c} \qquad (6\text{-}2\text{-}1)$$

the treatment was confined to completely dissociated electrolytes at extreme dilutions.   The equation will now be tested under these conditions. Later, it will be shown that the theory is also applicable to the *ions* of incompletely dissociated electrolytes.

Onsager[18] evaluated the parameters of the equation

$$\Lambda = \Lambda^0 - A\sqrt{c} + Bc \qquad (6\text{-}2\text{-}2)$$

from data of Kohlrausch at high dilutions.   The agreement between A[19] and $\mathcal{S}_{(\Lambda)}$ was within 5 and 13 % for 1-1 and 2-1 electrolytes.   In a more comprehensive test, Lange[20] demonstrated that the equation

$$\Lambda = \Lambda^0 - \mathcal{S}_{(\Lambda)}\sqrt{c} + Bc \qquad (6\text{-}2\text{-}2a)$$

with one less adjustable parameter, adequately represents the data for 560 strong electrolytes in a variety of solvents, and at concentrations up to 0.05 to 0.1 molar.   He showed that that B is proportional to Λ^0.

The data for some 1-1 electrolytes are compared with the theoretical limiting functions in Fig. (6-2-1).   The dependence of the slope of these graphs upon the temperature and the magnitude of Λ^0 is very striking indeed.   The value of Λ^0 for hydrochloric acid at 25° is almost three times that for potassium chloride at the same temperature.   The temperature appears explicitly in the theoretical slope as the product, $D_0 T$, which decreases only about 18 per cent in water between 0 and 100°.   The most pronounced temperature effect is the rapid decrease in viscosity, which acts to increase both Λ^0 and β^*.

The influence of valence type upon conductance is illustrated in Fig. (6-2-2).   The data used in this figure were all obtained at 25°, and the values of Λ^0 for the various salts are roughly equal.   All the results except those for zinc sulfate are in excellent accord with theory.   Throughout the entire experimental concentration range, the decrease in the conductance of zinc sulfate with $\sqrt{c}$ is more rapid than the theory predicts.   This behavior is characteristic of weak electrolytes.   Figure (6-2-2) shows that

[18] L. Onsager, *Physik. Z.*, **28**, 277 (1927); J. Lange, *Z. Physik. Chem.*, **A188**, 284 (1941).

[19] P. Walden [*Z. physik. Chem.*, **144**, 297, 434 (1929); *Ibid.*, **147 A**, 1 (1930)] showed that $A \simeq 65.7/D_0\eta_0$ by an extension of the empirical Ostwald-Walden-Bredig rule. This relation gives values of the same order as $\mathcal{S}_{(\Lambda)}$ for a surprising variety of electrolytes in various solvents.

[20] J. Lange, *Z. Physik. Chem.*, **A188**, 284 (1941).   *Cf* equation (6-11-1)

at moderate concentrations the conductance of potassium nitrate also falls below the limiting function, but to a less marked degree. This effect will be considered later.

Values of Λ and Λ^0 in water are given in Table (6-2-1A), and of Λ^0 in another medium of high dielectric constant are given in Table (6-2-2A).

As a further direct test of the theory, the effect of dielectric constant is shown in Fig. (6-2-3), where $(\Lambda - \Lambda^0)\eta_0$ for tetraethylammonium picrate in nitromethane,[21] methanol,[22] ethanol,[23] and acetone[24] is plotted against $\sqrt{c}$. The temperature of each system is 25°. The inclusion of the factor η_0 in

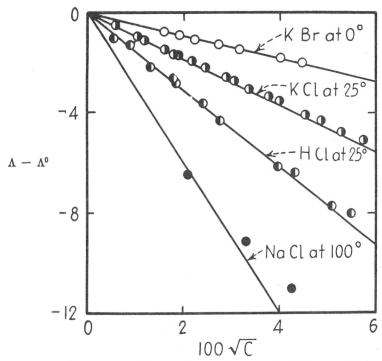

Fig. (6-2-1). Comparison of theoretical equation (6-2-1) with data for 1-1 electrolytes. The straight lines represent the theoretical equation (6-2-1).

the ordinates eliminates the effect of the widely different viscosities of the solvents, since both $\Lambda^0\eta_0$ and $\mathfrak{S}_{(\Lambda)}\eta_0$ are independent of η_0 for solutes, such as tetraethylammonium picrate, which obey Walden's rule [Equation (7-1-4)]. Consequently, the differences in the limiting slopes and in the character of the plots in the figure are almost entirely due to differences in dielectric con-

[21] C. P. Wright, D. M. Murray-Rust and H. Hartley, *J. Chem. Soc. (London)*, **134**, 199 (1931).

[22] A. Unmack, E. Bullock, D. M. Murray-Rust and H. Hartley, *Proc. Roy. Soc. London*, **A132**, 427 (1931).

[23] M. Barak and H. Hartley, *Z. physik. Chem.*, **A165**, 272 (1933).

[24] P. Walden, H. Ulich and G. Busch, *Ibid.*, **123**, 429 (1926).

stants. Specific solvent effects, which strongly influence the conductance of small ions, are minimized by our choice of solute.[25]

Figure (6-2-3) emphasizes the point that the predictions of the theoretical equation are verified by experimental results obtained under the conditions postulated in the theory, namely high dilution and complete dissociation. A number of phenomena indicate that ionization is far from complete in media of low dielectric constants. The tendency of Λ to fall more and more below the theoretical function as the dielectric constant is decreased must be due largely to incomplete dissociation. These negative

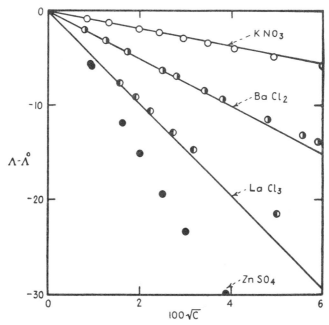

Fig. (6-2-2). The influence of valence upon the equivalent conductance in aqueous solutions at 25°. The straight lines represent the theoretical equation (6-2-1). Note that $\mathfrak{S}_{(\Lambda)}$ for LaCl₃ and ZnSO₄ are indistinguishable on this scale.

departures from the limiting equation are discussed in the following section and in Chapter (7).

The general equation (4-3-51) for the equivalent conductance of an ion constituent in the presence of an arbitrary mixture of ions is

$$\lambda_j = \lambda_j^0 - \left[\frac{1.981 \times 10^6}{(D_0 T)^{3/2}} \lambda_j^0 z_j \sum_0^\infty c_n r_j^{(n)} + \frac{29.16 z_j}{\eta_0 (DT)^{1/2}} \right] \sqrt{\Gamma} \quad (6\text{-}2\text{-}3)$$

In this equation $z_j \sum_0^\infty c_n r_j^{(n)}$ replaces the factor $| z_1 z_2 | q^* / (1 + \sqrt{q^*})$ in equation (4-3-42), derived for only two kinds of ions. The difference

[25] H. Ulich, *Z. angew. Chem.*, **41**, 1141 (1928).

between the effects of these two factors upon the numerical value of λ_j is not large in any case, and becomes zero as the mobilities of the various ions of like charge approach equality. Therefore, a rigorous experimental test of the "mixture effect" is more difficult than the tests of equation (6-2-1). The most readily verified prediction of equation (6-2-3) is that wide departures from the Kohlrausch principle of independent ionic mobilities should appear in mixtures containing ions of like sign but very

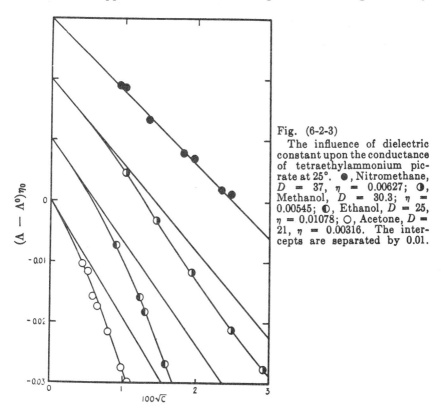

Fig. (6-2-3)

The influence of dielectric constant upon the conductance of tetraethylammonium picrate at 25°. ●, Nitromethane, $D = 37$, $\eta = 0.00627$; ◑, Methanol, $D = 30.3$; $\eta = 0.00545$; ◐, Ethanol, $D = 25$, $\eta = 0.01078$; ○, Acetone, $D = 21$, $\eta = 0.00316$. The intercepts are separated by 0.01.

different mobilities. In a mixture of hydrochloric acid and potassium chloride, the theory predicts that the hydrogen-ion mobility will be smaller, and the potassium-ion mobility larger than in solutions of the pure single electrolytes at the same ionic strength. This effect is clearly shown in Figs. (6-2-4) and (6-2-5). The ordinates represent the difference (in % of λ_j) between the cation conductance in the mixture and in a solution of the single electrolyte at the same ionic strength. The solid lines are the theoretical curves at 25° calculated by Onsager and Fuoss.[26] The circles represent the observed[27] effects at the same temperature. The

[26] L. Onsager and R. M. Fuoss, *J. Phys. Chem.*, **36**, 2689 (1932).
[27] L. G. Longsworth, *J. Am. Chem. Soc.*, **52**, 1897 (1930).

crosses represent an independent series of measurements[28] at 18°. The observed and theoretical effects are seen to agree in sign and order of magnitude. Exact numerical agreement could not be expected at the concentration involved ($\Gamma = 0.2$). The results given in Table (6-2-1) indicate more complete concordance at high dilution. The measurements upon which this table is based could not be expressed in terms of individual ionic

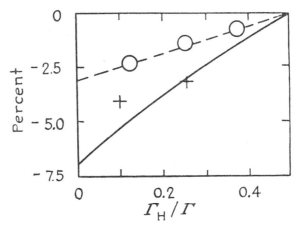

Fig. (6-2-4). Variation in hydrogen ion conductance in HCl-KCl mixtures

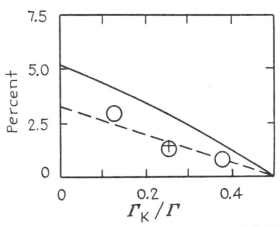

Fig. (6-2-5). Variation in potassium ion conductance in HCl-KCl mixtures

conductances, because the transference numbers are not known in sodium chloride-hydrochloric acid mixtures. The comparison with theory was therefore made on the basis of specific conductivities. In the column headed % obs., we have recorded the percentage difference between observed specific conductivities of the mixtures and values calculated by the

[28] K. Bennewitz, C. Wagner and K. Küchler, *Physik. Z.*, **30**, 623 (1929).

Kohlrausch law from measurements on solutions of the pure electrolytes. The % calc. column contains the corresponding changes in specific conductivity predicted by equation (6-2-3). The last column shows that the difference between the observed and calculated mixture effects disappears at high dilution. Similar results were obtained in mixtures of lithium and potassium chlorides by Krieger and Kilpatrick.[29]

The careful measurements of Renholm[30] on mixtures of potassium chloride with barium nitrate or copper sulfate, clearly demonstrate a "mixture effect" of the conductance at quite low concentrations (10^{-3} to 10^{-4}). A comparison of his results with the predictions of equation (6-2-3) has not been attempted because of the incomplete ionization of barium nitrate and copper sulfate.

TABLE (6-2-1).* COMPARISON OF OBSERVED WITH CALCULATED MIXTURE EFFECTS ON THE SPECIFIC CONDUCTIVITY OF HCl-NaCl MIXTURES AT 25°.

$\dfrac{c_{NaCl}}{c_{HCl}}$	r	% obs.	% calc.	Δ
1	0.400	1.99	3.31	1.32
1	.080	1.02	1.38	.36
1	.020	.76	.66	− .10
2	.300	1.72	3.29	1.57
2	.060	.98	1.35	.37
2	.015	.62	.65	.03
5	.240	1.44	2.50	1.06
5	.048	.88	1.03	.15
5	.012	.49	.49	.00

* Taken from Table VII in the paper of L. Onsager and R. M. Fuoss [*J. Phys. Chem.*, **36**, 2689 (1932)]. The measurements are by W. C. Bray and F. L. Hunt [*J. Am. Chem. Soc.*, **33**, 781 (1911)].

(3) EXTENSIONS OF THE ONSAGER EQUATION. EVALUATION OF Λ^0

Three distinct methods have been used for extending the range of the Onsager equation to somewhat higher concentrations. The first applies only to electrolytes for which the conductance falls below the limiting law in dilute solutions, and interprets this "conductance deficiency" in terms of finite ionization constants. The second assumes infinite ionization constants (complete dissociation), and attempts to account for all departures from the limiting equation by more elaborate theoretical treatments designed to include higher terms in the mathematical approximations, or inclusion of the "mean distance of closest approach" in the physical picture. The third method is the purely empirical addition of terms in higher powers of c than the one-half. To prevent confusion, these methods will be discussed separately.

[29] K. A. Krieger and M. Kilpatrick, *J. Am. Chem. Soc.*, **59**, 1878 (1937); Correction, *Ibid.*, **60**, 3601 (1938).
[30] J. E. Renholm, "Dissertation," Helsingfors, 1925.

The Introduction of Finite Dissociation Constants

The manner in which the limiting law is approached in dilute solutions is of considerable theoretical importance. Onsager[31] pointed out that completely dissociated electrolytes should approach the limiting tangent asymptotically from above, whereas incompletely dissociated electrolytes should approach it from below. Ionic association restricts the concentration range over which the limiting slope may be used, but does not influence its numerical value because the effect of association is proportional to the first power of the concentration at high dilution. This can be readily shown by combining the expression

$$K = \frac{(y_\pm \alpha)^2 c}{(1 - \alpha)} \qquad (6\text{-}3\text{-}1)$$

for the dissociation constant of a binary electrolyte, with equation (6-2-1). At extreme dilution, it is permissible to set both α^2 and the activity coefficient, $y_\pm^2$, equal to unity in the numerator, so that

$$1 - \alpha \simeq c/K \qquad (6\text{-}3\text{-}2)$$

Since the decrease in conductance due to ionic association is $\Lambda(1 - \alpha)$, or $\Lambda^0(1 - \alpha)$ in the limit, we may write

$$\Lambda = \Lambda^0 - (\alpha^*\Lambda^0 + \beta^*)\sqrt{c} - c\Lambda^0/K \qquad (6\text{-}3\text{-}3)$$

which is equation (62) given by Onsager. Although equation (6-3-3) is of theoretical interest, its use in the evaluation of ionization constants is subject to serious difficulties. This equation can represent the conductance of a partially dissociated electrolyte only throughout the concentration range in which (6-2-1) is valid for completely dissociated electrolytes. Reference to Figs. (6-2-1) and (6-2-2) shows that, in the region where the experimental curves for potassium nitrate and zinc sulfate are clearly concave downward, the curves for the typical strong electrolytes become concave upward. Any determination of the degree of dissociation of potassium nitrate, or zinc sulfate, should therefore take both of these effects into account. The first method of doing this is illustrated below.

Onsager assumed that the curve for potassium chloride represents the normal[32] deviation of strong 1-1 electrolytes from the limiting law. On this assumption, the difference, $\Lambda_{(obs.)} - \Lambda_{(lim.\ law.)}$, for potassium nitrate subtracted from the corresponding difference for potassium chloride, at the same concentration, would be the "conductance deficiency" attributed to the association of potassium nitrate. In terms of this deficiency, Δ, the associated fraction of the electrolyte would be

$$1 - \alpha = \Delta/\Lambda_{(obs.)} \qquad (6\text{-}3\text{-}4)$$

[31] L. Onsager, *Physik. Z.*, **28**, 277 (1927).

[32] In Section (11) the initial departure from the limiting law is expressed in terms of the a-parameter.

From this, K may be evaluated by (6-3-1) if the activity coefficient is known. In this connection, it should be noted that the stoichiometric activity coefficients calculated from freezing-point depressions, and other colligative properties, are actually the product, $y_\pm \alpha$, occurring in (6-3-1). The activity coefficient of un-ionized KNO_3 is assumed to be unity.

Table (6-3-1) gives the values of K, and the data required in their calculation. K is seen to be essentially constant over the whole concentration range considered. This independence of K upon concentration is a necessary, but not a sufficient, condition for the validity of the hypothesis that the conductance of potassium nitrate (in dilute solutions) falls below the limiting law because of ionic association. This is an important point, and will be referred to later in this section.

TABLE (6-3-1).[*] ESTIMATION OF THE DISSOCIATION CONSTANT OF KNO_3 AT 25° BY ONSAGER'S METHOD.

c	.005	.01	.02	.05	.07	.1
$\Lambda_{(obs.)}$; KNO_3	138.48	135.82	132.41	126.31	123.55	120.39
$\Lambda_{(obs.)} - \Lambda_{(L.L)}$; KCl	0.45	0.89	1.79	4.50	6.22	8.77
$\Lambda_{(obs.)} - \Lambda_{(L.L)}$; KNO_3	0.08	0.14	0.56	2.08	3.13	4.77
"Deficiency", Δ	0.37	0.75	1.23	2.42	3.09	4.00
Degree of Association $1 - \alpha$	.0027	.0055	.0093	.0192	.0250	.0332
$y_\pm \alpha$; KNO_3[†]	.927	.899	.862	.794	.763	.726
K	1.59	1.47	1.60	1.64	1.63	1.59

[*] All conductances are the smoothed values of T. Shedlovsky [*J. Am. Chem. Soc.*, **54**, 1411 (1932)] corrected to the standard of G. Jones and B. C. Bradshaw.

[†] G. Scatchard, S. S. Prentiss and P. T. Jones, *J. Am. Chem. Soc.*, **54**, 2690 (1932).

Davies[33] has made a large number of calculations of this nature,[34] and has tabulated[35] the dissociation constants of a variety of salts, especially complex valence types. Some typical results are given in Table (6-3-2). Values of K for more complex species are given in Table (6-3-1A). Judging from the magnitude of K for many of these salts, it appears that dissociation is far from complete in solutions of electrolytes of high valence types. However, we do not wish to accept this view entirely without reservation, because the evaluation of K depends upon the arbitrary selection of some conductance curve to represent the behavior of the

[33] C. W. Davies, *Trans. Faraday Soc.*, **23**, 351 (1927). Later references are given in Table (6-3-2).

[34] If the conductance of the salt departs seriously from the limiting law (*e.g.*, zinc sulfate), an accurate value of Λ^0 cannot be obtained from the simple extrapolation of Λ against $\sqrt{c}$. In this case, Davies determines, by trial, the value of Λ^0, which leads to the most nearly constant values of K at low concentrations. If accurate activity coefficients are not available, this process yields no completely consistent values of Λ^0 and K over any experimental concentration range, and therefore allows considerable latitude in evaluating either of these constants.

[35] C. W. Davies, *J. Chem. Soc.*, **140**, 2093 (1938); W. H. Banks, E. C. Righellato and C. W. Davies, *Trans. Faraday Soc.*, **27**, 621 (1931).

hypothetical completely dissociated electrolyte. In our calculations, we used the curve for potassium chloride and obtained very self-consistent values of K for potassium nitrate. If we had used almost any other experimental curve as standard, the values of K would have shown more variation with concentration. This difficulty is magnified in the case of a salt such as zinc sulfate, because no 2-2 electrolyte has yet been found to have a conductance curve which approaches the limiting law from above.

TABLE (6-3-2). DISSOCIATION CONSTANTS OF SALTS AND COMPLEX IONS IN WATER ESTIMATED FROM CONDUCTANCE DATA AT 25°* AND 18°. SEE TABLE (6-3-1A).

	K	Ref.		$100K$	Ref.
KClO$_3$	1.4	(1)	(Ca Acetate)$^+$	100*	(3)
KNO$_3$	1.4	(1)	(CaOH)$^+$	3.1*	(4)
AgNO$_3$	1.2	(1)	(BaOH)$^+$	23*	(4)
TlNO$_3$	.52	(1)	MgSO$_4$	0.78	(5)
TlCl	.300	(1)	CaSO$_4$	.53	(6)
(CdNO$_3$)$^+$	.394	(2)	CuSO$_4$	.50	(5)
(CdCl)$^+$	.0101	(2)	ZnSO$_4$	.53	(5)
(PbNO$_3$)$^+$	.0647	(2)	CdSO$_4$	.49	(5)
(PbCl)$^+$	.0304	(2)	MgSO$_4$	.63*	(6)
(CaNO$_3$)$^+$	.521	(2)	CoSO$_4$	.34*	(6)
(SrNO$_3$)$^+$	.150	(2)	NiSO$_4$	.40*	(6)
(BaNO$_3$)$^+$	.121	(2)	CuSO$_4$	.43*	(7)
(LiSO$_4$)$^-$	.229	(2)	ZnSO$_4$	.49*	(7)
(NaSO$_4$)$^-$	.198	(2)	Cu Malonate	.00025*	(6)
(KSO$_4$)$^-$	.151	(2)	Zn Malonate	.021*	(6)
(AgSO$_4$)$^-$	.05	(2)	Cd Malonate	.051*	(6)
(TlSO$_4$)$^-$	.0472	(2)	(KFe(CN)$_6$)$^≡$	.55*	(8)

* Values followed by an asterisk were estimated at 25°.

(1) C. W. Davies, *Trans. Faraday Soc.*, 23, 351 (1927).

(2) E. C. Righellato and C. W. Davies, *Ibid.*, 26, 592 (1930); compare J. Zirkler, *Z. physik. Chem.*, 163A, 1 (1932).

(3) C. W. Davies, *J. Chem. Soc.* (*London*), 140, 277 (1938). The ionization of calcium acetate is exceptionally high. The values of $100K$ for the calcium ions of nine other monobasic organic acids lie between 2 and 30. The association of alkaline-earth metal cations with carboxylic acid radicals has been investigated potentiometrically by R. K. Cannan and A. Kibrick, [*J. Am. Chem. Soc.*, 60, 2314 (1938)] and by N. E. Topp and C. W. Davies, *J. Chem. Soc.*, 142, 87 (1940).

(4) C. W. Davies, *Ibid.*, 141, 349 (1939).

(5) C. W. Davies, *Ibid.*, 140, 2093 (1938). Compare Ref. (1).

(6) R. W. Money and C. W. Davies, *Trans. Faraday Soc.*, 28, 609 (1932).

(7) B. B. Owen and R. W. Gurry, *J. Am. Chem. Soc.*, 60, 3074 (1938).

(8) C. W. Davies, *Ibid.*, 59, 1760 (1937).

Consequently, the physical interpretation of such values of K is somewhat obscure at present, although it may be clarified eventually in terms of the more complete conductance equation (6-11-1).

This situation is greatly improved if we are not required to calculate K at experimental concentrations, but may evaluate K and Λ^0 simultaneously by a suitable extrapolation to infinite dilution. Two similar and convenient extrapolation functions have been proposed by Fuoss[36] and by Shedlovsky.[37] These are considered in detail in Chapters (7), (11) and

[36] R. M. Fuoss, *J. Am. Chem. Soc.*, 57, 488 (1935).

[37] T. Shedlovsky, *J. Franklin Inst.*, 225, 739 (1938).

(13).   Fuoss assumes that the hypothetical completely ionized electrolyte would obey the Onsager limiting law at all concentrations; but Shedlovsky uses equation (6-3-10), which allows small departures above the limiting law in the experimental concentration range.   Both of these procedures, in common with that of Onsager and Davies, require some knowledge of the activity coefficient of the electrolyte as a function of the concentration.   In calculations involving 1-1 electrolytes, the Debye-Hückel limiting law may be satisfactorily employed in many cases, but for high valence type electrolytes it is not yet possible to estimate sufficiently trustworthy activity coefficients for this purpose from theory alone.   Furthermore, the experimental determinations of the activity coefficients of complex electrolytes are neither so accurate nor so numerous as those for simpler salts. For this reason, it is particularly desirable to avoid the introduction of activity coefficients, and to evaluate Λ^0 for complex electrolytes from conductivity data alone.   It will now be shown how this can be done by means of a theoretical extension of the limiting law (6-3-5).

Theoretical Extensions Based Upon The Assumption of Complete Dissociation

In one of his earlier papers,[38] and later with Fuoss,[39] Onsager estimated the effect of the mathematical simplifications involved in the derivation of his limiting equation.   The deviation of Λ from linearity with $\sqrt{c}$ is represented by the addition of two terms.   Thus in dilute solutions[40]

$$\Lambda = \Lambda^0 - S_{(\Lambda)}\sqrt{c} + Ac \log c + Bc \qquad (6\text{-}3\text{-}5)$$

As originally proposed, this expression was semi-empirical in that the numerical values of the constants A and B had not yet been completely[41] evaluated from theoretical considerations.   Recently derived[42] expressions for these constants are considered in Section (11), but unfortunately these are only applicable to symmetrical valence type electrolytes.   In this section, the *formal* validity of equation (6-3-5) will be verified for a variety of valence types, but A and B will be treated as empirical parameters whose evaluation is merely incidental to extrapolation.   The role of these two parameters becomes increasingly important in extrapolating the conductance of the higher valence types because the deviations from the limiting slopes become more pronounced.   Rearranging equation (6-3-5) to read

$$\left[\frac{\Lambda + (\alpha^*\Lambda^0 + \beta^*)\sqrt{c} - \Lambda^0}{c}\right] = A \log c + B \qquad (6\text{-}3\text{-}6)$$

[38] L. Onsager, *Physik. Z.*, **28**, 277 (1927).

[39] L. Onsager and R. M. Fuoss, *J. Phys. Chem.*, **36**, 2689 (1932).

[40] This equation applies to completely dissociated electrolytes.   The linear term, Bc, is not to be confused with the additional term, $-c\Lambda^0/K$, resulting from ionic association.   [*Cf.* equation (6-3-3)].

[41] R. M. Fuoss, *Physik Z.*, **35**, 59 (1934).

[42] R. M. Fuoss and L. Onsager, *J. Phys. Chem.*, **61**, 668 (1957).

the constants A and B can be evaluated from a plot of the bracketed terms against log c. It is clear that when the correct value of Λ^0 is used, a plot of the left-hand member of this equation against log c must be a straight line of slope A and intercept B. The selection of the correct value of Λ^0 can be done very readily by trial, because the value used in calculating the term $\alpha^*\Lambda^0$ is not a very important factor in determining the shape of the plot. A preliminary value of Λ^0 (and α^*) is therefore obtained from a rough extrapolation of a plot of Λ against $\sqrt{c}$. This value is used to

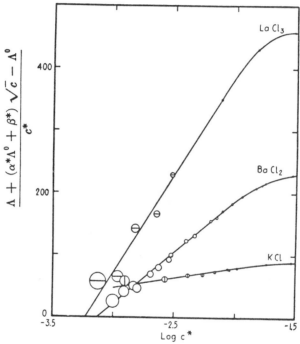

Fig. (6-3-1). Graphical evaluation of the parameters A and B of equation (6-3-5). The radii of circles correspond to an experimental error of 0.01 in Λ.

calculate values of $\Lambda + (\alpha^*\Lambda^0 + \beta^*)\sqrt{c}$, which remain unaltered during the selection of a value of Λ^0 roughly satisfying the graphical requirements of equation (6-3-6). The latter value is then used to calculate more accurate values of $\Lambda + (\alpha^*\Lambda^0 + \beta^*)\sqrt{c}$, and the process repeated until a self-consistent value of Λ^0 is found which will express the data by equation (6-3-6) up to about $0.01N$ within the probable experimental error. The final plots[43] for potassium, barium, and lanthanum chlorides are shown in Fig. (6-3-1). In order to make it possible to plot all three curves in a small space we have expressed the concentration c^* as equivalents per liter in the abscissa and in the denominator of the ordinate. It is apparent

[43] B. B. Owen, J. Am. Chem. Soc., 61, 1393 (1939).

from the figure that equation (6-3-5) fits the experimental results very closely in dilute solutions. The diameters of the circles representing the data correspond to an error of only 0.02 unit in the determination of $\Lambda^0 - \Lambda$. The plots are all linear below $0.008N$,[44] and pass through a maximum at about $0.03N$.

The values of A, B, and Λ^0, obtained from Fig. (6-3-1) and similar plots for other electrolytes, are recorded in Table (6-3-3). Because of the magnitudes[45] of the parameters for the last three electrolytes, the best

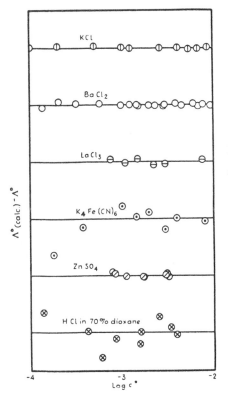

Fig. (6-3-2)
  Deviations: Diameters of circles are 0.06 conductance unit; distance between plots is 0.6 unit.

method of illustrating the accuracy of equation (6-3-5) is to use it to calculate Λ^0 from A and B and each experimental value of Λ. Figure (6-3-2) shows the difference between the values of Λ^0 calculated in this manner and the values of Λ^0 used in the graphical evaluation of A and B. Since the diameters of the circles in the figure represent an uncertainty

---

[44] Five results are available for barium chloride below $0.000985N$, but were omitted from the figure because the apparent uncertainty in $\Lambda^0 - \Lambda$ was several times greater than at higher concentrations.

[45] For reasons to be discussed later, the physical significance of the numerical values of these parameters is obscure.

of 0.06 conductance unit, it is clear that equation (6-3-5) fits the data for potassium, barium and lanthanum chlorides and zinc sulfate within about 0.02 unit. For the other two electrolytes, the deviations are as much as five to ten times as great, but are apparently without consistent trends. For the most part, these larger deviations result from the fact that the data for potassium ferrocyanide were combined from two different sources, and the data for hydrochloric acid involve measurements in two independent preparations of the 70 per cent dioxane solutions used as solvent. From this, it appears that equation (6-3-5) satisfactorily expresses the results for electrolytes of widely different valence types at high dilutions. Recalling that equation (6-3-5) is based upon the assumption of complete dissociation, we note that the conductance of several of these electrolytes can also be interpreted in terms of finite ionization constants [Table (6-3-2)]. This ambiguity in interpretation arises from the arbitrary selection of a standard conductance curve in the calcula-

TABLE (6-3-3).* PARAMETERS OF EQUATION (6-3-5) AT 25°.

Electrolyte	A	B	Λ°
KCl	31.8	144	149.87
BaCl$_2$	175	540	140.00
LaCl$_3$	320	1030	145.8
K$_4$Fe(CN)$_6$	3345	6170	185.0
ZnSO$_4$	5736	10627	132.92
HCl (70% dioxane)	4800	9800	93.1

* In evaluating A and B by equation (6-3-5), the concentration in the terms, $Ac^* \log c^* + Bc^*$, was arbitrarily expressed in equivalents per liter. All results are consistent with the primary standard of G. Jones and B. C. Bradshaw [*J. Am. Chem. Soc.*, **55**, 1780 (1933)].

tion of K, and from the purely empirical evaluation of A and B. For this reason, it is difficult to distinguish between the effects of non-conducting ion pairs, postulated in the estimation of K, and the higher electrostatic terms represented by $Ac \log c$ and Bc in (6-3-5), until A and B are evaluated theoretically. The equations in Section (11) express A and B in terms of ionic radii. The numerical values of these radii, calculated from different kinds of measurements[46], are in substantial agreement for 1-1 electrolytes even though they are subject to the effects of different approximations and experimental errors. The evaluation of a-parameters for higher valence types is not so satisfactory in this respect, but they are known to order of magnitude at least, and the standard conductance curve for a hypothetical completely dissociated 2-2 electrolyte approaches physical reality.

Consideration of various theoretical attempts to explain the specificity of conductance curves in terms of ionic radii will be found in Section (11).

---

[46] Compare values of a from Section (11) with those of Section (8) of Chapter (8), and Section (5) of Chapter (12).

One such attempt[47] is discussed in Section (4) because it leads to an expression which does not reduce to the Onsager limiting equation (6-2-1).

Purely Empirical Extensions

In studying the conductance of 1-1 electrolytes, Shedlovsky[48] noted that, if the limiting equation (6-2-1) is rearranged so that Λ^0 may be calculated directly from individual values of Λ, the difference between successive values of Λ^0 is proportional to the difference in concentration. The values of Λ^0 computed in this manner will henceforth be designated $\Lambda^{0'}$, so as to differentiate them from the true limiting conductances, Λ^0, obtained by extrapolation to infinite dilution. In mathematical form, Shedlovsky's observation can be written

$$\Lambda^{0'} \equiv \frac{\Lambda + \beta^*\sqrt{c}}{1 - \alpha^*\sqrt{c}} = \Lambda^0 + Bc \qquad (6\text{-}3\text{-}7)$$

or

$$\Lambda = \Lambda^0 - \mathcal{S}_{(\Lambda)}\sqrt{c} + Bc - \alpha^* Bc^{3/2} \qquad (6\text{-}3\text{-}8)$$

The positive empirical constant, B, is characteristic of each electrolyte, and of the same order of magnitude as $\mathcal{S}_{(\Lambda)}$. The conductance of strong 1-1 electrolytes can usually be expressed by this equation up to $0.1N$ within experimental error. Potassium chloride is a noteworthy exception. The conductance of high valence type electrolytes cannot be expressed by the equation, but it is apparent from Figure (6-3-3) that a plot of $\Lambda^{0'}$ against concentration allows a satisfactory extrapolation of the data for barium and lanthanum chlorides. This figure also illustrates the slight, though measurable, departure of the values of $\Lambda^{0'}$ for potassium chloride from the linear relationship (6-3-7). The approximately linear portion of the curves is the result of an inflection. At high concentrations, the curves are strongly concave downward. These plots permit the evaluation of Λ^0 within very narrow limits, even though the curvatures cause extra weight to be given to the data at the lowest concentrations. For higher valence types, such as potassium ferrocyanide and zinc sulfate, this extrapolation is impractical. Figure (6-3-4) shows that the plots for these salts are sharply curved as they approach the axis.

The initial decrease in $\Lambda^{0'}$ with concentration, observed in Figure (6-3-4), is predicted theoretically by equation (6-3-5) for all valence types,[49] because when c approaches zero as a limit, we find that

$$\frac{d\Lambda^{0'}}{dc} = \frac{\Lambda^{0'} - \Lambda^0}{c} = \frac{A \log c + B}{1 - \alpha^*\sqrt{c}} = -\infty \qquad (6\text{-}3\text{-}9)$$

Fortunately this result does not seriously affect the usefulness of the extrapolations illustrated in Figure (6-3-3). Calculations based upon the

[47] M. H. Gorin, *J. Chem. Phys.*, **7**, 405 (1939).

[48] T. Shedlovsky, *J. Am. Chem. Soc.*, **54**, 1405 (1932).

[49] B. B. Owen, *J. Am. Chem. Soc.*, **61**, 1393 (1939).

values of A and B, given in Table (6-3-3), for potassium, barium and lanthanum chlorides show that $\Lambda^{0\prime}$ passes through a rather flat minimum at a concentration just below the experimental range. Furthermore, the value of $\Lambda^{0\prime}$, corresponding to this minimum, is only slightly less than the

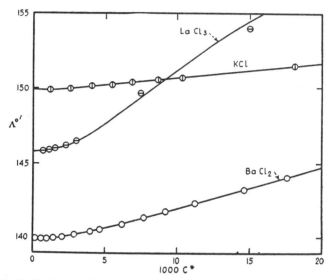

Fig. (6-3-3). Variation of $\Lambda^{0\prime}$ with concentration (equivalents per liter) in aqueous solutions at 25°; evaluation of Λ^{0} by extrapolation

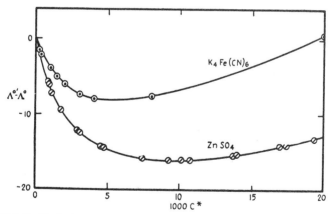

Fig. (6-3-4). Variation of $\Lambda^{0\prime}$ with concentration (equivalents per liter) in aqueous solutions at 25°.

value of Λ^{0} which satisfies equation (6-3-5). The difference is approximately 0.00015, 0.021 and 0.031 conductance unit for potassium, barium and lanthanum chlorides, respectively. This indicates that satisfactory values of Λ^{0} are obtained for these salts by simply extending the curves in Figure (6-3-3) horizontally beyond the lowest experimental points.

Shedlovsky[50] has proposed another extension of the Onsager equation which may be more readily applied to certain calculations than equation (6-3-8). He found that, up to $c \simeq 0.01$, the conductance of typical 1-1 strong electrolytes in water may be very accurately represented by the equation

$$\Lambda = \Lambda^0 - \frac{\Lambda}{\Lambda^0}(\alpha^*\Lambda^0 + \beta^*)c^{1/2} \qquad (6\text{-}3\text{-}10)$$

which allows for a gradual decrease in slope with increasing concentration. In the above form, this equation is not suitable for interpolation, but it may be rearranged as the series

$$\Lambda = \Lambda^0 - \mathcal{S}_{(\Lambda)}c^{1/2} + \frac{\mathcal{S}_{(\Lambda)}^2}{\Lambda^0}c - \frac{\mathcal{S}_{(\Lambda)}^3}{\Lambda^{02}}c^{3/2} + \cdots \qquad (6\text{-}3\text{-}11)$$

which, for the number of terms shown, is formally equivalent to (6-3-8), and has the advantage of avoiding the empirical parameter, B.

As an extrapolation function, equation (6-3-10) can be used in the form[51]

$$\frac{1}{\Lambda} = \frac{1}{\Lambda^0} + \left(\frac{\alpha^*\Lambda^0 + \beta^*}{\Lambda^{02}}\right)c^{1/2} \qquad (6\text{-}3\text{-}12)$$

according to which $1/\Lambda^0$ may be obtained by extrapolating a plot of $1/\Lambda$ against $c^{1/2}$. The obvious convenience of such a plot does not, however, make it superior to those shown in Figure (6-3-3), because extrapolation by (6-3-12) is longer and steeper.

(4) OTHER CONDUCTANCE EQUATIONS. CRITICAL SUMMARY

Among the numerous empirical equations which have been suggested for the extrapolation of conductivity data for strong electrolytes, the square root law of Kohlrausch[52]

$$\Lambda = \Lambda^0 - A\sqrt{c} \qquad (6\text{-}4\text{-}1)$$

has rendered the most noteworthy service in aqueous solutions, and is formally in agreement with the interionic attraction theory. Because of the success of this equation at extreme dilutions, most of the interpolation equations proposed for use at higher concentrations reduce to (6-4-1) in the limit. The simplest of these is the relation

$$\Lambda = \Lambda^0 - A\sqrt{c} + Bc \qquad (6\text{-}4\text{-}2)$$

[50] T. Shedlovsky, *J. Franklin Inst.*, **225**, 739 (1938).

[51] R. Lorenz [*Z. anorg. Chem.*, **108**, 191 (1919)] proposed a similar equation which can be written, $1/\Lambda = 1/\Lambda^0 + (A\Lambda^{p-1})c^{1/2}$. Unfortunately, he found the value of p characteristic of the electrolyte at moderate concentrations ($c \leq 0.1$), thereby missing a very important feature of equation (6-3-10), namely, $p = 1$ at high dilutions.

[52] For a comprehensive discussion of the application of this equation, consult F. Kohlrausch and L. Holborn "Das Leitvermögen der Elektrolyte," Teubner, Leipzig, 1916.

previously referred to in section (2). Walden[53] proposed the equation

$$\Lambda = \frac{\Lambda^0}{1 + B\sqrt{c}} \tag{6-4-3}$$

containing only two constants. This is considerably less accurate than (6-4-2), but covers the same concentration range ($<0.01M$). Lattey[54] combined features of both of these equations by writing

$$\Lambda = \Lambda^0 - \frac{A\sqrt{c}}{1 + B\sqrt{c}} \tag{6-4-4}$$

This expression is fairly successful at concentrations below 0.1N. By the addition of a linear term in concentration, Jones and Dole[55] showed that the relation

$$\Lambda = \Lambda^0 - \frac{A\sqrt{c}}{1 + B\sqrt{c}} + Dc \tag{6-4-5}$$

will describe their data for barium chloride up to 2N within the very small experimental error. The results for potassium bromide[56] can be expressed with equal success at 0° and 25°. All the foregoing equations have the property in common that

$$\left(\frac{d\Lambda}{d\sqrt{c}}\right)_{c \to 0} = -(\text{constant}) \tag{6-4-6}$$

but the value of this constant differs for each equation, and differs in general from the theoretical limiting slope given by equation (6-2-1). In view of the evident validity of the Onsager equation, none of the foregoing empirical equations should be used for extrapolation. Since the interionic attraction theory has demonstrated the inapplicability of the Ostwald dilution formula,[57]

$$K = \frac{\Lambda^2 c}{\Lambda^0(\Lambda^0 - \Lambda)} \tag{6-4-7}$$

to aqueous solutions of strong electrolytes, the numerous conductance equations incorporating this relation[58] have dropped into disuse.

The general equation

$$\Lambda = \Lambda^0 - Ac^n \tag{6-4-8}$$

[53] P. Walden, *Z. physik. Chem.*, **108**, 341 (1924).

[54] R. T. Lattey, *Phil. Mag.* [7], **4**, 831 (1927).

[55] G. Jones and M. Dole, *J. Am. Chem. Soc.*, **52**, 2245 (1930).

[56] G. Jones and C. F. Bickford, *J. Am. Chem. Soc.*, **56**, 602 (1934).

[57] W. Ostwald, *Z. physik. Chem.*, **2**, 36 (1888).

[58] Most of these equations are discussed by C. A. Kraus and W. C. Bray, *J. Am. Chem. Soc.*, **35**, 1315 (1913). See also E. W. Washburn, *Ibid.*, **40**, 150 (1918); and J. R. Partington in H. S. Taylor "Treatise on Physical Chemistry," Vol. I, p. 657, Van Nostrand Co., New York, 1931.

in which the exponent, n, is treated as an empirical parameter characteristic of each electrolyte (or group of electrolytes) was studied by Lorenz,[59] and, in spite of the success of the Onsager equation, is still used to some extent.[60] According to (6-4-8), a plot of log $(\Lambda^0 - \Lambda)$ against log c should be a straight line of slope n if Λ^0 is properly chosen. Ferguson and Vogel[61] have fitted this equation to their data for a large number of electrolytes, and find that both A and n are characteristic of the electrolyte. The individuality of A is in accord with theory, since the theoretical slope $(\alpha^*\Lambda^0 + \beta^*)$ contains the term Λ^0. Davies[62] has pointed out that, with few exceptions, the supposed variation of n, from one electrolyte to another $(0.4 < n < 0.6)$, is of the same order as that observed between duplicate series of measurements on a single electrolyte. This emphasizes the futility of using such an equation for extrapolation.

As an illustration of the large errors which may be produced by purely empirical extrapolation, we shall apply the foregoing equations to the data for a typical 2-1 electrolyte at 25°. Jones and Dole[63] found that, at high dilution, their measured molecular conductivities of barium chloride could be represented numerically as follows:

$$\Lambda_m = 278.75 - 449.9\sqrt{c} \tag{6-4-1a}$$

$$\Lambda_m = 280.64 - 550.12\sqrt{c} + 1265.1c \tag{6-4-2a}$$

$$\Lambda_m = 278.69/(1 + 1.715\sqrt{c}) \tag{6-4-3a}$$

$$\Lambda_m = 281.22 - 602.8\sqrt{c}/(1 + 4.069\sqrt{c}) \tag{6-4-4a}$$

$$\Lambda_m = 282.13 - 636.3\sqrt{c}/(1 + 4.628\sqrt{c}) - 31.13c \tag{6-4-5a}$$

$$\Lambda_m = 288.18 - 227.32c^{0.3276} \tag{6-4-8a}$$

Table (6-4-1) shows the concentration ranges throughout which the equations will reproduce the data. The figures in parentheses are the values of the limiting molecular conductivities, Λ_m^0, which satisfy these equations. The discordance of these values is proof enough of the im-

[59] R. Lorenz, *Z. anorg. Chem.*, **108**, 191 (1919); **114**, 209 (1920). The theoretical deductions of P. Hertz [*Ann. Phys.* [4], **37**, 37 (1912)] and of I. C. Ghosh [*J. Chem. Soc.*, **113**, 449 *et seq.* (1918)] gave considerable impetus to the study of the equation $\Lambda = \Lambda^0 - Ac^{1/3}$. Cf. R. Lorenz (*loc. cit.*), R. Lorenz and P. Osswald, [*Z. anorg. Chem.*, **114**, 209 (1920)], R. Lorenz and W. Michael, [*Ibid.*, **116**, 161 (1921)], and P. Walden and H. Ulich [*Z. physik. Chem.*, **106**, 49 (1923)].

[60] A. Ferguson and I. Vogel, *Phil. Mag.* [4], **50**, 971 (1925); [7], **4**, 1, 233, 300 (1927).

[61] A. Ferguson and I. Vogel, *Trans. Faraday Soc.*, **33**, 404, 414 (1927); I. Vogel, *Phil. Mag.* [7], **5**, 199 (1928).

[62] C. W. Davies, "The Conductivity of Solutions," Chapman and Hall, London, p. 84, 1930. Further discussion of the applicability of (6-4-8) may be found in the polemical papers of A. Ferguson and I. Vogel [*Trans. Faraday Soc.*, **27**, 285 (1927)], C. W. Davies, A. R. Martin, and A. W. Porter [*Ibid.*, **27**, 547 (1927)].

[63] G. Jones and M. Dole, *J. Am. Chem. Soc.*, **52**, 2245 (1930).

portance of an exact theoretical limiting function. The correct value[64] of Λ_m^0 is undoubtedly close to 280.00, which is twice the equivalent conductance recorded in Table (6-3-3). We note that the greatest departure from this value is the result (288.18) obtained by equation (6-4-8), which involves an arbitrary power of c. It is also significant that, among the remaining equations, the average discrepancy is 1.3 units in spite of their common property expressed by (6-4-6). Equation (6-4-5), which contains the greatest number of empirical constants, leads to an error of over 2 units in Λ_m^0.

TABLE (6-4-1). REPRESENTATION OF THE MOLECULAR CONDUCTANCE OF BARIUM CHLORIDE AT 25° BY EMPIRICAL EQUATIONS.

c	Λ_m(obs.)	(6-4-1a)	(6-4-2a)	(6-4-3a)	(6-4-4a)	(6-4-5a)	(6-4-8a)
0		(278.75)	(280.64)	(278.69)	(281.22)	(282.13)	(288.18)
.001	264.53	264.53	264.51	264.25	264.33	264.55	264.53
.0025	256.25	256.25	256.30	256.65	256.16	256.22	256.25
.005	248.11	246.94	248.07	248.56	248.10	248.03	248.11
.01	238.27	233.76	238.28	237.89	238.37	238.32	237.89
.025	223.25	207.61	225.29	219.24	223.22	223.26	220.29
.05	210.65		220.89	201.44	210.64	210.65	202.99
.1	197.36		233.19	180.69	197.86	197.36	181.27
.25	178.39				181.90	178.35	
.5	161.20				171.28	161.26	
1.00	137.96					137.94	

Gorin[65] has made an interesting addition to the list of conductance equations which do not reduce to the Onsager limiting law. In the derivation of his equation

$$\Lambda = \frac{\Lambda^0 + (a_-\lambda_+^0 + a_+\lambda_-^0)\kappa}{1 + (a_+ + a_-)\kappa} \qquad (6\text{-}4\text{-}9)$$

for binary electrolytes, Gorin makes use of the Debye-Hückel theory to calculate the potential at the surface of an ion, but he assumes that an applied external field does not sensibly distort the ionic atmospheres. This assumption neglects the asymmetry potential, ψ_i'. It will be recalled that ψ_i' is an essential feature of the Onsager equation, and leads to a satisfactory description of high field and frequency effects. In spite of its theoretical inadequacy, Gorin's equation is capable of representing conductance and transference data over a considerable concentration range. This is undoubtedly caused by the inclusion of two additional constants, the ionic radii, a_+ and a_-.

[64] Values between the limits 279.6 and 280.0 are obtained from three different plots based upon the Onsager equation. Two of these are illustrated in Figures (6-3-1) and (6-3-3). The third is a simple plot of Λ against $\sqrt{c}$ which is made to approach the theoretical limiting slope at extreme dilution. The latter plot involves a relatively long extrapolation, and yields 279.8 with an uncertainty of two or three tenths of a unit.

[65] M. H. Gorin, J. Chem. Phys., **7**, 405 (1939).

In common with the other equations in this section, (6-4-9) reduces to equation (6-4-6) in the limit. The limiting slope, in this case, becomes

$$\frac{d\Lambda}{d\kappa} = -(a_+\lambda_+^0 + a_-\lambda_-^0) \tag{6-4-10}$$

in terms of the variable κ. Table (6-4-2) shows the results of some calculations based upon the application of equation (6-4-9) to the data of Shedlovsky[66] and Longsworth.[67] The values of a_+ are not unreasonable for hydrated radii, and a_{Cl} is practically independent of the nature of the cation. Gorin has pointed out that the order and variation in a_+ is consistent with classic hydrodynamic theory.

TABLE (6-4-2). IONIC RADII (IN ÅNGSTROMS) ESTIMATED BY EQUATION (6-4-9) AT 25°.

Electrolyte	Λ^0	λ_+^0	λ_-^0	$\dfrac{d\Lambda}{d\sqrt{c}}$ $c \to 0$	d_+	d_-
HCl	426.06	349.73	76.33	−156.5	0.945	1.921
KCl	149.86	73.53	76.33	−96.1	1.978	1.933
NaCl	126.45	50.12	76.33	−90.6	2.562	1.937
LiCl	115.03	38.70	76.33	−88.7	3.095	1.976

(5) TRANSFERENCE NUMBERS* BY THE MOVING BOUNDARY METHOD. FUNDAMENTAL EQUATIONS

Lodge[68] demonstrated the possibility of directly observing ionic motion, and Whetham,[69] Nernst,[70] Masson,[71] and particularly Denison and Steele[72] have developed the method by which transference numbers can be quantitatively determined from the observed velocities of moving boundaries. In subsequent investigations by Cady,[73] E. R. Smith,[74] MacInnes,[75] and

[66] T. Shedlovsky, *J. Am. Chem. Soc.*, **54**, 1411 (1932).

[67] L. G. Longsworth, *Ibid.*, **54**, 2741 (1932); see also D. A. MacInnes, T. Shedlovsky and L. G. Longsworth, *Ibid.*, **54**, 2758 (1932).

* For bibliography of early literature bearing upon the general subject of transference numbers see D. J. LeRoy, Univ. Toronto Studies, Papers Chem. Lab., No. 156, (1939); J. W. McBain, *Ibid.*, No. 67 (1907).

[68] O. Lodge, *Brit. Assn. Advancement Sci.*, p. 389, Birmingham, (1886).

[69] W. C. D. Whetham, *Phil. Trans.*, **184 A**, 337 (1893); *Z. physik. Chem.*, **11**, 220 (1893).

[70] W. Nernst, *Z. Elektrochem.*, **3**, 308 (1897).

[71] D. O. Masson, *Phil. Trans.*, **192 A**, 331 (1899).

[72] R. B. Denison, and B. D. Steele, *J. Chem. Soc.*, **89**, 999 (1906).

[73] E. C. Franklin and H. P. Cady, *J. Am. Chem. Soc.*, **26**, 499 (1904); H. P. Cady and L. G. Longsworth, *Ibid.*, **51**, 1656 (1929).

[74] E. R. Smith and D. A. MacInnes, *J. Am. Chem. Soc.*, **46**, 1398 (1924); *Ibid.*, **47**, 1009 (1925); E. R. Smith, *Bureau of Standards J. Research*, **6**, 917 (1931).

[75] D. A. MacInnes and E. R. Smith, *J. Am. Chem. Soc.*, **45**, 2246 (1923); D. A. MacInnes, I. A. Cowperthwaite, and T. C. Huang, *Ibid.*, **49**, 1710 (1927); L. G. Longsworth and D. A. MacInnes, *Rev. Sci. Inst.*, **19**, 50 (1929).

Longsworth,[76] the method has been subjected to steady technical improvement, and is now capable of yielding data of very high accuracy. In view of the importance of these results for verifying[77] the interionic attraction theory, and their practical application to conductance and electromotive force studies, we shall outline the calculation of transference numbers from observed boundary velocities relative to the apparatus.

The first step is the calculation of a preliminary or apparent transference number by neglecting the effects of conductance of the solvent and volume changes at the electrodes. Then the true transference number is obtained by the application of appropriate corrections for these effects. Figure (6-5-1) represents a vertical section through a tube in which the boundary at x_0 is formed by juxtaposition of two solutions of electrolytes,

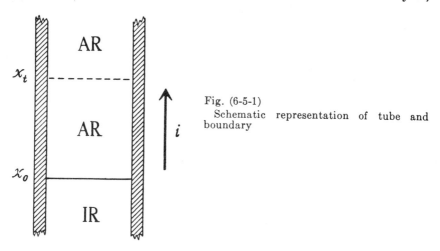

Fig. (6-5-1)
Schematic representation of tube and boundary

AR and IR, with a common ion, R. After the passage of a steady current, i, for t seconds, the boundary attains the position indicated by x_t. If c_A^* is the normality of the ion constituent A, and V the volume (in liters) swept out by the boundary in passing from x_0 to x_t, then the migration of A ions up the tube must have transferred Fc_A^*V coulombs past an arbitrary reference plane across the tube above x_t. Accordingly, the apparent transference number, T_A', of the A ion is given by

$$T_A' = \frac{Fc_A^*V}{it} \qquad (6\text{-}5\text{-}1)$$

[76] L. G. Longsworth, *J. Am. Chem. Soc.*, **54**, 2741 (1932).

For a comprehensive review of the theory, technique, and results of the modern moving boundary method, see D. A. MacInnes and L. G. Longsworth, *Chem. Rev.*, **11**, 171 (1932).

[77] With the exception of a few isolated data, transference numbers determined by the well known Hittorf analytical method are generally of insufficient accuracy for this purpose.

where the product (it) is the total quantity of electricity passed through the tube.

At very low concentrations an appreciable portion of the current is carried by ions resulting from ionization of the solvent and traces of impurities such as carbonic acid. The recognition of this effect and the calculation of its magnitude is due to Longsworth.[78] For a 1-1 electrolyte, AR, at concentration c^*, it can be shown that, if a is the area of the tube, the true transference number, $T_A = \bar{u}_A/(\bar{u}_A + \bar{u}_R)$, is given by

$$T_A = \frac{F\bar{u}_A c^*/1000}{i/a} + T_A' \frac{L_0}{L} \qquad (6\text{-}5\text{-}2)$$

Since mobilities are referred to a stationary solvent, $\bar{u}_A$ is the distance traveled by the A ions per second through the solution in unit field. If volume changes caused by electrolysis and ion migration produce motion of the solvent relative to the tube in which the boundary positions are determined, the volume which appears in equation (6-5-1) is given by

$$V = \frac{\bar{u}_A ta}{1000} + \Delta V \qquad (6\text{-}5\text{-}3)$$

Here ΔV represents the contribution (in liters) of the motion of the solvent to the observed volume swept out by the boundary in t seconds. Combination of equations (6-5-1) and (6-5-3) with (6-5-2) gives the expression

$$T_A = T_A' - \frac{Fc^*\Delta V}{it} + T_A' \frac{L_0}{L} \qquad (6\text{-}5\text{-}4)$$

The necessity of the correction term containing ΔV was pointed out by Miller.[79] ΔV can be measured experimentally,[80] or estimated from the densities of the solutions and the components of the electrodes.[81]

If the leading and indicator solutions are properly chosen, restorative effects limit the extent of diffusion across the boundary.[82]

Although the moving boundary method as just described is limited to the study of ions for which suitable (slower) indicator ions are available, it is capable of an interesting extension by which the transference numbers of the latter may also be directly determined. Kohlrausch[83] showed that one of the conditions of a stable boundary is proportionality between the concentrations and transference numbers of the leading and indicator ions. Since these ions must have the same velocity at the boundary,

[78] L. G. Longsworth, *J. Am. Chem. Soc.*, **54**, 2741 (1932).

[79] W. L. Miller, *Z. physik. Chem.*, **69**, 436 (1909).

[80] E. R. Smith, *Bur. Standards J. Research*, **8**, 457 (1932).

[81] G. N. Lewis, *J. Am. Chem. Soc.*, **32**, 862 (1910); L. G. Longsworth, *Ibid.*, **54**, 2741 (1932); A. R. Gordon and R. L. Kay, *J. Chem. Phys.*, **21**, 131 (1953).

[82] D. A. MacInnes and I. A. Cowperthwaite, *Proc. Nat. Acad. Sci.*, **15**, 18 (1929); L. G. Longsworth, *J. Am. Chem. Soc.*, **52**, 1897 (1930); W. L. Miller, *Z. physik. Chem.*, **69**, 436 (1909).

[83] F. Kohlrausch, *Ann. Physik.*, **62**, 209 (1897).

the volume swept out per faraday is not only equal to T_A/c_A^*, but must also equal T_I/c_I^*. Therefore

$$\frac{T_A}{c_A^*} = \frac{T_I}{c_I^*} \qquad (6\text{-}5\text{-}5)$$

If the concentration of the indicator solution was initially $c_I^{*'}$, not very different from c_I^*, the concentration in the region swept out by the boundary is automatically adjusted to c_I^* according to equation (6-5-5). The concentration disturbance produced by this adjustment remains near the initial boundary position as an observable concentration gradient. In more complex systems, sharp multiple boundaries appear. The observation and prediction of boundaries formed between mixtures of strong electrolytes have been developed by Longsworth[84a] and Dole[84b], and the complications introduced by weak electrolytes have been investigated by Svensson[85a] and Alberty[85b]

Hartley[86] applied equation (6-5-5) to the measurement of T_I/T_A, where T_I, the transference number of a very slow indicator ion, is evaluated in terms of the known value, T_A, of some reference ion. With improvements in technique and proper solvent corrections, Gordon[87] and his colleagues obtained ratios, T_I/T_A, in excellent agreement with the results of Longsworth[88]. From such ratios, extrapolated to infinite dilution, it is practicable to obtain[87] both T_I^0 and T_A^0 from values of Λ_{IX}^0 and Λ_{AX}^0 alone.

Although the Hittorf[89] method of determining transference numbers presents serious difficulties of chemical analysis when high precision is required, MacInnes and Dole[90] obtained values by this method with an accuracy of about 0.2 per cent. Within this experimental error, their results were in complete agreement with the corresponding moving boundary values. Jones and Bradshaw[91] reported data on lithium chloride which agree with moving boundary results to within ±0.7 per cent.

[84] (a) L. G. Longsworth, J. Am. Chem. Soc., 67, 1109 (1945); Natl. Bur. Standards Circular 524, 59 (1953). See also E. B. Dismukes and E. L. King, J. Am. Chem. Soc., 74, 4798 (1952). (b) V. P. Dole, Ibid., 67, 1119 (1945).

[85] (a) H. Svensson, Acta Chimica Scand., 2, 841 (1948); I. Brattsten and H. Svensson, Ibid., 3, 359 (1940). (b) R. A. Alberty and J. C. Nichol, J. Am. Chem. Soc., 70, 2297 (1948); Ibid., 72, 2361, 2367 (1950); R. A. Alberty and E. L. King, Ibid., 73, 517 (1951); E. B. Dismukes and R. A. Alberty, Ibid., 76, 191 (1954).

[86] G. S. Hartley, Trans. Faraday Soc., 30, 648 (1934); E. Drew and G. S. Hartley, Idem., p. 657; G. S. Hartley, B. Collie and C. S. Samis, Ibid., 32, 795 (1936).

[87] D. R. Muir, J. R. Graham and A. R. Gordon, J. Am. Chem. Soc., 76, 2157 (1954); A. R. Gordon and R. L. Kay, J. Chem. Phys., 21, 131 (1953).

[88] L. G. Longsworth, J. Am. Chem. Soc., 54, 2741 (1932).

[89] W. Hittorf, Ann. Physik., 89, 177 (1853); 98, 1 (1856); 103, 1 (1858); 106, 337, 513 (1859). An extensive bibliography of the method is given by J. R. Partington in H. S. Taylor, "A Treatise on Physical Chemistry," Vol. I, pp. 678–683, Van Nostrand Co., New York, 1931.

[90] D. A. MacInnes and M. Dole, J. Am. Chem. Soc., 53, 1357 (1931).

[91] G. Jones and B. C. Bradshaw, J. Am. Chem. Soc., 54, 138 (1932).

The true transference numbers are obtained by correcting[92] these Hittorf numbers for net transfer, per faraday, of ΔN_w mols of water, from anode to cathode. Thus

$$T_+ = T_{+(\text{Hittorf})} + 0.018\Delta N_w c^* \qquad (6\text{-}5\text{-}6)$$

Since ΔN_w is of the order of unity,[93] this correction becomes important at moderate concentrations.

(6) The Onsager Limiting Equation for Transference Numbers. Comparison with Experimental Results

The definition of the transference number of an ion constituent, in a solution containing a single electrolyte, can be written

$$T_j \equiv \lambda_j/\Lambda; \qquad T_j^0 \equiv \lambda_j^0/\Lambda^0 \qquad (6\text{-}6\text{-}1)$$

By limiting the discussion to electrolytes composed of only two kinds of ions (i, j) the values of λ_j and Λ given by equations (5-3-10) and (6-2-1) may be combined with the above to give the expression

$$T_j = T_j^0 + \mathcal{S}_{(T_j)} \sqrt{c}(\Lambda^0/\Lambda') \qquad (6\text{-}6\text{-}2)$$

predicted by the Onsager theory. In this and subsequent equations, values of the equivalent conductance calculated by (6-2-1) are written Λ', so as to differentiate them from observed values, Λ. Thus,

$$\Lambda' \equiv \Lambda^0 - (\alpha^*\Lambda^0 + \beta^*)\sqrt{c} \qquad (6\text{-}6\text{-}3)$$

Since Λ^0/Λ' approaches unity at high dilution, the limiting equation is

$$T_j = T_j^0 + \mathcal{S}_{(T_j)}\sqrt{c} \qquad (6\text{-}6\text{-}4)$$

where

$$\mathcal{S}_{(T_j)} = \left(\frac{T_j^0(|z_j| + |z_i|) - |z_j|}{(|z_j| + |z_i|)\Lambda^0}\right)\beta^* \qquad (6\text{-}6\text{-}4a)$$

Note that the slope does not contain the parameter α^*. Since only the numerical magnitudes of the valences appear in $\mathcal{S}_{(T_j)}$, it is immaterial whether the j ion is chosen to represent the anion or cation. In either case the condition, $T_j + T_i = 1$, requires that $\mathcal{S}_{(T_j)} = -\mathcal{S}_{(T_i)}$.

Some of the most accurate experimental values, obtained by the moving boundary method at 25°, are given in Table (6-6-1A). Figures (6-6-1) and (6-6-2) show the observed variation of the cation transference number, T_+, with $\sqrt{c}$ in aqueous solutions of electrolytes at 25°. The limiting expressions given by (6-6-4) are represented by straight lines with inter-

---

[92] E. W. Washburn, "Principles of Physical Chemistry", p. 277, McGraw-Hill Book Co., New York, 1921; *J. Am. Chem. Soc.*, **31**, 322 (1909); A. A. Noyes and K. G. Falk, *ibid.*, **33**, 1436 (1911).

[93] *E.g.*, $1/4 < \Delta N_w < 3/2$ for the chlorides of hydrogen and the alkalies.

cepts, T_+^0. The data for the chlorides are in striking agreement with theory, and this result is typical of 1-1 electrolytes which show positive departures from the limiting conductance equation (6-2-1) in dilute solutions. For such salts, the limiting law is approached from below if $\mathfrak{S}_{(T)}$ is positive, and from above if $\mathfrak{S}_{(T)}$ is negative. In the case of potassium nitrate, the observed transference numbers do not merge with the theoretical expression at experimental concentrations, and although $\mathfrak{S}_{(T_+)}$

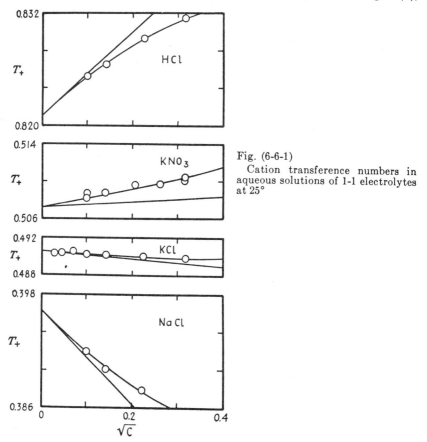

Fig. (6-6-1)

Cation transference numbers in aqueous solutions of 1-1 electrolytes at 25°

is positive, the limiting law is approached from above. The conductance of this salt shows negative departures from the conductance equation (6-2-1), as can be seen in Figure (6-2-2). The behavior of the transference numbers and conductance of silver nitrate is similar to that of potassium nitrate in all respects.

Figure (6-6-2) shows the experimental results for two complex valence type electrolytes, calcium chloride and erbium chloride. In these examples, $\mathfrak{S}_{(T_+)}$ is negative and the limiting law is approached from above, but convergence is not attained at the lowest experimental concentrations.

To account for this behavior of polyvalent ions theoretically it would be necessary to extend equation (4-3-26) and retain higher order and inhomogeneous terms as explained in Section (9) of Chapter (4). This has been done analytically for symmetrical electrolytes only, and is illustrated for 1-1 type electrolytes in Section (11). Dye and Spedding[94] have contributed to our knowledge of unsymmetrical types by evaluating some of the terms of the more general conductance equation by graphical integration with an assumed (constant) value of the a-parameter for a series of values of c. They used values of the mean ionic diameter, a, derived

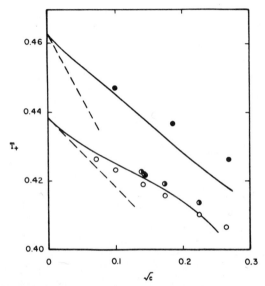

Fig. (6-6-2). Cation transference numbers of unsymmetrical electrolytes in water at 25°. ○; CaCl₂, data of A. G. Keenan, H. G. McLeod and A. R. Gordon, *J. Chem. Phys.*, **13**, 466 (1945). ◑; CaCl₂, data of L. G. Longsworth, *J. Am. Chem. Soc.*, **57**, 1185 (1935). ●; ErCl₃, data of F. H. Spedding and J. L. Dye quoted in Ref. (94).

from activity coefficient data for calcium[95] and erbium[96] chlorides for such graphical integrations, and estimated from them the ionic conductances from which transference numbers could be derived. These calculated transference numbers are represented by the solid curves in Figure (6-6-2), and the corresponding limiting tangents are shown as broken lines. The calculated curves are not in complete accord with the experimental points, but the improvement over the limiting law is remarkable. Closer agreement could be obtained if a were treated as an adjustable parameter derivable from the transference data themselves, but it is doubtful that this refinement would be meaningful in view of neglect of the inhomogeneous terms that appear in equation (4-9-1).

[94] J. L. Dye and F. H. Spedding, *J. Am. Chem. Soc.*, **76**, 888 (1954).

[95] H. G. McLeod and A. R. Gordon, *Ibid.*, **68**, 58 (1946): $a = 4.575$.

[96] F. H. Spedding and J. L. Dye, *Ibid.*, **76**, 879 (1954): $a = 5.92$.

The results of the tests of the theoretical equation (6-6-4) may be summarized as follows. The experimental results for 1-1 valence type electrolytes investigated by the moving boundary method tend to merge with the theoretical limiting tangent. The available data for higher valence type electrolytes do not show convergence with the theoretical limiting tangent at experimental concentrations. Consequently, their extrapolation requires extension of the limiting equations, either by consideration of higher terms, which is exceedingly onerous mathematically, or by addition of simpler, purely empirical terms, which is rarely completely satisfactory.

TABLE (6-6-1).* CATION TRANSFERENCE NUMBERS IN AQUEOUS POTASSIUM CHLORIDE SOLUTIONS.

$t°C$	Λ^0†	$\mathfrak{S}_{(T_+)}$	T_+^0	Concentration (mols/liter)				
				.005	.01	.02	.05	.10
15	121.1	-0.0027_7	0.4928	0.4926	0.4925	0.4924	0.4923	0.4921
25	149.9	$-.0037_9$	.4905	.4903	.4902	.4901	.4900	.4900
35	180.5	$-.0046_0$	.4889	.4887	.4886	.4885	.4885	.4888
45	212.5	$-.0054_3$	.4872	.4869	.4868	.4868	.4869	.4873

* R. W. Allgood, D. J. LeRoy and A. R. Gordon, *J. Chem. Phys.*, **8**, 418 (1940).
† H. E. Gunning and A. R. Gordon, *Ibid.*, **10**, 126 (1942).

TABLE (6-6-2).* CATION TRANSFERENCE NUMBERS IN AQUEOUS SODIUM CHLORIDE SOLUTIONS.

$t°C$	Λ^0†	$\mathfrak{S}_{(T_+)}$	T_+^0	Concentration (mols/liter)				
				.005	.01	.02	.05	.10
15	101.2	-0.0492_4	0.3929	0.3897	0.3885	0.3870	0.3846	0.3820
25	126.5	$-.0491_2$	.3962	.3930	.3918	.3903	.3878	.3853
35	153.9	$-.0485_3$	.4002	.3970	.3958	.3943	.3919	.3892
45	182.7	$-.0478_5$	.4039	.4008	.3996	.3982	.3957	.3932

* R. W. Allgood and A. R. Gordon, *J. Chem. Phys.*, **10**, 124 (1942).
† H. E. Gunning and A. R. Gordon, *Ibid.*, **10**, 126 (1942).

Although independent measurements of transference numbers at higher temperatures than 25° are not completely in accord, there is good evidence that those electrolytes which obey equation (6-6-4) in the limit of 25° do likewise at other temperatures. Cation transference numbers in aqueous potassium chloride and sodium chloride[97a] solutions[97] at several temperatures are given in Tables (6-6-1) and (6-6-2), and similar results for hydrochloric acid[98] in various media are collected in Table (11-9-1A). The

[97] R. W. Allgood, D. J. LeRoy and A. R. Gordon, *J. Chem. Phys.*, **8**, 418 (1940).
[97a] R. W. Allgood and A. R. Gordon, *Ibid.*, **10**, 124 (1942).
[98] Two of these electrolytes were studied by C. S. Samis, *Trans. Faraday Soc.*, **33**, 469 (1937). His results have not been included because it was pointed out in Reference 97 that they may contain inaccuracies due to peculiarities of the indicator solutions at high temperatures.

effect of temperature upon the transference numbers in potassium chloride solutions is exceptional, in that the difference between T_+ and T_- increases with temperature. As a rule,[99] the higher ionic mobilities have the lower temperature coefficients, so that transference numbers generally become more nearly equal[100] with rising temperature.

(7) Equations for Transference Numbers at Moderate Dilutions. Evaluation of T_i^0

A number of useful equations have been proposed for representing transference data from the lowest experimental concentrations ($\sim 0.01\ N$) up to 0.2 N, or higher. Three of these equations reduce to the theoretical limiting law at extreme dilution, and will be considered first.

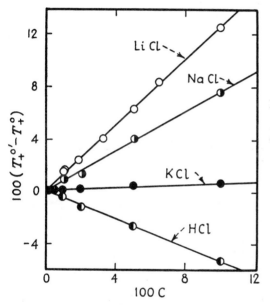

Fig. (6-7-1)
Verification of equation (6-7-1) for aqueous solutions of 1-1 chlorides at 25°

(a) Longsworth[101] found that values of T_+^0, calculated by equation (6-6-2), from experimental values of T_+ for the alkali chlorides and hydrochloric acid, vary linearly with c. Representing such calculated values by $T_+^{0'}$, so as to retain the usual meaning for the symbol T_+^0, Longsworth's observation can be written

$$T_+^{0'} \equiv \frac{T_+ \Lambda' + (1/2)\beta^* \sqrt{c}}{\Lambda' + \beta^* \sqrt{c}} = T_+^0 + Bc \qquad (6\text{-}7\text{-}1)$$

[99] F. Kohlrausch and L. Holborn, "Das Leitvermögen der Elektrolyte," Teubner, Leipzig and Berlin, 1916.
[100] See H. S. Taylor, *J. Chem. Phys.*, **6**, 331 (1938) and Reference 97.
[101] L. G. Longsworth, *J. Am. Chem. Soc.*, **54**, 2741 (1932).

for 1-1 electrolytes. The empirical constant B is characteristic of each electrolyte. Solution of this equation for T_+ gives

$$T_+ = T_+^0 + \mathbb{S}_{(T_+)}\sqrt{c}(\Lambda^0/\Lambda') + B(1 + \beta^*\sqrt{c}/\Lambda')c \qquad (6\text{-}7\text{-}2)$$

Figure (6-7-1) shows the high accuracy with which equation (6-7-1) fits those experimental results which merge with the theoretical limiting law. Tables (6-6-1) and (6-6-2) confirm this result at other temperatures. The extrapolated values of T_+^0, obtained from this figure, are completely in accord with the limiting conductances of the electrolytes and the principle of independent limiting mobilities. For the particular electrolytes involved, these considerations confirm the predictions of theory. On the other hand, equation (6-7-1) cannot be applied to potassium and silver nitrates, or to electrolytes of higher valence types.

(b) Shedlovsky[102] proposed the general empirical equation

$$\frac{1}{T_i} = \frac{1}{T_i^0} + A\sqrt{c} - B^*c \qquad (6\text{-}7\text{-}3)$$

which fits the data up to 0.2 N for a variety of electrolytes. When this equation is applied to the results for electrolytes such as calcium chloride and silver nitrate, both of the parameters, A and B^*, must be evaluated from the transference data. A theoretical value of A, consistent with equation (6-6-4), can be used in dealing with the alkali halides and other 1-1 electrolytes. In this case

$$A = -\mathbb{S}_{(T_i)}(1/T_i^0)^2 \qquad (6\text{-}7\text{-}4)$$

Since equation (6-7-3) contains only one arbitrary constant, B^*, under this condition, a plot of $[1/T_i + \mathbb{S}_{(T_i)}(1/T_i^0)^2\sqrt{c}]$ *vs.* c may be used to obtain $1/T_i^0$ by extrapolations involving a series of successive approximations. All of the limiting transference numbers obtained in this manner are in excellent agreement with those obtained by Longsworth's extrapolation. If the theoretical value of A, given by (6-7-4) is disregarded, correct values of T_i^0 for calcium chloride and silver nitrate can be derived from equation (6-7-3) by the method of least squares.

(c) The equation[103]

$$T_i = T_i^0 + \mathbb{S}_{(T_i)}\sqrt{c}(\Lambda^0/\Lambda')[1 - (1 - \alpha^*\sqrt{c})\sqrt{2c}] \qquad (6\text{-}7\text{-}5)$$

has been proposed for estimating T_i in dilute solutions of 1-1 electrolytes for which direct measurements are not available. The right-hand member contains no terms which cannot be determined from conductivity measurements and known limiting ionic conductance. Equation (6-7-5) yields values of T_i at 25° with an accuracy of 0.2 to 0.3 per cent when applied to dilute solutions ($c < 0.15$) of the 1-1 electrolytes for which equation

[102] T. Shedlovsky, *J. Chem. Phys.*, **6**, 845 (1938).
[103] B. B. Owen, *J. Am. Chem. Soc.*, **57**, 2441 (1935).

(6-6-2) is valid as a limit. It is unsatisfactory for other electrolytes. The most interesting feature of equation (6-7-5) is the fact that the empirical bracketed term accounts for the deviations of a whole group of electrolytes from the limiting equation. These deviations are more accurately represented by equations (6-7-2) and (6-7-3) because they contain an additional empirical parameter, B, or B^*, characteristic of each electrolyte. A comparison of equations (6-7-2) and (6-7-5) leads to the relation

$$B = -\sqrt{2}\,\mathbb{S}_{(T_i)} \qquad (6\text{-}7\text{-}6)$$

at 25°. Insufficient data are available to determine to what extent this equation is independent of temperature, but the indications are that it fails at higher temperatures. It is probable that the factor $\sqrt{2}$ which appears in equations (6-7-5) and (6-7-6) must be replaced by a parameter which varies with the temperature (and the nature of the solvent), if these equations are to have more general application.

(d) Gorin[104] deduced the equation

$$\frac{T_+}{T_-} = \frac{T_+^0}{T_-^0}\left(\frac{1 + a_- \kappa}{1 + a_+ \kappa}\right) \qquad (6\text{-}7\text{-}7)$$

for the ratio of the transference numbers of a symmetrical electrolyte. The derivation of this equation is based upon the same assumptions involved in equation (6-4-9). The values of a_+ and a_- can be calculated by equation (6-4-10) from a knowledge of the experimental limiting slopes of conductance curves and the limiting ionic mobilities. It is significant that, in spite of the two parameters, a_+ and a_-, equation (6-7-7) will not represent the experimental results over as wide a concentration range as the three equations, (6-7-2), (6-7-3), and (6-7-5), which reduce to the theoretical limiting law.

(e) Jones and Dole[105] found that the empirical equation

$$T_i = \frac{A}{1 + B\sqrt{c}} - 1 \qquad (6\text{-}7\text{-}8)$$

represented their results for barium chloride at 25° with an average deviation of only 0.0002 up to a concentration of one molar. Such high accuracy and long range make this two-constant equation useful for interpolation, but it is not suitable for extrapolation. The value $T_i^0 = A - 1$ derived from the data on barium chloride is not in accord with the known limiting conductances of the barium and chloride ions.

[104] M. H. Gorin, *J. Chem. Phys.*, **7**, 405 (1939).
[105] G. Jones and M. Dole, *J. Am. Chem. Soc.*, **51**, 1073 (1929).

(8) Limiting Ionic Conductance. Kohlrausch's Law

As a result of the classic investigation of the conductance of electrolytic solutions, Kohlrausch[106] showed that the limiting equivalent conductance of an electrolyte is the sum of two independent factors characteristic of the anion and cation respectively. Thus the relation

$$\Lambda^0 = \lambda^0_+ + \lambda^0_- \tag{6-8-1}$$

is known as the Kohlrausch law. The complete independence of the limiting ionic conductances is demonstrated by Figure (6-8-1) based upon

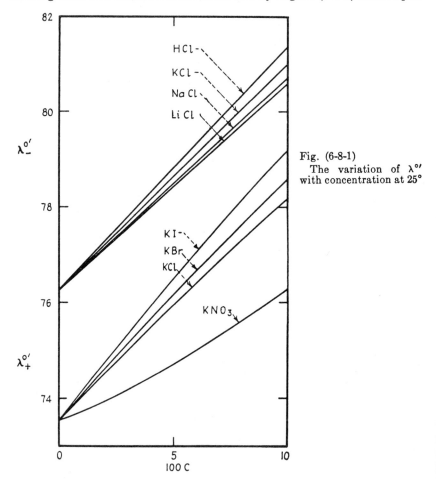

Fig. (6-8-1)
The variation of $\lambda^{0\prime}$ with concentration at 25°

the results of MacInnes, Shedlovsky and Longsworth[107] for some 1-1 electrolytes. The quantity $\lambda^{0\prime}_i$ used as ordinate in this figure represents

[106] F. Kohlrausch, *Ann. Physik.*, **50**, 385 (1893); **66**, 785 (1898).
[107] D. A. MacInnes, T. Shedlovsky, and L. G. Longsworth, *J. Am. Chem. Soc.*, **54**, 2758 (1932); *Chem. Rev.*, **13**, 29 (1933).

an "apparent" value of λ_i^0, calculated directly from the Onsager equation (5-3-10) by the introduction of an experimental value, $\lambda_i = T_i \Lambda$. At infinite dilution, $\lambda_i^{0'}$ equals the true limiting conductances, λ_i^0. The plots are all practically straight, except for potassium nitrate, indicating that $\lambda_i^{0'}$ is linear in c at low concentrations. Accordingly, the relation

$$\lambda_i^{0'} \equiv \frac{\lambda_i + (1/2)\beta^* \sqrt{c}}{1 - \alpha^* \sqrt{c}} = \lambda_i^0 + bc \tag{6-8-2}$$

for ionic conductances in 1-1 electrolyte solutions has the same form as equation (6-3-7) for the equivalent conductance. The empirical constant b is determined by the slopes of the curves.

The most important result to be derived from Figure (6-8-1) is the determination of λ_{Cl}^0 and λ_K^0 from a number of concordant and independent studies. All these values of λ^0, obtained by extrapolation of the individual curves, agree within ± 0.02 per cent, and the sum of the mean

TABLE (6-8-1). λ_{Cl} IN $0.05N$ SOLUTIONS OF SODIUM AND LITHIUM CHLORIDES IN METHANOL-WATER MIXTURES AT 25°.

Mol fraction of alcohol	0	0.1	0.2	0.4	0.6	0.8
λ_{Cl} (in NaCl)...........	68.01	45.87	36.19	30.45	29.69	30.82
λ_{Cl} (in LiCl)...........	67.99	45.85	36.24	30.46	29.77	30.82

values, $\lambda_{Cl}^0 = 76.34$ and $\lambda_K^0 = 73.52$, is exactly equal to $\Lambda_{KCl}^0 = 149.86$ determined by direct experiment. The limiting conductances of all the ions must therefore be known to ± 0.02 per cent by virtue of their common intercepts. This figure also demonstrates that the additivity expressed by equation (6-8-1) is very closely maintained up to a concentration as high as $c = 0.02$ for all the electrolytes shown, except potassium nitrate. This observation is of importance, as the applicability of the Kohlrausch principle to solutions at finite dilution is assumed in the determination of the ionization constants of weak electrolytes from conductivity measurements. It should be kept in mind that only 1-1 electrolytes are represented in Figure (6-8-1).

The additivity of univalent ionic conductances has also been found to exist in mixed solvents of relatively high dielectric constants. The results of Longsworth and MacInnes[108] given in Table (6-8-1) show that the chloride ion conductance in methanol-water solutions of sodium and lithium chloride is practically independent of the univalent cation.

The dependence of conductance of an ion constituent upon the valence of its co-ion is shown[109] in Figure (6-8-2). The theoretical limiting laws for the chloride ion conductance in the three salt solutions are

[108] L. G. Longsworth and D. A. MacInnes, *J. Phys. Chem.*, **43**, 239 (1939).
[109] L. G. Longsworth and D. A. MacInnes, *J. Am. Chem. Soc.*, **60**, 3070 (1938).

$$\lambda_{Cl}^{NaCl} = 76.34 - 47.2\sqrt{c^*} \qquad (6\text{-}8\text{-}3)$$

$$\lambda_{Cl}^{CaCl_2} = 76.34 - 74.0\sqrt{c^*} \qquad (6\text{-}8\text{-}4)$$

$$\lambda_{Cl}^{LaCl_3} = 76.34 - 99.1\sqrt{c^*} \qquad (6\text{-}8\text{-}5)$$

in terms of the concentration, c^*, in equivalents per liter. This concentration unit is used to prevent the curves from crowding on the figure. They are brought much closer together if the ionic strength is used as abscissa, but they do not superpose in any concentration range. In

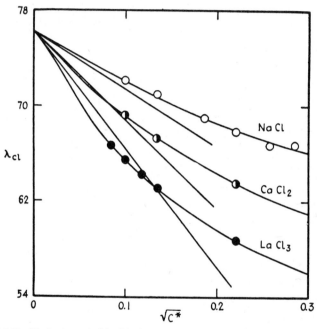

Fig. (6-8-2). Variation of chloride-ion conductance with concentration at 25°

addition to the individuality of these curves in dilute solutions which is predicted by theory, the departures from the theoretical relation depend to a high degree upon the valence of the co-ion. It clearly follows from this, and from the discussion of mixtures [Section (2)] that the principle of independent ionic mobilities can be used only as a rough approximation at experimental concentrations of high valence type, or mixed electrolytes.

In Table (6-8-2), we have collected representative values of limiting ionic conductances determined at 25°. The values for most of the univalent ions and for the alkaline earths are accurate to a few hundredths of one per cent. Some of the values for polyvalent ions are in considerable doubt, as is indicated by the number of significant figures. The values for some of the alkali and halide ions have been slightly changed from those

TABLE (6-8-2).* LIMITING IONIC CONDUCTANCES IN WATER AT 25°.

Cation	λ_+^0	Ref.	Anion	λ_-^0	Ref.
h$^+$	349.8	(1), (13)	OH$^-$	197.8	(8), (22)
Li$^+$	38.66	(1), (30)	Cl$^-$	76.35	(1), (30), (31)
Na$^+$	50.11	(1), (13), (30)	Br$^-$	78.20	(9), (2), (30), (31)
K$^+$	73.52	(1), (30), (31)	I$^-$	76.9	(10), (2), (30), (31)
Rb$^+$	77.8	(21)	NO$_3^-$	71.44	(1)
Cs$^+$	77.3	(21)	ClO$_3^-$	64.6	(29b)
Ag$^+$	61.92	(1)	BrO$_3^-$	55.8	(24), (28)
Tl$^+$	74.7	(3)	IO$_3^-$	40.5	(26), (27)
NH$_4^+$	73.4	(2)	ClO$_4^-$	67.3	(28), (29a), (3)
MeNH$_3^+$	58.7	(23)	IO$_4^-$	54.5	(28), (29c)
Me$_2$NH$_2^+$	51.9	(23)	HCO$_2^-$	54.6	(18)
Me$_3$NH$^+$	47.3	(23)	HOCO$_2^-$	44.5	(11)
Me$_4$N$^+$	45.0	(24)	CH$_3$CO$_2^-$	40.9	(1), (13)
Et$_4$N$^+$	32.7	(24)	ClCH$_2$CO$_2^-$	39.8	(12), (13)
Pr$_4$N$^+$	23.5	(24)	CNCH$_2$CO$_2^-$	41.8	(18)
Bu$_4$N$^+$	19.2	(24)	CH$_3$CH$_2$CO$_2^-$	35.8	(14)
$\frac{1}{2}$Mg^{++}	53.06	(4)	CH$_3$(CH$_2$)$_2$CO$_2^-$	32.6	(14), (18)
$\frac{1}{2}$Ca^{++}	59.50	(4)	HCO$_2$CO$_2^-$	40.2	(20)
$\frac{1}{2}$Sr^{++}	59.46	(4)	Benzoate$^-$	32.3	(15), (16)
$\frac{1}{2}$Ba^{++}	63.64	(4)	Picrate$^-$	30.4	(24)
$\frac{1}{2}$Cu^{++}	54	(5)	$\frac{1}{2}$C$_2$O$_4^{--}$	24.0	(20)
$\frac{1}{2}$Zn^{++}	53	(5)	$\frac{1}{2}$SO$_4^{--}$	80.0	(2), (7), (19)
$\frac{1}{3}$La^{+++}	69.5	(6), (2), (25)	$\frac{1}{3}$Fe(CN)$_6^{---}$	100	(7)
$\frac{1}{3}$Ce^{+++}	69.9	(25)	$\frac{1}{4}$Fe(CN)$_6^{----}$	111	(17)

* All values conform to the standard of Jones and Bradshaw.

(1) D. A. MacInnes, T. Shedlovsky and L. G. Longsworth, *J. Am. Chem. Soc.*, **54**, 2758 (1932).
(2) D. A. MacInnes, *J. Franklin Inst.*, **225**, 661 (1938).
(3) R. A. Robinson and C. W. Davies, *J. Chem. Soc.*, **139**, 574 (1937)..
(4) T. Shedlovsky and A. S. Brown, *J. Am. Chem. Soc.*, **56**, 1066 (1934).
(5) B. B. Owen and R. W. Gurry, *Ibid.*, **60**, 3074 (1938).
(6) G. Jones and C. F. Bickford, *Ibid.*, **56**, 602 (1934). See Table (6-3-3).
(7) G. S. Hartley and G. W. Donaldson, *Trans. Faraday Soc.*, **33**, 457 (1937).
(8) V. Sivertz, R. E. Reitmeier, and H. V. Tartar, *J. Am. Chem. Soc.*, **62**, 1379 (1940).
(9) G. Jones and C. F. Bickford, *J. Am. Chem. Soc.*, **56**, 602 (1934).
(10) P. A. Lasselle and J. G. Aston, *Ibid.*, **55**, 3067 (1933).
(11) T. Shedlovsky and D. A. MacInnes, *Ibid.*, **57**, 1705 (1935).
(12) T. Shedlovsky, A. S. Brown and D. A. MacInnes, *Trans. Electrochem. Soc.*, **66**, 165 (1935).
(13) B. Saxton and T. W. Langer, *J. Am. Chem. Soc.*, **55**, 3638 (1933).
(14) D. Belcher, *Ibid.*, **60**, 2744 (1938).
(15) B. Saxton and H. F. Meier, *Ibid.*, **56**, 1918 (1934). These authors also report 30.3 and 31.0 for the *ortho*- and *meta*-chlorobenzoate ions respectively.
(16) F. G. Brockman and M. Kilpatrick, *Ibid.*, **56**, 1483 (1934).
(17) G. Jones and F. C. Jelen, *Ibid.*, **58**, 2561 (1936); C. W. Davies, *Ibid.*, **59**, 1760 (1937). See Table (6-3-3).
(18) B. Saxton and L. S. Darken, *J. Am. Chem. Soc.*, **62**, 846 (1940).
(19) I. L. Jenkins and C. B. Monk, *J. Am. Chem. Soc.*, **72**, 2695 (1950).
(20) L. S. Darken, *Ibid.*, **63**, 1007 (1941).
(21) W. E. Voisenet, Thesis, Yale (1951); B. B. Owen, *J. chim. phys.*, **49**, C-72 (1952).
(22) L. S. Darken and H. F. Meier, *J. Am. Chem. Soc.*, **64**, 621 (1942).
(23) J. H. Jones, F. J. Spuhler and W. A. Felsing, *Ibid.*, **64**, 965 (1942).
(24) H. M. Daggett, E. J. Blair and C. A. Kraus, *Ibid.*, **73**, 799 (1951).
(25) F. H. Spedding, P. E. Porter and J. M. Wright, Ibid., **74**, 2055 (1952); F. H. Spedding and I. S. Yaffe, Idem., p. 4751. Consult these authors for data on other rare earth elements.
(26) M. Spiro, *J. Phys. Chem.*, **60**, 976 (1956).
(27) K. A. Krieger and M. Kilpatrick, *J. Am. Chem. Soc.*, **64**, 7 (1942).
(28) C. B. Monk, *Ibid.*, **70**, 3281 (1948).
(29) (a) J. H. Jones, *Ibid.*, **67**, 855 (1945); (b) *Ibid.*, **69**, 2065 (1947); (c) *Ibid.*, **68**, 240 (1946).
(30) R. E. Jervis, D. R. Muir, J. P. Butler and A. R. Gordon, *Ibid.*, **75**, 2855 (1953).
(31) B. B. Owen and H. Zeldes, *J. Chem. Phys.*, **18**, 1085 (1950).

of earlier editions.   This revision is not so much the result of new data as it is the result of consideration of Tables (6-8-4) and (6-11-3).

Although very precise values of the limiting conductances of many salts in non-aqueous solvents are now available in the literature, ionic conductances of comparable accuracy are not yet calculable because of the absence of appropriate transference numbers.   Gordon* and his collaborators have applied the moving boundary method to the measurement of transference numbers in sodium and potassium chloride solutions in pure methanol, and in 50 mole percent methanol-water mixtures.   Combination of these results with very careful DC conductance measurements in the same, and other, alkali halide solutions, yields the limiting ionic conductance values collected in Table (6-8-3).   The experimental evidence

TABLE (6-8-3). LIMITING IONIC CONDUCTANCES IN METHANOL* AT 25°.

Cation	λ^0_+	Ref.	Anion	λ^0_-	Ref.
Li+	39.82	(1), (2)	Cl-	52.38	(3), (2)
Na+	45.22	(3), (2)	Br-	56.55	(1), (2)
K+	52.40	(3), (2)	I-	62.75	(1), (2)

* In 50 mole percent methanol-water mixtures at 25°, the values λ^0_j = 29.56, 38.06 and 37.05 for Na, K and Cl, respectively, result from combination of the conductance measurements of H. I. Schiff and A. R. Gordon [J. Chem. Phys., **16**, 336 (1948)] with the transference numbers of L. W. Shemilt, J. A. Davies and A. R. Gordon [*Ibid.*, **16**, 340 (1948)].   In pure ethanol at 25°, the values λ^0_j = 17.05, 20.31, 23.55 and 21.85 for Li, Na, K and Cl, respectively, result from the conductance measurements of J. R. Graham, G. S. Kell and A. R. Gordon [*J. Am. Chem. Soc.*, **79**, 2352 (1957)] and the transference measurements of J. R. Graham and A. R. Gordon [*Idem.*, 2350] and of J. W. Lorimer, J. R. Graham and A. R. Gordon [*Idem.*, 2347].
(1) R. E. Jervis, D. R. Muir, J. P. Butler and A. R. Gordon, *J. Am. Chem. Soc.*, **75,** 2855 (1953).
(2) J. A. Davies, R. L. Kay and A. R. Gordon, *J. Chem. Phys.* **19,** 749 (1951).
(3) J. P. Butler, H. I. Schiff and A. R. Gordon, *Ibid.*, **19,** 752 (1951).

suggests that these values are as precise as any of those in aqueous solutions recorded in Table (6-8-2).   Less accurate ionic conductances can be derived from the limiting equivalent conductances given in Tables (6-2-2A) and (7-2-1A) by making reasonable assumptions regarding the necessary transference numbers.   For example, for a salt such as tetra-*n*-butylammonium triphenylborofluoride, composed of two large, nearly symmetrical ions of about the same size, the transference numbers can be assumed to be equal. Experimental verification of such an assumption is, however, a matter of considerable importance, because it can be seen in Figure (6-8-3) that even the simplest ions exhibit marked specificity in aqueous solutions, and it will be shown in Section (5) of the next chapter that the specific interac-

* References will be found at the bottom of Table (6-8-3), where attention is called to very recent measurements in pure ethanol.

tions between ions and non-aqueous solvents is exceedingly complicated. It will also be shown in the next chapter that, for those non-aqueous solvents having dielectric constants much lower than that of water, the evaluation of Λ^0 itself is not so precise as in aqueous solutions because of ionic association. In this case the numerical value of Λ^0 may depend to some extent upon the particular extrapolation function chosen for the simultaneous determination of Λ^0 and the ionization constant, K. The slopes of the extrapolations which lead to Λ^0 in solvents of low dielectric constants are functions of K, and are quite high, as can be seen in the typical example illustrated in Figure (7-2-1).

Within the last 20 years, the conductances and transference numbers of several salts and hydrochloric acid have been carefully measured over temperature ranges of 40 to 60 degrees. These measurements are so numerous that they will not be tabulated as functions of both temperature and concentration, but the values of infinite dilution are given in Table (6-8-3). Values at concentrations up to 0.01 or 0.02 normal may be found in the original literature referred to in the table. These limiting values and those at 25° for the same electrolytes, and sodium iodide, which appear in Tables (6-2-1A) and (6-6-1A) are enough to permit the construction of a reasonably consistent set of "preferred" limiting mobilities of seven simple ions over a 50 degree temperature range. These preferred values and their variation with temperature can be represented by the cubic equation

$$\lambda^0 = \lambda^0_{(25°)} + a(t - 25) + b(t - 25)^2 + c(t - 25)^3 \qquad (6\text{-}8\text{-}6)$$

the parameters of which are recorded in Table (6-8-4).

TABLE (6-8-4). PARAMETERS OF EQUATION (6-8-6) EXPRESSING THE TEMPERATURE DEPENDENCE OF LIMITING IONIC MOBILITIES BETWEEN 5 AND 55°C.

Ion	$\lambda^0_{(25°)}$	a	$b \times 10^2$	$c \times 10^4$
H+	349.85	4.81595	−1.03125	−0.7670
Li+	38.64	0.88986	+0.44075	−0.2042
Na+	50.15	1.09160	0.47150	−0.1150
K+	73.50	1.43262	0.40563	−0.3183
Rb+	77.81	1.47953	0.38400	−0.4533
Cs+	77.26	1.44790	0.38250	−0.2050
Cl−	76.35	1.54037	0.46500	−0.1285
Br−	78.17	1.54370	0.44700	−0.2300
I−	76.90	1.50993	0.43750	−0.2170

Values of Λ^0 and T^0_+, calculated by equation (6-8-6) and the parameters in Table (6-8-4), are compared in Table (6-8-5) with the observed values. The difference between calculated and observed values of Λ^0 is less than 0.02 per cent on the average, and exceeds 0.04 per cent only in the case

TABLE (6-8-5). COMPARISON OF CONSISTENT SET OF VALUES OF Λ^0 AND T^0_+ WITH THE EXPERIMENTAL VALUES* FROM WHICH THEY WERE DERIVED

		5°	15°	25°	35°	45°	55°	Source
HCl,	Λ^0	297.53	362.16	426.16	489.11	550.34	609.38	a
		297.57	362.07	426.24	489.15	550.30	609.47	b
				426.16				c
	T^0_+	.8403	.8304	.8209	.8115	.8021	.7926	a
		.842	.831	.821	.811	.801		k
				.8210				l
LiCl,	Λ^0	70.28	91.62	114.99	140.17	166.94	195.15	a
		70.30	91.60	114.99	140.18	166.92	195.14	d
				115.03				c
				114.95				e
	T^0_+	.3240	.3296	.3360	.3422	.3476	.3523	a
				.3368				l
NaCl,	Λ^0	77.81	101.14	126.50	153.74	182.69	213.23	a
		77.84		126.49			213.28	d
			101.18	126.45	153.75	182.65		f
				126.45				g
	T^0_+	.3894	.3927	.3964	.4002	.4039	.4072	a
			.3929	.3962	.4002	.4039		m
				.3963				l
KCl,	Λ^0	94.23	121.03	149.85	180.41	212.43	245.67	a
		94.26		149.88			245.69	h
			121.07	149.85	180.42	212.41		f
				149.86				g
	T^0_+	.4959	.4925	.4905	.4889	.4873	.4855	a
			.4928	.4905	.4889	.4872		n
				.4906				l
KBr,	Λ^0	95.99	122.81	151.67	182.23	214.17	247.15	a
		96.00		151.68			247.15	h
			122.81	151.64	182.24	214.17		f
				151.63				i
	T^0_+	.4868	.4854	.4846	.4840	.4834	.4826	a
				.4847				o
KI,	Λ^0	95.35	121.87	150.40	180.62	212.20	244.82	a
		95.32	121.83	150.34	180.60	212.13	244.73	h
				150.47				q
				150.38				j
	T^0_+	.4901	.4891	.4887	.4883	.4878	.4872	a
				.4887				p

* All values have been adjusted to the primary standard of G. Jones and B. C. Bradshaw, *J. Am. Chem. Soc.*, **55**, 1780 (1933).

a Calculated from equation (6-8-6) and the parameters in Table (6-8-4).

b Data of B. B. Owen and F. H. Sweeton [*J. Am. Chem. Soc.*, **63**, 2811 (1941)] re-extrapolated by equation (6-3-6).

c T. Shedlovsky, *J. Am. Chem. Soc.*, **54**, 1411 (1932).

d F. W. Tober, Dissertation, Yale University (1948).

e K. A. Krieger and M. Kilpatrick, Jr., *J. Am. Chem. Soc.*, **59**, 1878 (1937).

f G. C. Benson and A. R. Gordon, *J. Chem. Phys.*, **13**, 473 (1945).

g T. Shedlovsky, A. S. Brown and D. A. MacInnes, *Trans. Electrochem. Soc.*, **66**, 165 (1934).

h B. B. Owen and H. Zeldes, *J. Chem. Phys.*, **18**, 1083 (1950).

i G. Jones and C. F. Bickford, *J. Am. Chem. Soc.*, **56**, 602 (1934).

j L. G. Longsworth, Private Communication, quoted by H. E. Gunning and A. R. Gordon, *J. Chem. Phys.*, **10**, 126 (1942).

k H. S. Harned and E. C. Dreby, *J. Am. Chem. Soc.*, **61**, 3113 (1939).

l L. G. Longsworth, *Ibid.*, **54**, 2741 (1932).

m R. W. Allgood and A. R. Gordon, *J. Chem. Phys.*, **10**, 124 (1942).

n R. W. Allgood, J. D. LeRoy and A. R. Gordon, *Ibid.*, **8**, 418 (1940).

o A. G. Keenan and A. R. Gordon, *Ibid.*, **11**, 172 (1943).

p L. G. Longsworth, *J. Am. Chem. Soc.*, **57**, 1185 (1935).

q R. E. Jervis, D. R. Muir and A. R. Gordon, *Ibid.*, **75**, 2855 (1953).

of the value for potassium bromide at 25° recorded in Table (6-2-1A). Therefore, Λ^0 for this salt, 151.9, was disregarded in constructing the set of preferred mobilities. Bearing in mind that the experimental values of T^0_+ for hydrochloric acid (Ref. *k*) are expressed to only three places, the agreement between the calculated and observed results of T^0_+ appears satisfactory. One value, 0.4837 (Ref. *p*), for potassium bromide was, however, rejected in favor of 0.4847 (Ref. *o*) in order to obtain maximum consistency for the whole set.

Although the limiting mobilities in Table (6-8-5) are adjusted so as to represent a considerable body of data from independent sources within 0.02 %, the uncertainty in some values of λ^0_j calculated by equation (6-8-6) might be of the order of 0.1 unit. It will be recalled that some available data were not considered in evaluating the parameters of this equation because they were not consistent (within 0.05 %) with the bulk of the data. The precision of modern electrical measurements is so high that the factors which determine the accuracy of Λ and T_j are the estimation of solvent and polarization corrections, the purification and desiccation of salts, and sometimes the difficulties of chemical analysis. On the basis of the concordance of the *measured* values of Λ and T_j obtained in different laboratories, and often by different techniques, it seems reasonable to assign an accuracy of about 0.02 % to some of these quantities reported at experimental concentrations. On the other hand, the accuracies of the quantities Λ^0 and T^0_j can not be estimated so easily because the evaluation of these quantities requires judgment in both curve-fitting and choice of extrapolation function. Even for 1-1 electrolytes, extrapolations of a given series of data by different authors have often resulted in discrepancies exceeding 0.05 % in Λ^0. For this simplest type of electrolyte the uncertainty in extrapolation can now be reduced by the use of the *a*-parameter as outlined in Section (11), but for higher types (unsymmetrical) the available equations containing this parameter are less satisfactory from a theoretical point of view. Furthermore, the treatment of the experimental data on higher valence. types often involves rather large corrections for hydrolysis at the highest dilutions, so that the numerical values which are finally extrapolated are also less satisfactory. For these reasons we have not attempted to extend Tables (6-8-4) and (6-8-5) to include higher valence types.

An interesting property of ionic mobilities is illustrated by the intersecting curves in Figure (6-8-3), where the difference between the mobilities of several ions and that of the chloride ion is plotted against the temperature. It is evident that the relative magnitudes of mobilities vary with temperature in a complicated manner. Since these ions approach most closely to the simple hydrodynamic picture of uniformly charged spheres, Figure (6-8-3) underlines the difficulty of developing a satisfactory theory of ion-solvent interaction.

The temperature coefficients of ionic mobilities also show no simple correspondence with ionic radii, as follows from comparison of the values of a in Table (5-1-6). A roughly parallel family of curves is obtained, however, if $\partial \ln \lambda^0/\partial T$ is plotted against the temperature*.

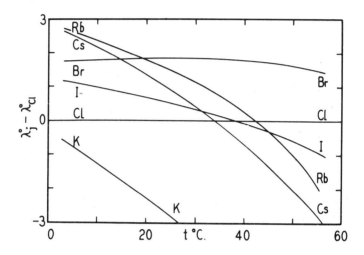

Fig. (6-8-3). The limiting mobilities of several simple ions compared with that of the chloride ion at various temperatures.

(9) Viscosity of Solutions of Strong Electrolytes and Its Dependence Upon Concentration

Since the pioneer investigations of Poiseuille,[110] an extensive literature[111] dealing with the viscosity, or its reciprocal, the fluidity, of solutions has appeared. With the development of the interionic attraction theory much of the interest in this subject has been directed toward very accurate determinations[112] of the viscosities of dilute solutions of electrolytes,

* B. B. Owen, *J. Chim. Phys.*, **49**, C-72 (1952).

[110] J. L. M. Poiseuille, *Ann. chim. phys.* [3], **21**, 76 (1847).

[111] See E. C. Bingham, "Fluidity and Plasticity", McGraw-Hill Book Co., New York, 1922; E. Hatschek, "The Viscosity of Liquids", D. Van Nostrand Co., New York, 1928.

[112] E. Grüneisen, *Wiss. Abh. phys. tech. Reichsanstalt*, **4**, 159, 241 (1904); E. W. Washburn and G. V. Williams, *J. Am. Chem. Soc.*, **35**, 737 (1913); E. C. Bingham and R. F. Jackson, *Bull. Bureau of Standards*, **14**, 59 (1918-19); G. Jones and S. K. Talley, *Physics*, **4**, 215 (1933); G. Jones and H. J. Fornwalt, *J. Am. Chem. Soc.*, **60**, 1683 (1938); G. Jones and R. E. Stauffer, *Ibid.*, **59**, 1630 (1937).

and the theoretical interpretation of the results. Grüneisen[113] appears to have been the first to make very accurate measurements at high dilutions, and he showed, in contradiction to earlier views,[114] that the viscosity

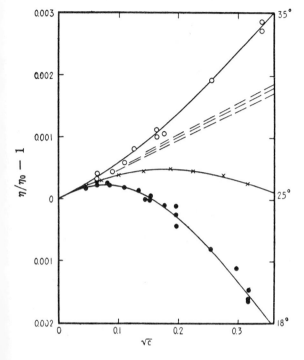

Fig. (6-9-1)
Relative viscosity of aqueous KCl solutions at 18, 25, and 35°; the theoretical limiting law gives the broken lines

is not a linear function of the concentration in dilute solutions. Moreover, the departures from linearity increase rapidly as the concentration is reduced. This behavior of electrolytes appears to be general,[115] and has been termed[116] the Grüneisen effect. It is absent in solutions of nonelectrolytes.

It was shown experimentally by Jones and Dole,[117] and Joy and Wolfenden[118] that the viscosities of solutions of strong electrolytes vary linearly

[113] E. Grüneisen, *Wiss. Abh. phys. techn. Reichsanstalt*, **4**, 151, 237 (1905).

[114] A. Sprung, *Pogg. Ann. Phys. Chem.*, **159**, 1 (1876); S. Arrhenius, *Z. physik. Chem.*, **1**, 285 (1887).

[115] M. P. Appelbey, *J. Chem. Soc.*, **97**, 2000 (1910); T. R. Merton, *Ibid.*, **97**, 2454 (1910).

[116] G. Jones and S. K. Talley, *J. Am. Chem. Soc.*, **55**, 624 (1933).

[117] G. Jones and M. Dole, *J. Am. Chem. Soc.*, **51**, 2950 (1929). See also G. Jones and S. K. Talley, *Ibid.*, **55**, 624 (1933).

[118] W. E. Joy and J. H. Wolfenden, *Proc. Roy. Soc. London*, **A 134**, 413 (1931).

with the square root of the concentration at high dilutions. This result is illustrated in Figure (6-9-1) and its generality is supported by recent studies of a large number of salts. It was pointed out[117] that the viscosities of many solutions can be accurately represented by the equation

$$\eta/\eta_0 = 1 + A\sqrt{c} + Bc \qquad (6\text{-}9\text{-}1)$$

up to concentrations as high as $0.1N$.

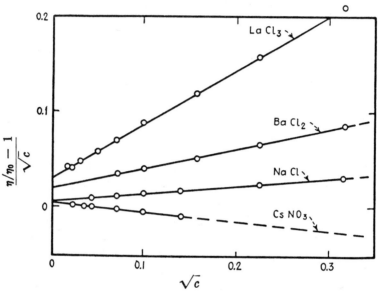

Fig. (6-9-2). Evaluation of the limiting slopes for relative viscosity at 25°

The experimental values of the parameters A and B are determined by plotting the left-hand member of the equation

$$\frac{\eta/\eta_0 - 1}{\sqrt{c}} = A + B\sqrt{c} \qquad (6\text{-}9\text{-}2)$$

against $\sqrt{c}$. Figures (6-9-2) and (6-9-3) illustrate such plots for a variety of electrolytes. The intercepts and slopes of the linear plots are A and B, respectively. The curved plots [Figure (6-9-3)] can be used to obtain satisfactory values of A if the data extend to very high dilutions, but it is clear that B is not constant within the experimental concentration range. Fortunately, such plots are unusual for aqueous solutions and are confined to partially dissociated, or high valence type (particularly 2-2) electrolytes. The behavior of electrolytes in non-aqueous solvents is similar, but the range of validity of equation (6-9-1) is limited to more dilute solutions.

The constant B is highly specific, and is an approximately additive[119, 120] property of the ions. Note that B is negative for cesium nitrate at 25°. Negative B-values are obtained at low temperatures for many salts composed of large, relatively unhydrated, ions. On the other hand, the observed temperature coefficients of B are always positive, so the effect of salts at high temperatures would be to increase the viscosity of the solution throughout the entire range covered by equation (6-9-1). Figure (6-9-1) shows that, for potassium chloride, this change of B from minus to plus takes place between 25 and 35°. So far, no satisfactory theoretical

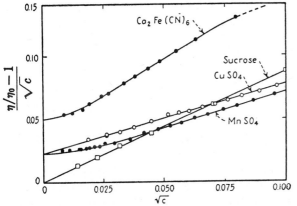

Fig. (6-9-3)
Evaluation of the limiting slopes for relative viscosity at 25°

interpretation of the B parameter has been found, but its approximate additivity can be used to develop empirical methods for calculating the viscosities of solutions containing one[121] or more[122] electrolytes. Ionic "fluidities" can also be used for this purpose.[123]

Although the individuality of A, and its variation with temperature, are much less pronounced than for those of B, the numerical values of A are of very great theoretical interest. Since $\eta/\eta_0 = 1 + \eta^*/\eta_0$, the theoretical value of the parameter, A, is obtainable from equation (4-2-28), which applies to solutions of a single electrolyte dissociating into only two kinds of ions. By combination of equations (3-1-2), (4-1-15) and

119 W. M. Cox and J. H. Wolfenden, *Proc. Roy. Soc. London,* **A 145,** 475 (1934).

120 V. D. Laurence and J. H. Wolfenden, *J. Chem. Soc.,* **136,** 1144 (1934).

121 W. M. Cox and J. H. Wolfenden, *Proc. Roy. Soc. London,* **A 145,** 475 (1934).

122 H. Tollert, *Z. physik. Chem.,* **A 172,** 129 (1935); **A 174,** 239 (1935); **A 180,** 383 (1937).

123 E. C. Bingham, *J. Phys. Chem.,* **45,** 885 (1941).

(4-2-25) to (4-2-28), the limiting law for the relative viscosity can be written

$$\eta/\eta_0 = 1 + \mathcal{S}_{(\eta)}\sqrt{c} \qquad (6\text{-}9\text{-}3)$$

where

$$\mathcal{S}_{(\eta)} = \frac{\beta^*}{80(|z_1| + |z_2|)^2}\left\{\frac{\lambda_1^0 z_2^2 + \lambda_2^0 z_1^2}{\lambda_1^0\lambda_2^0}\right. \\ \left. - \frac{4}{\lambda_1^0\lambda_2^0}\left[\frac{|z_2|\lambda_1^0 - |z_1|\lambda_2^0}{(\Lambda^0)^{1/2} + (\Lambda^0 + \lambda_1^0|z_2/z_1| + \lambda_2^0|z_1/z_2|)^{1/2}}\right]^2\right\} \qquad (6\text{-}9\text{-}4)$$

This is the equation, in slightly altered form, for the limiting slope as originally derived by Falkenhagen and Vernon.[124] Numerical values of the coefficient β^* are given in Tables (5-3-1) and (11-1-1A). For binary electrolytes

$$\mathcal{S}_{(\eta)} = \frac{\beta^*}{320}\frac{\Lambda^0}{\lambda_1^0\lambda_2^0}\left[1 - 0.6863\left(\frac{\lambda_1^0 - \lambda_2^0}{\Lambda_0}\right)^2\right] \qquad (6\text{-}9\text{-}5)$$

and in the special case where $\lambda_1^0 = \lambda_2^0$ this equation reduces to the relation,

$$\mathcal{S}_{(\eta)} = \frac{\beta^*}{160\lambda^0} \qquad (6\text{-}9\text{-}6)$$

derived by Falkenhagen and Dole.[125]

A comparison of the observed and theoretical limiting slopes is made in Table (6-9-1) for aqueous solutions at 25°. The agreement is very satisfactory indeed, and appears to be as good for complex valence types as for simple 1-1 salts. The relative viscosity can be calculated, within the experimental error, from the values of A and B and equation (6-9-1) up to, and often beyond, the concentrations indicated in the next to the last column. The non-electrolytes, sucrose and urea, are included in the table to show that the limiting slope is zero for solutes of zero charge. The influence of temperature upon the limiting slope has been shown to be completely in accord with theory[126]. A recent comparison of theoretical and experimental limiting slopes has been made over a 30° temperature

[124] H. Falkenhagen and E. L. Vernon, *Physik. Z.*, **33**, 140 (1932); *Phil. Mag.* [7] **14**, 537 (1932). See also H. Falkenhagen, *Nature*, **127**, 439 (1931); *Physik. Z.*, **32**, 745 (1931); *Z. physik. Chem.*, **B 6**, 159 (1931).

[125] H. Falkenhagen and M. Dole, *Physik. Z.*, **30**, 611 (1929); *Z. physik. Chem.*, **B 6**, 159 (1929).

[126] Results are available at 0° for all the salts in Table (6-9-1) which were studied by G. Jones and his students. W. E. Joy and J. H. Wolfenden [*Proc. Roy. Soc. London*, **A 134**, 413 (1913)] and W. M. Cox and J. H. Wolfenden [*Ibid.*, **A 145**, 475 (1934)] investigated a number of electrolytes, including nitric acid, at 18 and 35°. Data at 35° and higher temperatures are given by A. S. Chakravarti and B. Prasad [*Trans. Faraday Soc.*, **35**, 1466 (1939)], J. D. Ranade and G. R. Paranjpe [*J. Univ. Bombay*, **7**, 41 (1938)] and in standard handbooks.

range for salts of several valence types. These results are shown in Table (6-9-2).

TABLE (6-9-1). PARAMETERS A AND B OF THE VISCOSITY EQUATION (6-9-1) FOR AQUEOUS SOLUTIONS AT 25°. THE THEORETICAL LIMITING SLOPES.

Solute*	Type	$S_{(\eta)}10^4$	$A\ 10^4$	B	Range	Ref.
Sucrose....................	0	0	0	0.8786	0.02	(g)
Urea......................	0	0	0	0.0378	0.2	(g)
NH₄Cl.....................	1-1	50	57	−0.0144	0.2	(g)
NaCl......................	1-1	60	67	0.0244	0.2	(c)
KCl.......................	1-1	50	52	−0.0140	0.2	(g)
KBr.......................	1-1	49	47.4	−0.0480	0.1	(f)
KNO₃......................	1-1	52	50	−0.053	0.1	(g)
KClO₃.....................	1-1	55	50	−0.031	0.1	(g)
KBrO₃.....................	1-1	58	58	−0.001	0.1	(g)
KMnO₄....................	1-1	56	58	−0.066	0.1	(e)
CsI.......................	1-1	48	39	−0.118	0.2	(e)
CsNO₃.....................	1-1	51	43	−0.092	0.02	(g)
AgNO₃.....................	1-1	56	63	0.045	0.1	(a)
K₂SO₄.....................	1-2	131	140.6	0.194	0.1	(a)
K₂CrO₄....................	1-2	131	133	0.152	0.1	(a)
BaCl₂.....................	2-1	147	201	0.207	0.1	(h)
LaCl₃.....................	3-1	284	304	0.567	0.1	(b)
K₄Fe(CN)₆.................	1-4	330	370	0.366	0.1	(d)
MgSO₄.....................	2-2	228	225	—	—	(i)
MnSO₄.....................	2-2	227	231	—	—	(i)
CuSO₄.....................	2-2	228	230	0.540	0.01	(i)
ZnSO₄.....................	2-2	225	229	—	—	(i)
CdSO₄.....................	2-2	225	232	—	—	(i)
Cr₂(SO₄)₃.................	3-2	507	495	—	—	(i)
Ca₃[Fe(CN)₆]₂.............	2-3	464	467	—	—	(i)
Ca₂Fe(CN)₆................	2-4	490	495	—	—	(i)

* For additional solutes see V. D. Laurence and J. H. Wolfenden, *J. Chem. Soc.*, **136**, 1144 (1934).
(a) G. Jones and J. H. Colvin, *J. Am. Chem. Soc.*, **62**, 338 (1940).
(b) G. Jones and R. E. Stauffer, *Ibid.*, **62**, 335 (1940).
(c) G. Jones and S. M. Christian, *Ibid.*, **59**, 484 (1937).
(d) G. Jones and R. E. Stauffer, *Ibid.*, **58**, 2548 (1936).
(e) G. Jones and H. J. Fornwalt, *Ibid.*, **58**, 619 (1936).
(f) G. Jones and S. K. Talley, *Ibid.*, **55**, 4124 (1933).
(g) G. Jones and S. K. Talley, *Ibid.*, **55**, 624 (1933).
(h) G. Jones and M. Dole, *Ibid.*, **51**, 2950 (1929).
(i) E. Asmus, *Ann. Physik*, **35**, 1 (1939).

TABLE (6-9-2).* COMPARISON OF THEORETICAL WITH EXPERIMENTAL LIMITING SLOPES IN AQUEOUS SOLUTIONS AT VARIOUS TEMPERATURES.

t, °C.	NaCl		Li₂SO₄		FeCl₃		CeCl₃	
	$10^4\ S_{(\eta)}$	$10^4\ A$	$10^4\ S_{(\eta)}$	$10^4\ A$	$10^4\ S_{(\eta)}$	$10^4\ A$	$10^4\ S_{(\eta)}$	$10^4\ A$
12.5	58	58	...	...	...ᵃ	...ᵃ	...	...
15	59	58	160	160	163ᵃ	150ᵃ	...	303
25	60	62	166	167	167	164	300	310
35	62	65	171	170	170	172	...	315
42.5	64	71	172	173	174ᵇ	178ᵇ	...	321

* M. Kaminsky, *Z. Physik. Chem.*, *Neue Folge* **8**, 173 (1956). (a) 15.5°C. (b) 40°C.

The effect of the dielectric constant in non-aqueous solvents is more difficult to verify.   The experimental limiting slopes are subject to errors caused by accidental absorption of moisture by hygroscopic solvents, and the theoretical limiting slopes themselves may be inaccurate because the limiting ionic conductivities are not known with certainty in these media.

TABLE (6-9-3).   LIMITING SLOPES FOR VISCOSITY IN NON-AQUEOUS SOLVENTS AT 25°

Salt	Solvent	$A\ 10^4$	$\mathcal{S}_{(\eta)}10^4$	Ref.
LiCl	acetone	240	237	(a)
KCl	methanol	151	173	(b)
KBr	"	142	165	(b)
KI	"	159	158	(b)
NH₄Cl	"	183	165	(b)
NaI	ethanol	270	255	(c)

(a) G. R. Hood and L. P. Hohlfelder, *J. Phys. Chem.*, **38**, 979 (1934).
(b) G. Jones and H. J. Fornwalt, *J. Am. Chem. Soc.*, **57**, 2041 (1935).
(c) W. M. Cox and J. H. Wolfenden, *Proc. Roy. Soc. London*, **A145**, 475 (1934).

Table (6-9-3) shows some representative results obtained in acetone and alcohols.   In attempting to evaluate A in these solvents, it is necessary to obtain measurements at very low concentrations.   Dalian and Briscoe[127] found that the extrapolation of their data at relatively high concentrations ($c \geq 0.04$) leads to negative values of A for solutions of nickel and aluminum chlorides in ethanol, and zero values of A for the chlorides of cobalt, copper, iron, tin, cadmium and mercury* in this solvent.   Reference to Fig. (6-9-3) strongly suggests that the anomalous A-values reported by Dalian and Briscoe are without physical significance.

(10) DIFFUSION OF ELECTROLYTES AND SELF-DIFFUSION OF IONS

We shall restrict the immediate discussion to the consideration of two types of diffusion in electrolytic solutions, that of a single salt and the special case of diffusion of an ion at a very low concentration in a solution containing three or more kinds of ions.

In Chapter (4), Section (4), the theory of the diffusion of a single electrolyte in dilute solutions has been developed in detail. In this case, electrical neutrality requires that both positive and negative ions move with the same velocity.   Under these conditions the ionic atmospheres suffer no deformation and the time of relaxation effect vanishes. Further, since the electrolyte moves in one direction and the solvent by replacing it moves in the opposite direction, an "electrophoretic" effect exists. Finally, since the

---

[127] F. E. Dalian and H. T. Briscoe, *J. Phys. Chem.*, **41**, 1129 (1937).
* Even in dilute aqueous solutions mercuric chloride behaves as a typical non-electrolyte.   See F. Prasad, A. S. Chakravarti and B. Prasad, *J. Indian Chem. Soc.*, **15**, 301 (1938).

activity coefficient of the electrolyte is not constant throughout the diffusing system, it appears in the theoretical equation for the diffusion coefficient as a thermodynamic term $(1 + c\, \partial \ln y_{\pm}/\partial c)$.

Self-diffusion is a special kind of diffusion in a solution containing three or more species of ions. The simplest case of self-diffusion is that of a single ion at very low concentration (radioactive tracer ion) in a solution containing the non-radioactive species of this ion. For example, the net effect of the diffusion of radioactive sodium ion in a sodium chloride solution is the replacement of the inactive ion by the tracer-ion. Solvent displacement is negligible so that the effect of electrophoresis vanishes. On the other hand since positive and negative ions move relatively to one another the "time of relaxation effect" is the important factor in self-diffusion. Finally, the thermodynamic term reduces to unity since the activity coefficient of a species at very low concentration in a medium of constant ionic strength does not vary sensibly with its concentration [See Fig. (14-4-1)].

Equations for the Theoretical Computation of Diffusion Coefficients of Single Salts

According to the theory developed in Chapter (4), Section (4), the diffusion coefficient in dilute solution is expressed by

$$\mathfrak{D} = (\nu_1 + \nu_2)1000RT\left(1 + c\frac{\partial \ln y_{\pm}}{\partial c}\right)$$

$$\left(1.0741 \times 10^{-20}\frac{\lambda_1^0\lambda_2^0}{\nu_1\,|\,z_1\,|\,\Lambda^0} + \frac{\Delta\mathfrak{M}'}{c} + \frac{\Delta\mathfrak{M}''}{c}\right) \tag{6-10-1}$$

where the electrophoretic terms, $\Delta\mathfrak{M}'$ and $\Delta\mathfrak{M}''$, are given by equations (4-4-20) and (4-4-21). The thermodynamic factor may be evaluated by differentiation of the equation

$$\log y_{\pm} = -\frac{\mathbb{S}_{(f)}\sqrt{c}}{1 + A'\sqrt{c}} + Bc - \log\left[\frac{d + 0.001c(\nu M_1 - M_2)}{d_0}\right] \tag{6-10-2}$$

which results from combination of equations (3-8-2) and (1-8-14). Thus

$$\left(1 + c\frac{\partial \ln y_{\pm}}{\partial c}\right) = 1 - \frac{1.1514\mathbb{S}_{(f)}\sqrt{c}}{(1 + A'\sqrt{c})^2} + 2.303Bc - c\psi\,(d) \tag{6-10-3}$$

The density term, resulting from the differentiation of equation (6-10-2)

$$\psi\,(d) = \frac{\partial d/\partial c + 0.001(\nu M_1 - M_2)}{d + 0.001c(\nu M_1 - M_2)} \tag{6-10-4}$$

is not negligible except at high dilutions.

If we combine equations (6-10-1) and (6-10-3) after introducing the values of $\Delta\mathfrak{M}'$ and $\Delta\mathfrak{M}''$, and note that $c\phi(\kappa a)$ or $c\phi(A'\sqrt{c})$ and its first derivative with respect to $\sqrt{c}$ approach zero as c approaches zero, we obtain the limiting equation

$$\mathfrak{D} = \mathfrak{D}_0 - \mathfrak{S}_{(\mathfrak{D})}\sqrt{c} \qquad (6\text{-}10\text{-}5)$$

where

$$\mathfrak{S}_{(\mathfrak{D})} = \frac{1.3273 \times 10^{-3}}{D^{3/2}T^{1/2}} \frac{(\Sigma\nu_i z_i^2)^{3/2}}{\nu_1 \mid z_1 \mid} \left(\frac{\lambda_1^0\lambda_2^0}{\Lambda^0}\right)$$

$$+ \frac{2.604 \times 10^{-8}}{\eta_0 D^{1/2}T^{-1/2}} \frac{(\Sigma\nu_i z_i^2)^{1/2}}{\mid z_1 z_2 \mid} \left(\frac{\mid z_2 \mid\lambda_1^0 - \mid z_1 \mid\lambda_2^0}{\Lambda^0}\right)^2 \qquad (6\text{-}10\text{-}6)$$

and

$$\mathfrak{D}_0 = 8.936 \times 10^{-10}T \frac{(\nu_1 + \nu_2)}{\nu_1 \mid z_1 \mid} \left(\frac{\lambda_1^0\lambda_2^0}{\Lambda^0}\right) \qquad (6\text{-}10\text{-}7)$$

The Limiting Equation for Self-Diffusion

Onsager[128] has obtained a limiting equation for the diffusion coefficient of an ion at very small concentrations in an electrolytic solution of otherwise constant composition. Thus, if $\mathfrak{D}_j$ is the diffusion coefficient of the jth ion whose transference number, t_j, is very small

$$\mathfrak{D}_j = \omega_j \left[kT - \frac{\kappa e_j^2}{3D} \left(1 - \sqrt{d(\omega_j)} \right) \right] \qquad (6\text{-}10\text{-}8)*$$

where

$$d(\omega_j) = \frac{\bar{\lambda}}{\bar{\Gamma}} \sum_i \frac{t_i}{(\omega_i + \omega_j)} \qquad (6\text{-}10\text{-}9)$$

$$\bar{\lambda} = \sum_i n_i e_i^2 \omega_i \qquad (6\text{-}10\text{-}10)$$

$$t_i = n_i e_i^2 \omega_i / \bar{\lambda} \qquad (6\text{-}10\text{-}11)$$

$$\kappa^2 = \frac{4\pi}{DkT} \bar{\Gamma} \qquad (6\text{-}10\text{-}12)$$

$$\bar{\Gamma} = \sum_i n_i e_i^2$$

By introducing the limiting ionic conductance, λ_j, in Coulombs sec. cm.$^{-1}$ volt^{-1}, the Faraday, F, in coulombs, R in joules deg.$^{-1}$ mol.$^{-1}$, and c_i for concentration in mols of ion per liter, Gosting and Harned[129] and Wang[130] have shown that equation (6-10-8) becomes

---

* Compare equations (4-3-7) and (4-3-38).

[128] L. Onsager, *Ann. N. Y. Acad. Sci.*, **46**, 241 (1945).

[129] L. J. Gosting and H. S. Harned, *J. Am. Chem. Soc.*, **73**, 159 (1951).

[130] J. H. Wang, *ibid.*, **74**, 1182 (1952).

$$\mathfrak{D}_j = \frac{RT\lambda_j^0}{|z_j|\,\mathbf{F}^2} - \frac{\lambda_j^0\,|z_j|\,\mathbf{F}}{3ND}\,2.694 \times 10^{16}\,\sqrt{\frac{4\pi}{DRT}} \qquad (6\text{-}10\text{-}13)$$

$$[1 - \sqrt{d(\omega_j)}]\,\sqrt{\Gamma}$$

The first term on the right of this equation is the limiting value of the diffusion coefficient of the tracer-ion. The negative term expresses the time of relaxation effect and the coefficient of the square root of the ional concentration is the limiting slope of the theory. The quantity $d(\omega_j)$ depends on the number and types of ions present. For example, for the diffusion of ion of type (1) present at very low concentration, into a solution containing ions of types (2) and (3), $c_1 \cong 0$, $c_2|\,z_2\,| = c_3|\,z_3\,|$

$$d(\omega_1) = \left(\frac{|\,z_1\,|}{|\,z_2\,| + |\,z_3\,|}\right)\left(\frac{|\,z_2\,|\,\lambda_2^0}{|\,z_1\,|\,\lambda_2^0 + |\,z_2\,|\,\lambda_1^0} + \frac{|\,z_3\,|\,\lambda_3^0}{|\,z_1\,|\,\lambda_2^0 + |\,z_3\,|\,\lambda_1^0}\right) \qquad (6\text{-}10\text{-}14)$$

It is important to note that equation (6-10-13) is a limiting equation to be approached by experimental results as the concentrations of all the ions in the solution approaches zero.

The Diffusion Coefficients of Electrolytes in Dilute Aqueous Solutions

Of the various methods proposed for the measurement of diffusion coefficients,[131] only one has been developed which yields precise results at electrolyte concentrations below 0.01 molar. This method which utilizes the differences in conductance at the top and bottom of a cell in which restricted diffusion is taking place was devised by Harned and French[132] and in an improved form has been described in detail by Harned and Nuttall.[133]

Theoretically, the conductometric method is capable of very high accuracy, but in actual practice it is necessary that the diffusion process be steady over a period of six to ten days under gradients of concentration of electrolyte of the order of a few thousandths of a mol per centimeter or less. It is indeed surprising that in many experiments such steadiness has been obtained. Any mechanical disturbance caused by vibration, local heating when balancing the conductance bridge etc. will cause inconsistencies, which in the great majority of cases become apparent. In Table (6-10-1A) all the experimental results by the conductance method, in which no appreciable variations from steadiness were apparent, are compiled. No attempt has been made to smooth the results or subject them to statistical analysis. We shall find that the magnitude of the theoretical electro-

---

[131] Reviews of this subject which contain extensive bibliographies have been written by L. G. Longsworth, *Ann. N. Y. Acad. Sci.*, **46**, 211 (1945) and by H. S. Harned, *Chem. Rev.*, **40**, 461 (1947).

[132] H. S. Harned and D. M. French, *Proc. N. Y. Head. Sci.*, **46**, 267 (1945).

[133] H. S. Harned and R. L. Nuttall, *J. Am. Chem. Soc.*, **69**, 736 (1947).

phoretic effect is small and that the experimental verification of its correctness is very difficult. For this reason, we considered it advisable at this stage in the development of the subject not to resort to smoothing the results.

The theoretical calculations of the diffusion coefficients have been effected by the use of equations (6-10-1) and (6-10-2). The density term given by equation (6-10-4) is negligible at concentrations below 0.01 molar. The electrophoretic term, $\Delta\overline{\mathfrak{M}}'$ was computed by equation (4-4-20) and the other electrophoretic term $\Delta\overline{\mathfrak{M}}''$ by equation (4-4-21) with the use of Table

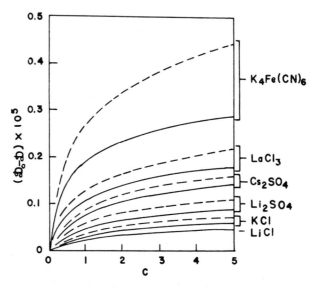

Fig. (6-10-1). Concentration dependence of diffusion coefficients in dilute aqueous solutions at 25°. The solid curves were computed by equation (6-10-1) and the dashed curves by equation (6-10-15). For a given salt the difference between the dashed and solid graphs represents the theoretical electrophoretic contribution. Concentration in millimols per liter.

(5-3-2). The equivalent conductances, λ_1^0 and λ_2^0 and the parameters, $\mathring{a}$, A' and 2.303B, employed in these calculations are compiled in Table (6-10-2A). The sources of the data for the evaluation of the activity coefficient term are to be found in the references recorded at the bottom of Table (6-10-1A). The last column of Table (6-10-2A) contains the limiting slopes of the theory as computed by equation (6-10-6).

To illustrate the result of these calculations we have recorded in the parentheses immediately following the observed results in Table (6-10-1A) the differences in the third decimal place between the calculated and observed values. These differences are positive when the calculated results are larger than the experimental ones. A preliminary survey of these deviations shows that for the alkali metal chlorides, silver and potassium nitrates most of the observed results are within 0.2 to 0.3 per cent of the calculated values. A similar agreement occurs for lithium and cesium sulphates, and magnesium, strontium and barium chlorides.   Lithium and potassium perchlorates, sodium sulphate and calcium and lanthanum chlorides at concentrations below 0.01 molar show deviations of the order of one percent.   Due to ion-pair formation, magnesium and zinc sulphates are to be considered as special cases while the agreement for potassium ferrocyanide is largely fortuitous, partly because of the uncertainty of evaluating the thermodynamic term.

The magnitudes of the thermodynamic and electrophoretic contributions are illustrated by Fig. (6-10-1) where the values of $(\mathfrak{D}_0 - \mathfrak{D}) \times 10^5$ are

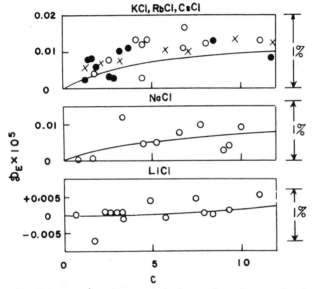

Fig. (6-10-2).   Calculated and observed electrophoretic contributions for the alkali metal chlorides.   In the top figure, the crosses, circles and dots represent the observed values for potassium, rubidium and cesium chlorides, respectively.   Concentration in millimols per liter.

plotted against the concentrations for a number of salts of different valence types.   If no electrophoretic effect exists equation (6-10-1) reduces to

$$\mathfrak{D} = \mathfrak{D}_0 \left(1 + c \frac{\partial \ln y_\pm}{\partial c}\right) \qquad (6\text{-}10\text{-}15)$$

The dashed curves in the figure represent values calculated by this latter equation for the salt solutions designated.   The solid graphs represent the diffusion coefficients computed by equation (6-10-1) and therefore the differences between the two plots for each salt represent the electrophoretic contributions which will be denoted by $\mathfrak{D}_E$.   It is to be noticed that $\Delta\overline{\mathfrak{M}}'$ is a negative electrophoretic term and $\Delta\overline{\mathfrak{M}}''$ is a positive one.   In some cases, as for example lithium chloride solutions, these terms are nearly the same magnitude and their sums are too small to be indicated in this figure. For potassium chloride, the theoretical electrophoretic contribution at

0.005 molar amounts to about 0.4 % of the value of the diffusion coefficient of this electrolyte. For electrolytes of higher valence types, the electrophoretic contributions as calculated are larger than 1-1 types but, unfortunately, with these solutions we encounter the difficulties which arise from ion-pair formations in solutions containing ion of charges greater than unity.

The proof of the existence of the electrophoretic term is a difficult one but the results so far obtained indicate that the calculated electrophoretic contribution appears to be of the right sign and magnitude for uniunivalent and biunivalent electrolytes. This conclusion is illustrated by the plots in Figs. (6-10-2) and (6-10-3) in which the electrophoretic

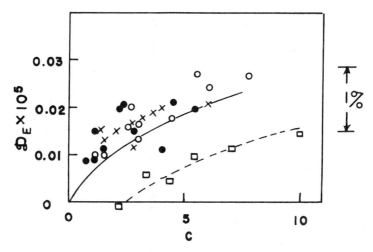

Fig. (6-10-3). Calculated and observed electrophoretic terms for the alkaline earth chlorides. The crosses, squares, circles and dots represent the values for magnesium, calcium, strontium and barium chlorides, respectively. Concentration in millimols per liter.

contributions for the alkali metal and alkaline earth chlorides as calculated are represented by the curves. The experimental values represented in these figures were computed by subtracting $\mathfrak{D}$ evaluated by equation (6-10-1) from the observed values. This procedure constitutes a very severe test of the data.[134] One percent of the magnitude of the diffusion coefficients is indicated on the extreme right of these figures. All the experimental results at concentrations below 0.012 molar are included in these figures.

Fig. (6-10-2) shows that at 0.01 molar concentration the magnitudes of the electrophoretic contributions are 0.5 % of the diffusion coefficients for potassium, rubidium and cesium chlorides, 0.4 % for sodium chloride and

---

[134] See E. A. Guggenheim, *Trans. Faraday Soc.*, **50**, 1048 (1954) who carried out this calculation for sodium chloride solutions.

0.1 % for lithium chloride.   It is to be observed that as predicted by theory a positive electrophoretic effect is indicated by the experimental data for all the salts with the exception of lithium chloride.   Figure (6-10-3) shows the more pronounced effect for the alkaline earth chlorides.   The results in all cases confirm a positive electrophoretic effect which is of the right magnitude for magnesium, strontium and barium chlorides.   The calcium chloride results lie about 0.8 % below the theoretical prediction.[135]   A

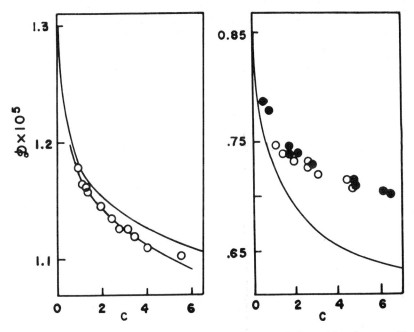

Fig. (6-10-4).   Observed and calculated diffusion coefficient of lanthanum chloride in dilute aqueous solution at 25°.   Upper curve represents theoretical values. Concentration in millimols per liter.

Fig. (6-10-5).   The diffusion coefficients of zinc (circles) and magnesium (dots) sulphates in dilute aqueous solutions at 25°.   Lower curve represents the calculation according to equation (6-10-1).   Concentration in millimols per liter.

similar calculation for lithium and cesium sulphate solutions reveals conformity with the theory.   On the contrary, the observed results for sodium sulphate are about one per cent higher than the theoretical prediction, a behavior opposite in sign and of the same magnitude as that found for calcium chloride solutions.

Figures (6-10-4) and (6-10-5) illustrate two contrasting types of deviations from the predictions of the theory which presupposes complete dissociation.   The diffusion of lanthanum chloride is plotted against the

[135] Attempts to explain this discrepancy have been made by A. W. Adamson, *J. Phys. Chem.*, **58**, 514 (1954) and R. H. Stokes, *J. Am. Chem. Soc.*, **75**, 4563 (1953). See also R. A. Robinson and R. H. Stokes, *Electrolyte Solutions*, Butterworths Scientific Publications, London (1955).

concentration in figure (6-10-4). The observed results for this salt lie below those calculated by equation (6-10-1) and appear to approach the theoretical values as the concentration approaches zero. Quite otherwise, the experimental results for the diffusion coefficients of magnesium and zinc sulphates are considerable higher than those computed by theory although they approach the limiting value satisfactorily as the concentration decreases. Harned and Hudson[136] have suggested that the deviations from theory for these 2-2 sulphates can be explained by ion-pair formation.

The influence of ion-pair formation on the diffusion coefficient may be may be computed readily for an electolyte which dissociates into two ions. If c_1, c_2 and c_m are the concentrations, ω_1, ω_2 and ω_m, the mobilities of the cation, anion and ion-pair, respectively, then the total flow J at constant temperature is expressed by

$$\mathbf{J} = -(c_1\omega_1\nabla\bar{\mu}_1 + c_2\omega_2\nabla\bar{\mu}_2) - c_m\omega_m\nabla\mu \qquad (6\text{-}10\text{-}16)$$

where $\bar{\mu}_1$, and $\bar{\mu}_2$ are the electrochemical potentials of the ions and μ is the chemical potential of the ion-pair. Since in diffusion of a single salt, the ions migrate with the same velocity $\omega_1\nabla\bar{\mu}_1 = \omega_2\nabla\bar{\mu}_2$. Utilizing this equality, the mass action law, $\mu = \mu_1 + \mu_2$, and noting that according to the definition of the electrochemical potential [Eq. (1-15-5)], $\mu = \bar{\mu}_1 + \bar{\mu}_2$, equation (6-10-16) becomes

$$\mathbf{J} = -\left[c_1 \frac{\omega_1\omega_2}{\omega_1 + \omega_2} + c_m\omega_m \right] \nabla\mu \qquad (6\text{-}10\text{-}17)$$

since c_1 equals c_2. The total concentration c equals $c_1 + c_m$ and $c_m/c = 1 - \alpha$ where α is the degree of dissociation of the ion-pair. So that equation (6-10-17) may be rearranged to give

$$\mathbf{J} = -c \frac{\omega_1\omega_2}{\omega_1 + \omega_2} \left[1 + (1 - \alpha) \left(\omega_m \Big/ \frac{\omega_1\omega_2}{\omega_1 + \omega_2} - 1 \right) \right] \nabla\mu \qquad (6\text{-}10\text{-}18)$$

The term within the brackets is a correction factor to be applied to the values of the diffusion coefficient, $\mathfrak{D}_{(\text{calc})}$, calculated by equation (6-10-1). Thus

$$\mathfrak{D}_{\text{obs}}/\mathfrak{D}_{\text{calc}} = 1 + (1 - \alpha) \left[\lambda_m^0 \Big/ \frac{\lambda_1^0\lambda_2^0}{\lambda_1^0 + \lambda_2^0} - 1 \right] \qquad (6\text{-}10\text{-}19)$$

upon substituting the equivalent conductances, λ_1^0, λ_2^0 of the ions and the corresponding equivalent quantity λ_m^0 for the ion-pair.

Harned and Hudson computed λ_m^0 at various concentrations from the limiting conductances in Table (6-8-2) and values of the degree of dissociation computed by Owen and Gurry[137] from conductance data. The

---

[136] H. S. Harned and R. M. Hudson, *J. Am. Chem. Soc.*, **73**, 3781, 5880 (1951).
[137] B. B. Owen and R. W. Gurry, *J. Am. Chem. Soc.*, **60**, 3078 (1938).

quantity, λ_m^0, was found to be constant over the concentration range from 0.0005 to 0.006 molar. The mean value of this quantity was 46 for magnesium sulphate and 44 for zinc sulphate. The mean mobility for the ions, $\lambda_1^0\lambda_2^0/(\lambda_1^0 + \lambda_2^0)$ of both these salts is 31.9.

Activity Coefficients from Diffusion Data[138]

The calculations in the preceding section were made by computing the thermodynamic term from activity coefficient data. Since very few accurate experimental determinations of activity coefficients at concentrations below 0.01 molar were available, it was necessary to rely on extrapolations of data at concentrations above 0.1 molar by means of equation (6-10-2). It appeared that at concentrations less than 0.01 molar the electrophoretic terms, $\Delta\mathfrak{M}'$ and $\Delta\mathfrak{M}''$, in equation (6-10-1) were of the correct sign and order of magnitude of the observed results. If these terms can be calculated accurately, then activity coefficients in very dilute solutions may be accurately computed from diffusion data in the following manner.

For simplicity, equation (6-10-1) will be written in the form

$$\mathfrak{D} = \nu 1000RT\left(\frac{\mathfrak{M}}{c}\right)\left(1 + c\frac{\partial \ln y_{\pm}}{\partial c}\right) \qquad (6\text{-}10\text{-}20)$$

where $(\mathfrak{M}/c)$ is the whole mobility term. Rearrangement of this equation yields

$$\frac{\mathfrak{D}}{\nu 1000RT(\mathfrak{M}/c)} - 1 \equiv \mathfrak{D}' = c\frac{\partial \ln y_{\pm}}{\partial c} \qquad (6\text{-}10\text{-}21)$$

whence

$$\ln y_{\pm} = \int_0^c \frac{\mathfrak{D}'}{c}\,dc = \int_0^c \frac{2\mathfrak{D}'}{c^{1/2}}\,dc^{1/2} \qquad (6\text{-}10\text{-}22)$$

and

$$\log y_{\pm} = \frac{\ln y_{\pm}}{2.3026} = 0.8686\int_0^c \frac{\mathfrak{D}'}{c^{1/2}}\,dc^{1/2} \qquad (6\text{-}10\text{-}23)$$

Fortunately, the value of $\mathfrak{D}'/c^{1/2}$ may be evaluated at the limit since the theoretical limiting slope of equation (5-2-2) is known. Thus

$$\lim_{c\to 0}\left[\frac{\mathfrak{D}'}{c^{1/2}} = \frac{\partial \ln y_{\pm}}{2\partial c^{1/2}} = \frac{2.3026\partial \log y_{\pm}}{2\partial c^{1/2}} = -\frac{2.3026}{2}\,\mathfrak{S}_{(f)}\right. \qquad (6\text{-}10\text{-}24)$$

By plotting $\mathfrak{D}'/c^{1/2}$ versus $c^{1/2}$, evaluation of $\log y_{\pm}$ at suitable concentrations may be achieved by graphical integration. Such a graph for sodium chloride solutions shown in Fig. (6-10-6). This method is very favorable for the determination of the activity coefficient since the whole area under the curve is involved.

[138] H. S. Harned, *Proc. Nat. Acad. Sci.*, **40**, 551 (1954).

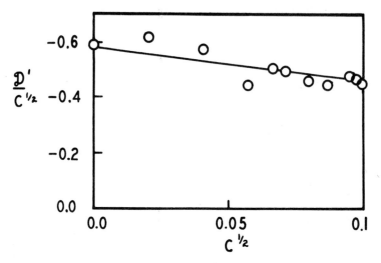

Fig. (6-10-6). Plot for computing activity coefficients according to equations (6-10-23) and (6-10-24).

Table (6-10-1) contains values of the activity coefficients calculated from the diffusion data. In parentheses are given the activity coefficients determined by MacInnes and Shedlovsky from the electromotive forces of cell with liquid junctions and transference number data. This method which is described in detail in Chapter (12), Section (1) is the only one in which accurate measurements have been made at concentrations in the range of

TABLE (6-10-1).   ACTIVITY COEFFICIENTS OF ELECTROLYTES IN DILUTE AQUEOUS SOLUTIONS AT 25° FROM DIFFUSION DATA.

$c \times 10^3$	0.1	0.4	0.5	1	2	5	7	10
LiCl	—	—	0.975	0.966	0.952	0.929	—	0.905
NaCl	—	—	.975	.9653	.9516	.9279	—	.9027
NaCl[a]	—	—	—	(.9651)	(.9519)	(.9273)	—	(.9022)
KCl	—	—	.975	.9651	.9517	.9276	—	.9016
KCl[a]	—	—	—	(.9650)	(.9516)	(.9270)	—	(.9015)
RbCl	—	—	.975	.966	.951	.928	—	.901
CsCl	—	—	.975	.965	.951	.927	—	.899
KNO$_3$	—	—	.975	.964	.951	.926	—	.900
AgNO$_3$	—	—	.974	.963	.949	.922	—	.894
AgNO$_3$[b]	—	—	—	—	—	(.922)	—	(.894)
Li$_2$SO$_4$	0.961	0.925	—	.887	.848	.779	.749	.717
Cs$_2$SO$_4$	.961	.925	—	.886	.845	.774	.742	.707
MgCl$_2$	.961	.926	—	.890	.954	.792	.765	—
CaCl$_2$	.961	.926	—	.888	.850	.784	.755	.724
CaCl$_2$[a]	—	—	—	(.889)	(.852)	(.789)	—	(.731)
SrCl$_2$	.961	.926	—	.889	.853	.790	.762	.732
BaCl$_2$	.961	.926	—	.888	.850	.783	.754	—
LaCl$_3$	.921	.853	—	.785	.722	.623	.583	.546
LaCl$_3$[a]	—	—	—	(.790)	—	(.638)	—	(.559)
K$_4$Fe(CN)$_6$	.867	.761	—	.663	.575	.449	.433	—

(a) T. Shedlovsky, *J. Am. Chem. Soc.*, **72**, 3680 (1950).
(b) D. A. MacInnes, *The Principles of Electrochemistry*, p. 164, Reinhold Publishing Corp., New York (1939).

0.002 to 0.005 molar.   For the 1-1 electrolytes the agreement between the values derived by these entirely different methods is very encouraging. For calcium and lanthanum chloride solutions, as previously noted, deviations become increasingly large as the concentrations increase.

Diffusion Coefficients of Electrolytes in Concentrated Solutions

Of the various ingenious methods[139] employed for determining diffusion coefficients at concentrations above 0.05 molar, the one which has yielded the most precise results, known as the Gouy interference method, utilizes the interference phenomena which accompany the deflection of light by gradients of the refractive index in a freely moving boundary.   Longsworth[140] suggested that a quantitative treatment of this phenomenon would yield a precise method for the study of diffusion.   Subsequently, the theory of this method was developed by Kegeles and Gosting,[141] by Coulson, Cox, Ogston and Philpot,[142] and in a more general manner by Gosting and Onsager.[143]   The experimental procedure has been described by Gosting, Hanson, Kegeles and Morris.[144]   Gosting and Morris[145] applied this method to the measurement of the diffusion coefficient of sucrose in water and proved that it was capable of an accuracy of the order of ±0.1 per cent.

The first determination of the diffusion coefficient of an electrolyte by the Gouy interference method was made by Gosting[146] whose values for potassium chloride as well as the conductometric results of Harned and Nuttall are plotted in Fig. (6-10-7).   The agreement in the region where the results of the two methods overlap is within 0.1 percent.   The curve in this figure was computed by equation (6-10-1) and is seen to represent

---

[139] Extensive bibliographies of methods for measuring diffusion coefficient are contained in reviews by L. G. Longsworth, *Ann. N. Y. Acad. Sci.*, **46,** 211 (1945), and H. S. Harned, *Chem. Rev.*, **40,** 461 (1947).   Determinations of a high order of accuracy have been made by E. Cohen and H. R. Bruins (*Z. Physik. Chem.*, **103,** 337, 349, 404 (1923); **113,** 157 (1924)), by the layer analysis method, by O. Lamm (*Z. physik. Chem.*, **A138,** 138, 313 (1928); **A143,** 177 (1929); *Nova Acta Regiae Soc. Sci. Upsaliensis*, (4) **10** (6) (1937); *Svensk. Kem. Tid.*, **51,** 139 (1939); **55,** 263 (1943)), by the optical scale displacement method and by B. W. Clack (*Proc. Roy. Soc. (London)*, **21,** 374 (1908); **24,** 40 (1912); **27,** 56 (1914); **24,** 49 (1916); **33,** 259 (1921)) who employed an optical system for steady state diffusion.

[140] L. G. Longsworth, *Am. N. Y. Acad. Sci.*, **46,** 211 (1945); *J. Am. Chem. Soc.*, **69,** 2510 (1947).

[141] G. Kegeles and L. J. Gosting, *Ibid.*, **69,** 2517 (1947).

[142] C. A. Coulson, J. T. Cox, A. G. Ogston and J. St. L. Philpot, *Proc. Roy. Soc.*, **192A,** 382 (1948).

[143] L. J. Gosting and L. Onsager, *J. Am. Chem. Soc.*, **74,** 6066 (1952).

[144] L. J. Gosting, E. Hanson, G. Kegeles and M. S. Morris, *Rev. Sci. Instr.*, **20,** 209 (1949).

[145] L. J. Gosting and M. S. Morris, *J. Am. Chem. Soc.*, **71,** 1998 (1949).

[146] L. J. Gosting, *J. Am. Chem. Soc.*, **72,** 4418 (1950).

the results within the error experiment from 0 to 0.1 molar concentration. This behavior is unusual as evidenced by Fig. (6-10-8) in which the diffusion coefficient of sodium chloride is plotted. It is apparent that a sharp deviation from the theoretical prediction occurs at 0.01 molar. Such a behavior is to be expected since equation (6-10-1) does not incorporate the influences of changing viscosity, dielectric constant and hydration.

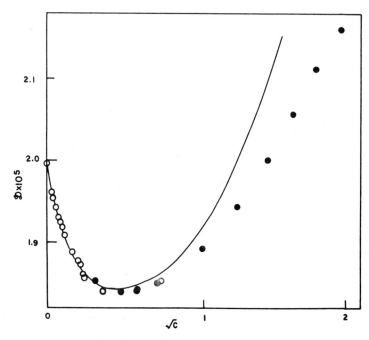

Fig. (6-10-7). The diffusion coefficient of potassium chloride in aqueous solutions at 25° by the conductometric (circles) and Gouy interference methods.

Fig. (6-10-8) includes results obtained at low concentrations by the conductometric method, by Vitagliano and Lyons by the Gouy interference method and by Stokes[147] who used the Northrup-McBain diaphragm type of cell.[148] The results given by values at the very low concentrations agree satisfactorily with those obtained by both the optical and diaphragm cell measurements. At concentrations above two molar, the values obtained by the Gouy interference method are somewhat greater than those by the

[147] R. H. Stokes, *J. Am. Chem. Soc.*, **72**, 2243 (1950).

[148] J. H. Northrup and M. L. Anson, *J. Gen. Physiol.*, **12**, 543 (1929); J. W. McBain and T. H. Liu, *J. Am. Chem. Soc.*, **53**, 59 (1931); J. W. McBain and C. R. Dawson, *Ibid.*, **56**, 1021 (1934); *Proc. Roy. Soc. London*, **A148**, 32 (1935). See also the careful studies with diaphragm cells made by G. S. Hartley and D. F. Runnicles, *ibid.*, **A168**, 401 (1938); A. R. Gordon, *J. Chem. Phys.*, **5**, 552 (1937); *Ann. N. Y. Acad. Sci.*, **46**, 285 (1945); W. A. James, E. A. Hollingshead and A. R. Gordon, *J. Chem. Phys.*, **7**, 89 (1937); W. A. James and A. R. Gordon, *Ibid.*, **7**, 763 (1939); E. A. Hollingshead and A. R. Gordon, *ibid.*, **9**, 152 (1941).

diaphragm cell method.   In Table (6-10-2), we have recorded the diffusion coefficients for five salts obtained from graphs of the conductometric and optical results as being the most accurate now available.   In Table (6-10-1A) are given the values for other electrolytes obtained by Stokes et alia by diaphragm cell measurements at high concentrations.

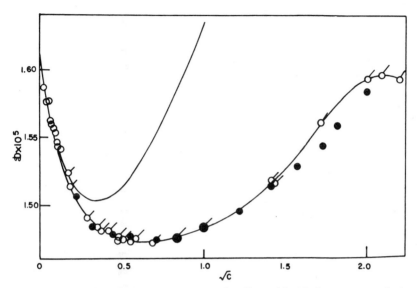

Fig. (6-10-8). The diffusion coefficient of sodium chloride in aqueous solutions at 25° by the conductometric method (circles), Gouy interference method (circles with dash) and diaphragm cell method (dots).

TABLE (6-10-2). DIFFUSION COEFFICIENTS OF ALKALI AND ALKALINE EARTH METAL CHLORIDES OVER ENTIRE CONCENTRATION RANGES AT 25°.

$\mathfrak{D} \times 10^5$

c	NaCl[1]	KCl[2]	CsCl[3]	CaCl$_2$[3]	BaCl$_2$[1]
0.0	(1.611)	(1.994)	(2.044)	(1.335)	(1.386)
.001	1.585	1.962	2.009	1.258	1.317
.002	1.574	1.951	1.996	1.239	1:298
.005	1.559	1.933	1.975	1:210	1.263
.01	1.545	1.915	1.954	1.188	1.238
.02	1.530	1.892	1.930	1.161	1.212
.05	1.507	1.862	1.892	1.137	1.176
.1	1.482	1.842	1.870	1.122	1.160
.2	1.473	1.835	1.856	1.122	1.150
.5	1.473	1.850	1.860	1.150	1.160
1.	1.485	1.893	1.902	1.220	1.177
2.	1.518	2.001	2.029	1.308	—
3.	1.565	2.111	2.173	1.278	—
4.	1.594	2.207	2.111	1.078	—
5.	1.590	—	2.363	0.725	—
6.	—	—	2.335	0.402	—

(1) V. Vitagliano and P. A. Lyons, J. Am. Chem. Soc., **78**, 1549 (1956).

(2) L. J. Gosting, Ibid., **72**, 4418 (1950).

(3) P. A. Lyons and J. F. Riley, ibid., **76**, 5216 (1954).

Self-Diffusion of Ions

Equations (6-10-13) and (6-10-14) reduce to the simple expression

$$\mathfrak{D}_j = \mathfrak{D}_j^0 - \mathfrak{S}_{(\mathfrak{D}_j)}\sqrt{c} \qquad (6\text{-}10\text{-}25)$$

where $\mathfrak{D}_j^0$ is the limiting value of the diffusion coefficient of the ion and $\mathfrak{S}_{(\mathfrak{D}_j)}$ the limiting theoretical constant. Since this equation represents a limiting law like equation (5-3-1) for the equivalent conductance of an electrolyte, its quantitative validity can be tested only by measurements in very dilute solutions. Examination of the plots of equivalent conductances in Figure (6-2-1) and (6-2-2) suggests that precise results of the self-diffusion coefficients at concentrations below 0.005 normal will be required to establish the theoretical prediction.

Since radioactive tracers of many ions have become available, the experimental knowledge of ion self-diffusion has increased considerably. Free diffusion,[149] diaphragm cell[150] and open-end capillary tube[151] methods of determination have been employed. So far, the agreement between the results by the different methods and the consistency of a single series of results by one method indicates that the overall reliability is of the order of 2 % at electrolyte concentrations from 0.05 normal to very concentrated solutions. At concentrations below 0.05 normal the results so far obtained are unreliable. In spite of this lack of precision, the recent pioneer investigations of self-diffusion of alkali metal and halide ions in salt solutions have contributed valuable information concerning the mobility of ions in concentrated aqueous electrolytic solutions.[152]

Harned and Gosting[153] were the first to compute $\mathfrak{S}_{(\mathfrak{D}_j)}$ in equation (6-10-25) by means of equations (6-10-13) and (6-10-14) and apply the result to the existing data. Although exact quantitative agreement between theory and experiment was not obtained, two qualitative predictions from the

---

[149] J. H. Wang and J. W. Kennedy, *J. Am. Chem. Soc.*, **72**, 2080 (1950).

[150] A. W. Adamson, *J. Chem. Phys.*, **15**, 760 (1947); A. W. Adamson, J. W. Cobble and J. M. Nielson, *Ibid.*, **17**, 740 (1944); J. M. Nielson, A. W. Adamson and J. W. Cobble, *J. Am. Chem. Soc.*, **74**, 446 (1952).

[151] J. A. Anderson and K. Saddington, *J. Chem. Soc.*, S 381 (1949).

[152] J. H. Wang and J. W. Kennedy, *J. Am. Chem. Soc.*, **72**, 2080 (1950); Sodium and iodide ion in sodium iodide solutions. R. Mills and J. W. Kennedy, *ibid.*, **75**, 5695 (1953); Iodide, Potassium and Rubidium Ions in Iodide and Hydriodic Acid Solutions. J. H. Wang, *J. Am. Chem. Soc.*, **74**, 1182 (1952); Sodium Ion in Potassium Chloride Solutions; J. H. Wang and S. Miller, *Ibid.*, **74**, 1611 (1952); Sodium Ion in Sodium Chloride Solutions. J. H. Wang, *Ibid.*, **74**, 1612 (1952); Chloride Ion in Sodium Chloride Solutions. J. H. Wang, *Ibid.*, **75**, 1769 (1953; Calcium and chloride Ions in Calcium Chloride Solutions. J. H. Wang and F. M. Polestra, *Ibid.*, **76**, 1584 (1954); Thallous ion in potassium chloride solutions. S. G. Whiteway, D. F. MacLennan and C. C. Coffin, *J. Chem. Phys.*, **18**, 229 (1950); Silver ion in silver nitrate solutions. J. M. Nielson, A. W. Adamson and J. W. Cobble, *J. Am. Chem. Soc.*, **74**, 446 (1952); Sodium and chloride ions in sodium chloride and sodium ions in sodium sulphate solutions.

[153] H. S. Harned and L. J. Gosting, *J. Am. Chem. Soc.*, **73**, 159 (1951).

theory were confirmed. All the results approached the calculated value, $\mathfrak{D}_i^0$, as the concentration tended toward zero. Secondly, the diffusion coefficient in dilute solutions decreases with increasing concentration of the electrolyte. This typical behavior is well illustrated by Fig. (6-10-9) in which the self-diffusion coefficient of the iodide ion in potassium iodide solutions determined by Mills and Kennedy[154] is plotted against the square

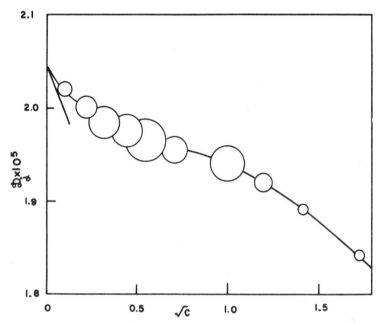

Fig. (6-10-9). The self-diffusion coefficient of the iodide ion in potassium iodide solutions at 25°. Radii of circles represent the estimated experimental error.

root of the concentration. For this case, equations (6-10-13) and (6-10-14) reduce to the simple numerical limiting expression

$$\mathfrak{D}_I \times 10^5 = 2.046 - 0.473\sqrt{c} \qquad (6\text{-}10\text{-}25\text{a})$$

which is represented by the straight line drawn from the limiting value at zero concentration. This tendency of the experimental results to approach the limiting equation is confirmed by the results compiled in the references previously listed.[152] The exact proof of the validity of the limiting law offers a difficult challenge to the experimenter since very precise results will be required at concentrations well below 0.01 molar.

A more precise indication of the validity of the limiting law for the self-diffusion of ions has been obtained by Longsworth[154a] from the exchange diffusion which occurs at the boundary between two equimolar solutions of potassium chloride and potassium iodide or sodium chloride and sodium

[154] R. Mills and J. W. Kennedy, *J. Am. Chem. Soc.*, **75**, 5695 (1953).
[154a] L. G. Longsworth, *J. Phys. Chem.*, **61**, 244 (1957).

TABLE (6-10-3). EXCHANGE DIFFUSION COEFFICIENTS OF CHLORIDE
AND IODIDE IONS IN AQUEOUS SOLUTIONS AT 25°

| | $\mathfrak{D} \times 10^5$ | |
c	KI-KCl	NaI-NaCl
0.01	2.011	2.006
.02	2.004	1.996
.05	1.997	1.981
.1	1.989	1.966
.2	1.982	1.943
.5	1.981	1.903
1.0	1.980	1.844

iodide. By utilizing the large difference in equivalent refractions between
iodides and chlorides, the exchange diffusion coefficients were. measured
with high precision by Rayleigh interferometry. The results for these two
systems are given in Table (6-10-3). The overall average deviation of the
results was of the order of 0.1 percent.

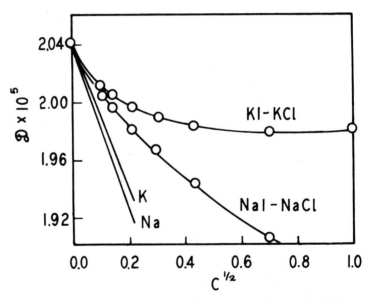

Fig. (6-10-10). The Cl⁻-I⁻ exchange diffusion coefficient with different common ions.

In Fig. (6-10-10), these results have been plotted against $c^{1/2}$. The
straight lines represent the limiting law of the theory expressed by equations
(6-10-13) and (6-10-14). The intercept at zero concentration is ($\mathfrak{D}_I^0 +$
$\mathfrak{D}_{Cl}^0$)/2. The observed results approach the limiting slopes from above.
Further, the results for solutions containing the potassium ion are higher
than those containing the sodium ion as predicted by the theory. These
results do not establish the theory numerically. However, the manner

in which the observed results approach the theoretical predictions as the concentration decreases is evidence that if observations could be extended to very low concentrations, the limiting law would be confirmed.

Viscosity and Diffusion in Concentrated Solutions

The general characteristics of self-diffusion and the salt diffusion of a strong electrolyte in water is well illustrated by Fig. (6-10-11).   In this figure the diffusion coefficient of calcium chloride determined in dilute solutions by the conductometric method[155] and in concentrated solutions by the Gouy interference method[156], as well as the self-diffusion coefficients[157] of the ions measured by the capillary method, are plotted against the

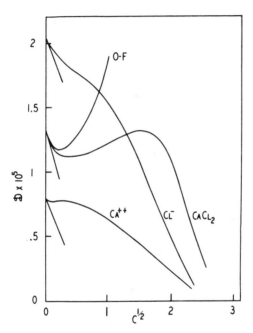

Fig. (6-10-11). Diffusion coefficient of calcium chloride and the self-diffusion coefficients of the calcium and chloride ions in aqueous solutions at 25°.

square root of the molar concentration.   The straight lines represent the limiting theoretical tangents for the salt diffusion and self-diffusion according to equations (6-10-5) and (6-10-13), respectively.   The curve designated O-F was computed by equation (6-10-1).   It is apparent that only in the very dilute solutions do the values of the self-diffusion coefficients approach the limiting equations of the theory, although they do converge toward the limiting values.   This behavior is not surprising, since conductance data of very high accuracy in the region of concentrations well below 0.002 molar

[155] H. S. Harned and H. W. Parker, *J. Am. Chem. Soc.*, **77**, 265 (1955).
[156] P. A. Lyons and J. F. Riley, *Ibid.*, **76**, 5216 (1954).
[157] J. H. Wang, *Ibid.*, **73**, 1769 (1953).

were required to verify the limiting law for the equivalent conductance of electrolytes. In this connection, see Figs. (6-2-1) and (6-2-2). The large departure from theory at high concentrations is certainly caused in part by the increase in viscosity of the solution, an effect recognized by Onsager and Fuoss and introduced by Gordon [158] in his empirical equation for the calculation of diffusion coefficients. For these calcium chloride solutions, Wang [157] has pointed out that the ratios of the self-diffusion coefficients at infinite dilution to those at 5.36 molar are 13 and 8 for the chloride ion and calcium ion, respectively, while the ratio of the macroscopic viscosity of a 5.36 molar calcium chloride solution to that of pure water is eleven.

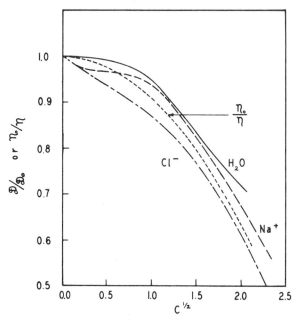

Fig. (6-10-12). Comparison of the self-diffusion coefficients of water and the sodium and chloride ions in aqueous sodium chloride solutions with the viscosity at 25°.[159]

A further illuminating illustration of the effect of viscosity due to Wang is illustrated by Figure (6-10-12). Here the ratios of the self-diffusion coefficients of water, the sodium ion and the chloride ion to their values at infinite dilution are plotted against the square root of the salt concentration. Comparison of these curves with the plot of the viscosity ratio, η_0/η, also drawn in the figure, leaves no doubt as to the importance of viscosity. One fact of unusual interest is that from 0 to 0.5 molar sodium chloride ion concentration, the self-diffusion of water is affected only slightly, if at all, by the presence of this salt. The first addition of salts

[158] A. R. Gordon, *J. Chem. Phys.*, **5**, 522 (1937); W. A. James and A. R. Gordon, *Ibid.*, **7**, 963 (1939); E. A. Hollingshead and A. R. Gordon, *Ibid.*, **9**, 152 (1941).
[159] J. H. Wang, *J. Phys. Chem.*, **58**, 686 (1954).

with larger ionic radii, such as potassium iodide, increases the self-diffusion of the water molecules.   These large ions appear to be good lubricants for water.

Mills and Kennedy[154] have found that plots of $\mathfrak{D}_j(\eta_0/\eta)$ against the square root of the concentration of salt are straight lines for concentration ranges from 0.05 to 2, or 3 molar.   These lines have slopes of considerable magnitudes which are characteristic of the ions.   They showed that plots of $\mathfrak{D}_j(\eta_0/\eta)$ for the iodide ion in rubidium, potassium, sodium and hydrogen iodides against the Debye-Hückel function, $\sqrt{c}/(1 + \kappa a)$, fall near each other if the values of a given in Table (12-5-2) are used.

The Hartley-Crank Equation and its Application

If the diffusion of each of the components in a system of s components is expressed in volume flows in respect to a fixed plane of reference, it can be shown that there will be $(s - 1)^2$ independent coefficients of diffusion.[160] Therefore, a system of two components can be described by a single diffusion coefficient, a result clearly expressed by Hartley and Crank.[161]   The volume transfers of components A and B in unit time across unit area in a fixed plane will be $-\mathfrak{D}_A^V \bar{V}_A \nabla c_A$ and $-\mathfrak{D}_B^V \bar{V}_B \nabla c_B$, respectively.   Since there is no net transfer of volume through this plane

$$\mathfrak{D}_A^V \bar{V}_A \nabla c_A + \mathfrak{D}_B^V \bar{V}_B \nabla c_B = 0 \qquad (6\text{-}10\text{-}26)$$

where $\bar{V}_A$ and $\bar{V}_B$ represent partial specific volumes [Note equation (4-4-2)] of the components subject to the condition

$$\bar{V}_A c_A + \bar{V}_B c_B = 1 \qquad (6\text{-}10\text{-}26a)$$

which upon differentiation becomes

$$\bar{V}_A \nabla c_A + \bar{V}_B c_B = 0 \qquad (6\text{-}10\text{-}26b)$$

If both equations (6-10-26) and (6-10-26b) are to be satisfied

$$\mathfrak{D}_A^V = \mathfrak{D}_B^V \equiv \mathfrak{D}^V \qquad (6\text{-}10\text{-}26c)$$

except for the trivial case where the partial volumes are zero.

Hartley and Crank proceed to show that for two component systems $\mathfrak{D}^V$ can be described by the equation

$$\mathfrak{D}^V = \frac{RT}{N} \frac{d \ln f_A N_A}{d \ln N_A} \left(\frac{N_B}{\sigma_A \eta} + \frac{N_A}{\sigma_B \eta} \right) \qquad (6\text{-}10\text{-}27)$$

Here η represents the viscosity and the thermodynamic term is expressed in terms of the mole fractions and rational activity coefficients.   The quantities, σ_A and σ_B, are characteristic of each of the diffusing

[160] L. Onsager, Am. N. Y. Acad. Sci., **46**, 241 (1945).
[161] G. S. Hartley and J. Crank, Trans. Faraday Soc., **45**, 801 (1949).

components which, by analogy with the quantity, $6\pi a_j$, in Stokes' equation (7-1-1), are related to the velocities of the diffusing species. Singular values of the parameters, σ_A and σ_B, in non-electrolytic systems of two components can be obtained by extrapolation of the measured diffusion coefficients to zero concentrations. It is not to be expected that these mobility parameters remain constant throughout the entire range of concentrations. If this constancy were valid then $\mathfrak{D}^v/(d \ln f_A N_A/d \ln N_A)1/\eta$ would be a linear function of N_A, a condition which experiment contradicts.

From precise measurements of the diffusion coefficients in the system diphenyl-benzene, Sandquist and Lyons[162] found that the quantity $\mathfrak{D}/(1 + c\partial \ln y/dc) (\eta_0/\eta)$ is a linear function of $(\eta - \eta_0)/\eta$. In completely miscible systems the intercepts at $N_B = 1$ and at $N_A = 1$ would be $\mathfrak{D}_{0,A}$ and $\mathfrak{D}_{0,B}$, respectively, and hence in dilute solutions and on the molefraction scale

$$\mathfrak{D}_A/(d \ln N_A f_A/d \ln N_A)\eta_{0,A}/\eta = \mathfrak{D}_{0,A} + k_1\Delta\eta_A/\eta_{0,A} \quad (6\text{-}10\text{-}28)$$

where $\Delta\eta_A = \eta - \eta_{0,A}$ and k_1 is a constant. Similarly

$$\mathfrak{D}_B/(d \ln N_B f_B/d \ln N_B)\eta_{0,B}/\eta = \mathfrak{D}_{0,B} + k_2\Delta\eta_B/\eta_{0,B} \quad (6\text{-}10\text{-}29)$$

Now, from equation (6-10-27), if σ_A is of the same order of magnitude as σ_B

$$\mathfrak{D}^v/(d \ln N_A f_A/d \ln N_A) \cong \frac{RT}{N\sigma_B\eta} \quad (6\text{-}10\text{-}30)$$

as N_B approaches zero. Hence

$$\frac{1}{\sigma_B} = \frac{N}{RT}\left[\mathfrak{D}_{0,A} + k_1\frac{\Delta\eta_A}{\eta_{0,A}}\right]\eta_{0,A} \quad (6\text{-}10\text{-}31)$$

Similarly

$$\frac{1}{\sigma_A} = \frac{N}{RT}\left[\mathfrak{D}_{0,B} + k_2\frac{\Delta\eta_B}{\eta_{0,B}}\right]\eta_{0,B} \quad (6\text{-}10\text{-}32)$$

Upon substitution of these values of σ_A and σ_B in the Hartley-Crank equation, we obtain

$$\mathfrak{D}^v = \frac{d \ln N_A f_A}{d \ln N_A}\frac{1}{\eta}\left[N_A\left(\mathfrak{D}_{0,A} + k_1\frac{\Delta\eta_A}{\eta_{0,A}}\right)\eta_{0,A} + N_B\left(\mathfrak{D}_{0,B} + k_2\frac{\Delta\eta_B}{\eta_{0,B}}\right)\eta_{0,B}\right] \quad (6\text{-}10\text{-}33)$$

as a formal expression for the variation of the diffusion (coefficient) over the entire range of concentration, $N_A = 0$ to $N_A = 1$.

For the system cyclohexane and benzene, the diffusion coefficients of

[162] C. L. Sandquist and P. A. Lyons, *J. Am. Chem. Soc.*, **76**, 4641 (1954).

each of the components in their dilute solutions have been determined experimentally by Lyons and Rodwin.[163] From these results by suitable plots of equations (6-10-28) and (6-10-29), $\mathfrak{D}_{0,A}$, $\mathfrak{D}_{0,B}$ and the parameters, k_1 and k_2, have been evaluated. Table (6-10-4) contains the experimental values of the diffusion coefficient, $\mathfrak{D}^V$, and those computed by equation (6-10-33). The values of the limiting diffusion coefficients and k_1 and k_2 are included in the table. The agreement of calculated with the observed values is good over the entire range of concentration. This computation is an unusually interesting one since the viscosities of benzene and cyclohexane are quite different and the viscosities of the mixtures exhibit a pronounced minimum when the mol fraction of benzene is 0.76.

TABLE (6-10-4). OBSERVED AND CALCULATED DIFFUSION COEFFICIENTS FOR THE SYSTEM: BENZENE (A)-CYCLOHEXANE (B) AT 25°.

$$\mathfrak{D}_{0,A} = 21.01 \times 10^{-6}; \qquad \mathfrak{D}_{0,B} = 18.76 \times 10^{-6}$$
$$k_1 = 5.4 \times 10^{-6}; \qquad k_2 = 53.2 \times 10^{-6}$$

N_B	$\mathfrak{D}^V \times 10^6$ (obs)	$\mathfrak{D}^V \times 10^6$ (calc)	N_B	$\mathfrak{D}^V \times 10^6$ (obs)	$\mathfrak{D}^V \times 10^6$ (calc)
0.0000	21.01	21.01	0.3961	18.15	17.95
.0100	20.90	20.92	.5205	17.96	17.76
.0501	20.44	20.43	.6418	17.99	17.98
.0911	19.99	20.01	.7795	18.29	18.40
.1101	19.78	19.84	.9299	18.66	18.70
.2000	19.03	19.06	.9800	18.76	18.83
.3017	18.45	18.53	1.0000	18.76	18.76
.3658	18.22	18.09	—	—	—

Robinson and Stokes[164] have employed a modified form of equation (6-10-27) for the calculation of diffusion coefficients of electrolytes in concentrated solutions. The effect of solvation is introduced upon the assumption that some of the ions transport a fixed number, n, of solvent molecules during their migration. For a uniunivalent electrolyte in water, the equation for the diffusion coefficient becomes

$$\mathfrak{D} = (\mathfrak{D}_0 + \Delta_1 + \Delta_2)\left(1 + m\,\frac{d\log y_\pm}{dm}\right)$$
$$\left[1 + 0.036m\left(\frac{\mathfrak{D}_{H_2O}}{\mathfrak{D}_0} - n\right)\right]\frac{\eta_0}{\eta} \tag{6-10-34}$$

where Δ_1 and Δ_2 represent the contributions of electrophoresis and $\mathfrak{D}_{H_2O}$ the self-diffusion coefficient of water. With a suitable value of the hydration parameter, n, the diffusion coefficients of the alkali metal halides can be computed with an accuracy of about 0.5 percent. A similar equation adapted for calcium chloride solutions yielded the form of the experimental

---

[163] P. A. Lyons and L. Rodwin, Private communication. The thermodynamic data employed in this calculation were derived from the vapor pressure measurements of G. Scatchard, S. E. Wood and J. M. Mochel, *J. Phys. Chem.*, **43**, 119 (1934).

[164] R. A. Robinson and R. H. Stokes, *Electrolyte Solutions*, p. 309–322, Butterworth Scientific Publications, London (1955).

results shown in Fig. (6-10-11) including the rapid decrease of the diffusion coefficient with increasing concentration of the salt in the concentrated solutions.

From a theoretical point of view, there are many uncertainties inherent in the application of equation (6-10-34). The electrophoretic corrections, applicable to dilute solutions, may be far from valid in concentrated ones. Secondly, it is known [Fig. (6-10-12)] that the self-diffusion coefficient of water varies considerably with salt concentration, a factor neglected in calculating the solvation parameter, n. It is not strange, therefore, that hydration values determined in this manner differ widely from those determined from thermodynamic data [Chapter (12), Section (9)]. Indeed, the concept of solvation will remain vague until a satisfactory statistical theory of the interaction of ions with the solvent has been developed.

Vitagliano and Lyons[165] have shown from precise Gouy interference measurements of the diffusion coefficient of acetic acid that at concentrations above 0.4 molar a plot of $\mathcal{D}/(d \ln N_A f_A/d \ln N_A)\eta_0/\eta$ versus $(\eta - \eta_0)/\eta_0$ is a straight line, a fact in accord with equation (6-10-28). This line represents the behavior of the undissociated acid molecules. At concentrations less than 0.4, the values derived from experiment lie above this plot to an amount with increases with decreasing concentration. This deviation is due to the presence of the ions whose mean diffusion coefficient is greater than that of the undissociated molecule. From the values of the degree of dissociation of acetic acid derived from conductance measurements and the limiting equivalent conductances of the ions, the magnitude of this deviation can be computed. As a result of these procedures, the limiting diffusion coefficient of the undissociated molecule of the acid and its value through the concentration range, 0 to 12.5 molar may be computed accurately.

(11) Applications of the Conductance Equation with Inclusion of Higher Order Inhomogeneous Terms and the Ionic Size Parameter

In Section (9) of Chapter (4) it was shown that by inclusion of the a-parameter and all terms of order c in the deviation of the conductance equation, Fuoss and Onsager[166, 167] deduced the equation

$$\Lambda = \Lambda^0 - (\alpha^*\Lambda^0 + \beta^*)\sqrt{c} + cB(\kappa a) \qquad (6\text{-}11\text{-}1)$$

where

$$B(\kappa a) = B_1\Lambda^0 + B_2 \qquad (6\text{-}11\text{-}2)$$

[165] V. Vitagliano and P. A. Lyons, *J. Am. Chem. Soc.*, **78**, 4538 (1955).
[166] R. M. Fuoss and L. Onsager, *Proc. Nat. Acad. Sci.*, **41**, 274 (1955).
[167] R. M. Fuoss and L. Onsager, *J. Phys. Chem.*, **61**, 668 (1957).

$$B_1 = 24\,\alpha'(b^{-2}(1 + 2b)\phi_1 - \phi_2) \tag{6-11-3}$$

$$B_2 = \alpha^*\beta^* + 16\beta'(\phi_3 - b^{-1}\phi_4) \tag{6-11-4}$$

$$\alpha' = \kappa^2 a^2 b^2/24c \tag{6-11-5}$$

$$\beta' = \beta^*\kappa ab/16\sqrt{c} \tag{6-11-6}$$

and b is the familiar variable defined by equation (3-7-7). Convenient numerical expressions for α^*, β^*, α', β' and b will be found in Chapter (5) Section (3). The functions

$$\phi_1(\kappa a) = (1 + \kappa a)^{-1}(1/12p_2) \cong 1/12p_3 \tag{6-11-7}$$

$$6\phi_2(\kappa a) = (1 + \kappa a)^{-2}(F(\kappa a) + (11\sqrt{2} - 3)/24\,p_2 p_3 + 1/4p_2) \tag{6-11-8}$$

$$\phi_3(\kappa a) = (1 + \kappa a)^{-2}(F(\kappa a)/4 + (\sqrt{2} + 5)/32p_2) \tag{6-11-9}$$

$$\phi_4(\kappa a) = (1 + \kappa a)^{-1}(1 - 11/96p_2) \cong 8/9(1 + \kappa a) \tag{6-11-10}$$

have been calculated at intervals of 0.01 in κa, and are given in Table (5-3-1a). The auxiliary functions are

$$p_1 = 1 + \kappa a + \kappa^2 a^2/2 \cong e^{\kappa a} \tag{6-11-11}$$

$$p_2 = 1 + q^*\kappa a + \kappa^2 a^2/4 \cong e^{q^*\kappa a} \tag{6-11-12}$$

$$p_3 = 1 + q^*\kappa a + \kappa^2 a^2/6 \tag{6-11-13}$$

$$F(\kappa a) = (1/8p_2)\,(7T_2 + p_1 T_1 - 4p_1 p_2 T_0) \tag{6-11-14}$$

The quantity q^*, defined by equation (4-3-43), becomes simply $\sqrt{2}/2$ for symmetrical electrolytes.

The integral

$$Tr(x) = e^x \int_x^\infty e^{-t}\, dt/t$$

defines the functions T_0, T_1 and T_2 when the variable x is κa, $(1 + q^*)\kappa a$ and $(2 + q^*)\kappa a$, respectively.

Although equation (6-11-1) expresses in elegant form the initial departures from the limiting tangent in terms of Λ^0, a and the properties of the solvent, it must be modified before it can be used to evaluate Λ^0 and a from conductivity data. For this purpose Fuoss and Onsager introduce the approximate forms of equations (6-11-11) and (6-11-12) into (6-11-14) to obtain

$$F(\kappa a) = (\tfrac{1}{8})e^{-q^*\kappa a}(7T_2 + e^{\kappa a}T_1 - 4e^{(1+q^*)\kappa a}T_0) + O(\kappa^3 a^3)$$

$$\cong (\tfrac{1}{8})e^{2\kappa a}[7Ei((2 + q^*)\kappa a) + Ei((1 + q^*)\kappa a) - 4Ei(\kappa a)] \tag{6-11-15}$$

Then making use of two additional approximations

$$(1 + \kappa a)^2 \cong e^{2\kappa a} \tag{6-11-16}$$

$$Ei(x) = -0.5772 - \ln x + x + O(x^2) \tag{6-11-17}$$

they write

$$(1 + \kappa a)^{-2} F(\kappa a) \cong -1.2269 - (\tfrac{1}{2}) \ln (\kappa a) + O(\kappa a) \tag{6-11-18}$$

for $q^* = \sqrt{2}/2$. Combination of this equation and the approximate forms of equations (6-11-7) to (6-11-10) with equations (6-11-1) to (6-11-6) finally leads to [168]

$$\Lambda''' = \Lambda'' - J_1 c + J_2 c^{3/2} \tag{6-11-19}$$

Λ''' is therefore an approximation for Λ^0 derived from the limiting form (6-11-1) for low (but non-zero) concentrations. The terms in equation (6-11-19) are defined by

$$\Lambda'' \equiv \frac{\Lambda + \beta^* \sqrt{c}}{1 - \alpha^* \sqrt{c}} - (\alpha' \Lambda^0 - \beta') \frac{c \ln c}{1 - \alpha^* \sqrt{c}} \tag{6-11-20}$$

$$J_1 \equiv \theta_1 \Lambda^0 + \theta_2 \tag{6-11-21}$$

$$J_2 \equiv \theta_3 \Lambda^0 + (8\beta^*/9)\,(\kappa^2 a^2/c) \tag{6-11-22}$$

$$\theta_1(a) \equiv 2\alpha'(b^{-2}(1 + 2b) + \ln (\kappa a/\sqrt{c}) + 0.9074) \tag{6-11-23}$$

$$\theta_2(a) \equiv \alpha^*\beta^* + (8\beta^*/9)\,(\kappa a/\sqrt{c}) - 2\beta'(\ln (\kappa a/\sqrt{c}) + 0.8504) \tag{6-11-24}$$

$$\theta_3(a) \equiv \alpha'\sqrt{2}(\kappa a/\sqrt{c})\,(b^{-2}(1 + 2b) - 1.0774) \tag{6-11-25}$$

The application of the above equations to the exact evaluation of Λ^0 and a involves a short series of successive approximations. The first step is to make a preliminary estimate of Λ^0 by one of the simpler extrapolations based on equations described earlier in this chapter. The Shedlovsky[48] equation (6-3-7)

$$\Lambda^{0\prime} \equiv \frac{\Lambda + \beta^* \sqrt{c}}{1 - \alpha^* \sqrt{c}} = \Lambda^0 + Bc \tag{6-11-26}$$

or some extension, such as

$$\Lambda^{0\prime} = \Lambda^0 + Bc + Ac \log c \tag{6-11-27}$$

suggested by equation (6-3-5), are both satisfactory for this purpose. This first approximation of Λ^0 can now be used to calculate the first set of values of Λ'', J_1 and J_2 for an assumed value of a. If by chance Λ^0 and a

---

[168] The term $J_2 c^{3/2}$ is dropped in a revised treatment outlined by R. M. Fuoss and F. Accascina in *Electrolytic Conductance*, Interscience Publishers, New York (1959). The theory is also undergoing revision. Compare R. M. Fuoss and L. Onsager, *Proc. Nat. Acad. Sci.*, **47**, 818 (1961) and current papers by Fuoss.

satisfy equation (6-11-19), then Λ''' must equal the preliminary value of Λ^0 within the experimental error for all values of c below about 0.008 normal, and a plot of Λ''' against c would be a horizontal straight line. In the more usual case the preliminary value of Λ^0 is very close to the true value of this quantity, but a_1 does not satisfy equation (6-11-19) exactly. Under these circumstances the plot of Λ''' against c approximates a straight line, but its slope is not zero. Figure (6-11-1) illustrates such plots constructed[169]

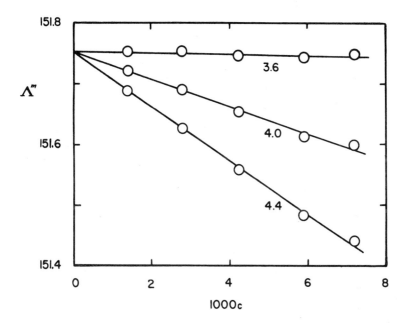

Fig. (6-11-1). The influence of the a-parameter in the application of equation (6-11-19) to the determination of Λ^0 for potassium bromide in water at 25°.

from the data on potassium bromide[170] with three assumed values of a, and Λ^0(prelim.) = 151.68 derived by means of equation (6-11-27). The common intercept of the three plots in Figure (6-11-1) is 151.75, which is within 0.05 % of Λ^0 (prelim.). The numerical values which enter into this plot for $a = 3.6$ Å are collected in Table (6-11-1). Note that the term $J_2 c^{3/2}$ is not negligible, and without it the plots would exhibit some curvature [See Figure (6-11-2)]. The exact value of a which satisfies equation (6-11-19) is readily determined by graphical interpolation against the slopes of the plots in Figure (6-11-1). This interpolation is approximately linear, and yields $a = 3.58$ Å for zero slope.

The determination of this exact value of a is not essential for a precise determination of Λ^0, because the intercepts of the plots in Figure (6-11-1) are insensitive to the value of a within a range of 0.8 Å, but an exact a

[169] R. M. Fuoss and L. Onsager, *J. Phys. Chem.*, **61**, 668 (1957).
[170] B. B. Owen and H. Zeldes, *J. Chem. Phys.*, **18**, 1083 (1950).

permits a precise calculation of Λ from equation (6-11-1) and the functions in Table (5-9-1) for comparison with experiment. Table (6-11-2) contains the results of such a calculation based upon $a = 3.58$ Å and $\Lambda^0 = 151.75$ for potassium bromide. The agreement between Λ(calc.) in Table (6-11-2) and Λ(obs.) in Table (6-11-1) is excellent, and judging from similar calculations by Fuoss and Onsager for other alkali halides, it is evident that equation (6-11-1) represents the data for these 1-1 electrolytes within the experimental error up to about 0.012 normal.

TABLE (6-11-1). NUMERICAL VALUES[a] OF THE TERMS IN EQUATION (6-11-19) WHEN APPLIED TO POTASSIUM BROMIDE[b] IN WATER AT 25°. $\Lambda^0 = 151.68$ (PRELIMINARY); $a = 3.6 \times 10^{-8}$ (ASSUMED)

$c \times 10^3$	Λ (obs.)	$\beta^*\sqrt{c}$	Λ''	J_1c	$J_2c^{3/2}$	Λ'''
1.3949	148.27	2.248	152.056	0.309	0.004	151.751
2.7881	146.91	3.179	152.356	.618	.013	151.751
4.2183	145.88	3.909	152.657	.935	.023	151.745
5.9269	144.90	4.634	153.018	1.314	.039	151.743
7.1698	144.30	5.097	153.286	1.590	.052	151.748

[a] Calculated values from Reference 169.
[b] Observed conductivities from Reference 170.

TABLE (6-11-2). CONDUCTANCE OF POTASSIUM BROMIDE IN WATER AT 25° CALCULATED[a] FROM EQUATION (6-11-1). $\Lambda^0 = 151.75$; $a = 3.58 \times 10^{-8}$.

$c \times 10^3$	$B_1\Lambda^0$	B_2	$B(\kappa a)$	$(\alpha^*\Lambda^0+\beta^*)\sqrt{c}$	$\alpha^*\sqrt{c}$	Λ (calc).
1.3949	−67.34	114.31	46.97	3.545	0.00855	148.27
2.7881	−45.65	107.20	61.55	5.013	.01209	146.91
4.2183	−32.21	102.89	70.68	6.165	.01487	145.89
5.9269	−21.28	99.20	77.92	7.308	.01762	144.91
7.1698	−15.27	97.13	81.86	8.038	.01938	144.30

[a] See Reference 169, Table II.

In Table (6-11-3) comparison is made between the results of extrapolations according to equations (6-11-19), (6-11-26) and (6-11-27). The agreement between values of Λ^0 derived from (6-11-19) and equation (6-11-27) with two adjustable parameters, A and B, is excellent. This is to be expected because (6-11-19) can be re-arranged to read

$$\Lambda^{0\prime} = \Lambda^0 + 2.303 \left(\frac{\alpha'\Lambda^0 - \beta'}{1 - \alpha^*\sqrt{c}} \right) c \log c + (J_1 - J_2\sqrt{c})c \qquad (6\text{-}11\text{-}28)$$

or

$$\Lambda = \Lambda^0 - \mathbb{S}_{(\Lambda)}\sqrt{c} + 2.303(\alpha'\Lambda^0 - \beta')c \log c \\ + (1 - \alpha^*\sqrt{c})(J_1 - J_2\sqrt{c})c \qquad (6\text{-}11\text{-}29)$$

and these equations are practically indistinguishable experimentally from equations (6-11-27) and (6-3-5) because the coefficients of c and $c \log c$ are very insensitive to changes in $\sqrt{c}$ over the short range of low concentrations considered here.

Unfortunately the practical success of equation (6-11-27) and (6-3-5) in extrapolating data for completely dissociated 1-1 electrolytes does not make it safe to assume that these equations will lead to equally reliable values of Λ^0 for higher valence types, or for 1-1 electrolytes which show evidence of association. It can be seen in Table (6-3-3) that the empirically evaluated parameters of equation (6-3-3) are very large when association is probable. Under this condition the evaluation of the parameters becomes less accurate, and B must account for the coefficient of c in the last term of equation (6-11-29) as well as the coefficient, Λ^0/K, which accounts approximately for ionic association* in equation (6-3-3).

TABLE (6-11-3). LIMITING CONDUCTANCES OF POTASSIUM HALIDES IN WATER. COMPARISON OF EXTRAPOLATIONS BY SEVERAL EQUATIONS.

Salt	t	$a \times 10^8$	Λ°			
			(6-11-1)[a]	(6-11-27)	(6-11-26)	(R & S)[d]
KCl[b]	5	3.29	94.27	94.26	...	94.21
KCl[b]	25	3.50	149.89	149.88	...	149.82
KCl[b]	55	3.39	245.97	...	245.69	245.73
KBr[b]	5	3.58	96.01	96.00	...	95.92
KBr[b]	25	3.58	151.75	...	151.68	151.60
KBr[b]	55	3.61	247.32	...	247.15	247.04
KI[b]	5	3.94	95.33	95.32	...	95.25
KI[b]	15	3.95	121.87	121.83	...	121.78
KI[b]	25	3.90	150.49	...	150.34	150.32
KI[b]	35	4.01	180.70	...	180.60	180.53
KI[b]	45	3.98	212.27	...	212.13	212.06
KI[b]	55	4.19	244.86	...	244.73	244.65
KCl[c]	15	3.55	121.04	121.09	...	120.98
KCl[c]	25	3.60	149.90	149.88	...	149.80
KCl[c]	35	3.60	180.54	180.50	...	180.39
KCl[c]	45	3.60	212.53	212.49	...	212.38

[a] Reference 169.
[b] Data of Reference 170.
[c] Data of H. E. Gunning and A. R. Gordon, *J. Chem. Phys.*, **11**, 18 (1943).
[d] Extrapolation by equation (6-11-30) performed by R. A. Robinson and R. H. Stokes, *J. Am. Chem. Soc.*, **76**, 1991 (1954).

If the value of a can be approximated independently, as for example by setting it equal to a derived from activity data, then it becomes practical to treat an incompletely dissociated electrolyte by equation (6-11-1), and to estimate its ionization constant. At the end of this Section it is shown how a value of a for sodium bromate, readily evaluated in dioxane-water mixtures of low dielectric constant, can be used with equation (6-11-19) to

---

* Since comparison of equations (6-3-5) and (6-11-29) shows that the theoretical value of A should be $2.303 \ (\alpha'\Lambda^\circ - \beta')$, this parameter can be evaluated from the data in Tables (6-3-3), (11-1-1) and (11-1-1A). This calculation leads to $A = 4,110$ which is not very different from 4,800 found empirically. A similar calculation of B is not so satisfactory because B is not truly independent of $\sqrt{c}$ and contains an (approximate) contribution, Λ°/K, from association. The approximation $B \cong J_1 - \Lambda^\circ/K$ leads to 17,400 instead of 9,800 found empirically.

obtain a value of K for this salt in water. It is probable that this procedure may be applied to a higher symmetrical valence type such as zinc sulfate, as indicated in Section (3), but in the present state of the theory it is impossible to make a rigorous numerical distinction between the effects of a and K upon the conductivities of unsymmetrical valence type electrolytes. We therefore must rely upon equations such as (6-3-6) and (6-11-27) for the extrapolation of the unsymmetrical types, but with the realization that in this case the uncertainty in Λ^0 may be many times greater than the experimental errors in Λ.

The results in Table (6-11-3) show that values of Λ^0 derived from equation (6-11-19) are significantly greater than those based upon the Shedlovsky equation (6-11-26). The explanation of this difference was discussed in Section (3) under equation (6-3-7), where it was pointed out that the Shedlovsky plot must pass through a minimum and turn upward as it approaches the axis of zero concentration. The figures in the last column of Table (6-11-3) were evaluated from the same data by Robinson and Stokes making use of the equation

$$\Lambda = \Lambda^0 - \mathcal{S}_{(\Lambda)}\sqrt{c}/(1 + \kappa a) \qquad (6\text{-}11\text{-}30)$$

Comparison shows that these values of Λ^0 are even lower than those derived from the Shedlovsky equation (6-11-26). It is clear that, although the introduction of the factor $(1 + \kappa a)^{-1}$ into the limiting law should extend the limiting law as an interpolation function at moderate dilutions and offer reasonable representation of the specificity of Λ for salts of a given valence type, it can not take account of the complicated terms considered in the development of the theoretical equation (6-11-1), and should not be relied upon for accurate extrapolation to infinite dilution. The considerable literature dealing with equation (6-11-30) and similar equations which involve κa, but in somewhat more complicated functions, is very thoroughly reviewed in a recent monograph by Robinson and Stokes to which the reader is referred.*

Figure (6-11-2) presents a graphical comparison of several extrapolations. The plots have all been derived from equation (6-11-1) with $\Lambda^0 = 151.75$ and $a .= 3.58$ Å, and represent the theoretical behavior of potassium bromide below 0.008 normal in water at 25°. The plot of Λ''' against c represents, of course, the "perfect" extrapolation because it is a rigorously straight line of zero slope, but it is important to note that within the range $0.010 > c > 0.001$ it does not differ by more than 0.02 from similar plots of $(\Lambda^{0'} - Ac \log c - Bc)$ or $(\Lambda + \mathcal{S}_{(\Lambda)}\sqrt{c} - Ac \log c - Bc)$ if the parameters are properly chosen. For the case under discussion satisfactory values are $A = 50.7$ and $B = 192.3$, both evaluated empirically, and $A = 59.73$ calculated from $2.303 \, (\alpha'\Lambda^0 - \beta')$ and $B = 191.0$ evaluated empirically.

---

* R. A. Robinson and R. H. Stokes, *Electrolyte Solutions*, Butterworths Scientific Publications, London, 1955.

The plot of $(\Lambda'' - J_1 c)$ permits an accurate determination of Λ^0, but since the curvature caused by neglect of $J_2 c^{3/2}$ interferes with the evaluation of a, the inclusion of this term is amply justified. The uppermost plot of Λ'' is very nearly linear, but its slope is so steep that the full calculation of Λ''' is recommended. The Shedlovsky plot of $\Lambda^{0'}$ against c is definitely inferior to the others for precise evaluation of Λ^0 because of the minimum, but for convenient interpolation this equation plays an important role in the determination of ionization constants of weak electrolytes [See Section (6) of Chapter (7)].

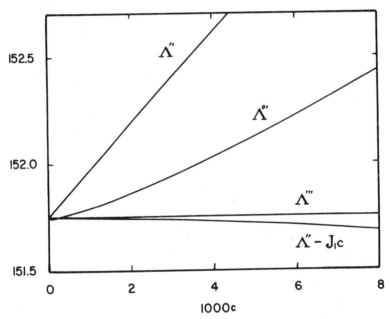

Fig. (6-11-2). Comparison of various extrapolations to determine Λ^0 for potassium bromide in water at 25°.

Conductance Equation with Higher Terms Applied to Determination of Ionic Association

The conductance equation with higher terms has recently been applied to the problem of determining ionic association in salt solutions where $K \geq 10^{-2}$ by Fuoss[172] and Fuoss and Kraus.[173] They make use of the data of Martel and Kraus[174] on sodium bromate and several quarternary ammonium salts in water and dioxane-water mixtures at 25°. Because some of the ions comprising these salts are large in comparison with the solvent molecules, Fuoss has modified the conductance equation to take this into

[172] R. M. Fuoss, *J. Am. Chem. Soc.*, **79**, 3301 (1957).
[173] R. M. Fuoss and C. A. Kraus, *Ibid*, **79**, 3304 (1957).
[174] R. W. Martel and C. A. Kraus, *Proc. Nat. Acad. Sci.*, **41**, 9 (1955).

account.   The more bulky ions are considered to interfere with the motion of the oppositely charged ions by causing them to move in a medium of viscosity, η, somewhat greater than the viscosity, η_0, of the pure solvent. To correct for this effect, Fuoss divides the terms $\Lambda^0 - \mathcal{S}_{(\Lambda)}\sqrt{c}$ by the relative viscosity.   This latter quantity he assumes to be given by the Einstein[175] equation

$$\eta/\eta_0 = 1 + \phi 5/2 \qquad (6\text{-}11\text{-}31)$$

in which ϕ is the volume fraction of the solute.   This is connected with the concentration, c, by the relation

$$\phi = (4\pi r_i^3/3)\,(Nc/1000) = \delta c \qquad (6\text{-}11\text{-}32)$$

where r_i is the hydrodynamic radius of the bulky ion.

It should be remarked at this point that introduction of the term δc into the conductance equation does not justify the presence of a term in $\sqrt{c}$ also.   Equation (6-11-31) refers to the viscosity which affects, at short range, the flow of ions through the solution.   The term $\mathcal{S}_{(\eta)}\sqrt{c}$ of equation (6-9-3) is the limiting, long range, effect of the presence of ions upon the bulk of flow of the solution*.

Neglecting, then, the term in $\mathcal{S}_{(\eta)}\sqrt{c}$, the effect of the increase in viscosity is represented to a first approximation by a small linear term in c, so that the conductance equation (6-11-29) becomes

$$\Lambda = \Lambda^0 - \mathcal{S}_{(\Lambda)}\sqrt{c} + \mathfrak{a}c \log c + Jc - (\Lambda^0 \delta 5/2)c \qquad (6\text{-}11\text{-}33)$$

where the theoretical coefficient of the $c \log c$ term is

$$\mathfrak{a} = 2.303(\alpha'\Lambda^0 - \beta') \qquad (6\text{-}11\text{-}34)$$

and

$$J = (1 - \alpha^*\sqrt{c})\,(1 - (J_2/J_1)\sqrt{c})J_1 \qquad (6\text{-}11\text{-}35)$$

For the ions of sodium bromide considered earlier in this Section, the term $(\Lambda^0 \delta 5/2)c$ in equation (6-11-33) is negligible compared with the others. For sodium bromate this term is likewise negligible, but for the quarternary ammonium salts its neglect leads to unrealistically small values of $\mathfrak{a}$.

The evaluation of the unknowns Λ^0, K and $\mathfrak{a}$ from conductance data requires the combination of equation (7-2-10) for the thermodynamic ionization constant, and equation (5-2-8) for the activity coefficient of the ions, with the conductivity equation (6-11-33).   In these last two equations the stoichiometric concentration, c, must be replaced by the actual concentration of the ions, $c_i = \alpha c$.   It is assumed that the conductance, Λ_i, of one equivalent of free ions in dilute solutions is given by equation (6-11-33) in the form

---

* For further discussion of this matter, see B. F. Wishaw and R. H. Stokes, *J. Am. Chem. Soc.*, **76**, 2065 (1954).

[175] A. Einstein, *Ann. Physik.*, **19**, 289 (1906); *Ibid.*, **34**, 591 (1911).

$$\Lambda_i = \Lambda^0 - \mathcal{S}_{(\Lambda)}\sqrt{c_i} + \alpha c_i \log c_i + Jc_i - (\Lambda^0 \delta 5/2)c_i \quad (6\text{-}11\text{-}36)$$

Consequently, the fraction of the electrolyte present as free ions is

$$\alpha = c_i/c = \Lambda/\Lambda_i \quad (6\text{-}11\text{-}37)$$

where Λ is the observed equivalent conductance.   Combination of equations (6-11-37) and (7-2-10) yields

$$\Lambda = \Lambda_i - K^{-1}\Lambda c_i y_{\pm}^2 \quad (6\text{-}11\text{-}38)$$

and combination of this equation with (6-11-36) leads to

$$y = J_1 - K^{-1}x - J_2\sqrt{c_i} - (\Lambda^0 \delta 5/2)(1 - \alpha^*\sqrt{c_i}) \quad (6\text{-}11\text{-}39)$$

where*

$$y \equiv \Delta\Lambda/c_i(1 - \alpha^*\sqrt{c_i}) \quad (6\text{-}11\text{-}40)$$

$$\Delta\Lambda \equiv \Lambda + \mathcal{S}_{(\Lambda)}\sqrt{c_i} - \alpha c_i \log c_i - \Lambda^0 \quad (6\text{-}11\text{-}41)$$

and

$$x \equiv \Lambda y_{\pm}^2/(1 - \alpha^*\sqrt{c_i}) \quad (6\text{-}11\text{-}42)$$

At low concentrations the term $J_2\sqrt{c_i}$ is negligible compared to J_1, and the denominator of the term in δ can be set equal to unity.   Therefore, as a first approximation we write

$$y \cong J_1 - K^{-1}x - \Lambda^0 \delta 5/2 \quad (6\text{-}11\text{-}43)$$

and a plot of y against x would be expected to be linear at high dilutions. The slope of such a plot is K^{-1}, and the term J_1 is given by equation (6-11-43) in the limiting form rearranged to read

$$J_1 = y(0) + K^{-1}\Lambda^0 + \Lambda^0 \delta 5/2 \quad (6\text{-}11\text{-}44)$$

where $y(0)$ is the value of y at infinite dilution $(x(0) = \Lambda^0)$.   From this value of J_1 the determination of a follows by graphical interpolation on a plot of J_1 calculated by equation (6-11-21) for a series of values of a.   It is clear that the evaluation of the three unknown quantities, Λ^0, K and a, from the equations just developed will require a reiterative procedure. Two of these are outlined below because they apply to different ranges of ionic association.

We consider first the determination of ionization constants which fall within the range[176] $1 > K > 10^{-3}$, and finally those greater than unity. In either case it is convenient to begin the calculation with a preliminary extrapolation of the conductance data by one of the methods described in

---

* The subscript, $\pm$, will always distinguish between the letter, $y_\pm$, used in general to represent activity coefficients on the c-scale, and y used in this Section as the special conductance function (6-11-40).

[176] For $K < 10^{-3}$ a number of practical extrapolations are described and criticized in Chapter (7).

Section (3).   The value, Λ^0(prelim), so obtained may be expected to fall within 0.1 or 0.2 % of the desired final value Λ^0, because the experimental conductance curves are close to the limiting law within the ranges of K and c considered here.   Furthermore, the function y is so sensitive to an error in Λ^0 as c approaches zero, that it is usually not difficult to adjust slightly the value of Λ^0 so as to obtain a linear plot of y against x.

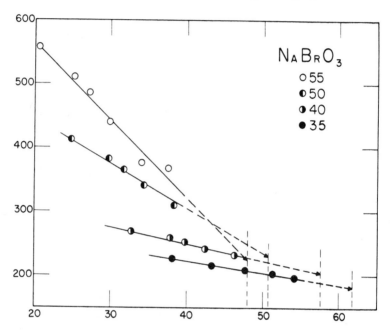

Fig. (6-11-3).   The evaluation of $y(0)$ by extrapolations conforming with equation (6-11-43).   Sodium bromate in dioxane-water mixtures at 25°.

For a preliminary value of α, the approximation

$$\Lambda/(\Lambda^0 - \mathcal{S}_{(\Lambda)}\sqrt{c\Lambda/\Lambda^0}) \qquad (6\text{-}11\text{-}45)$$

can be used.   Then having preliminary values of c_i it is possible to estimate $y_{\pm}$ by equation (5-2-8), and to calculate and plot preliminary values of y and x. J_1 can be evaluated from this plot and equation (6-11-44).   Knowing J_1, and hence a, to a first approximation, more exact values of α are obtained from the combination of equations (6-11-36) and (6-11-37).   New values of x and y calculated from these more exact values of α permit in turn a more exact determination of J_1 and a.   Another repetition of this calculation is hardly necessary, because the values of Λ^0, K and a obtained by the second approximation are not very different from the first.   The results of the calculations (second approximation) made by Fuoss and Kraus[173] on the data[174] for sodium bromate in 35, 40, 50 and 55 % dioxane-water mixtures are illustrated by the plots in Figure (6-11-3), and collected at the bottom of Table (6-11-4).

In the mixtures containing less than 35 % dioxane, the association of sodium bromate is so slight ($K \geq 1$) that the slopes of the plots of y against x are too small to permit reliable determination of K. The nearly constant ordinate, y, evaluates the sum of the terms on the right of equation (6-11-43), but does not lead to their accurate separation. In this case the value of a, about 4 Ångstroms, already obtained in mixtures of lower

TABLE (6-11-4).* SODIUM BROMIDE IN DIOXANE-WATER MIXTURES AT 25°.

Dioxane %(wt)	D[a]	K	J_1	$10^8 a$	Λ°
0	78.48	2.0	191	(4.00)	105.755
10	70.33	1.47	202	(4.00)	90.415
20	61.86	1.11	225	(4.00)	77.315
30	53.28	.75	272	(4.00)	66.47
35	48.91	.475	307	3.96	61.785
40	44.54	.366	360	3.94	57.66
50	35.85	.1455	579	4.03	50.74
55	31.53	.0847	790	4.17	47.92

* R. M. Fuoss and C. A. Kraus, *J. Am. Chem. Soc.*, **79**, 3304 (1957).
[a] The values of the dielectric constants are those of F. E. Critchfield, J. A. Gibson, Jr., and J. L. Hall, *J. Am. Chem. Soc.*, **75**, 1991 (1953), and were used by Fuoss and Kraus in determining the quantities which appear in this table.

dielectric constant may be assumed* to be independent of the dioxane-water ratio, and used to calculate J_1 and J_2, and subsequently Λ''' by equation (6-11-19).

Combination of equations (6-11-13) and (6-11-38) with the definitional equation (6-11-19) for Λ''' yields an expression

$$\Lambda''' - c\Lambda^0 \delta 5/2(1 - \alpha^*\sqrt{c}) = \Lambda^0 - K^{-1}z \qquad (6\text{-}11\text{-}46)$$

for Λ''' in terms of a new variable

$$z \equiv c\Lambda y_\pm^2/(1 - \alpha^*\sqrt{c}) \qquad (6\text{-}11\text{-}47)$$

The slope and intercept of a plot of the left hand member of equation (6-11-46) against z determine K^{-1} and Λ^0. Plots of this type, constructed without regard for the term containing δ, are illustrated in Figure (6-11-4) for 0, 10, 20 and 30 % dioxane-water mixtures. The numerical results are collected in Table (6-11-4). Although the first four values of K were derived from Λ''' vs. z plots, and the last four from y vs. x plots, the combined results are self-consistent. In Figure (6-11-5), the lower curve shows the two sets of constants represented satisfactorily by a single straight line on a plot of $-\log K$ against $1/D$. The equation for this line can be written in the form

* Although this can not be justified on the basis of the Bjerrum model for ion pair formation [See Chapter (7), Sections (3) and (5)], this assumption is given strong support by the results here considered in terms of the Denison and Ramsey proposal to count as associated only pairs of ions in actual contact [See Chapter (7), Section (3a)].

$$-\log K = -\log K_0 + C/D \qquad (6\text{-}11\text{-}48)$$

which is considered in some detail in Section (3a) of Chapter (7). If the electrostatic free energy is assumed[177] to be simply a charge-charge energy, as in the derivation of equation (7-3-4), the slope of this line is $C = \epsilon^2/akT$, and leads to $\mathring{a} = 3.30$ instead of the value 4.00 derived from the values of J_1 obtained from Figure (6-11-3). Fuoss and Kraus[178] point out that by considering the dipolar nature[179] of the bromate ion, the electrostatic free

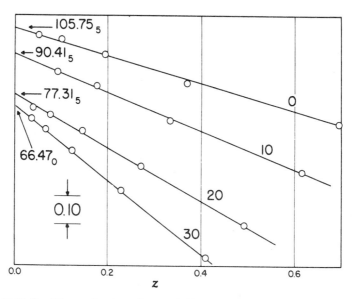

Fig. (6-11-4). The evaluation of Λ^0 and K^{-1} by extrapolations conforming with equation (6-11-46). Sodium bromide in dioxane-water mixtures at 25°. The plots are shifted vertically by arbitrary amounts for convenience in representation.

energy should contain a term $\mu\epsilon/d^2D$, in which μ is the dipole strength and d the distance from the center of the cation to the electrostatic center of the anion dipole with which it forms an ion pair. On this basis, the slope of the lower plot in Figure (6-11-5) should be the sum

$$C = \epsilon^2/akT + \mu\epsilon/d^2kT \qquad (6\text{-}11\text{-}49)$$

and equation (6-11-48) can be written

$$K^{-1} = K_0^{-1}e^{\epsilon^2/akDT}e^{\mu\epsilon/d^2DkT} \qquad (6\text{-}11\text{-}50)$$

for the special case where one of the ions in the ion pair contains a dipole. From the value of C corresponding to the slope of the plot and the value 4.00 Ångstroms for the a-parameter, it follows that the ratio μ/d^2 for the

[177] J. T. Denison and J. B. Ramsey, *J. Am. Chem. Soc.*, **77**, 2615 (1955).
[178] R. M. Fuoss and C. A. Kraus, *Ibid* **79**, 3304 (1957).
[179] J. C. Slater, *Phys. Rev.*, **38**, 325 (1931).

ion pair sodium-bromate is about 1/400, which is the expected order of magnitude.

The conductance data for tetrabutylammonium iodide and tetraiso-amylammonium nitrate have also been used to construct y vs. x plots as described above.   For the purpose of illustrating the determination of the viscosity correction, $c\Lambda^0\delta 5/2$, the results for the first of these salts are reproduced in Table (6-11-5).   The slopes of the y vs. x plots were used to determine the values of K.   Since, for the large quarternary ammonium ions, the viscosity correction in equation (6-11-44) can not be neglected in the calculation of J_1 without resulting in variable and absurdly small

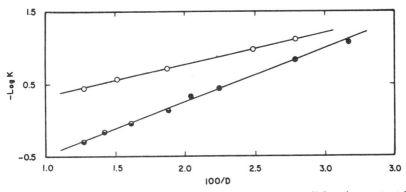

Fig. (6-11-5).   Dependence of the dissociation of salts upon dielectric constant in dioxane-water mixtures at 25°.   O; Tetrabutylammonium iodide.   ●; Sodium bromate by equation (6-11-43).   ◐; Sodium bromate by equation (6-11-46).

values of a, it becomes necessary in this case to determine realistic values of both the a-parameter and the hydrodynamic radius r for such ions.   The latter quantity is determined by equation (6-11-31) if the viscosity data are available, or a good estimate of r may be made for symmetrical ions from known interatomic distances and bond angles.   In the case of tetra-butylammonium iodide, Fuoss and Kraus chose to determine a from the plot of $-\log K$ against $1/D$ shown in Figure (6-11-5).   For this salt neither ion contains a dipole, so the slope of the plot, $C = \epsilon^2/akT$, leads to $\mathring{a} = 5.55$ for the distance between centers of the nitrogen and iodine atoms in anion

TABLE (6-11-5).* TETRABUTYLAMMONIUM IODIDE IN DIOXANE-WATER MIXTURES AT 25°.

Dioxane % (wt)	D^a	K	$J_1{}^b$	δ	$10^8 \, r$	Λ^0
0	78.48	0.366	245	0.98	7.3	96.30
15	66.10	.274	253	1.03	7.3	70.74
30	53.28	.196	303	1.30	8.0	53.84
45	40.20	.105	476	1.46	8.3	43.81
50	35.85	.077	604	1.56	8.5	41.69

* R. M. Fuoss and C. A. Kraus, *J. Am. Chem. Soc.*, **79,** 3304 (1957).

ª The values of the dielectric constants are those of F. E. Critchfield, J. A. Gibson, Jr., and J. L. Hall, *J. Am. Chem. Soc.*, **75,** 1991 (1953), and were used by Fuoss and Kraus in determining the quantities which appear in this table.

ᵇ Calculated for $a = 5.5 \times 10^{-8}$.

pair. Using this a to calculate J_1, equation (6-11-44) was then used to obtain the values of δ and r given in Table (6-11-5). These values are seen to vary slowly with the dioxane-water ratio, but they are of the expected order of magnitude.[180]

(12) Transference Numbers by the Electromotive Force Centrifuge

The determination of transference numbers from potential differences observed between similar electrodes at different positions in a gravitational field had its beginnings in the last century. Des Coudres[181] studied chloride solutions by means of calomel electrodes separated by heights of less than four meters, yet the resulting very small potential differences lead to transference numbers in approximate agreement with Hittorf values. The increase in sensitivity to be gained by replacing gravity by more intense centrifugal fields invited investigation with the electromotive force centrifuge, and Des Coudres and many others attempted to develop such an instrument. This early work is summarized by Tolman[182] who clarified the underlying theory, and attained an experimental accuracy that was not to be improved upon for nearly forty years. In spite of this noteworthy work by Tolman, there remained serious technical difficulties in the method. Frictional heating of the spinning cell in air caused temperature gradients which could be neither eliminated nor measured with much success, and there was difficulty in maintaining and measuring constant speeds of rotation. For a while, these problems seemed so serious that interest was revived in the gravity cell, which Grinnell and Koenig[183] developed to a remarkable degree. With a special potentiometer, constructed for this work, they measured potential differences of the order of 3 microvolts to within about 0.1 %, and obtained reproducible transference numbers agreeing within 0.5 % with the moving boundary values.

Recently MacInnes and Ray[184] have made use of the modern techniques of motor-driven centrifuges and multi-junction thermocouples, and by ingenious improvements in cell design, and in temperature* and speed

* The distribution and measurement of temperatures in high speed rotors is discussed by A. Biancheria and G. Kegeles, *Ibid.*, **76**, 3737 (1954).

[180] R. M. Fuoss, Unpublished viscosity measurements in this laboratory indicate that r is about 6 Ångstroms, and r is about 7 when scaled from a Hershfelder model for the tetrabutylammonium ion.

[181] Des Coudres, *Ann. Physik.*, **49**, 284 (1893); *Ibid.*, **55**, 213 (1895).

[182] R. C. Tolman, *J. Am. Chem. Soc.*, **33**, 121 (1911).

[183] S. W. Grinnell and F. O. Koenig, *J. Am. Chem. Soc.*, **64**, 682 (1942); F. O. Koenig and S. W. Grinnell, *J. Phys. Chem.*, **44**, 463 (1940).

[184] D. A. MacInnes and B. R. Ray, *J. Am. Chem. Soc.*, **71**, 2987 (1949). Factors affecting the precision of the method are carefully analyzed in *J. Phys. Chem.*, **61**, 657 (1957).

control and measurement, they have developed the electromotive force centrifuge to the status of practical research tool. The fundamental equations and some experimental results of this method are the subject of this section. For a description of the technique[184], the apparatus [185] and the measurement of speeds [186] the reader is referred to the original literature.

When the fundamental equation (1-15-52) is applied to a centrifugal field in which changes need only be considered along the radius, r, perpendicular to the axis of rotation, the gradients become partial derivatives with respect to r, and we can write

$$-\mathbf{F}\frac{\partial \psi}{\partial r} = \sum_{j=1}^{s} \frac{T_j}{z_j}\left[\frac{\partial \mu_j}{\partial r} + M_j'\frac{\partial \phi}{\partial r}\right] \qquad (6\text{-}12\text{-}1)$$

at constant T and P. In the experimental study of this equation it was found that the difference in potential, $\psi(r_2) - \psi(r_1)$, between electrodes at two points along the radius r is not zero, and that its value is independent of time for periods of half an hour or more[184]. This indicates that at the relatively slow speeds (7,200 r.p.m., or less) used in the determination of T_j for components of low molecular weight, the tendency toward sedimentation of the solute is effectively counteracted by diffusion. Accordingly, we write

$$\frac{\partial \mu_j}{\partial r} \cong 0 \qquad (6\text{-}12\text{-}2)$$

as a good approximation, and neglect this term in equation (6-12-1).

Corrected for the buoyancy effect of the solvent, the mass of a gram molecular weight of any solute component in the centrifugal field is

$$M_j' = M_j - d\,\bar{V}_j \qquad (6\text{-}12\text{-}3)$$

where M_j is the molecular weight and $\bar{V}_j$ the partial molal volume of the solute component, and d is the density of the solution. In the present application, the quantity ϕ, which appears first in equation (1-15-2), is the centrifugal potential*, and its derivative, $\partial \phi/\partial r$, is the centrifugal force* per unit mass. Accordingly

$$\frac{\partial \phi}{\partial r} = \omega^2 r = 4\pi^2 n^2 r \qquad (6\text{-}12\text{-}4)$$

at any distance, r, from the axis of rotation. Here the angular velocity, ω, is also expressed in terms of n, the number of revolutions per second.

Combination of the preceeding equations leads to

---

* In the articles by MacInnes referred to in this section the symbol ϕ is used to represent the centrifugal *force*.

[185] B. R. Ray and D. A. MacInnes, *Rev. Sci. Inst.*, **20**, 52 (1949).

[186] D. A. MacInnes, *Ibid.*, **14**, 14 (1943).

$$-F \frac{\partial \psi}{\partial r} = 4\pi^2 n^2 r \sum_{j=1}^{s} \frac{T_j}{z_j} [M_j - d\ \bar{V}_j] \tag{6-12-5}$$

In intergrating this equation over the interval $r_2 - r_1$ we note that $\psi(r_2) - \psi(r_1)$ is the measured electromotive force. Consequently,

$$-FE = 2\pi^2 n^2 (r_2^2 - r_1^2) \sum_{j=1}^{s} \frac{T_j}{z_j} [M_j - d\ \bar{V}_j] \tag{6-12-6}$$

upon the assumption that the quantities T_j, $\bar{V}_j$ and d_0 are independent of r. This condition is approximately fulfilled at low speeds where the pressure gradient along r is not large.

MacInnes and Ray[187] applied equation (6-12-6) to the study of 0.1941 normal solutions of potassium iodide to which iodine was added in varying amounts. From their measurements they derived the transference number of the potassium ion in a pure 0.1941 normal solution of potassium iodide, and demonstrated conclusively that $J = 2$ for the reaction

$$JI^0 + I^- \rightarrow I_{J+1}^0 \tag{6-12-7}$$

by which complex negative ions are formed in the ternary solutions. This reaction must be taken into account in the summation which occurs in Equation (6-12-6), because the electric current is carried by complex ions as well as by potassium and chloride ions. In order to reduce this equation to the convenient form used by MacInnes and Ray, we note that the valence, z_j, carries the sign of the charge, and that the transference number, molecular weight and partial molal volume of the complex ions are given by

$$T_{c^-} = 1 - T_{K^+} - T_{I^-} \tag{6-12-8}$$

$$M_{c^-} = J M_{I^0} + M_{I^-} \tag{6-12-9}$$

and

$$\bar{V}_{c^-} = J \bar{V}_{I^0} + \bar{V}_{I^-} \tag{6-12-10}$$

Combination of these equations with (6-12-6) results in the equation

$$-FE = 2\pi^2 n^2 (r_2^2 - r_1^2)[T_{K^+}(M_{KI} - d_0 \bar{V}_{KI})$$
$$- (1 + J T_{c^-})(M_{I^0} - d_0 \bar{V}_{I^0})] \tag{6-12-11}$$

Since the term $(r_2^2 - r_1^2)$ is fixed for a cell, this equation predicts that E be proportional to n^2 at constant T and P and for any given concentrations of potassium iodide and iodine. This prediction has been confirmed.

[187] D. A. MacInnes and B. R. Ray, *J. Am. Chem. Soc.*, **71**, 2987 (1949). For further applications to potassium- and sodium iodide-iodine solutions, see D. A. MacInnes and M. O. Dayhoff, Natl. Bur. Standards Circular **524**, 41 (1953).

Table (6-12-1) summarizes the results of measurements reported by Mac-Innes and Ray.   The value (6.71) for E/n^2 given in the fourth column was obtained by a short extrapolation to zero concentration of iodine.   Since T_{c-} is zero under this condition, the term JT_{c-} drops out of equation (6-12-11) when the limiting value of E/n^2 is introduced.   Furthermore, the partial molal volumes of potassium iodide and iodine in these solutions have been very accurately determined[188] for the purpose, so that equation (6-12-11) may be solved for the transference number of the potassium ion in 0.1941 normal potassium iodide.   The resulting value, $T_{K+} = 0.4873$, is within 0.3 % of the value 0.4887 derived from moving boundary measurements[189] described in Section (5).   Because of its high accuracy and relative simplicity, the moving boundary method is to be preferred in dealing with aqueous solutions, but the centrifugal method just described offers important advantages in the study of poorly conducting non-aqueous solutions in which convection produced by Joule heat limits the moving boundary and Hittorf methods to concentrated solutions.

TABLE (6-12-1).   RESULTS OF MEASUREMENTS* IN THE ELECTROMOTIVE FORCE CENTRIFUGE.   0.1941 N AQUEOUS SOLUTIONS OF POTASSIUM IODIDE CONTAINING IODINE OF VARYING CONCENTRATIONS AT 25°.

Iodine (Normality)	d	Λ_m	$10^8\ E/n^2$	
			obs.	calc.
0	1.02037	126.70	(6.71)	6.684
0.00165	1.02053	126.57	6.738	6.712
.00990	1.02135	125.91	6.874	6.853
.01981	1.02230	125.09	6.967	7.005
.03961	1.02418	123.49	7.380	7.341
.07922	1.02798	120.31	8.049	8.047
.1188	1.03178	117.15	8.851	8.790
.1585	1.03558	114.05	9.586	9.604

* D. A. MacInnes and B. R. Ray, J. Am. Chem. Soc., 71, 2987 (1949).

In closing this brief account of the electromotive force centrifuge, we return to equation (6-12-7) for the formation of the complex iodide ion. It is now possible to determine the mole number, J, from equation (6-12-11), since all of the quantities in this equation are either known, or can be closely approximated.   Thus, the measured equivalent conductance in the mixture, Λ_m , can be represented by

$$\Lambda_m = \lambda_{K+} + (1 - R/J)\lambda_{I-} + (R/J)\lambda_{c-} \qquad (6\text{-}12\text{-}12)$$

where R is the concentration ratio, c_{I_0}/c_{KI} .   This equation, of course, assumes additivity of ionic mobilities at 0.2 N, and will be satisfactory for our purpose so long as the last term on the right is small.   Consequently, we can closely approximate the quantities

188 D. A. MacInnes and M. O. Dayhoff, J. Am. Chem. Soc., 74, 1017 (1952).
189 L. G. Longsworth, J. Am. Chem. Soc., 57, 1185 (1935).

$$\lambda_{C-} = \lambda_{I-} - (J/R)(\Lambda_{KI} - \Lambda_m) \qquad (6\text{-}12\text{-}13)$$

$$T_{K+} = \lambda_{K+}/\Lambda_m \qquad (6\text{-}12\text{-}14)$$

and

$$T_{C-} = (R/J)\lambda_{C-}/\Lambda_m \qquad (6\text{-}12\text{-}15)$$

in the ternary solutions. With the aid of the value 0.4887 for T_{K+} in 0.2 N potassium iodide[189] and 126.70 for Λ_m from Table (6-12-1) the ionic conductances λ_{K+} and λ_{I-} are found to be 61.92 and 64.78 respectively. Substitution of these values into equations (6-12-13) to (6-12-15) results in

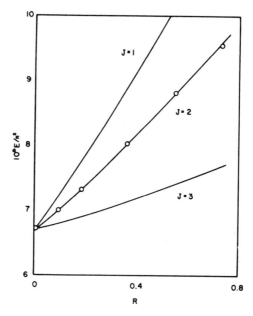

Fig. (6-12-1). Application of equation (6-12-11) to the determination of the mole number, J, in the complex iodide ion, I_{J+1} .

values of T_{K+} and T_{C-} for the mixture, so that the only remaining unknown term in equation (6-12-11) is the mole number J. MacInnes and Ray[177] illustrate the determination of this number very strikingly by calculating the ratio E/n^2 from this equation and their data for several values of J. The results of their calculations are shown in Fig. (6-12-1), where $10^8 E/n^2$ is plotted against the ratio $R = c_{I^0}/c_{KI}$ for $J = 1$, 2, and 3. It is very clear that their results require that $J = 2$, in complete accord with other experimental evidence[190]. The values of E/n^2 given in the last column of Table (6-12-1) were calculated for $J = 2$, and they are seen to agree satisfactorily with the experimental values over the entire range of iodine concentrations.

[190] See G. Jones and B. B. Kaplan [*J. Am. Chem. Soc.*, **50**, 1845 (1928)] for bibliography.

Chapter (7)

Coulomb Forces and Ion Association; Weak Electrolytes; Frequency and Field Effects

In the preceding chapter, the conductance of highly ionized electrolytes in a medium of high dielectric constant was discussed in considerable detail. On the basis of the Onsager conductance equation, the behaviors of most of these solutions indicated complete ionization of the solute at low concentrations. In media other than water, Bjerrum's theory of ionic association [Chapter (3), Section (7)] has indicated, and the experimental results about to be discussed will confirm, that the ions of all electrolytes tend to associate more and more as the dielectric constants of the solvent media decrease. Accordingly, all electrolytes are partially associated, or "weak," in media of low dielectric constants, and classification of electrolytes into strong and weak becomes somewhat arbitrary. Nevertheless, the characterization of electrolytes as strong and weak, depending upon whether they are highly or slightly ionized in aqueous solutions, is commonly retained in describing the electrolytes, regardless of the medium in which they may be dissolved. The title of the present chapter, dealing with non-aqueous solutions of the alkali halides, quarternary ammonium salts, etc., conforms with this convention.

(1) Stokes' Law and Walden's Rule

When strong electrolytes are dissolved in solvents of very low dielectric constants, the simple Coulomb forces are sufficient to cause ionic association at extremely low ionic concentrations. In this case, the ions not acting as part of an associated ion-pair, or more complex aggregate, are so far apart that short-range repulsive forces are negligible and the effect of the ionic atmospheres is also very small. For example, in a dioxane-water mixture having a dielectric constant of 2.3 (0.343 per cent H_2O), the ionic concentration present in a 10^{-3} N solution of tetraisoamyl ammonium nitrate (a strong electrolyte in water) is only of the order of 10^{-8}. In spite of the large limiting slopes, $S_{(\Lambda)}$, resulting from the low dielectric constant, the total effect of the ionic atmosphere is less than 0.2 per cent of Λ and may be neglected.

Exceedingly low ionic dissociation precludes the determination of Λ^0 by direct extrapolation of experimental data. In aqueous solutions, Λ^0 is indirectly evaluated for weak electrolytes by combining the data for suitable strong electrolytes in accordance with Kohlrausch's law. This procedure is obviously impossible in solvents of such low dielectric constants that all electrolytes dissolved in them are highly associated. In this case, it has generally been necessary to employ an approximation known as Walden's rule. This rule, as originally[1] proposed, was empirical, but it can be shown to be a direct consequence of the application of Stokes' law [Equation (4–3–9)] to the motion of ions. Since Walden's rule is most strictly applicable to systems which closely approach the conditions postulated in the derivation of Stokes' law, it will be of interest to consider these two relationships together.

According to Stokes' law, an electric force, $Xz_j\epsilon$, acting upon a spherical ion of radius a_j, would maintain it at a velocity[2]

$$\mathbf{v}_j = \frac{Xz_j\epsilon}{6\pi\eta_0 a_j} \tag{7-1-1}$$

in a homogeneous medium of viscosity, η_0. Ions are often far from spherical, and since they are of the same order of magnitude as the solvent molecules, it is questionable whether the retarding effect of the latter can be accurately described by the macroscopic viscosity. As a first approximation, we can regard the conditions required by equation (7-1-1) as fulfilled by large, spherical ions. By combining this equation with (4-1-15) and $\omega_j = \mathbf{v}_j/Xz_j\epsilon$, we obtain the relation,

$$\lambda_j^0\eta_0 = \frac{F|z_j|\epsilon}{6c \times 10^{-8}\pi a_j} = \frac{0.8147 \times 10^{-8}|z_j|}{a_j} \tag{7-1-2}$$

Therefore, if Λ^0 is the limiting equivalent conductance of an electrolyte dissociating into p kinds of ions, we write

$$\Lambda^0\eta_0 = 0.8147 \times 10^{-8} \sum_{j=1}^{p} \frac{|z_j|}{a_j} \tag{7-1-3}$$

Ionic radii calculated by (7-1-2) are of the order of one to three Ångstroms for the elementary ions,[3] which is in agreement with estimates of (solvated) ionic radii deduced from other data.[4] Since solvation of ions is clearly indicated by a variety of phenomena, a_j (and hence $\lambda_j^0\eta_0$) would be expected to depend to some extent upon the nature of the solvent, and to

[1] P. Walden, *Z. physik. Chem.*, **55**, 207, 246 (1906).

[2] J. J. Hermans [*Z. physik.*, **97**, 681 (1935)] derived a more exact equation for the velocity of an ion by taking the interaction of solvent dipoles into account.

[3] The value thus calculated for the hydrogen ion is a noteworthy exception, being about ¼Ångstrom in water. Since there is independent evidence that the high conductance of these ions is mainly due to successive exchanges between solvent molecules, the inapplicability of Stokes' law could be anticipated. In this connection, the experiments of L. E. Baker and V. K. La Mer [*J. Chem. Phys.*, **3**, 406 (1935)] and of M. Kilpatrick *et al.* [*J. Am. Chem. Soc.*, **78**, 5190, 5186 (1956).] are of particular interest.

[4] H. Ulich, *Z. Elektrochem.*, **36**, 497 (1930).

a lesser degree upon the temperature. This subject has been thoroughly investigated by Walden,[5] who showed that the products, $\lambda_j^0 \eta_0$ and $\Lambda^0 \eta_0$, are

TABLE (7-1-1).*   THE EFFECT OF TEMPERATURE UPON $\lambda_j^0 \eta_0$ AND $\Lambda^0 \eta_0$.

Ion	Solvent	$\lambda_j^0 \eta_0$		
H+.................	Water	3.99 (0°)	3.14 (25°)	1.81 (100°)
Na+.................	"	0.466 "	0.459 "	0.43 "
Cl⁻.................	"	.741 "	.682 "	.59 "
(C₂H₅)₄N+...........	"	.287 "	.295 "	.293 "
Picrate⁻.............	"	.269 "	.274 "	.27 "
½ SO₄⁻⁻.............	"	.73 "	.724 "	—

Electrolyte		$\Lambda^0 \eta_0$		
NaI.................	Ethanol	.529 (0°)	.524 (25°)	.527 (50°)
(CH₃)₄NCl...........	"	.524 "	.549 "	.555 (56°)
(C₂H₅)₄N Picrate......	"	.567 "	.559 "	.564 "
(C₂H₅)₄N Picrate......	Acetone	.568 "	.568 "	.560 (50°)
NaI.................	"	.557 "	.578 "	.570 (40°)
NaI.................	Isobutanol	.489 "	.488 "	.471 (50°)
NaI.................	Pyridine	.638 "	.637 (20°)	.640 "
KI.................	Nitromethane	.765 "	.77 (25°)	.75 (55°)

* H. Ulich, *Fortschritte Chem.*, **18**, No. 10 (1926).

TABLE (7-1-2).*   THE PRODUCT $\lambda_j^0 \eta_0$ IN VARIOUS SOLVENTS AT 25°.

Solvent	K+	Na+	I⁻	CNS⁻	(C₂H₅)₄N+	Picrate⁻
Water.................	0.668	0.459	0.686	0.598	0.295	0.269
Methanol...............	.292	.251	.332	.327	.294	.267
Ethanol................	.267	.238	.285	.28	.295	.263
Acetone................	.222	.217	.366	.40	.294	.266
Furfural	.215	.190	.424	—	.293	—
Acetonitrile	.31	.28	.38	.44	.294	—
Pyridine...............	.27	.22	.42	.45	.294	—

* H. Ulich and E. R. Birr, *Z. Angew. Chem.*, **41**, 443 (1928). See also H. Ulich, *Trans. Faraday Soc.*, **23**, 388 (1927).

practically independent of the temperature,[6] and exhibit less than a two-fold variation from solvent to solvent. This approximate constancy,

$$\left. \begin{array}{l} \lambda_j^0 \eta_0 = \\[1em] \Lambda^0 \eta_0 = \end{array} \right\} \text{constant} \qquad (7\text{-}1\text{-}4)$$

[5] A comprehensive review is given by P. Walden, "Elektrochemie nicht-wässeriger Lösungen," Barth, Leipzig, 1924. For more recent discussions, consult P. Walden and H. Ulich, *Z. physik. Chem.*, **114**, 297 (1925); P. Walden, H. Ulich, and G. Busch, *Ibid.*, **113**, 429 (1926); H. Ulich, *Fortschritte Chem.*, **18**, No. 10 (1926); H. Schmick, *Z. physik.*, **24**, 56 (1924); R. T. Lattey, *Phil. Mag.*, **6**, 258 (1928). *Cf.* M. Born, *Z. Physik.*, **1**, 221 (1920); E. Gonick, *J. Phys. Chem.*, **50**, 291 (1946).

[6] P. Walden and H. Ulich, *Z. physik. Chem.*, **107**, 219 (1923); H. Ulich, *Fortschritte Chem.*, **18**, No. 10 (1926). The most pronounced variations with temperature are found in systems containing hydrogen ions, or highly associated or highly viscous solvents.

was discovered experimentally,[7] and is known as Walden's rule. Very large spherical ions would be nearly free from solvation because of the low charge density on their surfaces, and the magnitude of their radii would be independent of the nature of the solvent. Such ions would most nearly approximate the ideal condition of spheres moving through homogeneous media, as required by Stokes' law. Ions of small size, or of unsymmetrical shape or distribution of charge, would be expected to show most serious departures from Walden's rule, especially when compared in solvents of widely differing polarizability and molecular volume. An idea of the magnitudes of the effects of these factors may be gained from inspection of Tables (7-1-1) and (7-1-2).

(2) Association into Ion Pairs. Estimation of Dissociation Constants

Although the Ostwald dilution function

$$K = \frac{\Lambda^2 c}{\Lambda^0 (\Lambda^0 - \Lambda)} \qquad (7\text{-}2\text{-}1)$$

is unsatisfactory when applied to aqueous solutions of strong electrolytes, it is a close approximation to the behaviors of dilute solutions of weak electrolytes in water, or of strong electrolytes in solvents of low dielectric constants. In these solvents, strong electrolytes are all highly associated, even at the lowest experimentally attainable concentrations. This condition makes it necessary to determine Λ^0 and K simultaneously from the same data. This can be done by assigning successive values to Λ^0 until K, calculated by (7-2-1), is independent of the concentration in dilute solution; but graphical methods are more satisfactory. Kraus and Bray[8] rearranged equation (7-2-1) to read

$$\frac{1}{\Lambda} = \frac{1}{\Lambda^0} + \frac{c\Lambda}{K(\Lambda^0)^2} \qquad (7\text{-}2\text{-}2)$$

and determined $1/\Lambda^0$ and $1/K(\Lambda^0)^2$ as intercept and slope, respectively, of a plot of $1/\Lambda$ against $c\Lambda$. They prepared plots of this nature for a large number of salts, both organic and inorganic, in liquid ammonia, liquid sulfur dioxide, and in many organic solvents. They surveyed the literature up to 1912, and concluded that the mass action expression [Equation (7-2-1)] is obeyed in *all* solutions of electrolytes in which the ion concentration is less than 10^{-3} or 10^{-4} N. They also pointed out that the divergence from the equation, which becomes increasingly apparent at higher concentrations, is a function of the ion concentration rather than of the total concentration of the solute.*

[7] P. Walden, *Z. physik. Chem.*, **55**, 207, 249 (1906). *Cf.* G. Angel, *Ibid.*, **A 170**, 81 (1934).

[8] C. A. Kraus and W. C. Bray, *J. Am. Chem. Soc.*, **35**, 1315 (1913).

* On the basis of insufficiently precise transference numbers, they rejected the suggestion of A. Schanov [*Z. physik. Chem.*, **83**, 129 (1913)] that the presence of complex ions and molecules,

Precise modern measurements, as well as theory, show that equation (7-2-1) is not exact, even at ionic concentration as low as $10^{-4}N$, because of the neglect of long-range interionic attraction upon the conductance and the activities of the ion. Fuoss and Kraus[9] developed a graphical method which took account of these effects by successive approximation. Since much of the laboriousness of this method is eliminated by the use of a table given by Fuoss,[10] the original method will not be given.

For a completely dissociated electrolyte, the conductance would be $\Lambda^0 - \mathcal{S}_{(\Lambda)}\sqrt{c}$ at high dilution [Equation (5-3-1)]. If the fraction of the electrolyte present as ions is α, then the mean ionic concentration is αc, and the equivalent conductance would be

$$\Lambda = \alpha(\Lambda^0 - \mathcal{S}_{(\Lambda)}\sqrt{\alpha c}) \qquad (7\text{-}2\text{-}3)$$

and the degree of dissociation is

$$\alpha = \frac{\Lambda}{\Lambda^0(1 - \mathcal{S}_{(\Lambda)}\sqrt{\alpha c}/\Lambda^0)} \qquad (7\text{-}2\text{-}4)$$

In the limit, these equations reduce to $\alpha = \Lambda/\Lambda^0$ upon which (7-2-1) is based. By the simple expedient of successive substitution of equation (7-2-4) back into its own correction term, $1 - \mathcal{S}_{(\Lambda)}\sqrt{\alpha c}/\Lambda^0$, the latter may be replaced by the continued fraction

$$F(Z) = 1 - Z\{1 - Z[1 - Z(\text{etc.})^{-1/2}]^{-1/2}\}^{-1/2} \qquad (7\text{-}2\text{-}5)$$

in which

$$Z = \mathcal{S}_{(\Lambda)}\sqrt{\Lambda c}(\Lambda^0)^{-3/2} \qquad (7\text{-}2\text{-}6)$$

Fuoss[11] tabulated numerical values of $F(Z)$, for $0 \le Z \le 0.209$, by intervals of 0.001, so that α can be calculated by

$$\alpha = \frac{\Lambda}{\Lambda^0 F(Z)} \qquad (7\text{-}2\text{-}7)$$

$$
\begin{array}{ll}
(CA)_2 \rightleftharpoons 2(CA) & \text{(A)} \\
(CA)_2 \rightleftharpoons C^+ + CA_2^- & \text{(B)} \\
CA \rightleftharpoons C^+ + A^- & \text{(C)}
\end{array}
$$

might explain the deviation from the mass action law for the simple ionization represented by (C). Twenty years later, Kraus, with Fuoss, brilliantly applied these equilibria to the interpretation of the conductance curves of salts in solvents of low dielectric constants.

[9] R. M. Fuoss and C. A. Kraus, *J. Am. Chem. Soc.*, **55**, 476 (1933).

[10] R. M. Fuoss, *J. Am. Chem. Soc.*, **57**, 488 (1935).

[11] R. M. Fuoss, *J. Am. Chem. Soc.*, **57**, 488 (1935).

$$F(Z) = \frac{4}{3}\cos^2 \frac{1}{3}\cos^{-1}\left(\frac{-3\sqrt{3}Z}{2}\right)$$

Cf. D. J. Mead, R. M. Fuoss and C. A. Kraus, *Trans. Faraday Soc.*, **32**, 594 (1936).

when Λ^0 is known. The evaluation of Λ^0 usually requires a short series of approximations, which may begin with a rough value of Λ^0 obtained by free-hand extrapolation of the conductance data, or the application of Walden's rule. This preliminary value of Λ^0 leads to approximate values of $F(Z)$ and α. These values of α are used to estimate the activity coefficient by the limiting law*

$$\log y_\pm = -\mathfrak{S}_{(f)}\sqrt{\alpha c} \tag{7-2-8}$$

or by equation (5-2-8). The expression

$$\frac{F(Z)}{\Lambda} = \frac{1}{\Lambda^0} + \frac{[c\Lambda y_\pm^2/F(Z)]}{K(\Lambda^0)^2} \tag{7-2-9}$$

obtained by combining the thermodynamic ionization constant

$$K = \frac{c\alpha^2 y_\pm^2}{1 - \alpha} \tag{7-2-10}$$

with equation (7-2-7), requires that $1/(K(\Lambda^0)^2)$ be the slope of a plot[12] of $F(Z)/\Lambda$ against $c\Lambda y_\pm^2/F(Z)$, and that $1/\Lambda^0$ be the intercept obtained by extrapolation. Such an extrapolation, based on the first approximate values of $F(Z)$ and $y_\pm$, yields a value of Λ^0 from which more accurate values of $F(Z)$ and $y_\pm$ may be obtained and a new plot constructed. This process is repeated until a final value of Λ^0 is found to satisfy all the equations (7-2-7), (7-2-8) and (7-2-9), and then K is derived from the plot based upon this value of Λ^0.

The use of equation (7-2-9) is illustrated in Figure (7-2-1). The plot is based upon the final values of α calculated by Shedlovsky and Uhlig[13] from their measurements of the conductance of sodium guaiacolate in wet guaiacol solutions at 25°. The experimental data are represented by a straight line whose intercept is 0.143 and whose slope is 416. These values correspond to $\Lambda^0 = 7.5$ and $K = 4.27 \times 10^{-5}$. It will be shown later in this section that this method is not satisfactory for values of K much greater than 10^{-5}, because its application is restricted by the use of equation (5-3-1) at the higher ionic strengths produced by higher K.

Shedlovsky[14] defines α by the expression

$$\Lambda = \alpha\Lambda^0 - \frac{\Lambda}{\Lambda^0}\mathfrak{S}_{(\Lambda)}\sqrt{\alpha c} \tag{7-2-11}$$

---

* Compare equations (5-2-2) and (1-8-14).

[12] Fuoss concluded that this plot should be linear for concentrations less than $3 \times 10^{-7}D^3$.

[13] T. Shedlovsky and H. H. Uhlig, *J. Gen. Physiol.*, **17**, 549 (1934).

[14] T. Shedlovsky, *J. Franklin Inst.*, **225**, 739 (1938).

which reduces to (6-3-10) for completely dissociated electrolytes. From this we write the quadratic function

$$\alpha = \frac{\Lambda}{\Lambda^0} + \left(\frac{\mathcal{S}_{(\Lambda)}}{(\Lambda^0)^2}\right)\Lambda\sqrt{\alpha c} \qquad (7\text{-}2\text{-}11a)$$

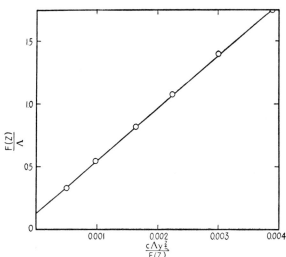

Fig. (7-2-1). Evaluation of K and Λ^0 by equation (7-2-9). Sodium guaiacolate in wet guaiacol solutions at 25°.

instead of the cubic equation (7-2-4). Solution of (7-2-11) for α in terms of the variable Z, defined by (7-2-6), leads to

$$\alpha = \frac{\Lambda}{\Lambda^0}\left[\frac{Z}{2} + \sqrt{1 + \left(\frac{Z}{2}\right)^2}\right]^2 \equiv \frac{\Lambda}{\Lambda^0} S(Z) \qquad (7\text{-}2\text{-}12)$$

The bracketed term may be used in the expanded form

$$S(Z) = 1 + Z + \frac{Z^2}{2} + \frac{Z^3}{8} - \cdots \qquad (7\text{-}2\text{-}13)$$

for small values of Z. Ordinarily, it is not necessary to employ terms higher than Z^2 in evaluating $S(Z)$. A table of $S(Z)$ is given by Daggett.[15] Combination of equation (7-2-12) with (7-2-10) gives the expression

$$\frac{1}{\Lambda S(Z)} = \frac{1}{\Lambda^0} + \frac{(c\Lambda y_{\pm}^2 S(Z))}{K(\Lambda^0)^2} \qquad (7\text{-}2\text{-}14)$$

[15] H. M. Daggett, *J. Am. Chem. Soc.*, **73**, 4977 (1951).

corresponding to (7-2-9). In Figure (7-2-2) the applications of these equations are compared for zinc sulfate[16] in the forms

$$\Lambda/F(Z) = \Lambda^0 - (c\alpha^2 y_\pm^2)\Lambda^0/K \qquad (7\text{-}2\text{-}15)$$

$$\Lambda S(Z) = \Lambda^0 - (c\alpha^2 y_\pm^2)\Lambda^0/K \qquad (7\text{-}2\text{-}16)$$

Although the two curves converge to a common intercept, $\Lambda^0 = 132.8$, the difference between their limiting slopes is

$$\Lambda^0/K(7\text{-}2\text{-}16) - \Lambda^0/K(7\text{-}2\text{-}15) = \mathcal{S}_{(\Lambda)}^2/\Lambda^0 \qquad (7\text{-}2\text{-}17)$$

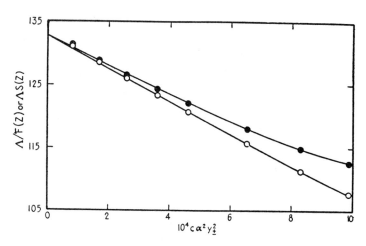

Fig. (7-2-2). Evaluation of Λ^0 and K for zinc sulfate in water at 25°. ●, by equation (7-2-15); ○, by equation (7-2-16); The product, $\alpha y_\pm$, was made equal to the stoichiometrical activity coefficient [Table (13-5-2)].

as was shown by Fuoss and Shedlovsky[17]. For zinc sulfate $K(7\text{-}2\text{-}16)$ is 0.0049 and $K(7\text{-}2\text{-}15)$ is 0.0052, which differ by 6 %. In this case the value 0.0049 from (7-2-16) is preferred[17], but for much weaker electrolytes ($< 10^{-5}$) equation (7-2-15) is also satisfactory*.

Tables (7-2-1A) to (7-2-8A) contain values of Λ^0 and and K for a large number of uniunivalent salts in solvents for which the dielectric constant is equal to, or greater than, 10.

An alternative extrapolation in terms of specific conductivities has recently been proposed by Shedlovsky[18]. He substitutes $1000(L - L_0)/c$

---

[16] B. B. Owen and R. W. Gurry, *J. Am. Chem. Soc.*, **60**, 3074 (1938).

[17] R. M. Fuoss and T. Shedlovsky, *Ibid.*, **71**, 1496 (1949).

* This is borne out by the calculations of D. Belcher, *J. Am. Chem. Soc.*, **60**, 2745 (1938). The limitations of this procedure have been carefully analyzed by M. L. Kilpatrick, *J. Chem. Phys.*, **8**, 306 (1940).

[18] T. Shedlovsky and R. L. Kay, *J. Phys. Chem.*, **60**, 151 (1956).

for Λ in equation (7-2-14), and solves for $1000L$. The resulting equation

$$1000L = 1000L_0$$
$$+ \Lambda^0 K^{1/2}\{(1 - 1000(L' - L_0)S(Z)/\Lambda^0 c)^{1/2}c^{1/2}/S(Z)y_\pm\} \quad (7\text{-}2\text{-}18)$$

yields $\Lambda^0 K^{1/2}$ and $1000L_0$ from the slope and intercept of a plot of $1000L$ against the bracketed terms. Such a plot is illustrated in Figure (7-2-3), based upon Shedlovsky's data for acetic acid in methanol-water mixtures.

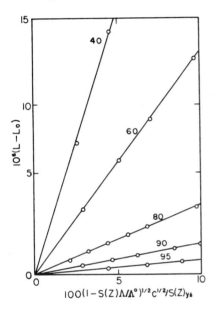

Figure (7-2-3)
Evaluation of $1000L_0$ and $\Lambda^\circ K^{1/2}$ by equation (7-2-18) for acetic acid in methanol-water mixtures.

Although L_0 is directly measurable, it was pointed out under equation (6-1-1) that the solvent correction usually varies in an unknown manner with c. In extrapolations based upon equation (7-2-18) the solvent correction is handled empirically, for L_0 plays the role of an empirical parameter which appears as the intercept and as a correction term within the brackets. Shedlovsky neglects L_0 in calculating the bracketed terms, so in the abscissa of Figure (7-2-3) the quotient $1000(L' - L_0)/c$ has been replaced by Λ. To obtain K from the slope, $\Lambda^0 K^{1/2}$, it is necessary to determine Λ^0 for acetic acid by combination of values of Λ^0 for hydrochloric acid, sodium acetate and sodium chloride as explained in Section (6).

(3) CONFIRMATION OF BJERRUM'S EXTENSION OF THE THEORY OF INTERIONIC ATTRACTION. IONIC PAIR FORMATION AS A FUNCTION OF THE DIELECTRIC CONSTANT

Bjerrum's equation

$$K^{-1} = \frac{4\pi N}{1000}\left(\frac{|z_1 z_2|\epsilon^2}{DkT}\right)^3 Q(b) \quad (3\text{-}7\text{-}13)$$

was deduced [Chapter (3) Section (7)] by considering the effect of Coulomb forces upon ion pair formation. K is the equilibrium constant for the ion pair dissociation,

$$[C^+A^-]^0 \rightleftharpoons C^+ + A^-$$

and b is the parameter

$$b = \frac{|z_1 z_2| \, \epsilon^2}{aDkT} \tag{3-7-7}$$

Numerical values of the function $Q(b)$ are given in Table (5-2-3).

A very important experimental verification of Bjerrum's theory and a proof of the validity of equation (3-7-13) have been presented by Fuoss and Kraus.[19] Their investigations have proved particularly important because, through them, the theory of ionic interaction has been extended to media varying from that of water ($D = 78.54$) to that of dioxane ($D = 2.1$). For this purpose, they employed their extensive conductance data on tetraisoamyl ammonium nitrate in dioxane-water mixtures. Ionic association was noticeable, but not very pronounced in a solution containing 53 per cent H_2O ($D = 38$ at $25°$). It was therefore practicable to extrapolate the data according to Onsager's approximate equation (6-3-3) to obtain Λ^0, and a rough estimate of K. A more accurate value of K was then obtained by consideration of activity coefficients at several low concentrations. In the solvent mixtures in which the dielectric constant was 11.9 and 8.5 (20.2 and 14.95 per cent H_2O), Λ^0 and K were evaluated by the intercept method described in the preceding section. Their data did not extend to sufficiently high dilutions to use this method at lower dielectric constants, so for the mixtures in which the dielectric constant is 5.84, or less, they assumed "reasonable values" of Λ^0 based on Walden's rule (7-1-4), and estimated the corrections due to interionic attraction. Values of K calculated in this manner increased with concentration, because of triple ion formation, and had to be extrapolated to zero concentration.

These values of K may be used to calculate the parameter a by equations (3-7-13) and (3-7-7) in conjunction with a plot of log $Q(b)$ against log b [Table (5-2-3)]. By introduction of the numerical values of the constants used by Fuoss and Kraus[19], these equations become

$$- \log K = 6.120 - 3 \log D + \log Q(b) \tag{7-3-1}$$

and

$$- \log b = 5.254 + \log D + \log a \tag{7-3-2}$$

at $25°$. The results of these calculations of Fuoss and Kraus are given in Table (7-3-1). In spite of the difficulties involved in the estimation of

[19] R. M. Fuoss and C. A. Kraus, *J. Am. Chem. Soc.*, **55**, 1019 (1933).

K in the solvents of lowest dielectric constants, the variation of K with D is sufficiently pronounced in these media to permit a significant test of the theory. It will be observed that the calculated values of a are fairly constant over the entire range of the mixtures. The maximum difference between any two values is 11 per cent, so it seems possible that the average value of a $(= 6.4 \times 10^{-8})$ would represent all the data within the com-

TABLE (7-3-1). CONSTANTS FOR TETRAISOAMYLAMMONIUM NITRATE IN
DIOXANE-WATER MIXTURES AT 25°.

Wt. % H_2O	D^*	$- \log K$	K	$a \times 10^8$
0.60	2.38	15.7	2×10^{-16}	6.01
1.24	2.56	14.0	1×10^{-14}	6.23
2.35	2.90	12.0	1×10^{-12}	6.36
4.01	3.48	9.6	2.5×10^{-10}	6.57
6.37	4.42	7.53	3.0×10^{-8}	6.65
9.50	5.82	5.78	1.65×10^{-6}	6.45
14.95	8.50	4.00	1.00×10^{-4}	6.50
20.2	11.9	3.08	9.0×10^{-4}	6.70
53.0	38.0	0.60	2.5×10^{-1}	6.15

* These values of D used by Fuoss and Kraus are somewhat higher than those in Table (5-1-4).

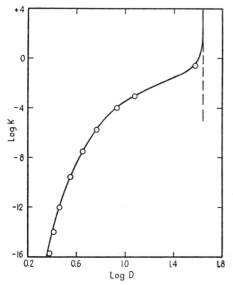

Fig. (7-3-1)
Dissociation of ion pairs as a function of the dielectric constant. Tetraisoamylammonium nitrate in dioxane-water mixtures at 25°

bined uncertainties of the calculations and the experimental measurements.

Accordingly the single value a $(= 6.4 \times 10^{-8})$ was used to calculate K by equations (7-3-1) and (7-3-2) for various values of D. These calculated values are represented graphically by the smooth curve in Fig. (7-3-1). The experimental points taken from Table (7-3-1) are seen to be in striking agreement with the general course of this curve throughout a range of fifteen powers of ten in the constant K. The curve has a vertical asymptote* corresponding to D = 43.6, which implies that tetraisoamylammonium nitrate cannot form stable ion pairs in dioxane-water mixtures when the dielectric constant is equal to, or greater than, this critical value.

(3a) FURTHER CONSIDERATION OF ION PAIR FORMATION AS A FUNCTION OF DIELECTRIC CONSTANT. THE EQUATIONS OF DENNISON AND RAMSEY[19a] AND OF GILKERSON[19b].

Although the variation of the dissociation constant of an ion pair with D and T in a given solvent closely follows the Bjerrum equation (3-7-13), as can be seen in Tables (7-3-1) and (7-4-3), the interpretation of a large number of ion association studies in terms of this equation leads to some puzzling contradictions and anomalies in the a-parameter†. The most noteworthy shortcoming of the Bjerrum model is its inability to follow the variation of K with D without sometimes requiring highly specific dependence of a upon the solvent. It is true that in Table (6-3-1) the value of a for tetraisoamylammonium nitrate is essentially constant over a wide range of composition in dioxane-water mixtures, but this system is in one sense a special case. Fuoss and Kraus pointed out that in all of the solvent mixtures included in the table, the molar water concentration is always much greater than that of the solute, and in view of the high polar moment of water (1.85) compared to that of dioxane (<0.4), we might expect the relative hydration of the solute ions, and therefore their effective diameter, to be practically constant. The specific dependence of a upon solvent becomes very evident when we compare values of K in different pure solvents, and in mixtures of non-aqueous solvents.

The organic solvents ethylene chloride (D = 10.23); ethylidene chloride (D = 10.00) and orthodichlorobenzene (D = 9.93) have practically the same dielectric constant, yet the values of K for salts in these media differ in general by factors of from 3 to 13. Table (7-3-2) contains ratios of the dissociation constants of various salts is these solvents identified by subscripts. In terms of the Bjerrum model the a-parameter of any one of these salts must vary from solvent to solvent. Such a variation is not altogether unreasonable for the model because ion pairs are considered associated up to the characteristic distance

$$q = |z_1 z_2| \, \epsilon^2 / 2DkT \qquad (3\text{-}7\text{-}4$$

---

* In the alternative treatment immediately following, this vertical asymptote is replaced by a horizontal one which is approached at infinite D.

[19a] J. T. Denison and J. B. Ramsey, *J. Am. Chem. Soc.*, **77**, 2615 (1955).

[19b] W. R. Gilkerson, *J. Chem. Phys.*, **26**, 1199 (1956). For a simpler derivation see R. M. Fuoss, *J. Am. Chem. Soc.*, **80**, 5059 (1958).

† Some of these anomalies are considered in Section (5) of this chapter. See also C. A. Kraus, *J. Phys. Chem.*, **60**, 129 (1956) for a complete resumé of the subject.

and can contain solvent molecules between them.   On the other hand, if it be assumed that we need count as associated *only* those ion pairs that are in actual contact, then the absence of solvent molecules between them implies constancy of the *a*-parameter from solvent to solvent.   This assumption underlies the equations derived in this section.

TABLE (7-3-2).* RATIOS OF DISSOCIATION CONSTANTS IN (1) ETHYLENE CHLORIDE, (2) ETHYLIDENE CHLORIDE, AND (3) *o*-DICHLOROBENZENE AT 25°.

Salt	K_1/K_2	K_1/K_3	K_2/K_3
Et₄NPi	13.9	4.9	3.05
Pr₄NPi	14.7	4.9	3.01
Bu₄NPi	13.2	5.0	2.62
Am₄NPi	13.1	4.8	2.73
Octad.Me₃NPi	26.6	5.8	4.42
Et₄NNO₃	. . .	9.9	. . .
Bu₄NNO₃	25.6	. . .	. . .

* Table from Ref. (19b) based upon the data of F. Acascina, E. L. Swarts, P. L. Mercier, and C. A. Kraus, *Proc. Natl. Acad. Sci.*, **39**, 917 (1953).

On the basis of the Born[19c] cycle, Denison and Ramsey[19a] calculated the electrical work

$$W = \epsilon^2/aD \tag{7-3-3}$$

required to separate a pair of ions from contact ($r = a$) to a very large distance ($r \gg a$), and neglecting all interaction except that between pairs of uniformly and oppositely charged ions, they set ΔF^0 equal to NW. Accordingly, for this simple case

$$K^{-1} = \exp \ (\epsilon^2/aDkT) = e^b \tag{7-3-4}$$

as a first approximation.   A more complete equation*

$$K^{-1} = K_0^{-1}e^b, \tag{7-3-5}$$

was derived by Gilkerson[19b] who estimated the entropy contribution to ΔF^0 from the partition functions of the free and paired ions in terms of the zeroth approximation of Kirkwood's[19d] theory.   In this equation

$$K_0 = (2\pi mkT/h^2)^{3/2}(gv\sigma) \exp \ (-U_s/kT) \tag{7-3-6}$$

* At the end of Section (11) of Chapter (6) it was pointed out that this equation could be further extended to take account of ions containing dipoles (*e.g.*, bromate) by the inclusion of a suitable factor.

[19c] M. Born, *Z. Physik*, **1**, 45 (1920).
[19d] J. G. Kirkwood, *J. Chem. Phys.*, **18**, 380 (1950).

where m is the function $m_+m_-/(m_+ + m_-)$ of the masses of the ions, and

$$(gv\sigma) = (gv\sigma)_+(gv\sigma)_-/(gv\sigma)_\pm \qquad (7\text{-}3\text{-}7)$$

In this last equation g represents the internal rotational and vibrational contributions to the partition functions, v is the free volume available to each particle, and σ is a factor varying from unity for solids to e for gases. The important parameter

$$U_s = U_+ + U_- - U_\pm \simeq A\mu_s \qquad (7\text{-}3\text{-}8)$$

is the difference between the solvent-ion and solvent-ion pair interaction energies, and to a first approximation it should be proportional to the dipole moment, μ_s, of the solvent. Equation (7-3-5) contains therefore one adjustable constant, a, characteristic of the ions alone, and in addition to μ_s and the dielectric constant, two parameters, U_s and $(gv\sigma)$, which can be considered properties of the pure solvent as a useful approximation.

For the above three solvents of nearly the same dielectric constants and similar chemical compositions, we might assume that the values of A and $(gv\sigma)$ are constant, and apply equations (7-3-5) to (7-3-8) to the ratios given in Table (7-3-2), and predict that

$$\frac{\log (K_1/K_2)}{\log (K_1/K_3)} = \frac{\mu_{s1} - \mu_{s2}}{\mu_{s1} - \mu_{s3}} \qquad (7\text{-}3\text{-}9)$$

The results of this prediction are compared with the experimental results in Table (7-3-3). The concordance seems much too good to be fortuitous because the calculation by equation (7-3-9) is very sensitive to the experimental values of μ_s.

TABLE (7-3-3).* THE EFFECT OF THE DIPOLE MOMENT OF SOLVENT MOLECULES UPON ION PAIR FORMATION. TEST OF EQUATION (7-3-9).

Salt	$\dfrac{\log K_1/K_2}{\log K_2/K_3}$	$\dfrac{\log K_1/K_3}{\log K_1/K_2}$
Et$_4$NPi	2.36	1.73
Pr$_4$NPi	2.44	1.69
Bu$_4$NPi	2.65	1.60
Am$_4$NPi	2.56	1.64
Octad.Me$_3$NPi	2.20	1.86
Equation (7-3-9)[a]	2.20	1.83

* From Gilkerson, Ref. 19b.

[a] Using $\mu_s = 1.75$ debyes for ethylene chloride (1), 2.05 for ethylidene chloride (2), and 2.30 (3) for o-dichlorobenzene.

By adjusting the parameters of equations (7-3-5) to (7-3-8) to fit the results for Bu$_4$NPi in four solvents at various temperatures, Gilkerson[19b] showed that a constant value of a ($=2.51 \times 10^{-8}$) leads to reasonable values of U_s and $(gv\sigma)$ for ethylene chloride, ethylidene chloride, propylene chloride and anisole. On the other hand, 2.51×10^{-8} seems too small for the a-parameter of a salt such as Bu$_4$NPi. It is only about half as great as the values obtained from the Bjerrum equation [see Table (7-5-2)], and is less than the value, 3.73×10^{-8}, derived from dipole measurements[19e]. It is not unlikely that this small value of a results, in part at least, from too small a value of K. It has been pointed out by Fuoss[19f] that when the ion size is large compared to that of solvent molecules, a viscosity correction should be applied to the conductance equation, and this correction has the effect of increasing the value of K. The details of such a calculation for sodium bromate are given in Section (11) of Chapter (6).

(4) Association into Complex Aggregates. Triple Ions, Quadrupoles, and the Conductance Minimum

As shown by Figure (7-4-1), when the dielectric constant of the solvent is of the order of 10 or less, a minimum is observed in the conductance curves in dilute solution. With further decrease in dielectric constant, the minimum becomes more distinct and its position shifts in the direction of increasing dilution. To account for the increase in the number of ions, per mol, as the solute concentration increases, Fuoss and Kraus[20] postulated the combination of ions with ion pairs to form "triple ions" according to the scheme

$$[A^+B^-A^+]^+ \rightleftharpoons A^+ + [A^+B^-]^0 \tag{7-4-1}$$

$$[B^-A^+B^-]^- \rightleftharpoons B^- + [A^+B^-]^0 \tag{7-4-2}$$

They pointed out that triple ions should be stable because the excess potential energy due to the third ion is several times as great as the mean thermal energy of the ions in a solvent of low dielectric constant.

If the simple ions are spherical, and the same size, the two triple-ion combinations should be formed to an equal extent, and we may write[21]

$$\frac{(AB)(B^-)}{(BAB^-)} = \frac{(AB)(A^+)}{(ABA^+)} = K_3 \tag{7-4-3}$$

If we consider the simple equilibrium,

$$[A^+B^-]^0 \rightleftharpoons A^+ + B^-; \qquad y_\pm^2 \frac{(A^+)(B^-)}{(AB)} = K \tag{7-4-4}$$

and let $\alpha = (A^+)/c$ and $\alpha_3 = (ABA^+)/c$, then all the equilibria may be considered simultaneously, and the concentrations of single ions, double ions, and triple ions will be $c\alpha$, $c(1 - \alpha - 3\alpha_3)$, and $c\alpha_3$, respectively. Sub-

[19e] J. A. Geddes and C. A. Kraus, *Trans. Faraday Soc.*, **180**, 585 (1936); C. A. Kraus, *J. Phys. Chem.*, **60**, 129 (1956).

[19f] R. M. Fuoss, *J. Am. Chem. Soc.*, **79**, 3301 (1957).

[20] R. M. Fuoss and C. A. Kraus, *J. Am. Chem. Soc.*, **55**, 2387 (1933).

[21] The assumption of equal ion size avoids the complication of considering two different triple-ion constants, which could not, at present, be independently evaluated. Whatever approximation is involved in this assumption will appear in the average ion size computed from K_3. See M. Dole, *Trans. Electrochem. Soc.*, **77**, 385 (1940). C. B. Wooster, *J. Am. Chem. Soc.*, **60**, 1609 (1938).

stituting these terms in the above equations, and solving for α and α_3, we obtain

$$\alpha_3 = \frac{c\alpha}{K_3}(1 - \alpha - 3\alpha_3) = (\sqrt{Kc}/K_3)(1 - \alpha - 3\alpha_3)^{3/2}y_\pm^{-1} \qquad (7\text{-}4\text{-}3a)$$

and

$$\alpha = \sqrt{K/c}\,(1 - \alpha - 3\alpha_3)^{1/2}y_\pm^{-1} \qquad (7\text{-}4\text{-}4a)$$

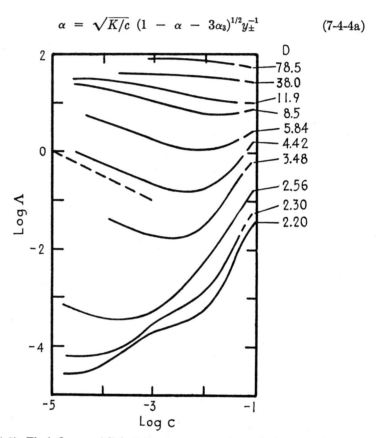

Fig. (7–4–1). The influence of dielectric constant upon the variation of conductance with concentration. Tetraisoamylammonium nitrate in dioxane-water mixtures at 25°. Dielectric constants are indicated at the right hand margin. Experimental curves after Fuoss and Kraus

Writing Λ_3^0 for the sum of the limiting conductances of the two kinds of triple ions, the function

$$\Lambda = (\alpha\Lambda^0 + \alpha_3\Lambda_3^0)(1 - \mathbb{S}_{(\Lambda)}\sqrt{c(\alpha + \alpha_3)}/\Lambda^0) \qquad (7\text{-}4\text{-}5)$$

should approximately express the conductance in dilute solutions. According to equation (7-2-8),

$$y_\pm^{-1} = \exp\,(2.303\mathbb{S}_{(f)}\sqrt{c(\alpha + \alpha_3)}) \qquad (7\text{-}4\text{-}6)$$

In order to combine these four equations, it will be necessary to introduce an additional approximation. Fuoss and Kraus assume that

$$c(\alpha + \alpha_3) \simeq c\Lambda/\Lambda^0 \qquad (7\text{-}4\text{-}7)$$

and

$$(1 - \alpha - 3\alpha_3) \simeq (1 - \Lambda/\Lambda^0) \qquad (7\text{-}4\text{-}8)$$

so that their final combined equation, rearranged for extrapolation, becomes

$$\Lambda\sqrt{c}\cdot g(c) = \sqrt{K}\Lambda^0 + (\sqrt{K}\Lambda_3^0/K_3)(1 - \Lambda/\Lambda^0)c \qquad (7\text{-}4\text{-}9)$$

where

$$g(c) \equiv \frac{\exp\left(-2.303\, \mathbb{S}_{(f)}\sqrt{c\Lambda/\Lambda^0}\right)}{(1 - \mathbb{S}_{(\Lambda)}\sqrt{c\Lambda/\Lambda^0}/\Lambda^0)(1 - \Lambda/\Lambda^0)^{1/2}} \qquad (7\text{-}4\text{-}10)$$

Since both c and Λ/Λ^0 are ordinarily much less than unity, this equation may be used in the approximate form[22]

$$\log g(c) \simeq \left[\frac{0.4343\, \mathbb{S}_{(\Lambda)} - \mathbb{S}_{(f)}\Lambda^0}{(\Lambda^0)^{3/2}}\right]\sqrt{c\Lambda} + \frac{0.2171\Lambda}{\Lambda^0} \qquad (7\text{-}4\text{-}10a)$$

The term $g(c)$ accounts for the effects of the ionic atmosphere upon the mass action expression and the conductance. If the conductance minimum occurs above $10^{-3}N$, the approximations involved in equation (7-4-9) are too crude for a quantitative treatment of the data unless the measurements extend to very low concentrations.

It is apparent from equation (7-4-9) that a plot of $\Lambda\sqrt{c}g(c)$ against $(1 - \Lambda/\Lambda^0)c$ will be a straight line with intercept, $\Lambda^0\sqrt{K}$, and slope, $\Lambda_3^0\sqrt{K}/K_3$. Such a plot is shown in Fig. (7-4-2). In order to estimate the individual values of K and K_3, Λ^0 and Λ_3^0 must be known. Λ^0 cannot be directly determined in solvents of very low dielectric constants, but Walden's rule (7-1-4) yields a good approximation for Λ^0. The product, $\Lambda^0\eta_0$, can be determined in solvents of sufficiently high dielectric constants to allow extrapolation. The value of Λ_3^0 cannot be directly determined in any medium, but the ratio Λ_3^0/Λ^0 may be estimated from a study of the temperature coefficient of the conductance,[23, 24] if it be assumed that Λ_3^0/Λ^0 is independent of T. Since the variation of K_3 with temperature and dielectric constant is of greater theoretical interest than its absolute magnitude, it is sufficient for most purposes to set Λ_3^0/Λ^0 equal to some

---

[22] Compare D. J. Mead and R. M. Fuoss, *J. Am. Chem. Soc.*, **62**, 1720 (1940), footnote (5).

[23] R. M. Fuoss, *J. Am. Chem. Soc.*, **56**, 1857 (1934); footnote (7).

[24] G. S. Bien, C. A. Kraus and R. M. Fuoss, *Ibid.*, **56**, 1860 (1934).

"reasonable" constant fraction, say 1/3 or 1/2, in all media and at all temperatures.[25]

A simpler, but somewhat less accurate, estimate of K_3 in terms of Λ^0/Λ_3^0 depends upon the numerical values of the minimum conductance and the concentration at which it appears. If we neglect $g(c)$ and the factor, $1 - \Lambda/\Lambda^0$, in equation (7-4-9), differentiate, and impose the condition for a minimum, we obtain the relation

$$K_3 = c_{\min}\Lambda_3^0/\Lambda^0 \qquad (7\text{-}4\text{-}11)$$

which, upon recombination with (7-4-9), yields

$$\sqrt{K} = \frac{(c\Lambda)_{\min}}{2\Lambda^0} \qquad (7\text{-}4\text{-}12)$$

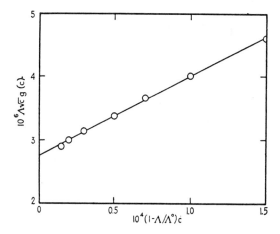

Fig. (7-4-2)
Plot according to equation (7-4-9) with $g(c)$ estimated by equation (7-4-10a). Tetraisoamylammonium nitrate in dioxane solutions containing 1.24 per cent water ($t = 25°$, $D = 2.56$)

Since the graphical determination of $c_{\min}$ and $\Lambda_{\min}$ is not very precise, and the correction term, $g(c)$, is neglected in the derivation of equation (7-4-11), K_3 is more accurately evaluated from the slopes and intercepts of plots such as the one illustrated in Figure (7-4-2). The experimental values of $- \log K_3$ given in Table (7-4-1) were obtained in this manner. Note that K_3 and the concentration at the minimum increase rapidly with the dielectric constant.

We are now in a position to apply the theory of "triple ion formation" developed in Chapter (3), Section (7). According to this theory, K_3 may be computed by the equation

$$K_3^{-1} = \frac{2\pi Na_3^3}{1000} I(b_3) \qquad (7\text{-}4\text{-}13)$$

[25] M. Born, *Z. Physik.*, **1**, 221 (1920); H. Schmick, *Ibid.*, **24**, 56 (1924); R. T. Lattey, *Phil. Mag.*, **6**, 258 (1928). The coefficient $d\lambda_j^0/dT$ is practically the same for most large ions.

where

$$b_3 = \frac{|z_+ z_-| \epsilon^2}{a_3 D k T} \qquad (7\text{-}4\text{-}14)$$

and $I(b_3)$ as a function of b_3 is given in Table (5-2-4). Consideration of boundary conditions leads to the conclusion that triple ions are unstable ($K_3 = \infty$) with respect to thermal agitation when $b_3 \leq 8/3$. Therefore, according to equation (7-4-14), triple ion formation can not take place in solvents in which

$$D \geq \frac{3|z_+ z_-| \epsilon^2}{8 a_3 k T} \qquad (7\text{-}4\text{-}15)$$

The existence of such a critical value of D is indicated in Figure (7-4-1) by the disappearance of the conductance minimum with increasing dielectric constant.

TABLE (7-4-1).* TETRAISOAMYLAMMONIUM NITRATE IN DIOXANE-WATER MIXTURES AT 25°.

Wt. % H_2O	D	$-\log c_{(min)}$	$-\log K_{3(exp)}$	$-\log K_{3(calc)}$
0.60	2.38	4.10	4.68	4.34
1.24	2.56	3.60	4.12	4.03
2.35	2.90	3.15	3.50	3.56
4.01	3.48	2.60	3.00	3.02
6.37	4.42	2.30	2.5	2.50
9.50	5.84	2.05	2.0	2.06
14.95	8.50	1.60	—	1.56

* Taken from Table III of the paper by R. M. Fuoss and C. A. Kraus, *J. Am. Chem. Soc.*, **55**, 2387 (1933).

In fitting equation (7-4-13) to the data for tetraisoamylammonium nitrate in dioxane-water mixtures, Fuoss and Kraus[26] used the value $a_3 = 9 \times 10^{-8}$ cm. The figures recorded in the last column of Table (7-4-1) as $-\log K_{3(calc)}$ are based upon this value. They are in very good agreement with $-\log K_{3(exp)}$. Referring to Table (7-3-1), we note that it was necessary to use the value $a \simeq 6.4 \times 10^{-8}$ cm to represent ion pair formation in the same solutions. In Figure (7-4-3), the values of $\log K_{3(exp)}$ given in Table (7-4-1) are shown as circles. The curve is derived from equation (7-4-13) for $a_3 = 9 \times 10^{-8}$ cm. According to equation (7-4-15), the theoretical limit of triple ion formation for this value of a_3 should appear at a dielectric constant of 23.2.

By combination with equations (7-4-11) and (7-4-14), equation (7-4-13) may be put in the form

$$\frac{D^3}{c_{min}} = \left(\frac{\Lambda_3^0 \, 2\pi N \epsilon^6}{\Lambda^0 \, 1000 \, k^3 \, T^3} \right) \frac{I(b_3)}{b_3^3} \qquad (7\text{-}4\text{-}16)$$

[26] R. M. Fuoss and C. A. Kraus, *J. Am. Chem. Soc.*, **55**, 2387 (1933).

Fuoss and Kraus suggested this relation as a probable explanation of the empirical rule, D^3/c_{min} = constant ($\simeq 3 \times 10^4$), discovered by Walden,[27] because the ratio $I(b_3)/b_3^3$ is not very sensitive to the value of b_3 within the region of the inflection [Fig. (7-4-3)].*

Association into more complex aggregates than triple ions would be expected in solvents of very low dielectric constant, and progress has already been made in the numerical consideration of quadrupole formation from ion pairs. The existence of quadrupoles is implied by inflections just above the minima in the conductance concentration curves for alkylammonium salts in benzene[28] and dioxane,[29] and by the apparent molecular weights of the solutes derived from cryoscopic data.[30] Moreover, the observed conductance is so small that it can be assumed, as a first approximation, that the concentrations of single ions, triple ions, and other charged aggregates are negligible compared to the concentrations of

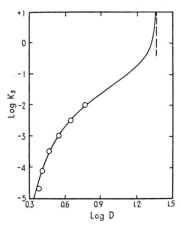

Fig. (7-4-3)
The influence of dielectric constant upon the dissociation of triple ions. Tetraisoamylammonium nitrate in dioxane-water mixtures at 25°

neutral ion pairs and quadrupoles. Over the limited concentration range in which this approximation is valid, we need only consider the equilibrium

$$[A^+B^-]^0[A^+B^-]^0 \rightleftharpoons 2[A^+B^-]^0 \qquad (7\text{-}4\text{-}17)$$

[27] P. Walden, *Z. physik. Chem.*, **147 A,** 1 (1930).

* Numerically, (7-4-16) becomes

$$\frac{D^3}{c_{min}} = 0.66 \times 10^6 \frac{\Lambda_3^0}{\Lambda^0} \frac{I(b_3)}{b_3^3} \text{ at } 25°$$

For large ions, say $a_3 = 10^{-7}$ cm and $D = 3$, or 4, $I(b_3)/b_3^3$ is of the order of 0.1 to 0.5. Since Walden found that $D^3/c_{min} \simeq 3 \times 10^4$, it follows that Λ_3^0/Λ^0 is of the order $\frac{1}{2}$ to 1. This is certainly a physically reasonable result.

[28] R. M. Fuoss and C. A. Kraus, *J. Am. Chem. Soc.*, **55,** 3614 (1933); W. F. Luder and C. A. Kraus, *Ibid.*, **58,** 255 (1936).

[29] R. M. Fuoss and C. A. Kraus, *Ibid.*, **55,** 21 (1933).

[30] F. M. Batson and C. A. Kraus, *J. Am. Chem. Soc.*, **56,** 2017 (1934); C. A. Kraus and R. A. Vingee, *Ibid.*, **56,** 511 (1934).

which defines the constant

$$K_4 = \frac{(AB)^2}{([AB][AB])} \qquad (7\text{-}4\text{-}18)$$

By introducing the assumption that a quadrupole can be represented by an ellipsoid (of axes a and λa), containing a point dipole of strength μ at its center, and parallel to the major axis, Fuoss and Kraus[31] derived the expression

$$K_4^{-1} = \frac{N}{2000} \left(\frac{\pi}{3}\right)^{3/2} \frac{\mu^2}{DkT} \frac{e^\nu}{y^{7/2}} (1/(2\lambda^2) - 1)^{-1/2} \qquad (7\text{-}4\text{-}19)$$

previously given as equation (3-7-27). The function, y, is defined by

$$y = \frac{\mu^2}{(\lambda a)^3 DkT} \qquad (7\text{-}4\text{-}20)$$

Freezing point measurements[32] on benzene solutions of tri-isoamylammonium picrate can be satisfactorily represented in terms of equation (7-4-18), leading to the relation[33]

$$K_4 = \frac{c(1 - 2j)^2}{j} \qquad (7\text{-}4\text{-}21)$$

where j, for an undissociated solute, is given by equation (9-5-21) when $\nu = 1$. It was found graphically that $K_4 = 0.105$ mol per liter at 5.5°. Substitution of this value in (7-4-19) results in the physically reasonable value, $\lambda a = 5.54 \times 10^{-8}$. In this case, the approximations underlying equation (7-4-21) seem justified by the data throughout the concentration range, 0.002 to 0.03N.

Making use of the same elliptical model postulated in the derivation of equation (7-4-19), Fuoss[34] showed that the limiting slope for a plot of the molecular polarization, P_2, of the solute against concentration should be

$$\left(\frac{dP_2}{dc}\right)_{c\to0} = -\frac{4\pi}{D} \left(\frac{\pi}{3}\right)^{3/2} \left(\frac{N\mu}{3kT}\right)^2 \frac{\mu^2}{1000} \frac{e^\nu}{y^{7/2}} \left(\frac{1}{2\lambda^2} - 1\right)^{-1/2} \qquad (7\text{-}4\text{-}22)$$

This equation may be combined with (7-4-19) to express K_4 as a function of P_2, but the numerical value of K_4 is too sensitive to errors in estimating μ and dP_2/dc to be of much interest. The results derived from some of these dielectric constant studies in benzene solutions are recorded in Table (7-4-2). The large limiting molecular polarizations, P_2^0, of the solutes, and the corresponding polar moments (in Debye units) are given in the second and third columns. The limiting slopes dP_2/dc were obtained

[31] R. M. Fuoss and C. A. Kraus, J. Am. Chem. Soc., 57, 1 (1935).
[32] F. M. Batson and C. A. Kraus, J. Am. Chem. Soc., 56, 2017 (1934).
[33] R. M. Fuoss and C. A. Kraus, J. Am. Chem. Soc., 57, 1 (1935).
[34] R. M. Fuoss, J. Am. Chem. Soc., 56, 1031 (1934).

graphically. The lengths, λa, of the minor axes depend upon the assumption that $\lambda = \frac{1}{2}$. The values obtained from dielectric constant data and equation (7-4-22) are given in the next to last column. They are of the expected order of magnitude, and agree satisfactorily with the two values derived from freezing point data by the use of equations (7-4-21) and (7-4-19). Unfortunately, no quantitative application of the ion pair-quadrupole equilibrium to the interpretation of conductance data has yet been made.

Fuoss[35] has derived the approximate equation

$$\frac{d \ln \Lambda}{d \ln T} = -\frac{d \ln \eta_0}{d \ln T} + \frac{1}{2}\left(1 + \frac{d \ln D}{d \ln T}\right)\left(b - 1 - \frac{4}{b}\right)$$
$$- \frac{\frac{1}{2}}{(1 + K_3 \Lambda^0/\Lambda_3^0 c)}\left(1 + \frac{d \ln D}{d \ln T}\right)\left(b_3 - 4 - \frac{16}{3b_3}\right) \quad (7\text{-}4\text{-}23)$$

TABLE (7-4-2).[1] PROPERTIES OF ELLIPSOIDAL DIPOLE MODELS.

Electrolyte	P_2^0(cc)	$\mu \times 10^{18}$	$\left(\dfrac{dP_2}{dc}\right)_{c\to 0} \times 10^{-6}$	$a \times 10^8$	
				(D)	(F.P.)
Tetra-n-butylammonium hydroxytri-phenylboron.	8270	19.7	−14.30	6.37	—
Tetra-iso-amylammonium picrate.	7090	18.3	−2.86	6.28	—
Tetra-n-butylammonium picrate.	6740	17.8	−1.52	6.28	—
Tri-iso-amylammonium picrate.	3830	13.3	−1.12	5.05	5.54[2]
Tri-n-butylammonium picrate.	3670	13.1	−0.71	5.02	5.59[3]
Tetra-n-butylammonium acetate.	2690	11.2	−0.27	4.59	—

[1] J. A. Geddes and C. A. Kraus, *Trans. Faraday Soc.*, 32, 585 (1936); See also G. S. Hooper and C. A. Kraus, *J. Am. Chem. Soc.*, 56, 2265 (1934); *Proc. Nat. Acad. Sci.*, 19, 939 (1933).
[2] R. M. Fuoss and C. A. Kraus, *J. Am. Chem. Soc.*, 57, 1 (1935).
[3] D. A. Rothrock and C. A. Kraus, *Ibid.*, 59, 1699 (1937).

for the temperature dependence of the conductance of strong electrolytes in media of low dielectric constants. It is based upon equation (7-4-9), and is therefore valid only when $\alpha \ll 1$, and at values of c less than the concentration at which Λ is a minimum. It is further restricted to systems for which $b_3 > 10$, because use is made of an asymptotic expansion of equation (7-4-13). The assumption of three physical restrictions is also made, namely

$$\frac{d(\Lambda^0 \eta_0)}{dT} = \frac{d(\Lambda_3^0 \eta_0)}{dT} = 0 \quad (7\text{-}4\text{-}24)$$

$$\frac{da}{dT} = \frac{da_3}{dT} = 0 \quad (7\text{-}4\text{-}25)$$

and

$$\frac{d(\Lambda^0/\Lambda_3^0)}{dT} = 0 \quad (7\text{-}4\text{-}26)$$

[35] R. M. Fuoss, *J. Am. Chem. Soc.*, 56, 1857 (1934).

The application of equation (7-4-23) to conductance data requires a series of plots and successive approximations, and also involves Walden's rule (7-1-4) in the estimation of Λ^0. The details of this calculation are given by Bien, Kraus and Fuoss,[36] who verified equation (7-4-23) with their measurements of the conductance of tetrabutylammonium nitrate and picrate in anisole ($D = 4.29$ at 25°) at temperatures between -33 and 95°. They plotted their data, as in Figure (7-4-2), and obtained $\Lambda_3^0\sqrt{K}/K_3$ and $\Lambda^0\sqrt{K}$ from the slopes and intercepts. These quantities are recorded in Table (7-4-3) for tetrabutylammonium nitrate. Λ^0 was estimated by the relation, $\Lambda^0\eta_0 = 0.508$, based on measurements in ethylene chloride[37] at 25°. The values of K were calculated from the figures given in columns (2) and (4) of the table, and the corresponding values of a computed by equations (3-7-13) and (3-7-7). The constancy of a may be taken as an indication of the correctness of the values of Λ^0.

The estimation of K_3 was performed in such a manner that the ratio, Λ_3^0/Λ^0, assumed to be independent of the temperature, could be determined

TABLE (7-4-3).* CONSTANTS FOR TETRABUTYLAMMONIUM NITRATE IN ANISOLE.

$t°C$	$\Lambda^0\sqrt{K} \times 10^4$	$\Lambda_3^0\sqrt{K}/K_3$	Λ^0	$K \times 10^{11}$	$a \times 10^8$	$K_3 \times 10^4$	$a_3 \times 10^8$
-33	0.650	0.115	14.22	2.08	4.88	4.61	5.79
0	2.34	.324	31.8	5.42	4.95	5.89	5.79
25	4.75	.550	49.5	9.20	4.96	7.05	5.84
61.3	10.50	.950	82.1	16.30	4.91	9.04	5.82
80.2	14.70	1.145	102.1	20.65	4.89	10.47	5.88
95.1	18.10	1.288	118.9	23.2	4.85	11.48	5.88

* Taken from Table III of the paper by G. S. Bien, C. A. Kraus and R. M. Fuoss *J. Am. Chem. Soc.*, **56**, 1860 (1934).

from the data. The average value of Λ_3^0/Λ^0 ($= 0.82$) was then employed to calculate K_3 from each experimental value of $K_3\Lambda^0/\Lambda_3^0$. These values of K_3, together with the corresponding values of a_3, calculated from them, are given in the last two columns of Table (7-4-3). The constancy of a_3 is very satisfactory.

With the aid of empirical equations, fitted to their data on the fluidity and molecular polarization of anisole, Bien, Kraus and Fuoss estimated analytically the terms $d \ln \eta_0/dT$ and $d \ln D/d \ln T$. Using the average values of a and a_3, it was then possible to calculate $d \ln \Lambda/dT$ by equation (7-4-23) and compare the results with experimental values read directly (as chord slopes) from a plot of $\ln \Lambda$ against T. This comparison is illustrated by curve I in Fig. (7-4-4). Although the theoretical curve only represents the general course of the experimental values, this is all that could be expected in the light of the complexity of the calculation and the approximations involved. The slope of the theoretical curve is mainly

[36] G. S. Bien, C. A. Kraus and R. M. Fuoss, *J. Am. Chem. Soc.*, **56**, 1860 (1934).
[37] N. L. Cox, C. A. Kraus and R. M. Fuoss, *Trans. Faraday Soc.*, **31**, 749 (1935).

due to the term $d \ln \eta_0/dT$, which suggests that departures from equation
(7-4-24) may be an important factor in the observed discrepancy.

The combination of equation (7-4-23) with (7-4-11) and (7-4-12) permits
a comparison with values of $\log c_{min}$ and $\log \Lambda_{min}$, read from logarithmic
plots of the original data at each temperature. Curves II and III in
Fig. (7-4-4) are derived from the foregoing equations, and the observed
$\log (c_{min})$ and $\log (\Lambda_{min})$ are represented by dots and circles, respectively.

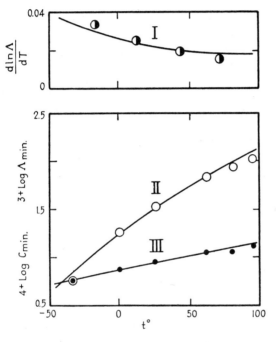

Fig. (7-4-4)
The effect of temperature
upon the conductance of
tetrabutylammonium ni-
trate in anisole

(5) The Influence of Ionic Size and Structure upon Conductance and Association

Since the extent of ionic association depends upon the potential energy
of an ion pair (or more complex aggregate), and this in turn depends upon
how close the charges on the ions may be brought together, ionic size is a
very important factor in determining the individuality of dissociation
constants. The effect of the "a" parameter has been given quantitative
expression in the equations of Bjerrum (3-7-13), and of Fuoss and Kraus
(7-4-13).

Unfortunately, it is not possible to check the equations by precise independent determination of "a", and this quantity has not been clearly
defined in terms of actual ionic dimensions, or structure. In the derivation of the equations, "a" is interpreted as the distance between centers
(charges) of uniformly charged spheres in contact. Ions are, in general,

neither spherical nor uniformly charged, especially when in contact. The difficult questions of solvation, and the correct value of the dielectric constant in the immediate vicinity of an ion, or between an ion pair, have not yet been satisfactorily answered. Nevertheless, it is possible to draw several qualitative conclusions from the systematic comparison of the magnitude of the "a" parameters, calculated from equations (3-7-13) and (7-4-13), with the results of studies of unrelated properties, such as crystal lattice constants, ionic mobilities, polar moments, and freezing-point lowerings.

In a qualitative way, we would expect this over-simplified physical picture to be most nearly approached in systems composed of large spherically symmetrical ions in media of low polarizability. Systems of this type have been investigated by Fuoss and Kraus,[38] who measured the conductance of tetraisoamylammonium halides in benzene. By locating the conductance minimum graphically, they could determine $K(\Lambda^0)^2$, and $K_3\Lambda^0/\Lambda_3^0$ by equation (7-4-12) and (7-4-11). Λ^0, and of course Λ_3^0, could

TABLE (7-5-1). CONSTANTS FOR SALTS IN BENZENE AT 25°.

	$-\log K(\Lambda^0)^2$	$-\log K$†	$a \times 10^8$	$-\log (K_3\Lambda^0/\Lambda_3^0)$	$-\log K_3$*	$a_3 \times 10^8$
$(C_5H_{11})_4NI$	13.30	17.30	5.67	4.90	5.40	7.36
$(C_5H_{11})_4NBr$	13.45	17.45	5.62	4.80	5.30	7.52
$(C_5H_{11})_4NCl$	13.90	17.90	5.47	4.70	5.20	7.67
$(C_5H_{11})_4NF$	14.20	18.20	5.25	4.60	5.10	7.85
$(C_5H_{11})_4NSCN$	13.25	17.25	5.68	4.65	5.15	7.76
$(C_5H_{11})_4NOC_6H_2(NO_2)_3$	13.05	17.05	5.75	4.35	4.85	8.34
$(C_5H_{11})_3HNOC_6H_2(NO_2)_3$	16.60	20.60	4.74	2.90	3.40	16.3

† Λ^0 assumed equal to 100.
* Λ^0/Λ_3^0 assumed equal to 3.

not be determined experimentally because of the minuteness of the degree of dissociation of electrolytes in benzene. The results for the halides, as well as for the thiocyanate and two picrates,[39] are given in Table (7-5-1). In a non-polar solvent such as benzene, where solvation is presumably absent, the size of the halide ions in solution should vary with atomic number in the same order as ionic radii calculated from X-ray crystal studies [Table (5-1-6)]. It is apparent from the table that $K(\Lambda^0)^2$ decreases steadily from iodide to fluoride, which may be taken as proof that K decreases in the same order, because Λ^0 should increase somewhat in passing from the large iodide ion to the small (hence more mobile) fluoride ion. Since the values of $\log K$ given in the table are calculated on the assumption that $\Lambda^0 = 100$ for all the salts, the "observed" variation of K with electrolyte is undoubtedly too small.

Λ^0/Λ_3^0 probably varies but slightly in any series of similar salts. There-

[38] R. M. Fuoss and C. A. Kraus, J. Am. Chem. Soc., 55, 3614 (1933).
[39] R. M. Fuoss and C. A. Kraus, J. Am. Chem. Soc., 55, 21 (1933).

fore K_3 varies as $K_3\Lambda^0/\Lambda_3^0$, which is seen to increase with decreasing atomic number of the halide ion. This is to be expected because the larger ions should be most loosely bound (lower potential energy) into triple ions, and therefore have the highest value of K_3. It should be remarked that the values of a_3 differ from those of "a" in both magnitude and order of increase with composition of electrolyte. A similar difference is illustrated in Table (7-4-3), where a single system is considered at various temperatures. In view of the simplicity of the physical picture of triple-ion formation upon which the theoretical equation (7-4-13) is based, we are hardly justified in attaching more significance to "observed" values of a_3 than to note that dimensions within the range 5 to 10 Å are physically reasonable for the ions under discussion. Certainly, the theory in its present form is inadequate to account for the observation[40] that a_3 for n-tetrabutylammonium picrate increases by 1 Å between -33 and $95°$.

TABLE (7-5-2). THE DISSOCIATION CONSTANT AND a-PARAMETER OF n-TETRABUTYLAMMONIUM PICRATE IN VARIOUS SOLVENTS.

Solvent	t	D	Λ^0	K	$a \times 10^8$
Ethylene chloride[1]	25	10.23	57.40	2.28×10^{-4}	5.75
Tricresyl phosphate[2]	40	6.92	1.92	1.014×10^{-5}	5.80
Chlorobenzene[3]	25	5.63	60	1.88×10^{-8}	4.75
Anisole[4]	25	4.29	43	1.16×10^{-9}	5.61
Diphenylether[5]	50	3.53	24.5	2.70×10^{-11}	5.33

[1] C. A. Kraus, *J. Franklin Inst.*, **225**, 687 (1938).
[2] M. A. Elliott and R. M. Fuoss, *J. Am. Chem. Soc.*, **61**, 294 (1939).
[3] R. L. McIntosh, D. J. Mead and R. M. Fuoss, *Ibid.*, **62**, 506 (1940).
[4] N. L. Cox, C. A. Kraus and R. M. Fuoss, *Trans. Faraday Soc.*, **31**, 749 (1935).
[5] D. J. Mead and R. M. Fuoss, *J. Am. Chem. Soc.*, **61**, 2047 (1939).

Although values of "a" are practically independent of temperature, there is no doubt that they depend upon the nature of the solvent as well as that of the solute. The variation of "a" shown in Table (7-5-2) is one of several examples which might have been selected to show that ion-solvent interaction[41] must be considered in any adequate theory dealing with polarizable solvents. Specific solvent effects are generally more pronounced when the solute is an incompletely substituted ammonium salt. The a-value of n-tributylammonium picrate is 4.66 Å in tricresyl phosphate,[42] but only 2.4 Å in ethylene chloride.[43]

The influence of ion structure upon this type of electrolytic dissociation

[40] G. S. Bien, C. A. Kraus and R. M. Fuoss, *J. Am. Chem. Soc.*, **56**, 1860 (1934).
[41] See R. L. McIntosh, D. J. Mead and R. M. Fuoss, *J. Am. Chem. Soc.*, **62**, 506 (1940); E. Swift, Jr., *Ibid.*, **60**, 2611 (1938); W. F. Luder, P. B. Kraus, C. A. Kraus and R. M. Fuoss, *Ibid.*, **58**, 255 (1936).
[42] M. A. Elliott and R. M. Fuoss, *J. Am. Chem. Soc.*, **61**, 294 (1939).
[43] D. J. Mead, C. A. Kraus and R. M. Fuoss, *Ibid.*, **61**, 3257 (1939).

has been brought out in a number of studies.[44] Some indications of structural effects may be obtained from Table (7-5-1) by considering the substitution of the larger, but more unsymmetrical, picrate ion for one of the halide ions. The localization of negative charge around the oxygen atom at one end of the picrate ion will decrease the tendency to form ion pairs because of the unsymmetrical screening effect of the trinitrobenzene group. This same localization of charge would, on the other hand, endow ion pairs, once formed, with additional stability, because the charges could be brought more closely together than if symmetrically distributed over the ionic surfaces. The net result of these opposing effects is not always clearly predictable in terms of K; but since the screening effect would be doubly effective in the formation of triple ions, and would decrease the potential energy contributed by the addition of a third ion to an ion pair, we expect a considerable increase in K_3 with the introduction of pronounced dissymmetry. The transition from quaternary ammonium iodide to thiocyanate to picrate is accompanied by an almost four-fold increase in K_3, and a two-fold increase in K. The substitution of ternary for quaternary ammonium picrate introduces dissymmetry into both ions with the result that the increase in K_3 is thirty-fold, while K is decreased by a factor of 3,500. The high increase in stability, accompanying the replacement of the large isoamyl radical by hydrogen, can be attributed partly to the ability of the charge-bearing atoms (O and N) to approach each other very closely, and partly to proton interaction with the solvent.[45]

The absolute magnitude of "a" is more significant than that of a_3, because "a" is associated with a simpler physical process, and can be evaluated by independent experimental methods. Thus, for tri-isoamylammonium picrate in benzene, $a \times 10^8$ was found to be 4.74 by conductance, 5.05 by dielectric constant, and 5.54 by freezing-point measurements [Tables (7-5-1) and (7-4-2)]. According to Table (7-1-2), the Stokes' law constant is 0.265 for the picrate ion, and about 0.295 for the tri-isoamylammonium ion (assuming the conductance of this ion equal to that of the tetraethylammonium ion). Substitution of these values into equation (7-1-2) yields 3.1 and 2.7 Å for the individual ionic radii, or 5.8 Å for the a-value estimated from mobilities. Since "a" is rather loosely defined in a physical sense, and approximations, as well as experimental errors of various kinds, are involved in its several determinations, the discordance of these independently derived values does not appear excessive. Our discussion of the effects of differences in ion size and structure is not concerned with this uncertainty in absolute magnitude, because

[44] C. A. Kraus, *J. Phys. Chem.*, **60**, 129 (1956). The scope of this important article exceeds that of the present discussion. Micellar electrolytes, and the effects of complexing agents are included.

[45] C. A. Kraus, *Science*, **90**, 281 (1939).

the observed effects are larger than the relative accuracy with which "a" can be determined conductometrically.

(6) The Ionization of Weak Electrolytes

The transformation of the thermodynamic mass action expression for the ionization of a binary weak electrolyte,

$$K = \frac{y_{\pm}^2 \alpha^2 c}{y_u(1 - \alpha)} \tag{7-6-1}$$

into the Ostwald dilution law, [Equation (7-2-1)], involves the approximations, $y_{\pm}^2/y_u = 1$ and $\alpha = \Lambda/\Lambda^0$, which ignore ionic interaction. At high dilutions, these approximations introduce small errors of the same order of magnitude and of opposite sign, so that the agreement of the Ostwald dilution law with the earlier measurements on weak electrolytes was sufficiently close to be considered a triumph of the Arrhenius[46] theory of electrolytic dissociation. Ostwald[47] recognized that there was a slight but reproducible trend in the values of K with c when calculated by his equation. He suggested that the assumption of constant ionic mobilities, introduced by setting $\alpha = \Lambda/\Lambda^0$, might be improved by considering the change in the viscosity of the solutions with concentration. In some cases, the trend in K could be eliminated over a considerable concentration range by the use of $\alpha = \Lambda\eta/\Lambda^0\eta_0$, but the improvement was by no means general. Before the advent of the interionic attraction theory, many other modifications of the original dilution law were proposed[48] on empirical grounds, but none of these was important in the final development of the subject.

Any exact determination of ionization constants of weak electrolytes by the conductance method must take into account the dependence of both activity coefficients and mobilities upon concentration. Sherrill and Noyes,[49] and MacInnes[50] were the first to perfect the method. They evaluated K in dilute solutions by employing the limiting law of Debye and Hückel for $y_{\pm}$, and defined the degree of ionization by

$$\alpha = \Lambda/\Lambda_e \tag{7-6-2}$$

[46] S. Arrhenius, *Z. physik. Chem.*, **1**, 631 (1887); M. Planck, *Ibid.*, **1**, 577 (1887).

[47] W. Ostwald, *Z. physik. Chem.*, **2**, 270 (1888).

[48] For a complete account of these "dilution laws" see J. R. Partington, Chapter XI, in H. S. Taylor's "Treatise on Physical Chemistry", Vol. I, D. Van Nostrand Co., New York.

[49] M. S. Sherrill and A. A. Noyes, *J. Am. Chem. Soc.*, **48**, 1861 (1926).

[50] D. A. MacInnes, *Ibid.*, **48**, 2068 (1926). See also C. W. Davies, *J. Phys. Chem.*, **29**, 977 (1925).

Λ_e is the equivalent conductance of the hypothetical completely ionized electrolyte at the ion concentration[51]

$$c_i = \alpha c \qquad (7\text{-}6\text{-}2a)$$

corresponding to the observed equivalent conductance, Λ. The evaluation of Λ_e is based upon the assumption[52] that the ionic mobilities are additive at the concentrations involved. For a weak acid, HR, dissociating as

$$HR \rightleftharpoons H^+ + R^-$$

the value of Λ_e can be obtained by combination of the measured conductances of the strong electrolytes, HCl, NaR, and NaCl, all at the concentration c_i, as follows:

$$\Lambda_{e_{HR}} = \Lambda_{HCl} + \Lambda_{NaR} - \Lambda_{NaCl} \qquad (7\text{-}6\text{-}3)$$

The determination of the ionic concentration, c_i, is performed by a short series of successive approximations. A first approximation to c_i is obtained as $c_i' = c\Lambda/\Lambda^0$, and a value Λ_e' calculated from (7-6-3) at this concentration. A second approximation is then given by $c_i'' = c\Lambda/\Lambda_e'$, from which, in turn, a value of Λ_e'' is obtained. Since Λ_e does not change very rapidly with c_i, a third or fourth approximation is seldom required to yield self-consistent values of c_i and Λ_e, within the experimental error of the best measurements.

For convenience in calculation, MacInnes expressed the conductances of the strong electrolytes by means of equation (6-3-8). Thus,

$$\Lambda_{HCl} = \Lambda_{HCl}^0 - \mathcal{S}_{HCl}\sqrt{c_i} + B_{HCl}c_i(1 - \alpha^*\sqrt{c_i}) \qquad (7\text{-}6\text{-}4)$$

$$\Lambda_{NaR} = \Lambda_{NaR}^0 - \mathcal{S}_{NaR}\sqrt{c_i} + B_{NaR}c_i(1 - \alpha^*\sqrt{c_i}) \qquad (7\text{-}6\text{-}5)$$

$$\Lambda_{NaCl} = \Lambda_{NaCl}^0 - \mathcal{S}_{NaCl}\sqrt{c_i} + B_{NaCl}c_i(1 - \alpha^*\sqrt{c_i}) \qquad (7\text{-}6\text{-}6)$$

From these, the parameters in the equation,

$$\Lambda_{e_{HR}} = \Lambda_{HR}^0 - \mathcal{S}_{HR}\sqrt{c_i} + B_{HR}c_i(1 - \alpha^*\sqrt{c_i}) \qquad (7\text{-}6\text{-}7)$$

are obtained by linear combination according to equation (7-6-3). This analytical expression of $\Lambda_{e_{HR}}$ has come into general use, and appears to give satisfactory results.* Before closing the discussion of the evaluation

---

[51] The first substitution of a hypothetical conductance of this nature for Λ^0 seems to have been due to F. Kohlrausch [Z. physik. Chem., **64**, 129 (1908)] who determined the solubility of silver chloride from the relation, $c = 1000 \, \kappa/\Lambda_e$, instead of $c = 1000 \, \kappa/\Lambda^0$. Here κ is the specific conductivity of the saturated solution, and c is the solubility.

[52] F. Kohlrausch, *Wied. Ann.*, **6**, 1 (1879); **26**, 161 (1885). See Chapter (6) Section (8).

* The objection might be raised that, in the preceding chapter, it was shown that equation (6-3-8) is not strictly valid at extreme dilutions. This objection is more academic than practical, however, as this equation satisfactorily expresses the results for 1-1 electrolyte within the concentration range employed in the determination of ionization constants. This procedure is therefore just as accurate, and presumably more convenient than a more refined analytical treatment.

of c_i, it should be made clear that, although Λ/Λ_e is a much closer approximation to the true ionic concentration than Λ/Λ^0, it cannot be considered exact, because the quantity Λ is measured in a medium containing $c_u = c - c_i$ mols per liter of undissociated weak electrolyte, whereas Λ_e is evaluated in pure water. It might appear at first glance that the effect of this variation in the solvent medium could be taken into account by writing $c_i = \Lambda\eta/\Lambda^0\eta_0$. As variations from Stokes' law are most pronounced where hydrogen ions are concerned, and the viscosity of a c_u normal solution of the weak electrolyte *free from ions* is unmeasurable, conductance measurements lead to apparent values of c_i. These values, however, will yield an accurate extrapolation of K_A. In addition to these objections to the use of the viscosity ratio, it has the property of being very helpful in certain cases[53] and superfluous in others. It is generally avoided because it requires additional experimental data.

The evaluation of K_A from a series of values of c and c_i can be conveniently performed in a number of ways. If experimental results are available at very high dilutions, it is sufficient to calculate

$$k_A = \frac{c_i^2}{c - c_i} = \frac{c_i^2}{c_u} \tag{7-6-8}$$

for various values of c_i, and extrapolate to infinite dilution by a plot of $\log k_A$ against $\sqrt{c_i}$. Fig. (7-6-1) shows a plot of this kind used by MacInnes and Shedlovsky[54] to obtain the ionization constant of acetic acid at 25°. The equation for the straight line drawn through the experimental points at high dilution is

$$\log k_A = \log K_A + 1.013\sqrt{c_i} \tag{7-6-9}$$

and a comparison of this equation with (7-6-1) and (7-6-8) shows that

$$2\log y_\pm - \log y_u = -1.013\sqrt{c_i} \tag{7-6-10}$$

At the high dilutions concerned, the activity coefficient of a neutral solute would be expected to be so close to unity[55] that $\log y_u$ can be safely disregarded, and we see that the limiting slope of the plot is in exact numerical agreement with the limiting slope predicted by the Debye-Hückel theory for aqueous solutions at 25°.

The departures of the experimental results from the limiting tangent in the more concentrated range cannot be accounted for by experimentally determined values of $\log y_u$, or by the introduction of reasonable ionic radii into the expression for $\log y_\pm$. Assuming $\mathring{a} = 4$ for ionized acetic acid, MacInnes and Shedlovsky calculated $\log y_\pm^2$ by equation (3-5-8), and $\log y_u$ from freezing-point measurements. The variation of $\log k_A$ with

[53] C. W. Davies, *J. Am. Chem. Soc.*, **54**, 3776 (1932).
[54] D. A. MacInnes and T. Shedlovsky, *J. Am. Chem. Soc.*, **54**, 1429 (1932).
[55] W. D. Larson and W. J. Tomsicek, *J. Am. Chem. Soc.*, **61**, 65 (1939).

$\sqrt{c_i}$, predicted by this calculation, falls slightly below the dashed line in Fig. (7-6-1), but departs widely from the experimental curve at the higher concentrations.

Although the failure of the Kohlrausch law and the increasing lack of exact physical definition of c_i at these concentrations undoubtedly account for some of the descrepancies observed above, an important factor is the neglect of the "medium effect" of the neutral molecules of acetic acid upon $\log y_{\pm}^2$ of its ions.   Quantitative information regarding this particular effect is not available.   The effect is probably not very different from that of acetic acid molecules upon $\log y_{\pm}^2$ of hydrochloric acid, which is known[56] to be about $0.106c_u$.   Without stressing the numerical magnitude of the effect, we may merely assume that it is proportional to c_u and write

$$\log \ (y_{\pm}^2/y_u) \ = \ -1.013\sqrt{c_i} \ + \ \beta c_u \qquad (7\text{-}6\text{-}11)$$

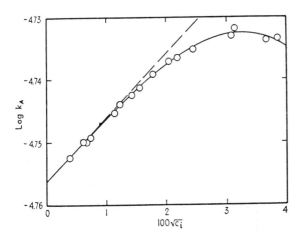

Fig. (7–6-1)
    Graphical evaluation of the ionization constant of acetic acid in water at 25° according to equation (7–6–9)

where $\log y_u$ has also been assumed linear in c_u.   Combination of this equation with equation (7–6–1) leads to[57]

$$\log k_A \ - \ 1.013 \ \sqrt{c_i} = \log K_A \ - \ \beta c_u \qquad (7\text{-}6\text{-}12)$$

In Fig. (7-6-2), the left-hand member of this equation is plotted for the data of MacInnes and Shedlovsky at concentrations above $0.005N$.   The radii of the circles represent an uncertainty of 0.1 per cent in k_A, which seems to be the experimental reproducibility of this quantity.   It is ap-

[56] B. B. Owen, *J. Am. Chem. Soc.*, **54**, 1758 (1932). By the conditions of the measurements, the ionization of the acetic acid, at the concentrations with which we are here concerned, was so depressed by the presence of HCl that we may consider its stoichiometrical concentration equal to c_u. $0.106 \, c_u$ has been written for 5.87 times the mole fraction of acetic acid.

[57] B. Saxton and T. W. Langer, *J. Am. Chem. Soc.*, **55**, 3638 (1933); B. Saxton and H. F. Meier, *Ibid.*, **56**, 1918 (1934); B. Saxton and L. S. Darken, *Ibid.*, **62**, 846 (1940).

parent that the linearity predicted by equation (7-6-12) is fulfilled over the concentration range considered, and the value of β is about 0.134.

To the factors already mentioned which contribute to the term βc_u an interesting addition has been made by Katchalsky, Eisenberg and Lifson.[58] They point out that there is ample evidence that the carboxylic acids are appreciably polymerized in aqueous solutions, and make the reasonable assumption that, at the concentrations with which we are concerned, we need consider only the two equilibria

$$2HA \rightleftharpoons H_2A_2 \tag{7-6-13}$$

and

$$HA \rightleftharpoons H^+ + A^- \tag{7-6-14}$$

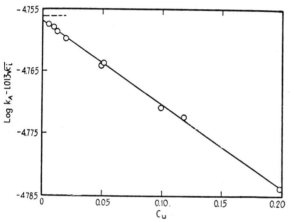

Fig. (7-6-2)
Graphical evaluation of the ionization constant of acetic acid at 25° according to equation (7-6-12)

On this basis they show that the equilibrium constant for the dimerization reaction (7-6-13) must contribute to the term βc_u of equation (7-6-12). Since it is not possible at present to assign numerical values to all of the various individual contributions to β, the magnitude of this parameter is not subject to rigorous analysis. This situation is closely paralleled by other empirical parameters which appear in the numerous expressions used to represent initial departures from theoretical limiting equations.

The extrapolated value of K_A from Figure (7-6-2) is 1.750×10^{-5}, while the value derived from Fig. (7-6-1) is 1.753×10^{-5}. The difference between these values is 0.17 per cent, almost twice the apparent experimental reproducibility of the individual data, but well within the agreement which we might expect between values of K_A determined by different investigators, or by different methods, under the best conditions. The choice between the two extrapolations is mainly a matter of experimental

[58] A. Katchalsky, H. Eisenberg and S. Lifson, *J. Am. Chem. Soc.*, **73**, 5889 (1951).

convenience, rather than of accuracy, and on this basis the method of Fig. (7-6-2) is unquestionably to be preferred. It can be observed from the plots that the concentration range that might be used to determine the straight line is *below* 0.003 in Fig. (7-6-1), but *above* 0.005 in Fig. (7-6-2), and the latter extrapolation is much shorter.

Table (7-6-1) contains ionization constants derived from conductance data by the methods outlined in this section.

In the conductometric evaluation of ionization constants which are much smaller than those in Table (7-6-1), the method of this Section can be combined with that of Section (2). For example, Λ^0 for completely ionized

TABLE (7-6-1). IONIZATION CONSTANTS OF WEAK ELECTROLYTES DETERMINED CONDUCTOMETRICALLY IN WATER AT 25°.

	K(m-scale)	Ref.
Formic acid	1.830×10^{-4}	1
Acetic acid	1.758×10^{-5}	2
n-Propionic acid	1.347×10^{-5}	3
n-Butyric acid	1.512×10^{-5}	3, 1
Chloroacetic acid	1.400×10^{-3}	4, 5
Cyanoacetic acid	3.370×10^{-3}	1
Lactic acid	1.391×10^{-4}	6
Sulfuric acid (K_{2A})	1.18×10^{-2}	7
Phosphoric acid (K_{1A}, 18°)	8.31×10^{-3}	7
α-Crotonic acid	1.981×10^{-5}	8
Benzoic acid	6.313×10^{-5}	9, 10
o-Chlorobenzoic acid	1.200×10^{-3}	9, 10
m-Chlorobenzoic acid	1.510×10^{-4}	9, 10
p-Chlorobenzoic acid	1.043×10^{-4}	9, 10
Carbonic acid (K_{1A})	4.323×10^{-7}	11
Monoethanolammonium hydroxide	3.19×10^{-5}	12
Oxalic acid (K_{1A})	5.376×10^{-2}	13

1. B. Saxton and L. S. Darken, *J. Am. Chem. Soc.*, **62**, 846 (1940).
2. D. A. MacInnes and T. Shedlovsky, *Ibid.*, **54**, 1429 (1932).
3. D. Belcher, *Ibid.*, **60**, 2744 (1938).
4. T. Shedlovsky, A. S. Brown and D. A. MacInnes, *Trans. Electrochem. Soc.*, **66**, 165 (1935).
5. B. Saxton and T. W. Langer, *J. Am. Chem. Soc.*, **55**, 3638 (1933).
6. A. W. Martin and H. V. Tartar, *Ibid.*, **59**, 2672 (1937), 0 to 50°.
7. M. S. Sherrill and A. A. Noyes, *Ibid.*, **48**, 1861 (1926).
8. B. Saxton and G. W. Waters, *Ibid.*, **59**, 1048 (1937).
9. B. Saxton and H. F. Meier, *Ibid.*, **56**, 1918 (1934).
10. F. G. Brockman and M. Kilpatrick, *Ibid.*, **56**, 1483 (1934).
11. T. Shedlovsky and D. A. MacInnes, *Ibid.*, **57**, 1705 (1935).
12. V. Sivertz, R. E. Reitmeier and H. V. Tartar, *Ibid.*, **62**, 1379 (1940).
13. L. S. Darken, *Ibid.*, **63**, 1007 (1941).

acetic acid can be obtained from equation (7-6-3) applied to limiting conductances, and used to calculate K from the slopes, $\Lambda^0 K^{1/2}$, of plots illustrated in Figure (7-2-3). Values of the ionization constant of acetic acid in methanol-water mixtures derived in this manner are given in Table (7-6-2).

TABLE (7-6-2).* IONIZATION CONSTANTS OF ACETIC ACID DETERMINED
CONDUCTOMETRICALLY IN WATER-METHANOL MIXTURES AT 25°.

Vol. % MeOH	K c-scale	Vol. % MeOH	K c-scale
10	1.31 10^{-5}	80	3.96 10^{-7}
20	9.59 10^{-6}	90	9.71 10^{-8}
40	4.52 10^{-6}	95	2.07 10^{-8}
60	1.82 10^{-6}	100	2.37 10^{-10}

* T. Shedlovsky and R. L. Kay, *J. Am. Chem. Soc.*, **60**, 151 (1956).

(7) EXPERIMENTAL INVESTIGATIONS OF THE EFFECT OF FREQUENCY ON
CONDUCTANCE AND DIELECTRIC CONSTANT

Wien[59] was the first to demonstrate the variation of conductivity with the frequency. Sack,[60] however, was the first to obtain sufficiently accurate data at high frequencies to show that the increase in conductivity with frequency is of the order predicted by theory. A number of different experimental methods have been employed by Sack,[61] Zahn,[62] Deubner,[63] Wien[64] and Malsch.[65] The method of Wien measures the effect of high frequency on either the conductance or the dielectric constant.

The theory of Debye and Falkenhagen[66] is verified by these experiments for cases of many electrolytes. Magnesium sulfate in water has been selected by Falkenhagen as the best example available. In Fig. (7-7-1), $100\Lambda_{\bar{\omega}}/\Lambda_m^0$ has been plotted against $\sqrt{c^*}$, where c^* is the equivalent concentration and Λ_m^0 is the molecular conductance when $\bar{\omega}$ is zero. According to equation (4-5-20),

$$\Lambda_{\bar{\omega}} = \Lambda_m^0 - \Lambda_{I\bar{\omega}} - \Lambda_{II} \qquad (7\text{-}7\text{-}1)$$

The solid line in the figure represents the plot of $100\Lambda_{I(\bar{\omega}=0)}/\Lambda_m^0$ for the stationary case derived from Onsager's equation. The dotted line is that calculated by the Debye and Falkenhagen theory. The latter is in good agreement with the experimental results of Wien which are given by the circles.

[59] M. Wien, *Ann. Phys.*, [4], **83**, 840 (1927).

[60] H. Sack, *Physik. Z.*, **29**, 627 (1928).

[61] B. Brendel, O. Mittelstaedt, and H. Sack, *Physik. Z.*, **30**, 576 (1929); H. Sack and B. Brendel, *Ibid.*, **31**, 345 (1930); B. Brendel, *Ibid.*, **32**, 327 (1931).

[62] H. Zahn, *Z. Physik.*, **51**, 350 (1928); H. Rieckhoff and H. Zahn, *Ibid.*, **53**, 619 (1929).

[63] A. Deubner, *Physik. Z.*, **30**, 946 (1929); *Ann. Physik.* [5], **5**, 305 (1930); *Physik. Z.*, **33**, 223 (1932).

[64] M. Wien, *Physik. Z.*, **31**, 793 (1930); **32**, 183 (1931); *Ann. Physik.* [5], **11**, 429 (1931).

[65] J. Malsch, *Physik. Z.*, **33**, 19 (1932); *Ann. Physik.* [5], **12**, 865 (1932).

[66] P. Debye and H. Falkenhagen, *Physik. Z.*, **29**, 121, 401 (1928); *Z. Elektrochemie*, **34**, 562 (1928).

In Fig. (7-7-2) the frequency effect on the conductance of a 0.001 N magnesium sulfate solution is illustrated. Here the solid line represents the plot of the percentage dispersion effect against the wave length in meters. The solid line is the calculated effect, and the points represent the experimental results of various investigators. This leaves little doubt of the fundamental validity of the theory.

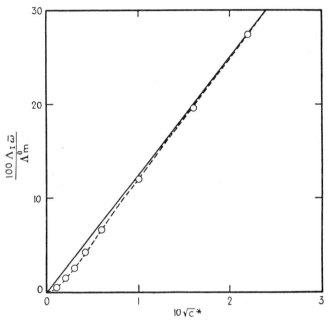

Fig. (7-7-1). Frequency effect upon the conductance of magnesium sulfate solutions at 18°. —— $\dfrac{100\,\Lambda_{\mathrm{I}(0)}}{\Lambda_m^0}$, or $l = \infty$; ---- $\dfrac{100\,\Lambda_{\mathrm{I}}(\bar{\omega})}{\Lambda_m^0}$, theoretical, $l = 10$; $\bigcirc$ experimental, $l = 10$

The theory of Debye and Falkenhagen of the lowering of the dielectric constant is interesting since it goes beyond the Onsager theory of conductance, and predicts a change in dielectric constant with the concentration at zero frequency. Equation (4-5-25) may be reduced to

$$D_{(\bar{\omega}=0)} - D_0 = \frac{1.97 \times 10^6 \, |z_1 z_2| (|z_1| + |z_2|)^{1/2}}{2 D_0^{1/2}\, T^{3/2} (1 + 1/\sqrt{q^*})^2} \, (q^* c^*)^{1/2} \qquad (7\text{-}7\text{-}2)$$

for the special case when $\bar{\omega} = 0$. Equation (4-3-43) defines q^*, and $c^* = \nu_1\,|z_1|\,c = \nu_2\,|z_2|\,c$. For simplicity, this equation may be written,

$$D_{(\bar{\omega}=0)} - D_0 = \mathbb{S}_{(D)}\sqrt{c} \qquad (7\text{-}7\text{-}3)$$

In water at 18°, $\mathfrak{S}_{(D)}$ was found by Falkenhagen to be 3.79, 10.9, 13.8 and 30.3 for potassium, magnesium, and lanthanum chlorides, and magnesium sulfate solutions, respectively.

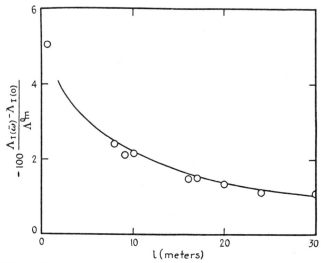

Fig. (7-7-2). Frequency effect upon the conductance of magnesium sulfate solutions at 18°; $c^* = 0.001$; —— theoretical

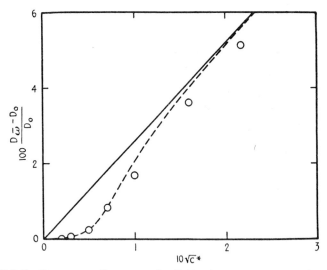

Fig. (7-7-3). Frequency effect upon the dielectric constant of magnesium sulfate solutions at 18°. —— $100(D_{(\bar{\omega}=0)} - D_0)/D_0$; ---- $100(D_{\bar{\omega}} - D_0)/D_0$; theoretical, $l = 10$; $\bigcirc$, experimental, $l = 10$

A good agreement with the theory is again obtained by comparison with measurements of Wien of the dielectric constant in dilute magnesium sulfate solutions. Fig. (7-7-3) contains a plot of $100 (D_{\bar{\omega}} - D_0)/D_0$ against

$\sqrt{c^*}$. The solid line represents the effect at zero frequency, and the dotted line that calculated from Table (5-3-4) at a wave length of 10 meters. The circles represent the values of Wien. Considering the difficulties of measuring dielectric constants in dilute salt solutions, the agreement is satisfactory.

(8) THE EFFECT OF HIGH ELECTRIC FIELDS UPON THE CONDUCTANCE OF ELECTROLYTES

In 1927 Wien[67] announced the important generalization that the conductivities of electrolytic solutions always increase with electrical field strength. He showed that this increase was a function of the concentration, the valence, and the specific nature of the solution. Furthermore, the equivalent conductance of strong electrolytes seems to approach a constant limiting value asymptotically in very high fields. In solutions containing weak electrolytes,[68] it was found that the relative increase in conductance with the field strength was many times greater than for strong electrolytes. Gemant[69] observed a similar effect in solvents of very low dielectric constant $(D \simeq 3)$. Wien correctly interpreted this behavior by suggesting that the field increased the dissociation of the electrolyte.

Since high fields produce considerable heating effects, the ordinary method of conductance measurement must be replaced by impulse methods whereby the field is applied for very short periods of time ($\sim 10^{-5}$ to 10^{-7} sec.). The difficulties of measurement have been largely overcome by Wien and his collaborators, so that accurate results are available. An excellent discussion of the experimental methods can be found in a review by Eckstrom and Schmelzer.[70]

The Wien Effect for Strong Electrolytes

In Fig. (7-8-1) the observed[71] relative increase in the equivalent conductance of various strong electrolytes is plotted against the field strength in kilovolts per cm. These plots refer to solutions of such concentrations that they have a common value of $\Lambda_{(x=0)}$. The relative increase in equivalent conductance is roughly proportional to $(z_+z_-)^2$, and seems to approach a constant value in very high fields.

The effect of concentration and the general character of the phenomenon are illustrated by Fig. (7-8-2), which shows the theoretical behavior predicted by equation (4-6-55) for a hypothetical 2-2 strong electrolyte in water. In low fields the Wien effect is vanishing small, as the curves are horizontal when $X = 0$. As the field strength is increased, the conductance

[67] M. Wien, *Ann. Physik.* [4], **83**, 327 (1927); *Ibid.*, **85**, 795 (1928); *Physik. Z.*, **28**, 834 (1927); *Ibid.*, **29**, 751 (1928).

[68] M. Wien and J. Schiele, *Physik. Z.*, **32**, 545 (1931).

[69] A. Gemant, *Physik. Z.*, **29**, 289 (1928).

[70] H. C. Eckstrom and C. Schmelzer, *Chem. Rev.*, **24**, 367 (1939).

[71] M. Wien, *Ann. Physik.*, **83**, 327 (1927).

increases more and more rapidly, passes through an inflection, and finally approaches a limiting value asymptotically.   This limiting value, $\Lambda_{(x=\infty)}$, is less than Λ^0, the limiting conductance at infinite dilution, because the destruction of the ionic atmosphere by the high field is not accompanied

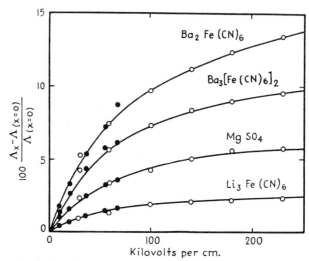

Fig. (7–8–1).   Wien effect on strong electrolytes. $L_{(x=0)} = 4.5 \times 10^{-5}$; ● and ○ refer to results obtained with two different cells

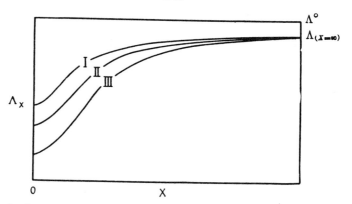

Fig. (7–8–2). General characteristics of Wien effect.   Curves I, II and III represent effects for solutions of three different concentrations of an electrolyte, $C_{III} > C_{II} > C_{I}$

by complete elimination of the electrophoretic effect.   The theoretical equation (5-3-14) for the conductance of symmetrical electrolytes in a field of strength, X, can be written,

$$\Lambda_x = \Lambda^0 - \left[\frac{\epsilon^2 |z_1 z_2| \Lambda^0}{2kDT} g(x) + \frac{F\epsilon(|z_1| + |z_2|) f(x)}{6\pi\eta_0\ \mathbf{c} \times 10^{-8} \sqrt{2}} \right] \kappa \qquad (7\text{-}8\text{-}1)$$

and recalling [Chapter (4), Section (6)] that $g(\infty) = 0$, and $f(\infty) = 1$, we see that the difference between Λ^0 and Λ_x is given by

$$\Lambda^0 - \Lambda_{(X=\infty)} = \frac{F\epsilon(|z_1| + |z_2|)}{6\pi\eta_0 \, c \times 10^{-8} \sqrt{2}} \kappa \qquad (7\text{-}8\text{-}2)$$

In low fields, equation (7-8-1) can be reduced to the quadratic form originally found by Joos and Blumentritt.[72] Thus, for $x^2 < 1$, and neglecting higher powers in x, Eckstrom and Schmelzer[72a] obtained

$$\frac{\Lambda_x - \Lambda_{(X=0)}}{\Lambda_{(X=0)}} = \left[\frac{(0.0172)(z\epsilon)^2 \Lambda^0 \kappa}{\Lambda_{(X=0)} DkT} + \frac{(0.0243)(643.34)|z\epsilon|\kappa}{\Lambda_{(X=0)} 6\sqrt{2}\pi\eta_0}\right] x^2 \qquad (7\text{-}8\text{-}3)$$

in formal agreement with the first term of the Joos and Blumentritt[72] equation* (4-6-2):

$$\frac{\Lambda_x - \Lambda_{(X=0)}}{\Lambda_{(X=0)}} = AX^2(1 - BX^2) \qquad (7\text{-}8\text{-}4)$$

Since the derivation of equation (7-8-3) limits it to binary electrolytes, the measurements of Wien[73] on magnesium sulfate yield the only data on high valence type electrolytes available for a comparison of theory with experiment. Eckstrom and Schmelzer have made the necessary calculations in both the high and the low field regions. The constants employed in the high fields are $c = 3.7 \times 10^{-4}$ and $\Lambda_{(X=0)} = 105.5$; and in the low fields $c = 1.22 \times 10^{-3}$ and $\Lambda_{(X=0)} = 99.0$. Further, $T = 291$, $D = 81$, $\eta_0 = 0.0105$, and $\Lambda^0 = 114$. The required values of $g(x)$ and $f(x)$ calculated by Wilson are given in Tables (5-3-5) and (5-3-6). The comparison is illustrated graphically in Fig. (7-8-3), where the circles represent the experimental data in low fields, and the dots those in high fields. The solid curves, representing the predictions of equations (7-8-1) and (7-8-3), are in remarkably good agreement with experiment below 50 kv./cm.

Falkenhagen, Frölich and Fleischer[74] have found that their theory of the effects of frequency upon conductance in high fields are in qualitative agreement with the data of Michels.[75] Since the experimental results in this field are very few, further investigation will be interesting.

The Wien Effect for Weak Electrolytes, or The Dissociation Field Effect

The Onsager theory of the effect of high fields on the dissociation of weak electrolytes led to the quantitative expression (4-7-29),

$$\frac{K(X)}{K(0)} = 1 + \bar{b} + \frac{\bar{b}^2}{3} + \frac{\bar{b}^3}{18} + \frac{\bar{b}^4}{180} + \cdots \qquad (7\text{-}8\text{-}5)$$

[72] G. Joos and M. Blumentritt, *Physik. Z.*, **28**, 836 (1927); M. Blumentritt, *Ann. Physik.*, **85**, 812 (1928).

[72a] H. C. Eckstrom and C. Schmelzer, *Chem. Rev.*, **24**, 367 (1939).

* The numerical coefficients in their equation correspond to 0.0133 and 0.0973 instead of 0.0172 and 0.0243 which appear in (7-8-3).

[73] M. Wien, *Ann. Physik.*, **85**, 795 (1928); *Physik. Z.*, **29**, 751 (1928).

[74] H. Falkenhagen, F. Frölich and H. Fleischer, *Naturwiss.*, **25**, 446 (1937).

[75] F. Michels, *Ann. Physik.*, **22**, 735 (1935).

where $K(X)$ and $K(0)$ represent the ionization constant with and without external field, respectively. The variable, $\bar{b}$, is given by equation (4-7-28),

$$\bar{b} = 9.695\ V/DT^2 \qquad (7\text{-}8\text{-}6)$$

for 1-1 electrolytes when V is in volts per centimeter. When the degree of ionization is small ($\alpha \ll 1$), then, by equation (4-7-34),

$$\frac{\Lambda_X}{\Lambda_{(X=0)}} = \frac{\alpha}{\alpha_0} = \sqrt{\frac{K(X)}{K(0)}} = 1 + \tfrac{1}{2}\bar{b} + \tfrac{1}{24}\bar{b}^2 + \cdots \qquad (7\text{-}8\text{-}7)$$

These equations have been verified by Onsager[76] with data in media of high and low dielectric constant.

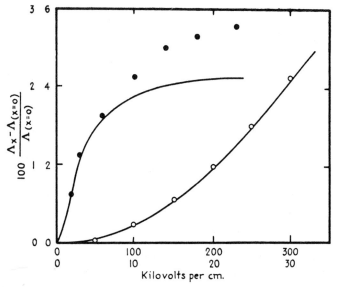

Fig. (7-8-3). Wien effect on magnesium sulfate solutions. —— Theory; ○ Weak fields; ● Strong fields

In Fig. (7-8-4), due to Onsager, the points represent the experimental results of Schiele[77] for acetic acid and chloroacetic acid in water ($D = 78.57$). The lines represent theoretical computations of the relative change in conductance. Here the effect depends largely on the value of α, and is greater the weaker the acid. In fields greater than 50 kilovolts per cm, the agreement is excellent. In lower fields, the lack of agreement is explained by the fact that the ionic atmosphere effect was omitted in the development of the theory which can be expected to be valid only in fields strong enough to destroy the ionic atmospheres. This discrepancy is in the right direction, but a theoretical calculation of this effect would be very difficult.

[76] L. Onsager, *J. Chem. Phys.*, **2**, 599 (1934).

[77] J. Schiele, *Ann. Physik* [5], **13**, 811 (1932).

Onsager first showed that his theory is confirmed in media of low dielectric constant by the data of Gemant[77a] who measured the effects of high fields upon a solution of picric acid in a mixture of 5 per cent ethyl alcohol and 1 per cent mineral oil in benzene ($D = 2.7$).

Mead and Fuoss[78] measured the conductance at 60 cycles of solutions of tetrabutylammonium picrate in diphenyl ether ($D = 3.53$) at 50° in fields ranging from 0 to 20 kv/cm. Measurements were made at a sufficient number of concentrations for the evaluations of the dissociation constants of both $[C^+A^-]^0$, and $[C^+A^-C^+]^+$ by the methods described in Sections (2) and (4). They obtained 2.70×10^{-11} and 1.00×10^{-3} for K and K_3, respectively.

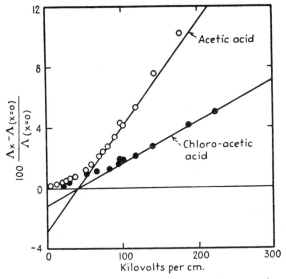

Fig. (7-8-4). Wien effect for acetic and chloroacetic acids; ———, theoretical

The field effects at a very low, and at a higher concentration, are shown in Figs. (7-8-5) and (7-8-6) in which specific conductance is plotted against field. When the solute is present at very low concentrations, the plot is very nearly linear, but as the concentration is increased, the initial part of the curve (Fig. 7-8-6) is concave upward and approaches linearity at higher field strengths. As previously mentioned, this deviation from linearity is due to the presence of ionic atmospheres which are broken up in the higher fields. If the linear parts of the graphs are extrapolated to zero field, the low voltage conductance which the ions would have if the

[77a] A. Gemant, "Electrophysik der Isolierstoffe," pp. 78–80, Springer, Berlin (1930); *Physik. Z.*, **29**, 289 (1928).

[78] D. J. Mead and R. M. Fuoss, *J. Am. Chem. Soc.*, **61**, 2047 (1939); Correction, *Ibid.*, **61**, 3589 (1939).

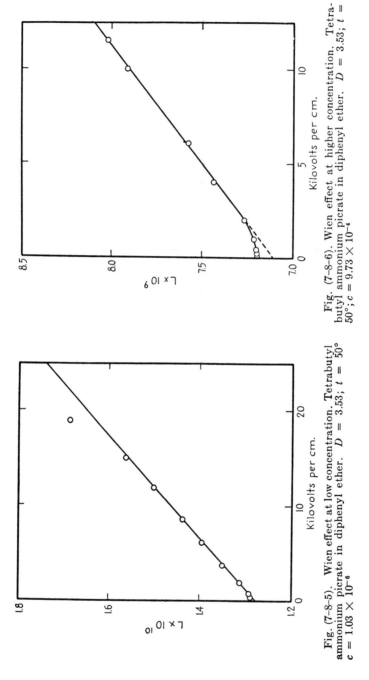

Fig. (7–8–6). Wien effect at higher concentration. Tetra-butyl ammonium picrate in diphenyl ether. $D = 3.53$; $t = 50°$; $c = 9.73 \times 10^{-4}$

Fig. (7–8–5). Wien effect at low concentration. Tetrabutyl ammonium picrate in diphenyl ether. $D = 3.53$; $t = 50°$; $c = 1.03 \times 10^{-6}$

activity coefficients were unity (dashed line) is obtained. The ratio of the conductance obtained from the actual results at zero field to the linearly extrapolated values is a measure of the activity coefficient. Mead and Fuoss computed the activity coefficient in this manner with the result shown in Fig. (7-8-7). The dashed line represents the limiting function, $\log f_{\pm} = -33.8c_i^{1/2}$, and the experimental results are indicated by the circles. The correct order of magnitude is obtained proving that Onsager's interpretation of the curvature in lower fields (Fig. 7-8-6) is correct.

According to equation (7-8-7)

$$\Lambda_X/\Lambda_{(X=0)} = 1 + \tfrac{1}{2}\bar{b} + \cdots = 1 + 0.0132(10^{-3}V) + \cdots \quad (7\text{-}8\text{-}8)$$

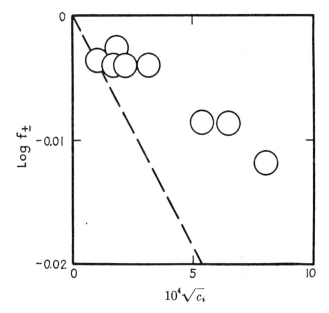

Fig. (7-8-7)
Activity coefficient of tetrabutylammonium picrate in diphenyl ether, estimated from the Wien effect

when $D = 3.53$, and $T = 323$. Mead and Fuoss found that the limiting value of their slopes at zero electrolyte concentration was in exact agreement with theory.

The slopes of the curves of conductance against field were found to decrease with increasing electrolyte concentration. This departure from the theoretical prediction occurs at a concentration where triple ion formation causes the $\log \Lambda$ vs. $\log c$ plot to begin to deviate from linearity. The theory does not include the effects of field on triple ion formation. Several series of measurements, made at 500 to 1500 cycles, showed that the slopes of the conductance-field strength curves decreased considerably with increasing frequency. Mead and Fuoss[79] have investigated this effect more thoroughly.

[79] D. J. Mead and R. M. Fuoss, *J. Am. Chem. Soc.*, **62**, 1720 (1940).

The change in slope with frequency is illustrated in Figure (7-8-8) for a single concentration. The ordinates are the ratios of the high voltage conductivity to the low voltage* conductivity at the same frequency. The abscissae are the field strengths in kilovolts per centimeter. The

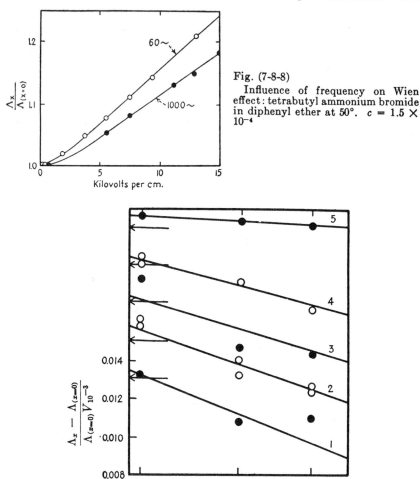

Fig. (7-8-8)
Influence of frequency on Wien effect: tetrabutyl ammonium bromide in diphenyl ether at 50°. $c = 1.5 \times 10^{-4}$

Fig (7-8-9). Influence of frequency and concentration upon Wien effect. Tetrabutyl ammonium bromide in diphenyl ether at 50°. The ordinate scale is shifted vertically (0.02 unit) for each concentration. The numbers on the right-hand margin represent $c \times 10^4$

effect of frequency† is most pronounced at high dilutions, and gradually disappears as the concentration is increased. The influence of concentra-

* A voltage so low that doubling it causes no detectable change in conductivity.

† Note that at low voltages the conductivity becomes independent of frequency, which indicates that polarization is negligible.

tion is observable in Figure (7-8-9) which shows the variation in the slope, $(\Lambda_x/\Lambda_{(x-0)} - 1)/(10^{-3}V)$ with frequency. The theoretical value (0.0132) is indicated, for each concentration, by the horizontal line at the left.

At low frequencies the observed slopes[80] are in excellent agreement with the theoretical, and for the highest concentration this agreement persists at 1000 cycles. This behavior is predictable from consideration of the Langevin time lag [Equation (4-7-36)]. For the most dilute solutions $(c = 10^{-4})$, τ' is about 5×10^{-4} sec, and the field-sensitive ionization reaction is unable completely to follow the field alternating at intervals of the same order (1000 cycles). Consequently, the field effect decreases sharply with increasing frequency. At higher concentrations, the time lag is shorter, and the ionic distribution can more completely adjust itself to the field. When $c = 5 \times 10^{-4}$, $\tau' \simeq 8 \times 10^{-5}$ sec, and the normal low frequency Wien effect is approximately maintained up to 1000 cycles.

(9) MEASUREMENTS OF THE HIGH FIELD CONDUCTANCE OF ELECTROLYTES BY A DIFFERENTIAL PULSE TRANSFORMER BRIDGE

Gledhill and Patterson[81] have designed a bridge by which the conductance of electrolytes can be measured in fields as high as two hundred kilovolts per centimeter with an accuracy of 0.03 %. They employed this means of measurement to obtain the Wien effect for magnesium and zinc sulphates. These measurements have been extended to include the Wien effects for magnesium and zinc sulphates as a function of temperature[82], copper sulphate[83], lanthanum ferricyanide[84], cadmium chloride[85], aqueous solutions of ammonia[86], glycine[87], amino-n-caproic acid[88], and aqueous solutions of carbonic acid[89].

Fig. (7-9-1) contains plots of the experimental relative increases in conductance, $\Delta\lambda/\lambda_{(0)}$, versus field strength for lanthanum ferricyanide at three concentrations (curves A, B, C) and copper, zinc and magnesium sulphates (curves E, F and G, respectively) at 25°. Curve D represents the theoreti-

[80] The slopes in Fig. (7-8-9) have been multiplied by $\frac{3}{4}$ to allow for the harmonic analysis made by the filter and amplifier which were used in the measuring circuit. See D. J. Mead and R. M. Fuoss, *J. Am. Chem. Soc.*, **61**, 3589 (1939).

[81] J. A. Gledhill and A. Patterson, Jr., *Rev. Sci. Instruments*, **20**, 960 (1949); *J. Phys. Chem.* **56**, 999 (1952).

[82] F. E. Bailey, Jr. and A. Patterson, Jr., *J. Am. Chem. Soc.*, **74**, 4426, 4428 (1952).

[83] D. Berg and A. Patterson, Jr., *Ibid.*, **74**, 4704 (1952).

[84] D. Berg and A. Patterson, Jr., *Ibid.*, **75**, 1484 (1953).

[85] F. E. Bailey, Jr. and A. Patterson, Jr., *Ibid.*, **75**, 1471 (1953).

[86] D. Berg and A. Patterson, Jr., *Ibid.*, **75**, 5731 (1953).

[87] D. Berg and A. Patterson, Jr., *Ibid.*, **75**, 1483 (1953).

[88] D. Berg and A. Patterson, Jr., *Ibid.*, **75**, 4834 (1953).

[89] D. Berg and A. Patterson, Jr., *Ibid.*, **75**, 5197 (1953); K. F. Wissbrun, D. M. French and A. Patterson, Jr., *J. Phys. Chem.*, **58**, 693 (1954).

cal calculation according to equation (5-3-15) and Tables (5-3-5) and (5-3-6) for lanthanum ferricyanide, and curve H shows a similar calculation for magnesium sulphate. In accord with the less accurate results shown in Fig. (7-8-3), the observed values are considerably greater than those computed by the theory which is based upon the assumption of complete ionization. This behavior is to be expected if a dissociation field effect upon the ion-pairs of these 2-2 and 3-3 electrolytes occurs. Such a correction to the calculation has been applied by Bailey and Patterson[90] in the

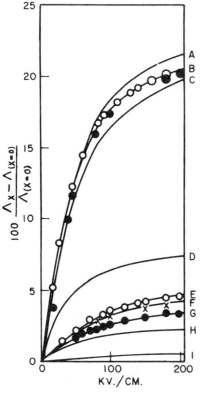

Fig. (7-9-1)
High field conductances of 2-2 and 3-3 electrolytes.
A. Lanthanum ferricyanide, $c = 1.032 \times 10^{-4}$.
B. Lanthanum ferricyanide, $c = 1.025 \times 10^{-4}$; circles represent experimental results, dots represent corrected Onsager-Wilson computation using $K(0) = 3.702 \times 10^{-4}$.
C. Lanthanum ferricyanide, $c = 1.023 \times 10^{-4}$.
D. Lanthanum ferricyanide, theoretical computation uncorrected for incomplete dissociation.
E. Copper sulfate, $c = 1.77 \times 10^{-4}$; curve represents corrected theoretical computation using $K(0) = 0.0043$.
F. Zinc sulfate, $c = 1.64 \times 10^{-4}$; curve represents corrected theoretical computation using $K(0) = 0.0049$.
G. Magnesium sulfate, $c = 1.39 \times 10^{-4}$; curve represents corrected theoretical computation using $K(0) = 0.0063$.
H. Magnesium sulfate; computation by the Onsager-Wilson equations uncorrected for incomplete dissociation.
I. Potassium chloride; theoretical computation by Onsager-Wilson equations.

following manner. Equation (5-3-15) was modified to include the degree of dissociation. Thus

$$\Lambda_X = \left\{ \Lambda^0 - \left(\frac{\alpha^* 3g(x)\Lambda^0}{2 - \sqrt{2}} + \frac{\beta^* f(x)}{\sqrt{2}} \right) \sqrt{\alpha c} \right\} \alpha \qquad (7\text{-}9\text{-}1)$$

The degree of dissociation when the field is zero was calculated by the mass action law including activity coefficients. The ratio of the dissociation constant in the field, $K(X)$, to that in the absence of the field, $K(0)$, was

[90] F. E. Bailey, Jr. and A. Patterson, Jr., *J. Am. Chem. Soc.*, **74**, 4428 (1952).

computed by equation (4-7-29). From these values of $K(X)$, the degree of dissociation in the field was obtained by means of the mass action law in the form

$$K(X) = \frac{c\alpha^2}{1 - \alpha}; \quad \text{or} \quad \alpha = 1 - \frac{c}{K(X)} + 2\left(\frac{c}{K(X)}\right)^2$$

$$- 5\left(\frac{c}{K(X)}\right)^3 + \tag{7-9-2}$$

We note that the activity coefficients are taken to equal unity in the latter calculation which assumption is of course an approximation. However, since the ionic atmospheres are broken up by the high fields, one would expect the activity coefficients to approach unity as the field increases.

By employing the dissociation constants of the 2-2 electrolytes in Table (6-3-2), the calculation by equations (7-9-1) and (7-9-2) yields the result shown by curves E, F and G in Fig. (7-9-1). It is apparent that the theoretical calculation which includes the effect of the field upon the dissociation of these electrolytes is in much closer agreement with experiment than the result represented by curve H, which omits the dissociation field effect. Bailey and Patterson extended their high field conductance measurements of magnesium sulphate over the temperature range, 5 to 55°, and found no significant variation in their results with temperature. Within the limits of experimental error, this result was shown to be in accord with theory. Berg and Patterson[91] were able to compute their high field conductance results for lanthanum ferricyanide by assuming that the dissociation constant of this electrolyte to be 3.7×10^{-4}. The dots near curve B in Fig. (7-9-1) represent these calculated values and are seen to accord closely with the results of experiment. The Onsager-Wilson theory without correction for the dissociation field effect is given by curve D in the figure.

It is to be noted that the above value of the dissociation constant is about twice the value of 1.82×10^{-4} obtained by Davies and James[92] from the usual low field conductance measurements. Berg and Patterson found that the theoretical result obtained by using this latter value of the dissociation constant was considerably greater than their observed result. A discrepancy of this amount is not unexpected because of lack of exact knowledge of the activity coefficients of this 3-3 electrolyte.

Berg and Patterson[93] have employed measurements of high field conductances of aqueous solutions of carbon dioxide and ammonia to determine the ionization constants present in these solutions. This method

[91] D. Berg and A. Patterson, Jr., *J. Am. Chem. Soc.*, **75**, 1484 (1953).

[92] C. W. Davies and J. C. James, *Proc. Roy. Soc.*, **A195**, 116 (1948).

[93] D. Berg and A. Patterson, Jr., *J. Am. Chem. Soc.*, **75**, 5197, 5732 (1953).

is particularly valuable for carbon dioxide solutions for by it one obtains the ionization constant of carbon dioxide in the hydrated form. Because of the slow rate of attainment of equilibrium between the hydrated and unhydrated forms, the high field conductance method which is performed in a period of time of a few microseconds is suitable for the measurement of the equilibrium constant of the reaction

$$H_2CO_3 \rightleftharpoons H^+ + HCO_3^-$$

Electromotive force and low field conductance measurements yield determinations of the equilibrium

$$H_2O + CO_2 \rightleftharpoons H^+ + HCO_3^-$$

and do not permit the evaluation of the ionization constant of hydrated carbon dioxide.

Berg and Patterson have described in detail how, by use of the Onsager theoretical equation (4-7-29), the ionization constant of a weak electrolyte can be computed from the relative increase in conductance as a function of the field[94]. Further discussion of the high field conductance measurements of weak electrolytes will be summarized in Chapter 15, Section (11).

---

[94] Some typographical errors and omissions in the paper by Berg and Patterson have been rectified by K. F. Wissbrun, D. M. French and A. Patterson, Jr., *J. Phys. Chem.*, **58**, 693 (1954).

Chapter (8)

Thermochemical Quantities, Partial Molal Volumes, and the Coefficients of Expansion and Compressibility

(1) Introduction

This chapter marks the beginning of a systematic discussion of the thermodynamics of electrolytic solutions. As indicated by the formal treatment of this subject in Chapter (1), this will require a study of all the partial molal quantities of the components of the solutions. These partial quantities may be divided into two types. (1) Those which may be derived from the determination of the pressure and temperature coefficients of the relative partial molal free energy or activity, such as the relative partial molal heat content, heat capacity, and volume [Equations (1-7-5), (1-7-7) and (1-7-11)]; these can be measured without the knowledge of the partial molal free energy, but it is impossible to derive this latter quantity from them without further information. (2) The partial molal free energy of the solute or the solvent.

Although it may seem somewhat arbitrary, we have found it to be more convenient to reserve the treatment of the free energy for later chapters, and to consider first the quantities which can be derived from it. The most important of these, the relative partial molal heat content, and its integral counterpart, the relative apparent molal heat content (heat of dilution) will be discussed first. Then, the partial molal heat capacity, which may be evaluated in an absolute sense, will be treated in considerable detail. Heats of neutralization will also be included so that all these calorimetric quantities can be discussed in immediate relation with one another. The concluding sections will deal with partial molal volumes, expansibility and compressibility.

(2) The Relative Apparent Molal Heat Content, Heat of Dilution, and Relative Partial Molal Heat Content

Thermochemical measurements have always been a major concern of physical chemists, but it is only by the recent development of multi-junction thermocouples, and successive refinements of the adiabatic thermal balance technique, that the small heat changes occurring in dilute solutions have been satisfactorily measured. For many purposes, it is necessary to know the heat contents of the components of a solution relative to their corresponding values at infinite dilution. The determination of such

331

quantities requires the extrapolation of experimental data in very dilute solutions. By the application of the Debye-Hückel equation, a theoretical limiting slope has been derived [Equation (5-2-14)] which increases the reliability of these extrapolations. Conversely, the verification of the limiting slope has magnified the importance of measurements at extreme dilutions. Before we can give an account of such measurements and their interpretation, it will be necessary to extend the treatment of partial molal quantities, given in Chapter (1), by defining several new quantities.

Dropping the generalized formulation of equation (1-7-2), we obtain for two components, •

$$H = n_1 \bar{H}_1 + n_2 \bar{H}_2 \tag{8-2-1}$$

which gives the total heat content of a solution, composed of n_1 mols of solvent and n_2 mols of solute, in terms of the partial molal heat contents of its components. A similar equation,

$$H = n_1 \bar{H}_1^0 + n_2 \phi_H \tag{8-2-2}$$

gives the heat content in terms of the partial molal heat content of the solvent at infinite dilution, $\bar{H}_1^0$, and the apparent molal heat content of the solute, ϕ_H. Comparison of these equations shows that

$$\phi_H^0 = \bar{H}_2^0 \tag{8-2-3}$$

at infinite dilution. Since the absolute values of heat contents are experimentally undefined, it is necessary to employ the corresponding relative properties, which, unless otherwise noted, will be referred to the infinitely dilute solution. Thus, by equation (1-7-6), the expression

$$H - H^0 = n_1(\bar{H}_1 - \bar{H}_1^0) + n_2(\bar{H}_2 - \bar{H}_2^0) = n_2(\phi_H - \phi_H^0) \tag{8-2-4}$$

follows from equations (8-2-1) and (8-2-2). Upon substituting the definitions, $L \equiv H - H^0$, $\bar{L}_1 \equiv \bar{H}_1 - \bar{H}_1^0$, $\bar{L}_2 \equiv \bar{H}_2 - \bar{H}_2^0$, and $\phi_L \equiv \phi_H - \phi_H^0$, this equation becomes

$$L = n_1 \bar{L}_1 + n_2 \bar{L}_2 = n_2 \phi_L \tag{8-2-5}$$

The relative apparent molal heat content, $\phi_H - \phi_H^0$, is equal to, and of opposite sign to, the heat of dilution, ΔH_D, for the isothermal isobaric addition of an infinite quantity of pure solvent to a solution containing one mol of solute in n_1/n_2 mols of solvent. Consequently,

$$n_2 \Delta H_D = -n_1 \bar{L}_1 - n_2 \bar{L}_2 = -n_2 \phi_L \tag{8-2-6}$$

According to this definition ΔH_D is positive when the dilution process is accompanied by the absorption of heat. This convention regarding sign is contrary to that adopted by Lange and other European writers to whom we shall presently refer.

Differentiating the first and last members of equation (8-2-5) with respect to n_2 at constant temperature, pressure, and n_1, and recalling that $\frac{\partial L}{\partial n_2}$ defines $\bar{L}_2$ under these conditions, we obtain

$$\bar{L}_2 = \phi_L + n_2 \frac{\partial \phi_L}{\partial n_2} \qquad (8\text{-}2\text{-}7)$$

This is the fundamental equation upon which calorimetric determination of $\bar{L}_2$ is based. The quantity ϕ_L cannot be measured directly, but is readily obtained by measuring the heat changes accompanying successive finite dilutions, and by extrapolating from the lowest experimental concentrations to infinite dilution. Thus for the dilution of a binary solution, from a

TABLE (8-2-1). THE HEAT OF DILUTION OF NaCl AT 25°.

c (mols/liter)		$\Delta H_D(c_{\mathrm{In}} \rightarrow c_{\mathrm{Fi}})$ cals/mol	Final concs.		$\Delta H_{(0.1 \rightarrow c)}$	ΔH_D
Initial	Final		c	$\sqrt{c}$		
0.1	0.00308	−61.5	0.05	0.2236	−12.8	−70.2
.1	.00605	−52.9	.025	.1581	−27.8	−55.2
.05	.00154	−54.9	.0125	.1118	−42.9	−40.1
.05	.00302	−48.7	.00605	.0778	−52.9	−30.1
.025	.000770	−45.6	.00305*	.0552	−61.5	−21.5
.025	.001515	−39.9	.00153	.0391	−67.4	−15.6
.0125	.000385	−33.1	.00076	.0276	−73.1	−9.9
.0125	.000754	−30.5	.00039	.0197	−75.7	−7.3
			0	0	(−83.0)	0

* The heat effect from $c = 0.00308$ to $c = 0.00302$ is negligible; hence both of these concentrations are set equal to their mean, and lower concentrations in the table are treated likewise.

solute concentration m (mols per kilogram of solvent) to m', and from m' to m'', etc., the corresponding heat effects may be written,

$$\Delta H_{(m \rightarrow m')} = \phi_H' - \phi_H \qquad (8\text{-}2\text{-}8)$$

$$\Delta H_{(m' \rightarrow m'')} = \phi_H'' - \phi_H' \qquad (8\text{-}2\text{-}9)$$

and so on, for successive dilutions. Linear combination of these equations leads to values of $\phi_H' - \phi_H$, $\phi_H'' - \phi_H$, $\phi_H''' - \phi_H$, etc., which may be extrapolated to infinite dilution in order to evaluate $\phi_H^0 - \phi_H$. Finally, by subtracting $\phi_H' - \phi_H$, $\phi_H'' - \phi_H$, etc., from this extrapolated value, the corresponding heats of dilution at m', m'', etc., are obtained throughout the whole experimental range. An example of such a calculation is given in Table (8-2-1). The data are for sodium chloride in aqueous solutions at 25°, the first three columns in the table being taken from the computations of Robinson.[1]

The extrapolation by which the value, $\Delta H_{(0.1 \rightarrow 0)} = -83.0$, is obtained,

[1] A. L. Robinson, *J. Am. Chem. Soc.*, **54**, 1311 (1932).

is illustrated in Fig. (8-2-1). A more elaborate procedure is outlined in Section (8). The limiting slope follows from equation (5-2-14),

$$\bar{L}_2 = \mathcal{S}_{(H)} \sqrt{c} = \sqrt{d_0}\, \mathcal{S}_{(H)} \sqrt{m} \qquad (8\text{-}2\text{-}10)$$

applied to a 1-1 strong electrolyte at such high dilutions that c may be replaced by $d_0 m$. Combination of this equation with (8-2-7) leads to

$$\phi_L = (2/3)\sqrt{d_0}\, \mathcal{S}_{(H)} \sqrt{m} \qquad (8\text{-}2\text{-}11)$$

or, in simpler terms

$$\Delta H_D = -(2/3)\, \mathcal{S}_{(H)} \sqrt{c} \qquad (8\text{-}2\text{-}12)$$

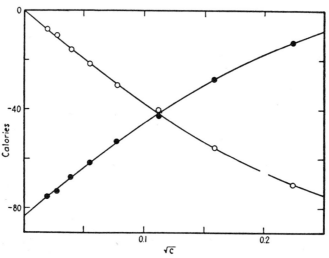

Fig. (8-2-1). Heats of dilution of sodium chloride in water at 25°; ● $\Delta H_{D(0.1\to c)}$ ○ ΔH_D. Compare Fig. (8-8-2).

This is the limiting function which the plot of ΔH_D should approach as c decreases. Accordingly, the limiting law for the experimental quantity $\Delta H_{(0.1 \to c)}$ is the equation,

$$\Delta H_{(0.1\to c)} = \Delta H_{(0.1\to 0)} + (2/3)\, \mathcal{S}_{(H)} \sqrt{c} \qquad (8\text{-}2\text{-}13)$$

which can be obtained by subtracting $\phi_{H(0.1)}$ from both sides of equation (8-2-11) and rearranging terms.

The method of extrapolation just described is that used by Lange.* Although his estimate of an error in extrapolation of ±2 calories per mol is usually justified, the "experimental" limiting slopes which he derived from his most dilute measurements show considerable deviations from the theoretical values. This contradiction to theory has been eliminated by more recent methods of computation. Before discussing these, it will

---

* Table (8-2-1A).

be profitable to describe briefly the remarkable experimental technique employed in these measurements.

The first accurate measurement of heats of dilution at very low concentrations were made by Nernst and Orthmann,[2] but the development of the method to its present high precision is largely due to Lange[3] who applied a number of ingenious refinements to the Joule-Pfaundler twin calorimeter technique. Their most striking innovation is the use of a flat thermocouple as a partition separating the two halves of the calorimeter.[4] A 1000 to 1500 junction iron-constantan thermel, employed in this manner, is capable of measuring small temperature differences with an accuracy of about 2×10^{-7} degree. Since the heat conductivity of such a thermel precludes the measurement of temperature differences greater than 10^{-3} in dilute solutions, the rise in temperature, accompanying the dilution of the solution in one half of the calorimeter, must be largely counterbalanced by electrical heating of the pure solvent in the other half. The function of the thermel is to determine the difference between the heat of dilution and the precisely measured electrical heating. In the ideal case, the thermel would operate as a null instrument. Making use of a Paschen galvanometer and a specially constructed potentiometer, Gucker, Pickard and Planck[5] have been able to decrease the heat conduction by employing a copper-constantan thermel of only 60 junctions. This permits a greater separation of the two halves of the calorimeter system. By delicate regulation of the thermostat, the temperature difference between the calorimeter and its surroundings is reduced to about 10^{-4} degree, and since this is the order of the temperature changes produced by dilutions at the lower concentrations, the measurements may properly be considered adiabatic and isothermal. A good example of the sensitivity of the measurements and the reproducibility of the data is furnished by a comparison of the work of Lange and Streeck,[6] and Lange and Monheim[7] on calcium sulfate at extreme dilutions. A plot of their results is given in Fig. (8-2-2) which shows the two independent series fitted to a common curve. The plot for magnesium sulfate is distinguishable from that for calcium sulfate at concentrations as low as $0.0005M$.

The specificity of heats of dilution at the lowest accessible concentrations is a general phenomenon not confined to any particular valence type

[2] W. Nernst and W. Orthmann, *Sitzber. preuss. Akad. Wiss.*, 51, (1926); *Z. physik. Chem.*, **135**, 199 (1928).

[3] A review of this technique is given by E. Lange and A. L. Robinson [*Chem. Rev.*, **9**, 89 (1931)], and a complete bibliography of earlier developments can be found in the paper by T. W. Richards and F. T. Gucker, Jr. [*J. Am. Chem. Soc.*, **47**, 1876 (1925)].

[4] E. Lange and J. Monheim, *Z. physik. Chem.*, **149 A**, 51 (1930).

[5] F. T. Gucker, Jr., H. G. Pickard and R. W. Planck, *J. Am. Chem. Soc.*, **61**, 459 (1939).

[6] E. Lange and H. Streeck, *Z. physik. Chem.*, **157 A**, 1 (1931).

[7] E. Lange and J. Monheim, *Z. physik. Chem.*, **150 A**, 349 (1930).

electrolytes. Fig. (8-2-3) illustrates the behavior of some typical 1-1 electrolytes studied by Lange.[8] These results raise two important questions. Is the theoretical slope actually approached by all of the curves at infinite dilution, and why is the individuality of the salts at high dilution so much more pronounced for heat data than for activity coefficients? The answer to the latter question is obtained by differentiation of the complete Debye-Hückel equation (3-8-2),

$$\log f_{\pm} = -\frac{\mathbf{S}_{(f)}\sqrt{\Gamma}}{1 + A\sqrt{\Gamma}} + B\Gamma \qquad (8\text{-}2\text{-}14)$$

from which it appears that the temperature coefficients of both A and B make important contributions at high dilutions.* Earlier attempts[9] to

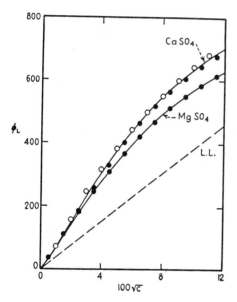

Fig. (8-2-2)
Relative apparent molal heat contents of calcium sulfate and magnesium sulfate in water at 25°. O Lange and Monheim; ● Lange and Streeck

explain the specificity of heat data on the basis of the A parameter alone, either in the above form, or including the extended terms of equations (3-6-4) and (3-6-5), led to some curious anomalies in the magnitudes of the ionic parameter, $\mathring{a}$. It was found[10] that if a series of electrolytes with a common ion is arranged in the order of increasing $\mathring{a}$-values, derived from heats of dilution, the order is usually the reverse of that which would have

[8] Bibliography of experimental papers will be given in connection with tables of ΔH_D and $\bar{L}_2$ in this chapter, and in the appendix.

* See Chapters (11) and (12).

[9] G. B. Bonino and V. Vaglio [*Nuovo Cimento*, **5**, 4 (1928)] attempted to account for the individuality of heats of dilution curves by a semi-empirical treatment.

[10] E. Lange and H. Streeck, *Naturwiss.*, **19**, 359 (1931). E. Lange and A. L. Robinson, *Chem. Rev.*, **9**, 89 (1931).

been obtained if $å$-values, derived from activity coefficient data, had been used. Furthermore, the nature of the common ion plays an important part in this connection, and may even reverse the order in certain series. Thus, $å_{MgSO_4}$ is greater than $å_{CaSO_4}$, while $å_{MgCl_2}$ is less than $å_{CaCl_2}$. These apparent discrepancies in the order and magnitudes of the a-parameters derived from heat data and activity coefficients disappear when the temperature coefficients of both A and B are properly considered. This subject will be elaborated in Section (8).

The reported discrepancies between the "experimental" limiting slopes and those required by theory were largely due to the difficulty of reading off a truly representative limiting slope from plots such as the one illustrated by Fig. (8-2-1). Graphs of this nature seemed to be linear over a considerable range within the accuracy of the data, but since pronounced de-

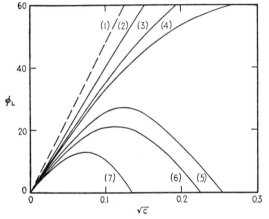

Fig. (8-2-3)

Relative apparent molal heat contents of potassium salts in water at 25°. (1) Theoretical limiting law; (2) KF; (3) KCl; (4) KBr; (5) KClO₃; (6) KNO₃; (7) KClO₄

partures from linearity appear at higher concentrations [Fig. (8-2-3)], the experimental limiting slope was a function of the concentration range employed in its evaluation. From their data on sodium chloride at 10, 15, 20 and 25°, Gulbransen and Robinson[11] concluded that the heat of dilution was linear with $\sqrt{m}$ up to $\sqrt{m} = 0.1$, although they state that "there is some evidence of continuously changing slope to $m = 0$, but the heat effects below $\sqrt{m} = 0.1$ are too small to decide this question definitely." According to their treatment of these results, Gulbransen and Robinson found that the limiting slopes are from 33 per cent (at 10°) to 12 per cent (at 25°) smaller than the theoretical. Later, by an analytical adaptation of the chord-area method,[12] Young and Groenier[13] found that the same data yielded slopes within 5 per cent of the theoretical.

[11] E. A. Gulbransen and A. L. Robinson, *J. Am. Chem. Soc.*, **56**, 2637 (1934).
[12] T. F. Young and O. G. Vogel, *J. Am. Chem. Soc.*, **54**, 3030 (1932).
[13] T. F. Young and W. L. Groenier, *Ibid.*, **58**, 187 (1936).

In the application of this method, the chord

$$P_i = \frac{\Delta H_{(m_1 \to m_2)}}{\sqrt{m_2} - \sqrt{m_1}}$$ (8-2-15)

represents the average value of the slope, S, of the ΔH_D vs. $\sqrt{m}$ curve throughout the concentration range, $\sqrt{m_2} \to \sqrt{m_1}$. The expansion of equation (3-8-5) implies that S may be represented in dilute solutions by

$$S = S^0 + B''\sqrt{m} + C''m$$ (8-2-16)

and preliminary plots show that the inclusion of higher powers of $\sqrt{m}$ are unnecessary below $\sqrt{m} = 0.64$. S^0, B'' and C'' are empirical constants which are to be evaluated from the experimental data after S has been properly expressed in terms of $\overline{P}_i$. If the data are in accord with theory, the value of S^0 so determined should be equal to $(2/3)\sqrt{d_0}\,S_{(H)}$. Repre-

TABLE (8-2-2). CONSTANTS FOR SODIUM CHLORIDE.

	Chord-area method			Theory S^0	Gulbransen and Robinson S^0
	$-B''$	C''	S^0		
25°	1452.2	730.4	476.1	477(472)*	418
20°	1585.7	894.8	451.3	434(442)	370
15°	1650.8	924.5	413.6	393(414)	340
10°	1531.5	591.8	355.7	355(387)	239

* Values in parentheses were calculated from $S_{(H)}$ given in Table (5-2-5). All other values are those reported by Young and Groenier.

senting the value of $(1/2)(\sqrt{m_2} + \sqrt{m_1})$ for the ith chord by x_i, and the value of S at x_i by P_i, then

$$P_i = S^0 + B''x_i + C''x_i^2$$ (8-2-17)

and the difference between P_i and $\overline{P}_i$ is given by

$$P_i - \overline{P}_i = -\frac{d^2S}{d(\sqrt{m})^2}\frac{\delta_i^2}{24} = -\frac{C''\delta_i^2}{12}$$ (8-2-18)

where δ_i is the change in $\sqrt{m}$ corresponding to the ith dilution. Elimination of P_i between equations (8-2-18) and (8-2-17) results in the desired equation,

$$\overline{P}_i = S^0 + B''x_i + C''(x_i^2 + \delta_i^2/12)$$ (8-2-19)

which allows the evaluation of S^0, B'' and C'' by the method of least squares. In carrying out this operation, Young and Groenier used m_2 as a weighting factor.

The constants obtained by this procedure are given in Table (8-2-2), where the values of S^0 are compared with those originally derived from the same data by Gulbransen and Robinson,[14] and the theoretical values,

[14] E. A. Gulbransen and A. L. Robinson, *J. Am. Chem. Soc.*, **56**, 2637 (1934).

$(2/3)\sqrt{d_0}\,\mathfrak{S}_{(H)}$. To show that this excellent agreement between the theoretical slopes and those calculated by the chord-area method is not fortuitous, Young and Seligmann[15] extended the application of this method to all the salts of the alkali metals for which adequate data are available. In these later calculations, m was replaced by c in equations (8-2-15) to (8-2-19). Since this alters the numerical values of B'' and C'', we shall designate these constants B' and C' when the c-scale is used. Their plots of P_i, calculated by equation (8-2-17) from the experimental values of $\overline{P}_i$ and empirical values of C', are reproduced in Figs. (8-2-4) and (8-2-5). The smooth curves represent the equations (8-2-16) for S obtained by the procedure described above. The intercepts, S^0, obtained in this manner are in good agreement with theory, the average of the deviations being only ± 5.6 per cent. The sum of the positive and negative deviations for twenty-one salts is only $+10.2$ per cent. The individual values of the deviation, $\Delta = 100\,[S^0_{(exp)} - S^0_{(theo)}]/S^0_{(theo)}$, are given in the sixth column of Table (8-2-3). In view of this concordance, Young and Seligmann considered the theory completely verified within the probable error of the data and the extrapolation method. They therefore accepted the theoretical value of S^0 in all cases, and re-evaluated the constants B' and C' by the method of least squares. The values obtained in this manner are recorded in Table (8-2-3). The use of these parameters in the expression,

$$\phi_L = -\Delta H_D = S^0\sqrt{c} + (1/2)B'c + (1/3)C'c^{3/2} \qquad (8\text{-}2\text{-}20)$$

leads to accurate values of the relative apparent molal heat content, or heat of dilution, up to $\sqrt{c} = 0.2$ in general, and up to $\sqrt{c} = 0.4$ for sodium and potassium chlorides. For all the salts considered in Table (8-2-3), the limiting slope is given by

$$S^0 = (2/3)\mathfrak{S}_{(H)} \qquad (8\text{-}2\text{-}21)$$

in accordance with theory. With regard to the remaining salts for which data are available at high dilution, Young and Seligmann found that the few measurements on lithium chloride[16] and potassium fluoride[17] are in accord with equation (8-2-21), although the data are insufficient to justify least squaring. They also reported, "An incomplete investigation of salts of the alkaline earth metals of the 2-1 valence type indicates similar agreement, at least at 25°. The extrapolations seem to be of poorer precision, and afford less definite support of the Debye-Hückel theory, but no data point to failure of the theory. Existing data for salts of the 2-2 valence type *if treated by the methods described above*, certainly do not lead to limiting values in agreement with theory."[18] Since there is evidence

[15] T. F. Young and P. Seligmann, *J. Am. Chem. Soc.*, **60**, 2379 (1938).

[16] E. Lange and J. Messner, *Z. Elektrochem.*, **33**, 431 (1927).

[17] E. Lange and A. Eichler, *Z. physik. Chem.*, **129**, 285 (1927).

[18] T. F. Young and P. Seligmann, *J. Am. Chem. Soc.*, **60**, 2379 (1938), footnote 19. *Cf.* T. F. Young, *Science*, **85**, 48 (1937).

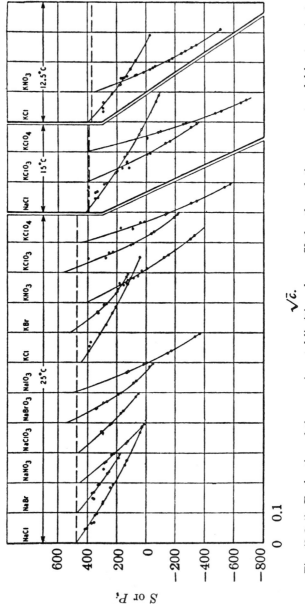

Fig. (8-2-4). Evaluation of the experimental limiting slopes, $S°$, for the relative apparent molal heat contents of 1-1 electrolytes in water at several temperatures

that salts of the 2-2 valence type are incompletely dissociated in solution [Table (6-3-2)], the behavior of these salts does not constitute a serious exception to the general conformity of heat of dilution data with theory.

The evaluation of the relative partial molal heat content, $\bar{L}_2$, from heats of dilution follows from equation (8-2-7) in the form

$$\bar{L}_2 = -\Delta H_D - n_2 \frac{\partial \Delta H_D}{\partial n_2} = -\Delta H_D - \tfrac{1}{2}\sqrt{m}\,\frac{\partial \Delta H_D}{\partial \sqrt{m}} \qquad (8\text{-}2\text{-}22)$$

In dilute solutions, where m is proportional to c, this equation may be combined with (8-2-20) to yield

$$\bar{L}_2 = (3/2)S^0\sqrt{c} + B'c + (5/6)C'c^{3/2} \qquad (8\text{-}2\text{-}23)$$

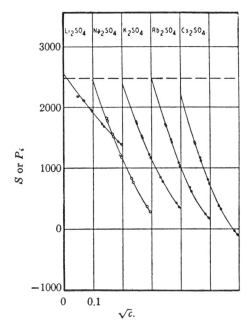

Fig. (8–2–5)

Evaluation of the experimental limiting slopes, S^0, for the relative apparent molal heat contents of 1-2 electrolytes in water at 25°

This expression may be used to calculate $\bar{L}_2$ up to concentrations of the order $0.05N$.

For practical reasons, particularly in relating the results of freezing-point measurements to a standard temperature, it is often necessary to calculate $\bar{L}_1$. The general relation for this quantity is

$$\bar{L}_1 = \frac{n_2^2}{n_1}\frac{\partial \Delta H_D}{\partial n_2} = \frac{M_1 m^{3/2}}{2000}\frac{\partial \Delta H_D}{\partial \sqrt{m}} \qquad (8\text{-}2\text{-}24)$$

and follows from equations (8-2-6) and (8-2-7). In sufficiently dilute solutions md_0 may replace c and this equation becomes

$$\bar{L}_1 = -\frac{M_1}{2000d_0}(S^0 c^{3/2} + B'c^2 + C'c^{5/2}) \qquad (8\text{-}2\text{-}25)$$

when ΔH_D is eliminated by (8-2-20).

In Tables (8-2-1A) and (8-2-2A), we have compiled values of ϕ_L and $\bar{L}_2$ derived from calorimetric data on strong electrolytes at 25°. Additional values, derived from electromotive force measurements, are given in Chapters (11) and (12). Comprehensive tabulations at other temperatures, particularly at 18°, can be found in standard handbooks, and in the monograph of Bichowsky and Rossini.[19]

Since the theoretical limiting slope was disregarded in the original extrapolations of most of the data used in the preparation of Table (8-2-1A),

TABLE (8-2-3). PARAMETERS OF EQUATION (8-2-20).

Salt	t^0	S^{0a}	$-B'$	C'	Δ	Ref.[c]
NaCl[b]	25	472	1,532	1,154	0.9	(1)
NaCl[b]	15	414	1,411	335	0	(1)
NaBr	25	472	1,888	1,770	−0.4	(2)
NaNO₃	25	472	2,961	2,834	−3.8	(3)
NaClO₃	25	472	2,708	2,701	−2.1	(3)
NaBrO₃	25	472	3,562	4,831	14.4	(3)
NaIO₃	25	472	5,635	6,913	6.1	(3)
KCl	25	472	1,893	2,144	−5.9	(4)
KCl	12.5	400	1,569	273	−1.5	(4)
KBr	25	472	2,541	3,902	8.9	(2)
KNO₃	25	472	5,006	6,079	−13.6	(5)
KNO₃	12.5	400	5,753	7,522	−12.5	(5)
KClO₃	25	472	4,527	5,334	20.3	(6)
KClO₃	15	414	4,681	4,602	−1.2	(6)
KClO₄	25	472	7,492	10,510	−6.8	(6)
KClO₄	15	414	8,086	11,011	0.7	(6)
Li₂SO₄	25	2,453	6,022	2,305	−3.9	(7)
Na₂SO₄	25	2,453	15,576	21,482	−0.9	(7)
K₂SO₄	25	2,453	16,022	25,599	−2.2	(7)
Rb₂SO₄	25	2,453	17,896	31,381	2.4	(7)
Cs₂SO₄	25	2,453	22,169	44,570	−9.1	(7)

[a] $S^0 = (2/3)\mathfrak{S}_{(H)}$.

[b] The parameters for NaCl refer to concentrations expressed as molality. The parameters for all of the other salts refer to concentrations expressed in mols per liter of solution.

[c] The references listed below give the origin of the data.
(1) E. A. Gulbransen and A. L. Robinson, *J. Am. Chem. Soc.*, **56**, 2637 (1934).
(2) H. Hammerschmid and A. L. Robinson, *Ibid.*, **54**, 3120 (1932).
(3) E. Lange and A. L. Robinson, *Z. physik. Chem.*, **148A**, 97 (1930).
(4) E. Lange and P. A. Leighton, *Z. Elektrochem.*, **34**, 566 (1928).
(5) E. Lange and J. Monheim, *Z. physik. Chem.*, **150A**, 349 (1930).
(6) M. Andauer and E. Lange, *Ibid.*, **165A**, 89 (1933).
(7) E. Lange and H. Streeck, *Ibid.*, **157A**, 1 (1931).

we have re-extrapolated the results for all salts, to make the curves of ϕ_L against $\sqrt{m}$ approach the origin with the theoretical slope, $(2/3)\sqrt{d_0}\mathfrak{S}_{(H)}$. This slope is greater than most of those previously employed, so it was usually necessary to bend the curves more strongly as the axis was approached. The resulting curves were then displaced vertically until they passed through the origin, and values of ϕ_L and $d\phi_L/d\sqrt{m}$ read off at round concentrations. $\bar{L}_2$ was calculated by equation (8-2-22) from these

[19] F. R. Bichowsky and F. D. Rossini, "Thermochemistry of Chemical Substances," Reinhold Publishing Corp., New York, 1936.

values, and smoothed graphically to eliminate irregularities due to the difficulty of estimating $d\phi_L/d\sqrt{m}$. Part I of Table (8-2-2A) contains these recalculated and smoothed values of $\overline{L}_2$. The results given in Part II of this table were not all recalculated, but were adjusted in every case to fall smoothly upon the extensions of plots of the corresponding values in Part I.

In dilute solutions, our values of ϕ_L and $\overline{L}_2$ agree closely with those calculated by equations (8-2-20) and (8-2-23) and the constants given in Table (8-2-3). In concentrated solutions, our values are usually greater than those[20] derived from the original extrapolations. This difference is recorded as Δ in the last column in Table (8-2-1A), and positive values of Δ represent the upward displacement required to bring the new extrapolation curves to the origin.

It will be seen that Δ does not exceed 7 cal except for lithium chloride, and the 2-2 salts. The large displacement for lithium chloride is due to the absence of data below $0.139M$. Our extrapolation is based upon the close similarity of the curves for lithium chloride and lithium bromide at moderate dilutions, and, although it is much less certain than those for the other 1-1 salts, it is to be preferred to that of Lange and Dürr.[21]

The extrapolation of the heat data for 2-2 salts is very uncertain, because the slopes of the experimental curves at the highest dilutions are two or three times greater than the theoretical. In forcing the extrapolation curves to conform with theory in the limit, it is necessary to introduce so much curvature[22] in the region below the experimental concentration range that the estimation of Δ is a rough approximation at best. Furthermore, the experimental results for these hydrolyzable salts are subject to corrections which may seriously influence the extrapolations.

Doehlemann and Lange[23] pointed out that measureable heat effects

[20] Some of the thermodynamic quantities, tabulated in the various German papers by Lange and his collaborators, can be simply transposed into the conventional American nomenclature used in these chapters by the relations,

$$- \phi_L = \Delta H_D = L_m - L_0 = - V_m$$

$$L_2 = \Lambda_0 - \Lambda_m = V_m + \frac{55.51}{m}\phi_m$$

$$L_1 = -\phi_m; \qquad L_{2(s)} = L_0 = \Lambda_0$$

Here $-L_m$ is the total (integral) heat of solution, and $-\Lambda_m$ is the partial (differential) heat of solution, and $L_{2(s)}$ is the relative partial heat content of the solid solute. For a more complete comparison of the American and German nomenclature and conventions, compare G. N. Lewis and M. Randall, "Thermodynamics", McGraw-Hill Book Co., New York, 1923, with W. Schottky, "Thermodynamik", Julius Springer, Berlin, 1929.

[21] E. Lange and F. Dürr, *Z. physik. Chem.*, **121**, 361 (1926).

[22] Experimental evidence of such curvature is provided by the calculations of A. L. Robinson and W. E. Wallace, *J. Am. Chem. Soc.*, **63**, 1582 (1941).

[23] E. Doehlemann and E. Lange, *Z. physik. Chem.*, **170A**, 391 (1934).

are produced by changes in ionic equilibria which accompany the process of dilution. In dilute neutral salt solutions, the effect of changing the ionization of water is small (<2 cal per mol of salt), but the heat effects produced by changes in the hydrolysis or dissociation of a salt, such as zinc sulfate, are unknown, and may be quite large. For the completely dissociated salt, ammonium chloride, the hydrolysis correction is of the same order as the displacement ($\Delta = 7$) involved in the re-extrapolation. It is probable that the effects of the hydrolysis of potassium and rubidium fluorides are only partially compensated by the displacements recorded for these salts. As an extreme example of the uncertainty which may be involved in the extrapolation of heat data which are influenced by changes

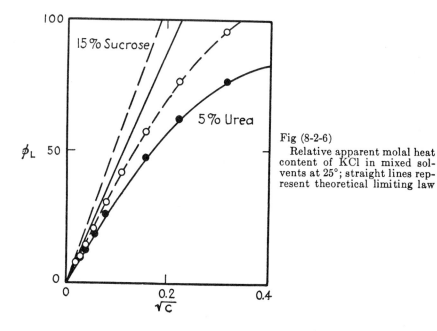

Fig (8-2-6)
Relative apparent molal heat content of KCl in mixed solvents at 25°; straight lines represent theoretical limiting law

in ionic equilibria, it is shown in Chapter (13), Section (13), that a displacement of the order of -450 cal is required to bring the calorimetric values of $\bar{L}_2$ for sulfuric acid into agreement with theory. Values of $\bar{L}_2$ for this acid may be computed at various temperatures from the parameters given in Table (13-13-1A).

Lange and Robinson[24] measured the heat of dilution of potassium chloride in aqueous sugar and urea solutions to see if variation of the dielectric constant by the presence of non-electrolytes would have the effect predicted by theory. Their results are shown in Fig. (8-2-6) along with the appropriate limiting slopes. In calculating the latter, the

[24] E. Lange and A. L. Robinson, *J. Am. Chem. Soc.*, **52,** 4218 (1930).

dielectric constants of Wyman were used for water[25] and the urea solution.[26] Wyman has published no data on sucrose solutions, but we may take Åkerlöf's[27] experience as an indication that Kockel's data are, in this case, consistent with Wyman's other measurements. Kockel's[28] data have, therefore, been used in calculating this theoretical slope for the sugar solution. Since dV/dT is not known with certainty for urea solutions, this term was omitted in evaluating all three slopes. It can be seen from the figure that the observed slopes are all about 25 per cent lower than required by theory, but this simple regularity must be regarded as fortuitous until dD/dT is more accurately known.[29] We note that the experimental limiting slopes estimated in this manner for 1-1 electrolytes in pure water were generally found to be from 10 to 50 per cent lower than the theoretical, and that the success of the chord-area method in clearing up this discrepancy would presumably extend to sucrose and urea solutions as well.

The heats of dilution and relative partial molal heat contents of a few non-electrolytes have been determined in dilute solutions. Because of the lack of charge, the square root term in the expression for the heat of dilution of an electrolyte should vanish for a non-electrolyte. There is no adequate theory by which the numerical magnitude of the coefficients of the linear or higher concentration terms may be predicted. For this reason, there has been but little interest in the calorimetry of solutions of non-electrolytes, and we are fortunate in having data on the sucrose-water system of an accuracy comparable to that attained with solutions of electrolytes. Gucker, Pickard and Planck[30] have measured the heat of dilution of sucrose at high dilutions in water at 20 and 30°, and Naudé[31] has made similar measurements at 18°. Data are available at higher concentrations through the work of Porter and Wood,[32] Pratt,[33] and Vallender and Perman.[34] Gucker[30] determined the chords $\Delta H/\Delta m$ experimentally and treated his results by an adaptation of the method of

[25] J. Wyman, Jr., *Phys. Rev.*, **35**, 623 (1930).

[26] J. Wyman, Jr., *J. Am. Chem. Soc.*, **55**, 4116 (1933).

[27] G. Åkerlöf, *J. Am. Chem. Soc.*, **54**, 4125 (1932).

[28] L. Kockel, *Ann. Physik.*, **77**, 417 (1925).

[29] Above 30 to 35°, urea solutions undergo a slow, irreversible change in conductivity and dielectric constant, and it was only by rapid manipulation that Wyman obtained reproducible temperature coefficients. An earlier value of dD/dT, obtained by L. Kockel [*Ann. Physik.*, **77**, 417 (1925)], actually gave a slope of opposite sign to that shown in Fig. (8-2-6).

[30] F. T. Gucker, Jr., H. G. Pickard and R. W. Planck, *J. Am. Chem. Soc.*, **61**, 459 (1939). See also the study of urea solutions by F. T. Gucker, Jr., and H. G. Pickard, *Ibid.*, **62**, 1464 (1940).

[31] F. M. Naudé, *Z. physik. Chem.*, **135**, 209 (1928).

[32] Results quoted by A. W. Porter, *Trans. Faraday Soc.*, **13**, 123 (1917).

[33] F. R. Pratt, *J. Franklin Inst.*, **185**, 663 (1918).

[34] R. B. Vallender and E. P. Perman, *Trans. Faraday Soc.*, **27**, 124 (1931).

Young and Vogel.[35] He found that, between $m = 0.002$ and $m = 0.2$, $\Delta H/\Delta m$ was constant within the experimental accuracy, the average deviation from the mean corresponding to about 3 micro-degrees. The limiting equations are

$$-\Delta H_D = \phi_L = 128.9m; \quad \text{at } 20° \qquad (8\text{-}2\text{-}26)$$

and

$$-\Delta H_D = \phi_L = 140.2m; \quad \text{at } 30° \qquad (8\text{-}2\text{-}27)$$

When the available data at higher concentrations were consistently treated to yield values of ϕ_L, it was found necessary to add a term in m^2 to the analytical expression for ϕ_L, but the coefficient of the linear term in m was practically the same as that evaluated from the data at high dilutions alone. Terms in m^2 were added to equations (8-2-26) and

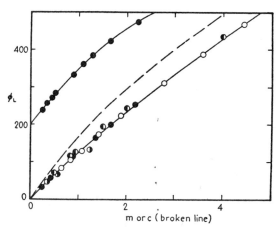

Fig. (8-2-7)
Relative apparent molal heat content of sucrose in aqueous solutions at 20 and 30°. The plot for 30° has been shifted upward 200 cals.

(8-2-27), and the coefficients adjusted to give a satisfactory representation of all the data. The final equations are

$$-\Delta H_D = \phi_L = 128.9m - 6.917m^2; \quad \text{at } 20° \qquad (8\text{-}2\text{-}28)$$

up to $m = 5.9$, and

$$-\Delta H_D = \phi_L = 140.2m - 7.08m^2; \quad \text{at } 30° \qquad (8\text{-}2\text{-}29)$$

up to $m = 2.2$. In Fig. (8-2-7) Gucker, Pickard and Planck[36] plot values calculated by these equations as heavy solid lines which may be compared with the experimental results. The broken line represents the results at 20° plotted against c instead of m. This change in the concentration scale has little effect upon the curvature in concentrated solutions.

[35] T. F. Young and O. G. Vogel, *J. Am. Chem. Soc.*, **54**, 3030 (1932).
[36] F. T. Gucker, Jr., H. G. Pickard and R. W. Planck, *J. Am. Chem. Soc.*, **61**, 459 (1939).

(3) Heats of Neutralization and Heats of Ionization

In considering the heats of neutralization of various acids and bases, we shall deal with both strong and weak electrolytes. The latter are discussed in Chapter (15), Section (6). Our chief concern will be with the determination of the limiting values approached by these quantities at infinite dilution. In the case of heats of neutralization of strong acids by strong bases, this limiting value is the heat of formation of water from its ions, or the negative of the heat of ionization of water, as determined from the temperature coefficient of its ionization constant. We shall now show how calorimetric data are employed to evaluate the heat of ionization of water, and record the best values so obtained for comparison with those derived from electromotive force measurements of the ionization constant.

The reaction between a strong acid and a strong base at finite and equal concentrations is given by

$$HB \cdot xH_2O + MOH \cdot xH_2O = MB \cdot (2x + 1)H_2O \qquad (8\text{-}3\text{-}1)$$

where $x = 55.5/m$. This reaction represents the formation of one mol of water from its ions at the initial concentration, $m = 55.5/x$, and also the dilution of one mol each of M^+ and B^- ions from m to $m' = 55.5/(2x + 1)$. The increase in heat content for the process is

$$\Delta H_n = \phi'_{H(s)} + \bar{H}^0_{H_2O} - \phi_{H(a)} - \phi_{H(b)} \qquad (8\text{-}3\text{-}2)$$

The subscripts refer to salt, water, acid and base, respectively, and the prime indicates that the salt concentration is m'. If we rewrite this equation for infinite dilution, and subtract from equation (8-3-2), we obtain

$$\Delta H_n = \Delta H^0_n - \Delta H'_{D(s)} + \Delta H_{D(a)} + \Delta H_{D(b)} \qquad (8\text{-}3\text{-}3)$$

Since the hydrogen and hydroxyl ions are uninfluenced by the ions of the salt at infinite dilution, we may write,

$$-\Delta H^0_n \equiv \Delta H^0_i \qquad (8\text{-}3\text{-}4)$$

where ΔH^0_i is the heat of ionization of water. This quantity is readily obtained from a single heat of neutralization if the corresponding heats of dilution are known. Richards and Hall[37] found that $\Delta H_n = -13,924$ for the combination of $HCl \cdot 100H_2O$ with $NaOH \cdot 100H_2O$ at 20°. Using heats of dilution which they considered most reliable, equation (8-3-3) becomes $-13,924 = -\Delta H^0_i + 15 - 266 - 20$, or $\Delta H^0_i = 13,653$. Rossini[38] has made a careful recalculation of fifty-two heats of neutralization obtained by Richards and Rowe,[39] and seven obtained by Gillespie, Lam-

[37] T. W. Richards and L. P. Hall, *J. Am. Chem. Soc.*, **51**, 731 (1929).

[38] F. D. Rossini, *Bur. Standards J. Research*, **6**, 847 (1931).

[39] T. W. Richards and A. W. Rowe, *J. Am. Chem. Soc.*, **44**, 684 (1922).

bert, and Gibson.[40] By combining these with appropriate values of ΔH_D and $\bar{C}_{p_2}$, which he obtained from a critical examination of all of the available data,[41] he derived a "best" value of 13,721 for ΔH_i^0 at 18°. The average individual deviation from this "best" value is less than 20 cals. At 20°, ΔH_i^0 becomes 13,606, according to Rossini.

The consistency of these results, derived from a large number of experiments with different combinations of reagents, is a strong indication of the essential accuracy of their mean. There is, however, an element of uncertainty introduced into the calculations by the use of individual heats of dilution, each of which involves extrapolation to infinite dilution. The data upon which we base our estimates of ΔH_D for acids and bases are either confined to concentrations above $0.1M$, or are too erratic at high dilutions to allow reliable extrapolation, except in a few isolated cases.

Sulfuric acid has been studied calorimetrically at high dilution by Lange, Monheim, and Robinson[42] at 25°, and their results have been closely checked by the electromotive force measurements of Harned and Hamer.[43] Hydrochloric acid[44] and sodium hydroxide[45] have been studied electrometrically over a wide range of temperatures.

ΔH_i^0 can be calculated from the same neutralization data of Richards and Rowe by a method which employs only directly measurable (intermediate) heats of dilution, and a single extrapolation of ΔH_n to infinite dilution. If we substitute the limiting law [Equation (8-2-12)] for the heats of dilution in equation (8-3-3), and remember that $m' = 0.5\ m$ in dilute solution, we obtain

$$\Delta H_n = -\Delta H_i^0 - (2 - \sqrt{0.5})\,[(2/3)\,\sqrt{d_0}\,\mathfrak{S}_{(H)}]\,\sqrt{m} \qquad (8\text{-}3\text{-}5)$$

Thus, if we have a series of observed (or calculated) values of ΔH_n at various concentrations, the plot of ΔH_n against $\sqrt{m}$ should be a straight line at extreme dilutions, and its intercept is $-\Delta H_i^0$. The slope of this line may be reduced, and the curvature somewhat modified by introducing the observed intermediate heat of dilution of the salt from m to m'. Lambert and Gillespie[46] calculated $\Delta H_n - \Delta H_{D(s)(m \to m')}$ at the five concentrations investigated, and plotted this function against $\sqrt{m}$ as illustrated in Fig. (8-3-1). Their plots are moderately curved, and converge toward a common tangent for which the equation is

$$\Delta H_n^* \equiv [\Delta H_n - \Delta H_{D(s)(m \to m')}]$$
$$= -\Delta H_i^0 - [(2/3)\,\sqrt{d_0}\,\mathfrak{S}_{(H)}]\,\sqrt{m} \qquad (8\text{-}3\text{-}6)$$

[40] L. J. Gillespie, R. H. Lambert, and J. A. Gibson, Jr., *J. Am. Chem. Soc.*, **52**, 3806 (1930).

[41] F. D. Rossini, *Bur. Standards J. Research*, **6**, 791 (1931); *Ibid.*, **7**, 47 (1931).

[42] E. Lange, J. Monheim, and A. L. Robinson, *J. Am. Chem. Soc.*, **55**, 4733 (1933).

[43] H. S. Harned and W. J. Hamer, *J. Am. Chem. Soc.*, **57**, 27 (1935).

[44] H. S. Harned and R. W. Ehlers, *J. Am. Chem. Soc.*, **55**, 2179 (1933).

[45] H. S. Harned and J. C. Hecker, *J. Am. Chem. Soc.*, **55**, 4838 (1933).

[46] R. H. Lambert and L. J. Gillespie, *J. Am. Chem. Soc.*, **53**, 2632 (1931).

We have introduced ΔH_n^* to represent the bracketed terms for which Lambert and Gillespie have coined the expression "heat of neutralization at constant concentration." From the intercept in Fig. (8-3-1), they obtain the value $\Delta H_i^0 = 13,650$ at $20°$, which is 44 cal. above the value obtained from the same data by the use of extrapolated heats of dilution, and 42 cal. below that derived from electromotive force measurements in Chapter (15), Section (3). As we might expect from the behavior of heats of dilution, the individuality of the curves persists well below $0.1M$.

Although the heat of ionization of pure water is equal to $-\Delta H_n^*$ at infinite dilution, $-\Delta H_n^*$ has no clear-cut physical significance at finite concentrations because, in writing $\Delta H_{D(s)(m \to m')}$ for $\phi'_{H(B)} + \phi'_{H(M)} - \phi_{H(B)} - \phi_{H(M)}$, it is tacitly assumed that $\phi_{H(MB)}$, in the neutral salt solution, is equal to the sum of the terms $\phi_{H(M)}$ and $\phi_{H(B)}$, in the basic and acid solution, respectively. A similar assumption is also made regarding

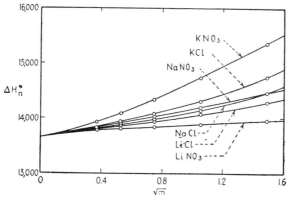

Fig. (8-3-1). Extrapolation of heats of neutralization at constant concentration to obtain the heat of ionization of water at $20°$; the salt produced by neutralization is indicated on each curve

$\phi_{H(H)}$ and $\phi_{H(OH)}$. We have no means of verifying this assumption because individual ionic heat contents are not thermodynamically defined.

(4) The Partial Molal Heat Capacity at Constant Pressure

The fundamental equations relating the total heat capacity, C_p, of a binary solution of the partial molal heat capacities, $\bar{C}_{p_1}$ and $\bar{C}_{p_2}$, of both components, or to the molal heat capacity, $\bar{C}_{p_1}^0$, of the pure solvent, and the apparent molal heat capacity, ϕ_{c_p}, of the solute, are analogous to those already discussed in section (2), and can be derived from them by partial differentiation with respect to temperature at constant pressure. Thus, referring to equations (8-2-1) and (8-2-2), the heat capacity of the solution is given by

$$C_p = n_1 \bar{C}_{p_1} + n_2 \bar{C}_{p_2} \tag{8-4-1}$$

or

$$C_p = n_1 \bar{C}_{p_1}^0 + n_2 \phi_{c_p} \tag{8-4-2}$$

and it is clear that

$$\phi_{c_p}^0 = \bar{C}_{p_2}^0 \tag{8-4-3}$$

at infinite dilution. The corresponding relative quantities are connected by the equation,

$$C_p - C_p^0 = n_1(\bar{C}_{p_1} - \bar{C}_{p_1}^0) + n_2(\bar{C}_{p_2} - \bar{C}_{p_2}^0) = n_2(\phi_{c_p} - \phi_{c_p}^0) \tag{8-4-4}$$

obtained by combinations of equations (8-4-1) and (8-4-2), or by differentiation of equation (8-2-4). Although the absolute values of C_p, $\bar{C}_{p_1}$, and $\bar{C}_{p_2}$ may be determined from available specific heat data, it is only the relative values which can be obtained from the temperature variation of activities. For these quantities, we shall employ the symbols given by the definitions $J \equiv C_p - C_p^0$, $\bar{J}_1 \equiv \bar{C}_{p_1} - \bar{C}_{p_1}^0$, $\bar{J}_2 \equiv \bar{C}_{p_2} - \bar{C}_{p_2}^0$ and $\phi_J \equiv \phi_{c_p} - \phi_{c_p}^0$, and rewrite equation (8-4-4) as

$$J = n_1\bar{J}_1 + n_2\bar{J}_2 = n_2\phi_J \tag{8-4-5}$$

J, $\bar{J}_1$ and $\bar{J}_2$ are the partial derivatives, $(\partial L/\partial T)_P$, $(\partial \bar{L}_1/\partial T)_P$ and $(\partial \bar{L}_2/\partial T)_P$, of the corresponding relative heat contents [Equation (1-7-7)]. The determination of these quantities from relative molal heat contents is therefore too simple to need elaboration, but the determination of absolute values of $\bar{C}_{p_1}$, $\bar{C}_{p_2}$, and ϕ_{c_p} requires discussion.

According to equation (8-4-2), the apparent molal heat capacity of the solute is given by

$$\phi_{c_p} = \frac{(1000 + mM_2)c_p - 1000\,c_p^0}{m} \tag{8-4-6}$$

if m is the molality of the solute of molecular weight, M_2, and c_p and c_p^0 are the specific heats of the solution and pure solvent respectively.

The calculation of $\bar{C}_{p_1}$ and $\bar{C}_{p_2}$ from ϕ_{c_p} is so similar to that described in section (2) that we need only record the fundamental equations

$$\bar{C}_{p_2} = \phi_{c_p} + n_2\frac{\partial\phi_{c_p}}{\partial n_2} = \phi_{c_p} + m\frac{\partial\phi_{c_p}}{\partial m} \tag{8-4-7}$$

or

$$\bar{C}_{p_2} = \phi_{c_p} + \frac{\sqrt{m}}{2}\frac{\partial\phi_{c_p}}{\partial\sqrt{m}} \tag{8-4-8}$$

and

$$\bar{J}_1 = -\frac{n_2^2}{n_1}\frac{\partial\phi_{c_p}}{\partial n_2} = -\frac{m^2}{1000/M_1}\frac{\partial\phi_{c_p}}{\partial m} \tag{8-4-9}$$

or

$$\bar{J}_1 = -\frac{m\sqrt{m}}{2000/M_1}\frac{\partial\phi_{c_p}}{\partial\sqrt{m}} \tag{8-4-10}$$

Since ϕ_{c_p}, as well as other apparent molal quantities, is often expressed in terms of c rather than m, the equations[47]

$$\bar{C}_{p_2} = \phi_{c_p} + \left[\frac{1000 - c\phi_V}{2000 + c^{3/2}\,\partial\phi_V/\partial\sqrt{c}}\right]c^{1/2}\frac{\partial\phi_{c_p}}{\partial\sqrt{c}} \tag{8-4-11}$$

[47] F. T. Gucker, Jr., *J. Phys. Chem.*, **38**, 312 (1934); F. T. Gucker, Jr., F. D. Ayres and T. R. Rubin, *J. Am. Chem. Soc.*, **58**, 2118 (1936).

and

$$\bar{C}_{p_1} = \bar{C}^0_{p_1} - \frac{M_1}{d_0}\left[\frac{c}{2000 + c^{3/2}\,\partial\phi_v/\partial\sqrt{c}}\right]c^{1/2}\frac{\partial\phi_{c_p}}{\partial\sqrt{c}} \qquad (8\text{-}4\text{-}12)$$

are found to be convenient. These equations may be adapted for the estimation of $\bar{L}_2$, and other partial molal quantities. The differential coefficients are, for the most part, determined graphically from plots of ϕ_{c_p} against m for non-electrolytes, or against $\sqrt{m}$ for electrolytes. In the latter case, the limiting slopes of the plots are given by theory according to equation (5-2-15), which may be written

$$\bar{J}_2 = \mathbb{S}_{(c_p)}\sqrt{c} = \mathbb{S}_{(c_p)}\sqrt{d_0 m} \qquad (8\text{-}4\text{-}13)$$

for (1-1) electrolytes. Combination of this equation with equations (8-4-8) and (8-4-3) yields

$$\phi_J = 2/3\ \mathbb{S}_{(c_p)}\sqrt{d_0 m} = 2/3\ \mathbb{S}_{(c_p)}\sqrt{c} \qquad (8\text{-}4\text{-}14)$$

upon integration and subsequent rearrangement.

The accurate determination of specific heats of solutions utilizes the twin calorimeter method of Joule[48] and Pfaundler,[49] greatly improved by later investigators.* This method is essentially a thermal balance. Two practically identical calorimeters, equipped with similar electrical heating elements, are submerged in a thermostat. One calorimeter contains water, and the other contains the solution under investigation. The relative weights of water and solution are adjusted so that the passage of a current through the heating elements, connected in series, produces the same rise in temperature in the two calorimeters. At the same time, the temperature of the thermostat is carefully increased in such a way that heat transfer through the calorimeter walls is practically eliminated, making the process adiabatic.

The calculation of c_p for a solution from such an experiment requires very accurate values of the ratio of the resistances of the heating elements, and of the water equivalent of each calorimeter system. The resistance ratio can be determined with high precision,[50] but completely satisfactory values for the water equivalents of the calorimeter systems are not readily obtainable. This difficulty can be eliminated by always using the same amount of water in one calorimeter, designated the tare, and determining

[48] J. P. Joule, *Mem. Manchester Lit. Phil. Soc.*, **2**, 559 (1845).

[49] L. Pfaundler, *Sitzsb. Akad. Wiss. Wien.*, **59**, 2145 (1869).

* A bibliography of over fifty references in this connection may be found in the paper by Richards and Gucker [*J. Am. Chem. Soc.*, **47**, 1876 (1925)], and a number of more recent papers will be referred to later in this section.

[50] F. T. Gucker, Jr., F. D. Ayres and T. R. Rubin [*J. Am. Chem. Soc.*, **58**, 2118 (1936)] employed variable heating elements whose resistance ratio could be accurately measured *during the course of* the experiments. This innovation has important technical advantages in the adjustment of the system to produce equal increases in temperature in the two calorimeters.

successively the weights of water and of solution which will produce a temperature rise in the other (working) calorimeter equal to that produced in the tare. If the absolute magnitude of the specific heat is to be determined with high precision, it is necessary to employ air-free water.[51] The complete numerical treatment of the experimental data, including the several small correction terms is considered in detail by Randall and Rossini.[52]

Although the twin calorimeter technique is capable of yielding specific heats with an accuracy of 0.01 per cent, or better, the values of ϕ_{c_p} and $\bar{C}_{p_2}$ which may be derived from these data are far from satisfactory at high dilutions. The unavoidable magnification of the experimental error which results from the use of equation (8-4-6) can be readily seen by differentiating this equation, and rearranging it in the forms

$$\delta\phi_{c_p} = \left[\frac{1000}{m}(c_p^0 - c_p)\right]\frac{\delta m}{m} \tag{8-4-15}$$

and

$$\delta\phi_{c_p} = \left[\frac{1000}{m}c_p^0 + \phi_{c_p}\right]\frac{\delta c_p}{c_p} \tag{8-4-16}$$

which show that ϕ_{c_p} is much more sensitive to errors in c_p than in m. Gucker and Schminke[53] point out that the term, $\frac{1000}{m}(c_p^0 - c_p)$, is nearly constant over a wide range in aqueous solutions, and is approximately equal to 50. An error of 0.1 per cent in m would therefore amount to only 0.05 calorie per degree in ϕ_{c_p}. On the other hand, the factor corresponding to the bracketed terms in equation (8-4-16) is of the order $1000/m$, which requires that an error of only 0.01 per cent in c_p would cause an uncertainty of 10 calories per degree in ϕ_{c_p}, when $m = 0.01$. Because of this magnification of the experimental errors, it is practically useless to carry out heat capacity measurements as low as $0.01M$ by present methods.

One practical solution of this difficulty is the combination of $\bar{C}_{p_2}$ with the corresponding values of $\bar{J}_2$, derived from the temperature coefficient of $\bar{L}_2$, or the second temperature derivative of activity coefficients. Since

$$\bar{C}_{p_2}^0 = \bar{C}_{p_2} - \bar{J}_2 \tag{8-4-17}$$

must be independent of m, we may confine the calculations to the concentration range in which both sets of data are most trustworthy. Table (8-4-1) contains the results of this calculation for the several electrolytes which yield essentially constant values of $\bar{C}_{p_2}^0$. It appears probable from inspection of the table that $\bar{C}_{p_2}^0$ is known to better than 0.5 cal. for the

[51] R. Jessel, *Proc. Phys. Soc. London*, **46**, 759 (1934).
[52] M. Randall and F. D. Rossini, *J. Am. Chem. Soc.*, **51**, 323 (1929).
[53] F. T. Gucker, Jr., and K. H. Schminke, *J. Am. Chem. Soc.*, **54**, 1358 (1932).

first three electrolytes, and to about 1 cal. for sodium hydroxide. It may be remarked that several theoretical attempts[54] to estimate $\bar{C}^0_{p_2}$ for electrolytes, on the basis of the electrostriction[55] of the solvent, have predicted the order of magnitude of this quantity without allowing for the specific differences observed experimentally.

It is a convenient experimental fact that $\bar{C}_{p_2}$, and many other partial molal properties of strong electrolytes vary linearly with $c^{1/2}$ or $m^{1/2}$ over a concentration range (0.2 to $3M$) far beyond the dilutions at which the limiting laws might be expected to hold. This behavior permits the expression of the experimental results in terms of the parameters of the equation,

$$\bar{C}_{p_2} = \bar{C}^0_{p_2} + S_{c_p} m^{1/2} \tag{8-4-18}$$

TABLE (8-4-1).   VALUES OF $\bar{C}^0_{p_2}$ CALCULATED BY EQUATION (8-4-17) AT 25°.

m	HCl[a,b]	KCl[c,d]	KOH[e,b]	NaOH[f,g]
0.2	−29.50	−28.30	. . . . . .	. . . . . .
.25	. . . . . .	. . . . . .	−30.3	−28.08
.5	−29.15	−28.75	−30.2	−27.74
1.0	−29.25	−29.25	−30.62	−28.37
1.5	−29.17	−28.78	−30.85	−27.52
2.0	−29.75	−30.05	−31.36	−26.24
2.5	. . . . . .	−28.45	. . . . . .	−26.30
ave.	−29.4	−28.8	−30.7	−27.4

[a] H. S. Harned and R. W. Ehlers, *J. Am. Chem. Soc.*, **55**, 2179 (1933).
[b] F. T. Gucker Jr. and K. H. Schminke, *Ibid.*, **54**, 1358 (1932).
[c] H. S. Harned and M. A. Cook, *Ibid.*, **59**, 1290 (1937).
[d] M. Randall and F. D. Rossini, *Ibid.*, **51**, 323 (1929).
[e] H. S. Harned and M. A. Cook, *Ibid.*, **59**, 496 (1937).
[f] H. S. Harned and J. C. Hecker, *Ibid.*, **55**, 4838 (1933).
[g] F. T. Gucker Jr. and K. H. Schminke, *Ibid.*, **55**, 1013 (1933).

although the experimental slopes, S_{c_p}, may differ considerably from the theoretical, $\mathfrak{S}_{(c_p)}$. This equation will represent the observed values of $\bar{C}_{p_2}$ for the electrolytes included in Table (8-4-2) within the experimental error throughout the concentration range $m = 0.2$ to $m = 3$. Since the parameters are not evaluated from data at high dilutions, the intercept and slope may differ numerically from the correct value of the property, $\bar{C}^0_{p_2}$, and the limiting slope given by theory. For the intercept, this difference is usually small, as is indicated by comparison of the values of $\bar{C}^0_{p_2}$ in Table (8-4-1) with those in Table (8-4-2). On the other hand, the experimental slopes, S_{c_p}, for these 1-1 electrolytes differ widely among themselves and from the theoretical limiting slope, $\mathfrak{S}_{(c_p)}$, which is about 13.36 at 25°. These differences are not in contradiction with theory, as determinations of $\bar{J}_2$ from $\partial \bar{L}_2/\partial T$ and $\partial^2 \ln \gamma_\pm/\partial T^2$ show that S_{c_p} varies

[54] F. Zwicky, *Physik Z.*, **26**, 664 (1925); *Ibid.*, **27**, 271 (1926); *Proc. Nat. Acad. Sci.*, **12**, 86 (1926); H. M. Evjen and F. Zwicky, *Phys. Rev.*, **33**, 860 (1929).
[55] T. J. Webb, *J. Am. Chem. Soc.*, **48**, 2589 (1926).

considerably with concentration below $c = 0.2$, and approaches the predicted limiting value at high dilutions. This is clearly demonstrated by the calculations of Young and Machin,[56] and is illustrated in Figs. (11-8-1) and (12-2-2).

Only a few precise calorimetric studies of the heat capacities of electrolytes of higher valence types have been reported, and the results of

TABLE (8-4-2). PARAMETERS OF THE INTERPOLATION EQUATION $\bar{C}_{p_2} = \bar{C}_{p_2}^0 + S_{C_p}\sqrt{m}$ VALID AT 25° FROM 0.2 TO 3 M.

Electrolyte[*]	S_{C_p}	$\bar{C}_{p_2}^0$
HCl[a]	7.50	−29.20
LiCl[a]	7.88	−15.63
NaCl[b]	21.6	−23.8
KCl[b]	16.8	−29.0
NaBr[b]	20.4	−24.3
KBr[b]	16.2	−29.5
NaI[b]	24.9	−25.0
KI[b]	20.4	−30.2
NaNO$_3$[b]	30.0	−12.6
KNO$_3$[b]	28.65	−17.8
NH$_4$NO$_3$[c]	12.1	−2.5
LiOH[d]	18.80	−19.98
NaOH[d]	26.24	−26.59
KOH[a]	19.88	−32.10

[a] F. T. Gucker Jr. and K. H. Schminke, *J. Am. Chem. Soc.*, **54**, 1358 (1932).
[b] F. D. Rossini, *Bur. Standards J. Research*, **7**, 47 (1931) recalculated from M. Randall and F. D. Rossini, *J. Am. Chem. Soc.*, **51**, 323 (1929). See also C. M. White, *J. Phys. Chem.*, **44**, 494 (1940), and C. B. Hess, *Ibid.*, **45**, 755 (1941).
[c] F. T. Gucker Jr., F. D. Ayres and T. R. Rubin, *J. Am. Chem. Soc.*, **58**, 2118 (1936).
[d] F. T. Gucker Jr. and K. H. Schminke, *Ibid.*, **55**, 1013 (1933).
[*] A similar table for these and several additional electrolytes at 18°, 21.5°, and 25° is given in Reference (b).

TABLE (8-4-3). $\bar{C}_{p_2}$ FOR HIGH VALENCE TYPE ELECTROLYTES AT 25°.

m	Na$_2$SO$_4$[a]	K$_2$SO$_4$[a]	BaCl$_2$[b]
0	(−50)	(−60.6)	(−74.36)
0.1	−22.6	−41.0	−57.5
.2	−8.5	−31.8	−50.5
.35	5.8	−21.4	−42.9
.5	15.8	−13.4	−36.7
1.0	39.0	......	−21.1
1.5	55.0	......	......
Slope	76	62	54

[a] M. Randall and F. D. Rossini, *J. Am. Chem. Soc.*, **51**, 323 (1929).
[b] C. M. White, *Ibid.*, **58**, 1615 (1936).

these investigations do not, in general, follow the simple linear relationship of equation (8-4-18). The smoothed values of $\bar{C}_{p_2}$ have been recorded in Table (8-4-3), along with the intercepts and apparent limiting slopes, obtained from the experimental data at high dilutions. The results for barium chloride were obtained from two different sources, and were considered adequately represented by equation (8-4-18).

[56] T. F. Young and J. S. Machin, *J. Am. Chem. Soc.*, **58**, 2254 (1936).

The pronounced variation observed in the values of S_{c_p}, [Table (8-4-2)], in a series of electrolytes of the same valence type, is illustrated graphically in Fig. (8-4-1) taken from a paper by Gucker and Rubin.[57] Those authors estimated the difference between the isopiestic and isochoric apparent molal heat capacities by means of the equation

$$\phi_{c_p} - \phi_{c_v} = \frac{\alpha^2}{\beta} v T - \frac{\alpha_0^2}{\beta_0} v_0 T \qquad (8\text{-}4\text{-}19)$$

in which α and β represent the coefficients of expansibility and compressibility respectively. The subscript zero refers to pure solvent. Their results are summarized in Table (8-4-4). The limiting values were derived from the equation

$$\phi_{c_p}^0 - \phi_{c_v}^0 = \frac{\alpha_0 T}{\beta_0}\left[2\phi_E^0 - \frac{\alpha_0}{\beta_0}\phi_K^0\right] \qquad (8\text{-}4\text{-}20)$$

TABLE (8-4-4). VALUES OF $\phi_{c_p} - \phi_{c_v}$ AT 25°.

Solute	$\sqrt{c} = 0$	0.25	0.50	0.75	1.00	1.25	1.50
HCl	2.90	2.91	2.71	2.85	3.01	3.10	3.23
LiCl	2.94	2.74	2.70	2.57	2.49	2.41	2.31
NaCl	8.60	8.33	8.14	8.11	8.25	8.48	8.71
KCl	7.82	7.32	7.16	6.98	6.89	6.82	6.72
LiOH	5.36	4.92	4.71	4.44	4.23	3.99	3.69
NaOH	11.36	10.66	10.59	10.63	10.78	10.98	11.12

TABLE (8-4-5). OBSERVED VALUES OF $\left(\dfrac{\partial\phi_{c_p}}{\partial\sqrt{c}} - \dfrac{\partial\phi_{c_v}}{\partial\sqrt{c}}\right)_{c\to 0}$ AT 25°.

HCl	LiCl	NaCl	KCl	LiOH	NaOH
-0.081	-0.72	-1.94	-2.04	-1.82	-3.27

in which ϕ_E^0 and ϕ_K^0 are the limiting values of the apparent molal expansibility and apparent molal compressibility. Gucker and Rubin also deduced the equation

$$\frac{\partial\phi_{c_p}}{\partial\sqrt{c}} - \frac{\partial\phi_{c_v}}{\partial\sqrt{c}} = \frac{\alpha_0 T}{\beta_0}\left[2\frac{\partial\phi_E}{\partial\sqrt{c}} - \frac{\alpha_0}{\beta_0}\frac{\partial\phi_K}{\partial\sqrt{c}}\right] \qquad (8\text{-}4\text{-}21)$$

for the condition $c \to 0$, which gives the difference in the limiting slopes of the isopiestic and isochoric systems. The observed values of this difference are highly specific, as can be seen in Table (8-4-5). Their magnitudes and signs are such that the limiting slopes of the plots in the isochoric system would show even more individuality than those in the isobaric system. In the experimental concentration range, however, the isopiestic system exhibits greater individuality in slopes. The most pronounced difference

[57] F. T. Gucker, Jr., and T. R. Rubin, J. Am. Chem. Soc., 57, 78 (1935).

in the two systems is that ϕ_{c_v} is always more negative than ϕ_{c_p} and there is a much greater spread in the values of $\phi_{c_v}^0$. Both of these effects are clearly indicated by a comparison of Fig. (8-4-1) with Fig. (8-4-2).

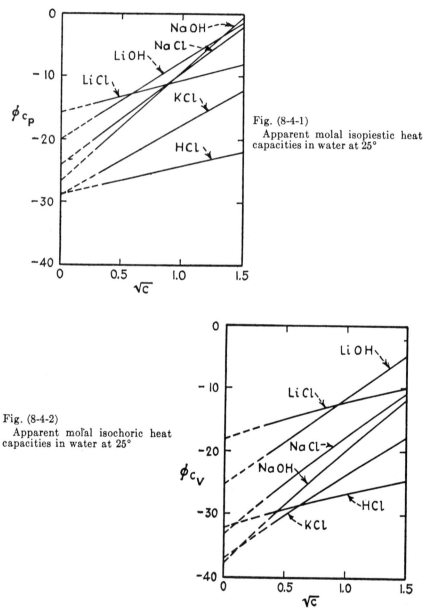

Fig. (8-4-1)
    Apparent molal isopiestic heat capacities in water at 25°

Fig. (8-4-2)
    Apparent molal isochoric heat capacities in water at 25°

By way of contrast with the properties of solutions of electrolytes, it will be useful to consider the behavior of a typical non-electrolyte. For this purpose we have reproduced in Fig. (8-4-3) a plot of ϕ_{c_p} for sucrose from a paper by Gucker and Ayres,[58] which represents the most accurate series of measurements available over a wide concentration range. The limiting slope of the plot against $\sqrt{c}$ is apparently zero. This is in accord with theory which attributes the $\sqrt{c}$ term to the effect of ionic interaction. The plot against c is linear within the experimental error up to about $c = 1$.[59] Essentially the same situation is maintained if the concentration scale is changed to mol fraction or molality, but the curvature is reversed and increased about 50 per cent. For convenience in computing $\bar{C}_{p_2}$

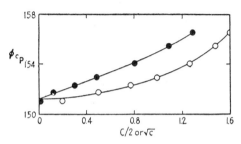

Fig. (8-4-3). Apparent molal heat capacity of sucrose at 25° plotted against $c/2$ (upper curve), and $\sqrt{c}$ (lower curve)

and $\bar{C}_{p_1}$, the results were expressed as a function of m according to the equation

$$\phi_{C_p} = 145.87 + 1.950m - 0.1182m^2 \qquad (8\text{-}4\text{-}22)$$

at 20°, and

$$\phi_{C_p} = 151.20 + 1.325m - 0.0704m^2 \qquad (8\text{-}4\text{-}23)$$

at 25°. The coefficient of the linear term is small, and decreases with temperature so fast that, at about 40°, ϕ_{C_p} would be nearly independent of concentration in dilute solutions. In this respect sucrose would behave as an ideal solute. This matter is considered in some detail by Gucker and Ayres, and especially by Bennewitz and Kratz.[60]

Although the limiting slopes, $(\partial \phi_{C_p}/\partial m)_{c \to 0}$, obtained from equations (8-4-22) and (8-4-23), were derived from experimental results above $0.04M$, the slope at 25° is in close agreement with the value derived from the temperature coefficient of heats of dilution at lower concentrations. Thus, from equations (8-2-28) and (8-2-29) for ϕ_L at 20 and 30°,

$$\frac{\partial \phi_{C_p}}{\partial m} = \frac{\partial}{\partial T}\left(\frac{\partial \phi_L}{\partial m}\right) \cong \frac{140.2 - 128.9}{10} = 1.13 \qquad (8\text{-}4\text{-}24)$$

[58] F. T. Gucker, Jr., and F. D. Ayres, *J. Am. Chem. Soc.*, **59**, 447 (1937).

[59] Similar plots for urea solutions show no such clear cut differentiation between the c and $\sqrt{c}$ plots. F.T. Gucker, Jr., and F. D. Ayres, [*J. Am. Chem. Soc.*, **59**, 2152 (1937)], and C. M. White, [*Ibid.*, **58**, 1620 (1936)].

[60] K. Bennewitz and L. Kratz, *Physik. Z.*, **37**, 496 (1936).

Gucker, Pickard and Planck[61] considered this a more accurate determination of the limiting slope, and used this value to re-evaluate the other parameters in equation (8-4-23) from the specific heat data. Their final equation,

$$\phi_{C_p} = 151.50 + 1.130m - 0.0466m^2 \qquad (8\text{-}4\text{-}25)$$

represents the experimental specific heats to within 1 part in 20,000 on the average.

(5) Partial Molal Volumes, Apparent Molal Volumes and the Densities of Solutions of Electrolytes

Partial molal and apparent molal volumes are derived from the densities of solutions. The apparent molal volume is given by

$$\phi_V = \frac{V - n_1 \bar{V}_1^0}{n_2} \qquad (8\text{-}5\text{-}1)$$

in general, which becomes

$$\phi_V = \frac{1000}{cd_0}(d_0 - d) + \frac{M_2}{d_0} \qquad (8\text{-}5\text{-}2)$$

if $n_2 = c$, the number of mols of solute in $V = 1000$ cc. of solution. Also,

$$\phi_V = \frac{1000}{mdd_0}(d_0 - d) + \frac{M_2}{d} \qquad (8\text{-}5\text{-}3)$$

if $n_2 = m$, the number of mols of solute per 1000 grams of solvent.

It was found by Masson[62] that ϕ_V varies linearly with $\sqrt{c}$ in dilute solutions, and that this simple relationship often extends to concentrated solutions. Thus, if

$$\phi_V = \phi_V^0 + S_V \sqrt{c} \qquad (8\text{-}5\text{-}4)$$

over the range in which the densities are known, the latter must be given by the equation

$$d = d_0 + \frac{(M_2 - d_0\phi_V^0)c}{1000} - \frac{(S_V d_0)c^{3/2}}{1000} \qquad (8\text{-}5\text{-}5)$$

which follows by combination of equations (8-5-2) and (8-5-4). This equation was first derived by Root.[63] According to theory, the coefficient, $S_V d_0/1000$, should be common to all strong electrolytes of the same valence type in a given solvent, and the coefficient of the c term should be an

[61] F. T. Gucker, Jr., H. G. Pickard and R. W. Planck, *J. Am. Chem. Soc.*, **61**, 459 (1939).

[62] D. O. Masson, *Phil. Mag.* [7], **8**, 218 (1929). See also A. F. Scott, *J. Phys. Chem.*, **35**, 2315 (1931); W. Geffcken, *Z. physik. Chem.*, **A155**, 1 (1931); and O. Redlich and P. Rosenfeld, *Z. Elektrochem.*, **37**, 705, (1931); *Z. physik. Chem.*, **A155**, 65 (1931).

[63] W. C. Root, *J. Am. Chem. Soc.*, **55**, 850 (1933).

additive property of the ions. The experimental values of S_V, however, show considerable individuality within a series of similar electrolytes, and are only of the order of magnitude of the theoretical slope [Equation (3-9-6)]. Root reported that the experimental coefficients are both additive. This additivity is considered later in Section (9).

Wirth[64] determined the apparent (and partial) molal volumes of potassium chloride, bromide, and sulfate in sodium chloride solutions, and found that equation (8-5-4) would express the results for the 1-1 type salt mixtures up to $1N$, if c represents the total solute concentration. The results for potassium sulfate can also be represented by this equation if $c^{1/2}$ is replaced by $\Gamma^{1/2}$. This confirms the theoretical equation (3-9-6) insofar as the variable, $\Gamma^{1/2}$, is concerned.

ϕ_V is not seriously influenced by ordinary experimental errors in the determination of concentration, but is very sensitive to experimental uncertainties in the density at high dilutions. Differentiation of equation (8-5-2) at constant d, and combination with (8-5-5), shows that

$$\delta\phi_V = \left[\frac{M_2}{d_0} - \phi_V^0\right]\frac{\delta c}{c} \qquad (8\text{-}5\text{-}6)$$

in dilute solutions. The bracketed terms are independent of c, and of the order, M_2 to $1/2\ M_2$. At constant c, the corresponding equation is

$$\delta\phi_V = -\frac{1000}{c}\frac{\delta d}{d_0} \qquad (8\text{-}5\text{-}7)$$

so that an error of 0.001 per cent in d would cause an uncertainty of 1 cc. in ϕ_V when $c = 0.01$.

Because of the linear relationship [Equation (8-5-4)], the most convenient calculation of partial molal volumes makes use of the c-scale. The equations are[65, 66, 67]

$$\bar{V}_2 = \phi_V + \left[\frac{1000 - c\phi_V}{2000 + c^{3/2}\,\partial\phi_V/\partial\sqrt{c}}\right]c^{1/2}\frac{\partial\phi_V}{\partial\sqrt{c}} \qquad (8\text{-}5\text{-}8)*$$

and

$$\bar{V}_1 = \left[\frac{2000\ \bar{V}_1^0}{2000 + c^{3/2}\,\partial\phi_V/\partial\sqrt{c}}\right] \qquad (8\text{-}5\text{-}9)$$

[64] H. E. Wirth, *J. Am. Chem. Soc.*, **59**, 2549 (1937); **62**, 1128 (1940).

[65] W. Geffcken, *Z. physik. Chem.*, **A155**, 1 (1931).

[66] F. T. Gucker, Jr., *J. Phys. Chem.*, **38**, 311 (1934). *Cf. J. Am. Chem. Soc.*, **60**, 2582 (1938).

[67] R. E. Gibson, *J. Phys. Chem.*, **38**, 320 (1934).

* At $c = 1$, the error caused by neglecting the concentration terms within the brackets is less than 0.1 cc. for most 1-1 and 2-1 electrolytes.

which follow from the more familiar equations

$$\bar{V}_2 = \phi_v + \frac{m^{1/2}}{2\partial\sqrt{m}}\frac{\partial\phi_v}{}$$ (8-5-10)

and

$$\bar{V}_1 = \bar{V}_1^0 - \frac{M_1}{2000}m^{3/2}\frac{\partial\phi_v}{\partial\sqrt{m}}$$ (8-5-11)

by combination with the useful relationship

$$\frac{c}{m} = d_0\left[1 - \frac{c\phi_v}{1000}\right]$$ (8-5-12)

Equation (8-5-12) is deduced from (8-5-2).

Values of the parameters, S_V and ϕ_v^0, derived by several investigators from density data at 25°, are recorded in Table (8-5-1). The values for all of the alkali halides, except potassium fluoride, were derived by Scott[68] from the data of Baxter and Wallace.[69] Geffcken[70] combined the same data with his own and some from other sources.[71, 72, 73, 74] The values obtained by Scott and by Geffcken are nearly identical. We have selected Scott's values wherever possible because they have been used in the estimation of some derived quantities which appear later in Table (8-5-2). Both authors tabulated values of S_V and ϕ_v^0 at 0, 25, 50 and 70°, and Geffcken includes some at 35 and 45°. Further results at 25° are given elsewhere.[75]

Table (8-5-1) shows that the difference between S_V and ϕ_v^0 for any pair of 1-1 type salts with a common ion is practically independent of the nature of the common ion. This additivity of ϕ_v^0 persists, less accurately, for salts of higher valence types. Scott[76] showed that the average deviation from additivity, derived from all possible combinations of alkali halides with a common ion, was about 0.07 cc. Geffcken's values lead to about the same figure, but the corresponding deviation derived by LaMer and Gronwall,[77] from the same data, is about twice as great. Instead of equation (8-5-4), a power series of the third order in m was used by the latter investigators, and it appears that this more complicated treatment

[68] A. F. Scott, *J. Phys. Chem.*, **35**, 2315 (1931).

[69] G. P. Baxter and C. C. Wallace, *J. Am. Chem. Soc.*, **38**, 70 (1916).

[70] W. Geffcken, *Z. physik. Chem.*, **A155**, 1 (1931).

[71] H. Hüttig, *Z. Elektrochem.*, **34**, 14 (1928).

[72] H. Köhner, *Z. physik. Chem.*, **B1**, 427 (1928).

[73] P. Hölemann and H. Köhner, *Ibid.*, **B13**, 338 (1931).

[74] Z. Shibata and P. Hölemann, *Ibid.*, **B13**, 347 (1931).

[75] L. G. Longsworth, *J. Am. Chem. Soc.*, **57**, 1185 (1935); B. B. Owen and S. R. Brinkley Jr., *Chem. Rev.*, **29**, 461 (1941); K. Fajans and O. Johnson, *J. Am. Chem. Soc.*, **64**, 668 (1942).

[76] A. F. Scott, *J. Phys. Chem.*, **35**, 2315 (1931).

[77] V. K. LaMer and T. H. Gronwall, *J. Phys. Chem.*, **31**, 393 (1927).

tends to exaggerate the deviations. In any event, the additivity of ϕ_V^0 is surprisingly exact when it is recalled that all the extrapolations are made from relatively concentrated solutions ($c \geq 0.25$). This matter will be discussed later in connection with the approximate additivity of S_V.

The theoretical limiting slope is not accurately known because of the uncertainty in the experimental value of $\partial D/\partial P$ required in equation

TABLE (8-5-1)*. VALUES OF THE PARAMETERS OF EQUATION (8-5-4) FOR AQUEOUS SOLUTIONS AT 25°.

Electrolyte	$\phi_V^0 (= \overline{V}_2^0)$	S_V	Electrolyte	$\phi_V^0 (= \overline{V}_2^0)$	S_V
LiCl[a]	17.00 (17.06)[b]	1.488	HCl[b]	18.20 (18.07)[g]	0.83
LiBr[a]	24.08	1.159	LiOH[i]	−6.0	3.00
LiI[a]	35.50	0.841	NaOH[i]	−6.7	4.18
NaCl[a]	16.40 (16.61)[d]	2.153	KOH[i]	2.9	4.35
			NH₄Cl[j]	35.98	1.45†
NaBr[a]	23.51 (23.48)[c]	1.760	NH₄NO₃[h]	47.56 (47.24)[c]	0.97
NaI[a]	35.10	1.346	AgNO₃[l]	28.01	2.61†
KF[b]	6.60	3.35	KNO₃[e]	38.18	2.30
KCl[a]	26.52 (26.81)[c]	2.327	K₂CrO₄[l]	37.13	11.70
			K₂SO₄[f]	32.28	18.11
KBr[a]	33.73	1.939	Na₂SO₄[c]	11.47 (11.52)[c]	12.16
KI[a]	45.36	1.556	Na₂CO₃[c]	−6.70 (−6.74)[c]	11.30
RbCl[a]	31.87	2.219			
RbBr[a]	38.71	2.038			
RbI[a]	50.31	1.607	CaCl₂[i]	18.25	5.99
CsCl[a]	39.15	2.172	SrCl₂[d]	17.94	9.90†
CsBr[a]	46.19	1.901	BaCl₂[i]	23.60	6.83
CsI[a]	57.74	1.579	LaCl₃[k]	16.02	11.87

* Where two values of ϕ_V^0 are given, the one in parentheses was evaluated from data at high dilution, and is the most accurate value of the physical quantity, ϕ_V^0. Such values were not used in evaluating S_V, and therefore should not be used for estimating ϕ_V at high concentrations by equation (8-5-4).

† Evaluated in dilute solutions, $c < 0.5$.

[a] A. F. Scott, *J. Phys. Chem.*, **35**, 2315 (1931).
[b] W. Geffcken, *Z. physik. Chem.*, **155A**, 1 (1931); *Naturwiss.*, **19**, 321 (1931).
[c] W. Geffcken and D. Price, *Z. physik. Chem.*, **26B**, 81 (1934).
[d] A. Kruis, *Ibid.*, **34B**, - (1936)
[e] R. E. Gibson and J. F. Kincaid, *J. Am. Chem. Soc.*, **59**, 25 (1937).
[f] H. E. Wirth, *Ibid.*, **59**, 2549 (1937).
[g] H. E. Wirth, *Ibid.*, **62**, 1128 (1940).
[h] F. T. Gucker Jr. and T. R. Rubin, *Ibid.*, **58**, 2118 (1936).
[i] F. T. Gucker Jr., *Chem. Rev.*, **13**, 111 (1933). *Cf.* R. M. Rush and G. Scatchard, *J. Phys. Chem.*, **65**, 2240 (1961).
[j] G. Jones and S. K. Talley, *J. Am. Chem. Soc.*, **55**, 624 (1933).
[k] G. Jones and R. E. Stauffer, *Ibid.*, **62**, 335 (1940).
[l] G. Jones and J. H. Colvin, *Ibid.*, **62**, 338 (1940).

(3-9-2). The experimental slopes, S_V, determined from the results above 0.25N, are specific, and do not yield an experimental verification of the limiting law. For this reason it is important to have precise measurements of densities at higher dilutions. To overcome the unfavorable magnification of the experimental error, according to equation (8-5-7), Geffcken, Beckmann and Kruis[78] developed a differential float method for deter-

[78] W. Geffcken, C. Beckmann and A. Kruis, *Z. physik. Chem.*, **B20**, 398 (1933).

mining relative densities with very high precision. The method is a refinement of the procedure used by Lamb and Lee,[79] and others,[80, 81] in which the bouyancy of a submerged float containing an iron core is delicately counterbalanced by the pull of a solenoid. The differential method, making use of duplicate float systems in the same thermostat, minimizes the effect of uncertainties in temperature control by simultaneously measuring the densities of solution and pure solvent. In addition, modern pycnometric studies of high precision have led to reliable values of ϕ_V in dilute solutions.[82] Geffcken and Price[83] have collected and analyzed the best data from various sources, and conclude that, for potassium and sodium chlorides and sodium bromide, there is convergence toward a common limiting slope at high dilutions. The value of this slope, 1.9 is approximately $(\frac{2}{3})\bar{S}_{(V)}$, which has been variously estimated as 1.9^{84} to 2.5, depending upon the values of $\partial \ln D/\partial P$ employed [Cf. Table (5-2-5)]. In Fig. (8-5-1) we have plotted $\phi - 1.9c^{1/2}$ against c for several salts. In this plot the data obtained by the differential float method are seen to be in excellent agreement with results obtained by an ingenious dilatometric method used by Kruis[85] and by Geffcken, Kruis and Solana.[86] Although the data for the salts shown in Fig. (8-5-1) are in satisfactory accord with theory, the results for sodium sulfate, sodium carbonate and ammonium nitrate, obtained by the same authors, are doubtful in this respect. The plot of $\phi_V - 1.9c^{1/2}$ for ammonium nitrate[87] against c is curved in dilute solutions, and the corresponding plots for sodium carbonate (corrected for hydrolysis) and sodium sulfate cannot be made to appear linear at high dilutions without assigning different values, 11.3 and 12.2, to the limiting slopes.* The theoretical slope for the 1-2 type electrolytes should fall between 13.1, from Table (5-2-5), and 9.9, which is the value used in Fig. (8-5-1) for strontium chloride. Considered

---

[79] A. B. Lamb and R. E. Lee, *J. Am. Chem. Soc.*, **35**, 1666 (1913).

[80] F. Kohlrausch and W. Hallwach, *Wied. Ann.*, **53**, 14 (1894).

[81] N. Reggiani, *Rend. Reale Accad. dei Lincei* [4], **6**, 99 (1890).

[82] Several very sensitive methods of detecting small density differences have been developed for estimating the isotopic composition of water. So far as we know, these methods have not yet been applied to the determination of ϕ_V at high dilutions. For bibliography see P. C. Vincent, *Proc. Phys. Soc. London*, **45**, 833 (1933); H. E. Wirth, T. G. Thompson and C. L. Utterback, *J. Am. Chem. Soc.*, **57**, 400 (1935); and O. E. Frivold, *Physik. Z.*, **21**, 529 (1920).

[83] W. Geffcken and D. Price, *Z. physik. Chem.*, **B26**, 81 (1934).

[84] O. Redlich, *J. Phys. Chem.*, **44**, 619 (1940).

[85] A. Kruis, *Z. physik. Chem.*, **B34**, 1 (1936).

[86] W. Geffcken, A. Kruis and L. Solana, *Ibid.*, **B35**, 317 (1937).

[87] F. T. Gucker, Jr., and T. R. Rubin [*J. Am. Chem. Soc.*, **58**, 2118 (1936)] found that their data for this salt at somewhat higher concentrations indicated a limiting slope of only 0.966.

* The slopes here given conform to our equation (8-5-4) in which ϕ_V is the apparent *molal* volume and c is in *mols* per liter.

as a whole, the results obtained by the float and dilatometer methods appear to support the interionic attraction theory for typical strong electrolytes. On the other hand the hydrolyzable salts show significant departures at the most dilute solutions studied. In the case of sodium carbonate, in which hydrolysis is most pronounced, the values of ϕ_V, calculated from the densities of Lamb and Lee,[88] pass through a minimum at about $0.01N$. The plot of ϕ_V against $\sqrt{c}$ approaches the axis at zero

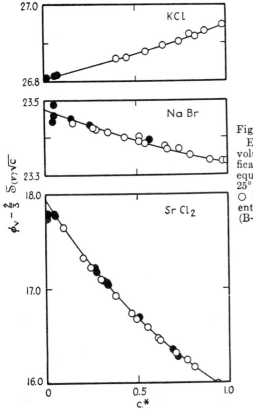

Fig. (8-5-1)
Evaluation of apparent molal volumes at infinite dilution. Verification of the theoretical limiting equation for aqueous solutions at $25°$; $c^* =$ equivalent per liter. ○ Dilatometer method; ● Differential float method. Compare Fig. (B-4-1).

concentration with a *negative* slope. Lamb and Lee attributed this effect to hydrolysis, and Geffcken and Price[89] estimated its numerical magnitude at each experimental concentration. At the lowest concentration, the hydrolysis correction is about 1.7 cc.; this not only eliminates the minimum but also brings the results into approximate agreement with theory. The agreement is within the estimated uncertainty of the hydrolysis corrections, and it is quite possible that the relatively small departures noted in the case of ammonium nitrate, and sodium sulfate might be eliminated

[88] A. B. Lamb and R. E. Lee, *J. Am. Chem. Soc.*, **35**, 1666 (1913).
[89] W. Geffcken and D. Price, *Z. physik. Chem.*, **B26**, 81 (1934).

in the same way.* With higher valence type salts such as zinc sulfate, the correction would have to take ionic association as well as hydrolysis into account. Geffcken and Price, and others,[90] have shown that ϕ_V for weak acids may be quantitatively interpreted in terms of their known dissociation constants. [See Section (9)].

In Fig. (8-5-2), we have plotted ϕ_V against $c^{1/2}$ for strontium chloride to show the S-shaped character of the curves in the transition from the limiting law, at high dilution, to Masson's equation (8-5-4), in more concentrated solutions. It appears that the first significant departures from

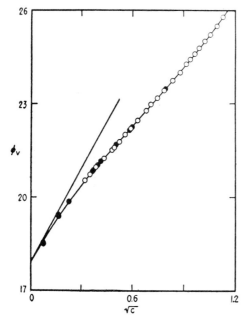

Fig. (8-5-2)
    Apparent molal volume of strontium chloride in water at 25°; departures from theoretical limiting law at moderate dilutions. O Dilatometer method; ● Differential float method

Masson's equation take place at such low concentrations that it makes little difference whether the data extend to extreme dilutions or not. More satisfactory extrapolations, which involve both the å-parameter and a linear term in c, are discussed in Section 8, and illustrated by Fig. (8-8-1).

No satisfactory explanation of the validity of equation (8-5-4) has yet been proposed, but a number of interesting speculations regarding it may be noted. Masson[91] postulated that, if the plots of ϕ_V against $c^{1/2}$ were to remain linear for supersaturated solutions, the hypothetical maximum

    [90] R. C. Hoather and C. F. Goodeve, *Trans. Faraday Soc.*, **30**, 630 (1934); I. M. Klotz and C. F. Eckert, *J. Am. Chem. Soc.*, **64**, 1878 (1942).
    * Cationic hydrolysis tends to reduce ϕ_V contrary to the effect produced by anionic hydrolysis (Na₂CO₃).
    [91] D. O. Masson, *Phil. Mag.* [7], **8**, 218 (1929).

value of ϕ_V would occur when c became the concentration of electrolyte in the pure crystalline salt. Using the subscript max. for this maximum, we have,

$$\phi_{V_{\text{max.}}} = \phi_V^0 + S_V \sqrt{c_{\text{max.}}} \qquad (8\text{-}5\text{-}13)$$

where $1000/c_{\text{max.}}$ is the molal volume, V_2, of the pure crystalline salt. A plot of $\phi_{V_{\text{max.}}}$ against V_2 for the alkali halides yields two straight lines, with the lithium and cesium salts on one line, and the remaining salts on the other. The intercepts of both lines are about 6 cc. The slope of the lithium and cesium plot is unity, while the other is 0.86 ($\cong \sqrt{3/4}$), which suggests a purely geometrical interpretation of the volume relationships in solutions. Scott[92] pointed out that equation (8-5-4) is valid for lithium salts over a limited range, and that, if the data at the highest concentrations only are used in evaluating ϕ_V^0 and S_V, the lithium salts would have lower values of $\phi_{V_{\text{max.}}}$. This would place them more nearly in line with the other alkali halides of the rock salt (face-centered cubic) crystalline structure than with the cesium salts, which have a body-centered cubic lattice. Furthermore, if hypothetical values of V_2 are calculated for cesium salts on the basis of a rock-salt lattice, these salts lie on the common plot with the sodium, potassium and rubidium salts.

Scott goes an important step further. He objects to the use of the pure crystalline solid as the hypothetical upper limit to the concentration of the solution, maintaining that if the properties of the solid salt are to be included in the interpretation of this limiting solution we should use the "critical disruptive volume," V^*, of the solid. The method of estimating V^*, is given by Scott.[93] For our purposes it will be sufficient to remark that the cohesive forces reach a maximum when the crystal is expanded from its normal equilibrium volume to V^*, and decrease thereafter with further expansion. Hence V^* marks the transition from rigid crystalline structure to the more mobile condition of liquids, and may be assumed to correspond to the hypothetical maximum concentration attainable in a (supersaturated) solution of a given salt.

In Table (8-5-2) we have given Scott's values of V^* for the alkali halides at 25°, and the corresponding values of

$$\phi_V^* = \phi_V^0 + S_V \sqrt{1000/V^*} \qquad (8\text{-}5\text{-}14)$$

derivable from equation (8-5-4), and the parameters in Table (8-5-1). To these, we have added values for potassium fluoride at 25°, and for the function

$$\psi^* \equiv \frac{\phi_V^*}{V^*} = \frac{S_V\sqrt{1000/V^*} + \phi_V^0}{V^*} \qquad (8\text{-}5\text{-}15)$$

---

[92] A. F. Scott, *J. Phys. Chem.*, **35**, 3379 (1931).

[93] See A. F. Joffé, "The Physics of Crystals," McGraw-Hill Book Co., New York, 1928.

at other temperatures. This fraction was estimated from values of S_γ and ϕ_V^0 obtained from the work of Scott,[94] Geffcken[95] and Pesce,[96] and upon the assumption that

$$V^* \cong V_{25}^*[1 + 1.2 \times 10^{-4}(t - 25)] \tag{8-5-16}$$

for all the salts. The effect of the temperature variation of V^* upon ϕ_V^* and ψ^* is so small that the coefficient of expansion need not be known accurately.

TABLE (8-5-2). PROPERTIES OF THE CRITICAL DISRUPTIVE CONDITION.

Salt	$V^*(25°)$	$\phi_V^*(25°)$	$\psi^* = \phi_V^*/V^*$					
			0°	25°	35°	45°	50°	70°
LiCl	32.4	25.3		0.78				
LiBr	39.1	30.0		.77				
LiI	51.2	39.2		.77				
NaCl	41.6	26.9	0.68	.65	0.64	0.65	0.64	0.64[b]
NaBr	49.0	31.5	.66	.64	.64	.64	.64	.65
NaI	61.1	40.6		.66				
KF	37.2	24.0		.65				
KCl	56.6	36.3	.65	.64	.64	.64	.64	.64[b]
KBr	64.7	41.3	.65	.64	.64	.64	.64	
KI	78.0	51.0		.65				
RbCl	63.8	40.7	.65	.64			.64	
RbBr	72.7	46.3	.64	.64			.64	
RbI	86.7	55.9		.64				
CsCl[a]	73.4	47.2		.64				
CsBr[a]	82.6	52.8		.64				
CsI[a]	97.5	62.7		.64				
CsCl	62.4	48.0		.77				
CsBr	70.4	53.4		.76				
CsI	83.3	63.2		.76				

[a] Hypothetical rock-salt type lattice structure.
[b] 85°.

From equation (8-5-15) we obtain

$$S_\gamma = (\psi^*V^* - \phi_V^0)\sqrt{V^*/1000} \tag{8-5-17}$$

for the rate of change of ϕ_γ with $c^{1/2}$. This result is peculiar since it makes no provision for the effect of an ionic atmosphere in the usual sense. The terms ψ^* and V^* apply to such a close-packed system of ions that their distribution presumably follows a crystal lattice pattern, and ϕ_V^0 implies the disappearance of the atmosphere by infinite separation of the ions. Two consequences of this empirical equation are of considerable interest. In the first place, it follows from the data in Tables (8-5-1) and (8-5-2), that both ϕ_V^0 and ϕ_V^* are additive. Therefore, for salts of the same crystalline structure (identical ψ^* values), it follows from equation (8-5-17) that $S_\gamma\sqrt{1000/V^*}$ must be additive in so far as V^* fulfills this condition

[94] A. F. Scott, *J. Phys. Chem.*, **35**, 3379 (1931).
[95] W. Geffcken, *Z. physik. Chem.*, **A155**, 1 (1931).
[96] B. Pesce, *Gazz. chim. ital.*, **66**, 99 (1936).

[Table (8-5-2), column 2]. The approximate additivity of S_V, noted by Root and others, should, however, be used with caution because the presence of ψ^* in equation (8-5-17) may completely obliterate this additivity if ψ^* varies considerably with crystal structure. A second consequence of equation (8-5-17) follows from the fact that ψ^* and V^* are nearly independent of the temperature over a considerable range, and therefore the relation

$$\frac{\partial S_V}{\partial T} \cong -\left(\frac{V^*}{1000}\right)^{1/2} \frac{\partial \phi_V^0}{\partial T} \tag{8-5-18}$$

is a fairly close approximation.

Fig. (8-5-3) shows a plot of ϕ_V^* against V^* at 25°. The arrows indicate the effect of using rough values of S_V and ϕ_V^0 for the lithium salts obtained

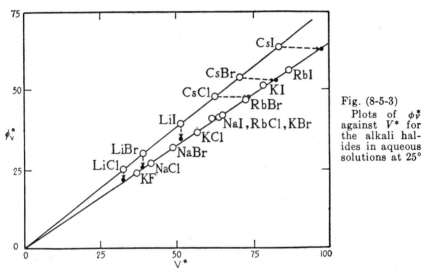

Fig. (8-5-3)
Plots of ϕ_V^* against V^* for the alkali halides in aqueous solutions at 25°

from data at the highest concentrations only,[97] and the effect of calculating V^* for the cesium salts on the basis of a rock-salt structure. It seems evident from the plot that ψ^*, the slope of the solid line, is a function of the spatial arrangement in the lattice, and this is supported by the fact that ψ^* is quite insensitive to variations in temperature. This conclusion is important, because, if the relationship between S_V and ϕ_V^0 given by equation (8-5-15) is governed only by the geometry of the critical disruptive state, it suggests that the geometry of this state is maintained, statistically at least, over the entire range of validity of equation (8-5-4). If this is the case, the concept of the ionic atmosphere might be replaced by a statistical lattice structure, except at high dilutions. This point deserves more detailed investigation, since X-ray studies also indicate a corre-

[97] There is evidence of abrupt changes in S_V in passing from low to high concentrations. *Cf.* A. F. Scott and G. L. Bridger, *J. Phys. Chem.*, **39**, 1031 (1935).

spondence between S_V and the rate of variation of the liquid structure of the solvent with ionic concentration.[98]

Precise density measurements on dilute solutions of urea[99] and sucrose[100] have been used to show that ϕ_V for non-electrolytes varies linearly with c rather than $c^{1/2}$ in dilute solutions. Examination of Fig. (8-5-4), from the work of Gucker, Gage and Moser,[99] will leave little doubt as to the validity of this conclusion.

So far our attention has been focussed upon ϕ_V rather than $\bar{V}_2$ because the former quantity is more directly obtained from the density data, and is more simply expressed by empirical equations, such as (8-5-4). The quantity $\bar{V}_2$ is no less important, but since its behavior is so similar to that of ϕ_V, it will be discussed briefly.

At extreme dilutions $\bar{V}_2$ varies linearly with $c^{1/2}$ wherever ϕ_V exhibits this behavior, and the slope $\partial \bar{V}_2/\partial c^{1/2}$ is $3/2$ times the corresponding slope,

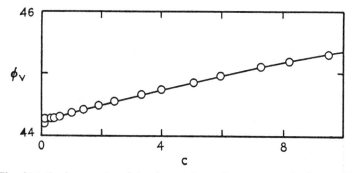

Fig. (8-5-4). Apparent molal volume of urea in aqueous solutions at 25°

$\partial \phi_V/\partial c^{1/2}$, a result obtained by differentiation of equation (8-5-8). Consequently, agreement with the theoretical limiting law in one case requires agreement in both. At moderate dilutions the S-shaped feature of ϕ_V shown in Fig. (8-5-2) is somewhat exaggerated by the requirements of equation (8-5-8), and in concentrated solutions, where ϕ_V is again linear with $c^{1/2}$ for many salts, the plot of $\bar{V}_2$ shows a slight curvature, which usually becomes quite pronounced at high concentrations.

The values of ϕ_V^0 given in Table (8-5-1) are equal to the corresponding values of $\bar{V}_2^0$. For many practical purposes $\bar{V}_2$ may be estimated at moderate concentrations by multiplying the last term in equation (8-5-4) by $3/2$ and using the values of S_V ($= \partial \phi_V/\partial c^{1/2}$) recorded in the same table.

The temperature and pressure variations of $\bar{V}_2$ are considered in detail

[98] G. W. Stewart, *J. Chem. Phys.*, **7**, 869 (1939).

[99] F. T. Gucker, Jr., F. W. Gage and C. E. Moser, *J. Am. Chem. Soc.*, **60**, 2582 (1938). Cf. O. K. Skarre, S. G. Demidenko and A. I. Brodskiĭ, *Acta Physicochim. U.R.S.S.*, **6**, 297 (1937).

[100] F. Plato, J. Domke and H. Harting, *Wiss. Abh. Normaleichungskommission*, 2 Hefte, Berlin, Springer, 1900, quoted by O. Redlich and H. Klinger, *Monatshefte für Chemie*, **65**, 137 (1934).

in Sections (6) and (7) which deal with expansibility and compressibility, but there are several interesting effects of these variations which are relevant to the present discussion. A number of recent studies[101-105] suggest the generalization that ϕ_v^0 for electrolytes in aqueous solutions passes through a maximum between 60 and 70°. This maximum also appears in plots of ϕ_v, and the effect of increasing concentration is usually a small increase in the temperature of the maximum, and a considerable decrease in the curvature of the plot in its neighborhood. The behavior

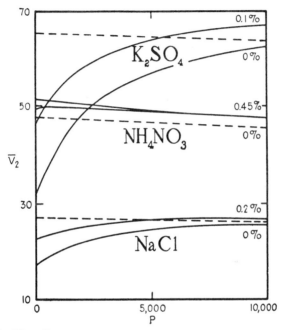

Fig. (8-5-5). The effect of pressure upon the partial molal volumes of salts in aqueous solutions at 25°. Molal volumes of pure solid salts are represented by broken lines. The numbers at the right-hand margin indicate the salt concentrations in weight per cent.

of $\bar{V}_2$ is quite similar. The maximum values of ϕ_v^0 or $\bar{V}_2^0$ are approximately additive.

The effect of pressure on ϕ_v and $\bar{V}_2$ is particularly interesting because an increase in pressure increases the apparent molal and partial molal volumes. The negative sign and order of magnitude of $\partial \bar{V}_2^0/\partial P$ is predictable[106, 107]

[101] W. R. Bousfield and T. M. Lowry, *Trans. Faraday Soc.*, **6**, 15 (1910).

[102] W. Geffcken, *Z. physik. Chem.*, **A155**, 1 (1931).

[103] A. F. Scott, *J. Phys. Chem.*, **35**, 2315 (1931).

[104] B. Pesce, *Gazz. chim. ital.*, **66**, 99 (1936).

[105] O. Redlich and H. Klinger, *Monatsh.*, **65**, 137 (1934).

[106] W. Geffcken, *Z. phys. Chem.*, **A167**, 240 (1933).

[107] I. R. Krichevskii, *Acta Physico-chem. U.R.S.S.*, **8**, 181 (1938); *J. Phys. Chem. (U.S.S.R.)*, **11**, 305 (1938).

from the simple electrostatic theory which led to equation (3-10-13). Adams[108] has shown that this curious effect persists at pressures as high as 10,000 atmospheres for solutions of sodium chloride and potassium sulfate, but becomes less pronounced at high pressures and high concentrations. Fig. (8-5-5) illustrates the behavior of these salts in comparison with that of ammonium nitrate.[109]   The broken lines in the figure, representing the molal volumes of the pure crystalline salts, are approached by the partial molal volumes at high concentrations and high pressures.   The increase in partial molal volume with pressure presumably results from a compression of the solvent caused by the solute when the process of solution is accompanied by a net contraction in volume.   Equation (8-5-1) shows that, if an increase in pressure decreases $\bar{V}_1^0$ much more rapidly than V, ϕ_V may increase with pressure.   This is the case in dilute aqueous solutions of electrolytes at low pressures, for the compressibility of water decreases rapidly with pressure under this condition.   At high pressures, where the compressibility decreases very little with pressure, or in concentrated solutions, where the magnitude of P_e[110] approaches that of P, the change in ϕ_V with P will decrease, and eventually become negative.   Furthermore these excessive conditions of high pressure, or high concentrations, should allow the compressibility of the pure salt to be an important factor in characterizing the compressibility of the solution.   The fact that ϕ_V and its variation with pressure approach the corresponding molal values of the pure solute under these conditions should therefore not be regarded as a sufficient condition of ideality.[111]

(6) The Partial Molal Expansibility, Apparent Molal Expansibility, and the Coefficient of Thermal Expansion of Solutions of Electrolytes

The partial molal expansibilities of the components of a binary solution are defined by

$$\bar{E}_1 \equiv \left(\frac{\partial \bar{V}_1}{\partial T}\right)_P \tag{8-6-1}$$

and

$$\bar{E}_2 \equiv \left(\frac{\partial \bar{V}_2}{\partial T}\right)_P \tag{8-6-2}$$

The apparent molal expansibility of the solute is defined by

$$\phi_E \equiv \left(\frac{\partial \phi_V}{\partial T}\right)_P \tag{8-6-3}$$

[108] L. H. Adams, *J. Am. Chem. Soc.*, **53**, 3769 (1931); *Ibid.*, **54**, 2229 (1932).

[109] L. H. Adams and R. E. Gibson, *J. Am. Chem. Soc.*, **54**, 4520 (1932).

[110] The effective pressure, P_e, is defined in the text immediately before equation (8-7-21).

[111] R. E. Gibson, *J. Am. Chem. Soc.*, **59**, 1521 (1937).

Combination of this equation with (8-5-1) leads to

$$\phi_E = \frac{\left(\dfrac{\partial V}{\partial T}\right)_P - n_1 \left(\dfrac{\partial \bar{V}_1^0}{\partial T}\right)_P}{n_2} = \frac{\alpha V - \alpha_0 n_1 \bar{V}_1^0}{n_2} \tag{8-6-4}$$

where

$$\alpha \equiv \frac{1}{V}\left(\frac{\partial V}{\partial T}\right)_P = -\frac{1}{d}\left(\frac{\partial d}{\partial T}\right)_P = -\frac{1}{c}\left(\frac{\partial c}{\partial T}\right)_P \tag{8-6-5}$$

is the coefficient of thermal expansion of the solution, and

$$\alpha_0 \equiv \frac{1}{\bar{V}_1^0}\left(\frac{\partial \bar{V}_1^0}{\partial T}\right)_P = -\frac{1}{d_0}\left(\frac{\partial d_0}{\partial T}\right)_P \tag{8-6-6}$$

is the coefficient of thermal expansion of the pure solvent. The apparent molal expansibility may be readily calculated from densities and their temperature coefficients by the equations

$$\begin{aligned}
\phi_E &= \frac{1000}{c d_0}(d_0 \alpha - d \alpha_0) + \frac{M_2}{d_0}\alpha_0 \\
&= \frac{1000}{c}(\alpha - \alpha_0) + \alpha_0 \phi_V
\end{aligned} \tag{8-6-7}$$

and

$$\begin{aligned}
\phi_E &= \frac{1000}{m d d_0}(d_0 \alpha - d \alpha_0) + \frac{M_2}{d}\alpha \\
&= \frac{1000}{m d_0}(\alpha - \alpha_0) + \alpha \phi_V
\end{aligned} \tag{8-6-8}$$

obtained by combination of equations (8-6-5) and (8-6-6) with (8-5-2) or (8-5-3). In practice the density data available for this purpose have usually been used to obtain ϕ_V, and therefore it is a simple matter to calculate ϕ_E from the latter by equation (8-6-3). Gucker[112] constructed plots of the values of ϕ_V calculated from the density data[113] for sodium and potassium chlorides. The tangents were estimated graphically, and are plotted against $\sqrt{c}$ at three temperatures in Fig. (8-6-1). With the exception of the results for sodium chloride at 0°, the points are satisfactorily represented by straight lines. Accordingly, ϕ_E is given by

$$\phi_E = \phi_E^0 + S_E \sqrt{c} \tag{8-6-9}$$

within the experimental concentration range. Because of the wide difference in S_E exhibited by salts of the same valence type, the values of ϕ_E^0, obtained by fitting this equation to the available data, may differ considerably from the true limiting partial molal expansibilities.

[112] F. T. Gucker, Jr., *J. Am. Chem. Soc.*, **56**, 1017 (1934).

[113] W. Geffcken, *Z. physik. Chem.*, **A155**, 1 (1931); G. P. Baxter and C. C. Wallace, *J. Am. Chem. Soc.*, **38**, 70 (1916).

In dilute solutions, equation (8-6-9) follows from differentiation of (8-5-4). Thus,

$$\phi_E = \frac{\partial \phi_V^0}{\partial T} + \left[\frac{\partial S_V}{\partial T} - \frac{\alpha S_V}{2} \right] c^{1/2} \tag{8-6-10}$$

within the range of validity of (8-5-4). Further, Gucker[114] points out that the effect of replacing α by α_0 in this equation is negligible for most 1-1 electrolytes up to concentrations as high as "several molal". Consequently we may write

$$S_E \cong \left[\frac{\partial S_V}{\partial T} - \frac{\alpha_0 S_V}{2} \right] \tag{8-6-11}$$

as a close approximation. The graphical advantages of a linear plot could be extended to more concentrated solutions by transferring the concen-

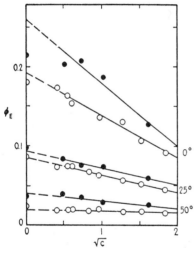

Fig. (8-6-1)
Variation of the apparent molal expansibility with temperature and composition in aqueous solutions. ● NaCl; ○ KCl

tration dependent term in α to the left side of equation (8-6-10), and plotting $[\phi_E + 1/2\, \alpha S_V c^{1/2}]$ against $c^{1/2}$. The estimation of S_E by substitution of the approximate relation (8-5-18) in (8-6-1) yields values .001 to .002 unit too low in the few cases for which the data are available.

Combination of equations (8-6-9) and (8-5-4) with the second form of (8-6-7) yields the expression

$$\alpha = \alpha_0 + \left[\frac{\phi_E^0 - \alpha_0 \phi_V^0}{1000} \right] c + \left[\frac{S_E - \alpha_0 S_V}{1000} \right] c^{3/2} \tag{8-6-12}$$

similar to the density equation (8-5-5). The values of the bracketed coefficients in this equation are readily determined from the slope and intercept of a plot of $(\alpha - \alpha_0)/c$ against $c^{1/2}$, and ϕ_E^0 and S_E can be estimated if ϕ_V^0 and S_V are known. These latter quantities are recorded for a number of electrolytes in Table (8-5-1), and Gucker[114] has added other values calculated from densities given in the "International Critical Tables", and from Gibson's[115] data on sodium sulfate. Gucker's values for the coefficients of equations (8-6-9) and (8-6-12) at 25° are given in Table (8-6-1). Values at 0° and 50° for lithium, sodium and potassium chlorides have also been compiled by Gucker. A plot of the apparent

TABLE (8-6-1). NUMERICAL COEFFICIENTS FOR ϕ_E AND α AT 1 ATMOSPHERE AND 25°

Electrolyte	$\phi_E = \phi_E^0 + S_E c^{1/2}$		$\alpha = \alpha_0 + Ac + Bc^{1/2}$[a]	
	$10^2 \phi_E^0$	$10^2 S_E$	$10^4 A$	$10^4 B$
HCl	3.4	−0.02	0.29	−0.004
LiCl	2.5	− .65	.21	− .069
LiOH[b]	4.5	−1.8	.47	− .19
NaCl	9.30	−2.10	.89	− .216
KCl	8.50	−2.20	.78	− .226
NaOH	11.7	−3.5	1.19	− .36
Na₂SO₄	22.19	−9.33	2.19	− .966

[a] $\alpha_0 = 2.55 \times 10^{-4}$.
[b] Values for LiOH must be considered rather tentative.

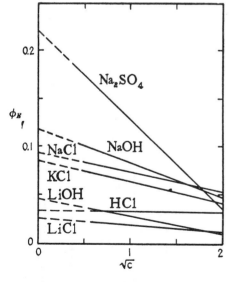

Fig. (8-6-2)
Apparent molal expansibilities in water at 25°

molal expansibility of these electrolytes is given in Fig. (8-6-2). At 25°, it is seen that ϕ_E^0 is positive and ϕ_E decreases with concentration. At lower temperatures, ϕ_E^0 becomes more positive, and the decrease with concentration is more pronounced. At higher temperatures, the opposite is true. Thus, at 50°, Gucker found that ϕ_E^0 was negative, and S_E was

[114] F. T. Gucker, Jr., *J. Am. Chem. Soc.*, **56**, 1017 (1934).
[115] R. E. Gibson, *J. Phys. Chem.*, **31**, 496 (1927); *Ibid.*, **38**, 319 (1934).

positive for lithium chloride. At the concentrations used in evaluating S_E, the electrolytes of the same valence type exhibit no tendency to share a common slope.

$\bar{E}_2$ and $\bar{E}_1$ may be obtained in terms of ϕ_E and $\partial\phi_E/\partial m^{1/2}$ by differentiation of equations (8-5-10) and (8-5-11). If it is more convenient to use the c-scale for this purpose, the corresponding equations are

$$\bar{E}_2 = \phi_E + \left[\frac{1000 - c\phi_V}{2000 + c^{3/2}\,\partial\phi_V/\partial\sqrt{c}}\right]c^{1/2}\frac{\partial\phi_E}{\partial\sqrt{c}} \qquad (8\text{-}6\text{-}13)$$

and

$$\bar{E}_1 = \bar{E}_1^0 - \frac{M_1}{d_0}\left[\frac{1}{2000 + c^{3/2}\,\partial\phi_V/\partial\sqrt{c}}\right]c^{3/2}\frac{\partial\phi_E}{\partial\sqrt{c}} \qquad (8\text{-}6\text{-}14)$$

Both of these equations are general, but Gucker[114] expresses equation (8-6-13) in the form

$$\bar{E}_2 = \phi_E^0 + \left[\frac{3000 - c\phi_V^0}{2000 + c^{3/2}\,\partial\phi_V/\partial\sqrt{c}}\right]c^{1/2}\frac{\partial\phi_E}{\partial\sqrt{c}} \qquad (8\text{-}6\text{-}15)$$

which is valid only over a concentration range in which both ϕ_E and ϕ_V vary linearly with $c^{1/2}$. Consequently, if ϕ_E is linear in $c^{1/2}$, $\bar{E}_2$ cannot be. For the electrolytes for which data are available the departures of $\bar{E}_2$ from linearity would be only 3 or 4 per cent up to $c = 9$, and it is difficult to decide which, if either, of the quantities, ϕ_E and $\bar{E}_2$, is strictly linear in $c^{1/2}$. In any case, the plots of $\bar{E}_2$ against $(3/2)c^{1/2}$ would fall so closely upon those shown in Fig. (8-6-2) that no further illustration is necessary.

The quantities α, ϕ_E, $\bar{E}_2$ and $\bar{E}_1$ have been estimated[116] for aqueous solutions of urea at 27.5° from density data at 25 and 30°. Since the densities at both temperatures were expressed by

$$d = d_0 + A_1 c + A_2 c^2 + A_3 c^3 + \cdots \qquad (8\text{-}6\text{-}16)$$

it follows [Equation (8-6-5)] that the equation for α must take the same form. The relationships between the coefficients of the similar equations for d and α have been derived by Gucker and Moser.[117] Their final expressions for the coefficient of thermal expansion and apparent molal volume of urea at 27.5° are

$$\alpha \times 10^6 = 281.2 + 52.0c - 4.71c^2 \qquad (8\text{-}6\text{-}17)$$

and

$$\phi_V = 44.385 + 0.1203c \qquad (8\text{-}6\text{-}18)$$

[116] F. T. Gucker, Jr., and C. E. Moser, J. Am. Chem. Soc., 61, 1558 (1939).

[117] F. T. Gucker, Jr., and C. E. Moser, J. Am. Chem. Soc., 61, 1558 (1939). The numerical factor of the third term in the coefficient of c^3 in their equation (6) should be unity.

Hence, by equation (8-6-7),

$$\phi_E = 0.0645 - 0.00468c \tag{8-6-19}$$

When account is taken of this linearity in c instead of $c^{1/2}$, these equations lead to

$$\bar{E}_2 = 0.0645 - 0.00936c + 0.00208c^2 \tag{8-6-20}$$

and

$$\bar{E}_1 = 0.005085 + 0.0000846c^2 - 10^{-8}c^4 \tag{8-6-21}$$

The absence of a term in $c^{1/2}$, in the expressions for $\bar{E}_2$, ϕ_E and ϕ_V, or of a term in $c^{3/2}$, in the expressions for $\bar{E}_1$, α and d, was to be expected for a solution of a non-electrolyte. The fact that the numerical values of ϕ_E and $\bar{E}_2$ for urea are approximately the same as the corresponding magnitudes for 1-1 type strong electrolytes is without explanation at present, and is probably coincidental. This non-ideal behavior of urea is very peculiar since the behavior of ϕ_V [Equation (8-6-18)] is almost ideal. The molal volume of solid urea is 45.19 cc. at 25°, and $\bar{V}_2$, at the same temperature, is within 2 per cent of this value up to $c = 10$.

(7) THE PARTIAL MOLAL COMPRESSIBILITY, APPARENT MOLAL COMPRESSIBILITY, AND COEFFICIENT OF COMPRESSIBILITY OF SOLUTIONS OF ELECTROLYTES

The partial molal compressibilities of the components of a binary solution are defined by

$$-\bar{K}_1 \equiv \left(\frac{\partial \bar{V}_1}{\partial P}\right)_T \tag{8-7-1}$$

and

$$-\bar{K}_2 \equiv \left(\frac{\partial \bar{V}_2}{\partial P}\right)_T \tag{8-7-2}$$

The apparent molal compressibility is

$$-\phi_K \equiv \left(\frac{\partial \phi_V}{\partial P}\right)_T \tag{8-7-3}$$

which, by combination with (8-5-1), becomes

$$-\phi_K = \frac{\left(\frac{\partial V}{\partial P}\right)_T - n_1 \left(\frac{\partial \bar{V}_1^0}{\partial P}\right)_T}{n_2} = \frac{-V\beta + n_1 \bar{V}_1^0 \beta_0}{n_2} \tag{8-7-4}$$

The coefficients of compressibility are defined by

$$\beta \equiv -\frac{1}{V}\left(\frac{\partial V}{\partial P}\right)_T = \frac{1}{d}\left(\frac{\partial d}{\partial P}\right)_T = \frac{1}{c}\left(\frac{\partial c}{\partial P}\right)_T \tag{8-7-5}$$

and

$$\beta_0 \equiv -\frac{1}{\bar{V}_1^0}\left(\frac{\partial \bar{V}_1^0}{\partial P}\right)_T = \frac{1}{d_0}\left(\frac{\partial d_0}{\partial P}\right)_T \tag{8-7-6}$$

for the solution and pure solvent respectively.

In practice, the apparent molal compressibility may be calculated from compressibility and density data by one of the equations,

$$\phi_K = \frac{1000}{c d_0}(d_0\beta - d\beta_0) + \beta_0\frac{M_2}{d_0}$$
$$= \frac{1000}{c}(\beta - \beta_0) + \beta_0\phi_V \tag{8-7-7}$$

and

$$\phi_K = \frac{1000}{m d d_0}(d_0\beta - d\beta_0) + \beta\frac{M_2}{d}$$
$$= \frac{1000}{m d_0}(\beta - \beta_0) + \beta\phi_V \tag{8-7-8}$$

as well as by equation (8-7-3).

As in the case of ϕ_S, we would expect the concentration dependence of ϕ_K to follow closely the simple form

$$\phi_K = \phi_K^0 + S_K\sqrt{c} \tag{8-7-9}$$

because differentiation of equation (8-5-4) leads to

$$\phi_K = \phi_K^0 - \left[\left(\frac{\partial S_V}{\partial P}\right)_T + \frac{\beta S_V}{2}\right]c^{1/2} \tag{8-7-10}$$

Furthermore

$$S_K = -\left[\left(\frac{\partial S_V}{\partial P}\right)_T + \frac{\beta_0 S_V}{2}\right] \tag{8-7-11}$$

so long as β may be replaced by β_0 in equation (8-7-10) without causing a large error. For 1-1 electrolytes, this condition is fulfilled below $3N$, at which concentration the difference in ϕ_K, as calculated by equation (8-7-9) and (8-7-10) amounts to approximately 1 per cent. A linear relationship with $\sqrt{c}$ may be maintained up to the highest concentrations, if equation (8-7-10) is rearranged to read

$$[\phi_K + \tfrac{1}{2}\beta S_V c^{1/2}] = \phi_K^0 - \left(\frac{\partial S_V}{\partial P}\right)_T c^{1/2} \tag{8-7-12}$$

and the bracketed member considered the dependent variable instead of ϕ_K. Scott[118, 119] uses this equation almost exclusively for both numerical

[118] A. F. Scott and R. W. Wilson, *J. Phys. Chem.*, **38**, 951 (1934).
[119] A. F. Scott and G. L. Bridger, *Ibid.*, **39**, 1031 (1935).

and theoretical purposes, and there can be no doubt as to its advantages over equation (8-7-9), if one considers Masson's rule strictly valid. At the present stage of the subject, we feel justified in using the simpler equation (8-7-9) for purposes of tabulation. We shall see later that, for some electrolytes, it is preferable to avoid the c-scale altogether, and make use of molalities or weight fractions.

Through the range in which both ϕ_K and ϕ_V vary as $c^{1/2}$, the combination of equations (8-7-9), (8-7-11) and (8-5-4) with (8-7-7) leads to an expression of the form

$$\beta = \beta_0 + Ac + Bc^{3/2} \qquad (8\text{-}7\text{-}13)$$

in which

$$1000A = \phi_K^0 - \beta_0\phi_V^0 \qquad (8\text{-}7\text{-}14)$$

and

$$1000B = S_K - \beta_0 S_V \qquad (8\text{-}7\text{-}15)$$

If equation (8-7-10) had been used instead of equations (8-7-9) and (8-7-11), the right-hand member of (8-7-15) would be increased by $\frac{1}{2}S_V (\beta_0 - \beta)$. The addition of this term would cause a difference of only about $\frac{1}{2}$ per cent in the calculated value of β in $3N$ solutions of 1-1 electrolytes.

In Table (8-7-1), we have recorded the parameters from which ϕ_K and β may be calculated by means of equations (8-7-9) and (8-7-13). The values of A and B were computed by Gucker and Rubin,[120] who converted the mean compressibility data of Lanman and Mair,[121] between 100 and 300 bars, to compressibility coefficents at one bar. For this calculation they employed the accurate method of Gibson[122] which will be considered later. ϕ_K^0 and S_K were estimated by equations (8-7-14) and (8-7-15) from the values of A and B given in the same table. The required values of ϕ_V^0 and S_V were taken from Table (8-5-1). ϕ_K^0 and S_K, for the salts and bases given in Table (8-7-1), are all about 16 and 23 per cent higher respectively than those obtained by Gucker[123] before he had converted the compressibility results from 200 bars to one atmosphere. Our values of ϕ_K^0 and S_K for hydrochloric acid are 26 and 30 per cent higher than his. The behavior of ϕ_K at high concentrations is illustrated in Fig. (8-7-1). A discussion of the results in more dilute solutions will be reserved for the end of this Section. Values of K_2^0 derived from compression measurements are collected in Table (8-7-1A).

The problem of calculating the compressibility coefficient at one atmosphere from direct measurement of the pressure-volume relationships of solutions is a difficult one. The pressure dependence of β is such that β

[120] F. T. Gucker, Jr., and T. R. Rubin, *J. Am. Chem. Soc.*, **57**, 78 (1935).

[121] E. H. Lanman and B. J. Mair, *J. Am. Chem. Soc.*, **56**, 390 (1934).

[122] R. E. Gibson, *J. Am. Chem. Soc.*, **56**, 4 (1934).

[123] F. T. Gucker, Jr., *Chem. Rev.*, **13**, 111 (1933).

decreases most rapidly at low pressures, where it is most difficult to obtain experimental results of high accuracy. The usual measurement involves determining the contraction in volume attending an increase in pressure of the order of 200 to 1000 atmospheres. If the initial pressure is P_0,

TABLE (8-7-1).   PARAMETERS FOR EQUATIONS (8-7-9) AND (8-7-13) AT 25° AND
1 ATMOSPHERE*

Electrolyte	$\phi_K^0 \times 10^4$†	$S_K \times 10^4$	$A \times 10^6$	$B \times 10^6$
HCl	−8.3	3.0	−1.66	0.26
LiCl	−42.0	9.1	−4.97	0.84
NaCl	−51.6	11.4	−5.91	1.04
KCl	−45.2	12.4	−5.73	1.13
LiOH	−77.9	17.0	−7.52	1.56
NaOH	−89.0	20.9	−8.59	1.90

* $\beta_0 = 45.5 \times 10^{-6}$.
† Additional values of ϕ_K^0 are tabulated by B. B. Owen and S. R. Brinkley Jr., *Chem. Rev.*, **29**, 461 (1941).

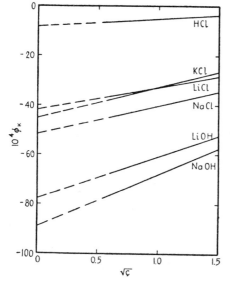

Fig. (8-7-1)
Apparent molal compressibilities of 1-1 electrolytes in water at 25° and one atmosphere.

usually one atmosphere, the result of a single measurement is the bulk compression, k_0, defined by*

$$k_0 \equiv -\frac{v_0^{(P)} - v_0^{(P_0)}}{v_0^{(P_0)}} \tag{8-7-16}$$

for a pure liquid. By dropping the subscript, 0, this equation becomes the definition of the bulk compression, k, of a solution. If k_0 is accurately

* From this point to the end of the chapter, we shall use specific volumes, etc., rather than the corresponding molal quantities, so that our treatment will not differ too greatly from Gibson's.

determined at a large number of pressures, it should be possible to express its pressure dependence by a power series in the pressure increase, such as

$$k_0 = a_1(P - P_0) + a_2(P - P_0)^2 + a_3(P - P_0)^3 + \ldots \quad (8\text{-}7\text{-}17)$$

and evaluate the parameters by suitable means.[124, 125] Furthermore, it follows from equation (8-7-17) that

$$\left(\frac{\partial k_0}{\partial P}\right)_T = a_1 + 2a_2(P - P_0) + 3a_3(P - P_0)^2 + \cdots \quad (8\text{-}7\text{-}18)$$

at any pressure. The true compressibility, β_0, at atmospheric pressure $(P = P_0 = 1)$ is equal to a_1. The difficulty of obtaining the numerous data essential to the success of this simple empirical treatment is very great. In the following paragraphs, the equations described are possibly less convenient for numerical computation, but they allow a very satisfactory estimation of β_0 over a wide pressure range from a single experimental value of k_0.

In 1888 Tait[126] discovered a simple $P\text{-}V$ relationship for water which may be written

$$\beta_0^{(P)} v_0^{(P)} = -\left(\frac{\partial v_0}{\partial P}\right)_T^{(P)} = \frac{0.4343C}{B + P} \quad (8\text{-}7\text{-}19)$$

or, in integrated form,

$$k_0 v_0^{(P_0)} = -(v_0^{(P)} - v_0^{(P_0)}) = C \log\left(\frac{B + P}{B + P_0}\right) \quad (8\text{-}7\text{-}20)$$

where C and B are positive constants. Gibson[127,128] has made a very thorough study of the Tait equation, and reports that it closely fits the experimental results of Adams[129] on water at 25° up to 10,000 bars, and Bridgman's[130] data on numerous non-volatile liquids at different temperatures over the same range. It also fits Bridgman's data for fifteen volatile liquids between 4,000 and 12,000 bars, and the data for some solids as well.

[124] A. L. T. Moesveld, *Z. physik. Chem.*, **105**, 442, 450 (1923).

[125] T. W. Richards and W. N. Stull, Carnegie Inst. Pub. #7 (1903); *Ibid.*, #76 (1907).

[126] P. G. Tait, "Report on some of the physical properties of fresh-water and of sea-water." 1888. From the "Physics and Chemistry" of the voyage of H. M. S. *Challenger*. Vol. II, Part IV. S. P. LXI.

[127] R. E. Gibson, *J. Am. Chem. Soc.*, **56**, 4 (1934); *Ibid.*, **57**, 284 (1935).

[128] R. E. Gibson and J. F. Kincaid, *Ibid.*, **60**, 511 (1938). See also J. F. Kincaid and H. Eyring, *J. Chem. Phys.*, **5**, 587 (1937) and L. J. Hudleston, *Trans. Faraday Soc.*, **33**, 98 (1937).

[129] L. H. Adams, *J. Am. Chem. Soc.*, **53**, 3769 (1931).

[130] P. W. Bridgman, *Proc. Am. Acad. Arts Sci.*, **66**, 185 (1931); *Ibid.*, **67**, 1 (1932); *Ibid.*, **68**, 1 (1933).

Some of Gibson's most recent* values, B and C/v_0, are given in Table (8-7-2). Note that C/v_0 varies very little with composition of the liquid, and is independent of the temperature.[131] The theoretical significance of the parameters has been discussed by Gibson and Kincaid.[132] The term

TABLE (8-7-2). PARAMETERS OF EQUATIONS (8-7-19) AND (8-7-20).

Substance	$\dfrac{C}{v_0}$	B (in bars)			
		25°	45°	65°	85°
Water[a,e]................	0.3150	2,996	3,081	3,052.2	2,939.0
Methanol[b]................	.2208	764	...	...	...
Ethylene glycol[a]................	.21763	2,544	2,363	2,186	2,011
Benzene[c]................	.21591	970	829	701	...
Chlorobenzene[d]................	.21591	1,249.1	1,097.8	960.9	835.0
Bromobenzene[d]................	.21591	1,404.4	1,247.3	1,103.3	972.0
Nitrobenzene[d]................	.21591	1,865.2	1,678.8	1,504.5	1,341.6
Aniline[d]................	.21591	2,006.6	1,798.3	1,605.6	1,429.4
Carbon tetrachloride[a]................	.21290	867.0	737.7	622.1	...

[a] Private communication from Dr. Gibson.
[b] R. E. Gibson, *J. Am. Chem. Soc.*, **59**, 1525 (1937).
[c] R. E. Gibson and J. F. Kincaid, *Ibid.*, **60**, 511 (1938). $B = 970 - 7.37 (t - 25) + 0.016 (t - 25)^2$.
[d] R. E. Gibson and O. H. Loeffler, *Ibid.*, **61**, 2517 (1939).
[e] R. E. Gibson, *Am. J. Sci.* [5], **35A**, 49 (1938).
Note that by our choice of symbols it is C/v_0, and not C, that is independent of temperature.

TABLE (8-7-3). COMPARISON OF VALUES OF $\beta_0 \times 10^6$ AT ONE BAR CALCULATED BY EQUATION (8-7-19) WITH VALUES DERIVED FROM MEASUREMENTS OF THE VELOCITY OF SOUND

Liquid	t	Equation	Sound
Benzene................	10	86.5	86.4[a]
Benzene................	20	93.1	93.7[a]
Benzene................	30	100.4	101.2[a]
Benzene................	40	108.6	108.6[a]
Benzene................	50	117.8	118.3[a]
Methanol................	25	125.3	125.6[a]
Water................	25	45.7	$\left\{ \begin{array}{l} 45.2^b \\ 45.9^c \end{array} \right.$

[a] E. B. Freyer, J. C. Hubbard and D. H. Andrews, *J. Am. Chem. Soc.*, **51**, 759 (1929). High frequencies.
[b] J. C. Hubbard and A. L. Loomis, *Phil. Mag.* [7], **5**, 1177 (1928). High frequencies.
[c] L. G. Pooler, *Phys. Rev.*, **35**, 832 (1930). Low frequencies.

$0.4343C$ may be regarded as the compression produced by a pressure interval, $B + P$, and B represents the difference between the expansive

* In Gibson's earlier papers, B and C should be replaced by $B + 1$ and $0.4343\ C$ to conform with the present meaning attached to these symbols.
[131] H. Carl, *Z. physik. Chem.*, **101**, 238 (1922).
[132] R. E. Gibson and J. F. Kincaid, *J. Am. Chem. Soc.*, **60**, 511 (1938). See also J. F. Kincaid and H. Eyring [*J. Chem. Phys.*, **5**, 587 (1938)], and L. J. Hudleston [*Trans. Faraday Soc.*, **33**, 98 (1937)] for discussions of equations of state similar to (8-7-19).

pressure, due to thermal energy, and the cohesive pressure, due to temperature-independent attraction between the molecules. Therefore, B decreases with the temperature, and increases with the intermolecular forces, as can be seen from Table (8-7-2).

The results in Table (8-7-3) illustrate the ability of equation (8-7-19) to represent the properties of liquids at atmospheric pressure by means of constants derived from compression measurements at high pressures. Values of β_0 at one bar are calculated from the constants given in Table (8-7-2), and compared with results derived from measurements of the velocity of sound through liquids at atmospheric pressures [Equations (8-7-29) and (8-7-30)]. The value for water, 45.7×10^{-6}, calculated by equation (8-7-19), is only 1/3 per cent higher than the mean of the results obtained from velocity measurements. A slightly lower value, 45.5×10^{-6}, previously reported by Gibson,[133] will be used in subsequent calculations.

Gibson[134] has applied the Tait equation to solutions by the introduction of a single additional parameter. This important extension is based upon Tammann's[135] hypothesis that, in the presence of an ionized solute, the water in an aqueous solution behaves as though it were subjected to a constant effective pressure, P_e, in addition to the atmospheric. The contraction in volume and decrease in compressibility which accompanies the solution of an electrolyte is thereby ascribed to a compression of the water rather than to any alteration in the properties of the solute (as a liquid).

In accordance with this idea the volume of one g. of solution containing x_1 g. of solvent and x_2 g. of solute may be represented by

$$v^{(P)} = x_1\psi_1^{(P)} + x_2\psi_2^{(P)} \qquad (8\text{-}7\text{-}21)$$

where ψ_2 is the specific volume of the pure solute (as a liquid), and ψ_1 is the apparent specific volume of the solvent in solution.* Further, the addition of an ionic solute (as a liquid) to one g. of pure water would cause the contraction, $v_0^{(P)} - \psi_1^{(P)}$, in the total volume of the system. In terms of the Tait equation (8-7-20), this volume change becomes

$$-[\psi_1^{(P)} - v_0^{(P)}] = C \log\left(\frac{B + P + P_e}{B + P}\right) \qquad (8\text{-}7\text{-}22)$$

at any pressure, P. This useful expression will be referred to as the Tait-Gibson equation.

[133] R. E. Gibson, *J. Am. Chem. Soc.*, **56**, 4 (1934).

[134] R. E. Gibson, *J. Am. Chem. Soc.*, **56**, 4 (1934); *Ibid.*, **57**, 284 (1935).

[135] G. Tammann, "Über die Beziehungen zwischen den inneren Kräften und Eigenschaften der Lösungen," p. 36, Voss, Leipzig, 1907.

* For moderate pressures and concentrations, where $x_2\psi_2$ is considerably less than $x_1\psi_1$, it is not essential to be able to evaluate ψ_2 exactly. The interpretation of this quantity will be referred to later.

Eliminating $\psi_1^{(P)}$ between the foregoing equations, we obtain

$$- v^{(P)} = x_1 C \log(B + P + P_e) - x_2 \psi_2^{(P)} - x_1[v_0^{(P)} + C \log(B + P)]$$

$$(8\text{-}7\text{-}23)$$

According to equation (8-7-20), the last term on the right drops out for variations in pressure at constant composition; hence

$$k v^{(P_0)} = -[v^{(P)} - v^{(P_0)}] = x_1 C \log \frac{(B + P + P_e)}{(B + P_0 + P_e)} - x_2[\psi_2^{(P)} - \psi_2^{(P_0)}]$$

$$(8\text{-}7\text{-}24)$$

By differentiation at constant temperature and composition, we obtain

$$\beta^{(P)} v^{(P)} = \frac{0.4343 \, x_1 C}{B + P + P_e} - x_2 \frac{\partial \psi_2^{(P)}}{\partial P} \qquad (8\text{-}7\text{-}25)$$

for the compressibility of the solution at any pressure, P. At moderate pressures and concentrations the terms containing ψ_2 are negligible. Since B and C are characteristic of the solvent alone, P_e is the only parameter dependent upon the properties of the solution, and may be evaluated from the measurement of a single compression over any convenient pressure range. P_e is directly related to the partial molal volume of the solute. From the definition, $\bar{v}_1 M_1 = (\partial V/\partial n_1)_{P, T, n_2}$, the proportion $x_1/x_2 = n_1 M_1/n_2 M_2$, and equation (8-7-21) it follows that

$$\bar{v}_1^{(P)} = x_1 x_2 \frac{\partial \psi_1^{(P)}}{\partial x_1} + \psi_1^{(P)} \qquad (8\text{-}7\text{-}26)$$

By combining this equation with the fundamental relation

$$v^{(P)} = x_1 \bar{v}_1^{(P)} + x_2 \bar{v}_2^{(P)} \qquad (8\text{-}7\text{-}27)$$

and equations (8-7-21) and (8-7-22), Gibson[136] derived the expressions

$$\bar{v}_2^{(P)} - \psi_2^{(P)} = \frac{0.4343 \, x_1^2 C}{B + P_e + P} \frac{\partial(B + P_e)}{\partial x_1} \qquad (8\text{-}7\text{-}28)$$

and

$$\bar{V}_2^{(P)} - M_2 \psi_2^{(P)} = \frac{- 434.3 C}{B + P_e + P} \frac{\partial(B + P_e)}{\partial m} \qquad (8\text{-}7\text{-}28a)$$

The last equation shows that the magnitude of the partial molal volume of the solute is largely governed by two factors. The first, $\partial(B + P_e)/\partial m$, is the rate of change of total internal pressure with concentration, and is a function of both solvent and solute. The second, $C/(B + P_e + P)$, is related to the compressibility of the solvent at the pressure, $P + P_e$, and is independent of the solute.

[136] R. E. Gibson, *Am. J. Sci.*, [5], **35A**, 49 (1938).

In the calculation of the values of β, corresponding to the parameters given in Table (8-7-1), the pressure increment of 200 bars was from an initial pressure, P_0, of 100 bars instead of atmospheric. In this case, the argument of the logarithmic term in equation (8-7-24) is $(B + P_e + 300)/(B + P_e + 100)$, and the last term represents the compression of the pure liquid solute between 100 and 300 bars. The interval 1 to 1000 bars was used by Gibson[137] in his investigation of the concentration dependence of P_e for a large number of electrolytes. Some of his results[138] are reproduced in Fig. (8-7-2). Since the term P_e evidently arises from attractive forces between the ions and the induced or residual charges on the water molecules, it would be expected to increase with the charge density on the ions.

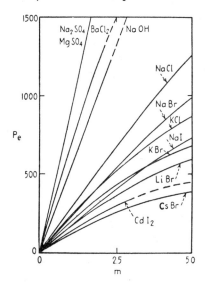

Fig. (8-7-2)
Effective pressure (bars) of salts in aqueous solutions at 25°

This expectation is borne out, with a few exceptions, by the curves in the figure, where it can be seen that in a series of salts with a common ion the value of P_e is highest for the salts with the smaller, or more highly charged uncommon ion. It should be remarked, however, that the *smallest* ions, Li^+, Be^{++} and Mg^{++}, constitute exceptions to these rules. The polarization produced by small ions of high charge density has been shown by Bernal and Fowler[139] to strengthen the forces responsible for the relatively open structure of water, in which each molecule is surrounded tetrahedrally by four others. This would counteract some of the normal tendency of the ions to compress the solvent, and give rise to abnormally low values of P_e. A more detailed description of this process is given by Gibson,[138] who also suggests that much of the specificity exhibited by P_e for similar

[137] R. E. Gibson, *J. Am. Chem. Soc.*, **57**, 290 (1935).
[138] R. E. Gibson, *Sci. Monthly*, **46**, 103 (1938).
[139] J. D. Bernal and R. H. Fowler, *J. Chem. Phys.*, 1, 540 (1933).

ions may be due simply to the effect of the volumes of the ions in increasing the average distance-between water molecules. This diminishes the contribution of water-water molecule interaction to the total internal pressure, $B + P_e$, of the solution. This volume effect would increase with the size of the ions. He proposed to take this effect into account by comparing the total internal pressures of solutions divided by the square of the water concentration rather than comparing the effective pressures alone. Thus, if the function, $(B + P_e)/C_W^2$, is plotted as ordinate in Fig. (8-7-2) instead of P_e, the individuality of the plots is greatly reduced. Indeed, the results for all of the 1-1 salts, except those of lithium, are surprisingly well represented by a single curve. This fact leaves little doubt as to the importance of pure ionic volume effects.

The role of the solvent is emphasized by the fact that the anomalous behavior of lithium salts in respect to P_e in water disappears in glycol solutions, and the plots of P_e against m for dilute solutions of sodium and lithium bromides, and sodium and cadmium iodides superimpose in methanol, but are widely divergent in water and in glycol.[140]

Another empirical relation governing the variation of P_e with composition is[141]

$$P_e = Lc_1c_2 + i \qquad (8\text{-}7\text{-}28\text{b})$$

where L and i are characteristic of the electrolyte. The constant i is so small that it may be neglected for most purposes. It is introduced into the equation to call attention to the fact that plots of P_e against c_1c_2 do not pass exactly through the origin for all salts. This equation suggests that P_e may be considered a measure of the departure of the volume relationships of solutions from ideality, because it has been shown[141] that the relative departures from the simple law of mixtures for the compressions of a number of solutions are also directly proportional to the product c_1c_2. It follows from equation (8-7-28b) that P_e varies inversely with the square of the volume. This brings out the analogy between P_e and the cohesive pressure in gases, which are responsible for the a/v^2 term in the van der Waals equation. It also implies that P_e is a function of the pressure. This may become an important consideration in the study of liquids of relatively high compressibilities. Under the conditions of the present applications of equations (8-7-24) and (8-7-25), P_e is considered a constant characteristic of a given system at constant composition and temperature. This simplification is justified by the ability of the equations to represent compression data over the entire experimental range, and to effect extrapolations to atmospheric pressure. In Table (8-7-4) some compressibilities, calculated at 1 bar by equation (8-7-25) from values of P_e derived

[140] R. E. Gibson, *J. Am. Chem. Soc.*, **59**, 1521 (1937).

[141] R. E. Gibson, *J. Am. Chem. Soc.*, **57**, 284 (1935). The concentrations of the water, c_1, and the electrolyte, c_2, are in mols per liter of solution.

from compressions at 1000 bars, are compared with values determined at one atmosphere from the velocity of sound[142] through the solutions. The agreement leaves little to be desired.

In concluding this discussion of the Tait equation, and its extension to solution of electrolytes, some implications regarding the actual volume of the dissolved solute will be briefly noted. Equation (8-7-23) may be used to compute ψ_2 at one atmosphere from values of P_e estimated from the contraction accompanying the process of solution. Values of ψ_2 obtained in this manner[143] are practically independent of the concentration, and are equal to, or a little greater (5 to 30 per cent) than the specific volume of the pure crystalline solute. If equation (8-7-28a) is used to estimate ψ_2 from P_e and $\bar{V}_2$, it is found that ψ_2 diminishes slightly with concentration. If,

TABLE (8-7-4).* COMPARISON OF COMPRESSIBILITIES ESTIMATED BY TWO INDEPENDENT METHODS AT 1 BAR AND 25°.

$100x_2$ (Wt.%)	$\beta \times 10^6$ (From compressions at 1000 bars)				$\beta \times 10^6$ (From sound velocities at 1 bar)			
	KCl	KBr	KI	NaCl	KCl	KBr	KI	NaCl
6	41.8	43.2	44.3	40.6	41.7	43.5	44.3	40.4
10	39.5	41.7	....	37.6	39.4	41.9	....	37.5
16	36.3	....	41.7	33.2	36.2	....	41.7	33.4
20	34.3	38.1	....	30.7	34.2	38.4	....	31.0
24	32.4	....	....	28.4	32.4	....	....	28.8
30	....	34.6	37.8	....	....	34.8	38.0	....
40	....	31.1	....	....	....	31.4	....	....
45	....	....	33.4	....	....	....	33.7	....

* R. E. Gibson, *J. Am. Chem. Soc.*, **57**, 284 (1935). Table IV, p. 291.

however, it is assumed that the compressibility of the solute in solution is three times as great as in the solid state, then ψ_2 is quite independent of concentration.[144] Thus, the specific volume of the pure solute, or more accurately the pure melted solute, appears to be closely associated with the "actual" volume of the solute in solution. The same conclusion is to be drawn from the discussion [Section (5)] of the critical disruptive volume, V^*, but it should be noted that V^* is considerably larger than the calculated values of $M_2\psi_2$. The exact relationship between these two quantities is by no means obvious.

So far the experimental data under consideration have been confined to relatively concentrated solutions ($c \geq 0.5$). Direct compression measurements are not well suited to the investigation of dilute solutions, so other means have been resorted to in an effort to determine accurate compressibilities, at sufficiently high dilutions, to make a significant comparison of the experimental results with the predictions of the interionic attraction

142 E. B. Freyer, *J. Am. Chem. Soc.*, **53**, 1313 (1931).
143 R. E. Gibson, *J. Am. Chem. Soc.*, **56**, 4 (1934); *Ibid.*, **57**, 284 (1935).
144 R. E. Gibson, *Am. J. Sci.* [5], **35A**, 49 (1938).

theory.   As was the case for the other second derivatives of the Debye-Hückel equation, $\bar{J}_2$ and $\bar{E}_2$, we are prepared not to expect close agreement of ϕ_K or $\bar{K}_2$ with the theoretical limiting law at dilutions within the present experimental range.   However, it is a matter of some interest to ascertain whether there is any tendency of the experimental curves to converge toward the predicted slopes at the highest accessible dilutions, or at least to group themselves unambiguously with regard to valence type.   It will be recalled that the experimental slopes S_K given in Table (8-7-1) show a seven-fold variation among the few 1-1 electrolytes represented.

The most accurate method of determining compressibilities at atmospheric pressure and low concentrations depends upon measurements of the velocity of sound through the solutions.   The velocity, u, in cm. sec.$^{-1}$, through a medium of density, d, in g. cm.$^{-3}$, is given by

$$u^2 = \frac{10^6}{\beta_s \, d} = \frac{10^6 c_p/c_v}{\beta \, d} \tag{8-7-29}$$

when the adiabatic and isothermal compressibilities, β_s and β, are expressed in bars^{-1}.   Since the ratio of the specific heats, c_p/c_v, is usually not known for salt solutions, we will make use of the difference, $\beta - \beta_s$, given by the thermodynamic formula

$$\delta \equiv \beta - \beta_s = 0.0239\alpha^2 T/\zeta \tag{8-7-30}$$

here α is the coefficient of thermal expansion of the solution, and ζ, the specific heat at constant pressure in cal. deg.$^{-1}$ cm.$^{-3}$, has been written for the familiar product $c_p \, d$ so as to avoid complicated subscripts in later equations.   Because of the factor α^2, the difference δ vanishes at the temperature of maximum density.   In aqueous solutions δ is only about 1 % of β at 25°, but the neglect of this small difference can affect the value of ϕ_V for 1-1 electrolytes by as much as 10 %.   In Tables (8-7-3) to (8-7-5) this difference has been taken into account, and isothermal values are recorded.

The determination of ϕ_V and $\bar{K}_2^0$ from sound velocity measurements requires considerable auxilliary data, as the following development will show.   If the quantity, $\phi_{K(s)}$, defined by

$$\phi_{K(s)} \equiv \frac{1000}{c} (\beta_s - \beta_{0s}) + \beta_{0s}\phi_V \tag{8-7-31}$$

is subtracted from the true apparent molal compressibility, ϕ_K, given by equation (8-7-7), we obtain

$$\phi_K = \phi_{K(s)} + \frac{1000}{c} (\delta - \delta_0) + \delta_0\phi_V \tag{8-7-32}$$

where δ_0 corresponds to equation (8-7-30) applied to the pure solvent. The last four equations lead to the evaluation of ϕ_K from sound velocities if the quantities δ, δ_0 and ϕ_V are known.   Subsequent extrapolation of a series of values of ϕ_K would lead to the limiting value, ϕ_K^0 , which is identical with the standard partial molal quantity, $\bar{K}_2^0$. If this procedure relies upon the extrapolation of the several apparent molal quantities against $c^{1/2}$, rather than functions involving the a-parameter discussed in the next section, the dependence of $\bar{K}_2^0$ upon the various factors entering into its calculation can be simply formulated.

The following set* of apparent molal properties, $\phi_X(X = K_2, E_2, C_{p_2}, C_{V_2}$ and $M_2)$ may be represented by the equation

$$\phi_X = \frac{1000}{c} (x - x_0) + x_0\phi_V \tag{8-7-33}$$

in which $x = \beta, \alpha, c_p d(\equiv \varsigma), c_v d$ and d, are the corresponding directly measurable specific properties. Throughout the concentration range in which the equation

$$\phi_X = \phi_X^0 + S_X c^{1/2} \tag{8-7-34}$$

is valid, the specific properties will be given by

$$x = x_0 + A_x c^{1/2} + B_x c^{3/2} \tag{8-7-35}$$

where

$$1000A_x = \phi_X^0 - x_0\phi_V^0 \tag{8-7-36}$$

and

$$1000B_x = S_X - x_0 S_V \tag{8-7-37}$$

These equations, generalizations of equations such as (8-7-13) to (8-7-15), can be combined with equation (8-7-30) to yield a series representation of δ in which the first three terms have the same forms as those of equation (8-7-35). Thus,

$$\delta = \delta_0 + A_\delta c + B_\delta c^{3/2} + \cdots \tag{8-7-38}$$

where

$$A_\delta = \delta_0(2A_\alpha/\alpha_0 - A_\varsigma/\varsigma_0) \tag{8-7-39}$$

and

$$B_\delta = \delta_0(2B_\alpha/\alpha_0 - B_\varsigma/\varsigma_0) \tag{8-7-40}$$

Similarly, the velocity of sound can be represented by

$$u = u_0 + A_u c + B_u c^{3/2} + \cdots \tag{8-7-41}$$

where

$$2A_u = -u_0(A_\beta/\beta_{s0} - A_\delta/\beta_{0s} + A_d/d_0) \tag{8-7-42}$$

* To complete the set and include equation (8-5-2), it is only necessary to observe that M_2 and the "apparent molal weight", ϕ_M , are identically equal.

and

$$2B_{\dot{u}} = -u_0(B_\beta/\beta_{0s} - B_\delta/\beta_{0s} + B_d/d_0) \qquad (8\text{-}7\text{-}43)$$

Combination of the above equations with (8-7-32) yields

$$\phi_K^0 = \phi_{K(s)}^0 + \delta_0\phi_V^0 + \delta_0(2000A_\alpha/\alpha_0 - 1000A_\zeta/\zeta_0) \qquad (8\text{-}7\text{-}44)$$

or, explicitly in terms of sound velocity parameters,

$$\phi_K^0 = 1000A_\delta + \delta_0\phi_V^0 + \beta_{0s}(2\phi_V^0 - M_2/d_0 - 2000A_u/u_0) \qquad (8\text{-}7\text{-}45)$$

The first term of the right hand member of the last equation accounts for about 7 % of ϕ_K^0 for sodium and potassium chlorides[145] in aqueous solutions at 25°. Values of ϕ_K^0 for several alkali halides have been determined by means of these equations, and are reported in Table (8-7-5). Comparison between the results derived from measurements of compressions and of sound velocities shows discrepancies of the order of 10 %. We believe that the values derived from sound velocities are the more accurate, but so long as the extrapolations are based upon equations, such as (8-7-34), which do not contain the a-parameter, it seems unwise to assume that any of the values of $\bar{K}_2^0$ is known to better than 2 % regardless of the precision of the basic data.

The experimental measurement of sound velocities began with the relatively crude experiments of Kundt[146] and developed very slowly until Pierce[147] realized the possibilities of ultrasonics as a research tool. The development of ultrasonics has been so rapid in recent years that the reader must be referred to monographs[148] on the subject for the bibliography. The main instrumental developments in applications to the study of solutions have been the reflector type and the optical type interferometers.

The first reflector type instruments made use of ultra-sound of fixed frequency, and the measurement involved determining its wave-length by moving a reflector between nodes. Hubbard and Loomis[149] began the use of this popular instrument. Later, Hubbard and Zartman[150] suggested the fixed reflector-variable frequency modification of the apparatus. Pulse[151] techniques have been introduced in recent years, but the movable

[145] B. B. Owen and H. L. Simons, *J. Phys. Chem.*, **61**, 479 (1957).

[146] A. Kundt, *Pogg. Ann.*, **127**, 497 (1866).

[147] G. W. Pierce, *Proc. Am. Acad. Arts Sci.*, **59**, 81 (1923); *Ibid.*, **60**, 271 (1923).

[148] L. Bergmann, "Der Ultraschall und Seine Anwendung in Wissenschaft und Technik," Sixth Edition, S. Hirzel Verlag, Stuttgart (1954); E. G. Richardson, "Ultrasonic Physics", Elsevier Publishing Co., New York (1952); P. Vigoureux, "Ultrasonics", John Wiley and Sons, New York (1951).

[149] J. C. Hubbard and A. L. Loomis, *Nature*, **120**, 189 (1927); *Phil. Mag.*, **75**, 1177 (1928); *Phys. Rev.*, **31**, 158 (1928).

[150] J. C. Hubbard and I. F. Zartman, *Rev. Sci. Inst.*, **10**, 382 (1939). *Cf.* H. I. Leon, *J. Acoust. Soc. Am.*, **27**, 1107 (1955).

[151] J. R. Pellman and J. K. Galt, *J. Chem. Phys.*, **14**, 608 (1946).

reflector type is considered[152] the most generally satisfactory of the reflector instruments.

The most sensitive and elegant acoustic interferometers are of the optical type based upon the discovery of Debye and Sears[153] and of Lucas and Biquard[154] that ultrasonic waves traversing a liquid set up a periodical inhomogeneity which can act as an optical grating. Szalay[155] made use of this instrument when he attempted to verify the valence factor in the theoretical slope $S_{(K)}$. His results were inconclusive because he only recorded values of $1 - \beta_s/\beta_{0s}$, and at the single concentration, 0.1 N.

TABLE (8-7-5).* VALUES OF $-10^4 \phi_K^0$ DERIVED FROM ULTRASONIC MEASUREMENTS AND EQUATION (8-7-45).

t°C.	NaCl	KCl	NaBr	KBr	%
30	42.4	37.1	34.0	28.6	±4.7
25	46.3ᵃ	40.4ᵃ	37.7	31.9	2.9
20	50.7	44.4	42.0	35.7	2.1
15	55.7	49.0	46.9	40.2	1.5
10	61.5	54.4	52.6	45.5	1.0
5	68.1	60.7	59.1	51.6	0.6
0	75.9	68.0	66.7	58.9	0.7

* B. B. Owen and P. L. Kronick, *J. Phys. Chem.*, **65**, 84 (1961). The figures given in the last column are the uncertainties in the values of ϕ_K^0 estimated by Kronick as resulting from the sum of the terms in equation (8-7-45).

ᵃ B. B. Owen and H. L. Simons[145] reported the values 46.6_5 and 40.7_2 for NaCl and KCl, respectively.

The valence effect was correctly considered by Gucker,[156] and by Falkenhagen[157] and Bachem,[158] but not verified. Gucker's values of $10^4 S_K$ recorded in Table (8-7-1) are seen to vary from 3 to 20 for a series of 1-1 type electrolytes. This variation is quite contrary to theory, but it must be remembered that in this case the experimental data were extrapolated from high pressures and high concentrations. Bachem's[158] measurements at 1 atmosphere extend to somewhat lower concentrations, but they can not at present be corrected for the difference for $\beta - \beta_s$ in the case of the higher valence type electrolytes. In view of the very high dilutions that

[152] V. A. Del Grosso, E. J. Smura and P. F. Fougere, "Accuracy of Ultrasonic Interferometer Velocity Determinations", Naval Research Laboratory Report 4439, Washington (1954).

[153] P. Debye and F. W. Sears, *Proc. Nat. Acad. Sci.*, **18**, 409 (1932); P. Debye, *Physik. Z.*, **33**, 849 (1932).

[154] R. Lucas and P. Biquard, *J. Phys. Radium*, **3**, 464 (1932).

[155] A. Szalay, *Physik. Z.*, **35**, 639 (1934).

[156] F. T. Gucker, Jr., *Chem. Rev.*, **13**, 111 (1933); *J. Am. Chem. Soc.*, **55**, 2709 (1933); F. T. Gucker, Jr., and T. R. Rubin, *Ibid.*, **57**, 78 (1935).

[157] H. Falkenhagen and C. Bachem, *Z. Electrochem.*, **41**, 570 (1935).

[158] C. Bachem, *Z. Physik*, **101**, 541 (1936).

must be attained before the limiting slopes $\mathcal{S}_{(H)}$ and $\mathcal{S}_{(V)}$ are approached, it seems probable that Bachem's lowest concentrations (about 0.03 N) should be considered "concentrated" in so far as agreement with $\mathcal{S}_{(K)}$ for higher valence types is concerned. In this respect the three quantities, $\bar{K}_2$, $\bar{E}_2$ and $\bar{C}_{p_2}$, all second derivatives of $\bar{F}_2$, present a challenging experimental problem to the next generation of physical chemists.

The compressibilities of some non-electrolyte solutions appear to possess the same concentration dependence as solutions of electrolytes. Gucker[159] obtained linear plots of ϕ_K against $\sqrt{c}$ from the data of Perman and Urry[160] on urea and sucrose. Bachem's[161] data on sucrose are more nearly linear in c than in $\sqrt{c}$, but two points at the lowest concentrations are inconsistent with either plot. Gibson[162] found that within the experimental error, ϕ_K for resorcinol is linear in $\sqrt{c}$. In methanol-water mixtures this relationship definitely does not apply to the methanol, but is very closely followed by the water.[162] In solutions of incompletely ionized electrolytes the results are contradictory. For acetic acid[163] in aqueous solutions ϕ_K is linear in $\sqrt{c}$ up to 40 per cent acid, while the values for cadmium iodide[164] in glycol and in methanol are linear in c up to 50 per cent salt.

In the face of the material presented in this and the two preceding sections, it seems evident that the interionic attraction theory in its present form in inadequate to deal with the volume relationships of aqueous solutions within the experimentally accessible concentration range. It is true that, by the development of an elaborate precision technique, partial molal volumes have been shown to agree with the Debye-Hückel theory at high dilutions, but the explanation of Masson's rule and the similar linear relationships obeyed by the expansibility and compressibility seem to require an intimate knowledge concerning the structure of liquids and quite possibly a much more detailed concept of ionic distribution than the ionic atmosphere.

(8) Inclusion of the a-Parameter in the Theoretical Limiting Equations for Apparent Molal Properties

The uncertainties involved in the extrapolation of plots of apparent molal properties against $c^{1/2}$ have been emphasized throughout this chapter. In Section (1) dealing with ϕ_L it was pointed out that the introduction of the a-parameter, without a term in the first power in c, would account for the observed individuality among salts of the same valence type, but that the magnitudes of a and the order in which these values arrange themselves

[159] F. T. Gucker, Jr., *J. Am. Chem. Soc.*, **55**, 2709 (1933); *Chem. Rev.*, **13**, 111 (1933). *Cf.* Ref. 30 and 90.

[160] E. P. Perman and W. D. Urry, *Proc. Roy. Soc. London*, **A126**, 44 (1929).

[161] C. Bachem, *Z. Physik*, **101**, 541 (1936).

[162] R. E. Gibson, *J. Am. Chem. Soc.*, **57**, 1551 (1935).

[163] R. E. Gibson, *J. Am. Chem. Soc.*, **57**, 284 (1935).

[164] R. E. Gibson, *J. Am. Chem. Soc.*, **59**, 1521 (1937).

were not the same as when the a-parameters were derived from activity coefficient data. In Section (5) it was shown that the use of a term in the first power in c, without consideration of the a-parameter, appeared to result in a satisfactory extrapolation of ϕ_V. Thus, it is apparent that Figure (8-5-1) that for three typical strong electrolytes, plots of $\phi_V - \mathcal{S}_{(V)}c^{1/2}$ against c were nearly linear, providing that $\mathcal{S}_{(V)}$ be given the value 1.9 for potassium chloride and sodium bromide, and $1.9(3)^{3/2}$, or 9.9, for strontium chloride. Unfortunately, these numerical values for the limiting slopes do not result in satisfactory extrapolations for other salts of the same valence types, and according to our estimated limiting slopes recorded in Table (5-2-5), the theoretical value of $(\frac{2}{3})\mathcal{S}_{(V)}$ at 25° should be nearer 2.5 than 1.9. Furthermore, the disregard of the a-parameter is quite indefensible theoretically.

Owen and Brinkley[165] showed that the use of both the a-parameter and a term in c results in linear extrapolations which appear to be consistent with the values of $\mathcal{S}_{(V)}$ and $\mathcal{S}_{(H)}$ in Table (5-2-5) and with the a-parameters derived from activity coefficient data. After an outline of the derivation of the limiting equations, their application to extrapolations will be illustrated at the conclusion of this section.

For a solution containing n_1 moles of solvent and n_2 moles of solute electrolyte, it can be shown that the Coulomb forces between the ions contributes the amount[166]

$$\Delta F(el) = -n_2 \frac{N\epsilon^2}{3D} \tau\kappa\Sigma\nu_j z_j^2 \qquad (8\text{-}8\text{-}1)$$

to the free energy of the solution. The function τ is given by

$$\tau = \frac{3}{\kappa^3 a^3}\left[\frac{1}{2}\kappa^2 a^2 - \kappa a + \ln(1 + \kappa a)\right] \qquad (8\text{-}8\text{-}2)$$

$$= 1 - \tfrac{3}{4}\kappa a + \tfrac{3}{5}\kappa^2 a^2 - \cdots ; \qquad \kappa a \leq 1. \qquad (8\text{-}8\text{-}2a)$$

The electrolytic contribution to the volume and enthalpy of the solution can be obtained from $\Delta F(el)$ by the thermodynamic equations

$$\Delta V(el) = \left(\frac{\partial \Delta F(el)}{\partial P}\right)_T \qquad (8\text{-}8\text{-}3)$$

$$\Delta H(el) = -T^2\left(\frac{\partial \Delta F(el)/T}{\partial T}\right)_P \qquad (8\text{-}8\text{-}4)$$

For the binary solution postulated, we can identify $\Delta V(el)$ and $\Delta H(el)$ with the total departures of the ionized solute from ideal behavior with respect to volume and enthalpy, and write

[165] B. B. Owen and S. R. Brinkley, Jr., *Ann. N. Y. Acad. Sci.*, **51**, 753 (1949).
[166] P. Debye and E. Hückel, *Physik. Z.*, **24**, 185 (1923).

$$\Delta V(el) = (n_1 V_1 + n_2 \phi_v) - (n_1 V_1 + n_2 \phi_v^0) = n_2(\phi_v - \phi_v^0) \qquad (8\text{-}8\text{-}5)$$

$$\Delta H(el) = (n_1 H_1 + n_2 \phi_H) - (n_1 H_1 + n_2 \phi_H^0) = n_2(\phi_H - \phi_H^0) \qquad (8\text{-}8\text{-}6)$$

Combination of these equations yields the expressions

$$\phi_V - \phi_V^0 = -\frac{\epsilon^2 N}{3D} \Sigma \nu_j z_j^2 \left[\sigma \frac{\partial \ln \kappa a}{\partial P} - \tau \frac{\partial \ln Da}{\partial P} \right] \kappa \qquad (8\text{-}8\text{-}7)$$

$$\phi_H - \phi_H^0 = T \frac{\epsilon^2 N}{3D} \Sigma \nu_j z_j^2 \left[\sigma \frac{\partial \ln \kappa a}{\partial T} - \frac{\tau}{T} - \tau \frac{\partial \ln Da}{\partial T} \right] \kappa \qquad (8\text{-}8\text{-}8)$$

in which the function σ is defined by

$$\sigma = \frac{\partial(\tau \kappa a)}{\partial \kappa a} \qquad (8\text{-}8\text{-}9)$$

Carrying out the indicated differentiation in terms of equation (8-8-2), σ can be expressed in terms of κa, thus

$$\sigma = \frac{3}{\kappa^3 a^3} [1 + \kappa a - (1 + \kappa a)^{-1} - 2 \ln (1 + \kappa a)] \qquad (8\text{-}8\text{-}10)$$

$$= 1 - \tfrac{9}{4}\kappa a + \tfrac{9}{5}\kappa^2 a^2 - \cdots ; \qquad \kappa a \le 1 \qquad (8\text{-}8\text{-}10a)$$

From equation (5-2-7), applied to a binary solution, we write

$$\kappa a = (\Sigma \nu_j z_j^2)^{\frac{1}{2}} \left(\frac{4\pi N \epsilon^2}{1000 k D T} \right)^{\frac{1}{2}} a c^{\frac{1}{2}} = A' c^{\frac{1}{2}} \qquad (8\text{-}8\text{-}11)$$

$$\frac{\partial \ln \kappa a}{\partial P} = -\frac{1}{2}\frac{\partial \ln D}{\partial P} + \frac{1}{2}\beta + \frac{\partial \ln a}{\partial P} \qquad (8\text{-}8\text{-}12)$$

$$\frac{\partial \ln \kappa a}{\partial T} = -\frac{1}{2}\frac{\partial \ln D}{\partial T} - \frac{1}{T} - \frac{1}{2}\alpha + \frac{\partial \ln a}{\partial T}. \qquad (8\text{-}8\text{-}13)$$

By combining equations (8-8-7) through (8-8-13), properly rearranging the terms in τ and σ and introducing the linear terms in c, which will be justified later, we obtain

$$\phi_V - \phi_V^0 = \tfrac{2}{3}\mathbb{S}_{(V)}\tau c^{1/2} + \tfrac{1}{2}W_{(V)}\theta c + \tfrac{1}{2}K_{(V)}c \qquad (8\text{-}8\text{-}14)$$

$$\phi_H - \phi_H^0 = \tfrac{2}{3}\mathbb{S}_{(H)}\tau c^{1/2} + \tfrac{1}{2}W_{(H)}\theta c + \tfrac{1}{2}K_{(H)}c. \qquad (8\text{-}8\text{-}15)$$

The function θ is defined by

$$\theta = \frac{4}{3}\left(\frac{\tau - \sigma}{\kappa a} \right) \qquad (8\text{-}8\text{-}16)$$

$$= 1 - \tfrac{8}{5}\kappa a + \tfrac{12}{6}\kappa^2 a^2 - \cdots ; \qquad \kappa a \le 1. \qquad (8\text{-}8\text{-}16a)$$

The theoretical coefficients $\mathbb{S}$, W and K are the same as those appearing in the equations for the corresponding partial molal quantities in a binary solution, viz.,

$$\bar{V}_2 - \bar{V}_2^0 = \frac{\mathbb{S}_{(V)}c^{\frac{1}{2}}}{1 + \kappa a} + \frac{W_{(V)}c}{(1 + \kappa a)^2} + K_{(V)}c \qquad (8\text{-}8\text{-}17)$$

$$\mathbb{S}_{(V)} = 2.303 \nu R T \mathbb{S}_{(f)} \frac{3}{2} \left[\frac{\partial \ln D}{\partial P} - \frac{1}{3} \beta \right] \qquad (8\text{-}8\text{-}17a)$$

$$W_{(V)} = -2.303 \nu R T \mathbb{S}_{(f)} A' \frac{1}{2} \left[\frac{\partial \ln D}{\partial P} - \beta - 2 \frac{\partial \ln a}{\partial P} \right] \qquad (8\text{-}8\text{-}17b)$$

$$K_{(V)} = 2.303 \nu R T B \left[\frac{\partial \ln B}{\partial P} + \beta \right] \qquad (8\text{-}8\text{-}17c)$$

and

$$\bar{H}_2 - \bar{H}_2^0 = \frac{\mathbb{S}_{(H)}c^{\frac{1}{2}}}{1 + \kappa a} + \frac{W_{(H)}c}{(1 + \kappa a)^2} + K_{(H)}c \qquad (8\text{-}8\text{-}18)$$

$$\mathbb{S}_{(H)} = -2.303 \nu R T^2 \mathbb{S}_{(f)} \frac{3}{2} \left[\frac{\partial \ln D}{\partial P} + \frac{1}{T} + \frac{1}{3} \alpha \right] \qquad (8\text{-}8\text{-}18a)$$

$$W_{(H)} = 2.303 \nu R T^2 \mathbb{S}_{(f)} A' \frac{1}{2} \left[\frac{\partial \ln D}{\partial T} + \frac{1}{T} + \alpha - 2 \frac{\partial \ln a}{\partial T} \right] \qquad (8\text{-}8\text{-}18b)$$

$$K_{(H)} = -2.303 \nu R T^2 B \left[\frac{\partial \ln B}{\partial T} - \alpha \right] \qquad (8\text{-}8\text{-}18c)$$

The effect of the a-parameter upon the apparent molal quantities is contained in the complicated functions τ and θ instead of the simpler more familiar terms $(1 + A'\sqrt{c})^{-1}$ and $(1 + A'\sqrt{c})^{-2}$.

In order to justify the terms in $K_{(V)}c$ and $K_{(H)}c$ we can combine the equations

$$\phi_V - \phi_V^0 = \frac{1}{m} \int_0^m (\bar{V}_2 - \bar{V}_2^0) \, dm \qquad (8\text{-}8\text{-}19)$$

$$\phi_H - \phi_H^0 = \frac{1}{m} \int_0^m (\bar{H}_2 - \bar{H}_2^0) \, dm \qquad (8\text{-}8\text{-}20)$$

and

$$m = \frac{c}{d_0} \left[1 - \frac{c\phi_V}{1000} \right]^{-1}. \qquad (8\text{-}8\text{-}21)$$

which follow from definitions, with (8-8-17) and (8-8-18), which follow from the Debye-Hückel equation (3-8-2) applied to binary solutions. The forms of the resulting integrals are too complicated to be of much practical use except to show, by expansion in series, that equations (8-8-14) and (8-8-15) must be valid at high dilutions, and that the terms $\frac{1}{2}K_{(V)}c$ and $\frac{1}{2}K_{(H)}c$ satisfactorily represent the integrals

$$\frac{1}{m}\int_0^m K_{(V)}c\, dm \quad \text{and} \quad \frac{1}{m}\int_0^m K_{(H)}c\, dm$$

for simple electrolytes at concentrations up to about 1 molar.

When equations (8-8-14) and (8-8-15) are rearranged to read

$$[\phi_V - \tfrac{2}{3}S_{(V)}\tau c^{1/2} - \tfrac{1}{2}W_{(V)}\theta c] = \phi_V^0 + \tfrac{1}{2}K_{(V)}c \tag{8-8-22}$$

and

$$[\phi_H - \phi_H' - \tfrac{2}{3}S_{(H)}\tau c^{1/2} - \tfrac{1}{2}W_{(H)}\theta c] = \phi_H^0 - \phi_H' + \tfrac{1}{2}K_{(H)}c. \tag{8-8-23}$$

they are in forms suitable for extrapolation.* Equation (8-8-22) has, in fact, been used to extrapolate the data for perchloric acid,[167] but for other

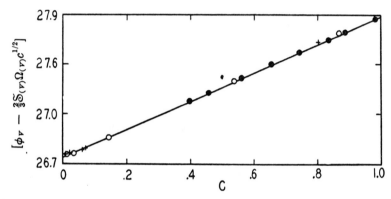

Fig. (8-8-1). Apparent molal volume of potassium chloride in water at 25°. ● and ○, Data of Kruis.　+, Data of Geffcken and Price.

electrolytes extrapolated by this method, the much simpler equations

$$[\phi_V - \tfrac{2}{3}S_{(V)}\Omega_{(V)}c^{1/2}] = \phi_V^0 + \tfrac{1}{2}K_{(V)}c \tag{8-8-24}$$

and

$$[\phi_H - \phi_H' - \tfrac{2}{3}S_{(H)}\Omega_{(H)}c^{1/2}] = \phi_H^0 - \phi_H' + \tfrac{1}{2}K_{(H)}c \tag{8-8-25}$$

are to be preferred.　The new functions

$$\Omega_{(V)} = \left[\frac{1}{1+\kappa a}\frac{\partial \ln D}{\partial P} - \frac{\sigma}{3}\beta\right]\left[\frac{\partial \ln D}{\partial P} - \frac{1}{3}\beta\right]^{-1} \tag{8-8-26}$$

$$\Omega_{(H)} = \left[\frac{1}{1+\kappa a}\left\{\frac{\partial \ln D}{\partial T} + \frac{1}{T}\right\} + \frac{\sigma}{3}\alpha\right]\left[\frac{\partial \ln D}{\partial T} + \frac{1}{T} + \frac{1}{3}\alpha\right]^{-1}. \tag{8-8-27}$$

---

* In the last equation ϕ_H' represents the apparent molal heat content at some convenient experimental concentration to which all heats are temporarily referred pending extrapolation.

[167] H. E. Wirth and F. N. Collier, Jr., *J. Am. Chem. Soc.*, **72**, 5292 (1950).

result from the rearrangement* of the terms in τ and θ of equations (8-8-22) and (8-8-23) if the a-parameter is assumed to be independent of T and P. Expressions for $\Omega_{(V)}$ and $\Omega_{(H)}$ suitable for convenient numerical calculations are given in equations (5-2-23) and (5-2-25), and values of σ are to be found in Table (5-2-6).

Applications of these last two equations† are illustrated in Figures (8-8-1) and (8-8-2) in which the left-hand members of equations (8-8-24) and (8-8-25) are plotted against c. Both plots appear to be linear within the experimental error, and both are based upon values of a taken from Table (12-5-2) which were derived independently from activity data. The equations derived from the slopes and intercepts of these plots are

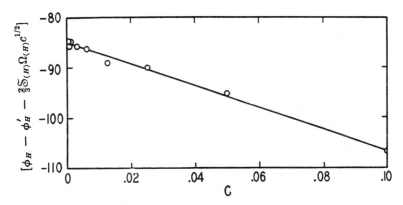

Fig. (8-8-2). Relative apparent molal heat content of sodium chloride in water at 25°. ◯, Data of Robinson.

$$\phi_V = 26.742 + 2.517\,\Omega_{(V)}c^{1/2} + 0.85c; \qquad \mathring{a} = 3.8 \qquad (8\text{-}8\text{-}28)$$

for potassium chloride at 25°, and

$$\phi_H - \phi_H^0 = 471.8\,\Omega_{(H)}c^{1/2} - 217c; \qquad \mathring{a} = 4.0 \qquad (8\text{-}8\text{-}29)$$

for sodium chloride at 25°. The results of similar plots are collected in Table (8-8-1). The values of ϕ_V in this table were obtained in every case by the use of values of a derived from activity data. The success of these independently determined a-values to represent appropriate density data is quite striking, but the possibility remains that this result is not general. Relatively few extrapolations have been made in this manner, and the

---

* The relation $2\tau + \sigma = 3(1 + \kappa a)^{-1}$ is helpful in regrouping terms.

† These equations take no account of the extended terms of Section (6), Chapter (2), and have been applied to ϕ_V and ϕ_H for $1 - 1$ type electrolytes only. They should not be applied to higher valence type electrolytes until the contributions of extended terms and association have been thoroughly investigated. Furthermore, the derivatives $\partial \ln a/\partial T$ and $\partial \ln a/\partial P$, which are both unknown, are assumed to be zero.

TABLE (8-8-1). THE EXTRAPOLATION OF APPARENT MOLAL VOLUMES BY MEANS OF EQUATIONS CONTAINING THE a-PARAMETER. AQUEOUS SOLUTIONS AT 25°.

Solute	ϕ_V^0	$\frac{1}{2}K_{(V)}$	$a \times 10^8$	Data
HCl	17.755	−0.32	4.4	(a)
NaCl	16.538	.76	4.0	(b)
KCl	26.742	.85	3.8	(c)
NaBr	23.420	.57	4.1	(c)
HClO₄*	44.039	−0.15	4.8	(d)
NaClO₄	42.847	.75	4.4	(d)

* For this electrolyte equation (8-8-22) was used with the value -2.68×10^{-5} (bar⁻¹) for the derivative $\partial \ln a/\partial P$.
(a) O. Redlich and J. Bigeleisen, *J. Am. Chem. Soc.*, **64**, 758 (1942).
(b) A. Kruis, *Z. physik. Chem.*, **B34**, 1 (1936).
(c) W. Geffcken and D. Price, *Ibid.*, **B26**, 81 (1934).
(d) H. Wirth and F. N. Collier, Jr., *J. Am. Chem. Soc.*, **72**, 5292 (1950).

exact value of the important quantity $\mathbb{S}_{(V)}$ is not known, and will not be known until a comprehensive study is made upon the effect of pressure on the dielectric constant of water. Pending such a study, the use of the above equations with the numerical values of $\mathbb{S}_{(V)}$, $\Omega_{(V)}$, $\mathbb{S}_{(H)}$ and $\Omega_{(H)}$ from Chapter (5), and of a as illustrated in this section, is recommended. This procedure is time-consuming, but is justified when very precise data are available, because it avoids the obvious theoretical objection to the simpler plot of ϕ_V against $\sqrt{c}$.

(9) ADDITIVITY OF IONIC VOLUMES. APPLICATIONS TO SYSTEMS OF MORE THAN TWO COMPONENTS, AND TO SOLUTIONS OF WEAK ELECTROLYTES

In this Section, various empirical relationships concerning the additivity of apparent molal, or partial molal volumes are considered. Their application to practical problems, such as the calculation of pressure effects in sea water and the extrapolation of ϕ_V for partially ionized, or hydrolyzed, electrolytes will then be illustrated. In Section (5) it was pointed out that the empirical slopes, S_V, of the Masson equation (8-5-4) are approximately additive for a number of 1-1 type electrolytes. This implies that ϕ_V, as well as ϕ_V^0, is an additive property of the individual ions. The concentration range over which ionic volumes may be considered independent of one another is surprisingly great for the case of the alkali and halide ions.

If for binary solutions the equation

$$\phi_V = \phi_V^0 + S_V c^{1/2} + bc^{3/2} \tag{8-9-1}$$

be written for the apparent molal volume of the solute, and similar equations

$$\phi_i = \phi_i^0 + S_i c^{1/2} + b_i c^{3/2} \tag{8-9-2}$$

be written for the individual ionic species, then additivity of ionic volumes would require that

$$\phi_V^0 = \sum \nu_i \phi_i^0 ; \qquad S_V = \sum \nu_i S_i ; \qquad b = \sum \nu_i b_i \qquad (8\text{-}9\text{-}3)$$

To test this requirement objectively, Zeldes[168] determined the parameters of equation (8-9-1) for each of fifteen alkali halides† by the usual method of least squares. He then employed a special least square procedure[169] by which the parameters of equations of the form of (8-9-2) for the eight individual ionic species could be simultaneously evaluated. The results of these calculations are given in Tables (8-9-1) and (8-9-2). The third, fourth and fifth columns in Table (8-9-2) contain "observed" values of

TABLE (8-9-1). PARAMETERS OF EQUATION (8-9-2) FOR AQUEOUS SOLUTIONS AT 25°

Ion	ϕ_i^0	S_i	b_i
Li⁺	−1.09	1.254	−0.0530
Na⁺	−1.55	1.784	.0015
K⁺	8.54	1.926	.0050
Rb⁺	13.74	1.936	.0044
Cs⁺	21.09	1.877	0
Cl⁻	18.10*	0.281	.0096
Br⁻	25.05	.060	−0.0035
I⁻	36.68	−0.341	−0.0061

* ϕ_i^0 for Cl⁻ is given the arbitrary value 18.10 to conform with Table 3 of Owen and Brinkley [*Chem. Rev.*, **29**, 461 (1941)].

TABLE (8-9-2). PARAMETERS OF EQUATION (8-9-1) FOR AQUEOUS SOLUTIONS AT 25°

Salt	$c(\text{max})^*$	Observed from equation (8-9-1)			Computed from equation (8-9-2)		
		ϕ_V^0	S_V	b	ϕ_V^0	S_V	b
LiCl	13.8	17.06	1.456	−0.0271	17.01	1.536	−0.0434
LiBr	13.2	23.97	1.375	−0.0595	23.96	1.314	−0.0565
LiI	8.4	35.53	0.931	−0.0725	35.59	0.913	−0.0591
NaCl	5.3	16.50	2.034	.0121	16.55	2.065	.0111
NaBr	5.5	23.50	1.765	0	23.50	1.844	−0.0020
NaI	6.7	35.14	1.330	0	35.13	1.443	−0.0046
KCl	3.8	26.66	2.190	.0150	26.64	2.207	.0146
KBr	4.6	33.62	2.006	0	33.59	1.986	.0015
KI	5.6	45.23	1.620	0	45.22	1.585	−0.0011
RbCl	6.0	31.94	2.127	.0133	31.84	2.217	.140
RbBr	5.17	38.70	2.030	0	38.79	1.996	.0009
RbI	2.78	50.40	1.650	0	50.42	1.595	−0.0017
CsCl	7.5	39.08	2.192	0	39.19	2.158	.0096
CsBr	4.18	46.20	1.900	0	46.14	1.937	−0.0035
CsI	2.9	57.82	1.540	0	57.77	1.536	−0.0061

* Upper limit of concentrations considered in evaluating the parameters.

[168] Private Communication from Dr. Henry Zeldes, Oak Ridge National Laboratories, Oak Ridge, Tenn. B. B. Owen, *Natl. Bur. Standards Circular* **524**, 193 (1953).

[169] S. Kaneko, *J. Chem. Soc. Japan.* **57**, 665 (1936).

† The sources of the data were essentially those referred to in Table (8-5-1).

ϕ_V^0, S_V and b derived directly from equation (8-9-1). The last three columns contain these quantities computed by combination of the individual ionic parameters given in Table (8-9-1). The differences between these two sets of values of ϕ_V^0 and S_V are very small. The considerable differences between the two sets of values of b is largely due to the sensitivity of this parameter to the upper limit of the concentration range of the data selected for curve-fitting. For example, if no concentrations above 1 normal are used for curve-fitting, it would be satisfactory to set all of the values of b and b_i equal to zero. The result of these calculations is the demonstration that, within the experimental errors of the density data for the alkali halide solutions, the individual ionic volumes appear to be additive over a wide concentration range. This gives some assurance that in ternary mixtures, and in more complicated solutions, such as those in which the ions are polyvalent, polarizable, partially associated, or highly solvated, the additivity principle

$$m\phi_V = \sum m_i \phi_i \qquad (8\text{-}9\text{-}4)$$

may be expected to be fulfilled very closely at high dilutions, and to be a useful approximation at moderate concentrations. This assurance will be reinforced by direct evidence considered later in this Section.

In the application of the principle of additivity of ionic volumes to ternary and more complicated systems, it is convenient to define the mean apparent molal volume by the relation

$$\Phi_V = \frac{V - n_1 V_1}{n_2 + n_3 + \cdots} = \frac{V - 1000/d_0}{m_2 + m_3 + \cdots} \qquad (8\text{-}9\text{-}5)$$

which may be easily and directly determined from the experimental data. The use of capital Φ for this quantity allows the familiar ϕ to represent apparent molal volumes of solutes in binary solutions. In terms of these symbols, the additivity principle, equation (8-9-4) extended to solutions of any number of electrolytes, is expressed by

$$(m_2 + m_3 + \cdots)\Phi_V = m_2\phi_2 + m_3\phi_3 + \cdots \qquad (8\text{-}9\text{-}6)$$

in which ϕ_2, ϕ_3, etc., are the apparent molal volumes of the solute species 2, 3, etc., in their binary solutions at the ionic strength

$$\mu = \mu_2 + \mu_3 + \cdots = \omega_2 m_2 + \omega_3 m_3 + \cdots \qquad (8\text{-}9\text{-}7)$$

of the ternary or more complicated system being considered in the calculation of Φ_V. The valence factors ω_2, ω_3, etc., are $\frac{1}{2}\sum \nu_i z_i^2$ for the electrolyte indicated by the subscript. It is important to note that although equation (8-9-6) reduces to (8-9-4) for the special case of a binary solution, equation (8-9-6) is not obtained from (8-9-4) without the introduction of the principle of ionic strength. In a binary solution it is not possible to change the ratio of the ionic strength to total molality, but the equations for ternary or more complicated systems must take such a change into account. Equation (8-9-6) requires that the volume change upon mixing two or more solutions of the same ionic strength is zero. There are theoretical as well as some experimental bases[170] for believing that ionic volumes are more exactly additive if ϕ_2, ϕ_3, etc., are each taken at the same ional concentration, Γ, but the use of the m-scale has important practical advantages to recommend its use. Furthermore, small deviations[171] from strict additivity can be readily taken into account by addition of a term which includes the volume change of mixing. Thus,

$$(m_2 + m_3 + \cdots)\Phi_V = m_2\phi_2 + m_3\phi_3 + \cdots + \psi \qquad (8\text{-}9\text{-}8)$$

where

$$\psi \equiv (m_2 + m_3 + \cdots)\Delta V_{\text{mix}}. \qquad (8\text{-}9\text{-}8a)$$

For a ternary solution, combination of equations (8-9-8) and (8-9-5) results in an expression for V which, when differentiated* with respect to m_3 at constant m_2, yields for the partial molal volume of the solute (3) in

$$\bar{V}_3 = \phi_3 + m_3\left(\frac{\partial\phi_3}{\partial m_3}\right)_{T,P} + \frac{\omega_3}{\omega_2}m_2\left(\frac{\partial\phi_2}{\partial m_2}\right)_{T,P} + \left(\frac{\partial\psi}{\partial m_3}\right)_{T,P,m_2} \qquad (8\text{-}9\text{-}9)$$

the ternary solution. The derivatives $\partial\phi_3/\partial m_3$ and $\partial\phi_2/\partial m_2$, refer, of course, to binary solutions. The first two terms on the right can be simply expressed in terms of $\bar{V}_{3(0)}$, the partial molal volume of the solute (3) in its binary solution (absence of (2)) at the ionic strength μ. Accordingly, we may write

$$\bar{V}_3 = \bar{V}_{3(0)} + m_2\left\{\frac{\omega_3}{\omega_2}\left(\frac{\partial\phi_2}{\partial m_2}\right)_{T,P} - \frac{\omega_2}{\omega_3}\left(\frac{\partial\phi_3}{\partial m_3}\right)_{T,P} + \frac{1}{m_2}\left(\frac{\partial\psi}{\partial m_3}\right)_{T,P,m_2}\right\}$$

$$(8\text{-}9\text{-}10)$$

The first term within the brackets is constant, because it refers to a binary solution at constant ionic strength. The function ψ is known for only a few simple systems. For the systems KCl-NaCl-H_2O and KBr-NaCl-H_2O, ψ is zero, for Young and Smith[172] have demonstrated conclusively that the data of Wirth[170] and of Wirth and Collier[173] conform to equation (8-9-6). The data of Drucker[174] seem to exhibit some departures

---

* Note that in this differentiation m_2 is held constant, but the ionic strength is increased by the amount $d\mu = \omega_3 dm_3$, and both ϕ_2 and ϕ_3 in their binary solutions must change accordingly. Also, in the two binary solutions at any particular ionic strength, $dm_3 = d\mu/\omega_3 = \omega_2 dm_2/\omega_3$.

170 H. E. Wirth, *J. Am. Chem. Soc.*, **59**, 2549 (1937); *Ibid.*, **62**, 1128 (1940).
171 T. F. Young, *Record of Chem. Progress*, **12**, 81 (1951).
172 T. F. Young and M. B. Smith, *J. Phys. Chem.*, **58**, 716 (1954).
173 H. E. Wirth and F. N. Collier, Jr., *J. Am. Chem. Soc.*, **72**, 5292 (1950).
174 C. Drucker, *Arkiv. Kemi, Mineral Geol.*, **14A**, No. 15 (1941).

from this equation, but they were obtained at only two concentrations of one of the components and were expressed in very different terms from ours. It is certain that ψ is not zero for the system HCl-NaCl-H$_2$O. In this case it has been shown[172] that

$$\psi = Km_2m_3 \qquad (8\text{-}9\text{-}11)$$

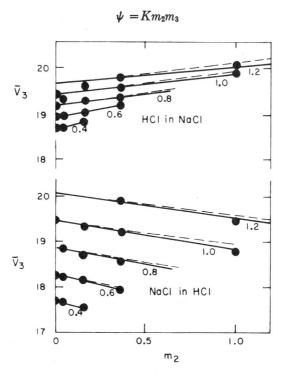

Fig. (8-9-1). Partial molal volumes of hydrochloric acid and of sodium chloride in ternary solutions at constant ionic strength.

where K is a constant. In the absence of sufficient experimental data it would be unwise to attribute any generality to this equation, but for the particular system for which it was derived it allows the very simple result

$$\frac{1}{m_2}\frac{\partial \psi}{\partial m_3} = \frac{1}{m_3}\frac{\partial \psi}{\partial m_2} = K \qquad (8\text{-}9\text{-}12)$$

Consequently, equation (8-9-10) requires that a plot of $\bar{V}_3$ against m_2 should be practically linear. In Figure (8-9-1), taken from the paper of Young and Smith,[172] the solid lines represent the partial molal volumes of HCl and NaCl in their ternary solution as calculated by equation (8-9-10). The dashed lines result if ψ is neglected in this calculation. The small difference between the solid and dashed lines is a measure of the failure of this system to obey the principle of ionic strength exactly, but in terms of the partial molal volumes this failure represents only about 0.1 cc. mole^{-1} in 1 molal solutions.

The dashed line in the upper half of Figure (8-9-1) can be predicted from the known behavior of the activity coefficient of hydrochloric acid in solutions of sodium chloride. Thus, if we make the subscripts in equations (14-4-3) consistent with those of this Section, we can represent the linear variation of the log $\gamma_\pm$ for HCl, with the concentration of NaCl at constant total ionic strength, by the equation

$$\log \gamma_3 = \log \gamma_{3(0)} - \omega_2 m_2 \alpha_{32} \tag{8-9-13}$$

By differentiation of this equation with respect to pressure at constant temperature and composition, we obtain

$$\bar{V}_3 = \bar{V}_{3(0)} - 2.303 \nu R T \omega_2 m_2 \left(\frac{\partial \alpha_{32}}{\partial P}\right)_{T,\mu} \tag{8-9-14}$$

and comparison with equation (8-9-10) shows that

$$-2.303 \nu R T \omega_2 \left(\frac{\partial \alpha_{32}}{\partial P}\right)_{T,\mu} = \frac{\omega_3}{\omega_2}\left(\frac{\partial \phi_2}{\partial m_2}\right)_{T,P} - \frac{\omega_2}{\omega_3}\left(\frac{\partial \phi_3}{\partial m_3}\right)_{T,P}$$
$$+ \frac{1}{m_2}\left(\frac{\partial \psi}{\partial m_3}\right)_{T,P,m_2} \tag{8-9-15}$$

The pressure derivative of α_{32} has never been determined directly, but it must be constant at a given ionic strength and temperature, because α_{32} is independent of m_2 and m_3 under these conditions.

Direct, precise information concerning ternary systems containing salts of higher valence types is supplied by Wirth's[175] study of the system K_2SO_4-NaCl-H_2O. In this mixture the partial molal volume of potassium sulfate varies linearly with $\sqrt{\Gamma}$ up to about $\Gamma = 2$ at 25°. The slopes of these lines depend to some extent upon the concentration of sodium chloride, but up to $\Gamma \simeq 1.5$ the partial molal volume of potassium sulfate in sodium chloride solutions differs from its value in the binary solution at the same ional concentration by only 0.3 cc. mole^{-1}.

The Estimation of Standard Partial Molal Volumes in Sea Water

In the general problem of calculating the effect of pressure upon ionic equilibria in sea water, it has been shown[176] convenient to consider an idealized sea water (referred to hereafter as salt water) as the solvent, and to shift the reference state from pure water to salt water so that the activity coefficients of all added solutes become unity at infinite dilution in salt water. Since the ionic strength[177] of normal[178] sea water is about

[175] H. E. Wirth, *J. Am. Chem. Soc.*, **59**, 2549 (1937).

[176] B. B. Owen and S. R. Brinkley, Jr., *Chem. Rev.*, **29**, 461 (1941).

[177] H. Wattenberg, *Wiss. Ergebn. Deutsch. Atlantischen Exped. "Meteor"*, **8**, 198 (1925–1927).

[178] Calculated on the basis of a chlorinity of 19.430 ‰. *Cf.* L. Lyman and R. H. Fleming, Sears Foundation, *J. Marine Research*, **3**, 134 (1940).

0.725, the solvent will be considered to be a 0.725 molal solution of sodium chloride (0.713 normal at 25°), and the problem becomes one of estimating the standard partial molal volumes of various solutes at infinite dilution in this solvent. These, and other quantities which make use of infinite dilution in salt water as reference state, will be designated by an asterisk. In pure water, the relation

$$\bar{V}_2 = \bar{V}_2^0 + A_V\sqrt{\Gamma} \tag{8-9-15}$$

is a useful approximation over a wide concentration range. It follows from equation (8-5-4) that A_V is very closely equal to $\frac{3}{2}S_V(\nu z_+ z_-)^{-1/2}$ up to ional concentrations of about unity. The experimental data considered above show that the presence of sodium chloride in solutions of potassium

TABLE (8-9-3).* STANDARD PARTIAL MOLAL VOLUMES AND PARTIAL MOLAL COMPRESSIBILITIES IN "SALT WATER" (0.725 M NaCl) AT 25° AND 1 ATMOSPHERE.

Compounds	$\bar{V}^{0*}{}_2$	$10^4\bar{K}^{0*}{}_2$	Ions	$\bar{V}^{0*}{}_i$	$10^4\bar{K}^{0*}{}_i$
H₂O	18.86ᵃ	6.89ᵃ	H⁺	0	0
HCl	19.6ᵃ	−7	Na⁺	−0.6	−37
NaCl	19.0ᵃ	−45	K⁺	9.7	−32
KCl	29.3ᵃ	−39	NH₄⁺	19.6	
KBr	36.2ᵃ	−30	Mg⁺⁺	−21	−73
KI	47.3	−16	Ca⁺⁺	−16.6	−62
KNO₃	41.1	−26	Ba⁺⁺	−12.1	−86
KOH	8.4	−71	Cl⁻	19.6	−7
KHCO₃	36	−30	Br⁻	26.4	2
K₂SO₄	41.4ᵃ	−122	I⁻	37.5	16
Na₂CO₃	1.5	−150	OH⁻	−1	−38
CaCl₂	22.6	−76	NO₃⁻	31	6
BaCl₂	27.1	−100	HCO₃⁻	26	2
MgCl₂	18.4		CO₃⁻	2.7	−74
MgSO₄		−133	SO₄⁻	22	−60

* From Ref. 174, Table 6.   ᵃ Evaluated directly from experimental data

chloride, or potassium bromide (and in potassium sulfate, or hydrochloric acid, as a close approximation), affects the partial molal volumes of the latter electrolytes only by its contribution to Γ, the numerical value of A_V remaining unchanged. Upon the *assumption* that this behavior is characteristic of all electrolytes in the presence of sodium chloride, we write

$$\bar{V}_2^{0*} = \bar{V}_2^0 + A_V\sqrt{2 \times 0.713} \tag{8-9-17}$$

by substituting the value of Γ corresponding to 0.725 molal sodium chloride at 25°. This equation will serve as a good approximation, but it is not likely to be strictly valid, even for salts. For hydrochloric acid in sodium chloride solutions it yields a value of $\bar{V}_2^{0*}$ which is about 0.3 cc. mole⁻¹ lower than the direct experimental[179] value, 19.6.

[179] H. E. Wirth, *J. Am. Chem. Soc.*, **62**, 1128 (1940).

In order to calculate the effect of pressure upon an ionic equilibrium in salt water, the standard volume change ΔV^{0*} for the reaction which appears in the equation

$$\left(\frac{\partial \ln K^*}{\partial P}\right)_{T,m} = -\frac{\Delta V^{0*}}{RT} \qquad (8\text{-}9\text{-}18)$$

must be expressed as a function of pressure. There appear to be no measurements on solutions of mixed electrolytes which would permit the direct evaluation of the standard partial molal compressibilities, $\bar{K}_2^{0*}$, but the two assumptions made in the estimation of $\bar{V}_2^{0*}$ should enable us to approxi-

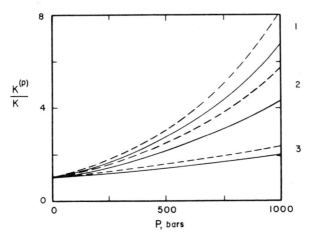

Fig. (8-9-2). Comparison of the effects of pressure upon ionic equilibria in pure water (- - -) and in salt water (——) at 25°. (1) $CaCO_3 \rightleftharpoons Ca^{++} + CO_3^{=}$. (2) $CaSO_4 \rightleftharpoons Ca^{++} + SO_4^{=}$. (3) $H_2O \rightleftharpoons H^+ + OH^-$.

mate this quantity. Thus the equation

$$\bar{K}_2 = \bar{K}_2^0 + A_K\sqrt{\Gamma} \qquad (8\text{-}9\text{-}19)$$

in which A_K is characteristic of the electrolyte, may be assumed applicable to mixtures containing sodium chloride without changing the value of A_K. Accordingly,

$$\bar{K}_2^{0*} \simeq \bar{K}_2^0 + A_K\sqrt{2 \times 0.713} \qquad (8\text{-}9\text{-}20)$$

in salt water at 25°. This quantity has also been estimated[180] from considerations based upon the effective pressure, P_e, discussed in Section (7). The final approximation

$$\bar{K}_2^{0*} \simeq 0.87\bar{K}_2^0 \qquad (8\text{-}9\text{-}21)$$

based upon $P_e = 207$ bars for 0.725 m NaCl in water at 25°, leads to values of $\bar{K}_2^{0*}$ which agree with those calculated from equation (8-9-20) within

[180] B. B. Owen and S. R. Brinkley, Jr., Chem. Rev., 29, 461 (1941).

about 10 to 20%. This agreement is close enough for most calculations of pressure effects, because ΔK^{0*} is much less important than ΔV^{0*}. Table (8-9-3) contains values of $\bar{V}_2^{0*}$ and $\bar{K}_2^{0*}$ estimated with the aid of equations (8-9-17) and (8-9-21). As an illustration of the use of these quantities, the effect of pressure upon several important ionic equilibria have been calculated and plotted in Figure (8-9-2) where it is seen that in every case the effect is somewhat less pronounced in salt water than it is in pure water.

Apparent Molal and Partial Molal Volumes of Weak Electrolytes

The application of the ionic strength principle and the additivity of ionic volumes to the problem of properly extrapolating the apparent molal volumes of hydrolyzed, or incompletely dissociated electrolytes, was carefully described by Geffcken and Price,[181] who corrected the apparent molal volumes determined in sodium carbonate solutions for hydrolysis, and of acetic acid solutions for partial dissociation. The following calculation for acetic acid will serve as an illustration of the procedure.

If the ionization reaction

$$HA \rightleftharpoons H^+ + A^-$$

proceeds very far at experimental concentrations, the ions must contribute to the apparent molal volume calculated from the density and stoichiometric molality of the solutions. The apparent molal volume, ϕ_u, of the undissociated acid may be expressed in terms of the mean (measured) apparent molal volume, ϕ_V, and a correction term, $\Delta\phi_V$, defined below. The application of equation (8-9-4), extended to include the undissociated acid molecules, leads to

$$m\phi_V = m\alpha\sum\phi_i + m(1 - \alpha)\phi_u \qquad (8\text{-}9\text{-}22)$$

where α is the degree of dissociation of the acid. This equation can be written in the form

$$\phi_u = \phi_V - \alpha\Delta\phi_V \qquad (8\text{-}9\text{-}23)$$

in which the correction term is defined by

$$\Delta\phi_V = \sum\phi_i - \phi_u \qquad (8\text{-}9\text{-}24)$$

for the reaction considered. In order to calculate $\Delta\phi_V$, a rough estimate of ϕ_u may be made to begin a series of successive approximations. It is usually satisfactory to begin with ϕ_u(prelim.) $\simeq \phi_V$. The ionic apparent molal volumes are obtained by linear combination of values of ϕ_V for simple binary solutions. Thus,

$$\sum\phi_i = \phi_V(\text{HCl}) + \phi_V(\text{NaA}) - \phi_V(\text{NaCl}) \qquad (8\text{-}9\text{-}25)$$

[181] W. Geffcken and D. Price, *Z. physik. Chem.*, **B26**, 81 (1934).

With these values of $\sum \phi_i$ and ϕ_u(prelim.), and the known ionization constant for the acid, the correction term $\Delta \phi_V$ can be estimated to a first approximation, and values of ϕ_u calculated by equation (8-9-23). This procedure is repeated until a self-consistent set of values of ϕ_u is obtained.

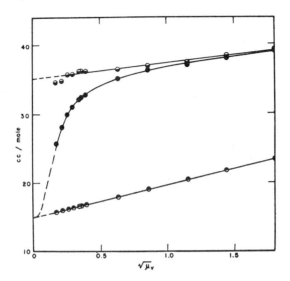

Fig. (8-9-3). Plots of the apparent molal volumes of sulfuric acid and its constituents against volume ionic strength in water at 25°. Data of I. M. Klotz and C. F. Eckert, *J. Am. Chem. Soc.*, **64**, 1878 (1942). ●, Observed values. ◓, Calculated values for $2H^+ + SO_4^{--}$. ◒, Calculated values for $H^+ + SO_4^{--}$.

These are subsequently plotted against the concentration of undissociated acid, $c_u = (1 - \alpha)c$, and extrapolated linearly to infinite dilution to evaluate ϕ_u^0, the standard partial molal volume of the undissociated acid. For a partially dissociated ion, such as HSO_4^-, the apparent molal volume (corrected as above for partial dissociation) should be plotted against $\sqrt{\Gamma}$ for a linear extrapolation. A plot of this kind, taken from the work of Klotz and Eckert[182] on sulfuric acid, is shown in Figure (8-9-3).

TABLE (8-9-4). STANDARD CHANGES, ΔV^0 AND ΔK^0, ACCOMPANYING THE DISSOCIATION OF WEAK ACIDS AND ACID RADICALS IN WATER AT 25°.

Reaction	ΔV^0	$10^4 \Delta K^0$	Ref.
$H_2O \rightleftharpoons H^+ + OH^-$	−23.4	−52	180
$H_2CO_3 \rightleftharpoons H^+ + HCO_3^-$	−29	...	180
$HCO_3^- \rightleftharpoons H^+ + CO_3^{--}$	−27.8	−87	180
$CH_3CO_2H \rightleftharpoons H^+ + CH_3CO_2^-$	−9.2*	−17	180
$H_2SO_4 \rightleftharpoons H^+ + HSO_4^-$	−20.2	...	182
$H_3PO_4 \rightleftharpoons H^+ + H_2PO_4^-$	−16.2	...	184
$H_2PO_4^- \rightleftharpoons H^+ + HPO_4^{--}$	−28.1	...	184

* O. Redlick and J. Bigeleisen, *Chem. Rev.*, **30**, 171 (1942), report the value −11.47.

[182] I. M. Klotz and C. F. Eckert, *J. Am. Chem. Soc.*, **64**, 1878 (1942).

There are only a small number of undissociated weak electrolytes for which ϕ_u^0 is known.[183, 184]   Table (8-9-4) contains values of ΔV^0 and ΔK^0 for their dissociation reactions.   By equation (8-9-24) it follows that ΔV^0 is also the limiting value of the correction term $\Delta \phi_V^0$.

[183] B. B. Owen, *Natl. Bur. Standards Circular* **524,** 193 (1953).
[184] J. S. Smith, *Dissertation*, Yale University (1943).

Chapter (9)

The Calculation of Activity and Osmotic Coefficients from Freezing Points, Boiling Points and Vapor Pressures

All the partial molal quantities except $\Delta \bar{F}$ and $\Delta \bar{S}$† were considered in the preceding chapter. Changes in the partial molal free energy, or activity, of dissolved electrolytes may be directly investigated by measurements of the electromotive forces of suitable cells, or calculated by the Gibbs-Duhem equation (1-4-5) from observed changes in the free energy, or activity, of the solvent. The present chapter is concerned with the most important methods of determining free energy changes of the solvent, and the derived quantities, the activity and osmotic coefficients. The electromotive force method will be considered in Chapter (10).

(1) Introduction

When the solute is non-volatile, the activity of the solvent can be determined from measurements of the lowering of its vapor pressure caused by the presence of the solute. This method has the advantage of not being limited to any particular temperature, but cannot attain the accuracy of the freezing-pont or boiling-point methods without elaborate experimental precautions. Accurate determinations of vapor pressure lowerings can be made with a sensitive differential manometer,[1,2,3] or calculated from the amount of solvent vapor required to saturate a given volume of inert gas.[4] The development of the static (manometric) method of studying solutions is largely due to Frazer and Lovelace.[5] The dynamic (air-saturation) method is simpler experimentally, and has been used in a large

---

† $\Delta \bar{S}$ is too rarely used to require detailed consideration. The variation of $\Delta \bar{F}$ with temperature is almost invariably expressed in terms of $\Delta \bar{H}$ rather than $\Delta \bar{S}$.

[1] C. Dieterici, *Ann. Physik* [3], **50**, 47 (1893); **62**, 616 (1897); **67**, 859 (1899).

[2] Lord Rayleigh, *Z. physik. Chem.*, **37**, 713 (1901); *Trans. Roy. Soc. London*, **196**, 205 (1901).

[3] A. Smits, *Z. physik. Chem.*, **39**, 386 (1906).

[4] J. Walker, *Z. physik. Chem.*, **2**, 602 (1888).

[5] J. C. W. Frazer and B. F. Lovelace, *Z. physik. Chem.*, **89**, 155 (1914); *J. Am. Chem. Soc.*, **36**, 2439 (1914); J. C. W. Frazer, B. F. Lovelace and E. Miller, *Ibid.*, **38**, 515 (1916); J. C. W. Frazer, B. F. Lovelace and T. H. Rogers, *Ibid.*, **42**, 1793 (1920); J. C. W. Frazer, B. F. Lovelace and V. B. Sease, *Ibid.*, **43**, 102 (1921); J. C. W. Frazer, B. F. Lovelace and W. H. Bahlke, *Ibid.*, **45**, 2930 (1923).

number of investigations, among which those of Berkeley,[6] Washburn[7] and Pearce[8] are particularly noteworthy.

The determination of freezing point depression is highly developed. The first investigator to abandon the original supercooling method of Raoult,[9] and Beckmann,[10] appears to have been Roloff,[11] and the use of thermocouples was introduced by Hausrath,[12] and Osaka.[13] More recently, the measurement of freezing point lowering has become a precision method through continuous improvements in technique and in potentiometer design. Some of the more important refinements are due to White,[14] Adams,[15] Randall,[16] Harkins,[17] and Scatchard.[18] The various sources of experimental errors and their magnitudes have been reviewed by these investigators.[19] Certain minor errors inherent in the calculation of activity coefficients from the experimental data will be discussed in this chapter.

The precise determination of boiling point elevations is much more difficult than the measurement of freezing-point depressions because of the phenomenon of super-heating, and the necessity of close pressure control. Furthermore, the molal boiling point elevation is less than the corresponding freezing-point depression, and, therefore, the uncertainties in temperature measurement produce greater errors in the calculated thermodynamic properties. The development of the successful method of overcoming the most serious difficulty, super-heating, began with the work of Cottrell,[20] and of Washburn and Read,[21] and culminated in that of Smith.[22] We need not discuss the many contributions of the intervening twenty years in detail, as they are exhaustively reviewed in a recent monograph,[23] and have progressed on a parallel course with the development of the freezing-point technique.

[6] Earl of Berkeley, E. G. J. Hartley and C. V. Burton, *Phil. Trans. Roy. Soc. London*, **A209**, 177 (1909); *Ibid.*, **A218**, 295 (1919).

[7] E. W. Washburn and E. O. Heuse, *J. Am. Chem. Soc.*, **37**, 309 (1915).

[8] J. N. Pearce and R. D. Snow, *J. Phys. Chem.*, **31**, 231 (1927); J. N. Pearce and A. F. Nelson, *J. Am. Chem. Soc.*, **54**, 3544 (1932); *Ibid.*, **55**, 3075 (1933); J. N. Pearce and L. E. Blackman, *Ibid.*, **57**, 24 (1935); J. N. Pearce and H. C. Eckstrom, *Ibid.*, **59**, 2689 (1937); *J. Phys. Chem.*, **41**, 563 (1936).

[9] F. M. Raoult, *Ann. chim. phys.* [5], **20**, 217 (1880).

[10] E. Beckmann, *Z. physik. Chem.*, **2**, 638 (1888); 7, 323 (1891).

[11] M. Roloff, *Z. physik. Chem.*, **18**, 572 (1895).

[12] H. Hausrath, *Ann. Physik*. [4], **9**, 522 (1902).

[13] Y. Osaka, *Z. physik. Chem.*, **41**, 560 (1902).

[14] W. P. White, *J. Am. Chem. Soc.*, **36**, 1859, 1876, 2011, 2292, 2313 (1914).

[15] L. H. Adams, *Ibid.*, **37**, 481 (1915).

[16] M. Randall and A. P. Vanselow, *J. Am. Chem. Soc.*, **46**, 2418 (1924).

[17] R. E. Hall and W. D. Harkins, *Ibid.*, **38**, 2658 (1916).

[18] G. Scatchard, P. T. Jones and S. S. Prentiss, *Ibid.*, **54**, 2676 (1932).

[19] See also, C. Robertson and V. K. LaMer, *J. Phys. Chem.*, **35**, 1953 (1931).

[20] F. G. Cottrell, *J. Am. Chem. Soc.*, **41**, 721 (1919).

[21] E. W. Washburn and J. W. Read, *J. Am. Chem. Soc.*, **41**, 729 (1919).

[22] R. P. Smith, *Ibid.*, **61**, 497 (1939).

[23] W. Swietoslawski, "Ebulliometry," Chemical Publishing Co. New York, 1937.

(2) General Equations for Calculating the Activity of the Solvent and the Osmotic Coefficient from Freezing-Point Depressions

At the temperature T', corresponding to the freezing point of a solution containing m mols of solute per kilogram of solvent, we shall represent the activity of the solid solvent by a'_s, the activity of the liquid solvent by $a_1^{0'}$, and the activities of the solvent and solute in the solution by a'_1 and a'_2, respectively. The increase in $\bar{F}_1$ accompanying the isothermal transfer of one mole of solvent from pure liquid to solid is $RT' \ln a'_s/a_1^{0'}$, and from pure liquid to solution is $RT' \ln a'_1/a_1^{0'}$ [Equations (1-6-1) and (1-6-2)]. Adopting the pure solvent as the common standard state to which all activities are referred, we may write $a_1^{0'} = 1$. Accordingly*

$$a'_s = a'_1 \qquad (9\text{-}2\text{-}1)$$

and

$$\left(\frac{a'_2}{m''}\right)_{m\to 0} = 1 \qquad (9\text{-}2\text{-}2)$$

The application of equation (1-7-5) to the transfer of one mol of solvent from pure liquid to solid permits the derivation of a functional relationship between a'_s, and hence a'_1, and the freezing point depression,

$$\vartheta \equiv T_0 - T' \qquad (9\text{-}2\text{-}3)$$

T_0 is the freezing point of the pure solvent. ΔH for this transfer is the difference between the relative molal heat contents for the solid and pure liquid solvent. Since the pure liquid solvent is in the standard state, its relative molal heat content is zero. Therefore,

$$d \ln a'_s = -\frac{L'_s}{RT'^2} dT' = \frac{L'_s d\vartheta}{R(T_0 - \vartheta)^2} \qquad (9\text{-}2\text{-}4)$$

where L'_s is the relative molal heat content of the solid at T'. Although temperature is a variable in this equation, we shall persist in the use of the primes as a constant reminder that the calculations are carried out at the freezing point of the solution. L'_s must be expressed as a function of T', or ϑ, before integrating this equation.

If the molal heat capacities of solid and pure liquid solvent are expressed as power series in ϑ, then

$$C_{p_s} - \bar{C}_{p_1}^0 = \sum_1^\infty A_{n-1} \vartheta^{n-1} \qquad (9\text{-}2\text{-}5)$$

* Since the conditions of the measurements require only that solid solvent and a certain solution be in equilibrium at T', it is immaterial that solid and pure liquid solvent cannot exist in equilibrium at any temperature but T_0. It is necessary to employ pure solvent as standard state so that the usual conventions represented by (9-2-1) and (9-2-2) may be retained at all temperatures.

if A_n is the difference between the numerical coefficients of the nth terms in the two series. A_0 is identical with $\Delta \bar{C}_{p_1}$ at T_0. Then, by the application of equation (1-7-7),

$$\int_{T_0}^{T'} dL_s = \int_{T_0}^{T'} (C_{p_s} - \bar{C}_{p_1}^0) \, dT = - \int_0^\vartheta \sum_1^\infty A_{n-1} \vartheta^{n-1} \, d\vartheta \qquad (9\text{-}2\text{-}6)$$

whence*

$$L_s' = L_{s(0)} - \sum_1^\infty \frac{1}{n} A_{n-1} \vartheta^n \qquad (9\text{-}2\text{-}7)$$

Substituting this value in equation (9-2-4), replacing a_s' by a_1', and expanding $(T_0 - \vartheta)^{-2}$, we obtain

$$d \ln a_1' = \frac{L_{s(0)}}{RT_0^2} \sum_1^\infty n C_n \vartheta^{n-1} \, d\vartheta = \frac{-M_1}{1000 \lambda} \sum_1^\infty n C_n \vartheta^{n-1} \, d\vartheta \qquad (9\text{-}2\text{-}8)$$

where

$$C_n = T_0^{1-n} - \frac{T_0^{1-n}}{L_{s(0)}} \sum_{s=1}^{s=n} \left(\frac{n-s}{ns} \right) T_0^s A_{s-1} \qquad (9\text{-}2\text{-}9)$$

and

$$\lambda = \frac{-M_1 RT_0^2}{1000 L_{s(0)}} \qquad (9\text{-}2\text{-}10)$$

It can be shown [Equation (9-5-22)] that $\nu\lambda$ is the lowering of the freezing point per mol of solute as m approaches zero. Numerical values† of this important quantity are given in Table (9-2-1) for several solvents. For aqueous solutions, the first four coefficients, calculated by equation (9-2-9) are $C_1 = 1$, $C_2 = 5.2 \times 10^{-4}$, $C_3 = -8.5 \times 10^{-6}$, and $C_4 \backsimeq -5 \times 10^{-8}$.

---

* Perhaps the first attempt to generalize equation (9-2-4) (using N_1 for a_1) by combining it with an equation analogous to (9-2-7) was that of J. J. van Laar, [*Kon. Akad. Wetten. Amsterdam, Verslog Wis.-en Natuur.*, **11**, 478 (1902)]. He expressed the variation of L_s as a power series in N_2, and determined the numerical coefficients from the freezing-point data themselves. Later [*Ibid.*, **11**, 576 (1903)], by an elaborate derivation, he expressed this variation in terms of the coefficients of the van der Waals equation of state for a binary mixture [*Z. physik. Chem.*, **8**, 188 (1891)]. E. W. Washburn [*J. Am. Chem. Soc.*, **32**, 653 (1910)] employed a power series in temperature similar to equation (9-2-7), but upon substitution in equation (9-2-4) (N_1 replacing a_1), his expansion included the logarithmic term, and is therefore not directly comparable with ours. His subsequent "general integration", retaining the logarithmic form, unfortunately neglects all coefficients beyond the second in equation (9-2-7). In comparing Washburn's equations with ours, we must remark the errata [*Ibid.*, p. 1636]. The signs of ΔC_p and L must be changed to conform with the present conventions.

† The necessary values of T_0 and $L_{s(0)}$ are taken from the "International Critical Tables," Vol. V, p. 130, McGraw-Hill Book Co., New York, 1931.

TABLE (9-2-1). FREEZING-POINT CONSTANTS OF VARIOUS SOLVENTS AT ONE ATMOSPHERE.

Solvent	t (F.P.)	λ^a
Ammonia	−75	0.72
Water	0	1.858
Acetic acid	16.6	3.73
Dioxane	11.7	4.63^b
Benzene	5.4	5.08
Phenol	25.4	6.11
Stannic chloride	−33	13.6
Carbon tetrachloride	−24	29.6
Camphor	178.4	37.7^c
Cyclohexanol	23.2	41.6^d

^{a} Evaluated by equation (9-2-10).
^{b} Determined from freezing points by C. A. Kraus and R. A. Vingee, *J. Am. Chem. Soc.*, **56**, 511 (1934).
^{c} Determined from freezing points by M. Frandsen, *Bur. Standards J. Research*, **7**, 477 (1931).
^{d} Compare E. Schreiner and O. E. Frivold, *Z. physik. Chem.*, **124**, 1 (1926).

In integrated form equation (9-2-8) becomes

$$\ln a_1' = \frac{-M_1}{1000\lambda} \sum_1^\infty C_n \vartheta^n \tag{9-2-11}$$

and comparison with equation (1-9-9) leads to the expression

$$\phi' = \frac{1}{\nu m \lambda} \sum_1^\infty C_n \vartheta^n \tag{9-2-12}$$

for the osmotic coefficient at the freezing point of the solution. For dilute aqueous solutions the first two terms in the summation yield

$$-\ln a_1' = 9.696 \times 10^{-3}\vartheta + 5.1 \times 10^{-6}\vartheta^2 \tag{9-2-13}$$

and

$$\phi' = \frac{\vartheta}{1.858\,\nu m} (1 + 0.54 \times 10^{-3}\vartheta) \tag{9-2-14}$$

(3) GENERAL EQUATIONS FOR CALCULATING THE ACTIVITY OF THE SOLVENT AND THE OSMOTIC COEFFICIENT FROM BOILING-POINT ELEVATIONS

At the boiling point, T', of a solution containing m mols of solute per kilogram of solvent, the activity of the solvent vapor is represented by a_v', and that of the solvent in solution by a_1'. Choosing the pure liquid solvent as reference state for both phases, a_v' is made equal to a_1' under the vapor pressure, p_0, of the pure solvent at T_0. According to equation (1-7-5), the activity of the solvent is therefore given by

$$d \ln a_1' = -\frac{L_v' dT'}{RT'^2} = -\frac{L_v' d\theta}{R(T_0 + \theta)^2} \tag{9-3-1}$$

in terms of the heat of vaporization, L'_v, of the solvent, and the elevation in the boiling point

$$\theta \equiv T' - T_0 \tag{9-3-2}$$

If the power series

$$C_{p_v} - C_{p_1} = \sum_1^\infty A^*_{n-1}\theta^{n-1} \tag{9-3-3}$$

represents the difference between the molal heat capacities of vapor and pure solvent under the constant[24] pressure, p_0, equation (1-7-7) requires that

$$L'_v = L_{v(0)} + \sum_1^\infty \frac{1}{n} A^*_{n-1}\theta^n \tag{9-3-4}$$

Substituting this equation in equation (9-3-1), and expanding $(T_0 + \theta)^{-2}$, we obtain

$$d \ln a'_1 = - \frac{L_{v(0)}}{RT_0^2} \sum_1^\infty nC^*_n \theta^{n-1}\, d\theta = - \frac{M_1}{1000\lambda^*} \sum_1^\infty nC^*_n \theta^{n-1}\, d\theta \tag{9-3-5}$$

where

$$C^*_n = (-T_0)^{1-n} + \frac{(-T_0)^{1-n}}{L_{v(0)}} \sum_{s=1}^{s=n} \left(\frac{n-s}{ns}\right) A^*_{s-1}(-T_0)^s \tag{9-3-6}$$

and

$$\lambda^* = + \frac{M_1 R T_0^2}{1000 L_{v(0)}} \tag{9-3-7}$$

Table (9-3-1) contains the molal elevation of the boiling point, λ^*, for common organic solvents at their normal boiling points. Values of λ^* and

TABLE (9-3-1).   BOILING-POINT CONSTANTS[a] OF SOLVENTS AT ONE ATMOSPHERE.

Solvent	t (B.P.)	λ^*
Ammonia	−33.4	0.349
Water	100.0	0.513
Methanol	64.7	0.862
Ethanol	78.3	1.214
Sulfur dioxide	−10.1	1.45
Carbon disulfide	46.3	2.41
Benzene	80.2	2.628
Cyclohexanol	116.1	2.78
Acetic acid	118.3	3.15

[a] Calculated by equation (9-3-7) from data in "International Critical Tables," Vol. V, p. 135, McGraw-Hill Book Co., New York, 1931.

[24] The computation of the temperature dependence of L_v at a fixed pressure, p_0, from the results obtained at the continuously varying saturation pressure, is carefully described by George C. Johnson, Dissertation, Yale University (1940). The results of this computation are given by G. C. Johnson and R. P. Smith, *J. Am. Chem. Soc.*, **63**, 1351 (1941).

the first three coefficients, C_n^*, for water at several pressures are given in Table (9-3-2).

TABLE (9-3-2). BOILING-POINT CONSTANTS[a] FOR WATER AT VARIOUS PRESSURES.

t	p_0	λ°	C_1^*	$10^5 C_2^*$	$10^8 C_3^*$	$10^{10} C_4^*$
60	149.4	0.39108	1	−347.900	1072.12	−325.2
70	233.7	.41931	1	−339.201	992.13	−284.1
80	355.2	.44905	1	−331.029	915.88	−245.9
90	525.8	.48007	1	−323.132	822.64	−198.2
100	760.0	.51276	1	−316.017	784.24	−184.4

[a] Calculated from the numerical constants used by R. P. Smith, *J. Am. Chem. Soc.*, **61**, 500 (1939); Table I: $T = 273.1 + t$; $R = 8.3126$ int. joules.

Integrating equation (9-3-5) and recalling equation (1-9-9), we obtain

$$\ln a_1' = -\frac{M_1}{1000\lambda^*} \sum_1^\infty C_n^* \theta^n \qquad (9\text{-}3\text{-}8)$$

and

$$\phi' = \frac{1}{\nu m \lambda^*} \sum_1^\infty C_n^* \theta^n \qquad (9\text{-}3\text{-}9)$$

(4) GENERAL EQUATIONS FOR CALCULATING THE ACTIVITY OF THE SOLVENT AND THE OSMOTIC COEFFICIENT FROM VAPOR PRESSURE MEASUREMENTS AND FROM ISOPIESTIC COMPARISONS

Equation (1-2-6) and the definitional equation for the activity of a pure gas at constant temperature, $RT\, d \ln a = dF$, lead to

$$\left(\frac{\partial \ln a_v}{\partial P}\right)_T = \frac{V}{RT} \qquad (9\text{-}4\text{-}1)$$

for the variation of the activity of water vapor with pressure. At equilibrium, the total pressure P is equal to the vapor pressure p. The molal volume is conveniently expressed by

$$V = \frac{RT}{P} - \alpha \qquad (9\text{-}4\text{-}2)$$

where α is, in general, a function of P and T, but reduces to a function of T alone when P is small. Combining the above equations and making use of the proportionality between the activity of the solvent in the vapor phase and in a solution in equilibrium with it, we obtain

$$d \ln a_1 = d \ln P - \frac{\alpha}{RT}\, dP \qquad (9\text{-}4\text{-}3)$$

Integrating between p and p_0, the vapor pressure of the pure solvent, gives

$$\ln a_1 = \ln p/p_0 - \int_{p_0}^p \frac{\alpha\, dP}{RT} \qquad (9\text{-}4\text{-}4)$$

The osmotic coefficient [Equation (1-9-9)] is therefore given by

$$\phi = - \frac{1000}{\nu m M_1} \ln \frac{p}{p_0} + \frac{1000}{\nu m M_1 RT} \int_{p_0}^{p} \alpha dP \qquad (9\text{-}4\text{-}5)$$

In practice the terms containing α are neglected as being smaller than the experimental errors in vapor pressure measurements at room temperatures.*

If the osmotic coefficient or activity of the solvent is known as a function of concentration in some reference solution, it may be readily determined in other solutions by isopiestic comparison.[25] Samples of a reference solution and of a solution under investigation are weighed into silver dishes, and kept in good thermal contact in a vacuum desiccator. After equilibrium is attained, the vapor pressure of the solvent is the same for all solutions. The equilibrium concentrations are determined by re-weighing the dishes and their contents. The properties of the solution being studied, at the concentration m, are given by

$$a_{1(m)} = a_{1R(m_R)} \qquad (9\text{-}4\text{-}6)$$

and

$$\phi_{(m)} = \frac{\nu_R m_R}{\nu m} \phi_{R(m_R)} \qquad (9\text{-}4\text{-}7)$$

in terms of the corresponding properties of the reference solution at the concentration m_R. Values of ϕ_R for important reference solutions are given in Table (9-4-1). Potassium chloride, or sodium chloride, forms the usual reference solution for comparison with other electrolytes.

(5) Calculation of the Activity Coefficient of the Solute from the Osmotic Coefficient or Activity of the Solvent

This calculation, which involves the integration of equation (1-8-1), has been performed by a variety of analytical and graphical methods. We shall illustrate representative methods by their applications to data from several sources. Rearrangement of equations (1-9-10) and (1-9-11) gives the fundamental relations

* It is also customary to disregard the fact that the values of a_1 and ϕ calculated from direct manometric measurements are derived under a pressure, p, which varies with the composition of the solution. Considering the magnitude of $\bar{V}_1/RT$, it is clear from equation (1-7-11) that the correction required to bring these values to a constant pressure, p_0, or to one atmosphere, is much less than the experimental error.

[25] D. A. Sinclair, *J. Phys. Chem.*, **37**, 495 (1933); R. A. Robinson and D. A. Sinclair, *J. Am. Chem. Soc.*, **56**, 1830 (1934).

$$d \ln \gamma_\pm = - \frac{1000}{\nu m M_1} d \ln a_1 - d \ln m \qquad (9\text{-}5\text{-}1)$$

and

$$d \ln \gamma_\pm = - \frac{1}{m} d\{m(1 - \phi)\} \qquad (9\text{-}5\text{-}2)$$

which are to be integrated. Since the values of $\ln a_1$, or ϕ, may be expressed empirically as functions of m, they may be eliminated from these equations.

TABLE (9-4-1). OSMOTIC COEFFICIENTS OF REFERENCE SOLUTIONS AT 25°.

m	NaCl[a]	KCl[a]	H$_2$SO$_4$[b]	Sucrose[c]
0.1	0.9319	0.9257	0.6800	1.0073
.2	.9246	.9129	.6680	1.0151
.3	.9212	.9062	.6672	1.0234
.5	.9217	.9002	.6748	1.0410
.7	.9265	.8979	.6888	1.0596
1.0	.9378	.8994	.7195	1.0897
1.5	.9594	.9056	.7823	1.1415
2.0	.9862	.9148	.8488	1.1929
2.5	1.0170	.9274	.9185	1.2436
3.0	1.0498	.9409	.9960	1.2923
3.5	1.0847	.9552	1.0725	1.3379
4.0	1.1219	.9698	1.1523	1.3805
4.5	......	.9854	1.2298	1.4186
5.0	......	.9958*	1.3041	1.4541
5.5	......	......	1.3766	1.4881
6.0	......	......	1.4485	1.5216
7.0	......	......	1.5817	......
8.0	......	......	1.6998	......

[a] These values were kindly furnished by Dr. R. A. Robinson. They have been adjusted to conform as closely as possible with the best electromotive force and vapor pressure determinations of the activity coefficients of the chlorides and bromides of sodium and potassium (ten independent series), and with the most recently determined isopiestic ratios. The values are given to four places as an aid to drawing consistent smooth curves. The last place is not physically significant, and differences in the third place sometimes result from variations in the graphical treatment of the same data. Compare, "Electrolyte Solutions" by R. A. Robinson and R. H. Stokes, Butterworths Scientific Publications, London (1955).

[b] Calculated from the values in columns (2) and (3) and the isopiestic ratios of G. Scatchard, W. J. Hamer and S. E. Wood, J. Am. Chem. Soc., **60**, 3061 (1938); H. Scheffer, A. A. Janis and J. B. Ferguson, Canadian J. Research, **17B**, 338 (1939); and R. A. Robinson, Trans. Faraday Soc., **35**, 1229 (1939). Above $3M$, the values of ϕ are based upon the data of S. Shankman and A. R. Gordon, J. Am. Chem. Soc., **61**, 2370 (1939).

[c] Calculated from the values in column (3) and the isopiestic ratios of G. Scatchard, W. J Hamer and S. E. Wood (loc. cit.); and R. A. Robinson and D. A. Sinclair, J. Am. Chem. Soc., **56**, 1830 (1934); and recent unpublished results of R. A. Robinson.

* $m = 4.81$.

Unfortunately, the absolute accuracy with which $\ln \gamma_\pm$ is determined by this procedure is strongly influenced by the form of these functions, if the lower limit of the integration is $m = 0$. The Debye-Hückel equation supplies a logical basis for the selection of proper functions by which the properties of solutions may be expressed from infinite dilution up to the lowest experimental concentrations.

Combination of equations (5-2-8) and (1-8-13) leads to

$$\log \gamma_\pm = - \frac{\mathcal{S}_{(f)} \sqrt{c}}{1 + A' \sqrt{c}} - \log \left(1 + \frac{\nu m M_1}{1000}\right) \qquad (9\text{-}5\text{-}3)$$

Since the present use of this equation is confined to dilute solutions, the last term may be neglected. Accordingly, if we let $x = A' \sqrt{c}$, and $k' = 2.303 \, \mathbb{S}_{(f)}/A'$, then

$$d \ln \gamma_\pm = - k'(1 + x)^{-2} \, dx \tag{9-5-4}$$

Substitution of this equation into (9-5-2) gives

$$1 - \phi = \frac{k'}{m} \int_0^x m \, \frac{dx}{(1 + x)^2} = \frac{k'}{x^2} \int_0^x x^2 \, \frac{dx}{(1 + x)^2} \tag{9-5-5}$$

since m is proportional to x^2 at high dilution.

Integration and rearrangement yield

$$1 - \phi = \frac{k'x}{3} \left\{ \frac{3}{x^3} \left(1 + x - 2 \ln (1 + x) - \frac{1}{1 + x} \right) \right\} \equiv \frac{k'x\sigma}{3} \tag{9-5-6}$$

The function σ defined by this equation may be expressed by

$$\sigma = \sum_{n=1}^{\infty} \frac{3n}{n + 2} (-x)^{n-1} = \sum_{n=1}^{\infty} \frac{3n}{n + 2} (-A' \sqrt{c})^{n-1} \tag{9-5-7}$$

when $x \leq 1$. Substituting the value of k' into (9-5-6), we obtain

$$1 - \phi = 0.7676 \mathbb{S}_{(f)} \sigma \sqrt{c} \tag{9-5-8}$$

Any expression which is used to represent experimental values of $1 - \phi$ as a function of composition should reduce to this equation at high dilutions. Numerical values of $\mathbb{S}_{(f)}$ and A' are given in Table (5-2-1) and values of σ are given in Tables (9-5-1) and (5-2-6).

Since the above equation is restricted to dilute solutions, we may write $\sqrt{c} = \sqrt{md_0}$, and define

$$\mathbb{S}_{m(f)} \equiv \mathbb{S}_{(f)} \sqrt{d_0} \tag{9-5-9}$$

$$A'_m \equiv A' \sqrt{d_0} \tag{9-5-10}$$

and

$$\sigma_m = \sum_{n=1}^{\infty} \frac{3n}{n + 2} (-A'_m \sqrt{m})^{n-1} \tag{9-5-11}$$

Accordingly,

$$1 - \phi = 0.7676 \mathbb{S}_{m(f)} \sigma_m \sqrt{m} \tag{9-5-12}$$

This convenient expression reduces to (9-5-8) in the limit, and differs from it by a negligible amount at moderate dilutions.

Smith[26] calculated ϕ' at the boiling points of solutions of sodium chloride, and used the expression

$$1 - \phi' = 0.7676 \mathbb{S}_{m(f)} \sigma_m \sqrt{m} - 0.5Bm \tag{9-5-12a}$$

[26] R. P. Smith, *J. Am. Chem. Soc.*, **61**, 500 (1939).

The term $0.5Bm$ is included to represent the data at high concentrations [Compare equation (3-8-2)]. Numerical values of A'_m and B can be chosen so that the deviation

$$\delta\phi' = -(1 - \phi') + 0.7676 \mathcal{S}_{m(f)}\sigma_m \sqrt{m} - 0.5Bm \qquad (9\text{-}5\text{-}13)$$

TABLE (9-5-1)*. THE FUNCTION σ. SEE TABLE (5-2-6)

$A'\sqrt{c}$	σ	$A'\sqrt{c}$	σ	$A'\sqrt{c}$	σ
0.00	1.0000	0.40	0.5986	0.80	0.4036
.05	.9293	.45	.5668	.85	.3863
.10	.8662	.50	.5377	.90	.3703
.15	.8097	.55	.5108	.95	.3552
.20	.7588	.60	.4860	1.00	.3411
.25	.7129	.65	.4631	1.05	.3279
.30	.6712	.70	.4418	1.10	.3154
.35	.6332	.75	.4220	1.15	.3037

* The column heading may be replaced by $A'_m\sqrt{m}$ and σ_m for use on the m-scale.

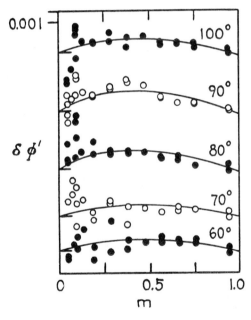

Fig. (9-5-1)
The deviation function, $\delta\phi'$, for sodium chloride in water at various temperatures. Diameter of circles equals 0.0005

is not large at any concentration. Comparison of equations (9-5-13) and (9-5-12) shows that $\delta\phi'$ must become zero at infinite dilution. Combining equations (9-5-13) with (9-5-2) and integrating, we obtain

$$\ln \gamma'_\pm = -\frac{2.303 \mathcal{S}_{m(f)} \sqrt{m}}{1 + A'_m \sqrt{m}} + Bm + \int_0^m \frac{\delta\phi'}{m}\, dm + \delta\phi' \qquad (9\text{-}5\text{-}14)$$

The two terms containing $\delta\phi'$ are evaluated graphically. From Fig. (9-5-1) which contains Smith's values of $\delta\phi'$ for sodium chloride solutions

($T_0 = 60, 70, 80, 90$ and $100°$), it appears that the maximum contribution of these terms to $\gamma'_\pm$ is only 2 or 3 per cent.

It should be noted that the quantity designated $\gamma'_\pm$ is not a true activity coefficient because equation (9-5-2) was used under non-isothermal conditions. It is converted to a true activity coefficient by correcting all values of ϕ' to some standard temperature, T'', before integrating equation (9-5-2). Writing equation (1-7-5) in the integrated forms

$$\log a_1'' = \log a_1' + X \tag{9-5-15}$$

and

$$\phi'' = \phi' - \frac{2{,}303X}{\nu m M_1} \tag{9-5-16}$$

where

$$X \equiv - \int_{T'}^{T''} \frac{\bar{L}_1 \, dT}{2.303RT^2} \tag{9-5-17}$$

we obtain the expression

$$\log \gamma'' = \log \gamma' - \frac{1000}{\nu M_1} \int_0^X \left(\frac{1}{m}\right) dX \tag{9-5-18}$$

used by Lewis and Randall.[27]

The calculation of activity coefficients from equations (9-5-14) and (9-5-18) is largely analytical, because the terms in $\delta\phi'$ and dX contribute very little to the final result. Although a formal and completely analytical method of calculating osmotic and activity coefficient is described by Scatchard,[28] it is more usual to emphasize graphical procedures. Integrating equation (9-5-2), the activity coefficient is given by

$$\ln \gamma_\pm = - (1 - \phi) - 2 \int_0^m \left(\frac{1 - \phi}{m^{1/2}}\right) dm^{1/2} \tag{9-5-19}$$

when dm is replaced by $2m^{1/2}dm^{1/2}$. A plot of $(1 - \phi)/m^{1/2}$ against $m^{1/2}$ is sufficient to evaluate both terms in ϕ. The value of $(1 - \phi)/m^{1/2}$ is so sensitive to experimental errors in dilute solutions that some form of the Debye-Hückel equation must be used to extend the plot from about 0.1M to infinite dilution. Equation (9-5-12) leads to

$$(1 - \phi)/m^{1/2} = 0.7676 S_{m(f)} \sigma_m \tag{9-5-20}$$

in dilute solutions. In using this equation to complete the plot of $(1 - \phi)/m^{1/2}$ against $m^{1/2}$, it is necessary to know A'_m in order to calculate

[27] G. N. Lewis and M. Randall, "Thermodynamics," p. 350, McGraw-Hill Book Co., New York, 1923. See also M. Randall and L. E. Young, *J. Am. Chem. Soc.*, **50**, 989 (1928).

[28] G. Scatchard, *Chem. Rev.*, **8**, 321 (1931); G. Scatchard and S. S. Prentiss, *J. Am. Chem. Soc.*, **56**, 1486 (1934).

σ_m. Since $\mathring{a}$ is usually unknown, a value of A'_m is selected, by trial, which makes equation (9-5-20) fit the, experimental data at the lowest concentrations. The evaluation of A'_m is illustrated in connection with the j-function [Equations (9-5-21)]. Equations (9-5-19) and (9-5-20) are usually employed in calculating activity coefficients from osmotic coefficients derived from vapor pressures, or isopiestic comparisons. Tables (12-3-1A) and (13-1-2A) contain values of $\gamma_\pm$ obtained in this manner.

In the estimation of activity coefficients from freezing-point depression, the graphical integration of the Gibbs-Duhem equation commonly involves the variable*

$$j \equiv 1 - \frac{\vartheta}{\nu m \lambda} \qquad (9\text{-}5\text{-}21)$$

of Lewis and Randall.[29] Combining equations (9-2-8), (9-5-1) and (9-5-18), we obtain

$$d \log \gamma''_\pm = 0.4343 \frac{d\vartheta}{\nu m \lambda} \sum_1^\infty n C_n \vartheta^{n-1} - d \log m - \frac{1000}{\nu M_1} \frac{dX}{m} \qquad (9\text{-}5\text{-}22)$$

Since differentiation of equation (9-5-21) gives

$$\frac{d\vartheta}{\nu m \lambda} = (1 - j) d \ln m - dj \qquad (9\text{-}5\text{-}23)$$

and the coefficient C_1 is unity, equation (9-5-22) may be written

$$d \log \gamma''_\pm = -0.4343 dj - j d \log m$$
$$+ \frac{0.4343 d\vartheta}{\nu m \lambda} \sum_2^\infty n C_n \vartheta^{n-1} - \frac{1000}{\nu M_1} \frac{dX}{m} \qquad (9\text{-}5\text{-}24)$$

whence

$$\log \gamma''_\pm = -0.4343 j - 0.8686 \int_0^m \left(\frac{j}{m^{1/2}} \right) d\sqrt{m}$$
$$+ \frac{0.4343}{\nu \lambda} \int_0^\vartheta \frac{1}{m} \sum_2^\infty n C_n \vartheta^{n-1} d\vartheta - \frac{1000}{\nu M_1} \int_0^X \frac{dX}{m} \qquad (9\text{-}5\text{-}25)$$

Calorimetric data are generally not available for evaluating C_n beyond C_1, or C_2. For water the data justify the use of C_3 when accurate freezing-point measurements are considered at moderate concentrations.[30] For

---

* The quantity $j^* \equiv 1 - \theta/\nu m \lambda^*$ may be applied to boiling-point calculations in an analogous manner.

[29] G. N. Lewis and M. Randall, "Thermodynamics," p. 347, McGraw-Hill Book Co., New York, 1923.

[30] T. F. Young [*Chem. Rev.*, **13**, 103 (1933)] has shown that the effect of the various terms upon the activity coefficient of $5.2M$ sodium chloride is about 0.58 per cent for the C_3 term, 0.06 per cent for C_4, and 0.006 per cent for C_5. These effects decrease rapidly with dilution.

most purposes the summation is neglected beyond C_2, and equation (9-5-25) takes the approximate but more familiar form

$$\log \gamma_{\pm}'' = -0.4343j - 0.8686 \int_0^m \left(\frac{j}{m^{1/2}}\right) d\sqrt{m}$$

$$+ 0.8686C_2 \int_0^\vartheta (1-j) \, d\vartheta - \frac{1000}{\nu M_1} \int_0^X \frac{dX}{m} \tag{9-5-26}$$

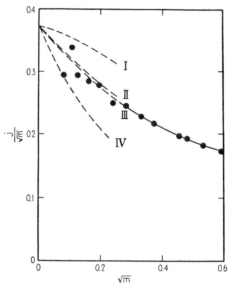

Fig. (9–5–2). Extrapolation of $j/m^{1/2}$ for potassium chloride solutions. Broken curves I, II, and IV by equation (9–5–29) with $d = 2, 3.6, 7$, respectively. Broken curve III by equation (9–5–28) with $d = 3.6$.

In dilute solutions, where the right-hand member of equation (9-5-24) may be represented by the first two terms, $d \log \gamma_{\pm}''$ can be eliminated by (9-5-4), and we obtain

$$j = 0.7676 \mathfrak{S}_{(f)} \sigma \sqrt{c} \tag{9-5-27}$$

and

$$j = 0.7676 \mathfrak{S}_{m(f)} \sigma_m \sqrt{m} \tag{9-5-28}$$

by the procedure used to derive equations (9-5-8) and (9-5-12). Obviously, $j = 1 - \phi$ within the concentration range covered by these equations.

The use of these equations and the selection of a proper value of A_m' from which to calculate σ_m are illustrated in Figure (9-5-2). The experimental[31] values of $j/m^{1/2}$ for aqueous potassium chloride solutions are plotted against $m^{1/2}$. The solid curve representing these values can be located with high accuracy down to concentrations as low as $m^{1/2} = 0.3$,

[31] G. Scatchard and S. S. Prentiss, *J. Am. Chem. Soc.*, **55**, 4355 (1933).

and with reasonable certainty down to $m^{1/2} = 0.2$. Below the latter concentration the experimental results are of little value in determining the shape of the curve which must bridge the gap between $m^{1/2} = 0.2$ and infinite dilution. This portion of the curve, represented by a broken line, was calculated by equation (9-5-28) for a value of A'_m corresponding to $å = 3.6$. In selecting the proper value of $å$, or A'_m, the experimental value of $j/m^{1/2}$, read from the plot at about $m^{1/2} = 0.2$, can be used to calculate $A'_m m^{1/2}$, and hence A'_m, from equations (9-5-11) and (9-5-28) by successive approximations. Spencer[32] published a table of theoretical values of $j/m^{1/2}$ and $m^{1/2}$ in aqueous solutions corresponding to various values of $å$ (1 to 8 Å). The equation he used was*

$$j = 0.3738\sigma_m\sqrt{m} - 0.1640(z^2/å)^3 10^3[X_3(x) - 6Y_3(x)]$$
$$- 0.0780(z^2/å)^5 10^5[X_5(x) - 10Y_5(x)] \tag{9-5-29}$$

which includes the contributions of the extended terms of equation (3-6-4) for symmetrical electrolytes. The three dashed curves in Figure (9-5-2) were constructed from Spencer's values corresponding to $å = 2, 3.6$, and 7 Å, respectively. The effect of the extended terms in aqueous potassium chloride solutions can be seen in the figure, where the curves based on equations (9-5-29) and (9-5-28) are clearly distinguishable. It is apparent from the figure that, if equation (9-5-29) had been used to extrapolate the experimental curve, we would have chosen a value of $å$ greater than 3.6. The difference between the values of $å$ (actually about 0.1 Å) derived from these two equations is not physically important, because both equations are employed at such high concentrations ($m^{1/2} = 0.2$) that the $å$ parameter has been forced to absorb the effect of writing $c = d_0 m$, and the effect of neglecting the last two terms in equation (9-5-25). To this extent, the extrapolation in Figure (9-5-2) is empirical except for the theoretical value of the intercept. Scatchard[33] has recently emphasized the empirical aspects of this calculation by employing the function*

$$j = \frac{0.3738 m^{1/2}}{1 + B m^{1/2}} + Cm \tag{9-5-30}$$

for 1-1 electrolytes which, although reducing to equation (9-5-28) at infinite dilution, does not agree with the Debye-Hückel theory at higher concentrations. This function has the merit, however, of conveniently approximating the freezing-point data up to $1M$. When used in conjunction with a plot of the deviation, δj, of values calculated by (9-5-30) from the experimental values, it puts a minimum of burden upon theory.

[32] H. M. Spencer, *J. Am. Chem. Soc.*, **54**, 4490 (1932).

[33] G. Scatchard, P. T. Jones and S. S. Prentiss, *J. Am. Chem. Soc.*, **54**, 2676, 2690 (1932).

* The coefficient 0.3738 would be 0.3747 in terms of the values of D and the physical constants of Chapter (5).

This procedure has certain advantages. It is usually a simple matter to assign values to the empirical constants, B and C, such that the deviation

$$\delta j = j - \frac{0.3738 m^{1/2}}{1 + B m^{1/2}} - C m \qquad (9\text{-}5\text{-}31)$$

is less than 0.01, or 0.02. A plot of δj against m, or $m^{1/2}$, therefore affords a very sensitive and compact means of smoothing the data, and obtaining representative j-values for use in evaluating the integrals of equation (9-5-25), or (9-5-26).

Figure (9-5-3) was constructed from the data of Scatchard and Prentiss[34] on potassium chloride. The solid curve was considered by them to repre-

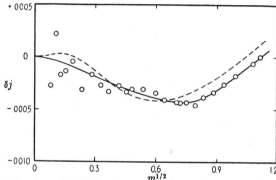

Fig. (9-5-3). δj values for KCl; $\delta j = j - (0.3738\ m^{1/2})/(1 + 1.7\ m^{1/2}) + 0.0149\ m$; Solid line used by Scatchard to obtain smoothed j-values from experimental data; broken line from Spencer's computation of earlier data

sent their data, shown as circles. For comparison, the j-values, obtained by Spencer[35] from a composite plot of earlier data, have been used to construct the broken curve. The agreement between the two curves is nearly everywhere better than ±0.001 in j, which is quite satisfactory for data derived from different sources.

From this and similar figures, the extensive measurements of Scatchard and Prentiss have been used to calculate the values of $-\log \gamma'_\pm$ for numerous 1-1 electrolytes. These are given in Table (9-5-1A), and will be referred to in the general discussion in Chapter (12).

[34] G. Scatchard and S. S. Prentiss, *J. Am. Chem. Soc.*, **55**, 4355 (1933).

[35] H. M. Spencer, *J. Am. Chem. Soc.*, **54**, 4490 (1932).

Chapter (10)

The Thermodynamics of Galvanic Cells

This chapter will begin with the elementary principles of the electromotive force method. The symbols for the representation of cells and the conventions regarding the signs of the electromotive force and standard electrode potentials will be stated. The thermodynamics of cells, without and with liquid junctions, in its relation to solution investigations will be developed. The hypothetical liquid-junction potential, the concept of electrical potential at phase boundaries, and the problem of individual ionic chemical potentials and activities will receive close attention. Finally, limitations of the use of cells with liquid junctions and a suitable method of eliminating liquid-junction potentials will be discussed.

(1) General Thermodynamic Properties of Cells. Definition of the Standard Electrode Potential

It has been shown that, at constant pressure, temperature and composition, the free energy change is related to the reversible electrical work according to equation (1-5-1), or

$$(dF)_{P,T,n} = \mp (\psi' - \psi'')de \qquad (1\text{-}5\text{-}1)$$

The mechanism which fulfills the conditions required by this equation is a galvanic cell, consisting of two reversible electrodes connected by a solution of appropriate electrolytes. The difference, $(\psi' - \psi'')$, is the electrical potential between two pieces of identical metal connected to the electrodes, and de is the charge transferred, which corresponds to a change in free energy dF. Equation (1-5-1) is valid for reversible changes only, a condition rigorously fulfilled if:

(1) No changes take place within the cell without the passage of the current.

(2) Every change which actually takes place during the passage of the current may be reversed by reversing the direction of the current.

Furthermore a cell is valuable for thermodynamic investigations only when the net result of all the chemical changes which take place is known. When all these conditions are fulfilled, we are in a position to measure the reversible electrical work, $(\psi' - \psi'')de$, and hence the free energy change, dF, corresponding to a known reaction. If a cell with an electromotive force, $\pm E$, is exactly balanced against an external electromotive force, so that no charging or discharging of the cell is taking place, then $\pm E$

is the electromotive force of the cell when the entire system is in equilibrium. If we imagine the cell to discharge against this electromotive force until a quantity of electricity, de, has passed through, the cell process will have taken place reversibly, performing the reversible electrical work, $\pm \mathbf{E} de$. The difference in potential, $(\psi' - \psi'')$, is equal to $+\mathbf{E}$ or $-\mathbf{E}$, depending on the convention adopted concerning the sign of the electromotive force. Equation (1-5-1) now becomes

$$(dF)_{P,T,n} = \pm \mathbf{E} de \qquad (10\text{-}1\text{-}1)$$

In dealing with chemical reactions, we are interested in changes of molar quantities of the substances and, therefore, according to Faraday's laws, are concerned with the passage of a Faraday, $\mathbf{F}$, of electricity, or a simple multiple of a Faraday, $\mathbf{NF}$, through the cell. Since dF is proportional to de, by equation (10-1-1),

$$(-\Delta F)_{P,T,n} = \mathbf{NFE} \qquad (10\text{-}1\text{-}2)$$

if $\mathbf{NF}$ coulombs pass through the cell. In writing this equation, we have now adopted the convention of Lewis and Randall that a positive $\mathbf{E}$ corresponds to a decrease in free energy.

The total free energy change of any chemical reaction in terms of the activities of the reactants and reaction products is given by equation (1-10-3). If we write $\Pi'a$ and Πa for the appropriate activity products of the resultants and reactants, respectively, and $\Pi'\gamma$, $\Pi\gamma$, $\Pi'm$, and Πm for the corresponding activity coefficients and concentration products, equation (1-10-3) may be written

$$\Delta F - \Delta F^0 = RT \ln \frac{\Pi'a}{\Pi a} = RT \ln \frac{\Pi'\gamma \Pi'm}{\Pi\gamma \Pi m} \qquad (10\text{-}1\text{-}3)$$

ΔF is the free energy of the reaction in general, and ΔF^0 is the free energy change when the activities of all reacting and resulting species are unity.

If the free energy of reaction is measured by means of a cell, then this equation may be combined with equation (10-1-2) to yield

$$\mathbf{E} = \mathbf{E}^0 - \frac{RT}{\mathbf{NF}} \ln \frac{\Pi'a}{\Pi a} = \mathbf{E}^0 - \frac{RT}{\mathbf{NF}} \ln \frac{\Pi'\gamma \Pi'm}{\Pi\gamma \Pi m} \qquad (10\text{-}1\text{-}4)$$

where

$$\mathbf{E}^0 = -\Delta F^0 / \mathbf{NF} \qquad (10\text{-}1\text{-}4a)$$

$\mathbf{E}^0$ is termed the standard electromotive force of the cell. Obviously, $\mathbf{E}$ equals $\mathbf{E}^0$ when the activities of all constituents are equal to unity. Since the composition of the solid components (or pure liquid phase) of the cell are ordinarily independent of the concentration of the electrolyte solution, it is customary to assign the value unity to the activities of such components, and consider them in their standard states at all temperatures under a pressure of one atmosphere.* The standard state for the components of liquid solutions is ordinarily selected so that $m = a$, or $\gamma = 1$, for each solute at infinite dilution. Since partial pressures are proportional to concentrations in gaseous mixtures, and the perfect gas law may be applied for practical purposes over small pressure changes in the neighborhood of one atmosphere, the activity of a gaseous component will be written equal to its partial pressure. Therefore, a gas is in its standard state at any temperature when its partial pressure is one atmosphere.† On the basis of this selection of standard states it will be seen, by rearranging equation (10-1-4) to the form

$$E + \frac{RT}{NF} \ln \frac{\Pi'm}{\Pi m} = E^0 - \frac{RT}{NF} \ln \frac{\Pi'\gamma}{\Pi\gamma} \tag{10-1-5}$$

that E^0 is numerically equal to the sum of the terms on the left-hand side of the equation at infinite dilution of the electrolyte solution, for under this condition the term in γ is zero. Various methods of evaluating the important quantity,

$$\left[E + \frac{RT}{NF} \ln \frac{\Pi'm}{\Pi m} \right]_{(m \to 0)} = E^0 \tag{10-1-5a}$$

will be discussed in Section (3) and in later chapters.

(2) Conventions Regarding the Representation of Cells and Electrodes, and the Signs of Their Electromotive Forces

Since most American chemists are accustomed to the system of conventions adopted by Lewis and Randall[1] for writing electrode and cell reactions, and the signs of their corresponding electromotive forces, their system will be adhered ·to. Regarding the schematic representation of cells by chemical symbols, etc., some variations will be introduced, and several additional conventions are required to describe the more complex cells recently appearing in the literature. Conventions of limited use will be announced at the time of their introduction, but those of general application will now be summarized.

(a) Contact between separate phases (electrode and solution) is usually indicated by a vertical line, but, in the representation of individual elec-

---

* Because of the small molal volumes of solids (and liquids), they may be considered to have unit activity at any pressure of the order of one atmosphere, [Equation (1-7-11)]. For gases, the pressure must be designated.

† These conventional standard states will always be implied except in a few special studies where the proper alternatives will be specifically mentioned.

[1] G. N. Lewis and M. Randall, "Thermodynamics," McGraw-Hill Book Co., New York, 1923.

trodes,* a hyphen is used between the phases.   Thus, Pt-Ag-AgCl | MCl(m) represents a silver-silver chloride electrode in contact with a chloride solution.

(b) The physical nature of a phase, when not self-evident, is indicated by (s), (l), or (g) for solid, liquid, or gas.   The symbols (m), (c), etc., expressing concentration, indicate liquid solutions.   Solid solutions are seldom used for electrodes except when mercury is a component and then two saturated solid solutions are usually present.   In such cases, the expression "two-phase amalgam" is used.   Thus, Pt-Pb-Hg(2-phase)-PbSO$_4$(m) | represents an electrode composed of saturated solutions of Hg in Pb, and of Pb in Hg.

(c) The partial pressure of a gas is indicated by (p), or (1 atm.), etc. The omission of a specific designation of pressure implies a partial pressure of one atmosphere.

(d) The concentration of solutes will usually be expressed in mols per kilogram of solvents, and represented by (m).   When several solutes are present in solution, their concentrations will be differentiated as (m_1), (m_2), etc., or sometimes m_{KCl}, m_{H^+}, etc.   Co-solutes are separated by commas to indicate that they are present in the same phase.

(e) Unless otherwise specified, the solvent is water.   When mixed solvents are employed, their composition will usually be expressed in weight percentages, X and Y. X will represent the non-aqueous component if water is present.

(f) A positive sign over an electrode of a cell indicates that negative electricity is transferred from the electrode to the electrolyte during the spontaneous operation of the cell in its standard state.   The positive sign will frequently be omitted, because cells written in general terms without specifying the numerical value of $\mathbf{E}^0$, or limiting the concentrations in any way, cannot be given a definite polarity.

(g) The electromotive force, $\mathbf{E}$, will be taken as positive when the spontaneous operation of the cell involves the transfer of negative electricity from right to left within the cell as written.

Most of the conventions so far enumerated can be illustrated by the cell,

$$H_2(1 \text{ atm.}) \mid HA(m_0), NaA(m_1), NaCl(m_2), CH_3OH(X), H_2O(Y) \mid AgCl\text{-}Ag^+$$

containing sodium chloride and some weak acid, HA, and its sodium salt. The solvent is X per cent methanol, and Y per cent water.   The silver-silver chloride electrode is indicated as positive.   Thus, by (10-1-4),

$$\mathbf{E} = \mathbf{E}^0 - \frac{RT}{\mathbf{NF}} \ln a_{H^+} a_{Cl^-}$$

---

* In representing these electrodes, Pt- is customarily omitted.   Thus, Ag-AgCl | MCl(m); Pb-Hg(2-phase)-PbSO$_4$ | etc.   Furthermore, amalgam electrodes are often written, M-Hg(sat.) and M$_x$Hg, to differentiate between a 2-phase and single-phase amalgam.

E^0 would be the electromotive force of this cell if we could make $a_H a_{Cl} = 1$. As we shall see later, E^0 is also the electromotive force of the cell,

$$H_2(1 \text{ atm.}) \mid HCl(m), \; CH_3OH(X), \; H_2O(Y) \mid AgCl\text{-}Ag$$

at the same temperature when $a_H a_{Cl} = 1$.

(h) All single electrodes will be written with the electrolyte on the right. Thus, for the hydrogen electrode,

$$H_2(p \text{ atm.}) \mid H^+(m_{H^+})$$

or, more simply

$$H_2(p) \mid H^+(m)$$

the electromotive force will be positive when negative electricity is transferred from right to left through the electrode. The operation of the above electrode corresponds to the reaction,

$$\tfrac{1}{2}H_2(p) = H^+(m) + \ominus \tag{10-2-1}$$

where the symbol, $\ominus$, represents one Faraday of negative electricity. By always writing electrode reactions so that $\ominus$ appears as a product of the reaction, the general equation for the potential, π, of a single electrode is given by

$$\pi = \pi^0 - \frac{RT}{NF} \ln \frac{\Pi' a}{\Pi a} \tag{10-2-2}$$

and for the electrode just considered, this becomes

$$\pi = \pi^0 - \frac{RT}{F} \ln \frac{a_{H^+}}{p_H^{1/2}} \tag{10-2-3}$$

since $N = 1$.

(i) The standard (or normal) electrode potential, π^0, is the potential when all the activities involved in the electrode reaction are unity. Since single electrode potentials are incapable of independent measurement, it is customary to compute their values relative to $\pi_H^0 = 0$.

(j) In combining any two single electrodes to form a galvanic cell, the electromotive force of the cell is the algebraic difference between the potentials of the electrodes. The electrode potential of the right-hand electrode is subtracted from that on the left. Thus, if we combine the electrode,

$$Ag\text{-}AgCl \mid Cl^-(m)$$

with the hydrogen electrode, we may write

$$H_2(p) \mid HCl(m) \mid AgCl\text{-}Ag, \qquad\qquad\qquad \text{I}$$

The electrode reactions are

$$\tfrac{1}{2}H_2(p) \;=\; H^+(m) \;+\; \ominus \tag{10-2-4}$$

and

$$Ag + Cl^-(m) = AgCl(s) + \ominus \tag{10-2-5}$$

The corresponding potentials are

$$\pi_{H(p)} = 0 - \frac{RT}{F} \ln \frac{a_H}{p^{1/2}} \tag{10-2-6}$$

and

$$\pi_{AgCl} = \pi^0_{AgCl} - \frac{RT}{F} \ln \frac{1}{a_{Cl}} \tag{10-2-7}$$

The cell reaction and electromotive force are

$$\tfrac{1}{2}H_2(p) + AgCl(s) \;\rightarrow\; Ag + HCl(m) \tag{10-2-8}$$

and

$$\pi_{H(p)} - \pi_{AgCl} = 0 - \pi^0_{AgCl} - \frac{RT}{F} \ln \frac{a_H a_{Cl}}{p^{1/2}} \tag{10-2-9}$$

or

$$E_{I(p)} = E_I^0 - \frac{RT}{F} \ln \frac{a_H a_{Cl}}{p^{1/2}} \tag{10-2-10}$$

for cell I as written. Under ordinary conditions, the spontaneous tendency for negative electricity to pass through this cell is from right to left, and therefore E_I and E_I^0 are positive. If we had chosen to combine the same two electrodes in the order,

$$\text{Ag-AgCl} \mid HCl(m) \mid H_2(p) \qquad\qquad \text{II}$$

it would be necessary to write

$$HCl(m) + Ag \rightarrow AgCl(s) + \tfrac{1}{2}H_2(p) \tag{10-2-11}$$

and

$$E_{II(p)} = E_{II}^0 + \frac{RT}{F} \ln \frac{a_H a_{Cl}}{p^{1/2}} \tag{10-2-12}$$

In this case, $E_{II(p)} = -E_{I(p)}$, and $E_{II}^0 = -E_I^0$. Obviously, it is immaterial whether we write cell I or cell II, so long as we associate the electromotive force and its sign with the appropriate cell reaction.

It should be emphasized at this point that the nature of the chemical reaction, corresponding to a particular electrode or cell, cannot be determined by electromotive force measurements alone. Cell reactions, no matter how simple and obvious, must be treated as hypothetical until it can be shown that thermodynamic quantities calculated from the electromotive force, ΔF, ΔH, equilibrium constants, etc., have been checked by other evidence.

To avoid the necessity of recording the partial pressures of gases involved in cell reactions, it has become customary to convert electromotive forces, measured at a partial pressure, p, to values corresponding to a partial pressure of exactly one atmosphere, and record the latter as an "observed" electromotive force. If we arrange equation (10-2-10) for cell I in the form

$$ \mathbf{E}^0 - \frac{RT}{F} \ln a_H \, a_{Cl} = \left[\mathbf{E}_{(p)} - \frac{RT}{2F} \ln p \right] = \mathbf{E} \qquad (10\text{-}2\text{-}13) $$

it is seen that the bracketed expression equals the electromotive force of the cell when $p = 1$. This electromotive force is designated $\mathbf{E}$.

TABLE (10-2-1). BAROMETRIC CORRECTION: $\frac{RT}{2F} \ln [760/(P - p_W)]$ FOR DILUTE AQUEOUS SOLUTIONS (VOLTS $\times 10^5$).

P	0°	5°	10°	15°	20°	25°	30°	35°	40°	45°	50°	55°	60°
780	−24	−21	−17	−12	−4	7	20	40	64	98	140	195	269
770	−8	−6	−1	4	12	24	38	58	82	115	160	217	291
760	7	10	15	21	29	41	56	76	101	136	181	239	314
750	23	26	31	38	46	59	74	95	121	156	202	261	338
740	39	43	48	55	64	76	92	113	141	176	223		

Table (10-2-1) contains values of the correction factor

$$ -\frac{RT}{2F} \ln p = \frac{RT}{2F} \ln \frac{760}{P - p_w} \qquad (10\text{-}2\text{-}14) $$

for aqueous solution. This quantity, sometimes written $\mathbf{E}_{(Bar.)}$, should be added to $\mathbf{E}_{(p)}$ to obtain $\mathbf{E}$. Here, the total barometric pressure, P, and the vapor pressure of pure water, p_w, are expressed in millimeters. The vapor pressure of water over a dilute solution does not differ enough from that of pure water to affect $\mathbf{E}$ appreciably, since a change of $\frac{1}{2}$ mm. in p_w affects the figures in Table (10-2-1) by about 0.01 mv. at room temperature. Linear interpolation is satisfactory. For concentrated solutions, however, it is necessary to employ equation (10-2-14) for each concentration, and make use of the appropriate values of p_w.

There remains one further matter. Since no boundary between two solutions of the same electrolyte at different concentrations, or between two solutions of different electrolytes, is specified in cells of the type considered in this section, these cells are designated "cells without liquid junction." However, such cells are not absolutely free from concentration gradients since the silver halide is slightly soluble. If the solution is saturated throughout with the halide, silver will deposit on the hydrogen electrode, and affect its electromotive force. If the solution is not saturated with the halide, a concentration gradient of silver and halide ions will be present which will give rise to a liquid junction potential of a small magnitude. This condition prevails in all cells containing electrodes of this kind. Obviously, the lower the solubility of the salt under consideration, the more nearly the actual cell approaches the ideal cell without liquid junction.

(3) EXTRAPOLATION OF ELECTROMOTIVE FORCE DATA AND EVALUATION OF THE STANDARD MOLAL ELECTRODE POTENTIAL

In general, the electromotive force of a cell is given by equation (10-1-4)· We shall be particularly interested in a specialized form of this equation. In the first place, we shall consider the electromotive force, $\mathbf{E}$, to be that at which any gas involved in the cell reaction is at unit pressure [Equation (10-2-13)]. Secondly, we shall consider only that kind of cell reaction in which the electrolyte is formed at a concentration, m [Equation (10-2-8)]. In this case, equation (10-1-4) reduces to

$$\mathbf{E} = \mathbf{E}^0 - \frac{RT}{\mathbf{NF}} \ln \gamma_+^{\nu^+} \gamma_-^{\nu^-} m_+^{\nu^+} m_-^{\nu^-}$$

or

$$\mathbf{E} = \mathbf{E}^0 - \frac{\nu RT}{\mathbf{NF}} \ln \gamma_\pm m_\pm \tag{10-3-1}$$

according to the definitional equations (1-6-3) and (1-8-5). Upon rearrangement of this equation, we obtain

$$\left[\mathbf{E} + \frac{\nu RT}{\mathbf{NF}} \ln m_\pm \right] = \mathbf{E}^0 - \frac{\nu RT}{\mathbf{NF}} \ln \gamma_\pm \tag{10-3-2}$$

The bracketed terms must equal $\mathbf{E}^0$ when $m = 0$, since $\gamma_\pm = 1$ at infinite dilution. Therefore, the problem of extrapolation reduces to the evaluation of the left side of this equation when $m = 0$. Since the equation (3-4-9), without the logarithmic term on the right,

$$\log \gamma_\pm = -\mathbf{S}_{(f)} \sqrt{\Gamma} \tag{10-3-3}$$

permits the elimination of $\gamma_\pm$ from equation (10-3-2), $\mathbf{E}^0$ might be calculated from a single, accurate measurement at very high dilution, or a series of measurements at various concentrations. In the latter case, the left side of equation (10-3-2) can be plotted against $\sqrt{\Gamma}$, and extrapolated to $c = 0$ so as to approach the limiting slope of the theory asymptotically. Such a plot was originally used by Lewis and Randall[2] before the advent of the

[2] G. N. Lewis and M. Randall, *J. Am. Chem. Soc.*, **43**, 1112 (1921).

Debye and Hückel theory. They assumed the linearity of the left side of equation (10-3-2) with $\sqrt{m}$ at infinite dilution, and extrapolated with an arbitrary slope which seemed to fit the data at high dilution. This type of extrapolation is not very satisfactory because it exhibits a curvature at the lowest concentrations, and too much weight must be given to the most dilute solutions where the measurements are least trustworthy.

A simple practical extrapolation[3] which fits the data closely at moderate concentrations may be obtained by using equation (10-3-3) with an additional term, or

$$\log \gamma_{\pm} = -\mathcal{S}_{(f)}\sqrt{\Gamma} + B'm \tag{10-3-4}$$

When combined with equation (10-3-2) and arranged in a suitable manner,

$$\left[\mathbf{E} + \frac{\nu RT}{\mathbf{NF}} \ln m_{\pm} - \frac{\nu RT}{\mathbf{NF}} \mathcal{S}_{(f)}\sqrt{\Gamma} \right] = \mathbf{E}^0 - \frac{\nu RT}{\mathbf{NF}} B'm \tag{10-3-5}$$

According to this equation, a plot of the bracketed term against m should be linear, and the intercept at $m = 0$ must be $\mathbf{E}^0$. Numerous examples of this and similar kinds of extrapolations will be found in Chapters (11) to (15).

We have made no attempt to compile comprehensive tables of standard potentials, but have recorded values of $\mathbf{E}^0$ which have a direct bearing on the immediate subject matter. Tables[4] of standard ionic free energies and entropies have been omitted entirely.

(4) Determination of Activity Coefficients by Extrapolation of the Electromotive Forces of Concentration Cells Without Liquid Junctions

There is another type of extrapolation which, although not as important as that just described, has proved useful in the development of this subject. Sometimes for experimental purposes it is convenient to combine two cells of the kind described above. An important example is the amalgam cell of the type

$$\mathrm{M}_x\mathrm{Hg} \mid \mathrm{MX}(m_1) \mid \mathrm{Ag}X\text{-}\mathrm{Ag} \tag{10-4-1}$$

where M is an alkali metal, and MX an alkali halide. The cell reaction is taken to be

$$\mathrm{M}(\mathrm{M}_x\mathrm{Hg}) + \mathrm{Ag}X = \mathrm{Ag} + \mathrm{M}X(m_1) \tag{10-4-2}$$

[3] D. I. Hitchcock, *J. Am. Chem. Soc.*, **50**, 2076 (1928); N. Bjerrum and A. Unmack, *Det. Kg. Danske Videnskab. Math. fys. Medd.*, **9**, 1 (1929).

[4] For recent tabulations see W. M. Latimer, "The Oxidation States of the Elements and Their Potentials in Aqueous Solutions," Prentice-Hall, New York, 1938. See also W. M. Latimer, K. S. Pitzer and W. V. Smith, *J. Am. Chem. Soc.*, **60**, 1829 (1938).

Consider another cell of this type,

$$M_zHg \mid MX(m_2) \mid AgX\text{-}Ag \tag{10-4-3}$$

in which the electrolyte is at a different concentration, m_2. The cell reaction is

$$M(M_zHg) + AgX = Ag + MX(m_2) \tag{10-4-4}$$

If these two cells are combined to form

$$Ag\text{-}AgX \mid MX(m_2) \mid M_zHg \mid MX(m_1) \mid AgX\text{-}Ag \tag{10-4-5}$$

the cell reaction is obtained by subtracting (10-4-4) from (10-4-2) so that the net effect of the cell reaction corresponds to the transfer of MX from a solution of concentration, m_2, to a solution of concentration m_1. This is represented by

$$MX(m_2) = MX(m_1) \tag{10-4-6}$$

From equation (1-6-2), we immediately obtain for the transfer of one mol,*

$$-\mathbf{N}FE = \int_{\bar{F}_2}^{\bar{F}_1} dF = \bar{F}_1 - \bar{F}_2 = \nu RT \ln \frac{\gamma_1 m_1}{\gamma_2 m_2} \tag{10-4-7}$$

This equation also results by applying equation (10-1-4) to cells (10-4-1) and (10-4-3), and subtracting. Since the ratio m_1/m_2 is known, the measurement of the electromotive force of a double cell of this kind yields an activity coefficient ratio. In order to determine γ, it is usually customary to keep m_1 constant at a reference concentration (0.1M), and determine $\gamma/\gamma_{0.1}$, where γ is the activity coefficient at any other concentration, m. The extrapolation is then effected by means of Hückel's extended Debye and Hückel equation, which is derived by adding a linear term in c to equation (3-5-8). Thus, recalling equation (1-8-13), we may write

$$\log \gamma = -\frac{\mathbf{S}_{(f)} \sqrt{\Gamma}}{1 + A \sqrt{\Gamma}} + Bc - \log(1 + 0.01802\nu m) \tag{10-4-8}$$

A and B are empirical constants at a given temperature. This equation has been shown to fit activity data with high precision from low concentrations to 1M, or sometimes to 2M, and for this reason is suitable for extrapolating data obtained at high concentrations.[5] A and B may be determined in a number of ways, the simplest of which is the solution of two

---

* For remainder of this section, γ will represent the mean activity coefficient, $\gamma_\pm$, and the subscripts 1 and 2 simply represent two different concentrations of the same electrolyte.

[5] E. Hückel, *Physik. Z.*, **26**, 93 (1925); G. Scatchard, *J. Am. Chem. Soc.*, **47**, 2098 (1925); H. S. Harned, *Ibid.*, **48**, 326 (1926); **51**, 416 (1929); H. S. Harned and G. Åkerlöf, *Physik. Z.*, **27**, 411 (1926).

simultaneous equations for activity coefficient ratios. Thus, according to equation (10-4-8),

$$\log \frac{\gamma_2}{\gamma_1} = - \frac{\mathcal{S}_{(f)} \sqrt{\Gamma_2}}{1 + A \sqrt{\Gamma_2}} + \frac{\mathcal{S}_{(f)} \sqrt{\Gamma_1}}{1 + A \sqrt{\Gamma_1}} + B(c_2 - c_1)$$

$$- \log \left(\frac{1 + 0.01802 \nu m_2}{1 + 0.01802 \nu m_1} \right) \tag{10-4-9}$$

If γ_2/γ_1 is written for two different values of c_2, c_1 and γ_1 remaining constant, two simultaneous equations are obtained from which A and B may be evaluated. Upon substituting these values of A and B in equation (10-4-8), γ may be computed at any desired concentration.

If good data are available at concentrations from 0.1 to $1M$, γ can be extrapolated by this method with an accuracy of the order of ± 0.002 in the activity coefficient, which corresponds to an error of ± 0.1 mv. The failure of equation (10-4-8) to represent the data accurately at concentrations much greater than $1M$ will sometimes result in an extrapolation error considerably in excess of this estimate.

(5) THE COMPUTATION OF THE RELATIVE PARTIAL MOLAL HEAT CONTENT, AND RELATIVE PARTIAL MOLAL HEAT CAPACITY OF ELECTROLYTES FROM ELECTROMOTIVE FORCE DATA

According to equations (3-8-1) and (10-3-1)

$$\frac{\nu \partial \ln \gamma_\pm}{\partial T} = - \frac{\bar{L}_2}{RT^2} \tag{3-8-1}$$

and

$$\frac{(E - E^0)NF}{\nu RT} = - \ln \gamma_\pm - \ln m. \tag{10-3-1}$$

Therefore, at constant composition,

$$\frac{\partial \ln \gamma_\pm}{\partial T} = - \frac{NF}{\nu R} \frac{\partial}{\partial T} \frac{(E - E^0)}{T} = - \frac{\bar{L}_2}{\nu RT^2} \tag{10-5-1}$$

and

$$\bar{L}_2 = NFT^2 \frac{\partial}{\partial T} \left(\frac{E - E^0}{T} \right) \tag{10-5-2}$$

which is the Gibbs-Helmholtz equation analogous to (1-3-4). Upon differentiation, this equation reduces to the more familiar form

$$\bar{L}_2 = - NF(E - E^0) + NFT \frac{\partial(E - E^0)}{\partial T} \tag{10-5-3}$$

These equations show that the determination of $\bar{L}_2$ from electromotive-force measurements depends on the accuracy with which the temperature coefficient of electromotive force can be determined.

The relative partial molal heat capacity may be computed from these relations by equation (1-7-7), or

$$\bar{J}_2 \equiv (\bar{C}_p - \bar{C}_p^0) = \frac{\partial \bar{L}_2}{\partial T} \tag{10-5-4}$$

Upon substituting the value of $\bar{L}_2$ given by equation (10-5-3), and performing the differentiation, we obtain

$$\bar{J}_2 = \mathbf{N}F T \frac{\partial^2 (\mathbf{E} - \mathbf{E}^0)}{\partial T^2} \tag{10-5-5}$$

The question now arises as to the kind of function which should be employed for the computation of the variation of $(\mathbf{E} - \mathbf{E}^0)$ with the temperature. Although it is known that $\bar{J}_2$ does not vary rapidly with temperature, we shall assume as a first approximation that it varies linearly, or that

$$\bar{J}_2 = \bar{J}_{2(0)} + c'''(T - T_0) \tag{10-5-6}$$

where $\bar{J}_{2(0)}$ refers to some reference temperature, T_0, and c''' is a constant. By integrating (10-5-4) between the limits of T and T_0, we obtain

$$\bar{L}_2 = \bar{L}_{2(0)} + \int_{T_0}^{T} \bar{J}_2 \, dT \tag{10-5-7}$$

which when combined with equation (10-5-6) yields

$$\bar{L}_2 = a'' + b''T + c''T^2 \tag{10-5-8}$$

where

$$\left. \begin{aligned} a'' &= \bar{L}_{2(0)} - \bar{J}_{2(0)} T_0 + c''' T_0^2/2 \\ b'' &= \bar{J}_{2(0)} - c''' T_0 \\ c'' &= c'''/2 \end{aligned} \right\} \tag{10-5-9}$$

Upon substitution of the value of $\bar{L}_2$ given by equation (10-5-8) in equation (10-5-2), and subsequent integration, we obtain

$$(\mathbf{E} - \mathbf{E}^0) = \frac{1}{\mathbf{N}F} (-a'' + IT + b''T \ln T + c''T^2) \tag{10-5-10}$$

$$= (a' - a_0') + (b' - b_0')T + (c' - c_0')T^2 + (d' - d_0')T \ln T \tag{10-5-11}$$

where I is an integration constant.

In actual practice it has been found that, over limited temperature ranges

(0° to 50°), both **E** and E^0 for many cells may be expressed to within ±0.05 mv. by the quadratic equations

$$\mathbf{E} = a + bT + cT^2 \qquad (10\text{-}5\text{-}12)$$

$$\mathbf{E}^0 = a_0 + b_0T + c_0T^2 \qquad (10\text{-}5\text{-}13)$$

without the logarithmic term.

If $(\mathbf{E} - \mathbf{E}^0)$ is expressed by equation (10-5-11), then according to (10-5-2)

$$\bar{L}_2 = -\mathbf{N}\mathbf{F}[(a' - a_0') - (d' - d_0')T - (c' - c_0')T^2] \quad (10\text{-}5\text{-}14)$$

and if the quadratic equations (10-5-12) and (10-5-13) are employed,

$$\bar{L}_2 = -\mathbf{N}\mathbf{F}[(a - a_0) - (c - c_0)T^2] \qquad (10\text{-}5\text{-}15)$$

The corresponding equations for $\bar{J}_2$ are

$$\bar{J}_2 = \mathbf{N}\mathbf{F}[(d' - d_0') + 2(c' - c_0')T] \qquad (10\text{-}5\text{-}16)$$

and

$$\bar{J}_2 = 2\mathbf{N}\mathbf{F}(c - c_0)T \qquad (10\text{-}5\text{-}17)$$

If we are dealing with a concentration cell without liquid junction [Equation (10-4-5)], then $\bar{L}_2$ and $\bar{J}_2$ can be computed only relative to a reference concentration. If the electromotive force of this cell is expressed by a quadratic formula as follows

$$\mathbf{E}_m - \mathbf{E}_R = a + bT + cT^2$$

then

$$\bar{H}_{2(m)} - \bar{H}_{2(R)} = \bar{L}_{2(m)} - \bar{L}_{2(R)} = -\mathbf{N}\mathbf{F}(a - cT^2) \quad (10\text{-}5\text{-}18)$$

where $\bar{L}_{2(m)}$ is the relative partial molal heat content at a concentration, m, and $\bar{L}_{2(R)}$ is its value at the reference concentration. The partial molal heat capacity relative to the reference concentration is given by

$$\bar{C}_{p_2(m)} - \bar{C}_{p_2(R)} = \bar{J}_{2(m)} - \bar{J}_{2(R)} = 2\mathbf{N}\mathbf{F}cT \qquad (10\text{-}5\text{-}19)$$

Since the constants a, b, c, etc., are usually obtained by the method of least squares, the labor of calculation is greatly reduced by using the simpler quadratic equations. If the accuracy of the electromotive forces is not greater than ±0.05 mv., and the temperature range not greater than 40°, the use of a term in $T \ln T$, or higher powers of T is scarcely justified.

(6) THE CONCENTRATION CELL WITH LIQUID JUNCTION

The general equation for the electromotive force of a concentration cell with transference across a liquid junction may be obtained in the following manner as shown by Taylor.[6] We represent such a cell by

Electrode (1) $| m_1, m_2, \cdots m_i, \cdots m_s | m_1', m_2', \cdots m_i', \cdots m_s' |$ Electrode (1)

$$(10\text{-}6\text{-}1)$$

[6] P. B. Taylor, *J. Phys. Chem.*, **31**, 1478 (1927).

where $m_1, \cdots m_s$, and $m_1', \cdots m_s'$ are the molalities of the ions on the two sides of the boundary of the two solutions, and where electrode (1) is reversible to ion (1). The odd subscripts refer to cations and the even to anions. A reversible discharge of the cell involving the passage of one Faraday would correspond to the transfer of one equivalent of ion (1) from one solution to the other. In addition to this, every ion in the solution is transferred across the boundary in amounts determined by their concentrations and transference numbers. Therefore, if the concentrations on the two sides of the boundary differ by infinitesimals, we obtain

$$\mathbf{F}\, d\mathbf{E}_{1(T)} = d\bar{F}_1 - T_1\, d\bar{F}_1 + T_2\, d\bar{F}_2 - T_3\, d\bar{F}_3 + \cdots \qquad (10\text{-}6\text{-}2)$$

$$= d\bar{F}_1 - \sum_1^s T_i\, d\bar{F}_i \qquad (10\text{-}6\text{-}3)$$

$$= d\bar{F}_1 - \mathbf{F}\, d\mathbf{E}_J \qquad (10\text{-}6\text{-}4)$$

$\mathbf{E}_{1(T)}$ is the electromotive force of the cell and can be obtained by direct measurement. $\mathbf{E}_J$ is commonly called the liquid-junction potential. In regard to the "hypothetical" partial free energies of the ions on the right of equation (10-6-3), it is important to recall the discussion in Chapter (1) in which it was stressed that thermodynamics permits the evaluation of only partial free energies, activities, etc., of the molecular components in the sense in which Gibbs defined them, and does not allow the actual determination of these quantities for the individual ionic species.

The above expression for $d\mathbf{E}_{1(T)}$ is very convenient for obtaining the relation between the electromotive forces of concentration cells with and without liquid junctions. For suppose we place an electrode reversible to ion (2) between the two solutions of the above cell (10-6-1), and thus construct the cell without liquid junction, namely

Electrode (1) | $m_1, \cdots m_s$ | Electrode (2) | $m_1', \cdots m_s'$ |

Electrode (1)   (10-6-5)

it follows that the electromotive force corresponds to a transfer of ions (1) and (2) from one solution to the other. Therefore, if the concentrations of the two solutions differ by infinitesimals, the electromotive force, $d\mathbf{E}_{12}$, is given by

$$\mathbf{F}\, d\mathbf{E}_{12} = d\bar{F}_1 + d\bar{F}_2, \quad \text{or} \quad d\bar{F}_2 = -d\bar{F}_1 + \mathbf{F}\, d\mathbf{E}_{12} \qquad (10\text{-}6\text{-}6)$$

Similarly, if electrode (2) is replaced by an electrode (3) reversible to ion 3, the electromotive force of the resulting cell, $d\mathbf{E}_{13}$, will be

$$\mathbf{F}\, d\mathbf{E}_{13} = d\bar{F}_1 - d\bar{F}_3, \quad \text{or} \quad d\bar{F}_3 = d\bar{F}_1 - \mathbf{F}\, d\mathbf{E}_{13} \qquad (10\text{-}6\text{-}7)$$

Similar equations may be obtained for the other ions.

By substituting these values of $d\bar{F}_2$, $d\bar{F}_3$, etc., in equation (10-6-2), we obtain

$$\mathbf{F}d\mathbf{E}_{1(T)} = d\bar{F}_1 - T_1 d\bar{F}_1 - T_2 d\bar{F}_1$$
$$+ T_2 \mathbf{F}d\mathbf{E}_{12} - T_3 d\bar{F}_1 + T_3 \mathbf{F}d\mathbf{E}_{13} \pm \cdots \quad (10\text{-}6\text{-}8)$$

or

$$\mathbf{F}d\mathbf{E}_{1(T)} = d\bar{F}_1 - (T_1 + T_2 + \cdots + T_s)d\bar{F}_1$$
$$+ T_2 \mathbf{F}d\mathbf{E}_{12} + T_3 \mathbf{F}d\mathbf{E}_{13} + \cdots \quad (10\text{-}6\text{-}9)$$

and, therefore,

$$dE_{1(T)} = T_2 dE_{12} + T_3 dE_{13} + \cdots \quad (10\text{-}6\text{-}10)$$

since the sum of the transference numbers of all-the ions is unity. A similar formula may be obtained when the ion transferred is an anion if the cation and anion subscripts are permuted. Thus, if the electrode in cell (10-6-1) is reversible to ion (2), then

$$dE_{2(T)} = T_1 dE_{21} + T_3 dE_{23} + \cdots \quad (10\text{-}6\text{-}11)$$

The result expressed by equations (10-6-10) and (10-6-11) is important, because we find that all ionic partial free energies, $d\bar{F}_i$, have been eliminated, and the electromotive forces of the cells have been expressed in terms of the quantities, E_{21}, E_{23}, etc., corresponding to sums of the partial free energies of the positive and negative ions. Such sums are simply the molecular free energies of the electrolytes.

Since we have shown that equation (10-6-2) will not yield ionic partial free energies, we are forced to the conclusion that measurements of the electromotive forces of cells with transference can yield no information whatsoever regarding ionic activities and partial free energies.

The exact thermodynamic result expressed by equations (10-6-10) and (10-6-11) is an important one, since it enables us to determine the transference number from measurements of cells with and without a liquid junction.[7] Suppose we consider cells of these kinds which contain a single electrolyte. If the electrode is reversible to the anion, equation (10-6-11) yields

$$dE_{2(T)} = T_1 dE_{21} \quad (10\text{-}6\text{-}12)$$

where T_1 is the cation transference number. It is apparent from this equation that if $E_{2(T)}$ is known as a function of E_{21}, T_1 may be evaluated. If such a function is not known, $E_{2(T)}$ may be plotted against E_{21} and the slope, T_1, determined. This method of determining the transference number was developed with a fair degree of accuracy by MacInnes and

[7] See H. v. Helmholtz, *Wied. Ann.*, **3**, 201 (1878); *Ber.*, **7**, 27 (1882); *Ges. Abhl.*, **1**, 840; **2**, 979.

Parker[8] and MacInnes and Beattie.[9, 10]   Since the limiting equation of Onsager for the transference was available, Jones and Dole[11] and others[12] have also applied this method, but the results so far obtained are of a much lower order of accuracy than those derived by the moving-boundary method [Chapter (6)].

Brown and MacInnes[13] have taken advantage of the high precision of moving boundary data by developing a method for determining the activity coefficient of a halide from measurements of cells with transference.   They employed the cell

$$\text{Ag-AgCl} \mid \text{NaCl}(c_1) \mid \text{NaCl}(c_2) \mid \text{AgCl-Ag} \qquad (10\text{-}6\text{-}13)$$

Upon integration of equation (10-6-12), the electromotive force of this cell is

$$\mathbf{E}_{2(T)} = T_{\text{Na}} \int_{\text{I}}^{\text{II}} d\mathbf{E}_{21} = -\frac{2RT}{\text{F}} \int_{\text{I}}^{\text{II}} T_{\text{Na}} d \ln y_{\pm} c \qquad (10\text{-}6\text{-}14)$$

If T_{Na} is known at various concentrations, $y_{\pm}$ can be very accurately determined by this relation.   The details of the calculation will be discussed in chapter (12), section (1).

The preceding discussion of cells with liquid-junction potentials, although adequate for our purposes, is too brief to exhaust this complicated and profound subject.   Recently contributions have been made by Hermans,[14] and especially by Koenig,[15] who has extended the theory to include the effects of gravitational, electrical and magnetic fields.

The Hypothetical Liquid Junction Potential

The deductions in the preceding paragraphs have shown that the measurements of cells with liquid junctions lead to the determination of partial molal free energies, or linear combinations of "hypothetical" ionic free energies.   This thermodynamic result is very important in its relation to the so-called liquid-junction potential.   Equations (10-6-3) and (10-6-12) lead to

$$\text{F}T_2 d\mathbf{E}_{12} = \text{F}d\mathbf{E}_{1(T)}$$

$$= d\bar{F}_1 - \sum_{1}^{s} T_i d\bar{F}_i = d\bar{F}_1 - RT \sum_{1}^{s} T_i d \ln a_i \qquad (10\text{-}6\text{-}15)$$

[8] D. A. MacInnes and K. Parker, *J. Am. Chem. Soc.*, **37**, 1445 (1915).

[9] D. A. MacInnes and J. A. Beattie, *Ibid.*, **42**, 1117 (1920).

[10] W. W. Lucasse, *Ibid.*, **47**, 743 (1925).

[11] G. Jones and M. Dole, *Ibid.*, **51**, 1073 (1929).

[12] W. J. Hamer, *Ibid.*, **57**, 662 (1935); H. S. Harned and E. C. Dreby, *Ibid.*, **61**, 3113 (1939).

[13] A. S. Brown and D. A. MacInnes, *J. Am. Chem. Soc.*, **57**, 1356 (1935).

[14] J. J. Hermans, *Rec. trav. chim.*, **56**, 635, 658 (1937); *Ibid.*, **58**, 99, 2419 (1939).

[15] F. O. Koenig, *J. Phys. Chem.*, **44**, 101 (1940); F. O. Koenig and S. W. Grinnell, *Ibid.*, **44**, 463 (1940); **46**, 980 (1942).

The only quantity which can be measured by the cell with liquid junction is $\mathbf{F}d\mathbf{E}_{1(T)}$, where $d\mathbf{E}_{1(T)}$ is the difference in potential between two wires of the same metal attached to the electrodes. $d\bar{F}_1$ is purely hypothetical, and impossible to evaluate by any thermodynamic method. Therefore, $\sum_1^s T_i d\bar{F}_i$ is equally arbitrary, and the liquid-junction potential given by the second term on the right of these equations is also entirely arbitrary. If a convention be adopted to fix the ionic free energy of one of the ions in the solution, then the ionic free energies of the other ions are also fixed through knowledge of the molecular free energies. So we are at liberty to adopt such a convention, whether or not it serves any useful end. For example, it has been proposed[16] to let $\bar{F}_K = \bar{F}_{Cl}$, and refer other ionic free energies to this conventional standard. But according to the relations given by (10-6-15), any other convention such as $\bar{F}_K = n\bar{F}_{Cl}$, where n is any finite positive number, would serve equally well. This was proved to be the case by Harned[17] by a numerical method, and by Taylor[18] by means of the analytical method just developed. Since this is the case, there is no more reason to choose the potassium and chloride ions as reference than the ions of any other electrolyte.

Equations for liquid-junction potentials, such as Planck's and Henderson's, do not solve the difficulties. This can be shown in a simple manner by writing the equation for the hypothetical liquid-junction potential, $\mathbf{E}_J$, in the integrated form

$$\mathbf{E}_J = -\frac{RT}{\mathbf{F}} \sum_1^s \int_{\mathrm{I}}^{\mathrm{II}} T_i \, d\ln \gamma_i - \frac{RT}{\mathbf{F}} \sum_1^s \int_{\mathrm{I}}^{\mathrm{II}} T_i \, d\ln m_i \qquad (10\text{-}6\text{-}16)$$

where the integration is between the limits corresponding to the two solutions (I and II) forming the liquid junction. Planck's[19] and Henderson's[20] formulas for $\mathbf{E}_J$ were obtained by evaluating the last term on the right of this equation. Assuming such an evaluation to be correct, only part of the liquid-junction potential would be evaluated, as the part involving the hypothetical ionic activity coefficients would still remain. This is true at all finite concentrations of ions, and the difficulty only disappears when the solutions on the two sides of the junctions have the same composition.

The use of salt bridges consisting of solutions of electrolytes at high concentrations (sat. KCl) may reduce the numerical value of the second term on the right of equation (10-6-16), but again leaves us with the purely arbitrary first term.

[16] D. A. MacInnes, *J. Am. Chem. Soc.*, **41**, 1086 (1919); H. S. Harned, *Ibid.*, **42**, 1808 (1920); *J. Phys. Chem.*, **30**, 433 (1926).

[17] H. S. Harned, *J. Phys. Chem.*, **30**, 433 (1926).

[18] P. B. Taylor, *J. Phys. Chem.*, **31**, 1478 (1927).

[19] M. Planck, *Wied. Ann.*, **39**, 161 (1890); **40**, 561 (1890).

[20] P. Henderson, *Z. physik. Chem.*, **59**, 118 (1907); **63**, 325 (1908); Compare J. J. Hermans, *Rec. trav. chim.*, **57**, 1373 (1938).

The Concept of Electrical Potential at Phase Boundaries

The conclusion of Taylor that measurements of cells with or without liquid junctions can yield no information whatsoever concerning ionic free energies has been extended by Guggenheim.[21] He has analyzed the concept of electric potential difference between two points in different media, and has arrived at the negative result that such a quantity is entirely arbitrary, and has not yet been defined in terms of physical realities (measurable quantities). Guggenheim shows the difference between this electrostatic potential and the one which is defined in electrostatics. The latter science is based "on a mathematical theory of an imaginary fluid electricity, whose equilibrium and motion is determined entirely by the electric field. 'Electricity' of this kind does not exist; only electrons and and ions have physical existence, and these differ fundamentally from the hypothetical fluid electricity in that the particles are at all times in movement relative to one another; their equilibrium is thermodynamic, not static." The criteria of thermodynamic equilibria in these systems at constant temperature and pressure may be developed from equation (1-5-2),

$$dF = \sum_{1}^{p} \sum_{1}^{s} \mu_i \, dn_i + (\psi' - \psi'') \, de \qquad (1\text{-}5\text{-}2)$$

We recall that $(\psi' - \psi'')$, applied to the reversible cell, is the difference in electrical potential of two wires attached to the electrodes of the cell; $(\psi' - \psi'') \, de$ represents the electrical work; and the μ_i are the chemical potentials of the components in a given phase. We shall now express that part of the work term corresponding to a phase as $\sum_{1}^{\sigma} \psi e_j \, dn_j$, where ψ is the potential at a particle, ion or electron, of charge e_j, and the summation is for all such particles in the phase. The potential ψ is purely conventional. $(\psi' - \psi'') \, de$ is equal to the summation, $\sum_{1}^{p} \sum_{1}^{\sigma} \psi e_j \, dn_j$. Equation (1-5-2) for a single phase becomes

$$dF_p = \sum_{1}^{s} \mu_i \, dn_i + \sum_{1}^{\sigma} \psi e_j \, dn_j \qquad (10\text{-}6\text{-}17)$$

where the first summation is over all the molecular and electrical species (s), and the second summation is over all the electrical species (σ). If we now consider a process which involves only the electrified particles, we may divide the chemical potential of the molecular component, μ_i, into arbitrary chemical potentials of the electrified species, μ_j, and write,

$$dF_e = \sum_{1}^{\sigma} \mu_j \, dn_j + \sum_{1}^{\sigma} \psi e_j \, dn_j$$

[21] E. A. Guggenheim, *J. Phys. Chem.*, **33**, 842 (1929); **34**, 1540 (1930).

or

$$dF_e = \sum_1^\sigma (\mu_j + \psi e_j)\, dn_j \qquad (10\text{-}6\text{-}18)$$

Now let, $\bar{\mu}_j \equiv \mu_j + \psi e_j$; then $\qquad\qquad (10\text{-}6\text{-}19)$

$$dF_e = \sum_1^\sigma \bar{\mu}_j\, dn_j \qquad (10\text{-}6\text{-}20)$$

analogous to

$$dF = \sum_1^c \mu_i\, dn_i \qquad (1\text{-}4\text{-}2)$$

whence it is apparent that $\bar{\mu}_j$ plays a role in the electrochemical system similar to that of μ_i in the molecular system. Applied to equilibria in a polyphase system at constant pressure, temperature and charge, this latter relation leads to the equality of the chemical potential of a component throughout all the phases, as shown by equation (1-2-8). Analogously, $\bar{\mu}_j$, the electrochemical potential (Guggenheim-Brönsted) of a given electrified species, determines the equilibria in the electrochemical systems, provided that it is distributed throughout all phases. Thus

$$\begin{array}{cccc} \bar{\mu}_1' = & \bar{\mu}_1'' = & \cdots & \bar{\mu}_1^p \\ \vert & \vert & & \vert \\ \bar{\mu}_\sigma' = & \bar{\mu}_\sigma'' = & \cdots & \bar{\mu}_\sigma^p \end{array} \qquad (10\text{-}6\text{-}21)$$

if $\bar{\mu}_1'$, $\bar{\mu}_1'' \cdots \bar{\mu}_1^p$, represent the electrochemical potentials of the first species, and $\bar{\mu}_2'$, $\bar{\mu}_2'' \cdots \bar{\mu}_2^p$, those of the second species, etc. throughout the p-phases.[22] For a single ionic species, the partial molal free energy, or μ_j, has been shown in the preceding discussion to be entirely arbitrary; consequently, ψe_j has no thermodynamic significance.

These relations will lead directly to the previous conclusion that, although μ_j is arbitrary, certain linear combinations of μ_j are not. For suppose we consider an electrolyte dissociating into two ions in the same phase. Then, as shown by Guggenheim,

$$\bar{\mu}_j = \mu_j + e_j \psi \qquad (10\text{-}6\text{-}22)$$

$$\bar{\mu}_k = \mu_k + e_k \psi$$

from which it follows by elimination of ψ that

$$\frac{\bar{\mu}_j}{e_j} - \frac{\bar{\mu}_k}{e_k} = \frac{\mu_j}{e_j} - \frac{\mu_k}{e_k} \qquad (10\text{-}6\text{-}23)$$

so that $\left(\dfrac{\mu_j}{e_j} - \dfrac{\mu_k}{e_k}\right)$ is definitely defined in terms of measurable quantities. Guggenheim shows that it is a simple matter to prove that the phenomena

[22] The above treatment of the electrochemical potential is essentially the same as that given by J. N. Brönsted, who uses the symbol λ for this quantity. [*Z. physik. Chem.*, **143**, 301 (1929)].

of diffusion, partition between two media, membrane equilibria, cells with and without liquid junctions, and reaction velocities can all be completely described in terms of the electrochemical potentials, and that the chemical potentials, μ_i, and the ψe_i terms never occur separately. This proves that no known measurements yield any knowledge regarding these latter quantities. Guggenheim goes as far as to say that "the electrical potential difference between two points in different media can never be measured."

These considerations are of great interest in relation to the century-old problem of the seat of the electrical potential in a galvanic cell, as for example the Daniell cell,

$$\text{Cu} \mid \text{Zn} \mid \text{ZnSO}_4 \ (m) \mid \text{CuSO}_4 \ (m) \mid \text{Cu}$$

The total measured electrical potential may be regarded as the sum of the differences of potentials at the boundaries, $\text{Cu} \mid \text{Zn}$, $\text{Zn} \mid \text{ZnSO}_4 \ (m)$, $\text{ZnSO}_4 \ (m) \mid \text{CuSO}_4 \ (m)$, and $\text{CuSO}_4 \ (m) \mid \text{Cu}$. Since we have shown that the potentials at points within the phases are neither defined nor capable of measurement by known methods, it is impossible at present to estimate the contributions at any individual phase boundary.

The point of view resulting from this analysis was anticipated by Gibbs[23] when he wrote, "Again, the consideration of the electrical potential in the electrolyte, and especially the consideration of the difference of potential in electrolyte and electrode, involves the consideration of quantities of which we have no apparent means of physical measurement, while the difference of potential in pieces of metal of the same kind attached to the electrodes is exactly one of the things which we can and do measure."

(7) The Use of Cells with Liquid Junctions. Determination of pH. Elimination of Liquid-Junction Potentials

There are two types of liquid junctions commonly encountered in electrochemical studies: homoionic junctions formed by juxtaposition of solutions differing only in ionic concentrations; and heterionic junctions involving differences in ionic species, or in both ionic species and concentrations. It was shown in section (6) that homoionic junction potentials are subject to exact thermodynamic definition [Equation (10-6-14)] and that cells containing them may be used in thermodynamic calculations [Chapter (11), Section (9), and Chapter (12), Section (1)]. The present section deals with the use of cells with heterionic liquid junctions. Their measurement has widespread applications in pH control procedures, and may, under very special conditions, yield results of thermodynamic significance. These special conditions are experimental, and are concerned with the elimination of liquid-junction potentials, but not with their evaluation.

[23] "The Collected Works of J. Willard Gibbs," Vol. I, p. 429, Longmans Green Co., New York, 1928.

We shall discuss first the modern measurement[24] of pH, and the uncertainty that liquid junctions produce in the definition of this quantity. It will then be shown that the junction potentials of certain cells, or combinations of cells, may be reduced to negligible values by causing the two solutions comprising the junction to approach identity. In this case the cells may be said to come under the usual definition* of cells without liquid junctions. Finally, we shall examine the limiting case in which complete identity of these two solutions may be attained only by extrapolations based upon a series of measurements. The use of such extrapolated results is thermodynamically rigorous, but the possibility of a practical extrapolation method must be established experimentally.

The pH of a solution was originally defined[25] as the negative of the common logarithm of the hydrogen-ion concentration, but it later became identified with this function of the hydrogen-ion activity.[26] We employ the equation

$$pH = -\log a_{H^+} \qquad (10\text{-}7\text{-}1)$$

with the understanding that this is a purely formal relationship, because a_{H^+} is itself undefined [Section (6)]. The ultimate definition of pH is made in terms of the method used in determining it. For this purpose the cell

$$H_2 \mid \text{Test Solution} \mid KCl_{(sat.)} \mid \text{Reference Electrode} \qquad I$$

is typical. The reference electrode is usually a saturated, or $N/10$ calomel electrode.[27] For special purposes, the hydrogen gas electrode is replaced by secondary standards such as the quinhydrone, antimony-antimony trioxide, and glass electrodes. In any case, the pH may be defined by

$$pH = \frac{E - E^0_{pH}}{2.3RT/F} = \frac{E - E^0_{pH}}{k} \qquad (10\text{-}7\text{-}2)$$

where E is the observed electromotive force of Cell I. If E^0_{pH} is a constant which depends only upon the temperature, the pressure, and the nature of

---

[24] For a more extensive discussion of electrometric methods, and for details concerning techniques, see R. G. Bates, "Electrometric pH Determinations", John Wiley & Sons, New York (1954). For comprehensive digests of earlier methods, see H. T. S. Britton, "Hydrogen Ions", Van Nostrand Co., New York (1929); I. M. Kolthoff and H. A. Laitinen, "pH and Electrotitrations", John Wiley & Sons, New York (1941).

* See the concluding paragraph of Section (2), p. 429.

[25] S. P. L. Sørensen, *Compt. Rend. Lab. Carlsberg*, **8**, 1 (1909).

[26] S. P. L. Sørensen and K. Linderstrøm-Lang [*Compt. Rend. Lab. Carlsberg*, **15**, 40 (1924)] proposed the term paH for use when hydrogen-ion activity is involved but we shall designate this quantity pH in keeping with current usage.

[27] This selection is arbitrary, and is governed largely by convenience. D. I. Hitchcock [*J. Am. Chem. Soc.*, **58**, 855 (1936)], and O. Redlich and H. Klinger [*Ibid.*, **61**, 2983 (1939)] discussed the possible advantage of employing reference electrodes which are reversible with respect to a univalent cation.

the electrodes, this equation completely defines a useful pH number, about which no confusion need arise unless an attempt is made to interpret it in terms of equation (10-7-1). It is clear that the numerical value of this pH number depends upon the nature of the liquid junction, and the manner in which it is formed. This number cannot be identified with $-\log a_{H^+}$ by equation (10-7-1) without also imputing a dependence of a_{H^+} upon the properties of the junction. In the effort to eliminate this difficulty in interpreting pH, or a_{H^+}, without eliminating the liquid junction itself,[28] attempts have been made to correct either E or E_{pH}^0 for the liquid-junction potentials. Neither of these is thermodynamically sound, and the "correction" of each measured E by Henderson's[29] equation, for example, is always laborious and usually impractical in routine control work.

Recently, new values of E_{pH}^0 have been proposed, for the various types of calomel electrodes, which presumably include the greater part of the junction potential. They should prove very convenient and useful in determining ionization and other equilibrium constants where the greatest accuracy is not required. These values of E_{pH}^0 were determined by replacing the test solution in Cell I by buffer solutions of acids, for which the ionization constants have been accurately evaluated conductometrically, or from cells without liquid junctions. This may be illustrated by considering a buffer solution of the weak acid, HA, and its sodium salt. If pK_A is the negative logarithm of its thermodynamic ionization constant,* then, by equations (10-7-1) and (7-2-10),

$$\text{pH} = pK_A + \log \frac{c_{A^-}}{c_{HA}} + \log \frac{y_{A^-}}{y_{HA}} \tag{10-7-3}$$

MacInnes, Belcher and Shedlovsky[30] write $-S\sqrt{\mu}$ for $\log y_{A^-}/y_{HA}$ and rearrange this equation to read

$$\frac{E - E_{pH}^0}{k} - \log \frac{c_{A^-}}{c_{HA}} = pK_A - S\sqrt{\mu} \tag{10-7-4}$$

They select a value of E_{pH}^0 by trial, so that a plot of the left-hand member against $\sqrt{\mu}$ is linear in dilute solutions ($\mu \sim 0.001$ to 0.01) and yields the intercept, pK_A. Two such plots are illustrated in Fig. (10-7-1). The val-

[28] The definition of pH in terms of cells without liquid junctions has been urged by D. I. Hitchcock [*J. Am. Chem. Soc.*, **58**, 855 (1936)], W. J. Hamer [*Trans. Electrochem. Soc.*, **72**, 45 (1937)], W. J. Hamer and S. F. Acree [*Bur. Standards J. Research*, **23**, 647 (1939)], E. A. Guggenheim [*J. Phys. Chem.*, **34**, 1758 (1930)], and others.

[29] P. Henderson, *Z. physik. Chem.*, **59**, 118 (1907); **63**, 325 (1908). *Cf.* N. Bjerrum and A. Unmack, *K. Danske Videnskab. Selskab Math-fys. Medd.*, **9**, 1 (1929), and E. A. Guggenheim and T. D. Schindler, *J. Phys. Chem.*, **38**, 533 (1934).

* It appears unnecessary to consider the difference between the values of K_A on a molality or a molarity basis because its effect on E_{pH}^0 is ordinarily less than 0.1 mv.

[30] D. A. MacInnes, D. Belcher and T. Shedlovsky, *J. Am. Chem. Soc.*, **60**, 1094 (1938).

ues of S determined from the slopes of the plots are 10 to 25 per cent higher than the Debye-Hückel slope, $S_{(f)}$, for an univalent ion.

Hitchcock and Taylor[31] replace $\log (y_{A^-}/y_{HA})$ in equation (10-7-3) by $-S_{(f)}\sqrt{\mu} + B\mu$, and rearrange this equation in the form

$$\mathbf{E}_{pH}^{0'} \equiv \mathbf{E} - kpK_A - k \log \frac{c_{A^-}}{c_{HA}} + kS_{(f)}\sqrt{\mu} = \mathbf{E}_{pH}^0 + kB\mu \quad (10\text{-}7\text{-}5)$$

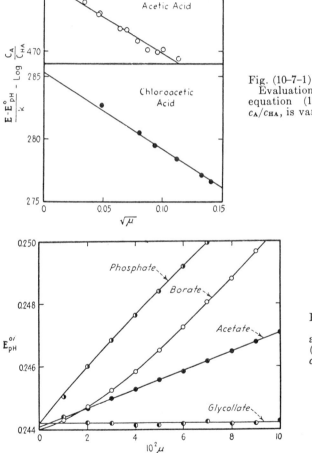

Fig. (10-7-1)
Evaluation of $\mathbf{E}_{pH}^{\circ}$ at 25° by equation (10-7-4). The ratio, c_A/c_{HA}, is variable

Fig. (10-7-2)
Evaluation of $\mathbf{E}_{pH}^{\circ}$ at 25° by equation (10-7-5). The ratio c_A/c_{HA} is unity

$\mathbf{E}_{pH}^0$ is determined as the intercept of the plot of the left-hand member against μ. For this purpose, values of μ between 0.01 and 0.1 are used, and the plots exhibit some curvature, as can be seen in Fig. (10-7-2).

Table (10-7-1) contains values of $\mathbf{E}_{pH}^0$ at 25° obtained by both of these

[31] D. I. Hitchcock and A. C. Taylor, *J. Am. Chem. Soc.*, **59**, 1812 (1937).

methods. The hydrogen electrode, in various buffer solutions, is used with the saturated calomel electrode* as reference.

The variation observed in the values of E_{pH}^0 given in Table (10-7-1) is presumably a measure of the difference between the liquid-junction potentials produced by the various test solutions in contact with saturated potassium chloride. The first seven values determined in buffered solutions are all within 0.1 mv of their average (0.2441). Hydrochloric acid, in the presence of nine parts of sodium chloride, also leads to this value. Pure hydrochloric acid solutions give a much higher result. There is a significant difference between the values of E_{pH}^0 obtained in essentially the same acetic acid buffers by the two different methods. Some of this discordance may be due to minor differences in the saturated calomel electrodes used in the two sets of measurements.

TABLE (10-7-1). E^0_{pH} AT 25° FOR THE CELL:
H_2 | ACID(m_1), SALT(m_2) | KCl(sat), HgCl, Hg

Acid	Salt	m_2/m_1*	E^0_{pH}
CH_3CO_2H	CH_3CO_2K	1	0.2442[a]
CH_3CO_2H	CH_3CO_2Na	4	.2441[a]
CH_3CO_2H	CH_3CO_2Na	1	.2441[a]
CH_3CO_2H	CH_3CO_2Na	1/4	.2440[a]
KH_2PO_4	Na_2HPO_4	1	.2442[a]
HBO_2	$NaBO_2$	1	.2440[a]
HCl	CH_2OHCO_2Li	2	.2442[a]
HCl	. . . .	. .	.2450[a]
HCl	KCl	9	.2445[a]
HCl	NaCl	9	.2441[a]
CH_3CO_2H	CH_3CO_2Na	1	.2446[b]
$ClCH_2CO_2H$	$ClCH_2CO_2Na$	1	.2445[b]

* The values of m_2/m_1 are only approximate.
[a] D. I. Hitchcock and A. C. Taylor, *J. Am. Chem. Soc.*, **59**, 1812 (1937).
[b] D. A. MacInnes, D. Belcher and T. Shedlovsky, *Ibid.*, **60**, 1094 (1938).

To avoid preparing reference electrodes according to exact specifications, it is recommended that E_{pH}^0 of each electrode system used be determined at the time. The standard solutions given in Table (10-7-2) are to be used for this purpose. The pH of these solutions has been calculated from the values of E_{pH}^0 given in Table (10-7-1). In determining E_{pH}^0 for any particular electrode system, it is desirable to employ a standard solution for which the pH is comparable with that of the test solution. The pH of standard solutions determined at the National Bureau of Standards over a wide temperature range are recorded in Table (10-7-1A).

If the standard and test solutions are of equal ionic strength, and very

* The results by MacInnes, Belcher and Shedlovsky were actually determined with the $N/10$ calomel electrode, but they have been reduced to conform with the common reference electrode by subtracting their value (0.0912) for the difference between the saturated and N/10 electrode potentials.

similar in composition,* the junction potentials against the reference electrode systems will be essentially equal, and may be assumed to cancel for most practical purposes. This experimental method of overcoming the effect of liquid junctions was used by Harned and Robinson,[32] Güntelberg and Schiödt,[33] and Larsson and Adell,[34] and may be illustrated by the following cells:

$$\text{H}_2 \left| \begin{array}{l} \text{HA}(m_1) \\ \text{NaCl}(m - m_\text{H}) \end{array} \right| \text{KCl}_\text{(sat.)}, \text{HgCl-Hg} \qquad\qquad \text{II}$$

$$\text{H}_2 \left| \begin{array}{l} \text{HCl}(m_0) \\ \text{NaCl}(m - m_0) \end{array} \right| \text{KCl}_\text{(sat.)}, \text{HgCl-Hg} \qquad\qquad \text{III}$$

TABLE (10-7-2). THE pH VALUES OF SOME STANDARD SOLUTIONS FOR USE IN DETERMINING E_pH^0 BY EQUATION (10-7-2). SEE ALSO TABLE (10-7-1A).

Solution Composition in mols/liter*		pH (25°)			pH (38°)	
		a, b	c	d	b	c
0.1	HCl	1.085	...	1.10	1.082	...
.1	KH$_3$(C$_2$O$_4$)$_2$ (tetroxalate)	1.480	...	1.52	1.495	...
.01	HCl + 0.09 NaCl	2.058	...	...	...	...
.01	HCl + 0.09 KCl	2.078	...	2.10	2.075	...
.03	KHC$_4$H$_4$O$_6$ (tartrate)	3.567	...	3.56	...	...
.1	KH$_2$C$_6$H$_5$O$_7$ (citrate)	3.719	...	3.72	...	...
.05	KHC$_8$H$_4$O$_4$ (phthalate)	4.008	4.000	4.01	4.025	4.015
.1	HC$_2$H$_3$O$_2$ + 0.1 NaC$_2$H$_3$O$_2$	4.648	4.640	4.65	4.655	4.635
.01	HC$_2$H$_3$O$_2$ + 0.01 NaC$_2$H$_3$O$_2$	4.714	4.700	4.71	...	4.710
.025	KH$_2$PO$_4$ + 0.025 Na$_2$HPO$_4$	6.857	...	6.86	6.835	...
.05	Na$_2$B$_4$O$_7$	9.180	...	9.18	9.070	...

* Compositions of solutions used by [a] and [b] were determined at 21 to 23°C.
[a] D. I. Hitchcock and A. C. Taylor, *J. Am. Chem. Soc.*, **59**, 1812 (1937).
[b] D. I. Hitchcock and A. C. Taylor, *Ibid.*, **60**, 2710 (1938).
[c] D. A. MacInnes, D. Belcher and T. Shedlovsky, *Ibid.*, **60**, 1094 (1938).
[d] R. G. Bates, "Electrometric pH Determinations", John Wiley & Sons, New York (1954), p. 74.

Since the electromotive force of Cell II yields a rough value of m_H in the solution of the weak acid, HA, by the application of equations (10-7-1) and (10-7-2), it is possible to adjust the concentrations in Cell III so that the ionic strengths in both acid solutions are equal to m.† The combination of these cells leads to the cell

$$\text{H}_2 \left| \begin{array}{l} \text{HA}(m_1) \\ \text{NaCl}(m - m_\text{H}) \end{array} \right| \left. \begin{array}{l} \text{HCl}(m_0) \\ \text{NaCl}(m - m_0) \end{array} \right| \text{H}_2 \qquad\qquad \text{IV}$$

* The preponderant electrolytes are identical, and at equal concentrations in the two solutions.
[32] H. S. Harned and R. A. Robinson, *J. Am. Chem. Soc.*, **50**, 3157 (1928).
[33] E. Güntelberg and E. Schiödt, *Z. physik. Chem.*, **135**, 393 (1928).
[34] E. Larsson and B. Adell, *Z. physik. Chem.*, **A156**, 352 (1931).

† In practice, m_0 may be kept constant at about $0.01M$, as it is sufficient that $m_\text{H} \simeq m_0$. Cell III is likely to give erratic results if $m_0 < 0.001$, but this is an experimental, not a theoretical, limitation of the method.

for which the electromotive force is practically free from liquid-junction potential if m_0 is small, and m is relatively large.

Assuming that the hydrochloric acid is completely ionized, the electromotive force of Cell IV is a measure of the hydrogen-ion concentration in the solution of the weak acid. Thus

$$E_{IV} = -k \log \frac{m_H}{m_0} \qquad (10\text{-}7\text{-}6)$$

since the activity coefficients of the hydrogen ions in the two solutions cancel because of the symmetry of the cell. Values of

$$k_A = \frac{m_H m_A}{m_{HA}} = \frac{m_H^2}{m_1 - m_H} \qquad (10\text{-}7\text{-}7)$$

in salt solutions, determined by this method,[34] are in close agreement with those obtained from cells without liquid junctions.[35] The corresponding thermodynamic ionization constants,

$$K_A = k_A(\mu \to 0) \qquad (10\text{-}7\text{-}8)$$

are also in accord with values obtained by other methods [Table (15-6-2)].

The practically complete elimination of liquid-junction potential attained in Cell IV, by making m_1 and m_0 small, can be made absolutely complete if it is possible to obtain the value of an appropriate function of **E** and of the concentrations as m_1 and m_0 approach zero as a limit.[36] The experimental determination of this limiting value of the function involves the study of a series of cells containing solutions of varying compositions, but maintained at constant total ionic strength by the presence of an electrolyte which takes no part in the electrode reactions.[37] Extrapolation to zero concentration of the dissimilar ions eliminates the junction potential. The conditions of extrapolation have been analyzed by Owen and Brinkley.[36a] The effect of the inert electrolyte is eliminated by subsequent extrapolation to zero ionic strength. The method will be illustrated by considering the cell

$$\text{Ag-AgCl} \begin{array}{|c|} KCl(x)m \\ KNO_3(1-x)m \end{array} \begin{array}{|c|} KNO_3(m) \end{array} \begin{array}{|c|} AgNO_3(x)m \\ KNO_3(1-x)m \end{array} \text{AgCl-Ag} \quad V$$

The total ionic strength in each solution is m, but a fraction, x, of this is composed of chloride ion in the left-hand compartment, and silver ion in the right. The electromotive force of the cell is given by

$$E = k \log a'_{Ag}/a_{Ag} \pm E_J \qquad (10\text{-}7\text{-}9)$$

[35] H. S. Harned and G. M. Murphy, *J. Am. Chem. Soc.*, **53**, 8 (1931).

[34] This notion was implied in the work of G. A. Linhart [*J. Am. Chem. Soc.*, **38**, 2356 (1916)], and used by S. Popoff and A. H. Kunz [*Ibid.*, **51**, 382 (1929)].

[36a] B. B. Owen and S. R. Brinkley, Jr., *Ibid.*, **64**, 2171 (1942).

[37] B. B. Owen, *J. Am. Chem. Soc.*, **60**, 2229 (1938).

E_J is the sum of the unknown liquid-junction potentials, $k = 2.303RT/F$, and a'_{Ag} and a_{Ag} represent the activities of the silver ion in the right-hand and left-hand solutions, respectively. The solubility product

$$K_{AgCl} = a_{Ag}a_{Cl} \qquad (10\text{-}7\text{-}10)$$

can be used to eliminate a_{Ag}, and equations (10-7-9) becomes

$$E - k \log a'_{Ag}a_{Cl} = -k \log K_{AgCl} \pm E_J \qquad (10\text{-}7\text{-}11)$$

The introduction of the concentrations, xm, and the individual activity coefficients leads to

$$E - 2k \log xm = -k \log K_{AgCl} + k \log \gamma_{Cl}\gamma'_{Ag} \pm E_J \qquad (10\text{-}7\text{-}12)$$

Note that the last two terms of this equation are not independently defined by thermodynamics alone.

Inspection of equation (10-7-12), and consideration of the symmetry of the electrochemical system it represents, shows that if m is held constant while x is varied, extrapolation to $x = 0$ must yield

$$[E - 2k \log xm]_{x=0} = -k \log K_{AgCl} + [k \log \gamma_{Cl}\gamma'_{Ag}]_{x=0} \qquad (10\text{-}7\text{-}13)$$

because E_J becomes zero under this condition. Since it is no longer necessary to retain the prime on γ'_{Ag} when $x = 0$, the last term is amenable to thermodynamic treatment, and can be expressed as a function of m, similar to that for any 1-1 strong electrolyte. Accordingly, $k \log \gamma_{Cl}\gamma_{Ag}$ is replaced by $-2k\mathcal{S}_{(f)}\sqrt{md_0}$, and equation (10-7-13) takes the form

$$[E - 2k \log xm + 2k\mathcal{S}_{(f)}\sqrt{md_0}]_{x=0} = -k \log K'_{AgCl} \qquad (10\text{-}7\text{-}14)$$

The determination of the bracketed member of this equation by extrapolation at several values of m is illustrated in Figure (10-7-3).[37] The determination of $-k \log K_{AgCl}$, by subsequent extrapolation of these intercepts $(-k \log K'_{AgCl})$ to $m = 0$, is shown in Figure (10-7-4). Both of these extrapolations appear to be linear*, and the extrapolated result has been checked very closely by an independent method†. Similar linear relationships were found to represent the results obtained with the cells[38]

$$\begin{array}{c} AgAc(x)m \\ H_2 \mid HAc(m),\ NaAc(m) \mid HAc(m),\ NaAc(1-x)m \mid Ag \end{array} \qquad VI$$

---

* The linearity apparent in Figure (10-7-3) is probably a consequence of equation (14-4-3), and the high symmetry of the electrolyte systems. The linearity of the plots in Figure (10-7-4) is predicted from consideration of equations (10-3-4) and (10-3-5).

† Conductometric titration by J. A. Gledhill and G. McP. Malan, *Trans. Faraday Soc.*, **48**, 258 (1952).

[38] B. B. Owen and S. R. Brinkley, Jr., *J. Am. Chem. Soc.*, **60**, 2233 (1938).

and[39]

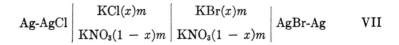

$$\text{Ag-AgCl} \left| \begin{array}{c} \text{KCl}(x)m \\ \text{KNO}_3(1-x)m \end{array} \right| \begin{array}{c} \text{KBr}(x)m \\ \text{KNO}_3(1-x)m \end{array} \right| \text{AgBr-Ag} \qquad \text{VII}$$

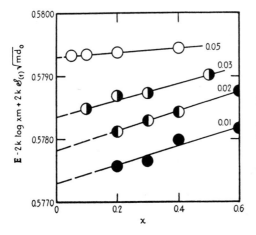

Fig. (10–7–3)
Elimination of E_J at 25° at constant total molalities indicated on the right

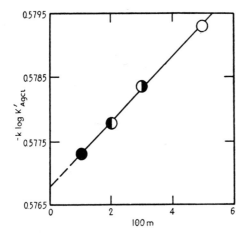

Fig. (10–7–4)
Evaluation of $(-k \log K_{\text{AgCl}})$ at 25°.

TABLE (10-7-3).   STANDARD ELECTRODE POTENTIAL OF SILVER DERIVED
FROM CELLS V AND VI

t	Cell V	Cell VI	Equation (10-7-16)
5	-0.8185_5	-0.8187	-0.8185_8
15	$-.8087$	$-.8090$	$-.8089_1$
25	$-.7990$	$-.7992$	$-.7991_0$
35	$-.7891$	$-.7892$	$-.7891_5$
45	$-.7788$	$-.7791_5$	$-.7790_8$

[39] B. B. Owen and E. J. King, *J. Am. Chem. Soc.*, **63**, 1711 (1941).

The simplicity of the function plotted in Figure (10-7-3) is important, as its form and the possibility of its extrapolation constitute the essential extra-thermodynamic hypothesis upon which this method of eliminating liquid-junction potentials is based.

The validity of the extrapolation by which the liquid-junction potentials are eliminated can be verified by comparing the calculated thermodynamic quantities with those obtained by independent procedure. Where such comparisons are possible, the agreement appears quite satis-factory.[37,38] The difference between the values of the standard potentials of the silver-silver chloride and silver-silver bromide electrodes, obtained from Cell VII, is in exact agreement with the difference between the corresponding values, directly obtained from cells without liquid junctions. It was also found that the results obtained from Cells V and VI are in excellent agreement, although the slopes of the extrapolations employed in the two systems differ in sign, and in order of magnitude. The standard electrode potential of silver may be calculated by the equation

$$\pi^0_{Ag} = k \log K_{AgCl} + \pi^0_{Ag-AgCl} \qquad (10\text{-}7\text{-}15)$$

from the values of K_{AgCl} obtained from Cell I. Cell II yields π^0_{Ag} directly. The comparison is illustrated in Table (10-7-3). These results are well represented by the quadratic equation

$$\pi^0_{Ag} = -0.7991 + 0.000988(t - 25) + 7 \times 10^{-7}(t - 25)^2 \qquad (10\text{-}7\text{-}16)$$

The temperature coefficient derived from this equation leads to a value of the entropy of the silver ion at 25°, in excellent agreement with the most recent calorimetric[40] determinations.

[40] W. M. Latimer, K. S. Pitzer and W. V. Smith, *J. Am. Chem. Soc.*, **60**, 1829 (1938); K. S. Pitzer and W. V. Smith, *Ibid.*, **59**, 2633 (1937).

Chapter 11

Hydrochloric Acid

The properties of hydrochloric acid in aqueous and nonaqueous solutions, and in water-nonaqueous solvent mixtures have been investigated more comprehensively than those of any other electrolyte, and they may be used to illustrate the fundamental characteristics of ionic solutions without introducing the difficulties caused by the presence of ions of charge greater than unity. The subject will be introduced with a discussion of the extent of ionization of this acid in media of varying dielectric constant as derived from conductance data. The thermodynamics of hydrochloric acid, as determined from the electromotive force of the cell,

$$H_2 \mid HCl(m) \mid AgCl\text{-}Ag$$

will then be developed in considerable detail. Comparison of the results obtained from electromotive forces will be made with similar results from freezing point, heat of dilution, and specific heat data. In this way, a comprehensive view of the properties of a single electrolyte as a function of its concentration, the temperature, and the dielectric constant may be obtained. All these results will be considered in relation to the predictions of the interionic attraction theory.

(1) CONDUCTANCE OF HYDROCHLORIC ACID IN DIOXANE-WATER MIXTURES

Previous discussion [Chapter (6) Section (2)] of the conductance of hydrochloric acid in water showed that it is a typically strong electrolyte. The criterion for this conclusion is that the equivalent conductance, Λ, is greater than that predicted by Onsager's equation,

$$\Lambda = \Lambda^0 - (\alpha^*\Lambda^0 + \beta^*\sqrt{c}) \tag{6-2-1}$$

in dilute solutions, and approaches the result predicted by this equation in the limit. The behavior of this acid in media of lower dielectric constant is illustrated clearly by the results of Owen and Waters,[1] who measured the conductance in dioxane-water mixtures of 20, 45, 70 and 82 per cent dioxane from 15 to 45°. At 25°, the dielectric constants of these mixtures, according to Åkerlöf and Short,[2] are 60.79, 38.48, 17.69 and 9.53, respectively. Fig. (11-1-1) contains plots of the equivalent conductance, Λ, against $c^{\frac{1}{2}}$. The experimental points are represented by the circles,

---

[1] B. B. Owen and G. W. Waters, *J. Am. Chem. Soc.*, **60**, 2371 (1938).

[2] G. Åkerlöf and O. A. Short, *J. Am. Chem. Soc.*, **58**, 1241 (1936).

whereas the straight lines are the theoretical plots of Onsager's equation. In the 20 per cent dioxane mixtures, the result is very similar to that in water, since the observed curve lies above the theoretical one [Fig. (6-2-1)]. Even the result for the most dilute solution (0.0004N) is slightly above the theoretical result. In the 45 per cent mixtures ($D \sim 40$), there is evidence for ionic association. The theoretical result is approached from below, although this effect is barely noticeable. In the case of the 70 per cent dioxane solutions, ionic association appears to be present to a considerable extent. In the 82 per cent dioxane mixtures, hydrochloric acid shows the characteristic behavior of a weak electrolyte.

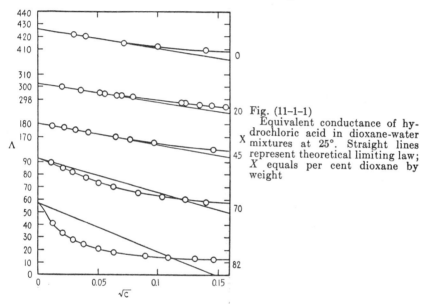

Fig. (11–1–1)
Equivalent conductance of hydrochloric acid in dioxane-water mixtures at 25°. Straight lines represent theoretical limiting law; X equals per cent dioxane by weight

To evaluate the limiting conductance in the 20 and 45 per cent mixtures, the extrapolation which utilizes the function,

$$\Lambda^{0\prime} = \frac{(\Lambda + \beta^* \sqrt{c})}{(1 - \alpha^* \sqrt{c})} \qquad (6\text{-}3\text{-}7)\dagger$$

was employed. For the 70 and 82 per cent mixtures, the method of Fuoss and Kraus,[3] improved by Fuoss,[4] which involves the use of equations (7-2-3) to (7-2-9), was used.

The dissociation constants obtained by Owen and Waters are given in Table (11-1-1). No accurate estimate can be made of the results in the 20 and 45 per cent dioxane solutions, although these investigators judge that K is of the order of unity in the latter.

---

† Values of α^* and β^* for these dioxane-water mixtures are given in Table (11-1-1A).
[3] R. M. Fuoss and C. A. Kraus, *J. Am. Chem. Soc.*, **55**, 476 (1933).
[4] R. M. Fuoss, *J. Am. Chem. Soc.*, **57**, 488 (1935).

The general nature of these results is in accord with Bjerrum's theory of ionic association. By employing this theory [Equation (3-7-13)], Owen and Waters obtained the values in Ångstroms of the sums of the ionic radii given in the table. Greater weight should be given to the values in the case of 82 per cent mixtures, since the values of K are somewhat more certain than those in the more dilute dioxane mixtures.

TABLE (11-1-1). DISSOCIATION CONSTANTS OF HYDROCHLORIC ACID IN DIOXANE-WATER MIXTURES*

t	70% Dioxane			82% Dioxane		
	D_0	$K \times 10^3$	$a \times 10^8$	D_0	$K \times 10^4$	$a \times 10^8$†
15	18.72	11	9.1	10.01	2.5	6.6
25	17.69	8	7.9	9.53	2.0	6.3
35	16.72	7	7.7	9.06	1.6	6.2
45	15.80	6	7.4	8.62	1.1	5.8

* Values of parameters α^* and β^*, and the required viscosities are to be found in Table (11-1-1A).
† Sum of ionic radii.

(2) THE STANDARD POTENTIAL OF THE CELL: $H_2 \mid HCl\ (m) \mid AgCl\text{-}Ag$ IN AQUEOUS SOLUTIONS

The reaction corresponding to the cell,

$$H_2 \mid HCl\ (m) \mid AgCl\text{-}Ag \qquad (11\text{-}2\text{-}1)$$

is taken to be

$$\tfrac{1}{2}H_2 + AgCl = Ag + HCl\ (m) \qquad (11\text{-}2\text{-}2)$$

Since one mol of hydrochloric acid is formed, the electromotive force of the cell is given by equation (10-3-2). Thus, for a 1-1 electrolyte,

$$E + 2k \log m = E^0 - 2k \log \gamma_\pm \qquad (11\text{-}2\text{-}3)$$

where k has been substituted for the factor $2.3026\ RT/F$. For purposes of extrapolation, equation (10-3-5) will be employed, namely,

$$E + 2k \log m - 2k \mathcal{S}_{(f)}\sqrt{\Gamma} = E^0 - 2kB'm \qquad (11\text{-}2\text{-}4)$$

In Fig. (11-2-1), the left side of this equation has been plotted against m. It is clear that these data can be represented by straight lines at the lower concentrations, and that the extrapolation can be made with high precision. Since the electrode potential of the hydrogen electrode at one atmosphere is taken to be zero at all temperatures, the value of E^0, thus obtained, becomes the standard potential of the silver-silver chloride electrode merely by changing its sign.

Many attempts have been made to determine this standard electrode potential. We shall discuss those which appear to be the most accurate.

Several different kinds of electrodes have been used. Linhart[5] employed an electrode made by introducing a platinum wire into a mixture of precipitated silver chloride, and silver prepared by electrolysis of silver nitrate at high current density. Carmody[6] used a platinum gauze electrode upon which silver had been deposited electrolytically. Silver chloride was formed on this by electrolysis of hydrochloric acid.[7] Ellis,[8] Roberts,[9] and Harned and Ehlers[10] used electrodes prepared by heating silver oxide on a platinum spiral to 500°. The silver thus formed was coated with silver chloride by electrolysis in hydrochloric acid solution.[11]

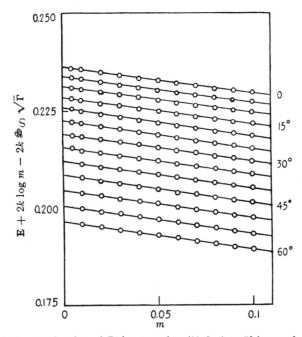

Fig. (11–2–1). Evaluation of E^0 by equation (11–2–4) at 5° intervals.

The values of E^0 have usually been determined by graphical methods. Prentiss and Scatchard[12] have recently computed E^0 from the measure-

[5] G. A. Linhart, *J. Am. Chem. Soc.*, **41**, 1175 (1919).

[6] W. R. Carmody, *J. Am. Chem. Soc.*, **51**, 2905 (1929).

[7] A similar electrode was employed by G. Scatchard, *J. Am. Chem. Soc.*, **47**, 641 (1925).

[8] A. A. Noyes and J. H. Ellis, *Ibid.*, **39**, 2532 (1917).

[9] E. J. Roberts, *Ibid.*, **52**, 3877 (1930).

[10] H. S. Harned and R. W. Ehlers, *Ibid.*, **54**, 1350 (1932); **55**, 2179 (1933).

[11] Somewhat different types of this electrode are described by E. Güntelberg, *Z. physik. Chem.*, **123**, 199 (1926); H. S. Harned, *J. Am. Chem. Soc.*, **51**, 416 (1929); D. A. MacInnes and J. A. Beattie, *Ibid.*, **42**, 1117 (1920); A. S. Brown, *Ibid.*, **56**, 646 (1934).

[12] S. S. Prentiss and G. Scatchard, *Chem. Rev.*, **13**, 139 (1933).

ments of the above investigators by using the method of least squares. In Table (11-2-1), we have compiled the results at 25°.

Considering the variety in technique and in type of electrodes used, the agreement between the results of the different investigators is excellent. Further, the results obtained graphically compare favorably with those computed by the least squares method.

TABLE (11-2-1). THE STANDARD POTENTIAL OF THE SILVER-SILVER CHLORIDE ELECTRODE AT 25°. INT. VOLTS

Observer	Graphical	Least Square (7)
Carmody.....................................	−0.2223 (1)	
"	−0.2222 (2)	−0.22222
Linhart.....................................	−0.2226 (3)	− .22253
"	−0.2224 (4)	
Roberts.....................................	−0.22240 (5)	− .22241
"	....	− .22237
Harned and Ehlers.........................	−0.22239 (6)	− .22244
MacInnes....................................	−0.2225 (8)	....

Computed by: (1) W. R. Carmody, *loc. cit.*; (2) H. M. Spencer, *J. Am. Chem. Soc.*, **54**, 3647 (1933); (3) G. Scatchard, *J. Am. Chem. Soc.*, **47**, 641 (1925); (4) D. I. Hitchcock, *Ibid.*, **50**, 2076 (1928); (5) E. J. Roberts, *loc. cit.*; (6) H. S. Harned and R. W Ehlers, *loc. cit.*; (7) S. S. Prentiss and G. Scatchard, *loc. cit.*; (8) D. A. MacInnes, "The Principles of Electrochemistry," p. 187, Reinhold Publishing Corp., New York, 1939 from the data of Harned and Ehlers, *loc. cit.*

TABLE (11-2-2). THE STANDARD POTENTIAL IN ABSOLUTE VOLTS OF THE SILVER CHLORIDE ELECTRODE FROM 0° TO 95°.

t	$-\pi°_{AgCl} = E°$	$-\pi°_{AgCl} = E°$	$-\pi°_{AgCl} = E°$	$E°$(Eq. 11-2-6)
0	0.23655	0.23642	0.23652	0.23654
5	.23413	.23400	.23405	.23408
10	.23142	.23134	.23137	.23140
15	.22857	.22855	.22849	.22856
20	.22557	.22558	.22549	.22557
25	.22234	.22246	.22239	.22240
30	.21904	.21919	.21908	.21910
35	.21565	.21570	.21570	.21566
40	.21208	.21207	.21207	.21207
45	.20835	.20828	.20833	.20834
50	.20449	.20444	.20449	.20449
55	.20056	.20042	—	.20051
60	.19649	.19636	—	.19641
70	.18782	—	—	.18785
80	.17873	—	—	.17885
90	.16952	—	—	.16946
95	.16511	—	—	—

By employing a vacuum technique and using the method of extrapolation shown in Fig. (11-2-1) Harned and Ehlers obtained the results in the third column of Table (11-2-2). The second column in this table contains the values resulting from the very comprehensive study of Bates and Bowers,[13] who made the extrapolations by the use of the more refined equation (11-3-1). To remove oxygen, they swept the cells with nitrogen. The fourth column of the table contains values of nitrogen swept cells containing hydrochloric acid and strontium chloride by Harned and Paxton.[14] The final column contains values calculated by the equation

$$\mathbf{E}^0 = 0.23659 - 4.8564 \times 10^{-4}t$$
$$- 3.4205 \times 10^{-6}t^2 + 5.869 \times 10^{-9}t^3 \qquad (11\text{-}2\text{-}6)$$

given by Bates and Bower.

(3) The Standard Potential of the Cell: $H_2 \mid HCl(m)$, $S(X)$, H_2O $(Y) \mid$ AgCl-Ag in Organic Solvent-Water Mixtures

The electromotive forces of these cells containing methanol-,[15] ethanol-,[16] 2-propanol-,[17] glycerol-,[18] ethylene glycol-,[19] sucrose-,[20] d-glucose-,[21] and fructose-[21] water mixtures have been determined with sufficient accuracy in dilute solutions for a precise determination of the standard potentials. The most comprehensive series of measurements of this kind has been made using dioxane water mixtures.[22] These include precise measure-

---

[13] R. G. Bates and V. E. Bower, *J. Research, Nat. Bur. Stds.*, **53**, 283 (1954).

[14] H. S. Harned and T. R. Paxton, *J. Phys. Chem.*, **57**, 531 (1953).

[15] G. Nonhebel and H. Hartley, *Phil. Mag.*, (6) **50**, 729 (1925); H. S. Harned and Thomas, *J. Am. Chem. Soc.*, **57**, 1666 (1935); **58**, 761 (1936).

[16] J. W. Woolcock and H. Hartley, *Phil. Mag.*, (7) **5**, 1133 (1928); P. S. Danner, *J. Am. Chem. Soc.*, **44**, 2832 (1922); H. S. Harned and M. H. Fleysher, *Ibid.*, **47**, 82 (1925); A. Patterson and W. A. Felsing, *Ibid.*, **64**, 1478 (1942); H. S. Harned and D. S. Allen, *J. Phys. Chem.*, **58**, 191 (1954); H. S. Harned, C. Calmon, *Ibid.*, **61**, 1491 (1939).

[17] R. L. Moore and W. H. Felsing, *Ibid.*, **69**, 1076 (1947); H. S. Harned and D. S. Allen, *loc. cit.*

[18] W. W. Lucasse, *Ibid.*, **48**, 627 (1926); *Z. physik. Chem.*, **121**, 254 (1926); H. S. Harned and F. H. M. Nestler, *J. Am. Chem. Soc.*, **68**, 665 (1946).

[19] H. D. Crockford, S. B. Knight and H. Seaton, *Ibid.*, **72**, 2164 (1950); S. B. Knight, J. F. Masi and D. Roesel, *Ibid*, **68**, 661 (1946).

[20] G. Scatchard, *Ibid.*, **48**, 2026 (1926).

[21] J. P. Williams, S. B. Knight and H. D. Crockford, *Ibid.*, **72**, 1277 (1950) H. D. Crockford *et alia*, unpublished results.

[22] H. S. Harned and J. O. Morrison, *Am. J. Sci.*, **33**, 161 (1937); *J. Am. Chem. Soc.*, **58**, 1908 (1936).

H. S. Harned and C. Calmon, *Ibid.*, **60**, 334 (1938). Densities.

H. S. Harned, *Ibid.*, **60**, 336 (1938). Extrapolations (20% and 45%).

H. S. Harned and J. G. Donelson, *Ibid.*, **60**, 339 (1938). Properties (20%); **60**, 2128 (1938). Properties (45%).

ments of the cells at 5° intervals from 0 to 50°, at concentrations of acid from $0.001M$ to the highest practical concentration in 20, 45, 70, and 82 per cent dioxane-water mixtures, which correspond to values of the solvent dielectric constant of approximately 60, 40, 20, and 10. The dielectric constants of the media have been determined by Åkerlöf and Short,[23] and the vapor pressures by Hovorka, Shaefer, and Dreisbach.[24]

As the dielectric constant of the solvent decreases, the effect of the higher-order terms of the interionic attraction theory, given by equations (3-6-4) and (3-6-5), must be taken into consideration in the extrapolations. In order to illustrate this effect, and at the same time show this method of extrapolation for media containing 20, 45 and 70 per cent dioxane, we shall employ the function, $\mathbf{E}^{0'}$, defined by

$$\mathbf{E}^{0'} \equiv \mathbf{E} + 2k \log m - \frac{2k \mathbb{S}_{(f)} \sqrt{c}}{1 + A'\sqrt{c}}$$

$$- 2k \log(1 + 0.002 M_{XY} m) = \mathbf{E}^0 + f(m) \qquad (11\text{-}3\text{-}1)$$

$\mathbf{E}$ is the observed electromotive force of the cell at a concentration m, $\mathbf{E}^0$ the standard potential of the cell, A' is the parameter which involves the apparent ionic diameter, $\mathring{a}$ [(Equation (3-5-9)], and M_{XY} is the average molecular weight of the solvent [Equation (1-8-16)]. $\mathbf{E}^{0'}$ was first calculated by employing a preliminary value of $\mathring{a}$. Then, the Gronwall, LaMer and Sandved extended-term contribution, corresponding to this value of $\mathring{a}$, was computed from their functions in Table (5-2-2). This quantity, multiplied by $2k$, will be denoted as $\mathbf{E}_{\text{Ext.}}$. The functions, $\mathbf{E}^{0'}$ and $\mathbf{E}^{0'} - \mathbf{E}_{\text{Ext.}}$, were plotted, and, if $\mathbf{E}^{0'} - \mathbf{E}_{\text{Ext.}}$ was not constant at the lower concentrations $(m < 0.02M)$, other values of $\mathring{a}$ were employed until constancy was obtained. Values of c were obtained from Table (11-3-2A).

Fig. (11-3-1) clearly shows the extrapolation and the extended-term effects. In it are the plots of $\mathbf{E}^{0'}$, and $\mathbf{E}^{0'} - \mathbf{E}_{\text{Ext.}}$ versus the molality, m, at 25^0 for solvents containing 20, 45, and 70 per cent dioxane. The dielectric constants of these solutions are 60.79, 38.48, and 17.69, respectively. We note that the plots of $\mathbf{E}^{0'}$ have "humps" near the origin which are characteristic of this function. Their magnitude increases with decreasing dielectric constant. That the extended-term theory accounts

H. S. Harned and C. Calmon, *Ibid.*, **60**, 2130 (1938). Extrapolations. (70%)

H. S. Harned, J. G. Donelson, and C. Calmon, *Ibid.*, **60**, 2133 (1938). Properties (70%).

H. S. Harned, F. Walker, and C. Calmon, *Ibid.*, **61**, 44 (1939). Extrapolations (82%).

H. S. Harned and F. Walker, *Ibid.*, **61**, 48 (1939). Properties (82%).

H. S. Harned, J. O. Morrison, F. Walker, J. G. Donelson, and C. Calmon, *Ibid.*, **61**, 49 (1939). Summary and Critique.

[23] G. Åkerlöf and O. A. Short, *J. Am. Chem. Soc.*, **58**, 1241 (1936).

[24] F. Hovorka, R. A. Schaefer, and D. Dreisbach, *J. Am. Chem. Soc.*, **58**, 2264 (1936).

for these results at low concentrations is shown by the graphs of the function $E^{0'} - E_{Ext.}$, which for the values of $\mathring{a}$ of 5.0, 5.4, and 5.6, respectively, are straight with zero slopes $[f(m) = 0]$ below $0.02M$. The contribution of the extended terms in the case of the 20 per cent solutions is so small that the extrapolation without them yields the same E^0 within very narrow limits ($\sim$0.1 mv). These values of $\mathring{a}$ agree closely with 5.6, obtained by Shedlovsky and MacInnes[25] from measurements of cells with liquid junction in water, and with 5.3, obtained from the data of Harned and Ehlers from cells without liquid junction in the same medium. The constancy of the function, $E^{0'} - E_{Ext.}$, in the concentration range from $0.002M$ to $0.02M$ is shown clearly by the data in Table (11-3-1).

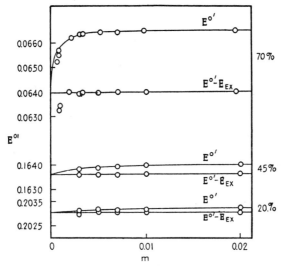

Fig. (11-3-1). Extrapolation in dioxane-water mixtures (at 25°) according to equation (11-3-1). Weight percent of dioxane is indicated at right.

The evaluation of the standard potential in solutions of dielectric constant as low as those containing 82 per cent dioxane cannot be carried out with certainty. There are a number of reasons for this. The Gronwall, LaMer and Sandved extension of the Debye and Hückel theory is not satisfactory in media of dielectric constant of the magnitude 10 or less, since the second term of the extended term series is large. In fact, it is greater than the first term at acid concentrations of the order of $0.001M$. In the second place, reliable electromotive forces at acid concentrations less than $0.001\ M$ have not yet been obtained. For an empirical extrapolation, results in the region of concentrations as low as $0.00005M$, or less, will be required. In view of these difficulties, a tentative method, which involves the law of mass action and dissociation constants derived from

[25] T. Shedlovsky and D. A. MacInnes, *J. Am. Chem. Soc.*, **58**, 1970 (1936).

conductance measurements, will be employed. This procedure is not altogether satisfactory, but seems as good as any method available at the moment.

According to equation (11-3-1), the deviation function, $\mathbf{E}^{0'} - \mathbf{E}^0$ is given by

$$\mathbf{E}^{0'} - \mathbf{E}^0 = \mathbf{E} - \mathbf{E}^0 + 2k \log m - \frac{2k\mathfrak{S}_{(f)}\sqrt{c}}{1 + A'\sqrt{c}} = f(m) \qquad (11\text{-}3\text{-}2)$$

if we neglect the term containing M_{XY}. If $\mathbf{E}^{0'} - \mathbf{E}^0$ can be computed by some means which is theoretically sound when m equals 0, then $\mathbf{E}^0$ may be evaluated from the known values of $\mathbf{E}^{0'}$. In order to utilize the known

TABLE (11-3-1). VALUES OF EXTRAPOLATION FUNCTION, $\mathbf{E}^{0'} - \mathbf{E}^0_{\text{Ext.}}$ [b]

m	$X = 20\%$ $\mathring{d} = 5.0$	$X = 45\%$ $\mathring{d} = 5.4$	$X = 70\%$ $\mathring{d} = 5.6$
0.000	(0.20303)	(0.16358)	(0.06395)
.001	....	....	(.0634)[a]
.002	....	....	.06400
.003	.20298	.16357	.06393
.005	.20304	.16358	.06389
.007	.20303	.16359	.06391
.01	.20305	.16361	.06399
.02	.20305	.16360	.06400

[a] At concentrations below 0.002 M, the accuracy of the results decreases greatly, as indicated by this result. This matter has been discussed in detail by H. S. Harned and C. Calmon, *J. Am. Chem. Soc.*, **60**, 2130 (1938).

[b] Values of $\mathfrak{S}_{(f)}$, used in these computations, are given in Table (11-3-1A). Densities of solutions are given in Table (11-3-2A).

values of the dissociation constant, K, we may express the cell electromotive force by the equation,

$$\mathbf{E} - \mathbf{E}^0 = -2k \log \alpha m \gamma_\alpha \qquad (11\text{-}3\text{-}3)$$

where α is the degree of dissociation, and γ_α, the activity coefficient of the acid as a strong electrolyte at an ionic concentration, αm. Combining this equation with equation (11-3-2), the deviation factor becomes

$$\mathbf{E}_\alpha \equiv \mathbf{E}^{0'} - \mathbf{E}^0 = -2k \log \alpha \gamma_\alpha - \frac{2k\mathfrak{S}_{(f)}\sqrt{c}}{1 + A'\sqrt{c}} = f(m) \qquad (11\text{-}3\text{-}4)$$

so that the problem becomes one of computing α and γ_α. In terms of the thermodynamic dissociation constant [Equation (7-6-1)], α is given by

$$\alpha = \frac{1}{2}\left[-\frac{K}{\gamma_\alpha^2 m} \pm \sqrt{\frac{K^2}{\gamma_\alpha^4 m^2} + \frac{4K}{\gamma_\alpha^2 m}}\right] \qquad (11\text{-}3\text{-}5)$$

By employing the theoretical equation with extended terms, γ_α was computed and a suitable plot of γ_α versus $\sqrt{m}$ drawn. The above equation

was then solved by arithmetical approximation, using the values of K†
determined from conductance data in Table (11-1-1). The characteristics
of the extrapolation at 25° are illustrated by Fig. (11-3-2) where both $\mathbf{E}^{0'}$
and $\mathbf{E}^{0'} - \mathbf{E}_\alpha$ are plotted against m. Both of these functions equal $\mathbf{E}^0$
when m equals zero. The plot of the Debye and Hückel function, $\mathbf{E}^{0'}$, is
deceptive because it is nearly straight, and, if the effect of ionic association
is not taken into consideration, would be extrapolated as shown by the
upper dashed line. This leads to a value of $\mathbf{E}^0$ about 20 mv. too high.

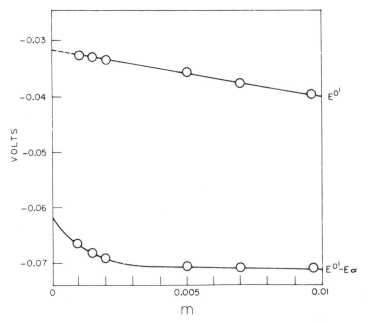

Fig. (11-3-2). Extrapolation in 82% dioxane-water mixtures at 25° according to
equations (11-3-4) and (11-3-5)

Recently, Janz, Taniguchi and Danyluk[26] have revised the earlier estimate of $\mathbf{E}^0$ by Harned and Calmon. The graph in Fig. (11-3-2) represents
the revised extrapolation at 25°. The subsequent calculations of activity
coefficient, partial molal heat content and specific heat in the 82% dioxane-
water mixtures are based on these new estimates.

Values of the standard potentials at 25° on the m-, c-, and N-scales in
some of these media are collected in Table (11-3-2) and specially designated

† Since at best this calculation is crude, the distinction between K on the c- and
m-scales has been ignored.

[26] G. J. Janz, H. Taniguchi and S. S. Danyluk, *J. Phys. Chem.*, in press. We are
grateful to Professor Janz and his colleagues for allowing us access to their results
prior to publication.

by a superscript asterisk to conform with equations (11-3-8) and (11-3-9). According to equation (1-8-10), these three quantities, $\mathbf{E}_m^{0*}$, $\mathbf{E}_c^{0*}$, and $\mathbf{E}_N^{0*}$, are related at 25° by the equations,

$$\mathbf{E}_c^{0*} = \mathbf{E}_m^{0*} + 0.1183 \log d_0 \tag{11-3-6}$$

$$\mathbf{E}_N^{0*} = \mathbf{E}_m^{0*} - 0.1183 \log (1000/M_{XY}) \tag{11-3-7}$$

In Fig. (11-3-3), $\mathbf{E}_m^{0*}$ is plotted against $1/D$ for media of high dielectric constant ($D \sim 80$ to 60). The origin of the plots on the left of the figure represents $\mathbf{E}_m^0$ for pure water. None of these plots is a straight line. Fur-

TABLE (11-3-2). STANDARD POTENTIALS OF THE CELLS: $H_2 \mid HCl$ (m), SOLVENT $X(N_2)$, H_2O $(N_1) \mid$ AgCl-Ag AT 25° [a,b]. N_1, N_2 = MOL FRACTION

Solvent	X	N_2	D_0	E_m^{0*}	E_c^{0*}	E_n^{0*}
Water	0	0	78.54	0.22246	0.22158	0.01602
Methanol-Water	10	.0588	74.0	.21552	.21438	.01124
	20	.1233	69.2	.20888	.20699	.00710
Methanol	100	1.0	31.5	−.0101		
Ethanol-Water	10	.0417	72.8	.21449	.21347	.01123
	20	.0891	67.0	.20743	.20568	.00763
	30	.1436	61.1	.20033	.17773	.00424
	40	.2069	55.0	.19454	.19089	.00239
	50	.2813	49.0	.18588	.18103	−.00189
Ethanol[c]	100	1.0	24.3	−.0814		
2-propanol-Water	5	.0168	74.9	.21814		.01350
	10	.0332	71.4	.21370	.21273	.01095
	20	.0704	64.1	.2060	.2043	.0073
Ethylene glycol-Water	5	.0152	76.9	.21912		.01455
	10	.0311	75.7	.21642		.01380
	15	.0486	74.2	.21337		.01275
	20	.0678	72.8	.21026		.01177
	30	.1110	69.8	.20367		.00955
	40	.1623	66.6	.19726		.00800
	60	.2991	59.4	.18076		.00285
Glycerol-Water	3.06	.01	77.1	.2197	.2207	.0146
	10	.0211	75.5	.21657		.01448
	21.2	.05	72.5	.2085	.2113	.0117
	30	0.077	70.1	.20228		.01005
	50	.165	64.0	.18404		.00407
Dioxane-Water	20	.0487	60.8	.20310	.20382	.00554
	45	.1433	38.5	.16357	.16518	−.02002
	70	.3231	17.7	.06397	.06586	−.10049
	82	.4823	9.5	−.0611	−.0594	−.21346
d-Glucose-Water	5	.0057	77.3	.21870		.01468
	10	.0106	76.1	.21426		.01271
	20	.0246	73.4	.20457		.00835
	30	.0413	70.5	.19361		.00336
d-Fructose-Water	5	.0057	77.3	.21907		.01449
	10	.0106	76.1	.21509		.01354

(a) See H. D. Crockford, Chap. 12, "Electrochemical Constants," Nat. Bur. Stds. Circular 524, Washington (1953). X = wt. percent of organic solvent.

(b) Standard potentials at other temperatures may be obtained from Table (11-3-3A).

(c) H. Taniguchi and G. J. Janz, *J. Phys. Chem.*, **61**, 688 (1957).

ther, they exhibit pronounced individual behavior. Plots of $\mathbf{E}_c^{0*}$, or $\mathbf{E}_N^{0*}$, versus $1/D$ have similar characteristics.

The phenomenon of transfer of the acid from water to the water-solvent mixture can be treated conveniently in the following manner. The electromotive force of these cells may be represented by two fundamental equations [Equation (11-2-3)] at 25°

$$E = \mathbf{E}_m^0 - 0.05915 \log m_H m_{Cl} - 0.05915 \log \gamma_H \gamma_{Cl} \qquad (11\text{-}3\text{-}8)$$

$$E = \mathbf{E}_m^{0*} - 0.05915 \log m_H m_{Cl} - 0.05915 \log \gamma_H^* \gamma_{Cl}^* \qquad (11\text{-}3\text{-}9)$$

In these, $\mathbf{E}_m^0$ is the standard potential in water, $\gamma_H \gamma_{Cl}$ is the activity coefficient in any of these solutions relative to unity at infinite dilution in water, $\mathbf{E}_m^{0*}$ is the standard potential in any mixture relative to unit activity coefficient, $\gamma_H^* \gamma_{Cl}^*$, at infinite dilution in that solvent. Combination of these equations yields,

$$\mathbf{E}_m^0 - \mathbf{E}_m^{0*} = 0.05915 \log \frac{\gamma_H \, \gamma_{Cl}}{\gamma_H^* \, \gamma_{Cl}^*} \qquad (11\text{-}3\text{-}10)$$

The superscript star is a special symbol used when a transfer of an electrolyte from one medium to another is under consideration. It appears in this section and in Chapter (15), Section (7).

Further, by using the thermodynamic relationships of the reaction, $H^+ + Cl^- + H_2O \rightleftharpoons H_3O^+ + Cl^-$, which prevails in solutions of high water content, equations (11-3-8) and (11-3-9) may be converted to

$$\mathbf{E}_m^0 - (\mathbf{E}_m^{0*} - 0.05915 \log a_w) = 0.05915 \log \frac{\gamma_{H_3O} \, \gamma_{Cl}}{\gamma_{H_3O}^* \, \gamma_{Cl}^*} \qquad (11\text{-}3\text{-}11)$$

where a_w is the activity of the water in any mixture. Similarly,

$$\mathbf{E}_N^0 - (\mathbf{E}_N^{0*} - 0.05915 \log a_w) = 0.05915 \log \frac{f_{H_3O} f_{Cl}}{f_{H_3O}^* f_{Cl}^*} \qquad (11\text{-}3\text{-}12)$$

The activity of pure water is always taken to be unity. Partial vapor pressure data indicate that as an approximation, N_1, the mol fraction of water, may be substituted for a_w in solutions of high water content. A plot of $(\mathbf{E}_m^{0*} - 0.05915 \log N_1)$ versus $1/D$ is shown on the right of Fig. (11-3-3).

For the monohydric alcohols and dioxane the plot of $(\mathbf{E}_m^0 - 0.05915 \log N_1)$ versus $1/D$ on the right of Fig. (11-3-3) lies closer to the experimental values than does a similar plot of $\mathbf{E}_m^{0*}$ on the left side of this figure. However, as shown by the precise work of Crockford,[26a] the structure of the

[26a] H. D. Crockford, Natl. Bur. Stds., Circular, **524**, 153 (1953).

molecules has a most pronounced effect, increasing in the order of the hydroxyl groups in the solvent-molecule system. This situation cannot be explained by the simple electrostatic theory involving the dielectric constant, although it will now be shown that such a theory gives the correct order of magnitude of the phenomenon.

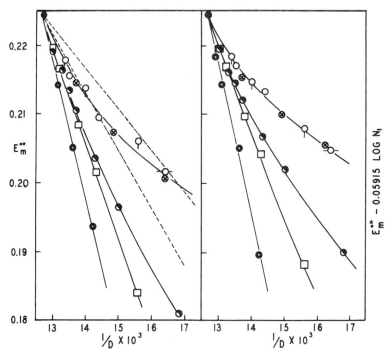

Fig. (11-3-3). Plots of E_m^{0*} and $E_m^{0*} - 0.05915 \log N_1$ against $1/D$. ●, water. ○, Methanol-water. ⊗, Ethanol-water. ϙ, 2-Propanol-water. □, Glycerol-water. ◑, Ethylene glycol-water. -o-, Dioxane-water. ◎, d-Glucose and d-fructose-water.

The transfer corresponding to equations (11-3-10), (11-3-11), and (11-3-12) is at unit activity and activity coefficient (hypothetical ideal solution at unit molality) and is therefore independent of the effect of the ionic atmosphere. The electrostatic theory of this effect has been developed in Chapter (3), Section (10), and shown to lead to the Born equation (3-10-13). For a 1-1 electrolyte at 25°, this equation becomes

$$\frac{E_N^0 - E_N^{0*}}{0.05915} = 1.210 \times 10^2 \frac{D_1 - D_2}{D_1 D_2} \sum \frac{1}{b_j} \qquad (11\text{-}3\text{-}13)$$

if $\ln f_{\pm(t)}$ be replaced by the corresponding expression for the electromotive force. Results given by this equation are indicated by the dashed lines in Figures (11-3-3) and (11-3-4). The lower plots have been computed using 1.2 for $\sum 1/b_j$, which corresponds roughly to values derived from crystallographic radii. The upper dashed graphs represent the result obtained from equation (11-3-13) when $\sum 1/b_j = 0.8$, which results from a mean ionic diameter 5 Å, if the radii of both ions are assumed to be equal. Although the agreement with this rough procedure is not good, the result shows that the theoretical result is of the right order of magnitude. The phenomenon is too complicated to be completely explained by so simple an electrostatic theory.

The characteristics of the variation of E_m^{0*} over wider ranges of dielectric constants are shown in Fig. (11-3-4). Curve (2) represents E_m^{0*} versus $1/D$ for ethanol-water mixtures, from pure water to pure alcohol. The intermediate values of E_m^{0*}, not given in Table (11-3-2), were derived from the data of Harned and Fleysher.[26b] Curve (1) for methanol-water mixtures

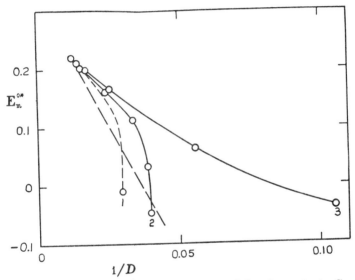

Fig. (11-3-4). E_m^{0*} versus $1/D$ over wide variation of dielectric constant. Curve (1), methanol-water; Curve (2), ethanol-water; Curve (3), dioxane water. Dashed line is a plot of equation (11-3-13)

was drawn tentatively to the value in pure alcohol. Curve (3) represents the results of the dioxane-water mixtures. The final point is in solution of dielectric constant 9.6, and is still quite far from a pure dioxane solution which possesses a dielectric constant of 2.1. The dashed straight line represents the result computed from Born's equation. We note that this equation is more than sufficient to account for the large change of E_m^{0*} in media containing from 100 to 2 per cent water. The very rapid decrease of E_m^{0*} with $1/D$, as the water content of the mixture becomes small, takes place under conditions where the oxonium ion, H_3O^+, is being replaced by (solvent)H^+ according to the reaction, $H_3O^+ + $ (solvent) $\rightleftharpoons H_2O + $ (solvent)H^+. The concentration of the dioxane in the dioxane-water

[26b] H. S. Harned and M. H. Fleysher, *J. Am. Chem. Soc.*, **47**, 82 (1925).

mixtures is not sufficient to show this effect.   This subject will be further amplified in subsequent discussions of medium effects [Chapter (15)].

(4) THE ACTIVITY COEFFICIENT OF HYDROCHLORIC ACID IN AQUEOUS SOLUTIONS

A comprehensive discussion of the activity coefficient and other thermo-dynamic properties of hydrochloric acid, computed from electromotive measurements, will now be undertaken.   The results will indicate to what extent the interionic attraction theory applies, and what additional parameters are required to express the actual results.

The most extensive investigation of cell (11-2-1) has been carried out by Harned and Ehlers.[27]   They extended their measurements from 0 to 60° at 5° intervals, and from 0.004 to 4 M concentration.   The accuracy

TABLE (11-4-1).   OBSERVED AND CALCULATED MEAN ACTIVITY COEFFICIENTS

m	0°			25°†		60°	
	(E.M.F.)	(F.P.)	(Calc.)	(E.M.F.)	(Calc.)	(E.M.F.)	(Calc.)
0.001	0.9668	0.9661	0.9667	0.9656	0.9654	0.9632	0.9628
.002	.9541	.9534	.9541	.9521	.9524	.9491	.9489
.005	.9303	.9300	.9311	.9285	.9285	.9235	.9235
.01	.9065	.9064	.9080	.9048	.9045	.8987	.8975
.02	.8774	.8772	.8798	.8755	.8751	.8666	.8660
.05	.8346	.8341	.8366	.8304	.8299	.8168	.8170
.1	.8027	.8021	.8032	.7964	.7946	.7813	.7780
.2	.7756	.7754	.7749	.7667	.7650	.7437	.7437
.5	.7761	.774	.7753	.7571	.7563	.7237	.7234
1.	.8419	.840	.8415	.8090	.8091	.7541	.7567
1.5	.9452	.....	.9465	.8962	.8960	.8178	.8196
2.	1.078	.....	1.081	1.0090	1.0085	.9072	.9059
3.	1.452	.....	1.454	1.316	1.313	.....	.....
4.	2.006	.....	2.005	......	......	....	.....

† T. Shedlovsky and D. A. MacInnes, *J. Am. Chem. Soc.*, **58**, 1970 (1936), have obtained values at 25° below 0.1 M from cells with liquid junctions.

obtained by them was of the order of ±0.05 mv.   The smoothed results, over the temperature range, were expressed by the equation

$$E = E_{25} + a(t - 25) + b(t - 25)^2 + c(t - 25)^3 \qquad (11\text{-}4\text{-}1)$$

and the constants of this equation are given in Table IV of their second communication.   The results from 0.0001 to 0.002 M inclusive were obtained from the graphs of the left side of equation (11-2-4) which were employed in evaluating E^0.

Upon rearrangement of equation (11-2-3), we obtain,

$$\log \gamma_{\pm} = - \log m - \frac{(E - E^0)}{2k} \qquad (11\text{-}4\text{-}2)$$

The values of $\gamma_{\pm}$ given in Table (11-4-1A) were computed from E obtained by equation (11-4-1), and E^0 from Table (11-2-2).   The results in parenthe-

[27] H. S. Harned and R. W. Ehlers, *J. Am. Chem. Soc.*, **54**, 1350 (1932); **55**, 652 (1933); **55**, 2179 (1933).

sis were obtained from extrapolated electromotive forces, and are not in the range of concentration of the observed results. Values at intermediate temperatures may be obtained by interpolation. An error of ± 0.05 mv corresponds to an error of the order of ± 0.001 in the activity coefficient. The values at 20 and 25° agree very closely with those obtained from electromotive force measurements by Güntelberg,[28] and by Randall and Young.[29] Åkerlöf and Teare[30] have extended the measurements of cell (11-2-1) to include acid concentrations from 3 to 16 M. Their values of $\log \gamma_{\pm}$ from 0 to 50° are given in Table (14-9-1A).

An important confirmation of the reliability of these results is obtained by comparing them with values of the activity coefficient, at the freezing point, $\gamma'_{\pm}$, computed by Randall and Young from the freezing point measurements of Randall and Vanselow.[31] Table (11-4-1) shows the agreement between values computed from electromotive force and freezing point data and leaves little doubt that our assumption regarding the nature of the cell reaction is a very close approximation to the actual cell process.

(5) Calculation of the Activity Coefficient of Hydrochloric Acid in Water by the Extended Debye and Hückel Theory

By combining equations (1-8-13), (3-5-8), and (3-6-4), we obtain for a 1-1 electrolyte

$$\log \gamma_{\pm} = -\frac{\mathcal{S}_{(f)}\sqrt{c}}{1 + A'\sqrt{c}} + \text{Ext.} - \log(1 + 0.01802\nu m) \qquad (11\text{-}5\text{-}1)$$

where Ext. represents the total contribution of the extended terms. This equation represents the total effect of Coulomb forces on the activity coefficient of a completely dissociated electrolyte, if the dielectric constant of the medium, acid and water, remains constant. The activity coefficient of an actual electrolyte approaches the theoretical prediction as its concentration approaches zero. To describe the behavior of a real electrolyte, it is necessary to add a linear term in c, [Equation (10-4-8)], or terms of a power series in c. Thus,

$$\log \gamma_{\pm} = -\frac{\mathcal{S}_{(f)}\sqrt{c}}{1 + A'\sqrt{c}} + \text{Ext.} + Bc$$
$$+ \sum_{n>2} A_n c^{n/2} - \log(1 + 0.01802\nu m) \qquad (11\text{-}5\text{-}2)$$

where B and A_n are constants at constant temperature and pressure. Experimental values of activity coefficients of strong electrolytes up to 1 M concentration can be represented with high accuracy without the terms

[28] E. Güntelberg, *Z. physik. Chem.*, **123**, 199 (1926).
[29] M. Randall and L. E. Young, *J. Am. Chem. Soc.*, **50**, 989 (1928).
[30] G. Åkerlöf and J. W. Teare, *J. Am. Chem. Soc.*, **59**, 1855 (1937).
[31] M. Randall and A. P. Vanselow, *J. Am. Chem. Soc.*, **46**, 2418 (1924).

of powers higher than unity.[32]   The determination of the parameters A' and B can be accomplished by solving two equations as outlined in Chapter (10), Section (4) [Equation (10-4-9)]. In the earlier calculations of these parameters, Hückel,[33] Harned,[34] and Harned and Åkerlöf[35] used results from 0.1 to 3 M, and the equation with the term linear in c only. Their values for A', and consequently [Equation (3-5-9)] their values of the mean distance of approach, $å$, are somewhat low. Better values of $å$ may be obtained if the constants of the equation be derived from the experimental results in the region from 0.01 to 1 M. This determination is very sensitive since, for example, a change in $å$ from 4.2 to 4.3 causes a change in the first term on the right of equation (11-5-1) of only one in the third decimal place of the activity coefficient at 0.1 M.

Harned and Ehlers solved the equation for $å$ directly from the experimental results at temperatures from 0 to 60°, at 5° intervals. All their values for $å$ were in the range 4.3 ± 0.2, while nine of the thirteen results (from 10 to 50° inclusive) were 4.33 ± 0.03. This is an important result since it indicates that the mean distance of approach varies little, if at all, with the temperature. We note that this value of $å$ is considerably greater than the sum of the ionic radii determined from crystallographic data. This result is to be expected in dilute solutions since the ions are hydrated. Shedlovsky and MacInnes[36] obtained 4.6 from cells with liquid junction when they used equation (11-5-2) with the first, third and fifth terms only. By using the expression $D'c^2$ in place of $\Sigma A_n c^{n/2}$ in equation (11-5-2), Harned and Ehlers obtained a very close fit with the results from 0 to 60°, and from 0.005 M to 2, or 4 M. Their computations were made by employing the values of $\mathfrak{S}_{(f)}$ and $\kappa/c^{1/2}$ given in Table (5-2-1), and $å = 4.3$. B and D' were found to vary linearly with the temperature. Thus,

$$B = 0.1390 - 0.000392t \qquad (11\text{-}5\text{-}3)$$

$$D' = 0.0070 - 0.000033t \qquad (11\text{-}5\text{-}4)$$

In Table (11-4-1), the observed activity coefficients, and the values computed by equation (11-5-2) are given at 0, 25 and 60°. In Table (11-5-1), an equation and constants, a_1 and b_1, are given by means of which c may be computed from m. This table also includes values of the parameters A', B and D', and the slopes $\mathfrak{S}_{(f)}$ at 5° intervals from 0 to 60°. This completes the data necessary for the employment of equation (11-5-2). The concordance of calculated and observed results shown in Table (11-4-1) is excellent, since with very few exceptions the maximum deviation is of

[32] Scatchard and Prentiss have employed a power series in c of the form, $\mathfrak{S}_{(f)}\sqrt{c} + Bc + Cc^{3/2} + Dc^2 + \cdots$

[33] E. Hückel, *Physik. Z.*, **26**, 93 (1925).

[34] H. S. Harned, *J. Am. Chem. Soc.*, **48**, 326 (1926).

[35] H. S. Harned and G. Åkerlöf, *Physik. Z.*, **27**, 411 (1926).

[36] T. Shedlovsky and D. A. MacInnes, *J. Am. Chem. Soc.*, **58**, 1970 (1936).

TABLE (11-5-1). DATA FOR THE CALCULATION OF THE ACTIVITY COEFFICIENT OF HYDROCHLORIC ACID ACCORDING TO EQUATION (11-5-2),

$$\log \gamma_\pm = -\frac{S_{(f)}\sqrt{c}}{1 + A'\sqrt{c}} + \text{Ext.} + Bc + D'c^2 - \log(1 + 0.03604\,m)$$

where

$$\frac{c}{m} = a_1 - b_1 m$$

Valid from 0 to 4 M (0 to 25°); from 0 to 2 M (30 to 60°)

t	0	5	10	15	20	25	30	35	40	45	50	55	60
$S_{(f)}$	0.487	0.490	0.494	0.498	0.502	0.506	0.512	0.517	0.522	0.528	0.534	0.541	0.547
A'	1.395	1.398	1.402	1.405	1.409	1.414	1.418	1.423	1.428	1.433	1.439	1.445	1.450
B	.1390	.1371	.1351	.1332	.1312	.1292	.1272	.1253	.1233	.1214	.1194	.1175	.1155
D'	.0070	.0068	.0067	.0065	.0063	.0061	.0060	.0058	.0057	.0055	.0054	.0052	.0050
a_1	0.9998	1.0000	0.9995	0.9990	0.9982	0.9972	0.9958	0.9941	0.9922	0.9901	0.9879	0.9855	0.9832
$b_1 \times 10^2$	1.707	1.742	1.760	1.782	1.805	1.817	1.822	1.825	1.825	1.815	1.815	1.805	1.805

Values of Ext.

m	0°	25°	60°
0.001	−0.00009	−0.00010	−0.00011
.002	−.00015	−.00018	−.00019
.005	−.00027	−.00030	−.00036
.01	−.00041	−.00045	−.00053
.02	−.00055	−.00061	−.00072
.05	−.00071	−.00077	−.00091
.1	−.00075	−.00080	−.00094

m	0°	25°	60°
0.2	−0.00067	−0.00072	−0.00085
.5	−.00045	−.00049	−.00057
1	−.00027	−.00028	−.00032
1.5	−.00017	−.00019	−.00020
2	−.00012	−.00013	−.00015
3	−.00007	−.00007	−.00008
4	−.00004	−.00005	−.00006

the order of ± 0.001 in $\gamma_{\pm}$, which corresponds to ± 0.05 mv error. The results at the lower temperatures (0 and 5°, from 0.01 to 0.1 M) are not quite as good as those at the higher temperatures. In view of the agreement of the observed results with the results from freezing point measurements, we are not inclined to ascribe this discrepancy to experimental error only.

From a few general considerations of equation (11-5-2), it is possible to describe the behaviors of highly dissociated electrolytes. For 1-1 electrolytes in water, Ext., the contribution of the extended terms is very small, amounting at most to about one in the third decimal place of the activity coefficient, and neet not concern us for the present. A typical completely dissociated 1-1 electrolyte will possess a mean distance of approach, $\mathring{a}$, of about 4. If we consider a number of electrolytes with this value of $\mathring{a}$, the first term on the right of equation (11-5-2) will be the same for each of

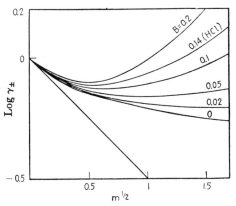

Fig. (11-5-1). Illustrating the magnitudes of the different terms of equation (11-5-1) at 25° ($\mathring{a}$ = 4)

them. On the other hand, the values of B may vary widely (from 0.01 to 0.2 for halides), and may be used to distinguish the individual characteristics of electrolytes in the more concentrated solutions. This behavior is very well illustrated in Fig. (11-5-1), in which are plotted the total contributions to log $\gamma_{\pm}$, due to the limiting law [Equation (3-4-9)], to the first term on the right of equation (11-5-2), and to the sum of this term and the linear term, Bc. It is to be noticed that the higher the value of B, the sharper the minimum characteristic of many strong electrolytes.

It is also a matter of importance to consider the order of magnitude of the terms in equation (11-5-2) in the case of an actual electrolyte such as hydrochloric acid. In very dilute solutions, the terms in c, or higher powers of c, are very small compared to the Debye and Hückel contribution, but even at 0.001 M, they are detectable. For example, at 0.002 M and 0° the first, second, and remaining terms contribute -0.02050, -0.00015, and $+.00028$, respectively. Thus, the terms, $Bc + \cdots$, are twice the magnitude of Ext. At $0.1\ M$, these terms contribute -0.10680, -0.00075, $+0.01394$, respectively, while at $4\ M$ the respective contributions are -0.25458, -0.00004, and $+0.6153$. We note that at $0.1\ M$, the term linear in c is about fifteen times the contribution of the extended terms.

(6) The Activity Coefficient of Hydrochloric Acid in Media Containing Organic Solvents

The characteristics of the variation of the activity coefficient with acid concentration, temperature, and dielectric constant (or solvent composition) may be illustrated strikingly by the extensive investigations of

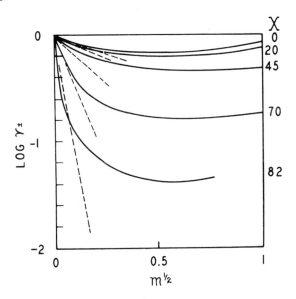

Fig. (11–6–1). Mean activity coefficient of hydrochloric acid in dioxane-water mixtures. $X =$ weight percent of dioxane.

dioxane-water mixtures [Data in Table (11-6-1A)]. In Fig. (11-6-1), all of the values of $\log \gamma_\pm$ at $25°$, and some of those, given in Table (11-6-1A) at 0 and $50°$, have been plotted against $m^{1/2}$ for mixtures containing 0, 20, 45, 70 and 82 per cent dioxane. The straight lines represent the plots of the limiting law of the interionic attraction theory at $25°$. Values of the limiting slopes, $\mathfrak{S}_{(f)}$, are given in [Table (11-3-1A)].

The most striking characteristic of these results is the general agreement of the observed values with those predicted by theory in dilute solutions. The limiting slope, $\mathfrak{S}_{(f)}$, in the 82 per cent dioxane solutions ($D = 9.53$; $\mathfrak{S}_{(f)} = 11.98$) is 23 times that in water ($D = 78.54$; $\mathfrak{S}_{(f)} = 0.506$), so that the term $\mathfrak{S}_{(f)} \sqrt{c}$, due to Coulombic forces is very large in the former. Thus, the theory predicts a change of a ten-fold variation in $\gamma_\pm$ between 0

and 0.1 N acid.   If no ionic association occurs, the observed plot lies above the limiting slope, an effect predicted by the theory which includes the mean distance of approach of the ions.   In media containing 0, 20, and 45 per cent, the results conform with this prediction, and at all concentrations lie above the limiting slope.   As the dielectric constant decreases, the observed plot in dilute solutions approaches the theoretical curve until, as illustrated by the 70 per cent dioxane mixtures, it superimposes at acid concentrations below 0.002 M.   In the 82 per cent dioxane mixtures, the plot of log $\gamma_\pm$ may lie below the limiting slope, as indicated by the results at 0.001 and 0.0015 M acid.   This behavior parallels that observed from conductance, shown in Fig. (11-1-1).   The activity coefficients at all concentrations and temperatures decrease with increasing temperature. Consequently, the relative partial molal heat content, $\bar{L}_2$, is always positive.

In the more concentrated solutions, all the plots in Fig. (11-6-1) show minima.   This indicates that the combined effect of restriction of Coulomb forces due to the sizes of the ions, and the concentrated solution effect, which increases the activity of the acid, is very large in the 82 per cent solutions.   For example, the limiting law predicts a value log $\gamma_\pm$ of -8.569 at 0.5 M, whereas the observed value is -1.2173.   If $\mathring{a}$ is taken to be 6, log $\gamma_\pm$ equals -1.697 which helps considerably to reduce this discrepancy.

The activity coefficient of hydrochloric acid has been determined in some methanol-, ethanol-, isopropanol-, and glycerol-water mixtures, and in pure methanol and ethanol solutions [Table (11-6-2A)].   The characteristics of this function in these media seems to be normal, and conforms to a pattern similar to that found in aqueous solutions.   The results may be computed from 0 to 1 M by the equation,

$$\log \gamma_\pm = -\frac{\mathbb{S}_{(f)}\sqrt{c}}{1 + A'\sqrt{c}} + B'm - \log\left(1 + 0.002 M_{XY}m\right) \qquad (11\text{-}6\text{-}1)$$

In the solutions of higher dielectric constant ($D \geq 60$), the accuracy of the computation is ± 0.002 in $\gamma_\pm$, if 4.3 is employed for $\mathring{a}$.   The values of B' for 10 and 20 per cent methanol-, 10 and 20 per cent ethanol-, and 10 per cent isopropanol-water mixtures suitable for the calculation are 0.1315, 0.1293, 0.1345, 0.1376, and 0.1373, respectively.   In pure methanol and ethanol solutions, other values of the parameters $\mathring{a}$ and B' are required.[37,38]

(7) THE RELATIVE PARTIAL MOLAL HEAT CONTENT OF HYDROCHLORIC ACID.   NUMERICAL METHODS FOR COMPUTING $\bar{L}_2$ FROM ELECTROMOTIVE FORCES

The calculation of heat data from electromotive force measurements is very sensitive to experimental errors.   If, for 1-1 electrolytes, the temperature coefficient of electromotive force be determined to within ± 0.001

[37] G. Scatchard, *J. Am. Chem. Soc.*, **47**, 2098 (1925).
[38] W. W. Lucasse, *Z. physik. Chem.*, **121**, 254 (1926).

mv/deg., then the error in $\bar{L}_2$ is ± 7 cal. The best results are not as accurate as this. If an accuracy of ± 30 cal. is obtained, the result may be considered very satisfactory. Since the best calorimetric values have a relative accuracy in $\bar{L}_2$ of ± 10 cal., they are better than those derived from electromotive force.

The customary procedure for evaluating $\bar{L}_2$ from electromotive forces requires measurements at many temperatures. The results are smoothed graphically against concentration, and values are obtained at convenient round concentrations. The constants of some suitable function, such as equation (10-5-12), are obtained from these results at each concentration by the method of least squares, or by plotting first order differences.[39] In the case of hydrochloric acid, Harned and Ehlers employed equations (10-5-12), and evaluated $\bar{L}_2$ by equation (10-5-15). They also computed $\bar{L}_2$ by the differentiation of the Debye and Hückel equation (11-5-2) in a manner similar to that by which equation (3-8-5) was derived. The resulting equation is

$$\bar{L}_2 = \frac{2 \mathfrak{s}_{(\bar{H})}\sqrt{2c}}{1 + A\sqrt{2c}} - \frac{2.3481 \times 10^7\, T^{1/2}}{(1 + A\sqrt{2c})^2\, D^{3/2}}\left[c\frac{\partial A}{\partial T} + \frac{A}{2}\frac{\partial c}{\partial T}\right]$$
$$- 4.6052 \times RT^2\left[(B + 2D'c)\frac{\partial c}{\partial T} + c\left(\frac{\partial B}{\partial T} + c\frac{\partial D'}{\partial T}\right)\right] \qquad (11\text{-}7\text{-}1)$$

Table (11-7-1) contains values of $\bar{L}_2$ at 10, 25, 40, and 60°, obtained by the two methods of calculation. Table (11-7-2) contains an equation and parameters by means of which $\bar{L}_2$ may be computed at all temperatures from 0 to 60°. The values obtained by the first method were smoothed by plotting against $m^{\frac{1}{2}}$. At all temperatures from 10 to 60°, the two series of results exhibit a maximum deviation of 40 cal. At 0°, the discrepancy is somewhat greater. The second method is more complicated, but yields more reliable results. The term, $\partial c/\partial T$, is readily computed from density data, $\partial B/\partial T$ and $\partial D'/\partial T$ are known from equations (11-5-3) and (11-5-4), and we have shown that $\mathring{a}$ may be considered independent of the temperature.

It is instructive to investigate the contribution to $\bar{L}_2$ due to the first, second, and final terms of equation (11-7-1). The first term, designated (1) in Fig. (11-7-1), is always positive, and contributes the most to $\bar{L}_2$ in the dilute solutions. The second term is negative in the case of hydrochloric acid, since $c\partial A/\partial T > A\partial c/2\partial T$. The sum of the first and second terms is indicated by (1) + (2) in the figure. Since both $\partial B/\partial T$ and $\partial D'/\partial T$ are negative in the case of hydrochloric acid, the third term is positive, and constitutes the major contribution to $\bar{L}_2$ in concentrated solutions. The curve designated (1) + (2) + (3) represents the right member of equation (11-7-1).

[39] H. S. Harned and L. F. Nims, *J. Am. Chem. Soc.*, **54**, 423 (1932).

TABLE (11-7-1). THE RELATIVE PARTIAL MOLAL HEAT CONTENT OF HYDROCHLORIC ACID. (1) COMPUTED BY EQUATION (10-5-15); (2) COMPUTED BY EQUATION (11-7-1)

m		10°	25°	40°	60°
0.001	(1)	16	22	27	39
.005	(1)	18	37	60	90
	(2)	34	45	59	79
.01	(1)	19	46	75	117
	(2)	48	63	81	108
.02	(1)	27	64	101	155
	(2)	64	·85	109	145
.05	(1)	74	120	169	238
	(2)	99	130	165	219
.1	(1)	101	160	221	300
	(2)	135	175	222	295
.2	(1)	172	238	307	414
	(2)	189	242	306	395
.5	(1)	319	402	488	614
	(2)	319	391	483	608
1.	(1)	502	626	748	944
	(2)	503	611	728	900
1.5	(1)	676	840	1000	1230
	(2)	698	831	975	1184
2.0	(1)	866	1040	1236	1506
	(2)	900	1059	1230	1470
3.0	(1)	1264	1510	....	....
	(2)	1302	1507	....	....
4.0	(1)	1696	1982	....	....
	(2)	1735	1991	....	....

TABLE (11-7-2)[a]. CONSTANTS OF THE EQUATION $\bar{L}_2 = \bar{L}_2(0°) + \alpha t + \beta t^2$ Valid from 0 to 60°[b]

m	$\bar{L}_2 (0°)$	α	β
0.005	28	0.70	0.003
.01	39	1.00	.003
.02	52	1.30	.004
.05	82	1.85	.006
.1	113	2.50	.008
.2	159	3.20	.009
.5	272	4.70	.011
1.	427	6.80	.015
1.5	615	8.20	.019
2.	791	10.00	.023
3.	1175	12.45	.031
4.	1604	14.70	.040

[a] G. Åkerlöf and J. W. Teare [*J. Am. Chem. Soc.*, **59**, 1855 (1937)] have evaluated L_2 from 0 to 50°, and from 3 to 16 M from electromotive force date.

[b] Values of $\bar{L}_2$ obtained from cells are in good agreement with the recent calorimetric results of J. M. Sturtevant [*J. Am. Chem. Soc.*, **62**, 584 (1940)]. Maximum deviation is 31 cal. at 3 M.

Further consideration of the variation of the B and D' parameters with temperature is helpful in summarizing the general behavior of $\bar{L}_2$ for different electrolytes in concentrated solutions. For hydrochloric acid, $\partial B/\partial T$ and $\partial D'/\partial T$ are both negative, and the third term is positive. It is sometimes found that these coefficients are positive, and the third term of equation (11-7-1) is negative. The curve designated by $(1) + (2) - (3)$ illustrates an electrolyte which possesses values of these coefficients equal in magnitude, but opposite in sign to the values for hydrochloric acid, and which possesses an $\mathring{a}$-value equal to 4.3. Curves $(1) + (2) + (3)$ and $(1) + (2) - (3)$ represent extreme cases. The values of $\bar{L}_2$ for most 1-1 electrolytes are between these curves. As an example, we have in-

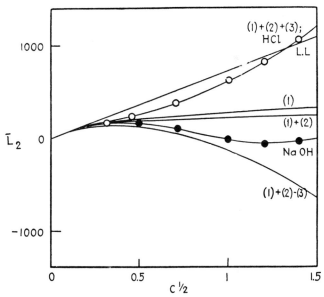

Fig. (11-7-1). Variation of $\bar{L}_2$ with $c^{1/2}$ at 25° according to equation (11-7-1). $\mathring{a} = 4$.

cluded on the graph the values of $\bar{L}_2$ for sodium hydroxide in aqueous solution. Since the $\mathring{a}$ value is approximately 3.5, the curve is slightly higher than the corresponding hydrochloric acid curve in dilute solution. The curve passes through a maximum when $m^{1/2}$ equals 0.4 ,indicating that $\partial B/\partial T$ is positive. Then, there appears a minimum when $m^{1/2}$ equals 1.2, which indicates that $\partial D'/\partial T$ is negative. This illustrates, in a general way, the behavior of $\bar{L}_2$ for 1-1 electrolytes in water.

The characteristic behavior of the relative partial molal heat content as a function of the dielectric constant is apparent from the graphs in Fig. (11-7-2). $\bar{L}_2$ at 25° in dioxane-water mixtures is plotted against $m^{1/2}$. The straight lines, drawn from the origin, represent values computed by the limiting theoretical equation, $\bar{L}_2 = \mathcal{S}_{(H)} \sqrt{c}$. Values of $\mathcal{S}_{(H)}$, computed by equation (3-8-6), are to be found in Table (11-7-1A). We note that there is an increasing tendency for the experimental curves to be higher than the limiting values in dilute solution as the dioxane content of the mixtures increases. All the curves have similar characteristics. After the first rapid rise in dilute solutions, their slopes decrease, and rise again as the solutions become more concentrated.

The uncertainty, due chiefly to the difficulties of extrapolation, increases with increasing dioxane concentration. In the 82 per cent dioxane mixture, the error may amount to several hundred calories. The accuracy relative to a given concentration is better than this, and is estimated to be of an order of 100 cal. Equations for the calculation of $\bar{L}_2$ in these mixtures are given in Table (11-7-2A).

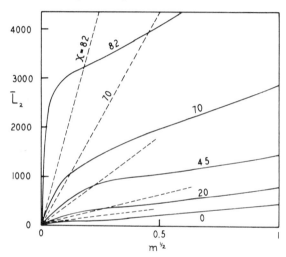

Fig. (11–7–2). Relative partial molal heat content of hydrochloric acid in dioxane-water mixtures at 25°. Straight lines represent limiting law. X = weight percent of dioxane.

(8) THE RELATIVE PARTIAL MOLAL HEAT CAPACITY OF HYDROCHLORIC ACID

The relative partial molal heat capacity may be determined by equation (10-5-17),

$$\bar{J}_2 = 46,120(c - c_0)T \qquad (11\text{-}8\text{-}1)$$

where c and c_0 are the constants of equations (10-5-12) and (10-5-13). Since the determination of this quantity involves the second differential coefficient of the original electromotive force data, high accuracy cannot be expected. On the other hand, values obtained by this method are of real interest for purposes of comparison with calorimetric determinations. In Table (11-8-1) values of $(c - c_0)$ are given from which $\bar{J}_2$ may be computed at temperatures from 0 to 60°. Harned and Ehlers also computed this quantity from values of $\bar{L}_2$, calculated by equation (11-7-1). The results at 25° are given in the table.

TABLE (11-8-1). THE RELATIVE PARTIAL MOLAL HEAT CAPACITY OF
HYDROCHLORIC AND HYDROBROMIC ACIDS

m	HCl $(c - c_0) \times 10^6$	HBr $(c - c_0) \times 10^6$	$\bar{J}_2(25°)$		
			HCl[1]	HCl[2]	HCl[3]
0.001	0.03	0.04	0.3	...	0.3
.005	.08	.10	.9	...	1.1
.01	.11	.15	1.2	...	1.5
.02	.15	.20	1.5	...	2.1
.05	.22	.26	2.1	...	3.1
.1	.28	.31	2.9	2.4	3.8
.2	.34	.35	3.7	3.4	4.8
.5	.43	...	5.3	5.3	6.0
1.	.58	...	7.5	7.5	8.1
1.5	.74	...	9.1	9.2	10.1
2.	.87	...	11.2	10.6	12.0
3.	1.14	...	14.1	13.0	15.8
4.	1.4	...	16.7	15.0	19.1

[1] Equation (11-7-1).
[2] Equation (11-8-1).
[3] Calorimetric Values. F. T. Gucker Jr., and K. H. Schminke, *J. Am. Chem. Soc.*,
54, 1358 (1932).

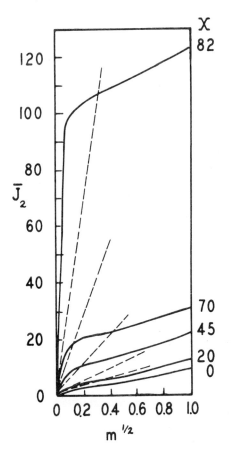

Fig. (11–8–1).
Relative partial molal heat capacity of hydrochloric acid in
dioxane-water mixtures at 25°.
Straight lines represent limiting
law. X = weight percent of
dioxane.

Gucker and Schminke[40] have determined this quantity in concentrated solutions at 25° by calorimetric measurements. Their results may be represented by the equation, $\bar{J}_2(25°) = 7.5m^{1/2}$, and values computed by this expression are included in the table. The agreement between these results and those derived from the electromotive forces is very good, considering the difficulties encountered in obtaining these quantities.

Values of $\bar{J}_2(25°)$ in water, and in the dioxane-water mixtures designated, are plotted against $m^{1/2}$ in Fig. (11-8-1). The straight lines represent the limiting equation (5-2-15), $\bar{J}_2(25°) = \mathbb{S}_{(c_p)}\sqrt{c}$, for the relative partial molal heat capacity, resulting from the interionic attraction theory. Relative to a given acid concentration, these results are valid to within a few calories (± 2). The extrapolation in the case of the 82 percent dioxane mixtures, represented by the dashed line, may be subject to a large error (~ 10 cal.). The rapid increase in this quantity in the media of low dielectric constant is illustrated strikingly by these results.

(9) The Transference Numbers of Hydrochloric Acid in Water and Dioxane-Water Mixtures from 0 to 50°

In Chapter (6), Section (6), the transference numbers of a few electrolytes determined by the very accurate moving boundary method, were discussed in relation to the limiting equation of the interionic attraction theory. In Chapter (10), Section (6), it was shown that the transference number of an electrolyte may be obtained from measurements of the electromotive forces of cells with and without liquid junctions by equation (10-6-12). This method has been employed by Harned and Dreby[41] in an extensive study of the cation transference number of hydrochloric acid in water, and in dioxane-water mixtures from 0 to 50°. The results constitute the most extensive survey of the transference number of an electrolyte as a function of its concentration, the temperature, and solvent composition.

The required data were obtained from the electromotive forces, $\mathbf{E}_T$ and $\mathbf{E}$, of the cells,

$$\text{Ag-AgCl} \mid \text{HCl } (m), \text{Dioxane } (X), \text{H}_2\text{O } (Y) \mid \text{HCl } (m_R), \text{Dioxane } (X),$$

$$\text{H}_2\text{O } (Y) \mid \text{AgCl-Ag};$$

and

$$\text{Ag-AgCl} \mid \text{HCl } (m), \text{Dioxane } (X), \text{H}_2\text{O } (Y) \mid \text{H}_2 \mid \text{HCl } (m_R), \text{Dioxane } (X),$$

$$\text{H}_2\text{O } (Y) \mid \text{AgCl-Ag};$$

with and without liquid junctions, respectively. The electromotive forces of the cells with liquid junction were measured by Harned and Dreby,

[40] F. T. Gucker Jr. and K. H. Schminke, *J. Am. Chem. Soc.*, **54**, 1358 (1932).

[41] H. S. Harned and E. C. Dreby, *J. Am. Chem. Soc.*, **61**, 3113 (1939).

and those of the cells without liquid junction were computed by them from the measurements of the cells

$$H_2 \mid HCl\ (m),\ Dioxane\ (X),\ H_2O\ (Y) \mid AgCl\text{-}Ag$$

discussed in section (3). HCl (m_R) denotes a fixed reference concentration.

According to equation (10-6-12), the cation transference number, T_+, is given by

$$T_+ = d\mathbf{E}_T/d\mathbf{E} \qquad (11\text{-}9\text{-}1)$$

T_+, at any particular concentration, is the slope of the plot of $\mathbf{E}_T$, the electromotive force of the cell with liquid junction, versus $\mathbf{E}$, the electromotive force of the cell without liquid junction. It is well known that the accuracy of this method, which requires the evaluation of a slope, is not as great as that of the moving boundary method, but it is reliable and rapid, and therefore suitable for an extensive investigation.

The actual evaluation of the slope of $\mathbf{E}$ against $\mathbf{E}_T$ may be carried out by expressing these quantities by empirical functions, and performing the differentiation,[42] or by a purely graphical method. Hamer,[43] and Harned and Dreby[41] found the following graphical method to be more satisfactory than any other method, graphical or analytical, which they could devise.

Since the range of values of $\mathbf{E}_T$ and $\mathbf{E}$ is large, plotting them directly causes the loss of significant figures, necessary for the accurate determination of the slope. Harned and Dreby used a method whereby values of $\mathbf{E}$ at equally spaced intervals of $\mathbf{E}_T$ were determined without the loss of significant figures. Furthermore, the results in this form made it possible to determine the slope analytically, and hence improve the accuracy.

Deviation functions, defined by the relations,

$$X \equiv \mathbf{E} + 2k \log m/m_R; \qquad X_T \equiv \mathbf{E}_T + 2k \log m/m_R \qquad (11\text{-}9\text{-}2)$$

gave values of X_T and X corresponding to the values of $\mathbf{E}_T$ and $\mathbf{E}$. These values of X_T and X covered a very small range, so that they could be plotted very accurately with no loss of significant figures. Values of X_T were interpolated graphically to the round concentrations at which values of X were known. These results were then used to make a plot of $X - X_T$ versus X. It is to be noted that $X - X_T$ is simply $\mathbf{E} - \mathbf{E}_T$. From this graph, $X - X_T$ was read off for values of X_T corresponding to values of $\mathbf{E}_T$ spaced at equal intervals of 0.01 v. The latter were obtained from a plot of $\mathbf{E}_T$ against X_T. Adding together the appropriate values of $X - X_T$ and $\mathbf{E}_T$ gave the desired results, namely, $\mathbf{E}$ corresponding to $\mathbf{E}_T$, spaced at intervals of 0.01 v. The data were then in a form for the analytical determination of the slope.

[41] D. A. MacInnes and J. A. Beattie, *J. Am. Chem. Soc.*, **42**, 1117 (1920).
[43] W. J. Hamer, *J. Am. Chem. Soc.*, **57**, 662 (1935).

A derivative function obtained by Rutledge[44] was employed for the determination. It is of the form

$$\frac{dE}{dE_r} = f(E) = \frac{1}{12h}(C_{-2}E_{-2} + C_{-1}E_{-1} + C_0E_0 + C_1E_1 + C_2E_2) \quad (11\text{-}9\text{-}3)$$

where dE/dE_r is the slope at a value, E, of the dependent variable; h is the magnitude of the chosen interval in the independent variable; E_{-2}, E_{-1}, etc., are consecutive values of the dependent variable; and C_{-2}, C_{-1}, etc.,

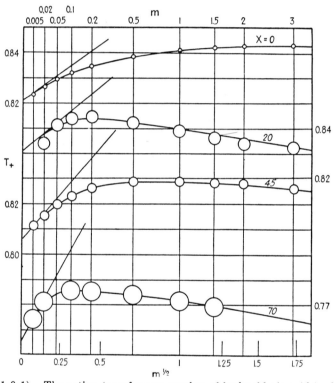

Fig. (11-9-1). The cation transference number of hydrochloric acid in dioxane-water mixtures at 25°. Gross error equals diameter of circles. $X = \%$ dioxane by weight. Limiting theoretical law is represented by the straight lines from the origin of each plot.

are constants. There are three sets of constants, the choice of any one being dependent on whether the slope is to be determined at E_{-1}, E_0, or E_1. Except at the extremes, the values of the slope were determined by taking the average of the results obtained by placing the Rutledge formula in the three possible positions.

T_+ obtained in this manner were plotted against E_T, and from this graph, smoothed values of T_+ at round acid concentrations were obtained.

[44] G. Rutledge, *J. Math. Phys. M. I. T.*, **8**, 1 (1929); *Phys. Rev.*, **40**, 262 (1932).

From these results, the limiting value of the transference number was determined by the method of Longsworth,[45] described in Chapter (6), Section (7). This consists in plotting the function

$$T_+^{0'} = \frac{T_+\Lambda' + 1/2\beta^*\sqrt{c}}{\Lambda' + \beta^*\sqrt{c}} \qquad (11\text{-}9\text{-}4)$$

where

$$\Lambda' = \Lambda^0 - (\alpha^*\Lambda^0 + \beta^*)\sqrt{c} \qquad (11\text{-}9\text{-}5)$$

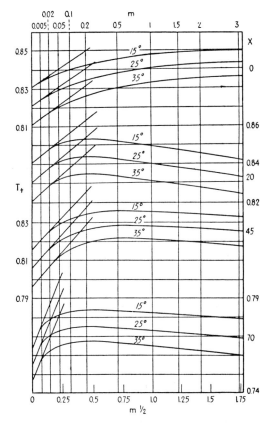

Fig. (11-9-2)

The cation transference number of hydrochloric acid at 15°, 25°, and 35° in dioxane-water mixtures. Straight lines represent theoretical limiting law. X = weight percent of dioxane.

against the acid concentration, c, and extrapolating to zero concentration. The actual plots of Harned and Dreby were straight lines at concentrations from 0.01 to $0.1N$,[46] and were satisfactory for extrapolation. The values of T_+ at concentrations less than $0.01N$ were more erratic. This behavior is due to the difficulty of obtaining slopes at the extreme ends of the curve.

From a consideration of the Rutledge derivative function, it can be shown

[45] L. G. Longsworth, *J. Am. Chem. Soc.*, **54**, 2741 (1932).

[46] In the case of the 20 percent dioxane solution, this plot was straight from 0.03 to $0.1N$. The results below $0.03N$ were erratic.

that an error of 0.01 mv. in $\mathbf{E}$, or $\mathbf{E}_T$, causes an error of 0.001 in T_+. From the mean deviations of the observed electromotive forces, or from the average deviations of the observed points from the smoothed graphs, the average error in T_+ may be estimated. A representation of extent of error is contained in Fig. (11-9-1). T_+ at 25° is plotted for pure water, and 20, 45 and 70 percent dioxane-water mixtures. The estimated gross error is given by the diameters of the circles, and is 0.002 in water, and 0.005, 0.004 and 0.008 for the three dioxane-water mixtures, respectively.

The final smoothed values of T_+^0 and T_+ in these solvents and at 5° intervals from 0 to 50° are contained in Table (11-9-1A), and plots of this quantity at 15, 25, and 35° are shown in Fig. (11-9-2). The straight

TABLE (11-9-1). T_+ OF HYDROCHLORIC ACID FROM ELECTROMOTIVE FORCES AND BY
THE MOVING BOUNDARY METHOD AT 25°

c	0.005	0.01	0.02	0.05	0.100
T_+ (M.B.)	0.8239	0.8251	0.8266	0.8292	0.8314
T_+ (E.M.F.)	(.824)	(.825)	(.827)	(.830)	(.830)

lines represent values calculated by the Onsager limiting equation for the transference number,

$$T_+ = \mathcal{S}_{(T)}\sqrt{c} = \frac{(2T_+^0 - 1)\beta^*}{2\Lambda^0}\sqrt{d_0}\sqrt{m} \qquad (11\text{-}9\text{-}6)$$

Values of $\mathcal{S}_{(T)}$ are given at the bottom of Table (11-9-1A). The results conform with theory since all the curves converge towards the predicted slopes as the concentration of electrolyte decreases.

According to Fig. (11-9-1), the best results were obtained with solutions of the acid in pure water. That the error is no greater than one or two in the third decimal place is shown in Table (11-9-1), in which the values obtained by Longsworth, by the more accurate moving boundary method, are compared with those obtained by Harned and Dreby from electromotive forces. In this, the most favorable case, the agreement is good, and the deviations are of the order of magnitude predicted from the mean deviations of the original electromotive forces.

Harned and Dreby also measured the electromotive forces of the cells with liquid junction in 82 percent dioxane-water mixtures. The results were less accurate than those in the mixtures of lower dioxane content, particularly when the cells contained acid at concentrations less than 0.05M. Since no transference number data are available in media of dielectric constant as low as these ($D(25°) = 9.57$), the results have a value, and are included in Table (11-9-1A).

(10) ADDITIONAL CONSIDERATIONS AND COMPARISONS

From electromotive forces measurements of some six hundred cells over a temperature range from 0° to 90° and at concentrations from 0.001 to 0.1 molal, Bates and Bower[47] have computed the thermodynamic properties of hydrochloric acid. The standard potentials obtained from these data are given in Table (11-2-2) and the derived thermodynamic quantities at some of the temperatures are recorded in Table (11-10-1).

Comparison of these results with those in Tables (11-4-1), (11-4-1A), (11-7-1) and (11-8-1) reveals surprisingly good agreement for $\bar{L}_2$ and $\bar{J}_2$. The maximum difference in activity coefficient between these two sets of values occurs at 60° and is 0.6 per cent which corresponds to a difference of 0.3 mv. A thorough examination of the data by different investigators has been made by Bates and Bower but the causes of the discrepancies are still unknown.[48] At 25°, the present state of the subject is well illustrated

TABLE (11-10-1). THERMODYNAMIC PROPERTIES OF HYDROCHLORIC ACID
ACCORDING TO BATES AND BOWER
Activity Coefficients

m	0°	20°	60°	90°
0.001	0.9670	0.9654	0.9631	0.961
.002	.9540	.9524	.9493	.946
.005	.9313	.9289	.9249	.920
.01	.9081	.9054	.9000	.893
.02	.8805	.8766	.8700	.860
.05	.8381	.8331	.8227	.810
.1	.8067	.8000	.7828	.765

Relative Partial Molal Heat Content, $\bar{L}_2$ (Cals.)

.001	19	23	31	37
.002	20	29	45	63
.005	30	42	63	86
.01	35	54	90	130
.02	45	72	122	180
.05	72	113	234	269
.1	111	177	295	400

Relative Partial Molal Heat Capacity, $\bar{J}_2$

.001	0.17	0.19	0.24	0.29
.002	.32	.41	.53	.67
.005	.43	.53	.69	.84
.01	.69	.88	1.17	1.46
.02	.96	1.25	1.7	2.1
.05	1.46	1.87	2.6	3.1
.1	2.35	3.0	4.1	5.1

[47] R. G. Bates and V. E. Bower, J. Research, N.B.S., **53**, 283 (1954).

[48] See also G. J. Janz and H. Taniguchi, Chem. Rev., **53**, 397 (1953), for a comprehensive review of the methods of preparation and reproducibility of the silver-silver halide electrodes.

by Table (11-10-2) prepared by Bates and Bower in which the activity coefficients obtained by different investigators are recorded.

TABLE (11-10-2). ACTIVITY COEFFICIENT OF HYDROCHLORIC ACID AT 25°

m	(1)	(2)	(3)	(4)	(5)
0.001	0.9656	0.9646	0.9653	0.9650	0.9650
.002	.9521	.9516	.9525	.9519	.9520
.005	.9285	.9285	.9287	.9280	.9283
.01	.9048	.9044	.9049	.9040	.9045
.02	.8755	.8755	.8757	.8747	.8753
.05	.8304	.8303	.8301	.8296	.8308
.1	.7964	.7969	.7938	.7958	.7967

(1) Harned and Owen from the data of Harned and Ehlers.
(2) Bates and Bowers recalculation of the data of Harned and Ehlers.
(3) Shedlovsky[49] from transference numbers and the electromotive forces of cells with liquid junction.
(4) Hills and Ives[50] from electromotive forces of the hydrogen-calomel cells.
(5) Bates and Bowers.

The characteristics of a number of electrodes in aqueous solutions at temperatures above 100° have been investigated by Lietski and his colleagues[51, 52] and by Choudbury and Bonilla.[53] They found that the silver-silver chloride and silver-silver sulphate electrodes were the more satisfactory at the higher temperatures and pressures. As an illustration, Lietzke estimated from the measurements of Choudbury and Bonilla that the cells

$$H_2 \text{ (P atms.)} \mid HCl \text{ } (0.01689M) \mid AgCl\text{-}Ag$$

at pressures of 7.8 and 18 atmospheres functioned satisfactorily from 25 to 200°. Due to hydrolysis, it was found that the mercury-mercurous salt electrodes were much less promising.

[49] Shedlovsky, *J. Am. Chem. Soc.*, **72**, 3680 (1950).

[50] G. J. Hills and D. J. G. Ives, *J. Chem. Soc.*, 305–323 (1951); *Nature*, **163**, 997 (1949).

[51] M. H. Lietzke and R. W. Stoughton, J. Am. Chem. Soc., **75**, 5226 (1953). Silver-silver sulphate and mercury-mercurous sulphate electrodes. M. H. Lietzke and J. V. Vaughan, *Ibid.*, **77**, 876 (1955): Silver-silver chloride and mercury-mercurous chloride electrodes.

[52] M. H. Lietzke, *Ibid*, **77**, 1344 (1955). The hydrogen-silver chloride cell.

[53] R. N. Choudbury and C. F. Bonilla, MSc. Thesis, by R. N. Choudbury, Columbia University, May (1952).

Chapter (12)

Strong 1-1 Electrolytes in Aqueous Solution

In Chapter (9), the important and extensive determinations of freezing point lowerings of 1-1 electrolytes have been described, and in Chapter (8), the recent very valuable determinations of the heat data of these solutions have been discussed. In the present survey, a more general discussion of the results obtained from measurements of the thermodynamic properties of these solutions will be given.

The importance of a systematic study of the activity coefficients of electrolytes was first emphasized by Lewis.[1] By the use of an empirical extrapolation function, containing two constants, Lewis and Linhart,[2] and Lewis and Randall[3] made the first systematic attempt to compute activity coefficients from the existing data. A similar attempt was made by Harned,[4] who employed an empirical equation for $\gamma_{\pm}$ which contained three empirical constants. These investigations, made before the limiting law of the Debye and Hückel theory was known, were subject to large errors in extrapolation, and the activity coefficients computed at that time had an accuracy not greater than ± 0.01.

When the limiting law of Debye and Hückel was used, rapid advances were made in improving the accuracy of the extrapolations. Hückel,[5] Scatchard,[6] Harned[7] and Randall and Young,[8] by employing the limiting law, or extended forms of the Debye and Hückel theory, were able to improve considerably the accuracy of the extrapolations. A general survey of the results obtained before 1929 was made by Harned.[9] More recently, knowledge of activity and osmotic coefficients has been greatly increased by the vapor pressure measurements of Robinson and Stokes.[9a]

In the following discussion, a summary based on the available data on 1-1 electrolytes will be given. Further, the heat data in relation to activity coefficients will be discussed. Sodium and potassium chlorides will be

[1] G. N. Lewis, *J. Am. Chem. Soc.*, **34**, 1631 (1912).

[2] G. N. Lewis and G. A. Linhart, *J. Am. Chem. Soc.*, **41**, 1951 (1919).

[3] G. N. Lewis and M. Randall, *Ibid.*, **43**, 1112 (1921). See also "Thermodynamics," McGraw-Hill Book Company, New York (1923).

[4] H. S. Harned, *J. Am. Chem. Soc.*, **42**, 1808 (1920); **44**, 252 (1922). See also H. S. Harned, H. S. Taylor, "Treatise on Physical Chemistry," 1st Edition, p. 744-747, Van Nostrand and Company, New York, (1924).

[5] E. Hückel, *Physik. Z.*, **26**, 93 (1925).

[6] G. Scatchard, *J. Am. Chem. Soc.*, **47**, 648 (1925); **47**, 2098 (1925).

[7] H. S. Harned, *Ibid.*, **48**, 326 (1926).

[8] M. Randall and L. E. Young, *Ibid.*, **50**, 989 (1928).

[9a] R. A. Robinson and R. H. Stokes, "Electrolyte Solutions", Butterworths Scientific Publications, London (1955).

treated first, since they have been investigated most thoroughly, both at 25° and at other temperatures. The activity coefficients of these electrolytes may then be employed as reference for the computation of the activity coefficients of other electrolytes by the isopiestic vapor pressure method [Section (3)]. Sections (5) to (8) and Section (12) include a survey of the activity coefficients of 1-1 electrolytes in relation to the theory of Debye and Hückel, its modifications, and extensions to concentrated solutions.

In addition, Section (10) is devoted to the "salting effects" of electrolytes upon neutral molecules, and Section (11) to the surface tension of ionic solutions. Both of these phenomena are discussed in relation to the theories developed in Chapter (3), Sections (10) and (11).

(1) THE THERMODYNAMICS OF SODIUM CHLORIDE SOLUTIONS FROM ELECTROMOTIVE FORCE AND CALORIMETRIC DATA

(a) The Activity Coefficient in Dilute Solutions at 25°

Extensive measurements of electromotive forces of cells without liquid junction containing 1-1 halides and hydroxides have been made.[10] It was found that the flowing amalgam electrodes behaved very well in solutions at concentrations higher than $0.05M$. At lower concentrations, these electrodes exhibit erratic behaviors.

In order to avoid this difficulty, Brown and MacInnes[11] have measured very carefully the cell

$$\text{Ag-AgCl} \mid \text{NaCl} (c_1) \mid \text{NaCl} (c_2) \mid \text{AgCl-Ag}$$

It has been shown [Equation (10-6-14)] that the electromotive force of this cell is given by

$$\mathbf{E} = -\frac{2RT}{\mathbf{F}} \int_{\mathrm{I}}^{\mathrm{II}} T_+ \, d \ln a_{\pm} \tag{12-1-1}$$

where the integration extends from the concentration of the solution at electrode (I) to the solution at electrode (II). Due to the very accurate knowledge of transference numbers obtained by MacInnes and Longsworth [Chapter (6)], and to the fact that the above cells may be measured

[10] D. A. MacInnes and K. Parker, *J. Am. Chem. Soc.*, **37**, 1445 (1915); D. A. MacInnes and J. A. Beattie, *Ibid.*, **42**, 1117 (1920); M. Knobel, *Ibid.*, **45**, 70 (1923); H. S. Harned and F. E. Swindells, *Ibid.*, **48**, 126 (1926); H. S. Harned, *Ibid.*, **47**, 676 (1925); **51**, 416 (1929); H. S. Harned and S. M. Douglas, *Ibid.*, **48**, 3095 (1926); H. S. Harned and O. E. Schupp Jr., *Ibid.*, **52**, 3886 (1930); H. S. Harned and L. F. Nims, *Ibid.*, **54**, 423 (1932); H. S. Harned and J. C. Hecker, *Ibid.*, **55**, 4838 (1933); H. S. Harned and M. A. Cook, *Ibid.*, **59**, 497 (1937); H. S. Harned and C. C. Crawford, *Ibid.*, **59**, 1903 (1937); G. Åkerlöf and G. Kegeles, *Ibid.*, **62**, 620 (1940).

[11] A. S. Brown and D. A. MacInnes, *J. Am. Chem. Soc.*, **57**, 1356 (1935); similar measurements from 15 to 45° have been made by G. J. Janz and A. R. Gordon, *Ibid.*, **65**, 218 (1943). Revised values are given by Shedlovsky, *Ibid.*, **72**, 3680 (1950).

at low concentrations, a good extrapolation can be made, and accurate activity coefficients obtained.

In differential form, equation (12-1-1) at 25° becomes

$$dE = -0.1183T_+ (d\log c + d\log y_\pm) \tag{12-1-2}$$

Instead of expressing T_+ as a function of c and performing the integration, a simpler method due to Longsworth was employed. The transference number at any concentration is given by

$$T_+ \equiv T_R + \Delta T_+ \tag{12-1-3}$$

where T_R is its value at a reference concentration, in this case, $0.1N$. By substituting this value of T_+ in (12-1-2), rearranging the terms and integrating, we obtain

$$-\Delta \log y_\pm \equiv \log y_\pm - \log y_R = -\frac{E}{0.1183T_R} - \log \frac{c}{c_R}$$
$$\tag{12-1-4}$$
$$-\frac{1}{T_R}\int_{c_R}^{c} \Delta T_+ \, d\log c - \frac{1}{T_R}\int_{y_R}^{y_\pm} \Delta T_+ \, d\log y_\pm$$

The first two terms on the right of this equation may be evaluated immediately from the experimental data. The third term may be obtained by graphical integration. The last term, which is relatively small, was obtained by graphical integration, using preliminary values of $\Delta \log y_\pm$ obtained from the first three terms. The preliminary values of $\Delta \log y_\pm$ were then corrected, and the process repeated until further approximations were found unnecessary. Since $y_\pm$ equals unity at infinite dilution, we may write

$$\log y_\pm = C' - \Delta\log y_\pm \tag{12-1-5}$$

where C' is the constant, $\log y_R$. Substituting for $\log y_\pm$ the value given for $\log f_\pm$ in equation (5-2-8), and rearranging terms, we obtain

$$\Delta \log y_\pm - S_{(f)}\sqrt{c} = C' + A'(C' - \Delta\log y_\pm)\sqrt{c} \tag{12-1-6}$$

By plotting the left-hand member of this equation against $(C' - \Delta\log y_\pm)\sqrt{c}$, the constants C' and A' can be evaluated after a few approximations. By this procedure Brown and MacInnes obtained -0.1081 and -0.1088 for $\log y_\pm$ and $\log \gamma_\pm$, respectively, at the concentration $0.1M$. Their values of $y_\pm$ and $\gamma_\pm$ are given in Table (12-1-1). The last column contains values of $y_\pm$ computed by equation (10-4-8).

(b) The Relative Partial Molal Heat Content of Sodium Chloride in Water

In Table (8-2-2A) we have given values of $\bar{L}_2$ of sodium chloride in aqueous solution at 25°. These data have been supplemented by Gulbransen and Robinson[12] who reported calorimetric measurements at 10, 15, 20, and 25°. Their results are given in Table (12-1-2).

[12] E. A. Gulbransen and A. L. Robinson, *J. Am. Chem. Soc.*, **56**, 2637 (1934).

(c) The Activity Coefficient of 0.1M Sodium Chloride from 0 to 100°

From the value of 0.7784 for $\gamma_\pm$ at $0.1M$ and 25°, and the values of $\bar{L}_2$ at this concentration, given in Table (12-1-2), $\gamma_{0.1}$ may be calculated at other temperatures by means of the equation

$$\frac{2\partial \ln \gamma_{0.1}}{\partial T} = -\frac{\bar{L}_{2(0.1)}}{RT^2} \tag{3-8-1}$$

TABLE (12-1-1).   ACTIVITY COEFFICIENT OF SODIUM CHLORIDE AT 25°

m	$y_\pm$	$\gamma_\pm$	$y_\pm$ (calc.)[1]
.005	0.9283	0.9283	0.9281
.007	.9171	.9171	.9169
.01	.9034	.9032	.9034
.02	.8726	.8724	.8724
.03	.8513	.8509	.8515
.04	.8354	.8348	.8354
.05	.8221	.8215	.8224
.06	.8119	.8111	.8115
.08	.7940	.7927	.7938
.1	.7796	.7784	.7796

[1] Calculated by equation in (10-4-8); $\mathring{a} = 4$; $B = 0.047$.

TABLE (12-1-2).   THE RELATIVE PARTIAL MOLAL HEAT CONTENT OF SODIUM CHLORIDE FROM HEATS OF DILUTION†

$$\bar{L}_2 \left(\frac{\text{cal}}{\text{mol}}\right)$$

m	10°	15°	20°	25°
0.0001	3.0	4.7	5.3	6.3
.0005	8.3	12.0	13.1	14.8
.001	11.5	16.5	17.9	20.1
.005	25.6	35.8	38.1	42.2
.01	34.8	46.0	51.0	55.8
.05	43.2	65.0	76.3	93.7
.1	30.2	57.7	76.6	99.6
.2	−20.	9.4	54.2	85.0
.404	−130.	−89.9	−19.4	30.0
.816	......	......	−169.7	−123.3

† These are the values originally reported by Gulbransen and Robinson. The results at 25° differ slightly from those in Table (8-2-2A).

$\bar{L}_{2(0.1)}$ is given as a function of the temperature by the equation

$$\bar{L}_{2(0.1)} = -1277 + 4.62T \tag{12-1-7}$$

Upon substitution of $\bar{L}_{2(0.1)}$ in equation (3-8-1), integration, and evaluation of the integration constant by employing the value of 0.7784 for $\gamma_{0.1}$ at 25°, we obtain

$$-\log \gamma_{0.1} = \frac{139.56}{T} + 1.1625 \log T - 3.2358 \tag{12-1-8}$$

This should yield an accurate value of $\gamma_{0.1}$ over a wide temperature range, provided that the relative partial heat capacity ($= 4.62$) changes not at all or little with temperature. Values of $\gamma_{0.1}$ computed in this manner at various temperatures are given in Table (12-1-3).

Harned and Nims[13] have measured the cells without liquid junction

$$\text{Ag-AgCl} \mid \text{NaCl } (m) \mid \text{Na}_x \text{ Hg} \mid \text{NaCl } (0.1) \mid \text{AgCl-Ag}$$

at 5° intervals from 0 to 40°. These flowing amalgam cells are not reliable at concentrations below $0.05M$, and, therefore, the extrapolation must be made from the results at higher concentrations. To this end the Debye and Hückel functions [Equations (10-4-8) or (10-4-9)] may be used. Experience has shown that a good extrapolation can be effected by this method if the results from 0.1 to $1M$ are employed. If these equations are

TABLE (12-1-3). $\gamma_{0.1}$ OF SODIUM CHLORIDE BY INDEPENDENT METHODS

t	Eq. (12-1-8)†	Eq. (10-4-9)	B.P
0	0.7809	0.781	. . . . .
5	.7809	.782	. . . . .
10	.7807	.782	. . . . .
15	.7802	.7815	. . . . .
20	.7793	.781	. . . . .
25	.7784	.779	. . . . .
30	.7773	.776	. . . . .
35	.7757	.774	. . . . .
40	.7743	.773	. . . . .
50	.770	. . . . .	. . . . .
60	.766	. . . . .	0.766
70	.761	. . . . .	.762
80	.756	. . . . .	.757
90	.751	. . . . .	.752
100	.745	. . . . .	.746

† H. S. Harned, *J. Franklin Inst.*, **225**, 623 (1938); E. R. Smith and J. K. Taylor, *Bur. Standards J. Res.*, **25**, 731 (1940).

applied over a greater concentration range (0.1 to $3M$), somewhat low values of $\mathring{a}$ and $\gamma_{\pm}$ will be obtained. In the third column of Table (12-1-3) are given the results obtained from these data by Harned and Cook.[14] The value of the mean distance of approach of the ions was found to be 4.0 ± 0.1 Å at all temperatures. The agreement of these values of $\gamma_{0.1}$ with those in the first column is satisfactory.

By employing equation (10-4-9), in combination with the equations for the osmotic coefficient obtained from elevation of the boiling point, Smith[15] obtained the values in the last column of Table (12-1-3). He also employed 4.0 for the mean distance of approach of the ions. The agreement with the results obtained by equation (12-1-8) is very satisfactory.

[13] H. S. Harned and L. F. Nims, *J. Am. Chem. Soc.*, **54**, 423 (1932).

[14] H. S. Harned and M. A. Cook, *J. Am. Chem. Soc.*, **61**, 495 (1939).

[15] R. P. Smith, *J. Am. Chem. Soc.*, **61**, 500 (1939).

The use of cells with liquid junctions combined with transference number experiments has been extended by Gordon[15a] and his colleagues to evaluate the activity coefficients of some uniunivalent electrolytes and calcium chloride in dilute solutions from 15 to 45°. The results agree very closely at $0.1M$ concentration with those obtained from cells without liquid junctions which are listed in Table (13-1-2A). These results may be computed by means of the data compiled in Table (12-1-3a) by the equation

$$\log \gamma_\pm = - \frac{\mathbb{S}_{(f)} \sqrt{d_0} \sqrt{m}}{1 + A' \sqrt{m}} + Bm \tag{12-1-9}$$

TABLE (12-1-3a). PARAMETERS OF EQUATION (12-1-9) FOR THE COMPUTATION OF ACTIVITY COEFFICIENTS. VALIDITY RANGE = 0 TO $0.1M$.

	15°	25°	35°	45°
1. *Sodium Chloride*; $d = 4.12$*				
$\mathbb{S}_{(f)} \sqrt{d_0}$	0.4966	0.5049	0.5141	0.5254
A'	1.343	1.350	1.357	1.364
B	0.022	0.031	0.034	0.033
2. *Potassium Chloride*; $d = 3.97$†				
A'	1.300	1.307	1.314	1.321
B	-0.014_0	-0.007_5	-0.005_5	-0.004_0
3. *Calcium Chloride*; $d = 4.575$ Å‡				
$\mathbb{S}_{(f)} \sqrt{d_0}$	1.7321	1.7615	1.7925	
A'	2.588	2.600	2.613	
B	0.198	0.203	0.185	
4. *Potassium Bromide*§				

$$t = 25°; \; d = 4.3 \text{ Å}; \; \mathbb{S}_{(f)} \sqrt{d_0} = 0.5049; \; A' = 1.420$$
$$B = -0.014$$

* G. J. Janz and A. R. Gordon, *J. Am. Chem. Soc.*, **65**, 218 (1943). Transference numbers by R. W. Allgood and A. R. Gordon, *J. Chem. Phys.*, **10**, 124 (1942).

† W. J. Hornibrook, G. J. Janz and A. R. Gordon, *J. Am. Chem. Soc.*, **64**, 513 (1942). Transference numbers by R. W. Allgood, D. J. LeRoy and A. R. Gordon, *J. Chem. Phys.*, **8**, 418 (1940).

‡ H. G. McLeod and A. R. Gordon, *J. Am. Chem. Soc.*, **68**, 58 (1946); Transference numbers by A. G. Keenan, H. G. McLeod and A. R. Gordon, *J. Chem. Phys.*, **13**, 466 (1945).

§ E. A. MacWilliam and A. R. Gordon, *J. Am. Chem. Soc.*, **65**, 984 (1943); Transference numbers by A. G. Keenan and A. R. Gordon, *J. Chem. Phys.*, **11**, 172 (1943).

Butler and Gordon have used the same method to make the first accurate determination of an activity coefficient of a salt in dilute organic solvent-water mixtures. They determined $y_\pm$ of sodium chloride in 50 mole percent methanol-water mixtures.

[15a] J. P. Butler and A. R. Gordon, *J. Am. Chem. Soc.*, **70**, 2276 (1948).

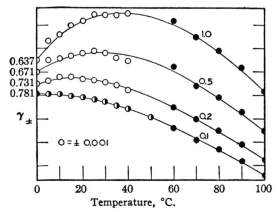

Fig. (12-1-1). The mean activity coefficient of sodium chloride in 0.1, 0.2, 0.5 and 1M solutions as a function of temperature. ◑, Calculated by equation (12-1-8); ○, electromotive force; ●, boiling point. Diameter of circles equals 0.002.

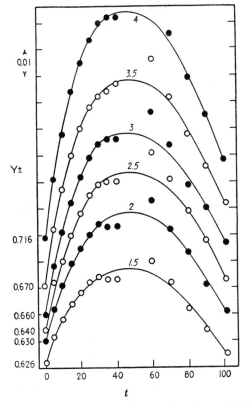

Fig. (12-1-2). The mean activity coefficient of sodium chloride from 1.5 to 4 molal concentration as a function of temperature. 0 to 40°, Electromotive force; 60 to 100°, Boiling point. Diameter of circles equals 0.002.

In Table (12-1-1A), simple equations and their constants for computing c from m are given for solutions of 1-1 electrolytes. These will be found useful in certain theoretical computations.

(d) The Osmotic and Activity Coefficients of Sodium Chloride from 0 to 100°

From the electromotive force data,[16] and boiling point data,[17, 18] the activity coefficient and osmotic coefficient of sodium chloride from 0 to 100° and from 0.1 to 4M have been computed. The activity coefficient

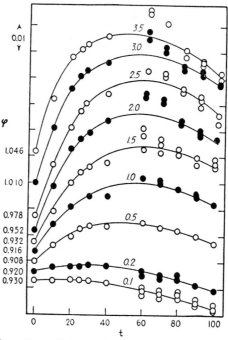

Fig. (12-1-3). Osmotic coefficients of sodium chloride solutions from 0.1 to 3.5M. 0 to 40°, Electromotive force; 60 to 100°, Boiling point. Diameter of circles equals 0.002.

is plotted against the temperature in Figs. (12-1-1) and (12-1-2), respectively. Similar plots for the osmotic coefficients are given in Fig. (12-1-3). The results from 0 to 40° were obtained from the electromotive forces, and those from 60 to 100° from the boiling points. We note that the results indicate a small error in both types of measurement. At 35 and 40, the values of $\gamma_\pm$ from the electromotive force measurements appear to be too low in some cases, while at 60 and 70° the values obtained by

[16] H. S. Harned and L. F. Nims, *J. Am. Chem. Soc.*, **54**, 423 (1932).

[17] R. P. Smith, *Ibid.*, **61**, 497 (1939).

[18] R. P. Smith and D. S. Hirtle, *Ibid.*, **61**, 1123 (1939). Similar results for potassium bromide from 60 to 100° have been obtained by G. C. Johnson and R. P. Smith, *Ibid.*, **63**, 1351 (1941). See Table (12-2-5A).

the boiling point method appear somewhat too high. This is most apparent for the results at 60°, and at high concentrations (1.5 to 4M). The same remarks apply to the osmotic coefficients. Values of $\gamma_\pm$ are given in Table (12-1-2A). These results were smoothed in the range of 35 to 70° according to the plots shown in the figures so that the graphs may be reproduced. The diameter of the circles in these plots equals 0.002 in $\gamma_\pm$, which corresponds to about 0.15 mv, or 0.0003° in the boiling point rise. At 40° the maximum deviation of the observed results from the curve is 0.004, or about 0.3 mv.

(e) **Relative Partial Molal Heat Content and Heat Capacity of Sodium Chloride**

The best estimate of the relative partial molal heat content from the electromotive force and boiling point measurements has been made by Smith and Hirtle.[18] Equation (3-8-1) may be written in the form

$$\frac{\partial \ln \gamma_\pm}{\partial(1/T)} = \frac{\bar{L}_2}{2R} \qquad (3\text{-}8\text{-}1)$$

from which it is apparent that $\bar{L}_2$ may be determined from the slopes of the tangents to the curves of $\ln \gamma_\pm$ plotted against $1/T$. The results at 0° are practically the same as those determined from the electromotive force measurements by Harned and Cook. The results at 100° are not so reliable since the slope at the end of the curve is not well defined. Fig. (12-1-4) contains the plots of these results together with the calorimetric results of Robinson,[19] Gulbransen and Robinson[20] and Rossini.[21] These data are given in (12-1-3A). The values obtained from the electromotive forces and boiling points are represented in the figure by circles, and the calorimetric results by dots. The dotted line was obtained from Rossini's values at 18°. The agreement between the results derived by these entirely independent methods is very satisfactory from 10 to 25°. At the higher temperatures no calorimetric data are available for comparison. The results at the higher temperatures are only an approximate estimate, but they serve to give a comprehensive view of the behavior of $\bar{L}_2$ over a wide temperature range.

The values of relative partial molal heat capacity, $\bar{J}_2$, obtained by Smith and Hirtle from the temperature coefficient of $\bar{L}_2$ are given with those obtained by calorimetric methods in Table (12-1-4). Up to 1M, the results obtained from the boiling point and electromotive force measurements agree with those of Gulbransen and Robinson, and at higher temperatures show a trend towards those obtained by Rossini.[22]

[19] A. L. Robinson, *J. Am. Chem. Soc.*, **54**, 1311 (1932).
[20] E. A. Gulbransen and A. L. Robinson, *Ibid.*, **56**, 2637 (1934).
[21] F. D. Rossini, *Bur. Standards J. Research*, **7**, 47 (1931); *Ibid.*, **6**, 791 (1931).
[22] F. D. Rossini, *Bur. Standard J. Research*, **7**, 47 (1931).

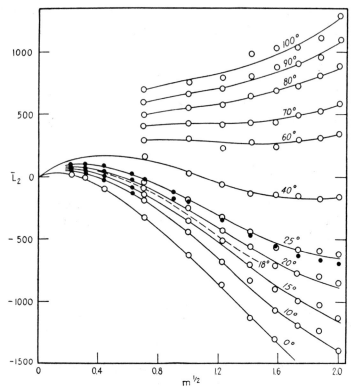

Fig. (12-1-4). L_2 of sodium chloride in aqueous solution. $\bigcirc$, Electromotive force and boiling point (diameter = 50 cal.); $\bullet$, Calorimetric (diameter = 30 cal.)

TABLE (12-1-4).   THE RELATIVE PARTIAL MOLAL HEAT CAPACITY OF SODIUM
CHLORIDE

m	$\overline{J_2}^1$			$\overline{J_2}^2$	$\overline{J_2}^3$
	0°	25°	60°	25°	25°
.05	....	3.3	....	3.5	4.8
.1	....	5.4	....	5.	6.8
.2	....	7.	....	7.1	9.6
.5	10	10.	10	11.2	15.3
1.	20	16.	12	15.6	21.6
1.5	25	20.	15	....	26.4
2.	33	24.	19	....	31.0
2.5	35	32.	21	....	34.2
3.	45	35.	21	....	37.2
3.5	51	38.	22	....	40.5
4.	53	41.	24	....	43.2

[1] Boiling point and electromotive force.
[2] Derived by Gulbransen and Robinson from values of L_2 determined calorimetrically.
[3] Derived by Rossini from heat capacity measurements of M. Randall and F. D. Rossini, *J. Am. Chem. Soc.*, **51**, 323 (1929).

(2) The Thermodynamics of Hydrobromic Acid, Potassium Chloride, Sodium Bromide, and Sodium and Potassium Hydroxides in Aqueous Solution

(a) The Standard Potential of the Cell H_2 | HBr (m) | AgBr-Ag

Since the earlier work of Lewis and Storch,[23] and Harned and James[24] on cells with hydrogen and silver-silver bromide electrodes at 25°, extensive measurements have been made[25] over a wide temperature range of the cells containing the acid solutions only,[26] or acid solutions containing a bromide.[27, 28] Two kinds of silver-silver bromide electrodes have been employed. One of these was prepared by heating a mixture of 90 per cent silver oxide and 10 per cent silver bromate to 650°. The other was prepared by heating silver oxide on a platinum spiral to 450°, and then forming silver bromide by electrolyzing hydrobromic acid or a bromide solution. Harned, Keston and Donelson showed that if oxygen is excluded these two types of electrodes give essentially the same result.

Three independent determinations of the standard potential of the silver-silver bromide electrode have been made recently.

(i) E^0 of the above cell, containing hydrobromic acid only, was determined by the method of graphical extrapolation described in Chapter (11), Section (2).

(ii) From the cells

$$H_2 \mid HBr\ (0.01),\ LiBr\ (m) \mid AgBr\text{-}Ag$$

Harned and Donelson obtained E^0 by a similar method.

(iii) That a direct comparison between the silver-silver bromide and chloride electrodes can be made in buffered solutions has been shown by Owen.[29] Consider the cells,

$$H_2 \mid HBO_2\ (m),\ NaBO_2\ (m),\ NaBr\ (m) \mid AgBr\text{-}Ag$$

$$H_2 \mid HBO_2\ (m),\ NaBO_2\ (m),\ NaCl\ (m) \mid AgCl\text{-}Ag$$

measured by Owen and Foering.[30] Their electromotive forces, E^m_{HBr} and E^m_{HCl} are given by the equations

$$E^m_{HBr} = E^0_{HBr} - \frac{RT}{F} \ln \gamma_H \gamma_{Br}\, m_H\, m_{Br}$$

$$E^m_{HCl} = E^0_{HCl} - \frac{RT}{F} \ln \gamma_H \gamma_{Cl}\, m_H\, m_{Cl}$$

[23] G. N. Lewis and H. Storch, *J. Am. Chem. Soc.*, **35**, 2544 (1917).

[24] H. S. Harned and G. M. James, *J. Phys. Chem.*, **30**, 1060 (1926).

[25] A. S. Keston, *J. Am. Chem. Soc.*, **57**, 1671 (1935).

[26] H. S. Harned, A. S. Keston and J. G. Donelson, *Ibid.*, **58**, 989 (1936).

[27] H. S. Harned and W. J. Hamer, *Ibid.*, **55**, 4496 (1933).

[28] H. S. Harned and J. G. Donelson, *Ibid.*, **59**, 1280 (1937).

[29] B. B. Owen, *J. Am. Chem. Soc.*, **57**, 1526 (1935).

[30] B. B. Owen and L. Foering, *J. Am. Chem. Soc.*, **58**, 1575 (1936).

Upon eliminating $\gamma_H m_H$ from these equations by means of the thermodynamic equation for the boric acid equilibrium,

$$K_A = \frac{\gamma_H \gamma_{BO_2}}{\gamma_{HBO_2}} \frac{m_H m_{BO_2}}{m_{HBO_2}}$$

and rearranging, we obtain

$$E^0_{HBr} - f(\gamma) = E^m_{HBr} + \frac{RT}{F} \ln K_A + \frac{RT}{F} \ln m$$

and

$$E^0_{HCl} - f(\gamma) = E^m_{HCl} + \frac{RT}{F} \ln K_A + \frac{RT}{F} \ln m$$

These equations may be employed individually to obtain K_A, and then E^0_{HBr}, or K_A may be eliminated, provided that all three electrolytic com-

TABLE (12-2-1).   THE STANDARD POTENTIAL OF THE SILVER-SILVER BROMIDE ELECTRODE BY THREE METHODS*

$$-\pi^0_{Ag\text{-}AgBr} = E^0_{HBr}$$

t	(i)	(ii)	(iii)
0	0.0813	0.08165	. . . . . .
5	.0796	.07991	0.07986
10	.0777	.07801	.07800
15	.0756	.07593	.07596
20	.0734	.07377	.07374
25[a]	.0711	.07127	.07134[a]
30	.0685	.06872	.06876
35	.0658	.06602	.06600
40	.0629	.06300	.06306
45	.0600	.05995	. . . . . .
50	.0569	.05666	. . . . . .

[a] G. Jones and S. Baeckström [*J. Am. Chem. Soc.*, **56**, 1524 (1934)] found 0.0712 at 25°.

* All results in Int. Volts = 0.99967 Abs. Volt.

ponents are at the same concentration. Thus, subtraction of the second of these equations from the first gives

$$E^0_{HBr} = E^0_{HCl} + E^m_{HBr} - E^m_{HCl} \qquad (12\text{-}2\text{-}1)$$

Knowing the standard potential of the silver-silver chloride electrode, $-E^0_{HCl}$, and measuring E^m_{HBr} and E^m_{HCl} at one low concentration, E^0_{HBr} can readily be evaluated. In this connection, see Fig. (15-4-2). The values of E^0 determined by these methods are given in Table (12-2-1). The values of E^0_{HCl}, necessary for the computation by equation (12-2-1), were obtained by equation (11-2-6). Excellent agreement is found between the results in the last two columns, while those in the first column are somewhat lower. The equation

$$-\pi_{Ag-AgBr} = E^0_{HBr} = 0.07131 - 4.99 \times 10^{-4}(t - 25)$$
$$- 3.45 \times 10^{-6}(t - 25)^2 \qquad (12\text{-}2\text{-}2)$$

expresses the results in columns (ii) and (iii) to within a few hundredths of a millivolt.

(b) The Thermodynamics of Hydrobromic Acid from Electromotive Force Measurements

The activity coefficient, relative partial molal heat content, and heat capacity of hydrobromic acid have been measured up to $1M$ concentration and from 0 to 60° by Harned, Keston, and Donelson.[31] Values of $\gamma_{\pm}$ over these temperature and concentration ranges are given in Table (12-2-1A) as well as values of $\bar{L}_2$ and $\bar{J}_2$ at 25°. Since the properties of this acid are very similar in magnitude and character to those of hydrochloric acid, further discussion is not required.

(c) The Thermodynamics of Potassium Chloride in Aqueous Solution

Aqueous solutions of potassium chloride have been investigated by various methods. The electromotive force of the cells

$$\text{Ag-AgCl} \mid \text{KCl}(m) \mid \text{K}_x\text{Hg} \mid \text{KCl}(m_0) \mid \text{AgCl-Ag}$$

have been measured at 25° by MacInnes and Parker,[32] and Harned,[33] at 0° by Smith,[34] and from 0 to 40° by Harned and Cook.[35] The cell

$$\text{Ag-AgCl} \mid \text{KCl}(c_1) \mid \text{KCl}(c_2) \mid \text{AgCl-Ag}$$

has been investigated by Shedlovsky and MacInnes[36] at 25°.

Spencer[37] has computed the activity coefficient from freezing point data at 0°, and Scatchard and Prentiss[38] have made a similar calculation of their own results. Saxton and Smith[39] have computed $\gamma_{\pm}$ at 100° from boiling determinations. The vapor pressures of potassium chloride solutions at 20° have been measured by Lovelace, Frazer and Sease.[40]

Comparisons of results by these methods are shown in Table (12-2-2). The agreement between the results obtained by the various methods is very good. A more complete set of values of the activity coefficient covering a wider range in temperature is given in Table (12-2-2A).

In Table (12-2-3A), the constants of equations by means of which $\bar{L}_2$ and $\bar{J}_2$ may be computed from 0 to 40° have been compiled. This material will be considered later in this section.

[31] H. S. Harned, A. S. Keston and J. G. Donelson, *J. Am. Chem. Soc.*, **58**, 989 (1936).

[32] D. A. MacInnes and K. Parker, *J. Am. Chem. Soc.*, **37**, 1445 (1915).

[33] H. S. Harned, *Ibid.*, **51**, 416 (1929).

[34] R. P. Smith, *J. Am. Chem. Soc.*, **55**, 3279 (1933).

[35] H. S. Harned and M. A. Cook, *Ibid.*, **59**, 1290 (1937).

[36] T. Shedlovsky and D. A. MacInnes, *J. Am. Chem. Soc.*, **59**, 503 (1937).

[37] H. M. Spencer, *J. Am. Chem. Soc.*, **54**, 4490 (1932).

[38] G. Scatchard and S. S. Prentiss, *J. Am. Chem. Soc.*, **55**, 4355 (1933).

[39] B. Saxton and R. P. Smith, *J. Am. Chem. Soc.*, **44**, 2826 (1932).

[40] B. F. Lovelace, J. C. W. Frazer and V. B. Sease, *J. Am. Chem. Soc.*, **43**, 102 (1921).

TABLE (12-2-2). THE ACTIVITY COEFFICIENT OF POTASSIUM CHLORIDE BY VARIOUS METHODS

m	0°				20°		25°	
	$\gamma_\pm$ (E.M.F.)[1]	$\gamma_\pm$ (E.M.F.)[2]	$\gamma_\pm$ (F.P.)[3]	$\gamma_\pm$ (F.P.)[4]	$\gamma_\pm$ (E.M.F.)[1]	$\gamma_\pm$ (V.P.)[5]	$\frac{\gamma_\pm}{(E.M.F.)^1}$	$\frac{\gamma_\pm}{(E.M.F.)^6}$
0.005	(0.929)		0.929	0.929			(0.927)	(0.9275)
.01	(.904)		.903	.904			(.901)	.902
.05	(.819)		.818	.819	(0.816)		(.815)	.817
.1	.768	.770	.771	(.770)	.770		.769	.770
.2	.717	.717	.719	.717	.718	.721	.719	.719
.3	.683				.688		.688	
.5	.642	.642	.645	.644	.651	.651	.651	.652
.7	.613	.615		.618	.627		.628	
1.	.588	.589	.590	.588	.604	(.604)	.606	.607
1.5	.563	.562	.561		.582		.585	
2.	.547	.548			.573	.573	.576	.578
2.5	.540	.541			.568		.572	
3.	.539	.540			.567	.569	.573	.574
3.5	.540	.542			.571		.574	.576
4.					.574	.572	.582	.581

[1] H. S. Harned and M. A. Cook, cells without liquid junction, *J. Am. Chem. Soc.*, **59**, 1290 (1937); H. S. Harned, *Ibid.*, **41**, 416 (1929).
[2] R. P. Smith, cells without liquid junction, *Ibid.*, **55**, 3279 (1933).
[3] H. M. Spencer, freezing point, *Ibid.*, **54**, 4490 (1932).
[4] G. Scatchard and S. S. Prentiss, freezing point, *Ibid.*, **55**, 4355 (1933).
[5] B. F. Lovelace, J. C. W. Frazer and V. B. Sease, vapor pressure, *Ibid.*, **43**, 102 (1921).
[6] T. Shedlovsky and D. A. MacInnes, cells with liquid junction, *Ibid.*, **59**, 503 (1937).

TABLE (12-2-3). ACTIVITY COEFFICIENTS OF ALKALI HYDROXIDES AT 25°.

m	LiOH[1]	NaOH[2]	KOH[3-5]	CsOH[4]
0.05	(0.803)	(0.818)	(0.824)	(0.831)
.1	.760	.766	.790	.802
.2	.702	.727	.757	.761
.5	.616	.693	.728	.748
1	.554	.679	.756	.780
1.5	.528	.683	.814	....
2.	.513	.698	.888	....
2.5	.501	.729	.974	....
3.	.494	.774	1.081	....
3.5	.487	.826	1.215	....
4.	.481	.888	1.352	....

[1] H. S. Harned and F. E. Swindells, *J. Am. Chem. Soc.*, **48**, 126 (1926).
[2] H. S. Harned and J. C. Hecker, *Ibid.*, **55**, 4838 (1933) (0.05 to 2 M); G. Åkerlöf and G. Kegeles, *Ibid.*, **62**, 620 (1940) (2 to 4 M).
[3] H. S. Harned and M. A. Cook, *Ibid.*, **59**, 496 (1937).
[4] H. S. Harned and O. E. Schupp, Jr., *Ibid.*, **52**, 3886 (1930).
[5] G. Akerlof and P. Bender, *Ibid.*, **70**, 2366 (1948).

(d) The Thermodynamics of Sodium Bromide in Aqueous Solutions from Electromotive Force Measurements

The flowing amalgam cell with silver-silver bromide electrodes has been employed in obtaining the activity coefficient, relative partial molal heat content, and heat capacity by Harned and Crawford.[41] The activity

[41] H. S. Harned and C. C. Crawford, *J. Am. Chem. Soc.*, **59**, 1903 (1937).

coefficients obtained by them are given in Table (12-2-4A). Equations and their constants are given in Table (12-2-5A) from which $\bar{L}_2$ and $\bar{J}_2$ can be computed from 0 to 40°.

(e) The Activity Coefficients of the Alkaline Hydroxides at 25°

The reaction of the cell

$$\text{H}_2 \mid \text{MOH}(m_2)\mid \text{M}_x\text{Hg} \mid \text{MOH}(m_1)\mid \text{H}_2; \qquad \text{M} = \text{Li, Na, etc.}$$

may be represented by

$$\text{MOH}(m_2) + \text{H}_2\text{O}(m_1) = \text{MOH}(m_1) + \text{H}_2\text{O}(m_2)$$

and its electromotive force by

$$\mathbf{E} = 2k \log \frac{\gamma_2 m_2}{\gamma_1 m_1} + k \log \frac{a_{w(m_1)}}{a_{w(m_2)}} \tag{12-2-4}$$

where k equals $2.3026RT/\mathbf{F}$, and $a_{w(m_1)}$ and $a_{w(m_2)}$ are the activities of water in the two solutions designated.

The activity coefficients of potassium, sodium, lithium and cesium hydroxides have been computed from measurements of these cells at 25° by Knobel,[42] Harned,[43] Harned and Swindells,[44] and Harned and Schupp.[45] More recently, Harned and Hecker[46] investigated cells containing sodium hydroxide, and Harned and Cook[47] cells containing potassium hydroxide from 0 to 35°. Harned has shown how the correction for the water transfer may be computed from the electromotive forces by employing an equation for $\gamma_{\pm}$. Harned and Hecker, and Harned and Cook employed a graphical method which is somewhat similar. According to equation (1-8-1), the relation between the activity of the solvent and that of the solute is given by

$$d \ln a_w = -\frac{N_2}{N_1} d \ln a_2 \tag{12-2-5}$$

Since $d \ln a_2 = \nu d \ln \gamma m$

$$d \ln a_w = -\frac{2m}{55.51} d \ln \gamma m \tag{12-2-6}$$

for 1-1 electrolytes in water, and consequently

$$-\frac{1}{2} d \ln a_w = \frac{dm}{55.51} + \frac{m}{55.51} d \ln \gamma \tag{12-2-7}$$

[42] M. Knobel, *J. Am. Chem. Soc.*, **45**, 70 (1923).
[43] H. S. Harned, *J. Am. Chem. Soc.*, **47**, 676 (1925).
[44] H. S. Harned and F. E. Swindells, *Ibid.*, **48**, 126 (1926).
[45] H. S. Harned and O. E. Schupp Jr., *Ibid.*, **52**, 3886 (1930).
[46] H. S. Harned and J. C. Hecker, *J. Am. Chem. Soc.*, **55**, 4838 (1933).
[47] H. S. Harned and M. A. Cook, *J. Am. Chem. Soc.*, **59**, 496 (1937).

Upon integration between the limits m_1 and m_2, the desired logarithm of the activity ratio is given by

$$\frac{1}{2} \log \frac{a_{w(m_R)}}{a_{w(m)}} = \frac{m - m_R}{2.303 \times 55.51} + \frac{1}{55.51} \int_{m_R}^{m} m d \log \frac{\gamma_{\pm}}{\gamma_R} \qquad (12\text{-}2\text{-}8)$$

Let γ_R and m_R represent a reference activity coefficient and molality. Harned and Hecker used $0.05M$ as a fixed reference concentration. The desired term on the left of this equation may be evaluated by arithmetical approximation. As a first approximation the second term on the right is omitted. The values of the left side at various concentrations are computed and substituted in equation (12-2-4), along with E and m. Provisional values of $\log \gamma_{\pm}/\gamma_R$ are calculated by equation (12-2-4), and used to evaluate the second term of (12-2-8) by graphical integration. This process gives new values of the left side of equation (12-2-8), which may be employed in obtaining more accurate values of the activity coefficient ratio. This procedure is repeated until the equations are satisfied.* Three or four repetitions will satisfy the equations to within 0.01 mv, which is considerably less than the experimental error. This leads to final values of the ratio $\gamma_{\pm}/\gamma_R$. By appropriate application of the equation of the Debye and Hückel theory (10-4-8), these results may be extrapolated, and a value of γ_R, at the reference concentration, and subsequently $\gamma_{\pm}$ at the other concentrations, may be found.

Values of $\gamma_{\pm}$ at 25° determined by this method are given in Table (12-2-3). The extrapolation should be reliable for all but the lithium hydroxide, for which the results are relatively inaccurate.

(f) The Thermodynamics of Aqueous Sodium and Potassium Hydroxides from Electromotive Force Measurements

The activity coefficient, relative partial molal heat content, and heat capacity of sodium hydroxide in water up to $4M$ and from 0 to 35° have been determined by Harned and Hecker.[48] Åkerlöf and Kegeles[49] have made a very extensive investigation of these solutions which covers concentration and temperature ranges from 0.1 to $17M$ and 0 to 70°. Potassium hydroxide solutions have been studied by Akerlof and Bender and Harned and Cook.[50] The activity coefficients of these hydroxides are given in Tables (12-2-6A) and (12-2-7A). Constants of equations by means of which $\bar{L}_2$ and $\bar{J}_2$ may be computed are given in Tables (12-2-8A) and (12-2-9A).

---

* G. Åkerlöf and G. Kegeles [*J. Am. Chem. Soc.*, **62**, 620 (1940)] employ an analytical procedure which avoids successive approximations, but which requires the representation of E as a function of m by the method of least squares.

[48] H. S. Harned and J. C. Hecker, *J. Am. Chem. Soc.*, **55**, 4838 (1933).

[49] G. Åkerlöf and G. Kegeles, *Ibid.*, **62**, 620 (1940).

[50] H. S. Harned and M. A. Cook, *J. Am. Chem. Soc.*, **59**, 496 (1937); G. Akerlof and P. Bender, *Ibid.*, **70**, 2266 (1948).

(g) **Comparison of the Relative Partial Molal Heat Content and Heat Capacity as Determined from Electromotive Force and Calorimetric Measurements**

In Fig. (12-2-1), $\bar{L}_2$ obtained from heat of dilution data and electromotive forces is plotted against $m^{1/2}$ for hydrochloric acid, potassium chloride, and sodium and potassium hydroxides at 18°. The solid lines represent the values determined by electromotive forces, and the dashed lines those obtained calorimetrically. The maximum discrepancy between the two sets of data is about 60 cals. This agreement is good since the flowing amalgam cells employed in the three cases are among those most difficult to operate. The straight line represents the limiting law of the interionic

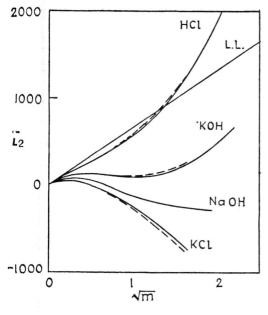

Fig. (12–2–1)
The relative partial molal heat contents of some 1-1 electrolytes at 18°. ———, electromotive force; ----, calorimetry.

attraction theory. Similarly, $\bar{L}_2$ for sodium bromide solutions, determined from the electromotive forces, is in good agreement with the calorimetric results of Hammerschmid and Robinson,[51] if allowance is made for a difference of 25 cals., due to the difficulty of extrapolation.

Fig. (12-2-2) contains plots of $\bar{J}_2$ of potassium chloride, potassium hydroxide and hydrochloric acid as determined by the two methods. The dashed lines represent the calorimetric results whereas the solid lines represent the values obtained from suitable cells. The agreement is excellent since the maximum deviation is of the order of two calories. The values for sodium hydroxide, not included in the figure, agree equally well.

[51] A. L. Robinson, *J. Am. Chem. Soc.*, **60**, 1265 (1938); H. Hammerschmid and A. L. Robinson, *Ibid.*, **54**, 3120 (1932).

These illustrations suffice to show that the electromotive force method can be used for obtaining a comprehensive view of the behaviors of $\bar{L}_2$ and $\bar{J}_2$ for quite a number of electrolytes. It should be borne in mind that the electromotive method measures directly $(\bar{F}_2 - \bar{F}_2^0)$ and $\gamma_\pm$. When attempt is made to determine $\bar{L}_2$ and $\bar{J}_2$ by this method, the original data are subjected to a very severe test, since these determinations involve the first and second differential coefficients of the original data. For this reason, the calorimetric determinations should yield the better result, except in cases where the electromotive forces can be measured with extreme accuracy. The agreement noted in the preceding illustrations indicates that the postulated cell mechanisms approach very closely the actual ones.

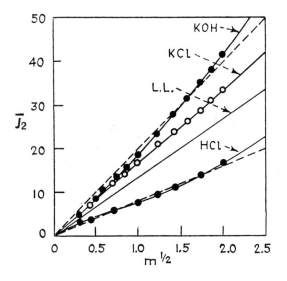

Fig. (12-2-2) The relative partial molal heat capacities of some 1-1 electrolytes at 25°. ———, electromotive force; ----, calorimetry.

(3) THE ACTIVITY COEFFICIENTS OF 1-1 ELECTROLYTES FROM ISOPIESTIC VAPOR PRESSURE MEASUREMENTS

(a) Activity Coefficients at 25°

The electromotive force method has been shown to be good when applicable, but is limited to the electrolytes which possess ions for which reversible electrodes may be found. For concentrated solutions, a vapor pressure method is generally applicable, but so far the absolute vapor pressures of only a few electrolytic solutions have been accurately measured. A very valuable contribution to this subject has been made by Robinson and Sinclair,[52] and Robinson,[53] who have greatly improved the isopiestic

[52] D. A. Sinclair, *J. Phys. Chem.*, **37**, 495 (1933).

[53] R. A. Robinson and D. A. Sinclair, *J. Am. Chem. Soc.*, **56**, 1830 (1934); R. A. Robinson, *Ibid.*, **57**, 1161 (1935); **57**, 1165 (1935); **59**, 84 (1937); *Trans. Faraday Soc.*, **35**, 1217 (1939); R. A. Robinson and R. H. Stokes, "Electrolyte Solutions", Butterworth Scientific Publications, London (1955).

vapor pressure comparison method of Bousfield[54] [Chapter (9), Section (4)]. If solutions of two different salts are allowed to equilibrate through the vapor phase and then analyzed, and if the activity of one of the salts at its concentration is known, then the activity coefficient of the other salt may be computed. Let m_R, γ_R, m, and $\gamma_\pm$ be the molalities and activity coefficients of the two salts under the above isopiestic condition, and let a_R represent the activity of the reference salt. Then, since the solvent activities of the two solutions are the same, we have [Equation (1-8-1)]

$$\frac{m_R}{55.51} d\ln a_R = -d\ln a_w = \frac{m}{55.51} d\ln a_2 \qquad (12\text{-}3\text{-}1)$$

or

$$d\ln \gamma_\pm = d\ln \gamma_R + d\ln \frac{m_R}{m} + \left(\frac{m_R}{m} - 1\right) d\ln \gamma_R m_R \qquad (12\text{-}3\text{-}2)$$

Since

$$d\ln \gamma_R m_R = 2\frac{d\sqrt{a_R}}{\sqrt{a_R}}$$

we obtain upon integration

$$\ln \gamma_\pm = \ln \gamma_R + \ln \frac{m_R}{m} + 2\int_0^{a_R} \left(\frac{m_R}{m} - 1\right)\frac{d\sqrt{a_R}}{\sqrt{a_R}} \qquad (12\text{-}3\text{-}3)$$

from which $\gamma_\pm$ may be evaluated provided that γ_R and a_R are known. The ratio of the concentrations of the isopiestic solutions, m_R/m, may be plotted against m, and the second term on the right evaluated at round concentrations. The third term on the right may be evaluated graphically from a plot of $(m_R/m - 1)/\sqrt{a_R}$ versus $\sqrt{a_R}$. Since $a_R = 0$ when $m = 0$, the plot proceeds to zero.

The problem of obtaining a suitable reference electrolyte still remains. Robinson and Sinclair employed potassium chloride solutions as reference, whereas Scatchard, Hamer and Wood[55] used sodium chloride solutions. The latter placed more weight on vapor pressure measurements and less on electromotive force measurements than the former, and their standard values differ considerably from Robinson's [Table (9-4-1)]. In Table (12-3-1A) Robinson's values of $\gamma_\pm$ at 25° for all the alkali metal halides, nitrates, acetates, and many other uniunivalent electrolytes are compiled. These are based on potassium or sodium chloride solutions as standards. The values of $\gamma_\pm$ which he employed for these salts are practically the same as those recorded in Tables (12-1-2A) and (12-2-2A). Robinson's is the most extensive work of this kind at 25°.[55a]

The isopiestic vapor pressure measurement is quite accurate, and the results obtained by it agree satisfactorily with those obtained by the

[54] W. R. Bousfield and E. Bousfield, *Proc. Roy. Soc. (London)*, **A, 103**, 429 (1923).
[55] G. Scatchard, W. J. Hamer and S. E. Wood, *J. Am. Chem. Soc.*, **60**, 3061 (1938).
[55a] See compilation by R. H. Stokes, *Trans. Faraday Soc.*, **45**, 612 (1949).

electromotive force method. This is clearly illustrated by the data in Table (12-3-1), in which the ratios of the activity coefficients of several salts to that of potassium chloride, determined by both methods, are compiled. From 0.1 to $3M$, the agreement is excellent. The discrepancies at the higher concentrations may be due to solubility effects on the electrodes. This is not certain since this region of concentration has not been investigated as thoroughly with flowing amalgam cells as the region 0.1 to $3M$. Lithium amalgam electrodes are not as reproducible as those of the other alkali metals. Consequently, the agreement with the isopiestic measurements for lithium chloride and bromide is not as good.[56]

TABLE (12-3-1). MEAN ACTIVITY RATIOS AT 25° DETERMINED BY THE ISOPIESTIC VAPOR PRESSURE AND ELECTROMOTIVE FORCE METHODS

m	$\dfrac{\gamma_{NaCl}{}^{c}}{\gamma_{KCl}}$		$\dfrac{\gamma_{NaBr}}{\gamma_{KCl}}$		$\dfrac{\gamma_{KBr}}{\gamma_{KCl}}$		$\dfrac{\gamma_{CsCl}}{\gamma_{KCl}}$	
	V.P.	E.M.F.	V.P.	E.M.F.	V.P.	E.M.F.[a]	V.P.	E.M.F.[b]
0.1	1.012	1.013	1.016	1.017	1.003	1.004	0.982	0.984
.2	1.024	1.020	1.031	1.029	1.006	1.004	.967	.966
.3	1.033	1.032	1.044	1.044	1.007	1.006	....	....
.5	1.049	1.046	1.069	1.068	1.011	1.013	.929	.931
.7	1.067	1.068	1.097	1.094	1.018	1.018	.915	.916
1.	1.088	1.084	1.136	1.132	1.020	1.019	.898	.898
1.5	1.126	1.122	1.203	1.202	1.027	1.026	.879	.879
2.	1.167	1.165	1.273	1.274	1.037	1.032	.861	.859
2.5	1.210	1.210	1.346	1.352	1.042	1.039	.848	.843
3.	1.257	1.261	1.426	(1.447)	1.047	1.043	.838	.829
3.5	1.307	1.312	1.512	(1.530)	1.052	1.053	....	....
4.	1.361	1.368	1.612	1.613	1.057	1.061	....	....

[a] H. S. Harned, *J. Am. Chem. Soc.*, **51**, 416 (1929).
[b] H. S. Harned and O. E. Schupp Jr., *Ibid.*, **52**, 3886 (1930).
[c] Similar comparisons at 15 and 40° have been made by R. A. Robinson, *Trans. Faraday Soc.*, **35**, 1222 (1939) and P. Olynyk and A. R. Gordon, *J. Am. Chem. Soc.*, **65**, 224 (1943). For results at high concentrations see Table (12-3-2A).

(4) CALCULATION OF THE ACTIVITY COEFFICIENT AT VARIOUS TEMPERATURES AND PRESSURES FROM VALUES AT 25° AND ONE ATMOSPHERE

In Tables (8-2-2A) and (8-4-2) and (8-4-3), values of $\bar{L}_2$ and $\bar{J}_2$ are compiled. If the small variation of $\bar{J}_2$ with temperature be neglected, the approximate equation for $\bar{L}_2$,

$$\bar{L}_2 = \bar{L}_{2(T_R)} + \bar{J}_{2(T_R)}(T - T_R) \tag{12-4-1}$$

follows. T_R is some reference temperature. This result can be used to compute activity coefficients at various temperatures from values determined at a given temperature. Thus, according to equation (3-8-1),

$$\left(\frac{\partial \ln \gamma_{\pm}}{\partial T}\right)_{P,m} = \left(\frac{\partial \ln f_{\pm}}{\partial T}\right)_{P,m} = -\frac{\bar{L}_2}{\nu R T^2} \tag{3-8-1}$$

[56] For other similar comparisons see R. A. Robinson and H. S. Harned, *Chem. Rev.*, **28**, 419 (1941).

If this equation be combined with (12-4-1) and integrated, we obtain

$$\log \gamma_{\pm} = \frac{\bar{L}_{2(T_R)} - \bar{J}_{2(T_R)}T_R}{\nu 2.303RT} - \frac{\bar{J}_{2(T_R)}}{\nu R}\log T + I \qquad (12\text{-}4\text{-}2)$$

If γ_R at a given temperature, T_R, is known, the integration constant, I, may be computed. [See Section (1) of this chapter]. If the reference temperature is 25°, $T_R = 298.1$ may be substituted into the above equation, and the integration constant expressed in terms of $\log \gamma_{\pm}$ at this temperature. Thus

$$\log \gamma_{\pm} = \log \gamma_{\pm}(25°) + \frac{y}{\nu}\bar{L}_2(25°) - \frac{z}{\nu}\bar{J}_2(25°) \qquad (12\text{-}4\text{-}3)$$

when

$$y = \frac{298.1 - T}{2.303R \, 298.1T} \qquad (12\text{-}4\text{-}4)$$

$$z = 298.1y - \frac{1}{R}\log\left(\frac{298.1}{T}\right) \qquad (12\text{-}4\text{-}5)$$

Values of the variables, y and z, are given in Table (5-1-2) for temperatures between 0 to 100°C.

According to equation (3-9-1) the variation of the activity coefficient with pressure is given by

$$\left(\frac{\partial \ln f_{\pm}}{\partial P}\right)_{T,m} = \left(\frac{\partial \ln \gamma_{\pm}}{\partial P}\right)_{T,m} = \frac{\bar{V}_2 - \bar{V}_2^0}{\nu RT} \qquad (12\text{-}4\text{-}6)$$

Table (8-5-1) contains values of $\bar{V}_2^0$ and S_V at 25°, and $\bar{V}_2$, at this temperature, can be calculated from these quantities by the approximate equation

$$\bar{V}_2 = \bar{V}_2^0 + (3/2)S_V\sqrt{c} \qquad (12\text{-}4\text{-}7)$$

or by the more exact relation

$$\bar{V}_2 = \frac{\bar{V}_2^0 + (3/2)S_V\sqrt{c}}{1 + S_V c^{3/2}/2000} \qquad (12\text{-}4\text{-}8)$$

obtained from equation (8-5-8). $\bar{V}_2^0$ and $\bar{V}_2$ can be estimated at other temperatures by equations (8-6-2), (8-6-9), and (8-6-13), and the data given in Table (8-6-1).

In order to express $\bar{V}_2 - \bar{V}_2^0$ as a function of pressure before integrating equation (12-4-6), we may consider the partial molal compressibilities at one atmosphere, $\bar{K}_2$ and $\bar{K}_2^0$, to be constant over a small pressure range, and write

$$\bar{V}_2 - \bar{V}_2^0 = (\bar{V}_2 - \bar{V}_2^0)_{P=1} - (P-1)(\bar{K}_2 - \bar{K}_2^0)_{P=1} \qquad (12\text{-}4\text{-}9)$$

by equation (8-7-2). Accordingly, equation (12-4-6) yields

$$\log \gamma_{\pm} = (\log \gamma_{\pm})_{P=1} + \frac{(P-1)(\bar{V}_2 - \bar{V}_2^0)_{P=1}}{2.303\nu RT}$$

$$- \frac{(P-1)^2(\bar{K}_2 - \bar{K}_2^0)_{P=1}}{2 \times 2.303\nu RT} \qquad (12\text{-}4\text{-}10)$$

from which activity coefficients can be estimated at moderate pressures. For higher pressures, or greater accuracy, the variation of $\bar{K}_2 - \bar{K}_2^0$ with pressure must be taken into account. $\bar{K}_2 - \bar{K}_2^0$ is closely represented up to $1M$ by

$$\bar{K}_2 - \bar{K}_2^0 = (3/2)S_K\sqrt{c} \qquad (12\text{-}4\text{-}11)$$

and values of S_K for some salts are to be found in Table (8-7-1).

Robinson and Harned[57] have employed equation (12-4-2) in the form

$$\log \gamma_{\pm} = -\frac{A}{T} - B\log T + I \qquad (12\text{-}4\text{-}2a)$$

for the computation of the activity coefficient of sodium chloride from 0 to 100°. From the heat data discussed in Section (1) and the values of $\gamma_{\pm}$ at 25°, the values of A, B and I in Table (12-4-1) were obtained. The use of this equation is limited by the paucity of reliable thermal data at high concentrations. A comparison of the activity coefficients calculated by this equation with the values given in Table (12-1-2A) is made in Table (12-4-2) where the deviations of calculated from observed values are recorded. It will be observed that the equation represents the results with accuracy from 0 to 100° although, as is to be expected, somewhat greater discrepancies are to be found at the higher concentrations.

TABLE (12-4-1). DATA FOR CALCULATING THE ACTIVITY COEFFICIENT OF SODIUM CHLORIDE BETWEEN 0 AND 100°C.

$$\log \gamma_{\pm} = I - \frac{A}{T} - B\log T$$

m	I	A	B
0.1	3.5083	152.06	1.2557
0.2	5.0010	221.15	1.7755
0.3	6.1564	275.49	2.1748
0.5	7.9970	364.47	2.8051
0.7	9.5163	440.34	3.3199
1.0	11.4326	535.45	3.9679
1.5	14.0912	668.38	4.8619
2.0	16.3294	779.34	5.6128

[57] R. A. Robinson and H. S. Harned, *Chem. Rev.*, **28**, 419 (1941).

TABLE (12-4-2). COMPARISON OF OBSERVED ACTIVITY COEFFICIENTS OF SODIUM
CHLORIDE WITH THOSE COMPUTED BY EQUATION (12-4-2a)

$$(\gamma_{obsd.} - \gamma_{calcd.}) \times 10^3$$

t	$m = 0.1$	$m = 0.2$	$m = 0.5$	$m = 1.0$	$m = 1.5$	$m = 2.0$
0	+1	−2	−2	−1	−2	−2
10	+1	−1	−2	0	−1	0
20	0	−2	−2	−2	−3	−1
30	0	−2	−2	−3	−4	−1
40	0	−2	−2	−4	−4	−4
60	0	−1	0	0	−2	−2
80	+1	+2	+3	+1	+1	0
100	+2	+3	+4	+1	+4	+2

By elimination of $(\bar{V}_2 - \bar{V}_2^0)$ and $(\bar{K}_2 - \bar{K}_2^0)$ from equation (12-4-10) by means of equation (12-4-7) and (12-4-11), we obtain

$$\log \gamma_{\pm} = (\log \gamma_{\pm})_{P=1} + 0.888 \times 10^{-5}(\tfrac{3}{2}S_V)(P - 1)\sqrt{c}$$
$$- 0.444 \times 10^{-5}(\tfrac{3}{2}S_K)(P - 1)^2\sqrt{c} \qquad (12\text{-}4\text{-}12)$$

for a 1-1 electrolyte at 25°.

The magnitudes of the pressure effects upon the activity coefficients of hydrochloric acid at 1, 100 and 1000 atmospheres at four concentrations and for potassium chloride, sodium chloride and sodium hydroxide at unit

TABLE (12-4-3). EFFECT OF PRESSURE ON ACTIVITY COEFFICIENTS AT 25°

P	Activity Coefficients						
	HCl				KCl $c = 1$	NaCl $c = 1$	NaOH $c = 1$
	$c = 0.1$	$c = 0.5$	$c = 1.0$	$c = 2.0$			
1	0.797	0.757	0.807	0.991	0.605	0.6545	0.6775
100	0.7975	0.759	0.809	0.995	0.609	0.659	0.686
1000*	0.803	0.771	0.828	1.0275			
1000**	0.802	0.768	0.829	1.021	0.637	0.687	0.745
$(3/2) S_V$	1.25				3.49	3.23	6.27
$(3/2) S_K 10^4$	4.5				18.6	17.1	31.3

* Equation (12-4-12) neglecting term containing $(P - 1)^2$.
** Equation (12-4-12) complete.

concentration are illustrated in Table (12-4-3). At 100 atmospheres, the contribution due to the term containing the square of the pressure is negligible, but at 1000 atmospheres, it must be included. The last two rows of the table contain values of $3/2 S_V$ and $3/2 S_K$ from Tables (8-5-1) and (8-7-1).

The activity coefficient of hydrochloric acid is not influenced greatly by a change in pressure. Even in a $2M$ solution, only a 3 per cent change in $\gamma_{\pm}$ is produced by a change in pressure of 1000 atmospheres. For the other electrolytes, the influence of pressure is somewhat greater. The largest effect, of 10 per cent, occurs with the activity coefficient of sodium hydroxide.

(5) General Discussion of the Activity Coefficients of 1-1 Electrolytes in Relation to the Theory of Debye and Hückel

(a) The Mean Distances of Approach of the Ions, $\mathring{a}$

Numerous examples have been cited which show the agreement of the observed results with the limiting laws of the interionic attraction theory. Further, the equations resulting from the theory have been employed repeatedly for purposes of extrapolation. The limiting laws, however, are valid at infinite dilution only, and do not apply rigidly to a real ionic solution. The factors which cause deviations from the limiting laws are of great interest as are also the various theoretical interpretations of the properties of electrolytes at moderate or high concentrations.

Debye and Hückel realized that a restriction due to the finite sizes of the ions must be put on Coulombic forces, and introduced the parameter, $\mathring{a}$, defined as the "mean distance of approach of the ions, positive or negative." This led to the extension of the limiting law for activity coefficients, represented by equations (3-5-8) and (3-5-9), and may be written

$$\log f_{\pm} = -\frac{\mathfrak{S}_{(f)}\sqrt{\Gamma}}{1 + 35.57\mathring{a}(DT)^{-1/2}\sqrt{\Gamma}} \qquad (12\text{-}5\text{-}1)$$

Later Hückel[58] extended this theory by assuming that the dielectric constant of the medium varies linearly with the concentration of ions. Upon introducing this relation, Hückel deduced an equation of the form of (10-4-8), or

$$\log f_{\pm} = -\frac{\mathfrak{S}_{(f)}\sqrt{\Gamma}}{1 + 35.57\ \mathring{a}(DT)^{-1/2}\sqrt{\Gamma}} + Bc \qquad (12\text{-}5\text{-}2)$$

which we have frequently employed for the purpose of extrapolating electromotive force data. According to his theory, the term Bc represents the effect of change of dielectric constant with salt concentration. A lowering of D, produced by the addition of ions, has the effect of "salting out the ions," and causes an increase in the activity coefficient. This result corresponds to an effect of repulsive force between the ions, and is opposite in sign to the interionic attraction effect expressed by the first term on the right of equation (12-5-2). If, on the other hand, the dielectric constant is increased by salt addition, the ions are "salted in," Bc is negative, and the activity coefficient is decreased. These behaviors correspond to the salting effects which, according to Debye and McAulay [Chapter (3), Section (10)], vary directly as the sum of the reciprocals of the ion radii, $\Sigma\ 1/b_j$. Although there is no doubt that the dielectric con-

[58] E. Hückel, *Physik. Z.*, **26**, 93 (1925).

stant is altered by addition of ions, it is also certain that this effect is not the only important factor in concentrated solutions. Therefore, this equation must be regarded as mainly empirical.

When the parameters, $å$ and B are determined from the data, they are found to be different for each electrolyte. However, no exact significance can be attached to the values of $å$, although they are always of the right order of magnitude. In Table (12-5-1), values of $å$ for a few electrolytes evaluated from data over various concentration ranges by a number of different equations are compiled. In column (1), values[59] determined by equation (12-5-1), without the linear term, are given. In the next three columns values obtained by fitting equation (12-5-2) to the data over different concentration ranges are given. In column (5) are given values of $å$ computed from the equation

$$\log f_{\pm} = -\frac{\mathcal{S}_{(f)}\sqrt{\Gamma}}{1 + 35.57å(DT)^{-1/2}\sqrt{\Gamma}} + Bc + D'c^2 \qquad (12\text{-}5\text{-}3)$$

TABLE (12-5-1). MEAN DISTANCES OF APPROACH OF IONS, $å$

	(1) Equation (12-5-1)	(2) Equation (12-5-2)	(3)	(4)	(5) Equation (12-5-3)	(6) Equation (12-8-8)
		(0.005 – 0.1 M)	(0.1 – 1 M)	(0.1 – 3 M)	(0.1 – 4 M)	(0.1 – 3 M)
HCl............	5.6	4.6	4.3	3.6	4.3	
KCl............	4.1	4.1	3.6	3.4	3.95	3.2
NaCl..........	4.4	4.4	4.0	3.6	4.2	3.7

which contains an additional term in c^2 and which was used [Chapter (11), Section (5)] for computing the activity coefficient of hydrochloric acid. The last column contains values computed by Van Rysselberghe and Eisenberg[60] by equation (12-8-8) which is similar in form to (12-5-3). We note that the different methods of computation do not lead to the same result, but that the values obtained are always of the right magnitude, usually somewhat larger than crystal dimensions, and that the values of $å$ are in the same order, HCl > NaCl > KCl, whichever way the calculation is made.

In the above cases, the simple equation without the linear term, and with a constant value of $å$, expresses the data over a considerable range of concentration (0.005 to 0.1M). This is not always the case. Gronwall, LaMer and Sandved[61] have shown that for potassium nitrate, $å$ varies

[59] A. S. Brown and D. A. MacInnes, *J. Am. Chem. Soc.*, **57**, 1356 (1935); T. Shedlovsky and D. A. MacInnes, *Ibid.*, **59**, 503 (1937).

[60] P. Van Rysselberghe and S. Eisenberg, *J. Am. Chem. Soc.*, **61**, 3020 (1939).

[61] T. H. Gronwall, V. K. LaMer and K. Sandved, *Physik. Z.*, **29**, 358 (1928).

with concentration when computed by this equation, and that a constant value of d was obtained when their extended theory was employed.

In Table (12-5-2), values of the parameters d and B of equation (12-5-2) and d, B' and D' of equation (12-5-3) for the 1-1 halides, halide acids and sodium and potassium hydroxides at 25° are recorded. We have pointed out in Section (1) that good extrapolations may be obtained by equation (12-5-2), if it be fitted to the experimental results at concentrations up to $1M$, but not to higher concentrations of electrolytes. Activity coefficients at $0.1M$ computed by the use of these parameters are identical with those in Table (12-3-1A). From 0.1 to $1M$, the agreement between the observed activity coefficients and those computed by equation (12-5-2)

TABLE (12-5-2).   PARAMETERS OF EQUATIONS (12-5-2) AND (12-5-3) AT 25°

	Equation (12-5-2) Valid to 1M		Equation (12-5-3). Valid to 4M				$(r_+ + r_-)$
	d	B	d	B	D'	Max. Dev.	
HI	5.0	0.197	5.5	0.1725	0.0128	0.007	
HBr	4.4	.165					
HCl	4.3	.133	4.3	.1292	.00615	.003	
LiI	5.05	.165	5.0	.155	.0113	.015	2.77
LiBr	4.3	.130	4.3	.126	.0099	.002	2.56
LiCl	4.25	.121	4.25	.111	.0070	.002	2.41
NaI	4.2	.100	4.2	.090	.0058	.008	3.13
NaBr	4.1	.0687	4.2	.0590	.0064	.002	2.91
NaCl	4.0	.0521	4.2	.0410	.0053	.001	2.76
KI	3.94	.0462	3.95	.0440	.0016	.002	3.50
KBr	3.84	.0282	3.85	.0247	.0035	.001	3.28
KCl	3.8	.0202	3.85	.0187	.0034	.001	3.14
RbCl	3.6	.010	3.2	.0235	.0023	.003	3.29
RbBr	3.55	.010	3.2	.0193	.0021	.005	3.43
RbI	3.5	.0085	3.2	.0162	.0031	.004	3.65
CsCl	3.0	0	2.5	.0229	.0024	.006	3.46
CsBr	2.93	0	2.5	.0162	.0033	.008	3.61
CsI	2.87	0	2.5	.0140	0	.006	3.82
NaOH	3.24	.0460					
KOH	3.7	.1294					

is within ± 0.002 in $\gamma_\pm$ with three exceptions. For lithium iodide, the agreement is not good; for lithium bromide and cesium chloride, the calculated and observed results are within the above limit up to $0.7M$.

The middle columns of Table (12-5-2) contain the parameters d, B and D' of equation (12-5-3). The next to last column records the maximum deviations of the observed results [Table (12-3-1A)] from those calculated by this equation whose range of validity extends to $4M$. It will be observed that in nearly all cases the agreement is excellent, and is particularly good for the results in which most confidence may be placed. The most serious discrepancies are found with lithium and sodium iodide, both of which salts require further experimental investigation.[62]

[62] R. A. Robinson and H. S. Harned, *Chem. Rev.*, **28**, 419 (1941).

The last column of this table contains the sum of the crystallographic radii of the salts. The values of $\mathring{a}$ are all of the expected order of magnitude. For most of the salts, $\mathring{a}$ is greater than the sum of the crystallographic radii. This can be explained by the effect of the hydration of the ions. For cesium, salts, $\mathring{a}$ is less than $(r_+ + r_-)$. Since there is some doubt as to the absolute magnitude of $\mathring{a}$, it is inadvisable to draw any inference from this result.

Judging from Bjerrum's theory of ionic association [Chapter (3), Section (7)] all of these electrolytes are strong, because most of the $\mathring{a}$ values are greater than q ($= 3.5$), indicating that the probability of ionic association is very small. Ion pair formation may occur to some extent in the cases of the cesium salts, but even in these solutions, it is doubtful.

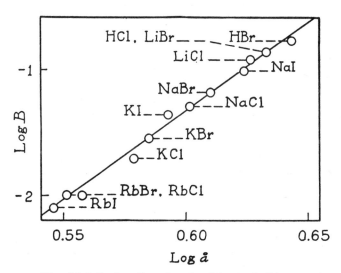

Fig. (12–5–1). Log B against log $\mathring{a}$ for 1-1 halides at 25°.

It will be observed from Table (12-5-2) that $\mathring{a}$ and B obtained from equation (12-5-2) are in the same order and it is probable that some relation can be found between them. If this is so, then all these results can be expressed up to $1M$ by a single parameter equation and constitute a single family of curves. In Fig. (12-5-1) we have plotted log $\mathring{a}$ against log B and find that a linear relation between the two holds within the limits within which $\mathring{a}$ and B can be evaluated. The equation of this straight line is

$$\log B = 14\log \mathring{a} - 9.75 \qquad (12\text{-}5\text{-}4)$$

which leads to the result that B is proportional to the 14th power of $\mathring{a}$, a very sensitive relation indeed if we desire to compute B from values of $\mathring{a}$. The reverse calculation of $\mathring{a}$ from B is satisfactory. We do not consider significant the exact numerical value found for the power of $å$. It merely suggests that the repulsive forces between the ions depend on a power of $å$ and that two equations, such as equations (12-5-2) and (12-5-4) are sufficient for the representation of the single family of curves for the alkali and hydrogen halides between 0.1 and 1.0 M.*

Any relationship between $å$ and B, calculated from data between 0.1 and $4M$ by means of equation (12-5-3), is obscured by the introduction of the third term, $D'c^2$. Nor does this constant D' appear to be related to B but, with so sensitive a three-parameter equation, it is doubtful if any quantitative relation can be found by induction. The tendency of $å$ and B to increase together, however, is still found. We shall return in Section (8) to a consideration of a relation similar in form to equation (12-5-3) which has some theoretical support.

If the B values are plotted against $\Sigma\ 1/r_i$, separate curves are obtained from the chlorides, bromides and iodides, respectively. Although the result does not confirm the Debye and McAulay equation (3-10-10), it indicates that the activity coefficients in concentrated solutions may be largely determined by the ionic radii. More careful consideration of this possibility will be reserved for Section (7).

(b) Specific Behaviors of 1-1 Electrolytes

In Fig. (12-5-2), $\gamma_\pm$ is plotted against $\sqrt{m}$ for the chlorides, bromides and iodides of the alkali metals up to high concentrations. The spread of the results is great, and very pronounced individual differences, corresponding to large differences in the B-values, occur as the concentration increases. Since all the plots lie above that which represents the limiting law of the theory, there is no definite evidence of ionic association. The graphs show regularity except in one respect. The order for the cations is lithium, sodium, potassium, rubidium, and cesium. For the anions it is iodide, bromide and chloride for the lithium, sodium, and potassium salts, but the reverse for the rubidium and cesium salts. The situation would have been more complicated had the less accurate results of the fluorides been included, because the cation order appears to be reversed for the fluorides.

* H. I. Stonehill and M. A. Berry, [*J. Am. Chem. Soc.*, **64**, 2724 (1942)] express doubt that any relation, such as equation (12-5-4), would exist if $\mathbb{S}_{(f)}$ were altered from 0.5065 to 0.5103. The calculations which they present are misleading, in that the concentration range which they have chosen, 0.01 to 0.10, is not suitable for the determination of B because the contribution of the linear term is less than the experimental error at 0.01M, and of the order of the experimental error at 0.10M. Had they chosen the range 0.1 to 1.0M employed by us, the effect of this change in $\mathbb{S}_{(f)}$ would have been 0.138 in $å$ and -0.0034 in B instead of 0.63 and -0.0528 as given in their example. In calculations of this kind using other values of $\mathbb{S}_{(f)}$, we have always found, for a series of 1-1 halides, that B is a fairly smooth, rapidly increasing function of $å$. Any equation which will express this function will serve to represent the results as a single family of curves.

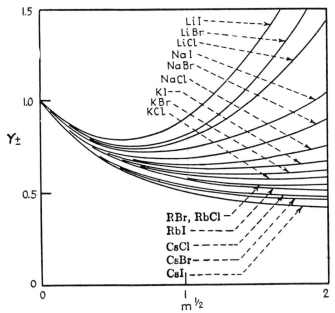

Fig. (12–5–2). Mean activity coefficients of 1-1 halides at 25°.

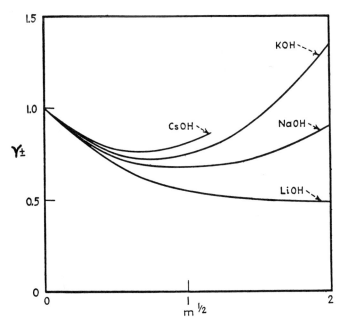

Fig. (12–5–3). Mean activity coefficients of 1-1 hydroxides at 25°.

The most pronounced example of reversal of order occurs with the hydroxides, as demonstrated by the graphs in Fig. (12-5-3). These plots show a wide spread with cesium hydroxide possessing the highest, and lithium hydroxide the lowest activity coefficient. This is exactly opposite to the behavior of the chlorides, bromides and iodides. This behavior may be interpreted partially by ionic interaction, and formation of associated ion pairs. According to Bjerrum's theory of ionic association [Chapter (3), Section (7)], a 1-1 electrolyte is strong if the distance of approach of the ions is equal to or greater than 3.5Å. The above values of $\gamma_\pm$ are consistent with values of mean distances of approach of 3, 3.5, 4, and 4.2Å, for lithium, sodium, potassium and cesium hydroxides, respectively. On the basis of this theory, all these hydroxides are strong electrolytes, although some ionic association may occur in the case of lithinm hydroxide. This observation agrees with indications derived from conductance measurements. A similar order of results is found with the acetates although the spread is not so great.

We suggest that the "normal order" for the halides and the reversal of this order for the hydroxides, acetates etc. has its explanation in solvent interaction with the ions. Owing to the more intense fields of the smaller ions (*i.e.*, the lithium ion), there will be strong interaction with the solvent dipoles. The formation of a sheath of water molecules around the ion will result in high values of $\mathring{a}$, compared with crystallographic radii. With the halides, the values of B [Equation (12-5-2)] are in the same order as the values of $\mathring{a}$, and the activity coefficients will be in the same order. Therefore, the hydration which decreases in the order Li > Na > K > Rb > Cs will account for the order of the activity coefficients found for the halides. But this kind of ion-solvent interaction can also lead to a "localized hydrolysis" by reaction with anions which are proton acceptors.[62a] The protons in these water molecules will be repelled from the hydration sheath and will tend to form linkages with proton acceptors such as hydroxyl or acetate ions. This tendency may be represented by

$$M^+ + H_2O \rightleftharpoons M^+ \cdots OH^- \cdots H^+$$

where the dotted lines represent the linkages due to ion-solvent molecule forces. The interaction with a proton acceptor may be represented by

$$M^+ \cdots OH^- \cdots H^+ + A^- \rightleftharpoons M^+ \cdots OH^- \cdots H^+ \cdots A^-$$

and the proton regarded as oscillating between extreme positions on the hydroxyl group and proton acceptor. Addition of these expressions gives

$$M^+ + H_2O + A^- \rightleftharpoons M^+ \cdots OH^- \cdots H^+ \cdots A^-$$

which resembles ion pair formation of the type

$$M^+ + A^- \rightleftharpoons M^+ \cdots + \cdots A^-$$

in that both lead to a reduction of the number of free ions in the solution. This mechanism leads to a lower activity coefficient than that calculated

[62a] R. A. Robinson and H. S. Harned, *Chem. Rev.*, **28**, 419 (1941).

upon the basis of complete ionization, and this lowering will be greater the smaller the radius of the cation. Thus, for compounds of the proton accepting hydroxides, acetates etc., the order of activity coefficients will be Cs > Rb > K > Na > Li. In some of these cases ordinary hydrolysis may occur but this does not lead to a change in the number of free ions.

(6) Brönsted's Postulates of Specific Ionic Interaction, and Guggenheim's Method of Computation of Osmotic and Activity Coefficients at Low Concentrations

The specificity of the properties of electrolytes has been amply illustrated by the behaviors of their activity coefficients, relative heat contents and heat capacities. The theory of Debye and Hückel does not account for such varied behaviors. Bjerrum's theory of ionic pair formation, supplemented by the theory of Fuoss and Kraus of triple ion formation [Chapter (7)], has proved of great value for interpreting the characteristics of ionic solutions in media of low dielectric constant, but adds little to the interpretation of ionic interaction of strong electrolytes in media of high dielectric constant.

An important contribution to the elucidation of the specific effects of ions of different kinds upon the activity coefficients of other electrolytes was made by Brönsted[63] before the advent of the Debye and Hückel theory. His investigations of the solubilities of higher valence type cobalt compounds in various salt solutions culminated in a generalization known as "the theory of specific ionic interaction". The fundamental postulate of Brönsted's theory is that "in dilute salt solutions of constant total concentrations, ions will be uniformily influenced by ions of like sign." Specific electrical effects take place between the ions and, in dilute solution, only the ions of unlike sign approach each other closely enough to produce these specific effects. Besides the interaction effect, Brönsted also recognizes that there are present solvent, or "salting out" effects. Since most of the experimental evidence in support of the principle of specific ionic interaction was obtained from the investigation of solutions of mixtures of two electrolytes, the detailed discussion of this theory will be reserved for Chapter (14), which deals with the properties of such mixtures.

Guggenheim[64] has employed a combination of the Debye and Hückel theory and a simplified theory of specific interaction for the treatment of 1-1 electrolytes at concentrations from 0 to $0.1M$. A standard electrolyte is chosen which has the characteristics of a "perfect Debye and Hückel electrolyte," or an electrolyte whose rational activity coefficient is deter-

[63] J. N. Brönsted, *J. Am. Chem. Soc.*, **42**, 761 (1920); **44**, 877 (1922); **44**, 938 (1922); **45**, 2898 (1923).

[64] E. A. Guggenheim, Rep. of Scandinavian Science Congress, Copenhagen (1929) p. 296; *Phil. Mag.* [7], **19**, 588 (1935); *Ibid.*, [7], **22**, 322 (1936); E. A. Guggenheim and L. A. Wiseman, *Ibid.*, [7], **25**, 45 (1938).

mined by the equation

$$\log f_{\pm} = -\frac{\mathcal{S}_{(f)}\sqrt{\Gamma}}{1 + A\sqrt{\Gamma}} \tag{3-5-8}$$

This electrolyte obeys Coulomb's law at all distances and its ions are rigid non-polarizable spheres. Further, for purposes of numerical simplicity, let the mean distance of approach of the ions be equal to 3.05 Å. at 25°. Then

$$\log f_{\pm} = -\frac{\mathcal{S}_{(f)}\sqrt{\Gamma}}{1 + \sqrt{\Gamma/2}} \tag{12-6-1}$$

or, for 1-1 electrolytes,

$$\log f_{\pm} = -\frac{\mathcal{S}_{(f)}\sqrt{c}}{1 + \sqrt{c}} \tag{12-6-2}$$

Guggenheim adds to this a linear term to account for the contribution due to all the specific effects which give the electrolyte its individual characteristics. Thus, the very simple and easily applied equation

$$\log f_{\pm} = -\frac{\mathcal{S}_{(f)}\sqrt{c}}{1 + \sqrt{c}} + \lambda c \tag{12-6-3}$$

is obtained. The term λc will include the contributions due to lowering of the dielectric constant (Hückel), to ionic pair formation (Bjerrum), to effects due to ion size, polarizability, etc. Guggenheim applied this equation to the computation of osmotic and activity coefficients from freezing point and electromotive force data at concentrations less than $0.1M$. The agreement with the freezing data is within ± 0.0002 to $\pm 0.0005°C$.

This equation is useful for the calculation of the activity coefficients in dilute solution because of its simplicity. Since at a given temperature the first term on the left is the same for all 1-1 electrolytes, it need only be computed once for each concentration, so that the calculation of $f_{\pm}$ merely involves that of the linear term. In Table (12-6-1A), Guggenheim's values of λ for a large number of electrolytes, and $f_{\pm}(\lambda = 0)$ of the standard electrolyte are tabulated at a number of concentrations. From these, $f_{\pm}$ may be computed up to $0.1M$ with an estimated accuracy of the order of 0.5 per cent, which is sufficient for most practical purposes.

From a theoretical point of view, this treatment is over simplified, even in the range of concentration specified ($<0.1M$). Applied to the activity coefficients of two electrolytes at the same concentration, equation (12-6-3) leads to the relation

$$\log \frac{f_1}{f_2} = \log \frac{\gamma_1}{\gamma_2} = (\lambda_1 - \lambda_2)c = B_{12}c \tag{12-6-4}$$

where $(\lambda_1 - \lambda_2)$ and hence B_{12} is not a function of c. The Debye and Hückel theory does not lead to this result unless the mean distance of approach of the ions is the same for all electrolytes. This would indeed be an unexpected result. According to this theory equation (3-5-8) would lead to

$$\log f_1/f_2 = -\mathscr{S}_{(f)}\sqrt{\Gamma}\left(\frac{1}{1 + A_1\sqrt{\Gamma}} - \frac{1}{1 + A_2\sqrt{\Gamma}}\right) \quad (12\text{-}6\text{-}5)$$

$$\neq B_{12}c$$

an expression which is not linear, but which requires B_{12} to vary with the concentration. The behavior of this function for two 1-1 electrolytes possessing $\mathring{a}$ values of 4.0 and 3.5, respectively, is shown by the curve in Fig. (12-6-1). Here, $\dfrac{\log (f_1/f_2)}{c}$ is plotted against c, and it is clear that it is a function of c.

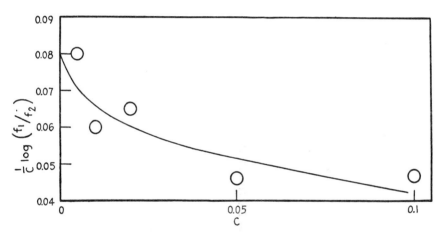

Fig. (12–6–1). Theoretical and experimental variation of $1/c \log (f_1/f_2)$. ——, theoretical; $\bigcirc$, experimental, (1) NaCl; (2) KCl.

Brown and MacInnes, and Shedlovsky and MacInnes obtained $\mathring{a}$ values of 5.6, 4.1, and 4.4 for hydrochloric acid, potassium chloride, and sodium chloride, respectively, when they fitted their accurate data to the Debye and Hückel equation [Table (12-5-1)], and 4.6, 3.7 and 4.0 by using this formula with a linear term [Equation (12-5-2)]. The range of concentration was from 0.005 to 0.1 M. This result is not in accord with Guggenheim's simplified equation. $(\lambda_{HCl} - \lambda_{KCl})$, computed from the observed values of $\log (\gamma_{HCl}/\gamma_{KCl})$, varies from 0.24 to 0.15. In the case of $\log (\gamma_{HCl}/\gamma_{NaCl})$, $(\lambda_{HCl} - \lambda_{NaCl})$ varies from 0.16 to 0.11 from 0.005 to 0.1M. The circles in Fig. (12-6-1) are the values of $(\lambda_{NaCl} - \lambda_{KCl})$ obtained from these results. Even though the computed $\mathring{a}$-values differ by only 0.3, there is an indication that this quantity decreases with increasing concentration.

These computations are extremely sensitive, and can only be verified by the most accurate experiments. We believe that these experiments are sufficiently accurate to indicate that Guggenheim's method is approximate, and of value for practical calculations where simplicity is desired.[65]

(7) The Theory of Concentrated Solutions of Alkali Halides According to Scatchard

In Section (5), we have mentioned the extension of the original Debye and Hückel theory by the addition of a "salting out" term produced by the change in dielectric constant of the medium with ionic concentration. We have also pointed out that although this factor must be considered in a theory of concentrated solutions, it alone is inadequate for their explanation. Indeed, Hückel's formula led to the result that in a hydrochloric acid solution at about $4M$, the dielectric constant would be zero and negative at higher concentrations.[66,67]

The most comprehensive theoretical study of concentrated solutions of strong electrolytes, particularly, the alkali halides, has been made by Scatchard.[68] The simplest case, ions of the noble gas type, is the one best suited for numerical treatment. Scatchard's equation for the activity coefficient is

$$\ln \gamma_\pm = -\ln (1 + \nu_s N_s/N_0) + \frac{\epsilon^2 N}{2RTD_0}\left[\frac{z_1 z_2 \kappa}{1 + \kappa a}\right.$$
$$\left. + \left(\frac{\kappa}{1 + \kappa a} + X\right) z_1 z_2 V_s m d_0 + \frac{4\nu_1 \nu_2}{\nu_s}\left(\frac{V_2 z_1^2}{b_1} + \frac{V_1 z_2^2}{b_2}\right) m d_0\right] \quad (12\text{-}7\text{-}1)$$
$$+ \frac{A m d_0 (2 + \nu_s m d_0)}{RT(1 + V_s m d_0)^2}$$

The extended terms of Gronwall, LaMer and Sandved are omitted. N_s is number of mols of electrolyte, and N_0 is the number of mols of solvent. V_1 and V_2 are the molal volumes of the ions, and V_0 is the molal volume of solvent. The parameters, b_1 and b_2, are the radii of the ions which are effective for "salting out". The other symbols are defined by the following equations in which "a" is the sum of the ionic radii effective in ionic collisions (mean distance of approach), and a_{12}, a_{10}, and a_{20} are the mutual cohesive energy densities.

[65] Additional evidence for this conclusion is discussed by R. A. Robinson and H. S. Harned, *Chem. Rev.*, **28**, 419 (1941).

[66] H. S. Harned, *J. Am. Chem. Soc.*, **48**, 326 (1926).

[67] E. Güntelberg, *Z. Physik. Chem.*, **123**, 199 (1926).

[68] G. Scatchard, *Physik. Z.*, **33**, 22 (1932); *Chem. Rev.*, **19**, 309 (1936). For the development leading to the deduction of equation (12-7-1), see Chapter (3) on "Thermodynamics and Electrostatic Theory" by G. Scatchard in E. J. Cohn and J. T. Edsall, "Proteins, Amino Acids and Peptides," Reinhold Publishing Corporation, New York (1943).

$$md_0 = N_s/V_0 N_0$$

$$\nu_s = \nu_1 + \nu_2$$

$$V_s = \nu_1 V_1 + \nu_2 V_2$$

$$D = D_0 V_0 N_0/V$$

$$\kappa^2 = -\frac{8\pi N^2 \epsilon^2 z_1 z_2 \nu_s N_s}{1000RTDV} = -\frac{8\pi N^2 \epsilon^2 z_1 z_2 \nu_s md_0}{1000RTD_0}$$

$$X = \frac{\kappa}{1 + \kappa a} - Y$$

$$Y = \left[1 + \kappa a - \frac{1}{1 + \kappa a} - 2\ln(1 + \kappa a)\right] \Big/ \kappa^2 a^3$$

$$A = 2\nu_1 \nu_2 V_1 V_2 (2a_{12} - a_{10} - a_{20})/\nu_s$$

We shall not go into detail in the discussion of this complicated expression, but simply describe the significance of each term.

Equation (12-7-1) represents an extension of the Debye and Hückel theory. The first term on the right is merely the usual expression for converting the rational activity coefficient, $f_\pm$, to the stoichiometrical activity coefficient, $\gamma_\pm$. The first two terms within the bracket are essentially those of Debye and Hückel for charge-charge interaction, except that κ is defined for changing dielectric constant, D, rather than for constant dielectric constant, D_0. Whereas Hückel assumes a linear variation of dielectric constant with molarity of electrolyte, Scatchard employs the relation, $D = D_0 V_0 N_0/V$ found by Wyman[69] for nonelectrolytic solutions. The influence of this difference in κ turns out to be small. The effect is proportional to the number of ions in unit volume of solvent. The third term within the brackets is the salting out term, or the charge-molecule term, and corresponds to the Debye and McAulay expression for this effect. These terms are similar to those of the Hückel extension of the theory. The final term outside the brackets is introduced to represent the non-electrolyte molecule-molecule interaction, or the departure of purely non-electrolyte solutions from the ideal solution.

For the application of the theory, it is necessary to know the temperature, the molal volume, and the dielectric constant of solvent, the valence, molal volume in solution, and the radius effective in salting out for each ion, the effective collision diameter of the pair of ions, a, and their molecule-molecule interaction coefficient, A. For alkali halides, the ions are assumed to be spheres. In this, $b = r$, and $a = r_1 + r_2$. The values of the radii were those obtained by Pauling[70] from crystallographic data. The ionic volume in solution was taken to be somewhat less than $4\pi r^3/3$, and the constant, A, was assumed to be the same for all these halides. Brönsted's

[69] J. Wyman Jr., J. Am. Chem. Soc., **58**, 1482 (1936).

[70] L. Pauling, J. Am. Chem. Soc., **50**, 1036 (1928). See Table (5-1-6).

theory of ionic interaction, which excludes short range interaction between ions of like sign, was also employed to simplify certain substitutions. Two parameters were determined empirically from osmotic coefficient data. These were the ratio of the volume in solution to the actual volume of the ions, and the coefficient A. Of these, the first agreed with the theoretically expected value while the second agreed approximately.

The calculations by this theory of the osmotic coefficients of the alkali halides agree, in general, satisfactorily with the data of Robinson and Sinclair, and Robinson. The most important result is that the properties of these noble gas type ions are characterized by their valences, and sizes as determined from crystallographic data. The order and magnitude of the results for the iodides, bromides and chlorides are in good agreement with theory. Further, the theory also predicts the reversal in order of cationic effects in the case of the fluorides as judged from freezing point data.

This investigation of Scatchard is the most determined attempt to obtain a theoretical knowledge of concentrated solutions by a detailed extension of the Debye and Hückel theory. Charge-charge, charge-molecule, and molecule-molecule interaction are considered separately, and relations between the individual thermodynamic properties of the electrolytes and the ionic radii, as determined by crystallographic data, are indicated.

(8) Interpretation of Concentrated Solutions of Electrolytes in Terms of a van der Waals' Co-Volume Effect

We have shown [Section (5)] that the activity coefficients of many 1-1 electrolytes from 0 to $4M$, may be calculated very accurately by the equation,

$$\log f_{\pm} = -\frac{\mathfrak{S}_{(f)}\sqrt{\Gamma}}{1 + 35.57 \mathring{a}(DT)^{-1/2}\sqrt{\Gamma}} + Bc + D'c^2 \qquad (12\text{-}8\text{-}1)$$

The numerator of the first term on the right represents the effect of Coulomb forces between ions considered as point charges. The denominator represents the effect of the restriction on Coulomb forces, imposed by the finite sizes of the ions. The terms Bc and $D'c^2$ are positive, and opposite in sign to the first term, and may be interpreted in terms of the short range repulsive forces which cause such large effects in very concentrated solutions.

As a result of an interesting analysis of the theory of concentrated solutions, Onsager[71] suggested that these repulsive force terms might be expressed as an ordinary van der Waals co-volume correction

$$\Delta \mu_i \approx kT \left(\sum \frac{4\pi}{3} \frac{\mathring{a}^3}{V} \right) \qquad (12\text{-}8\text{-}2)$$

[71] L. Onsager, *Chem. Rev.*, **13**, 73 (1933).

where $\mathring{a}$ is the "mean distance of approach of the ions" and V is the total volume. This amounts to the assumption that the repulsive forces decrease rapidly with the distance, and that these forces may be represented "by a large discontinuity of the potential energy at some distance $(r = \mathring{a})$." Since the parameter $\mathring{a}$ in the excluded volume term [Equation (12-8-2)] is the same as in the first term on the right of equation (12-8-1), this theory raises the possibility, mentioned in Section (5), of expressing the thermodynamic properties of electrolytes in terms of an equation with only one parameter.

This suggestion has been developed in greater detail by Van Rysselberghe and Eisenberg.[72] The problem of computing a suitable function, which represents the mutual exclusion from certain portions of space, in the case of N_1 and N_2 molecules of two kinds with diameters, d_1 and d_2, respectively, is a difficult one. The best treatment so far is that of Ursell[73] who has developed the theory of the general case for any number of molecules, and has obtained a complete solution for the case of two kinds of molecules. His result is greatly simplified by assuming that

$$d_1 = d_2 = d_{12} = d_+ = d_- = d_\pm = a$$

and by the relations

$$N_1 = N_+ = \nu_+ N; \qquad N_2 = N_- = \nu_- N$$

$$\nu_+ + \nu_- = \nu$$

$$N_i = (\nu_+ + \nu_-)N = \nu N$$

d_+, d_- and $d_\pm$ denote the cationic, anionic, and mean ionic diameters of the ions and electrolyte, respectively. We note that $d_\pm$ is equated to the mean distance of closest approach a, of the ions, and appears as a parameter, not a mean diameter derived from crystallographic data. For the case of a binary electrolyte, the excluded volume term (ln Y of Van Rysselberghe) is simply

$$\ln Y = -\frac{1}{2}\frac{N_i^2}{V}v - \frac{5}{64}\frac{N_i^3}{V^2}v^2 \tag{12-8-3}$$

where V is the volume, and $v = \frac{4}{3}\pi a^3$. The excluded volume effect contributes to the total van der Waals work content of the solution, A_w^*, the amount,

$$A_w^* = N_i\Delta\mu_i^* + N_0\Delta\mu_0^* = -kT \ln Y$$

$$= N_i kT \left[\frac{1}{2}\frac{N_i}{V}v + \frac{5}{64}\left(\frac{N_i}{V}\right)^2 v^2\right] \tag{12-8-4}$$

[72] P. Van Rysselberghe and S. Eisenberg, *J. Am. Chem. Soc.*, **61**, 3030 (1939); Correction, *Ibid.*, **62**, 451 (1940).

[73] H. D. Ursell, *Proc. Camb. Phil. Soc.*, **23**, 685 (1927); See R. H. Fowler, "Statistical Mechanics," 2nd edition, pp. 241 *et seq.*, Cambridge University Press (1936).

If, taking into consideration the small compressibility of ionic solutions, A_w^* be replaced by F_w^*, the van der Waals contribution to the activity coefficient, $\ln f_\pm^*$, may be obtained by differentiating with respect to N_i at constant P, T, and N_0. Thus,

$$\ln f_\pm^* = \frac{\Delta \mu_i^*}{kT} = \frac{1}{kT} \frac{\partial F_w^*}{\partial N_i}$$

$$= \frac{N_i}{V} v + \frac{15}{64} \left(\frac{N_i}{V}\right)^2 v^2 - \left[\frac{1}{2} \left(\frac{N_i}{V}\right)^2 v + \frac{10}{64} \left(\frac{N_i}{V}\right)^3 v^2\right] \frac{\partial V}{\partial N_i} \qquad (12\text{-}8\text{-}5)$$

Similarly, the activity coefficient of the solvent is given by

$$\log f_1^* = \frac{\partial F^*}{\partial V} \frac{\partial V}{\partial N_0} = - \left[\frac{1}{2} \left(\frac{N_i}{V}\right)^2 v + \frac{10}{64} \left(\frac{N_i}{V}\right)^3 v^2\right] \frac{\partial V}{\partial N_0} \qquad (12\text{-}8\text{-}6)$$

Expressing 'a' in Ånstrom units, converting to molar concentrations, and neglecting the last term in $\partial V/\partial N_i$, we obtain from equation (12-8-5) the result

$$\log f_\pm^* = 2.2063 \times 10^{-3} \mathring{a}^3 c + 2.6269 \times 10^{-6} \mathring{a}^6 c^2 \qquad (12\text{-}8\text{-}7)$$

for binary electrolytes. This is the theoretical result corresponding to the terms $Bc + D'c^2$ in equation (12-8-1).

It is hardly to be expected that this simplified picture is sufficient to give an accurate representation of the results. In the case of hydrochloric acid, we found that the experimental results at 25° could be expressed with an accuracy of ±0.001 in γ if $\mathring{a}$, B and D' were 4.3, 0.1292 and 0.00615, respectively. Using 4.3 for $\mathring{a}$, the theoretical equation (12-8-7) yields 0.1754 and 0.01661 for B and D', respectively. This indicates that the van der Waals co-volume effect is more than sufficient to account for the contribution corresponding to the net repulsive forces between the ions.

We have noted in Section (5) the possibility of obtaining a single parameter equation for the computation of activity coefficients of 1-1 electrolytes at a given temperature. Van Rysselberghe and Eisenberg found that the empirical equation

$$\log f_\pm = - \frac{0.5059 \sqrt{c}}{1 + \frac{\mathring{a}}{3.042} \sqrt{c}} \qquad (12\text{-}8\text{-}8)$$

$$+ 2.206 \times 10^{-3} \mathring{a}^3 c + 26.27 \times 10^{-7} \mathring{a}^6 c^2$$

similar in form to (12-8-1), nearly satisfies this possibility from 0.1 to $4M$. The application of this equation to 1-1 halides yields values of $\mathring{a}$ which do not differ greatly from those obtained by equation (12-5-2) from data in the concentration range from 0.05 to $3M$. They are lower than those evaluated from the best data from 0.005 to $1M$ [Table (12-5-2)], and lead to values of $\gamma_\pm$ at $0.1M$ which are somewhat too low. However, considering the complexity of the situation, the single parameter equation is a surprisingly good approximation.

(9) Ionic Hydration, Activity Coefficients and Osmotic Coefficients

In Sections (5) to (8), theories proposed to account for the behaviors of the activity coefficients of electrolytes in concentrated solutions were considered in detail. Two of these extensions of the Debye and Hückel theory, those of Hückel and of Scatchard, depended largely on the computation of the effects produced upon the activity coefficient by ion-ion, ion-solvent, and molecule-molecule interactions in relation to change in dielectric constant produced by varying concentration of electrolyte. Another theory, developed by Van Rysselberghe, was based upon the estimation of a van der Waals' co-volume effect. In 1920, before the advent of the Debye and Hückel theory, Bjerrum[74] proposed a theory of ionic hydration. We shall now discuss a version of Bjerrum's theory modernized and expanded by Stokes and Robinson.[75]

In deriving the equations of this theory, we shall not use the method of Stokes and Robinson, who employed the Gibbs-Duhem equation, but shall follow closely a derivation by Harned[76] based directly upon the law of mass action. We shall assume that the equilibria in an aqueous solution of an electrolyte are represented by the reactions and equations

$$(1) \ CA \rightleftharpoons C^+ + A^- \qquad \qquad ; K_1 = a_+a_-/a_2$$

$$(2) \ C^+ + h \ H_2O \rightleftharpoons C^+ \cdot h \ H_2O; \ K_2 = a_h/a_+a_w^h \qquad (12\text{-}9\text{-}1)$$

$$(3) \ A^- + j \ H_2O \rightleftharpoons A^- \cdot j \ H_2O \ ; \ K_3 = a_j/a_-a_w^j$$

where K_1, K_2 and K_3 are mass action constants; a_+, a_- are the activities of the non-hydrated ions; a_h, a_j, those of the hydrated ions; and a_w is the activity of water. Multiplication of the three mass action expressions yields

$$K_1K_2K_3 = \frac{a_ha_j}{a_2a_w^n}; \qquad K_2K_3 = \frac{a_ha_j}{a_+a_-a_w^n} \qquad (12\text{-}9\text{-}2)$$

where $n = (h + j)$. If the convention is adopted that $a_w = 1$ at infinite dilution of electrolyte, $K_2K_3 = 1$, and this expression becomes

$$a_+a_- = a_ha_j/a_w^n \qquad (12\text{-}9\text{-}3)$$

Upon introduction of the activity coefficients and molalities, and by conversion to logarithms

[74] N. Bjerrum, Z. anorg. Chem., **109**, 275 (1920).

[75] R. H. Stokes and R. A. Robinson, J. Am. Chem. Soc., **70**, 1870 (1948); R. A. Robinson and R. H. Stokes, Ann. N. Y. Acad. Sci., **51**, 593 (1949).

[76] H. S. Harned, in H. S. Taylor, "Treatise on Physical Chemistry," First Edition, Vol. 2, p. 776–8, D. Van Nostrand and Co., New York (1924).

$$\log \gamma_{\pm} m = \log \gamma'_{\pm} m' - \frac{n}{\nu} \log a_w \qquad (12\text{-}9\text{-}4)$$

is obtained. In this expression, $\gamma_{\pm}$ is the mean activity coefficient of the electrolyte, m its stoichiometric molality, $\gamma'_{\pm}$ the activity coefficient of the hydrated ions and m' their molality. If the electrolyte is assumed to be *completely dissociated at all concentrations* m' can be represented by

$$m' = \frac{55.51m}{55.51 - nm} = \frac{m}{1 - 0.018nm} \qquad (12\text{-}9\text{-}5)$$

As the concentration of the electrolyte tends toward zero, the mass action law requires that complete hydration of the ions is approached. Consequently, it is safe to assume that the Debye and Hückel equation (5-2-8) represents the activity coefficient of the hydrated ions or that

$$\log \gamma'_{\pm} = -\frac{\mathcal{S}_{(f)}\sqrt{c}}{1 + A'\sqrt{c}} - \log (1 + 0.018\nu m') \qquad (12\text{-}9\text{-}6)$$

If this result for $\log \gamma'_{\pm}$ is substituted in equation (12-9-4), m' eliminated by equation (12-9-5), and $A'\sqrt{c}$ expressed by equations (5-2-9) and (5-2-10), we obtain

$$\log \gamma_{\pm} = -\frac{\mathcal{S}_{(f)}\sqrt{c}}{1 + 0.3286\, å\sqrt{\Gamma/2}}$$
$$- \frac{n}{\nu} \log a_w - \log (1 - 0.018(n - \nu)m) \qquad (12\text{-}9\text{-}7)$$

which is the "modernized" Bjerrum equation as employed by Stokes and Robinson, except that they replace c and $\Gamma/2$ by m and μ, respectively.

This equation contains two adjustable parameters, $å$ and n, and is capable of representing the activity coefficient with an accuracy equal to that of equation (12-5-2), and over a wider range of concentration. For practical purposes, it is not as easy to use as equations (12-5-2) and (12-5-3), since it is necessary to evaluate a_w from the experimental activity coefficients. Table (12-9-1) contains some of the values of $å$ and n listed in the more extended table of Stokes and Robinson.

In Chapter (12), Sections (5) and (8), we noted the possibility of obtaining a single-parameter equation for computing the activity coefficient over a considerable range of concentration. To this end, Stokes and Robinson introduce the relation

$$å = \left[\frac{3}{4\pi} (30n + V_+) \right]^{1/3} + r_- - \Delta \qquad (12\text{-}9\text{-}8)$$

by which $å$ can be eliminated from equation (12-9-7). As a result, the hydration number, n, is the only parameter required. The justification of this equation rests on the conclusions of Bernal and Fowler[77] regarding

[77] J. D. Bernal and R. H. Fowler, *J. Chem. Phys.*, **1**, 515 (1933).

the apparent molal volumes of ions and water. It is assumed that the large anions, Cl^-, Br^-, I^-, are much less hydrated than the smaller cations, Li^+, Na^+ etc., so that r_- is the crystallographic radius of the anion. It is also assumed that the water molecule occupies an effective volume of 30 cubic Angström units, and therefore, if V_+ is the apparent ionic volume of the cation, $\left[\dfrac{3}{4\pi}(30n + V_+)\right]^{1/3}$ is the effective "idealized" radius, r_1, of the hydrated cation. To estimate V_+, Stokes and Robinson computed the apparent molal volumes of some electrolytes at 1 M concentration from density data. These can be represented by the empirical equation, $V_{app.} = 6.47\,(r_+^3 + r_-^3)$ where r_+ and r_- are the crystallographic radii [Table (5-1-6)]. If each anion contributes $6.47\,r_-^3$ cubic Angströms, the cation contribution is $V_+ = V_{app.} - 6.47\,\nu_- r_-^3/\nu_+$, where ν_-/ν_+ is the number of anions asso-

TABLE (12-9-1). CONSTANTS OF EQUATION (12-9-7), AND OF EQUATIONS (12-9-7) AND (12-9-8) COMBINED

Electrolyte	Equation (12-9-7)		Equation (12-9-7) and (12-9-8)		
	n	$å$	n	$å$	R
HCl	8.0	4.47	7.3	4.84	0.1-1
LiCl	7.1	4.32	6.5	4.66	.1-2
NaCl	3.5	3.97	3.5	3.97	.1-5
KCl	1.9	3.63	1.9	3.63	.1-4
RbCl	1.2	3.49	1.25	3.47	.1-2
$MgCl_2$	13.7	5.02	13.9	4.99	.1-1
$CaCl_2$	12.0	4.73	11.9	4.75	.1-1.8
$SrCl_2$	10.7	4.61	10.8	4.60	.1-1.8
$BaCl_2$	7.7	4.45	8.4	4.29	.1-1

R—Molal concentration range of validity of the single-parameter equation (12-9-7) combined with (12-9-8).

sociated with one cation. From this relation, V_+ is calculated, and r_1 evaluated from V_+. It is found that $(r_1 + r_-)$ exceeds the value of $å$, derived by the two parameter equation (12-9-7), by 0.7 Å. for alkali halides, and 1.3 Å for alkaline-earth halides. This quantity, Δ in equation (12-9-8), is interpreted as a penetration of the anion into the hydration shell of the cation,[78] or as a distortion of the ions in the field.

In the fourth column of Table (12-9-1) are listed the values of n which yielded the most satisfactory agreement with the experimental data. The fifth column contains values of $å$ computed by equation (12-9-8) and it is apparent that these agree closely with those in the third column. The agreement with the observed results is within ± 0.0015 in $\gamma_\pm$ over the concentration ranges listed in the last column, and is surprisingly good for calcium and strontium chlorides.

[78] H. S. Frank, *J. Am. Chem. Soc.*, **63**, 1789 (1941).

Glueckauf[79] has proposed a theory of hydration based upon volume fraction statistics. His equation is as effective as equation (12-9-7) for computing activity coefficients and yields values for the hydration numbers roughly one-half those in Table (12-9-1). Miller[80] has used a free volume theory to determine hydration numbers and obtains hydration numbers about twice those in Table (12-9-1).

Thermodynamic Properties of Ions in Relation to Their Size and Structure

As a result of the recent comprehensive investigations of the freezing points by Scatchard and Prentiss [Chapter (9)], and the isopiestic vapor pressure measurements of Robinson, sufficient knowledge of the thermodynamic coefficients of many 1-1 electrolytes has been obtained to permit a crude classification of them in terms of the structure of the ions.[81, 82] For convenience, the following scheme may be adopted:

Group I. Noble gas type cations with
　　　　　(1) Noble gas type anions.
　　　　　(2) Anions which are proton acceptors.
　　　　　　　(a) Small anions, F^-, OH^-, etc.
　　　　　　　(b) Unsymmetrical anions, $HCOO^-$, CH_3COO^-, etc.
　　　　　(3) Polyatomic anions of the type, NO_3^-, ClO_3^-, ClO_4^-, etc.
Group II. Polyatomic Cations, H_3O^+, NH_4^+, and organo-substituted ammonium ions.

The first class in Group I has been discussed in the preceding sections, and it appeared that the individual properties depended very largely on the size of the ions. The peculiar interaction which causes the reversal of the cationic effects in the presence of the fluoride and hydroxide ions depends also on the very small size of these according to Scatchard and Prentiss. Although little is known accurately about the fluorides, it would appear that the fluoride ion is a proton acceptor since the osmotic coefficient of $1M$ hydrofluoric acid is about the same as that of formic acid at this concentration. If this is the case, the mechanism of cationic reaction with the solvent water, discussed in Section (5), may be an important factor. An anion of large size such as the acetate probably has its charge at a considerable distance from its center. This would account for its proton accepting capability, and the reversal in the order of the cationic effects.

---

[79] E. Glueckauf, *Trans. Faraday Soc.*, **51**, 1235 (1955).

[80] D. G. Miller, *J. Phys. Chem.*, **60**, 1296 (1956).

[81] H. S. Harned and G. Åkerlöf, *Physik. Z.*, **27**, 411 (1926).

[82] Similar attempts have been made when fewer data were available by H. S. Harned [H. S. Taylor, "Treatise on Physical Chemistry," 2nd Edition, Chapter XII, p. 823 ff. Van Nostrand and Co., New York, (1929)]. The present discussion follows closely the summary given by G. Scatchard and S. S. Prentiss, *J. Am. Chem. Soc.*, **56**, 807 (1934).

The behavior of the salts of the polyatomic anions which are not proton acceptors (their acids are strong electrolytes) is more difficult to explain. The characteristics of the alkaline nitrates, chlorates or perchlorates are illustrated by Fig. (12-9-1), in which the activity coefficients of the nitrates are compared with the chlorides. Although the anion is complex, the cationic order is the same, but the spread of the curves for the nitrates is a little greater. Scatchard and Prentiss have pointed out that since the cationic order is the reverse of that of the acetates, etc., the effects cannot be explained by an unsymmetrical ionic charge distribution. Further, in regard to effects of dipole moments, Scatchard and Prentiss say, "The

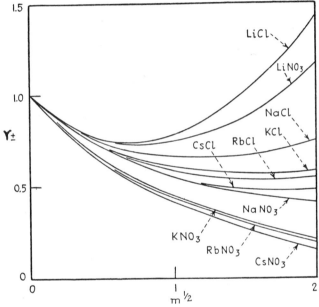

Fig. (12-9-1). Mean activity coefficients of 1-1 chlorides and nitrates at 25°.

fact that the difference from the halide ions is no greater for the chlorate, which should have a dipole, than for the nitrate and perchlorate which have no dipoles unless the structure in solution is very different from that in the crystal, eliminates the dipole moment as an important factor."

There is not sufficient knowledge of the properties of the polyatomic cations to throw much light on their behavior. The hydronium ion in strong acid solutions behaves nearly the same as the lithium ion, even though their sizes appear to be quite different.

The symmetrical ammonium ion in concentrated solutions acts similarly to the smaller sodium or potassium ions. Scatchard and Prentiss[83] found that the ammonium halides and nitrates behave uniquely in dilute solution

[83] G. Scatchard and S. S. Prentiss, *J. Am. Chem. Soc.*, **54**, 2696 (1932).

($< 0.04M$). They all show an effect similar to that of ionic association, which at higher concentrations disappears due to factors which increase the activity coefficient. No other 1-1 electrolytes have been found which possess this characteristic ion interaction. So far, a satisfactory explanation of the effect has not been found.

The freezing points of solutions of alkyl ammonium fluorides and chlorides have been measured accurately by Ebert and Lange,[84] and Lange.[85] Their values of the osmotic coefficients of these strong electrolytes are plotted in Fig. (12-9-2). The dashed line represents the Debye and Hückel limiting law. The chlorides are all strong electrolytes, whereas the fluoride ion appears to form ion pairs with these polyatomic cations, since their curves all lie below the limiting law.

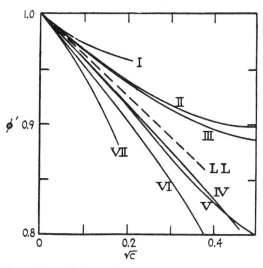

Fig. (12-9-2). Osmotic coefficients of alkyl ammonium chlorides and fluorides at the freezing point. I, $N(C_4H_9)_4Cl$; II, $N(C_3H_7)_4Cl$; III, $N(CH_3)_4Cl$; IV, $N(CH_3)_4F$; V, $N(CH_3)_3(C_5H_{11})F$; VI, $N(C_3H_7)_4F$; VII, $N(C_4H_9)_4F$. L.L., theoretical limiting law.

That the effect of ionic association may appear in the case of a monoatomic ion of a high electron complexity is evidenced by the behavior of thallous chloride. Cowperthwaite, LaMer and Barksdale[86] have measured the electromotive force of the cells,

$$Tl(s) \mid TlCl(m) \mid AgCl\text{-}Ag$$

from 0 to 50°. Their results indicated ion-pair formation with a dissociation constant of 0.3.

[84] L. Ebert and J. Lange, *Z. Physik. Chem.*, A, **139**, 584 (1928).

[85] J. Lange, *Ibid.*, A, **168**, 147 (1934).

[86] I. A. Cowperthwaite, V. K. LaMer and J. Barksdale, *J. Am. Chem. Soc.*, **56**, 544 (1934).

Transition from Simple Ions to Complex Aggregates and Polymer Electrolytes

The scope of material in this treatise has been purposefully limited to the theories and properties of solutions containing ions of comparatively simple structures. In view of the large quantity of contemporary research upon long-chain, multiple-charge electrolytes and proteins, we thought it appropriate to discuss briefly results which illustrate the transition in properties of typical series of salt solutions containing ions of increasing complexity.

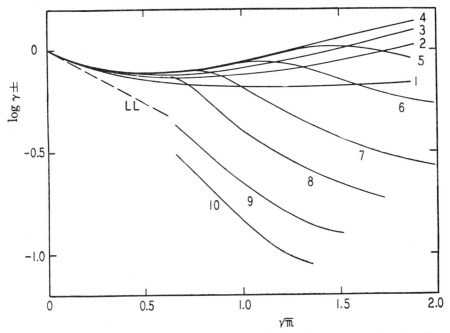

Fig. (12-9-3). Mean activity coefficients of sodium salts of monocarboxylic acids in water at 25°. 1, Formate; 2, acetate; 3, propionate; 4, butyrate; 5, valerate; 6, caproate; 7, heptylate; 8, caprylate; 9, pelargonate; and 10, caprate.

Fig. (12-9-3) contains graphs of the mean activity coefficients of the sodium salts of the first ten normal aliphatic acids.[87] The activity coefficients of the first four members of the series show the characteristic behavior of simple 1-1 type strong electrolytes in water, as illustrated by Figs. (12-5-2), (12-5-3) and (12-9-1). Sodium valerate is the first to exhibit a deviation from normal behavior, since the plot of its activity coefficient is seen to cross that of sodium butyrate. Beginning with sodium caproate, the difference in behavior is very pronounced, and becomes in-

[87] E. R. B. Smith and R. A. Robinson, *Trans. Faraday Soc.*, **38**, 70 (1942).

creasingly so as the number of carbon atoms in the salt increases. These results indicate the presence of micelle formation in all the solutions from the six- to ten-carbon atom salts. Extremely sharp bends occur with the salts containing nine and ten carbon atoms.

The abrupt transition from simple ions to micelles is very apparent in the variation of the equivalent conductivity with concentration. This is illustrated in **Fig.** (12-9-4) in which the appearance of characteristic breaks in the conductivity curves of the higher members of a series of alkylamine hydrochlorides[88, 89] indicate micelle formation. The break is very sharp for octadecylamine and hexadecylamine hydrochlorides, and becomes less pronounced with decreasing number of carbon atoms in the cation. The plot for octylamine hydrochloride is typical of normal 1-1

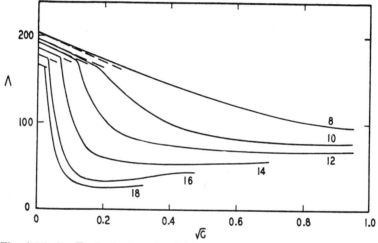

Fig. (12-9-4). Equivalent conductivities of alkylamine hydrochlorides in water at 25°. 8, Octyl-; 10, decyl-; 12, dodecyl-; 14, tetradecyl-; 16, hexadecyl-; and 18, octadecyl-amine hydrochloride.

type strong electrolytes. The concentration at which this transition from the behavior of typical electrolytes to that of micelles takes place is very sensitive to the structure of the solute and the nature of the solvent medium. The complex behaviors of the above type of electrolytes in mixed solvents and in the presence of added electrolytes of simpler structures have been the subject of many recent investigations[90] by Kraus, Tartar, Ralston, and

[88] A. W. Ralston and C. W. Hoerr, *J. Am. Chem. Soc.*, **64,** 772 (1942).

[89] A. W. Ralston, C. W. Hoerr and E. J. Hoffman, *Ibid.*, **64,** 97 (1942).

[90] For typical investigations of this kind, see P. F. Grieger and C. A. Kraus, *J. Am. Chem. Soc.*, **70,** 3803 (1948); A. B. Scott, H. V. Tartar and E. C. Lingafelter, *Ibid.*, **65,** 698 (1943); and A. W. Ralston and D. N. Eggenberger, *Ibid.*, **70,** 2918 (1948). A summary of some of this work is given by P. F. Grieger, *Ann. N. Y. Acad. Sci.*, **51,** 827 (1949).

their colleagues. An important theoretical interpretation of these effects has been proposed by Debye.[91]

(10) ACTIVITY COEFFICIENTS OF NEUTRAL MOLECULES IN AQUEOUS SALT SOLUTIONS

The computation of the activity coefficient of a neutral molecule in a salt solution may be made most readily from solubility determinations, or from partition measurements. Consider a gas in equilibrium with its aqueous solution according to a reaction such as: $O_2(g) = O_2(aq.)$. The equilibrium constant at constant P and T is

$$K = \frac{a_2(aq.)}{a_2(g)} = \frac{f_{(s)} N_{(s)}}{p} \tag{12-10-1}$$

if the pressure of the gas, p, is low enough to equal its fugacity. $N_{(s)}$ and $f_{(s)}$ are the mol fraction and activity coefficient of the gas in the salt solution. In pure water, let $f_{(s)} = f_{(0)} = 1$, and $\gamma_{(s)} = m_{(0)}/m_{(s)}$. Then, $f_{(s)} N_{(s)} = N_{(0)}$, and

$$f_{(s)} = \frac{N_{(0)}}{N_{(s)}} = \gamma_{(s)} \frac{55.5 + m_{(s)}}{55.5 + m_{(0)}} \tag{12-10-2}$$

Exactly the same relation would be obtained for the activity coefficient of a liquid or a solid solute in a salt solution, provided that the activity coefficients are taken to be unity in the saturated solution in pure water.

An exhaustive survey of the data previous to 1927 has been made by Randall and Failey.[92] This material, and more recent determinations of the activity coefficients of helium, argon, and more complicated molecules such as ethyl acetate[93] and diacetone alcohol, will be employed to illustrate the complicated nature of the effects.

Empirical equations for the salt effect upon neutral molecules have been proposed by a number of investigators.[94] Of these, we mention particularly that of Setchénow,

$$\log \frac{S^0}{S} = k_s c \tag{12-10-3}$$

[91] P. Debye, *Ann. N. Y. Acad. Sci.*, **51**, 575 (1949).
[92] M. Randall and C. F. Failey, *Chem. Rev.*, **4**, 271 (1927); **4**, 285 (1927); **4**, 291 (1927).
[93] G. Åkerlöf, *J. Am. Chem. Soc.*, **57**, 1198 (1935), He, A; *Ibid.*, **51**, 984 (1929), Diacetone alcohol; S. Glasstone and A. Pound, *J. Chem. Soc.*, **127**, 2660 (1925), S. Glasstone, D. W. Dimond and E. C. Jones, *Ibid.*, **128**, 2935 (1926), Ethyl acetate.
[94] M. Setchénow, *Ann. chim. phys.*, [6] **25**, 226 (1892); V. Gordon, *Z. Physik. Chem.*, **18**, 8 (1895); V. Rothmund, *Ibid.*, **33**, 401 (1900).

where S^0 and S are the solubilities of the neutral molecule in the pure solvent and the salt solution, respectively, c is the concentration in mols per liter, and k_s is a constant. Comparison with equation (12-10-2) indicates that the relations,

$$\log f_{(s)} = k_N \mu \qquad (12\text{-}10\text{-}4)$$

$$\log \gamma_{(s)} = k_m \mu \qquad (12\text{-}10\text{-}5)$$

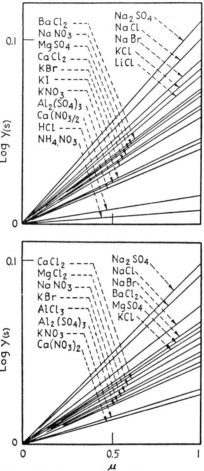

Fig. (12–10–1a). Various salt effects. Upper figure, N_2O; lower figure, C_2H_4.

where μ is the ionic strength, should serve as a useful means of expressing the results. That such a linear relationship is a first approximation, and not strictly valid, has been shown by Randall and Failey. On the other hand, it gives a fair representation of the data, and will be used as a basis for the present discussion.

In Table (12-10-1A), the salting coefficients, k_m [Equation (12-10-5)] for helium,[95] argon,[95] hydrogen,[96] oxygen,[96] nitrous oxide,[96] carbon dioxide,[96] iodine,[96] acetylene[96] in many salt solutions are compiled. Similar constants for the liquids ethyl acetate,[97] diacetone alcohol,[98] phenyl thiourea,[99] and phenol[100] are also given. The general nature of the phenomenon is shown in Fig. (12-10-1), in which log $\gamma_{(s)}$ for two gases and two liquid molecules in many salt solutions are plotted against the ionic strength.

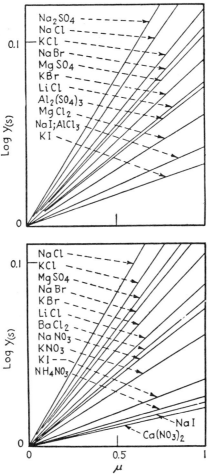

Fig. (12-10-1b). Various salt effects. Upper figure, diacetone alcohol; lower figure, ethyl acetate.

[95] G. Åkerlöf, *J. Am. Chem. Soc.*, **57**, 1196 (1935).

[96] M. Randall and C. F. Failey, *Chem. Rev.*, **4**, 271 (1927); **4**, 285 (1927).

[97] S. Glasstone and A. Pound, *J. Chem. Soc.*, **127**, 2660 (1925); S. Glasstone, D. W. Dimond and E. C. Jones, *Ibid.*, **128**, 2935 (1926).

[98] G. Åkerlöf, *J. Am. Chem. Soc.*, **51**, 984 (1929).

[99] W. Blitz, *Z. physik. Chem.*, **43**, 41 (1903); V. Rothmund, *Ibid.*, **33**, 401 (1900).

[100] W. Herz and F. Hiebenthal, *Z. anorg. Chem.*, **177**, 363 (1929).

We note immediately the similarity in nature of the graphs. The order of magnitude of the salting out is the same, and the order of the salt effects is approximately the same. Minor changes in order of the salt effects may be observed. The similarity between the order and magnitude of the effects upon such dissimilar molecules as nitrous oxide and diacetone alcohol should be noted.

In Chapter (3), Section (10), the Debye and McAulay equation (3-10-9) for the salting effect on neutral molecules by electrolytes,

$$\ln f_{(s)} = \frac{\bar{\beta}}{2kTD_0} \sum_1^i \frac{n_j e_j^2}{b_j} \qquad (12\text{-}10\text{-}6)$$

was obtained. The derivation showed that this equation is an approximation for dilute solutions, and cannot be expected to yield quantitative results at high concentrations. It will be interesting, however, to compare qualitatively the results of this theory with the experimental data.

We recall that $\bar{\beta}$ is a constant characteristic of the non-electrolyte, defined by the relation, $D = D_0 - \bar{\beta}n$, where n is the number of molecules of non-electrolyte. D is the dielectric constant of the mixture of non-electrolyte and solvent (water), D_0 is that of pure solvent. n_j is the number of ions of the kind, j, of radius, b_j. The summation is over all the ions present. The coefficient, $\bar{\beta}$, is positive when the non-electrolyte has a lower dielectric constant than that of the solvent. Since water has a high dielectric constant, $f_{(s)}$ of most neutral substances, should be increased in aqueous solutions. The data in Fig. (12-10-1) bear out this prediction. Further, the theory predicts that $\log f_{(s)}$ varies linearly with the ional concentration which again conforms with experimental observation, since $\Gamma \cong 2\mu$. Finally, the salt effects should be in the order of the sum of the reciprocals of the ionic radii. If crystallographic radii [Table (5-1-6)] are employed, this prediction is not followed, and many exceptions may be noted.

The salt effects of sodium and barium chlorides upon a number of neutral molecules are shown in Fig. (12-10-2). In the case of barium chloride solutions, the spread of the results is much smaller than in that of the sodium chloride, a fact which indicates that the constant $\bar{\beta}$ must vary from salt to salt in order to satisfy the results.

We may sum up this complicated situation in the following manner. The equation of Debye and McAulay has the form of the empirical equation (12-10-5), and leads to results of the right order of magnitude.[101] This shows that the electrostatic influence is an important part of the salting out effect. The role of the ionic radius is confused, and the theoretical prediction of the order of effects does not agree with the observed results. The theory requires salting out in aqueous solution, while numerous examples of salting in (ethyl acetate in cesium iodide) occur. These discrepancies might be partially eliminated if the investigations were confined to dilute solutions of both neutral molecules and salts.

[101] G. Scatchard, *Trans. Far. Soc.*, **23**, 454 (1927).

The Activity Coefficient of the Undissociated Part of Some Weak Acids in Salt Solutions

In Table (12-10-2A), the salting coefficients, k_m, of benzoic, o-toluylic, o-nitrobenzoic, salicylic, acetic and chloroacetic acids, as computed by Randall and Failey,[102] are recorded. The results for the first four of these

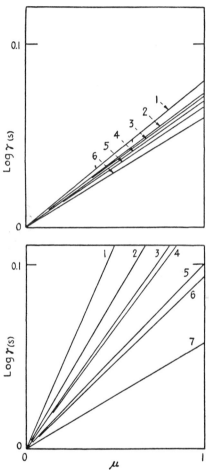

Fig. (12–10–2). Salt effects of barium and sodium chlorides upon various substances. Upper figure, barium chloride: 1, ethyl acetate; 2, phenylthiourea; 3, N_2O; 4, argon, phenol; 5, C_2H_4; 6, CO_2. Lower figure, sodium chloride: 1, phenol; 2, ethyl acetate; 3, phenylthiourea, diacetone alcohol; 4, O_2; 5, N_2O; 6, H_2, C_2H_4; 7, argon.

acids were obtained from the solubility data of Rördam,[103] and Hoffmann and Langebeck,[104] while those for acetic acid were compiled from the

[102] M. Randall and C. F. Failey, *Chem. Rev.*, **4**, 291 (1927).
[103] H. N. K. Rördam, *Thesis*, Copenhagen (1926).
[104] F. Hoffmann and K. Langebeck, *Z. physik. Chem.*, **51**, 385 (1905).

results of Sugden,[105] and McBain and Kam.[106] Sugden determined the distribution of acetic acid between amyl alcohol and water, whereas McBain and Kam obtained a quantity which was proportional to the partial pressure of acid over the solution, divided by the concentration of the undissociated molecules of the acid in the solution. Randall and Failey investigated the distribution of monochloro- and dichloro-acetic acids between dibutyl ether and aqueous salt solutions.

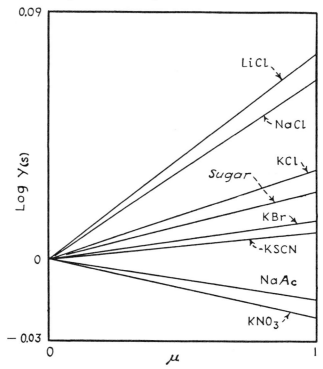

Fig. (12–10–3). Salt effects upon acetic acid.

In Fig. (12-10-3), values of $\log \gamma_{(s)}$ of acetic acid are plotted against the ionic strength. We note that these results are similar to those of other non-electrolytes shown in Figs. (12-10-1), and (12-10-2). Minor dissimilarities in order of the curves may be noted as well as salting in effects in sodium acetate and potassium nitrate solutions.

Partition of Acetone and Hydrocyanic Acid Between Aqueous Salt Solutions and Benzene. The Debye Theory of Salt Effects

A thorough investigation of the effects of salts on the activity coefficients of acetone and hydrocyanic acid has been conducted by Gross,[107] by measur-

[105] J. N. Sugden, *J. Chem. Soc.*, **128**, 174 (1926).

[106] J. W. McBain and J. Kam, *J. Chem. Soc.*, **115**, 1332 (1919).

[107] P. Gross and K. Schwarz, *Sitz. Akad. Wiss. Wien*, **139**, 179 (1930); P. Gross and M. Iser, *Ibid.*, **139**, 221 (1930).

ing the distribution of these substances between water, or aqueous salt solutions, and benzene. These measurements are particularly suitable for testing the Debye theory of the salting effect [Chapter (3), Section (11)], since acetone lowers, and hydrocyanic acid raises the dielectric constant of water.

From the partition coefficients between benzene and pure water, and freezing point measurements of the solutions in benzene combined with calorimetric data, the activity coefficients in benzene were calculated as a function of the concentration. From these, the activity coefficients of the compounds in the salt solutions may be computed. Gross tabulates the functions

$$f_c \equiv \left(\frac{c_B}{c_0}\right)_s \bigg/ \left(\frac{c_B}{c_0}\right)_0 \; ; \qquad f_m = \left(\frac{m_B}{m_0}\right)_s \bigg/ \left(\frac{m_B}{m_0}\right)_0 \qquad (12\text{-}10\text{-}7)$$

where the subscripts s and 0 indicate the presence and the absence of electrolytes, respectively, and B refers to the benzene solutions. In the partition experiments with dilute salt solutions, $[c_B]_s \cong [c_B]_0$, and the above ratios are nearly equal to the ratio of the activity coefficient in the salt solution to that in pure water. At higher concentrations of salt, a small correction can be made for the variation of the activity coefficient with concentration of the salted out substance in the benzene layer.

The salting effects were found to be dependent upon the nature of the non-electrolyte, but practically independent of its concentration and the temperature. Further, the equations

$$\frac{1}{f_c} = 1 - b_c c; \qquad \frac{1}{f_m} = 1 - b_m c \qquad (12\text{-}10\text{-}8)$$

in which c is the salt concentration, represent the results approximately.[108] In Fig. (12-10-4), some of Gross's results are plotted. The full and dashed lines represent the salting of acetone and hydrocyanic acid, respectively. For cesium and potassium nitrates, sodium chloride, and magnesium and lanthanum sulphates, a striking reversal in salt effect is observed. Acetone is salted out, and hydrocyanic acid is salted in. As an exception, we note the behavior in lithium nitrate solutions. Similar reversal in effects were found in the cases of lithium and potassium chloride, sodium nitrate and potassium sulphate solutions, but in magnesium chloride solutions another exception was found.

These results conform in a general way with the Debye theory of salt effects. In Chapter (3), Section (10), the equation

$$\frac{f^0}{f} = 1 - \frac{4\pi N}{1000} \Sigma J_j c_j \qquad (3\text{-}10\text{-}43)$$

was obtained. The functions, J_j, given by equations (3-10-44) to (3-10-46),

---

[108] This is approximately the same as equation (12-10-5) since $k_m \mu = \log \gamma_{(s)} \cong 1 - 1/\gamma_{(s)}$.

are themselves functions of the ionic radii, and a quantity, $\bar{R}_j$, defined by equation (3-10-38),

$$\bar{R}_j^4 = \frac{z_j^2 \epsilon^2}{8\pi RTD_1} \frac{1000}{} |\bar{\alpha}|$$ (3-10-38)

The constant, $|\bar{\alpha}|$, is defined by equation (3-10-37),

$$|\bar{\alpha}| = \frac{(D_1 - D_2)}{D_1} V_1$$ (3-10-37)

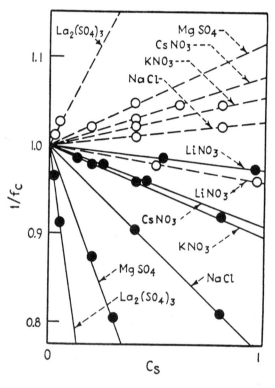

Fig. (12-10-4)
Salting in and out of hydrocyanic acid and acetone. ●, acetone; ○, hydrocyanic acid.

D_1 and D_2 are the dielectric constants of components (1) and (2), and V_1 is the molal volume of component (1). The component (2) is salted out or in. Applied to the systems under discussion, component (1) is water and component (2) is either acetone or hydrocyanic acid.

Since the functions J_j are constant functions depending on the values of $|\bar{\alpha}|$ and $\bar{R}_j$, and since f^0, the activity coefficient of the component (2), is taken to be unity in pure water, equation (3-10-43) is formally equivalent to (12-10-8). Consequently, the theory predicts the observed linear variation of $1/f_c$. Further, according to theory, hydrocyanic acid should be salted in, since its dielectric constant is greater than water while the reverse is true for acetone. With the exception of lithium nitrate and magnesium chloride, this prediction is verified by the results.

From measurements of the dielectric constants, Gross obtained

$$D = D_1(1 - 0.0367c) \qquad (12\text{-}10\text{-}9)$$

and

$$D = D_1(1 + 0.0039c) \qquad (12\text{-}10\text{-}10)$$

for solutions of acetone and hydrocyanic acid, respectively. Therefore, according to equations (3-10-39) and (3-10-41), $|\bar{\alpha}|$ equals 0.0367 and 0.0039, respectively, and $\bar{R}_j$ (acetone) $= 2.03 \times 10^{-8}$ cm., and $\bar{R}_j$ (HCN) $= 1.2 \times 10^{-8}$ cm., according to equation (3-10-38). For the limiting salting effects (dilute salt solutions), these values lead to the equations

$$1/f = 1 - \frac{0.13}{\mathring{a}} \Gamma \qquad (12\text{-}10\text{-}11)$$

$$1/f = 1 + \frac{0.0135}{\mathring{a}} \Gamma \qquad (12\text{-}10\text{-}12)$$

for acetone and hydrocyanic acid, respectively, where $1/\mathring{a} = \Sigma\, 1/\mathring{a}_j$.

These equations cannot be expected to hold quantitatively since they are limiting equations for very dilute solutions, and since, as evidenced by the anomalous results for lithium nitrate and magnesium chloride, they are probably complicated by chemical effects which are not purely electrostatic. The theoretical predictions are of the right order of magnitude since they yield values of $\mathring{a}$ of the order of 0.5 to 2 for many of the salts. The large effects for lanthanum sulphate and magnesium sulphate are striking, and agree approximately with theory.

The salting out of water from water-dioxane mixtures by potassium, sodium, and lithium chlorides has been investigated by Scatchard and Benedict[109] by freezing point measurements. Mixtures of dioxane with the salts in 1 to 2 and 2 to 1 ratios in water at concentrations from 0.01 to $2M$ were used. From the values of the osmotic coefficient, the salting out coefficients (molecule-salt interaction coefficients) were evaluated. Using crystallographic radii [Table (5-1-6)], excellent agreement was found between the results and Debye's theory of salting out, whereas the Debye and McAulay theory proved to be less satisfactory.

A thorough survey of salting effects of ions on nonelectrolyte solutes in aqueous solutions has been made by Long and McDevit.[110] A complete

[109] G. Scatchard and M. A. Benedict, *J. Am. Chem. Soc.*, **58**, 837 (1936).
[110] F. A. Long and W. F. McDevit, *Chem. Rev.*, **51**, 119 (1952).

bibliography of solubility determinations of the salting by ions of simpler structure is to be found in this contribution. The subject of salting by dipolar ions and proteins which has received detailed consideration by Cohn and Edsall[111] is not included in this review nor have the salting effects in polyelectrolyte solutions, ion-exchange resins, polymeric non-electrolytes been considered.

Long and McDevit reconsider the electrostatic theories of Debye[112] and Kirkwood[113] and show that although these theories predict the order of magnitude of the salting out of non-electrolytes by ordinary electrolytes like sodium or potassium halides, they do not predict the large differences in effects by different salts. As examples, the salting in of all non-electrolytes by large ions such tetramethyl-ammonium ion and naphalenesulphonate ion is a marked exception to the theoretical prediction.

McDevit and Long[114] have shown that the order of salting effects on non-polar molecules may be predicted by a theory based on the volume changes of the solvent produced by added salts. Thus, if the internal pressure of the solution causes the solvent to occupy a smaller volume, there is less room for the solute molecule which is salted out. A limiting expression is derived of the form

$$\lim_{\substack{c_s \to 0 \\ n_i \to 0}} \frac{d \ln f}{d c_s} = \lim_{c_s \to 0} \frac{\bar{V}_i^0}{RT} \frac{dP_e}{d c_s} \tag{12-10-4}$$

where f is the activity coefficient of the non-polar molecule, $\bar{V}_i^0$ is its partial volume, c_s the molar salt concentration and P_e is the effective pressure of Gibson [See Chap. (8), Section (7)]. According to this relation the order of the salt effects of non-polar molecules would be determined by the slopes of the curves in Fig. (8-7-2) and in fact this order, exemplified by $Na^+ > K^+ > Li^+$ is usually observed.

For acetic nonelectrolytes [(Fig. (12-10-3)], the order of salting out is $Li^+ > Na^+ > K^+$. Long and McDevit found the hypothesis of "localized hydrolysis" (Section (5) of this chapter) of considerable value in giving a qualitative explanation of this order of salt effects on phthallic, benzoic, succinic acids and the reverse order $K^+ > Na^+ > Li^+$ on the basic electrolytes, trimethylamine and aniline. We suggest that this hypothesis of ion-solvent interaction will afford a similar explanation for certain salt effects in ion-exchangers.

[111] "Proteins, Amino Acids and Peptides", 2nd. Ed., Reinhold Publishing Corp., New York (1949).

[112] See Chapter (3), Section (10b).

[113] J. G. Kirkwood, *J. Chem. Phys.*, **18**, 380 (1950).

[114] W. F. McDevit and F. A. Long, J. Am. Chem. Soc., **74**, 1773 (1952).

(11) The Surface Tension of Dilute Solutions of Electrolytes

The theoretical treatment of surface tension according to Wagner, and Onsager and Samaras, has been shown [Chapter (3), Section (11)], to lead to

$$\frac{\sigma}{\sigma_0} = 1 + \frac{1.012c}{\sigma_0} \log \frac{1.467}{c} \tag{12-11-1}$$

for the effect of 1-1 electrolyte addition upon the relative surface tension of water at 25°. Onsager and Samaras found that their theory agreed in order of magnitude with the results of Heydweiller and Schwenker. Exact agreement was not obtained, but this was probably due to experimental error, because the results of Heydweiller[115] were not in exact agreement with those of Schwenker.[116]

Jones and Ray[117] by employing a silica capillarimeter, have succeeded in measuring the relative capillary rise with a very high degree of accuracy. From their measurements, they derived a quantity $(\sigma/\sigma_0)'$ which we shall designate as an "apparent relative surface tension". The reproducibility of the measurements was extraordinary. The greatest deviation for any solution was 0.005 percent, and the average deviation was 0.002 percent.

Some of their results in very dilute solutions are illustrated in Fig. (12-11-1), in which the apparent relative surface tension is plotted against the concentration for potassium chloride, cesium nitrate and potassium sulphate. In each case, the upper curve represents the theoretical result according to equation (12-11-1). In the extremely dilute solutions, there is a rapid decrease in $(\sigma/\sigma_0)'$ until a sharp minimum occurs. After this, the curves rise at approximately the rate predicted by theory. It is obvious that if $(\sigma/\sigma_0)'$ is a relative surface tension, and nothing else, the theory is erroneous in very dilute solutions. Jones and Ray showed that this rapid decrease was a property of ionic solutions, and does not occur in solutions of sucrose in water.

Langmuir[118] has pointed out that, in very dilute solutions, the zeta potential of quartz causes the formation of a wetting layer in the fine quartz capillaries. This is of such a thickness as to reduce the diameters of the capillaries sufficiently to affect the measurements of the surface tension. As a result, the effect observed by Jones and Ray is not a measure of relative surface tension alone, but is an effect which includes both surface tension and the influence of the zeta-potential. Onsager[119] has made an extended theoretical investigation of wetting the surfaces with electrolytic

[115] A. Heydweiller, *Ann. Physik.* [4] **33**, 145 (1910); *Physik. Z.*, **3**, 329 (1902).

[116] G. Schwenker, *Ann. Physik.*, **11**, 525 (1931).

[117] G. Jones and W. A. Ray, *J. Am. Chem. Soc.*, **59**, 187 (1937); *Ibid.*, **63**, 288 (1941).

[118] I. Langmuir, *Science*, **88**, 430 (1937); *J. Chem. Phys.*, **6**, 873 (1938); An attempt to interpret the results as a pure surface tension effect has been made by M. Dole *J. Am. Chem. Soc.*, **60**, 904 (1938).

[119] L. Onsager, Private communication.

solutions, and has developed a quantitative theory of the influence of the zeta-potential on the capillary rise. His theory accounts largely for the difference between the results shown in Fig. (12-11-1), the rapid decrease in $(\sigma/\sigma_0)'$ in dilute solutions, and the minimum in the curves. It does not yet include the possible effects of London forces. However, from the actual surface tension measurements of Jones and Ray, Onsager calculates with accuracy the zeta-potential of quartz.

These considerations lead to the conclusion that the interionic attraction theory for the surface tension as developed by Wagner, and Onsager and Samaras, is a good first approximation.

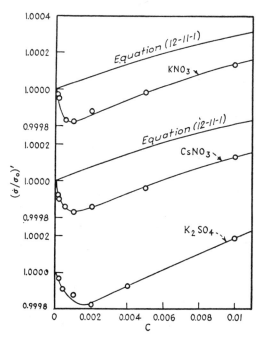

Fig. (12–11–1). Apparent relative surface tension of potassium nitrate, cesium nitrate, and potassium sulphate solutions at 25°. Theoretical curves for relative surface tension according to equation (12–11–1).

(12) ACTIVITY COEFFICIENTS AND THE CLUSTER SUM THEORY OF MAYER. CALCULATIONS BY POIRIER

By means of equations (3-6-7) to (3-6-10) and Table (5-2-2a) of Mayer's theory, Poirier[120] has computed $\ln y'_\pm$ as defined by equation (3-6-11) for 1-1, 2-1, 3-1 and 2-2 electrolytes in water at 25°. In Fig. (12-12-1), values of this quantity for different values of the distance parameter, A, are plotted against the square root of the molar concentration. As shown by Table (3-6-1), $\ln y'_\pm$ does not differ greatly from $\ln y_\pm$ so that the graphs in

120 J. C. Poirier, J. Chem. Phys., **21**, 972 (1953).

Fig. (12-12-1) should represent the general characteristics of activity coefficients. The straight lines are graphs of the Debye and Hückel limiting law.

It is immediately apparent from curve (a) that this theory predicts the general behavior of the activity coefficients of 1-1 electrolytes. We shall find in the next chapter that curves (b), (c) and (d) also represent the general characteristic of 2-1, 3-1 and 2-2 electrolytes. A very important feature of this theory is that the minima and upper trend of the activity coefficients at the higher values of A is predicted by computations of ionic interactions among the clusters. In other words, this upper trend is deduced without introducing additional factors such as change in dielectric

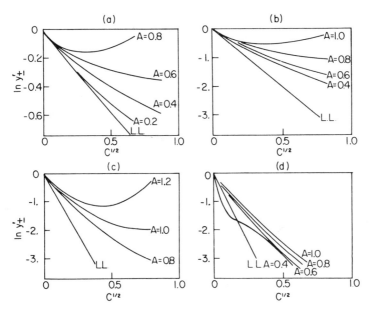

Fig. (12-12-1). Activity coefficients according to Mayer's theory. Graphs (a) (b), (c) and (d) represent the calculation for 1-1, 2-1, 3-1 and 2-2, electrolytes, respectively. L.L. represents the limiting law.

constant, co-volume effects or hydration. Another important feature is illustrated by the curve in figure (d) at $A = 0.4$ which shows the effect of interaction between two divalent ions of the kind denoted "ion-pair" formation. Qualitatively, the theory yields a remarkable representation of the observed results.

Table (12-12-1) contains Poirier's calculations of the activity coefficients of sodium, calcium, lanthanum chlorides and zinc sulphate. Excellent agreement with the experimental values is obtained for sodium chloride solutions up to 0.1 molar. The results of the calculation for the salts of higher valence types do not show so good an agreement.

The values of the closest distance of approach, $\overset{\circ}{a}$, are nearly the same as those determined by the modified Debye and Hückel theory and are greater than those derived from crystallographic radii. This result is in accord with the values in Table (12-5-2) which were obtained by equations (12-5-2) and (12-5-3).

TABLE (12-12-1).   COMPARISON OF OBSERVED ACTIVITY COEFFICIENTS WITH THOSE CALCULATED BY MAYER'S THEORY.

NaCl ($\overset{\circ}{a} = 3.9$)			CaCl$_2$ ($\overset{\circ}{a} = 5.68$)		
c	$-\log y_{\pm}^{(a)}$ (obs.)	$-\log y_{\pm}$ (calc.)	c	$-\log y_{\pm}^{(b)}$ (obs.)	$-\log y_{\pm}$ (calc.)
0.004984	0.0323	0.0327	0.00609	0.1100	0.1082
.009967	.0441	.0445	.00958	.1331	.1290
.019934	.0592	.0596	.02417	.1861	.1813
.03985	.0781	.0782	.03753	.2149	.2117
.05976	.0905	.0907	.05000	.2340	.2340
.07965	.1002	.1003	.09654	.2778	.2938
.09952	.1081	.1081	—	—	—
.1986	.1329	.1342	—	—	—
.2974	.1464	.1507	—	—	—
.3959	.1559	.1624	—	—	—

LaCl$_3$ ($\overset{\circ}{a} = 6.39$)			ZnSO$_4$ ($\overset{\circ}{a} = 3.74$)		
c	$-\log y_{\pm}^{(c)}$ (obs.)	$-\log y_{\pm}$ (calc.)	c	$-\log y_{\pm}^{(d)}$ (obs.)	$-\log y_{\pm}$ (calc.)
0.000607	0.084	0.080	0.000498	0.108	0.114
.001663	.127	.123	.000997	.155	.163
.003218	.166	.161	.001994	.216	.227
.004885	.195	.190	.004985	.321	.328
.010936	.260	.260	.00997	.412	.413
.017188	.302	.310	.01994	.526	.501
.033333	.368	.402	.04987	.695	.655

(a) A. S. Brown and D. A. MacInnes, *J. Am. Chem. Soc.*, **57**, 1356 (1935); (b) T. Shedlovsky and D. A. MacInnes, *Ibid.*, **59**, 505 (1937); (c) T. Shedlovsky, *Ibid.*, **77**, 3680 (1950); (d) V. B. Bray, *Ibid.*, **49**, 2372 (1927).

(13) FURTHER CONTRIBUTIONS TO THE THEORY OF CONCENTRATED ELECTROLYTIC SOLUTIONS

The preceding review of the theories proposed to explain the thermodynamic properties of electrolytic solutions in moderate or concentrated solutions serves to introduce the many factors, such as variation of dielectric constant, co-volume effects, hydration, etc., which influence these properties. Another view regarding the deviations from the limiting law of Debye and Hückel has been introduced by Frank,[121] which is based upon a model of Debye and Pauling,[122] originally intended to show that the limiting law for the chemical potential, or activity coefficient, was unaffected by changes in dielectric constant in the immediate neighborhood of the central ion.

[121] H. S. Frank, *J. Am. Chem. Soc.*, **63**, 1789 (1941); For further discussion of interactions of solutes with the water lattice, see: H. S. Frank, *J. Chem. Phys.* **13**, 479, 493, (1945); H. S. Frank and M. W. Evans *Ibid.*, **13**, 507 (1945).

[122] P. Debye and L. Pauling, *J. Am. Chem. Soc.*, **47**, 2129 (1925).

The Debye and Pauling model presupposes a central rigid spherical ion of radius, $r = a$ and of charge, $z\epsilon$, located at the center of the ion. The region between the ion and within a sphere of radius $r = A > a$ is assumed to be a domain of continuous variation of the dielectric constant, while outside this region, from $r = R$ to $R = \infty$, the dielectric constant is assumed to be constant. From this model and suitable boundary conditions, a complicated equation for the potential of the ion is derived, which, upon expansion in a power series of the concentration, reduces to the limiting law plus terms involving first and higher powers of the concentration.

Frank derives the Debye and Pauling equation by an alternative method and obtains an expression for the free energy of the ion in its atmosphere rather than the potential. He then examines the consequences of the theory in the region of moderate concentrations by assuming series of values for the dielectric constant within the sphere of radius R_1, and a single constant value of the macroscopic dielectric constant of water (78.54 at 25) outside this sphere. As a result of these calculations, Frank finds that, when the local dielectric constant within the sphere of radius R does not exceed 25, and the ions can approach each other to a distance equal to the sum of the crystal radii, $(r_+ + r_-)$, the theory yields very large negative deviations from the Debye and Hückel limiting equation in disagreement with experimental results. These deviations decrease as the difference between R and a decreases. If the ions are hydrated and the hydrated ions are rigid impenetrable spheres, then dielectric saturation is reached within this layer of water molecules, and $R = a$. This condition, and the removal by hydration of the water molecules as solvent, leads to positive deviations from theory. If, however, the ions are hydrated and if they can penetrate the hydration shells of oppositely charged ions, the theory can be made to conform with experiment.

Eigen and Wicke[123] have developed a theory of concentrated solutions by modifying the Boltzmann distribution equation (2-4-4) in such a way as to include hydration and volume influences. These effects restrict the number of possibilities for arrangement of the ions. In addition to this restriction, an ion can penetrate the hydration shell of an ion of opposite sign causing incomplete ionization. Eigen and Wicke succeed in representing the observed activity coefficients of a number of electrolytes of different valence types in concentrated solutions by means of suitable distance parameters, a, and mass action constants. Although in principle it may be advantageous to modify the fundamental charge distribution function to include other factors, the actual modification made by Eigen and Wicke has been seriously questioned.[124]

[123] M. Eigen and E. Wicke, *J. Phys. Chem.*, **58**, 702 (1954); E. Wicke and M. Eigen, *Naturwiss.*, **38**, 456 (1951); *Z. Electrochemie*, **56**, 551 (1952); *J. Phys. Chem.*, **58**, 702 (1954).

[124] G. Scatchard, *loc. cit.*, **58**, 712 (1954); E. Hückel, and G. Krafft, *Z. Physik. Chem., Neue. Folge*, **3**, 135 (1955).

In section (5) of this chapter, we mentioned Hückel's[125] interpretation of the linear effect represented by Bc in equation (12-5-2) as being caused by a lowering of the macroscopic dielectric constant of the solvent upon addition of salt. This matter has been re-examined by Hasted, Ritson and Collie[126] in the light of their measurements of the dielectric constants and loss angles of concentrated electrolytic solutions at wave-lengths of 10, 3 and 1.25 cm. Unfortunately, their experimental procedure did not permit the evaluation of these quantities in dilute solutions. They found that from 0.5 to $2M$ the results may be represented by the equation

$$D = D_0 - (\delta_+ + \delta_-)c \qquad (12\text{-}13\text{-}1)$$

where D is the static dielectric constant, D_0 is the dielectric constant of water, and δ_+ and δ_- are positive constants characteristic of the cations and anions, respectively. Above $2M$, the linear relationship is no longer valid, and the results indicate that above this concentration $(\delta_+ + \delta_-)$ decreases with the concentration. Hasted, Ritson, and Collie compute minimum hydration values from their data by assuming that ions attract water molecules to form inner hydration sheaths which effectively remove them from contributing to the value of the dielectric constant. If n is the minimum number of water molecules in the inner layer and M_1 is the molecular weight of water, then

$$D = D_0 - \frac{nM_1D_0}{1000}c = D_0 - (\delta_+ + \delta_-)c \qquad (12\text{-}13\text{-}2)$$

Outside this region, a relatively smaller lowering of the dielectric is caused by water molecules attracted to the ions. For sodium chloride, where $(\delta_+ + \delta_-) = 11$, the authors assume, on theoretical grounds regarding the rotation of water molecules bound by attraction to the ions, that $\delta_+ = 8$ and $\delta_- = 3$. Further, for sodium chloride, they assume that the contribution to the fall in dielectric constant caused by the ions in the outer water

TABLE (12-13-1).   THE CONSTANTS, δ_+ , δ_- , AND SOME MINIMUM HYDRATION VALUES.
OF POSITIVE IONS

Ion	H^+	Li^+	Na^+	K^+	Rb^+	Mg^{++}	Ba^{++}	La^{+++}	Cl^-
δ_+, δ_-	17	11	8	8	7	24	22	35	3
n_+	10.5	6	4	4	3.5	15.5	14	23	

layer is $\frac{1}{4}$ the contribution of the inner layer. Therefore, for the cation hydration number, n_+ , of sodium chloride, they obtain

$$n_+ = (\delta_+ - 2)\frac{1000}{M_1D_0} \qquad (12\text{-}13\text{-}3)$$

[125] E. Hückel, Physik. Z., 26, 93 (1925).
[126] J. B. Hasted, D. M. Ritson, and C. H. Collie, J. Cnem. Phys., 16, 1 (1948).

It is also assumed that this decrease of δ_+ by two units is common to all cations, so that equation (12-13-3) is considered to be general. We have recorded in Table (12-13-1) some values of δ_+, δ_-, and of n_+ computed by this equation

Ritson and Hasted[127] developed a theory of dielectric saturation in the neighborhood of the ion on the basis of the reaction field theory of Onsager[128] and also on an extension of the theory of Kirkwood.[129] They obtained qualitative agreement with the observed values of the lowering of the dielectric constant. They also re-examined the theories of concentrated solutions and estimated the contributions of the van der Waals' co-volume effect, of Bjerrum's ion association, of varying dielectric constant, and of the solvent structure-breaking effect. They conclude that the situation requires a determined theoretical attack on ion-solvent interaction.

The preceding account of the various theories of concentrated electrolytic solutions has had two purposes, the first to acquaint the reader with the present state of the subject through the different proposed methods of approach and the second to again emphasize the difficulties of extending the present theory to higher concentrations. Each of the theories described has some merit but all of them can be severely critized either upon fundamental grounds or because of failure to include all of the factors. In view of the extent of the mathematical analysis involved in Fuoss and Onsager's recent derivation of the *Limiting Law* of conductance (Chapter (4), Section (9)) the solution of the problem of concentrated solutions cannot be solved by an extension of the present theory based upon smoothed ionic distribution. As a clue to a possible definitive theory of concentrated solutions, we refer to the new element found by Kirkwood and Poirier by statistical mechanical theory (Chapter (2), Section (7)) which leads to stratification of average space-charge of alternating sign in the neighborhood of each ion. This conclusion points in the direction of a sound theory of fused salts and is in accord with the statement of Fuoss and Onsager that the approach to a theory of concentrated solution "must start by an adequate theory of fused salts, which must then be followed by the theoretical treatment of the effect on the radial distribution function of adding uncharged (solvent) molecules. At high concentrations, the distribution function must be a damped periodic function of the interionic distances."

[127] D. M. Ritson and J. B. Hasted, *J. Chem. Phys.*, **16**, 11 (1948).
[128] L. Onsager, *J. Am. Chem. Soc.*, **58**, 1486 (1936).
[129] J. G. Kirkwood, *J. Chem. Phys.*, **4**, 592 (1936).

Chapter (13)
Polyvalent Electrolytes in Aqueous Solution

The presence of ions of higher valence types introduces further complications in the thermodynamic properties, even in media of high dielectric constants. The theoretical considerations in Chapter (3), Sections (6) and (7), prove that, upon the basis of Coulomb's forces only, deviations from the original Debye and Hückel theory are to be expected. The higher order terms of the complete solution of the Poisson-Boltzmann equation are a function of the valences of the ions. As shown by Gronwall, LaMer and Sandved for symmetrical electrolytes, the contribution to $\ln f_{\pm}$ caused by the second and third terms on the right of equation (3-6-4), though practically negligible for 1-1 electrolytes in water, varies very markedly with the magnitude of z, since the terms which multiply the functions within the brackets involve z^6 and z^{10}, respectively. A similar result was obtained for the extended terms for unsymmetrical valence type electrolytes as indicated by equation (3-6-6). The exact determination of the effect of the extended terms is a matter of considerable difficulty, since it may be somewhat obscured and confused by other effects such as those caused by the series terms, $\sum_{n>2} A_n c^{n/2}$ [Equation (11-5-2)], which have been found necessary for the computation of the activity coefficients of 1-1 electrolytes.

It is illuminating to consider polyvalent electrolytes from the alternative point of view of Bjerrum's theory of ionic association [Chapter (3), Section (7)]. We have learned that if b, the minimum distance of approach of positive to negative ions, is greater than $q = \epsilon^2 |z_1 z_2|/2DkT$, then the probability of ionic association is negligible. For a 1-1 electrolyte in water at 25°, $q = 3.5$ Å. Therefore for 2-1, 3-1, 2-2, 3-2, and 3-3 electrolytes, q equals 7, 10.5, 14, 21, and 31.5 Å, respectively. Since these values are much greater than $å$ for many high valence type electrolytes, considerable ionic association of the Bjerrum type is to be expected. Judging from conductance data in dilute solution, calcium chloride and like electrolytes are strong, but electrolytes like zinc and magnesium sulfates are associated.

Other electrolytes which are unquestionably incompletely dissociated are the cadmium halides. In these cases, there is the possibility of equilibrium of the kind represented by

$$\text{MCl}_2 \rightleftharpoons \text{Cl}^- + \text{MCl}^+ \rightleftharpoons \text{M}^{++} + 2\text{Cl}^-$$

where the ionization is not completely determined by Coulomb's forces but by more complex fields such as those discussed in Chapter (3), Section (7).

In these cases, mass action type calculations have been found to fit the experimental results.

Of the abundant but scattered material in this field, we shall consider a limited amount which will illustrate the best attempts yet employed for treating the results. Examples of 2-1, 3-1, 2-2, and 3-2 electrolytes will first be discussed. The properties of solutions of the weaker electrolytes will then be considered with particular emphasis on cadmium halide solutions. Finally, the properties of aqueous sulphuric acid solutions will be considered in some detail.

(1) THE THERMODYNAMICS OF MAGNESIUM, CALCIUM, STRONTIUM AND BARIUM HALIDE SOLUTIONS

Lucasse[1] has measured the electromotive forces at 25° of the cells,

$$\text{Ag-AgCl} \mid \text{MCl}_2(m) \mid \text{M}_x\text{Hg} \mid \text{MCl}_2(m_R) \mid \text{AgCl-Ag}$$

containing calcium, strontium, and barium chlorides. Scatchard and Tefft[2] also employed this cell in order to investigate calcium chloride solutions at 25°. More recently, Tippetts and Newton[3] have extended the study of barium chloride solutions over the temperature range from 0 to 45° by the same kind of measurement.

From considerations similar to those employed in deriving equation (10-4-7), the electromotive force of this cell is given by

$$\text{E} = \frac{3RT}{2\text{F}} \ln \frac{\gamma_{\pm}m}{\gamma_R m_R} \tag{13-1-1}$$

from which it is clear that $\gamma_{\pm}$ relative to its value, γ_R, at a reference concentration may be computed. These data have been extrapolated in conformity with theory by Harned,[4] Scatchard and Tefft,[2] Jones and Dole,[5] and Tippetts and Newton by employing equation (10-4-9), or a similar function. The extended terms were not employed in any of these treatments. So far, experience indicates that both barium and strontium amalgam electrodes are reproducible, and that calcium amalgam electrodes are extremely erratic and lead to erroneous results. Tippetts and Newton report an average deviation of ±0.2 mv. with the barium amalgam electrodes, while Scatchard and Tefft's average deviation with the calcium electrodes was ±0.4 mv. Lucasse, and Scatchard and Tefft employed flowing amalgams, while stationary electrodes covered with an oil layer were used by Tippetts and Newton. Results at salt concentrations less than 0.01M have not been reported, since the consistency of the results decreases with decreasing concentration. Values of $\gamma_{\pm}$ at 25° for barium

---

[1] W. W. Lucasse, *J. Am. Chem. Soc.*, **47**, 743 (1925).

[2] G. Scatchard and R. F. Tefft. *J. Am. Chem. Soc.*, **52**, 2265 (1930).

[3] E. A. Tippetts and R. F. Newton, *J. Am. Chem. Soc.*, **56**, 1675 (1934).

[4] H. S. Harned, *J. Am. Chem. Soc.*, **48**, 326 (1926).

[5] G. Jones and M. Dole, *J. Am. Chem. Soc.*, **51**, 1084 (1929).

and strontium chlorides obtained from the amalgam cell measurements are given in Table (13-1-1). Tippetts and Newton's values for barium chloride from 0 to 45° are contained in Table (13-1-1A).

That cells containing barium amalgam can be accurately reproduced is shown by the agreement of the values of the activity coefficient at 25°, as determined by Tippetts and Newton, in column (3) with those computed from Lucasse's data in column (4). Newton and Tippetts[6] have also computed the activity of water in barium chloride solutions from their

TABLE (13-1-1). THE ACTIVITY COEFFICIENTS OF ALKALINE EARTH CHLORIDES AT 25°

m	BaCl$_2$			SrCl$_2$		CaCl$_2$
	V.P.[c]	E.M.F.		V.P.[c]	E M.F.[b]	V.P.[c]
	$\gamma_\pm$	$\gamma_\pm{}^a$	$\gamma_\pm{}^b$	$\gamma_\pm$	$\gamma_\pm$	$\gamma_\pm$
0.01	.....	0.723	0.723	.....	0.729	.....
.05	.....	.559	.554	.....	.571	.....
.1	(0.492)	.492	.495	(0.514)	.512	(0.531)
.2	.438	.436	.439	.463	.465	.482
.3	.411	.411	.....	.440	.....	.462
.4	.398	.....	.....	.430	.....	.456
.5	.390	.390	.395	.425	.427	.457
.6	.386	.....	.....	.426	.....	.462
.7	.384	.384	.....	.430	.....	.469
.8	.385	.....	.....	.436	.....	.479
.9	.388	.....	.....	.444	.....	.493
1.0	.392	.389	.395	.455	.449	.509
1.1	.397	.....	.....	.467	.....	.528
1.2	.402	.....	.....	.480	.....	.550
1.3	.409	.....	.....	.494	.....	.573
1.4	.416	.....	.....	.510	.....	.599
1.5	.423	.425	.425	.527	.526	.626
1.6	.431	.....	.....	.546	.....	.657
1.7	.440	.....	.....	.566	.....	.690
1.8	.450	.....	.....	.587	.....	.726
1.9	.....	.....	.....	.611	.....	.764
2.0	.....	.....	.....	.636	.638	.807
2.1	.....	.....	.....	.664	.....	.853
2.2	.....	.....	.....	.694	.....	.901
2.5	.....	.....	.....	.....	.772	.....
3.	.....	.....	.....	.....	1.003	.....

[a] E. A. Tippetts and R. F. Newton, *J. Am. Chem. Soc.*, **56**, 1675 (1934).
[b] H. S. Harned, *Ibid.*, **48**, 326 (1926) from the data of Lucasse, *Ibid.*, **47**, 743 (1925).
[c] R. A. Robinson and R. H. Stokes, *Trans. Faraday Soc.*, **36**, 735 (1940).

electromotive force measurements at 25°, and have compared the results obtained with values determined directly from their dynamic vapor pressure measurements. The agreement is a good indication of the fundamental correctness of both methods at this temperature.

The relative partial molal heat content, $\bar{L}_2$, of barium chloride has been computed from electromotive force measurements by Tippetts and Newton, and the result is in good agreement with values obtained from the

[6] R. F. Newton and E. A. Tippetts, *J. Am. Chem. Soc.*, **58**, 280 (1936); M. F. Bechtold and R. F. Newton, *Ibid.*, **62**, 1390 (1940).

calorimetric measurements of Richards and Dole[7] at 25°. On the other hand, their values at the other temperatures cannot be reliable, particularly those at their extreme temperatures, 0 and 45°, since values of the relative partial molal heat capacity, $\bar{J}_2$, computed from them, differ greatly from the calorimetric measurements. At 25° and 0.1M, Tippetts and Newton obtained 61 for $\bar{J}_2$, whereas the calorimetric value of White[8] is 17.1. This discrepancy may be caused largely by the difficulties of extrapolation of the electromotive force results rather than by large errors in the original measurements.

The osmotic and activity coefficients of manganese, cobalt, nickel, copper, magnesium, calcium, strontium and barium chlorides and magnesium bromide and iodide have been determined from isopiestic vapor pressure measurements by Robinson[9] from 0.1 to 1.6 or 2M. The standard solution to which all these isopiestic measurements are referred is sodium chloride [See pages 289 and 375]. The values of $\gamma_\pm$ at 25° are compiled in Table (13-1-2A). The agreement of the isopiestic measurements with the results obtained from electromotive forces for barium and strontium chlorides is made apparent by the results in Table (13-1-1). On the other hand, the values of $\gamma_\pm$ determined by the use of calcium amalgam differ greatly from those obtained from the vapor pressures.

(2) The Thermodynamics of Aqueous Lithium, Sodium and Potassium Sulphate Solutions

Cells of the type,

$$\text{Hg-Hg}_2\text{SO}_4 \mid \text{M}_2\text{SO}_4(m) \mid \text{M}_x\text{Hg} \mid \text{M}_2\text{SO}_4(m_R) \mid \text{Hg}_2\text{SO}_4\text{-Hg}$$

have been employed by Åkerlöf[10] for determining the activity coefficients of lithium, sodium, and potassium sulphates at 25°. More recently, Harned and Hecker[11] have measured the electromotive forces of the cells,

$$\text{Pb-Pb}_x\,\text{Hg-PbSO}_4 \mid \text{Na}_2\,\text{SO}_4(m) \mid \text{Na}_x\,\text{Hg} \mid \text{Na}_2\,\text{SO}_4(0.05) \mid \text{PbSO}_4\text{-Pb}_x\,\text{Hg-Pb}$$

in a more thorough investigation of the thermodynamics of aqueous sodium sulphate solutions. For this salt, accurate freezing point, heat of dilution, and specific heat data have been obtained by Randall and Scott,[12] Lange and Streeck,[13] and Randall and Rossini,[14] respectively.

[7] T. W. Richards and M. Dole, *J. Am. Chem. Soc.*, **51**, 794 (1931).

[8] C. M. White, *J. Am. Chem. Soc.*, **58**, 1620 (1936).

[9] R. A. Robinson and R. H. Stokes, *Trans. Faraday Soc.*, **36**, 733 (1940); R. A. Robinson, *Ibid.*, **36**, 735 (1940); R. A. Robinson and R. H. Stokes, *Ibid.*, **36**, 1137 (1940).

[10] G. Åkerlöf, *J. Am. Chem. Soc.*, **48**, 1160 (1926); H. S. Harned and G. Åkerlöf, *Physik. Z.*, **27**, 411 (1926).

[11] H. S. Harned and J. C. Hecker, *J. Am. Chem. Soc.*, **56**, 650 (1934).

[12] M. Randall and G. N. Scott, *J. Am. Chem. Soc.*, **49**, 647 (1927).

[13] E. Lange and H. Streeck, *Z. physik. Chem. A.*, **157**, 1 (1931).

[14] M. Randall and F. D. Rossini, *J. Am. Chem. Soc.*, **51**, 323 (1929).

Since the alkali metal amalgams are inaccurate in the dilute solutions ($m < 0.05M$), extrapolation to zero molality by the use of equation (10-4-9) is uncertain. In Table (13-2-1), the values of $\gamma_\pm$ from amalgam cell measurements are given. The reference values obtained by extrapolation with equation (10-4-9) are shown in brackets. In the third column, values of $\gamma'_\pm$ at the freezing point, computed by Randall and Scott, with the use of the Debye and Hückel limiting equation are given. Their value of 0.537 at $0.05M$ is not widely different from 0.532, obtained from electromotive forces by Harned and Hecker. This discrepancy is caused principally by the difficulties of extrapolation. Values at 25° determined by the isopiestic vapor pressure method, are in good agreement with those from the electromotive forces.

Harned and Hecker computed $\bar{L}_2$ and $\bar{J}_2$ from 0 to 35° and up to $2M$ from their electromotive forces. These results are of value in giving a general view of the behavior of these quantities as functions of electrolyte concentration and temperature, but are subject to large errors. Accurate determinations of these quantities by calorimetric measurements have been made at 15, 20 and 25° from very dilute solutions to $0.4M$ by Wallace and Robinson.[15] Their results for sodium sulphate may be computed by the following empirical equations:

$$15°; \quad \bar{L}_2 = 2650m^{1/2} - 11382m + 7080m^{3/2} \tag{13-2-1}$$

$$20°; \quad \bar{L}_2 = 3100m^{1/2} - 12164m + 8340m^{3/2} \tag{13-2-2}$$

$$25°; \quad \bar{L}_2 = 3644m^{1/2} - 15468m + 22475m^{3/2} - 15108m^2 \tag{13-2-3}$$

$$25°; \quad \bar{J}_2 = 84m^{1/2} \tag{13-2-4}$$

$$25°; \quad \bar{C}_{p_2} = 84m^{1/2} - 50 \tag{13-2-5}$$

(3) Halides of Zinc, Cadmium, and Lead in Aqueous Solution

The properties of solutions of these salts have been investigated by means of cells of the type,

$$\text{M}_x\text{Hg (single or 2-phase)} \mid \text{MX}_2(m) \mid \text{AgX-Ag}$$

According to equation (10-3-2) their electromotive force is given by

$$\mathbf{E} = \mathbf{E}^0 - \frac{3}{2}\frac{RT}{\mathbf{F}} \ln \gamma_\pm m_\pm = \mathbf{E}^0 - \frac{3}{2}\frac{RT}{\mathbf{F}} \ln \gamma_\pm m(4)^{1/3} \tag{13-3-1}$$

Upon rearrangement and substitution of the limiting law of Debye and Hückel with an added linear term, we obtain the particularized form of equation (10-3-5)

$$\mathbf{E}^{0'} \equiv \mathbf{E} + \frac{3RT}{2\mathbf{F}} \ln m(4)^{1/3} - \frac{3RT}{2\mathbf{F}} 2.303 \mathcal{S}_{(f)} \sqrt{c} = \mathbf{E}^0 - \frac{3RT}{2\mathbf{F}} Bm \tag{13-3-2}$$

which at 25° becomes

[15] W. E. Wallace and A. L. Robinson, *J. Am. Chem. Soc.*, **63**, 958 (1941).

TABLE (13-2-1). THE MEAN ACTIVITY COEFFICIENTS OF SODIUM, LITHIUM, AND POTASSIUM SULPHATES

m	Na_2SO_4							Li_2SO_4		K_2SO_4		$Na_2S_2O_3$
	0[a]	0[b]	15[a]	25[a]	25[d]	25[c]	35[a]	25[a]	25[d]	25[a]	25[d]	25[d]
0.01	(0.532)	(0.719)	(0.530)	(0.529)	.....	(0.529)	(0.523)	.....	.....	.....	.....	.....
.05	.482	.537	.482	.480	(0.445)	.480	.475	(0.468)	(0.468)	(0.441)	(0.441)	0.455
.075	.446	.....	.447	.445	.365	.445	.440	.398	.398	.361	.361	.382
.1	.359	.449	.364	.365	.320	.366	.363	.....	.362	.313	.317	.340
.2	.310	.374	.319	.322	.267	.322	.321	.323	.322	.265	.264	.292
.3	.250	.....	.263	.268	.234	.271	.270	.....	.299	.....	.233	.263
.5	.....	.....	.230	.234	.202	.237	.238	.276	.281	.....	.....	.236
.7	.....	.....	.....	.204	.187	.204	.208	.....	.....	.....	.....	.....
1.	.....	.....	.....	.189	.182	.187	.194	.....	.....	.....	.....	.....
1.2	.....	.....	.....	.182	.171	.180	.187	.....	.....	.....	.....	.....
1.3	.....	.....	.....	.....	.153	.....	.....	.272	.269	.....	.....	.212
1.5	.....	.....	.....	.....	.....	.....	.....	.267	.269	.....	.....	.200
2.	.....	.....	.....	.....	.....	.....	.....	.....	.....	.....	.....	.....

[a] Electromotive force.
[b] $\gamma_\pm$ from freezing point.
[c] Calculated by equation (10-4-9) with parameters, $A = 0.809$; $B = -0.014$; $\mathring{a} = 3.63$.
[d] Isopiestic vapor pressure measurements. R. A. Robinson, J. M. Wilson and R. H. Stokes, *J. Am. Chem. Soc.*, **63**, 1011 (1941).

$$\mathbf{E^{0'}} = \mathbf{E} + 0.08873 \log m + 0.01783 - 0.155\sqrt{m} = \mathbf{E^0} - f(m) \qquad (13\text{-}3\text{-}3)$$

if m is taken equal to c as a simplifying approximation. The behavior of $\mathbf{E^{0'}} - \mathbf{E^0}$ as a function of the concentration for some cadmium, lead and zinc halides are shown in Fig. (13-3-1). These curves are similar to those of Scatchard and Tefft,[16] whose method of treatment of these solutions will in a general way be followed. The measurements of cadmium chloride are those of Horsch,[17] and Harned and Fitzgerald,[18] and those on lead

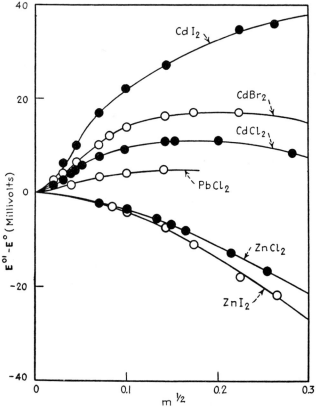

Fig. (13-3-1). Plots of $\mathbf{E^{0'}} - \mathbf{E^0}$ for halides of lead, zinc, and cadmium at 25°.

chloride were made by Carmody.[19] The zinc chloride results are those of Scatchard and Tefft. The zinc iodide,[20] cadmium bromide[21] and iodide[22]

[16] G. Scatchard and R. F. Tefft, *J. Am. Chem. Soc.*, **52**, 2272 (1930).

[17] W. G. Horsch, *J. Am. Chem. Soc.*, **41**, 1787 (1919).

[18] H. S. Harned and M. E. Fitzgerald, *J. Am. Chem. Soc.*, **58**, 2624 (1936).

[19] W. R. Carmody, *J. Am. Chem. Soc.*, **51**, 2905 (1929).

[20] R. G. Bates, *J. Am. Chem. Soc.*, **60**, 2983 (1938).

[21] R. G. Bates, *J. Am. Chem. Soc.*, **61**, 308 (1939).

[22] R. G. Bates *J. Am. Chem. Soc.*, **63**, 399 (1941).

plots were constructed from the data of Bates, and Bates and Vosburgh.[23] It is to be observed that the zinc chloride and zinc iodide plots possess no maxima, and as we proceed from this salt to cadmium chloride, bromide and iodide, a maximum appears which becomes increasingly pronounced.

There are two ways of treating these data. One is to employ the extended Debye and Hückel theory. LaMer, Gronwall, and Greiff have done this, and obtained for the mean distances of approach of the ions of zinc, lead, and cadmium chloride the values, 3.8, 1.75 and 1 Å, respectively. More recently, Bates[24] has applied the extended term theory for the purpose of extrapolating his electromotive force data of the cells containing cadmium bromide. Log $\gamma_{\pm}$ was computed by equations (3-6-3) and (3-6-5), and the data in Table (5-2-2) for a number of values of $\mathring{a}$.

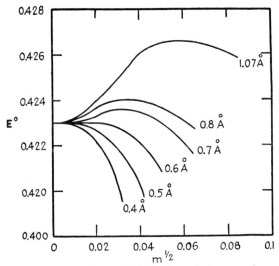

Fig. (13-3-2). Tentative values of $\mathbf{E}^0$ of the cadmium amalgam-silver bromide cell at 25°, calculated by the extended equation (3-6-5).

By substitution in equation (13-3-1), tentative values of $\mathbf{E}^0$ were computed at concentrations from 0.0005 to 0.01M salt. These are shown plotted versus $m^{1/2}$ in Fig. (13-3-2). The data are best represented by a value of $\mathring{a}$ equal to 0.6. Constant values of the tentative $\mathbf{E}^0$ are obtained only at concentrations below 0.001M. Since the theory only describes the results at such low concentrations, and since a value of $\mathring{a}$ of 0.6 seems to have little physical significance, it seems probable that factors other than those deducible from simple Coulombic interaction of the ions must be considered. The second method described by Scatchard and Tefft,[25] and modified by

[23] R. G. Bates and W. C. Vosburgh, *J. Am. Chem. Soc.*, **59**, 1188 (1937).

[24] R. G. Bates, *J. Am. Chem. Soc.*, **61**, 308 (1939).

[25] G. Scatchard and R. F. Tefft, *J. Am. Chem. Soc.*, **52**, 2272 (1930).

Harned and Fitzgerald,[26] is to assume that the effect is caused by incomplete dissociation of a kind represented by

$$MX_2 \rightarrow MX^+ + X^-$$

and

$$MX^+ \rightleftharpoons M^{++} + X^- \quad \text{or} \quad MX^+ + X^- \rightleftharpoons M^{++} + 2X^-$$

and then apply the law of mass action. In the cases of cadmium chloride and bromide, it is probable that both MX_2 and MX^+ are incompletely dissociated, but we shall assume that the first dissociation is complete. This assumption is not justifiable for cadmium iodide solutions. If α is the degree of dissociation of MX^+, and K the dissociation constant of this equilibrium, then the former is given by

$$\alpha = \frac{1}{2}\left\{ -\left(1 + \frac{K}{m\gamma_{\alpha(M)}}\right) + \sqrt{\left(1 + \frac{K}{m\gamma_{\alpha(M)}}\right)^2 + 4\frac{K}{m\gamma_{\alpha(M)}}} \right\} \quad (13\text{-}3\text{-}4)$$

if $\gamma_{\alpha(X)}$ is taken equal to $\gamma_{\alpha(MX)}$. $\gamma_{\alpha(M)}$ is the real activity coefficient of the M^{++} ion, or $a_M/\alpha m$, where αm is the actual concentration of the ion. This means that $\gamma_{\alpha(M)}$ will have a value comparable to that found for strong electrolytes such as barium chloride. Therefore, we may compute $\gamma_{\alpha(M)}$ in dilute solution according to the Debye and Hückel equation,

$$\log \gamma_{\alpha(M)} = -\frac{2\mathscr{S}_{(f)}\sqrt{2\mu'}}{1 + A\sqrt{2\mu'}} \quad (13\text{-}3\text{-}5)$$

We assign to $\mathring{a}$ the value of 5, which is of the order of magnitude found for barium chloride. Such a value of $\mathring{a}$ reduces the contribution of the extended terms of the theory to a magnitude small enough to be negligible for these computations. Note that $2\mu'$ equals $\Sigma m_i' z_i^2$ where m_i' is an estimated actual ionic concentration to be distinguished from stoichiometrical.† Values of α corresponding to given values of K and m may be obtained by the following procedure. An initial value of α is assumed for values of K and m. From this μ' is calculated by the relation,

$$\mu' = (2\alpha + 1)m \quad (13\text{-}3\text{-}6)$$

$\gamma_{\alpha(M)}$ is then obtained by equation (13-3-5). Then α is recalculated by equation (13-3-4) using this value of $\gamma_{\alpha(M)}$. From this value of α, $\gamma_{\alpha(M)}$ and μ' are recomputed, and equation (13-3-5) reapplied. This process is repeated until the same value of α, to 0.1 percent, is obtained.

Equation (13-3-1) has been written in terms of the stoichiometrical activity coefficient and molality. **E** may also be expressed by the alternative equation,

²⁶ H. S. Harned and M. E. Fitzgerald, *J. Am. Chem. Soc.*, **58**, 2624 (1936).
† This symbolism is used in Chapter (15).

$$\mathbf{E} = \mathbf{E}^0 - \frac{RT}{2\mathbf{F}} \ln \alpha (1 + \alpha)^2 m^3 \gamma_\alpha^3 \qquad (13\text{-}3\text{-}7)$$

where γ_α is the "real" mean activity coefficient, and $\alpha(\alpha + 1)^2 m^3$ is the product of the real concentrations. According to the definition of $\mathbf{E}^{0'}$ in equation (13-3-2)

$$\mathbf{E}^{0'} - \mathbf{E}^0 = \mathbf{E} - \mathbf{E}^0 + \frac{1}{2}\frac{RT}{\mathbf{F}} \ln 4m^3 - \frac{3}{2}\frac{RT}{\mathbf{F}} 2.303 \mathcal{S}_{(f)} \sqrt{2\mu} \qquad (13\text{-}3\text{-}8)$$

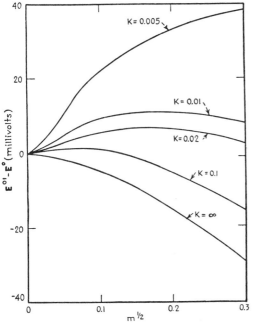

Fig. (13-3-3).
Plots of $\mathbf{E}^{0'}\text{-}\mathbf{E}^\circ$ according to equation (13-3-9) for various values of K.

which when combined with equation (13-3-7) gives

$$\mathbf{E}^{0'} - \mathbf{E}^0 = \frac{1}{2}\frac{RT}{\mathbf{F}} \ln 4 - \frac{1}{2}\frac{RT}{\mathbf{F}} \ln \alpha(1 + \alpha)^2$$

$$- \frac{3}{2}\frac{RT}{\mathbf{F}} \ln \gamma_\alpha - \frac{3}{2}\frac{RT}{\mathbf{F}} 2.303 \mathcal{S}_{(f)} \sqrt{2\mu} \qquad (13\text{-}3\text{-}9)$$

From the values of α, computed as above described for different values of K, and values of γ_α assumed to equal those derived from measurements on a strong 2-1 electrolyte such as barium chloride, the deviation factor, $\mathbf{E}^{0'} - \mathbf{E}^0$, may be computed. Such calculations are represented in Fig. (13-3-3) for values of K ranging from 0.01 to ∞. By comparison with Fig. (13-3-2), we note a close similarity, which indicates that barium, zinc, lead and cadmium chlorides in dilute solutions may be explained by this theory provided we assign ionization constants for the reaction, $MX^+ \rightleftharpoons$ $M^{++} + X^-$, of the order ∞, 0.1, 0.04, 0.01, respectively.

An illustration of the more careful application of this method is to be found in the work of Harned and Fitzgerald,[27] who made a comprehensive investigation of aqueous cadmium chloride solutions. In Fig. (13-3-4) are shown plots of the deviation factors, $E^{0'} - E^0$, at 0, 25, and 40°, calculated by this method, and which fitted closely the values of $E^{0'}$, computed from the experimental results expressed by equation (13-3-3). The values of

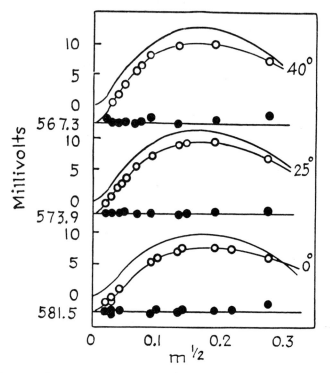

Fig. (13–3–4). Extrapolation functions at 0°, 25°, and 40° (scale in mv., diameters of circles equal 1 mv. Curves without points are calculated by equation (13-3-9). $E^{0'} - E^0$ is plotted. Circles represent plots of $E^{0'}$ according to equation (13-3-2). Dots represent E^0 according to equation (13-3-10). The ionization constants are 0.01, 0.011, and 0.013 at 40°, 25°, and 0°, respectively.

the ionization constants employed, which seemed to agree best with the results, are given.[28]

Upon rearrangement of equation (13-3-7), E^0 is given by

$$E^0 = E + \frac{3}{2}\frac{RT}{F} \ln \alpha (1 + \alpha)^2 m^3 \gamma_\alpha^3 \qquad (13\text{-}3\text{-}10)$$

[27] H. S. Harned and M. E. Fitzgerald, *J. Am. Chem. Soc.*, **58**, 2624 (1936).

[28] They are in approximate agreement with the value, 0.010, estimated from conductance data by E. C. Righellato and C. W. Davies, *Trans. Faraday Soc.*, **26**, 592 (1930).

The straight line plots used for extrapolation of E^0 were obtained by adding to the experimental values of E the second term on the right of this equation. This fit shows that the simple expedient of combining the law of mass action and the Debye and Hückel limiting law affords a satisfactory extrapolation method.

Bates[29] in an equally comprehensive investigation of cadmium bromide solutions by means of the cell,

$$Cd\text{-}Cd_xHg \mid CdBr_2(m) \mid AgBr\text{-}Ag$$

has also determined the standard potential from 0 to 40°. By combining these with the standard potentials of the silver-silver chloride, and silver-silver bromide electrodes [Equations (11-2-6) and (12-2-2), respectively], the standard potential of the electrode, $Cd\text{-}Cd_xHg \mid Cd^{++}$ $(a = 1)$, may be obtained. In Table (13-3-1A), the standard potentials obtained from these results are compiled. The last two columns contrast the values obtained by Harned and Fitzgerald, and Bates. The agreement at 25, 30, 35 and 40° is excellent, but an increasing difference is observed with decreasing temperature. This discrepancy is still unexplained.

Bates and Vosburgh measured the cell,

$$Cd\text{-}Cd_xHg \mid CdI_2(m) \mid Hg_2I_2\text{-}Hg$$

containing cadmium iodide solutions only, and also cells containing cadmium iodide-sulphate mixtures, and cadmium iodide-potassium iodide mixtures. The standard potential of the mercury-mercurous iodide electrode was obtained,[30] the activity coefficient of cadmium iodide[31] was evaluated, and the numerous equilibria involved in these solutions[32] were investigated at 25°.[33] The thermodynamic properties, $\gamma_\pm$, $\bar{L}_2$, and $\bar{J}_2$, have been determined by Bates[34] from measurements of the cells,

$$Cd\text{-}Cd_xHg \mid CdI_2(m) \mid AgI\text{-}Ag$$

from 5 to 40°.

Zinc chloride,[35] bromide[36] and iodide[37] solutions have been studied by means of the cells,

$$Zn\text{-}Zn_xHg \mid ZnX_2(m) \mid AgX\text{-}Ag$$

[29] R. G. Bates, *J. Am. Chem. Soc.*, **61**, 308 (1939).

[30] R. G. Bates and W. C. Vosburgh, *J. Am. Chem. Soc.*, **59**, 1188 (1937).

[31] R. G. Bates and W. C. Vosburgh, *J. Am. Chem. Soc.*, **59**, 1583 (1937).

[32] R. G. Bates and W. C. Vosburgh, *J. Am. Chem. Soc.*, **60**, 136 (1938).

[33] For earlier work on cadmium halides, see, W. G. Horsch, *J. Am. Chem. Soc.*, **41**, 1787 (1919); F. H. Getman, *J. Phys. Chem.*, **35**, 588 (1931); W. W. Lucasse, *J. Am. Chem. Soc.*, **51**, 2597 (1929).

[34] R. G. Bates, *J. Am. Chem. Soc.*, **63**, 399 (1941).

[35] G. Scatchard and R. F. Tefft, *J. Am. Chem. Soc.*, **52**, 2272 (1930); R. A. Robinson and R. H. Stokes, *Trans. Faraday Soc.*, **36**, 740 (1940); Transference numbers from cells with liquid junction are given by A. C. Harris and H. N. Parton, *Ibid.*, **36**, 1139 (1940).

[36] H. N. Parton and J. W. Mitchell, *Trans. Faraday Soc.*, **35**, 758 (1939); R. H. Stokes and J. M. Stokes, *Ibid.*, **41**, 488 (1945).

[37] R. G. Bates, *J. Am. Chem. Soc.*, **60**, 2983 (1938).

The work of Robinson and Stokes on zinc chloride, and of Bates on zinc iodide covers the temperature range from 5 to 40°, while that of Parton and Mitchell on zinc bromide is at 25° only. The standard potentials of these cells, as well as that of the two phase zinc amalgam electrode, are given in Table (13-3-2A). The agreement between the standard potentials of the latter electrode obtained from the different sources is excellent. From the standard potentials of the cells and their electromotive forces, values of $\gamma_{\pm}$ were computed by equation (13-3-1). These have been compiled in Table (13-3-3A).

By means of equations (10-5-15) and (10-5-17), the relative partial molal heat content, $\bar{L}_2$, and the relative partial molal heat capacity, $\bar{J}_2$, of zinc chloride and iodide, and cadmium chloride, bromide, and iodide, have been derived from electromotive forces. For zinc chloride and iodide, these quantities may be computed from the data in Table (13-3-4A).

Robinson and Wallace[37a] have determined $\bar{L}_2$ and $\bar{J}_2$ up to 0.2M from heat of dilution data. Their results differ considerably from those computed from the electromotive forces and, being unquestionably more accurate, are given in Table (13-3-5A). A re-examination of the methods employed for computing these quantities from electromotive force data may clarify the situation.

(4) General Considerations Regarding 1-2 and 2-1 Electrolytes in Aqueous Solutions

The activity coefficients at 25° of 1-2 and 2-1 halides and sulphates and barium hydroxide[38] are plotted against $m^{1/2}$ in Fig. (13-4-1). The upper group from barium chloride to magnesium iodide inclusive are strong electrolytes. Values of $\mathring{a}$, the mean distance of approach of the ions, for these salts are roughly between 4 for barium chloride and 6 for magnesium and zinc iodides. These are less than the value of $q = 7$ Å of Bjerrum's theory of ionic association for 2-1 or 1-2 electrolytes, and consequently, some ionic association may be expected to occur. $[M^{++}X^-]$ or $[MX]^+$ ions are not excluded in any of these solutions, and may be present to a considerable extent in concentrated solutions of barium chloride. The high activity coefficients of zinc iodide and cobalt chloride should be noted. The middle group containing the alkali sulphates and barium hydroxide, with $\mathring{a}$ values from 3 to 4, show more evidence of some kind of ionic association such as the presence of $[MSO_4]^-$, $[Ba(OH)]^+$ ions. Lead chloride and the incompletely ionized cadmium halides form a third group. By the method of treatment of electromotive forces outlined in the preceding section, Harned and Fitzgerald obtained 0.011 for the ionization constant of $[CdCl]^+$ at 25°. Similarly, Bates,[39] and Bates and Vosburgh,[40] obtained

[37a] A. L. Robinson and W. E. Wallace, *Chem. Rev.*, **30**, 195 (1942).

[38] H. S. Harned and C. M. Mason, *J. Am. Chem. Soc.*, **54**, 1439 (1932).

[39] R. G. Bates, *J. Am. Chem. Soc.*, **61**, 308 (1939).

[40] R. G. Bates and W. C. Vosburgh, *J. Am. Chem. Soc.*, **60**, 136 (1938).

0.006 and 0.004 for the ionization constants of $[CdBr]^+$ and $[CdI]^+$, respectively. Carmody's[41] results with lead chloride cells leads to a value of the ionization constant of $[PbCl]^+$ of the order of 0.03.

These observations are in accord with Onsager's and, particularly, with Righellato and Davies' interpretation of conductance data [Chapter (6), Section (3)]. They found that the group, barium chloride to magnesium chloride, was composed of very strong electrolytes. The estimated ionization constants of $[LiSO_4]^-$, $[NaSO_4]^-$, and $[KSO_4]^-$ were 0.23, 0.20, and 0.15, respectively, and are in the same order as indicated by their activity coefficients. $[CaNO_3]^+$, $[SrNO_3]^+$, and $[BaNO_3]^+$ possess ionization constants of the same order of magnitude. Finally, the values of 0.03 and 0.01 for $[PbCl]^+$ and $[CdCl]^+$ are in close agreement with those evaluated from the thermodynamic measurements.

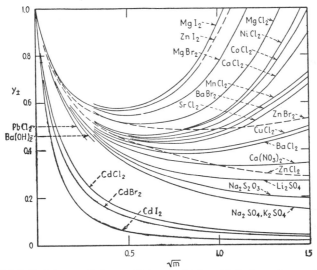

Fig. (13–4–1). Mean activity coefficients of 1-2 and 2-1 electrolytes at 25°.

The curves for zinc chloride and zinc bromide exhibit a curious feature. In dilute solutions both salts behave as strong electrolytes, electromotive force experiments leading to $\mathring{a}$ values of approximately 5 to 6, but above about $0.3M$ the activity coefficient curves begin to descend in such a way as to intersect the curves for many other electrolytes; the reason for this behavior is not clear.

(5) THE THERMODYNAMICS OF AQUEOUS ZINC SULPHATE SOLUTIONS

Bray[42] has measured the cells,

$$\text{Zn-Zn}_x\text{Hg} \mid \text{ZnSO}_4(m) \mid \text{PbSO}_4\text{-Pb}_x\text{Hg-Pb}$$

at 25° over a wide concentration range. More recently, Cowperthwaite

[41] W. R. Carmody, *J. Am. Chem. Soc.*, **51**, 2905 (1929).
[42] U. B. Bray, *J. Am. Chem. Soc.*, **49**, 2372 (1972).

and LaMer[43] investigated this cell at low concentrations (0.0005 to 0.01M) at temperatures from 0 to 50°. The relative partial heat content, $\bar{L}_2$, has been determined at low concentrations by Lange, Monheim, and Robinson.[44] These investigations will serve to illustrate some important characteristics of 2-2 electrolytes.

We shall employ the quantity, $\mathbf{E}^{0\prime}$, defined in terms of the equation for the cell by

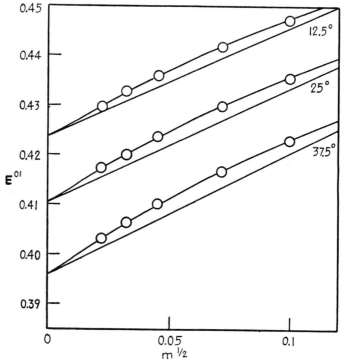

Fig. (13–5–1). Plots of $\mathbf{E}^{0\prime}$ [Equation (13–5–1)] for zinc sulfate solutions. Straight lines represent limiting law.

$$\mathbf{E}^{0\prime} \equiv \mathbf{E} + \frac{\nu RT}{\mathbf{NF}} \ln m = \mathbf{E}^0 - \frac{\nu RT}{\mathbf{NF}} \ln \gamma_{\pm} \qquad (13\text{-}5\text{-}1)$$

In Fig. (13-5-1), $\mathbf{E}^{0\prime}$, obtained from Cowperthwaite and LaMer's results, is plotted against $m^{1/2}$. The straight line represents the limiting equation of the Debye and Hückel theory. The noticeable departure from the limiting law, characterized by a "hump" agrees with the expectation of the extended Debye theory as developed by Gronwall, LaMer and Sandved. Indeed, this probably constitutes the most rigorous verification of the extended theory in aqueous solutions.

By employing equations (3-6-4), Cowperthwaite and LaMer obtained

[43] I. A. Cowperthwaite and V. K. La Mer, *J. Am. Chem. Soc.*, **53**, 4333 (1931).
[44] E. Lange, J. Monheim, and A. L. Robinson, *J. Am. Chem. Soc.*, **55**, 4733 (1933).

a value of $\mathring{a}$ which led to an exact agreement between the theory and their data, since their computed value of E^0 was constant throughout the concentration range, 0.0005 to 0.01M. Furthermore $\mathring{a}$ was found to have the constant value, 3.64, at all temperatures from 0 to 50°. Although the inclusion of additional effects, linear in concentration, might alter the numerical results slightly, the concentrations are too low for such effects to be comparable in magnitude to the contribution of the extended terms.

The values of $\bar{L}_2$ derived from these electromotive forces[45] are in good agreement with those obtained from the calorimetric data by Lange, Monheim and Robinson from 0.001 to 0.01M as shown by Table (13-5-1). The latter have been decreased uniformly by 25 cal. in accordance with our re-extrapolation explained in Chapter (8), Section (2).

The activity coefficients in concentrated solutions have been determined by the electromotive force method by Bray,[45] and the isopiestic vapor pressure method by Robinson and Jones.[47] In Table (13-5-2), values of this quantity at 25° are given. The value of $\gamma_\pm$ (0.387) at 0.01M from Cowperthwaite and LaMer's computations, is used for the recalculation of Bray's values. The vapor pressure results are based on the value of 0.150 at 0.1M also determined from electromotive forces. The agreement

TABLE (13-5-1). THE RELATIVE PARTIAL MOLAL HEAT CONTENT OF ZINC SULFATE AT 25° FROM ELECTROMOTIVE FORCE AND CALORIMETRIC DATA

m	0.0005	0.001	0.002	0.005	0.01
L_2 (E.M.F.)	(198)	385	480	674	772
L_2 (Cal.)	227	327	463	655	765

is quite good throughout the concentration range in which measurements by both methods were obtained.

For 2-2 electrolytes, $q = 14$ Å. Since Cowperthwaite and LaMer found $\mathring{a}$ to be 3.6 for zinc sulphate, it is to be expected that this salt will be incompletely dissociated. With this value of $\mathring{a}$, Bjerrum's equation (3-7-13) leads to 0.003 for K. Owen and Gurry[48] have measured the conductances of zinc and copper sulphates in water at 25°, and obtained 0.0049 and 0.0043 for the dissociation constants, respectively. Davies[49] reported 0.0045 at 18° for both these salts.

(6) ACTIVITY COEFFICIENTS OF THE SULFATES OF BIVALENT METALS IN AQUEOUS SOLUTION

Although the thermodynamics of aqueous solutions of cadmium, copper, magnesium, manganese, and nickel sulphates have not been studied as

[45] H. S. Harned, J. Am. Chem. Soc., **58**, 360 (1937).
[46] U. B. Bray, J. Am. Chem. Soc., **49**, 2372 (1927).
[47] R. A. Robinson and R. S. Jones, J. Am. Chem. Soc., **58**, 959 (1936).
[48] B. B. Owen and R. W. Gurry, J. Am. Chem. Soc., **60**, 3074 (1938).
[49] C. W. Davies, Trans. Faraday Soc., **23**, 351 (1927).

comprehensively as zinc sulphate solutions, sufficient data are available to indicate that the behavior of their activity coefficients is of considerable interest. In the first place the freezing point data in dilute solutions show that the activity coefficients of each of these electrolytes have nearly the same value. Thus, at $0.1M$ different investigators have obtained values of 0.149, 0.150, 0.166 and 0.160 for the activity coefficients of copper, cadmium, magnesium and zinc sulphate, respectively. Further, LaMer and Parks[49a] obtained, from electromotive force measurements, values of $\gamma_\pm$ for cadmium sulphate (0.699, 0.476, and 0.383 at $0.001M$, $0.005M$, and $0.01M$) which are nearly identical with those for zinc sulphate given in Table (13-5-2). The present uncertainty in the data, and also in the methods of extrapolation, is probably as great as the spread of the values

TABLE (13-5-2). THE MEAN ACTIVITY COEFFICIENT OF ZINC SULFATE IN AQUEOUS SOLUTION AT 25°

m	$\gamma_\pm$(E.M.F)	$\gamma_\pm$(V.P.)
0.0005	0.780	.....
.001	.700	.....
.002	.608	.....
.005	.477	.....
.01	.387	.....
.02	.298	.....
.05	.202	.....
.1	.150	(0.150)
.2	.104	.104
.5	.0634	.0626
1.	.0438	.0434
1.5	.0372	.0378
2.	.0354	.0350
2.5	.0368	.0360
3.	.0409	.0397
3.5	.0478	.0467

of $\gamma_\pm$, obtained from the freezing point results. In any case, the individuality is very slight indeed.

This conclusion is also substantiated by the isopiestic vapor pressure data of Robinson and Jones[50] in solutions of high concentration (0.1 to $4M$). If, for the purpose of illustration, we let $\gamma_\pm$ be 0.150 at $0.1M$ and 25° for all these sulphates, the result shown in Table (13-6-1) is obtained. Inspection of these values shows that, even in concentrated solutions, the individuality is very much less pronounced than that observed for 1-1 and 2-1 electrolytes.

(7) 1-3, 3-1, 3-2, AND 1-4 ELECTROLYTES

Accurate data on these unsymmetrical types of electrolytes are fragmentary. Only in one case, lanthanum chloride, have results been ob-

[49a] V. K. LaMer and W. G. Parks, *J. Am. Chem. Soc*, **53**, 2040 (1931); *Ibid.*, **55**, 4343 (1933).

[50] R. A. Robinson and R. S. Jones, *J. Am. Chem. Soc.*, **58**, 959 (1936).

tained in solutions sufficiently dilute for extrapolation.[51] From freezing point measurements, the activity coefficients of lanthanum nitrate,[52] potassium ferri-,[53] and cobalti-cyanide,[54] and lanthanum sulphate[55] have been computed. Isopiestic vapor pressure data on solutions of lanthanum chloride,[56, 57, 58] potassium ferrocyanide,[56] aluminum sulphate,[56] and some 3-1 rare earth chlorides[58] have been made. Aqueous indium sulphate solutions have been investigated from 0 to 35° by the use of the cell,

$$In \mid In_2(SO_4)_3(m) \mid Hg_2SO_4\text{-}Hg$$

by Hattox and DeVries.[59]

From measurements of the cells,

$$Ag\text{-}AgCl \mid LaCl_3(c_1) \mid LaCl_3(c_2) \mid AgCl\text{-}Ag$$

TABLE (13-6-1).   THE MEAN ACTIVITY COEFFICIENTS OF BIVALENT METAL SULFATES AT 25°

m	$ZnSO_4$	$CdSO_4$	$MnSO_4$	$MgSO_4$	$CuSO_4$	$NiSO_4$
0.1	(0.150)	(0.150)	(0.150)	(0.150)	(0.150)	(0.150)
.2	.104	.102	.1056	.1077	.1043	.1049
.3	.0831	.0815	.0850	.0877	.0834	.0841
.4	.0708	.0692	.0728	.0760	.0708	.0713
.5	.0626	.0609	.0643	.0678	.0624	.0628
.7	.0520	.0501	.0532	.0574	.0515	.0516
1.	.0434	.0411	.0441	.0488	.....	.0426
1.5	.0368	.0342	.0373	.0430	.....	.0360
2.	.0350	.0318	.0351	.0419	.....	.0343
2.5	.0360	.0315	.0353	.0441	.....	.0357
3.	.0397	.0327	.0375	.0495	.....	.....
3.5	.0467	.0351	.0416	.....	.....	.....
4.	.....	.....	.0478	.....	.....	.....
4.25	.....	.....	.0518	.....	.....	.....

and the transference numbers, Shedlovsky and MacInnes[60] have supplied the data for the determination of the activity coefficient of lanthanum chloride from 0.0006 to 0.03333 molar by the method described in Chapter (12), Section (1).   Due to an error in calculation, the erroneous conclusion was made that lanthanum chloride in water does not conform to theory in dilute solutions. We have repeated the computation and find that, as a first approximation, the observed results may be calculated by the Debye

[51] T. Shedlovsky and D. A. MacInnes, *J. Am. Chem. Soc.*, **61**, 200 (1939).

[52] R. E. Hall and W. D. Harkins, *J. Am. Chem. Soc.*, **38**, 2658 (1916).

[53] G. T. Bedford, *Proc. Roy. Soc.*, **83A**, 454 (1909).

[54] C. Robertson and V. K. LaMer, *J. Phys. Chem.*, **35**, 1953 (1931).

[55] F. Hovorka and W. H. Rodebush, *J. Am. Chem. Soc.*, **47**, 1614 (1925); W. H. Rodebush, *Ibid.*, **48**, 709 (1926).

[56] R. A. Robinson, *J. Am. Chem. Soc.*, **59**, 84 (1937).

[57] R. A. Robinson, *Trans. Faraday Soc.*, **35**, 1229 (1939).

[58] C. M. Mason, *J. Am. Chem. Soc.*, **60**, 1638 (1938).

[59] E. M. Hattox and T. DeVries, *J. Am. Chem. Soc.*, **58**, 2126 (1936).

[60] T. Shedlovsky and D. A. MacInnes, *J. Am. Chem. Soc.*, **61**, 200 (1939).

and Hückel formula

$$\log y_\pm = -\frac{3.7446 \sqrt{c}}{1 + 4.75 \sqrt{c}} \qquad (13\text{-}7\text{-}1)$$

which yields the reasonable value of 5.9Å. for the mean distance of approach of the ions. The theoretical functions in this equation were computed from the recent values of the universal constants given in Appendix B, Table (B-1-1). The average difference between the calculated and observed results is 0.0015 in $y_\pm$. The character of this deviation from theory indicates that this difference could be reduced by employing the extended terms of the theory.† Since there is no large difference between $y_\pm$ and $\gamma_\pm$ at the low concentrations, this equation has been employed to compute the value of 0.392 for $\gamma_\pm$ at $0.05M$.

TABLE (13-7-1). MEAN ACTIVITY COEFFICIENTS OF LANTHANUM CHLORIDE, POTASSIUM FERROCYANIDE, ALUMINUM AND INDIUM SULFATES AT 25°

m	LaCl₃	K₄Fe(CN)₆[a]	Al₂(SO₄)₃[a]	In₂(SO₄)₃[b]
0.001	0.788	.....	.....	.....
.005	.637	.....	.....	.....
.01	.559	.....	.....	0.142
.02	.484	.....	.....	.095
.03	.442	.....	.....	.071
.05	.392	(0.189)	.....	.054
.1	.336	.138	(0.0350)	.035
.2	.293	.107	.0223	.022
.3	.281	.088	.0174	.017
.4	.280	.076	.0151	.015
.5	.285	.067	.0115	.....
.7	.305	.055	.0133	.....
1.	.366	.048	.0176	.....
1.2	.426	.....	.....	.....
1.4	.503	.....	.....	.....
1.5	.554	.....	.....	.....

[a] R. A. Robinson, *J. Am. Chem. Soc.*, **59**, 84 (1937).
[b] E. M. Hattox and T. DeVries, *J. Am. Chem. Soc.*, **58**, 2126 (1936). Results obtained at 0°, 15° and 30°. L_2 estimated.

Robinson[61] and Mason[62] made isopiestic vapor pressure measurements on lanthanum chloride solutions at high concentrations (0.05 to 2M). Activity coefficients derived from these results have been brought into accord with the values at low concentration.[63] These are recorded in Table (13-7-1). Chlorides of aluminum, scandium, yttrium, cerium, praseo- and neodymium have also been investigated by this method in concentrated solutions by Mason. These are compiled in Table (13-7-1A).

† Dr. Shedlovsky has informed us that he has recomputed his results. By using the Debye and Hückel formula with an additional term, $Dc \log c$, he is able to reduce the average deviation to 0.0002.

[61] R. A. Robinson, *J. Am. Chem. Soc.*, **59**, 84 (1937).
[62] C. M. Mason, *J. Am. Chem. Soc.*, **60**, 1638 (1938).
[63] R. A. Robinson, *Trans. Faraday Soc.*, **35**, 1229 (1939).

The 1-4 and 3-2 electrolytes are represented in Table (13-7-1) by potassium ferrocyanide, aluminium sulphate[64] and indium sulphate.[65] In these cases, the extrapolations are uncertain, but the results are of the right order of magnitude, and serve to illustrate the behavior of electrolytes of these valence types. Further advance in this field will require much additional data in very dilute solutions.

(8) THE IONIZATION CONSTANT OF HSO_4^- FROM ELECTROMOTIVE FORCE MEASUREMENTS

The following sections will be devoted principally to a discussion of the activity coefficient, the relative partial molal heat content and heat capacity of sulphuric acid in aqueous solutions, derived from measurements of the cells,

$$H_2 \mid H_2SO_4(m) \mid PbSO_4\text{-}PbO_2\text{-}Pt$$

$$H_2 \mid H_2SO_4(m) \mid Hg_2SO_4\text{-}Hg$$

Since sulphuric acid is a partially weak electrolyte, difficulties arise in the determination of the standard potentials of these cells which can be overcome if the ionization constant

$$K_{2A} = \frac{m_H \, m_{SO_4} \, \gamma_H \, \gamma_{SO_4}}{m_{HSO_4} \, \gamma_{HSO_4}} \tag{13-8-1}$$

is known.

K_{2A} has been determined by Hamer[66] from measurements of the cells

$$H_2 \mid NaHSO_4(m_1), \ Na_2SO_4(m_2), \ NaCl(m_3) \mid AgCl\text{-}Ag$$

and by Davies, Jones and Monk[63a] from the cells

$$H_2 \mid HCl(m_1), \ H_2SO_4(m_2) \mid AgCl\text{-}Ag$$

Young, Klotz and Singleterry[67] used a spectrophotometric method for the same purpose. Sherill and Noyes[68] calculated K_{2A} at 25° from the conductance and transference data of Noyes and Stewart.[69] All their estimates of K_{2A} took into consideration the corrections given by the interionic attraction theory and yield a value of about 0.01 at 25°. We note that this value is considerably lower than 0.03, 0.02, and 0.017 previously reported by investigators[70] who did not make all the required corrections.

Values determined by these methods are recorded in Table (13-8-1).

[63a] C. W. Davies, H. W. Jones and C. S. Monk, *Trans. Faraday Soc.*, **48**, 921 (1952).

[64] R. A. Robinson, *J. Am. Chem. Soc.*, **59**, 84 (1937).

[65] E. M. Hattox and T. DeVries, *J. Am. Chem. Soc.*, **58**, 2126 (1936).

[66] W. J. Hamer, *J. Am. Chem. Soc.*, **56**, 860 (1934).

[67] Private communication from Professor T. F. Young based on the Dissertations of I. M. Klotz and C. R. Singleterry, University of Chicago (1940).

[68] M. S. Sherill and A. A. Noyes, *J. Am. Chem. Soc.*, **48**, 1861 (1926).

[69] A. A. Noyes and M. A. Stewart, *J. Am. Chem. Soc.*, **32**, 1133 (1910).

[70] R. S. Livingston, *J. Am. Chem. Soc.*, **48**, 45 (1926); C. Drucker, *Z. physik. Chem.*, **96**, 381 (1920); I. M. Kolthoff, *Rec. trav. chim.*, **43**, 207 (1924).

Hamer[71] used the limiting equation in the form

$$-\log f_i = \text{S}_{(f)} z_i^2 \sqrt{\mu} - B\mu \tag{13-8-2}$$

while Davies, Jones and Monk used the more refined formula

$$-\log f_i = \text{S}_{(f)} z_i^2 \sqrt{\mu}/(1 + A\sqrt{\mu}) - B\mu \tag{13-8-3}$$

and corrected for the partial ionization of $NaSO_4^-$. This procedure brings Hamer's results into somewhat closer agreement with their own measurements which are very close indeed to the values derived from spectrophotometry. The equation

$$-\log K_{2A} = 1.67 + 0.0127t \tag{13-8-4}$$

reproduces the last two series of results within the experimental error. From this equation, the heat of ionization is found to be 5.2 ± 0.1 kcals in agreement with Pitzer's[72] calorimetric estimate of 5.2 ± 0.5 kcals.

TABLE (13-8-1). THE IONIZATION CONSTANT OF HSO_4^-

t	E.M.F.[a]	E.M.F.[b]	E.M.F.[c]	Opatical[d]	Calc.
0	0.0148	0.0150	—	—	0.0214
5	.0143	.0140	0.0173	0.0180	.0185
10	.0139	.0133	.0158	—	.0160
15	.0134	.0123	.0143	.0136	.0138
20	.0127	.0110	.0120	—	.0119
25	.0120	.0103	.0103	.0101	.0103
30	.0113	.0098	.0090	—	.0089
35	.0105	.0087	.0078	.0075	.0077
40	.0097	.0083	.0067	—	.0064
45	.0089	.0074	—	.0056	.0057
50	.0079	.0069	.0050	—	.0050
55	.0070	.0059	—	.0041	.0043
60	.0060	.0051	—	—	.0037

a) Hamer, partial ionization of $NaSO_4^-$ neglected (Ref. 66)
b) Hamer's E.M.F.'s recalculated by Davies, Jones and Monk (Ref. 63a)
c) Davies, Jones and Monk from their E.M.F. data.
d) Young and Singleterry (Ref. 67)

(9) THE STANDARD POTENTIAL OF THE CELL,[73]

$$H_2 \mid H_2SO_4 \; (m) \mid PbSO_4\text{-}PbO_2\text{-}Pt$$

(a) Evaluation of the Standard Potential, E^0, by an Empirical Method.

The chemical reaction represented by the cell in question is taken to be

$$H_2 + PbO_2(s) + H_2SO_4(m) = PbSO_4(s) + 2H_2O$$

and the electromotive force is given by the equation,

$$\mathbf{E} = \mathbf{E}^0 + (RT/2F) \ln m_H^2 m_{SO_4} + (RT/2F) \ln \gamma_H^2 \gamma_{SO_4}$$
$$- (RT/2F) \ln a_w^2 \tag{13-9-1}$$

71 W. J. Hamer, *J. Am. Chem. Soc.*, **56**, 860 (1934).

72 K. S. Pitzer, *J. Am. Chem. Soc.*, **59**, 2365 (1937).

73 W. J. Hamer, *J. Am. Chem. Soc.*, **57**, 9 (1935).

where $\mathbf{E}$ is the measured electromotive force of the cell, and $\mathbf{E}^0$ is its standard potential. The activity of the water in a solution of m molal sulphuric acid is represented by a_w.

We shall first employ an empirical method of extrapolation.[74] Equation (13-9-1) may be rearranged in the form,

$$\mathbf{E} - (RT/2\mathbf{F}) \ln m_\mathrm{H}^2 m_{\mathrm{SO}_4} = \mathbf{E}^0 + (RT/2\mathbf{F}) \ln \gamma_\mathrm{H}^2 \gamma_{\mathrm{SO}_4} - (RT/2\mathbf{F}) \ln a_w^2$$

$$(13\text{-}9\text{-}2)^{[75]}$$

and if the left side is plotted against the square root of the molality, a straight line may be obtained in dilute solution. At zero concentration this function equals $\mathbf{E}^0$, since by definition the last two terms on the right vanish.

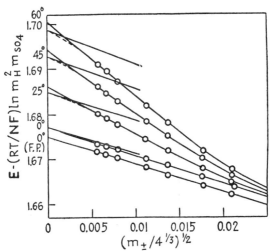

Fig. (13-9-1). Plots of left side of equation (13-9-2) against $(m_{\pm}/4^{1/3})^{1/2}$.

As a comparison with this extrapolation, the activity coefficients at $0°$ of Randall and Scott,[76] obtained from freezing point determinations, were used to evaluate the second term on the right of equation (13-9-2). The difference between this term and the left side of the same equation gives $\mathbf{E}^0$, when a_w, a very small term, is neglected. The electromotive force measurements are parallel to their curve as found for other electrolytes by Randall and Young.[77] The extrapolations of the left side of equation (13-9-2) against $(m_{\pm}/4^{1/3})^{1/2}$ are given in Fig. (13-9-1) at 0, 25, 45, and $60°$ from 0.0005 to $0.01M$. The lower curve is the one given by freezing point

[74] G. N. Lewis and M. Randall, "Thermodynamics," McGraw-Hill Book Company, New York (1923), p. 334.

[75] In very dilute solutions, these electromotive forces were corrected for the solubility of PbSO$_4$. W. J. Hamer, *J. Am. Chem. Soc.*, **57**, 9 (1935).

[76] M. Randall and G. N. Scott, *J. Am. Chem. Soc.*, **49**, 647 (1927).

[77] M. Randall and L. E. Young, *J. Am. Chem. Soc.*, **50**, 989 (1928).

measurements. For clear comparison with electromotive force measurements, 0.002v. has been subtracted from the function computed from freezing point measurements. The freezing point curve has a slight "hump" below 0.002M, but this may be due to the somewhat arbitrary extrapolation by Randall and Scott of their function, $j/m^{1/2}$, in dilute solutions. The points computed from the electromotive forces are not accurate enough to justify this slight "hump", and consequently straight lines have been drawn at the other temperatures. The standard potentials, determined in this manner, are given in the second column of Table (13-9-1). These were least squared to fit a quadratic equation, and the equation with numerical values is

$$\mathbf{E}^0 = 1.6769_4 + 342.17 \times 10^{-6}t + 83.11 \times 10^{-8}t^2 \quad (13\text{-}9\text{-}3)$$

Values of $\mathbf{E}^0$, calculated by this equation, agree with the observed values to less than 0.1 mv.

TABLE (13-9-1). STANDARD POTENTIALS OF THE CELL, $H_2 \mid H_2SO_4(m) \mid PbSO_4\text{-}PbO_2\text{-}Pt$

t	[Equation (13-9-2)]	[Equation (13-9-6)]	Δ(mv.)
0	1.67694	1.67694	0
5	1.67870	1.67846	0.24
10	1.68045	1.67998	.47
15	1.68228	1.68159	.69
20	1.68411	1.68322	.89
25	1.68597	1.68488	1.09
30	1.68800	1.68671	1.29
35	1.68991	1.68847	1.45
40	1.69196	1.69036	1.60
45	1.69396	1.69231	1.65
50	1.69616	1.69436	1.80
55	1.69831	1.69649	1.82
60	1.70044	1.69861	1.83

(b) Evaluation of the Standard Potential, E^0, by a Method Employing the Ionization Constant of HSO_4^-.

In the previous method of extrapolation, we have employed stoichiometrical concentrations. Sulfuric acid is known to be a moderately strong electrolyte, the second step in its ionization being incomplete. This is shown to be true in Fig. (13-9-1), since the experimental slopes are greater than those predicted by the limiting law of Debye and Hückel for a completely dissociated electrolyte.

This method of extrapolation possesses the advantage of simplicity, but is subject to two major criticisms. When $m^{1/2}$ is plotted, the extrapolation from the last experimental point to zero concentration is long. Secondly, for an electrolyte which is partially dissociated, the straight line extrapolation does not conform to the law of Debye and Hückel at zero concentration.

An alternative method, which has the advantage of including the limiting law, will now be described.

If the value of the real concentration of the hydrogen ion, given by the equation

$$K_{2A} = (m_H m_{SO_4} \gamma_H \gamma_{SO_4})/(m_{HSO_4} \gamma_{HSO_4}) \tag{13-9-4}$$

is substituted in equation (13-9-1), we obtain

$$\mathbf{E} = \mathbf{E}^0 + (RT/2F) \ln m_H m_{HSO_4} + (RT/2F) \ln \gamma_H \gamma_{HSO_4}$$
$$+ (RT/2F) \ln (K_{2A}/a_w^2) \tag{13-9-5}$$

In making this step a number of considerations are involved. In the first place, the assumption that sulfuric acid dissociates completely into the hydrogen and hydrosulfate ions is made. In the second place, we regard m as representing the true concentration of a species present, and not the stoichiometrical concentration. This permits the substitution of the limiting law of Debye and Hückel for the activity coefficients. Upon substitution of this law with an additional term, $\beta\mu'$, for the third term on the right of equation (13-9-5), the equation

$$\mathbf{E}^{0'} = \mathbf{E} - (RT/2F) \ln m_H m_{HSO_4} + 2.303 \, (RT/2F) \mathcal{S}_{(f)} \sqrt{2\mu'}$$

$$- (RT/2F) \ln K_{2A}$$

$$= \mathbf{E}^0 - (RT/2F) \ln a_w^2 + \beta\mu' \tag{13-9-6}$$

results. Since at very low concentrations all quantities on the left side may be either obtained experimentally or evaluated, an extrapolation of the left side against μ' gives $\mathbf{E}^0$. The ionic strength, μ', is computed from the real concentrations of the ionic species.

The ionic concentrations of each of the ions (H^+, HSO_4^- and SO_4^-) were estimated from equation (13-9-4), and the logarithm of the activity coefficient ratio was obtained from the limiting law of Debye and Hückel. In equation (13-9-4), $m_H = m + m_H'$, $m_{SO_4} = m_H' + S$, and $m_{HSO_4} = m - m_H'$, where m is the stoichiometrical concentration, and m_H' is the concentration of the sulfate or hydrogen ion produced in the ionization of HSO_4^-. S is the additional molality of the sulfate ion caused by the slight solubility of lead sulfate. The ionic strength is equal to ($m + 2m_H' + 4S$). The values of m_H', and the ionic strength were obtained by successive approximations. In these calculations, the experimental values of K_{2A}, given in Table (13-8-1), were employed. The values of the concentrations obtained by this method are only approximations in solutions of appreciable ionic strength, but in dilute solutions they approach the correct values, and should yield a correct extrapolation.

The extrapolation is shown by Fig. (13-9-2) in which the left side of equation (13-9-6), $\mathbf{E}^{0'}$, is plotted against μ'. The final results are given in the third column of Table (13-9-1).   These results may be computed by the equation

$$E^0 = 1.67699 + 0.000285t + 1.2467 \times 10^{-6}t^2 \qquad (13\text{-}9\text{-}7)$$

obtained by the method of least squares.   The fourth column contains the differences between these values and those obtained by the first method of extrapolation.   At 0° the plots have a slight curvature, but at higher temperatures they are straight lines, and it is a comparatively simple matter to make the short extrapolation.

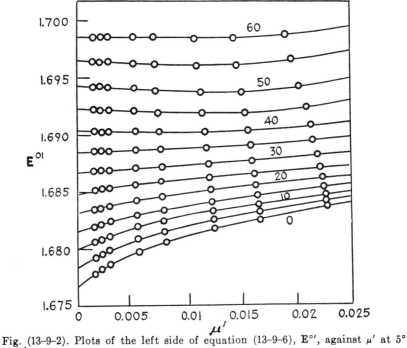

Fig. (13-9-2). Plots of the left side of equation (13-9-6), $E^{o\prime}$, against μ' at 5° intervals.

We are now in a position to compare the two methods of extrapolation. In Fig. (13-9-1), we have drawn lines (L. L.) to the values of E^0, obtained by the second method of extrapolation, which show the requirement of the limiting law of Debye and Hückel.   First, it is to be noticed that at zero degrees the slope of the Lewis and Randall extrapolation happens to be nearly the same as that required by the limiting law.   Consequently, at this temperature both methods of extrapolation give the same values of E^0.   At the higher temperatures, most noticeable at 60°, the slope of the Lewis and Randall graph is greater than that required by theory.   It is obvious that if we do not abandon the theory, the values of E^0 must be lower than those obtained by the first method.   Such conformity with theory is represented by the dotted lines drawn to the values of E^0, obtained by the second method. Somewhere in the region of concentration below $0.0005M$, the results should show a curvature, and the slopes of experimental graphs should approach the limiting slopes. Although the present results show no tendency to approach the limiting law, we think that this is simply due to the fact that reliable experiments have not been obtained from the cells in question at such extreme dilutions. In view of this well established theoretical requirement, there is no doubt that the values of E^0, obtained by the second method of extrapolation, are the better.

(10) THE ACTIVITY OF WATER IN AQUEOUS SULFURIC ACID FROM ELECTROMOTIVE FORCE AND VAPOR PRESSURE MEASUREMENTS

As pointed out in the preceding section, the electromotive forces of cells with the lead sulfate-dioxide electrode are given by equation (13-9-1), and the corresponding cell reaction by

$$H_2 + PbO_2 + H_2SO_4(m) = PbSO_4 + 2H_2O$$

To evaluate a_w, from the electromotive forces and equation (13-9-1), γ', a preliminary activity coefficient, obtained by neglecting the term containing a_w, was first computed. From these values of γ', a preliminary value of a_w may be computed by graphical integration of the general thermodynamic equation (1-8-1) which becomes

$$- \ln a_w = \ln \frac{p_0}{p} = \frac{m}{55.5} \left[\nu + \frac{\nu}{m} \int_0^{\ln \gamma} m \, d\ln \gamma \right] \qquad (13\text{-}10\text{-}1)$$

when the vapor pressures are introduced. These values of a_w were then substituted in equation (13-9-1), and new values of γ' computed. This process was repeated until the values of a_w satisfied this equation. This procedure was most convenient for concentrations below $0.1M$. At higher concentrations a simpler method was adopted.

The electromotive forces of the cells,

$$H_2 \mid H_2SO_4(m) \mid Hg_2SO_4\text{-}Hg \qquad\qquad I$$

are given by the equation[78]

$$E_I = E_I^0 - \frac{RT}{2F} \ln m_H^2 \, m_{SO_4} - \frac{RT}{2F} \ln \gamma_H^2 \, \gamma_{SO_4} \qquad (13\text{-}10\text{-}2)$$

where E_I^0 is the molal electrode potential of the cell. Upon addition of equations (13-9-1) and (13-10-2), we obtain

$$E + E_I - E^0 - E_I^0 = - \frac{RT}{2F} \ln a_w^2 \qquad (13\text{-}10\text{-}3)$$

[78] The subscript, I, differentiates the cell containing mercurous sulfate from that containing lead dioxide. It is used in this section only.

from which a_w may be computed easily. By employing the values of E^0 in Table (13-9-1), of E and E_I^0 given by Hamer,[79] and Harned and Hamer,[80] and E_I^0 in Table (13-12-1), a_w was computed. These are given at several temperatures in Table (13-10-1).

These results are in excellent agreement with the values from the direct vapor pressure measurements of Grollman and Frazer[81] for dilute solutions, and with the data of Collins[82] at somewhat higher concentrations (0.5 to $4M$), as shown by Fig. (13-10-1). On the other hand, the vapor pressure measurements of Shankman and Gordon[83] do not agree well with results derived from the electromotive forces in regions of concentration from 5 to $8M$, and from 12 to $17.5M$. Up to $4M$, the agreement is good as shown by the fourth column of Table (13-10-1), while at 5, 6 and $7M$ the deviations are of the order of 1 per cent in a_w. Recent results of Hornung and Giauque[83a] are in agreement with Shankman and Gordon's.

TABLE (13-10-1).   THE ACTIVITY OF WATER IN SULFURIC ACID SOLUTIONS

$m(H_2SO_4)$	0°	25°	25°(V.P.)[a]	40°	60°
0.0005	0.99998	0.99998	.....	0.99998	0.99998
.01	.99959	.99960	.....	.99961	.99962
.05	.99809	.99819	.....	.99822	.99823
.1	.99620	.9964	.....	.9964	.9964
.5	.9817	.9821	.9821	.9822	.9823
1	.9613	.9620	(.9620)	.9624	.9630
1.5	.9374	.9391	.9389	.9402	.9415
2	.9105	.9136	.9129	.9155	.9180
3	.8438	.8506	.8514	.8548	.8602
4	.7650	.7775	.7795	.7850	.7950
5	.6801	.6980	.7030	.7086	.7229
6	.5968	.6200	.6252	.6288	.6505
7	.5184	.5453	.5497	.5608	.5815

[a] S. Shankman and A. R. Gordon, *J. Am. Chem. Soc.*, **61**, 2370 (1939).

(11) THE ACTIVITY COEFFICIENT OF SULFURIC ACID

Upon eliminating the last term on the right of equation (13-9-1) and rearranging, we obtain,

$$E = E^0 - \frac{3RT}{2F} \ln m\gamma_\pm 4^{1/3} \qquad (13\text{-}11\text{-}1)$$

which may be used to compute $\gamma_\pm$ from the data of either cells containing the lead dioxide-lead sulfate-platinum electrode, or the mercurous sulfate-mercury electrode. The cells with the mercurous sulfate-mercury electrodes are not satisfactory at concentrations below $0.05M$, but from this concentration up to $17.5M$, they are quite reproducible. The values

[79] W. J. Hamer, *J. Am. Chem. Soc.*, **57**, 9 (1935).
[80] H. S. Harned and W. J. Hamer, *J. Am. Chem. Soc.*, **57**, 27 (1935).
[81] A. Grollman and J. C. W. Frazer, *J. Am. Chem. Soc.*, **47**, 712 (1925).
[82] E. M. Collins, *J. Phys. Chem.*, **37**, 1191 (1933).
[83] S. Shankman and A. R. Gordon, *J. Am. Chem. Soc.*, **61**, 2370 (1939).
[83a] E. W. Hornung and W. F. Giauque, *Ibid.*, **77**, 2744 (1955).

of $\gamma_{\pm}$, computed from the combined results, are given in Table (13-11-1) at several temperatures. The second column contains values obtained by Randall and Scott[84] from freezing point measurements. It is apparent that the agreement is excellent. At 25°, the values are much lower than those given by Lewis and Randall.[85] This is due principally to the fact that they employed in their calculation values of the relative partial molal heat content which were unquestionably too low. The present results

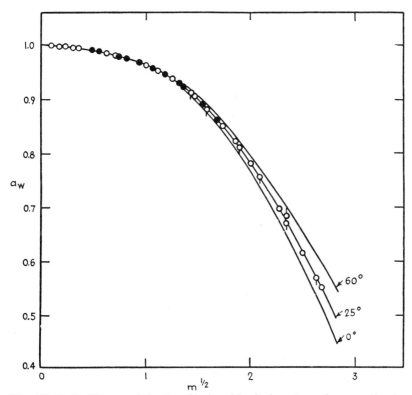

Fig. (13-10-1). Water activity in sulfuric acid solutions from electromotive force and vapor pressure measurements. ●, Grollman and Frazer (V.P.); ♀, Collins (V.P.); ○, Harned and Hamer (E.M.F.)

are 2.4 per cent higher than those obtained by Baumstark,[86] and those computed by Sherrill and Noyes.[87]

Values of $\gamma_{\pm}$ at 25°, computed from the vapor pressures of Shankman and Gordon using a common reference value at 1 M, are also given in Table

[84] M. Randall and G. N. Scott, *J. Am. Chem. Soc.*, **49**, 647 (1927).

[85] G. N. Lewis and M. Randall, "Thermodynamics," McGraw-Hill Book Co., New York, 1923, pp. 354 and 356.

[86] G. Baumstark, Dissertation, Catholic University of America. Baltimore, Md., 1933.

[87] M. S. Sherrill and A. A. Noyes, *J. Am. Chem. Soc.*, **48**, 1861 (1926).

(13-11-1).   The agreement is satisfactory from 1 to $4M$ and from 9 to $11M$ inclusive, but is poor from 5 to $8M$ and from 12 to $16M$.   The last column contains values of $\gamma_{\pm}$ obtained by the isopiestic vapor pressure method, using sodium chloride as standard.   Good agreement is obtained between 0.1 and $4M$.   In Table (13-11-1A), the activity coefficient from 0 to 60° at 5° intervals derived from the electromotive forces is given.

TABLE (13-11-1).   MEAN ACTIVITY COEFFICIENT OF SULFURIC ACID IN AQUEOUS SOLUTION

m	0°(F.P.)[1]	0°(E.M.F.)[2]	25°(E.M.F.)[2]	25°(V.P.)[3]	25°(V.P.)[4]
0.0005	0.912	0.908	0.885	.....	.....
.001	.876	.873	.830	.....	.....
002	.825	.825	.757	.....	.....
.005	.734	.734	.639	.....	.....
.01	.648	.649	.544	.....	.....
.02	.553	.554	.453	.....	.....
.05	.424	.426	.340	.....	.....
.1	.341	.341	.265	.....	(0.265)
.2	.272	.271	.209	.....	.207
.5	....	.202	.154	.....	.154
1.	....	.173	.130	(0.130)	.131
1.5	....	.167	.124	.124	.125
2	....	.170	.124	.125	.126
3	....	.201	.141	.141	.142
4	....	.254	.171	.168	.172
5	....	.330	.212	.206	....
6	....	.427	.264	.254	....
7	....	.546	.326	.315	....
8	....	.686	.397	.385	....
9	....	.843	.470	.466	....
10	....	1.012	.553	.557	....
11	....	1.212	.643	.643	....
12	....	1.431	.743	.763	....
13	....	1.676	.851	.850	....
14	....	1.958	.969	1.009	....
15	....	2.271	1.093	1.123	....
16	....	2.612	1.235	1.270	....
17	....	3.015	1.387	.....	....
17.5	....	3.217	1.473	.....	....

[1] M. Randall and G. N. Scott, *J. Am. Chem. Soc.*, **49**, 647 (1927).
[2] H. S. Harned and W. J. Hamer, *Ibid.*, **57**, 27 (1935).
[3] S. Shankman and A. R. Gordon, *Ibid.*, **61**, 2370 (1939).
[4] R. A. Robinson, *Trans. Faraday Soc.*, **35**, 1229 (1939).   From isopiestic ratios $m_{H_2SO_4}/m_{NaCl}$.   G. Scatchard, W. J. Hamer and S. E. Wood, *J. Am. Chem. Soc.*, **60**, 3061 (1938).

(12) THE STANDARD POTENTIAL OF THE CELL, $H_2 \mid H_2SO_4 \ (m) \mid Hg_2SO_4\text{-}Hg$

Since the electromotive forces of the cells of this type were insufficiently accurate in dilute solutions for suitable extrapolation, we employed the values of $\gamma_{\pm}$, derived from cells with lead sulphate-oxide electrodes, for the purpose of computing the molal electrode potential.   The values of $\gamma_{\pm}$ at 0.05, 0.07 and $0.1M$ were substituted in equation (13-11-1) as were also the values of E, and E^0 was computed at each concentration.   The mean value of the three determinations is given in Table (13-12-1). They may be expressed to within approximately ± 0.05 mv. by the quadratic equation

$$E^0 = 0.63495 - 781.44 \times 10^{-6}t - 426.89 \times 10^{-9}t^2 \quad (13\text{-}12\text{-}1)$$

The constants of this equation were computed by the method of least squares.

The result at 25° is 6 mv. lower than that computed by Lewis and Randall[88] from the data of Randall and Cushman.[89] It is also lower than the value calculated by Brodsky.[90] We are certain that the present value is better since the activity coefficients of the acid computed from the electromotive forces of the cells with mercurous sulphate electrodes agree with those of cells containing lead oxide from 0.05 to $7M$. These activity coefficients at 0° agree very well with those obtained from freezing point data of Randall and Scott.

TABLE (13-12-1). THE STANDARD POTENTIAL OF THE CELL,
$H_2 \mid H_2SO_4(m) \mid Hg_2SO_4\text{-}Hg$

t	E^0	t	E^0
0	0.63495	35	0.60701
5	.63097	40	.60305
10	.62704	45	.59900
15	.62307	50	.59487
20	.61930	55	.59051
25	.61515	60	.58659
30	.61107	..	......

(13) THE RELATIVE PARTIAL MOLAL HEAT CONTENT AND HEAT CAPACITY OF SULFURIC ACID IN AQUEOUS SOLUTION

Values of $\bar{L}_2$ from 0 to 60° were computed from the electromotive forces by Harned and Hamer. The results were expressed by the equation

$$\bar{L}_2 = \bar{L}_2(0°) + \alpha t + \beta t^2 \quad (13\text{-}13\text{-}1)$$

in which α and β are constants, and $\bar{L}_2(0°)$ is the value of $\bar{L}_2$ at 0°. The constants of this equation are given in Table (13-13-1A).

Lange, Monheim, and Robinson[91] determined $\bar{L}_2$ calorimetrically from 0.0001 to $0.05M$. In Fig. (13-13-1), their results (dots), and values of $\bar{L}_2 - \bar{L}_2(0.05)$, computed from the electromotive forces (circles), have been plotted against $m^{1/2}$. The agreement is excellent since most of the values agree within 20 cal.

[88] G. N. Lewis and M. Randall, "Thermodynamics," p. 407, McGraw-Hill Book Co., New York (1923).

[89] M. Randall and O. E. Cushman, *J. Am. Chem. Soc.*, **40**, 393 (1918).

[90] A. E. Brodsky, *Z. Elektrochem.*, **35**, 833 (1929).

[91] E. Lange, J. Monheim, and A. L. Robinson, *J. Am. Chem. Soc.*, **55**, 4733 (1938).

In this figure, two extrapolations are shown. The straight line represents an empirical extrapolation which Lange, Monheim, and Robinson used. This is in agreement with the empirical extrapolation of the electromotive forces [Equation (13-9-2); Fig. (13-9-1)]. The curved line represents an extrapolation consistent with theory, and the standard potentials obtained by the use of the limiting law [Equation (13-9-6); Fig. (13-9-2)]. We note that the theoretical requirement is approached only in very dilute solutions ($m < 0.0001M$). The difference between the two methods of extrapolation amounts to 460 cal. at 25°. In our opinion, the extrapolation in agreement with theory is preferable, although no measurements of electromotive force, or heats of dilution have been obtained at sufficiently low concentrations to prove the contention.

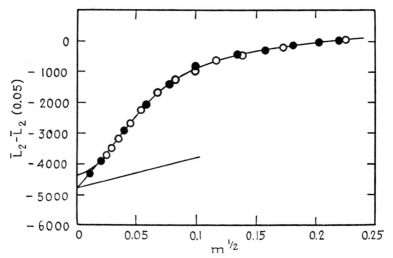

Fig. (13-13-1). $\bar{L}_2 - \bar{L}_2$ (0.05) of sulfuric acid in dilute aqueous solutions at 25°. ○, electromotive force; ●, calorimetry.

For further comparison, $\bar{L}_2$ at 25° has been plotted against $m^{1/2}$ over the entire concentration range in Fig. (13-13-2). The circles represent the results derived from electromotive forces, the dots the results of Lange, Monheim and Robinson, and the circles with vertical lines represent values computed by Brönsted from electromotive force measurements. Since Brönsted's data were not determined in sufficiently dilute solutions for purposes of extrapolation, it was necessary to add 2530 cal. to each of his results. The present results and those of Brönsted[92] possess the same characteristics although the maximum deviation is of the order of 300 cal. The dashed plot represents values determined from the calorimetric data

[92] J. N. Brönsted, *Z, physik. Chem.*, **68**, 693 (1910); G. N. Lewis and M. Randall, "Thermodynamics," p. 95, McGraw-Hill Book Co., New York, 1923.

by Craig and Vinal.[93]   They employed the experimental method of extrapolation and for this reason the curve lies about 400 cal. higher than the
one obtained from the electromotive forces.   If allowance is made for the
difference in method of extrapolation, the agreement is quite satisfactory.

The relative partial molal heat capacity, obtained from equation (13-13-1)
by differentiation, is given by

$$\bar{J}_2 = \alpha + 2\beta t \qquad (13\text{-}13\text{-}2)$$

Craig and Vinal have computed $\bar{J}_2$ at 25° from calorimetric data.[94]   Values
of this quantity at 25° from both the electromotive force and calorimetric

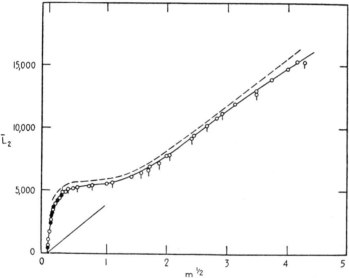

Fig. (13–13–2). L_2 of sulphuric acid in aqueous solutions at 25°.   O, Electromotive
force; ●, Calorimetry; ♀, Electromotive force (Brönsted).   Straight line from
origin represents limiting law.   Dashed line represents values computed by Craig
and Vinal from calorimetric data.

data are given in Table (13–13–1A).   The results from these sources are
plotted in Fig. (13-3-3).   Both series of results are characterized by a very
rapid increase in $\bar{J}_2$ with $m^{1/2}$ in dilute solutions after which $\bar{J}_2$ decreases,
passes through a minimum and then increases again in very concentrated
solutions.   The agreement is not good.   Both series of results may be
considerably in error.   The calorimetric values were derived from older
data of uncertain accuracy, and high accuracy is not to be expected from
results derived from the second differential coefficient of electromotive
force.

[93] D. N. Craig and G. W. Vinal, *Bur. Standards J. Research*, **24**, 475 (1940).
[94] E. Biron, *Russkoe Fiziko-Khimicheskoe Obshehestvo*, **31**, 201 (1899); S. Socolik,
Z. physik. Chem., **158**, 305 (1932); F. Bode, *Z. Angw. Chem.*, **2**, 244 (1889); P. Pascal
and Garnier, *Bull. Soc. Chim.*, **27**, 8 (1920); M. D. Taylor, Thesis, University of
California (1931).

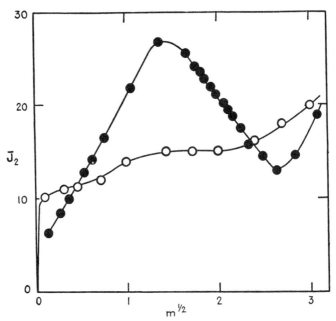

Fig. (13-13-3). Relative partial molal heat capacity of sulfuric acid in aqueous solutions at 25°. ○, electromotive force; ●, calorimetry.

(14) The Cation Transference Number of Sulfuric Acid in Aqueous Solutions

From the electromotive forces of the cells,

$$\text{Hg-Hg}_2\text{SO}_4 \mid \text{H}_2\text{SO}_4(m) \mid \text{H}_2 \mid \text{H}_2\text{SO}_4(m_R) \mid \text{Hg}_2\text{SO}_4\text{-Hg}; \; \mathbf{E},$$

derived from the results discussed in the preceding sections, and those of the cells,

$$\text{Hg-Hg}_2\text{SO}_4 \mid \text{H}_2\text{SO}_4(m) \mid \text{H}_2\text{SO}_4(m_R) \mid \text{Hg}_2\text{SO}_4\text{-Hg}; \; \mathbf{E}_T,$$

Hamer[95] has determined the cation transference number of sulphuric acid. The method he employed to evaluate T_+ by means of equation (10-6-12), or $T_+ = d\mathbf{E}_T/d\mathbf{E}$, was essentially the same as that described in Chapter (11), Section (9). The slopes of the graph of $\mathbf{E}$ versus $\mathbf{E}_T$ at various acid concentrations were determined by the Rutledge derivative function [Equation (11-9-3)]. These values of T_+ from 0.05 to $17M$, and from 0 to 60° are contained in Table (13-14-1A). This table also contains values of the limiting transference number, computed from conductance data and other transference number data, and values of the limiting slopes, $\mathbb{S}_{(T)}\sqrt{d_0}$, of the Onsager equation,

$$T_+ = T_+^0 + \mathbb{S}_{(T)}\sqrt{d_0}\,\sqrt{m} \tag{13-14-1}$$

[95] W. J. Hamer, *J. Am. Chem. Soc.*, **57**, 662 (1935).

Plots of T_+ versus $m^{1/2}$ are shown in Fig. (13-14-1). The theoretical limiting functions represented by the straight lines predict an increase in T_+ as the concentration increases. The experimental results were not obtained in solutions dilute enough to verify the theoretical prediction, nor can they be used satisfactorily for purposes of extrapolation. The results all show a tendency to approach a maximum as the concentration of acid decreases, and it is reasonable to suppose that they should approach the theoretical results in more dilute solutions. The theoretical lines have been drawn to values of the limiting transference numbers obtained from other sources.[95]

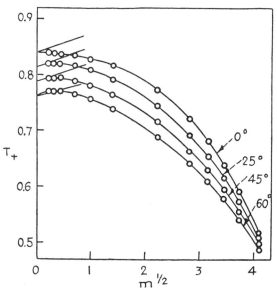

Fig. (13-14-1). Cation transference number of sulfuric acid in aqueous solutions. Straight lines represent limiting law.

(15) Dissociation of Strong Electrolytes as Derived from Raman Spectrum

The problem of the dissociation of moderately strong and very strong electrolytes has been the subject of an excellent review by Redlich,[96] who emphasized particularly the unequivocal evidence for the presence of undissociated molecules which can be derived from Raman spectra. The presence of vibration spectra is a criterion which can be used to distinguish sharply between molecules and interacting ions. Redlich and Rosenfeld[97]

[95] W. J. Hamer, *J. Am. Chem. Soc.*, **57**, 662 (1935).

[96] O. Redlich, *Chem. Rev.*, **39**, 333 (1946). Contains an extensive bibliography.

[97] O. Redlich and P. Rosenfeld, *Stizber. Acad. Wiss. Wien, Math.-Naturw. Klasse (Abt II b)* **145**, 87 (1936).

suggested that true ionic concentration can be determined by comparison of the spectrum of the solution with that of a completely dissociated electrolyte containing the same ion.   It is known that the intensity of the Raman spectra of alkali nitrates is proportional to their concentrations[98, 99], which is evidence of their complete dissociation.   Therefore, in order to find the concentration of the nitrate ions, αc, in nitric acid at a stoichiometrical concentration c, a sodium nitrate solution having Raman lines of equal intensity to the nitric acid solution is prepared.   Since the reference nitrate solution of concentration, c_R, is completely dissociated, c_R equals αc.

TABLE (13-15-1).   DEGREE OF DISSOCIATION OF NITRIC ACID IN THE NEIGHBORHOOD OF 25°

c	0.1	1	2	3	4	6	8	10	12	14
α	0.997	0.978	0.95	0.90	0.85	0.72	0.56	0.42	0.28	0.16

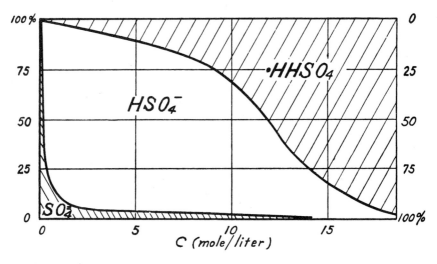

Fig. (13–15–1). Fractions of sulfuric acid present as undissociated acid, as bisulfate ion, and as sulfate ion, represented as vertical distances between adjacent lines.

Values of α determined in this manner are given in Table (13-15-1) from which the thermodynamic dissociation constant was estimated to be 21.4.

Young and Blatz[100] have utilized existing Raman spectrum measurements to unravel the complex equilibria occurring in sulphuric acid solutions at all concentrations. The SO_4^{--} and HSO_4^- band intensities may be compared with those of $(NH_4)_2SO_4$ and $KHSO_4$ solutions, while the band

[98] N. R. Rao, *Indian J. Phys.*, **15**, 185 (1941).

[99] O. Redlich and J. Bigeleisen, *J. Am. Chem. Soc.*, **65**, 1883 (1943); O. Redlich, E. K. Holt and J. Bigeleisen, *Ibid.*, **66**, 13 (1944).

[100] T. F. Young and L. A. Blatz, *Chem. Rev.*, **44**, 93 (1949).

of H_2SO_4 is identified by its maximum at 50 mole per cent of H_2O and SO_3. The result of this analysis is clearly demonstrated by Fig. (13-15-1) in which the relative percentages of $HHSO_4$, HSO_4^- and SO_4^{--} in a solution of sulphuric acid are plotted against c. On the basis of the degrees of dissociation, a reasonable quantitative interpretation of the heats of dilution, surface tensions[101] and apparent molal volumes may be made.

The Raman spectra of iodic acid[102], trichloroacetic acid[103] and perchloric acid[104] prove that these substances are incompletely dissociated. Important progress is to be expected from this type of optical measurement with improved methods of measuring relative intensities.

(15a) DISSOCIATION OF SOME MODERATELY STRONG ELECTROLYTES

Table (13-15-2) contains values of ionization constants of some moderately strong electrolytes, estimated by various methods, which are taken from the review of Redlich.[105]   These results supplement the data contained in Table (6-3-2).   The sources of this information, recorded by Redlich, are voluminous and have not been included.

TABLE (13-15-2). DISSOCIATION CONSTANTS OF SOME MODERATELY
STRONG ELECTROLYTES

Substance	K	Substance	K
HIO_3	0.17	$PbBr^+$	0.07
CCl_3COOH	.22−0.23	PbI^+	.035
Picric Acid	.16	H_2SO_3	.012−0.017
$CHCl_2COOH$	.14	$HSeO_4^-$	.01
$H_4P_2O_7$	.14	o-Nitrobenzoic acid	.006
$PbCl^+$	.06−0.1		

(16) RECENT EXPERIMENTAL CONTRIBUTIONS

The method of determination of activity coefficients by means of the ultracentrifuge has been analyzed carefully by Young, Kraus and Johnson[106] and applied to the investigation of cadmium iodide and uranyl fluoride solutions by Johnson, Kraus and Young.[107]   Recalling that $\nabla\phi = \nabla P/\rho$, equation (1-15-50) becomes upon integration

$$\ln(a_\beta/a_\alpha) = \nu \ln (m_{\pm\beta}/m_{\pm\alpha}) + \nu \ln (\gamma_{\pm\beta}/\gamma_{\pm\alpha})$$

$$= \frac{M\omega^2}{2RT} (x_\beta^2 - x_\alpha^2) - \frac{M}{RT} \int_{P_\alpha}^{P_\beta} \bar{V}_\beta \, dP \qquad (13\text{-}16\text{-}1)$$

[101] T. F. Young and S. R. Grinstead, *Ann. N. Y. Acad. Sci.*, **51**, 765 (1949).
[102] N. R. Rao, *Indian J. Phys.*, **16**, 71 (1942).
[103] N. R. Rao, *Ibid.*, **17**, 332 (1943).
[104] O. Redlich, E. K. Holt and J. Bigeleisen, *J. Am. Chem. Soc.*, **66**, 13 (1944).
[105] O. Redlich, *Chem. Rev.*, **39**, 333 (1946).
[106] T. F. Young, K. A. Kraus and J. S. Johnson, *J. Chem. Phys.*, **22**, 878 (1954).
[107] J. S. Johnson, K. A. Kraus and T. F. Young, *J. Am. Chem. Soc.*, **76**, 1436 (1954).

where

$$dP = \rho\omega^2 x \, dx \qquad (13\text{-}16\text{-}2)$$

M is the molecular weight of the electrolyte, ω is the angular velocity and $\bar{V}_\beta$ represents the partial molal volume at a concentration $m_{\pm\beta}$ at position x_β in the cell. If the position x_α is at the boundary of the solution in the cell where the pressure is one atmosphere, then the calculated activity will be comparable to those obtained at one atmosphere by the usual methods. The concentrations as a function of x may be determined from the refractive index gradients yielded by the apparatus and separately determined refractive index-concentration data.

The activity coefficient of cadmium iodide at 30° determined by the centrifuge method was found to be in close agreement with the electromotive force determination of Bates.[108] The activity coefficient of uranyl fluoride was determined at 30° by Johnson, Kraus and Young by ultracentrifugation and at 0° by Johnson and Kraus[109] by the freezing point method. Values of these activity coefficients are compiled in Table (13-3-3A). From the character of the results at concentrations between 0.1 and 5M it appears that uranyl fluoride is largely undissociated and tends to associate. By postulating the formation of a dimer, $(UO_2F_2)_2$, and assuming the logarithms of the activity coefficients of the monomer and dimer vary linearly with the concentration, the equilibrium constant of the reaction, $2UO_2F_2 \rightleftharpoons (UO_2F_2)_2$, was determined. The ultracentrifuge has also been applied to estimate the polymerization of tetravalent zirconium, hafnium and thorium in solutions of supporting electrolytes.[110, 111, 112]

Comprehensive investigations of the conductances, transference numbers and activity coefficients of rare earth chloride and bromide solutions have been carried out by Spedding, Porter and Wright.[113] The equation and the values of the distance parameter required for computation of the activity coefficients of these halides are listed in Table (13-3-3A). This table also contains activity coefficient ratios of indium sulphate solutions derived from electromotive forces of the cell,

$$\text{In} \mid \text{In}_2(SO_4)_3(m) \mid Ag_2SO_4\text{-Ag.}^{[114]}$$

[108] R. G. Bates, *J. Am. Chem. Soc.*, **63,** 399 (1941). Table (13-3-3A).

[109] J. S. Johnson and K. A. Kraus, *J. Am. Chem. Soc.*, **74,** 4436 (1932).

[110] K. A. Kraus and J. S. Johnson, *J. Am. Chem. Soc.*, **75,** 5769 (1953).

[111] J. S. Johnson, K. A. Kraus and R. W. Holmberg, *Ibid.*, **78,** 26 (1956).

[112] K. A. Kraus and R. W. Holmberg, *J. Phys. Chem.*, **58,** 325 (1954).

[113] F. H. Spedding, P. E. Porter and J. M. Wright, *J. Am. Chem. Soc.*, **74,** 2055, 2778, 2781, 4751 (1952).

[114] M. H. Lietzke and R. W. Stoughton, *Ibid.*, **78,** 4520 (1956).

Chapter (14)

Mixtures of Strong Electrolytes

The determination of a thermodynamic property such as the activity coefficient of one electrolyte in a solution of another electrolyte has been of considerable value in establishing the theory of interionic attraction, and in extending our knowledge of ionic equilibria. Two experimental methods have proved to be of prime importance in this field. The first is the determination of the solubility of salts in salt solutions, and the second the determination of the activity coefficient of one electrolyte in the presence of another by electromotive force measurements.

The investigation of the solubility of salts in salt solutions was begun by Noyes,[1] and continued by Bray,[2] and Harkins.[3] These results were employed by Lewis and Randall[4] to illustrate the value of their concept of ionic strength, and by Noyes[5] in his discussion of the Debye and Hückel theory.

The solubilities of the salts employed in these first studies were somewhat too great for an exact proof of the validity of the equations of the interionic attraction theory. This difficulty was surmounted by Brönsted[6] and his collaborators who determined the solubilities of many higher order cobalt compounds of very low solubility ($\sim 0.00005 M$) in various salt solutions. These investigations were the first to illustrate in a very striking manner the effects on the activity coefficients caused by the different valences of the ions. They also brought to light many complicated specific effects of electrolytes upon the properties of other electrolytes, and led Brönsted[6] to his theory of specific ionic interaction.

The cell without liquid junction containing a mixture of electrolytes was first employed by Harned,[7] who investigated the effect of varying concentrations of potassium chloride on the activity coefficient of $0.1M$ hydrochloric acid. Loomis, Essex and Meacham,[8] and Ming Chow[9] also in-

---

[1] A. A. Noyes, *Z. physik. Chem.*, **6**, 241 (1890); A. A. Noyes and W. C. Bray, *J. Am. Chem. Soc.*, **30**, 1643 (1908).

[2] W. C. Bray and W. J. Winninghof, *J. Am. Chem. Soc.*, **33**, 1663 (1911).

[3] W. D. Harkins and W. J. Winninghof, *J. Am. Chem. Soc.*, **33**, 1827 (1911); W. D. Harkins and H. M. Paine, *Ibid.*, **41**, 1155 (1919); W. D. Harkins and W. T. Pearce, *Ibid.*, **38**, 2679 (1916).

[4] G. N. Lewis and M. Randall, *J. Am. Chem. Soc.*, **43**, 1112 (1921).

[5] A. A. Noyes, *J. Am. Chem. Soc.*, **46**, 1098 (1924).

[6] J. N. Brönsted, *J. Am. Chem. Soc.*, **42**, 761 (1920); **44**, 877 (1922); **44**, 938 (1922); **45**, 2898 (1923); J. N. Brönsted and A. Petersen, *Ibid.*, **43**, 2265 (1921).

[7] H. S. Harned, *J. Am. Chem. Soc.*, **38**, 1986 (1916); **42**, 1808 (1920).

[8] N. E. Loomis, J. L. Essex, and M. R. Meacham, *J. Am. Chem. Soc.*, **39**, 1133 (1917).

[9] Ming Chow, *J. Am. Chem. Soc.*, **42**, 497 (1920).

vestigated a similar cell for the purpose of measuring the activity coefficient of hydrochloric acid in potassium chloride solutions at $0.1M$ total ionic strength. One result, shown by Harned to follow from these measurements, is that the activity coefficient, and also the relative partial molal heat content of a strong electrolyte in a solution of another electrolyte, is primarily a function of the total electrolyte concentration, or, as shown by Lewis and Randall, the total ionic strength. This conclusion is in accord with the general theoretical equations of the interionic attraction theory, because $\Gamma^{1/2}$, a function of all the ions and their valences, always appears. Since these earlier studies and the advent of the interionic attraction theory, very comprehensive electromotive force investigations of mixtures have been made. These results form a basis for an exact study of ionic equilibria of weak electrolytes which involve hydronium ions in salt solutions [Chapter (15)].

(1) Solubility Measurements and the Interionic Attraction Theory

The activity coefficient relationships of strong electrolytes in the presence of salts (co-solutes) of various types and concentrations can be deduced in a very simple manner from solubility measurements. The presence of the solid phase of the saturating solute requires that

$$\mathcal{P}_{(0)}\gamma'_{(0)} = \mathcal{P}\gamma'_{\pm} = (m_+^{\nu+})(m_-^{\nu-})(\gamma_+^{\nu+}\gamma_-^{\nu-}) \tag{14-1-1}$$

where $\mathcal{P}_{(0)}$ and $\mathcal{P}$ have been written for its stoichiometrical solubility product in water, and in the presence of the co-solute, respectively, and $\gamma_{(0)}$ and $\gamma_\pm$ are the corresponding mean activity coefficients. Therefore,

$$\frac{1}{\nu} \log \frac{\mathcal{P}}{\mathcal{P}_{(0)}} = \log \gamma_{(0)} - \log \gamma_\pm \tag{14-1-2}$$

in general. If the co-solute is a non-electrolyte, or has no ion in common with the saturating electrolyte, the left side of this equation may be replaced by $\log (S/S_{(0)})$, where S and $S_{(0)}$ are the stoichiometrical solubilities in the salt solution and pure water, respectively. We shall now discuss some results of solubility measurements, which we regard as particularly significant in their relation to the interionic attraction theory.

Immediately after the Debye and Hückel development of the interionic attraction theory, solubility data were employed extensively to test its validity. The measurements of Brönsted and LaMer[10] with cobalt-ammines of 1-1, 2-1, and 3-1 valence types, and more recent experiments with 2-2 and 3-3[11] types, leave little doubt as to the correctness of the valence factor in the theoretical equation, and show that $\log \gamma_\pm$ is very closely proportional to the square root of the ionic strength. In selected cases[12], the data confirm the numerical value of the theoretical slopes.

[10] J. N. Brönsted and V. K. LaMer, *J. Am. Chem. Soc.*, **46**, 555 (1924).

[11] J. N. Brönsted and N. J. Brumbaugh, *J. Am. Chem. Soc.*, **48**, 2015 (1926).

[12] V. K. LaMer, C. V. King, and C. F. Mason, *J. Am. Chem. Soc.*, **49**, 363 (1927).

Later LaMer and others have observed abrupt changes in slope at the concentration of the saturating solute in water. Baxter[13] has confirmed the theory at 75° from measurements of the solubility of silver iodate in salt solutions. Solubility measurements in organic solvents of low dielectric constant have not, in general, led to agreement with theory except in a qualitative manner.

Even when the complication of ionic association is reduced to a minimum, as in very dilute aqueous solutions, the activity coefficient relationships are highly specific in certain combinations of complex valence type electrolytes. This effect was first investigated by Brönsted and Petersen[14] and more recently by LaMer.[15] Fig. (14-1-1) illustrates the results obtained by LaMer and Mason for the solubility of the 1-3 salt, luteodinitrodi-

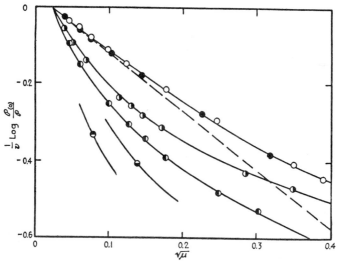

Fig. (14–1–1). The influence of various salts upon the solubility of $[Co(NH_3)_6]$ $[Co(NH_3)_2(NO_2)_2C_2O_4]$ in water at 25°. ●, KNO_3; ○, $BaCl_2$; ◐, K_2SO_4; ◑, $MgSO_4$; ◒, $K_3Fe(CN)_6$; ◓, $K_4Fe(CN)_6$. The broken line represents the limiting law.

ammino-oxalo cobaltiate, in various aqueous salt solutions at 25°. It will be observed that the co-solutes, potassium nitrate and barium chloride, yield curves which converge satisfactorily with the theoretical limiting slope, while the other salts produce characteristic "humps". The most abrupt changes in slope are observed with systems in which the ion of the highest valence in the saturating solute is of opposite sign to the ion of highest valence in the co-solute.[14] Pronounced "humps" are common to (3-1, 1-2) systems such as lanthanum iodate in potassium sulfate,[16] cerium

[13] W. P. Baxter, *J. Am. Chem. Soc.*, **48**, 615 (1926).

[14] J. N. Brönsted and A. Petersen, *J. Am. Chem. Soc.*, **43**, 2265 (1921).

[15] V. K. LaMer and C. F. Mason, *J. Am. Chem. Soc.*, **49**, 410 (1927).

[16] V. K. LaMer and F. H. Goldman, *J. Am. Chem. Soc.*, **51**, 2632 (1929).

iodate in potassium sulfate,[17] and 3-1 valence type cobaltammines in potassium sulfate.[15,18] Replacement of the potassium sulfate in these systems by a symmetrical valence type sulfate, such as magnesium sulfate, reduces the hump considerably, and it is absent in the presence of magnesium chloride. When no ions of valence greater than two are involved, the hump is small, and sometimes experimentally unrealizable. Thus, in the system calcium iodate-potassium sulfate, no hump was observed,[19] but it is definitely present in other (2-1, 1-2) systems.[20]

When the ions of highest valence of the saturating salt and co-solute are of the same sign, the hump is generally absent.[21] The most striking exception to this rule is the (3-3, 2-2) system studied by LaMer, King and Mason.[22]

Incomplete ionization would account for some of the above results in a qualitative way, and LaMer has found a close correlation between certain features of his results and Brönsted's principle of specific ionic interaction, but no quantitative treatment has been found. The relationships shown in Figs. (14-1-2) and (14-1-3) give some notion of the complexity of these ionic interactions, even at concentrations of the order of μ equal to 0.01, and for combinations of valence types as simple as (1-1, 1-2). Although it has been shown [Chapters (12) and (13)] that the Debye and Hückel equation in its extended form can closely account for the humps observed in the activity coefficients of simple electrolytes, it is inadequate for mixtures of salts of varying proportions if $å$ is to retain any physical significance. The specific parameter, $å_0$, of the saturating salt is generally different from that, $å_s$, of the co-solute, and the calculation, or even a satisfactory definition of $å$ in the mixtures in terms of $å_0$ and $å_s$ has not been made.[23] Since this is the case, it is not particularly significant that a constant value of $å$ can sometimes be found which will approximately fit the data. A more illuminating use of the theory would be to assume its validity in mixtures of any given concentration ratio, and calculate the values of $å$ which would give exact agreement with the observed solubilities in these mixtures. In this way, the variation in $å$ with the ionic strength may be studied.

In order to carry out such a computation, log $\gamma_{(0)}$ is obtained by the extended equation for some arbitrary value of $å_0$, such as 1, and is com-

[17] J. B. Chloupek, V. Z. Daneš and B. A. Danešova, *Coll. Czech.*, **5**, 21 (1933).

[18] V. K. LaMer and R. G. Cook, *J. Am. Chem. Soc.*, **51**, 2622 (1929).

[19] J. B. Chloupek, V. Z. Daneš, and B. A. Danešova, *Coll. Czech.*, **6**, 116 (1934).

[20] E. W. Neuman, *J. Am. Chem. Soc.*, **55**, 879 (1933); V. K. LaMer and F. H. Goldman, *Ibid.*, **51**, 2632 (1929).

[21] L. O'Neill and J. R. Partington, *Trans. Faraday Soc.*, **30**, 1134 (1934); V. K. LaMer and C. F. Mason, *J. Am. Chem. Soc.*, **49**, 410 (1927); J. B. Chloupek, V. Z. Daneš and B. A. Danešova, *Coll. Czech.*, **6**, 116 (1934).

[22] V. K. LaMer, C. V. King, and C. F. Mason, *J. Am. Chem. Soc.*, **49**, 363 (1927).

[23] J. R. Partington and H. J. Stonehill, *Phil. Mag.* [7], **22**, 857 (1936).

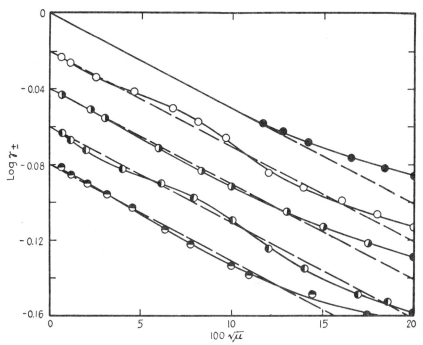

Fig. (14-1-2). Mean activity coefficients of silver chloride in aqueous salt solutions at 25°. ●, KNO₃; ○, K₂SO₄; ◐, La(NO₃)₃; ◑, La₂(SO₄)₃; ◓, MgSO₄. The ordinates have been displaced by multiples of 0.02.

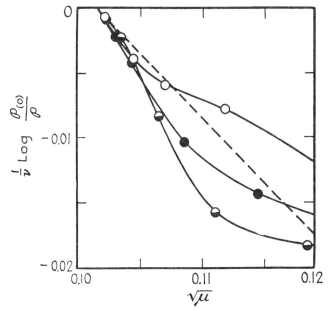

Fig. (14-1-3). The influence of various salts upon the solubility of [Co(NH₃)₄NCS] [NO₃]₂ in water at 25°. ○, KCNS; ●, NaCNS; ◓, Ba(CNS)₂. The broken line represents the limiting law.

bined with solubility data in equation (14-1-2) to give values of log $\gamma_{\pm}$. The extended equation is then solved, by successive approximations, for a-values corresponding to each log $\gamma_{\pm}$. The whole process is then repeated for values of $\mathring{a}_0$ equal to 2, 3, 4 etc. Partington and Stonehill[23] have made extensive calculations of this type on their data for 2-1 cobaltammines. They ascertained the value of $\mathring{a}_0$ for a given saturating salt which produced the minimum variation of $\mathring{a}$ in the presence of the given co-solute. These values of $\mathring{a}_0$, and the average of the corresponding $\mathring{a}$-values obtained in the mixtures, are recorded in Table (14-1-1). The numbers given in the second column are the cationic radii of the co-solutes derived from crystallographic data. Although the thiocyanate ion is common to all the co-solutes, it is seen that the order of $\mathring{a}$ is not the same as that of the crystallographic radii, and also varies with the nature of the saturating salt. The mean $\mathring{a}$ is therefore a function of both salts, without being characteristic of either one separately. This conclusion is not limited to cobaltamminethiocyanate systems, for a similar situation was found by Chloupek, Daneš, and Danešova[19] with cerium iodate and calcium iodate in the pres-

TABLE (14-1-1).   MEAN VALUES OF $\mathring{a}$ (EXTENDED EQUATION)

Co-Solute		Saturating Salt	
$M(SCN)_n$	r_M	$\left[\text{Co}\,{}^{NCS}_{(NH_3)_5}\right](NO_3)_2$ ($d_0 = 3.0$)	$\left[\text{Co}\,{}^{NCS}_{(NH_3)_5}\right]I_2$ ($d_0 = 4.0$)
NaSCN	0.96	$\mathring{a} = 2.85$	4.86
KSCN	1.33	3.03	4.07
$Ba(SCN)_2$	1.35	2.84	5.11
$La(SCN)_3$	1.15	3.88	5.34

ence of a variety of salts, although in these cases the variations of $\mathring{a}$ were not so pronounced.

Crockford and Thomas[24] derived a definition of $\mathring{a}$ in mixtures, based upon considerations of collision frequencies. Their expression,

$$\mathring{a} = \frac{\mathring{a}_1 k_1 c_1^2 + \mathring{a}_2 k_2 c_2^2}{k_1 c_1^2 + k_2 c_2^2} \qquad (14\text{-}1\text{-}3)$$

contains kinetic constants, k_1 and k_2, whose evaluation would require a knowledge of individual ionic radii in solutions. If k_1, $\mathring{a}_1$ and k_2, $\mathring{a}_2$ were characteristic of the individual salts, this equation predicts that the order of the $\mathring{a}$, obtained for a given series of co-solutes, would be independent of the saturating salt. This contradicts the results in Table (14-1-1). The same objection applies to the simpler equation,

$$\mathring{a} = \frac{\mathring{a}_1 c_1 + \mathring{a}_2 c_2}{c_1 + c_2} \qquad (14\text{-}1\text{-}4)$$

[24] H. D. Crockford and H. C. Thomas, *J. Am. Chem. Soc.*, **55**, 568 (1933).

suggested by MacDougall.[25] Therefore, neither equation properly defines $\mathring{a}$ in terms of parameters characteristic of the individual salts. It is possible that equation (14-1-3) would be satisfactory if data were available for evaluating k_1 and k_2 as properties of the mixtures.

The "a" parameter, which appears in the Debye-Hückel equation (3-5-9), is related to the individual values of a_j by

$$\frac{\sum_1^p \nu_j z_j^2}{1 + \kappa a} = \sum_1^p \frac{\nu_j z_j^2}{1 + \kappa a_j} \qquad (14\text{-}1\text{-}5)$$

At high dilutions, where $(1 + \kappa a)^{-1}$ may be replaced by $(1 - \kappa a)$, this equation may be written

$$\mathring{a} = \frac{\sum_1^p \nu_j z_j^2 \mathring{a}_j}{\sum_1^p \nu_j z_j^2} \qquad (14\text{-}1\text{-}6)$$

Neither of these relations gives a satisfactory physical picture of $\mathring{a}$, because $\mathring{a}_j$ is not clearly defined.

(2) THE ACTIVITY COEFFICIENTS OF HYDROCHLORIC, HYDROBROMIC, AND SULFURIC ACIDS, AND OF ALKALI METAL HYDROXIDES IN SALT SOLUTIONS FROM ELECTROMOTIVE FORCE MEASUREMENTS

One very important advantage of the electromotive force method, as applied to the measurement of the activity coefficient of one electrolyte in the presence of another, is that the concentrations of both electrolytes may be varied at will. The solubility method has the disadvantage that one concentration, that of the saturating electrolyte, is fixed. It is possible to employ electromotive forces either to determine the activity coefficient of one electrolyte, at a fixed concentration, in the presence of another electrolyte of varying concentration, or to measure this quantity, at varying concentration of both electrolytes, in a medium of constant total molality.

The fundamental equations of the cells,

$$H_2 \mid HX(m_1), MX_n(m_2) \mid AgX\text{-}Ag$$

$$H_2 \mid H_2SO_4(m_1), M_2SO_4(m_2) \mid Hg_2SO_4\text{-}Hg$$

are

$$E = E^0 - \frac{2.303RT}{F} \log \gamma_H \gamma_X m_1(nm_2 + m_1) \qquad (14\text{-}2\text{-}1)$$

$$E = E^0 - \frac{2.303RT}{2F} \log \gamma_H^2 \gamma_{SO_4}(2m_1)^2(m_1 + m_2) \qquad (14\text{-}2\text{-}2)$$

[25] F. H. MacDougall, *Thermodynamics and Chemistry*, p. 279, John Wiley and Sons, New York (1926).

respectively. Thus, if their standard potentials are known, γ_{HX} and $\gamma_{H_2SO_4}$ may be readily determined in the halide and sulfate solutions.

We have already shown [Chapter (11), Section (2) and Chapter (13), Section (12)] that these standard potentials may be evaluated from measurements of the cells of these types containing acid solutions only. Although the salt-free cells are most favorable for this purpose, good determinations of E^0 may be effected by the cells containing salts. By rearranging equation (14-2-1), and introducing the Debye and Hückel limiting

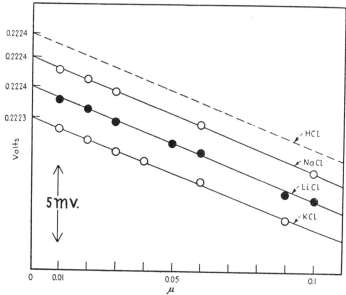

Fig. (14-2-1). Extrapolation of E^0 at 25° according to equation (14-2-3).

equation, we obtain a modified form of equation (11-2-4), suitable for this purpose. Thus,

$$E^{0'} \equiv E + \frac{2.303RT}{F} \log m_1(nm_2 + m_1) - \frac{4.605RT\mathfrak{S}_{(f)}\sqrt{\mu d_0}}{F}$$
$$= E^0 + f(\mu)$$

(14-2-3)

where $E^{0'} = E^0$, when $\mu = 0$. In Figure (14-2-1), plots of $E^{0'}$ against μ for cells containing lithium, sodium, and potassium chlorides are shown. Since these plots are practically superimposable, they have been separated in the figure. We note that they all extrapolate to nearly the same value of E^0, and that this value agrees with that previously obtained with the cell containing acid alone. The plot for this latter cell is represented by the dashed line. The cell employed for determining the thermodynamics of hydroxide solutions [Chapter (12), Section (2)];

$$H_2 \left| MOH(m_1), \begin{cases} MX, \text{ or} \\ M_x(SO_4)_y \end{cases} (m_2) \right| M_x Hg \mid MOH(m_R) \mid H_2$$

may be utilized for measuring the activity coefficients of hydroxides in halide and sulfate solutions. Its electromotive force in a halide solution is given by

$$E = \frac{2.303RT}{F} \log \frac{\gamma_M \gamma_{OH} \, a_{H_2O(m_R)} \, m_1(m_1 + m_2)}{\gamma_{M(m_R)} \gamma_{OH(m_R)} \, a_{H_2O} \, m_R^2} \qquad (14\text{-}2\text{-}4)$$

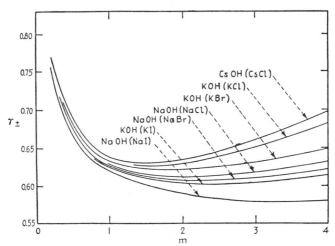

Fig. (14-2-2). Mean activity coefficients of hydrochloric and hydrobromic acids in alkali halide solutions at 25°.

Fig. (14-2-3). Mean activity coefficients of hydroxides in corresponding halide solutions at 25°.

The characteristics of these results are illustrated in Figs. (14-2-2), (14-2-3), and (14-2-4) where the activity coefficients of the acids and bases are plotted at low concentrations (0.1 or 0.01M or less) in the salt solutions of the strengths designated.[26] In general, these curves are similar

[26] The sources of the material used in these figures are: H. S. Harned, *J. Am. Chem. Soc.*, **42**, 1808 (1920); H. S. Harned and N. J. Brumbaugh, *Ibid.*, **44**, 2729 (1922); H. S.

in form to those of the single electrolytes. They show characteristic minima, and many increase very rapidly in concentrated solutions.

The specific behaviors of the activity coefficients may be summarized in a general way by two statements.

(i) At a given ionic strength and acid concentration, the activity coefficient of a strong acid is greater in the solution of a salt, of a given valence type, which in the pure solvent possesses the greater activity coefficient. Thus, from Fig. (14-2-2), it is seen that

$$\gamma_{HCl(LiCl)} > \gamma_{HCl(NaCl)} > \gamma_{HCl(KCl)} > \gamma_{HCl(CsCl)}$$

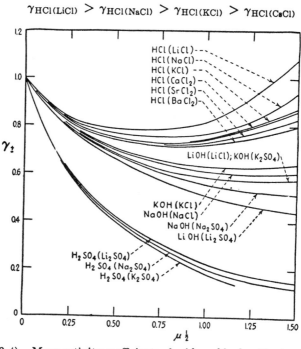

Fig. (14-2-4). Mean activity coefficients of acids and hydroxides in salt solutions at 25°.

and, from Fig. (12-5-2)

$$\gamma_{LiCl} > \gamma_{NaCl} > \gamma_{KCl} > \gamma_{CsCl}$$

Also, from Fig. (14-2-4),

$$\gamma_{H_2SO_4(Li_2SO_4)} > \gamma_{H_2SO_4(Na_2SO_4)} > \gamma_{H_2SO_4(K_2SO_4)}$$

and, from Fig. (13-4-1)

$$\gamma_{Li_2SO_4} > \gamma_{Na_2SO_4} > \gamma_{K_2SO_4}$$

Harned and F. E. Swindells, *Ibid.*, **48**, 126 (1926); H. S. Harned and G. M. James, *J. Phys. Chem.*, **30**, 1060 (1926); G. Åkerlöf, *J. Am. Chem. Soc.*, **48**, 1160 (1926); M. Randall and C. T. Langford, *Ibid.*, **49**, 1445 (1927); M. Randall and G. F. Breckenridge, *Ibid.*, **49**, 1435 (1927); H. S. Harned and O. E. Schupp, Jr., *Ibid.*, **52**, 3892 (1930); H. S. Harned and G. Åkerlöf, *Physik. Z.*, **27**, 411 (1926).

(ii) Strong hydroxides in the halide solutions exhibit the opposite behavior. As shown in Fig. (14-2-3),

$$\gamma_{MOH(CsCl)} > \gamma_{MOH(KCl)} > \gamma_{MOH(KBr)} > \gamma_{MOH(NaCl)} >$$

$$\gamma_{MOH(NaBr)} > \gamma_{MOH(KI)} > \gamma_{MOH(NaI)}$$

which is in the reverse order to the activity coefficients of the individual salts in water. Further, Fig. (14-2-4) indicates that

$$\gamma_{MOH(K_2SO_4)} > \gamma_{MOH(Na_2SO_4)} > \gamma_{MOH(Li_2SO_4)}$$

which also conforms to this rule. Ionic interaction in solutions containing hydroxides and acids is a very interesting one, and will receive further attention. Recently, the activity coefficients of hydrochloric and hydrobromic acid in solutions containing lithium, sodium, potassium and barium chlorides, and lithium, sodium and potassium bromides, respectively, have been evaluated over wide temperature ranges ($\sim$ 0 to 50°) with an accuracy of ± 0.001. These results will appear later to be of considerable importance in the calculation of the ionization of water and weak electrolytes in salt solutions [Chapter (15), Sections (2) and (8)]. Therefore, they are incorporated in Table (14-2-1A) along with the bibliography.

(3) The Relative Partial Molal Heat Content of $0.01M$ Hydrochloric and Hydrobromic Acids in Halide Solutions

From the electromotive force data of the cells considered in the last section, it is possible to compute the partial molal heat content, $\bar{L}_2 - \bar{L}_2(0.01)$, of the acid relative to its value at $0.01M$, by employing equation (3-8-1), or a suitable form of the Gibbs-Helmholtz equation. In Fig. (14-3-1), plots of $\bar{L}_2$ of these acids in some of their corresponding halide solutions are shown as well as the values for hydrochloric acid in pure water. The similarity in form and magnitude of these results should be noted. Indeed, the relative heat contents of the acids in lithium chloride and bromide solutions are nearly the same as that of hydrochloric acid in water.

(4) The Variation of the Activity Coefficient of One Electrolyte in the Presence of Another at Constant Total Ionic Strength

Extensive measurements have been made with cells of the type,

$$H_2 \mid HX(m_1), MX_n(m_2) \mid AgX\text{-}Ag$$

in which the ionic strength, μ, is maintained constant. From these measurements, the activity coefficient of the halide acid in the mixtures has been determined, and surprisingly simple empirical relationships have been discovered in both dilute and concentrated solutions.

At $0.1M$ total concentration and at 20 and 25°, Güntelberg[27] has made

---

[27] E. Güntelberg, *Z. physik. Chem.*, **123**, 199 (1926); *Studier over Elektrolyt-Activiteter* G. E. C. Gads Forlag, København (1938).

extraordinarily accurate measurements of the above cell containing lithium, sodium, potassium and cesium chlorides. Owing to the fact that Güntelberg found an error due to presence of traces of bromide ion in the chloride solutions, the earlier work was repeated except for the cells containing cesium chloride. In this work, two types of silver-silver chloride electrodes were used which differed from each other by a constant amount (0.185 mv.). The one which gave the higher electromotive force was prepared from silver obtained by precipitation from a silver nitrate solution upon addition of ferrous sulphate. The second by electrolytic precipitation of silver from a silver nitrate solution. The cell, containing the first of these types of electrodes and $0.1M$ hydrochloric acid, had an electromotive force of 0.35316 at 20° and 0.35233 at 25°. Harned and

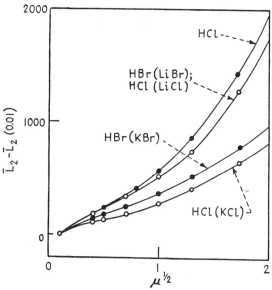

Fig. (14-3-1). Relative partial molal heat contents of halide acids in some halide solutions.

Ehlers[28] obtained 0.35322 and 0.35239 at these temperatures using electrodes made by electrolytic formation of silver chloride upon silver, obtained by thermal decomposition of silver oxide. The reproducibility of Güntelberg's cells was of the order of ±0.02 mv. and the mean values possessed a relative accuracy within ±0.01 mv.

From the equation for the cell, we may define $\mathbf{E}^{0'}$ by the equation,

$$\mathbf{E}^{0'} \equiv \mathbf{E} + \frac{RT}{\mathbf{F}} \ln m_{\mathrm{H}} m_{\mathrm{Cl}} = \mathbf{E}^0 - \frac{2RT}{\mathbf{F}} \ln \gamma_{\pm} \qquad (14\text{-}4\text{-}1)$$

where $\mathbf{E}$ is the electromotive force of the cell at constant total molality, and varying acid and salt composition. If $m_{\mathrm{MCl}} = 0.1\ x$, where x has all

[28] H. S. Harned and R. W. Ehlers, *J. Am. Chem. Soc.*, **55**, 2179 (1933).

values between zero and 1, then the results may be expressed by the simple relation,

$$\mathbf{E}^{0\prime} = \mathbf{E}^{0\prime}_{(x=0)} + kx \tag{14-4-2}$$

where k is an isothermal constant. Table (14-4-1) contains the values of $\mathbf{E}^{0\prime}_{(x=0)}$ and k, which Güntelberg found satisfied his results obtained with the electrodes prepared from chemically precipitated silver. The excellent agreement between the observed results and those computed by equation (14-4-2) is illustrated in the lower part of the table. The values of k obtained in the earlier contribution were 0.00008, 0.00049, and 0.00098 at 25°. By employing similar cells with calomel electrodes, Harned[29] obtained results of less accuracy which lead to values of k at 25° of 0.0002, 0.0005 and 0.0009 for lithium, sodium and potassium chloride with an error of the order of 0.0001.

TABLE (14-4-1).   CONSTANTS OF EQUATION (14-4-2), AND PROOF OF THE LINEAR VARIATION OF $\mathbf{E}^{0\prime}$

	$t = 20°$	$t = 25°$
LiCl	$\mathbf{E}^{0\prime} = 0.23683_0 + 0.00014x$	$\mathbf{E}^{0\prime} = 0.23401_5 + 0.00011x$
NaCl	$\mathbf{E}^{0\prime} = .23683_0 + .00054x$	$\mathbf{E}^{0\prime} = .23401_5 + .00051x$
KCl	$\mathbf{E}^{0\prime} = .23683_0 + .00096x$	$\mathbf{E}^{0\prime} = .23401_5 + .00093x$
CsCl	$\mathbf{E}^{0\prime} = .23683_0 + .00170x^a$	

Salt	x	$t = 25°$ $\mathbf{E}^{0\prime}(calc.)$	$t = 25°$ $\mathbf{E}^{0\prime}(obs.)$
	0	0.23401_5	0.23402_0
LiCl	0.5	$.23407_0$	$.23407_0$
	.9	$.23411_4$	$.23411_0$
NaCl	.5	$.23427_0$	$.23427_0$
	.9	$.23447_4$	$.23445_5$
KCl	.5	$.23448_0$	$.23448_5$
	.9	$.23485_2$	$.23485_2$

^{a} 0.00170 was taken from Güntelberg's earlier contribution. $2RT/F\ 0.4343 = 0.116324$ and 0.118310 at 20 and 25°, respectively.

Since $\mathbf{E}^0$ is a constant at a given temperature, it is apparent from equation (14-4-1) that the observed linear variation of $\mathbf{E}^{0\prime}$ requires that log $\gamma_\pm$ vary linearly with acid, or salt concentration at constant total molality. This simple empirical rule is not restricted to dilute solutions in many cases.

Fig. (14-4-1) shows the variation of $\gamma_\pm$ of hydrochloric acid, in a few chloride solutions at total molalities of $1M$ and $3M$, with the logarithm of the acid concentration. It is important to note that as the concentration of the acid decreases, $\gamma_\pm$ approaches constancy. In Fig. (14-4-2), log $\gamma_\pm$ for the acid is plotted against the acid concentration. These plots are straight lines. In fact, Hawkins[30] has shown that, for hydrochloric acid-uniunivalent halide mixtures, this linearity persists at constant total

[29] H. S. Harned, *J. Am. Chem. Soc.*, **48**, 326 (1926).
[30] J. E. Hawkins, *J. Am. Chem. Soc.*, **54**, 4480 (1932).

molalities as high as $6M$. Bates and Urmston,[31] and Murdock and Barton[32] have also found a linear variation for hydrochloric acid in sodium and potassium perchlorates, and perchloric acid. The error of these experi-

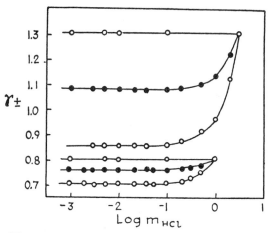

Fig. (14–4–1). Mean activity coefficients of hydrochloric acid in chloride solutions against the logarithm of its molality at 1 and 3 total molalities. Upper three curves at $3M$, lower three curves at $1M$. The upper curve of each series of three refers to lithium chloride; the center (dots) to sodium chloride and the lower to potassium chloride.

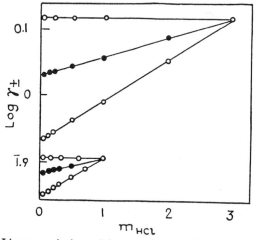

Fig. (14–4–2). Linear variation of log $\gamma_\pm$ of hydrochloric acid in 1–1 chloride solutions at constant total molality. Upper three plots at $3M$, lower three at $1M$. The upper curve of each series of three refers to lithium chloride; the center (dots) to sodium chloride and the lower to potassium chloride.

ments is of the order of ±0.1 mv. It is very important to note that these results can be extrapolated to zero acid concentration. This permits the

[31] S. R. Bates and J. W. Urmston, *J. Am. Chem. Soc.*, **55**, 4068 (1933).
[32] P. G. Murdock and R. C. Barton, *J. Am. Chem. Soc.*, **55**, 4074 (1933).

evaluation of log $\gamma_\pm$ of the acid at zero concentration in the pure salt solution.

In Fig. (14-4-3), log $\gamma_\pm^2$ of hydrochloric acid in pure aqueous solutions (curve), and in cesium chloride solutions[33] of fixed total concentrations (straight lines), are plotted against μ. The straight lines are drawn through the corresponding points at the same total molality. These

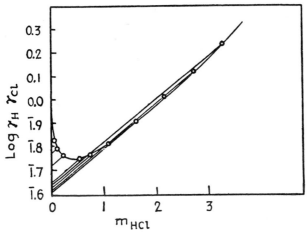

Fig. (14-4-3). Plots of log $\gamma_H\gamma_{Cl}$ versus m_{HCl} in hydrochloric acid-cesium chloride solutions. Straight lines represent variations at constant total molalities.

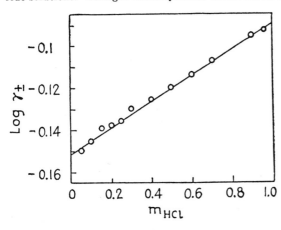

Fig. (14-4-4). Plot of log $\gamma_\pm$ of hydrochloric acid against acid concentration in hydrochloric acid-aluminum chloride solutions at constant ionic strength (unity).

plots appear to be parallel, and indeed are nearly so at the higher concentrations. This behavior is characteristic of hydrochloric acid in halide solutions.

The same linear variation is found frequently in cases of solutions containing electrolytes of higher valence types. This is verified by Fig. (14-4-4) in which the activity coefficient of hydrochloric acid in aluminum

[33] H. S. Harned and O. E. Schupp, Jr., *J. Am. Chem. Soc.*, **52**, 3892 (1930).

chloride solutions[34] at constant total ionic strength is plotted against its molality (ionic strength). Similar results have been obtained for the activity coefficient of this acid in cerium chloride,[35] barium and lanthanum chlorides[36] and sodium dithionate.[37] Determinations of the solubility of silver sulfate[38] in mixtures of salts also indicate a linear variation of log $\gamma_\pm$ of the saturating salt at constant total ionic strength. It is important to observe that the linear relationship is valid only when the ionic strengths of the salts are plotted. Thus, log $\gamma_\pm$ of silver sulfate in magnesium and cadmium sulfate mixtures, in magnesium and lithium sulfate mixtures, and in aluminum and zinc sulfate solutions varies linearly with the ionic strength of the silver sulfate.

The linear variation of log $\gamma_\pm$ of each of two electrolytes in a mixture may be represented in detail by the equations,

$$\log \gamma_1 = \log \gamma_{(0)1} + \alpha_{12}\mu_1 = \log \gamma_{1(0)} - \alpha_{12}\mu_2 \qquad (14\text{-}4\text{-}3)$$

$$\log \gamma_2 = \log \gamma_{(0)2} + \alpha_{21}\mu_2 = \log \gamma_{2(0)} - \alpha_{21}\mu_1 \qquad (14\text{-}4\text{-}4)$$

where the subscripts (1) and (2) refer to electrolytes (1) and (2), respectively. The mean activity coefficients of electrolytes (1) and (2) in a mixture of any composition at constant total molality are written γ_1 and γ_2. In these expressions, $\gamma_{(0)1}$ is the activity coefficient of electrolyte (1) at zero concentration in the presence of electrolyte (2) at a given ionic strength μ, and $\gamma_{(0)2}$ is the activity coefficient of electrolyte (2) at zero concentration in the presence of electrolyte (1) at the same ionic strength, μ. Further, $\gamma_{1(0)}$ and $\gamma_{2(0)}$ are the activity coefficients of electrolytes (1) and (2) in the pure solutions of (1) and (2), respectively. The constants, α_{12} and α_{21}, represent the slopes of the plots shown in the figures. This symbolism is important, and necessary for the subsequent theoretical developments.

An interesting and valuable extension of this behavior of concentrated solutions of mixtures is to be found in an investigation of Åkerlöf, Teare and Turck[39]. In Fig. (14-4-5) the logarithm of the activity coefficient of hydrochloric acid in sodium chloride solutions at $1M$ total ionic strength, and, at the temperatures indicated, is plotted against the molality of the acid. The six solvents are 10, 20, 30, 40, 50 and 60% by weight methyl alcohol-water mixtures. The plots are straight lines within an error of ± 0.1 mv. Further, at a given temperature the slopes of these lines $(-\alpha_{12})$ are independent of the alcohol concentration, which is an unexpectedly simple result. It is obvious that α_{12} is a function of the temperature.

[34] H. S. Harned and C. M. Mason, *J. Am. Chem. Soc.*, **53**, 3377 (1931).
[35] C. M. Mason and D. B. Kellam, *J. Phys. Chem.*, **38**, 689 (1934).
[36] M. Randall and G. F. Breckenridge, *J. Am. Chem. Soc.*, **49**, 1435 (1927).
[37] P. G. Murdock and R. C. Barton, *J. Am. Chem. Soc.*, **55**, 4074 (1933).
[38] G. Åkerlöf and H. C. Thomas, *J. Am. Chem. Soc.*, **56**, 593 (1934).
[39] G. Åkerlöf, J. W. Teare and H. E. Turck, *J. Am. Chem. Soc.*, **59**, 1916 (1937).

The linear relationship expressed by equation (14-4-3) is not a universal law, and cases are known where it is necessary to employ equations with higher powers of μ_2 and μ_1 to account for the results.   This has been shown by Harned and Harris,[40] and Harned and Cook,[41] who measured the activity coefficients of sodium and potassium hydroxides in their corresponding chloride solutions by means of the cells,

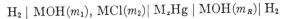

$$H_2 \mid MOH(m_1),\ MCl(m_2) \mid M_zHg \mid MOH(m_R) \mid H_2$$

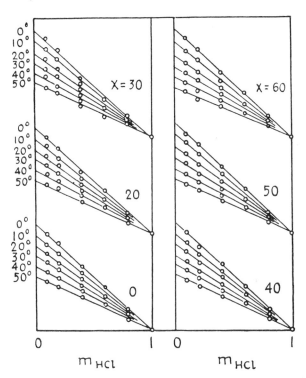

Fig. (14-4-5).   Plots of log $(\gamma_{(0)}/\gamma_{\pm})$ for hydrochloric acid in sodium chloride solutions at 1 M total molality against molality of acid.   The activity coefficient in the salt-free acid solutions is $\gamma_{(0)}$. X = weight per cent of methanol.   Diameter of circles equals 0.002.

In Fig. (14-4-6), log $\gamma_{\pm}$ of sodium hydroxide in sodium chloride solutions at 3 and 5 total molalities is plotted against the hydroxide concentration. The deviations from the linear variation of this quantity are clearly seen.

All these results indicate that the linear variation of log $\gamma_{\pm}$, as expressed by equations (14-4-3) and (14-4-4), affords a first approximation which can be utilized in the treatment of many such mixtures.   Certainly, a considerable simplification of a complicated subject is made possible by this fact.

[40] H. S. Harned and J. M. Harris, *J. Am. Chem. Soc.*, **50**, 2633 (1928).
[41] H. S. Harned and M. A. Cook, *Ibid.*, **59**, 1890 (1937).

In cases where incompletely ionized electrolytes are present, deviations from the above empirical relationship may be expected. As an illustration, Güntelberg[42] has measured the cells,

$$Pb_xHg \mid PbCl_2(m_1), \; MCl(m_2) \mid AgCl\text{-}Ag$$

at $\mu = 0.1$. He found that instead of the linear relationship given by equation (14-4-2), $\mathbf{E}^{0'}$ could be expressed by the equation

$$\mathbf{E}^{0'} = \mathbf{E}^{0'}_{(x=0)} - ax + bx^{3/2} \qquad (14\text{-}4\text{-}5)$$

where a and b are constants. The degree of ionization of lead chloride in the halide solutions was estimated.

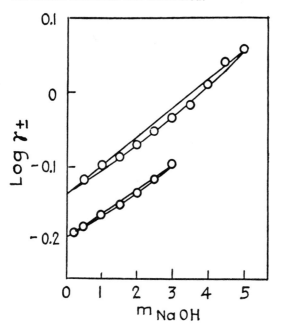

Fig. (14-4-6).

Log $\gamma_{\pm}$ of sodium hydroxide, in sodium hydroxide-chloride mixtures of 5 molal (upper curves), and 3 molal (lower curves) total concentrations, against molality of hydroxide.

(5) THERMODYNAMIC THEORY OF MIXTURES AT CONSTANT TOTAL MOLALITY*

For the purpose of reducing our discussion to its simplest form, we shall consider only solutions of mixtures of two 1-1 electrolytes, denoted (1) and (2), at constant total molality. Further, we shall consider only those mixtures where the logarithm of the activity coefficient of each electrolyte may be assumed to vary linearly with its molal concentration. According

[42] E. Güntelberg, *Studier over Elektrolyt-Activiteter*, G. E. C. Gads Forlag, København (1938).

* The following treatment follows closely that of H. S. Harned [*J. Am. Chem. Soc.,* **51**, 1865 (1935)]. A number of important ramifications suggested by the excellent work of E. Güntelberg [*Studier over Elektrolyt-Actitiviteter*, G. E. C. Gads Forlag København (1938)] have been incorporated. A treatment of mixtures of higher valence type electrolytes is given in Section (10) of this Chapter.

to equations (14-4-3) and (14-4-4), the linear variation of $\log \gamma_{\pm}$ for electrolytes (1) and (2) is given by the equations,

$$\log \gamma_1 = \log \gamma_{(0)1} + \alpha_{12} m_1 = \log \gamma_{1(0)} - \alpha_{12} m_2 \qquad (14\text{-}5\text{-}1)$$

$$\log \gamma_2 = \log \gamma_{(0)2} + \alpha_{21} m_2 = \log \gamma_{2(0)} - \alpha_{21} m_1 \qquad (14\text{-}5\text{-}2)$$

Relations between α_{12} and α_{21}, and other thermodynamic quantities may be obtained from the Gibbs-Duhem equation (1-8-1), or

$$N_1 \, d \ln a_1 + N_2 \, d \ln a_2 + N_w \, d \ln a_w = 0 \qquad (1\text{-}8\text{-}1)$$

where N_1, N_2, N_w and a_1, a_2, a_w are the mol fractions and activities of electrolytes, (1), (2), and water, respectively. This equation becomes

$$2 m_1 \, d \log \gamma_1 + 2 m_2 \, d \log \gamma_2 = -55.51 \, d \log a_w \qquad (14\text{-}5\text{-}3)$$

upon substitution of activity coefficients and molalities. According to equations (14-5-1) and (14-5-2), $d \log \gamma_1 = \alpha_{12} \, dm_1$, $d \log \gamma_2 = \alpha_{21} \, dm_2$, whence equation (14-5-3) becomes

$$2 \alpha_{12} m_1 \, dm_1 + 2 \alpha_{21} m_2 \, dm_2 = -55.51 \, d \log a_w \qquad (14\text{-}5\text{-}4)$$

Let $m = m_1 + m_2$, and $m_1 = mx$, where x can have any value between 0 and 1. Then $m_2 = (1 - x)m$. Substitution of these in the last equation leads to,

$$2(\alpha_{12} + \alpha_{21}) x \, dx - 2\alpha_{21} \, dx = -\frac{55.51}{m^2} \, d \log a_w = \frac{2 \, d\phi}{2.303 m} \qquad (14\text{-}5\text{-}5)$$

since

$$d \log a_w = -\frac{2m \, d\phi}{55.51(2.303)}$$

by differentiation of equation (1-9-9) at constant m and T. Upon integration of the left side of equation (14-5-5), we obtain

$$(\alpha_{12} + \alpha_{21}) x^2 - 2\alpha_{21} x = -\frac{55.51}{m^2} \int_0^x d \log a_w$$

$$= -\frac{55.51}{m^2} \log \frac{a_{w(x)}}{a_{w(0)}} \qquad (14\text{-}5\text{-}6)$$

$$= \frac{2}{2.303 m} \int_0^x d\phi = \frac{2}{2.303 m} (\phi_x - \phi_0)$$

which is fundamental to much of the subsequent discussion.

If either α_{12} or α_{21} is known (by experiment), the other may be evaluated from osmotic and activity coefficients by the following simple procedures. Substituting the upper limit $(x = 1)$ into equation (14-5-6), we obtain

$$\alpha_{21} = \alpha_{12} + \frac{55.51}{m^2} \log \frac{a_{w(1)}}{a_{w(2)}} = \alpha_{12} + \frac{2}{2.303 m} (\phi_{2(0)} - \phi_{1(0)}) \qquad (14\text{-}5\text{-}7)$$

where $a_{w(1)}$, $a_{w(2)}$, $\phi_{1(0)}$ and $\phi_{2(0)}$ are the activities of water and the osmotic coefficients in pure binary solutions of the electrolytic components, (1) or (2), respectively.

Further, we have found [Chapter (1), Section (9)] that the osmotic coefficient is related to the activity coefficient of the solute by the equation,

$$\phi = 1 + \frac{1}{m} \int_1^{\gamma_\pm} m \, d \ln \gamma_\pm \qquad (1\text{-}9\text{-}12)$$

Upon substitution for ϕ in equation (14-5-7), we readily obtain

$$\alpha_{21} = \alpha_{12} + \frac{2}{m^2} \left[\int_1^{\gamma_{2(0)}} m \, d \ln \gamma_{2(0)} - \int_1^{\gamma_{1(0)}} m \, d \ln \gamma_{1(0)} \right]$$

$$= \alpha_{12} + \frac{2}{m^2} \left[\int_0^m m \, d \ln \frac{\gamma_{2(0)}}{\gamma_{1(0)}} \right] \qquad (14\text{-}5\text{-}8)$$

Equations (14-5-7) and (14-5-8) show the relation between the slopes, α_{12} and α_{21}, and the osmotic coefficients and activity coefficients of the solutions of the unmixed electrolytes at a total concentration, m. The validity of these relationships is determined by the accuracy of the linear variation of the logarithms of the activity coefficients of the solutes at constant total molality, as expressed by equations (14-5-1) and (14-5-2). The deductions from these relations depend on exact thermodynamic methods.

(a) In general, we see from equation (14-5-6) that the linear variation of $\log \gamma_\pm$ with x, at constant total molality, leads to a quadratic variation of the osmotic coefficient except for the case when $\alpha_{12} = -\alpha_{21}$. For the latter it is obvious that,

$$(\phi_x - \phi_0) = 2.303 m \alpha_{21} x \qquad (14\text{-}5\text{-}9)$$

which represents a linear variation of ϕ. The general result without any additional restriction is illustrated by Fig. (14-5-1) (a). Here $\alpha_{12} \neq -\alpha_{21}$, $\log \gamma_{(0)1} \neq \log \gamma_{(0)2}$, and ϕ is quadratic in x.

(b) If we superimpose the restriction that

$$\log \frac{\gamma_{1(0)}}{\gamma_{2(0)}} = B_{12} m \qquad (14\text{-}5\text{-}10)$$

where $B_{12} \neq f(m)$, a relation which Åkerlöf and Thomas[43] have found to be approached at high concentrations, we obtain the result shown in Fig. (14-5-1) (b). By substituting this relation in equation (14-5-8), and integrating, we obtain

$$\alpha_{12} - \alpha_{21} = B_{12} \neq f(m) \qquad (14\text{-}5\text{-}11)$$

Further, from this and equations (14-5-1) and (14-5-2), we find that

$$(\alpha_{12} - \alpha_{21}) m = \log \frac{\gamma_{1(0)}}{\gamma_{2(0)}} \qquad (14\text{-}5\text{-}12)$$

[43] G. Åkerlöf and H. C. Thomas, J. Am. Chem. Soc., **56**, 593 (1934).

and

$$\log \gamma_{0(1)} = \log \gamma_{0(2)} \qquad (14\text{-}5\text{-}13)$$

a relation shown in Fig. (14–5–1b).

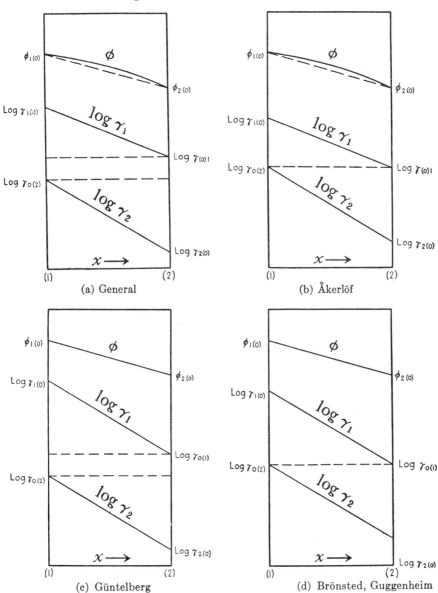

(a) General

(b) Åkerlöf

(c) Güntelberg

(d) Brönsted, Guggenheim

Fig. (14-5-1). Qualitative illustrations of various interpretations of the properties of two strong electrolytes in solution.

(c) Brönsted's theory of specific ionic interaction [Chapter (12) Section (6)] introduces different restrictions. In order to understand clearly the application of this theory, it is convenient to choose a concrete case, for example, a mixture of hydrochloric acid and potassium chloride. We may write for the logarithm of the activity coefficients of hydrochloric acid and potassium chloride in solutions of potassium chloride and hydrochloric acid, respectively, the following expressions,

$$\ln \gamma_{HCl(KCl+HCl)} = \ln \gamma_{H(H)}\gamma_{Cl(Cl)}\gamma_{H(K)}\gamma_{Cl(K)}\gamma_{H(Cl)}\gamma_{Cl(H)}\gamma^2_{(H+K)}\gamma^2_{(Cl)} \quad (14\text{-}5\text{-}14)$$

$$\ln \gamma_{KCl(HCl+KCl)} = \ln \gamma_{K(H)}\gamma_{Cl(Cl)}\gamma_{K(K)}\gamma_{Cl(K)}\gamma_{K(Cl)}\gamma_{Cl(H)}\gamma^2_{(K+H)}\gamma^2_{(Cl)} \quad (14\text{-}5\text{-}15)$$

where $\gamma_{H(H)}$, $\gamma_{Cl(K)}$, etc. are specific interaction coefficients, and $\gamma_{(H+K)}$ and $\gamma_{(Cl)}$ are salting out coefficients. Brönsted's theory may be summarized by two postulates:

(i) Ions of unlike sign react differently upon one another, while ions of like sign react identically with one another.

(ii) Each ion has a characteristic "salting out effect" which acts upon all other ions in the solution.

Consider a change in $x = m_{HCl}/m$ at constant molality, m. According to postulate (i), $\gamma_{H(H)} = \gamma_{H(K)} = \gamma_{Cl(Cl)} = \gamma_{K(K)} = $ a constant. Further, at constant chloride concentration, the interaction coefficients of the chloride ion on the cations, $\gamma_{H(Cl)}$ and $\gamma_{K(Cl)}$, will remain constant with change in composition. Differentiation of equations (14-5-14) and (14-5-15) will yield, respectively, the relations,

$$d \ln \gamma_{HCl(HCl+KCl)} = d \ln \gamma_{Cl(K)}\gamma_{Cl(H)} + 2d \ln \gamma_{(H+K)}\gamma_{(Cl)} \quad (14\text{-}5\text{-}16)$$

$$d \ln \gamma_{KCl(HCl+KCl)} = d \ln \gamma_{Cl(K)}\gamma_{Cl(H)} + 2d \ln \gamma_{(K+H)}\gamma_{(Cl)} \quad (14\text{-}5\text{-}17)$$

at any given value of x from 0 to 1. Therefore,

$$d \ln \gamma_{HCl(HCl+KCl)} = d \ln \gamma_{KCl(HCl+KCl)} \quad (14\text{-}5\text{-}18)$$

Referring to our earlier treatment, this is equivalent to the statement that $\alpha_{12} = -\alpha_{21}$. This result always follows from the Brönsted theory of specific ionic interaction.

Let us now consider the limiting values of $\ln \gamma_{HCl(KCl)}$ and $\ln \gamma_{KCl(HCl)}$, where the subscripts indicate that the acid and salt are at zero concentrations in the solutions of the salt and acid, respectively. For this extreme case, equations (14-5-14) and (14-5-15) reduce to

$$\ln \gamma_{HCl(KCl)} = \ln \gamma_{H(K)}\gamma_{H(Cl)}\gamma_{Cl(K)}\gamma_{Cl(Cl)}\gamma^2_{(KCl)} \quad (14\text{-}5\text{-}19)$$

$$\ln \gamma_{KCl(HCl)} = \ln \gamma_{K(H)}\gamma_{K(Cl)}\gamma_{Cl(H)}\gamma_{Cl(Cl)}\gamma^2_{(HCl)} \quad (14\text{-}5\text{-}20)$$

where $\gamma_{(KCl)}$ and $\gamma_{(HCl)}$ are the salting out coefficients of the electrolytes, $\gamma_{(K)}\gamma_{(Cl)}$ and $\gamma_{(H)}\gamma_{(Cl)}$, respectively. From these equations, it is clear that

$$\ln \gamma_{HCl(KCl)} - \ln \gamma_{KCl(HCl)} = 2 \ln \gamma_{(KCl)} - 2 \ln \gamma_{(HCl)} \quad (14\text{-}5\text{-}21)$$

if we introduce the postulated relations, $\gamma_{H(K)} = \gamma_{Cl(Cl)} = \gamma_{K(H)}$, and if we assume that $\gamma_{H(Cl)} = \gamma_{Cl(H)}$, and $\gamma_{K(Cl)} = \gamma_{Cl(K)}$. Güntelberg[44] has dis-

[44] E. Güntelberg, *Z. physik. Chem.*, **123**, 199 (1926).

cussed the fundamental nature and plausibility of this assumption. It depends on the basic assumption of the linear superposition of ionic atmospheres which requires that the average force acting upon the ion is given by the potential of atmosphere of the other ion [Equation (2-4-7)].

Equation (14-5-21) shows that Brönsted's postulates do not require that $\ln \gamma_{HCl(KCl)}$ equal $\ln \gamma_{KCl(HCl)}$, the result obtained from Åkerlöf's relation, and expressed by (14-5-13). Another result from Brönsted's theory may be readily obtained by integrating equation (14-5-18) from $x = 0$ to $x = 1$. By this means, we find that,

$$\ln \gamma_{HCl(KCl)} + \ln \gamma_{KCl(HCl)} = \ln \gamma_{KCl} + \ln \gamma_{HCl} \qquad (14\text{-}5\text{-}22)$$

The Brönsted result is represented by Fig. (14-5-1) (c). Here, $\alpha_{12} = -\alpha_{21}$, ϕ is linear with change in composition according to (14-5-7), and $\log \gamma_{0(1)} \neq \log \gamma_{0(2)}$.

(d) If we neglect the salting out coefficients of Brönsted in equation (14-5-21), it follows immediately from equation (14-5-22) that

$$\ln \gamma_{HCl(KCl)} = \ln \gamma_{KCl(HCl)} = \tfrac{1}{2}(\ln \gamma_{HCl} + \ln \gamma_{KCl}) \qquad (14\text{-}5\text{-}23)$$

which in our general symbolism means that, $\alpha_{12} = -\alpha_{21}$, and $\log \gamma_{0(1)} = \log \gamma_{0(2)}$. This condition is represented by Fig. (14-5-1) (d), and follows from Guggenheim's treatment of the theory of specific interaction. Guggenheim's[45] equation (12-6-3) leads to the expression, for the logarithm of the ratio of the activity coefficients of two electrolytes, which is the same as the Åkerlöf and Thomas relation (14-5-10), except that it is in c units, not m units, and the rational activity coefficient is employed. Thus,

$$\log \frac{f_{1(0)}}{f_{2(0)}} = Bc \qquad (12\text{-}6\text{-}4)$$

where B is a constant. This will lead to the result given by equation (14-5-13), namely, $\log \gamma_{0(1)} = \log \gamma_{0(2)}$.

(6) General Survey of the Experimental Investigations of 1-1 Halide Mixtures

As an introduction to the discussion of the theories and rules developed in the preceding section, the extensive experimental investigations of hydrochloric acid in chloride solutions will be reviewed. From the measurements cited in Sections (2) and (4), $\log \gamma_1$ of the acids in the halide solutions is obtained, and, consequently, the characteristic slopes, α_{12}, may be evaluated at different concentrations and temperatures. From these and the activity, or osmotic coefficients of the acids and the salts in pure water, α_{21} may be computed by means of equations (14-5-7), or (14-5-8).[46] Since α_{12} is computed from only two experimental values, that

[45] E. A. Guggenheim, *Phil. Mag.* [7], **19**, 588 (1935).
[46] H. S. Harned, *J. Am. Chem. Soc.*, **37**, 1865 (1935).

in pure acid and that in the $0.01M$ acid-salt solution of the same molality, the highest accuracy is not to be expected. Further, the error in the computation of α_{12} is proportional to $1/m$, and consequently its evaluation at concentrations below $0.5M$ is not of a high order of accuracy, and has been omitted. Errors in the electromotive forces of ± 0.1, ± 0.2 and ± 0.2 mv. at 0.5, 1 and $3M$, respectively, cause an error in α_{12} equal to ± 0.0034, ± 0.0034, and ± 0.0011 at these concentrations. Since the results come from many sources, it is difficult to estimate the errors, but judging from the consistency of the results, an accuracy of ± 0.001 is probably obtained. The evaluation of α_{21} is less certain and is of the order of ± 0.002 in the most favorable cases. Table (14-6-1) contains these values, and the sources of the data from which α_{12} and α_{21} were

TABLE (14-6-1).*   VALUES OF α_{12} AND α_{21} FOR 1-1 CHLORIDE-HYDROCHLORIC ACID MIXTURES AT $25°$

m	$LiCl^b$		$NaCl^c$		KCl^d		$CsCl^e$	
	α_{12}	$-\alpha_{21}$	α_{12}	$-\alpha_{21}$	α_{12}	$-\alpha_{21}$	α_{12}	$-\alpha_{21}$
0.1	0.0013^a	.....	0.043^a	.....	0.077^a	.....	0.143^b	.....
.5	.006	0.011	.037	0.057	.062	0.074	.105	0.070
1.	.005	.012	.032	.058	.056	.072	.100	.060
1.5	.005	.011	.....	.058	.055	.069	.099	.053
2.	.005	.012	.031	.058	.057	.064	.099	.046
3.	.004	.013	.031	.058	.062	.054	.098	.041
$4.^f$	$-$ .0025	.....	.030	.....	.066	.050	.....	.....
$5.^f$	....	.....	.030	.....	.072	.....	.....	.....
$6.^f$	$-$ .0086	.....	.029	.....	.....	.....	.....	.....

[a] E. Güntelberg, *Z. physik. Chem.*, **123**, 199 (1926).
[b] H. S. Harned and H. R. Copson, *J. Am. Chem. Soc.*, **55**, 2206 (1933).
[c] H. S. Harned, *Ibid.*, **57**, 1865 (1935).
[d] H. S. Harned and W. J. Hamer, *Ibid.*, **55**, 2194 (1933).
[e] H. S. Harned and O. E. Schupp Jr., *Ibid.*, **52**, 3892 (1930).
[f] J. E. Hawkins, *Ibid.*, **54**, 4480 (1932).
* The values employed for log $\gamma_{\pm}$ for hydrochloric acid and the halides were those in Tables (11-4-1A) and (12-3-1A), respectively.

obtained. The effects of temperature may be seen from the values of these quantities for sodium chloride-hydrochloric acid mixtures given in Table (14-6-2). That ± 0.001 is the magnitude of the error in determining α_{12} from these measurements is proved by the more recent results of Åkerlöf, Teare and Turck,[47] who obtained values at $1M$ from 0 to $40°$ which agree with those in the table to within this limit.

The characteristics of the behaviors of α_{12} and α_{21} as functions of the concentration are shown in Figs. (14-6-1) and (14-6-2). As the concentration increases, it appears [Fig. (14-6-1)] that in some cases (CsCl, NaBr, NaCl) that α_{12} approaches constancy. This tendency led Åkerlöf and Thomas to the rule that this quantity as well as α_{21} are not functions of the concentration in concentrated solutions. Due to the fact, however,

[47] G. Åkerlöf, J. W. Teare and H. E. Turck, *J. Am. Chem. Soc.*, **59**, 1916 (1937).

that there is distinct evidence that this rule is not valid in all cases (KBr, KCl, etc.), it must be regarded as a first approximation. At the lower concentrations ($<0.5M$), it is obvious that the rule is invalid for all of these mixtures.

TABLE (14-6-2). VALUES OF α_{12} AND α_{21} FOR HYDROCHLORIC ACID-SODIUM CHLORIDE MIXTURES FROM 10 TO 40°

	α_{12}					
	m = 0.1	0.3	0.5	1	2	3
10	.....	.044	.040	.038	.037	.037
20	0.046[a]	.040	.036	.034	.033	.033
25	.043[a]	.038	.034	.032	.031	.031
30	.....	.035	.032	.030	.029	.029
40	.....	.030	.028	.026	.025	.025
	$-\alpha_{21}$					
10	.....	.068	.070	.069	.066	.064
20	.....	.060	.062	.062	.060	.064
25	.....	.057	.059	.058	.058	.059
30	.....	.054	.055	.055	.055	.057
40	.....	.047	.047	.048	.049	....

[a] E. Güntelberg, *Z. physik. Chem.*, **123**, 199 (1926)

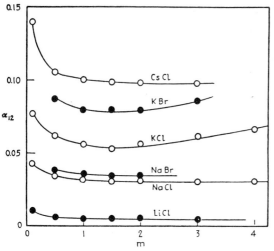

Fig. (14-6-1).
Variation of the parameter, α_{12}, with molality:

In Fig. (14-6-2), plots of both α_{12} and α_{21} are given for cesium chloride and sodium chloride. The parameter, α_{12} is not equal to $-\alpha_{21}$ although in the case of sodium, the value of α_{12} appears to approach that of $-\alpha_{21}$ as the concentration decreases.

If we consider these results in relation to the theory of the preceding section, we find that they conform to the case which we have designated as general [Fig. (14-5-1) (a)]. This fact is illustrated by Fig. (14-6-3) in which both $(\alpha_{12} - \alpha_{21})$ and B_{12}, defined by the equation,

$$\log \frac{\gamma_{1(0)}}{\gamma_{2(0)}} = B_{12} m \qquad (14\text{-}5\text{-}10)$$

are plotted against m. We note that B_{12} is a function of m in dilute solutions, and hence according to theory, $\log \gamma_{0(1)}$ does not equal $\log \gamma_{0(2)}$, nor does $\alpha_{12} - \alpha_{21}$ equal B_{12} except in the cases of lithium bromide and

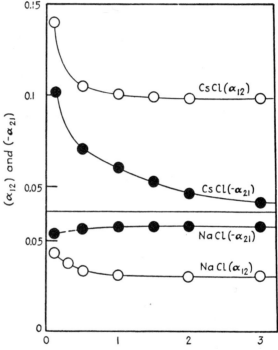

Fig. (14-6-2). Variation of parameters, α_{12} and $(-\alpha_{21})$, with molality for cesium and sodium chloride solutions.

chloride. This equality may not be exact but is well within the experimental error. As the concentration increases, B_{12} and $\alpha_{12} - \alpha_{21}$ approach each other in magnitude, a fact which indicates that the empirical rule that $B_{12} \neq f(m)$ is a good approximation in the very concentrated solutions, and that the condition represented by Fig. (14-5-1) (b) is approached.

A direct proof that the osmotic coefficient does not vary linearly in lithium chloride-potassium chloride mixtures at total molalities of 1, 2 and $3M$, has been obtained by Owen and Cooke.[48] By utilizing the iso-

[48] B. B. Owen and T. F. Cooke, Jr., *J. Am. Chem. Soc.*, **59**, 2273 (1937).

piestic vapor pressure method, they obtained directly the change in osmotic coefficient, and were able to test equation (14-5-6), or

$$(\phi_x - \phi_0) = -2.303\alpha_{21}mx + 1.151(\alpha_{12} + \alpha_{21})mx^2 \qquad (14\text{-}6\text{-}1)$$

In this system, the concentration of the lithium chloride is mx, and of potassium chloride is $m(1 - x)$, where m is the total molality. In terms of the vapor pressure, this equation may be rearranged to read

$$\frac{\log p_0 - \log p_x}{xm^2} = -0.036\alpha_{21} + 0.018(\alpha_{12} + \alpha_{21})x \qquad (14\text{-}6\text{-}2)$$

If a plot of the left side of this equation versus x is a straight line, then a quadratic variation of the osmotic coefficient will express the results. In

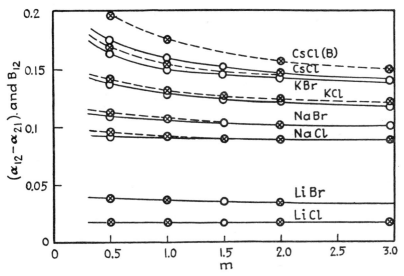

Fig. (14-6-3). Plots of B_{12} and $(\alpha_{12}-\alpha_{21})$ against molality for 1-1 halide solutions; $\otimes$, B_{12}; $\bigcirc$, $(\alpha_{12}-\alpha_{21})$.

Fig. (14-6-4), this function is plotted. The diameters of the circles represent an error of ± 0.1 percent in m, which is the estimated error of the measurements. The plots are evidently linear within this limit of error, which indicates a formal agreement with equations (14-6-1) and (14-6-2).

Since α_{12} does not equal $-\alpha_{21}$ in the concentrated solutions ($0.5M$ or greater), the theory of specific ionic interaction in its simplest form [Figs. (14-5-1) (c) or (d)] is not strictly valid. This fact is illustrated by Fig. (14-6-5) in which $\alpha_{12} + \alpha_{21}$ is plotted against m for hydrochloric acid-chloride mixtures. Since $\alpha_{12} + \alpha_{21}$ does not equal zero, the conditions superimposed by specific interaction do not hold. This, of course, is not surprising in solutions of these concentrations.

Although the computation becomes very sensitive at $0.1M$, it seems from the present data that the correct distribution of the curves is obtained

at this concentration.   Thus, taking values of 0.0980, 0.1135, 0.1088, and
0.1238 for $-\log \gamma_{0.1}$ of hydrochloric acid, potassium chloride, sodium

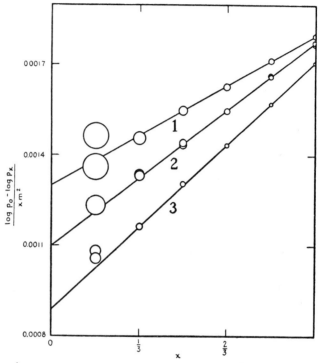

Fig. (14-6-4).   Formal verification of equations (14-6-1) and (14-6-2).   The numbers indicate the total molality for each series.   The ordinates of the 3 M series have
been lowered by 0.0001 to avoid overlapping.

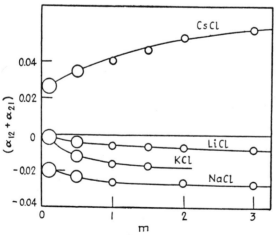

Fig. (14-6-5).   Plots of $(\alpha_{12} + \alpha_{21})$ against m.   Radii of circles represent the magnitudes of the errors.

chloride and cesium chloride, respectively [Tables (11-4-1A) and (12-3-1A)],
and the values of α_{12} in Table (14-6-1), we obtain $+0.028$, -0.001 and

-0.020 for $\alpha_{12} + \alpha_{21}$ in the cases of cesium, potassium, and sodium chloride mixtures. The small difference between $\alpha_{12} - \alpha_{21}$ and B_{12} has been neglected in this computation. As seen by the plots in Fig. (14-6-5), these results show the same distribution as those at higher concentrations. There seems to be a tendency for $\alpha_{12} + \alpha_{21}$ to approach zero, but this condition is not reached at $0.1M$, although it is very nearly valid in the lithium and potassium chloride mixtures.

Owen and Cooke[49] have determined log $\gamma_{\pm}$ for hydrobromic acid in hydrochloric acid solutions from the cells,

$$\text{H}_2 \mid \text{HBr}(m_1), \text{HCl}(m_2) \mid \text{AgBr-Ag}$$

at $m_1 + m_2$ equal to 0.5 from 0 to 45°. Log γ_{HBr} was found to vary linearly with the molality of hydrobromic acid. The slopes, α_{12}, were evaluated, and the slopes, α_{21}, for the variation of hydrochloric acid in these mixtures was estimated and found to be nearly equal in magnitude but opposite in sign to α_{12}. The sum, $\alpha_{12} + \alpha_{21}$, is small at all temperatures.

The preceding considerations indicate that the original treatment of specific ionic interaction of Brönsted, developed in the preceding section, is somewhat oversimplified. This point is established by the comprehensive analysis of the freezing measurements of mixtures of potassium nitrate, potassium chloride, lithium nitrate, and lithium chloride carried out by Scatchard and Prentiss.[50] By application of his extended equation (12-7-1), which includes the effects of change in dielectric constant with salt concentration, ion-molecule salting out, and molecule-molecule effect to the mixtures, Scatchard's investigations indicate that the theory of specific ionic interaction is confirmed at concentrations above $0.1M$, and possibly at concentrations of $1M$.

(7) Further Considerations of the Theory of Specific Ionic Interaction

Although the results in the last section show the extremely complicated nature of these systems, and the difficulty of obtaining exact verification of the theory of specific ionic interaction, Brönsted and Güntelberg have obtained much evidence for its essential validity. Of this, we shall choose a few illustrations from experimental results of a high degree of accuracy.

One of the requirements which follows readily from the application of the theory is that

$$\log \frac{\gamma_{\text{TlCl(HCl)}}}{\gamma_{\text{TlCl(MCl)}}} = \log \frac{\gamma_{\text{AgCl(HCl)}}}{\gamma_{\text{AgCl(MCl)}}} = \log \frac{\gamma_{\text{RCl(HCl)}}}{\gamma_{\text{RCl(MCl)}}} = \log \frac{\gamma_{\text{HCl(HCl)}}}{\gamma_{\text{HCl(MCl)}}} \quad (14\text{-}7\text{-}1)$$

$$= \text{etc.}$$

[49] B. B. Owen and T. F. Cooke, Jr., *J. Am. Chem. Soc.*, **59**, 2277 (1937).

[50] G. Scatchard and S. S. Prentiss, *J. Am. Chem. Soc.*, **56**, 2320 (1924); G. Scatchard, *Chem. Rev.*, **19**, 309 (1936).

By measuring the solubility of the slightly soluble salt, $[Co(NO_2)(CNS)$ $(NH_3)_4]Cl$, in chloride solutions, Güntelberg[51] was able to relate solubility determinations with his electromotive force measurements of hydrochloric acid in the same halide solutions. From the last two of these relations, we obtain,

$$\frac{1}{2} [\log S_{RCl(MCl)} - \log S_{RCl(HCl)}] = \log \gamma_{HCl(HCl)} - \log \gamma_{HCl(MCl)}$$ (14-7-2)

$$= \alpha_{12} m$$

The results at 20° are shown in Table (14-7-1), where the left side of this equation divided by m is given in the third column, and the values of α_{12}

TABLE (14-7-1).   PROOF OF EQUATION (14-7-2). $m = 0.1$

	S_{RCl}	$\frac{1}{2m}[\log S_{RCl(MCl)} - \log S_{RCl(HCl)}]$	α_{12}
HCl	0.01216	.....	....
LiCl	.01219	0.006	0.012
NaCl	.01238	.039	.046
KCl	.01264	.084	.081
CsCl	.01301	.147	.146

TABLE (14-7-2).   RATIO OF THE SOLUBILITY OF TETRANITRO-DIAMMINE-COBALTIATES IN 0.1 M KNO$_3$ TO THAT IN 0.1 M NaNO$_3$ AT 20°

Cations	$r = S_{RX_n(KNO_3)}/S_{RX_n(NaNO_3)}$
$Co(NH_3)_4(C_2O_4)^+$	1.034
$Co(NH_3)_4CO_3^+$	1.032
Ag^+	1.034
$N(CH_3)_4^+$	1.033
$Co(NH_3)_5Cl^{++}$	1.041
$Co(NH_3)_5NO_2^{++}$	1.041
$Co(NH_2C_2H_4NH_2)_3^{+++}$	1.045
$Co(NH_3)_5H_2O^{+++}$	1.047

from electromotive force measurements are given in the last column. The agreement between the results from these entirely different sources is good.

Another excellent example of the proof of the relationship given by equation (14-7-1) is the solubility measurements of complex salts with the common anion, $[Co(NH_3)_2(NO_2)_4]^-$. According to theory, r, the ratio of the solubilities of these salts, of a given valence type, in potassium and sodium nitrates should be the same. This is shown clearly by the results in Table (14-7-2)[52]. Further, it follows from Guggenheim's[53] treatment of the theory that

$$r_0 = (r_{RX})^2 = (r_{RX_2})^{3/2} = (r_{RX_3})^{4/3}$$ (14-7-3)

[51] E. Güntelberg, Z. physik. Chem., **123**, 199 (1926).
[52] J. N. Brönsted, J. Am. Chem. Soc., **44**, 877 (1922).
[53] E. A. Guggenheim, Phil. Mag., [7] **19**, 588 (1935).

where r_0 is a constant, which, if assigned the value 1.064, satisfies this relation. This procedure yields 1.032, 1.042 and 1.047 for r for uni-, bi-, and trivalent cations, respectively. This checks well with the results in Table (14-7-2).

(8) Hydroxide-Chloride Mixtures

As pointed out in Section (4) [Fig. (14-4-6)], Harned and Harris showed that in some hydroxide-chloride mixtures, the logarithm of the activity coefficients of the hydroxides did not vary linearly with the concentration

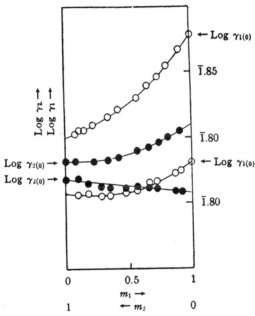

Fig. (14-8-1). Log γ_1 and log γ_2 against m_2 and m_1 at a constant molality of $1M$. Two curves at top represent KOH-KCl mixtures; two curves at bottom NaOH-NaCl mixtures. Diameter of circles equals 0.5 mv.

of hydroxide at constant total molality. Recently, Harned and Cook[54] by measurements of the cells,

$$H_2 \mid MOH(m_1), MX(m_2) \mid M_xHg \mid MOH(m_R) \mid H_2$$

and

$$Ag\text{-}AgX \mid MOH(m_1), MX(m_2) \mid M_xHg \mid MX(m_R) \mid AgX\text{-}Ag$$

have been able to determine the activity coefficients of both the hydroxide and chloride in the mixtures. This is the first time that the activity coef-

[54] H. S. Harned and M. A. Cook, *J. Am. Chem. Soc.*, **59**, 1890 (1937).

ficients of both electrolytic components in a mixture have been directly evaluated. Indeed, there are not many cells suitable for such a determination.

The characteristics of the results are illustrated in Fig. (14-8-1). The two curves at the upper part of the figure represent the behavior of the potassium hydroxide-chloride mixtures while the two curves at the bottom of the figure represent the sodium hydroxide-chloride mixtures, both at $1M$. At the top (circles) the logarithm of the activity coefficient of potassium hydroxide in the chloride solutions is plotted against its concentration. The curve below this (dots) represents the logarithm of the activity coefficient of the chloride in the hydroxide solution. Log $\gamma_{1(0)}$, the activity coefficient of the hydroxide, and log $\gamma_{2(0)}$, that of the chloride, both in pure water, are indicated on the margins. Similarly, the two lower curves represent the behavior of the sodium hydroxide-chloride system. The circles represent the values of the logarithm of the activity coefficient of sodium hydroxide in the chloride solution, and the dots represent the activity coefficient of the sodium chloride in the same mixtures.

It is clear that neither log γ_1 nor log γ_2 vary linearly with m_2 or m_1. Harned and Cook were able to express the variation within the error of experiment by the quadratic equations,

$$\log \gamma_1 = \log \gamma_{1(0)} - \alpha_{12}m_2 - \beta_{12}m_2^2$$
$$\log \gamma_2 = \log \gamma_{2(0)} - \alpha_{21}m_1 - \beta_{21}m_1^2 \qquad (14\text{-}8\text{-}1)$$

Upon substitution in equation (14-5-4) and integration, the change in osmotic coefficient becomes

$$\frac{\phi_{(x_1=0)} - \phi_{(x_1=x)}}{2.303m} = \alpha_{21} x_1 - \frac{1}{2}(\alpha_{12} + \alpha_{21})x_1^2 - m(\beta_{12} - \beta_{21})x_1^2$$
$$+ \frac{2}{3} m(\beta_{12} - \beta_{21})x_1^3 \qquad (14\text{-}8\text{-}2)$$

where $m = m_1 + m_2$ is constant, and $x_1 = m_1/m$.

There is one peculiarity of the sodium hydroxide-chloride mixtures. The curves slope in the opposite direction, a fact which leads to the same sign for α_{12} and α_{21}. This has not proved to be characteristic of most of the other systems, although there is evidence that the lithium hydroxide chloride mixtures behave in like manner.

Harned and Cook computed by equation (14-8-2) the change in osmotic coefficients between the pure hydroxides and chlorides, or $(\phi_{(x_1=1)} - \phi_{(x_1=0)})$. They compared these differences with values computed from electromotive force measurements by graphical integration of equation (14-5-8), and with similar values calculated from freezing point measurements. The differences, computed from these entirely independent series of results, agreed within satisfactory limits.

(9) EXTRAPOLATION OF ACTIVITY COEFFICIENTS TO SATURATED SOLUTIONS. CALCULATION OF THE SOLUBILITY OF HIGHLY SOLUBLE SALTS IN SOLUTIONS OF ELECTROLYTES

The knowledge of the thermodynamic properties of electrolytes and their mixtures may be applied to the calculation of the solubility of highly soluble salts in salt solutions. This calculation requires some method of extrapolation by which the activity coefficient of the saturating solute may be estimated at the high total ionic strengths of the mixed salt solutions. For this purpose, Åkerlöf and Thomas,[55] and Åkerlöf[56] employed the approximate empirical equation (14-5-10), which we write in the form[57]

$$\log \frac{\gamma_{1(0)}}{\gamma_{R(0)}} = B_{R1}\,\mu \qquad (14\text{-}9\text{-}1)$$

The subscript (0) serves as a reminder that this equation applies only to simple binary solutions of the individual electrolytes, (1) and (R), at the same ionic strength, μ.[58] Hydrochloric acid is used as the reference electrolyte (R) because its activity coefficient is known over a very wide concentration range. Åkerlöf and Teare[59] have determined this quantity from 0 to 50°, and from 3 to 16M. Their values are given in Table (14-9-1A). The isothermal constant, B_{R1}, may be determined from known values of $\gamma_{1(0)}$ and $\gamma_{R(0)}$ in simple unsaturated solutions, or from solubility data by a method outlined later.

The solubility product of an electrolyte which dissociates into two kinds of ions will be written

$$\mathcal{P}_{(0)} = (m_+^{\nu_+} m_-^{\nu_-})_{(0)} = (\nu_+^{\nu_+} \nu_-^{\nu_-}) m_{(0)}^{\nu} \qquad (14\text{-}9\text{-}2)$$

when the solvent is pure water, and

$$\mathcal{P} = (m_+^{\nu_+} m_-^{\nu_-}) \qquad (14\text{-}9\text{-}3)$$

when the solvent is a solution containing other electrolytes. If these other electrolytes have no ions in common with the saturating salt, $\mathcal{P}$ is also equal to $(\nu_+^{\nu_+}\nu_-^{\nu_-})m^{\nu}$.

In saturated solutions of electrolyte (1), the ionic activity product of this electrolyte is constant at a given temperature, and therefore

$$\frac{1}{\nu_1}\log K_1 = \frac{1}{\nu_1}\log \mathcal{P}_{1(0)} + \log \gamma_{1(0)} = \frac{1}{\nu_1}\log \mathcal{P}_1 + \log \gamma_1 \quad (14\text{-}9\text{-}4)$$

---

[55] G. Åkerlöf and H. C. Thomas, *J. Am. Chem. Soc.*, **56**, 593 (1934).

[56] G. Åkerlöf, *Ibid.*, **56**, 1439 (1934); *J. Phys. Chem.*, **41**, 1053 (1937). See also G. Åkerlöf and H. E. Turck, *J. Am. Chem. Soc.*, **56**, 1875 (1934); H. S. Harned, *J. Franklin Institute*, **225**, 623 (1938).

[57] In some cases, it is necessary to include a small constant term, because the plot of $\log \gamma_{1(0)}/\gamma_{R(0)}$ extrapolated from high concentrations to $\mu = 0$, does not always pass through the origin. Occasionally, the plot exhibits a distinct curvature at high concentrations, and a term in μ^2 should be added to equation (14-9-1).

[58] In solutions of mixed electrolytes the subscript (0) is omitted.

[59] G. Åkerlöf and J. W. Teare, *J. Am. Chem. Soc.*, **59**, 1855 (1937).

Since $\log \gamma_{1(0)}$ in this equation refers to a saturated solution of electrolyte (1) in pure water, this term is given directly by equation (14-9-1).[60] Denoting the ionic strength of this solution by $\mu_{1(0)}$, we obtain

$$\frac{1}{\nu_1} \log K_1 = \frac{1}{\nu_1} \log \mathcal{P}_{1(0)} + \log \gamma_{R(0)} + B_{R1}\,\mu_{1(0)} \qquad (14\text{-}9\text{-}5)$$

The term $\log \gamma_1$ in equation (14-9-4) refers to a saturated solution of (1) in the presence of one or more additional electrolytes at a total ionic strength, μ_T. For simplicity, we shall consider only a single co-solute, designated electrolyte (2), so that $\mu_T = \mu_1 + \mu_2$. The calculation of $\log \gamma_1$ involves two steps. Equation (14-9-1) is assumed to hold in supersaturated solutions of (1) in pure water, so that it may be used to calculate $\log \gamma_{1(0)}$ at the ionic strength, μ_T. At this ionic strength equation (14-5-1) is used to express $\log \gamma_1$ in terms of $\log \gamma_{1(0)}$ and μ_2. Thus,

$$\log \gamma_1 = \log \gamma_{1(0)} - \alpha_{12}\mu_2 \qquad (14\text{-}9\text{-}6)$$

Combination with equation (14-9-1), also at μ_T, yields[61]

$$\log \gamma_1 = \log \gamma_{R(T)} + B_{R1}\mu_T - \alpha_{12}\mu_2 \qquad (14\text{-}9\text{-}7)$$

Accordingly, equation (14-9-4) becomes

$$\frac{1}{\nu_1} \log K_1 = \frac{1}{\nu_1} \log \mathcal{P}_{1(0)} + \log \gamma_{R(0)} + B_{R1}\,\mu_{1(0)}$$
$$\qquad (14\text{-}9\text{-}8)$$
$$= \frac{1}{\nu_1} \log \mathcal{P}_1 + \log \gamma_{R(T)} + B_{R1}\,\mu_T - \alpha_{12}\,\mu_2$$

This equation contains three independent constants, B_{R1}, α_{12}, and $\mathcal{P}_{1(0)}$ (or K_1), which must be evaluated before $\mathcal{P}_1$, and subsequently the solubility of electrolyte (1), can be calculated in the presence of the co-solute (2). There are many possible combinations of data from which these constants can be evaluated. The following three are of particular interest.

(i) If B_{R1} and α_{12} are known from measurements in dilute solutions, and $\mathcal{P}_{1(0)}$ is obtained by a single solubility determination in pure water, equation (14-9-8) predicts[62] the solubility of electrolyte (1) in mixed solutions containing the co-solute at any ionic strength, μ_2. This is an interesting

---

[60] In this equation μ is any experimental ionic strength within the range of validity of the equation. The use of equation (14-9-1) at $\mu_{1(0)}$ usually constitutes an extrapolation, as activity coefficients of highly soluble salts are rarely measured up to saturation.

[61] The validity of equation (14-9-6) appears less general in concentrated solutions than that of (14-9-1). It is frequently necessary to add a term $\beta_{12}\mu_2^2$ to equations (14-9-6) to (14-9-8). We have avoided a completely general formulation of these relationships because each additional empirical parameter tends to obscure the physical significance of the rest.

[62] The solution of this equation is obtained by a short series of successive approximations because, in this calculation, μ_T is not known at the start.

result because no solubility measurements in the mixtures would be required.

(ii) If the activity coefficient of electrolyte (1) is known in pure water over a sufficiently high concentration range to evaluate B_{R1}, then $\mathcal{P}_{1(0)}$ and α_{12} can be determined from one solubility measurement in the pure solvent, and one in the presence of the co-solute. These activity coefficient data are frequently available.

(iii) If B_{R1} is not known, the constants can be obtained from three solubility measurements in the presence of the co-solute. This result is noteworthy because, through B_{R1} and equation (14-9-1), solubility data in mixtures at high ionic strength are seen to predict the activity coefficient of the saturating solute in pure water. Unfortunately, activity coefficients obtained in this manner are subject to large errors, because uncertainties in the data and departures from equation (14-9-8) are magnified by the form of this equation.

It is important to note that the application of equation (14-9-8) to actual solubility calculations requires that neither B_{R1} nor α_{12} varies with the total ionic strength, μ_T. In Section (6), we have shown that for some electrolytes at high concentrations, B_{R1} fulfills this condition very closely [Fig. (14-6-3)]. That part of the computations which depends upon this equation may be expected to be quite accurate for many electrolytes. On the other hand, the assumption that α_{12} is not a function of the concentration may introduce considerable error in some cases. For example, Tables (14-6-1) and (14-6-2), and Figs. (14-6-1) and (14-6-2) show that although α_{12} and α_{21} very little with m at high concentrations in sodium chloride-hydrochloric acid mixtures, they vary considerably in potassium chloride-hydrochloric acid mixtures. These facts are in agreement with the recent calculations of Åkerlöf[63] of the solubility of sodium and potassium chlorides in hydrochloric acid solutions. He found that the equations,

$$\tfrac{1}{2} \log m_{\text{NaCl}} = 0.7782 + 0.0875\mu_T - \tfrac{1}{2} \log \mu_T - \log \gamma_{R(T)}$$
$$- 0.0530 m_{\text{HCl}} + 0.0005 m_{\text{HCl}}^2 \tag{14-9-9}$$

and

$$\tfrac{1}{2} \log m_{\text{KCl}} = 0.4621 + 0.118\mu_T - \tfrac{1}{2} \log \mu_T - \log \gamma_{R(T)}$$
$$- 0.0512 m_{\text{HCl}} + 0.00167 m_{\text{HCl}}^2 \tag{14-9-10}$$

will represent accurately the solubilities, m_{NaCl} and m_{KCl}, at 25°. These are identical with (14-9-8) except for the additional terms in m_{HCl}^2. The first terms on the right of these equations are the values of $1/2 \log K_1$, and -0.0875 and -0.118 are the values of B_{R1} for these systems, respectively. The last two terms in each of these equations replace the last term in

[63] G. Åkerlöf, Private communication.

equation (14-9-8). This not only indicates that the parameter, α_{12}, varies with concentration, but that it changes more rapidly in the potassium than in the sodium chloride system. This result is in accord with the data in Table (14-6-1) which indicate the $(-\alpha_{21})$[64] decreases more rapidly in the potassium than in the sodium chloride system. The numerical values of these quantities, determined from the solubility data and the data in more dilute solutions, are in rough agreement, but, up to the present, an accurate fit of the material from these two sources has not been obtained.

Åkerlöf[65] has applied extended forms of equations (14-9-8) to a number of ternary and quaternary systems, and the quinary system, NaCl-KCl-MgCl$_2$-MgSO$_4$-water.

(10) Application of Cross Differentiation Equations to Solutions Containing Two Electrolytes

The thermodynamic treatment of systems containing two electrolytes and the solvent component has been advanced considerably by Glueckauf,[66] McKay[67-69] and their colleagues. Their contributions demonstrate the value of introducing the cross differentiation equations (1-12-2). We shall consider two aspects of the application of these equations, the extension and generalization of the theory given in Section (6) of this Chapter and the ingenious methods of treatment of McKay.[70]

We rewrite equations (14-4-3) and (14-4-4) in the form

$$\log \gamma_1 = \log \gamma_{1(0)} - \alpha_{12}\mu_2 + \Delta_1 \qquad (14\text{-}10\text{-}1)$$

$$\log \gamma_2 = \log \gamma_{2(0)} - \alpha_{21}\mu_1 + \Delta_2 \qquad (14\text{-}10\text{-}2)$$

$$\mu_1 + \mu_2 = \mu = \text{constant} \qquad (14\text{-}10\text{-}3)$$

The quantities Δ_1 and Δ_2 represent deviations to be determined experimentally for each individual system.[71] For the present, we shall omit any speculation regarding the nature or magnitude of these deviations.

Consider the cross differentiation equation (1-12-2).

$$\nu_1\left(\frac{\partial \log \gamma_1}{\partial m_2}\right)_{m_1} = \nu_2\left(\frac{\partial \log \gamma_2}{\partial m_1}\right)_{m_2} \qquad (14\text{-}10\text{-}4)$$

---

[64] Note that α_{21} in Table (14-6-1) corresponds to α_{12} in equation (14-9-8).

[65] G. Åkerlöf, *J. Phys. Chem.*, **41**, 1053 (1937).

[66] E. Glueckauf, H. A. C. McKay and A. R. Mathieson, *J. Chem. Soc.*, S. 299 (1949); *Trans. Faraday Soc.* **47**, 428 (1951).

[67] H. A. C. McKay, *Ibid.*, **48**, 1103 (1952); **49**, 237 (1953).

[68] H. A. C. McKay and A. R. Mathieson, *Ibid.*, **47**, 428 (1951).

[69] I. L. Jenkins and H. A. C. McKay, *Ibid.*, **50**, 107 (1954).

[70] H. A. C. McKay and Perring, *Ibid.*, **49**, 163 (1953); H. A. C. McKay, *Ibid.*, **51**, 903 (1955).

[71] H. S. Harned and R. Gary, *J. Am. Chem. Soc.*, **76**, 5924 (1954).

To extend the theory to two electrolytes of all types, we let

$$\mu_1 = (\mu - \mu_2) \equiv jm_1; \qquad \mu_2 = (\mu - \mu_1) \equiv km_2 \qquad (14\text{-}10\text{-}5)$$

in which j and k are constants each of which is characteristic of the valence type of electrolyte. Using this notation, equation (14-10-4) becomes,

$$\nu_1 k \left(\frac{\partial \log \gamma_1}{\partial \mu} \right)_{\mu_1} = \nu_2 j \left(\frac{\partial \log \gamma_2}{\partial \mu} \right)_{\mu_2} \qquad (14\text{-}10\text{-}6)$$

If both equations (14-10-1) and (14-10-2) are valid ($\Delta_1 = \Delta_2 = 0$)

$$\log \gamma_1 = \log \gamma_{1(0)} - \alpha_{12}(\mu - \mu_1) \qquad (14\text{-}10\text{-}7)$$

$$\log \gamma_2 = \log \gamma_{2(0)} - \alpha_{21}(\mu - \mu_2) \qquad (14\text{-}10\text{-}8)$$

then

$$\nu_1 k \left[\frac{d \log \gamma_{1(0)}}{d\mu} - \alpha_{12} - (\mu - \mu_1) \frac{d\alpha_{12}}{d\mu} \right]$$
$$= \nu_2 j \left[\frac{d \log \gamma_{2(0)}}{d\mu} - \alpha_{21} - \mu_1 \frac{d\alpha_{21}}{d\mu} \right] \qquad (14\text{-}10\text{-}9)$$

where total may replace the partial coefficients since $\gamma_{1(0)}$, $\gamma_{2(0)}$, α_{12} and α_{21} are functions of μ only. As a further consequence of this latter condition the coefficient of μ_1 must vanish if the equality is to hold for all values of μ and μ_1. Thus

$$\frac{d(\nu_1 k \alpha_{12} + \nu_2 j \alpha_{21})}{d\mu} = 0 \qquad (14\text{-}10\text{-}10)$$

$$\nu_1 k \alpha_{12} + \nu_2 j \alpha_{21} = \text{constant} \equiv S' \qquad (14\text{-}10\text{-}11)$$

This result, first established by Glueckauf, is most useful as a criterion for deciding whether equation (14-10-8) is obeyed when equation (14-10-7) is known to be valid from experimental data.

TABLE (14-10-1). SUM OF PARAMETERS ($\alpha_{12} + \alpha_{21}$) FOR THE SYSTEMS, HX + MX, IN WATER AT 25°

$-(\alpha_{12} + \alpha_{21})$

System	$t \setminus \mu$	0.5	1	1.5	2	3
HCl-LiCl	25	0.005	0.007	0.007	0.007	0.009
HCl-NaCl	10	.030	.031	.029	.027	—
	20	.026	.028	.027	.031	—
	25	.025	.026	.027	.027	.027
	30	.023	.025	.026	.028	
HCl-KCl	25	.012	.016	.014	.007	−.008
HCl-CsCl	25	−.035	−.040	−.046	−.048	−.047
HBr-LiBr	25	.029	.025	.025	.026	—
HBr-NaBr	25	.032	.032	.031	.026	—
HBr-KBr	25	−.012	−.011	−.015	−.015	—

Equation (14-10-11) can be applied to the data recorded in Tables (14-6-1) and (14-6-2). We recall that α_{12} was determined experimentally and α_{21} was computed upon the assumption that $\log \gamma_2$ of the salt varied linearly according to equation (14-10-8). For 1-1 electrolytes, equation (14-10-11) requires that $S' = \alpha_{12} + \alpha_{21}$ be constant at constant temperature. Values of this quantity are given in Table (14-10-1). An observed constancy of these values of $(\alpha_{12} + \alpha_{21})$, particularly at ionic strengths greater than one is good evidence for the linear variation rule for both electrolytes. However, the variation of $(\alpha_{12} + \alpha_{21})$ with the total ionic strength for the hydrochloric acid-potassium chloride and -cesium chloride systems is sure evidence that deviations from the linear relations (14-10-7) and (14-10-8) occur. The deviation may be expressed by quadratic terms [Equation (14-8-1)] but when the complicated nature of the possible interactions in mixtures of this kind is contemplated, it seems probable that the quadratic form may prove inadequate.

(11) Extension of Thermodynamic Theory to Include Higher Valence Type Electrolytes

The theory outlined in Section (5) of this chapter has been extended by Harned and Gary[72] to include solutions of two electrolytes of any valence types to which equations (14-10-7) and (14-10-8) apply. The Gibbs-Duhem equations becomes

$$\frac{\nu_1\mu_1}{j} d \ln \gamma_1 + \frac{\nu_2\mu_2}{k} d \ln \gamma_2 + \frac{\nu_1}{j} d\mu_1 + \frac{\nu_2}{k} d\mu_2 = -55.51 \, d \ln a_w \quad (14\text{-}11\text{-}1)$$

by utilizing the relations (14-10-5). Now, introduce the variable $0 \leqq x \leqq 1$ so that

$$\mu_1 = x\mu \quad (14\text{-}11\text{-}2)$$

$$\mu_2 = (1 - x)\mu \quad (14\text{-}11\text{-}3)$$

$$d \log \gamma_1 = -\alpha_{12} \, d\mu_2 = \alpha_{12}\mu \, dx \quad (14\text{-}11\text{-}4)$$

$$d \log \gamma_2 = -\alpha_{21} \, d\mu_1 = -\alpha_{21}\mu \, dx. \quad (14\text{-}11\text{-}5)$$

$$d\mu_1 = -d\mu_2 \quad (14\text{-}11\text{-}6)$$

If these relations are employed, equation (14-11-1) becomes

$$\left(\frac{\nu_1}{j}\alpha_{12} + \frac{\nu_2}{k}\alpha_{21}\right) x \, dx + \left(\frac{\nu_1}{2.3j\mu} - \frac{\nu_2}{2.3k\mu} - \frac{\nu_2}{k}\alpha_{21}\right) dx$$

$$= -\frac{55.5}{2.3\mu^2} d \ln a_w \quad (14\text{-}11\text{-}7)$$

upon suitable rearrangement. Integrating between the limits $x = 0$ and x

[72] H. S. Harned and R. Gary. *J. Am. Chem. Soc.*, **76**, 5924 (1954).

$$\left(\frac{\nu_1}{j}\alpha_{12} + \frac{\nu_2}{k}\alpha_{21}\right)\frac{x^2}{2} + \left(\frac{\nu_1}{2.3j\mu} + \frac{\nu_2}{2.3k\mu} - \frac{\nu_2}{k}\alpha_{21}\right)x$$

$$= -\frac{55.5}{2.3\mu^2}\ln\frac{a_{w(x)}}{a_{w(0)}} \tag{14-11-8}$$

This equation expresses the solvent activity in all solutions at constant pressure, temperature at a fixed total ionic strength providing α_{12} and α_{21} which are functions of μ are known. For convenience in the subsequent calculations, it is customary to express the water activity in terms of the practical osmotic coefficient, ϕ.

The practical osmotic coefficient for aqueous solutions is defined by

$$\mu_w = \mu_w^0 - \frac{\phi RT}{55.5}\Sigma m_i \tag{14-11-9}$$

where μ_w is the chemical potential of the solvent, μ_w^0 is its chemical potential in a chosen standard state and the summation is over the molalities of all the ionic species present. Since the solvent activity is defined by the expression

$$\mu_w = \mu_w^0 + RT\ln a_w \tag{14-11-10}$$

it follows that

$$\ln a_w = -\frac{\phi}{55.5}\Sigma m_i \tag{14-11-11}$$

$$\ln a_w = -\frac{\phi_1}{55.5}\nu_1 m_1 \tag{14-11-12}$$

$$\ln a_w = -\frac{\phi_2}{55.5}\nu_2 m_2 \tag{14-11-13}$$

for the single electrolytes 1 and 2, respectively. In a solution containing both electrolytes 1 and 2

$$\mu_1 = x\mu = \frac{m_1}{2}(\nu_{1+}z_{1+}^2 + \nu_{1-}z_{1-}^2) \tag{14-11-14}$$

$$\mu_2 = (1 - x)\mu = \frac{m_2}{2}(\nu_{2+}z_{2+}^2 + \nu_{2-}z_{2-}^2) \tag{14-11-15}$$

Electrical neutrality requires the equalities

$$\nu_{1+}z_{1+} = \nu_{1-}z_{1-}, \quad \nu_{2+}z_{2+} = \nu_{2-}z_{2-} \tag{14-11-16}$$

and since $\nu_1 = \nu_{1+} + \nu_{1-}$, $\nu_2 = \nu_{2+} + \nu_{2-}$

$$m_1 = \frac{2x\mu}{\nu_1 z_{1+}z_{1-}} \tag{14-11-17}$$

$$m_2 = \frac{2(1 - x)\mu}{\nu_2 z_{2+}z_{2-}} \tag{14-11-18}$$

Therefore

$$\Sigma m_i = \nu_1 m_1 + \nu_2 m_2 = 2\mu \left[\frac{x}{z_{1+}z_{1-}} + \frac{(1-x)}{z_{2+}z_{2-}} \right] \tag{14-11-19}$$

In these equations the subscripts $1+$, $1-$, $2+$, $2-$, indicate, respectively, the cations and anions of electrolytes 1 and 2. As a consequence of equations (14-11-4), (14-11-5) and (4-11-9)

$$- \log a_{w(x)} = \frac{2\mu\phi_x}{(2.3)(55.5)} \left[\frac{x}{z_{1+}z_{1-}} + \frac{(1-x)}{z_{2+}z_{2-}} \right] \tag{14-11-20}$$

This equation in combination with (14-11-8) yields the expression

$$\left(\frac{\nu_1}{j} \alpha_{12} + \frac{\nu_2}{k} \alpha_{21} \right) \frac{x^2}{2} + \left(\frac{\nu_1}{2.3j\mu} - \frac{\nu_2}{2.3k\mu} - \frac{\nu_2}{k} \alpha_{21} \right) x$$

$$= \frac{2}{2.3\mu} \frac{\phi_2}{z_{2+}z_{1-}} + \frac{2\phi_x}{2.3\mu} \left[\frac{x}{z_{1+}z_{1-}} + \frac{(1-x)}{z_{2+}z_{2-}} \right] \tag{14-11-21}$$

which may be used to calculate the osmotic coefficient and, hence, the water activity and vapor pressure for a solution of any composition of two strong electrolytes provided that α_{12} and α_{21} are known at a particular total ionic strength, μ, of the mixture, that the osmotic coefficient ϕ_2 for electrolyte 2 alone is available, and that both linearity rules (14-10-7) and (14-10-8) are obeyed.

In the next section, we shall consider electromotive force investigations which lead to the accurate determination of α_{12}. To determine α_{21} from α_{12} and the osmotic coefficients ϕ_1 and ϕ_2 of electrolytes 1 and 2 in pure water, equation (14-11-21) is integrated over the entire range of x, that is, from $x = 0$, corresponding to a solution of electrolyte 1 alone, to $x = 1$, which corresponds to a solution of electrolyte 2. The result is

$$\frac{1}{2} \left(\frac{\nu_1}{j} \alpha_{12} + \frac{\nu_2}{k} \alpha_{21} \right) + \left(\frac{\nu_1}{2.3j\mu} - \frac{\nu_2}{2.3k\mu} - \frac{\nu_2}{k} \alpha_{21} \right)$$

$$= \frac{2}{2.3\mu} \left(\frac{\phi_1}{z_{1+}z_{1-}} - \frac{\phi_2}{z_{2+}z_{2-}} \right) \tag{14-11-22}$$

which, after replacing j and k by their equivalents μ_1/m_1 and μ_2/m_2 and rearranging, reduces to

$$\frac{\alpha_{21}}{z_{2+}z_{2-}} = \frac{\alpha_{12}}{z_{1+}z_{1-}}$$

$$- \frac{2}{2.3\mu} \left[\left(\frac{\phi_1}{z_{1+}z_{1-}} - \frac{\phi_2}{z_{2+}z_{2-}} \right) - \left(\frac{1}{z_{1+}z_{1-}} - \frac{1}{z_{2+}z_{2-}} \right) \right] \tag{14-11-23}$$

analogous to (14-5-7) which we applied to 1-1 electrolyte mixtures.

(12) The Activity Coefficient of Hydrochloric Acid in Chloride Solutions of the Types, MCl_n, at Constant Total Ionic Strength

Since the use of cells of the types

$$H_2 \mid HCl(m_1), MX_n(m_2) \mid AgCl\text{-}Ag$$

had not been fully exploited for studying mixtures containing unsymmetrical type electrolytes, measurements of high accuracy of cells containing the systems HCl-$BaCl_2$, HCl-$SrCl_2$, HCl-$AlCl_3$, HCl-$ThCl_4$, and HCl-$CdCl_2$ have been made with the purpose of testing the limits of validity of the linear relationships given by equation (14-10-7) and (14-10-8).

Since the electromotive force method leads to the determination of the activity coefficient, γ_1, of one of the components, hydrochloric acid, the method of computation employed in Section (5) of this chapter is a suitable one. If $\log \gamma_1$ varies linearly with $m_1(\Delta_1 = 0)$, the assumption will be made that the logarithm of the activity coefficient of the salt, $\log \gamma_2$, also varies linearly with its concentration, m_2. Then, from the measured coefficient, α_{12}, α_{21} is computed from ϕ_1 and ϕ_2 by equation (14-11-23). For these mixtures of hydrochloric acid and higher valence type chlorides, $z_{1+} = z_{1-} = z_{2-} = 1$ and as a result equation (14-11-23) reduces to

$$\frac{\alpha_{21}}{z_{2+}} = \alpha_{12} - \frac{2}{2.303\mu}\left[\left(\phi_1 - \frac{\phi_2}{z_{2+}}\right) - \left(1 - \frac{1}{z_{2+}}\right)\right] \qquad (14\text{-}12\text{-}1)$$

The extent of the validity of the assumption regarding the linear variation of $\log \gamma_2$ may then be tested by equation (14-10-11) which requires that S' is not a function of the total molality.

Table (14-12-1) contains some and Table (14-2-1A) all of the results of

Table (14-12-1). Observed and Calculated Activity Coefficients of Hydrochloric Acid in Chloride Solutions of the Types, MCl_n.

m_1 = molality of hydrochloric acid.
$\Delta\gamma_1$ = (γ obs. − γ calc.) $\times 10^4$; $t = 25°$

BaCl₂($\mu = 1$)			SrCl₂($\mu = 5$)			AlCl₃($\mu = 5$)	
m_1	γ_1	$\Delta\gamma_1$	m_1	γ_1	$\Delta\gamma_1$	γ_1	$\Delta\gamma_1$
1.0	0.8111	−1	5.0	2.380	0	2.380	−10
.9	.7972	−20	4.5	2.224	−10	2.216	20
.8	.7881	9	4.0	2.080	−10	2.059	0
.7	.7755	0	3.5	1.949	30	1.916	20
.6	.7640	0	3.0	1.821	10	1.780	0
.5	.7529	3	2.5	1.701	−10	1.657	20
.4	.7413	−1	2.0	1.592	0	1.537	−20
.3	.7302	2	1.5	1.489	10	1.431	0
.2	.7201	6	1.	1.489	−10	1.322	−90
.1	.7077	−11	0.5	—	—	1.225	−130
.01	.6990	0	—	—	—	—	—

Equations used for calculations:
$BaCl_2(\mu = 1)$; $\log \gamma_1 = -0.09086 - 0.0651\ \mu_2$
$SrCl_2(\mu = 5)$; $\log \gamma_1 = +0.37651 - 0.0582\ \mu_2$
$AlCl_3(\mu = 5)$; $\log \gamma_1 = +0.37651 - 0.0631\ \mu_2$

Harned and Gary[73] which characterize the behaviors of the systems HCl-BaCl$_2$, HCl-SrCl$_2$ and HCl-AlCl$_3$. In Table (14-12-1), the molalities and the activity coefficient of the acid, the equation used for its calculation, and the deviations in the fourth decimal place of log γ_1 from the linear formula are recorded. For the barium and strontium chloride systems, the linear variation rule holds with surprising accuracy. The same agreement is found for the barium chloride system at 2 and 3 total μ, for the strontium chloride system at 1 and 3 total μ, and for aluminum chloride system at 1 and 3μ.

TABLE (14-12-2). OSMOTIC COEFFICIENTS, PARAMETERS, α_{12} AND α_{21}, AND S'

(1) BaCl$_2$

μ	$\phi_1^{(a)}$	ϕ_2	α_{12}	$-\alpha_{21}$	S'
1	1.039	0.864	0.0651	0.0716	0.176
2	1.188	.996	.0653	.0824	.145
3	1.348	.934	.0672	.0866	.143

(2) SrCl$_2$

1	1.039	0.869	0.0581	0.0646	0.155
3	1.348	1.009	.0579	.0836	.097
5	1.680	1.192	.0582	.0868	.089

(3) AlCl$_3$

1	1.039	0.831	0.0614	0.0636	0.482
2(b)	1.188	.905	.062	.099	.348
3	1.348	1.007	.0629	.1113	.310
5	1.680	1.272	.0631	.1179	.286

(4) CeCl$_3$

1	1.039	0.795	0.0870	0.0177	0.973
2	1.188	.847	.0908	.0426	.919
3	1.348	.914	.0918	.0510	.898

(a) The osmotic coefficients were obtained from the data in Tables (13-1-2A) and (13-7-1A).

(b) Computed from the data of Harned and Mason, Ref. (34).

An observable deviation occurs with the aluminum chloride system at 5μ as evidenced by the deviation in the last column of the table.

In Table (14-12-2), values of α_{21} computed from the observed value of α_{12} and the osmotic coefficients of the acid and salt in water, ϕ_1 and ϕ_2, respectively, are compiled. Similar values computed from the results of Mason and Kellam[74] are also recorded in this table. The last column con-

[73] H. S. Harned and R. Gary, *J. Am. Chem. Soc.* **76**, 5924 (1954); **77**, 1994 (1955); **77**, 4696 (1955).

[74] C. M. Mason and D. B. Kellam, *J. Phys. Chem.*, **38**, 689 (1934).

contains the values of S' computed by equation (14-10-11). It appears that this quantity is higher at 1μ than at the higher concentrations in all cases. This evidence indicates that the linear variation rule is not strictly valid for the variation of both activity coefficients at this concentration. In the next section, an examination of these results by an ingenious method due to McKay will be presented.

(13) Activity Coefficients in Mixtures Containing Two Electrolytes by the Methods of McKay[75, 76]

By application of the cross differentiation equations (1–12–1) in the form

$$\left(\frac{\partial \ln a_1}{\partial n_w}\right)_{n_1, n_2} = \left(\frac{\partial \ln a_w}{\partial n_1}\right)_{n_2, n_w} = \cdots \tag{14-13-1}$$

McKay and Perring have derived relations which are particularly useful for the computation of activity coefficients in mixtures from isopiestic vapor pressure measurements. Since it is very convenient to equilibrate a solution of constant mole ratios, n_1/n_2, at different concentrations with standard reference solutions, McKay and Perring choose n_1/n_2 and a_w as independent variables. Thus

$$\left[\frac{\partial \ln a_1}{\partial \left(\dfrac{n_w}{n_2}\right)}\right]_{n_1/n_2} = \left[\frac{\partial \ln a_w}{\partial \left(\dfrac{n_1}{n_2}\right)}\right]_{n_w/n_2} \tag{14-13-2}$$

Upon introducing the molalities and multiplying by

$$\left[\frac{\partial \left(\dfrac{1}{m_2}\right)}{\partial \ln a_w}\right]_{m_1/m_2}$$

one obtains

$$\left(\frac{\partial \ln a_1}{\partial \ln a_w}\right)_{m_1/m_2} = -55.51 \left[\frac{\partial \left(\dfrac{1}{m_2}\right)}{\partial \left(\dfrac{m_1}{m_2}\right)}\right]_{a_w} \tag{14-13-3}$$

Now, if $\dfrac{m_1}{m_2}$ is constant, it can be shown that

$$d \ln a_1 = \nu_1 d \ln \mu\gamma_1 \tag{14-13-4}$$

where

$$\mu = \mu_1 + \mu_2 = jm_1 + km_2 \tag{14-13-5}$$

[75] H. A. C. McKay and J. K. Perring, *Trans. Faraday Soc.*, **49**, 163 (1953).
[76] H. A. C. McKay, *Ibid.*, **51**, 903 (1955).

and where j and k are the valence factors defined by equation (14-10-5). If these latter two relations and the fractions

$$x_1 = jm_1/\mu; \qquad x_2 = km_2/\mu$$

be introduced in equation (14-13-2),

$$0.018\nu_1 \left(\frac{\partial \ln \mu\gamma_1}{\partial \ln a_w}\right)_{x_1} = -\left(\frac{j}{\mu^2}\right)\left(\frac{\partial \mu}{\partial \ln x_2}\right)_{a_w} - \frac{j}{\mu} \qquad (14\text{-}13\text{-}6)$$

The integrands of this equation are not convenient for extrapolation to infinite dilution. However, if a solution of the first electrolyte whose activity coefficient is designated γ_R at concentration m_R in pure solvent is equilibrated isopiestically with the mixed solution, a useful expression can be obtained by introducing the Gibbs-Duhem equation in the form

$$\nu_1 \, d \ln \gamma_R m_R = -\frac{55.51j}{m_R} \, d \ln a_w \qquad (14\text{-}13\text{-}7)$$

into equation (14-13-6). The result upon integration at constant x_1 is

$$0.018\nu_1 \ln \frac{\mu\gamma_1}{m_R\gamma_R} = j \int_0^{\ln a_w} \left(-\frac{\partial \mu}{\mu^2 \partial \ln x_2}\right)_{a_w} - \left(\frac{1}{\mu} + \frac{1}{m_R}\right) d \ln a_w \qquad (14\text{-}13\text{-}8)$$

The isopiestic data yield $(\partial\mu/\partial \ln x_2)_{a_w}$, μ and m_R and since γ_R is known, γ_1 may be computed. Equation (14-13-8) is well calculated to yield valuable results in the study of mixtures by the isopiestic method.

McKay[77] has devised an alternative method to the one deduced in Sections (5) and (11) of this chapter for cases where the activity coefficient of one of the electrolytes in a solution containing two electrolytes may be determined experimentally. McKay considers the simple case where it is found that the activity coefficient, γ_1, varies according to the linear relationship (14-10-7). Knowing α_{12}, from experiment, he then proceeds to show that α_{21} may be evaluated without the assumption that the linear relationship (14-10-8) is valid for the second electrolyte.

By substituting equations (14-10-7) and (14-10-8) in cross differentiation equation (14-10-6) with no assumption regarding α_{21} we obtain

$$\nu_1 k \left[\left(\frac{\partial \log \gamma_{1(0)}}{\partial \mu}\right)_{\mu_1} - \alpha_{12} - \mu_2 \left(\frac{\partial \alpha_{12}}{\partial \mu}\right)_{\mu_1}\right]$$
$$= \nu_2 j \left[\left(\frac{\partial \log \gamma_{2(0)}}{\partial \mu}\right)_{\mu_2} - \left(\frac{\partial(\alpha_{21}\mu_1)}{\partial \mu}\right)_{\mu_2}\right] \qquad (14\text{-}13\text{-}9)$$

Since $\gamma_{1(0)}$, $\gamma_{2(0)}$ and α_{12} are functions of μ only, the partial can be replaced by total differential coefficients in all terms but the one containing α_{21}. Thus

---

[77] H. A. C. McKay, *Nature*, **169**, 464 (1952).

$$\nu_1 k \left[\frac{d \log \gamma_{1(0)}}{d\mu} - \alpha_{12} - \mu_2 \frac{d\alpha_{12}}{d\mu} \right]$$

$$= \nu_2 j \left[\frac{d \log \gamma_{2(0)}}{d\mu} - \left(\frac{\partial(\alpha_{21}\mu_1)}{\partial\mu} \right)_{\mu_2} \right] \tag{14-13-10}$$

Upon rearrangement and integration at constant μ_2 between the limits $\mu = \mu_2$ and $\mu = \mu$, we obtain

$$\nu_2 j \alpha_{21}\mu_1 = \nu_2 j \log \gamma_{2(0)} \Big]_{\mu_2}^{\mu} - \nu_1 k \log \gamma_{1(0)} \Big]_{\mu_2}^{\mu}$$

$$+ \nu_1 k \int_{\mu_2}^{\mu} \alpha_{12} \, d\mu + \nu_1 k \mu_2 \alpha_{12} \Big]_{\mu_2}^{\mu} \tag{14-13-11}$$

Thus, knowing α_{12} at a given total ionic strength, μ, α_{21} at this ionic strength can be computed at each value of μ_1 if the activity coefficients $\gamma_{1(0)}$ and $\gamma_{2(0)}$ are known. Further the method affords a means of determining the nature of the deviation Δ_2 in equation (14-10-2) provided Δ_1 in equation (14-10-1) is zero.

The limiting value of α_{21} at $\mu_1 = \mu$ and μ_2 approaches zero follows from equation (14-13-11) and and is given by

$$\nu_2 j \alpha_{21(\mu)} = \nu_2 j \log \gamma_{2(0)} - \nu_1 k \log \gamma_{1(0)} + \nu_1 k \int_0^{\mu} \alpha_{12} \, d\mu \tag{14-13-12}$$

The other limiting expression obtained when μ_1 tends to zero is

$$\nu_2 j \alpha_{21(0)} = \nu_2 j \frac{d \log \gamma_{1(0)}}{d\mu} + \nu_1 k \mu \frac{d\alpha_{12}}{d\mu} - \nu_1 k \frac{d \log \gamma_{2(0)}}{d\mu} + \nu_1 k \alpha_{12} \tag{14-13-13}$$

Equations (14-13-11) to (14-13-13) are equivalent to (14-5-7) when Akerlöf and Thomas' relation $\log (\gamma_{1(0)}/\gamma_{2(0)}) = B\mu$ holds and when α_{12} does not vary with μ.

Figure (14-13-1) represents this method of evaluating α_{21} from α_{12} for the hydrochloric acid-potassium chloride system for which both α_{12} and $(\alpha_{12} + \alpha_{21})$ vary with the total concentration. It appears that at 2, 3, 4, and 5 total molalities (ionic strength) that α_{21} is a linear function of m_2. The plots are straight lines within errors of evaluation and are parallel with equal slope -0.0065. This result furnishes direct evidence that for many systems containing 1-1 electrolytes the relation

$$\alpha_{21} = \alpha_{21(0)} + \beta_{21}\mu_1 = \alpha_{21(\mu)} - \beta_{21}\mu_2 \tag{14-13-14}$$

is a suitable one, consistent with equations of the type (14-8-1) containing quadratic terms. A summary of the β-coefficients for 1-1 electrolyte mixtures compiled by McKay is given in Table (14-13-1). For a number of these systems, the linear equations for both electrolytic components express the results. The hydroxide-salt systems discussed in Section (3), the hydrochloric acid-potassium chloride system and the lithium chloride-cesium chloride systems show the most pronounced deviations from the linear rules.

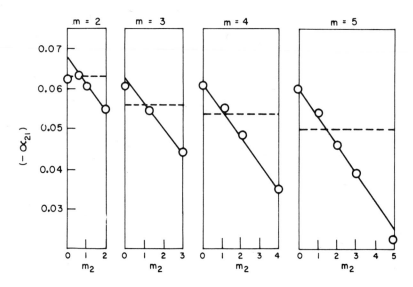

Fig. (14-13-1). Calculation of $-\alpha_{21}$ for the system, HCl-KCl-H$_2$O, according to the method of McKay.

TABLE (14-13-1). THE COEFFICIENTS β_{12} AND β_{21} FOR 1-1 ELECTROLYTE
MIXTURES IN WATER AT 25°

System	Total μ	β_{12}	β_{21}	Ref.
HCl, LiCl..........	1–2	0.000	0.000	(1)
	3–5	.000	(.002)*	(1)
HCl, NaCl.........	2–6	.000	.000	(1)
HCl, KCl..........	2–5	.000	.0065	(1)
LiCl, NaCl.........	2–6	−.001	−.001	(2)
LiCl, KCl..........	2–5	−.0025	−.0025	(2)
LiCl, CsCl.........	2–6	.001	.005	(3)
LiCl, LiNO$_3$......	2–10	−.0014	−.0014	(2)
NaCl, KCl.........	2–5	.000	.000	(4)
NaCl, CsCl........	2–6	.000	.000	(5)
NaCl, NaOH.......	0.5	−.080	.000	(6)
	1.	−.020	−.029	(6)
	3.	—	−.005	(7)
	5.	—	(−.002)*	(7)
KCl, CsCl..........	2–5	.000	.000	(3)
KCl, KOH......:..	1	−.034	−.056	(6)
	3–5	—	−.004	(7)

* Rough value.

(1) H. A. C. McKay, *loc. cit.* (2); R. A. Robinson and C. K. Lim, *Trans. Faraday Soc.*, **49**, 1144 (1953); (3) R. A. Robinson, *Ibid.*, **49**, 1147 (1953); (4) R. A. Robinson, *J. Am. Chem. Soc.*, **74**, 6035 (1952); (5) R. A. Robinson, "Electrochemical Constants," p. 171, National Bureau of Standards Circular 524 (1953); *J. Am. Chem. Soc.*, **74**, 6035 (1952); (6) H. S. Harned and M. A. Cook, *Ibid.*, **59**, 1870 (1937); (7) H. S. Harned and J. M. Harris, *Ibid.*, **50**, 2633 (1928).

Table (14-13-2) contains a calculation of α_{21} by McKay's method for hydrochloric acid-barium chloride and hydrochloric acid-strontium chloride systems. The constancy of these values of α_{21} indicates that these systems can be computed with high accuracy by use of the linear equations.

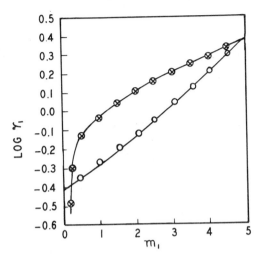

Fig. (14-13-2).

The activity coefficient of hydrochloric acid in cadmium chloride and thorium chloride solutions at a constant total stoichiometric ionic strength of 5.

$\otimes$, Thorium chloride.

$\bigcirc$, Cadmium chloride.

TABLE (14-13-2). THE LINEAR COEFFICIENTS α_{21} FOR THE SYSTEMS: $HCl\text{-}BaCl_2\text{-}H_2O$ AND $HCl\text{-}SrCl_2\text{-}H_2O$*

BaCl$_2$		SrCl$_2$			
$\mu = 3$		$\mu = 5$		$\mu = 3$	
μ_1	$-\alpha_{21}$	μ_1	$-\alpha_{21}$	μ_1	$-\alpha_{21}$
0.0	0.076	0.0	0.085	0.0	0.090
.3	.086	.8	.091	.3	.090
.9	.083	1.4	.096	.9	.089
1.5	.086	2.	.096	1.5	.087
1.8	.086	2.3	.096	1.8	.086
3.0	.085	2.6	.095	3.0	.078
$\mu = 2$		2.9	.094	$\mu = 1$	
.5	.085	3.5	.092	0.0	0.064
.8	.084	3.8	.092	1.0	0.063
2.	.081	5.0	.085	—	—

* Computed by Dr. Alan B. Gancy. *Dissertation,* Yale University, June (1956).

The hydrochloric acid-aluminum chloride system as anticipated from the results in Table (14-12-1) indicates a value of -0.007 for β_{21} at total ionic strength of 3.*

* W. J. Argersinger, Jr. and D. M. Mohilner (*J. Phys. Chem.*, **61**, 99 (1957)) have subjected these results to a careful numerical analysis and have reached the conclusion that the linear variation rule holds for the salt component within narrow limits, but that the small deviations found are significant.

In figure (14-13-2), the logarithm of the coefficient of hydrochloric acid in cadmium and thorium chlorides from the data in Table (14-12-1A) at a total stoichiometrical ionic strength of 5μ are plotted against the acid concentration. These curves illustrate the complications which result from ionic interactions such as the formation of $CdCl^+$ and the probable presence of complexes of high molecular weight which are present in the thorium chloride solutions.[78]   In these and other cases involving weak electrolytes, the stoichiometric ionic strength has little significance.

We have restricted the above treatment to the determination of the thermodynamic properties of these mixtures of concentrated solutions of electrolytes. More elaborate interpretations of the subject which make use of Brönsted's theory of specific ionic interaction are presented by Scatchard and Breckenridge[79] and by Guggenheim.[80]

[78] K. A. Kraus and R. W. Holmberg, *J. Phys. Chem.* **58**, 325 (1954).

[79] G. Scatchard and R. C. Breckenridge, *J. Phys. Chem.*, **58**, 596 (1954).

[80] E. A. Guggenheim, *Kgl. Danske Videnskab. Selskab, Mat.-fys. Medd.*, **30**, No. 14, 1–10 (1955).

Chapter (15)

The Ionization and Thermodynamic Properties of Weak Electrolytes*

In Chapter (7), the most recent methods of computing the ionization constants of strong electrolytes in media of low dielectric constant, and of weak electrolytes in aqueous solution from conductance measurements were considered. In most cases, the ionization constants from this source are known accurately at 25° only and, therefore, yield no knowledge regarding heats of ionization or other thermochemical quantities associated with the ionization reactions.

Most of the accurate data on the variation of ionization constants with temperature have been derived from measurements of cells without liquid junction containing weak electrolytes. Also, the only accurate ionization constants yet obtained in water-non-aqueous solvent mixtures, over considerable temperature ranges, have been derived from cells without liquid junction. In this chapter, the basis of this method and its application to the determination of the ionization constants of water, weak acids, and ampholytes in water, in aqueous salt solutions, and in organic solvent-water mixtures, will be discussed. Methods of computing the variation of ionization constants with temperature will be described, and tables of the thermochemical quantities associated with ionization reactions will be considered.

In general, two types of cells without liquid junction may be employed. The first type, which contains a buffer solution, is especially adapted for the determination of ionization constants in pure solvents, in mixed solvents and in salt solutions. The second type, containing unbuffered solutions yields additional information concerning medium effects. In several of these respects the electromotive force method is superior to the conductance method.

Cells involving unknown liquid junctions have been used in the study of weak electrolytes, but since these are usually unsuitable for rigorous thermodynamic purposes, they will be used in the present discussion as an occasional source of information to supplement that now available from the cells without liquid junction.†

---

* Parts of this chapter follow closely a review by H. S. Harned and B. B. Owen, *Chem. Rev.*, **25**, 31 (1939).

† Note discussion of the use of cells with liquid junction in Chapter (10), Section (7).

Quite recently, with the development of completely objective photoelectric technique, accurate determinations of ionization constants and ionization in salt solutions have been made. Some of these results will be discussed, and contrasted with those derived from electromotive force measurements.

(1) The Ionization Constant of Water

Since water is the most important weak electrolyte, the thermodynamics of its ionization process has received much attention. Early accurate determinations of its ionization constant were made by conductance measurements[1] and by electrometric measurements of cells with liquid junctions. In view of the great experimental difficulties, the values of K_w (0.59×10^{-14} at 18° and 1.04×10^{-14} at 25°) estimated conductometrically are in remarkable agreement with the most recent electrometric values (0.58×10^{-14} at 18° and 1.008×10^{-14} at 25°). Cells with liquid junctions similar to the one originally used by Arrhenius

$$H_2 \mid NaOH(m) \mid NaCl(m) \mid HCl(m) \mid H_2$$

have frequently been employed.[2] By the use of the Lewis and Sargent[3] equation for liquid junction potentials and the substitution of mean for individual ionic activities, Lewis, Brighton and Sebastian[4] obtained the value 1.012×10^{-14} for K_w at 25° in good agreement with 1.008×10^{-14} derived from cells without liquid junctions.

The first application of cells without liquid junction to the study of the ionization of water was the determination of the ionization product, $m_H m_{OH}$, and the activity coefficient function, $\gamma_H \gamma_{OH}/a_{H_2O}$, in salt solutions at 25°.[5] This latter quantity was shown to approach the limiting law for activity coefficients in dilute salt solutions.[6] The calculations involved the use of an ionization constant determined from other data. In subsequent investigations, the cells without liquid junction,

$$H_2 \mid HX(m) \mid AgX\text{-}Ag \qquad\qquad I$$

$$H_2 \mid MOH(m_1), MX(m_2) \mid AgX\text{-}Ag \qquad\qquad II$$

$$H_2 \mid HX(m_1), MX(m_2) \mid AgX\text{-}Ag \qquad\qquad III$$

[1] F. Kohlrausch and A. Heydweiller, *Z. physik. Chem.*, **14**, 317 (1894); *Ann. Physik.*, **53**, 209 (1894); F. Kohlrausch, *Z. physik. Chem.*, **42**, 193 (1903); A. Heydweiller, *Ann. Physik.*, [4], **28**, 503 (1909).

[2] S. Arrhenius, *Z. physik. Chem.*, **11**, 808 (1893); A summary of the early determinations of K_w is given by H. T. Beans and E. T. Oakes, *J. Am. Chem. Soc.*, **42**, 2116 (1920).

[3] G. N. Lewis and L. W. Sargent, *J. Am. Chem. Soc.*, **31**, 363 (1909).

[4] G. N. Lewis, T. B. Brighton, and R. L. Sebastian, *J. Am. Chem. Soc.*, **39**, 2245 (1917).

[5] H. S. Harned, *J. Am. Chem. Soc.*, **47**, 930 (1925); H. S. Harned and F. E. Swindells, *Ibid.*, **48**, 126 (1926); H. S. Harned and G. M. James, *J. Phys. Chem.*, **30**, 1060 (1926).

[6] H. S. Harned, *Trans. Faraday Soc.*, **23**, 462 (1927).

were employed in certain combinations for the determination of the ionization constant itself, as well as $m_H m_{OH}$ and $\gamma_H \gamma_{OH} / a_{H_2O}$ in salt solutions.

The electromotive forces of these cells are all expressed by the equivalent relations

$$E = E^0 - \frac{RT}{F} \ln a_H a_X \qquad (15\text{-}1\text{-}3)$$

and

$$E = E^0 - \frac{RT}{F} \ln \gamma_H \gamma_X m_H m_X \qquad (15\text{-}1\text{-}4)$$

where the subscript X refers to chloride, bromide, or iodide. The meaning to be attached to the quantities, γ_H, γ_X, m_H, and m_X, is largely derived from extra-thermodynamical considerations. Consider cell I containing only the halide acid. All of the evidence discussed in chapter (11) indicates that the halide acids are very strong electrolytes. We shall assume that they are completely ionized at all ionic strengths, and consequently that m_H is the sum of the (molal) concentrations of protons and solvated protons, and that m_X is the sum of the concentrations of the halide ion and solvated halide ion. Any deviations from this hypothesis will require corrections to the values we shall obtain for $m_H m_{OH}$ and $\gamma_H \gamma_{OH} / a_{H_2O}$ in salt solutions, but will not affect the determination of the ionization constant, K_w.[6a] Further, since m_H and m_X are actual stoichiometric molalities, $\gamma_H \gamma_X$ is the activity coefficient product of a completely ionized electrolyte, obeying the limiting law of the interionic attraction theory.

These considerations are equally applicable to the cell

$$\text{H}_2 \mid \text{MOH}(m_1), \text{MX}(m_2) \mid \text{AgX-Ag} \qquad \text{II}$$

used to determine the ionization constant of water. It is assumed that the strong base, MOH (usually an alkali hydroxide), and MX are completely ionized, so that m_{OH} is the sum of the molalities of the hydroxyl ions and hydrated hydroxyl ions. The electromotive force of this cell is given by equation (15-1-4). In this case, the hydrogen ion concentration is determined by the equation for ionization of water,

$$K_w = \frac{\gamma_H \gamma_{OH}}{a_{H_2O}^x} m_H m_{OH} \qquad (15\text{-}1\text{-}5)$$

and is now expressed in terms of the independent variable, m_{OH}. Since the subscripts, H and OH, include the hydrated ions, the exponent x is unity, or greater, depending upon the extent of hydration. There is evidence that the hydration of the proton is virtually complete in aqueous solutions, but in the absence of exact information regarding the hydration of ions, we shall adopt the convention of writing $x = 1$. This convention will introduce no error in subsequent thermodynamic computations, but

---

[6a] F. G. R. Gimblett and C. B. Monk, *Trans. Faraday Soc.*, **50**, 965 (1954), have estimated dissociation constants of the hydroxides from these data.

should not be overlooked in interpreting the mechanism of the ionization. Thus, if x is made unity, the elimination of m_H between equations (15-1-4) and (15-1-5), results in the expression

$$\frac{(E_{II} - E^0)F}{2.303RT} + \log \frac{m_X}{m_{OH}} = \log \frac{\gamma_{OH}}{\gamma_X \, a_{H_2O}} - \log K_w \qquad (15\text{-}1\text{-}6)$$

Since the term, $\log \gamma_{OH}/\gamma_X a_{H_2O}$, is proportional to the ionic strength in dilute solutions, a plot of the left-hand member against μ should yield $(-\log K_w)$ by linear extrapolation to infinite dilution. In Figure (15-1-1)

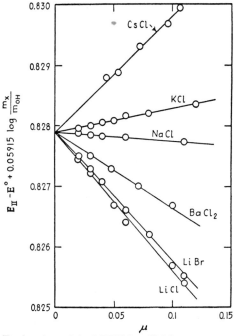

Fig. (15-1-1). Evaluation of $(-0.05915 \log K_w)$ by measurements in various salt solutions at 25°.

six independent extrapolations of this type are shown. If the experiment is limited to the evaluation of K_w only, it may be convenient to keep m_X/m_{OH} constant[7] throughout a series of dilutions. In the measurements represented in the figure,[8-13] however, m_X was varied, while m_{OH} was kept

[7] E. J. Roberts, *J. Am. Chem. Soc.*, **52**, 3877 (1930).

[8] H. S. Harned and O. E. Schupp Jr., *J. Am. Chem. Soc.*, **52**, 3892 (1930): CsOH-CsCl.

[9] H. S. Harned and W. J. Hamer, *Ibid.*, **55**, 2194 (1933): KOH-KCl.

[10] H. S. Harned and H. R. Copson, *Ibid.*, **55**, 2206 (1933): LiOH-LiCl.

[11] H. S. Harned and G. E. Mannweiler, *Ibid.*, **57**, 1873 (1935): NaOH-NaCl.

[12] H. S. Harned and J. G. Donelson, *Ibid.*, **59**, 1280 (1937): LiOH-LiBr.

[13] H. S. Harned and C. G. Geary, *Ibid.*, **59**, 2032 (1937): Ba(OH)₂-BaCl₂.

constant and equal to 0.01, so that the data could also be used in subsequent calculations of other quantities. The plots are all linear within the range shown, and their intercepts have been made identical without injustice to the data. The reproducibility of the electromotive forces is about 0.05 mv., and it is probable that the extrapolated value of K_w is accurate to 0.2% at 25°.

There is another combination of cells which yields the ionization constant of water without recourse to the standard potential, $\mathbf{E}^0$. By combining cells of types II and III,

$$\mathrm{H_2 \mid HX}(m_1),\ \mathrm{MX}(m_2) \mid \mathrm{AgX\text{-}Ag} \qquad\qquad \mathrm{III}$$

we obtain the expression

$$\frac{(\mathbf{E_{II}} - \mathbf{E_{III}})\mathbf{F}}{2.303RT} = \log \frac{(\gamma_\mathrm{H}\,\gamma_\mathrm{X}\,m_\mathrm{H}\,m_\mathrm{X})_\mathrm{III}}{(\gamma_\mathrm{H}\,\gamma_\mathrm{X}\,m_\mathrm{H}\,m_\mathrm{X})_\mathrm{II}} = \log \frac{(m_\mathrm{H}\,m_\mathrm{X})_\mathrm{III}}{(m_\mathrm{H}\,m_\mathrm{X})_\mathrm{II}} \qquad (15\text{-}1\text{-}7)$$

The second equality involves the premise that the activity coefficient of the acid is the same in the acid-salt solution as in the hydroxide-salt solution. This assumption is closely approximated under the experimental conditions, since both the acid and hydroxide concentrations are only $0.01M$. In the next section, a method is presented by which these concentrations may be made zero by a series of extrapolations at constant ionic strengths, but the correction is usually less than 0.03 mv. when $m_1 = 0.01$, and may be safely neglected. Accordingly the value of the function, $\gamma_\mathrm{H}\gamma_\mathrm{OH}/a_\mathrm{H_2O}$, in either of the cells II or III may be identified with its value in a pure solution of the salt, MX, at an ionic strength corresponding to $m_1 + m_2$. With this in mind, the elimination of $(m_\mathrm{H})_\mathrm{II}$ between equations (15-1-7) and (15-1-5) leads to the expression

$$\frac{(\mathbf{E_{II}} - \mathbf{E_{III}})\mathbf{F}}{2.303RT} - \log \frac{(m_\mathrm{H}\,m_\mathrm{X})_\mathrm{III}}{(m_\mathrm{X}/m_\mathrm{OH})_\mathrm{II}} = \log \frac{\gamma_\mathrm{H}\,\gamma_\mathrm{OH}}{a_\mathrm{H_2O}} - \log K_w \qquad (15\text{-}1\text{-}8)$$

in which $\gamma_\mathrm{H}\gamma_\mathrm{OH}/a_\mathrm{H_2O}$ appears without the designation II. According to the Debye-Hückel theory, this quantity can be represented by

$$\log \frac{\gamma_\mathrm{H}\,\gamma_\mathrm{OH}}{a_\mathrm{H_2O}} = -\frac{3.629 \times 10^6}{(DT)^{3/2}}\sqrt{\mu} + f(\mu) \qquad (15\text{-}1\text{-}9)$$

which, upon combination with (15-1-8), yields

$$-\log K_w' \equiv \frac{(\mathbf{E_{II}} - \mathbf{E_{III}})\mathbf{F}}{2.303RT} - \log \frac{(m_\mathrm{H}\,m_\mathrm{X})_\mathrm{III}}{(m_\mathrm{X}/m_\mathrm{OH})_\mathrm{II}}$$
$$+ \frac{3.629 \times 10^6}{(DT)^{3/2}}\sqrt{\mu} = -\log K_w + f(\mu) \qquad (15\text{-}1\text{-}10)$$

Since all of the terms making up the left side of this equation are known experimentally, a plot of this member against μ leads to $(-\log K_w)$ by extrapolation to infinite dilution. Several plots of this nature are shown in Figure (15-1-2), where it will be noticed that the slopes differ from those of the corresponding curves in Figure (15-1-1). This difference is a decided advantage in determining the intercept.[14] The most important property of the extrapolation represented by Figure (15-1-2) is its inde-

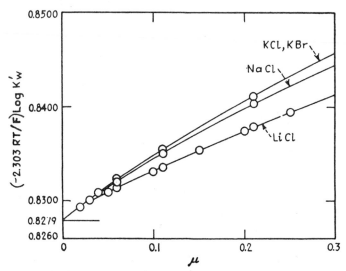

Fig. (15–1–2). Evaluation of K_w at 25° according to equation (15–1–10).

TABLE (15-1-1). THE IONIZATION CONSTANT OF WATER ($P = 1$ atm.)
$K_w \times 10^{14}$

t	KCl[1]	NaCl[2]	BaCl$_2$[3]	LiBr[4]	Weighted Mean
0	0.1142[a]	0.1134	(0.1125)	(0.1132)	0.1139
5	(.1860)	.1850	(.1834)	.1842	.1846
10	(.293)	.2919	(.2890)	.2921	.2920
15	(.452)	.4505	.4506	.4504	.4505
20	.681	.6806	.6815	.6806	.6809
25	1.008	1.007	1.009	1.007	1.008
30	1.471	1.470	1.466	1.467	1.469
35	2.088	2.091	2.090	(2.068)	2.089
40	2.916	2.914	2.920	....	2.919
45	4.016	4.017	4.023	....	4.018
50	5.476	5.482	5.465	....	5.474
55	7.297	......	....	....	7.297
60	9.614	......	....	....	9.614

[1] H. S. Harned and W. J. Hamer, *J. Am. Chem. Soc.*, **55**, 2194 (1933).
[2] H. S. Harned and G. E. Mannweiler, *Ibid.*, **57**, 1875 (1935).
[3] H. S. Harned and C. G. Geary, *Ibid.*, **59**, 2032 (1937).
[4] H. S. Harned and J. G. Donelson, *Ibid.*, **59**, 1280 (1937).
[a] Recalculated.

pendence of standard electrode potentials. It will be seen that the value of K_w is the same as that obtained from Figure (15-1-1).

A comparison of the values of K_w, obtained independently in several of the investigations quoted above, is given in Table (15-1-1). Those re-

[14] H. S. Harned and H. R. Copson, *J. Am. Chem. Soc.*, **55**, 2206 (1933).

sults which we believe to be of most doubtful accuracy are enclosed by parentheses, and are not included in estimating the mean value given in the last column.

(2) The Activity Coefficient Function, $\gamma_H\gamma_{OH}/a_{H_2O}$, and the Ionization Product, $m_H m_{OH}$, in Aqueous Salt Solutions

The first determinations[15–18] of the quantity, $\gamma_H\gamma_{OH}/a_{H_2O}$, required measurements on cells of the types

$$\text{H}_2 \mid \text{MOH}(m_1), \text{MX}(m_2) \mid \text{M}_x\text{Hg} \mid \text{MOH}(m_3) \mid \text{H}_2 \qquad \text{IV}$$

and

$$\text{Ag-AgX} \mid \text{MX}(m_2) \mid \text{M}_x\text{Hg} \mid \text{MX}(m_1) \mid \text{AgX-Ag} \qquad \text{V}$$

in addition to those discussed in the preceding section. The method depends upon the evaluation of the three quantities, $\gamma_H\gamma_X$, $\gamma_M\gamma_{OH}/a_{H_2O}$, and $\gamma_M\gamma_X$, in solutions of the pure salt, MX, at the same concentration. The combination of these quantities yields $\gamma_H\gamma_{OH}/a_{H_2O}$ in the salt solution at this particular concentration. Thus

$$(\gamma_H\gamma_X)(\gamma_M\gamma_{OH}/a_{H_2O})/(\gamma_M\gamma_X) = \gamma_H\gamma_{OH}/a_{H_2O} \qquad (15\text{-}2\text{-}1)$$

The evaluation of $\gamma_M\gamma_X$ is carried out with the aid of Cell V by methods outlined in Chapter (10), section (4). Cells I and III, or Cell III, and the value of $\mathbf{E}^0$ derived from Cell I, can be used to determine $\gamma_H\gamma_X$ in the mixture, HX-MX, in various proportions at a given constant total molality. Then, by making use of the linear variation of log $\gamma_H\gamma_X$ with m_{HX}, discussed in Chapter (14), Section (4), it is a simple matter to obtain $\gamma_H\gamma_X$ in the pure salt solution by extrapolation to zero concentration of acid. The application of the same procedure to the results derivable from Cell IV yields values of $\gamma_M\gamma_{OH}/a_{H_2O}$ in salt solutions at zero concentration of hydroxide.

The method just described is accurate and thermodynamically sound, but it is laborious since it requires the use of the inconvenient flowing amalgam electrode. This inconvenience is now avoided by the use of cells of types II and III. Since K_w is known, equation (15-1-8) may be rewritten

$$\frac{(\mathbf{E}_{II} - \mathbf{E}_{III})\mathbf{F}}{2.303RT} - \log\frac{(m_H m_X)_{III}}{(m_X/m_{OH})_{II}} + \log K_w = \log\frac{\gamma_H\gamma_{OH}}{a_{H_2O}} \qquad (15\text{-}2\text{-}2)$$

to give $\gamma_H\gamma_{OH}/a_{H_2O}$ directly. The ionization product, $m_H m_{OH}$, is obtained by dividing this quantity into K_w, in accordance with equation (15-1-5). This method has been used to determine the ionization of water in aqueous

[15] H. S. Harned, *J. Am. Chem. Soc.*, **47**, 930 (1925).
[16] H. S. Harned and F. E. Swindells, *Ibid.*, **48**, 126 (1926).
[17] H. S. Harned and G. M. James, *J. Phys. Chem.*, **30**, 1060 (1926).
[18] H. S. Harned and O. E. Schupp Jr., *J. Am. Chem. Soc.*, **52**, 3892 (1930).

solutions of the chlorides and bromides of sodium, potassium and lithium, and the chlorides of cesium, strontium and barium, over the concentration range 0 to $3M$, and at temperatures ranging from 0 to 50, or 60°.

It is very important to recall that in these calculations, we have assumed that all the strong electrolytes in the cells (HX, MOH and MX) are completely ionized at all concentrations. If this assumption is not true, then the values of $m_H m_{OH}$ are not strictly the product of the actual molali-

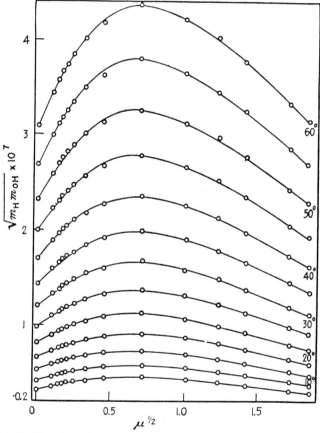

Fig. (15-2-1). The dissociation of water in potassium chloride solutions at 5° intervals.

ties of these ions in the salt solutions. The present results, however, may be corrected in the future for any deviations found from the assumption of complete ionization. However, the value of $m_H m_{OH}$ when the salt concentration is zero, or K_w, will not be altered because these deviations vanish on extrapolation.

The effect of temperature and concentration upon $m_H (= \sqrt{m_H m_{OH}})$ in potassium chloride solutions[19] is illustrated in Figure (15-2-1). It is seen

[19] H. S. Harned and W. J. Hamer, *J. Am. Chem. Soc.*, **55**, 2194 (1933).

that the ionization attains a maximum at about $0.7M$, and this maximum becomes increasingly pronounced at higher temperatures.

Values of both $\gamma_H\gamma_{OH}/a_{H_2O}$ and m_Hm_{OH} in a series of salt solutions at 25° are plotted against $\sqrt{\mu}$ in Figure (15-2-2). The complete results at various temperatures are compiled in Table (15-2-1A). They have been

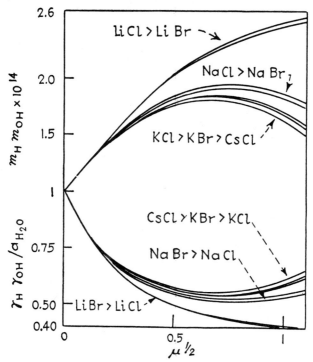

Fig. (15-2-2). The ionic activity coefficient product and ionization of water in some halide solutions at 25°.

TABLE (15-2-1). CONSTANTS FOR EQUATIONS (15-2-5) TO (15-2-7)

Salt	d	b_0	$b_1 \times 10^4$	c_0	$c_1 \times 10^4$	$\Delta_{ave.}$
KCl.............	3.6	0.266	5.20	−0.0350	−4.88	0.0027
NaCl............	3.6	.198	2.00	− .0085	−2.0	.0032
LiCl............	3.6	.039	2.00	+ .0325	−4.0	.0025
KBr............	4.2	.205	12.75	− .016	−9.0	.0022
NaBr............	4.2	.157	6.75	+ .010	−6.57	.0035
LiBr............	4.2	.000	0.000	+ .0475	−2.20	.0041

partially summarized by Harned and Cook[20] in terms of the Debye-Hückel equation,

$$\log \frac{\gamma_H \gamma_{OH}}{a_{H_2O}} = \frac{-2\mathfrak{S}_{(f)}\sqrt{\mu}}{1 + A'\sqrt{\mu}} + B\mu + C\mu^{3/2} \qquad (15\text{-}2\text{-}3)$$

[20] H. S. Harned and M. A. Cook, *J. Am. Chem. Soc.*, **59**, 2304 (1937).

in which

$$\mathbb{S}_{(f)} = 1.814 \times 10^6/(DT)^{3/2} \qquad (15\text{-}2\text{-}4)$$

and

$$A' = \mathring{a}50.30/(DT)^{1/2} \qquad (15\text{-}2\text{-}5)$$

Values of D are given in Table (5-1-3). For convenience in calculation and tabulation, it was assumed that the empirical parameters, B and C, vary linearly with temperature

$$B = b_0 + b_1 t \qquad (15\text{-}2\text{-}6)$$

$$C = c_0 + c_1 t \qquad (15\text{-}2\text{-}7)$$

and that $\mathring{a}$ is independent of temperature. The constants are recorded in Table (15-2-1). In spite of the arbitrary selection of common $\mathring{a}$-values for the chlorides and bromides, respectively, and a simple temperature dependence for the parameters, the constants given in Table (15-2-1) will reproduce the experimental results within $\frac{1}{2}$ to 1 percent at all concentrations up to $3M$, and at any temperature between 0 and 40°, except in lithium chloride solutions where the errors exceed 1% below 10°. In sodium and potassium chloride solutions, the representation may be satisfactorily extended to 50°. The average deviations, Δ_{ave}, between the observed values of log $\gamma_H\gamma_{OH}/a_{H_2O}$ and those calculated by equation (15-2-3) are recorded in the last column of Table (15-2-1). If we had allowed all of the parameters to be unrestricted, these deviations would not have exceeded the experimental errors.

The order in which the curves in Figure (15-2-2) arrange themselves deserves some comment. At a given concentration, the ionization of water is greater in solutions containing ions of smaller radii in the crystalline state. This effect could be predicted, qualitatively at least, from the greater polarization of the water molecules under the immediate influence of the high charge density of the smaller ions. The data are not sufficiently consistent to allow a determination of the exact functional dependence of solvent dissociation upon ionic radii, but the regular and inverse nature of this dependence can be seen in Figure (15-2-3). This effect has already been illustrated by Harned and Mannweiler[21] who arbitrarily used $\Sigma 1/a_i (\equiv 1/a_+ + 1/a_-)$ as the abscissa. We have used $\Sigma 1/a_i^2$ as a variable because the average charge density on the ions is proportional to this quantity. The ionic radii were taken from Table (5-1-6).

Although it would be unwise to draw any quantitative conclusions from Figure (15-2-3), the equation,

$$\log \frac{\gamma_H \gamma_{OH}}{a_{H_2O}} = \log \frac{K_w}{m_H m_{OH}} = A - B\Sigma \frac{1}{a_i^2} \qquad (15\text{-}2\text{-}8)$$

[21] H. S. Harned and G. E. Mannweiler, *J. Am. Chem. Soc.*, **57**, 1873 (1935).

representing the straight lines through the points, suggests that results of this kind may eventually be used to separate the effect of the salt into two distinct parts. The effect of interionic forces may be associated with the term A, while the effect of polarization of the solvent molecules may appear only in the term, $B\Sigma 1/a_i^2$, which is proportional to the mean charge densities. The plausibility of such a separation is increased by the fact that the parameter B increases steadily with concentration, while A first decreases with concentration, passes through a minimum at about $0.4M$, and thereafter increases with concentration according to the familiar behavior of the activity coefficient of a strong 1-1 electrolyte.

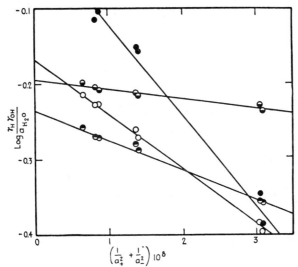

Fig. (15-2-3). Dependence of $\gamma_H\gamma_{OH}/a_{H_2O}$ in salt solutions upon ionic radii of the salts. $\bullet$, $2.01\,M$; $\bigcirc$, $1M$; $\ominus$, $0.5\,M$; $\ominus$, $0.11\,M$ ($t = 25°$).

(3) The Effect of Temperature and Pressure on the Ionization of Water. Thermochemical Quantities*

In view of the lack of an exact theoretical equation for expressing the ionization constant as a function of the temperature, and of the fact that ionization constants are known accurately only over comparatively short temperature ranges (0 to 60° at most), it is difficult to know which of the possible empirical equations to use. The usual method has been to assume that ΔH_i^0 can be expressed as a power series in T,

$$\Delta H_i^0 = A - BT - CT^2 + \cdots \tag{15-3-1}$$

$$\Delta C_{p_i}^0 = -B - 2CT + \cdots \tag{15-3-2}$$

whence

$$\ln K_w = -\frac{A}{RT} - \frac{B}{R}\ln T - \frac{C}{R}T + D + \cdots \tag{15-3-3}$$

* H. S. Harned and R. A. Robinson, *Trans. Faraday Soc.*, **36**, 973 (1940).

by substitution in equation (1-10-12), and subsequent integration. The signs of the terms are chosen so that the constants obtained from the experimental values are positive. For a series of results over a limited temperature range, it is never necessary to use terms beyond T^2 in the first of these equations. The evaluation of the constants of equation (15-3-3) from the experimental results by least squares is laborious, and therefore simpler expressions are desirable. One satisfactory simplification is to assume that $\Delta C^0_{p_i}$ is independent of T, or that ΔH^0_i varies linearly with T. Thus,

$$\Delta H^0_i = A - BT \tag{15-3-4}$$

$$\Delta C^0_{p_i} = -B \tag{15-3-5}$$

$$\ln K_w = -\frac{A}{RT} - \frac{B}{R}\ln T + D \tag{15-3-6}$$

Another equation for $\ln K$, which follows immediately from the nature of the original electromotive forces, deserves consideration. We have found that over the temperature range in question, the observed electromotive forces obey a quadratic equation in t within the error of experiment (± 0.05 mv.). Inspection of equation (15-1-6) shows immediately that if both $\mathbf{E}_{II}$ and $\mathbf{E}^0$ are quadratic in T, $\ln K_w$ may be expressed by

$$\ln K_w = -\frac{A}{RT} - CT + D \tag{15-3-7}$$

and, consequently,

$$\Delta H^0_i = A - CT^2 \tag{15-3-8}$$

$$\Delta C^0_{p_i} = -2CT \tag{15-3-9}$$

It is certainly not likely that $\Delta C^0_{p_i}$ is absolutely independent of T, nor that it varies linearly with T, as expressed by equations (15-3-5) and (15-3-9), respectively. We shall show, however, that both equations (15-3-6) and (15-3-7) may be used with equal accuracy for the computation of K_w from 0 to 60°. This will demonstrate that these calculations can not be used to prove or disprove how $\Delta C^0_{p_i}$ varies with T.

The constants in equations (15-3-3), (15-3-6) and (15-3-7) were evaluated by the method of least squares from the values of K_w in Table (15-1-1). The resulting numerical equations and those derived from equation (15-3-3) for computing ΔF^0_i, ΔH^0_i, $\Delta C^0_{p_i}$ and ΔS^0_i are given in the Table (15-3-1). A striking agreement is found with all three equations. Thus the mean deviations are only 0.00045, 0.0005, and 0.0005 in ($-\log K_w$) for the three equations, respectively, and the maximum deviations are 0.0014. The mean deviation corresponds to an error of 0.03 mv. and the maximum deviation to an error of 0.08 mv. which are no greater than the reproducibility of the original electromotive forces. This proves that these results cannot be used to decide whether $\Delta C_{p_i}^0$ is constant, or how this quantity varies with temperature.

The maximum variation in ΔH_i^0 computed by the three equations is 40 cal. at 0°. At 25°, the values of $\Delta C_{p_i}^0$ obtained from equations (15-3-2), (15-3-5) and (15-3-9) are -46.7, -47.0, and -46.5, respectively. However, at higher or lower temperatures, the differences are considerable. Thus at 0° the three equations yield -44.8, -47.0, and -42.6. Since all the equations fit the experiments equally well, it is impossible to say which one of these results is nearest the true value.

In Fig. (15-3-1), values of $(-\log K_w)$, calculated by equations (15-3-3a), (15-3-6a), and (15-3-7a), have been plotted against T. Each of these plots has a maximum in the neighborhood of 550°. The only determinations of K_w at such high temperatures were obtained by Noyes and Kato[22]

TABLE (15-3-1). NUMERICAL VALUES FOR THE COMPUTATION OF $(-\log K_w)$ BY EQUATIONS (15-3-3), (15-3-6) AND (15-3-7), AND OF ΔF_i^0, ΔH_i^0, $\Delta C_{p_i}^0$ AND ΔS_i^0 BY THE EQUATIONS RELATED TO (15-3-3)

(1) Equation (15-3-3) etc.

$$\log K_w = -\frac{5242.39}{T} + 35.3944 - 0.008530T - 11.8261 \log T \qquad \text{(15-3-3a)}$$

(Average deviation of observed from calculated results is 0.00045 in log K. Maximum deviation 0.0014).

$$\Delta F_i^0 = 23984.15 + 54.1047T \log T - 161.9308T + 0.039025T^2$$
$$\Delta H_i^0 = 23984.15 - 23.497T - 0.039025T^2 \qquad \text{(15-3-1a)}$$
$$\Delta C_{p_i}^0 = -23.497 - 0.07805T \qquad \text{(15-3-2a)}$$
$$\Delta S_i^0 = -54.1047 \log T - 0.07805T + 138.4338$$

(2) Equation (15-3-6)

$$\log K_w = -\frac{6013.79}{T} - 23.6521 \log T + 64.7013 \qquad \text{(15-3-6a)}$$

(Average deviation is 0.0005; maximum deviation 0.0014).

(3) Equation (15-3-7)

$$\log K_w = -\frac{4470.99}{T} + 6.0875 - 0.017060T \qquad \text{(15-3-7a)}$$

(Average deviation is 0.0005; maximum deviation 0.0014).

and Sosman[23] from investigations of the hydrolysis of ammonium acetate. These are represented by the circles in the figure, and indicate definitely that a maximum occurs in K_w at the temperature predicted by these equations.

Another unique application of these results is the calculation of ΔH_i, the heat of ionization of water in salt solutions. In a solution of concentration m, the heat of ionization of water is

$$\Delta H_i = \bar{H}_{H^+} + \bar{H}_{OH^-} - \bar{H}_{H_2O} \qquad \text{(15-3-10)}$$

or, in terms of the corresponding relative quantities

$$\Delta H_i = \Delta H_i^0 + \bar{L}_{H^+} + \bar{L}_{OH^-} - \bar{L}_{H_2O} \qquad \text{(15-3-11)}$$

[22] A. A. Noyes and Y. Kato, *Publications Carnegie Institution*, **63**, 153 (1907).
[23] R. B. Sosman, *Publications Carnegie Institution*, **63**, 193 (1907).

Thus, ΔH_i may be divided into two parts. The first part, ΔH_i^0, is independent of the salt concentration, and is related to the temperature coefficient of $\ln K$ by equation (1-10-12). The second part $(\overline{L}_{H^+} + \overline{L}_{OH^-} - \overline{L}_{H_2O})$ varies with the concentration, and is calculable by equation (1-7-5) from the temperature coefficient of the function, $\ln (\gamma_H \gamma_{OH}/a_{H_2O})$. Accordingly,

$$\Delta H_i = RT^2 \frac{\partial \ln K_w}{\partial T} - RT^2 \frac{\partial \ln (\gamma_H \gamma_{OH}/a_{H_2O})}{\partial T} \qquad (15\text{-}3\text{-}12)$$

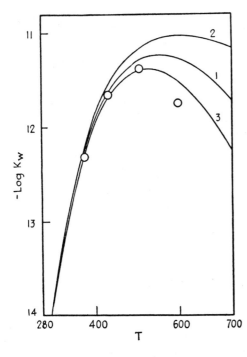

Fig. (15-3-1).
Ionization constant of water as a function of temperature. O, Experimental; 1, Equation (15-3-3a); 2, Equation (15-3-6a); 3, Equation (15-3-7a).

Comparison of this equation with (15-1-8) shows that ΔH_i can be obtained directly from the electromotive force data by the relation

$$\Delta H_i = FT^2 \frac{[\partial(E_{II} - E_{III})/T]}{\partial T} \qquad (15\text{-}3\text{-}13)$$

Similarly, the other quantities are given by

$$\Delta S_i = F \frac{\partial(E_{II} - E_{III})}{\partial T} \qquad (15\text{-}3\text{-}14)$$

and

$$\Delta C_{p_i} = FT \frac{\partial^2(E_{II} - E_{III})}{\partial T^2} \qquad (15\text{-}3\text{-}15)$$

The heats of ionization of water in various salt solutions have been calculated,[24-26] and found to vary linearly with $\mu^{1/2}$ at all concentrations within the experimental uncertainty of 30 to 80 calories. Such a relationship is predicted theoretically for $\bar{L}_{H^+} + \bar{L}_{OH^-} - \bar{L}_{H_2O}$ at high dilutions. Its unexpected validity at higher concentrations permits the determination of ΔH_i^0 by extrapolation of ΔH_i to infinite dilution. Figure (15-3-2) illustrates the behavior of ΔH_i in five different salt solutions at 20°. When the data in the individual salt solutions are extrapolated independently, the intercepts all occur within about ±30 calories of the value of ΔH_i^0 equal to 13,710, and the agreement is of the same order at other temperatures. To avoid confusion in the figure the data are omitted, and the

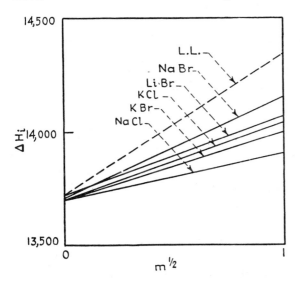

Fig. (15-3-2)
Total heat of ionization of water in some halide solutions at 20°.

results are represented by straight lines with the experimentally observed slopes. The theoretical limiting slope is indicated by the broken line.

In comparing Figure (15-3-2) with the corresponding calorimetric determination illustrated in Figure (8-3-1), it will be noted that the intercepts, ΔH_i^0, obtained by the two independent methods, differ by 40 calories, which appears within the combined uncertainties of the two determinations. The discussion in Chapter (8), Section (3) showed that $(-\Delta H_i)$ in a salt solution can not be identified with ΔH_n, a directly measured heat of neutralization, because of the dilution of the salt ions accompanying neutralization. Furthermore, although ΔH_n^* is ostensibly the heat of neutralization, corrected for the heat of dilution of the salt, it is not the

[24] H. S. Harned and W. J. Hamer, *J. Am. Chem. Soc.*, **55**, 4496 (1933).
[25] H. S. Harned and G. E. Mannweiler, *Ibid.*, **57**, 1873 (1935).
[26] H. S. Harned, *J. Franklin Inst.*, **225**, 623 (1938).

same as $(-\Delta H_i)$ unless the individual ionic heat contents are additive at all concentrations. Therefore, we have refrained from attempting to compare $(-\Delta H_i)$ with ΔH_n^* at any point other than their common limiting value at infinite dilution.[27]

According to equation (1-10-11), the effect of pressure upon the ionization of water is given by

$$\left(\frac{\partial \log K_w}{\partial P}\right)_T = \frac{-\Delta V_i^0}{2.3RT} \qquad (15\text{-}3\text{-}16)$$

where

$$\Delta V_i^0 = \bar{V}_{H^+}^0 + \bar{V}_{OH^-}^0 - \bar{V}_{H_2O}^0 \qquad (15\text{-}3\text{-}17)$$

The quantity, $\bar{V}_{H_2O}^0$, is equal to the molal volume of pure water, or 18.07 cc. at 25° and one atmosphere. The partial molal volume of ionized water may be calculated by linear combination of values of $\bar{V}_2^0$ for strong acids, bases, and salts, since ionic volumes are additive at infinite dilution. For example, we may write

$$\bar{V}_{H^+}^0 + \bar{V}_{OH^-}^0 = \bar{V}_{2(HCl)}^0 + \bar{V}_{2(KOH)}^0 - \bar{V}_{2(KCl)}^0$$

In the same way, $\bar{K}_{H^+}^0 + \bar{K}_{OH^-}^0$ can be obtained by combination of values of $\bar{K}_2^0$ for strong acids, bases and salts, and $\bar{K}_{H_2O}^0$ is equal to $18.02\,\beta_0/d_0$. If $\bar{K}_2^0$ be considered independent of P, then

$$\bar{V}_{2(P)}^0 = \bar{V}_2^0 - \bar{K}_2^0(P-1) \qquad (15\text{-}3\text{-}18)$$

by equation (8-7-2). Here $\bar{V}_{2(P)}^0$ represents a partial molal volume at any pressure, P, and $\bar{V}_2^0$ and $\bar{K}_2^0$ refer to values at $P = 1$. Combination of the preceding three equations leads to the approximate relation

$$\log \frac{K_w}{K_{w(P-1)}} = -\frac{\Delta V_i^0(P-1)}{2.3RT} + \frac{\Delta K_i^0(P-1)^2}{4.6RT} \qquad (15\text{-}3\text{-}19)$$

valid for low pressures.

Fortunately, it is not necessary to neglect the variation of ΔK_i^0 with pressure, for it has been shown[28] that, so long as $\bar{K}_2^0$ is large compared to the molal compression of the pure solute, the limiting partial molal volume of a solute at any pressure is given by

$$\bar{V}_{2(P)}^0 = \bar{V}_2^0 - \bar{K}_2^0 \left(\frac{B+1}{B+P}\right)(P-1) \qquad (15\text{-}3\text{-}20)$$

---

[27] Comparison of $(-\Delta H_i)$ and ΔH_n^*, however, shows a close correspondence. H. S. Harned and W. J. Hamer, *J. Am. Chem. Soc.*, **55**, 4496 (1933); H. S. Harned and G. E. Mannweiler, *Ibid.*, **57**, 1873 (1935); H. S. Harned, *J. Franklin Inst.*, **225**, 623 (1938).

[28] B. B. Owen and S. R. Brinkley Jr., *Chem. Rev.*, **29**, 461 (1941).

The factor, $(B + 1)/(B + P)$, which distinguishes this equation from (15-3-18), accounts for the pressure dependence of $\bar{K}_2^0$ over a considerable range. Combination of this equation with (15-3-16) and (15-3-17) yields the expression

$$\log \left(\frac{K_w}{K_{w\,(P-1)}} \right) = -\frac{\Delta V_i^0 (P - 1)}{2.3RT}$$
$$+ \frac{\Delta K_i^0 (B + 1)}{2.3RT} \left\{ (P - 1) - (B + 1) \ln \left(\frac{B + P}{B + 1} \right) \right\} \tag{15-3-21}$$

which may be used over a pressure range of several thousand atmospheres.

Table (15-3-2) contains average values of $\Delta \bar{V}_i^0$ and $\Delta \bar{K}_i^0$, and shows the results obtained by substituting these values into equation (15-3-21).

TABLE (15-3-2).[a] THE EFFECT OF PRESSURE UPON THE IONIZATION OF PURE WATER

P(bars)[c]	$K_w/K_w(P-1)$						
	5°	15°	25°	35°	45°	$\Delta H_i^0 (25°)$	$\Delta S_i^0 (25°)$
1	1	1	1	1	1	13,500	−18.7
200	1.246	1.225	1.202	1.180	1.163	13,200	−19.4
400	1.543	1.490	1.435	1.384	1.345	12,900	−20.1
600	1.896	1.800	1.703	1.612	1.545	12,600	−20.8
800	2.317	2.163	2.009	1.868	1.766	12,200	−21.8
1000	2.816	2.585	2.358	2.154	2.009	11,800	−22.8
ΔV_i^0	−26.1	−24.9	−23.4	−21.8	−20.6	......	......
ΔK_i^0	......	......	−0.00522[b]	......	......	....	......

[a] B. B. Owen and S. R. Brinkley Jr., *Chem. Rev.*, **29**, 461 (1941).
[b] The value of ΔK_i^0 at 25° was used at all temperatures.
[c] One bar = 0.9869 normal atms.

The ionization constant increases with pressure, and the relative increase is the greater the lower the temperature. At zero degrees, K_w undergoes a threefold increase between 1 and 1000 bars. The positive temperature coefficient of $\Delta \bar{V}_i^0$ (and $\Delta \bar{V}^0$ for some other ionization reactions) indicates that, at sufficiently high temperatures, $\Delta \bar{V}_i^0$ may become positive and cause a decrease in K_w with pressure. The effect of pressure upon ΔH_i^0 and ΔS_i^0 at 25° is shown in the last two columns of Table (15-3-2). These thermochemical quantities, as well as $\Delta C_{p_i}^0$, become more negative with increasing pressure.

Unfortunately, the data at hand are not sufficiently accurate to give us unambiguous information about the effect of pressure upon the temperature of the maximum value of K_w, or K_i for weak electrolytes in general. A brief discussion of this matter, and the effect of pressure upon ionization reactions in salt solutions, is given by Owen and Brinkley.[28]

(4) Determination of the Ionization Constants of Weak Acids and Bases

Ionization constants of weak acids can be derived from measurements of cells without liquid junction containing either an unbuffered solution, or a buffered solution. The unbuffered cell,

$$H_2 \mid HR(m_1), \; MX(m_2) \mid AgX\text{-}Ag \qquad\qquad VI$$

was first used to determine the ionization function, $m_H^2/(m_1 - m_H)$, and the activity coefficient function, $\gamma_H\gamma_{Ac}/\gamma_{HAc}$, in salt solutions,[29] and later for the determination of the ionization constant, K_A.[30] These results yielded a value of 1.75×10^{-5} for K_A for acetic acid at 25°, and further determinations[31] showed that this quantity varied little if at all between 20 and 30°. These values are consistent with recent ones of greater accuracy determined by means of cells containing buffered solutions. A comprehensive analysis of the unbuffered cell will be given in Section (7). It will be shown that activity coefficient, and ionization functions of weak acids in salt solutions as well as ionization constants may be determined by this cell. Further, the medium effects on the properties of the substances in the cells will be thoroughly investigated.

The most direct electrometric determination of the ionization constant of a weak acid makes use of cells of the type[32]

$$H_2 \mid HR(m_1), \; MR(m_2), \; MCl(m_3) \mid AgCl\text{-}Ag \qquad\qquad VII$$

Although such cells are limited to the determination of ionization constants only, they are peculiarly well adapted to this purpose. Buffer action permits accurate and easy measurements of small hydrogen ion concentrations at relatively low ionic strengths. The necessary extrapolation is short and practically linear. The concentrations of the weak acid, HR, and of the two salts, MR and MCl, are made approximately equal, and the cation, M, is usually sodium or potassium. The use of the silver-silver chloride electrode has many practical advantages, but other combinations can be used when this electrode is unsuitable.

The electromotive force of this cell is given by equation (15-1-4), in which $\gamma_H m_H$ may be eliminated by combination with the expression,

$$K_A = \frac{\gamma_H\gamma_R}{\gamma_{HR}} \frac{m_H m_R}{m_{HR}} \qquad\qquad (15\text{-}4\text{-}1)$$

[29] H. S. Harned and R. A. Robinson, *J. Am. Chem. Soc.*, **50**, 3157 (1928).

[30] H. S. Harned and B. B. Owen, *J. Am. Chem. Soc.*, **52**, 5079 (1930).

[31] H. S. Harned and G. M. Murphy *J. Am. Chem. Soc.*, **53**, 8 (1931).

[32] H. S. Harned and R. W. Ehlers, *J. Am. Chem. Soc.*, **54**, 1350 (1932).

for the ionization of the weak acid. The resulting equation is

$$\frac{(E_{VII} - E^0)F}{2.303RT} + \log \frac{m_{Cl}m_{HR}}{m_R} = -\log K_A - \log \frac{\gamma_{Cl}\gamma_{HR}}{\gamma_R} \qquad (15\text{-}4\text{-}2)$$

Since $m_{Cl} = m_3$, $m_{HR} = m_1 - m_H$, and $m_R = m_2 + m_H$, the left-hand member of this equation is known if m_H is negligible compared to m_1 and m_2. If m_H is too large to be neglected, it may be estimated as follows.[33-35] A preliminary value of K_A is obtained from equation (15-4-2) by using the limiting law for activity coefficients, and writing $m_{HR}/m_R = m_1/m_2$. If this value is less than 10^{-4}, m_H is given with sufficient accuracy by $m_H \simeq K_A m_1/m_2$. If necessary, more accurate values of m_H can be derived from a more exact value of K_A, obtained by extrapolation as described below. The number of such successive approximations required increases with the magnitude of K_A. Ionization constants of the order of 10^{-4}, or greater, can also be determined by this method, but the relatively large values of m_H encountered make it necessary either to employ a very long series of approximations,[36] or to avoid the use of equation (15-4-2) altogether. In the latter case, the procedure is based upon the calculation of "apparent" hydrogen ion concentrations[37] directly from the electromotive forces [Section (7)] and equation (15-1-4). Thus, if we rearrange this equation and express the activity coefficients by the limiting law, we obtain

$$- \log m_H' = \frac{(E_{VII} - E^0)F}{2.303\,RT} + \log m_{Cl} - 2\mathfrak{S}_{(f)}\sqrt{\mu d_0} \qquad (15\text{-}4\text{-}3)$$

The ionic strength is approximately

$$\mu \simeq m_2 + m_3 + m_H' \qquad (15\text{-}4\text{-}3)$$

The approximation introduced by the use of the limiting law, which neglects the medium effect of the unionized weak electrolyte, prevents the determination of the true m_H by this method, but the difference between m_H and m_H' decreases rapidly with dilution, and vanishes in the limit. Accordingly, we may calculate an apparent ionization constant, k_A', corresponding to m_H', from equation (15-4-1) and the limiting law. Thus,

$$\log k_A' = -2\mathfrak{S}_{(f)}\sqrt{\mu d_0} + \log \frac{m_H'(m_2 + m_H')}{(m_1 - m_H')} \qquad (15\text{-}4\text{-}5)$$

Log K_A may be obtained by extrapolation[38] of values of log k_A'.

[33] H. S. Harned and R. W. Ehlers, *J. Am. Chem. Soc.*, **54**, 1350 (1932).
[34] L. F. Nims, *Ibid.*, **55**, 1946 (1933).
[35] B. B. Owen, *Ibid.*, **56**, 1695 (1934).
[36] W. J. Hamer, *J. Am. Chem. Soc.*, **56**, 860 (1934); See Chapter (13), Section (8).
[37] H. S. Harned and B. B. Owen, *J. Am. Chem. Soc.*, **52**, 5079 (1930).
[38] L. F. Nims, *J. Am. Chem. Soc.*, **56**, 1110 (1934).

If, as in the case of boric acid, $K_A < 10^{-9}$, the hydrolysis of the acid anion, R, must be considered at high dilutions. Since m_H is quite negligible in solutions of such weak acids, we may write, $m_{HR} = m_1 + m_{OH}$, and, $m_R = m_2 - m_{OH}$, and estimate m_{OH} from the hydrolysis constant,

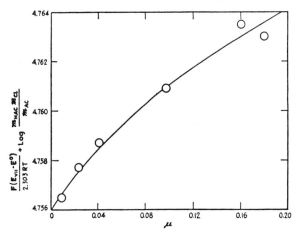

Fig. (15–4–1). Evaluation of ionization constant of acetic acid at 25° according to equation (15–4–2).   Diameters of circles equal 0.02 mv.

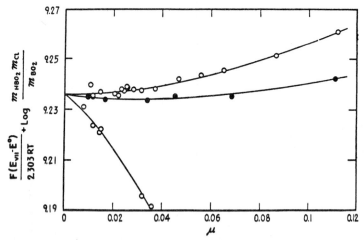

Fig. (15–4–2). Evaluation of the ionization constant of boric acid at 25° according to equation (15–4–2).   The ratio, m_{HBO_2}/m_{BO_2}, is 1 in the upper curve, 1.18 in the center curve, and 2.69 in the lower curve.

K_h, of the acid anion.   A sufficiently accurate value of m_{OH} is given by $m_{OH} \simeq K_h m_2/m_1$, and a suitable value of K_h is obtained from the ratio of K_w, and a rough estimate of K_A.

Returning to equation (15-4-2), it will be seen that the last term on the right contains the logarithm of the ratio of two activity coefficients of the same valence type, and the logarithm of the activity coefficient of a neutral molecule. Since both of these quantities vary little with the ionic strength at high dilution, a plot of the left hand member of equation (15-4-2) against μ permits the determination of $(-\log K_A)$. Figure (15-4-1) illustrates the extrapolation by which the ionization constant of acetic acid[40] is evaluated at 25°.

The tendency of boron to form complex polybasic ions, even in relatively dilute solutions, results in a peculiar plot for the extrapolation function for boric acid. The determination of the first ionization constant of boric acid (H_3BO_3) at 25° is illustrated in Figure (15-4-2). Variation in the ratio, m_1/m_2, has a much more pronounced effect upon the position and shape of the curves than would be observed for acetic acid. The upper curves in Figure (15-4-2) become horizontal at $\mu \simeq 0.01$. This makes extrapolation unnecessary below that concentration. Furthermore, equation (15-4-2) may be rearranged so that $\mathbf{E}^0$ may be determined if K_A is known. The combination of these circumstances, and the stability of iodides in alkaline solutions, has made it possible to determine the standard potential of the silver-silver iodide electrode[41] with much greater ease in borax buffers than by cells containing dilute hydriodic acid solutions. The use of buffer solutions has been found advantageous in determining other standard potentials[42,43] [See Chapter (12), Section (2)].

For polybasic acids, the extrapolation function is complicated by step-wise dissociation, and the presence of polyvalent ions, but this is of little practical importance if the ratios of the constants of the several dissociation processes are greater than 10^3 or 10^4. The second ionization constant of phosphoric acid will be used to illustrate the calculations.[44] The cell used is

$$H_2 \mid MH_2PO_4(m_1), M_2HPO_4(m_2), MCl(m_3) \mid AgCl\text{-}Ag \qquad \text{VIII}$$

and its electromotive force is represented by equation (15-1-4). The second ionization constant of phosphoric acid is given by

$$K_{2A} = \frac{\gamma_H \gamma_{HPO_4}}{\gamma_{H_2PO_4}} \frac{m_H m_{HPO_4}}{m_{H_2PO_4}} \qquad (15\text{-}4\text{-}6)$$

The elimination of $\gamma_H m_H$ between these two expressions leads to

$$\frac{(\mathbf{E}_{VIII} - \mathbf{E}^0)F}{2.303\,RT} + \log \frac{m_{Cl} m_{H_2PO_4}}{m_{HPO_4}} = -\log K_{2A} - \log \frac{\gamma_{Cl} \gamma_{H_2PO_4}}{\gamma_{HPO_4}} \qquad (15\text{-}4\text{-}7)$$

[40] H. S. Harned and R. W. Ehlers, *J .Am. Chem. Soc.*, **54**, 1350 (1932). *Ibid.*, **55**, 652 (1933).

[41] B. B. Owen, *J. Am. Chem. Soc.*, **57**, 1526 (1935); R. K. Gould and W. C. Vosburgh, *Ibid.*, **62**, 1817 (1940).

[42] B. B. Owen and L. Foering, *J. Am. Chem. Soc.*, **58**, 1575 (1936).

[43] R. G. Bates and W. C. Vosburgh, *Ibid.*, **59**, 1188 (1937).

[44] L. F. Nims, *J. Am. Chem. Soc.*, **55**, 1946 (1933).

The last term on the right contains the activity coefficients of two uni-valent ions in the numerator, and of a bivalent ion in the denominator. Application of the Debye-Hückel equation to this term allows its replacement by $- 2\mathcal{S}_{(f)}\sqrt{\mu d_0} \pm \beta\mu$ at high dilution, so that equation (15-4-7) may be written

$$\frac{(E_{VIII} - E^0)F}{2.303RT} + \log \frac{m_{Cl}\, m_{H_2PO_4}}{m_{HPO_4}} + 2\mathcal{S}_{(f)}\sqrt{\mu d_0} = -\log K_{2A} \pm \beta\mu \quad (15\text{-}4\text{-}8)$$

The determination of $(-\log K_{2A})$ by equation (15-4-8) is illustrated in Figure (15-4-3).[44] In the phosphate buffer solutions, the value of m_H is of the order 10^{-7}, which is so small relative to m_1 and m_2 that it was disre-

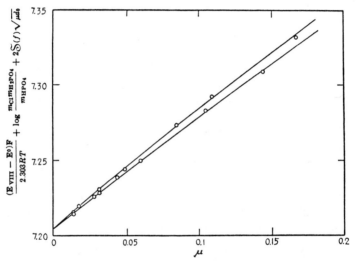

Fig. (15–4–3). Evaluation of the second ionization constant of phosphoric acid at 25° according to equation (15–4–8). Lower curve, sodium salts, $m_1 = m_2$. Upper curve, monosodium phosphate and dipotassium phosphate, $4\, m_1 = 3m_2$.

garded in computing $m_{H_2PO_4}$ and m_{HPO_4}. In general, it will be found that both m_H and m_{OH} may be neglected if $m_1/m_2 \simeq 1$, and K is between 10^{-5} and 10^{-9}.

The electrometric determination of the ionization constants of weak bases is analogous in principle to those just described, but some substitute for the silver-silver chloride electrode must be used in ammoniacal and other basic solutions in which silver chloride is quite soluble. The sodium amalgam electrode is known[45] to give results comparable with those of the silver-silver chloride electrode in a system where both can be used. The use of thallium amalgam has been suggested.[46] The silver-silver

[45] H. S. Harned and B. B. Owen, J. Am. Chem. Soc., **52**, 5091 (1930).
[46] E. J. Roberts, J. Am. Chem. Soc., **56**, 878 (1934).

iodide electrode is a convenient one for this purpose, and will be used to illustrate the method. The electromotive force of the cell,

$$H_2 \mid BOH(m_1), \; BI(m_2) \mid AgI\text{-}Ag \qquad\qquad IX$$

can be expressed by equation (15-1-4), if the substitution of I for Cl is taken into account. The product, $\gamma_H m_H$, can be eliminated by combination with the expressions

$$K_w = \frac{\gamma_H \gamma_{OH}}{a_{H_2O}} \, m_H m_{OH} \qquad\qquad (15\text{-}4\text{-}9)$$

and

$$K_B = \frac{\gamma_B \gamma_{OH}}{\gamma_{BOH}} \frac{m_B m_{OH}}{m_{BOH}} \qquad\qquad (15\text{-}4\text{-}10)$$

The resulting extrapolation function becomes

$$\frac{(E_{IX} - E^0)F}{2.303 \, RT} + \log K_w + \log \frac{m_B m_I}{m_{BOH}} - \mathcal{S}_{(f)}\sqrt{\mu d_0} = \log K_B \pm \beta\mu \qquad (15\text{-}4\text{-}11)$$

upon substitution of $-\mathcal{S}_{(f)}\sqrt{\mu d_0} \pm \beta\mu$ for $\log \gamma_B \gamma_I / \gamma_{BOH}$. Making use of some preliminary measurements[47] on ammonia-ammonium iodide solutions at 25°, it was found that a plot of the left hand member of equation (15-4-11) against μ was linear up to $\mu \simeq 0.1$. The value of K_B obtained by extrapolation, 1.75×10^{-5}, is of the expected order of magnitude. More reliable values of K_B have been derived for the basic ionization of amino-acids, and will be discussed in the next section.

The familiar methods of determining ionization constants by visual colorimetry, either directly, when the weak electrolyte or its ion is colored, or indirectly, by the use of colored indicators and standard buffer solutions, are quite inferior in accuracy to the modern conductometric and electrometric methods. If, however, the subjective visual matching of light intensities is replaced by the completely objective photoelectric technique[48] now available, the most important source of error is eliminated. The resulting "photoelectric colorimetry" is capable of very high accuracy indeed. The first application of the photoelectric method to the precise determination of an ionization constant is the investigation of picric acid by von Halban and Ebert.[49] The apparatus and experimental technique are described by von Halban and Siedentopf.[50] The method is very

[47] B. B. Owen, *J. Am. Chem. Soc.*, **56**, 2785 (1934).

[48] E. Meyer and H. Rosenberg, *Vierteljahres schr. Astron. Ges.*, **48**, 3 (1913).

[49] H. v. Halban and L. Ebert, *Z. physik. Chem.*, **112**, 359 (1924).

[50] H. v. Halban and K. Siedentopf, *Z. physik. Chem.*, **100**, 208 (1922); *Ibid.*, **103**, 71 (1922).

simple in principle, and makes use of the laws of Lambert and Beers in the integrated form,

$$\log \frac{I_0}{I} = \mathcal{E}cx \qquad (15\text{-}4\text{-}11\text{a})$$

Here, I_0 and I represent the intensity of the light before and after traversing x centimeters of the solution, and $\mathcal{E}$ is a constant characteristic of the solution, the temperature, and the wave length of the light. We will conform to the usage of von Halban, and refer to $\mathcal{E}$ as the extinction coefficient. The quantity, $\mathcal{E}c = (1/x) \log (I_0/I)$, will be designated the extinction.

The conditions underlying equation (15-4-11a) have been examined by von Halban,[51] and found to be fulfilled in his experiments. It is assumed that the absorption of light by the acid anion is independent of the nature of the cations present. This introduces an element of uncertainty, but the effect of varying the nature of added neutral salts is very small in dilute solutions, and the hydrogen ion concentrations involved are so small that the specific effects of this ion are presumably negligible.

Von Halban and Kortüm[52] determined the degree of ionization of α-dinitrophenol (1, 2, 4) by comparing the extinctions of solutions of this acid with those of its alkali salts at the same ionic strength. Since the extinction is $\mathcal{E}c\alpha$ in the acid solution and $\mathcal{E}c$ in the salt solution at a given stoichiometric concentration c, the degree of ionization, α, is the ratio of these quantities. In an unbuffered acid solution, the expression for the ionization of a weak acid, HR, is

$$K_A = \frac{y_H y_R}{y_{HR}} \frac{c_H c_R}{c_{HR}} = \frac{y_H y_R}{y_{HR}} \frac{c\alpha^2}{1 - \alpha} \qquad (15\text{-}4\text{-}12)$$

If we write $k_A \equiv c\alpha^2/(1 - \alpha)$, and represent the activity coefficients by the limiting law, this equation becomes

$$\log K_A = -2\mathcal{S}_{(f)}\sqrt{\mu d_0} + \log k_A \qquad (15\text{-}4\text{-}13)$$

The experimental values of $\log k_A$ in solutions of α-dinitrophenol, in pure water, and in various salt solutions[53,54] are plotted against $\sqrt{\mu d_0}$ in the upper portion of Figure (15-4-4), and the straight line is drawn with the theoretical slope 1.013. In the lower part of Fig. (15-4-4), values of log

[51] H. v. Halban and L. Ebert, *Z. physik. Chem.*, **112**, 321 (1924); H. v. Halban and J. Eisenbrand, *Ibid.*, **122**, 337 (1926); **146**, 294 (1930); H. v. Halban and G. Kortüm, *Ibid.*, **A170**, 212, 351 (1934); H. v. Halban and M. Seiler, *Ibid.*, **A181**, 70 (1937); G. Kortüm, *Ibid.*, **B33**, 243 (1936).
[52] H. v. Halban and G. Kortüm, *Z. physik. Chem.*, **A170**, 351 (1934).
[53] H. v. Halban and G. Kortüm, *Z. physik. Chem.*, **A170**, 351 (1934).
[54] H. v. Halban, G. Kortüm and M. Seiler, *Ibid.*, **A173**, 449 (1935).

$k_A - 1.013\sqrt{\mu d_0}$ are plotted against the concentration of undissociated acid, c_u, and the nearly horizontal straight line through these points is drawn to correspond to $\log K_A = \bar{5}.9103$. Although the data for the weak acid alone (upper curve) could be more closely represented by a slope some 20% higher than the theoretical, the results in salt solutions seem satisfactorily expressed by the theoretical value up to $\mu = 0.0004$, or higher. In view of the discussion concerning Figs. (7-6-1) and (7-6-2), we might expect some evidence of a discontinuity at $\mu \simeq 0.0002$, where the data for the pure acid meet the data for the acid in salt solutions, because the concentration of the undissociated molecules varies continuously below

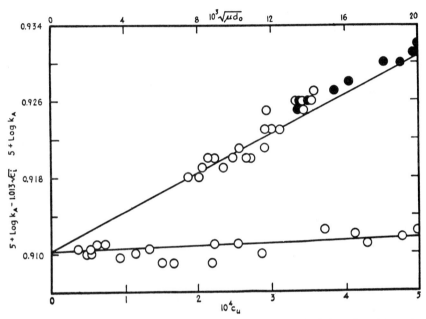

Fig. (15-4-4). Evaluation of the ionization constant of α-dinitrophenol in water at 25°. O, Weak acid alone; ●, Neutral salts present.

this point, but is practically constant above it. In Fig. (7-6-1), the medium effect of the neutral molecules is already appreciable at $\mu \simeq 0.0002$, and increases so rapidly that the data at higher concentrations cannot be used for extrapolation unless this effect is formally provided for, as in Figure (7-6-2). In Figure (15-4-4), however, the conditions are quite different. The medium effect is practically constant from $\mu = 0.0002$ upwards, so the results in the more concentrated range of the plot may furnish a more reliable test of the limiting law than those in the more dilute range. Therefore, it seems justifiable to employ data up to $\mu = 0.0004$ in determining the limiting slope, and to consider the data satisfactorily represented by the theoretical slope within the experimental uncertainty.

The average deviation of the points from the curves is about 1/4 per cent, and only five or six points deviate as much as 1/2 per cent. These deviations are of the same order as those encountered in electrometric determinations of ionization constants from cells without liquid junctions (0.05 mv. average, with 0.1 mv. maximum).[55] It should be remarked, however, that the colorimetric method is often applicable at concentrations outside the range which can be investigated by the use of cells.

(5) Determination of the Ionization Constants of Ampholytes

The determination of the ionization of the most important ampholyte, water, by cells without liquid junctions, has been discussed in Section (1). The other ampholytes which have been investigated by this method have all been aliphatic amino acids. The electrically neutral molecules of these compounds in solution have been shown[56-59] to be mainly zwitterions (amphions), bearing a positive and negative charge. Indicating such molecules by $Z^{\pm}$, the acidic and basic dissociation of a simple amino-acid may be represented by,

$$ZH^+ \rightleftharpoons Z^{\pm} + H^+ \tag{15-5-1}$$

and

$$ZOH^- \rightleftharpoons Z^{\pm} + OH^- \tag{15-5-2}$$

and the corresponding ionization constants by [60,61]

$$K_A = \frac{\gamma_Z \gamma_H}{\gamma_{ZH}} \frac{m_Z m_H}{m_{ZH}} \tag{15-5-3}$$

and

$$K_B = \frac{\gamma_Z \gamma_{OH}}{\gamma_{ZOH}} \frac{m_Z m_{OH}}{m_{ZOH}} \tag{15-5-4}$$

The most convenient determination of acidic ionization is performed with cells containing approximately equal concentrations of amino-acid and its hydrochloride. The electromotive force of the cell,

$$H_2 \mid Z^{\pm}(m_1), \; HCl(m_2) \mid AgCl\text{-}Ag \qquad\qquad X$$

[55] In comparing the two methods, H. v. Halban and G. Kortüm [*Z. physik. Chem.*, **A170**, 351 (1934)] unintentionally include the effects of impurities in sample, and neglect the medium effect in their estimate of the accuracy of the electrometric method, but omit these factors in estimating the accuracy of their photoelectric determination.

[56] E. Q. Adams, *J. Am. Chem. Soc.*, **38**, 1503 (1916).

[57] N. Bjerrum, *Z. physik. Chem.*, **104**, 147 (1923).

[58] J. T. Edsall and M. H. Blanchard, *J. Am. Chem. Soc.*, **55**, 2337 (1933).

[59] J. Wyman Jr. and T. L. McMeekin, *Ibid.*, **55**, 908, 915 (1933).

[60] N. Bjerrum, *Z. physik. Chem.*, **104**, 147 (1923).

[61] H. S. Harned and B. B. Owen, *J. Am. Chem. Soc.*, **52**, 5091 (1930).

is given by equation (15-1-4), and elimination of $\gamma_H m_H$ by (15-5-3) leads to

$$\frac{(E_x - E^0)F}{2.3\,RT} + \log \frac{m_{Cl}\,m_{ZH}}{m_Z} + \log \frac{\gamma_{Cl}\gamma_{ZH}}{\gamma_Z} = -\log K_A \qquad (15\text{-}5\text{-}5)$$

The last term of the left side may be replaced by $-2\mathbb{S}_{(f)}\sqrt{\mu d_0} \pm \beta\mu$, and the unknown linear term transposed to give an extrapolation function,

$$\frac{(E_x - E^0)F}{2.3\,RT} + \log \frac{m_{Cl}m_{ZH}}{m_Z} - 2\mathbb{S}_{(f)}\sqrt{\mu d_0} = -\log K_A \pm \beta\mu \qquad (15\text{-}5\text{-}6)$$

very similar to that used for phosphoric acid. Since $m_{Cl} = m_2$, $m_Z = m_1 + m_H$, and $m_{ZH} = m_2 - m_H$, the concentration term may be evaluated by successive approximations from a preliminary value of K_A, obtained by neglecting m_H altogether. Convergence of successive approximations is rather slow for the amino acids investigated to date, because their values of K_A are of the order 10^{-3} to 10^{-2}. It is perhaps more satisfactory to rewrite equation (15-1-4) as

$$-\log m_H = \frac{(E_x - E^0)F}{2.3\,RT} + \log m_{Cl} + \log \gamma_H\gamma_{Cl} \qquad (15\text{-}5\text{-}7)$$

and estimate m_H with the help of the approximation, $\log \gamma_H\gamma_{Cl} \simeq -2\mathbb{S}_{(f)}\sqrt{\mu d_0}$.

Figure (15-5-1) illustrates the use of equation (15-5-6) in evaluating K_A for dl-alanine.[62] At each temperature, the lower curve is the plot of the the left-hand member of (15-5-6) against μ. The upper, almost horizontal, curves represent an alternative function, obtained by replacing $-2\mathbb{S}_{(f)}\sqrt{\mu d_0}$ in equation (15-5-6) by known values of $\log \gamma_H\gamma_{Cl}$ in pure aqueous solutions at the ionic strength and temperatures in question. Since both extrapolation functions must give the same value of $(-\log K_A)$, their difference in slopes is of some practical advantage in accurately locating the common intercept.

The basic ionization constants of ampholytes can be determined by cells of the type,

$$\text{H}_2\,|\,Z^{\pm}(m_1),\ \text{MZOH}(m_2),\ \text{MCl}(m_3)\,|\,\text{AgCl-Ag} \qquad \text{XI}$$

in which the concentrations of the constituents are usually made equal. MZOH represents a convenient alkali (Na, or K) salt of the ampholyte, and MCl the corresponding chloride. Strictly speaking, the symbol, MZOH, indicates a hydrated form of the salt. Hydration affects the interpretation of K_B, but not its numerical evaluation.

Eliminating $\gamma_H m_H$ and $\gamma_{OH} m_{OH}$ between equations (15-1-4), (15-5-4), and the expression for the ionization of water, we obtain

$$\frac{(E_{XI} - E^0)F}{2.3\,RT} + \log \frac{m_{Cl}m_Z}{m_{ZOH}} + \log K_w = \log K_B - \log \frac{\gamma_{Cl}\gamma_Z a_{H_2O}}{\gamma_{ZOH}} \qquad (15\text{-}5\text{-}8)$$

[62] L. F. Nims and P. K. Smith, *J. Biol. Chem.*, **101**, 401 (1933).

The last term on the right involves only neutral molecules and the ratio of two similar ionic activity coefficients.   It is therefore linear in μ at high

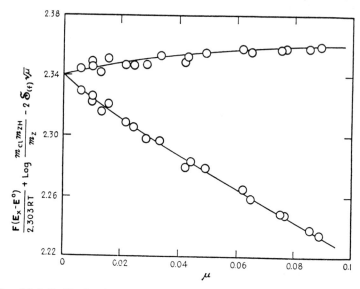

Fig. (15-5-1). Evaluation of the acidic ionization constant of dl-alanine at 25° according to equation (15-5-6).   In the upper curve, $-2\mathcal{S}_{(f)}\sqrt{\mu d_0}$ has been replaced by experimental values of $\log \gamma_H\gamma_{Cl}$ in pure sodium chloride solutions [Table (14-2-1A)].

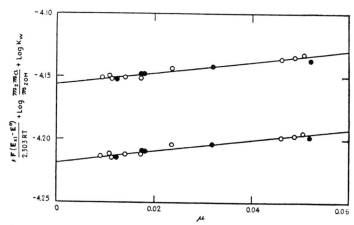

Fig. (15-5-2). Evaluation of the basic ionization constant of glycine at 25 and 35° (upper curve) according to equation (15-5-8).

dilution.   Fig. (15-5-2) illustrates the use of this extrapolation function to evaluate the basic ionization constant of glycine.[63]

If $\log K_B$ has been evaluated, the quantity $\gamma_{Cl}\gamma_Z a_{H_2O}/\gamma_{ZOH}$ in a salt

[63] B. B. Owen, *J. Am. Chem. Soc.*, **56**, 24 (1934).

solution may be evaluated by equation (15-5-8) since the left side may be computed from experimental data. Similarly, $\gamma_{Cl}\gamma_{ZH}/\gamma_Z$ may be estimated in a salt solution by equation (15-5-5).

Cells of the type

$$\text{Ag-AgCl} \mid \text{KCl}(m_2) \mid \text{KCl}(m_2), \text{ glycine } (m_3) \mid \text{AgCl-Ag}$$

have been employed by Roberts and Kirkwood[64] to determine both the activity coefficients of potassium chloride $y_\pm$ and glycine y_3 in aqueous solutions containing both these substances at molal concentrations m_2 and m_3, respectively. From the cell measurements $y_\pm/y_\pm^0$ is determined where $y_\pm^0$ is the activity coefficient of potassium chloride in the absence of glycine. From the equation

$$2\left(\frac{\partial \ln y_\pm}{\partial m_3}\right)_{T,P,m_2} = \left(\frac{\partial \ln y_3}{\partial m_2}\right)_{T,P,m_3} \tag{15-5-9}$$

which follows from the conditions of integrability of equation (1-2-7), y_3 may be computed. The values of these quantitities at 25° as determined by Roberts and Kirkwood are given by the empirical equations

$$\log \frac{y_\pm}{y_\pm^0} = -0.08942m_3 + 0.1226m_2^{1/2}/m_3 + 0.01074m_3^2 - 0.0628m_2m_3 \tag{15-5-10}$$

and

$$\log y_3 = -0.1789m_2 - 0.06278m_2^2 + 0.1635m_2^{3/2} \tag{15-5-11}$$

(6) THE CALCULATION OF IONIZATION CONSTANTS AND THE DERIVED THERMODYNAMIC FUNCTIONS, ΔH_i^0, ΔS_i^0, AND $\Delta C_{p_i}^0$.

Ionization constants, obtained by the methods described in the preceding sections are compiled in Tables (15-6-1A), (15-6-2A) and (15-6-3A). Table (15-6-1A) contains the observed ionization constants in water at various temperatures. Table (15-6-2A) contains the ionization constants of water, formic, acetic, propionic acids and glycine in dioxane-water mixtures at 5° intervals from 0° to 50°. In Table (15-6-3A), values of the acid and base constants of some amino-acids in water from 1 to 50° are recorded. In all cases, the references to the original sources are to be found in these tables.

The change in ionization constant with dielectric constant is large. For aliphatic acids and water, it amounts to a decrease in K of five powers of ten for a change in D from 80 (pure water) to 10 (82% dioxane-water). Since determinations have been made in only five solvent mixtures in water and dioxane [Table (15-6-2A)], these results cannot be interpolated accurately from a single graph. Harned and Fallon[65] have suggested a method

[64] R. M. Roberts and J. G. Kirkwood, *J. Am. Chem. Soc.*, **63**, 1373 (1941).

[65] H. S. Harned and L. D. Fallon, *J. Am. Chem. Soc.*, **61**, 2377 (1939).

of interpolation, based upon the fact that log K varies nearly linearly with the mol fraction of water, or dioxane. This is shown by Fig. (15-6-1) in which $\log K - \log K_{(N_2=0)}$ at 25° is plotted against the mol fraction of dioxane, N_2. The experimental values for water, acetic, and propionic acids indicate a maximum deviation from linearity of the order of 0.05 or

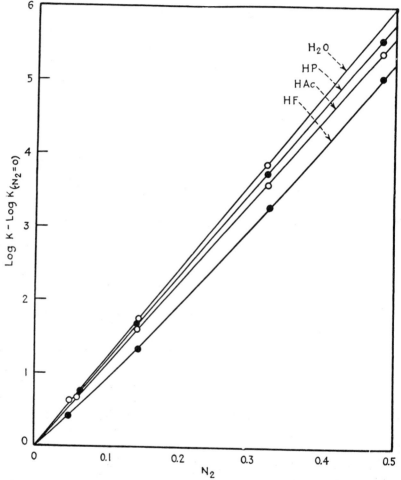

Fig. (15-6-1). Logarithm of ionization constants as a function of mol fraction of dioxane ($t = 25°$). HP, propionic; HAc, acetic; HF, formic acid.

about 1 per cent in log K. A plot of these deviations from the simple linear relationship may be employed for accurate interpolation. The graph for formic acid possesses the greater curvature.

As in the study of the ionization of water [Section (3)], many empirical equations have been employed for representing the ionization constants of weak electrolytes as a function of T, and for computing the thermochemical functions. The same difficulties in drawing conclusions from the observed results concerning the behavior of $\Delta C_{p_i}^0$ occur as those found with water. The data in Table (15-6-1) illustrate this point thoroughly. Here, observed values of $(-\log K_A)$ for formic acid are given in the second column. The other columns contain the deviations of these values computed by the five equations given at the bottom of the table. The constants of these equations were obtained by the method of least squares. We note that the first three of these equations have the same form as equations (15-3-3), (15-3-6), and (15-3-7), used for the calculation of the ionization constant of

TABLE (15-6-1). IONIZATION CONSTANT OF FORMIC ACID*

$$\Delta = [-\log K_A]\text{calc.} - [-\log K_A]\text{obs.}$$

$$\Delta \times 10^4$$

t	$-\log K_A$	(1)	(2)	(3)	(4)	(5)
0	3.7857	−5	−5	−6	−22	−32
5	3.7719	+6	+5	+7	+6	−5
10	3.7625	+5	+4	+6	+14	+3
15	3.7572	−7	−8	−5	+6	−4
20	3.7533	−2	−3	−2	+6	+2
25	3.7515	+5	+6	+4	+11	+5
30	3.7525	+13	+15	+10	+11	−11
35	3.7577	0	+3	−3	−6	−4
40	3.7655	−15	−13	−18	−25	−18
45	3.7734	−11	−9	−13	−21	−8
50	3.7825	+3	+5	0	−5	+15
55	3.7940	+11	+11	+11	+13	+39
60	3.8094	−2	−6	+1	+12	+49
Δ (total)		85	83	86	158	195
Δ (mean)		6.5	6.4	6.6	12	15

$$\text{(1)} \quad \log K_A = 30.9965 - \frac{2013.5}{T} - 0.0075841T - 10.4000 \log T \tag{15-6-1}$$

$$\text{(2)} \quad \log K_A = 56.7186 - \frac{2684.1}{T} - 20.8000 \log T \tag{15-6-2}$$

$$\text{(3)} \quad \log K_A = -\frac{1342.85}{T} + 5.2744 - 0.0151682T \tag{15-6-3}$$

$$\text{(4)} \quad \log K_A = -8.0502 + 0.028803T - 4.826 \times 10^{-5}T^2 \tag{15-6-4}$$

$$\text{(5)} \quad \log K_A = -8.1868 + 0.02978T - 5 \times 10^{-5}T^2 \tag{15-6-5}$$

* H. S. Harned and R. A. Robinson, *Trans. Faraday Soc.*, **36**, 973 (1940).

water [Table (15-3-1)]. The calculated and observed values show mean deviations of only 0.0007 in $\log K$, and are the same for all three equations. We arrive at the same conclusion found for the ionization of water, that from these results we cannot decide how $\Delta C_{p_i}^0$ varies with temperature. We have shown that existing evidence indicates that the ionization constant of water passes through a maximum in the neighborhood of 250°C, which is far from the region of temperature (0 to 60°) through which it is known accurately. The maxima for formic and other aliphatic acids occur at about room temperature. In the neighborhood of the maxima, it has been found that a quadratic equation in T is also satisfactory for the calculation of $\log K$. This is illustrated by the values of the deviations in the last two columns of Table (15-6-1). The first of these calculations was made with equation (15-6-4) in which all three constants were obtained by least squares. The last column contains deviations of observed values from those calculated by equation (15-6-5) in which the coefficient of the term in T^2 was taken to be 5×10^{-5}, and the other constants determined by least squares. The agreement is not so exact as with the first three equations, since the mean deviations (0.0012 and 0.0015 in log K, respectively) are about twice as great. This indicates definitely that for the computation of the most accurate results, equations (15-6-1) to (15-6-3) are better than the quadratic equations.

The ionization constants of a number of weak electrolytes [Table (15-6-1A)] exhibit maxima between 0 and 60°. Harned and Embree[66] suggested that this is a property of all weak electrolytes. They also showed that as a first approximation the equation

$$\log K - \log K_\theta = -p(t - \theta)^2 \qquad (15\text{-}6\text{-}6)$$

represents the results closely (± 0.002 in log K) provided that it is applied in the neighborhood of the temperature, θ, at which the ionization constant is a maximum, or. K_θ. Thus, the ionization constant is given in terms of two empirical constants, θ and K_θ, and a universal constant, p, which was found to be 5×10^{-5}. Expanded and rearranged, equation (15-6-6) becomes

$$\log K = [\log K_\theta - p\theta^2] + 2p\theta t - pt^2 \qquad (15\text{-}6\text{-}7)$$

This equation is the same as equation (15-6-5), and its applicability to formic acid has been illustrated in the last column of Table (15-6-1). Although this equation does not represent the best data as accurately as the other equations we have discussed, it yields a good approximation, and can be applied readily without resorting to least squares. Thus, upon rearranging,

$$\log K + pt^2 = [\log K_\theta - p\theta^2] + 2p\theta t \qquad (15\text{-}6\text{-}8)$$

is obtained. The left side of this equation is determined from the data, and then plotted against t. A straight line should be obtained with a slope, $2p\theta$, and an intercept at $t = 0$, [log $K_\theta - p\theta^2$]. Since p is known both θ and K_θ may be evaluated. Such graphs are given in Fig. (15-6-2), in which pt^2 plus the mantissa of log K for formic, acetic, propionic, and chloroacetic acids are plotted against t. From 0 to 45° the points fall on straight lines within the estimated accuracy of the observed ionization constants. Deviations occur from 50 to 60°.[67]

All of these equations have been employed at various times. Recently, systematic computations of the thermodynamic quantities from the ioniza-

[66] H. S. Harned and N. D. Embree, *J. Am. Chem. Soc.*, **56**, 1050 (1934).
[67] J. L. Magee, T. Ri and H. Eyring, *J. Chem. Phys.*, **9**, 419 (1941).

tion constants in Tables (15-6-1A), (15-6-2A), and (15-6-3A) have been made by Harned and Owen[68] by means of equation (15-6-6), and by Everett and Wynne-Jones[69] who employed equation (15-3-6). The latter equation represents the experimental results more accurately than the quadratic form, and is therefore somewhat more reliable for the computation of the thermodynamic properties.

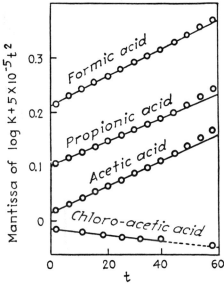

Fig. (15-6-2)
Graphs of the left side of equation (15-6-8) for acetic, propionic, formic, and chloro-acetic acids.

For this purpose, we have employed equation (15-3-7) in the form,[70]

$$\log K = -\frac{A^*}{T} - C^*T + D^* \qquad (15\text{-}6\text{-}9)$$

Whence

$$\Delta F_i^0 = A' - D'T + C'T^2 \qquad (15\text{-}6\text{-}10)$$

$$\Delta H_i^0 = A' - C'T^2 \qquad (15\text{-}6\text{-}11)$$

$$\Delta C_{p_i}^0 = -2C'T \qquad (15\text{-}6\text{-}12)$$

$$\Delta S_i^0 = D' - 2C'T \qquad (15\text{-}6\text{-}13)$$

$$T_\theta = \sqrt{\frac{A^*}{C^*}} \qquad (15\text{-}6\text{-}14)$$

$$\log K_\theta = D^* - 2\sqrt{C^*A^*} \qquad (15\text{-}6\text{-}15)$$

[68] H. S. Harned and B. B. Owen, *Chem. Rev.*, **25**, 31 (1939).

[69] D. H. Everett and W. F. K. Wynne-Jones, *Trans. Faraday Soc.*, **35**, 1380 (1939); **37**, 373 (1941); J. F. J. Dippy and H. O. Jenkins, *Ibid.*, **37**, 366 (1941).

[70] H. S. Harned and R. A. Robinson, *Trans. Faraday Soc.*, **36**, 973 (1940). We are greatly indebted to Dr. Robert A. Robinson for most of the following calculations.

where A', C', and D' equal 2.3026 R times A^*, C^* and D^*, respectively. Our choice of this method of treatment depends on the fact that all the experimental electromotive forces can be expressed within the estimated accuracy over the temperature ranges involved by a quadratic equation in T. Possibly, when more accurate results are obtained, or temperature ranges greater than 60° are investigated, the quadratic equation for $\mathbf{E}$ may be proved to be inadequate, but so far no further extension has been found necessary. As typical of the equations used in determining K by extrapolation, we may select equation (15-4-2) which, at $\mu = 0$, becomes

$$\frac{(\mathbf{E}_{VII} - \mathbf{E}^0)\mathbf{F}}{2.303\ RT} + \log \frac{m_{Cl}m_{HR}}{m_R} = -\ [\log K_A]_{\mu=0} \qquad (15\text{-}6\text{-}16)$$

Since both $\mathbf{E}^0$ and $\mathbf{E}_{VII}$ are quadratic in T, and the term containing the molalities is independent of the temperature, equations (15-6-9) and (15-6-10) for $\log K$ and ΔF_i^0 result. Equations (15-6-11) to (15-6-15) for the other thermodynamic quantities immediately follow.

The constants, A^*, C^*, D^*, A', C' and D' of equations (15-6-9) to (15-6-13) are recorded in Table (15-6-4A). Values of the temperatures of the maxima, T_θ, and $(-\log K_\theta)$ are also included. In Table (15-6-2), ΔF_i^0, ΔH_i^0, $\Delta C_{p_i}^0$, and ΔS_i^0 at 25°, calculated by equations (15-6-9) to (15-6-13), are compiled. These results agree well with those obtained by Everett and Wynne-Jones by use of equations (15-3-4), (15-3-5) and (15-3-6). The most notable exception is $\Delta C_{p_i}^0$ for water for which Everett and Wynne-Jones obtained -51 cal. compared with -46.5.

The most accurate results have been obtained with the aliphatic acids and water in aqueous solution, and in water-dioxane mixtures of higher dielectric constant ($D > 30$). In mixtures of high dioxane content, the greatest uncertainty resides in the determination of $\mathbf{E}^0$ [Chapter (11), Section (3)], and the error in the ionization constant increases progressively as the dielectric constant decreases. In 70 percent dioxane, the result is fairly reliable, but in the 82% mixtures, the values are approximate.

There is a discrepancy of 1 or 2 percent between the independently determined constants of dl-alanine that appear in Table (15-6-1A) and those in Table (15-6-3A). Whenever the absolute magnitude of K_A or K_B is required, the data in Table (15-6-1A) are preferable, because the results in Table (15-6-3A) were obtained with very limited amounts of material, and without the complete exclusion of air from the cell. On the other hand, the thermochemical quantities derived from the data in Table (15-6-3A) may be the more accurate because of the longer temperature range.

The determinations of ionization constants by cells with liquid junctions, or from electrometric titration curves, are very numerous.[71] Table

---

[71] *The International Critical Tables*, Vol. VI, pp. 259–304, McGraw-Hill Book Co., New York (1929).

TABLE (15-6-2). ΔF_i^0, ΔH_i^0, $\Delta C_{p_i}^0$, AND ΔS_i^0 AT 25° IN CALORIES

	ΔF_i^0	ΔH_i^0	$\Delta C_{p_i}^0$	ΔS_i^0
Acids				
Water	19089	13519	−46.5	−18.7
Formic	5117	−23	−41.7	−17.6
Acetic	6486	−92	−36.5	−22.1
Propionic	6647	−163	−38.3	−22.8
Butyric	6574	−693	−36.4	−24.4
Chloroacetic	3901	−1158	−40.0	−17.0
Lactic	5267	−99	−40.7	−18.0
Glycolic	5225	175	−38.8	−16.9
Sulphuric (2)	2721	−5200	−50.0	−26.5
Oxalic (2)	5846	−1577	−57.8	−24.9
Malonic (2)	7767	−1157	−60.0	−29.9
Phosphoric (1)	2896	−1773	−50.7	−15.7
(2)	9829	822	−45.1	−30.2
Boric	12596	3328	−45.0	−31.1
Amino-Acids				
Glycine A	3205	1156	−32.2	−6.9
B	5753	2713	−21.9	−10.2
dl-Alanine A	3191	714	−34.2	−8.3
	3203	773	−37.3	−8.2
B	5627	2787	−44.8	−9.5
	5631	2539	−29.9	−10.4
dl-α-Amino-*n*-Butyric A	3123	298	−34.1	−9.5
B	5681	2824	−29.9	−9.6
dl-α-Amino-*n*-Valeric A	3161	487	−34.2	−9.0
B	5714	2685	−38.7	−10.1
dl-Norleucine A	3183	528	−33.1	−8.9
B	4314	2593	−32.3	−5.8
dl-α-amino-isobutyric A	3215	492	−38.0	−9.1
B	5170	1988	−31.5	−10.7
Valine A	3118	59	−37.8	−10.3
B	5835	2872	−32.7	−9.9
dl-Leucine A	3176	382	−36.8	−9.4
B	5796	2705	−32.5	−10.4
dl-isoleucine A	3163	264	−38.1	−9.7
B	5786	2772	−28.6	−10.1

Water and Acids in Dioxane- and Methanol-Water Mixtures

		ΔF_i^0	ΔH_i^0	$\Delta C_{p_i}^0$	ΔS_i^0
Water in X per cent Dioxane	$X = 20$	19940	13515	−50.4	−21.5
	$= 45$	21470	13190	−54.0	−27.8
	$= 70$	24353	12662	−49.4	−39.2
Formic Acid in X per cent Dioxane	$X = 20$	5701	359	−43.4	−17.92
	$= 45$	6944	1067	−48.1	−19.72
	$= 70$	9569	1474	−46.2	−27.16
	$= 82$	12002	2509	−109.1	−31.84
Acetic Acid in X per cent Dioxane	$X = 20$	7217	−52	−44.0	−24.4
	$= 45$	8602	−442	−51.1	−30.3
	$= 70$	11348	−610	−51.7	−40.1
	$= 82$	13827	−1338	−124.5	−50.8
Propionic Acid in X per cent Dioxane	$X = 20$	7455	−48	−42.0	−25.5
	$= 45$	8937	−206	−46.8	−30.7
	$= 70$	11746	−201	−47.6	−40.1
	$= 82$	14203	−1064	−120.1	−51.2

TABLE (15-6-2).—*Continued*

		ΔF_i^0	ΔH_i^0	$\Delta C_{p_i}^0$	ΔS_i^0
Acetic Acid in X per cent $X = 10$		6690	30	−43.3	−22.3
Methanol $= 20$		6929	168	−47.1	−22.7
Glycine K_A in X per cent $X = 0$		3205	1156	−32.2	−6.9
Dioxane $= 20$		3586	1183	−34.1	−8.1
$= 45$		4233	993	−32.4	−10.9
$= 70$		5412	829	−30.9	−15.4
Glycine K_B in X per cent $X = 0$		5753	2713	−21.9	−10.2
Dioxane $= 20$		6428	2869	−27.4	−11.9
$= 45$		7511	3342	−19.5	−14.0
$= 70$		8968	3763	......	−17.5

(15-6-3) gives some values obtained from cells with liquid junctions, which seem representative of the best results of modern technique and extrapolations based upon the interionic attraction theory. The corresponding values from cells without liquid junction were interpolated to 18°. In the examples illustrated in Table (15-6-3), the two methods yield results within 1.5% on the average, which is unusually satisfactory. Discrepancies of ten times this magnitude are very common, and are probably due to uncertainties in corrections for liquid junction potentials

TABLE (15-6-3). COMPARISON OF IONIZATION CONSTANTS DERIVED FROM CELLS WITH, AND WITHOUT LIQUID JUNCTIONS AND FROM CONDUCTANCE

Acid	18°		25°	
	With L.J.[*]	Without L.J.	Without L.J.	Conductance
Formic..............	1.79 × 10⁻⁴	1.76 × 10⁻⁴	1.772 × 10⁻⁴	1.830 × 10⁻⁴
Acetic.............	1.73 × 10⁻⁵	1.75 × 10⁻⁵	1.754 × 10⁻⁵	1.758 × 10⁻⁵
Propionic..........	1.32 × 10⁻⁵	1.34 × 10⁻⁵	1.336 × 10⁻⁵	1.347 × 10⁻⁵
n-Butyric.........	1.53 × 10⁻⁵	1.56 × 10⁻⁵	1.515 × 10⁻⁵	1.512 × 10⁻⁵
Chloroacetic.......	1.49 × 10⁻³	1.44 × 10⁻³	1.379 × 10⁻³	1.400 × 10⁻³
α-Lactic...........	1.38 × 10⁻⁴	1.37 × 10⁻⁴	1.374 × 10⁻⁴	1.391 × 10⁻⁴
Glycolic..........	1.46 × 10⁻⁴	1.455 × 10⁻⁴	1.475 × 10⁻⁴	

[*] E. Larsson and B. Adell, *Z. physik. Chem.*, **A156**, 352, 381 (1931); *Ibid.*, **A157**, 342 (1931).

rather than to gross experimental errors. This emphasizes the advantage of employing cells without liquid junctions, or combinations of cells by which the junction potential may be eliminated. [Chapter (10), Section (7)]

Comparisons of ionization constants at 25° derived from cells without liquid junctions and from conductance [Table (7-6-1)] are shown in the last two columns of Table (15-6-3). The agreement is particularly good for acetic and butyric acids, and unsatisfactory for formic acid.[*]

[*] The discrepancy for formic acid is puzzling because the same sample of acid was used in both determinations.

It is very difficult to estimate the accuracy of the thermal data. All the difficulties, encountered in evaluating quantities such as $\bar{L}_2$ and $\bar{J}_2$ of strong electrolytes [Chapters (11), (12) and (13)] by differentiation, occur in determining ΔH_i^0 and $\Delta C_{p_i}^0$ of the ionization reactions. In the most favorable cases (water and aliphatic acids in water), ΔH_i^0 at 25° is probably known to within 50 cal. For the least reliable results (acid and base constants of the amino acids) the error may be as great as 250 cal. Thus, for the acid ionization of glycine, Sturtevant[72] obtains 906 cal. by calorimetric measurements which is 250 cal. lower than the value recorded in Table (15-6-1). The values of $\Delta C_{p_i}^0$ in the middle range of temperature (15 to 35°) may be known to within ± 1 cal. for the most accurate results. On the other hand, errors of the order of ± 7 cal., or greater probably occur in the most unfavorable cases. Further considerations of these uncertainties are to be found in the contributions of Walde,[73] Pitzer,[74] Everett and Wynne-Jones,[75] and Harned and Owen.[76]

A general discussion of the thermodynamics of ionization equilibria, and proposed theories of the variation of ionization constants with temperature, will be given [Section (10)] after the theoretical treatment of the unbuffered cell with liquid junction and the discussion of medium and salt effects [Sections (7) and (8)].

(7) Medium Effects. The Unbuffered Cell Without Liquid Junction

In Chapter (11), Section (3), the effect of changes in composition of water-organic solvent mixtures upon the standard potential of the cell

$$H_2 \mid HCl(m), \text{ Solvent } (X), \text{ Water } (Y) \mid AgCl\text{-}Ag$$

were considered. It was shown that the Born equation (3-10-13) predicts the order of magnitude of the effect, but cannot be relied upon for accurate calculations. A more general treatment of the subject of medium effects upon the properties of both strong and weak electrolytes remains to be undertaken.

In discussing the influence of the solvent medium upon the numerical value of the activity coefficient, or ionization constant of an ionized solute, it will be convenient to distinguish between a primary and a secondary medium effect. In a solution of an electrolyte in the presence of neutral (non-aqueous) molecules, the total medium effect is defined as the logarithm of the ratio of the activity coefficient of the electrolyte in the presence of the neutral molecules to that in pure water at the same con-

[72] J. M. Sturtevant, *J. Am. Chem. Soc.*, **62**, 1879 (1940).

[73] A. W. Walde, *J. Phys. Chem.*, **39**, 477 (1935).

[74] K. S. Pitzer, *J. Am. Chem. Soc.*, **59**, 2365 (1937).

[75] D. H. Everett and W. F. K. Wynne-Jones, *Trans. Faraday Soc.*, **35**, 1380 (1939).

[76] H. S. Harned and B. B. Owen, *Chem. Rev.*, **25**, 31 (1939).

centration of electrolyte. Both of the activity coefficients in this ratio are referred to unity at infinite dilution in pure water. The primary medium effect is the limit to which the total effect converges as the electrolyte concentration approaches zero. The secondary medium effect is always given by the difference between the total and primary effects.

To make use of these terms without confusion, we must be able to identify the reference state of any activity coefficient. Throughout this section, all activity coefficients in any medium are understood to be referred to unity at infinite dilution in pure water unless written with an asterisk (*viz.*, γ^*), in which case they are referred to infinite dilution in the medium in which the solute is dissolved. When this medium is pure water, a superscript zero will be used (*viz.*, γ^0). A subscript zero indicates that the concentration of electrolyte is zero. Thus for all concentrations, we may write

$$\log \gamma = \log \gamma_0 + \log \gamma^* \qquad (15\text{-}7\text{-}1)$$

or, adding $-\log \gamma^0$ to both sides

$$\log \frac{\gamma}{\gamma^0} = \log \gamma_0 + \log \frac{\gamma^*}{\gamma^0} \qquad (15\text{-}7\text{-}2)$$

is obtained. The three terms of this last equation give the definitional relationship between the total, primary and secondary medium effects,[77] respectively. The primary medium effect is the one with which equations (3-10-12) and (3-10-13) are concerned.

The values of $(-\log K_A)$ in water-organic solvent mixtures, given in Table (15-6-2A), were obtained from the cells

$$\text{H}_2 \mid \text{HR}(m_1),\ \text{NaR}(m_2),\ \text{NaCl}(m_3),\ \text{Solvent } (X),\ \text{H}_2\text{O } (Y) \mid \text{AgCl-Ag}$$

by employing equation (15-4-2). There are two simple equivalent ways of expressing the electromotive force of such a cell, namely

$$\frac{\text{F}(\text{E} - \text{E}^0)}{2.3\,RT} = -\log m_{\text{H}} m_{\text{Cl}} - \log \gamma_{\text{H}} \gamma_{\text{Cl}} \qquad (15\text{-}7\text{-}3)$$

and

$$\frac{\text{F}(\text{E} - \text{E}^{0*})}{2.3\,RT} = -\log m_{\text{H}} m_{\text{Cl}} - \log \overset{*}{\gamma}_{\text{H}} \overset{*}{\gamma}_{\text{Cl}} \qquad (15\text{-}7\text{-}4)$$

In the first expression, $-\text{E}^0$ is the standard potential of the silver-silver chloride electrode in pure water. In the second expression, $-\text{E}^{0*}$ is the standard potential in the mixed solvent. Combination of these two equations, and comparison with equation (15-7-1), shows that the primary

[77] B. B. Owen, *J. Am. Chem. Soc.*, **54**, 1758 (1932).

medium effect of the solvent upon the hydrogen and chloride ions is given directly by the two standard potentials. Thus

$$\log \gamma_{0HCl} = \frac{1}{2} \log \frac{\gamma_H \gamma_{Cl}}{\gamma_H^* \gamma_{Cl}^*} = \frac{F(E^0 - E^{0*})}{4.6\,RT} \qquad (15\text{-}7\text{-}5)$$

The primary medium effect of the organic solvent upon the activity coefficient or ionization constant of acetic acid can be determined by extrapolation of the data for the above cell in accordance with equation (15-4-2). Employing equation (15-7-4), we obtain a quantity, K_A^*, whose value is a function of the medium, because γ^* is always unity at infinite dilution. If we write,

$$\gamma_A^2 = \frac{\gamma_H \gamma_R}{\gamma_{HR}} \quad \text{and} \quad k_A = \frac{m_H m_R}{m_{HR}} \qquad (15\text{-}7\text{-}6)$$

the thermodynamic ionization constant in pure water, K_A, is related to the properties of the acid in the mixed solvent by the definitional equation,

$$K_A = \gamma_A^2 k_A = \gamma_{0A}^2 \gamma_A^{*2} k_A = \gamma_{0A}^2 K_A^* \qquad (15\text{-}7\text{-}7)$$

Accordingly,

$$\log \gamma_{0A} = \frac{1}{2} \log \frac{K_A}{K_A^*} \qquad (15\text{-}7\text{-}8)$$

Table (15-7-1) contains the values of E^{0*} obtained for the methanol-water and dioxane-water mixtures, and the corresponding values of $\log \gamma_{0HCl}$ and $\log \gamma_{0A}$. It will be noticed that the medium effect of acetic acid upon hydrochloric acid is greater than that of methanol or dioxane, and that the effects of the latter upon acetic acid are greater than upon hydrochloric acid. The medium effect of acetic acid molecules upon ionized acetic acid has not yet been determined experimentally.

If equation (15-7-3) be employed for extrapolation instead of equation (15-7-4), the situation would be similar to that encountered with cells containing unbuffered solutions of weak acids. Equation (15-7-3) can be written

$$\frac{F(E - E^0)}{2.3RT} + \log \frac{m_{HR}}{m_R} m_{Cl} = -\log K_A + 2 \log \gamma_A - 2 \log \gamma_{HCl} \qquad (15\text{-}7\text{-}9)$$

Extrapolation of the left-hand member to zero ionic strength yields $(-\log K_A + 2 \log \gamma_{0A} - 2 \log \gamma_{0HCl})$, so that knowing K_A, we obtain the difference between the primary medium effects of the solvent upon the weak acid and upon hydrochloric acid. From this, it is clear that $\log \gamma_{0A}$ cannot be obtained from the above cell unless either $\log \gamma_{0HCl}$ or E^{0*} is known [Equation (15-7-5)].

We are now in a position to consider unbuffered cells of the type,

$$H_2 \mid HR(m_1), NaCl(m_2) \mid AgCl\text{-}Ag$$

first used to determine ionization constants,[78] and the activity coefficients[79] of weak electrolytes in salt solutions. In such cells the weak acid concentration was maintained constant at some particular value of m_1, while the salt concentration, m_2, was varied. If the electromotive force expression

TABLE (15-7-1).   PRIMARY MEDIUM EFFECTS AT 25° IN ORGANIC SOLVENT-
WATER MIXTURES

X = Weight Per Cent Organic Solvent

Solvent	X	E^{0a}	Log $\gamma_0 HCl$	Log $\gamma_{0A}{}^b$		
				Formic Acid	Acetic Acid	Propionic Acid
Water	0	0.22239	0.0	0.0	0.0	0.0
Methanol	10	.21535	.0595	.....	.0741	......
	20	.20881	.1148	......	.1614	......
Dioxane	20	.20303	.1636	.2143	.2678	.2961
	45	.16352	.4976	.6200	.7755	.8392
	70	.06395	1.3392	1.6318	1.7823	1.869
	82	−.0415	2.230	2.52	2.69	2.77
Acetic Acid	10	.21050	.1005	......	....	......
	20	.19682	.2161	......	....	......
	30	.18091	.3506	......	....	......
	40	.16211	.5095	......	....	......
	50	.13945	.7010	......	....	......
	60	.11150	.9373	......	....	......

a Table (11-3-2); Acetic acid, B. B. Owen, *J. Am. Chem. Soc.*, **54**, 1758 (1932).
b From data in Table (15-6-2A).

for this cell is rearranged, and 2 log γ^0_{HCl} added to both sides of the equation, we obtain

$$\frac{F(E - E^0)}{2.3RT} + \log m_2 + 2 \log \gamma^0_{HCl} = -\log m_H - 2 \log \frac{\gamma_{HCl}}{\gamma^0_{HCl}} \quad (15\text{-}7\text{-}10)$$

The right-hand member contains the total medium effect of the weak acid upon the chloride and hydrogen ions. This quantity is ordinarily unknown. Consequently, it is useful to define an apparent hydrogen ion concentration, m'_H, by

$$\log m'_H = \log m_H + 2 \log \frac{\gamma_{HCl}}{\gamma^0_{HCl}} \quad (15\text{-}7\text{-}11)$$

which can be calculated directly from the left-hand member of equation (15-7-10). The corresponding apparent activity coefficient of the weak

[78] H. S. Harned and B. B. Owen, *J. Am. Chem. Soc.*, **52**, 5079 (1930); H. S. Harned and G. M. Murphy, *Ibid.*, **53**, 8 (1931).
[79] H. S. Harned and R. A. Robinson, *Ibid.*, **50**, 3157 (1928).

acid, γ'_A, is defined in terms of the thermodynamic ionization constant by the equation

$$K_A = \frac{\gamma'_H \gamma'_R}{\gamma'_{HR}} \frac{m'^2_H}{m_1 - m'_H} = \gamma'^2_A k'_A \qquad (15\text{-}7\text{-}12)$$

analogous to the expression,

$$K_A = \frac{\gamma_H \gamma_R}{\gamma_{HR}} \frac{m^2_H}{m_1 - m_H} = \gamma^2_A k_A \qquad (15\text{-}7\text{-}13)$$

which relates the real activity coefficient with the real hydrogen ion concentration. In both of these expressions all activity coefficients are referred to unity at infinite dilution in pure water.

Combining equations (15-7-11) to (15-7-13), we find that

$$\log \gamma'_A = \log \gamma_A - 2 \log \frac{\gamma_{HCl}}{\gamma^0_{HCl}} + \frac{1}{2} \log \frac{m_1 - m'_H}{m_1 - m_H} \qquad (15\text{-}7\text{-}14)$$

which shows that $\log \gamma'_A$ is expressed in terms of real activity coefficients, and indeed must simulate the properties of a real activity coefficient when the term containing m'_H is small. If the concentration, m_1, of the weak acid is kept constant while the ionic strength is altered by variations in salt concentration, m_2, we can obtain a series of values of m'_H and k'_A in a $(m_1 - m_H)$ molal solution of unionized weak electrolyte in water. So long as m_H is much smaller than m_1, the composition of the solvent is very nearly constant, and the primary medium effect, and, as a first approximation, the total medium effect may be considered independent of the salt concentration. It is therefore practicable to obtain

$$k_{0A} = \lim_{\mu \to 0} [k'_A] \qquad (15\text{-}7\text{-}15)$$

by extrapolation. The logarithm of the corresponding quantity,

$$\gamma'_{0A} = \lim_{\mu \to 0} [\gamma'_A] \qquad (15\text{-}7\text{-}16)$$

is of the nature of a primary medium effect, since it would equal

$$\log \gamma_{0A} - 2 \log \gamma_{0HCl}$$

by equation (15-7-14), if the concentration term is eliminated by the extrapolation.

The extrapolation of $\log k'_A$ is performed by means of the equations,

$$\log k'_A - 2 \mathcal{S}_{(f)} \sqrt{\mu' d_0} = \log k'_{0A} \pm 2\beta\mu' \qquad (15\text{-}7\text{-}17)$$

or

$$\log k'_A - \frac{2 \mathcal{S}_{(f)} \sqrt{\mu' d_0}}{1 + A' \sqrt{\mu' d_0}} = \log k'_{0A} \pm 2\beta\mu' \qquad (15\text{-}7\text{-}18)$$

in which μ' ($= m_2 + m_H'$) is used for $\mu(= m_2 + m_H)$ as a very close approximation. The use of the numerical value of $S_{(f)}$ for pure water neglects the secondary medium effect of the weak acid, but this approximation is unavoidable because the influence of HR molecules upon the dielectric

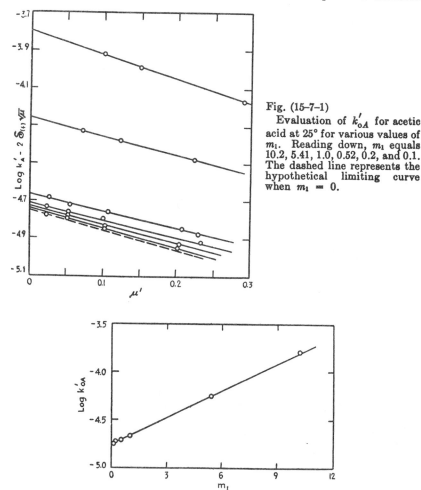

Fig. (15-7-1)

Evaluation of k_{oA}' for acetic acid at 25° for various values of m_1. Reading down, m_1 equals 10.2, 5.41, 1.0, 0.52, 0.2, and 0.1. The dashed line represents the hypothetical limiting curve when $m_1 = 0$.

Fig. (15-7-2). Evaluation of $\log K_A$ for acetic acid at 25°.

constant of the solvent is generally unknown. The extrapolation is illustrated in Fig. (15-7-1), in which $\log k_{oA}'$ is determined for acetic acid[80] for six values of m_1 by equation (15-7-17). A recent investigation[81] shows that it is necessary to use equation (15-7-18) if higher values of μ' are included.

[80] H. S. Harned and B. B. Owen, *J. Am. Chem. Soc.*, **52**, 5079 (1930).
[81] H. S. Harned and F. C. Hickey, *J. Am. Chem. Soc.*, **59**, 1284 (1937).

From the nature of γ'_{0A}, it is clear that it must become unity when $m_1 = 0$, for under this condition the medium is pure water. According to equation (15-7-12), extrapolation of k'_{0A} to $m_1 = 0$ must yield K_A. This second extrapolation is shown in Fig. (15-7-2). The fact that this extrapolation is linear within the experimental error is without theoretical significance, because it is impossible at present to evaluate the effects of the several approximations involved in the calculations. It is known that $\log \gamma_{0HCl}$ is not linear[82] when similarly plotted, but the behavior of $\log \gamma_{0A}$ is unknown.[83]

(8) THE ACTIVITY COEFFICIENTS OF WEAK ACIDS IN SALT SOLUTIONS

It was shown in Section (2) that the function, $\log (\gamma_H \gamma_{OH}/a_{H_2O})$, for water in salt solutions could be derived from the electromotive forces of suitable cells without liquid junctions. The electromotive force method is also applicable to the estimation of analogous functions for other weak electrolytes. Similar results may be obtained by the optical method described in Section (4). In this section, we shall illustrate the calculation of the function, $\log \gamma_H \gamma_R/\gamma_{HR}$, for acetic acid from electromotive force data, and for α-dinitrophenol from optical data. The electromotive force method will be considered first because it is based upon the results just discussed in Section (7).

The nearly parallel nature of the lines for low concentrations in Fig. (15-7-1) suggests that the broken line drawn from the intercept, $\log K_A$, would represent the properties of infinitely dilute acetic acid in sodium chloride solutions. In such solutions, the medium effect of the weak acid is zero. This illustrates a very important restriction upon the information which may be derived from the unbuffered cell without liquid junction. Without extra-thermodynamical information, this cell gives k_A, or $m_H^2/(m_1 - m_H)$, in salt solutions at zero concentration of weak acid $(m_1 = 0)$. It does not measure this quantity in a solution containing a finite amount of the weak electrolyte. On the other hand, the method points the way toward such knowledge because it shows that, in order to solve the problem, the medium effect of the weak acid, or the effect of change of m_1 upon k_A, must be known. As these studies are extended, and the general laws of the effects of change of solvent composition become known, it will be possible to obtain m_H in acid-salt solutions of various compositions. The important determination of m_H in buffered solutions will also be possible.

[82] B. B. Owen, *J. Am. Chem. Soc.*, **54**, 1758 (1932).

[83] In the original paper by H. S. Harned and B. B. Owen [*J. Am. Chem. Soc.*, **52**, 5079 (1932)] the third equality in equation (17) is invalid as it neglects the medium effect of acetic acid upon the real γ_A. The third sentence on p. 5081 of this paper is incorrect as it refers γ_A to "a given solvent" rather than to pure water. These mistakes were corrected by H. S. Harned and B. B. Owen, [*Chem. Rev.*, **25**, 31 (1939)] whose recent treatment has been followed in the text.

When the medium effect of the weak acid is zero ($m_1 = 0$), we drop the primes in equation (15-7-15), or (15-7-16). If we refer to equation (15-7-11), it follows that the slope of the broken line can be identified with 2β in an equation such as,

$$2 \log \gamma_A = \log K_A - \log k_A = \frac{-2\mathcal{S}_{(f)}\sqrt{\mu d_0}}{1 + A'\sqrt{\mu d_0}} + 2\beta\mu \quad (15\text{-}8\text{-}1)$$

This may be used to evaluate the ionization, or activity coefficient, γ_A, of the weak acid in salt solutions.

In Table (15-8-1), we have recorded values of k_A at 25° in some salt solutions obtained by Harned and Hickey.[84] These are plotted in Fig. (15-8-1), and we note the similarity to the plots of $m_H m_{OH}$ in halide solutions shown in Fig. (15-2-2). In concentrated solutions, the order of the

TABLE (15-8-1). THE IONIZATION OF ACETIC ACID AT INFINITE DILUTION
IN SALT SOLUTIONS AT 25°

$$k_A \times 10^5$$

μ	LiCl	NaCl	KCl	BaCl$_2$
0.	1.754	1.754	1.754	1.754
.02	2.290	2.292	2.302	2.292
.03	2.401	2.401	2.415	2.404
.06	2.630	2.622	2.650	2.635
.11	2.874	2.850	2.891	2.885
.21	3.167	3.101	3.151	3.190
.51	3.546	3.315	3.340	3.609
1.01	3.670	3.158	3.071	3.799
2.01	3.432	2.475	2.182	3.680
3.01	.....	1.824	.....	.....

salt effect is the same as that found for water, and agrees with the first, but less accurate, results of this kind found by Harned and Robinson,[85] who also obtained the same order for the weak hydroxide, monomethyl-amine. In alkali halide solutions, the greatest ionization occurs in the solution containing the cation of smallest radius, and the remarks in Section (2) concerning specific salt effects on the ionization of water also apply to weak acids and hydroxides. In general, the ionization of weak electrolytes in concentrated solutions depends to a large extent on the fields of the ions.

Harned and Hickey have determined k_A for acetic acid in sodium chloride solutions by this method from 0 to 40°. They found the temperature variation could be expressed by the relation,

$$\log k_A = \log k_\vartheta - 5 \times 10^{-5}(t - \vartheta)^2 \quad (15\text{-}8\text{-}2)$$

[84] H. S. Harned and F. C. Hickey, *J. Am. Chem. Soc.*, **59**, 1284 (1937); **59, 2303** (1937). The ionization of lactic acid in sodium chloride solutions from 0 to 37.5° has been determined by F. C. Hickey, *Ibid.*, **62**, 2916 (1940).

[85] H. S. Harned and R. A. Robinson, *J. Am. Chem. Soc.*, **50**, 3157 (1928).

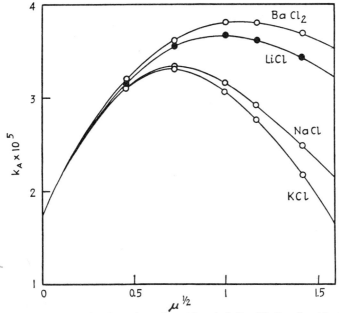

Fig. (15-8-1). The ionization of acetic acid at infinite dilution in chloride solutions at 25°.

TABLE (15-8-2). PARAMETERS OF EQUATION (15-8-2) FOR ACETIC ACID AT
INFINITE DILUTION IN SODIUM CHLORIDE SOLUTIONS

μ	$-\log k_{\vartheta}$	ϑ	Δ ave.
0.00	4.7544	22.6	0.0009
.02	4.6388	25.1	.0007
.03	4.6189	25.6	.0007
.06	4.5798	26.4	.0007
.11	4.5432	27.6	.0009
.21	4.5061	29.2	.0011
.51	4.4752	32.5	.0009
1.01	4.4957	35.7	.0012
2.01	4.5875	45.0	.0029
3.01	4.7132	50.9	.0038

similar to equation (15-6-6). This leads to the interesting conclusion that log γ_A varies linearly with temperature, for by combining equations (15-8-1) and (15-8-2) with (15-6-6), we obtain

$$\log \gamma_A = (1/2) \log (K_\theta/k_\vartheta)$$
$$+ 2.5 \times 10^{-5}(\vartheta^2 - \theta^2) - 5 \times 10^{-5}(\vartheta - \theta)t \qquad (15\text{-}8\text{-}3)$$

Values of log k_ϑ and ϑ are given in Table (15-8-2). The average deviations between observed values of log k_A and those calculated by equation (15-8-2) are indicated by Δ_{ave}.

The behavior of the activity coefficients of several weak electrolytes in sodium chloride solutions is illustrated in Fig. (15-8-2), where they are compared with the activity coefficient of the strong electrolyte, hydrochloric acid, in the same salt solutions. The results for α-dinitrophenol are due to von Halban and Kortüm.[86] Although the points for this acid differ from those of the other weak electrolytes by lying above the curve for hydrochloric acid, the difference is small. A close similarity in the behavior of 1-1 type weak acids in salt solutions appears to be quite general. The activity coefficient functions of twenty-four such acids, studied by Larsson and Adell[87] with the cells containing liquid junctions, would almost exactly fall within the upper and lower limits set by the points for α-dinitro-

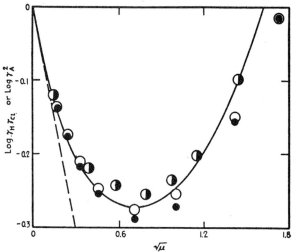

Fig. (15-8-2). Comparison of activity coefficients of electrolytes at infinite dilution in sodium chloride solutions at 25°. Smooth curve, $\log \gamma_H \gamma_{Cl}$; ●, $\log \gamma_H \gamma_{OH}/a_{H_2O}$; ○, $\log \gamma_H \gamma_{Ac}/\gamma_{HAc}$; ◑, $\log \gamma_H \gamma_{D_n}/\gamma_{HD_n}$ ($Dn = \alpha$-dinitrophenol ion)

phenol and water in Fig. (15-8-2). Judging from these results, it may be said that the activity coefficients of the normal fatty acids are practically indistinguishable, and that the introduction of a methyl, phenyl or hydroxyl group into the acid anion is without significant effect unless it occupies the α-position to the carboxyl group. Further discussion of constitutional effects are given by Larsson and Adell, and Güntelberg and Schiödt.[88]

The presence of the term, γ_{HR}, in the activity coefficient function, γ_A, of weak acids is of considerable importance in determining the order of the salt effects at high ionic strengths [Fig. (12-10-3)]. For α-dinitrophenol in sodium and potassium chloride solutions, the curves actually cross at

[86] H. v. Halban and G. Kortüm, *Z. physik. Chem.*, **A170**, 351 (1934).

[87] E. Larsson and B. Adell, *Z. physik. Chem.*, **A157**, 342 (1931); *Ibid.*, **A156**, 381 (1931).

[88] E. Güntelberg and E. Schiödt, *Z. physik. Chem.*, **135**, 393 (1928).

about $2M$, so that the order at high concentrations is the reverse of that at low concentrations.   This may be a very unusual phenomenon, because in dilute solutions the order of the salt effects upon α-dinitrophenol follows the order for the relatively non-deformable hydrogen halides.   Furthermore, von Halban, Kortüm and Seiler[89] have shown, from solubility

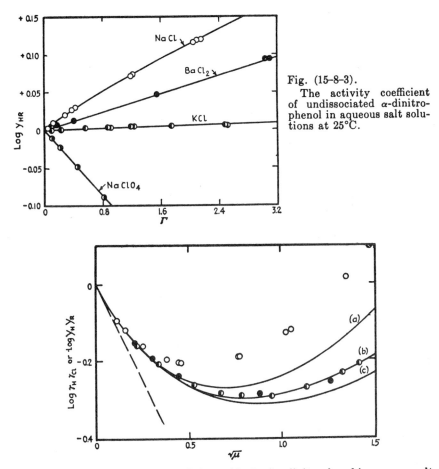

Fig. (15–8–3).
  The activity coefficient of undissociated α-dinitrophenol in aqueous salt solutions at 25°C.

Fig. (15–8–4).   The activity coefficient of ionized α-dinitrophenol in aqueous salt solutions at 25°.   O, NaCl; ◑, KCl; ●, BaCl₂.   The curves represent the activity coefficient of hydrochloric acid in the same salt solutions; (a) NaCl; (b) KCl; (c) BaCl₂

measurements, that the variation of y_{HR} for this acid is quite large.   Plots of their values of log y_{HR} against Γ in several salt solutions are reproduced in Fig. (15–8–3).   The difference in magnitudes of the salt effects of sodium and potassium chlorides upon y_{HR} is so great that if these results are used

[89] H. v. Halban, G. Kortüm and M. Seiler, *Z. physik. Chem.*, **A173**, 449 (1935).

to eliminate y_{HR} from the function, $y_H y_R / y_{HR}$, which exhibited a reversal in order of salt effect at about $2M$, it is found that there is no indication of a reversal in salt effect upon $y_H y_R$ at any concentration. In Fig. (15-8-4), the behavior of log $y_H y_R$ for α-dinitrophenol in sodium, potassium, and barium chloride solutions is compared with that of log $\gamma_H \gamma_{Cl}$ in the same salt solutions. It will be noticed that the order of the curves is the same for the two acids, and that curves for the weak acid are higher than the corresponding curves for hydrochloric acid. No explanation of these interesting anomalies has yet been offered.

Cells without liquid junction have. been employed by Batchelder and Schmidt[90] to determine the dissociation of alanine, aspartic acid, arginine and ornithine in potassium, sodium and barium chloride solutions.

(9) Hydrolysis of Organic Acid Anions in Salt Solutions

By combination of the activity coefficient functions, $\gamma_H \gamma_R / \gamma_{HR}$ and $\gamma_H \gamma_{OH} / a_{H_2O}$, the influence of salts upon the hydrolysis of the anion, R^- (at infinite dilution of HR), may be investigated. The relationships for the hydrolytic reaction,

$$R^- + H_2O \rightleftharpoons HR + OH^-$$

are

$$K_h = \frac{K_w}{K_A} = \frac{\gamma_{HR}\,\gamma_{OH}}{a_{H_2O}\,\gamma_R}\frac{m_{HR}\,m_{OH}}{m_R} = \frac{\gamma_w^2\,k_w}{\gamma_A^2\,k_A} = \gamma_h^2 k_h \qquad (15\text{-}9\text{-}1)$$

Since the four quantities, γ_w, k_w, γ_A, and k_A, are separately known in some salt solutions, γ_h and k_h may be evaluated in these solutions.

Table (15-9-1) contains values of k_h for the hydrolysis of the acetate ion in sodium chloride solution from 0 to 40°, and in potassium, lithium, and barium chloride solutions at 25°, obtained by Harned and Hickey. At a given ionic strength, barium chloride produces the greatest salt effect at 25°, and the other salt effects decrease in the order lithium, sodium and potassium chloride.

Values of the activity coefficient function, log γ_h, for sodium chloride at 25° are plotted in Fig. (15-9-1) as circles, the radii of which represent an uncertainty of 0.1 percent in γ_h. This figure illustrates two interesting points. The total variation of γ_h with salt concentration is very small, being less than 2 percent. This nearly ideal behavior of the hydrolysis reaction is maintained also at 30 and 40°, but tends to disappear at lower temperatures. The second point of interest is the form taken by the plot in dilute solutions. Since γ_h is $\gamma_{HAc}\gamma_{OH} / a_{H_2O}\gamma_{Ac}$ by equation (15-9-1), a plot of log γ_h against $\sqrt{\mu}$ must approach the intercept, log $\gamma_h = 0$, with

[90] A. C. Batchelder and C. L. A. Schmidt, *J. Phys. Chem.*, **44**, 880 (1940); **44**, 893 (1940).

zero slope. It is clear from the figure that this condition is not fulfilled at the lowest experimental concentration, $0.02M$. To illustrate the extreme dilutions which might be required before the plot shows definite signs of becoming horizontal, the curve is drawn for the ratio of two hypothetical univalent ions conforming to the Debye-Hückel equation.

TABLE (15-9-1). HYDROLYSIS FUNCTION, $k_h = k_w/k_A$, FOR THE ACETATE ION AT INFINITE DILUTION IN CHLORIDE SOLUTIONS

$$k_h \times 10^{10}$$

μ	NaCl						KCl	LiCl	BaCl$_2$
	0°	10°	20°	25°	30°	40°	25°	25°	25°
0.0	0.684	1.688	3.88	5.74	8.40	17.11	5.74	5.74	5.74
.02	.697	1.706	3.92	5.79	8.45	17.29	5.77	5.81	5.83
.03	.704	1.701	3.92	5.79	8.45	17.29	5.74	5.83	5.85
.06	.706	1.714	3.93	5.79	8.44	17.31	5.69	5.93	5.96
.11	.708	1.720	3.95	5.82	8.50	17.39	5.65	6.08	6.05
.21	.719	1.741	3.98	5.84	8.54	17.36	5.61	6.27	6.29
.51	.738	1.770	4.03	5.91	8.57	17.44	5.65	6.53	6.81
1.01	.761	1.820	4.09	5.96	8.65	17.68	5.57	6.87	7.43
2.01	.801	1.864	4.11	5.93	8.54	17.48	5.85	7.13	8.28
3.01	.818	1.858	4.02	5.74	8.27	17.05	....	....	9.02

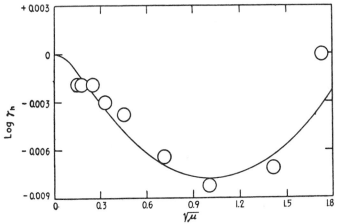

Fig. (15–9–1). Variation of log γ_h for hydrolysis of acetate ion at infinite dilution in sodium chloride solutions at 25°.

The $\dot{a}$-values were taken as 4.0 and 4.5, and a linear term, 0.005μ, was selected to give approximate agreement with the data at high ionic strengths. The numerical values of these parameters are too arbitrary to be significant, but they demonstrate the essential conformity of the data with theory, and their difference, 0.5 Å., calls attention to the very small magnitude of the effect which has been measured experimentally.

(10) Theoretical Considerations

The ionization constant data of weak electrolytes given in the preceding sections has been the subject of a number of recent discussions.[91] None of these yield an exact, or a complete solution of any of the numerous questions raised. In such a complicated situation, a further analysis of the experimental data in relation to the important variables and proposed theories will lead to interesting conclusions and problems.

In Fig. (15-10-1), $(-\log K)$ on the m-scale at 25° for water, formic, acetic, and propionic acids in dioxane-water mixtures is plotted against

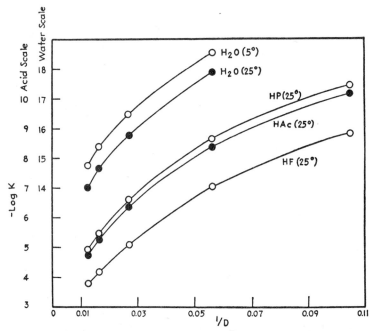

Fig. (15–10–1). Ionization constants as a function of dielectric constant in dioxane-water mixtures. HP, propionic acid; HAC, acetic acid; HF, formic acid.

$1/D$. As pointed out by Harned[92], these plots are not linear and, therefore, Born's equation [Equation (3-10-13)] is not valid. If the logarithm of the ionization constant on the c-scale or N-scale be plotted, the result is similar. This departure from the result required by the Born equation

[91] H. S. Harned and N. D. Embree, *J. Am. Chem. Soc.*, **56**, 1050 (1934); K. S. Pitzer, *Ibid.*, **59**, 2365 (1937); R. W. Gurney, *J. Chem. Phys.*, **6**, 499 (1938); E. C. Baughan, *Ibid.*, **7**, 951 (1939); D. H. Everett and W. F. K. Wynne-Jones, *Trans. Faraday Soc.*, **35**, 1380 (1939); D. H. Everett and C. A. Coulson, *Ibid.*, **36**, 633 (1940); J. F. J. Dippy, *Chem. Rev.*, **25**, 131 (1940); H. S. Harned and B. B. Owen, *Chem. Rev.*, **25**, 31 (1939); H. S. Harned and R. A. Robinson, *Trans. Faraday Soc.*, **36**, 973 (1940).

[92] H. S. Harned, *J. Phys. Chem.*, **43**, 275 (1939).

is not unexpected, since a similar result was noted for the standard potentials of the hydrogen-silver chloride cell [Chapter (11), Section (3)]. Further, similar results are obtained at all temperatures between 0 and 50°.

Gurney[93] has suggested a theory for the temperature variation of ionization constants which has been developed in a more suitable manner for calculation of these results by Baughan.[94] In the first place, consider two types of ionization reactions,

$$RNH_3^+ + H_2O \rightleftharpoons RNH_2 + H_3O^+ \qquad\qquad I$$

$$RCOOH + H_2O \rightleftharpoons RCOO^- + H_3O^+ \qquad\qquad II$$

Reactions of Type I involve a proton shift, but not the creation of a new field. They are isoelectric. Type II reactions involve both a proton shift, and the creation of a new field. A third type represented by

$$H_2PO_4^- + H_2O \rightleftharpoons HPO_4^{--} + H_3O^+ \qquad\qquad III$$

involves the creation of a new field, and additional work of separating a positively charged proton from a negative ion.

According to Born's equation, the electrical contribution to the standard free energy change of process II is given by

$$\Delta F^0(\text{El}) = \frac{N\epsilon^2}{2D}\left(\frac{1}{r_+} + \frac{1}{r_-}\right) \qquad (15\text{-}10\text{-}1)$$

If the total free energy, ΔF^0, is separated into a chemical, $\Delta F^0_{(D=\infty)}$, and an electrical part, $\Delta F^0(\text{El})$, then

$$\Delta F^0 = \Delta F^0_{(D=\infty)} + \Delta F^0(\text{El}) \qquad (15\text{-}10\text{-}2)$$

$$= -RT \ln K = -RT \ln K_{(D=\infty)} + \frac{N\epsilon^2}{2D}\left(\frac{1}{r_+} + \frac{1}{r_-}\right) \quad (15\text{-}10\text{-}3)$$

or

$$-\ln K = -\ln K_{(D=\infty)} + \frac{N\epsilon^2}{2DRT}\left(\frac{1}{r_+} + \frac{1}{r_-}\right) \qquad (15\text{-}10\text{-}4)$$

Upon substitution in equation (1-10-12), or

$$\frac{\partial \ln K}{\partial T} = \frac{\Delta H^0}{RT^2} \quad \text{and} \quad \frac{\partial \ln K_{(D=\infty)}}{\partial T} = \frac{\Delta H^0_{(D=\infty)}}{RT^2} \quad (15\text{-}10\text{-}5)$$

and differentiating, we obtain

$$\Delta H^0 = \Delta H^0_{(D=\infty)} + C\left[\frac{1}{D}\left(1 + T\frac{\partial \ln D}{\partial T}\right)\right] \qquad (15\text{-}10\text{-}6)$$

[93] R. W. Gurney, *J. Chem. Phys.*, **6**, 499 (1938).
[94] E. C. Baughan, *J. Chem. Phys.*, **7**, 951 (1939).

where

$$C = \frac{N\epsilon^2}{2}\left(\frac{1}{r_+} + \frac{1}{r_-}\right) \tag{15-10-7}$$

Equation (15-10-6) is the one employed by Baughan for representing reactions of types II and III.

The validity of equation (15-10-6) rests upon two factors. It presupposes the exactness of the Born equation from 0 to 60°, which, for aqueous solutions, involves a change in D from 88 to 67. The second factor involves an assumption regarding the variation of $\Delta H^0_{(D=\infty)}$ with temperature. From the recent measurements of Everett and Wynne-Jones[95] of the ionization of the ammonium ion, and of Pedersen[96] who determined the ionization constants of the anilinium and o-chloroanilinium ion, it appears that, for these isoelectric dissociations corresponding to Type I, log K varies with temperature according to the relation,

$$\log K = A - \frac{B}{T} \tag{15-10-8}$$

in which A and B are constants. If this is true, then ΔH^0_i is constant, and ΔC^0_{pi} is 0. More recent studies[97] reveal, however, that the mono-, di-, and tri-methyl ammonium ion dissociations are accompanied by changes in heat capacities of 7, 20, and 41 cals., respectively. Following Gurney, Baughan assumes that $\Delta H^0_{(D=\infty)}$ is independent of T for isoelectric reactions. In spite of the doubtful nature of this assumption, and the inexactness of Born's equation, Baughan succeeded in obtaining some results which lead to the right order of magnitude of the ionic radii. A few further computations will show that the situation is too complicated to be explained by this simplified treatment.

According to equation (15-10-6), if ΔH^0 be plotted against $\frac{1}{D}\left(1 + T\frac{\partial \ln D}{\partial T}\right)$, a straight line should be obtained with a slope, C, and an intercept, $\Delta H^0_{(D=\infty)}$. Such a plot is shown in Fig. (15-10-2) for water and acetic acid in aqueous solutions. Values of ΔH^0 were computed by equation (15-6-7), using the parameters in Table (15-6-4A). The plots are nearly straight lines, but each shows distinct curvatures. The deviations are greater than the estimated experimental errors. Similar results are obtained for water, formic, acetic and propionic acids in dioxane-water mixtures. From values of C, estimated roughly from the slopes of the curves, values of a mean radius, r, defined by the equation,

$$\frac{2}{r} = \frac{1}{r_+} + \frac{1}{r_-} \tag{15-10-8a}$$

[95] D. H. Everett and W. F. K. Wynne-Jones, *Proc. Roy. Soc. (London)*, **169A,** 190 (1938).

[96] K. Pedersen, *K. Danske Vidensk. Selsk. Skr.*, **14,** 9 (1937); **15,** 3 (1937).

[97] D. H. Everett and W. F. K. Wynne-Jones, *Trans. Faraday Soc.*, **35,** 1380 (1939).

have been determined, and recorded in Table (15-10-1). Similar results for these and other acids in water have been obtained by Baughan, who found values of r between 0.65 and 0.85.

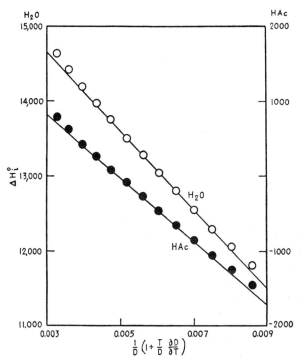

Fig. (15–10–2). Plot of ΔH_i^o according to equation (15–10–6) for water, O, and acetic acid, ●.

TABLE (15-10-1). VALUES OF MEAN IONIC RADII DERIVED BY MEANS OF
EQUATION (15-10-7)*
Solvent is Water-Dioxane Mixtures. X = Per Cent Dioxane; r (Å) by equation
(15-10-8)

X	H_2O	HCOOH	CH_3COOH	C_2H_5COOH
0	0.61	0.68	0.77	0.74
20	.86	1.00	.99	1.04
45	1.51	1.70	1.60	1.75
70	3.62	3.88	3.47	3.76
82	....	2.38	2.09	2.17

* H. S. Harned and T. R. Dedell, *J. Am. Chem. Soc.*, **63**, 3308 (1941).

Although the values of r are of the right order of magnitude, no convincing conclusions can be obtained from them. In water, they seem to be too small, and in 70% dioxane-water mixtures they are too large. Indeed, their variation with change in solvent will be difficult to explain.

It is interesting to note that by combining equations (15-10-4) and (15-10-6), the equation

$$\log K = A - \frac{B}{T} - \frac{C'}{DT} \tag{15-10-9}$$

is obtained where A, B, and C' are constants. This equation, different in form from the empirical equations discussed in Sections (3) and (6), fits the data fairly well.*

That a simplified electrostatic theory is inadequate in aqueous solutions becomes apparent from consideration of the heat capacities of the reactions. Examination of the values of $\Delta C_{p_i}^0$ in Table (15-6-2) leads to the following rough classification corresponding to the type reactions. Thus,

$$HA + H_2O \rightleftharpoons A^- + H_3O^+ \qquad\qquad \Delta C_{p_i}^0 \cong -(36 \to 41)$$

$$^+NH_3RCO_2H + H_2O \rightleftharpoons {}^+NH_3RCO_2^- + H_3O^+ \qquad \Delta C_{p_i}^0 \cong -36 \text{ (Mean)}$$

$$NH_2RCO_2^- + H_2O \rightleftharpoons {}^+NH_3RCO_2^- + OH^- \qquad \Delta C_{p_i}^0 \cong -32 \text{ (Mean)}$$

The heat capacities of the acid dissociations of ampholytes vary from -32 to -38, whereas those of the basic dissociation range from -29 to -39 if the anomalous result of -22 for the basic dissociation of glycine be omitted. It is important to note that although these reactions are of quite different electrical types, $\Delta C_{p_i}^0$ is roughly the same for all of them. These results may be stated in a more significant way by comparison with a common reference reaction. Thus, we have chosen

$$H_2O + H_2O \rightleftharpoons H_3O^+ + OH^- \qquad\qquad \Delta C_{p_i}^0 \cong -47$$

although other reactions such as the ionization of acetic acid would be suitable. Subtracting the above three reactions in turn from the water reaction, and including the first of them, we obtain

(a) $HA + H_2O \rightleftharpoons A^- + H_3O^+$ $\Delta C_{p_i}^0 \cong -(36 \to 41)$

(b) $A^- + H_2O \rightleftharpoons HA + OH^-$ $\Delta C_{p_i}^0 \cong -(6 \to 11)$

(c) $^+NH_3RCO_2^- + H_2O \rightleftharpoons {}^+NH_3RCO_2H + OH^-$ $\Delta C_{p_i}^0 \cong -11$

(d) $^+NH_3RCO_2^- + H_2O \rightleftharpoons NH_2RCO_2^- + H_3O^+$ $\Delta C_{p_i}^0 \cong -16$

The isoelectric reactions (b) are accompanied by appreciable changes in $\Delta C_{p_i}^0$ which is contrary to the assumption that $\Delta H_{(D-\infty)}$ is independent of the temperature, and to the result expressed by equation (15-10-8).

---

* V. K. LaMer and F. Brescia [*J. Am. Chem. Soc.*, **62**, 617 (1940)] on the basis of the preceding theory have obtained an expression for the empirical constant, p, in equation (15-6-6) of Harned and Embree. J. L. Magee, T. Ri and H. Eyring [*J. Chem. Phys.*, **9**, 419 (1941)] have extended the ideas of Gurney and Baughan to include a more detailed discussion of the mechanism of the ionization process and the influence of temperature and change of solvent media on ionization constants.

In Fig. (15-10-3), a plot of $\Delta C^0_{p_i}$ against the number of carbon atoms of the first four acids of the aliphatic series is shown. There is a definite decrease in $(-\Delta C^0_{p_i})$ with increasing complexity of the acids. This would not be the case if $\Delta C^0_{p_i}$ were zero for isoelectric reactions. If we subtract (c) from (d), we obtain another isoelectric reaction,

(e) $^+NH_3RCO_2H + OH^- \rightleftharpoons NH_2RCO_2^- + H_3O^+$ $\Delta C^0_{p_i} \cong -5$

in which $\Delta C^0_{p_i}$ is indeed low. Considering the errors involved, this value may be nearly zero.

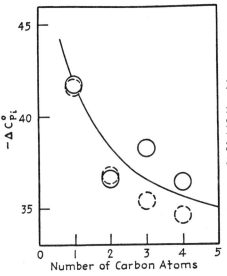

Fig. (15-10-3)

The heat capacity of ionization reactions as a function of the number of carbon atoms in aliphatic acids. Broken circles, Everett and Wynne-Jones, Equation (15-3-6). Circles, Table (15-6-1), Equation (15-6-9).; diameter of circles equals 1 cal.

Two general conclusions result from these considerations. (1) Values of $(-\Delta C^0_{p_i})$ for isoelectric reactions are considerably smaller than for other types. This indicates that the Coulombic forces are responsible for a considerable part of the effect. (2) It is also clear that the chemical type, as well as the electrical type, of these reactions, is important. This factor adds greatly to the complexity of the phenomena.

In view of the inadequacy of the Born expression for the interpretation of ionization equilibria and the thermodynamic properties of the ions, attempts have been recently made to compute these properties in terms of the orientation of water molecules around the ions. Bernal and Fowler,[98] from considerations of the structure of liquid water and its orientation around ions, have computed heats of solutions of ions in water. Eley and Evans[99] have extended this theory to the computation of the entropy of ions derived from the investigations of Latimer.[100] Everett and Coulson[101]

[98] J. D. Bernal and R. H. Fowler, *J. Chem. Phys.*, **1**, 515 (1933).

[99] D. D. Eley and M. G. Evans, *Trans. Faraday Soc.*, **34**, 1093 (1938).

[100] W. M. Latimer, K. S. Pitzer and C. M. Shansky, *J. Chem. Phys.*, **7**, 108 (1939).

[101] D. H. Everett and C. A. Coulson, *Trans. Faraday Soc.*, **36**, 633 (1940).

have attempted to employ this procedure for the computation of ionic heat capacities, and the estimation of the heat capacity changes of the ionization of a weak acid. After summing the orientation effect of the water molecules in the immediate neighborhood of the ions, and the Born electrostatic effect outside the tetrahedral shell of the water molecules, they obtain values of $(-\Delta C_{p_i}^0)$ which are less than those observed, even though values of the ionic radii of 1 $\mathring{A}$. are employed. They suggest that other effects, particularly that due to the "free volume" of the water molecules, may explain the discrepancy.*

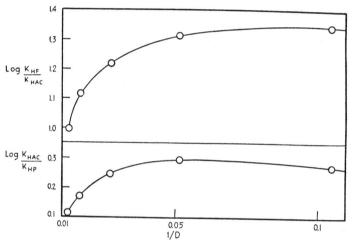

Fig. (15–11–1). Variations of the logarithms of ionization constant ratios as a function of dielectric constant in dioxane-water mixtures at 25°. HF, formic acid; HAc, acetic acid; HP, propionic acid.

(11) Additional Observations

These recent investigations of ionization constants as a function of the medium, and of the temperature, show that considerable care must be taken in attempting to develop a theory of the relation of ionization constants to the constitution of the weak electrolytes. Wynne-Jones[102] showed the ratio of the ionization constants of two weak electrolytes to be a function of the dielectric constant of the medium. His results (obtained in media of high dielectric constant) indicated that the logarithm of this ratio varied linearly with $1/D$. The more recent and more extended results do not

---

* Extensive investigations of relative strengths of acids in butyl alcohol have been made by L. A. Wooten and L. P. Hammett [*J. Am. Chem. Soc.*, **57**, 2289 (1935)] by the electrometric method, and R. B. Mason and M. Kilpatrick [*Ibid.*, **59**, 572 (1937)] who employed a photoelectric colorimeter. These studies have been extended to other solvents by L. J. Minnick and M. Kilpatrick [*J. Phys. Chem.*, **43**, 259 (1939)] and J. H. Elliott and M. Kilpatrick [*Ibid.*, **45**, 454 (1941); **45**, 466 (1941); **45**, 472 (1941); **45**, 485 (1941)].

102 W. F. K. Wynne-Jones, *Proc. Roy. Soc.*, **140**, 440 (1933).

confirm a linear variation.   In Fig. (15-11-1), the logarithm of the ratios of
the ionization constants of formic to acetic acids (upper curve), and acetic
to propionic acids (lower curve) have been plotted against $1/D$.   The
plots possess greater curvature as $1/D$ decreases, and their extrapolation
to $0(D = \infty)$ without an exact theoretical function is without significance.

It is also apparent from Fig. (15-11-2), in which $(-\log K_A)$ for acetic
and butyric acids is plotted against the temperature, that the ratio of the
ionization constants of two weak electrolytes changes considerably with

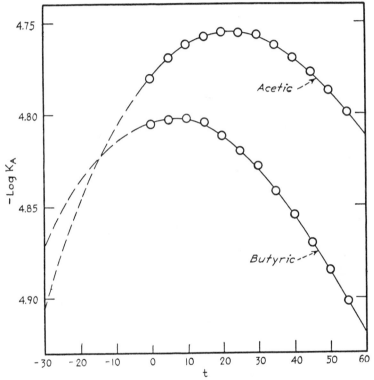

Fig. (15–11–2). Variation of ionization constants of acetic and butyric acids with
temperature.

temperature.   Indeed, if the curves be extended below 0°, they cross at
$-15°$.   Above this temperature, acetic acid is more highly dissociated than
butyric acid whereas below this temperature butyric acid is the stronger.

The ionization constant has usually been employed as a measure of the
strength of an electrolyte, and the ratio of ionization constants as a measure
of the relative strengths.   The preceding observations show that the
relative "strength" is a function of the nature of the medium and the
temperature, and is by no means a fixed quantity.   To adequately understand acid and base equilibria, it will be necessary to take into account the
effects of these and other variables, such as pressure and salt concentration.

(12) The Ionization Constants of Carbonic Acid in Water and in Aqueous Sodium Chloride Solutions from Electromotive Force, Calorimetric and High Field Conductance Measurements

The first ionization of carbonic acid,

$$H_2O + CO_2 \rightleftharpoons H_2CO_3 \rightleftharpoons H^+ + HCO_3^-$$

has been subjected to a comprehensive and consistent investigation by Harned and Davis,[103] and Harned and Bonner,[104] who measured the electromotive forces of the cell

$$Pt-H_2 \mid NaHCO_3(m_1), NaCl(m_2), CO_2(m_3) \mid AgCl-Ag$$

The general equation for the electromotive force of this cell is

$$E = E^0 - \frac{RT}{F} \ln m_H m_{Cl} \gamma_H \gamma_{Cl} - E_c \tag{15-12-1}$$

where $E_c = -(RT/2F) \ln P_{H_2}$. The term E_c is retained since the measurements were carried out with hydrogen-carbon dioxide gas mixtures which varied from 18 to 80 per cent carbon dioxide. The ionization constant may be defined by

$$K_{1A} \equiv \frac{a_H a_{HCO_3}}{a_{H_2O} a_{CO_2}} = \frac{\gamma_H \gamma_{HCO_3} m_H m_{HCO_3}}{a_{H_2O} \gamma_{CO_2} m_{CO_2}} = \frac{\gamma_H \gamma_{HCO_3}}{a_{H_2O} \gamma_{CO_2}} k_{1A} \tag{15-12-2}$$

As a reference state, the condition that $\gamma_H = \gamma_{HCO_3} = \gamma_{CO_2} = a_{H_2O} = 1$ in pure water was chosen, and therefore K_{1A} is an isothermal constant at all salt concentrations. By elimination of m_H between equations (15-12-1) and (15-12-2), we obtain

$$(E + E_c - E^0)\frac{F}{2.3026\,RT} + \log m_{CO_2} + \log \frac{m_{Cl}}{m_{HCO_2}}$$
$$= -\log K_{1A} - \frac{\log \gamma_H \gamma_{Cl} a_{H_2O} \gamma_{CO_2}}{\gamma_H \gamma_{HCO_3}} \equiv -\log K' \tag{15-12-3}$$

which defines the extrapolation function, $-\log K'$. Since the logarithmic term containing the activity coefficients is zero in pure water, $-\log K_{1A}$ may be obtained by extrapolating the right side of this equation to zero concentration of all solutes. An exact procedure requires two extrapolations, a first to zero ionic strength, and a second to zero concentration of carbon dioxide. The molality of the carbon dioxide may be obtained from Henry's law in the form

$$m_{CO_2} = S_0 P_{CO_2} \tag{15-12-4}$$

[103] H. S. Harned and R. Davis, Jr., *J. Am. Chem. Soc.*, **65**, 2030 (1943).
[104] H. S. Harned and F. T. Bonner, *Ibid.*, **67**, 1026 (1945).

Harned and Davis, by using gas mixtures of a wide range of concentrations of carbon dioxide, showed that its presence in the solution produced no appreciable medium effect on $-\log K'$. The establishment of this fact eliminates the necessity of double extrapolation, and greatly simplifies subsequent experimental procedures.

The ionization, k_{1A}, in the salt solutions may be obtained by elimination of K_{1A} from equations (15-12-2) and (15-12-3) whereby

$$-\log k_{1A}$$

$$= (E - E^0 + E_c) \frac{F}{2.3026\,RT} + \log \frac{m_{CO_2}m_{Cl}}{m_{HCO_3}} + \log \gamma_H\gamma_{Cl} \qquad (15\text{-}12\text{-}5)$$

is obtained. All quantities on the right-hand side of this equation are known, since $\sqrt{\gamma_H\gamma_{Cl}}$, the activity coefficient of hydrochloric acid at zero concentration in sodium chloride solutions [Table (14-2-1A)] has been determined. The carbon dioxide molality may be calculated by means of

$$m_{CO_2} = S_{(s)}P_{CO_2} \qquad (15\text{-}12\text{-}6)$$

if the Henry law constants for the salt solutions, determined by Harned and Davis, are employed. The observed values of K_{1A} and k_{1A} in sodium chloride solutions are given in Table (15-12-1), and the constants of equation (15-6-9) for computing their temperature variations are contained in Table (15-6-4A).

By taking the logarithm of equation (15-12-2) and substituting the Debye and Hückel formula, with an additional linear term for $\log \gamma_H\gamma_{HCO_3}$, we obtain

$$-\log k_{1A} = -\log K_{1A} - \frac{2S_{(f)}\sqrt{d_0\mu}}{1 + A'\sqrt{\mu}} + B'\mu - \log \gamma_{CO_2}a_{H_2O} \qquad (15\text{-}12\text{-}7)$$

It is found that from 0 to 1 M sodium chloride

$$\log \gamma_{CO_2} = \log \frac{S_0}{S_{(s)}} = \alpha\mu \qquad (15\text{-}12\text{-}8)$$

where α is an isothermal constant. Further, the approximation

$$-\log a_{H_2O} = \beta m \qquad (15\text{-}12\text{-}9)$$

represents the observed results within sufficiently narrow limits to permit us to reduce equation (15-12-7) to the simple form

$$-\log k_{1A} = -\log K_{1A} - \frac{2S_{(f)}\sqrt{d_0\mu}}{1 + \sqrt{\mu}} + B\mu \qquad (15\text{-}12\text{-}10)$$

by replacing A' by unity at all temperatures. The necessary quantities for the computation of k_{1A} from 0 to 50° and 0 to 1 M concentration are summarized in the following equations:

$$\log K_{1A} = -3404.71/T + 14.8435 - 0.032786T \qquad (15\text{-}12\text{-}11)$$

$$S_{(f)} \sqrt{d_0} = 0.4883 + 0.75545 \times 10^{-3}t + 0.1743 \times 10^{-5}t^2$$
$$+ 0.11665 \times 10^{-7}t^3 \qquad (15\text{-}12\text{-}12)^*$$

$$B = 0.066 + 1.92 \times 10^{-3}t - 0.0176 \times 10^{-3}t^2 \qquad (15\text{-}12\text{-}13)$$

Harned and Bonner found that these equations represent the observed results with average deviations in $-\log k_{1A}$ of 0.001 from 0 to 10°, of 0.001 to 0.002 from 15 to 30°, and of 0.002 to 0.004 from 35 to 50°. The maximum deviation is 0.0063 at 50° and 1 M sodium chloride.

The values of α in equation (15-12-8), which permit the calculation of $\log \gamma_{CO_2}$ at all temperatures and concentrations under consideration, are given by the equation

$$\alpha = 0.1190 - 0.833 \times 10^{-3} t + 0.666 \times 10^{-5}t^2 \qquad (15\text{-}12\text{-}14)$$

The carbon dioxide concentration is given by

$$\log m_{CO_2} = \log S_0 P_{CO_2} - \alpha\mu \qquad (15\text{-}12\text{-}15)$$

in which $\log S_0$ can be computed by the expression

$$- \log S_0 = -2385.73/T + 14.0184 - 0.015264 \, T \quad (15\text{-}12\text{-}16)$$

These investigations lead to the accurate evaluation of many important quantities involved in aqueous solutions of carbon dioxide. Besides the standard thermodynamic functions, ΔF_i^0, ΔH_i^0, $\Delta C_{p_i}^0$, and ΔS_i^0, the quantities, K_{1A}, k_{1A}, $\gamma_H\gamma_{HCO_3}/\gamma_{CO_2}a_{H_2O}$, $\gamma_H\gamma_{HCO_3}$, γ_{CO_2} and m_{CO_2} in the salt solutions, have been determined. However, it is important to note that this method does not yield any information regarding the ionization of the acid, H_2CO_3, but only that of $H_2O + CO_2$, or the sum of the reactions

$$H_2O + CO_2 \rightleftharpoons H_2CO_3$$

and

$$H_2CO_3 \rightleftharpoons H^+ + HCO_3^-$$

Roughton,[105] by means of kinetic calorimetric measurements, has been able to estimate the heat contents of both these reactions and the velocity constant of the second reaction. He employed the method of rapid mixing of solutions of sodium bicarbonate and hydrochloric acid. This mixture flowed at a known rate through an observation tube containing thermocouples at suitable distances. The temperature measurements showed conclusively that, with a strong acid, the reaction, $H^+ + HCO_3^- \rightarrow H_2CO_3$, was practically instantaneous, while the rate constant, k_0, of the slower reaction, $H_2CO_3 \rightarrow H_2O + CO_2$, was capable of measurement. Independent measurements[105a] of the rate of formation of carbon dioxide in bicar-

---

* G. Scatchard, *J. Am. Chem. Soc.*, **65**, 1249 (1943).

[105] F. J. W. Roughton, *J. Am. Chem. Soc.*, **63**, 2930 (1941).

[105a] R. Brinkman, R. Margaria and F. J. W. Roughton, *Phil. Trans. Roy. Soc.*, **A 332**, 65 (1933).

bonate-cacodylate buffers (P_H = 5.5 to 7) yielded the velocity constant, k_1, of the rapid reaction, $H^+ + HCO_3^- \rightarrow H_2O + CO_2$. From the ratio, k_0/k_1, the ionization constant of H_2CO_3 was estimated to be 2×10^{-4} at 27° in a 0.06 M sodium chloride solution.

TABLE (15-12-1). THE IONIZATION CONSTANTS, $K(0)$ AND K_{1A}, OF CARBONIC ACID IN WATER AND THEIR RATIOS.

t	$K(0) \times 10^4$	$K_{1A} \times 10^{7(a)}$	$10^2 K_{1A}/K(0)$
5	1.56	3.04	0.195
15	1.76	3.80	.216
25	1.72	4.45	.259
35	1.67	4.91	.294
38	1.59	5.01	.315
45	1.60	5.14	.323

(a) H. S. Harned and R. Davis, *J. Am. Chem. Soc.*, **65**, 2030 (1943).

As mentioned in Chapter (7), Section (9), high field conductance measurements of carbonic acid solutions yield the ionization constant $K(0)$ of H_2CO_3. This determination has been carried out by Berg and Patterson[106] at 25° and by Wissbrun, French and Patterson[107] from 5° to 45°. Table (15-12-1) contains their values of $K(0)$ and K_{1A} and the ratio $K_{1A}/K(0)$. Since $K(0)$ is the dissociation constant of the reaction, $H_2CO_3 \rightleftharpoons H^+ + HCO_3^-$ and K_{1A} is that of the reaction, $CO_2 + H_2O \rightleftharpoons H^+ + HCO_3^-$, the ratio $K_{1A}/K(0)$ is the equilibrium constant of the hydration reaction, $CO_2 + H_2O = H_2CO_3$. The value of $K(0)$ in the table refers to a salt-free carbon dioxide solution whereas Roughton's value of 2.5×10^{-4} was obtained in a 0.06 molar sodium chloride solution. Harned and Bonner found that the ratio of K_{1A} in 0.06 molar salt solution to K_{1A} in water was 1.51 at 15°. Assuming that the same ratio is valid for $K(0)$, then Roughton's value of $K(0)$ in the salt-free solution is $(2.5 \times 10^{-4})/1.51. = 1.66 \times 10^{-4}$. This result is in surprisingly good agreement with the result given in Table (15-12-1).

The values of $K(0)$ can be computed within the error of experiment by the equation of Harned and Embree[66]

$$\log K(0) = \log K_m - 5 \times 10^5(t - \theta)^2$$

The maximum value, K_m, was found to occur at 17°. Heat contents for the reactions involved in solutions of carbon dioxide were computed from these data and found to be in reasonable conformity with the results of other investigators.

A similar measurement of the high field conductance of ammonia in water by Berg and Patterson[108] yielded the value $6.3 \pm 0.5 \times 10^{-5}$ for the

[106] D. Berg and A. Patterson, Jr., *J. Am. Chem. Soc.*, **75**, 5197 (1953).

[107] K. F. Wissbrun, D. M. French and A. Patterson, Jr., *J. Phys. Chem.*, **58**, 693 (1954).

[108] D. Berg and A. Patterson, *J. Am. Chem. Soc.*, **75**, 5731 (1953).

dissociation constant of the ammonium hydroxide molecule according to the reaction, $NH_4OH \rightleftharpoons NH_4^+ + OH^-$ at 25°. The ionization constant of the reaction, $NH_3 + H_2O \rightleftharpoons NH_4^+ + OH^-$, according to the electromotive force measurements of Bates and Pinching[109] was found to be 1.77×10^{-5}.

(13) RECENT DETERMINATIONS OF IONIZATION CONSTANTS

In Tables (15-13-1A) and (15-3-2A) we have compiled accurate values of ionization constants in water, in salt solutions and in water-organic solvent mixtures which have been determined in recent years by cells without liquid junctions by the methods described in this chapter. Table (15-13-3A) contains the parameters of equations (15-6-9) to (15-6-15) which we have found suitable for the calculation of ionization constants as functions of the temperature and for the calculation of the standard thermodynamic functions corresponding to the ionization reactions.

The determination of the ionization of boric acid in sodium chloride solutions by Owen and King[110] was effected by means of buffered solutions in cells without liquid junctions. An interesting feature of this contribution consisted in their choice of a standard state which requires that the activity coefficients are unity at infinite dilution in each sodium chloride solution at concentration m. Thus, every salt solution is treated as an independent solvent. The mathematical procedure is analogous to that developed for organic solvent-water mixtures in Section (7) of this chapter. Although this method has certain formal and logical advantages, it does not yield information which cannot be obtained by the earlier procedures, as exemplified by the treatment of the carbonic acid equilibrium described in Section (12).

The fruitfulness of the thermodynamic method for the determination of ionization constants, and the ionization of weak acids in a given solvent and in salt solutions from electromotive measurements of cells without liquid junctions, is further exemplified by its extension by Bates[111] to the overlapping dissociation of weak acids. He shows how the method can be employed to determine the product K_1K_2 for dibasic acids, and both the products K_1K_2 and K_2K_3 for tribasic acids. Bates and Pinching[112] have illustrated this method by a comprehensive study of the three ionization constants of citric acid. Their results are listed in Table (15-13-1A) and the constants of the equations for computing the thermodynamic functions are incorporated in (15-13-3A). At 18, 25, and 37°, their values of $-\log K_{2A}$ and $-\log K_{3A}$ agree closely with those determined by Bjerrum and Unmack[113] from cells with liquid junctions, but the results for $-\log K_{1A}$

[109] R. G. Bates and G. D. Pinching, *J. Am. Chem. Soc.*, **72**, 1393 (1950).

[110] B. B. Owen and E. J. King, *Ibid.*, **65**, 1612 (1943).

[111] R. G. Bates, *J. Am. Chem. Soc.*, **70**, 1579 (1948).

[112] R. G. Bates and G. D. Pinching, *Ibid.*, **71**, 1274 (1949).

[113] N. Bjerrum and A. Unmack, *Kgl. Danske Videnskab, Selskab Math.-fys., Medd.* **9**, No 1 (1929).

by the two methods differ by approximately 0.06. Further illustrations of this procedure are the determinations of the first and second ionization constants of succinic acid by Pinching and Bates[114] and the resolution of the ionization constants of d-tartaric acid by Bates and Canham.[115]

Bates and Pinching[116] have employed the cells

$$H_2 \mid NH_4Cl(m), NH_3(m) \mid AgCl\text{-}Ag$$

and

$$H_2 \mid NH_3(m), KHP(m) \mid AgCl\text{-}Ag$$

where KHP is potassium hydrogen phenol sulphonate, to determine the acidic dissociation constant of the ammonium ion and the ionization of ammonia in aqueous solutions. Satisfactory agreement between the results obtained from both these types of cells was obtained. Values of the basic constant are recorded in Table (15-13-4A).

The determinations of dissociation constants by cells without liquid junctions can be used as criteria for the accuracy of similar determinations by cells with salt bridges. Some comparisons of results by the two methods have been recorded in Table (15-6-3). From the large number of measurements of cells with salt bridges in which accurate extrapolations have been possible, we cite the investigations of Everett and Wynne-Jones[117] and more recently the work of Everett and Pinsent[118] who determined the first and second dissociation constants of ethylene diammonium and hexamethylene diammonium ions from 0 to 60°. These results are recorded in Table (15-13-4A).

For evaluating the ionization constants of fatty acids, Everett, Landsman and Pinsent[119] have employed cells of the type

$$H_2 \mid HAc_1(m_1), NaAc_1(m_1), NaCl(m - m_1) \mid KCl(3.5\ M)$$

$$\cdot \mid HAc_2(m_1), NaAc_2(m_1)NaCl(m - m_1) \mid AgCl\text{-}Ag$$

which lead to precise determinations of the ratio, K_{HAc_2}/K_{HAc_1}. They assume that the sum of the two liquid junction is negligible. They choose the ionization constant of acetic acid as a standard of reference and carried their measurements over a range of temperature from 0 to 60°. Values of the ionization constants for fatty acids not given in Table (15-6-1A) are recorded in Table (15-13-4A).

[114] G. D. Pinching and R. G. Bates, *J. Research, Nat. Bureau of Stds.*, **45**, 322, 440 (1950).

[115] R. G. Bates and R. G. Canham, *Ibid.*, **47**, 343 (1951).

[116] R. G. Bates and G. D. Pinching, *Ibid.*, **42**, 419 (1949); *J. Am. Chem. Soc.*, **73**, 1393 (1950).

[117] D. H. Everett and W. F. K. Wynne-Jones, *Proc. Roy. Soc. A.* **169**, 190 (1938); **177**, 499 (1941); *Trans. Faraday Soc.*, **35**, 1380 (1939).

[118] D. H. Everett and B. R. W. Pinsent, *Proc. Roy. Soc., A*, **215**, 416 (1952).

[119] D. H. Everett, D. A. Landsman and B. R. W. Pinsent, *Proc. Roy. Soc., A*, **215**, 403 (1952).

The method of determination of ionization constants from electromotive forces of cells without liquid junction has been employed with considerable success in the study of dissociation equilibria of biologically important solutions. As illustrations, the precise determinations of the ionization constants of a number of N-acyl amino-acids,[120] sulphanilic,[121] metanilic[122] acid, glycerol-2-phosphoric acid,[123] glucose-1-phosphoric acid,[124] 2-amino-ethanol-1-phosphoric acid[125] and N-carbamoylamino-acids[126] may be cited. The parameters by means of which the ionization constants and derived thermodynamic functions may be computed from 0 to 50° are given in Table (15-13-5A).

Shedlovsky and Kay[127] have employed conductance to determine the ionization constant of acetic in water-methanol mixtures over the entire range of composition. These results, recorded in Table (15-13-1), should prove of considerable value for the determination of ionization constants of other acids in these media by the use of differential potentiometry.

TABLE (15–13–1). IONIZATION CONSTANTS OF ACETIC ACID IN WATER-METHANOL MIXTURES AT 25°.

Volume % Methanol	K_{1A}	Volume % Methanol	K_{1A}
0	1.753×10^{-5}	80	3.96×10^{-7}
10	1.31×10^{-5}	90	9.71×10^{-8}
20	9.59×10^{-6}	95	2.07×10^{-8}
40	4.52×10^{-6}	100	2.37×10^{-10}
60	1.82×10^{-6}	—	—

[120] E. J. King and G. W. King, *J. Am. Chem. Soc.*, **78**, 1089 (1956).

[121] R. O. MacLaren and D. F. Swinehart, *Ibid.*, **73**, 1822 (1951).

[122] R. D. McCoy, and D. F. Swinehart, *Ibid.*, **76**, 4708 (1954).

[123] J. H. Ashby, E. M. Crook and S. P. Datta, *Biochem. J.*, **56**, 190, 198 (1954).

[124] J. H. Ashby, H. B. Clarke and S. P. Datta, *Ibid.*, **59**, 203 (1955).

[125] H. B. Clarke, S. P. Datta and B. R. Rabin, *Ibid.*, **59**, 209 (1955).

[126] E. J. King, *J. Am. Chem. Soc.*, **78**, 6020 (1956).

[127] T. Shedlovsky and R. L. Kay, *J. Phys. Chem.*, **60**, 151 (1956).

Appendix A

TABLE (6-2-1A). THE EQUIVALENT CONDUCTANCES OF ELECTROLYTES IN AQUEOUS SOLUTIONS AT 25°. (INT. MHOS)

	$c^\circ = 0$	0.0005	0.001	0.005	0.01	0.02	0.05	0.1	Reference
HCl	426.16	422.74	421.36	415.80	412.00	407.24	399.09	391.32	1, 19
LiCl	115.03	113.15	112.40	109.40	107.32	104.65	100.11	95.86	1, 2, 3
NaCl	126.45	124.50	123.74	120.65	118.51	115.76	111.06	106.74	4, 20
KCl	149.86	147.81	146.95	143.55	141.27	138.34	133.37	128.96	1, 20
NH$_4$Cl	149.7	......	......		141.28	138.33	133.29	128.75	5
KBr	151.9	......	......	146.09	143.43	140.48	135.68	131.39	6, 7
NaI	126.94	125.36	124.25	121.25	119.24	116.70	112.79	108.78	8
KI	150.34	......	......	144.37	142.18	139.45	134.97	131.11	7
KNO$_3$	144.96	142.77	141.84	138.48	132.82	132.41	126.31	120.40	1
KHCO$_3$	118.00	116.10	115.34	112.24	110.08	107.22	......	......	9
NaO$_2$CCH$_3$	91.0	89.2	88.5	85.72	83.76	81.24	76.92	72.80	10
NaO$_2$C(CH$_3$)$_2$CH$_3$	82.70	81.04	80.31	77.58	75.76	73.39	69.32	65.27	11
NaOH	247.8	245.6	244.7	240.8	238.0	......	......	......	18
AgNO$_3$	133.36	131.36	130.51	127.20	124.76	121.41	115.24	109.14	1
MgCl$_2$	129.40	125.61	124.11	118.31	114.55	110.04	103.08	97.10	12
CaCl$_2$	135.84	131.93	130.36	124.25	120.36	115.65	108.47	102.46	12
SrCl$_2$	135.80	131.90	130.33	124.24	120.29	115.54	108.25	102.19	12
BaCl$_2$	139.98	135.96	134.34	128.02	123.94	119.09	111.48	105.19	12
Na$_2$SO$_4$	129.9	125.74	124.15	117.15	112.44	106.78	97.75	89.98	7
CuSO$_4$	133.6	121.6	115.26	94.07	83.12	72.20	59.05	50.58	13
ZnSO$_4$	132.8	121.4	115.53	95.49	84.91	74.24	61.20	52.64	13
LaCl$_3$	145.8	139.6	137.0	127.5	121.8	115.3	106.2	99.1	6, 14
K$_3$Fe(CN)$_6$	174.5	166.4	163.1	150.7	......	......	......	......	15
K$_4$Fe(CN)$_6$	184.5	......	167.24	146.09	134.83	122.82	107.70	97.87	16, 17

* Concentrations expressed in equivalents per liter.

(1) T. Shedlovsky, J. Am. Chem. Soc., 54, 1411 (1932).
(2) D. A. MacInnes, T. Shedlovsky and L. G. Longsworth, Ibid., 54, 2758 (1932).
(3) K. A. Krieger and M. Kilpatrick, Ibid., 59, 1878 (1937).
(4) T. Shedlovsky, A. S. Brown, and D. A. MacInnes, Trans. Electrochem. Soc., 66, 165 (1934).
(5) L. G. Longsworth, J. Am. Chem. Soc., 57, 1185 (1935).
(6) G. Jones and C. F. Bickford, Ibid., 56, 602 (1934).
(7) Unpublished measurements of T. Shedlovsky and L. G. Longsworth quoted by MacInnes in "Principles of Electrochemistry," Reinhold Publishing Corp., New York (1939), p. 339.
(8) P. A. Lasselle and J. G. Aston, J. Am. Chem. Soc., 55, 3067 (1933).
(9) T. Shedlovsky and D. A. MacInnes, Ibid., 57, 1705 (1935).
(10) D. A. MacInnes and T. Shedlovsky, Ibid., 54, 1429 (1932).
(11) D. Belcher, Ibid., 60, 2744 (1938).
(12) T. Shedlovsky and A. S. Brown, Ibid., 56, 1066 (1934).
(13) B. B. Owen and R. W. Gurry, Ibid., 60, 3074 (1938). These values have been corrected for presence of M(OH)$^+$ and HSO$_4^-$ ions.
(14) L. G. Longsworth and D. A. MacInnes, Ibid., 60, 3070 (1938).
(15) G. S. Hartley and G. W. Donaldson, Trans. Faraday Soc., 33, 457 (1937).
(16) G. Jones and F. C. Jelen, J. Am. Chem. Soc., 58, 2561 (1936).
(17) E. Swift Jr., Ibid., 60, 728 (1938).
(18) V. Sivertz, R. E. Reitmeier, and H. V. Tartar, Ibid., 62, 1379 (1940).
(19) Values up to c equal to 12 and at 10° intervals between 5 and 65° are given by B. B. Owen and F. H. Sweeton, Ibid., 63, 2811 (1941).
(20) Values from 15° to 45° are given by H. E. Gunning and A. R. Gordon, J. Chem. Phys., 10, 126 (1942).

TABLE (6-2-2A).* LIMITING CONDUCTANCES IN n-METHYLACETAMIDE† AT 40°.

Salt	Λ^0	Salt	Λ^0	Salt	Λ^0
LiCl	18.1	MeNH₃Cl	23.43	Me₄NCl	23.58
NaCl	19.6	Me₂NH₂Cl	25.23	Me₄NBr	24.80
NaBr	21.0	Me₃NHCl	24.40	Me₄NI	26.65
NaI	22.8	MeNH₃Br	24.73	Et₄NBr	24.50
KCl	20.1	Me₂NH₂Br	26.46	Et₄NI	26.25
KBr	21.1	Me₃NHBr	25.72	Pr₄NBr	22.01
KI	23.1	EtNH₃Cl	22.39	Pr₄NI	23.74
NH₄Cl	21.18	Et₂NH₂Cl	23.47	Bu₄NI	22.35
NH₄Br	22.50	BuNH₃Cl	21.33	Me₃PhNCl	21.80
NH₄I	24.30	Bu₂NH₂Cl	20.90	Me₃PhNI	24.80

* L. R. Dawson, P. G. Sears and R. H. Graves, Jr., *J. Am. Chem. Soc.*, **77**, 1986 (1955), the alkali halides; L. R. Dawson, E. D. Wilhoit and P. G. Sears, *Ibid.*, **78**, 1569 (1956), the ammonium and substituted ammonium halides.
† $D = 165.5$; $\eta = 0.03020$; $d = 0.9420$.

TABLE (6-3-1A).* DISSOCIATION CONSTANTS OF COMPLEX VALENCE TYPE SALTS AND IONS ESTIMATED FROM CONDUCTANCE DATA IN WATER AT 25°.

	$10^3 K$	Ref.		$10^3 K$	Ref.
(CaIO₃)⁺	130	(1)	(MgP₃O₉)⁻	0.489	(8)
(SrIO₃)⁺	1000	(2)	(CaP₃O₉)⁻	0.356	(8)
CaOxalate	1	(3)	(SrP₃O₉)⁻	0.444	(9)
BaOxalate	4.7	(3)	(BaP₃O₉)⁻	0.450	(8)
LaFe(CN)₆	0.182	(4)	(MnP₃O₉)⁻	0.272	(8)
LaCo(CN)₆	0.182	(5)	(NiP₃O₉)⁻	0.603	(8)
La₂(SO₄)₃	0.2	(6)	(NaP₃O₉)⁼	68	(10)
MgFe(CN)₆⁻	1.63	(7)	KFe(CN)₆⁻	20	(5)
CaFe(CN)₆⁻	1.47	(7)	KCo(CN)₆⁻	60	(5)
SrFe(CN)₆⁻	1.41	(7)	(SrP₄O₁₂)⁻	0.007	(9)
BaFe(CN)₆⁻	1.32	(7)	(NaP₄O₁₂)⁼	9	(10)

* Dissociation constants of numerous salts and ions, determined from solubility and pH data as well as conductivity, are collected and compared by H. W. Jones, C. B. Monk and C. W. Davies, *J. Chem. Soc.* (London), **1949**, 2693.

(1) C. W. Davies, *J. Chem. Soc.* (London), **1938**, 273.
(2) C. A. Colman-Porter and C. B. Monk, *Ibid.*, **1952**, 1312.
(3) R. W. Money and C. W. Davies, *Trans. Faraday Soc.*, **28**, 609 (1932).
(4) C. W. Davies and J. C. James, *Proc. Roy. Soc.* (London), A195, 116 (1948). The ionization of this salt has been studied in mixed solvents by J. C. James, *J. Chem. Soc.* (London), **1950**, 1094, and by H. S. Dunsmore and J. C. James, *Ibid.*, **1951**, 2925.
(5) J. C. James and C. B. Monk, *Trans. Faraday Soc.*, **46**, 1041 (1950).
(6) I. L. Jenkins and C. B. Monk, *J. Am. Chem. Soc.*, **72**, 2695 (1950).
(7) C. W. Gibby and C. B. Monk, *Trans. Faraday Soc.*, **48**, 632 (1952).
(8) H. W. Jones, C. B. Monk and C. W. Davies, *J. Chem. Soc.* (London), **1949**, 2693.
(9) C. B. Monk, *Ibid.*, **1952**, 1314.
(10) C. W. Davies and C. B. Monk, *Ibid.*, **1949**, 413.

TABLE (6-6-1A). CATION TRANSFERENCE NUMBERS IN AQUEOUS SOLUTIONS AT 25°
BY THE MOVING BOUNDARY METHOD

Electrolyte	Ref.	$\Lambda^\bullet$	$\mathcal{S}_{(T_+)}^\bullet$	T_+^0	Concentration (equivalents/liter)				
					.01	.02	.05	.10	.20
HCl..................	a	426.17	+0.04507	.8209	.8251	.8266	.8292	.8314	.8337
NaC₂H₃O₂...........	b	90.99	+ .03336	.5507	.5537	.5550	.5573	.5594	.5610
KC₂H₃O₂............	f	114.40	+ .07467	.6427	.6498	.6523	.6569	.6609	.....
KNO₃................	b	144.96	+ .00297	.5072	.5084	.5087	.5093	.5103	.5120
NH₄Cl...............	b	149.94	− .00363	.4909	.4907	.4906	.4905	.4907	.4911
KCl.................	a	149.86	− .00376	.4906	.4902	.4901	.4899	.4898	.4894
KI..................	b	150.29	− .00430	.4892	.4884	.4883	.4882	.4883	.4887
KBr.................	b	151.63	− .00596	.4849	.4833	.4832	.4831	.4833	.4841
AgNO₃..............	c	133.36	− .01604	.4643	.4648	.4652	.4664	.4682	.....
NaCl................	a	126.43	− .04910	.3963	.3918	.3902	.3876	.3854	.3821
LiCl................	a	115.03	− .08514	.3364	.3289	.3261	.3211	.3168	.3112
CaCl₂...............	b	135.84	− .26174	.4380	.4264	.4220	.4140	.4060	.3953
Na₂SO₄.............	b	129.9	+ .0632	.386	.3848	.3836	.3829	.3828	.3828
K₂SO₄..............	d	153.3	+ .1482	.479	.4829	.4848	.4870	.4890	.4910
LaCl₃..............	e	145.9	− .5491	.477	.4625	.4576	.4482	.4375	.4233

References to sources of data: (a) L. G. Longsworth, *J. Am. Chem. Soc.*, **54**, 2741 (1932); (b) L. G. Longsworth, *Ibid.*, **57**, 1185 (1935); (c) D. A. MacInnes and I. A. Cowperthwaite quoted by D. A. MacInnes and L. G. Longsworth, *Chem. Rev.*, **11**, 171 (1932); (d) G. S. Hartley and G. W. Donaldson, *Trans. Faraday Soc.*, **33**, 457 (1937); (e) L. G. Longsworth and D. A. MacInnes, *J. Am. Chem. Soc.*, **60**, 3070 (1938); (f) D. J. LeRoy and A. R. Gordon, *J. Chem. Phys.*, **6**, 398 (1938).

* These values of $\mathcal{S}_{(T_+)}$, calculated by equation (6-6-4a), require that the concentration be expressed in moles per liter. If the data are plotted against the square root of the equivalent concentration, the limiting slopes become −0.18508, +0.0447, +0.1048 and −0.3170 for the last four salts in the table.

TABLE (6-6-2A). CATION TRANSFERENCE NUMBERS IN ALCOHOLIC
SOLUTIONS AT 25° BY THE MOVING BOUNDARY METHOD.

Salt	Solvent	Λ^0	T_+^0	1000c (stoichiometric)				
				1	1.5	2	2.5	5
NaClᵃ.	Methanol	97.61	.4633	.4615	.4612	.4609	.4606	.4595
KClᵃ..	Methanol	104.78	.5001	.5002	.....	.5003	.....	.5007
NaClᵇ.	MeOH—H₂O*	66.62	.4437	.4425	.4423	.4421	.4420	.4415
KClᵇ.	MeOH—H₂O*	75.10	.5068	.5070	.....	.5071	.....	.5074
LiClᶜ.	Ethanol	38.90	.5607	.5657	.5674	.....	.5698	.....
NaClᶜ.	Ethanol	42.16	.5187	.5204	.5209	.5212	.5218	.....

* 50 mole per cent methanol.
(a) J. A. Davies, R. L. Kay and A. R. Gordon, *J. Chem. Phys.*, **19**, 749 (1951). Values of Λ^0 from J. P. Butler, H. I. Schiff and A. R. Gordon, *Idem.*, p. 752. (b) L. W. Schemilt, J. A. Davies and A. R. Gordon, *Ibid.*, **16**, 340 (1948). Values of Λ^0 from H. I. Schiff and A. R. Gordon, *Idem.*, p. 336. (c) J. R. Graham and A. R. Gordon, *J. Am. Chem. Soc.*, **79**, 2350 (1957). Values of Λ^0 from J. R. Graham, G. S. Kell and A. R. Gordon, *Idem.*, p. 2352.

TABLE (6–10—1A). OBSERVED DIFFUSION COEFFICIENTS OF ELECTROLYTES IN DILUTE AQUEOUS SOLUTIONS AT 25° UNLESS OTHERWISE SPECIFIED. (THE VALUES IN PARENTHESES ARE THE DIFFERENCES IN THE THIRD DECIMAL PLACE BETWEEN THE VALUES CALCULATED BY EQUATIONS (6–10–1) AND (6–10–3) AND ARE POSITIVE WHEN THE CALCULATED ARE GREATER THAN THE OBSERVED VALUES. THE DATA REQUIRED FOR THE CALCULATION ARE ASSEMBLED IN TABLE (6–10–2A) WHICH FOLLOWS IMMEDIATELY. THE CONCENTRATIONS, c, ARE IN MILLIMOLS PER LITER.)

LiCl[1]		NaCl[1]		KCl[2]		RbCl[3]		CsCl[4]	
c	$\mathfrak{D} \times 10^5$	c	$\mathfrak{D} \times 10^5$	c	$\mathfrak{D} \times 10^5$	c	$\mathfrak{D} \times 10^5$	c	$\mathfrak{D} \times 10^5$
0.000	(1.367)	0.000	(1.611)	0.00	(1.994)	0.00	(2.055)	0.00	(2.044)
.634	1.348(0)	.746	1.586(2)	1.25	1.961(−3)	1.76	2.012(0)	1.22	2.007(1)
1.79	1.331(7)	1.61	1.576(3)	1.94	1.954(−3)	2.55	2.008(−3)	1.31	2.012(−5)
2.29	1.335(−1)	3.3	1.516(−8)	3.25	1.943(−2)	4.08	2.001(−7)	1.34	2.011(−5)
2.35	1.335(−1)	4.5	1.562(0)	5.85	1.931(−3)	4.46	1.988(4)	1.79	2.002(−2)
2.63	1.334(−1)	5.2	1.559(0)	7.04	1.924(−2)	4.49	1.998(−6)	2.66	1.990(2)
3.02	1.331(−1)	6.5	1.557(−2)	9.80	1.918(−4)	4.60	1.998(−7)	2.75	1.988(3)
3.39	1.327(1)	7.7	1.555(−4)	12.61	1.908(−2)	6.77	1.985(−3)	3.14	1.994(−5)
4.96	1.326(−4)	9.0	1.544(4)	26.54	1.879(2)	6.87	1.989(−9)	3.68	1.990(−5)
5.68	1.319(1)	9.3	1.544(3)	39.92	1.877(−9)	7.97	1.979(−3)	8.49	1.965(−4)
7.32	1.320(−4)	10.0	1.547(−2)	46.20	1.872(−8)	11.10	1.969(−3)	12.87	1.946(2)
7.92	1.315(0)	14.73	1.542(−6)	54.50	1.860(−1)	.....	....	.....	....
8.34	1.313(1)	.....	....	60.74	1.856(0)	.....	....	.....	....
9.35	1.312(0)	.....	....	129.8	1.838(0)	.....	....	.....	....
11.00	1.313(−4)	.....	....	332.3	1.842(−5)	.....	....	.....	....

KCl(4°)[5]		KCl(20°)[6]		KCl(30°)[6]		LiClO₄[7]		KClO₄[7]	
0.0	1.134	0.00	1.763	0.00	2.231	0.0	1.308	0.0	1.871
16.6	1.080(1)	1.25	1.736(−4)	3.26	2.172(−1)	3.3	1.277(−2)	1.2	1.843(−3)
16.8	1.038(0)	2.48	1.724(−2)	6.50	2.154(−1)	4.3	1.278(−6)	1.8	1.842(−8)
30.7	1.036(−1)	3.67	1.719(−4)	8.96	2.146(−3)	4.5	1.275(−4)	2.3	1.839(−9)
37.9	1.037(−2)	4.51	1.710(1)	12.36	2.139(−8)	5.3	1.273(−4)	3.4	1.832(−9)
55.8	1.042(−3)	11.21	1.688(0)	.....	....	5.4	1.273(−6)	4.9	1.829(−12)
.....	....	.....	....	.....	....	.....	....	6.3	1.825(−13)
.....	....	.....	....	.....	....	.....	....	7.5	1.813(−4)
.....	....	.....	....	.....	....	.....	....	8.4	1.814(−6)
.....	....	.....	....	.....	....	.....	....	9.7	1.792(13)

KNO₃[8]		AgNO₃[9]		Li₂SO₄[10]		Na₂SO₄[10]		Cs₂SO₄[11]	
0.0	1.929	0.00	1.766	0.00	1.040	0.00	1.229	0.00	1.568
.90	1.902(−4)	2.85	1.718(1)	.64	1.000(−2)	.81	1.178(−3)	.96	1.490(−1)
1.21	1.894(−1)	3.22	1.719(−3)	.71	.997(−1)	.81	1.177(−2)	1.02	1.484(3)
1.63	1.887(2)	4.27	1.711(−1)	.71	.998(1)	1.47	1.170(−13)	1.12	1.489(−5)
2.68	1.878(2)	4.96	1.708(−2)	.85	.993(0)	1.99	1.160(−11)	1.20	1.481(−1)
4.03	1.869(1)	6.28	1.701(−1)	2.10	.973(1)	2.68	1.151(−10)	1.50	1.470(4)
4.52	1.868(−1)	.....	....	2.67	.968(−1)	3.56	1.137(−6)	2.51	1.441(12)
5.15	1.857(6)	.....	....	3.48	.960(1)	4.48	1.129(−6)	3.78	1.435(0)
7.28	1.856(−3)	.....	....	4.40	.954(0)	4.49	1.132(−9)	4.68	1.419(6)
8.68	1.847(0)	.....	....	5.73	.946(1)	4.79	1.124(−2)	4.72	1.424(1)

MgCl₂[12]		CaCl₂[13]		SrCl₂[14]		BaCl₂[12]		LaCl₃[15]	
0.00	1.250	0.00	1.335	0.00	1.335	0.00	1.386	0.00	1.293
1.29	1.187	1.70	1.251(2)	1.68	1.270(−6)	.68	1.332(−4)	.93	1.178(4)
1.53	1.180(−5)	2.10	1.236(12)	1.50	1.256(−1)	.97	1.319(−3)	1.16	1.162(14)
2.05	1.163(−4)	3.2	1.227(9)	2.50	1.243(−3)	1.09	1.321(−8)	1.27	1.163(6)
2.70	1.164(−4)	4.3	1.214(13)	2.72	1.244(−7)	1.39	1.368(−2)	1.40	1.159(6)

TABLE (6-10-1A)—*Continued*

MgCl₂[12]		CaCl₂[13]		SrCl₂[14]		BaCl₂[12]		LaCl₃[15]	
2.83	1.157(2)	5.4	1.209(10)	3.00	1.233(1)	2.14	1.302(−9)	1.95	1.146(8)
3.09	1.156(−4)	7.0	1.200(11)	3.00	1.237(−3)	2.29	1.301(−11)	2.40	1.135(11)
3.64	1.555(−4)	12.0	1.183(12)	4.45	1.222(0)	2.87	1.285(−2)	2.72	1.126(15)
4.00	1.554(−4)	13.9	1.175(14)	5.49	1.212(−7)	4.03	1.271(6)	3.07	1.127(9)
……	…………	16.2	1.167(16)	6.11	1.217(−6)	4.52	1.271(−4)	3.38	1.120(13)
……	…………	28.1	1.153(16)	7.74	1.208(−4)	5.42	1.261(0)	4.01	1.110(16)
……	…………	54.7	1.136(36)	……	…………	……	…………	5.52	1.104(8)
……	…………	102.0	1.122(50)	……	…………	……	…………	6.68	1.087(16)
……	…………	……	…………	……	…………	……	…………	26.0	1.021(31)

MgSO₄[16]				ZnSO₄[17]				K₄Fe(CN)₆[18]	
0.00	0.849	2.72	0.730	0.00	0.849	2.60	0.731	0.00	1.472
.48	.788	4.57	.716	1.08	.747	2.63	.732	2.69	1.218(2)
.80	.779	4.81	.709	1.39	.739	3.08	.721	3.84	1.197(2)
1.67	.739	6.10	.703	1.92	.733	4.39	.714	3.96	1.198(0)
1.70	.746	6.36	.702	2.56	.728	4.71	.707	4.74	1.183(0)
2.08	.740	……	…………	……	…………	……	…………	5.56.	1.178(0)

(1) H. S. Harned and C. L. Hildreth, Jr., *J. Am. Chem. Soc.*, 73, 650 (1951).
(2) H. S. Harned and R. L. Nuttall, *Ibid.*, 69, 736 (1947).
(3) H. S. Harned and M. Blander, *Ibid.*, 75, 2853 (1953).
(4) H. S. Harned, M. Blander and C. L. Hildreth Jr., *Ibid.*, 76, 4219 (1954).
(5) H. S. Harned and C. A. Blake Jr., *Ibid.*, 72, 2265 (1950).
(6) H. S. Harned and R. L. Nuttall, *Ibid.*, 71, 1460 (1949).
(7) H. S. Harned, H. W. Parker and M. Blander, *Ibid.*, 77, 2071 (1955).
(8) H. S. Harned and R. M. Hudson, *Ibid.*, 73, 652 (1951).
(9) H. S. Harned and C. L. Hildreth Jr., *Ibid.*, 73, 3292 (1951).
(10) H. S. Harned and C. A. Blake Jr., *Ibid.*, 73, 2448 (1951).
(11) H. S. Harned and C. A. Blake Jr., *Ibid.*, 73, 5882 (1951).
(12) H. S. Harned and F. M. Polestra, *Ibid.*, 76, 2064 (1954).
(13) H. S. Harned and A. L. Levy, *Ibid.*, 71, 2781 (1949); H. S. Harned and H. W. Parker, *Ibid.*, 77, 265 (1955).
(14) H. S. Harned and F. M. Polestra, *Ibid.*, 75, 4168 (1953).
(15) H. S. Harned and C. A. Blake Jr., *Ibid.*, 73, 4255 (1951).
(16) H. S. Harned and R. M. Hudson. *Ibid.*, 73, 5880 (1951).
(17) H. S. Harned and R. M. Hudson, *Ibid.*, 73, 3781 (1951).
(18) H. S. Harned and R. M. Hudson, *Ibid.*, 73, 5083 (1951).

TABLE (6-10-2A). DATA EMPLOYED IN THE CALCULATION OF THE DIFFUSION CO-
EFFICIENTS OF ELECTROLYTES IN DILUTE AQUEOUS SOLUTION AT 25 OR AT
TEMPERATURES SPECIFIED. LIMITING EQUIVALENT CONDUCTANCES
ARE IN ABS. OHMS.$^{-1}$ CM.^{2} EQUI.$^{-1}$

	λ_1^0	λ_2^0	$d(\text{Å})$	A'	$2.303B$	$\mathfrak{S}_{(\mathfrak{D})} \times 10^6$
LiCl.......	36.67	76.30	4.25	1.40	0.2740	0.89
NaCl......	50.09	76.30	4.0	1.31	.1287	.98
KCl........	73.48	76.30	3.8	1.25	.049	1.17
RbCl.......	78.01	76.30	3.6	1.18	.037	1.21
CsCl.......	77.23	76.30	3.0	0.99	.000	1.20
KCl(4°)....	45.48	46.15	3.6	1.17	.032	0.64
KCl(20°)...	66.21	68.53	3.8	1.24	.043	1.04
KCl(30°)...	80.73	84.14	3.8	1.25	.060	1.35
LiClO₄.....	36.67	67.28	5.0	1.63	.38	0.8
KClO₄......	73.48	67.28	5.0	1.63	.38	1.1
KNO₃......	73.48	71.41	3.5	1.14	−.288	1.13
AgNO₃.....	61.92	71.41	3.0	1.00	−.239	1.04
Li₂SO₄.....	36.67	79.8	3.9	2.22	.000	2.11
Na₂SO₄.....	50.09	79.8	3.5	1.98	−.128	2.5
Cs₂SO₄.....	77.23	79.8	3.7	2.13	−.157	3.34
MgCl₂......	53.03	76.30	4.9	2.8	.156	2.66
CaCl₂......	59.47	76.30	4.9	2.8	.338	2.78
SrCl₂......	59.43	76.30	4.9	2.8	.507	2.78
BaCl₂......	63.61	76.30	4.3	2.5	.183	2.94
LaCl₃......	69.6	76.30	6.8	5.5	$\begin{cases}0.536 \times 2.3\\ \log c + 1\end{cases}$†	6.35
MgSO₄.*...	53.03	79.8	3.6	2.39	....	4.05
ZnSO₄.*....	53.0	79.8	3.6	2.39	....	4.05
K₄Fe(CN)₆.	73.48	111.0	4.4	4.6	.599	10.9

t	4°	20°	25°	30°
$\eta_0 \times 10^3$..............	15.676	10.087	8.944	8.004
D_0................	86.43	80.36	78.54	76.75
$\mathfrak{S}_{(f)}$ (1–1).............	0.4913	0.5046	0.5091	0.5141
Valence types........	(1–2)(2–1)	(1–3)(3–1)	(1–4)(4–1)	(2–2)
$\mathfrak{S}_{(f)}$ (25°).............	1.764	3.74	6.44	4.88

* Special equation used: $\left(1 + c \dfrac{\partial \ln y_\pm}{\partial c}\right) = 1 + 28.48c - 6.187c^{1/2}$

† T. Shedlovsky, *J. Am. Chem. Soc.*, **72**, 3680 (1950).

TABLE (6-10-3A). DIFFUSION COEFFICIENTS OF CONCENTRATED ELECTROLYTES IN
AQUEOUS SOLUTIONS AT 25°.

c	0	0.1	0.2	0.5	1	2	3	4
HCl[1]	3.336	3.05	3.06	3.18	3.44	4.05	4.66	5.17
HBr[1]	3.400	3.15	3.19	3.39	3.97	—	—	—
LiCl[1]	1.367	1.27	1.27	1.27	1.30	1.36	1.43	—
LiBr[1]	1.378	1.28	1.28	1.33	1.40	1.54	1.65	—
LiNO₃[4]..............	1.336	1.24	1.24	1.26	1.29	1.33	1.33	1.29
NaBr[1]	1.626	1.52	1.51	1.54	1.60	1.67	—	—
NaI[2]................	1.615	1.52	1.53	1.58	1.67	1.85	1.99	—
KBr[1]	2.016	1.87	1.87	1.88	1.97	2.13	2.28	—
KI[2]	1.999	1.86	1.86	1.95	2.06	2.25	2.44	—
NH₄Cl[3].............	1.994	1.84	1.84	1.86	1.92	2.05	2.16	2.35
NH₄NO₃[4]..........	1.926	1.97	1.75	1.72	1.69	1.63	1.58	1.52
(NH₄)₂SO₄[4]........	1.525	0.825	0.867	0.938	1.01	1.07	1.11	1.13

(1) R. H. Stokes, *J. Am. Chem. Soc.*, **72**, 2243 (1950).
(2) P. J. Dunlop and R. H. Stokes, *Ibid.*, **73**, 5456 (1951).
(3) J. R. Hull, B. F. Wishaw and R. H. Stokes, *Ibid.*, **75**, 1556 (1953).
(4) B. F. Wishaw and R. H. Stokes, *Ibid.*, **76**, 2065 (1954).

TABLE (7-2-1A).* LIMITING EQUIVALENT CONDUCTANCES AND IONIZATION CONSTANTS IN ETHYLIDINE CHLORIDE† AT 25°.

Salt	Λ^0	$10^5 K$	Salt	Λ^0	$10^5 K$
Et₄NPi................	116.6	3.48	Et₄NSCN..........	137.4	1.17
Pr₄NPi................	103.7	3.97	Et₄NClO₄..........	128.9	1.76
Bu₄NPi................	96.9	4.54	OctdMe₃NPi........	86.4	0.84
Am₄NPi................	90.4	4.94	OctdBu₃NPi........	80:4	5.39
Et₄NNO₃..............	149.0	0.75	...	...	...

* F. H. Healy and A. E. Martell, *J. Am. Chem. Soc.*, **73**, 3296 (1951).
† D = 10.00; η = 0.00466; d = 1.1667. Me = methyl; Et = ethyl; Pr = *n*-propyl; Bu = *n*-butyl; Am = *n*-amyl; Octd = octadecyl; Pi = picrate.

TABLE (7-2-2A). LIMITING EQUIVALENT CONDUCTANCES AND IONIZATION CONSTANTS IN ETHYLENE CHLORIDE* AT 25°.

Salt	Λ^0	$10^4 K$	Salt	Λ^0	$10^4 K$
Me₄NPiª..............	73.81	0.32	Bu₄NClO₄[b,f]........	66.2	1.53
Et₄NPiᶜ..............	69.44	1.59	PrBu₃NPiᵇ..........	59.07	2.03
Pr₄NPiᶜ..............	62.66	1.94	MeBu₃NPiᵇ..........	60.30	1.20
Bu₄NPiª,ᵈ............	57.40	2.28	MeBu₃NClO₄ᵇ.......	68.30	0.80
Am₄NPiᶜ.............	54.50	2.38	Bu₄PPiᵈ............	57.27	1.60
i-Am₄NPiᶜ..........	55.00	2.39	Bu₄AsPiᵈ...........	57.14	1.42
PhPyrPiᶜ............	67.94	0.86	Bu₃SPiᵈ............	62.31	0.449
Et₄NNO₃ᶜ............	78.43	0.74	Bu₃SClO₄ᵈ..........	68.72	0.394
Pr₄NNO₃ᶜ............	71.48	0.95	EtPh₃PPiᵇ..........	58.63	3.77
Bu₄NNO₃ᶜ............	66.31	1.18	EtPh₃PClO₄ᵇ........	66.03	3.60
Am₄NNO₃ᶜ...........	63.33	1.29	EtPh₃PNO₃ᵇ	67.00	2.18
i-Am₄NNO₃ᶜ........	63.57	1.20	EtPh₃AsPiᵇ.........	58.63	3.45
Et₄NClᶜ..............	77.4	0.51	EtPh₃AsClO₄ᵇ.......	65.69	3.45
Et₄NBrᶜ..............	72.1	0.70	EtPh₃AsNO₃ᵇ.......	66.68	2.14
Et₄NBFₓᶜ............	81.0	1.05	Ph₂IPiᵈ............	62.50	0.023
Bu₄NSCNᶜ..........	68.6	1.40	Ph₂IClO₄ᵈ..........	70.42	0.115
Bu₄NAcᶜ............	53.5	1.34	OctdMe₃NAcᶠ......	63.1	0.062
Bu₄NClAcᶜ.........	50.5	1.94	OctdBu₃NAcᶠ......	57.2	1.33
MeBu₃NSCNᶜ.......	71.2	0.66	OctdBu₃NSCNᶠ.....	60.2	1.56

ª D. J. Mead, R. M. Fuoss and C. A. Kraus, *Trans. Faraday Soc.*, **32**, 594 (1936).
ᵇ L. F. Gleysteen and C. A. Kraus, *J. Am. Chem. Soc.*, **69**, 451 (1947).
ᶜ L. M. Tucker and C. A. Kraus, *Ibid.*, **69**, 454 (1947).
ᵈ E. R. Kline and C. A. Kraus, *Ibid.*, **69**, 814 (1947).
ᵉ W. E. Thompson and C. A. Kraus, *Ibid.*, **69**, 1016 (1947).
ᶠ E. J. Blair and C. A. Kraus, *Ibid.*, **73**, 2459 (1951).
* D = 10.23; η = 0.007870; d = 1.2455. PhPyr = phenylpyridonium; Octd = octadecyl; ClAc = chloroacetate; Pi = picrate.

TABLE (7-2-3A). LIMITING EQUIVALENT CONDUCTANCES AND IONIZATION CONSTANTS IN PYRIDINE* AT 25°.

Salt	Λ^0	$10^4 K$	Salt	Λ^0	$10^4 K$
LiPi[a]	58.6	0.83	Me$_3$HOC$_2$H$_4$NPi[a]	67.0	1.5
NaPi[a]	60.5	0.43	Me$_3$EtNPi[a]	75.5	8.2
NaI[a]	75.2	3.7	Me$_4$NPi[a]	76.7	6.7
KI[a]	80.4	2.1	Bu$_4$NAc[a]	76	1.7
NH$_4$I[a]	95.2	2.4	Bu$_4$NNO$_3$[a]	76.6	3.7
NH$_4$Pi[a]	80.5	2.8	Bu$_4$NBFPh$_3$[a]	48.0	13.2
AgNO$_3$[a,b]	86.9	9.3	Bu$_4$NPi[b]	57.7	12.8
AgPi[a]	68.0	30.6	Bu$_4$NBr[b]	75.3	2.5
AgClO$_4$[b]	81.9	19.1	Bu$_4$NI[b]	73.1	4.1
C$_5$H$_5$NHNO$_3$[a]	102.2	0.51	Ph$_3$EtAsPi[b]	57.7	19.4
C$_5$H$_5$PhNPi[a]	66.3	11.5	OctdMe$_3$NF[c]	53.88	2.93
C$_5$H$_{10}$NH$_2$NO$_3$[a]	91.1	0.18	OctdMe$_4$NCl[c]	73.3	0.36
Me$_2$PhOHNPi[a]	62.3	12.3	OctdMe$_3$NPi[c]	55.62	7.66
Me$_3$BrCH$_2$NPi[a]	71.5	4.8	OctdBu$_3$NAc[c]	68.94	3.88
Me$_3$BrC$_2$H$_4$NPi[a]	67.1	5.8	Octd$_2$Bu$_2$NI[c]	62.36	4.21

[a] D. S. Burgess and C. A. Kraus, *J. Am. Chem. Soc.*, **70**, 706 (1948).
[b] W. F. Luder and C. A. Kraus, *Ibid.*, **69**, 2481 (1947).
[c] E. J. Bair and C. A. Kraus, *Ibid.*, **73**, 2459 (1951).
* $D = 12.01$; $\eta = 0.008824$; $d = 0.97792$. Octd = octadecyl; Ph = phenyl.

TABLE (7-2-4A). LIMITING EQUIVALENT CONDUCTANCES AND IONIZATION CONSTANTS IN ACETONE* AT 25°.

Salt	Λ^0	$10^3 K$	Salt	Λ^0	$10^3 K$
LiPi[a]	158.1	1.03	Am$_4$NBr[b]	174.4	4.25
NaPi[a]	163.7	1.35	Me$_4$NF[a]	183.0	0.77
KPi[a]	165.9	3.43	Bu$_4$NBFPh$_3$[a]	134.2	19.7
KI[a]	192.8	8.02	Bu$_4$NPi[a]	152.4	22.3
KSCN[a]	201.6	3.83	Bu$_4$NClO$_4$[a]	182.4	9.58
NH$_4$Pi[b]	180.2	1.11	Bu$_4$NNO$_3$[a]	187.2	5.46
Me$_4$NPi[b]	183.1	11.2	Bu$_4$NBr[a]	183.0	3.29
Et$_4$NPi[a]	176.5	17.5	Bu$_4$NI[a]	179.4	6.48
Pr$_4$NI[b]	190.6	4.98	OctdBu$_3$NI[b]	163.6	5.99
Bu$_4$NCl[b]	172.3	2.28	Octd$_2$Bu$_2$NI[b]	157.2	6.77

[a] M. B. Reynolds and C. A. Kraus, *J. Am. Chem. Soc.*, **70**, 1709 (1948).
[b] M. J. McDowell and C. A. Kraus, *Ibid.*, **73**, 3293 (1951).
* $D = 20.47$; $\eta = 0.003040$; $d = 0.7845$.

TABLE (7-2-5A). LIMITING EQUIVALENT CONDUCTANCES AND
IONIZATION CONSTANTS IN NITROMETHANE* AT 25°.

Salt	Λ^0	$10^3 K$	Salt	Λ^0	$10^3 K$
NaPi[a]	32.30	0.028	Me₃NHPi[b]	34.8	0.15
KPi[a]	33.81	0.686	Me₃OHNPi[b]	33.1	0.017
NH₄Pi[a]	34.4	0.146	Me₃EtNPi[b]	33.3	44.0
BuNH₃ClO₄[a]	37.92	2.53	Me₃PhNPi[b]	31.6	41.0
BuNH₃Pi[a]	32.97	0.149	Me₃MxyNPi[b]	33.7	25.0
Bu₂NH₂Pi[a]	30.41	0.156	Me₄NPi[b]	33.3	40.0
Bu₃NHPi[a]	28.85	0.19	Et₄NPi[b]	32.4	140.0
Bu₄NPi[b]	27.9	—	Et₄NCl[a]	38.55	12.5
Bu₄NNO₃[a]	34.51	25.0	Pr₄NPi[b]	29.5	—
Bu₄NBr[a]	33.48	16.2	Me₂PhOHNPi[a,b]	28.0	0.02
Bu₄NAc[a]	35.5	6.7	Bu₄NBF₄[a]	33.96	51.0
Am₄NPi[b]	26.8	—	Bu₄NBFPh₃[b]	23.4	—
Bu₃NHI[a]	33.33	0.095	Me₃BrCH₂NPi[b]	32.3	12.0

[a] C. A. Witschanke and C. A. Kraus, *J. Am. Chem. Soc.*, **69**, 2472 (1947).
[b] E. G. Taylor and C. A. Kraus, *Ibid.*, **69**, 1731 (1947).
* $D = 34.5$; $\eta = 0.01811$; $d = 1.1986$. Mxy = methoxy.

TABLE (7-2-6A). LIMITING EQUIVALENT CONDUCTANCES AND
IONIZATION CONSTANTS IN ACETONITRILE* AT 25°.

Salt	Λ^0	$10^2 K$	Salt	Λ^0	$10^2 K$
Me₄NCl[a]	193.1	1.29	CsIBr₂[a]	187.1	—
Me₄NBr[a]	192.7	2.41	Me₄NI[b]	195.3	3.62
Me₄NI[a]	195.3	3.62	Me₄NI₃[b]	190.9	54.0
Me₄NIBrCl[a]	197.2	—	Pr₄NI[b]	171.6	11.0
Me₄NIBr₂[a]	193.0	—	Pr₄NI₃[b]	167.5	10.8

[a] A. I. Popov and N. E. Skelly, *J. Am. Chem. Soc.*, **76**, 5309 (1954).
[b] A. I. Popov, R. H. Rygg and N. E. Skelly, *Ibid.*, **78**, 5740 (1956).
* $D = 36.7$; $\eta = 0.00344$; $d = 0.7767$.

TABLE (7-2-7A).* LIMITING EQUIVALENT CONDUCTANCES
IN DIMETHYLFORMAMIDE† AT 25°.

Salt	Λ^0	$\mathcal{S}_{(\Lambda)}$	Salt	Λ^0	$\mathcal{S}_{(\Lambda)}$
KI....................	82.6	158	NaSCN............	89.5	163
NaI...................	81.9	158	KBr..............	84.1	159
KClO₄...............	82.7	158	NaBr.............	83.4	159
NaClO₄.............	82.1	158	KNO₃.............	88.5	162
KSCN..............	90.2	164	NaNO₃...........	87.9	162

* D. P. Ames and P. G. Sears, *J. Phys. Chem.*, **59**, 16 (1955). The results conformed
so closely with the theoretical limiting slopes that complete dissociation was assumed
† $D = 36.71$; $\eta = 0.00796$; $d = 0.9443$.

TABLE (7-2-8A).* LIMITING EQUIVALENT CONDUCTANCES OF POTASSIUM CHLORIDE
AND OF SODIUM CHLORIDE IN METHANOL-WATER MIXTURES AT 25°. (INT. MHOS)

Methanol % (wt.)	D^a	$10^3 \eta$	Λ^0 (KCl)	Λ^0 (NaCl)
0	78.49	8.949	149.85	126.45
25	67.5	14.75	90.45	77.95
50	56.31	15.4	74.75	65.65
75	45.0	11.5	77.95	70.25
100	32.64	5.41	104.45[b]	97.45[b]

* T. Shedlovsky, *private communication.*
ᵃ These values of the dielectric constants and viscosities were used in the extrapolations to obtain the limiting conductances.
ᵇ The values 104.78 for KCl, and 97.61 for NaCl, were obtained by J. P. Butler, H.
I. Schiff and A. R. Gordon, *J. Chem. Phys.*, **19**, 749 (1951).

TABLE (8-2-1A). ϕ_L, RELATIVE APPARENT MOLAL HEAT CONTENTS IN DILUTE AQUEOUS SOLUTIONS AT 25°

Part I

$\sqrt{m}$	Ref.	.01	.02	.04	.06	.08	.10	.15	.20	.25	.30	Δ*
HCl.........	(1)	4.8	9.6	19.2	29	38	48	71	93	114	134	0
LiCl.........	(2)	4.3	8.4	16.6	25	33	40	60	78	96	114	81
LiBr.........	(3, 16)	4.2	8.2	16.2	24	32	39	59	76	93	110	7
NaCl........	(4)	4.5	8.5	17.0	25	33	40	55	67	77	83	2
NaBr........	(5, 9)	4.2	8.4	16.4	24	31	38	52	62	69	73	2
NaNO₃........	(7)	4.3	8.5	16.5	23	29	34	43	44	40	31ᵃ	4.5
NaClO₃.......	(7)	4.2	8.4	17.0	24	30	35	43	49	48	43ᵃ	1
NaBrO₃.......	(7)	4.3	8.5	16.7	24	30	34	39	38	34	26ᵃ	1
NaIO₃........	(7)	4.0	7.5	14.0	19	21	21	16	0	−24	−57ᵃ	2
NaOH........	(8)	4.8	9.5	19.0	28	36	44	62	77	90	99	0
KF..........	(6)	4.7	9.2	18.3	27	36	45	66	83	99	113	6
KCl.........	(9, 10, 12)	4.5	8.5	16.0	24	31	38	54	65	72	77	2
KBr.........	(5, 9)	4.2	8.2	15.6	23	29	36	47	55	61	64	2
KNO₃........	(12)	4.1	8.0	15.1	20	23	24	22	12	−6	−29ᵇ	4
KClO₃.......	(13)	4.2	8.2	15.5	21	26	29	28	19	4	−19ᵃ	3
KClO₄.......	(13)	4.3	8.0	13.0	16	16	14	−3	−28	−59	−109ᵃ	3
RbF.........	(12)	4	8	14	20	26	31	44	57	69	80ᶜ	4
CsCl........	(16)	4	8	15	21	27	32	43	49	51	51ᵈ	2.5
NH₄Cl.......	(11)	4.4	8.6	17	25	33	39	53	66	78	88ᵉ	7
Li₂SO₄.......	(15)	24	47	91	135	177	218	307	377	438	488	3
Na₂SO₄.......	(15)	23	44	84	119	150	175	216	237	243	237	2
K₂SO₄.......	(15)	22	42	81	116	146	171	214	238	249	250	2
Rb₂SO₄.......	(15)	21	41	79	114	143	166	200	215	226	219	2
Cs₂SO₄.......	(15)	20	39	71	99	121	139	160	161	152	137	3
MgCl₂........	(14)	24	47	89	129	167	202	280	350	415	471	0
MgBr₂........	(14)	23	45	86	124	161	196	271	334	389	437	0
Mg(NO₃)₂.....	(15)	23	44	81	119	155	187	254	304	344	376	5
CaCl₂........	(14)	24	47	88	127	165	199	275	340	398	445	1
CaBr₂........	(14)	23	44	83	120	154	186	252	308	355	394	1
Ca(NO₃)₂.....	(15)	22	43	79	111	136	158	200	222	230	224	5
SrCl₂........	(14)	23	46	86	124	161	195	270	332	381	420	1
SrBr₂........	(14)	23	44	82	120	152	182	244	293	333	366	1
Sr(NO₃)₂......	(15)	21	40	72	99	122	140	166	169	159	135	5
BaCl₂........	(14)	23	46	86	124	160	194	268	329	375	412	2
BaBr₂........	(14)	22	43	81	117	150	180	240	287	325	356	1
Ba(NO₃)₂.....	(15)	19	36	59	70	72	66	20	−46	−128	−223	5
MgSO₄........	(15)	44	118	154	369	463	542	685	784	842		−25
CaSO₄........	(12)	47	125	283	415	523	611	700ᶠ				−25
ZnSO₄........	(17)	51	127	273	396	501	581	731	826	896	953	−25
CdSO₄........	(17)	70	180	386	554	693	807	1018	1150	1246	1324	−40
CuSO₄........	(17)	62	159	345	501	618	713	885	1012	1109	1183	−35

* Approximate increase involved in new extrapolation.

ᵃ At $\sqrt{m} = 0.3162$.

ᵇ At $\sqrt{m} = 0.35$, $\phi_L = −55$.

ᶜ At $\sqrt{m} = 0.35, 0.40, 0.45$, and 0.50, $\phi_L = 91, 101, 111$, and 120, respectively.

ᵈ At $\sqrt{m} = 0.35$, and 0.40, $\phi_L = 49$, and 44, respectively.

ᵉ At $\sqrt{m} = 0.4, 0.5, 0.6, 0.72, 0.88$, and 1, $\phi_L = 101, 111, 127, 136, 142$, and 143, respectively.

ᶠ At $\sqrt{m} = 0.125$.

(1) J. M. Sturtevant, *J. Am. Chem. Soc.*, **62**, 584 (1940); Corrections, *Ibid.*, **62**, 3265 (1940).

(2) E. Lange and F. Dürr, *Z. physik. Chem.*, **121,** 361 (1926).

(3) E. Lange and E. Schwartz, *Ibid.*, **133,** 129 (1928).

(4) A. L. Robinson, *J. Am. Chem. Soc.*, **54**, 1311 (1932).

(5) H. Hammerschmid and A. L. Robinson, *Ibid.*, **54,** 3120 (1932).

(6) E. Lange and A. Eichler, *Z. physik. Chem.*, **129,** 285 (1927).

(7) E. Lange and A. L. Robinson, *Ibid.*, **148A,** 97 (1930).

(8) J. M. Sturtevant, *J. Am. Chem. Soc.*, **62,** 2276 (1940).

(9) J. Wüst and E. Lange, *Z. physik. Chem.*, **116,** 161 (1925).

(10) E. Lange and P. A. Leighton, *Z. Elektrochem.*, **34,** 566 (1928).

(11) H. Streeck, *Z. physik. Chem.*, **169A,** 103 (1934). Data for the methylammonium chlorides are also given.

(12) E. Lange and J. Monheim, *Ibid.*, **150A,** 349 (1930).

(13) M. Andauer and E. Lange, *Ibid.*, **165A,** 89 (1933).

(14) E. Lange and H. Streeck, *Ibid.*, **152A,** 1 (1931).

(15) E. Lange and H. Streeck, *Ibid.*, **157A,** 1 (1931).

(16) E. Lange and J. Messner, *Z. Elektrochem.*, **33,** 431 (1927).

(17) E. Lange, J. Monheim, and A. L. Robinson, *J. Am. Chem. Soc.*, **55,** 4733 (1933).

TABLE (8-2-1A).* ϕ_L, RELATIVE APPARENT MOLAL HEAT CONTENTS IN WATER AT 25°

Part II

m	HCl	LiCl	LiBr	NaCl	NaBr	NaOH	KF	KCl	KBr
0.1	140	119	117	83	73	102	117	78	64
.2	191	162	156	90	72	117	143	81	70
.3	229	194	185	84	63	121	155	76	46
.4	261	220	210	72	53	119	163	63	29
.5	290	242	232	58	41	114	169	48	9
.6	317	263	252	42	27	108	174	33	−13
.7	342	283	271	26	13	101	179	18	−35
.8	368	300	289	9	−3	94	183	3	−58
.9	391	318	306	−7	−20	86	186	−12	−81
1.0	414	334	322	−23	−37	78	190	−26	−104
1.2	460	365	352	−57	−72	61	198	−55	−148
1.5	526	410	394	−105	−124	38	209	−99	−212
1.7	569	438	421	−136	−160	25	215	−128	−251
2.0	633	479	460	−177	−212	8	223	−169	−306
2.5	739	547	524	−224	−294	−10	234	−236	−394
3.0	847	615	588	−304	−364	−17	246	−300	−480
3.5	954^a	683	652	−355	−424	−12	260	−355	−559
4.0	...	758	716	−395	−482	3	279	−405	−631
4.5	...	838	780	−427	−533	36^a	305	−448	−697
5.0	...	921	849	−453	−578	...	334	−472^c	−760
5.5	...	1007	920	−470	−617	...	368	...	−819
6.0	...	1098	994	−483^b	−648	...	404	...	−839^d

* Sources of data are indicated in Part I of this table.

^{a} Extrapolated.

^{b} For sat. soln., $m = 6.12$.

^{c} For sat. soln., $m = 4.82$.

^{d} For sat. soln., $m = 5.68$.

TABLE (8-2-2A).* L_2, RELATIVE PARTIAL MOLAL HEAT CONTENTS IN DILUTE AQUEOUS SOLUTIONS AT 25°

Part I

$\sqrt{m}$	.01	.02	.04	.06	.08	.10	.15	.20	.25	.30
HCl............	7.2	14.3	28.6	43	57	71	105	136	165	193
LiCl............	6.4	12.5	24.7	37	49	60	89	115	141	165
LiBr............	6.3	12.2	24.0	35	47	59	86	111	136	159
NaCl............	6.5	12.5	24.0	35	46	57	77	92	100	104
NaBr............	6.3	12.2	24.2	35	45	54	70	79	83	82
NaNO₃..........	6.0	11.5	22.5	31	40	46	51	40	27	13ᵃ
NaClO₃.........	6.6	12.9	24.4	34	41	47	55	55	45	27ᵃ
NaBrO₃.........	6.5	12.7	24.2	33	39	43	42	33	22	8ᵃ
NaIO₃..........	5.8	11.0	19.8	24	24	20	0	−41	−88	−143ᵃ
NaOH..........	7.1	14.0	28.0	42	54	65	89	104	117	125
KF.............	7.0	13.8	27.4	41	54	66	94	117	136	151
KCl............	6.5	12.5	24.0	36	46	55	71	82	88	91
KBr............	6.1	12.1	23.0	33	41	48	62	69	71	68
KNO₃..........	5.7	11.0	20.3	26	29	28	12	−17	−57	−103ᵇ
KClO₃..........	6.7	12.3	21.7	28	32	32	20	−6	−37	−77ᵃ
KClO₄..........	6.2	11.3	16.6	17	13	4	−34	−86	−148	−228ᵃ
NH₄Cl..........	6.7	13	25	37	47	56	75	91	105	121ᵃ
Li₂SO₄..........	35	69	135	200	260	317	424	508	578	620
Na₂SO₄.........	33	64	122	170	206	229	261	264	241	287
K₂SO₄..........	32	62	119	164	200	226	262	272	266	233
Rb₂SO₄.........	31	61	115	162	195	216	233	233	225	201
Cs₂SO₄.........	29	57	102	136	161	176	172	152	124	87
MgCl₂..........	36	70	130	187	240	287	388	484	567	626
MgBr₂..........	34	67	125	181	233	278	372	453	519	564
Mg(NO₃)₂.......	32	62	121	175	224	264	339	393	437	465
CaCl₂..........	35	68	127	185	237	282	378	463	530	576
CaBr₂..........	34	65	120	172	219	260	340	410	462	498
Ca(NO₃)₂.......	31	62	114	152	183	212	245	250	234	191
SrCl₂...........	34	66	125	180	232	277	372	443	492	528
SrBr₂..........	33	64	119	170	216	254	324	383	423	452
Sr(NO₃)₂.......	30	58	102	137	159	180	185	161	116	46
BaCl₂..........	34	66	124	180	231	275	369	435	480	513
BaBr₂..........	33	64	118	169	214	251	317	372	412	439
Ba(NO₃)₂.......	27	51	75	80	68	37	−65	−195	−352	−528
MgSO₄..........	79	191	380	525	631	715	865	937	951	...
CaSO₄..........	80	208	418	588	712	802	882ᶜ	...	...	
ZnSO₄..........	86	202	415	595	698	765	893	989	1064	1120
CdSO₄..........	119	290	567	785	939	1071	1266	1380	1467	1542
CuSO₄	106	256	518	711	826	930	1115	1242	1321	1375

* Sources of data are indicated in Table (8-2-1A).

ᵃ At $\sqrt{m} = 0.3162$.

ᵇ At $\sqrt{m} = 0.35$, $L_2 = -149$.

ᶜ At $\sqrt{m} = 0.125$.

TABLE (8-2-2A).* L_2, RELATIVE PARTIAL MOLAL HEAT CONTENTS IN WATER AT 25°
Part II

m	HCl	LiCl	LiBr	NaCl	NaBr	NaOH	KF	KCl	KBr
0.1	202	173	166	102	78	127	155	91	70
.2	273	234	223	90	58	133	179	72	39
.3	332	279	267	62	31	122	190	44	1
.4	383	318	305	28	2	105	197	12	−42
.5	430	352	339	−10	−30	89	203	−21	−89
.6	475	384	371	−48	−66	69	209	−55	−136
.7	518	313	400	−85	−100	51	215	−85	−180
.8	560	440	424	−120	−136	33	220	−115	−224
.9	604	467	448	−156	−173	13	226	−146	−268
1.0	645	491	471	−188	−206	−4	231	−176	−309
1.2	728	540	515	−252	−280	−37	240	−233	−390
1.5	853	614	580	−343	−382	−70	254	−316	−507
1.7	934	665	625	−398	−448	−81	262	−370	−579
2.0	1055	744	696	−466	−538	−86	274	−446	−678
2.5	1269	885	821	−556	−654	−73	291	−558	−823
3.0	1484	1044	960	−626	−751	−24	318	−648	−956
3.5	1690ª	1205	1097	−671	−832	57	376	−721	−1076
4.0	....	1375	1237	−688	−897	180	456	−782	−1181
4.5	....	1524	1386	−683	−945	....	546	−828	−1269
5.0	....	1743	1544	−656	−981	....	643	−853ᶜ	−1345
5.5	....	1947	1700	−620	−1001	....	754	....	−1392
6.0	....	2163	1865	−570ᵇ	−992	....	884	....	−1412ᵈ

* Sources of data are indicated in Table (8-2-1A).
ª Extrapolated.
ᵇ For sat. soln., $m = 6.12$.
ᶜ For sat. soln., $m = 4.82$.
ᵈ For sat. soln., $m = 5.68$.

TABLE (8-7-1A).   STANDARD PARTIAL MOLAL COMPRESSIBILITIES
IN WATER AT 25° AND 1 ATMOSPHRE.*

Electrolyte	$10^4 \bar{K}_2^0$	Ref.	Electrolyte	$10^4 \bar{K}_2^0$	Ref.
HCl................	−8	(1)	Na_2CO_3	−171	(3)
LiOH...............	−78	(1)	K_2CrO_4............	−139	(3)
NaOH..............	−89	(1)	Li_2SO_4.............	−146	(5)
KOH...............	−81	(2)	Na_2SO_4.............	−154	(5)
LiCl...............	−42	(1, 3)	K_2SO_4.............	−139	(5)
NaCl...............	−50	(1, 3)	Cs_2SO_4............	−119	(5)
KCl................	−45	(1, 3)	$(NH_4)_2SO_4$........	−91	(5)
NaBr...............	−42	(3)	$BaCl_2$..............	−115	(3)
KBr................	−34	(3)	$CaCl_2$..............	−87‡	(6)
CsBr...............	−25	(3)	$MgCl_2$..............	−153	(5)
LiI................	−17	(3)	$CdSO_4$..............	−127	(5)
KI.................	−18	(3)	$CuSO_4$..............	−132	(5)
KCNS..............	−22	(3)	$ZnSO_4$..............	−140	(5)
KNO₃..............	−30	(3)	$BeSO_4$	−93	(5)
KHCO₃.............	−35	(4)	$CeCl_3$.............	−176	(3)
KO₂CCH₃...........	−47	(2)			
HO₂CCH₃...........	7	(3)	H_2O...............	8.22	(3)

* These values are all derived from measurements of bulk compression defined by equation (8-7-16). The requirement of two extrapolations (to $P = 1$, and to $c = 0$) introduces uncertainties into the values which may exceed 10% for the higher valence types.
‡ At 30° and 100 bars.

(1) F. T. Gucker, Jr., and T. R. Rubin, J. Am. Chem. Soc., 57, 78 (1935). (2) E. H. Lanman and B. J. Mair, Ibid., 56, 390 (1934). (3) R. E. Gibson, Ibid., 57, 284 (1935). (4) International Critical Tables. (5) R. E. Gibson, J. Am. Chem. Soc., 56, 4 (1934) (6) F. T. Gucker, Chem. Rev., 13, 111 (1933).

TABLE (9-5-1A).* VALUES OF $-\text{LOG } \gamma_\pm$ AT THE FREEZING POINTS OF AQUEOUS SOLUTIONS (1)

	Ref.	$m =$ 0.005	0.01	0.02	0.05	0.1	0.2	0.3	0.5	0.7	1.0
LiCl........	(4)	0.0343	0.0463	0.0605	0.0830	0.1017	0.1192	0.1262	0.1281	0.1220	0.1055
LiBr........	(4)	.0298	.0400	.0525	.0720	.0877	.1008	.1041	.0996	.0875	.0621
LiNO₃......	(2)	.0304	.0412	.0543	.0760	.0947	.1125	.1204	.1246	.1220	.1122
LiClO₃......	(5)	.0302	.0406	.0537	.0745	.0915	.1070	.1131	.1141	.1080	.0923
LiClO₄......	(5)	.0290	.0386	.0506	.0692	.0835	.0940	.0948	.0856	.0697	.0396
LiO₂CH.....	(6)	.0311	.0424	.0573	.0826	.1057	.1312	.1465	.1637	.1729	.1802
LiO₂CCH₃...	(6)	.0309	.0421	.0564	.0799	.1000	.1201	.1298	.1373	.1370	.1296
NaCl........	(4)	.0306	.0416	.0557	.0804	.1039	.1309	.1476	.1690	.1824	.1948
NaBr.......	(4)	.0282	.0377	.0503	.0721	.0928	.1161	.1300	.1465	.1554	.1622
NaNO₃......	(2)	.0311	.0428	.0584	.0870	.1165	.1543	.1812	.2214	.2525	.2907
NaClO₃.....	(5)	.0316	.0433	.0588	.0865	.1139	.1482	.1718	.2066	.2330	.2644
NaClO₄.....	(5)	.0321	.0439	.0588	.0857	.1116	.1429	.1640	.1936	.2151	.2393
NaO₂CH....	(6)	.0308	.0416	.0557	.0794	.1012	.1262	.1415	.1606	.1720	.1829
NaO₂CCH₃..	(6)	.0306	.0412	.0544	.0754	.0928	.1089	.1160	.1199	.1172	.1074
KCl........	(4)	.0317	.0434	.0587	.0857	.1121	.1430	.1632	.1903	.2093	.2302
KBr........	(4)	.0313	.0428	.0578	.0839	.1091	.1392	.1590	.1855	.2038	.2236
KNO₃.......	(2)	.0329	.0461	.0645	.1001	.1391	.1923	.2336	.2979	.3502	.4158
KClO₃......	(5)	.0301	.0418	.0583	.0913	.1277	.1771	.....	.....	.....	.....
KClO₄......	(5)	.0347	.0492	.0697	.....	.....	.....	.....	.....	.....	.....
KO₂CH.....	(6)	.0302	.0406	.0543	.0774	.0989	.1221	.1356	.1509	.1589	.1648
KO₂CCH₃...	(6)	.0306	.0411	.0544	.0750	.0915	.1061	.1113	.1107	.1034	.0867
NH₄Cl......	(3)	.0405	.0555	.0732	.1025	.1298	.1616	.1818	.2081	.2249	.2423
NH₄Br......	(3)	.0451	.0605	.0786	.1082	.1351	.1657	.1849	.2097	.2260	.2427
NH₄I.......	(3)	.0375	.0509	.0674	.0947	.1193	.1479	.1659	.1897	.2052	.2218
NH₄NO₃....	(3)	.0401	.0547	.0736	.1064	.1390	.1806	.2101	.2542	.2884	.3306
(NH₄)₂SO₄...	(3)	.1308	.1749	.2294	.3194	.4023	.4994	.5633	.6514	.7141	.7836

* Results for CsCl and the iodides of Li, Na, K, and Cs are available up to about 0.1 N. See J. Lange, *Z. physik. Chem.*, **177A**, 193 (1936).

(1) Calculated by equation (9-5-25), the term

$$-\frac{1000}{\nu M_1} \int_0^m \frac{dX}{m}$$

being neglected.

(2) G. Scatchard, P. T. Jones and S. S. Prentiss, *J. Am. Chem. Soc.*, **54**, 2690 (1932).

(3) G. Scatchard and S. S. Prentiss, *Ibid.*, **54**, 2696 (1932). For tetrasubstituted ammonium chlorides and iodides, see J. Lange, *Z. physik. Chem.*, **168A**, 147 (1934).

(4) G. Scatchard and S. S. Prentiss, *J. Am. Chem. Soc.*, **55**, 4355 (1933).

(5) G. Scatchard, S. S. Prentiss and P. T. Jones, *Ibid.*, **56**, 805 (1934).

(6) G. Scatchard and S. S. Prentiss, *Ibid.*, **56**, 807 (1934).

TABLE (10-7-1A).* THE pH VALUES OF SOME STANDARD SOLUTIONS FOR USE IN DETERMINING E^0_{pH} BY EQUATION (10-7-2) AT VARIOUS TEMPERATURES.

Solution	μ	pH 0°	pH 10°	pH 25°	pH 38°	$\delta pH\S$
HCl, 0.1 M	0.1	1.088	1.088	1.092	1.096	0.014
HCl, 0.01 M; KCl, 0.09 M	.1	2.101	2.101	2.102	2.104	.014
Sulfamic acid, 0.01 M	.0078	2.086	2.084	2.083	2.083	.002
KH$_3$(C$_2$O$_4$)$_2$, 0.1 M	.144	. . .	. . .	1.507	1.514	.019
KH$_3$(C$_2$O$_4$)$_2$, 0.05 M	.077	1.670	1.673	1.676	1.698	.012
KH$_3$(C$_2$O$_4$)$_2$, 0.025 M	.042	1.858	1.860	1.865	1.875	.008
KH$_3$(C$_2$O$_4$)$_2$, 0.01 M	.018	2.143	2.145	2.147	2.158	.004
Citric acid, 0.05 M	.0063	2.284	2.261	2.238	2.224	.001
Citric acid, 0.01 M	.0025	2.664	2.644	2.624	2.610	.000
KH tartrate, 0.03 M	.036	. . .	. . .	3.571	3.559	.007
KH$_2$ citrate, 0.1 M	.115	3.818	. . .	3.717	3.695	.016
KH$_2$ citrate, 0.02 M	.024	3.926	. . .	3.836	3.819	.005
KH phthalate, 0.05 M	.053	4.008	4.000	4.008	4.034	.009
Acetic acid, 0.1 M; NaAc, 0.1 M	.1	4.688	. . .	4.656	4.661	.014
Acetic acid, 0.05 M; NaAc, 0.05 M	.05	4.709	. . .	4.679	4.685	.009
Acetic acid, 0.01 M; NaAc, 0.01 M	.01	4.747	. . .	4.718	4.726	.003
NaHSuccinate, 0.05 M; Na$_2$Suc, 0.05 M	.202	5.405	5.369	5.343	5.344	.023
NaHSuc, 0.025 M; Na$_2$Suc, 0.025 M	.101	5.459	5.424	5.403	5.408	.015
NaHSuc, 0.01 M; Na$_2$Suc, 0.01 M	.041	5.526	5.494	5.474	5.480	.007
Na$_2$B$_4$O$_7$, 0.01 M	.02	9.466	9.331	9.181	9.085	.005
KHCO$_3$, 0.05 M; Li$_2$CO$_3$, 0.05 M	.2	10.212	10.070	9.902	9.793	.022
KHCO$_3$, 0.025 M; Li$_2$CO$_3$, 0.025 M	.1	10.302	10.159	9.993	9.882	.014
KHCO$_3$, 0.01 M; Li$_2$CO$_3$, 0.01 M	.04	10.402	10.258	9.088	9.972	.008
NaHCO$_3$, 0.05 M; Na$_2$CO$_3$, 0.05 M	.2	10.238	10.098	9.933	9.824	.022
NaHCO$_3$, 0.025 M; Na$_2$CO$_3$, 0.025 M	.1	10.325	10.184	10.018	9.907	.014
NaHCO$_3$, 0.01 M; Na$_2$CO$_3$, 0.01 M	.04	10.421	10.280	10.112	9.996	.008
Na$_2$CO$_3$, 0.01 M	.029	11.627	11.356	11.006	10.738	.006
Na$_2$CO$_3$, 0.025 M	.074	11.772	11.500	11.155	10.892	.012
Na$_2$CO$_3$, 0.05 M	.148	11.887	11.612	11.266	11.000	.019
Na$_3$PO$_4$, 0.01 M	.047	. . .	. . .	11.719	11.375	.009
Na$_3$PO$_4$, 0.05 M	.27	12.750	12.440	12.039	11.739	.026
NaOH, 0.01 M	.01	12.886	12.471	11.939	11.522	.003
NaOH, 0.05 M	.05	13.565	13.148	12.616	12.205	.009

* R. G. Bates, G. D. Pinching and E. R. Smith, *J. Research Nat. Bur. Stds.*, **45**, 418 (1950).

§ The quantity δpH represents the difference in pH obtained when the a-parameter is varied from 4 to 6 Ångstroms in the estimation of activity coefficients, and it serves as a measure of the relative uncertainty of the values of pH in the various solutions.

TABLE (11-1-1A). DIELECTRIC CONSTANTS AND VISCOSITIES OF DIOXANE-WATER MIXTURES. CONSTANTS OF EQUATIONS (5-3-4) AND (5-3-5)

Wt. % dioxane	t^0	D_0	$100\eta_0$	α^*	β^*
20	15	64.01	1.689	0.3258	35.73
20	25	60.79	1.292	.3345	47.17
20	35	57.73	1.017	.3439	60.42
20	45	54.83	0.8243	.3542	75.29
45	15	40.70	2.453	.6425	30.85
45	25	38.48	1.837	.6642	41.66
45	35	36.37	1.430	.6878	54.14
45	45	34.39	1.142	.7131	68.62
70	15	18.72	2.483	2.060	44.94
70	25	17.69	1.918	2.131	58.85
70	35	16.72	1.522	2.207	75.03
70	45	15.80	1.232	2.290	93.83
82	15	10.01	2.106	5.268	72.46
82	25	9.53	1.671	5.389	92.02
82	35	9.06	1.356	5.532	114.39
82	45	8.62	1.117	5.683	140.12

TABLE (11-3-1A). LIMITING SLOPES FOR ACTIVITY COEFFICIENTS IN DIOXANE-WATER MIXTURES. DIELECTRIC CONSTANTS
X = Weight Percent of Dioxane

t	$X = 20$		$X = 45$	
	D	$\mathbb{S}_{(f)}$	D	$\mathbb{S}_{(f)}$
0	69.16	0.6989	44.28	1.364
5	67.39	.7072	43.05	1.385
10	65.68	.7156	41.86	1.406
15	64.01	.7245	40.70	1.429
20	62.38	.7339	39.57	1.453
25	60.79	.7437	38.48	1.477
30	59.94	.7540	37.41	1.503
35	57.73	.7648	36.37	1.530
40	56.26	.7760	35.37	1.557
45	54.83	.7877	34.39	1.586
50	53.43	.7999	33.43	1.616

t	$X = 70$		$X = 82$	
	D	$\mathbb{S}_{(f)}$	D	$\mathbb{S}_{(f)}$
0	20.37	4.373	.....	.....
5	19.81	4.437	10.52	11.47
10	19.25	4.510	10.27	11.58
15	18.72	4.581	10.01	11.72
20	18.20	4.657	9.77	11.85
25	17.69	4.738	9.53	11.98
30	17.20	4.820	9.29	12.16
35	16.72	4.907	9.06	12.30
40	16.26	4.995	8.84	12.46
45	15.80	5.092	8.62	12.64
50	15.37	5.185	....	.....

TABLE (11-3-2A). DENSITIES OF PURE SOLVENTS, AND OF SOLUTIONS OF HYDRO-
CHLORIC ACID IN DIOXANE-WATER MIXTURES. PARAMETERS OF EQUATIONS
DESIGNATED. (c MAY BE OBTAINED FROM m BY, $c/m = d_0 - Am$, WITH AN ACCURACY
OF 0.1%.) Δ = PERCENTAGE DIFFERENCE BETWEEN CALCULATED AND OBSERVED
VALUES. Δ_1 REFERS TO EQUATION FOR d; Δ_2 REFERS TO EQUATION FOR c/m. X =
WEIGHT PERCENT OF DIOXANE[*]

$$X = 20$$
$$d = d_0 + am - bm^2 + em \log m; \text{ Valid to 3 } M$$

t	d_0	a	b	e	Δ_1	A	Δ_2
0	1.0271	0.0133	0.00032	0.008	0.02	0.02159	0.16
5	1.0245	.0142	.00035	.007	.02	.02116	.12
10	1.0219	.0149	.00025	.004	.02	.02077	.09
15	1.0193	.0154	.00005	.000	.02	.02038	.05
20	1.0167	.0160	.00013	....	.02	.02013	.03
25	1.0141	.0161	.00013	....	.01	.01989	.02
30	1.0115	.0167	.00019	....	.02	.01965	.01
35	1.0090	.0168	.00020	....	.01	.01954	.01
40	1.0063	.0168	.00018	....	.02	.01933	.01
45	1.0038	.0166	.00015	....	.02	.01922	.02
50	1.0014	.0164	.00014	....	.01	.01933	.02

$$X = 45$$
$$d = d_0 + am - bm^2; \text{ Valid to 3 } M$$

t	d_0	a	b	Δ_1	A	Δ_2
0	1.0484	......	....	....	(0.02267)[a]	0.07
5	1.0450	0.0143	0.00005	0.01	.02223	.05
10	1.0419	.0145	.00008	.01	.02209	.05
15	1.0386	.0144	.00002	.01	.02171	.07
20	1.0353	.0147	.00004	.01	.02148	.06
25	1.0319	.0150	.00010	.01	.02138	.04
30	1.0282	.0153	.00011	.01	.02109	.03
35	1.0246	.0156	.00012	.01	.02072	.02
40	1.0210	.0157	.00012	.01	.02052	.01
45	1.0175	.0160	.00013	.01	.02021	.02
50	1.0139	.0163	.00016	.01	.01995	.01

[a] Extrapolated.

$$X = 70$$
$$d = d_0 + am + em \log m; \text{ Valid to 1.5 } M$$

t	d_0	a	e	Δ_1	A	Δ_2
0	1.0619	......	......	....	(0.02559)[a]	....
5	1.0570	0.0123	0.0085	0.03	.02489	0.13
10	1.0522	.0128	.0080	.03	.02420	.12
15	1.0474	.0135	.0060	.02	.02352	.11
20	1.0426	.0142	.0040	.02	.02275	.07
25	1.0378	.0150	.0020	.02	.02200	.05
30	1.0332	.0155	.0015	.01	.02128	.05
35	1.0285	.0159	.0000	.01	.02077	.02
40	1.0239	.0165	.....	.01	.01998	.02
45	1.0194	.0167	.....	.01	.01968	.02
50	1.0148	.0169	.....	.01	.01926	.02

[a] Extrapolated.
[*] H. S. Harned and C. Calmon, J. Am. Chem. Soc., **60**, 334 (1938).

Tᴀʙʟᴇ (11-3-2A)—*Concluded*
$X = 82$
$d = d_0 + am$; Valid to 0.6 M

t	d_0	a	Δ_1	A	Δ_2
5	1.0540	0.0152	0.01	0.0224	0.01
10	1.0488	.0159	.02	.0220	.02
15	1.0436	.0165	.02	.0212	.02
20	1.0387	.0165	.01	.0210	.01
25	1.0338	.0166	.01	.0210	.01
30	1.0288	.0165	.01	.0206	.01
35	1.0236	.0173	.01	.0198	.01
40	1.0183	.0178	.01	.0198	.02
45	1.0130	.0183	.03	.0178	.05

Tᴀʙʟᴇ (11-3-3A). Sᴛᴀɴᴅᴀʀᴅ Pᴏᴛᴇɴᴛɪᴀʟs ᴏꜰ ᴛʜᴇ Cᴇʟʟ, $H_2 \mid HCl$ (m), Sᴏʟᴠᴇɴᴛ (X), H_2O $(Y) \mid AgCl$-Ag
X and Y are weight percentages

Dioxane-Water Mixtures

$X = 0$; $E^0 = 0.22237 - 639.64 \times 10^{-6}(t - 25) - 3.181 \times 10^{-6}(t - 25)^2$
$X = 20$; $E^{0*} = 0.20303 - 760.5 \times 10^{-6}(t - 25) - 3.70 \times 10^{-6}(t - 25)^2$
$X = 45$; $E^{0*} = 0.16352 - 1135 \times 10^{-6}(t - 25) - 3.70 \times 10^{-6}(t - 25)^2$
$X = 70$; $E^{0*} = 0.06395 - 1767 \times 10^{-6}(t - 25) - 3.70 \times 10^{-6}(t - 25)^2$
$X = 82$; $E^{0*} = -0.0611 - 2573 \times 10^{-6}(t - 25) - 9.65 \times 10^{-6}(t - 25)^2$

These have a range of validity from 0 to 50° inclusive.

Methanol-Water Mixtures

$X = 10$; $E^{0*} = 0.21818 - 555.63 \times 10^{-6}(t - 20) - 4.128 \times 10^{-6}(t - 20)^2$
$X = 20$; $E^{0*} = 0.21151 - 529.10 \times 10^{-6}(t - 20) - 4.706 \times 10^{-6}(t - 20)^2$

These have a range of validity from 0 to 40° inclusive.

Ethyl Alcohol-Water Mixtures[a]

$X = 10$; $E^{0*} = 0.21900 - 5.03 \times 10^{-4}(t - 20) - 3.82 \times 10^{-6}(t - 20)^2$
$X = 20$; $E^{0*} = 0.21025 - 4.19 \times 10^{-4}(t - 20) - 6.00 \times 10^{-6}(t - 20)^2$

Isopropyl Alcohol-Water Mixtures[b]

$X = 5$; $E^{0*} = 0.22110 - 5.7425 \times 10^{-4}(t - 20) - 3.8357 \times 10^{-6}(t - 20)^2$
$X = 10$; $E^{0*} = 0.21666 - 5.3324 \times 10^{-4}(t - 20) - 4.7405 \times 10^{-6}(t - 20)^2$
$X = 20$; $E^{0*} = 0.20905 - 4.9001 \times 10^{-4}(t - 20) - 6.8362 \times 10^{-6}(t - 20)^2$

Glycerol-Water Mixtures[c]

$X = 50$; $E^{0*} = 0.18392 - 7.45 \times 10^{-4}(t - 25) - 3 \times 10^{-6}(t - 25)^2$; Valid from 0 to 90° inclusive.

(a) A. Patterson and W. A. Felsing, *J. Am. Chem. Soc.*, **64,** 1478 (1942). Revised.
(b) R. L. Moore and W. A. Felsing, *Ibid.*, **69,** 1076 (1947).
(c) H. S. Harned and F. H. M. Nestler, *Ibid.*, **68,** 665 (1946).

TABLE (11-4-1A). MEAN ACTIVITY COEFFICIENT OF HYDROCHLORIC ACID IN WATER†

m	0°	5°	10°	15°	20°	25°	30°	35°	40°	45°	50°	55°	60°
0.0001	(0.9890)	(0.9886)	(0.9890)	(0.9890)	(0.9892)	(0.9891)	(0.9890)	(0.9886)	(0.9885)	(0.9883)	(0.9879)	(0.9879)	(0.9879)
.0002	(.9848)	(.9847)	(.9846)	(.9844)	(.9844)	(.9842)	(.9835)	(.9838)	(.9833)	(.9835)	(.9831)	(.9833)	(.9831)
.0005	(.9756)	(.9756)	(.9756)	(.9757)	(.9759)	(.9752)	(.9747)	(.9745)	(.9741)	(.9741)	(.9738)	(.9735)	(.9734)
.001	(.9668)	(.9662)	(.9666)	(.9661)	(.9661)	(.9656)	(.9650)	(.9647)	(.9643)	(.9644)	(.9639)	(.9636)	(.9632)
.002	.9541	.9539	.9544	.9530	.9527	.9521	.9515	.9513	.9505	.9504	.9500	.9497	.9491
.005	.9303	.9300	.9300	.9297	.9294	.9285	.9275	.9268	.9265	.9261	.9250	.9240	.9235
.01	.9065	.9056	.9055	.9055	.9052	.9048	.9034	.9025	.9016	.9008	.9000	.8990	.8987
.02	.8774	.8768	.8773	.8770	.8768	.8755	.8741	.8731	.8715	.8704	.8690	.8680	.8666
.05	.8346	.8344	.8338	.8329	.8317	.8304	.8285	.8265	.8246	.8232	.8211	.8195	.8168
.1	.8027	.8023	.8016	.8000	.7985	.7964	.7940	.7918	.7891	.7872	.7850	.7829	.7813
.2	.7756	.7756	.7740	.7717	.7694	.7667	.7630	.7604	.7569	.7538	.7508	.7474	.7437
.5	.7761	.7730	.7694	.7658	.7616	.7571	.7526	.7477	.7432	.7387	.7344	.7292	.7237
1.	.8419	.8363	.8295	.8229	.8162	.8090	.8018	.7942	.7865	.7790	.7697	.7628	.7541
1.5	.9452	.9365	.9270	.9154	.9065	.8962	.8849	.8740	.8601	.8517	.8404	.8276	.8178
2.	1.078	1.068	1.053	1.039	1.024	1.009	.9929	.9755	.9602	.9481	.9327	.9186	.9072
3.	1.452	1.427	1.401	1.373	1.345	1.316	......	......	......	......	......	......	......
4.	2.006	1.960	1.911	1.862	1.812	1.762	......	......	......	......	......	......	......

† From observed electromotive forces. Results at concentrations less than $M = 0.002$ were obtained from plots used for extrapolation. These values are based on the data of H. S. Harned and R. W. Ehlers, *J. Am. Chem. Soc.*, **55**, 2179 (1933). N. J. Anderson [Dissertation, University of Chicago (1934)] has made a very careful study of the hydrogen silver-silver chloride cell containing hydrochloric acid at concentrations between 0.00002 and 0.003 M. Corrections were made for the solubility of silver chloride and other effects. At 25°, the activity coefficient was found to be 0.9751, 0.9653 and 0.9523 at 0.0005, 0.001 and 0.002 M, respectively. These values agree remarkably well with the extrapolated results in the table. We are grateful to Professor T. F. Young for bringing this matter to our attention.

X = weight percent of dioxane

$X = 20$

m	0°	10°	20°	25°	30°	40°	50°
0.005	0.902	0.900	0.898	0.896	0.895	0.892	0.889
.007	.889	.886	.883	.880	.880	.876	.871
.01	.872	.869	.865	.862	.861	.857	.851
.02	.835	.830	.825	.821	.820	.814	.808
.03	.811	.805	.800	.796	.795	.788	.781
.05	.780	.774	.768	.763	.762	.755	.748
.07	.759	.753	.746	.740	.740	.732	.725
.1	.736	.729	.722	.720	.716	.708	.701
.2	.696	.688	.681	.676	.673	.665	.656
.3	.682	.675	.667	.661	.658	.649	.639
.5	.684	.675	.666	.660	.656	.646	.633
.7	.649	.690	.679	.672	.667	.655	.641
1.	.736	.725	.712	.704	.698	.683	.666
1.5	.830	.815	.797	.786	.777	.755	.732
2.	.959	.938	.913	.898	.885	.855	.823
3.	1.337	1.293	1.245	1.219	1.195	1.141	1.085

$X = 45$

m	0°	10°	20°	25°	30°	40°	50°
0.003	0.849	0.846	0.844	0.842	0.839	0.834	0.828
.005	.824	.817	.811	.808	.803	.795	.786
.007	.802	.793	.786	.782	.777	.767	.757
.01	.776	.766	.758	.753	.747	.737	.725
.02	.720	.707	.697	.692	.686	.673	.660
.03	.683	.671	.661	.654	.649	.635	.622
.05	.637	.624	.613	.607	.600	.586	.573
.07	.605	.593	.583	.577	.570	.557	.545
.1	.579	.566	.553	.547	.540	.525	.512
.2	.529	.514	.503	.496	.488	.474	.459
.3	.511	.496	.484	.476	.466	.453	.438
.5	.503	.487	.473	.465	.456	.440	.423
.7	.513	.495	.480	.471	.461	.443	.424
1.	.547	.526	.508	.497	.485	.463	.442
1.5	.640	.612	.585	.570	.555	.524	.496
2.	.773	.733	.695	.676	.655	.614	.575
3.	1.191	1.112	1.037	1.001	.962	.887	.818

$X = 70$

m	0°	10°	20°	25°	30°	40°	50°
0.001	0.719	0.713	0.705	0.700	0.696	0.686	0.675
.0015	.672	.665	.656	.651	.647	.636	.624
.002	.641	.633	.623	.618	.613	.601	.589
.003	.589	.582	.573	.568	.563	.552	.540
.005	.530	.521	.510	.505	.499	.487	.473
.007	.488	.479	.468	.462	.457	.444	.431
.01	.446	.436	.425	.418	.413	.401	.388
.02	.369	.359	.348	.342	.336	.324	.312
.03	.328	.318	.308	.303	.297	.286	.275
.05	.283	.274	.264	.258	.253	.243	.232
07	.259	.249	.239	.234	.229	.219	.208
.1	.236	.226	.217	.212	.207	.197	.188
.2	.204	.194	.185	.180	.175	.165	.156
.3	.193	.182	.173	.168	.163	.154	.144
.5	.191	.179	.169	.163	.158	.147	.137
.7	.200	.187	.175	.168	.162	.150	.139
1.0	.227	.211	.195	.187	.179	.165	.151
1.5	.303	.277	.252	.240	.228	.207	.187

TABLE (11-6-1A)—*Concluded*
$X = 82$

m	5°	15°	25°	35°	45°
0.001	.3063	.2843	.2698	.2540	.2272
.0015	.2690	.2497	.2364	.2221	.1978
.002	.2432	.2256	.2134	.2001	.1776
.003	.2067	.1914	.1818	.1708	.1504
.005	.1674	.1561	.1479	.1380	.1212
.007	.1459	.1361	.1288	.1199	.1047
.010	.1259	.1176	.1105	.1023	.0893
.015	.1063	.0991	.0930	.0858	.0744
.020	.0946	.0878	.0822	.0757	.0654
.030	.0804	.0741	.0691	.0633	.0547
.050	.0659	.0603	.0560	.0513	.0441
.070	.0563	.0521	.0484	.0441	.0377
.100	.0506	.0465	.0429	.0390	.0332
.150	.0453	.0412	.0378	.0343	.0291
.200	.0426	.0386	.0353	.0319	.0269
.300	.0407	.0367	.0333	.0297	.0248
.500	.0430	.0381	.0340	.0298	.0244

* For bibliography, see reference 22, chapter (11).

TABLE (11-6-2A). MEAN ACTIVITY COEFFICIENT OF HYDROCHLORIC ACID IN ORGANIC SOLVENTS, AND IN ORGANIC SOLVENT-WATER MIXTURES. N_2 = MOL FRACTION OF ORGANIC SOLVENT

I. Methanol

m	$N_2 = 0.0588^a$			$N_2 = 0.1233^a$		
	0°	25°	40°	0°	25°	40°
0.001	0.964	0.962	0.961	0.961	0.959	0.957
.002	.951	.948	.946	.946	.943	.941
.005	.926	.922	.919	.919	.915	.912
.01	.901	.897	.893	.893	.888	.884
.02	.872	.866	.861	.862	.856	.850
.05	.825	.819	.812	.814	.806	.798
.1	.790	.780	.772	.771	.762	.751
.2	.762	.747	.736	.741	.727	.715
.5	.754	.737	.718	.726	.708	.693
1.	.809	.783	.756	.772	.747	.722
1.5	.898	.861	.827	.855	.814	.781
2.	1.020	.966	.917	.965	.911	.860

$N_2 = 1^b$

m	25°	m	25°	m	25°
0.00236	0.826	0.01444	0.658	0.0733	0.470
.002683	.817	.01722	.638	.0751	.468
.002980	.809	.01986	.621	.0947	.443
.003161	.804	.02363	.601	.1155	.423
.00494	.766	.02549	.592	.4802	.325
.00542	.758	.04261	.532	.5574	.322
.00711	.732	.04356	.530	.....	....
.00986	.699	.05312	.507	.....	....

II. Ethanol

$N_2 = 0.0417^c$		$N_2 = 0.0891^c$		$N_2 = 0.5^{d,e}$		$N_2 = 1^f$	
m	25°	m	25°	m	25°	m	25°
0.00631	0.914	0.00470	0.915	0.005	0.815	0.005	0.587
.00758	.907	.00787	.894	.01	.757	.007	.540
.01088	.891	.01015	.883	.02	.676	.01	.490
.01987	.864	.01983	.850	.05	.586	.02	.402
.04210	.824	.04150	.809	.1	.521	.03	.355
.05100	.814	.05166	.794	.2	.471	.05	.300
.07085	.795	.07123	.775	.5	.432	.07	.263
.0800	.788	.0816	.770	1.	.449	.10	.232
.0885	.783	.0924	.761	1.5	.510	...	...
.1091	.773	.1042	.751	2.	.582	...	...
.1990	.744	.3038	.699	2.5	.697	...	...
.2999	.731	.4751	.698	...	...	...	...
.5050	.730	.7309	.709	...	...	...	...
.7014	.743	1.0216	.741	...	...	...	...
.9946	.776	1.549	.819	...	...	...	...
1.499	.856	2.079	.930	...	...	...	...
1.994	.954	....	....	...	...	...	...

TABLE (11-6-2A)—*Concluded*

III. Isopropanol[c]

$N_2 = 0.0323$

m	25°	m	25°	m	25°
0.001862	0.948	0.03558	0.830	0.2990	0.726
.004019	.927	.04855	.813	.4451	.723
.006356	.911	.06685	.795	.6993	.737
.008616	.899	.07947	.785	.8863	.757
.00892	.898	.1119	.766	1.	.770
.02089	.858	.1921	.740	. . . . .	. . . . .

IV. Glycerol[d]

m	$N_2 = 0.01$	$N_2 = 0.05$
	25°	25°
0.002	0.951	. . . . .
.005	.924	0.898
.01	.902	.885
.02	.873	.858
.05	.826	.810
.1	.798	.775
.2	.764	.744
.28	.756	.738
.38	.753	.738
.5	.755	.737
.7	.772	.760
1.	.810	.801
1.5	.901	.901
2.	1.019	1.030
2.5	1.161	1.190
3.	1.345	1.385
4.	1.792	1.914

[a] H. S. Harned and H. C. Thomas, *J. Am. Chem. Soc.*, **58,** 761 (1936).
[b] G. Nonhebel and H. Hartley, *Phil. Mag.*, [6] **50,** 298, 729 (1923).
[c] H. S. Harned and C. Calmon, *J. Am. Chem. Soc.*, **61,** 1491 (1939).
[d] H. S. Harned and M. H. Fleysher, *Ibid.*, **47,** 82 (1925).
[e] W. W. Lucasse, *Z. physik. Chem.*, **121,** 254 (1926).
[f] H. Tanaguchi and G. J. Janz, *J. Phys. Chem.*, **61,** 688 (1957).

TABLE (11-7-1A). LIMITING SLOPES, $\mathfrak{S}_{(L)}$, FOR L_2 IN DIOXANE-WATER MIXTURES

X = weight percent of dioxane

t	$X = 0$	$X = 20$	$X = 45$	$X = 70$	$X = 82$
0	433	945	2480	7480	. . . . .
10	537	1147	2930	8940	14630
20	654	1364	3440	10570	17610
25	717	1485	3720	11470	19210
30	785	1605	4010	12410	20910
40	931	1872	4640	14450	24520
50	1090	2173	5340	16730	. . . . .

TABLE (11-7-2A). PARAMETERS OF EQUATIONS, $L_2 = \alpha + \beta T^2$; $J_2 = 2\beta T$, AND L_2 AND J_2 AT 25°. VALID FROM 0 TO 50°[a]

X = weight percent of dioxane

$X = 20$

m	$-\alpha$	β	$\bar{L}_2 (25°)$	$\bar{J}_2 (25°)$
0.005	77	0.00208	108	1.2
.007	77	.00254	149	1.5
.01	72	.00277	169	1.7
.02	77	.00346	235	2.1
.03	87	.00393	262	2.3
.05	87	.00438	302	2.6
.07	96	.00485	335	2.9
.1	144	.00554	348	3.3
.2	298	.00808	420	4.8
.3	435	.01015	467	6.1
.5	682	.01384	548	8.3
.7	871	.01684	625	10.0
1.	1156	.02123	731	13.8
1.5	1517	.02723	903	16.2
2.	1753	.03207	1097	19.1
3.	2013	.03946	1494	23.5

$X = 45$

m	$-\alpha$	β	$\bar{L}_2 (25°)$	$\bar{J}_2 (25°)$
0.003	640	0.00923	180	5.5
.005	619	.01061	324	6.3
.007	630	.01154	395	6.9
.01	609	.01223	478	7.3
.02	651	.01408	600	8.4
.03	669	.01500	664	8.9
.05	703	.01638	753	9.8
.07	735	.01730	802	10.2
.1	754	.01823	866	10.9
.2	839	.02077	1007	12.4
.3	934	.02284	1096	13.6
.5	1179	.02723	1241	16.2
.7	1430	.03138	1359	18.7
1.	1704	.03646	1536	21.7
1.5	1999	.04292	1815	25.6
2.	2169	.04799	2095	28.6
3.	2285	.05561	2657	33.1

$X = 70$

m	$-\alpha$	β	$\bar{L}_2 (25°)$	$\bar{J}_2 (25°)$
0.001	701	0.0129	446	7.7
.0015	862	.0157	533	9.4
.002	994	.0180	606	10.7
.003	1121	.0196	621	11.7
.005	1233	.0228	793	13.6
.007	1266	.0242	884	14.4
.01	1270	.0254	987	15.1
.02	1299	.0282	1207	16.8
.03	1348	.0295	1273	17.6
.05	1389	.0316	1419	18.8
.07	1397	.0328	1518	19.6
.1	1413	.0341	1617	20.3
.2	1417	.0371	1880	22.1
.3	1477	.0397	2051	23.7
.5	1558	.0438	2334	26.1
.7	1635	.0475	2586	28.3
1.0	1697	.0519	2915	30.9
1.5	1700	.0579	3445	34.5

TABLE (11-7-2A)—*Concluded*

$X = 82$

m	$-\alpha$	β	$\overline{L}_2$ (25°)	$\overline{J}_2$ (25°)
.001	5990	0.0948	2438	56.5
.0015	6520	.1019	2539	60.8
.002	7345	.1115	2567	66.5
.003	8600	.1259	2592	75.1
.005	10050	.1433	2689	85.5
.007	10835	.1535	2811	91.5
.010	11350	.1608	2945	95.9
.015	11660	.1654	3044	98.6
.020	11800	.1677	3108	100.0
.030	11935	.1704	3213	101.6
.050	12060	.1735	3364	103.5
.070	12135	.1754	3458	104.6
.100	12235	.1779	3580	106.1
.150	12410	.1817	3743	108.3
.200	12590	.1854	3892	110.6
.300	12910	.1925	4203	114.8
.500	13630	.2075	4817	123.7

ᵃ For bibliography, see reference 22, chapter (11).

TABLE (11-9-1A). CATION TRANSFERENCE NUMBERS, T_+, OF HYDROCHLORIC ACID IN WATER AND DIOXANE-WATER MIXTURES[a]

X = weight percent of dioxane

m	0°	5°	10°	15°	20°	25°	30°	35°	40°	45°	50°
					$X = 0$						
0.0	.....	0.842	0.837	0.831	0.826	0.821	0.816	0.811	0.806	0.801	0.796
.005	.....	.844	.840	.834	.829	.824	.819	.814	.809	.804	.799
.01	.....	.845	.841	.835	.830	.825	.819	.816	.811	.806	.801
.02	.....	.846	.842	.836	.832	.827	.822	.818	.813	.808	.803
.05	.....	.848	.844	.838	.834	.830	.825	.821	.816	.811	.806
.1	.....	.850	.846	.840	.837	.832	.828	.823	.819	.814	.810
.2	.....	.851	.847	.843	.839	.835	.830	.827	.823	.818	.814
.5	.....	.854	.850	.846	.842	.838	.834	.831	.827	.822	.819
1.0	.....	.855	.852	.848	.844	.841	.837	.833	.829	.824	.821
1.5	.....	.857	.853	.849	.845	.842	.839	.835	.830	.825	.822
2.0	.....	.857	.853	.849	.846	.843	.839	.835	.831	.826	.822
3.0	.....	.858	.854	.850	.846	.843	.840	.836	.832	.827	.823
					$X = 20$						
0.0	0.856	.851	.846	.841	.836	.831	.825	.821	.816	.810	.805
.005	.861	.855	.850	.845	.840	.835	.829	.825	.820	.814	.809
.01	.862	.857	.851	.846	.841	.836	.831	.827	.821	.816	.811
.02	.865	.859	.853	.848	.843	.838	.833	.829	.824	.818	.813
.05	.867	.861	.856	.851	.846	.841	.837	.832	.827	.822	.816
.1	.868	.862	.857	.852	.848	.843	.839	.834	.829	.823	.818
.2	.869	.863	.858	.853	.849	.844	.840	.835	.830	.825	.820
.5	.867	.862	.857	.852	.847	.843	.838	.833	.829	.823	.818
1.0	.864	.860	.854	.849	.844	.840	.836	.831	.826	.821	.816
1.5	.862	.857	.852	.847	.842	.838	.834	.829	.824	.819	.814
2.0	.860	.855	.850	.845	.841	.836	.832	.828	.823	.818	.813
3.0	.856	.852	.847	.842	.838	.833	.829	.825	.820	.816	.811
					$X = 45$						
0.0	.828	.824	.820	.816	.811	.806	.801	.796	.791	.787	.783
.005	.833	.829	.825	.821	.816	.811	.807	.801	.797	.793	.788
.01	.835	.830	.827	.823	.818	.813	.809	.804	.799	.795	.790
.02	.838	.833	.829	.825	.820	.816	.811	.807	.802	.798	.793
.05	.842	.837	.833	.829	.824	.820	.816	.812	.807	.803	.798
.1	.845	.840	.836	.831	.827	.823	.819	.816	.811	.807	.803
.2	.849	.844	.840	.834	.830	.826	.823	.820	.816	.812	.807
.5	.851	.846	.842	.836	.833	.829	.826	.822	.819	.815	.811
1.0	.851	.846	.841	.836	.832	.828	.825	.822	.819	.815	.811
1.5	.850	.845	.840	.835	.832	.828	.824	.821	.818	.814	.810
2.0	.849	.844	.839	.835	.831	.827	.824	.820	.817	.813	.809
3.0	.847	.843	.838	.833	.830	.825	.822	.817	.814	.810	.807
					$X = 70$						
0.0	.....	.772	.768	.764	.760	.755	.750	.746	.742	.738	.734
.005	.....	.781	.778	.774	.770	.766	.761	.757	.753	.750	.747
.01	.....	.783	.780	.777	.773	.769	.764	.760	.756	.753	.751
.02	.....	.786	.783	.779	.776	.772	.767	.763	.760	.757	.755
.05	.....	.788	.785	.782	.778	.774	.770	.766	.763	.760	.758
.1	.....	.789	.786	.783	.780	.775	.771	.768	.765	.762	.759
.2	.....	.789	.786	.784	.780	.776	.771	.768	.765	.762	.759
.5	.....	.789	.786	.783	.779	.774	.770	.766	.764	.760	.757
1.0	.....	.788	.785	.782	.777	.772	.768	.764	.762	.758	.754
1.5	.....	.788	.784	.781	.776	.771	.766	.763	.760	.757	.752

[a] H. S. Harned and E. C. Dreby, *J. Am. Chem. Soc.*, **61**, 3113 (1939).

TABLE (11-9-1A)—*Concluded*

$X = 82$

m	5°	10°	15°	20°	25°	30°	35°	40°	45°
0.0	0.677	0.675	0.673	0.672	0.670	0.668	0.667	0.665	0.663
.05	.742	.735	.730	.726	.722	.717	.712	.708	.702
.1	.767	.764	.762	.759	.756	.754	.752	.750	.747
.2	.755	.751	.747	.744	.740	.738	.735	.732	.729
.3	.718	.715	.711	.708	.705	.702	.699	.696	.693
.5	.660	.657	.654	.651	.648	.645	.642	.639	.637

Theoretical Limiting Slopes, $\mathcal{S}_{(T)}\sqrt{d_0}$, of the Equation, $T_+ = \mathcal{S}_{(T)}\sqrt{d_0}\ \sqrt{m}$

	H_2O	20%	45%	70%
15°	0.04278	0.04906	0.06773	0.1629
25°	.04509	.05195	.07186	.1642
35°	.04714	.05507	.07492	.1664

TABLE (12-1-1A). FUNCTION FOR CONVERTING m TO c FOR 1-1 ELECTROLYTES IN WATER

$$c/m = d_0 - Am + Bm^2; \qquad d_0 = 0.9970$$

Accuracy $\simeq \pm 0.05\%$

I. 25°; Valid to 4 M[a]

		Cl	Br	I	NO$_3$
Li	A.............	0.0182	0.0247	0.0358	0.0289
	B.............	0	.0002	.0009	.0004
Na	A.............	.0183	.0245	.0356	.0288
	B.............	0	0	.0008	0
K	A.............	.0284	.0345	.0458	.0392
	B.............	.0003	.0005	.0014	.0007
Rb	A.............	.0331	.0395	.0508	.0439
	B.............	.0004	.0008	.0016	.0008
Cs	A.............	.0400	.0470	.0580	.0503
	B.............	.0008	.0015	.0021	0

II. $B = 0$ for all Substances Except Sodium Bromide

t	d_0	NaBr[b]		HCl[c]	HBr[d]	KCl[e]	NaCl[f]
		A	B	A	A	A	A
0	0.9999	0.0212	−0.0003	0.0171	0.0228	0.0263	0.0160
5	1.0000	.0222	− .0001	.0174	.0232	.0265	.0166
10	.9997	.0231	− .0000	.0176	.0236	.0266	.0171
15	.9991	.0237	.0000	.0178	.0239	.0267	.0176
20	.9982	.0244	.0001	.01805	.0241	.0270	.0180
25	.9970	.0248	.0002	.0182	.0243	.0272	.0183
30	.9957	.0252	.0002	.0182	.0244	.0273	.0186
35	.9940	.0255	.0003	.01825	.0245	.0274	.0188
40	.9922	.0257	.0004	.01825	.0245	.0276	.0189
45	.9901	.....	.....	.01815	.0245	.....	.....
50	.9879	.....	.....	.01815	.0245	.....	.....
55	.9855	.....	.....	.01805	.0244	.....	.....
60	.9832	.....	.....	.01805	.0244	.....	.....

[a] Dr. R. A. Robinson, Private communication.
[b] H. S. Harned and C. C. Crawford, *J. Am. Chem. Soc.*, **59**, 1903 (1937).
[c] H. S. Harned and R. W. Ehlers, *Ibid.*, **59**, 2179 (1933).
[d] H. S. Harned, A. S. Keston and J. G. Donelson, *Ibid.*, **58**, 989 (1936).
[e] H. S. Harned and M. A. Cook, *Ibid.*, **59**, 1290 (1937).
[f] H. S. Harned and M. A. Cook, *Ibid.*, **61**, 495 (1939).

TABLE (12-1-2A).   MEAN ACTIVITY COEFFICIENT OF SODIUM CHLORIDE FROM 0 TO 100°[d]

m	0°	0°[a]	5°	10°	15°	20°	25°[b]	25°[c]	30°	35°	40°	50°	60°	70°	80°	90°	100°[e]
0.1	0.781	0.781	0.781	.781	.780	0.779	0.778	0.778	0.777	0.776	0.774	0.770	0.766	0.762	0.757	0.752	0.746
.2	.731	.731	.733	.734	.734	.733	.732	.732	.731	.7295	.728	(.725)	.721	.717	.711	.705	.698
.5	.671	.673	.675	.677	.678	.679	.679	.678	.679	(.679)	(.678)	(.675)	(.671)	.667	.660	.653	.644
1.	.6375	.635	.6435	.649	.652	.654	.656	.654	.657	.657	.657	.656	.654	.648	.641	.632	.622
1.5	.626	.....	.6355	.6425	.648	.652	.6555	.658	.658	.660	.661	.662	.659	(.655)	.646	.638	.629
2.	.630	.....	.6425	.652	.659	.665	.670	.670	.674	.676	.678	.678	.676	.672	.663	.651	.641
2.5	.641	.....	.659	.667	.677	.684	.691	.....	.695	.697	.698	.699	.696	(.692)	.685	.674	.659
3.0	.660	.....	.677	.691	.702	.7115	.719	.718	.724	.7255	(.728)	(.728)	(.726)	(.721)	(.712)	.700	.687
3.5	.687	.....	.706	.721	.735	.744	.752	.....	.756	.759	.761	(.762)	(.760)	(.758)	.742	.730	.716
4.	.717	.....	.7395	.757	.772	.783	.791	.....	.797	.800	(.802)	(.802)	.799	.791	.777	.763	.746

[a] From freezing point. G. Scatchard and S. S. Prentiss, *J. Am. Chem. Soc.*, **55**, 4855 (1933).
[b] H. S. Harned and L. F. Nims, *Ibid.*, **54**, 423 (1932).
[c] H. S. Harned, *Ibid.*, **51**, 416 (1929).
[d] R. A. Robinson, *Trans. Faraday Soc.*, **35**, 1222 (1939).
[e] Values from 60 to 100° are based on the boiling point data of R. P. Smith and D. S. Hirtle, *J. Am. Chem. Soc.*, **61**, 1123 (1939).
Values in parenthesis were obtained from graphs in Figs. (12-1-1) and (12-1-2).

TABLE (12-1-3A). RELATIVE PARTIAL MOLAL HEAT CONTENT OF SODIUM CHLORIDE[a]

m	0°	10°	20°	25°	30°	40°	60°	70°	80°	90°	100°
0.5	− 330	− 185	− 90	− 45	15	170	300	400	500	600	700
1.	− 630	− 440	−250	−180	−100	30	310	430	550	670	760
1.5	− 860	− 680	−430	−330	−260	− 60	240	420	580	720	800
2.	−1120	− 840	−560	−450	−330	−130	280	450	650	820	1020
2.5	−1300	−1070	−710	−560	−380	−140	290	480	700	890	1040
3.	−1650	−1190	−770	−580	−400	−150	300	500	730	910	1040
3.5	−1800	−1230	−800	−590	−420	−170	310	520	820	960	1120
4.	−1850	−1380	−850	−620	−440	−150	360	590	890	1100	1300

[a] R. P. Smith and D. S. Hirtle, *J. Am. Chem. Soc.*, **61**, 1123 (1939). Combined calorimetric, electromotive force, and boiling point data.

TABLE (12-2-1A). MEAN ACTIVITY COEFFICIENT OF HYDROBROMIC ACID IN AQUEOUS SOLUTION[a]

$\bar{L}_2$ and $\bar{J}_2$ at 25°

m	0°	5°	10°	15°	20°	25°	30°	35°	40°	45°	50°	55°	60°	$\bar{L}_2$	$\bar{J}_2$
0.001	0.967	0.967	0.967	0.966	0.966	0.966	0.966	0.965	0.964	0.964	0.964	0.963	0.963	22	0.4
.005	.932	.932	.932	.930	.930	.930	.929	.928	.928	.927	.926	.924	.924	47	.8
.01	.910	.910	.909	.908	.907	.906	.906	.905	.904	.904	.902	.900	.898	64	1.
.02	.883	.883	.883	.882	.879	.879	.879	.878	.877	.875	.873	.871	.869	85	1.5
.05	.843	.843	.843	.842	.838	.838	.837	.834	.833	.831	.830	.827	.826	124	2.2
.1	.812	.812	.811	.808	.807	.805	.804	.802	.800	.797	.795	.791	.788	163	2.9
.2	.793	.791	.790	.787	.785	.782	.780	.777	.774	.772	.769	.765	.758	228	3.9
.5	.806	.803	.800	.797	.793	.790	.784	.781	.776	.772	.767	.764	.760	338	5.6
1.	.900	.894	.889	.888	.877	.871	.864	.856	.850	.844	.838	.831	.823	500	7.7

[a] H. S. Harned, A. S. Keston and J. G. Donelson, *J. Am. Chem. Soc.*, **58**, 989 (1936).

TABLE (12-2-2A). MEAN ACTIVITY COEFFICIENT OF POTASSIUM CHLORIDE IN AQUEOUS SOLUTION[a]

m	0°	5°	10°	15°	20°	25°	30°	35°	40°
0.1	0.768	0.769	0.769	0.769	0.770	0.769	0.768	0.767	0.765
.2	.717	.718	.718	.719	.718	.719	.718	.717	.715
.3	.683	.685	.687	.687	.688	.688	.687	.685	.682
.5	.642	.646	.648	.650	.651	.651	.651	.648	.646
.7	.613	.619	.623	.624	.627	.628	.629	.627	.626
1.	.588	.595	.598	.601	.604	.604	.604	.604	.603
1.5	.563	.570	.576	.579	.582	.585	.585	.585	.585
2.	.547	.554	.562	.568	.573	.576	.578	.579	.578
2.5	.540	.549	.556	.562	.568	.572	.574	.575	.575
3.	.539	.549	.556	.562	.567	.571	.573	.574	.573
3.5	.540	.550	.558	.565	.571	.574	.577	.578	.578
4.	....	....	.563	.569	.574	.579	.582	.584	.585

[a] H. S. Harned and M. A. Cook, *J. Am. Chem. Soc.*, **59**, 1290 (1937).

TABLE (12-2-3A). RELATIVE PARTIAL MOLAL HEAT CONTENT AND HEAT CAPACITY
OF POTASSIUM CHLORIDE IN AQUEOUS SOLUTION

$$\bar{L}_2 = \bar{L}_2(0°) + \alpha t + \beta t^2; \ \bar{J}_2 = \alpha + 2\beta t.^a \quad \text{Valid from 0 to 40°}$$

m	$\bar{L}_2(0°)$	α	β
0.05	(34)	2.0	0.014
.1	− 15	3.5	.025
.2	− 80	5.1	.030
.3	− 190	7.5	.034
.5	− 280	9.4	.037
.7	− 430	12.0	.040
1.0	− 570	14.4	.045
1.5	− 760	18.4	.049
2.0	− 920	22.2	.055
2.5	−1000	23.0	.060
3.0	−1025	25.4	.066
3.5	−1200	27.7	.072
4.0	−1270	29.6	.079

[a] H. S. Harned and M. A. Cook, *J. Am. Chem. Soc.*, **59**, 1290 (1937).

TABLE (12-2-4A). MEAN ACTIVITY COEFFICIENT OF SODIUM BROMIDE IN AQUEOUS
SOLUTION[a]

m	0°	5°	10°	15°	20°	25°	30°	35°	40°
0.1	(0.784)	(0.784)	(0.784)	(0.783)	(0.783)	(0.782)	(0.781)	(0.779)	(0.777)
.2	.738	.739	.741	.740	.741	.740	.739	.737	.734
.3	.713	.716	.718	.720	.718	.718	.717	.715	.712
.5	.685	.689	.693	.693	.695	.695	.694	.692	.689
.7	.670	.675	.681	.684	.683	.687	.686	.685	.685
1.	.659	.667	.675	.680	.684	.686	.687	.686	.686
1.5	.664	.673	.686	.693	.699	.703	.706	.7C8	.707
2.	.679	.693	.708	.719	.727	.734	.739	.741	.743
2.5	.708	.727	.745	.738	.769	.773	.784	.789	.791
3.	.745	.766	.787	.802	.815	.826	.834	.839	.842
3.5	.787	.811	.834	.852	.866	.878	.887	.893	.896
4.	.832	.858	.885	.905	.921	.934	.945	.951	.954

[a] H. S. Harned and C. C. Crawford, *J. Am. Chem. Soc.*, **59**, 1903 (1937).

MEAN ACTIVITY COEFFICIENT OF POTASSIUM BROMIDE IN AQUEOUS SOLUTIONS.[b]

m	60°	70°	80°	90°	100°
0.1	0.759	0.756	0.752	0.748	0.744
.3	0.684	0.681	0.677	0.673	0.668
.5	0.653	0.649	0.647	0.643	0.637
1.	0.623	0.621	0.618	0.613	0.607
2.	0.616	0.615	0.613	0.608	0.602
3.	0.631	0.630	0.629	0.625	0.619
4.	0.654	0.655	0.654	0.650	0.644

[b] G. C. Johnson and R. P. Smith, *J. Am. Chem. Soc.*, **63**, 1351 (1941).

TABLE (12-2-5A). RELATIVE PARTIAL MOLAL HEAT CONTENT AND HEAT CAPACITY OF SODIUM BROMIDE IN AQUEOUS SOLUTION[a]

$$\bar{L}_2 = \bar{L}_2(0°) + \alpha t + \beta t^2; \quad \bar{J}_2 = \alpha + 2\beta t. \quad \text{Valid from 0 to 40°}$$

m	$\bar{L}_2(0°)$	α	β
0.1	$-$ 23	4.6	0.015
.2	$-$ 140	8.2	.023
.3	$-$ 210	11.8	.027
.5	$-$ 400	15.5	.036
.7	$-$ 580	21.8	.044
1.	$-$ 830	23.5	.049
1.5	-1140	27.4	.055
2.	-1390	30.6	.061
2.5	-1600	33.6	.066
3.	-1790	37.0	.073
3.5	-1940	41.4	.079
4.	-2020	43.2	.086

[a] H. S. Harned and C. C. Crawford, *J. Am. Chem. Soc.*, **59**, 1903 (1937).

TABLE (12-2-6A). MEAN ACTIVITY COEFFICIENT OF SODIUM HYDROXIDE IN AQUEOUS SOLUTION[a]

m	0°	5°	10°	15°	20°	25°	30°	35°
0.05	0.820	0.821	0.820	0.820	0.819	0.818	0.818	0.816
.1	.767	.768	.768	.767	.766	.766	.765	.764
.25	.713	.715	.716	.717	.714	.713	.712	.712
.5	.684	.688	.690	.692	.693	.693	.693	.694
1.	.660	.668	.672	.676	.678	.679	.680	.678
1.5	.661	.669	.673	.681	.682	.683	.685	.683
2.	.674	.682	.689	.694	.696	.698	.700	.698
2.5	.696	.708	.717	.724	.727	.729	.730	.726
3.	.736	.751	.762	.769	.774	.774	.775	.772
3.5	.792	.801	.816	.822	.825	.826	.827	.822
4.	.857	.874	.882	.887	.889	.888	.888	.882

[a] 0.05 to 1.5M, H. S. Harned and J. C. Hecker, *J. Am. Chem. Soc.*, **55**, 4838 (1933); See also G. Åkerlöf and G. Kegeles, *Ibid.*, **62**, 620 (1940) and Table (B-5-2).

TABLE (12-2-7A). MEAN ACTIVITY COEFFICIENTS OF POTASSIUM
HYDROXIDE IN AQUEOUS SOLUTION.*

m	0°	10°	20°	30°	40°	50°	60°	70°	80°
0.1	0.796	0.794	0.792	0.787	0.783	0.780	0.772	0.765	0.759
.2	.761	.759	.756	.752	.747	.740	.733	.724	.718
.4	.737	.736	.733	.728	.722	.714	.704	.694	.683
1.	.757	.757	.755	.749	.740	.728	.713	.696	.680
1.5	.810	.814	.810	.802	.791	.774	.756	.732	.710
2.	.887	.890	.884	.874	.858	.837	.811	.782	.755
4.	1.42	1.41	1.39	1.35	1.30	1.24	1.177	1.109	1.043
6.	2.49	2.42	2.33	2.20	2.09	1.95	1.81	1.66	1.53
8.	4.48	4.24	3.98	3.70	3.40	3.11	2.82	2.54	1.82
10.	8.00	7.37	6.73	6.11	5.50	4.92	4.37	3.87	3.42
12.	13.88	12.45	11.10	9.85	8.68	7.62	6.65	5.78	5.11
14.	23.2	20.4	17.8	15.4	13.3	11.5	9.84	8.41	7.20
17.	47.8	40.7	34.5	28.4	24.4	20.3	16.8	13.8	11.4

* P. Bender, *Dissertation*, Yale University, June (1939); G. Akerlof and P. Bender, *J. Am. Chem. Soc.*, **70**, 2366 (1948); see also F. L. Shibata, F. Murata and Y. Toyoda, *J. Chem. Soc.* (Japan) **58**, 627 (1931); F. L. Shibata and F. Murata, *Ibid.*, **52**, 645 (1931).

TABLE (12-2-8A).[a] RELATIVE PARTIAL MOLAL HEAT CONTENT AND HEAT CAPACITY
OF SODIUM HYDROXIDE IN AQUEOUS SOLUTION[b]

$$\bar{L}_2 = \bar{L}_2(0°) + \alpha t; \quad \bar{J}_2 = \alpha$$

m	$-\bar{L}_2(0°)$	α
0.05	7	6
.1	70	9.5
.25	200	15
.5	400	20
1.	680	27
1.5	820	30.5
2.	940	35

[a] H. S. Harned and J. C. Hecker, *J. Am. Chem. Soc.*, **55**, 4838 (1933).
[b] Extensive tables of $\bar{L}_2$ and $\bar{J}_2$ from 0 to 70°, and to 17M sodium hydroxide are given by G. Åkerlöf and G. Kegeles, *J. Am. Chem. Soc.*, **62**, 620 (1940).

TABLE (12-2-9A). RELATIVE PARTIAL MOLAL HEAT CONTENT AND HEAT CAPACITY
OF POTASSIUM HYDROXIDE IN AQUEOUS SOLUTION[a]

$$\bar{L}_2 = \bar{L}_2(0°) + \alpha t + \beta t^2; \quad \bar{J}_2 = \alpha + 2\beta t. \quad \text{Valid from 0 to 40°}$$

m	$\bar{L}_2(0°)$	α	β
0.05	37	2.4	0.017
.1	41	3.6	.029
.15	30	4.7	.030
.25	− 1	6.4	.032
.35	− 35	8.2	.034
.5	− 95	10.4	.036
.75	−180	13.6	.040
1.0	−270	16.2	.043
1.5	−335	20.6	.050
2.0	−381	24.6	.057
2.5	−390	28.2	.063
3.0	−356	31.5	.070
3.5	−335	34.5	.078
4.0	−226	37.4	.081

[a] H. S. Harned and M. A. Cook, *J. Am. Chem. Soc.*, **59**, 496 (1937).

TABLE (12-3-1A). MEAN ACTIVITY COEFFICIENTS OF 1-1 ELECTROLYTES AT 25°

m	LiCl	NaCl	KCl	RbCl	CsCl
0.1	0.792	0.778	0.769	0.764	0.755
.2	.761	.734	.717	.709	.693
.3	.748	.710	.687	.675	.653
.5	.742	.682	.650	.634	.604
.7	.754	.668	.626	.607	.573
1.	.781	.658	.605	.583	.543
1.5	.841	.659	.585	.559	.514
2.	.931	.671	.575	.547	.495
2.5	1.043	.692	.572	.540	.485
3.	1.174	.720	.573	.538	.480
3.5	....	.753	.576	.539	.476
4.	....	.792	.582	.541	.474
4.5	....	....	.590	.544	.474
5.	....	....	....	.547	.476

m	LiBr	NaBr	KBr	RbBr	CsBr
0.1	0.794	0.781	0.771	0.763	0.754
.2	.764	.739	.721	.706	.692
.3	.757	.717	.692	.674	.652
.5	.755	.695	.657	.634	.603
.7	.770	.687	.637	.606	.570
1.	.811	.687	.617	.579	.537
1.5	.899	.704	.601	.552	.504
2.	1.016	.732	.596	.537	.486
2.5	1.166	.770	.596	.527	.474
3.	1.352	.817	.600	.521	.468
3.5	....	.871	.606	.518	.462
4.	....	.938	.615	.517	.460
4.5	....	....	....	.517	.459
5.	....	....	....	.518	.460

m	LiI	NaI	KI	RbI	CsI
0.1	0.811	0.788	0.776	0.762	0.753
.2	.800	.752	.731	.705	.691
.3	.799	.737	.704	.673	.651
.5	.819	.726	.675	.631	.599
.7	.848	.729	.659	.602	.566
1.	.907	.739	.646	.575	.532
1.5	1.029	.772	.639	.548	.495
2.	1.196	.824	.641	.533	.470
2.5	1.423	.889	.649	.525	.450
3.	1.739	.967	.657	.519	.434
3.5	....	1.060	.667	.518	....
4.	....	....	.678	.517	....
4.5	....	....	.692	.519	....
5.	....	....	....	.520	....

m	HNO₃	NH₄Cl	NH₄NO₃	NaCOOH	CH₃CH₂COONa
0.1	0.791	0.770	0.740	0.778	0.800
.2	.754	.718	.677	.734	.772
.3	.735	.687	.636	.710	.763
.5	.720	.649	.582	.685	.764
.7	.717	.625	.545	.671	.777
1.	.724	.603	.504	.661	.808
1.4	.745	.584	.564	.657	.864
2.	.793	.570	.419	.658	.966
3.	.909	.561	.368	.678	1.160
4.	....	.560	.330	....	....

TABLE (12-3-1A)—*Continued*

m	LiNO₃	NaNO₃	KNO₃	RbNO₃	CsNO₃
0.1	0.788	0.758	0.733	0.730	0.729
.2	.751	.702	.659	.656	.651
.3	.737	.664	.607	.603	.598
.5	.728	.615	.542	.534	.526
.7	.731	.583	.494	.484	.475
1.	.746	.548	.441	.429	.419
1.5	.783	.509	.378	.365	.354
2.	.840	.481	.327	.319	....
2.5	.903	.457	.293	.284	....
3.	.973	.438	.266	.256	....
3.5	1.052	.423	.244	.235	....
4.	....	.410	....	.216	....
4.5	....	.398	....	.200	....
5.	....	.388	....	....	....
5.5	....	.380	....	....	....
6.	....	.373	....	....	....

m	LiAc[a]	NaAc	KAc	RbAc	CsAc
0.1	0.782	0.791	0.796	0.797	0.798
.2	.740	.755	.767	.771	.773
.3	.718	.741	.752	.759	.763
.5	.698	.740	.751	.760	.765
.7	.691	.741	.755	.769	.777
1.	.690	.757	.779	.795	.802
1.5	.709	.799	.839	.859	.868
2.	.734	.854	.910	.940	.952
2.5	.769	.920	.993	1.034	1.046
3.	.807	.993	1.086	1.139	1.153
3.5	.847	1.070	1.187	1.255	1.277
4.	.893	....	....	....	....

m	NaF	KF	NaCNS	KCNS	HI
0.1	0.764	0.774	0.787	0.769	0.818
.2	.708	.727	.750	.716	.807
.3	.675	.701	.731	.685	.811
.5	.631	.672	.715	.646	.839
.7	.602	.657	.710	.623	.883
1.	.572	.649	.712	.600	.965
1.5	....	.649	.725	.574	1.139
2.	....	.663	.751	.558	1.367
2.5	....	.684	.784	.548	1.656
3.	....	.713	.820	.542	2.025
3.5	....	.748	.860	.537	....
4.	....	.790	.911	.533	....
4.5	....	....	....	.531	....
5.	....	....	....	.529	....

m	(1)	(2)	(3)	(4)	(5)
0.1	0.800	0.800	0.803	0.803	—
.2	.774	.776	.779	.780	—
.3	.769	.771	.775	.777	—
.5	.782	.790	.794	.783	—
.7	.812	.817	.826	.775	0.553
1.	.868	.907	.865	.562	.349
1.4	.952	.945	.855	.512	.309
2	1.083	1.030	.763	.398	.236
3	1.278	.982	.612	.306	.185

(1) Na-butyrate (2) Na-valerate (3) Na-caproate (4) Na-heptylate (5) Na-caprylate.   [a] Ac represents acetate radical.

TABLE (12-3-1A)—*Continued*

m	CsNO₃	LiS̄*	Na S̄	K S̄	TlNO₃	TlClO₄	TlAc	AgNO₃
0.1	0.729	0.773	0.764	0.760	0.701	0.730	0.748	0.731
0.2	0.651	0.729	0.708	0.701	0.605	0.652	0.684	.654
0.3	0.598	0.698	0.672	0.662	0.544	0.599	0.643	.603
0.5	0.526	0.664	0.624	0.607	....	0.527	0.588	.534
0.7	0.475	0.642	0.592	0.562	....	....	0.552	.483
1.0	0.419	0.621	0.551	0.509	....	....	0.513	.428
1.5	0.354	0.595	0.502	0.438	....	....	0.472	.362
2.0	....	0.574	0.460	0.387	....	....	0.444	.315
2.5	....	0.565	0.428	0.349	....	....	0.422	.280
3.0	....	0.563	0.403	0.318	....	....	0.405	.252
3.5	....	0.566	0.385	0.294	....	....	0.390	.229
4.0	....	0.573	0.368	....	....	....	0.377	.210
4.5	....	0.584	....	....	....	....	0.365	.194
5.0	....	....	....	....	....	....	0.354	.181
5.5	....	....	....	....	....	....	0.345	.169
6.0	....	....	....	....	....	....	0.336	.159
8.0	....	....	....	....	....	....	....	.129
10.0	....	....	....	....	....	....	....	.110
13.0	....	....	....	....	....	....	....	.0908

* S̄ = p-toluenesulfonate radical.

Bibliography: R. A. Robinson and D. A. Sinclair, *J. Am. Chem. Soc.*, **56**, 1830 (1934); R. A. Robinson, *Ibid.*, **57**, 1161 (1935); **57**, 1165 (1935); **59**, 84 (1937); R. A. Robinson, *Trans. Faraday Soc.*, **35**, 1217 (1939); R. A. Robinson, *J. Am. Chem. Soc.*, **62**, 3131 (1940); *Ibid.*, **63**, 628 (1941); H. S. Harned and R. A. Robinson, *Trans. Faraday Soc.*, **37**, 302 (1941); R. A. Robinson and H. S. Harned, *Chem. Rev.*, **28**, 419 (1941).

TABLE (12-3-1A)*—*Continued*

m	NaClO₃[1]	KClO₃[2]	NaBrO₃[3]	KBrO₃[3]	LiClO₄[4]	NaClO₄[5]	NaH₂PO₄[5]	KH₂PO₄[5]
0.1	0.772	0.749	0.758	0.745	0.812	0.775	0.744	0.731
.2	0.720	0.681	0.696	0.674	0.794	0.729	0.675	0.653
.3	0.688	0.635	0.657	0.625	0.792	0.701	0.629	0.602
.5	0.645	0.568	0.605	0.552	0.808	0.668	0.563	0.529
.7	0.617	0.518	0.569		0.834	0.648	0.517	0.477
1.0	0.589		0.528		0.887	0.629	0.468	0.421
1.4	0.563		0.489		0.979	0.616	0.420	0.369
2.0	0.538		0.450		1.158	0.609	0.371	
2.5	0.525		0.426		1.350	0.609	0.343	
3.0	0.515				1.582	0.611	0.320	
3.5	0.508				1.866	0.617	0.305	
4.0					2.18	0.626	0.293	
5.0						0.649	0.276	
6.0						0.677	0.265	

(1) J. H. Jones, *J. Am. Chem. Soc.*, **65**, 1353 (1943); (2) J. H. Jones, *Ibid.*, **66**, 1672 (1944); (3) J. H. Jones, *Ibid.*, **69**, 1066 (1947); (4) J. H. Jones, *J. Phys. Chem.*, **51**, 516 (1947); (5) J. M. Stokes, *Trans. Faraday Soc.*, **41**, 685 (1945). See summary of osmotic and activity coefficients by R. A. Robinson and R. H. Stokes, *Trans. Faraday Soc.*, **45**, 612(1949).

* For results at very high concentrations, see Table (12-3-2A).

TABLE (12-3-1A)*—*Concluded*

m	KH_2PO_4	NaH_2PO_4	KH_2AsO_4	NaH_2AsO_4	K_2HPO_4	Na_2HPO_4
0.1	0.743	0.752	0.750	0.767	0.482	0.480
.2	.667	.681	.679	.708	.398	.392
.3	.615	.632	.630	.667	.352	.340
.4	.574	.596	.593	.637	.319	.305
.5	.540	.565	.562	.611	.296	.277
.6	.512	.540	.537	.589	.278	.256
.7	.488	.519	.515	.569	.263	.238
.8	.466	.499	.495	.552	.250	.223
.9	.447	.483	.479	.537	.240	.216
1.0	.430	.468	.463	.522	.231	.200
1.1	.415	.454	.450	.509	.223	.190
1.2	.410	.442	.438	.498	—	—
1.3	.388	.431	.427	.486	—	—

m	K_2HAsO_4	Na_2HAsO_4	K_3PO_4	Na_3PO_4	K_3AsO_4	Na_3AsO_4
0.1	0.512	0.498	0.312	0.293	0.331	0.299
.2	.441	.419	.244	.216	.270	.225
.3	.404	.373	.211	.177	.242	.188
.4	.377	.341	.190	.151	.223	.165
.5	.357	.316	.175	.134	.212	.148
.6	.341	.296	.164	.12.	.202	.136
.7	.329	.280	.156	.109	.195	.126
.8	.318	.265	—	—	—	—
.9	.308	.254	—	—	—	—
1.0	.300	.243	—	—	—	—
1.1	.293	.233	—	—	—	—

* G. Scatchard and P. C. Breckenridge, *J. Phys. Chem.*, **58**, 596 (1954).

TABLE (12-3-2A). MEAN ACTIVITY COEFFICIENTS OF SOME 1-1 ELECTROLYTES, SULPHURIC ACID, CALCIUM CHLORIDE AND NITRATE AT 25° AND HIGH CONCENTRATIONS.

m	NaCl	NaOH	LiCl	LiBr	LiNO$_3$	H$_2$SO$_4$	CaCl$_2$	HClO$_4$	Ca(NO$_3$)$_2$
0.1	0.778	0.766	0.790	0.796	0.788	0.2655	0.518	0.803	0.485
.2	.735	.727	.757	.766	.752	.2090	.472	.778	.426
.5	.681	.693	.739	.753	.726	.1557	.448	.769	.363
1.	.657	.679	.774	.803	.743	.1316	.500	.823	.336
1.5	.656	.683	.838	.896	.783	....	....	.923	.336
2.	.668	(0.700)	.921	1.015	.835	.1276	.792	1.055	.345
3.	.714	.774	1.156	1.341	.966	.1422	1.483	1.448	.380
4.	.783	.890	1.510	1.897	1.125	.1700	2.934	2.08	.435
5.	.874	1.060	2.02	2.74	1.310	.2081	5.89	3.11	.507
6.	.986	1.280	2.72	3.92	1.515	.2567	11.11	4.76	.592
7.	....	1.578	3.71	5.76	1.723	.3166	18.28	7.44	.690
8.	....	1.979	5.10	8.61	1.952	.386	26.02	11.83	.801
9.	....	2.51	6.96	12.92	2.19	.467	34.20	19.11	.935
10.	....	3.18	9.40	19.92	2.44	.559	43.0	30.9	1.065
11.	....	4.04	12.55	31.0	2.69	.661	....	50.1	1.184
12.	....	5.11	16.41	46.3	2.95	.770	....	80.8	1.311
14.	....	7.91	26.2	104.7	....	1.017	....	205.	1.538
16.	....	11.38	37.9	198.0	....	1.300	....	500.	1.724
18.	....	15.15	49.9	331.	....	1.608	....	....	1.917
20.	....	19.0	62.4	485.	....	1.940	....	....	2.008
22.	....	22.7	....	....	....	2.300	....	....	....
24.	....	26.1	....	....	....	....	....	....	....
26.	....	29.0	....	....	....	....	....	....	....
29.	....	33.2	....	....	....	....	....	....	....
Ref.*	(1)	(2)	(3)	(4)	(5)	(6)	(7)	(8)	(9)

* Comprehensive tables of osmotic and activity coefficients are given by R. A. Robinson and R. H. Stokes, *Trans. Faraday Soc.*, **45**, 612 (1949).

(1) R. H. Stokes and B. J. Levien, *J. Am. Chem. Soc.*, **68**, 333 (1946).

(2) R. H. Stokes, *Ibid.*, **67**, 1689 (1945). Referred to 0.700 at 2 M.

(3) R. A. Robinson, *Trans. Faraday Soc.*, **41**, 756 (1945).

(4) R. A. Robinson and H. J. McCoach, *J. Am. Chem. Soc.*, **69**, 2244 (1947).

(5) R. A. Robinson, *Ibid.*, **68**, 2402 (1946).

(6) R. H. Stokes, *Trans. Faraday Soc.*, **44**, 295 (1948) (Review).

(7) R. H. Stokes, *Trans. Faraday Soc.*, **41**, 637 (1945).

(8) R. A. Robinson and O. J. Baker, *Trans. Roy. Soc., N. Z.*, **76**, 250 (1946).

(9) R. H. Stokes and R. A. Robinson, *J. Am. Chem. Soc.*, **70**, 1871 (1948).

TABLE (12-6-1A). CONSTANTS AND $f_\pm$ (STANDARD) OF GUGGENHEIM'S EQUATION, (12-6-3), $\log f_\pm = \log f_\pm(\lambda = 0) + \lambda c$. VALUES OF $\gamma_{0.1}$

	λ	$\gamma_{0.1}$	m	$f_\pm(\lambda = 0)$
HCl	+.240	0.801	0.001	0.966
LiCl	+.195	.793	.005	.927
NaCl	+.130	.781	.01	.901
KCl	+.072	.771	.02	.867
LiClO₃	+.243	.802	.03	.844
NaClO₃	+.035	.764	.04	.825
KClO₃	−.143	.734	.05	.810
LiClO₄	+.330	.818	.06	.797
NaClO₄	+.065	.770	.07	.786
KClO₄	−.435	....	.08	.776
LiNO₃	+.226	.799	.09	.767
NaNO₃	+.000	.758	.1	.758
KNO₃	−.206	.723	....	....
CsNO₃	+.00	(.758)	....	....
NaIO₃	−.35	.700	....	....
KIO₃	−.35	.700	....	....
LiOOCH	+.122	.780	....	....
NaOOCH	+.148	.785	....	....
KOOCH	+.165	.787	....	....
LiOOC·CH₃	+.183	.791	....	....
NaOOC·CH₃	+.252	.804	....	....
KOOC·CH₃	+.252	.804	....	....

TABLE (12-10-1A). SALTING COEFFICIENTS
k_m (25°) [Equation (12-10-5)]

	He (1)	A (1)	H₂ (2)	O₂ (2)	N₂O (2)	CO₂ (2)	C₂H₄ (2)	CH₃COOC₂H₅ (3)	C₆H₁₂O₂ (4)	$CS\langle^{NHC_6H_5}_{NH_2}$ (5)	C₆H₅OH (6)
HCl	....	....	.020	.022	.016	.006	....	....	....	....	....
LiCl	−.015	.037	.066	....	.081	....	....	.088	.077	....	.181
NaCl	.053	.058	.094	.132	.101	....	.093	.166	.139	.140	.220
NaBr	....	....	....	....	.089	....	.077	.119	.109	....	....
NaI	....	....	....	....	....	....	.024	.041	....	.029	....
NaNO₃	.050	.058	.080	....	.072	(I₂) .053	.050	.074	....	.019	....
Na₂SO₄	....	....	....	....	.110	(I₂) .100	.098	....	.159	.133	....
KCl	.055	.061	.078	....	.085	.059	.062	.143	.118	.118	.245
KBr	....	....	....	....	.063	.045	.049	.105	.090	.055	....
KI	....	....	....	....	.058	.032	....	.037	.034	.057	....
KNO₂	....	....	.061	....	.047	.025	.030	.060	....	.013	....
NH₄NO₃	....	....	....	....	.007	....	....	.027	....	−.057	....
BaCl₂	....	.070	....	....	.073	.060	.067	.080	....	.074	.069
SrCl₂	....	.033	....	....	....	....	....	....	....	....	.064
CaCl₂	....	.018	.065	....	.064	....	.058	....	....	....	.062
Ca(NO₃)₂	....	....	....	....	.041	....	.028	.022	....	....	.062
MgCl₂	....	.012	....	....	....	....	.055	....	.060	....	.060
MgSO₄	....	....	....	.057	.070	....	.064	.127	.105	.080	....
AlCl₃	....	.021	.028	....	....	....	.044	....	.043	.063	....
Al₂(SO₄)₃	....	....	....	....	.045	....	.043	....	.076	....	....
LiI	−.038	....	....	....	....						
HClO₄	−.048	−.022	....	....							

(1) G. Åkerlöf, J. Am. Chem. Soc., 57, 1196 (1935); (2) M. Randall and C. F. Failey, Chem. Rev., 4, 271 (1927); 4, 285 (1927); (3) S. Glasstone and A. Pound, J. Chem. Soc., 127, 2660, (1925); S. Glasstone, A. Dimond and D. W. Pound, Ibid., 128, 2935 (1926); (4) G. Åkerlöf, J. Am. Chem. Soc., 51, 984 (1929); (5) W. Biltz, Z. physik. Chem., 43, 41 (1903); V. Rothmund, Ibid., 33, 401 (1900); (6) W. Herz and F. Hiebenthal, Z. anorg. Chem., 177, 363 (1929).

TABLE (12-10-2A). SALTING COEFFICIENTS FOR SOME WEAK ACIDS.
k_m (25°) [Equation (12-10-5)]

	(a)	(b)	(c)	(d)	(e)	(f)
NaCl.............	0.191	0.232	0.180	0.196	0.066	0.088
KCl..............	.152	....	....	.140	.033	.026
NaNO$_3$...........	.064	.089	....	− .078	....	....
LiCl..............	....	....	....	....	.075	....
NaAc.............	....	....	....	....	− .014	....
NaOOC·CH$_2$Cl ...	....	....	....	....	....	− .016
BaCl$_2$.............	.100	.134	.105	....	....	.056
Ba(NO$_3$)$_2$.........	.030	.040	.004	....	....	....
KBr..............	....	....	....	....	.014	.008
KNO$_3$.............	.025	....	....	− .006	− .020	− .043
KSCN............	....	....	....	....	.010	....
C$_{12}$H$_{22}$O$_{11}$.........	....	....	....	....	.025	....

(a) Benzoic. (b) o-Toluylic. (c) o-Nitrobenzoic. (d) Salicylic. (e) Acetic.
(f) Chloro-acetic.

TABLE (13-1-1A). MEAN ACTIVITY COEFFICIENT OF BARIUM CHLORIDE[a]

m	0°	15°	25°	35°	45°
0.01	0.725	0.727	0.723	0.720	0.710
.05	.555	.565	.559	.554	.536
.1	.483	.498	.492	.492	.487
.2	.422	.442	.436	.436	.431
.3	.394	.416	.411	.411	.405
.5	.371	.395	.390	.390	.382
.7	.365	.390	.384	.384	.376
1.	.377	.395	.389	.389	.381
1.5	.410	.410	.425	.417	.409

[a] E. A. Tippetts and R. F. Newton, *J. Am. Chem. Soc.*, **56**, 1675 (1934).

TABLE (13-1-2A).   MEAN ACTIVITY COEFFICIENTS OF 2-1 SALTS AT 25°.

m	MnCl₂[e]	CoCl₂[e]	NiCl₂[e]	CuCl₂[c]	FeCl₂[f]	MgCl₂[a]	CaCl₂[b,c]	SrCl₂[b]	BaCl₂[b]	MgBr₂[a]	MgI₂[a]	BaBr₂[d]	Cd(NO₃)₂[d]	Ca(NO₃)₂[d]	Cu(NO₃)₂[g]	K₂CrO₄[g]
0.1	(0.522)	(0.526)	(0.526)	(0.501)	(0.525)	(0.565)	(0.531)	(0.514)	(0.492)	(0.582)	(0.599)	(0.513)	(0.517)	(0.480)	(0.513)	(0.455)
.2	.474	.482	.483	.447	.480	.520	.482	.463	.438	.546	.577	.465	.469	.421	.464	.379
.3	.454	.466	.468	.423	.463	.507	.462	.440	.411	.547	.585	.446	.448	.391	.443	.338
.4	.446	.463	.465	.409	.459	.508	.456	.430	.398	.560	.607	.438	.437	.373	.434	.311
.5	.446	.465	.468	.405	.460	.514	.457	.425	.390	.579	.637	.437	.433	.360	.432	.292
.6	.448	.473	.476	.403	.467	.527	.462	.426	.386	.604	.676	.439	.431	.351	.434	.276
.7	.455	.483	.489	.403	.475	.542	.469	.430	.384	.635	.723	.444	.432	.344	.438	.263
.8	.463	.496	.504	.405	.486	.563	.479	.436	.385	.671	.782	.452	.435	.339	.445	.253
.9	.474	.514	.522	.408	.501	.587	.493	.444	.388	.714	.851	.463	.438	.336	.453	.244
1.	.486	.538	.542	.411	.519	.613	.509	.455	.392	.764	.929	.473	.443	.334	.463	.236
1.2	.516	.578	.595	.419	.558	.680	.550	.480	.402	.885	1.112	.500	.455	.332	.485	.224
1.4	.554	.635	.660	.430	.607	.764	.599	.510	.416	1.032	1.353	.534	.469	.333	.513	.214
1.6	.596	.706	.737	.442	.668	.867	.657	.546	.431	1.214	1.651	.572	.487	.335	.541	.207
1.8	.637	.785	.826	.454	.739	.986	.726	.587	.450	1.440	.....	.616	.507	.339	.577	.201
2.	.682	.884	.938	.466	.817	1.143	.807	.636	.....	.....	.....	.666	.528	.343	.614	.197

[a] R. A. Robinson and R. H. Stokes, *Trans. Faraday Soc.*, **36**, 733 (1940).
[b] R. A. Robinson, *Ibid.*, **36**, 735 (1940).
[c] R. A. Robinson and R. H. Stokes, *Ibid.*, **36**, 1137 (1940).
[d] R. A. Robinson, *Ibid.*, **36**, 1135 (1940).
[e] T. Shedlovsky and D. A. MacInnes [*J. Am. Chem. Soc.*, **59**, 503 (1937)] have obtained values of $\gamma_\pm$ at 25°, and concentrations below 0.1 M from cells with liquid junctions.
[f] R. H. Stokes and R. A. Robinson, *Trans. Faraday Soc.*, **37**, 419 (1941).
[g] R. A. Robinson, Private communication.

TABLE (13-1-2A)—*Continued*

MEAN ACTIVITY COEFFICIENTS OF 2-1 AND 1-2 ELECTROLYTES AND THORIUM NITRATE AT 25°.

m	$MgCl_2$	$MgBr_2$	MgI_2	$CaBr_2$	CaI_2	$SrCl_2$	$SrBr_2$	SrI_2	BaI_2	$Mg(NO_3)_2$	$Sr(NO_3)_2$	$Ba(NO_3)_2$	$Co(NO_3)_2$
0.1	0.529	0.550	0.580	0.532	0.560	0.511	0.526	0.553	0.542	0.523	0.478	0.428	0.518
.2	.489	.519	.558	.492	.531	.462	.483	.520	.509	.481	.410	.342	.471
.5	.481	.545	.614	.491	.561	.430	.467	.536	.523	.470	.329	……	.445
.7	.506	.599	.698	.522	.614	.434	.484	.578	.562	.489	.302	……	.455
1.	.570	.723	.892	.597	.741	.461	.535	.680	.649	.537	.275	……	.490
1.4	.709	.975	1.291	.747	.992	.524	.643	.885	.814	.632	.253	……	.563
2.	1.053	1.614	2.43	1.121	1.640	.670	.906	1.407	1.221	.842	.232	……	.726
3.	2.32	4.26	7.93	2.54	……	1.126	……	……	……	……	……	……	1.182
4.	5.54	12.2	29.0	6.28	……	1.977	……	……	……	……	……	……	1.972

m	$ZnCl_2$	$ZnBr_2$	ZnI_2	$Zn(ClO_4)_2$	$Zn(NO_3)_2$	$Mg(ClO_4)_2$	Na_2Fu†	Na_2Ma‡	Rb_2SO_4	Cs_2SO_4	K_2CrO_4	Na_2CrO_4	$Th(NO_3)_4$
0.1	0.515	0.547	0.581	0.581	0.531	0.590	0.465	0.430	0.451	0.456	0.456	0.464	0.279
.2	.462	.510	.559	.564	.489	.578	.402	.354	.374	.382	.382	.394	.225
.5	.394	.511	.610	.629	.473	.647	.335	.272	.279	.291	.292	.307	.189
.7	.369	.528	.683	.720	.489	.739	.323	.250	.249	.262	.263	.280	.191
1.	.339	.552	.800	.929	.535	.946	.319	.231	.219	.235	.235	.253	.207
1.4	.309	.567	.928	1.386	.625	1.385	.323	.219	.196	.214	.214	.233	.246
2.	.289	.572	1.028	2.74	.817	2.65	.343	.213	……	……	.196	.222	.326
3.	.287	.598	1.123	9.99	1.363	9.19	……	.220	……	……	.190	.236	.486
4.	.307	.664	1.259	38.8	2.31	……	……	……	……	……	……	.285	.647

* R. H. Stokes, *Trans. Faraday Soc.*, **44**, 295 (1948). This contribution contains a complete bibliography of the original sources of these results.

† Na₂Fu = Sodium fumarate; ‡ Na₂Ma = Na₂ maleate; R. A. Robinson, P. K. Smith and E. R. B. Smith, *Trans. Faraday Soc.*, **38**, 63 (1942).

TABLE (13-1-2A)—Concluded

m	MgAc₂	BaAc₂	CoBr₂	CoI₂	Ca(ClO₄)₂	Sr(ClO₄)₂	Na₂S₂O₄	(NH₄)₂SO₄	Cd(NO₂)₂	Pb(NO₂)₂	Pb(ClO₄)₂	UO₂Cl₂	UO₂(NO₃)₂	UO₂(ClO₄)₂	UO₂SO₄	BeSO₄
0.1	0.450	0.450	0.546	0.58	0.565	0.532	0.457	0.439	0.513	0.395	0.524	0.544	0.551	0.626	(0.150)	(0.150)
.2	.389	.395	.513	.56	.540	.497	.382	.356	.464	.308	.482	.510	.520	.634	.102	.109
.3	.359	.370	.509	.57	.540	.491	.340	.311	.442	.260	.466	.520	.518	.669	.081	.0885
.4	.340	.356	.517	.59	.552	.497	.313	.280	.430	.228	.461	.505	.526	.723	.069	.0769
.5	.328	.347	.532	.62	.573	.511	.292	.257	.425	.205	.464	.517	.542	.790	.061	.0692
.6	.320	.340	.554	.66	.598	.529	.276	.240	.423	.187	.470	.532	.563	.871	.057	.0639
.7	.314	.335	.580	.71	.627	.550	.262	.226	.423	.172	.478	.549	.587	.969	.051	.0600
.8	.310	.331	.612	.77	.664	.577	.251	.214	.425	.160	.490	.571	.617	1.087	.048	.0570
.9	.308	.328	.648	.84	.706	.608	.242	.205	.428	.150	.505	.595	.651	1.226	.046	.0546
1.0	.307	.325	.690	.91	.754	.643	.234	.196	.433	.141	.522	.620	.689	1.390	.044	.0530
1.2	.308	.320	.789	1.09	.866	.723	.222	.182	.446	.127	.562	.678	.773	1.804	.041	.0506
1.4	.310	.315	.914	1.31	1.007	.818	.214	.171	.460	.115	.612	.744	.868	2.38	.039	.0493
1.6	.316	.311	1.069	1.59	1.179	.935	.207	.162	.478	.106	.668	.816	.975	3.17	.038	.0488
1.8	.321	.306	1.255	1.95	1.393	1.067	.202	.155	.495	.099	.733	.894	1.099	4.29	.037	.0490
2.0	.329	.301	1.478	2.4	1.659	1.229	.198	.149	.515	.093	.807	.978	1.237	5.91	.037	.0497
2.5	.351	.286	2.25	4.4	2.66	1.767	.195	.137	.570	—	1.043	1.228	1.626	13.37	.037	.0538
3.0	.378	.271	3.42	7.7	4.27	2.59	.199	.130	—	—	1.383	1.551	2.03	30.9	.038	.0613
3.5	.406	.256	5.10	13.6	6.86	3.71	.207	.124	—	—	1.827	—	2.41	70.4	.040	.0724
4.0	.436	—	7.62	24.	10.93	5.24	—	.120	—	—	2.39	—	2.68	160.2	.043	.0875
4.5	—	—	11.02	42.	17.28	7.35	—	—	—	—	3.21	—	2.89	358.	.046	—
5.0	—	—	13.36	62.	27.1	10.16	—	—	—	—	4.04	—	3.06	750.	.050	—
5.5	—	—	—	83.	42.3	13.83	—	—	—	—	5.22	—	3.25	1510.	.054	—
6.0	—	—	—	102.	64.7	18.56	—	—	—	—	6.66	—	—	—	.057	—

TABLE (13-3-1A). STANDARD POTENTIALS:

Cd-Cd$_x$Hg | CdCl$_2$(m) | AgCl-Ag; E^0(CdCl$_2$)

Cd-Cd$_x$Hg | CdBr$_2$(m) | AgBr-Ag; E^0(CdBr$_2$)

Cd-Cd$_x$Hg | Cd^{++} (a = 1)　　　; π^0

t	E^0(CdCl$_2$)	E^0(CdBr$_2$)	π^{0a}	π^{0b}
0	0.5815	......	0.3452	......
5	.5804	0.4250	.3465	0.3452
10	.5790	.4248	.3477	.3468
15	.5776	.4243	.3491	.3483
20	.5758	.4236	.3503	.3499
25	.5730	.4227	.3515	.3514
30	.5716	.4215	.3526	.3528
35	.5696	.4201	.3539	.3541
40	.5673	.4185	.3553	.3554

[a] H. S. Harned and M. E. Fitzgerald, *J. Am. Chem. Soc.*, **58**, 2624 (1936).
[b] R. G. Bates, *Ibid.*, **61**, 308 (1939).

TABLE (13-3-2A). STANDARD POTENTIALS:

Zn-Zn$_x$Hg | ZnCl$_2$ (m) | AgCl-Ag; E^0(ZnCl$_2$)

Zn-Zn$_x$Hg | ZnI$_2$ (m)　| AgI-Ag;　E^0(ZnI$_2$)

Zn-Zn$_x$Hg | Zn^{++} (a = 1);　　π^0

t	E^0(ZnCl$_2$)[a]	E^0(ZnI$_2$)[b]	π^{0b}	π^{0a}
5	......	0.6176	0.7646	......
10	0.9962	.6161	.7642	0.7639
15	.9919	.6145	.7637	.7635
20	.9885	.6126	.7632	.7630
25	.9848	.6105	.7627	.7625
30	.9810	.6083	.7622	.7619
35	.9770	.6059	.7617	.7614
40	.9728	.6038	.7612	.7608

Zn-Zn$_x$Hg | ZnBr$_2$ (m) | AgBr-Ag; t = 25°; E^0(ZnBr$_2$) = 0.8339; π^0 = 0.7628[c]
[a] R. A. Robinson and R. H. Stokes, *Trans. Faraday Soc.*, **36**, 740 (1940).
[b] R. G. Bates, *J. Am. Chem. Soc.*, **60**, 2983 (1938).
[c] H. N. Parton and J. W. Mitchell, *Trans. Faraday Soc.*, **35**, 758 (1939).

TABLE (13-3-3A). MEAN ACTIVITY COEFFICIENTS OF ZINC AND CADMIUM HALIDES, AND OF LEAD CHLORIDE
I. $\gamma_\pm$ at 25°

m	PbCl$_2^a$	ZnCl$_2^b$	ZnBr$_2^c$	ZnI$_2^d$	CdCl$_2^e$	CdBr$_2^f$	CdI$_2^g$
0.0005	0.902	....	....	....	0.880	0.855	....
.001	.859	....	....	....	.819	.787	....
.002	.803	....	....	0.851	.743	.699	....
.003	....	....	....	.833	....	....	....
.005	.704	0.789	....	.799	.623	.570	0.490
.007	....	....	....	.772	....	.520	.441
.01	.612	.731	....	.746	.524	.468	.379
.02	.497	.667	0.685	.690	.456	.370	.281
.05	....	.628	.605	.621	.304	.259	.167
.1	....	.575	.555	.578	.228	.189	.108
.2	....	.459	.517	.564	.163^h	.132	.0685
.5	....	.394	.490	.624	.1001	.0789	.0382
.7	....	.367	.485	.701	.0825	.0651	.0310
1.	....	.337	.492	....	.0664	.0533	.0254
1.5	....	.306 (1.49M)	.500	....	.0523	.0425	.....
2.	....	.282 (2.83M)	.516	....	.0439	....	.0183

a W. R. Carmody, *J. Am. Chem. Soc.*, **51**, 2905 (1929).
b R. A. Robinson and R. H. Stokes, *Trans. Faraday Soc.*, **36**, 740 (1940).
c H. N. Parton and J. W. Mitchell, *Ibid.*, **35**, 758 (1939).
d R. G. Bates, *J. Am. Chem. Soc.*, **60**, 2983 (1938).
e H. S. Harned and M. E. Fitzgerald, *Ibid.*, **58**, 2624 (1936).
f R. G. Bates, *Ibid.*, **61**, 308 (1939).
g R. G. Bates and W. C. Vosburgh, *Ibid.*, **59**, 1583 (1937).
h R. A. Robinson, *Trans. Faraday Soc.*, **36**, 1135 (1940).

TABLE (13-3-3A)—*Continued*
ACTIVITY COEFFICIENTS OF RARE EARTH HALIDES AT 25° ACCORDING TO EQUATION

$$\log \gamma_\pm = -\frac{3.745\sqrt{m}}{1 + 0.8049\, d\, \sqrt{m}}$$

	d		d		d		d
LaCl$_3$........	5.75	SmCl$_3$......	5.63	GdCl$_3$.......	5.63	GdBr$_3$.....	5.72
CeCl$_3$........	5.75	EuCl$_3$......	5.60	LaBr$_3$.......	6.20	HoBr$_3$.....	6.42
PrCl$_3$........	5.73	ErCl$_3$......	5.65	PrBr$_3$.......	6.10	ErBr$_3$.....	5.90
NdCl$_3$........	5.92	YbCl$_3$......	5.65	NdBr$_3$.......	6.06	—	—

Range of validity, 0 to 0.05 *M*. F. H. Spedding, P. E. Porter and J. M. Wright, *J. Am. Chem. Soc.*, **74**, 2055, 2778, 2781, 4751 (1952).

TABLE (13-3-3A)—*Continued*
II. $\gamma_\pm$ at Various Temperatures

m	ZnCl₂				ZnI₂			
	10°	20°	30°	40°	5°	15°	30°	40°
0.005	0.794	0.791	0.787	0.783	0.808	0.802	0.797	0.793
.007	....	....	....	....	.782	.775	.770	.765
.008	....	....	....	....	.772	.765	.759	.754
.01	.737	.733	.728	.723	.757	.750	.744	.738
.02	.673	.669	.663	.657	.701	.694	.687	.680
.03	.635	.631	.625	.617	.671	.664	.655	.648
.05	.587	.582	.575	.566	.634	.627	.617	.609
.07	.556	.551	.543	.532	.611	.604	.594	.585
.1	.525	.520	.510	.497	.592	.585	.574	.564
.2	.476	.465	.452	.434	.581	.572	.559	.546
.5	.453	.439	.419	.393	.650	.638	.614	.593
.7	.433	.409	.379	.347	.740	.723	.687	.656
.8	.415	.384	.349	.313	.787	.766	.724	.687
1.0	.394	.357	.318	.280	....	....	....	....

m	CdCl₂		CdBr₂			
	0°	40°	5°	15°	30°	40°
0.0005	0.885	0.872	0.850	0.854	0.855	0.853
.001	.834	.811	.777	.784	.787	.784
.002	.746	.739	.688	.696	.699	.696
.005	.659	.607	.553	.564	.571	.569
.007	....	....	.504	.514	.521	.518
.01	.545	.505	.453	.463	.468	.465
.02	.444	.408	.358	.366	.370	.367
.03	....	....	.309	.317	.320	.317
.05	.318	.292	.250	.257	.259	.256
.07	....	....	.215	.221	.223	.221
.1	.237	.218	.182	.187	.189	.186
.2	....	....	.127	.130	.132	.129
.5	....	....	.0753	.0779	.0787	.0772
.7	....	....	.0619	.0643	.0650	.0638
1.	....	....	.0505	.0526	.0532	.0522
1.2	....	....	.0449	.0467	.0473	.0465
1.5	....	....	.0400	.0418	.0424	.0417
1.8	....	....	.0359	.0376	.0383	.0376

TABLE (13-3-3A)—*Continued*
II. $\gamma_{\pm}$ at Various Temperatures.

m	CdI$_2$†					
	5°	15°	20°	25°	30°	40°
0.002	0.566	0.596	0.607	0.615	0.622	0.629
.005	.445	.472	.483	.492	.499	.506
.007	.391	.417	.428	.436	.443	.440
.01	.338	.364	.374	.382	.389	.397
.02	.243	.265	.274	.281	.287	.294
.05	.141	.156	.162	.167	.171	.177
.07	.113	.126	.131	.135	.139	.143
.1	.0891	.0989	.103	.107	.110	.113
.2	.0562	.0625	.0652	.0675	.0694	.0718
.5	.0307	.0342	.0356	.0369	.0379	.0393
.7	.0254	.0282	.0294	.0304	.0312	.0323
1.	.0210	.0233	.0242	.0250	.0257	.0265
1.5	.0173	.0191	.0198	.0205	.0210	.0216
2.	.0155	.0171	.0177	.0183	.0187	.0192

† R. G. Bates, *J. Am. Chem. Soc.*, **63**, 399 (1941).

TABLE (13-3-3A)—*Concluded*
ACTIVITY COEFFICIENTS OF URANYL FLUORIDE AND INDIUM SULPHATE.

UO$_2$F$_2$			In$_2$(SO$_4$)$_3$	
m	$\gamma_{\pm}(0°)^a$	$\gamma_{\pm}/\gamma_{0.1485}(30°)^b$	m	$\gamma_{\pm}/\gamma_{0.1}^c$
0.1	0.942	—	—	—
.15	—	1.00	0.3	0.421
.3	.801	.88	.5	.336
.5	.719	.78	.7	.337
.7	.666	.72	1.0	.363
1.	.613	.66	1.2	.415
2.	.545	.57	1.5	.530
3.	.543	.56	2.0	.775
4.	.570	.57	2.2	.890
5.	.615	.61	2.3	1.046

[a] J. S. Johnson and K. A. Kraus, *J. Am. Chem. Soc.*, **74**, 4436 (1952).
[b] J. S. Johnson, K. A. Kraus and T. F. Young, *Ibid.*, **75**, 1436 (1953).
[c] M. H. Lietzke and R. W. Stoughton, *Ibid.*, **78**, 4520 (1956).

TABLE (13-3-4A). L_2 AND J_2 OF $ZnCl_2$ AND ZnI_2 FROM ELECTROMOTIVE FORCE DATA.
CONSTANTS OF EQUATIONS:

$$L_2 = \alpha + \beta T^2; \text{ and } J_2 = 2\beta T$$

Valid from 0 to 40°

1. $ZnCl_2$[a]

m	$-\alpha$	β	$\bar{L}_2(25°)$	$\bar{J}_2(25°)$
0.005	295	0.0060	237	4
.01	718	.0116	316	7
.02	1540	.0219	403	13
.03	2140	.0295	485	18
.05	3380	.0453	644	27
.07	4400	.0587	812	35
.1	5700	.0752	981	45
.2	9340	.1224	1530	73
.3	12110	.1639	2450	98
.5	11760	.1773	3990	106
.7	11430	.1846	4970	110
1.	10290	.1846	6110	110

[a] R. A. Robinson and R. H. Stokes, *Trans. Faraday Soc.*, **36**, 740 (1940).

2. ZnI_2[b]

m	$-\alpha$	$\beta \times 10^4$	$\bar{L}_2(25°)$	$\bar{J}_2(25°)$
0.005	739	106	204	6
.007	848	125	259	7
.008	895	134	294	8
.01	1152	166	324	10
.02	1719	240	413	15
.03	2095	291	488	18
.05	2623	360	576	22
.07	3009	411	640	25
.1	3381	461	720	28
.2	4291	586	917	35
.5	6852	932	1432	56
.7	8740	1200	1922	72
.8	9405	1301	2160	78

[b] R. G. Bates, *J. Am. Chem. Soc.*, **60**, 2983 (1938).

TABLE (13-3-5A). RELATIVE PARTIAL MOLAL HEAT CONTENT OF CADMIUM HALIDE SOLUTIONS[†]

m	$CdCl_2$		$CdBr_2$		CdI_2	
	15°	25°	15°	25°	15°	25°
0.0001	47	67	−4	6	−287	−157
.0005	112	157	−74	−7	−819	−564
.001	162	232	−134	−23	−1148	−828
.005	362	634	−343	−108	−2155	−1587
.01	472	759	−414	−131	−2622	−1941
.05	702	993	−540	−127	−3700	−2789
.1	778	1134	−591	−70	−4074	−3108
.2	860	1323	−639	−9	......	......
.4	...	....	−686	−5	......	......

[†] A. L. Robinson and W. E. Wallace, *Chem. Rev.*, **30**, 195 (1942).

TABLE (13-7-1A).   ACTIVITY COEFFICIENTS OF TRIVALENT METAL CHLORIDES
AT 25°†

m	Activity Coefficients								
	AlCl₃	ScCl₃	YCl₃	LaCl₃	CeCl₃	PrCl₃	NdCl₃	SmCl₃	EuCl₃
0.05	0.409	0.395	0.392	0.392	0.392	0.390	0.389	0.385	0.389
0.1	0.360	0.342	0.336	0.336	0.331	0.333	0.332	0.331	0.335
0.2	0.308	0.297	0.293	0.292	0.292	0.292	0.291	0.290	0.294
0.3	0.323	0.302	0.288	0.281	0.279	0.278	0.279	0.280	0.283
0.5	0.354	0.319	0.297	0.285	0.282	0.280	0.282	0.284	0.288
0.7	0.415	0.363	0.328	0.305	0.306	0.301	0.308	0.306	0.313
1.0	0.578	0.474	0.412	0.366	0.366	0.362	0.368	0.373	0.383
1.2	0.750	0.582	0.494	0.426	0.423	0.423	0.431	0.442	0.453
1.4	1.002	0.724	0.606	0.503	0.502	0.500	0.514	0.526	0.543
1.6	1.374	0.913	0.750	0.600	0.598	0.597	0.617	0.643	0.666
1.8	1.946	1.165	0.946	0.724	0.732	0.722	0.753	0.795	0.830
2.0	.....	.....	1.216	0.883	0.906	0.883	0.928	0.997	1.076

† C. M. Mason, *J. Am. Chem. Soc.*, **60**, 1638 (1938); **63**, 220 (1942).   Recalculated by R. A. Robinson to conform with the new isopiestic vapor pressure standards (See Chapter (9), Section (5)) and referred by us to the value for LaCl₃ at 0.05M (See Table (13-7-1)).

TABLE (13-11-1A).   MEAN ACTIVITY COEFFICIENT OF SULFURIC ACID IN
AQUEOUS SOLUTIONS FROM ELECTROMOTIVE FORCES[a]

m	0°	10°	20°	25°	30°	40°	50°	60°
0.0005	0.912	0.901	0.890	0.885	0.880	0.869	0.859,	0.848
.0007	.896	.880	.867	.857	.854	.841	.828	.814
.001	.876	.857	.839	.830	.823	.806	.790	.775
.002	.825	.796	.769	.757	.746	.722	.701	.680
.003	.788	.754	.723	.709	.695	.669	.645	.622
.005	.734	.693	.656	.639	.623	.593	.566	.533
.007	.691	.647	.608	.591	.574	.543	.515	.489
.01	.649	.603	.562	.544	.527	.495	.467	.441
.02	.554	.509	.470	.453	.437	.407	.380	.356
.03	.495	.453	.417	.401	.386	.358	.333	.311
.05	.426	.387	.354	.340	.326	.301	.279	.260
.07	.383	.346	.315	.301	.290	.266	.246	.228
.1	.341	.307	.278	.265	.254	.227	.214	.197
.2	.271	.243	.219	.209	.199	.161	.166	.153
.5	.202	.181	.162	.154	.147	.133	.122	.107
1.	.173	.153	.137	.130	.123	.111	.101	.0922
1.5	.167	.147	.131	.124	.117	.106	.0956	.0869
2.	.170	.149	.132	.124	.118	.105	.0949	.0859
3.	.201	.173	.151	.141	.132	.117	.104	.0926
4.	.254	.215	.184	.171	.159	.138	.121	.106
5.	.330	.275	.231	.212	.196	.168	.145	.126
6.	.427	.350	.289	.264	.242	.205	.174	.150
7.	.546	.440	.359	.326	.297	.247	.208	.177
8.	.686	.545	.439	.397	.358	.296	.246	.206
9.	.843	.662	.527	.470	.425	.346	.285	.237
10.	1.012	.785	.618	.553	.493	.398	.325	.268
11.	1.212	.930	.725	.643	.573	.458	.370	.302
12.	1.431	1.088	.840	.742	.656	.521	.418	.339
13.	1.676	1.261	.965	.851	.750	.590	.471	.379
14.	1.958	1.458	1.104	.967	.850	.664	.525	.420
15.	2.271	1.671	1.254	1.093	.957	.741	.583	.462
16.	2.612	1.907	1.420	1.234	1.076	.828	.647	.511
17.	3.015	2.176	1.604	1.387	1.204	.919	.712	.559
17.5	3.217	2.316	1.703	1.471	1.275	.972	.752	.589

[a] H. S. Harned and W. J. Hamer, *J. Am. Chem. Soc.*, **57**, 27 (1935).   (Regions of confirmed validity 0 to 4 M and 9 to 11 M inclusive.)

TABLE (13-13-1A). THE RELATIVE PARTIAL MOLAL HEAT CONTENT OF
SULFURIC ACID.[a] CONSTANTS OF EQUATION:

$$L_2 = L_2(0°) + \alpha t + \beta t^2$$

m	$L_2(0°)$	α	$\beta \times 10^2$	$L_2(25°)$	$J_2(25°)$ (E.M.F.)	$J_2(25°)$ (Cal.)
0.0005	397	7.228	6.748	620	11	..
.001	858	7.678	6.706	1092	11	..
.002	1481	7.038	6.664	1699	10	..
.005	2503	6.948	6.676	2719	10	..
.01	3244	7.538	6.691	3474	11	6
.02	3729	7.328	6.713	3954	11	7
.05	4192	7.128	6.628	4411	10	8
.1	4672	7.748	6.712	4908	11	9
.2	4903	8.008	6.798	5145	11	11
.5	5063	8.268	6.828	5313	12	15
1.	5310	10.168	7.118	5608	14	21
2.	5766	11.068	7.658	6091	15	27
3.	6607	11.528	7.488	6942	15	25
4.	7464	11.908	7.458	7809	15	21
6.	9059	12.578	7.638	9421	16	16
8.	10399	13.898	7.908	10795	18	13
10.	11474	16.768	8.518	11946	21	20
12.	12434	18.218	8.748	12944	23	24
14.	13402	16.168	8.308	13858	20	26
16.	14320	12.438	7.388	14677	16	28
17.5	14961	11.508	7.488	15296	15	29

[a] H. S. Harned and W. J. Hamer, *J. Am. Chem. Soc.*, **57**, 27 (1935).

TABLE (13-14-1A). THE CATION TRANSFERENCE NUMBERS OF SULFURIC ACID[a]
IN WATER

m	0°	10°	15°	25°	35°	45°	60°
0.0	(0.840)	(0.829)	(0.824)	(0.813)	(0.801)	(0.788)	(0.761)
.05	.839	.834	.830	.819	.807	.793	.770
.10	.838	.834	.829	.819	.807	.793	.770
.20	.837	.833	.829	.819	.806	.792	.770
.50	.834	.828	.824	.815	.801	.787	.764
1.00	.828	.822	.818	.808	.793	.779	.755
2.00	.816	.808	.803	.793	.779	.763	.737
3.00	.803	.793	.788	.776	.762	.747	.720
5.00	.772	.762	.756	.744	.730	.715	.689
8.00	.720	.708	.702	.690	.676	.663	.641
10.00	.682	.672	.666	.655	.642	.629	.610
12.00	.638	.629	.625	.616	.605	.595	.578
14.00	.591	.584	.580	.573	.564	.556	.543
17.00	.512	.508	.506	.502	.498	.494	.488
$S_{(T)}\sqrt{d_0}$	.0331	.0362	.0370	.0375	.0363	.0331	.0250

[a] W. J. Hamer, *J. Am. Chem. Soc.*, **57**, 662 (1935).

TABLE (14-2-1A). THE MEAN ACTIVITY COEFFICIENTS OF HYDROCHLORIC AND
HYDROBROMIC ACIDS IN HALIDE SOLUTIONS. ACID CONCENTRATION
= $0.01M$. SALT CONCENTRATION = m

Part I. Hydrochloric Acid

m	0°	5°	10°	15°	20°	25°	30°	35°	40°	45°	50°
(1) Salt = KCl[a]											
0.0	0.906	0.906	0.906	0.905	0.905	0.905	0.904	0.903	0.902	0.901	0.900
.01	.876	.875	.875	.874	.874	.874	.873	.871	.871	.869	.866
.02	.856	.855	.853	.853	.853	.852	.851	.850	.850	.847	.844
.03	.841	.841	.840	.839	.838	.837	.836	.834	.834	.831	.828
.05	.819	.819	.817	.817	.816	.816	.814	.812	.812	.809	.806
.1	.786	.786	.786	.784	.783	.782	.780	.778	.777	.773	.769
.2	.753	.753	.752	.750	.749	.747	.746	.743	.742	.739	.734
.5	.712	.712	.711	.709	.708	.706	.704	.701	.699	.695	.690
1.	.731	.727	.728	.725	.723	.720	.716	.712	.709	.702	.697
1.5	.758	.757	.754	.750	.747	.743	.738	.732	.728	.722	.713
2.	.801	.799	.796	.791	.786	.781	.773	.767	.761	.753	.743
3.	.893	.890	.882	.875	.868	.860	.851	.841	.831	.820	.808
3.5	.939	.933	.926	.917	.908	.899	.888	.876	.867	.853	.839
(2) Salt = NaCl[b]											
0.01	0.877	0.876	0.876	0.875	0.874	0.874	0.873	0.872	0.871	0.870	0.869
.02	.856	.856	.856	.855	.855	.854	.853	.851	.850	.849	.847
.05	.821	.821	.821	.819	.819	.818	.816	.814	.812	.810	.807
.1	.789	.789	.788	.786	.785	.784	.781	.779	.777	.774	.771
.2	.758	.758	.757	.754	.753	.752	.749	.747	.745	.742	.739
.5	.738	.737	.736	.733	.732	.730	.727	.724	.721	.718	.715
1.	.765	.764	.762	.759	.756	.754	.750	.746	.742	.738	.733
2.	.898	.896	.893	.888	.883	.878	.871	.864	.856	.847	.838
3.	1.103	1.099	1.094	1.086	1.077	1.068	1.056	1.043	1.029	1.014	.999
(3) Salt = LiCl[c]											
0.01	.....	.....	.....	0.878	0.878	0.881	0.879	0.877	.....	.....	.....
.02	.....	.....	.....	.859	.859	.861	.859	.857	.....	.....	.....
.05	.....	.....	.....	.826	.826	.827	.824	.822	.....	.....	.....
.1	.....	.....	.....	.798	.797	.796	.793	.789	.....	.....	.....
.2	.....	.....	.....	.769	.767	.766	.762	.760	.....	.....	.....
.5	.....	.....	.....	.762	.759	.757	.753	.749	.....	.....	.....
1.	.....	.....	.....	.812	.806	.801	.793	.787	.....	.....	.....
1.5	.....	.....	.....	.896	.887	.879	.869	.858	.....	.....	.....
2.	.....	.....	.....	1.012	.999	.986	.972	.958	.....	.....	.....
3.	.....	.....	.....	1.334	1.308	1.284	1.257	1.232	.....	.....	.....
4.	.....	.....	.....	1.791	1.748	1.708	1.665	1.624	.....	.....	.....

(4) Salt = $BaCl_2$[d]; μ = Ionic strength of solution

μ	0°	5°	10°	15°	20°	25°	30°	35°	40°	45°	50°
0.01	0.906	0.906	0.905	0.905	0.905	0.905	0.903	0.903	0.902	0.901	0.900
.02	.876	.876	.875	.875	.875	.875	.873	.872	.871	.870	.869
.03	.855	.855	.855	.855	.855	.854	.853	.852	.851	.850	.848
.05	.829	.828	.827	.827	.827	.826	.825	.824	.823	.821	.820
.07	.808	.808	.808	.808	.808	.807	.805	.804	.802	.801	.799
.1	.788	.788	.787	.787	.787	.786	.784	.783	.781	.779	.777
.2	.747	.748	.748	.747	.747	.746	.744	.741	.739	.736	.733
.5	.710	.709	.709	.708	.707	.705	.702	.698	.694	.690	.686
.7	.704	.704	.703	.702	.700	.698	.694	.691	.686	.682	.677
1.	.707	.706	.705	.704	.702	.699	.693	.690	.685	.680	.675
2.	.760	.758	.756	.752	.748	.743	.737	.731	.724	.716	.708
3.	.847	.844	.841	.836	.830	.823	.815	.805	.796	.785	.774

TABLE (14-2-1A)—*Continued*

Part II. Hydrobromic Acid

m	0°	5°	10°	15°	20°	25°	30°	35°	40°	45°	50°
				(1)	Salt	=	KBr*				
0.0	0.910	0.910	0.909	0.908	0.907	0.906	0.906	0.905	0.904	0.903	0.902
.01	.881	.880	.879	.877	.876	.874	.874	.873	.871	.870	.868
.02	.861	.860	.858	.856	.855	.853	.852	.852	.849	.847	.846
.03	.845	.844	.843	.841	.834	.838	.837	.835	.833	.831	.829
.05	.824	.824	.822	.821	.820	.818	.817	.814	.812	.811	.810
.1	.792	.792	.790	.787	.785	.783	.782	.778	.776	.773	.771
.2	.760	.759	.757	.754	.752	.750	.748	.744	.741	.738	.736
.5	.728	.728	.725	.722	.722	.717	.714	.710	.705	.701	.697
1.	.748	.745	.741	.737	.732	.728	.724	.718	.712	.706	.700
1.5	.777	.774	.770	.765	.760	.756	.751	.743	.736	.729	.722
2.	.840	.836	.831	.825	.818	.810	.803	.794	.785	.776	.767
3.	.974	.967	.958	.948	.937	.926	.916	.903	.890	.874	.864
				(2)	Salt	=	NaBr*				
0.01	0.884	0.883	0.882	0.880	0.879	0.878	0.878	0.878	0.875	0.876	0.874
.02	.866	.866	.865	.863	.861	.859	.858	.858	.854	.852	.850
.03	.850	.850	.848	.846	.844	.842	.841	.841	.837	.835	.833
.05	.829	.828	.827	.824	.822	.821	.820	.818	.815	.813	.811
.1	.801	.799	.797	.795	.793	.791	.789	.788	.783	.781	.779
.2	.780	.778	.775	.772	.769	.767	.765	.765	.759	.756	.753
.5	.774	.772	.768	.764	.761	.756	.752	.747	.739	.735	.730
1.	.833	.827	.821	.814	.808	.801	.795	.788	.778	.770	.762
1.5	.934	.926	.916	.906	.895	.884	.875	.865	.852	.840	.828
2.	1.050	1.038	1.026	1.009	.995	.981	.967	.954	.936	.921	.905
3.	1.362	1.337	1.311	1.284	1.258	1.233	1.208	1.184	1.156	1.131	1.106
				(3)	Salt	=	LiBr*				
0.0	0.911	0.910	0.910	0.909	0.908	0.907	0.905	0.904	0.902	0.901	0.899
.01	.885	.885	.884	.883	.882	.880	.878	.877	.874	.872	.870
.02	.866	.867	.866	.865	.864	.863	.861	.858	.856	.853	.850
.03	.854	.854	.853	.852	.851	.849	.847	.844	.841	.838	.835
.05	.834	.834	.834	.833	.831	.829	.827	.824	.821	.817	.814
.07	.821	.821	.821	.820	.818	.816	.813	.811	.807	.804	.799
.1	.810	.809	.807	.807	.805	.802	.799	.796	.793	.789	.785
.2	.796	.794	.792	.789	.787	.783	.780	.776	.772	.767	.763
.3	.796	.793	.791	.788	.784	.780	.776	.772	.768	.763	.758
.4	.802	.799	.796	.792	.788	.784	.780	.775	.770	.765	.760
.6	.824	.822	.818	.814	.809	.805	.800	.794	.789	.783	.777
1.	.911	.905	.898	.892	.885	.878	.870	.863	.856	.848	.840
1.5	1.061	1.050	1.039	1.028	1.017	1.006	.996	.985	.974	.964	.954
2.	1.255	1.241	1.227	1.213	1.197	1.160	1.168	1.152	1.137	1.121	1.105
3.	1.775	1.748	1.720	1.694	1.667	1.641	1.615	1.589	1.564	1.538	1.514

TABLE (14-2-1A)—*Continued*

Part III.   Hydrochloric Acid at 25°

Acid concentration $= m_1$; salt concentration $= m_2$

m_2	$(m_1 = 0.01)$ $CsCl$[a]	m_2	$(m_1 = 0.05)$ $AlCl_3$[h]	m_2	$(m_1 = 0.01)$ $CeCl_3$[i]	m_2	$(m_1 = 0.01)$ $SrCl_2$[j]
0.0	0.905	0.0	0.830	0.0	0.904	0.0	0.904
.01	.875	.005	.809	.005	.839	.025	.797
.03011	.836	.075	.799	.01	.805	.05	.761
.07	.795	.01	.789	.03	.745	.075	.743
.1	.773	.02	.763	.05	.717	.1	.731
.2	.730	.03	.750	.075	.699	.2	.706
.4	.685	.05	.728	.1	.689	.3	.711
.7	.656	.07	.714	.165	.662	.5	.739
1.	.644	.1	.708	.25	.655	.75	.801
1.34	.638	.2	.716	.375	.664	1.	.888
1.5	.639	.4	.797	.5	.698	1.5	1.121
2.	.641	.6	.920	.75	.767	2.	1.460
3.	.672	1.	1.402	1.	.855	2.5	1.944
		2.	3.96				

[a] H. S. Harned and W. J. Hamer, *J. Am. Chem. Soc.*, **55**, 2194 (1933).
[b] H. S. Harned and G. E. Mannweiler, *Ibid.*, **57**, 1873 (1935).
[c] H. S. Harned and H. R. Copson, *Ibid.*, **55**, 2296 (1933).
[d] H. S. Harned and C. G. Geary, *Ibid.*, **59**, 2032 (1937).
[e] H. S. Harned and W. J. Hamer, *Ibid.*, **55**, 4496 (1933).
[f] H. S. Harned and J. G. Donelson, *Ibid.*, **59**, 1280 (1937).
[g] H. S. Harned and O. E. Schupp Jr., *Ibid.*, **52**, 3892 (1930).
[h] H. S. Harned and C. M. Mason, *Ibid.*, **53**, 3377 (1931).
[i] C. M. Mason and D. B. Kellam, *J. Phys. Chem.*, **38**, 689 (1934).
[j] J. E. Vance, *J. Am. Chem. Soc.*, **55**, 2729 (1933).

THE MEAN ACTIVITY COEFFICIENT OF HYDROCHLORIC ACID IN STRONTIUM CHLORIDE SOLUTIONS[a].

μ	0°	5°	10°	15°	20°	25°	30°	35°	40°	45°	50°
0.01	0.906	0.906	0.905	0.905	0.905	0.905	0.903	0.903	0.902	0.901	0.900
.02	.876	.876	.875	.875	.874	.874	.873	.872	.870	.868	.867
.03	.855	.855	.854	.853	.853	.852	.851	.850	.849	.847	.846
.05	.827	.827	.826	.826	.824	.824	.822	.820	.819	.817	.816
.07	.807	.807	.807	.807	.806	.805	.803	.801	.799	.797	.795
.1	.789	.789	.788	.787	.785	.785	.783	.781	.779	.776	.774
.2	.752	.752	.752	.751	.749	.746	.745	.743	.740	.737	.733
.3	.734	.733	.732	.731	.729	.726	.724	.721	.718	.715	.712
.5	.718	.717	.715	.712	.711	.708	.705	.701	.698	.695	.692
.7	.714	.714	.710	.708	.705	.702	.700	.696	.692	.688	.683
1.	.721	.721	.718	.716	.710	.709	.705	.700	.695	.692	.689
2.	.796	.794	.788	.785	.779	.772	.767	.759	.752	.745	.738
3.	.915	.910	.903	.897	.889	.877	.869	.860	.850	.740	.829

THE RELATIVE PARTIAL MOLAL HEAT CONTENT IN CALORIES OF 0.01 M HYDROCHLORIC ACID IN STRONTIUM CHLORIDE SOLUTIONS[a].

$$\bar{L_2} = \bar{L_2}(25°) + \alpha(t - 25) + \beta(t - 25)^2$$

μ	$\bar{L_2}$ (25°)	α	$\beta \times 10^3$	μ	$\bar{L_2}$ (25°)	α	$\beta \times 10^3$
0.02	16.8	0.4	0.7	0.3	167.2	4.4	7.4
.03	29.5	.8	1.4	.5	219.5	4.8	8.1
.05	49.3	1.8	3.0	.7	255.3	5.2	8.8
.07	66.4	2.3	3.9	1.	305.5	5.9	9.9
.1	81.6	3.0	5.1	2.	500.6	10.0	16.8
.2	136.5	3.9	6.5	3.	668.0	15.3	25.6

[a] H. S. Harned and T. R. Paxton, *J. Phys. Chem.*, **57**, 531 (1953).

TABLE (14-2-1A)—*Concluded*

ACTIVITY COEFFICIENTS OF HYDROCHLORIC ACID, $\gamma_\pm$, IN CHLORIDE SOLUTIONS OF THE TYPE, MCl_n AT CONSTANT TOTAL IONIC STRENGTHS.

$t = 25°$

	$\mu = 1$				$\mu = 2$		$\mu = 3$				$\mu = 5$	
m_1	BaCl₂	SrCl₂	AlCl₃	m_1	BaCl₂	m_1	BaCl₂	SrCl₂	AlCl₃	m_1	SrCl₂	AlCl₃
1.0	0.8111	0.8111	0.8111	2.0	1.008	3.0	1.318	1.318	1.318	5.0	2.380	2.380
0.9	.7972	.7985	.7994	1.7	.9647	2.7	......	1.267	1.254	4.5	2.224	2.216
.8	.7881	.7903	.7870	1.4	.9231	2.4	1.202	1.216	1.205	4.0	2.080	2.059
.7	.7755	.7794	.7781	1.1	.8812	2.1	......	......	1.157	3.5	1.949	1.916
.6	.7640	.7708	.7664	0.5	.8058	1.8	1.097	1.123	1.108	3.0	1.821	1.780
.5	.7529	.7596	.7555	.2	.7690	1.5	1.046	1.079	1.062	2.5	1.701	1.657
.4	.7413	.7495	.7458	...	......	1.2	.9994	1.038	1.015	2.0	1.592	1.537
.3	.7302	.7401	.7335	...	......	.9	.9541	.9955	......	1.5	1.489	1.431
.2	.7201	.7281	.7246	...	......	.6	......	.9557	.9286	1.0	1.391	1.322
.1	.7077	.7197	.7135	...	......	.3	.8696	.9175	.8872	0.5	.....	1.225
.01	.6990	......	......	...	......	.2	.8554	......	......	...	.....	.....
....	......	......	......	...	......	.1	.8419	......	......	...	.....	.....

	$\mu = 5$						$\mu = 3$		
m_1	CdCl₂	m_1	CdCl₂	m_1	ThCl₄	m_1	ThCl₄	m_1	ThCl₄
5.0	2.380	2.0	0.696	5.0	2.380	2.0	1.266	3.0	1.318	1.2	1.003
4.5	1.948	1.5	.615	4.5	2.167	1.5	1.096	2.7	1.275	.9	0.919
4.0	1.585	1.0	.522	4.0	1.953	1.0	.923	2.4	1.229	.6	0.831
3.5	1.289	0.5	.442	3.5	1.769	0.5	.756	2.1	1.182	.3	0.688
3.0	1.053	0.2	.....	3.0	1.598	0.2	.328	1.8	1.128	.1	0.283
2.5	.871	...	.....	2.5	1.427	...	.....	1.5	1.069	...	.....

TABLE (14-9-1A).[a] SMOOTHED VALUES OF LOG $\gamma_\pm$ FOR HYDROCHLORIC ACID IN CONCENTRATED AQUEOUS SOLUTIONS

m	0°	10°	20°	25°	30°	40°	50°
3	0.1544	0.1377	0.1205	0.1120	0.1028	0.0841	0.0650
4	.2955	.2732	.2503	.2389	.2269	.2025	.1775
5	.4427	.4145	.3857	.3714	.3564	.3260	.2951
6	.5922	.5581	.5233	.5059	.4879	.4516	.4146
7	.7413	.7011	.6603	.6400	.6190	.5765	.5335
8	.8877	.8415	.7948	.7714	.7475	.6990	.6500
9	1.0297	.9776	.9250	.8988	.8718	.8175	.7625
10	1.1661	1.1082	1.0498	1.0208	.9908	.9306	.8699
11	1.2962	1.2326	1.1684	1.1366	1.1036	1.0377	.9712
12	1.4196	1.3503	1.2803	1.2457	1.2097	1.1380	1.0657
13	1.5366	1.4613	1.3855	1.3479	1.3090	1.2314	1.1531
14	1.6476	1.5662	1.4841	1.4436	1.4016	1.3178	1.2334
15	1.7536	1.6656	1.5770	1.5333	1.4878	1.3975	1.3065
16	1.8559	1.7608	1.6650	1.6179	1.5687	1.4711	1.3730

[a] G. Åkerlöf and J. W. Teare, *J. Am. Chem. Soc.*, **59**, 1855 (1937). Extensive tables of L_2, J_2, etc. are also given in this contribution.

TABLE (15-2-1A). THE IONIC ACTIVITY FUNCTION OF WATER, $\gamma_H \gamma_{OH}/a_{H_2O}$, IN SALT SOLUTIONS

KCl[a]

μ	0°	5°	10°	15°	20°	25°	30°	35°	40°	45°	50°
0.01	0.819	0.818	0.818	0.818	0.817	0.816	0.816	0.812	0.809	0.809	0.808
.02	.765	.762	.764	.762	.759	.760	.760	.754	.753	.751	.750
.03	.732	.729	.726	.727	.726	.726	.725	.720	.718	.715	.713
.04	.707	.709	.706	.706	.704	.702	.700	.696	.694	.691	.687
.06	.672	.672	.669	.671	.669	.668	.667	.662	.661	.655	.655
.11	.621	.621	.622	.623	.619	.618	.617	.612	.611	.605	.602
.21	.574	.576	.576	.576	.572	.574	.573	.567	.565	.562	.558
.51	.534	.536	.537	.538	.535	.534	.534	.527	.524	.519	.514
1.01	.600	.596	.601	.599	.595	.592	.588	.580	.574	.563	.558
1.51	.698	.689	.696	.693	.677	.672	.665	.652	.643	.633	.620
2.01	.816	.815	.813	.807	.795	.787	.774	.761	.744	.728	.710
3.01	1.128	1.126	1.109	1.095	1.075	1.056	1.037	1.006	.979	.948	.925
3.51	1.313	1.301	1.285	1.264	1.234	1.205	1.183	1.147	1.109	1.075	1.043

NaCl[b]

0.02	0.764	0.764	0.763	0.763	0.760	0.759	0.759	0.756	0.752	0.752	0.751
.03	.726	.728	.732	.728	.726	.725	.725	.720	.717	.715	.715
.06	.663	.665	.666	.665	.664	.664	.663	.658	.653	.650	.649
.11	.612	.613	.613	.611	.608	.607	.605	.600	.595	.591	.589
.21	.562	.562	.559	.559	.557	.556	.553	.549	.544	.540	.538
.51	.519	.519	.520	.518	.516	.514	.513	.508	.502	.498	.497
1.01	.542	.543	.542	.541	.537	.535	.531	.524	.517	.511	.507
2.01	.694	.698	.699	.696	.691	.696	.681	.667	.654	.640	.629
3.01	.975	.982	.985	.982	.972	.962	.998	.925	.898	.878	.855

LiCl[c]

μ	15°	20°	25°	30°	35°	μ	15°	20°	25°	30°	35°
0.02	0.758	0.758	0.759	0.759	0.758	0.35	0.466	0.464	0.462	0.459	0.456
.03	.717	.718	.719	.718	.717	.40	.456	.454	.452	.449	.447
.05	.664	.663	.665	.664	.662	.45	.449	.446	.443	.440	.440
.06	.645	.646	.645	.644	.642	.50	.442	.439	.437	.433	.431
.10	.591	.590	.589	.587	.584	1.01	.409	.405	.400	.395	.390
.11	.581	.580	.579	.575	.572	1.51	.408	.402	.397	.390	.383
.15	.546	.544	.543	.540	.536	2.01	.427	.418	.410	.401	.393
.20	.515	.513	.511	.508	.505	2.51	.459	.449	.438	.427	.416
.25	.493	.491	.489	.486	.483	3.01	.496	.483	.470	.456	.442
.30	.478	.476	.474	.471	.468	....	....	....	....	....	....

KBr[d]

μ	0°	5°	10°	15°	20°	25°	30°	35°	40°
0.02	0.778	0.775	0.774	0.771	0.769	0.766	0.764	0.764	0.761
.03	.744	.739	.739	.736	.734	.731	.729	.728	.725
.04	.719	.715	.713	.709	.710	.709	.706	.704	.701
.06	.685	.683	.680	.678	.676	.675	.672	.671	.668
.11	.635	.633	.628	.630	.628	.624	.621	.621	.617
.21	.583	.583	.582	.582	.581	.579	.576	.574	.570
.51	.540	.540	.540	.540	.541	.536	.532	.529	.523
1.01	.601	.601	.600	.598	.595	.590	.584	.578	.570
1.51	.677	.677	.677	.672	.667	.661	.651	.642	.630
2.01	.798	.795	.795	.785	.776	.764	.752	.739	.721
3.01	1.062	1.053	1.045	1.029	1.009	.993	.971	.947	.921

TABLE (15-2-1A)—*Continued*

NaBr[d]

μ	0°	5°	10°	15°	20°	25°	30°	35°	40°
0.02	0.777	0.773	0.773	0.771	0.769	0.767	0.765	0.765	0.761
.03	.745	.742	.741	.737	.735	.731	.728	.726	.723
.04	.715	.711	.711	.707	.705	.703	.701	.699	.695
.06	.678	.675	.674	.670	.668	.666	.662	.660	.655
.11	.624	.622	.621	.618	.615	.612	.608	.606	.601
.21	.571	.569	.570	.568	.566	.565	.563	.561	.558
.51	.524	.525	.528	.527	.526	.524	.520	.518	.513
1.01	.552	.551	.553	.551	.550	.547	.542	.539	.532
1.51	.648	.640	.638	.633	.626	.618	.609	.600	.592
2.01	.752	.746	.740	.730	.718	.706	.693	.679	.662
3.01	1.044	1.020	1.007	.983	.959	.931	.905	.878	.847

LiBr[e]

μ	0°	5°	10°	15°	20°	25°	30°	35°	40°
0.02	0.778	0.778	0.777	0.773	0.771	0.769	0.770	0.769	0.767
.03	.736	.736	.738	.735	.733	.731	.733	.731	.729
.04	.707	.708	.709	.706	.704	.702	.704	.701	.698
.06	.659	.662	.663	.661	.660	.658	.659	.657	.653
.08	.624	.628	.630	.629	.628	.627	.628	.625	.622
.11	.590	.593	.594	.593	.592	.590	.591	.588	.584
.21	.525	.527	.528	.526	.524	.522	.522	.518	.513
.31	.492	.493	.494	.491	.489	.486	.484	.481	.476
.41	.469	.470	.469	.467	.464	.461	.460	.456	.451
.61	.442	.442	.441	.438	.435	.432	.430	.426	.421
1.01	.426	.426	.424	.420	.416	.412	.409	.404	.398
1.51	.442	.437	.436	.430	.425	.419	.415	.408	.400
2.01	.478	.472	.469	.462	.455	.449	.443	.434	.424
2.51	.553	.549	.544	.535	.527	.517	.509	.498	.486

BaCl₂[f]

μ	0°	5°	10°	15°	20°	25°	30°	35°	40°	45°	50°
0.03	0.727	0.728	0.723	0.720	0.716	0.716	0.719	0.716	0.711	0.710	0.713
.05	.676	.677	.671	.668	.665	.660	.665	.663	.658	.655	.658
.07	.637	.638	.637	.633	.629	.626	.628	.624	.619	.616	.617
.1	.597	.598	.594	.593	.589	.587	.589	.584	.579	.574	.574
.2	.516	.517	.515	.514	.511	.507	.507	.502	.495	.490	.488
.5	.426	.423	.421	.418	.416	.412	.410	.404	.397	.391	.385
.7	.391	.394	.392	.390	.386	.383	.381	.375	.368	.362	.358
1.	.364	.367	.364	.363	.361	.357	.354	.350	.343	.337	.333
2.	.337	.341	.339	.337	.334	.330	.326	.320	.313	.307	.301
3.	.339	.344	.344	.341	.337	.333	.328	.320	.310	.302	.292

Values in cesium chloride[g], strontium chloride[h], and sodium, potassium, and lithium sulfates[i] have been obtained at 25°.

[a] H. S. Harned and W. J. Hamer, *J. Am. Chem. Soc.*, **55**, 2194 (1933).
[b] H. S. Harned and G. E. Mannweiler, *Ibid.*, **57**, 1873 (1935).
[c] H. S. Harned and H. R. Copson, *Ibid.*, **55**, 2206 (1933).
[d] H. S. Harned and W. G. Hamer, *Ibid.*, **55**, 4496 (1933).
[e] H. S. Harned and J. G. Donelson, *Ibid.*, **59**, 1280 (1937).
[f] H. S. Harned and C. G. Geary, *Ibid.*, **59**, 2032 (1937).
[g] H. S. Harned and O. E. Schupp Jr., *Ibid.*, **52**, 3892 (1930).
[h] J. E. Vance, *Ibid.*, **55**, 2729 (1933).
[i] G. Åkerlöf, *Ibid.*, **48**, 1160 (1926).

TABLE (15-2-1A)—*Concluded*

THE IONIC ACTIVITY FUNCTION OF WATER, $\gamma_{HY_{OH}}/a_{H_2O}$, IN STRONTIUM
CHLORIDE SOLUTIONS[a]

μ	0°	5°	10°	15°	20°	25°	30°	35°	40°	45°	50°
0.02	0.755	0.751	0.749	0.746	0.746	0.744	0.748	0.744	0.740	0.737	0.737
.03	.714	.711	.709	.705	.705	.704	.706	.703	.698	.697	.695
.05	.660	.655	.654	.651	.650	.648	.650	.647	.642	.639	.637
.07	.622	.617	.616	.613	.611	.610	.611	.608	.603	.599	.597
.1	.581	.576	.574	.572	.573	.569	.568	.565	.560	.556	.554
.2	.499	.497	.493	.491	.489	.484	.484	.481	.475	.469	.466
.3	.452	.450	.447	.444	.442	.436	.437	.432	.425	.420	.416
.5	.400	.396	.394	.389	.388	.384	.381	.375	.368	.364	.360
.7	.370	.366	.363	.359	.357	.353	.349	.345	.338	.324	.328
1.	.343	.342	.339	.336	.331	.328	.324	.318	.311	.306	.300
2.	.317	.315	.312	.308	.304	.298	.294	.286	.278	.271	.264
3.	.323	.322	.316	.313	.307	.301	.295	.286	.277	.268	.261

THE HEAT OF IONIZATION OF WATER IN
STRONTIUM CHLORIDE SOLUTIONS
ACCORDING TO THE EQUATION:

$$\Delta H_i = \Delta H_1(25°)$$

$$+ A(t - 25) + B(t - 25)^2$$

THE IONIZATION CONSTANT AND HEAT
OF IONIZATION OF PURE WATER.

$$\Delta = \Delta H_i^0(obs) - \Delta H_i^0(calc)$$

$$\Delta H_i^0(calc) = 23984.15 - 23.497T$$

$$- 0.039025T^2$$

μ	ΔH_i (25°)	A	−B	t	$K \times 10^{14}$[b]	ΔH_i^0 (cal)	Δ
0.02	13558	45.7	0.077	0	0.1135	14645	−9
.03	13610	45.1	.076	5	.1847	14435	+6
.05	13626	44.1	.074	10	.2923	14198	−4
.07	13643	43.5	.073	15	.4521	13980	+7
.1	13667	42.6	.071	20	.6808	13744	+2
.2	13752	40.7	.068	25	1.008	13520	+11
.3	13811	38.9	.065	30	1.462	13272	−2
.5	13899	36.6	.061	35	2.084	13025	−12
.7	13936	34.9	.059	40	2.918	12768	−31
1.	14005	32.6	.055	45	4.012	12525	−33
2.	14190	25.6	.043	50	5.450	12275	−34
3.	14327	19.3	.032				

[a] H. S. Harned and T. R. Paxton, *J. Chem. Phys.*, **57**, 531 (1953).
[b] See Table (15-1-1).

Table (15-6-1A). Observed Ionization Constants in Water. All Values are on the m-Scale.

Acids		0°	5°	10°	15°	20°	25°	30°	35°	40°	45°	50°	55°	60°	Ref.
Formic	$K_A \times 10^4$	1.638	1.691	1.728	1.749	1.765	1.772	1.768	1.747	1.716	1.685	1.650	1.607	1.551	(1)
Acetic	$K_A \times 10^5$	1.657	1.700	1.729	1.745	1.753	1.754	1.750	1.728	1.703	1.670	1.633	1.589	1.542	(2)
Propionic	$K_A \times 10^5$	1.274	1.305	1.326	1.336	1.338	1.336	1.326	1.310	1.280	1.257	1.229	1.195	1.160	(3)
n-Butyric	$K_A \times 10^5$	1.563	1.574	1.576	1.569	1.542	1.515	1.484	1.439	1.395	1.347	1.302	1.252	1.199	(4)
Chloro-acetic	$K_A \times 10^3$	1.528		1.488	1.440†		1.379	1.308‡		1.230					(5)
Lactic	$K_A \times 10^4$	1.287		1.361*			1.374		1.336**			1.270			(6)
Glycolic	$K_A \times 10^4$	1.334		1.427*			1.475		1.471**			1.415			(7)
Sulfuric	$K_{2A} \times 10^2$		1.80		1.36		1.01		0.75		0.56		0.41		(7a)
Carbonic	$K_{2A} \times 10^{11}$	2.36	2.77	3.24	3.71	4.20	4.69	5.13	5.62	6.03	6.38	6.73			(7b)
Oxalic	$K_{2A} \times 10^5$	5.91	5.82	5.70	5.55	5.40	5.18	4.92	4.67	4.41	4.09	3.83			(8)
Malonic	$K_{2A} \times 10^6$	2.140	2.165	2.152	2.124	2.076	2.014	1.948	1.863	1.768	1.670	1.575	1.469	1.362	(8a)
Phosphoric	$K_{1A} \times 10^3$	8.968		8.394*			7.516		6.531**	6.471	6.475	6.439			(9)
Phosphoric	$K_{2A} \times 10^8$					6.056	6.226	6.349	6.430						(10)
Boric	$K_A \times 10^{10}$		3.63	4.17	4.72	5.26	5.79	6.34	6.86	7.38		8.32			(11)
Amino-Acids															
Glycine	$K_A \times 10^3$			3.94		4.31	4.47	4.50		4.81					(12)
Glycine	$K_B \times 10^5$			4.68	5.12	5.57	6.04	6.52	6.98	7.43	7.87				(12)
Alanine	$K_A \times 10^3$					4.47	4.57	4.66	4.71	4.74	4.76				(13)
Alanine	$K_B \times 10^5$					6.90	7.47	8.08	8.61	9.10	9.60				(13)

* At 12.5°; † At 18°; ‡ At 32°; ** At 37.5°.

(1) H. S. Harned and N. D. Embree, *J. Am. Chem. Soc.*, **56**, 1042 (1934).

(2) H. S. Harned and R. W. Ehlers, *Ibid.*, **55**, 652 (1933).

(3) H. S. Harned and R. W. Ehlers, *Ibid.*, **55**, 2379 (1933).

(4) H. S. Harned and R. O. Sutherland, *Ibid.*, **56**, 2039 (1934).

(5) D. D. Wright, *Ibid.*, **56**, 314 (1934).

(6) L. F. Nims and P. K. Smith, *J. Biol. Chem.*, **113**, 145 (1936).

(7) L. F. Nims, *J. Am. Chem. Soc.*, **58**, 987 (1936).

(7a) Private communication from Professor T. F. Young based on the Dissertations of I. M. Klotz and C. R. Singleterry, University of Chicago (1940).

(7b) H. S. Harned and S. R. Scholes, Jr., *J. Am. Chem. Soc.*, **63**, 1706 (1941).

(8) H. S. Harned and L. D. Fallon, *Ibid.*, **61**, 3111 (1939).

(8a) W. J. Hamer, J. O. Burton and S. F. Acree, *Bur. Standard J. Research*, **24**, 292 (1940).

(9) L. F. Nims, *J. Am. Chem. Soc.*, **56**, 1110 (1934).

(10) L. F. Nims, *Ibid.*, **55**, 1946 (1933).

(11) B. B. Owen, *Ibid.*, **56**, 1695 (1934); **56**, 2785 (1934).

(12) B. B. Owen, *Ibid.*, **56**, 24 (1934).

(13) L. F. Nims and P. K. Smith, *J. Biol. Chem.*, **101**, 401 (1933).

H. V. Tartar and H. H. Garretson [*J. Am. Chem. Soc.*, **63**, 808 (1941)] have determined the ionisation constants of sulphurous acid at 25° from cells without liquid junctions. K_{1A} and K_{2A} are found to be 1.72×10^{-2} and 6.24×10^{-8}, respectively.

TABLE (15-6-2A). IONIZATION CONSTANTS IN DIOXANE-WATER AND METHANOL-WATER MIXTURES. ALL VALUES ARE ON THE m-SCALE. SEE TABLE (15-13-2A).

X = Weight Percent of Organic Solvent

X		0°	5°	10°	15°	20°	25°	30°	35°	40°	45°	50°
					Water in Dioxane-Water Mixtures (1)							
0 (6)	$K_w \times 10^{14}$	0.1139	.1846	.2920	.4505	.6809	1.008	1.469	2.089	2.919	4.018	5.474
20	$K_w \times 10^{15}$	.2702	.4375	.6918	1.067	1.622	2.399	3.477	4.922	6.947	9.531	12.87
45	$K_w \times 10^{16}$	.2114	.3409	.5349	.8188	1.234	1.809	2.594	3.655	5.077	6.914	9.277
70	$K_w \times 10^{18}$	.1789	.2819	.4348	.6511	.9654	1.395	1.974	2.743	3.779	5.064	6.719
					Formic Acid in Dioxane-Water Mixtures (2)							
0 (7)	$K_A \times 10^4$	1.638	1.691	1.728	1.749	1.765	1.772	1.768	1.747	1.716	1.685	1.650
20	$K_A \times 10^5$	6.412	6.548	6.625	6.656	6.651	6.605	6.519	6.394	6.243	6.077	5.876
45	$K_A \times 10^6$	8.702	8.702	8.615	8.488	8.318	9.009	7.834	7.537	7.212	6.867	6.510
70	$K_A \times 10^8$	11.077	10.876	10.641	10.347	10.005	9.634	9.213	8.778	8.310	7.842	7.359
82°	$K_A \times 10^{10}$	.....	9.754	9.170	8.417	7.919	7.231	6.671	5.893	5.234	4.295	.....
					Acetic Acid in Dioxane-Water Mixtures (3)							
0 (7)	$K_A \times 10^5$	1.657	1.700	1.729	1.745	1.753	1.754	1.750	1.728	1.703	1.670	1.633
20	$K_A \times 10^6$	4.75	4.87	4.98	5.50	5.09	5.11	5.08	5.03	4.95	4.86	4.73
45	$K_A \times 10^7$	4.78	4.89	4.96	4.96	4.96	4.93	4.86	4.75	4.61	4.44	4.28
70	$K_A \times 10^9$	4.75	4.83	4.89	4.83	4.83	5.78	4.69	4.56	4.42	4.22	4.05
82°	$K_A \times 10^{11}$	.....	3.60	3.55	3.40	3.32	3.10	2.96	2.67	2.43	2.03	.....
					Propionic Acid in Dioxane-Water Mixtures (4)							
0 (7)	$K_A \times 10^5$	1.274	1.305	1.326	2.336	1.338	1.336	1.326	1.310	1.280	1.257	1.229
20	$K_A \times 10^6$	3.175	3.267	3.337	3.385	3.412	3.417	3.403	3.370	3.319	3.252	3.172
45	$K_A \times 10^7$	2.641	2.713	2.764	2.796	2.808	2.801	2.776	2.734	2.677	2.607	2.526
70	$K_A \times 10^9$	2.299	2.364	2.410	2.439	2.450	2.444	2.422	2.386	2.336	2.274	2.202
82°	$K_A \times 10^{11}$	....	1.986	1.965	1.886	1.862	1.771	1.702	1.587	1.439	1.220	.....

* Revised by S. S. Danyluk, H. Taniguchi and G. J. Janz private communication.

					Acetic Acid in Methanol-Water Mixtures (5)							
10	$K_A \times 10^5$	1.138	.....	1.200	.....	1.242	1.247	1.237	.....	1.214	.....	.....
20	$K_A \times 10^6$	7.38	.....	7.94	.....	8.24	8.34	8.30	.....	8.19	.....	.....

					Glycine in Dioxane-Water Mixtures (8)							
20	$K_A \times 10^3$	1.832	1.953	2.067	2.169	2.257	2.352	2.428	2.481	2.533	2.573	2.591
45	$K_A \times 10^4$	6.339	6.707	7.034	7.348	7.626	7.847	8.091	8.232	8.350	8.457	8.484
70	$K_A \times 10^5$	8.933	9.350	9.759	10.01	10.43	10.84	10.98	11.15	11.26	11.36	11.39
20	$K_B \times 10^5$	1.179	1.317	1.473	1.618	1.781	1.937	2.088	2.241	2.407	2.548	2.690
45	$K_B \times 10^6$	1.789	2.024	2.272	2.541	2.840	3.120	3.408	3.707	4.015	4.342	4.680
70	$K_B \times 10^7$	1.47	1.68	1.91	2.13	2.39	2.66	2.94	3.24	3.60	3.96	4.34

(1) H. S. Harned and L. D. Fallon, *J. Am. Chem. Soc.*, 61, 2374 (1939).
(2) H. S. Harned and R. S. Done, *Ibid.*, 63, 2579 (1941).
(3) H. S. Harned and G. L. Kazanjian, *Ibid.*, 58, 1912 (1936); H. S. Harned and L. D. Fallon, *Ibid.*, 61, 2377 (1939). Revised by H. S. Harned, *J. Phys. Chem.*, 43, 275 (1938).
(4) H. S. Harned and T. R. Dedell, *Ibid.*, 63, 3308 (1941).
(5) H. S. Harned and N. D. Embree, *Ibid.*, 57, 1669 (1935).
(6) **Table (15-1-1).**
(7) Table (15-6-1A).
(8) H. S. Harned and C. M. Birdsall, *J. Am. Chem. Soc.*, 65, 54 (1943) for values of K_A; *Ibid.*, 65, 1117 (1943) for values of K_B.

TABLE (15-6-3A). OBSERVED IONIZATION CONSTANTS OF AMINO-ACIDS[a] IN WATER. ALL VALUES ARE ON THE m-SCALE

	1°	12.5°	25°	37.5°	50°
dl-Alanine, $K_A \times 10^3$	3.75	4.14	4.49	4.68	4.66
$K_B \times 10^5$	4.83	6.10	7.40	8.73	9.86
dl-α-Amino-n-butyric acid, $K_A \times 10^3$	4.63	4.90	5.18	5.15	5.05
$K_B \times 10^5$	4.25	5.50	6.81	8.22	9.38
dl-α-Amino-n-valeric acid, $K_A \times 10^3$	4.21	4.57	4.81	4.91	4.86
$K_B \times 10^5$	4.04	5.18	6.47	7.64	8.63
dl-Norleucine, $K_A \times 10^3$	4.04	4.41	4.62	4.74	4.70
$K_B \times 10^4$	4.41	5.62	6.87	8.05	9.16
α-Aminoisobutyric acid, $K_A \times 10^3$	3.81	4.17	4.40	4.46	4.41
$K_B \times 10^4$	1.14	1.38	1.61	1.84	1.99
dl-Valine, $K_A \times 10^3$	4.79	5.05	5.18	5.11	4.90
$K_B \times 10^5$	3.24	4.21	5.27	6.28	7.28
dl-Leucine, $K_A \times 10^3$	4.14	4.49	4.70	4.71	4.65
$K_B \times 10^5$	3.57	4.52	5.60	6.71	7.59
dl-Isoleucine, $K_A \times 10^3$	4.32	4.59	4.81	4.82	4.66
$K_B \times 10^5$	3.61	4.57	5.77	6.79	7.85

[a] P. K. Smith, A. C. Taylor and E. R. B. Smith, *J. Biol. Chem.*, **122**, 109 (1937).

Table (15-6-4A). Constants of Equations (15-6-9) to (15-6-15) for Ionization Constants, ΔF_i^0, ΔH_i^0, $\Delta C_{p_i}^0$, ΔS_i^0, $-\log K_\theta$, and T_θ. See Table (15-13-3A).

$$\log K = -\frac{A^*}{T} + D^* - C^*T \qquad \begin{array}{l} A' = 2.3026\ RA^* \\ D' = 2.3026\ RD^* \\ C' = 2.3026\ RC^* \end{array}$$

$$\Delta F_i^0 = A' - D'T + C'T^2$$

$$\Delta H_i^0 = A' - C'T^2$$

$$\Delta C_{p_i}^0 = -2C'T$$

$$\Delta S_i^0 = D' - 2C'T$$

$$T_\theta = \sqrt{\frac{A^*}{C^*}}; \quad \log K_\theta = D^* - 2\sqrt{C^*A^*}$$

Part I. Aqueous Solutions

Acids	A^*	D^*	C^*	A'	D'	C'	T_θ	$-\log K_\theta$
Formic	1342.85	5.2743	0.015168	6143.59	24.1301	0.069395	297.5	3.7519
Acetic	1170.48	3.1649	.013399	5354.99	14.4795	.061301	295.6	4.7555
Propionic	1213.26	3.3860	.014055	5550.71	15.4911	.064302	293.8	4.8729
n-Butyric	1033.39	2.6215	.013334	4727.80	11.9935	.061004	278.4	4.8026
Chloroacetic	1049.05	5.0273	.014654	4799.45	23.0001	.067043	267.6	2.8143
Lactic	1304.72	4.9639	.014926	5969.15	22.7100	.068287	295.7	3.8620
Glycolic	1303.26	4.7845	.014236	5962.47	21.8893	.065130	302.6	3.8302
Carbonic (2)	2902.39	6.4980	.02379	13278.55	29.7286	.10884	349.3	10.121
Oxalic	1539.31	7.1966	.021200	7042.40	32.9247	.096991	269.5	4.2285
Malonic	1703.31	6.5810	.022014	7792.71	30.1083	.100715	278.2	5.6659
Phosphoric (1)	1264.51	7.6601	.018590	5785.18	35.0452	.085050	260.8	2.0368
(2)	1648.88	3.2542	.016534	7543.69	14.8880	.075644	315.8	7.1885
Boric	2193.55	3.0395	.016499	10035.58	13.9058	.075484	364.6	8.9923
Amino-Acids								
Glycine A	1300.53	5.5277	.011792	5949.98	25.2894	.053949	332.1	2.3045
B	1307.30	2.5629	.008038	5980.95	11.7254	.036773	403.3	3.9202
dl-Alanine A	(1383.06)	(6.3639)	(.013661)	(6327.55)	(29.1151)	(.062502)	(318.2)	(2.3297)
	1271.17	5.6650	.012548	5815.65	25.9176	.057408	318.3	2.3226
B	2069.10	7.7123	.01643	9466.22	35.2841	.075159	354.9	3.9481
	(1529.44)	(4.2704)	(.010966)	(6997.25)	(19.5373)	(.050168)	(373.5)	(3.9201)
dl-α-Amino-n-Butyric A	1174.74	5.3735	.012487	5374.48	24.5840	.057129	299.8	2.2866
B	1591.68	4.4429	.010965	7282.0	20.3264	.05017	381.0	3.9126
dl-α-Amino-n-Valeric A	1222.02	5.5238	.012553	5590.79	25.2716	.05743	312.0	2.3094
B	1852.42	6.2544	.014191	8474.9	28.6141	.064923	361.3	3.9999
dl-Norleucine A	1193.30	5.2850	.012130	5459.40	24.179	.055495	313.7	2.3242
B	1619.10	5.7984	.011842	7407.45	26.5279	.054178	369.8	2.9591
dl-α-Amino-isobutyric A	1344.95	6.3053	.013924	6153.20	28.8470	.063703	310.8	2.3497
B	1460.04	4.5471	.011540	6679.41	20.8032	.052796	355.7	3.6624
dl-Valine A	1245.31	6.0251	.013868	5697.34	27.5650	.063447	299.6	2.2863
B	1694.53	4.9842	.012004	7752.54	22.8029	.054919	375.7	4.0360
dl-Leucine A	1283.60	6.0027	.013505	5872.52	27.4626	.061786	308.3	2.3244
B	1651.61	4.8479	.011933	7556.18	22.1793	.054594	372.0	4.0310
dl-Isoleucine A	1298.09	6.1967	.013959	5938.81	28.3502	.063863	205.0	2.3169
B	1537.47	4.0396	.010482	7033.99	18.4813	.047956	383.0	3.9893

TABLE (15-6-4A)—*Concluded*

Part II.   Water and Acids in Dioxane- and Methanol-Water Mixtures. X = Weight Percent of Organic Solvent.

X	$A^\bullet$	$D^\bullet$	$C^\bullet$	A'	D'	C'	T_θ	$-\log K_\theta$
				Water in Dioxane-Water Mixtures				
0	4470.99	6.0875	0.01706	20454.96	27.8506	0.078050	511.9	11.3796
20	4596.78	6.3108	.0184867	21030.45	28.8722	.084577	498.7	12.1260
45	4641.08	5.7231	.019784	21233.13	26.1834	.090513	484.3	13.4414
70	4377.47	2.2289	.018116	20027.10	10.1973	.082882	491.6	15.5815
				Formic Acid in Dioxane-Water Mixtures				
20	1339.04	5.0628	.015983	6126.17	23.1626	.072917	289.8	4.1766
45	1333.79	4.6393	.017634	6102.16	21.2248	.080676	275.0	5.0602
70	1181.65	1.9920	.016922	5406.09	9.1135	.077419	264.2	6.9513
				Acetic Acid in Dioxane-Water Mixtures				
20	1423.45	4.2934	.016136	6512.34	19.6425	.073822	297.0	5.2917
45	1568.31	4.5387	.018736	7175.08	20.7650	.085718	289.3	6.3027
70	1549.12	2.5194	.018933	7087.29	11.5264	.086619	286.0	8.3119
				Propionic Acid in Dioxane-Water Mixtures				
20	1356.57	3.67038	.015384	6206.67	16.7930	.070385	297.0	5.4662
45	1480.12	3.52870	.017163	6771.94	16.1447	.078525	293.7	6.5516
70	1508.10	1.65390	.017466	6879.96	7.5670	.079914	293.8	8.6112
				Acetic Acid in Methanol-Water Mixtures				
10	1417.19	4.5806	.015874	6483.70	20.9564	.072624	298.8	4.9055
20	1572.21	5.3447	.017279	7192.92	24.4522	.079052	301.7	5.0796
				K_A of Glycine in Dioxane-Water Mixtures				
0	1300.53	5.5277	.011792	5949.98	25.2894	.053949	332.1	2.3043
20	1368.94	5.6875	.012493	6263.16	26.0216	.057161	331.0	2.5806
45	1273.49	4.7113	.011887	5826.47	21.5553	.054386	327.3	3.0702
70	1187.30	3.3894	.011322	5432.12	15.5073	.051801	323.8	3.9435
				K_B of Glycine in Dioxane-Water Mixtures				
0	1307.30	2.5629	.008038	5980.95	11.7254	.036673	403.3	3.9203
20	1519.89	3.3800	.010046	6953.78	15.4642	.045964	389.0	4.4350
45	1364.90	1.1999	.007139	6244.69	5.4898	.032663	437.2	5.0433
70	895.27	−3.328	.000818	4096.02	−15.227	.003743	.....	......

TABLE (15-13-1A). OBSERVED IONIZATION CONSTANTS IN WATER.
ALL VALUES ARE ON THE m-SCALE

Acid	Solvent		0°	5°	10°	15°	20°	25°	30°	35°	40°	45°	50°	Ref.
Carbonic	Water	$K_1 \times 10^7$	2.64	3.04	3.44	3.81	4.16	4.45	4.71	4.90	5.04	5.13	5.19	1
	0.1M NaCl	"	4.48	5.16	5.84	6.49	7.11	7.66	8.14	8.54	8.85	9.06	9.16	2
	0.2M NaCl	"	5.15	5.93	6.70	7.44	8.14	8.78	9.33	9.79	10.15	10.39	10.51	2
	0.5M NaCl	"	6.23	7.14	8.04	8.90	9.70	10.41	11.03	11.53	11.92	12.19	12.32	2
	0.7M NaCl	"	6.62	7.56	8.47	9.34	10.15	10.81	11.51	12.03	12.45	12.75	12.93	2
	1.0M NaCl	"	7.02	7.98	8.92	9.80	10.63	11.37	12.02	12.58	13.03	13.37	13.58	2
Phosphoric	Water	$K_{2A} \times 10^8$	4.85	5.24	5.57	5.89	6.12	6.34	6.46	6.53	6.58	6.59	6.55	3
Phenolsulphonic	"	$K_{2A} \times 10^{10}$	4.45	5.20	6.03	6.92	7.85	8.85	9.89	10.94	12.00	13.09	14.16	4
Glycine	"	$K_{1A} \times 10^7$	....	3.82	3.99	4.17	4.32	4.46	4.57	4.66	4.73	4.77	4.79	5
Benzoic	"	$K_{1A} \times 10^5$	....	....	....	....	6.24	6.29	6.27	6.24	....	....	....	6
Citric	"	$K_{1A} \times 10^4$	6.03	6.31	6.69	6.92	7.21	7.45	7.66	7.78	7.96	7.99	8.04	7
	"	$K_{2A} \times 10^5$	1.45	1.54	1.60	1.65	1.70	1.73	1.76	1.77	1.78	1.76	1.75	7
	"	$K_{3A} \times 10^7$	4.05	4.11	4.14	4.13	4.09	4.02	3.99	3.78	3.69	3.45	3.28	7

[1] H. S. Harned and R. Davis, Jr., J. Am. Chem. Soc., 65, 2030 (1943).

[2] H. S. Harned and F. T. Bonner, Ibid., 67, 1026 (1945).

[3] R. G. Bates and S. F. Acree, J. Res. Nat. Bur. Standards, 30, 129 (1943).

[4] R. G. Bates, G. L. Siegel and S. F. Acree, Ibid., 31, 205 (1943).

[5] E. J. King, J. Am. Chem. Soc., 67, 2178 (1945).

[6] A. V. Jones and H. N. Parton, Trans. Faraday Soc., 48, 8 (1952).

[7] R. G. Bates and G. D. Pinching, J. Am. Chem. Soc., 71, 1274 (1949).

TABLE (15-13-2A). IONIZATION CONSTANTS OF WEAK ACIDS IN ORGANIC SOLVENT-WATER MIXTURES. ALL VALUES ARE ON THE m-SCALE.
X = Weight Per Cent Organic Solvent

X		0°	5°	10°	15°	20°	25°	30°	35°	40°	45°	50°

Propionic Acid in Methyl Alcohol-Water Mixtures[2]

X		0°	5°	10°	15°	20°	25°	30°	35°	40°	45°	50°
0[1]	$K_A \times 10^5$	1.274	1.305	1.326	1.336	1.338	1.336	1.326	1.310	1.280	1.257	1.229
10	"	0.881	.....	0.885	.....	0.917	0.947	0.909	.....	0.838	....	....
20	"	0.603	.....	0.608	.....	0.586	0.578	0.553	.....	0.525	....	....

Propionic Acid in Ethyl Alcohol-Water Mixtures[2]

X		0°	5°	10°	15°	20°	25°	30°	35°	40°	45°	50°
10	$K_A \times 10^5$	0.870	.....	0.900	.....	0.900	0.900	0.906	.....	0.902	....	....
20	"	0.673	.....	0.755	.....	0.771	0.781	0.788	.....	0.780	....	....

Propionic Acid in Isopropyl Alcohol-Water Mixtures[3]

X		0°	5°	10°	15°	20°	25°	30°	35°	40°	45°	50°
5	$K_A \times 10^5$	1.015	1.038	1.052	1.061	1.060	1.053	1.044	1.032	1.012	....	....
10	"	0.780	0.803	0.815	0.823	0.824	0.820	0.812	0.800	0.785	....	....
20	"	0.431	0.448	0.459	0.466	0.466	0.466	0.462	0.454	0.444	....	....

n-Butyric Acid in Isopropyl Alcohol-Water Mixtures[4]

X		0°	5°	10°	15°	20°	25°	30°	35°	40°	45°	50°
5	$K_A \times 10^5$	1.190	1.197	1.189	1.177	1.157	1.133	1.104	1.077	1.040	....	....
10	"	0.922	0.929	0.925	0.916	0.907	0.888	0.864	0.839	0.813	....	....
20	"	0.466	0.475	0.476	0.473	0.465	0.456	0.446	0.432	0.417	....	....

Acetic Acid in Glycerol-Water Mixtures[5] (0 to 90°)

X		0°	5°	10°	15°	20°	25°	30°	35°	40°	45°	50°
50	$K_A \times 10^6$	4.78	4.96	5.10	5.22	5.32	5.35	5.38	5.37	5.33	5.27	5.18

X		55°	60°	65°	70°	75°	80°	85°	90°			
50	"	5.07	4.95	4.81	4.65	4.47	4.31	4.14	3.93	....	....	....

[1] H. S. Harned and R. W. Ehlers, *J. Am. Chem. Soc.*, **55**, 2379 (1933).
[2] A. Patterson and W. A. Felsing, *Ibid.*, **64**, 1480 (1942).
[3] R. L. Moore and W. A. Felsing, *Ibid.*, **69**, 2420 (1947).
[4] W. A. Felsing and M. May, *Ibid.*, **70**, 2904 (1948).
[5] H. S. Harned and F. H. M. Nestler, *Ibid.*, **68**, 966 (1946).

TABLE (15-13-3A). CONSTANTS OF EQUATIONS (15-6-9) TO (15-6-15) FOR
IONIZATION CONSTANTS, ΔF_i^0, ΔH_i^0, $\Delta C_{p_i}^0$, $-\log K_\theta$, AND T_θ

$$K = \frac{m_H m_{Ac}}{m_{HAc}} \frac{\gamma_H \gamma_{Ac}}{\gamma_{HAc}} = k \frac{\gamma_H \gamma_{Ac}}{\gamma_{HAc}}$$

$$\left. \begin{array}{l} \log K \\ \log k \end{array} \right\} = -\frac{A^*}{T} + D^* - C^*T \qquad \begin{array}{l} A' = 2.3026\,RA_*^* \\ D' = 2.3026\,RD^* \end{array}$$

$$\Delta F_i^0 = A' - D'T + C'T^2 \qquad C' = 2.3026\,RC^*$$

$$\Delta H_i^0 = A' - C'T^2$$

$$\Delta C_{p_i}^0 = D' - 2C'T$$

$$T_\theta = \frac{A^*}{C^*} \;;\; \log K_\theta = D^* - 2\sqrt{C^*A^*}$$

Part I. Aqueous Solutions

		A^*	D^*	C^*	A'	D'	C'	T_θ	$-\log K_\theta$
Phosphoric acid...	K_{2A}	1979.5	5.3541	0.019840	9055.0	24.491	0.090751	317	7.1795
Phenolsulphonic acid..............	K_{2A}	1961.2	1.1436	0.012139	8970.8	5.231	0.055525	402	8.3928
Benzoic acid.......	K_{1A}	1590.2	5.394	0.01765	7319.1	29.247	0.080733	301	4.2014
Citric acid........	K_{1A}	1255.6	4.5635	0.011673	5143.3	20.874	0.053394	328	3.094
" "	K_{2A}	1585.2	5.4460	0.016399	7250.9	24.911	0.074012	311	5.751
" "	K_{3A}	1814.9	6.3664	0.022389	8301.6	29.121	0.102410	285	6.383

Part II. Carbonic Acid (K_{1A}), (k_{1A}) in Aqueous NaCl Solutions[1]

mNaCl	A^*	D^*	C^*	mNaCl	A^*	D^*	C^*
0.0	3404.71	14.8435	0.032786	0.5	3158.38	13.5235	0.029892
.1	3266.11	14.0256	.030811	.7	2955.23	12.2139	.027721
.2	3228.50	13.8363	.030401	1.0	2786.18	11.1187	.025885

Boric Acid in Aqueous NaCl Solutions[2]

.0	2291.9	3.6865	.017560	0.725	1695.2	0.0750	.010799
.02	2221.1	3.2837	.016595	1.25	1496.2	−1.1962	.008662
.07	2136.4	2.7805	.015590	2.00	1264.9	−2.7439	.006053
.36	1881.8	1.2322	.012782	3.00	984.7	−4.7340	.002626

Glycine (K_A) in Aqueous NaCl Solutions[3]

.0	1259.9	5.3980	.011817	1.25	1277.1	5.2559	.011412
.1	1278.0	5.5030	.011974	2.00	1213.1	4.6187	.010234
.3	1292.4	5.5727	.012067	3.00	1026.6	3.0809	.007529
.725	1297.4	5.5234	.011931				

Propionic Acid in Isopropyl Alcohol-Water Mixtures

X				X			
0	1213.26	3.3860	.014055	10	1403.858	4.5143	.016406
5	1191.0865	3.1909	.013995	20	1771.125	6.7087	.020457

TABLE (15-13-3A)—*Concluded*
n-Butyric Acid in Isopropyl Alcohol-Water Mixtures

X	A*	D*	C*	X	A*	D*	C*
0	1033.39	2.6215	.013334	10	1217.523	3.6903	.015625
5	1048.516	2.6719	.013753	20	1459.369	5.0187	.018325

Acetic Acid in Glycerol-Water Mixture (0 to 90°)

50	1321.4256	3.4148	0.014268				

[1] H. S. Harned and F. T. Bonner, *J. Am. Chem. Soc.*, **67,** 1026 (1945).
[2] B. B. Owen and E. J. King, *Ibid.*, **65,** 1612 (1943).
[3] E. J. King. *Ibid.*, **67,** 2178 (1945).

TABLE (15-13-4A). OBSERVED IONIZATION CONSTANTS IN WATER.

		0°	10°	20°	25°	30°	40°	50°	60°	Ref.
Ammonia	$K_B \times 10^5$	1.374	1.570	1.710	1.774	1.820	1.862	1.892		1
Ethylene diammonium ion ⎰	$K_{1B} \times 10^8$	2.73	5.42	10.35	14.2	10.2	34.4	60.1	102.3	2
⎱	$K_{2B} \times 10^{11}$	1.94	4.14	8.41	11.8	16.5	30.9	56.0	98.8	2
Hexamethylamine	$K_{1B} \times 10^{11}$	1.73	4.22	9.68	14.8	21.2	44.3	88.7	171.0	2
Diammonium ion	$K_{2B} \times 10^{12}$	1.39	3.40	7.85	11.7	17.3	36.2	73.0	141.0	2
Valeric acid	$K_{1A} \times 10^5$	1.504	1.501	1.463	1.436	1.409	1.329	1.241	1.147	3
Hexoic acid	$K_{1A} \times 10^5$	1.445	1.448	1.416	1.390	1.364	1.287	1.201	1.110	3
Iso-butyric acid	$K_{1A} \times 10^5$	1.497	1.489	1.447	1.417	1.387	1.301	1.208	1.110	3
Iso-valeric acid	$K_{1A} \times 10^5$	1.879	1.810	1.709	1.657	1.605	1.477	1.345	1.216	3
Iso-hexoic acid	$K_{1A} \times 10^5$	1.491	1.491	1.455	1.429	1.402	1.322	1.235	1.141	3
Trimethylacetic acid	$K_{1A} \times 10^5$	0.965	0.968	0.944	0.929	0.911	0.858	0.797	0.732	3
Diethyl acetic acid	$K_{1A} \times 10^5$	2.384	2.169	1.948	1.835	1.744	1.540	1.353	1.181	3

(1) R. G. Bates and G. D. Pinching, *J. Am. Chem. Soc.*, **72,** 1393 (1950)
(2) D. H. Everett and B. R. W. Pinsent, *Proc. Roy. Soc.*, A, **215,** 416 (1952).
(3) D. H. Everett, D. A. Landsman and B. R. W. Pinsent, *Idem.*, p. 403.

TABLE (15-13-5A). CONSTANTS OF EQUATIONS (15-6-9) TO (15-6-15).

	$A^{\bullet}$	$D^{\bullet}$	$C^{\bullet}$	
Acetyl glycine, K_{1A}................	1284.54	4.8146	0.014411	(1)
Propionyl glycine, K_{1A}..............	1103.03	3.7708	.012730	(1)
Acetyl-dl-alanine, K_{1A}.............	908.48	2.8416	.011771	(1)
Acetyl-dl-α-amino-n butyric acid, K_{1A}	908.43	2.9315	.012096	(1)
Acetyl-β-alanine, K_{1A}.	1279.32	3.9494	.013763	(1)
γ-amino-butyric acid...........$\{$ K_{1A}	1209.07	3.7820	.012605	(2)
K_{2A}	2804.84	-0.5879	.0018797	(2)
Taurine, K_{2A}.......................	2458.49	0.0997	.0030689	(3)
Sulphamic acid, K_{1A}................	3792.8	24.122	.041544	(4)
Sulphanilic acid, K_{1A}...............	1143.71	1.2979	.0023142	(5)
Metanilic acid, K_{1A}................	1327.59	1.55334	.00281319	(6)
Orthanilic acid, K_{1A}...............	1106.68	3.2314	.0066339	(7)
Glycerol-2-phosphoric acid.....$\{$ K_{1A}	1891.9072	13.4799	.02841	(8)
K_{2A}	1667.4043	4.8394	.01978	(8)
Glycerol-1-phosphoric acid, K_{2A}.....	1432.1569	3.4213	.017177	(9)
2-Amino-ethanol-1-phosphoric acid, K_{2A}.............................	1228.3378	2.7328	.01493	(10)

(1) E. J. King and G. W. King, *J. Am. Chem. Soc.*, **78**, 1089 (1956).
(2) E. J. King, *Ibid.*, **76**, 1006 (1954).
(3) E. J. King, *Ibid.*, **75**, 2204 (1953).
(4) E. J. King and G. W. King, *Ibid.*, **74**, 1212 (1952).
(5) R. O. MacLaren and D. F. Swinehart, *Ibid.*, **73**, 1822 (1951).
(6) R. D. McCoy and D. F. Swinehart, *Ibid.*, **76**, 4708 (1954).
(7) R. N. Diebel and D. F. Swinehart, *J. Phys. Chem.*, **61**, 333 (1957).
(8) J. H. Ashby, E. M. Crook and S. P. Datta, *Biochem. J.*, **56**, 190, 198 (1954).
(9) J. H. Ashby, H. B. Clarke and S. P. Datta, *Ibid.*, **59**, 203 (1955).
(10) H. B. Clarke, S. P. Datta and B. R. Rabin, *Ibid.*, **59**, 209 (1955).

AUTHOR INDEX

ADDENDUM

SUBJECT INDEX

A

Activity coefficients of strong electrolytes, at the freezing point, 711
definition of, mean, molal, molar, practical, rational, and stoichiometrical, 10–11
extended equations for, 66–70
from boiling point elevations, 411–3, 491
from cells with liquid junctions, 438, 486–7
from cells without liquid junctions, 431–3, 466, 489, 497–500, 574, 591
from freezing point depressions, 409–11, 419–22, 711
from osmotic coefficients, 414–18
from vapor pressures, 413–18, 502–4
hydrochloric acid, from 0 to 60° in water, 466, 716, 751
  from 0 to 50° in mixed solvents, 717–20
in relation to concentration scales, 11–2
in relation to osmotic coefficient, 12–4
limiting law for (*See:* Limiting laws.)
  values of constants, in water, 164–5
  values of constants in dioxane-water mixtures, 713
polyvalent, 550, 553, 565–6, 576, 734–5, 737–46
pressure dependence of, 505–8
ratios of, 504, 516–7, 604–10, 681
representation of, as a function of concentration,
  by Debye-Hückel method, 467–71, 508–10
  by Guggenheim's method, 515–8, 736
  by Scatchard's method, 518–20
  by van der Waal's co-volume effect, 520–2
representation of, as a function of dielectric constant, 82
sodium chloride from 0 to 100° in water, 488–92, 726
temperature dependence of, 467–71, 504–7
uni-univalent, 486–92, 497–500, 716–33, 735–6, 748–51
valence factors for, 62–4, 164–6

verification of limiting law for, 313, 455, 471, 487, 657, 716
Activity coefficients of strong electrolytes in mixtures, acids in salt solutions, 591–616, 748–51
acids in acid solutions, 613
at constant ionic strength in water, 595–616
  in mixed solvents, 600–1
extrapolation to saturated solutions, 617–20
from solubility measurements, 586–90, 679
hydroxides in salt solutions, 592–5, 615–6
linear variation of, at constant ionic strength, 595–607
salts in salt solutions, 610–1, 618
Activity coefficients of neutral molecules in salt solutions, 531–40, 752–4
weak acids in salt solutions, 535–6, 657
Activity coefficients of weak electrolytes, acids in salt solutions, 675–80
glycine in potassium chloride solutions, 661
water in salt solutions, 639–43, 752–4
Activity, definition of, 6, 7
mean, definition of, 10
of water in sulfuric acid solutions, 574–5
standard states for, in cell measurements, 425, 463, 669–72
  in chemical equilibrium, 14, 15
  in cryoscopy, 411
  in ebullioscopy, 411
  in general, 7, 8
  in vapor pressure measurements, 413
variation of, with composition, 9
  with pressure, 9
  with surface tension, 16
  with temperature, 8
Adsorption equation of Gibbs, 16
Adsorption potential, 89–90
Amalgam cells, calculation of water correction, 499–500
containing, alkaline earth metal amalgams, 549–51
alkali metal amalgams, 489–94, 497–502, 551–3, 592–5, 615, 639, 654
cadmium amalgams, 551, 554–60

773

Crystals, critical disruptive condition of, 365

critical disruptive volume of, 365–7, 385

D

Debye and Hückel theory, 49–50, 59–66
constants for, 165–7, 713, 720
effect of ionic size, 65–6
extended, 66–70, 166
tables for, 167
limiting law of, 53, 62–4
See also: Extrapolation functions; Interionic attraction theory.
Demal unit of concentration, 197
Dielectric constant, effect of frequency on 127, 181–3, 318
of solutions of electrolytes, 81, 508, 519
of water, 159–62
of water-dioxane mixtures, 713
of water-nonaqueous solvent mixtures, 161–2
Diffusion, cell, 245, 254–5
activity coefficients from, 251–3
coefficients, extrapolation of, 245–6, 262
experimental test of theory, 246–50, 700–2
electrophoretic term, 247–9
exchange, coefficient of, 258
in concentrated solutions, 253–5, 259–64
ion-pair formation in, 250–1, 264
limiting law for, 243–4
of neutral molecules, 250–1, 261–4
self, 244, 256–9
tables of experimental values, 700–2
theoretical equations for, 243
theory of, 118–22, 181
thermodynamic term, 247
viscosity and, 259–64
Dissipation function, 20–2
definition of, 20
Dissociation constants, determination of, by extrapolation, 286–90
effects of high fields upon, 324–7
influence of ionic size upon, 306–10
of ion pairs and triple ions, 289–302
of salts and complex ions, 206, 698, 703–5
theory of ionic association and, 70–4
See also: Ionization constants.
Dissociation field effect, on alkyl ammonium salts in diphenyl ether, 324–6

on weak acids in water, 323
theory of, 138–46, 184
Distribution functions, change of, with time, 47–8
definition of, 44–6

E

Effective pressure, 370, 383–4
definition of, 381
equation for, 384
Electrochemical potential function, 33, 441–2
including gravitational field, 33
Electrodes, polarization and capacity effects of, 195
representation of, 425–7
Electrode potentials, conventions regarding, 425–8
pressure corrections for, 429
standard, definition of, 427
See also: Standard cell potentials; Standard electrode potentials.
Electromotive force centrifuge, 278–82
Electromotive force, definition of, 423
See also: Cells.
Electrophoresis, 107–10
in high fields, 134
Energy, of phase, 1
of separation of ion pairs and triple ions, 71, 297
total differential of, 2
Entropy, 2
increase in, for ionization reactions, 645, 667–8, 758–9
Equilibrium constant, general, 14–6
See also: Ionization constants; Dissociation constants.
Expansibility, coefficient of, concentration dependence of, 372
definition of, 371
of salt solutions, 372–4
Extended terms, 67–8, 166–7
applied to, electromotive forces, 459, 467–70, 555–63
freezing points, 420–1
mixtures, 588–91
Extinction coefficient, 656
Extrapolation functions for,
activity coefficients, 433, 487, 503
at high concentrations, 617–20
in mixtures, 598–602
apparent molal, compressibilities, 376
expansibilities, 371
volumes, 358, 362, 365
boiling point elevations, 417

CHEMICAL INDEX

A

Acetate ion, hydrolysis of, in salt solutions, 681

Acetic acid, apparent molal compressibility of, 390, 710
  conductance of, 291, 313–6, 668, 696, 756
  effect of high fields upon, 323
  diffusion coefficient of, 264
  free energy, entropy, heat capacity and heat content of ionization, 667
  ionization constant as a function of, dielectric constant, 682, 688, 758–9, 761, 763
    mole fraction of water, 662
    temperature, 758–9
  ionization constant of, from cells, with liquid junction, 668
    without liquid junction, (buffered), 652, 668, 755–8, 763
    (unbuffered), 650, 673–5
  ionization constant of, from conductance, 313–5, 668, 696
    in dioxane-water mixtures, 756
    in methanol-water mixtures, 291, 316, 696, 756
  ionization of, in salt solutions at 25°, 676–7
    as a function of temperature, 677
  medium effect upon ionization constant of, 313–4, 672, 674
  partial molal compressibility of, 710
  pH of solutions of, 447, 712
  polymerization of, 314
  salting effects by various electrolytes upon, 531–40, 737
  volume change of ionization, 405

Acetonitrile, conductance and association in, 705
  mobility-viscosity ratio in, 285

Acetone, conductance and association in, 704
  mobility-viscosity products in, 285

Acetone, salting effects of various salts on, 538–9

Acetone-water mixtures, dielectric constants of, 161

Acetyl-dl-alanine, ionization constant of, ·764

Acetyl-dl-amino-n-butyric acid, ionization constant of, 764

Acetyl-β alanine, ionization constant of, 764

Acetylglycine, ionization constant of, 764

dl-Alanine, acidic ionization constant of, 660, 755, 757–8
  basic ionization constant of, 755, 757–8
  entropy, free energy, heat capacity, and heat content of ionization of, 667, 758

Alkyl ammonium chlorides and fluorides, osmotic coefficients of, 528

Alkylamine hydrochlorides, equivalent conductances of, 530

Aluminum chloride, activity coefficient of, 566, 746
  hydrochloric acid in solutions of, 750–1
  effect on activity coefficient of hydrochloric acid, 599, 625
  salt effects on neutral molecules, 532, 736

Aluminum sulfate, activity coefficient of, 566
  salt effects on neutral molecules, 532–3, 736

dl-α-Amino-n-butyric acid, acidic and basic ionization constants of, 757–8
  entropy, free energy, heat capacity and heat content of ionization of, 667, 758

Amino-n-caproic acid, conductance in high fields, 327

γ-Amino-butyric acid, ionization constant of, 764

dl-α-Amino-isobutyric acid, acidic and basic ionization constants of, 757–8
  entropy, free energy, heat capacity and heat content of ionization of, 667, 758

2-Amino-ethanol-1-phosphoric acid, ionization constant of, 764

dl-α-Amino-n-valeric acid, acidic and basic ionization constants of, 757–8
  entropy, free energy, heat capacity and heat content of ionization of, 667, 758

Ammonium bromide, activity coefficient of, 711

Calcium sulphate, dissociation constant of, 206

effect of pressure on solubility product of, 403

relative apparent molal heat content of, 336, 707

relative partial molal heat content of, 709

Calcium perchlorate, activity coefficient of, 740

Carbon dioxide, salting effects upon, by various salts, 533–6, 736

Carbonic acid, conductance of, in high fields, 327–30

first ionization constant of, 315, 329, 690–4, 760, 762

second ionization constant of, 690–4, 755, 758

volume change of ionization of, 405

Carbamoylamino-acids, ionization constants, of, 696

Carbon tetrachloride, compressibility of, 380

Cerium chloride, activity coefficient of, 566, 742, 746

effect upon activity coefficient of hydrochloric acid, 750

partial molal compressibility of, 710

viscosity of solutions of, 241

Cesium acetate, activity coefficient of, 732

Cesium bromide, activity coefficient of, 513, 731

apparent molal volume of, 361, 397

densities of solutions of, 725

effective pressure of, 383

mean distance of approach of ions of, 510

partial molal compressibility of, 710

properties of critical disruptive condition of, 366–7

Cesium chloride, activity coefficient of, 252, 255, 513, 527, 731

apparent molal volume of, 361, 397

densities of solutions of, 725

diffusion of, 247–8, 700

effects upon activity coefficients of hydrochloric acid and cesium hydroxide, 593, 750

mean distance of approach of ions of, 510

properties of critical disruptive condition of, 366–7

relative apparent molal heat content of, 707

Cesium dibromoiodide, limiting conductance and ionization, constant of, 705

Cesium hydroxide, activity coefficient of, 498, 513

in presence of cesium chloride, 593

Cesium iodide, activity coefficient of, 513, 731

apparent molal volume of, 361, 397

densities of solutions of, 725

mean distance of approach of ions of, 510

properties of critical disruptive condition of, 366–7

viscosity of solutions of, 241.

Cesium nitrate, activity coefficient of, 527, 732–3, 736

densities of solutions of, 725

salting effect by, 538

surface tension of dilute solution of, 542

viscosity of, 238, 241

Cesium sulphate, activity coefficient of, 252, 739

diffusion of, 249, 700

partial molal compressibility of, 710

relative apparent molal heat content of, 707

relative partial molal heat content of, 341–2, 709

Chloroacetic acid, effect of high fields on conductance of, 323

entropy, free energy, heat capacity and heat content of ionization of, 667, 758

ionization constant of, 315, 668, 755, 758

salting effects upon, by various salts, 737

standard potentials in buffered solutions of, 446

Chlorobenzene, compressibility of, 380

conductance and association in, 308

m-Chlorobenzoic acid, ionization constant of, 315

o-Chlorobenzoic acid, ionization constant of, 315

p-Chlorobenzoic acid, ionization constant of, 315

Chromic sulfate, viscosity of solutions of, 241

Citric acid, ionization constants of, 760

pH of standard solutions of, 712

Cobaltammines, solubility of, in salt solutions, 585–90

Water (Cont'd)
bulk compression as a function of pressure, 378–9
changes in entropy, free energy, heat capacity and heat content of ionization of, 667
coefficient of compressibility of, 161, 163, 378, 381
coefficient of expansion of, 161, 163, 373
density of solutions of, 161
dielectric constant of, 159–61
mixtures with organic solvents, 161–2
heat of ionization of, 645–7, 649, 754
ionization of in salt solutions, 639–43
as a function of ionic radii, 639–43
ionization constant of, 485, 581, 584
as a function of dielectric constant, 682, 756, 759
as a function of mole fraction of dioxane, 662, 756
effect of pressure upon, 403–5, 648–9
effect of temperature upon, 643–6
from cells without liquid junction, 634–9
mean ionic radius of, from temperature variation of, 685
molal depression of the freezing point of, 411
molal elevation of boiling point of, 413
partial molal compressibility of, 390, 402, 710
relative partial molal, heat capacity of, 350–1
heat content of, 341–2
sea, estimation of thermodynamic properties, 401–3
self-diffusion of, 260–1
total heat of ionization of, in salt solutions, 645–8
vapor pressure of, 413
viscosity of solutions of, 161, 163
volume change of ionization, 405

Y

Ytterbium chloride, activity coefficient of, 742

Yttrium chloride, activity coefficient of, 566, 746

Z

Zinc, standard potential of, 741
Zinc bromide, activity coefficient of, 560–1, 742
extrapolation of amalgam cells containing, 554–60
relative partial molal heat capacity of, 560
relative partial molal heat content of, 560
Zinc chloride, activity coefficient of, 560–1, 739, 742–3
extrapolation of amalgam cells containing, 554–60
relative partial molal heat capacity of, 560, 745
relative partial molal heat content of, 560, 745
Zinc iodide, activity coefficient of, 560–1, 739, 742–3
extrapolation of amalgam cells containing, 554–60
relative partial molal heat capacity of, 560, 745
relative partial molal heat content of, 560, 745
Zinc malonate, dissociation of, 206
Zinc nitrate, activity coefficient of, 739
Zinc perchlorate, activity coefficient of, 739
Zinc sulfate, activity coefficient of, 544, 564–5
diffusion coefficient of, 249–51
equivalent conductance of, 200, 290, 697
in high fields, 327–8
ionization constant and limiting conductance of, 206, 290
in diffusion, 249–51, 701
partial molal compressibility of, 710
relative apparent molal heat content of, 707
relative partial molal heat content of, 563, 709
viscosity of solutions of, 241